# Living Humanism: Part Two

Having presented core and other principles underpinning our conduct and actions in part one of Living Humanism, and having discussed these principles and their application in several key contexts, part two of Living Humanism takes the discussion and application of core and other principles into further areas of our lives, focusing specifically on our conduct and actions in support of, and in relation to, our freedom, individuality and autonomy; education and learning; our need to support peace and cooperation, as well as avoiding violence; our personal action in relation to supporting our health and well-being, as well as examining our relationship with our non-human world and the actions we need to take in regard to that non-human world in order to support our own well-being and the well-being of others.

The final chapter of this second part of the guide, brings together the ideas discussed through parts one and two, summarising and consolidating the range of principles, the elements of personal conduct, and the forms of action we need to take, over the range of areas discussed, in order for us to support well-being, and in support of our efforts to reduce and prevent pain and suffering, for both ourselves and others.

# Living Humanism

A Guide to Personal Conduct and
Action for the 21st Century and Beyond

## Part Two

Philip Nathan

Copyright © 2018 Philip Nathan

The moral right of the author has been asserted.

Apart from any fair dealing for the purposes of research or private study, or criticism or review, as permitted under the Copyright, Designs and Patents Act 1988, this publication may only be reproduced, stored or transmitted, in any form or by any means, with the prior permission in writing of the publishers, or in the case of reprographic reproduction in accordance with the terms of licences issued by the Copyright Licensing Agency. Enquiries concerning reproduction outside those terms should be sent to the publishers.

Matador
9 Priory Business Park,
Wistow Road, Kibworth Beauchamp,
Leicestershire. LE8 0RX
Tel: 0116 279 2299
Email: books@troubador.co.uk
Web: www.troubador.co.uk/matador
Twitter: @matadorbooks

ISBN 978 1789010 176

British Library Cataloguing in Publication Data.
A catalogue record for this book is available from the British Library.

Printed and bound by CPI Group (UK) Ltd, Croydon, CR0 4YY
Typeset in 12pt Bembo by Troubador Publishing Ltd, Leicester, UK

Matador is an imprint of Troubador Publishing Ltd

# Contents

**Chapter Ten:** 1
Individuality, Autonomy,
Independence, Freedom and the Social

**Chapter Eleven:** 203
Upbringing, Education, Learning and
Personal Development

**Chapter Twelve:** 318
Pursuing Peace and Cooperation,
and Avoiding Violence

**Chapter Thirteen:** 524
Supporting Health, Wellness and Well-being

**Chapter Fourteen:** 787
Personal Conduct and the Non-Human World

**Chapter Fifteen:** 880
Bringing it All Together – Humanist Personal
Conduct, Well-being, Fulfillment and Happiness

**Coda** 915

**Acknowledgements** 917

**Appendix:** 919
The Principles

**Index** 955

# Ten

# Individuality, Autonomy, Independence, Freedom and the Social

While we are social beings, significantly dependent on others for the enjoyment of lives of well-being, fulfillment and happiness, living through others, supporting and receiving support from others, gaining an important sense of identity through our families and our affiliations and memberships of other groups, and gaining many of the joys and pleasures of life through our relationships with others, it is also the case that in order to support our personal well-being and happiness and the well-being and happiness of others, as required by the core principles set out in this guide, we need to have a strong sense of our own individual selves, our personal identity and individuality, a sense of our separateness, our individual identity aside from others, as well as a sense of our own uniqueness, our own special characteristics and special identity. Similarly our pursuit and achievement of well-being and happiness require us to have a strong sense of our own personal autonomy and independence, a strong sense and belief in our own ability to think, judge, evaluate and indeed take actions autonomously and independently, our actions being capable of being taken, and being taken, in a manner which is not determined, or inappropriately constrained by the thoughts, desires, wants and actions of others. Of course, our pursuit of well-being and happiness also requires our possession, in practice, of the capacities and abilities to determine our thoughts, beliefs and actions.

Possessing these senses, feelings, these various individual characteristics and features, in itself represents an element supportive of our personal well-being, yet also, through having such a strong sense of personal autonomy, a strong sense of our uniqueness and individuality, of personal identity and independence, through our having such abilities and capabilities in terms of independent thought and action, we are better able to contribute not only to our own personal well-being but we are also better able to contribute to the social, to others, to our communities and societies.

Closely tied to these more individually focused characteristics, we need the capacity, ability and self-confidence to assert and be comfortable with our differences from others and to express our difference where we desire to do this. Furthermore, while our difference from others and our individual character and uniqueness is to some degree inevitable given the multitude and complexity of influences on each of us, we will still likely, to some degree, wish and need to act to differentiate ourselves from others (though not always through explicit, conscious decisions and actions), in order to achieve such different states of being, such differential individuality, since our individuality, difference and unique identities are necessary for our well-being and indeed the well-being of others, our communities, societies and beyond, which benefit from our human diversity.

Through such capacities, abilities and self-confidence, as individuals, we will also be free to conform with the desires, expectations, conventions and norms of others, our communities and societies if we so wish and choose to so do, but we will furthermore, also be free from the need to conform inappropriately and sometimes painfully to those desires and expectations, those norms and conventions of others, our communities and societies.

Crucially, in support of our well-being, fulfillment and happiness, we need a strong sense of being free, being free to think and act, being free from unwarranted and unnecessary pressure and constraints, free from personally damaging pressure and constraints on our thoughts and actions, pressures and constraints which may be put in place by others, or may even be self-imposed. We need to be free from damaging constriction, constraint and oppression. And we need to take action to support such a sense of being free, and indeed to support the reality of being free, for ourselves as individuals and for all others.

Our desire for and wish for our personal and individual freedom, independence and autonomy does not dissolve the reality that we are social beings, who need others, who are dependent to an important degree on others, who largely realise our lives through others. Alongside our individuality, our awareness, knowledge and sense of our separate individuality, our separate individual identity, our sense of separateness and our sense of autonomy, we are also fundamentally and integrally part of the whole. We are social – all of us; it is part of our human identity, part of our humanity, whatever our sense of independence and separation, that we live with, engage with and interact with others in the world. We live day-to-day, month-to-month, year-to-year in our families, in our workplaces, in our more local communities and societies, as part of our global humanity.

Our need, want and possession of those characteristics relating to our personal independence, personal and individual identity, our separateness, our freedom, in themselves enhance our well-being and happiness and mean that we can be, in a sense, 'properly social', meaning that we are diverse as a group of individuals, which strengthens the group, and as individuals, we are strong and independent thinkers and actors who through our independence, freedom and autonomy can contribute effectively to others as individuals, and to our groups, and such that we can contribute optimally to both ourselves and all others.

Our actual degree of, and sense of, personal and individual freedom, independence and autonomy, from an individual perspective will be comprised of our varying degrees and levels of physical, emotional and psychological independence and autonomy but also will be influenced in practice by the level of resources we have available (which can mean money), the education, skills and expertise we have and the demand that exists for such skills and abilities. Yet of course our sense of freedom, independence and autonomy will also be influenced substantially by the nature of the community and social context in which we are embedded.

Also relating to our sense of freedom and independence, our personal well-being and happiness is supported by our opportunity, ability and capacity to make our own independent choices, our own decisions about the things we do in our lives, our own capacity to determine our thoughts, beliefs and actions in our own lives and, in the world beyond our immediate situations and circumstances, make our own decisions about for example, where we want to go, where we want to be and indeed who we want to be with. This capacity for individual choice again does not mean we are isolated and non-social human beings, but nevertheless places us with some level of influence and control as an individual over some, if not many of the individual and social happenings in our lives. The ability to make such important personal choices is central to our well-being, happiness and fulfillment. Without having such capacities, such room for personal choice and opportunities, without such room and space for manoeuvre in our lives, in regard to our emotional state, we are likely to experience pain and suffering sometimes, deep-seated frustration, pain, distress, unhappiness, even deep sadness and depression.

As competent adults or for that matter, as competent young adults, to have our choices made for us, is to denude us of an important element of our humanity, that is our autonomy, our freedom, our need and capacity to make such choices and our sense of self and our individuality. Being more specific about some of the choices we should make, we thus need to be able to make decisions about and have responsibility for big decisions in our lives, decisions about our careers, work, education and the more micro-level daily decisions in regard to such apparently small things as our apparel, our style, our look, our hair, our food and drink, the use of our time, those with whom we associate, where we spend our time. We need to be able to make or certainly have the capacity to influence decisions in regard to the things we do at work, in regard to where we go at work, when we go and with whom, and with regard to the vast range of other daily work and other-related decisions.

We certainly, at least the vast majority of us, need this sense of our own independence in order to support our well-being and happiness. Although complete independence is, as has already been suggested, literally, or to all intents and purposes, an impossibility, due to our human social nature and our need for others in both practical and emotional terms (and indeed their need for us), this sense and notion, need and desire for a substantial degree of personal independence has crucial importance and validity for well-being in our individual lives and the lives of our communities, societies and beyond.

Despite our social nature; despite our frequent and indeed general social need for others; despite our need to work and cooperate with others to achieve goals; despite all of this, tied to our general desire for autonomy, freedom and independence, we also have also need and desire for a level of resource-based, economic independence, involving our capacity to, in a metaphorical sense, stand on our own two feet. This, in a sense, gives us a feeling that we have significant personal control over our lives, and indeed is likely to mean that we, to some degree, actually do have an additional level of control over our lives, a consequence of our financial and economic independence being that we will be in a state of some independence from important factors which could undermine our personal security, well-being and happiness.

Yet, if we can achieve such a sense of financial and economic independence, as a consequence of feeling and indeed having such a sense of independence and control, having such a sense of what is in essence, additional freedom and autonomy, this puts upon us an important individual and personal responsibility not only for what we do ourselves and continue to do in order to support our own well-being, but also places on us important and additional responsibility for supporting others, additional significant and personal responsibility for supporting the well-being of others.

Of course such a sense of financial and economic independence does not mean that we are not dependent on others or that we do not need others, because of course, as social human beings we are dependent. Thus, whatever such feelings of financial and other independence and autonomy, in apparent contradiction to this, in practical terms, we will of course need others if we are to achieve anything of substance, and will always retain some dependence on others and will need their cooperation. Moreover with regard to apparent financial and economic independence, such a state of apparent financial and economic independence is likely to be to some degree illusory due to the complex nature of money and economics, with our fortunes and wealth, or that which supports our financial and economic independence, capable of rapidly disappearing for reasons which may be far beyond our control.

In practice, our desire and need to have a sense of control and independence, and to some extent our desire for a sense of freedom as well, means that in practice we need to seek out and acquire enough resources, material, emotional and otherwise, enough skills and abilities as adults, in order to achieve that which we wish to achieve, such that, as a consequence, we can feel that sense of control and such that we do not have too high a degree of need for, and too much dependence on others. And importantly, as such a significantly independent person, we will have the capacity to support and give to, to provide for and support others, our families, communities, societies, and beyond without significantly damaging our own well-being, having the capacity to support those in significant need and hopefully being happy to do so, all of this being admirable, desirable and consistent with core principles of supporting well-being and happiness.

Such independence is in an important sense, part of a state of adulthood, wherein we become, in the main, supporters of others, our communities and societies, of our broader humanity, rather than in the main being supported by others. That is not to say that we are being anti-social and operating outside of core principles if we are unable to express and enjoy such high levels of independence, if we are in a position where we need and receive some support from others, and indeed if we are substantially dependent on others. Indeed it is likely that we will all need some substantial support and help from others at some points in our lives.

Clearly, while our psychological, personal, physical and financial independence and support for such independence is desirable, there can be many reasons, reasons beyond our individual control, which may damage our individual lives and damage our capacity to be independent in these respects, be they more individually focused events such as accident, illness and disability, our own wrong choices and mistakes, or at a broader level, more societal and even global problems, such as those based in economic and political circumstances, unjust discrimination, war, natural disaster or otherwise.

Our sense and feeling of independence can thus, through such circumstances, clearly be compromised and damaged in various ways and if this occurs, we need to act, as far as we can, to regain our independence and self-sufficiency. We should reasonably expect help and support from others in regaining that independence. Where others are in such trying circumstances and need help, it is our role to support their well-being and happiness, to reduce their pain and suffering, and to act to encourage them and to support and move them, wherever we can, towards greater self-sufficiency, autonomy, personal freedom and independence.

More generally, our adulthood does in a sense represent that sense of independence and hopefully represents our having made our own way to such a more independent and self-supporting state. Such a state in which we are able to support ourselves independently in emotional, physical, psychological, financial and other terms, and where we are in a position to act substantially to support others and determine to provide such support, is a desirable state from our individual point of view, from the point of view of supporting our own sense of well-being and happiness and from the point of view of the interests of others, our communities, societies and our broader humanity.

The fact that we are not requiring of substantial financial, resource-based, psychological and practical support from others around us, even though others may wish to help us, and the fact that we are in a position to support others, relieves the need of others to provide us with support and frees the resources and efforts of ourselves and others to support those who are in real need. Of course, in our state of independence we are to some extent denying others the opportunity to be giving towards us, but under such circumstances, these others and ourselves can still fulfill that need to give us support in ways beyond provision of resources, and can give support to others anyway, beneficially and in a directed manner to those in true need, giving to and supporting our communities, societies and beyond in a broader sense in order to support others into the future.

In terms of our individual freedom and autonomy, our well-being requires that we have our own opportunities and freedom to express our thoughts, beliefs and ideas, as well as having such opportunities, freedom and capacity to devise, invent and challenge ideas, challenge versions of truth, challenge orthodoxy and accepted explanations, challenge orthodox and common beliefs and determine and express answers to important (and even less important) questions. We further need opportunities and the freedom to investigate truth and develop our own beliefs and opinions, our own thinking and frames of thinking, proposing our own answers and solutions based in rationality and evidence, with the allied need to be able to determine our own actions in regard to issues which affect our lives more broadly, such as our actions and decisions in relation to deciding our life goals and destinations, how those goals are pursued and how those destinations will be reached.

Making our own choices in the range of important matters in our lives will hopefully lead us to our own achievement of success, with our also contributing substantially to our communities and societies, and achieving our individual and more social goals with accompanying joy, pleasure, well-being and happiness. Of course making our own choices does not mean that we should not seek advice or help from others or that we should not educate ourselves in the range of ways possible, based for example on the spoken words and writings of others, based in our own experiences and the experiences of others, in regard to the choices we and others make. It does mean that we are responsible and we make the decisions and take responsibility for them, that we take responsibility for our wrong actions, our miscalculations and of course our successes and achievements.

Yet, of course, these decisions of ours may also lead to our not achieving our desired goals. We may achieve all of the things we wish to achieve; we may sometimes, if not often, not be successful and may feel an accompanying sense of disappointment and perhaps failure, even deep feelings of inadequacy and incapability. The success of our choices cannot always be assured. The making of choices and the dealing with consequent success and failures when they occur, as already stated, is an important element of our humanity, and is central to our well-being, our more everyday and our broader sense of happiness and fulfillment. Hopefully our successes and achievements will outweigh our failures, will outweigh our non-achievement of goals, and on the whole, for the vast majority of us, they surely will. Based sometimes in our incorrect choices, and sometimes in circumstances which are complex and beyond our control, or for other reasons, there will be errors and mistakes in all of our lives and we have to learn to cope with these and continue on, aiming to enjoy our own well-being and happiness and supporting the well-being and happiness of others, aiming to find more challenges, meeting the challenges we face, developing ourselves personally and hopefully overcoming these challenges.

The reality is that often we will have successes which we need to recognise and give weight to. And we will hopefully often be successful in achieving the things we have decided we wish to achieve. It is far better, in the main, and overall, to have influence over, be involved in and indeed ourselves make those choices which lead to us to success or failure, which determine the courses of our lives, than to have few or no choices and to be coerced or forced into a life which is not of our choosing, being coerced or forced to take actions against our will or volition, or to live in an infant-like acquiescence to the will, wishes, commands and desires of others, acquiescence at variance with our human feelings, our emotions and needs, a life in which, while in some cases, we may be get by and have some well-being, we are likely to feel substantially unhappy and dissatisfied, as if our lives have not been lived to the full.

Unhappiness and dissatisfaction are also of course possible with our living lives of substantial choice, though in the case of where decisions are not substantially our own, decisions which do not take into account who we are, what we want and how we feel, we are likely to more frequently suffer and to suffer more substantially than where we are making our own choices and where we can, for example, change our minds. Admittedly in situations where others are commanding, coercing and forcing, then, if we cannot throw off or prevent their coercion and force, we might perhaps have the unworthy consolation of blaming others for our pain and unhappiness, yet in some contexts and situations, our pain and suffering may be substantive, in certain conflict situations, sometimes final and terminal, with such capacity to blame, being effectively of no consequence.

As far as we can, we need to be ensuring we make or contribute to decisions that affect our lives, such that they are our either our own decisions, that they are substantially our own or at least in part our own. Our choices, our decisions, often taken after consultation with others, taken with advice from others, choices which are aimed at helping us achieve our wishes, our dreams, or which are perhaps contributing components of our group decisions which are aimed at achieving group and team goals, are a necessary part of our fulfillment as human beings, are core elements of our individuality and autonomy and are crucial for us to achieve maximal well-being and happiness.

Thus, beyond the decisions affecting our own more individual lives, as part of our individuality and as part of our need and desire for well-being and fulfillment, we need to ensure we have the opportunities to make choices, decisions, and important decisions not only about our own lives, but also have the opportunity and reality of making contributions to the decisions made by our families, organisations, communities and societies, and beyond, many, if not all of which decisions, in some way or other, will affect our own individual lives. And our social entities also need to ensure that we as individuals have the opportunity for contributions to decisions and considerations of our social groups, especially where these are of significant relevance to our individual well-being.

So with regard to the communities and societies we live in, as well as our broader human community, we need to be engaged in the decisions and decision processes which affect our lives and which affect our communities and societies more broadly. This again, is seen as a deeply human, personal and individual need, as well as representing a social need which must be met. That is not to say that our own personal and individual voices within our communities and societies will be louder than the voices of others or that it is our wants, needs and desires which will trump the wants needs and desires of others. Yet each of us needs to be listened to, and have the capacity to contribute in some manner to our communities' and societies' decisions and choices.

Thus, on the whole, we frequently if not perhaps, almost always, feel that need to comment on and contribute to the events that are taking place in our communities and societies and wish to feel consulted, included and taken account of, in regard to decisions being made, our being unable to do this being detrimental to our well-being and the well-being of our communities, societies and beyond. Being ignored and not taken account of is damaging to our well-being and happiness and, if frequent and widespread, creates a sense of alienation and division within our communities, and beyond, leading to anger, unrest, unhappiness. It also leads to the likelihood of poor decision-making because we are not all consulted and leads to ineffective action and implementation since those of us whose contributions, cooperation and agreement may be necessary or perhaps useful, have not engaged in the decision-making process.

The responsibility to contribute and participate lies with both ourselves and our wider communities, societies and beyond. If we have made no effort and provided ourselves with no time to engage and participate in choice-making and decision-making within our communities then we can have little grounds for reasonable complaint about decisions which are made. That being said, the demands of our relationships, our work, our daily lives can certainly serve to deprive us of important time and space to think about, contribute to and take actions within our communities and societies. However, while our lives may be busy with work, family and leisure pursuits amongst other things, whilst sometimes we may feel tired and distracted, we do need to give some priority to our broader community and social decision-making, and ensure that some time is set aside for our contributions to our communities and societies, and ensure that we do engage in some form or other of broader contribution in a continuous manner.

That being said, we also need to ensure that our communities and societies are organised such that we can make our contributions, such that that there is meaningful and effective consultation, and that we all do, in reality, have an opportunity to contribute. Work and our other concerns must not drain too much of our time such that we cannot be involved in our communities, societies and beyond. And we must also not focus so much on our immediate enjoyment of personal leisure and pleasure with the consequence that we have no time to meaningfully engage in important local and broader, community and societal decisions.

Not only is our personal wish and desire to contribute to the decisions of our families, communities, societies and beyond, a deep psychological need and want, but it is the case that without our contributions, our interests and concerns will most likely not be presented and discussed and they will not be influential in regard to social decisions, resulting in the already mentioned detriment to our well-being, with the potential, if not the likelihood, that our interests will be ignored. As a consequence we may become victims of these social decisions, perhaps even seriously damaged by these decisions, damage which can occur in a vast range of different ways.

Aside from our need and desire to make our own choices, our need and desire for a sense of independence, and our need and desire for freedom and autonomy, an important reality is that our well-being and happiness, in both the individual and personal sense, and in regard to the well-being and happiness of others in our communities, societies and beyond, also requires that, should we want it, at least at some times we have our own individual space, our own physical and mental space, our own space away from the crowd, away from the bombardment and welter of opinions and ideas we are exposed to and which are given, solicited or unsolicited by others. Sometimes we need space aside from the oppression of conformity and social convention; our own space in which we can be free to experiment in our actions, experiment with our thoughts and perhaps also, aspects of our behaviour, space in which we can be free to break conventions, to act irrationally if we choose to, in which we can make errors, our own errors; space where we can be free to enjoy silence without interruption and disturbance, where we can be free to think of nothing at all, if we so choose. Such personal space, available at least at some time, is necessary for our well-being and happiness. Our minds also need to be our private space, where we can experiment with thought, think what might be considered and may be perverse thoughts if we wish, where we can be and know ourselves, without unwanted and unwarranted intrusion, questioning and investigation. And we need to act to ensure that we, as individuals as well as all others have such physical and mental space available to us.

In addition to needing our own separate mental and physical space, our well-being and happiness require, by apparent contrast, that we have the freedom, capacity and ability to meet with others, to enjoy the company of others, the opportunity and freedom to pursue friendships, to have a sense of belonging and togetherness, and also that we have the opportunity to, with the consent of those others, access the experiences of these others, the thoughts, ideas produced by others, such that we can know of and enjoy those experiences and ideas, and as a consequence develop, learn and, if we so wish, modify or change what we do, who we are, how we conduct ourselves and how we live, enabling us to learn and grow throughout our lives, such learning providing us with opportunities and routes to improve our well-being. All of this is necessary for our individual well-being and the well-being of all, benefiting our personal health and enjoyment of life as well as enabling us to provide much to others, through our autonomy, freedom and independent action, these, in themselves, serving to support others, our communities, societies and beyond. We need to act to support such togetherness and sharing, such individual learning and personal growth and change. All of this is likely to support our own personal and individual well-being, our personal happiness and the broader well-being and happiness too.

In line with our social nature, our well-being not only requires our strong sense of autonomy and sense of independence and individuality, but it also requires that we engage with and interact with others, this engagement and interaction benefiting us in many ways. Unless we link with others, engage in joint enterprise with others, cooperate with others, the likelihood is that our own well-being and the well-being of others, our own positive actions to achieve our well-being and happiness and to support the well-being and happiness of others, are unlikely to result in the achievement of that well-being. And without these connections with others, our effective cooperative interactions, our well-being and happiness and the well-being and happiness of others are likely to be severely damaged.

In terms of both our social needs and our individuality, our well-being and happiness require that, alongside our sense of individuality and independence, together with our interactions and engagement with others, we have a sense of belonging, a sense and feeling of being part of the whole, that we feel connected to and a part of our families, our communities, societies, and additionally and perhaps most importantly, part of the world of people, part of the whole which is our humanity. As part of that sense of belonging, alongside our sense of individuality, autonomy and separateness, a high level of well-being and happiness will almost always require us to have some form of relationships, positive and caring relationships, and attachment to other people, these relationships being of crucial importance to us, to our well-being and happiness.

While solitude, being alone in our personal space, being free from demands, free to enjoy personal pleasures, having that space in which to be on our own and in which we can be our private selves, is generally necessary, healthy and enjoyable, our well-being is almost always likely to require us, at a minimum, to have functional, caring, intimate, as well as transactional everyday relationships with others. And as individuals, our recognising this, we need to do what we can to make sure we have, experience and enjoy all forms of relationship, especially the deeper, more supportive, positive and caring relationships, in our lives.

Indeed it is undoubtedly the case that, while we have our desire and need for autonomy, a desire for independence and freedoms from what may sometimes be the demanding, indeed oppressive demands of others, we are also vulnerable to pain and suffering through the absence of interactions with others, through being ignored, through feelings of being of no or little significance to others, through our rejection by others, in particular by those we are close to and love deeply.

Also, in an important sense, as more isolated individuals, aside from others, on our own, we can become vulnerable to the oppressive, callous, uncaring and sometimes violent and destructive actions of others. While we need our freedom, autonomy and independence, such positive characteristics of our life can only be fully enjoyed in truly secure environments which comprise and embody effective safe and secure social foundations in which we are safe from pain, suffering and oppressive action. Of course our freedom, autonomy and a degree of independence represent part of that effective social foundation.

This need of ours for others, for our social relationships, for social interaction, for self-protection and indeed for others to care for and sometimes or more often, to look after; our need for others whose well-being and happiness we can and indeed must support; all these needs mean that we cannot simply pursue our own personal goals in a negatively selfish manner, only looking after ourselves, but instead we need to cooperate with and support the well-being and happiness of others, something which of course benefits ourselves.

And relating to this need for others and our concern for not only our personal well-being but also for the well-being and happiness of others, we must take into account and take appropriate actions which enable us to live well with others in our families, communities and societies, indeed which enable us to live well in our world together with the rest of humanity. To an important degree, both in relation to supporting the well-being of others and ourselves, we therefore have to be aware of, take into account and, where appropriate, necessary and desirable, act to accommodate, at least to some extent, the wants, the needs, the feelings, the interests, the well-being and happiness of others. And we as individuals also need to reach accommodations consistent with core and other principles, where appropriate, such that our actions meet important social requirements of living in families, communities and societies. As a consequence, in regard to some actions we can take, there are, there need to be, and indeed must be, self-imposed or externally imposed constraints on the things we do as individuals, constraints on our personal conduct, on our actions. Our personal freedom cannot be total, allowing us to do all we wish to do.

More specifically, in regard to those constraints, in terms of our own personal well-being and the well-being of others, we clearly, cannot and should not act in ways which are significantly destructive, detrimental and damaging to others. We should not take actions where those actions are taken with the goal of achieving short-term or longer-term personal benefit for ourselves at the significant expense of, damage to, and detriment of others. Behaving in a manner motivated by perhaps our short-term negatively selfish impulses, our short-term or immediate negatively selfish desires, our personally, individual and negatively selfish, self-focused short or longer term goals, our negatively selfish short-term wishes and wants, acting in ways where there is some significant damage and harm or where there is likely potential significant harm to others, is entirely unacceptable.

Such negatively selfish actions, carried out by ourselves or by others will be damaging to both ourselves and others, damaging to our families, our communities and our societies, and will likely be damaging, to some degree, to our humanity as a whole. Such negatively selfish and self-focused actions harm the well-being of others and ourselves. They may cause real physical and emotional harm to others and through their effects on community and society, such actions run the risk of causing widespread and severe harm. Such actions, in their damage to well-being and happiness are inconsistent with core principles and we must take great care to avoid such actions.

As our negatively selfish actions can damage others (and ourselves), as a consequence, in order to function in a society, as already mentioned, there must clearly be some self-imposed or socially imposed limits and constraints on our personal and individual choices in terms of our individual actions and our personal freedoms and independence. These precise limits and constraints are undoubtedly in some respects complex and difficult to establish and define. And these difficult to define, complex limits must apply, in line with notions of justice and fairness, to all others in our communities, societies and beyond, as well.

To paraphrase this in clearer terms, we cannot do exactly as we wish in our lives; we cannot simply engage in acts which benefit ourselves without regard to the consequences of our actions for others, not only because that is not what we would normally wish to do as social beings, but significantly because our conduct affects others and can, if carried out without sufficient thought and care, or if inappropriate, substantially damage others. And others likewise, cannot do exactly as they wish, cannot simply engage in acts without regard to us as individuals and others, because their conduct affects us all as individuals. And the actions of these others can, if negatively selfish, if inappropriate and done without sufficient thought and care, damage us and damage others.

The broader well-being and the longer term well-being of both ourselves and others are not supported by such negatively selfish actions which damage others. While it is part of our humanity to be social, to interact with, to cooperate and work with others, to work with appropriate sociability, nevertheless our ability to cooperate with, interact with and support others needs to be taught and learn about. While growing up, indeed throughout our lives, we must be taught about, learn about, experience and furthermore develop, a knowledge and understanding of how to live well and socially, in a manner that not only promotes our own well-being but which also supports the well-being and happiness of others. We must also know and understand the nature of negatively selfish actions and the consequences of such negatively selfish actions, as well as ensuring that others are taught about and recognise the consequences of such actions.

While it might be the case, given our fundamental social and cooperative human character and nature, that we each of us has the capacity, in all cases to select, and as social entities we have the capacity to select, the correct and most appropriate actions to support our own well-being and happiness and the well-being and happiness of others, this, in reality would seem highly unlikely, especially given the frequency of decisions we need to make, given the complexity of many decisions and actions we need to take, given the complex nature of consequences, our capacity for misjudgments and a range of other factors.

Indeed we are all required and indeed must constrain and restrain ourselves, if we experience short-term and longer-term impulses, desires and wishes which, if we act upon them, will harm others and may harm ourselves. As emphasised through this guide, in support of our well-being and happiness and the well-being and happiness of others, as integrally social beings, we all need to take responsibility for our actions and conduct in order to avoid negatively selfish conduct, and will likely need to place constraints and restrictions on our own individual personal conduct and behaviour to some degree, in some, if not many cases, perhaps to a significant degree. In some, if not many cases in our daily lives and beyond, we must therefore apply significant self-control, self-regulation, and self-restraint and constraint, such that we ourselves and others can enjoy well-being and happiness in safe, cooperative, effective and functioning, communities, societies and in the wider world, our appropriate conduct serving to support not only our own well-being but the well-being of others too (something which of course in itself can promote our own well-being).

While certain anti-social negatively selfish individual actions, apparently open to us, may seem tempting, indeed substantially tempting, indeed in circumstances where there may be the opportunity for taking self-benefiting actions which we judge others may never even know about, we must in any case restrain and constrain ourselves from carrying out such acts, recognising their damaging consequences for others as individuals and for our communities and societies, as well as recognising in the longer term, potential damage for ourselves. Further, we need to develop our sense and understanding of both ourselves, others and the communities, societies, including our global community, that we live in, such that we can recognise and desist from the individual actions we might sometimes take which, sometimes without any selfish or damaging intent, might inadvertently or otherwise, result in harm to others.

And if we are unable to constrain and restrain ourselves and there are significantly damaging consequences or the prospect of such damaging consequences as a result of our actions or potential actions; if there is such severe harm to others or in prospect for others due to such unintended or negatively selfish actions; if self-restraint and our own personal awareness, sense of care for others; if our constraints on our own actions do not operate effectively, then it is likely that in support of ourselves and our own well-being, in support of the well-being of others, in order to support our communities and societies, there will be a need for our wider community and society or even our more global entities, to apply and enforce constraints and restrictions on us, preventing our negatively selfish and damaging conduct, in order to ensure the well-being of all, thereby avoiding substantial and unnecessary pain and suffering. And for ourselves as individuals, those not engaged in such negatively selfish actions, we will need to support others, our communities and societies in implementing such constraints and restraints on those committing such destructive and damaging acts, with the aim of supporting individual, community, societal and global well-being.

Living with others in any context therefore, is likely to require, and in all cases, in reality, does involve this self-imposition, self-restraint and where necessary imposition of certain constraints and restrictions on our own personal conduct and behaviour and the conduct and behaviour of others, or more specifically on those of our and others' personal and individual behaviours which would offer significant damage to ourselves and others. Such restraints and constraints may in some cases, in serious cases where others have been or may be damaged significantly, mean there is a need to place significant restrictions on individuals, restrictions which will be significantly detrimental to them such as incarceration away from ourselves and others, on account of the dangers and threats that their actions may offer to other individuals, to others, the rest of our community, society and in some cases globally.

Such restrictions are well known to us, often being presented, framed and interpreted as punishments and are applied in almost all cases for what are presented as and considered to be the most heinous acts and other socially and individually damaging acts. The obvious case in point, for example, is our response to those causing, or threatening to cause others deliberate physical injury. It is clear that those individuals who plan to physically injure others, who have physically injured others, perhaps murdered or committed rape and serious, damaging violent acts, and who may do so in the future, represent a threat to the well-being of all of us and will almost certainly need to be, through the use of force, kept out of community and society, away from others to whom they offer a threat, whom they might damage, this removal from community and society persisting at the minimum until such threats are disappeared and the individual understands the unacceptability, the damaging nature of their actions and until we are certain they will not, or it seems they are extremely unlikely, to commit such violent destructive threats or actions again. Such restraint and constraint are necessary for the benefit of us all. Such destructive and damaging actions by these individuals, or even by groups, cannot be allowed to go unchecked because of the damage, pain and suffering and potential damage, pain and suffering that has been caused or might be caused to other individuals, our communities, societies and to our broader humanity.

Such restrictions need to be imposed in a humane manner, without the unnecessary infliction of pain and suffering on those who are being restrained or constrained, providing them with opportunities for change, addressing their conduct, giving opportunities for education and personal development, offering routes to a better future, while ensuring, as far as possible, that these opportunities will not enhance their capacity for committing more damaging acts.

Similar such restrictions on freedoms and actions may be applied for lesser damaging actions by individuals, such as theft and fraud, criminal damage, threatening actions, corruption and a range of other socially unacceptable actions, contrary to core and other principles, which damage others significantly and substantially. Individuals committing such acts may well require some form of restriction, alongside the mentioned addressing of their conduct, efforts at education and provision of an opportunity to change, in order to ensure that such actions are not repeated or even promoted or encouraged through lack of such an appropriate and restrictive response from ourselves, community and society, as well as through lack of an educational and developmental response. For allowing damaging and destructive conduct and behaviour to go unchecked will not only mean such damaging and destructive conduct is likely to continue, but also runs the risk of encouraging such conduct and behaviour into the future, not only by those who have behaved in such ways, but also through the potential encouraging of others to engage in such conduct and behaviour into the future.

Damaging actions which may interfere with our own freedoms, our own individuality, our own well-being, can originate from a range of sources, and not simply from those we do not know or whom we are not familiar with. Clearly, those individuals in our families, communities and societies, and also these entities as social entities themselves, can in some instances, act to damage us as individuals, as well as damaging themselves through, for example, unwarranted and unnecessary efforts to constrain and restrict our individual actions, our expression of our feelings, opinions, attitudes and beliefs. These individuals and entities may implement such damaging and destructive restrictions on our actions and expression, perhaps with the goal of aiming to preserve personal or group power, and perhaps in some cases to preserve something termed as unity, which may in reality, represent that same desire for personal and group power. There may be efforts to constrain and restrict our thinking and action, efforts to damage or restrict our expression of our individual sense of self, efforts to damage our sense of self-value and self-respect, our sense and actuality of personal autonomy, separateness and independence, sometimes through taking actions which are violent, physically and emotionally threatening or otherwise destructive and restrictive which may directly inflict significant, damaging, physical and emotional pain on us, but which also in essence, unnecessarily, destructively and damagingly affect our independence, autonomy freedom and freedoms.

More specifically, and indeed often, such damage towards us may be inflicted through the motivations and actions of those individuals in positions of power and influence within families, communities and societies, those who may be unable to accept legitimate and reasonable challenge, those who feel personally and otherwise under threat in terms of their power and control and who wish to maintain and bolster their positions of authority and power. Such actions may be carried out to restrict the actions of, or harm those of us who do not conform to expectations, desired behaviours or social norms, who perhaps through our non-conformity, interpreted as a challenge to power and the powerful, are seen as threats to individuals, communities, systems and societies, even when we as individuals, through our speech and actions are caring for others, our communities and societies, and represent no such threat to others, and offer no threat of pain and suffering.

While those of us who challenge and promote the new and different may sometimes be wrong and misguided, it is frequently the case that such restraints and restrictions, such destructive actions against us, such threats of violence and social ostracism, additional to and alongside those mentioned motivations arising from wishing to exercise and maintain power, also arise from irrational and unevidenced beliefs and fears. Such restraints, restrictions, threats and indeed actions, may be imposed due to historic and false systems of thinking which themselves, in reality and in fact, serve to damage individuals, community and society. Such destructive and damaging actions may be pursued by those individuals and groups who may sincerely believe they are acting for the best, through the seriously mistaken beliefs they hold, through their fear of change and fear of difference, through a lack of knowledge or misjudgment, through fear of losing their own power and influence, through perhaps an emotional disconnect with the feelings of others or disconnect with and misunderstanding of the nature of well-being and happiness. Through their incorrect and destructive beliefs, such people and such groups may do us and others, our communities, societies and beyond, tremendous damage and cause significant if not vast levels of pain and suffering.

In some families, communities and other social contexts, such powerful and influential people may attempt to say they are emphasising the well-being of family, community and society as the basis for their decisions and actions in restricting freedoms, in restricting autonomy and independence. They may say that they are supporting stability. Yet, often, in fact they will be acting to retain their own personal power and the power of the groups they lead or represent, acting to suit their own personal economic interests, or sometimes simply opposing change through fear of such change and fear of an unknown and different future. Rather than pursuing dialogue with change, something which would be likely to support peacefulness and cooperation, well-being and happiness, they are in fact almost certain to be causing damage through the restrictions and constraints they impose, and the threats and violence they promote and carry out, causing damage not only to the specific individual or individuals directly affected but, in the medium and longer term, causing substantial damage to individuals, family, community and society and, in the end, to all.

Not only can it be the actual specific, unwarranted and unnecessary, damaging and destructive intention and goal to act to constrain and restrict the actions, freedoms, expression of feelings and beliefs of individuals, which lead to pain and suffering, but in particular the mechanisms that may be adopted to implement such unwarranted and unnecessary restrictions, many of these mechanisms representing in themselves direct attacks on our freedom, independence and autonomy. Such methods, which can also operate at the family and more community level as well as in wider contexts may involve coercion, threats to well-being, oppressive behaviour which may vary in degree, cruelty, violence and threats of violence, directly creating pain and suffering, placing people in poverty and more.

The reality is that we, as individuals, very probably almost everyone of us, and if not, very many if not the vast majority of us, place a great deal of value on our autonomy, our freedom of belief and expression of belief, our independence, and as a consequence, we often do not acquiesce easily to such restrictions, with some of us often acting vigorously to defend them. We will act, and should act in a robust manner to protect our sense of individuality, independence, freedoms and autonomy, these being crucial to our well-being and happiness.

With regard to the more legitimate restrictions and constraints on our conduct and behaviour, and these certainly do, and it is considered here, certainly should exist, these restrictions can be present in our lives informally as unwritten and unspoken shared mutual understandings, as unrecorded and unwritten practices, being found for example, within the home and family environment but also, to some extent, in wider cultural contexts. Yet in the modern world, on the wider scale (and also sometimes in families), optimally, such accepted ways of behaving are almost always present and codified to some degree in our laws or in the form of written codes of conduct and rules which establish for us the bounds of what it is considered we must not do and further, what we can do unconstrained, in relation to our actions within our communities, societies and beyond, in regard to our actions which affect others or which may be seen as affecting others.

Such codes, rules and laws where present, will also tend to lay down sanctions and responses and consequences for breach of these codes, rules and laws. These codes of conduct, rules and laws need to be designed to enhance our well-being and happiness, the well-being and happiness of us all, and need to serve to protect us from injury, harm, suffering and pain, and this well-being applies to those who transgress these rules and laws as well as the rest of our communities, societies and beyond. They further need to be formulated in a manner which encourages participation and support for these laws, rules and codes, in a manner which encourages well-being in our communities and societies, and formulated to maximise our spaces and our freedoms within the necessary social constraints. Such codes, rules and laws need to be consistent, indeed clearly consistent with core and other principles, and need also to be applied consistently in support of fairness and justice.

Where others significantly threaten the well-being and happiness of others, threatening or causing significant pain and suffering, then these rules, codes of conduct will state that their actions will need to be constrained. And this is likely to require, particularly in the case of those who offer or are engaged in violence and violent threat, the use of restraining force, if not overwhelming restraining and force to prevent their violent actions. Though such force will aim to restrain and constrain, it must not aim to cause direct painful physical harm, and must indeed aim to preserve, as far as possible, the physical and emotional well-being of those offering such threats, without placing those engaged in the constraint and restraint under unnecessary risk to themselves, ensuring that these people, indeed that all people, are as far as possible protected and safe.

While these codes of conduct, laws and rules should be used in support of our well-being and happiness and to protect us from suffering and pain, unfortunately they can be used by those who are powerful as routes to oppression and suppression incorporating the promotion of conformity and illegitimately restricting our conduct, freedoms and actions. Others, authorities, those in power, can impose such codes, rules and laws which harm us and harm others, which damage our individual well-being, the well-being of others, our communities and societies and the world beyond, and which aim to prevent us from opposing oppression and the destruction and damage it causes.

In such circumstances it is legitimate to act to aim to modify or to remove these unjust codes, rules and laws and indeed to refuse to follow them, as they are inconsistent with core principles, such rules, codes and laws being oppressive, damaging of our freedom, autonomy and independence and in particular because they are causing significant harm, suffering and pain to ourselves and others.

Apart from our formally written down, rules, codes of conduct and laws, we may also be limited, constrained and indeed restrained in our actions through the existence of the unwritten social and cultural norms and conventions already referred to above, behaviours which are not dealt with in written legislation, which do not appear to be actions which could seriously damage others, but which in fact comprise norms and conventions which we are expected to abide by.

Exemplifying the constraints placed upon us in such unwritten forms, our use of language and our actions are, for example, constrained by factors such as the social situation in which we are operating, with the use of certain taboo or uncustomary language, with challenging attitudes towards others as well as certain physical or behavioural habits, frowned upon, with moreover, certain topics or even political views and opinions considered to be inappropriate or beyond the pale, in social situations. The use of such language and the discussion of such topics as well as our engaging in other actions considered unacceptable in certain social situations, can lead to social opprobrium and even social ostracism for us, and in some places and cultures can even lead to violence, even though not identified by the community and society as worthy of legal sanction or specifically outlawed.

Use of appropriate, recognised, accepted and acceptable behaviour may be necessary in order for us to be accepted by a community and may often need to be understood and adopted in order to get things done and in order to achieve success. However, where possible and reasonable, we need to act to ensure that unnecessary and indeed, damaging norms and conventions, are challenged and changed. Cultural norms and conventions which are inappropriate and which contradict our desire and need for independence, freedom and autonomy, which damage our well-being and happiness, need to be removed or changed, even if they may be sometimes, if not often, deeply embedded in our communities, societies and cultures. Such change can sometimes take a significant time to achieve due to the deep embeddedness of certain views, behaviours and attitudes.

In what might be seen as an issue of individuality of less significance to our personal well-being and happiness, though it certainly is, in fact, of some significant importance, our dress, our clothing may be laid down or prescribed in certain contexts. In certain jurisdictions, the state, the government, the powerful set down what citizens can wear, something which is entirely unacceptable, indicating that most likely a wide range of other freedoms are denied to people in those jurisdictions. What we wear under such circumstances is not a matter of social and culture convention. But cultural norms and conventions may well apply in the work environment, with departing from these norms potentially earning substantial disapproval. Yet where such conventions are unnecessary for effective work performance, for safety or for other purposes it is certainly reasonable to challenge such norms.

On more social occasions the convention and norm may be that a suit or other item of formal clothing is expected of us if we attend, for example, a wedding. In such circumstances informal and untidy wear might be considered rude, insulting and anti-social, having the potential to be seen as an insult to those being married, stating in essence that the married couple didn't matter to us, as demonstrated through our lack of care and attention to our appearance on what, for the married couple and others, may well be a very special occasion. Our conformity to norms on such occasions does remain a matter of personal judgment and there may be important reasons for us as individuals, which underpin why we would wish to break with these norms and conventions. Nevertheless, we would certainly need to take into account the possible effects of our actions on others, that is, on the well-being and happiness of others.

There are many other social and cultural customs that we may do well to follow, especially when living and working in cultures which are not familiar to us. While others in those cultures might excuse our conduct if we are not a member of such a culture, should we not follow these customs, there may well be negative consequences for us, which may in some contexts, be very serious indeed. Yet if we are familiar with and practice such cultural conventions and norms, in cases where others break such conventions, we should not ourselves be too harsh or admonitory. Dependent on their perceived and real motives, these non-physically threatening, likely harmless breaches of norms and conventions, can be seen, and often need to be taken as, in reality minor transgressions, if transgressions at all, these being transgressions about which we should take little or no action beyond, perhaps, informative words, and even such informative words may be undesirable and unnecessary. It is highly unlikely that such peaceful transgression of conventions will do any real damage to ourselves or others. A peaceful response and understanding response is undoubtedly best.

If someone turns up in an unkempt state to a wedding, it may be seen as insulting and not good conduct, yet there may be many good reasons for this, which we could initially make an effort to investigate before uttering admonition and condemnation, and hopefully, though we and others may be a little upset, the actual real harm may be minimal, though alternately, as such a wedding is an important occasion, there may be those who are mortally offended and may disparage and disrespect us for a long time into the future should we dress ourselves in such a careless manner. For the rest of us, investigating, taking no or little notice of the person who is unkempt, and simply letting things be at the time will most likely be the best strategy, though making it known explicitly, quietly and peaceably, where appropriate, that offence has been taken, may well be advisable as not all of us realise when we are breaking such codes and customs.

Of course we can challenge social norms and conventions, and there should be no significant harm resulting for us if we refuse to conform to those expectations, as our actions will often be producing little real harm to anyone, with well-being and happiness generally, not significantly affected. Our challenge to rules and conventions may in some cases be appropriate and welcomed, serving to help remove over-conformity and over-conservatism though, of course, such challenge may well not be welcomed by some.

As already stated, but worthy of emphasising, we ourselves, in seeing and experiencing such breach of conventions by others, need to be tolerant of those who make such challenges, perhaps being questioning, and perhaps expressing a level of disapproval when this is legitimate, but also being tolerant and understanding where appropriate on the grounds of supporting the important freedom, independence, non-conformity and individuality which are crucial to the well-being of all of us, especially when these actions are in essence harmless and where they occur in a context in which such actions do little or no real damage to others.

Overall, however, it is clear that while we hope to have, and indeed should have, a high level of autonomy, independence and personal freedom, our individual choice of action cannot be unlimited, but may be legitimately under certain circumstances, constrained and restricted by ourselves and our own thinking and decisions, by our responsibilities in terms of supporting the well-being and happiness of others, supporting other individuals, families, communities and societies, and by the communities, societies and our humanity around us, also with the goal of supporting well-being and happiness, and supporting those families, communities and societies (as well as our broader humanity). It is hoped that in the broader sense, where our individual choice of action is constrained and restricted, this will, in reality support our own personal well-being and happiness in the round as well as the happiness and well-being of others. These restrictions may be determined by ourselves through our understanding of core and other principles and well-being, both the well-being of ourselves and others, but may also be imposed in systematic form by our families, communities and broader society.

In our daily lives we need to act to ensure that both ourselves and others are, as far as possible, able to act with independence, freedom and autonomy, that we support others and ourselves in developing individuality, identity and separateness, and that we and all others, have the personal and psychological space that we all need, within the essential constraints of our social needs, our social goals and our social identitie,s and in a manner consistent with the core principles, our well-being and happiness, and the well-being and happiness of others.

Within our close families, where we have children, we need to ensure that our children are supported in their learning and development, such that they can move successfully towards greater independence and personal autonomy. Our children need to be given every opportunity that we can give them, such that they can pursue their dreams, the goals that they choose, and such that they can learn and develop in line with their own personal interests and needs, moving towards a fulfilled life of well-being and happiness in which, at key points, and as they grow older, in an ongoing and increasing manner, they will have been critical in influencing, deciding and determining, the directions they have taken and the goals which they have decided to pursue in their lives.

We need to support and develop the capacities of our children as they grow, supporting them to make choices, appropriate and optimal choices, giving them opportunities to choose, which of course will sometimes mean them making the wrong choices and making wrong judgments. While certain choices may need to be restricted for the youngest, such opportunities to engage in choice-making need to be increased with age, with increasing levels of contribution to important life decisions. We need to provide a sense of real choices being available appropriate to age, where there are, for older children, important choices to be made, rather than offering trivial peripheral and unimportant choices as exercises in making choice, false and unimportant choices being something which children will easily sense as being unreal and unimportant. The capacity and requirement for making real decisions and for making choices which have real consequences, is part of our human experience. Allowing such to take place is an important element of education, which, of course, is not just a school-based formal educational system exercise, but is something which needs to run through and indeed inevitably runs through, our lives.

Of course, as parents, we will have views about the correctness and desirability of the directions chosen, the actions and life prospects of our children, and indeed we have a responsibility to help them, as far as we can, and as far as is reasonable, towards making the best decisions. We have a responsibility in supporting their well-being, happiness, success and achievement in terms of where they wish to go with their lives, their directions, their journeys, their careers, their futures. However, we are not our children, or the young adults, or the adults they will become. Our children are in the process of developing their own individuality, their own unique personalities, interests and goals, their own constellation of skills, abilities, wants and desires, and it is our role to support them, advise them and help them as far as we can, but it is not our role to decide their lives for them.

Yet, that being said, as parents, we need to ensure, as far as we can, that our children are able to and do, as far as we can reasonably determine, behave socially, that they are able, as far as we can ensure it, to understand and recognise the needs and interests of others, appreciating the differences between people, the uniqueness of others, such that they and those others are able to allow others room and personal space in which to make their own judgments and decisions. We need to support our children in their upbringing such that they understand and respect, indeed enjoy, the individuality of others, the differences between us, and further, we need to do what we can to ensure that they are not and do not become the oppressors of others themselves. We need to do as much as we can to ensure that our children are able to appreciate and enjoy individuality and differences (as well as commonalities), such that they are able to support those who act in caring, reasonable ways and indeed those who do not, both supporting themselves as individuals in terms of their own well-being and happiness and supporting the well-being and happiness of others, including those who do not wish to conform, and do not conform in ways which might sometimes find the disapproval of others.

During the period when our children are growing up, it is likely, if not a certainty, that at some point, particularly at younger ages, they will behave badly towards others, in particular other children, behaving in selfish ways, and sometimes, especially at a very young age, behaving aggressively, with negative selfishness, and perhaps with an unacceptable, though generally physically trivial, though not psychologically, trivial, level of violence towards others. Our children need to be taught and must learn as far as we can help them to learn, that such conduct is not acceptable. They must know and learn that there is no freedom to hurt others in such ways, to damage, to act aggressively towards, or seriously and otherwise hurt others, and we need to teach them, in as gentle and caring, but as effective a manner as is possible, of this unacceptability.

Aside from bringing up our children, as partners and parents, while we are part of our families, and though we are integral parts of our families, we still most likely wish to have our own sense of independence and individuality, our own personal mental and physical space, and we should therefore act to ensure that we have such space and should reasonably expect, commensurate with fulfilling our family and other social responsibilities, that others will accommodate our more individual needs. This separate personal independence and, to some extent, separateness is seen as supporting our own personal well-being and happiness, but is also seen as strengthening the family, strengthening togetherness, allowing us to be stronger individuals who can contribute better towards the family and support that family effectively. We clearly need to ensure this for our partners too, supporting them in achieving their personal and more individual dreams where we can. One of our dreams, one of our goals, will be of course to have a happy family, a wonderful relationship with our partner and to have good, if not wonderful and enjoyable, relationships with our more distant family. All of this is supported in families where we, as parents and partners, do our utmost to sustain and develop our identities and practices as capable, independent and autonomous adults, part of, embedded in and contributing to our families.

Our families and our other relationships need therefore to support our freedoms, our independence and autonomy, supporting us emotionally and otherwise in pursuing those goals and activities, consistent with core principles, which we wish to pursue and which are concomitant with having a family, with having partners to love and children to bring up and support. So we have to realise and recognise that, of course, our families and relationships can, and often do, directly or inadvertently place restrictions on our actions because of our responsibilities to our partners, to our children, sometimes to parents and also to other family members. We have responsibilities to meet their needs, and indeed their wants, and we will want to meet their needs and meet our responsibilities. There may be tensions at times between our different personal goals, our different wants and desires, but we may well need to sacrifice achieving some of our more separate and personal goals, reduce some of our more individual commitments, and commitments outside of the family, give up some of the freedoms of independent and more solitary living, perhaps sacrifice substantial personal freedoms, sacrifice personal time, because we have, have committed to and have taken on responsibilities towards our partners and our children, as well as needing, at times to look after and care for the well-being of other family members.

This is something which we, hopefully, have consciously decided to do, with full awareness of what we were deciding to do, with the knowledge of the effects this is likely to have on our personal lives, but recognising our families as supporting our own greater well-being and happiness including through our commitment and love for others, our love for our partners and families, and through, hopefully, their love and care for us. Thus we will have decided, hopefully, with full knowledge and understanding that, for our greater well-being and happiness, for our greater pleasure and reward, we are willing to give up some of our independence and separateness, some of our freedom of action, to meet those family needs and demands, the demands and needs of our partners and of our children. And indeed, in the round, we will do so gladly and happily because of the joy we feel in seeing the greater well-being and happiness of others, due to the joy we anticipate and feel from loving and supporting others and from the pleasure we feel in their love for us. In essence, we in the main wish to, and are often required within our families (and indeed within our communities and societies), to put the immediate needs and wants of others first, ahead of our own immediate wants and needs, though in the broader sense we are achieving and supporting our own wants and needs through supporting and loving our partners and children, and therefore also hopefully achieving greater well-being and happiness for ourselves.

That of course is an overview and summary and does not refer to the individual moments or longer periods of time where we may feel unloved and unappreciated even though we are within a family, living with a partner and children. And we may feel frustrations at what we are unable to do as individuals outside of the family and we may also feel at times under too much pressure within our families, to support our partner and children. Things may go wrong, our relationships may change, and we may, to one degree or another, stop loving our partners and find things too much to take. Hopefully, should we have such troubles and difficulties, then we will manage and survive through them and will feel loved and will be successful in our bringing up of our children and our loving of our partners.

Indeed, of course, many of our relationships, whether within or outside of the family, particularly the important, close and caring relationships, which bring us pleasure and warmth, a sense of belonging and being supported, are likely at some time to make demands on us, to place restrictions and constraints of one form or another, on our abilities and desires to do exactly what we want to do and on when we can do these things. For some, if not many of us, these relationships may be absolutely central to our well-being and happiness and we may actually feel no sense of restriction, with our recognising those relationships as being, in themselves, to all intents and purposes, our key to well-being and happiness, and with our more personal goals and desires fitting easily together with our family desires and responsibilities.

Yet for others of us, we may have a strong sense of wishing to follow other more personal goals and wish to achieve more personally and individually, while maintaining those important relationships and friendships which support our well-being and happiness, and at the same time supporting the well-being and happiness of those with whom we have such relationships. In such cases, we certainly need to accept and fulfill the relevant desires, duties and responsibilities which come with our relationships, accept the reasonable restrictions of such relationships, even though sometimes we may feel frustrated when faced with putting aside our more personal goals in order to spend such time with and care for others. We must do our best to fulfill the obligations which such close, caring and loving relationships place upon us, while also seeking to express ourselves, and while trying to do and achieve those other things which are of also of importance and personal and individual value to us in our lives.

Sometimes we may feel we wish time to ourselves, and may not perhaps feel like contacting or being with anyone else. In the case of more distant relatives or friends and acquaintances, we may sometimes feel, because of the looseness and distance of these more distant relationships, that we do not wish to make significant effort to see these relatives. Yet we may well need to do so, indeed in some cases we are obliged to do so, in order to support those relatives and help keep our families and friendships together, benefiting that relative or our more distant friends, and indeed our own closer families. Our more distant relatives, our friends, may feel alone and isolated and may well need our contact and support. And in fact we will likely feel better ourselves for having made such contact, for having supported them and taken the time to show we care. We do need to maintain such contacts and maintain an awareness of how important we may be to the lives of others, however geographically distant we are.

There may well be times when we are upset if not angry with those we love, our lovers, our partners, our friends, in part perhaps, or even substantially or wholly, because of the demands they are making on us, or the restrictions which they may appear to be placing on us, which we might see as unreasonable (but which they of course may not see in that way). It may be that we are not acting in a reasonable manner ourselves and that we are not meeting our obligations and responsibilities to partners and family, not expressing sufficient attention and love to our families, and in such circumstances, we certainly need to see the perspectives of others. Yet if upset and angry, and even if justifiably so, while stating our feelings and our reasons for our feelings, we must do out utmost to ensure that our anger, hurt and upset do not lead to painful and hate-filled argument and rancor, that they do not lead to bitterness and pain, to the saying of rash and offensive, ill-thought out things, said out of anger, which are hurtful and damaging but which we do not truly mean.

It is fine to express hurt, upset and anger if we feel that way, to let others know how we feel, but it is almost always better to exercise a significant level of self-control, show restraint and constrain ourselves in terms of what we say, looking to pursue those things which matter to us deeply wherever we can through a mutual and caring exchange, something which, of course, may be difficult if the other party, often a lover or partner, is themselves frustrated, angry and upset, if that other person is being self-focused and they themselves are not willing to empathise, listen and understand us and our frustrations in the way that we would hope for and in the way we should be doing ourselves. Hopefully we can avoid painful conflict, reach agreement, compromise and gain better, mutual understanding, having listened carefully to our partner or others, without causing any major rifts in our relationships, maybe deciding to give up something we would like to do, or on the other hand perhaps deciding not to do so and living with the frustration we feel, at least for a while. In any case, it is by far the best to avoid damaging rifts, rancor, deep resentments and prolonged frustration and bitterness if at all possible.

Wherever and whenever we can, should they arise, we need to heal such rifts in our relationships, investigate misunderstandings and solve problems in a caring, rational and reasoned manner, discuss issues of personal wants, needs and personal space, and avoid engaging in damaging and uncontrolled actions born in our personal upset and frustration, avoiding insult and abuse, which may create damaging and long-term fractures and fissures in our relationships, rifts and fissures which may last for years, arising through unnecessary, sometimes unintended, thoughtless and angry remarks, remarks which will be difficult, if not impossible to forget, insults which are painful, hurtful and difficult to forget and difficult to forgive (though which may perhaps at some point be forgiven, at least on the surface, following a heartfelt apology).

Of course within all of our relationships whenever we can, we need to be supportive of others, providing them where we can with the capacity and the freedom to follow their personal dreams, encouraging them in their search for their dreams, encouraging them in their search for self-realisation, helping them to develop their autonomy and attain and enjoy their freedoms to as great an extent as possible. Indeed the encouragement to pursue such personal desires and goals should apply to all, including those beyond our close relationships.

Freedoms, exploration, discovery, education for autonomy and independence, the development of self-identity, self-efficacy and indeed self-confidence (where appropriate) which enable autonomy and separateness, should all be encouraged in others, as well as developed within ourselves. We should not act as barriers placing ourselves in the way of others and their dreams. We should look to encourage and support where such encouragement and support is needed, and find ways, and support others in finding ways, to help others to achieve their reasonable and legitimate desires and success.

Yet, of course, as we have responsibilities to others, where we believe that such goals and desires may significantly damage those with these goals and desires, and others, we may well need to point out our view and such facts from our point of view, and indeed, where necessary, act to dissuade others from pursuing self-damaging and other-person damaging goals and from taking part in self-damaging and other-person damaging activities.

Considering issues of autonomy, independence and freedom specifically in regard to our work environments, we certainly need a real, if not a substantial degree of our own freedom, autonomy and independence in our work environments, something which should benefit the organisations, institutions and businesses we work in. We all feel the need for some room for personal manoeuvre, space in which our individual selves can make some sort of difference and contribution to the success of the work we do. While some of us may work more independently and autonomously, operating our own businesses and providing various services, many others of us are likely to work in complex organisations, businesses and other entities wherein we must operate in a more complex social environment, playing just one role amongst many other roles in the often multifaceted operations and functions of the organisation. Within the context of such complex, social organisations, if we are managers, we need to act, as far as it is reasonable and possible, to ensure that our employees and indeed we as employees ourselves, have some space and room for decision-making within that organisation, something which is likely, in itself to support the success of our work organisations and entities, enabling employees to act flexibility and meet the intricate and individual needs of those we are serving, of our customers and service receivers.

Our work organisations must, of course, operate effectively, fulfilling their functions such that they can remain in existence, and more than that, thrive and prosper, delivering whatever services or products are within our work organisation's area of concern and interest, and delivering them in a manner which suits and meets the needs of employees, employers, customers and clients. And through providing such services and products we will be acting to improve the well-being of individuals, our communities, societies and beyond. As a consequence, though we need autonomy, independence, space for decision-making in our work environment, it is in reality likely, and indeed quite rightly the case to an important extent, that our employers, whether in smaller organisations and businesses or in our larger more complex multi-employee organisations, will, throughout our working hours, for a large proportion of the time, or at least in the first place, set out, have expectations in regard to, and to some degree determine our work, our duties and responsibilities, and indeed not only the content, but to some extent or significantly, may wish to set out, to some extent, how these duties and responsibilities are carried out.

And we as individuals, will quite reasonably, in many circumstances, again at least in the first place when we start in jobs and organisations, may wish for guidance about how to do our work such that we can do that work well in the context in which we are operating, so that we can serve others (and ourselves) to the best of our ability. In response to such guidance we will aim to fulfill our duties and responsibilities, giving up to some extent, where appropriate, an element of our autonomy and independence, such that we can achieve and be successful in our work, both for the benefit of our organisations, for others, for our customers or clients and for our own personal benefit too. Of course, joining a new organisation, it is an expectation, (not always realised), that our managers and colleagues will have a better understanding of what the organisation requires and what we need to do in our work in order to support the organisation and carry out tasks effectively.

In the work context, as indeed may be the case elsewhere, as we develop in terms of our experience, personal knowledge and understanding of what we are doing, as we build relationships and gain in authority, our level of autonomy and independence is likely to need to increase. Indeed, while we are all likely to need training, support and direction, especially when starting out in a new job or in a new work context, as time goes on we do need to be assigned or assume greater responsibility and be given or act with greater flexibility, this, to some extent, being something which should, in the round, help the organisation in a range of ways, promoting organisational benefit and flexibility, organisational achievement, and in addition supporting our own individual sense of autonomy, independence and contribution to the whole, thereby supporting our well-being and happiness in our work context, which again should help to support the organisation.

As managers we need to help to support our staff, where appropriate, in taking on such responsibility, helping them to develop their skills, autonomy and independence, allowing others we work with, our staff members, the space in which to both succeed and fail, though clearly any failure to achieve goals, cannot be to too great a detriment to the organisation. This is not to say that there is no need for some or extensive continuous, organisational oversight, monitoring and assessment, including of course the oversight, monitoring, evaluation and assessment of others by ourselves if we are owners, investors, managers and organisers, though such monitoring can in some cases in itself be undermining and detrimental to performance. Of course, as with other employees, if we are owners, managers and organisers, we need to be continually monitoring, evaluating and looking to improve our own personal performance, this being essential to the effective working of our organisation, but also being supportive of the world beyond our organisation.

While being monitored and overseen may sometimes feel like, and may be seen as an infringement of our autonomy and independence, in our work contexts it may be in our own interests for what we do, to some extent, to be monitored by competent and able people who can help us improve our work and performance, our performance being something of legitimate concern to the organisation, a concern which is without doubt reasonable and warranted. In the work context, we are part of a social group to which we contribute and to which we need to contribute well. If we do not do that, this might well be to the detriment of our organisation, business or company, and to the detriment of ourselves and the others we work with.

Nevertheless, we should be sure to apply an appropriate degree of oversight, and not be unnecessarily over-zealous in our oversight as a general policy and principle, such an approach being capable of representing and demonstrating a lack trust and belief in others (though this sometimes can be reasonable and justified, and such detailed and zealous oversight and monitoring may be justified in some cases) and also being capable of, if not likely undermining the confidence, the self-efficacy and the performance of others, as well their sense of self, independence and autonomy. Nor as employees ourselves should we be simply accepting of such over-zealous conduct towards ourselves, such conduct being frequently not only undermining of ourselves, but undoubtedly capable of causing frustration, upset and pain, and impinging on our well-being. Heavy-handed oversight is likely to inhibit our contributions to an organisation, to the group, and runs the risk of demoralising us, encouraging cynicism and alienation and thereby reducing our desire to contribute to the whole. In many cases, dependent on the context, it may be reasonable, rather than implementing heavy-handed monitoring and oversight, or even in some cases, monitoring and oversight at all, to allow people to develop and grow in their roles, allowing substantial autonomy which may substantially enhance motivation and performance.

If applied significantly or too generally, such over-zealous and heavy handed conduct, such a lack of trust in others, may therefore also cause significant damage to the organisation in the longer term, with the organisation being denied access to our perceptions, our true abilities and other contributions, many of which could support the effectiveness of the organisation, such heavy-handedness also serving to likely demoralise and demotivate those of us working for the organisation, inhibiting achievement of organisational goals. In some hierarchical systems of organisation and management we may be demeaned by, and the organisation may suffer through the need of one senior manager or owner to contribute to and make many low level decisions, and in some cases, all decisions.

In the vast main, wherever reasonable and possible, there needs to be a sense of trust between us and those we work with, between those who are our bosses, managers and ourselves. As individuals we need to live up to that trust and, as members of such organisations, we need to work to build that trust and provide others and ourselves with the personal and human space where, as far as possible, there is an important degree of autonomy and independence.

As already mentioned in reference to all of our conduct, behaviour and actions, the reality of such autonomy is that, of course, such room for decisions and choices means that we can make the wrong decisions and wrong choices. Indeed such wrong decisions and choices are an inevitability for all of us at least on some occasions. We are human and cannot avoid mistakes, especially given the vast complexity and frequency of judgments we are required to make. Ideally we will reduce the number of mistakes we make through reflection on our errors over time, and through looking to improve ourselves and how we do our jobs and how we fulfill our work roles. Nevertheless, in terms of improving how we work, helping us develop and learn, and gain satisfaction from what we do, from our achievement, most of us will benefit from assistance from others in order to more frequently to make the right choices in terms of our workplace functions, though the receiving of such assistance may, in some respects mean that, at least at that moment, we have given up some of our sense of independence.

Indeed, in regard to our requesting and receiving assistance form others, achieving high levels of performance is often not practical without at least some teaching and oversight from those with more experience, or without support from those who can provide ideas or stimulate us to think about and perhaps rethink what we are doing and how we are doing it. Without such support we may sometimes feel we are floundering and not achieving (even in some cases when we may be achieving success). Of course, sometimes it will be ourselves who are assisting, helping and supporting others, grounded in our knowledge, understandings, our abilities and experience.

All of this being said, it has to be remembered that for all of our organisations, private businesses, public services and the like, in the main, and certainly dependent on circumstances, while we have an obligation to care for and look after those we work with and all others, we need to recognise that we could be taking substantial risks and damaging our operations and activities if we allow those individuals who are not contributing, those who are not doing their jobs, those who lack the capacity to fulfill their roles, those who are substantially lacking in terms of competence, and who refuse to change and improve or who are judged incapable of changing or improving in their contributions and efforts, to stay in such roles. More suitable and achievable roles need to be found for them or it will up to us, if we are such people, to find different jobs and roles. Maintaining such of us in these roles can threaten the well-being of others, the survival of businesses, the competence and perceptions of our administration and institutions, and much more, and in these respects is likely to damage well-being and happiness and potentially result in significant pain and suffering for the many. Of course these are complex, situationally and people-dependent matters, which assume the competence of those making such judgments about others, and these people, those of us making such judgments, may not be sufficiently competent ourselves. Nevertheless we have responsibilities to make our organisations and institutions work effectively for all.

Oversight and systems of oversight will be of particular importance, if not essential, in some contexts where trustworthiness is of the greatest importance, and where misunderstandings and errors could lead to intense mistrust and threats to well-being and job security. This will apply in particular for certain organisations and parts of organisations focusing on monetary and financial transactions, where checks and rechecks may be thought to be essential, but also in a range of other business areas, such that our businesses, our organisations, can be successful.

And while independence and autonomy to some extent in our work environments is necessary, in some if not many work contexts, failing to monitor and oversee what we do to a sufficient degree, in support of the goals of the organisational group, would be in itself a dereliction of duty, an avoidance of responsibility by those who are in positions of responsibility, in terms of the success and well-being of the overall organisation and of others in the organisation. Such inaction and lack of oversight can provide space for those of us who are in the process of learning (which may be all of us), those of us in the process of acquiring skills, abilities and expertise, to perform at below the levels we are capable of performing at with potentially substantial detriment resulting for ourselves and others.

Lack of oversight, indeed an absence of management, can lead to underperformance if not very poor or unacceptable performance from those of us who are not so committed in attitude and care, those of us who are perhaps negatively selfish and self-centred or lacking commitment to others, to our company or organisation. It may lead to underperformance or unacceptable performance from those of us who for other reasons work less effectively than we could do or who may even work highly ineffectively. Such poor, such ineffective or uncommitted work, generates damage at the expense of the organisation, clients, customers, the broader world, ourselves and others in the organisation, and in effect all others, our community and society.

Of course, as already alluded to when referring to the competence of those who manage, an issue in terms of our independence and autonomy in the work context and elsewhere is the oversight of those who oversee. Those who manage and oversee the work of others, the operation of systems, and who have other oversight roles, need to be people of integrity focused on core and other principles, interested in the well-being and success of our community, society and beyond, interested in the success of the organisations in which they operate, interested in the well-being of each of the individuals with whom they work, interested in the well-being and happiness of all. And optimally they will also have relevant thinking skills, personal and interactional skills as well as technical knowledge and skills relevant to what they do, though we may have to, in reality, make do with an optimal balance of attributes and skills amongst our managers and others. Oversight of what others do and influencing their actions such that the best outcomes are achieved for all is a crucial and worthy activity which must be carried out effectively but in a manner which as far as possible, in the relevant circumstances, enables individual autonomy.

Thus, in a work context, as in other social contexts, and as referred to above, in addition to having some autonomy and independence, we have to be prepared to accept some restrictions and constraints on our desired personal autonomy and independence. Through the effective consideration and care that we or others as managers can deploy, or through our being in receipt of such caring, considerate management in our role as employees, care and consideration which allows the appropriate degree of freedom, personal space and autonomy, commensurate with our roles and tasks, and which also supports the goals of the organisation, this should enable us as either managers and employees, to have sufficient room for our own autonomous action and to make personal contributions which will benefit the organisation and benefit us all.

In addition to restrictions on our specific task-based choices and actions in the context of our work roles, we may face what are in reality and in effect, restrictions on our dress. Dress restrictions have already been mentioned in terms of governments and states trying to control what we wear and also in terms of convention on social and other occasions. Additionally, in many organisations, there are rules about dress which we are required to follow, and in many contexts such rules are clearly necessary with specific dress considered essential to perform our work functions effectively and also to keep us and others safe (for example medical surgeons, nurses, chefs, microbiologists, those working on construction sites must wear appropriate protective clothing).

It is clearly consistent with core principles that we adopt the required clothing and safety equipment in such situations where ways of dressing are a necessary part of our job functions, such clothing clearly benefiting our own well-being and the well-being of others and supporting the prevention of pain and suffering. Of course the imposition of dress rules and dress codes might be seen as restriction on our autonomy to some extent, however our greater well-being is enhanced through the use of clothing which improves our safety at work and therefore, where there is reasonable justification, this comprises acceptable restriction on our autonomy and freedom. The core principles mean that it would not be acceptable to leave ourselves and as a consequence, possibly others, open to danger because we refused to wear appropriate safety clothing. More than that, in such contexts, if we are in managerial positions with responsibility for safety, and also ourselves as employees with our own responsibility for the safety of others, irrespective of roles and regulations, we should not be cavalier with concerns of safety but indeed need to be stern and to some degree officious in ensuring the safety not only of ourselves but of others, helping to maintain the personal and general rigour and discipline required to support safety for all.

Dependent on circumstances, a precautionary approach is almost always the best in terms of safety in order to support well-being and reduce and prevent pain and suffering. Careless and sloppy laxity, lack of thought, preparation, attention and care in regard to potential threats and difficulties in regard to issues and procedures relating to safety is totally unacceptable due to the dangers these offer to co-workers, colleagues and indeed to us all.

Yet, of course, on the other hand being over-zealous and too officious about threats which are to all intents and purposes, in reality, non-existent, is also unacceptable, inhibiting our autonomy, our capacity to experiment, explore and investigate, supporting inefficiency, inaction and indeed being seen as extraordinarily petty, annoying and frustrating when important work needs to be done. Such over-zealousness – in effect our having too much fear of danger from negligible risks – is also contrary to core principles, the delays, frustration and annoyance caused, militating against well-being and happiness. A reasonable balance needs to be established in general and in specific situations between our estimate of risks to our health and safety and the need to live life to the full and get things done which will support well-being and happiness.

Those who refuse to conform to practices designed for their own safety can and indeed most probably must be denied access to such dangerous forms of work, in particular as their refusal to adopt safety procedures may damage them, something of course which might be said to be something which is up to them, but their action is also likely to hurt and damage others, who may suffer through their obligations to support an 'unsafe' colleague and who may be harmed through the emotional and other consequences of working with someone who is willing, without good reason, to place their own safety, their own life at risk.

Those running organisations, businesses, community groups, government departments and the like must also conform with and follow safety laws, rules and regulations and need to ensure and have responsibility for ensuring these rules and regulations are put into place. There is no excuse for shortcutting on safety which is an integral part of our organisational operations, be that relating to the maintenance of vehicles, ensuring staff are supplied with and are using protective clothing, ensuring fire safety, ensuring safe surfaces for walking, protective fences, labeling of poisons, staff safety training, safe handling of chemicals and safe disposal of waste, amongst other things. Our resources may be under pressure but we cannot place our employees and staff in danger, and available resources must be allocated to ensure safety.

In other work contexts, we may also be subject to codes of dress, which may be compulsory (for example police officers, teams in sporting contests, nurses, military personnel, or firefighters), or we may also be subject to codes of dress which, while not formally compulsory, are considered important if not crucial elements by convention or otherwise, of success in our work, perhaps establishing our commitment to a profession and professionalism through for example wearing suits and ties for business people or for certain types of managers. Again there may, in many cases, though certainly not always, be a strong need or even a near absolute necessity in some contexts, if we decide to enter these fields of work and employment, to adopt these dress codes or to be prepared to adopt them.

That being said, it is probably worth recognising that the use of compulsory dress or uniform will, to some degree, in some cases, be reflective of the nature and culture of the organisation and also may be reflective of the significance and the role we will have and will be expected to play within that organisation. These dress codes, in some cases or frequently, may also suggest a degree of ranking in the work context, a degree of individual super- and subordination and as a consequence perhaps a lack of flexibility, independence and autonomy for those of us working in these organisations, a lack of flexibility and autonomy which, for some of us, we should be wary of.

For areas where there is unwritten agreement and no formal compulsion to adopt a dress code, our success may still be enabled by or perhaps also be dependent on conformity to such codes, since our progress, success and well-being may be heavily influenced by the views of others, our managers, our colleagues, as well as, or perhaps rather than, our success being viewed in terms of more concrete measures of performance which quantify how well we do our job (although our job performance may be hampered by our not conforming). Nevertheless, rationally and reasonably, justly and fairly, it is how well we do our job of work which needs to count, not conformity to a dress code or other norm, and if we are uncomfortable adopting such a code and can perform well without it, then that is what we need to do. Dependent on context, the nature and function of our organisation, acting outside that dress code needs to be acceptable and allowed for us to do where this is appropriate, and does not, in an evidenced manner, undermine the success of our organisations.

Again there would seem to be some arguments in terms of well-being for such conformity and consistency of dress in some contexts, to be the case, even though perhaps that conformity is not strictly necessary, and may even in some cases act to the detriment of the functions these organisations are required to perform. This kind of matter needs to be open to discussion with the focus on our service to others, on well-being and happiness, on personal autonomy and freedom, on reducing pain and suffering with our interpretations of core principles being the arbiter.

Despite the possible uses and possible value of conformity of attire and dress, this uniformity of dress, in some if not many contexts, might be seen by some as being against an important freedom, representing one of the outward signs of conformist, hierarchical and authoritarian systems, wherein we, frequently the individuals acting within the system, have little decision or input into our own actions, our actions perhaps being dictated in an authoritarian manner by bosses, by those with power, in charge. Under such systems, we, the uniformed individual, are simply required to follow the instructions and training given with frequently little flexibility for manoeuvre and little room for our own thinking and input.

Such systems may, in some cases, be necessary and important, with our actions determined by, and needing to be determined or influenced by those with greater expertise than ourselves, and indeed needing to conform to best practice and optimum procedures. Yet in other circumstances, those with apparent expertise may well be ineffective, out of touch and inefficient in important ways, since, with such little flexibility at the ground level, at the point at which a task is performed, our performance of the work or other function may be substantially damaged. Importantly, hierarchical and authoritarian systems conformist cultral systems, those systems which do not listen to the individual at the coalface, the individual doing the action, will often lack an important degree of effectiveness and may in fact, dependent on the goals of the system, not actually support the goals which those in positions of power and authority actually wish them to achieve. Many, of the systems we might accept as requiring uniform attire in particular, may not need uniformity of dress, with similar systems and practices able to operate in various organisations where no uniform or dress code is required.

For the many of us, we might well like to be significantly free or have an entirely free hand in making the decisions concerning our actions in the work context. Yet, as already referred to, linked to issues of conformity and the above points however, for a range of reasons, our organisations may well need to have consistency in procedures and actions in these professional and work contexts. There may be acknowledged better and more effective ways in which we should be operating in a work context in order to achieve organisational goals, to achieve best performance, as determined by research, expertise, experience and professionalism, and it is a reasonable expectation from all sides, from employers, employees, social representatives, community and society, as well as from our individual perspectives, that we should aim to work in these ways to benefit the organisation, its service users, clients and customers. Departures from this best performance and practice may serve to damage our business, our service, our clients, our customers, in other words ourselves and other people, reducing their well-being and happiness. Even so, what is considered a procedure or set of procedures which are known as general best practice are highly likely to need modifications or may even need to be cast aside, based in specific and variable circumstances and situations, which often require our individual decisions and judgments to ensure the best outcomes.

Thus, in the work and employment context, we should be judged by our performance at our work and not our conformity to a norm. Many in business and other areas have not conformed to such codes and norms, and have proved incredibly successful, such lack of conformity, in some, but not all contexts, being indicative of an ability to innovate and to break certain rules and conventions which may hold back individual as well as organisational progress and success.

A significant number of us, of course, do not work in the context of large complex organisations. We may not engage in work performance alongside or in concert with many fellow employees or work under the management and supervision of others. Instead, others of us, in many other contexts around the world, may earn our living as shopkeepers, traders, farmers, craft workers, stallholders, perhaps work in tiny family run operations or have our own individually run businesses of various kinds, with no other or few other employees, these representing contexts where we are in effect the bosses and managers and are our own bosses and managers.

In such situations, while sometimes significantly constrained by our business and other environments and our need to earn and survive, constrained by our need to provide our service or product and generate an income from customers and clients (this need for income generation sometimes placing us under enormous strain at times), we may have some, if not a great deal of, control over important areas of what we do. We may similarly feel that we have and indeed, we may in reality have, much autonomy in terms of our decisions over how we use our time, over where we go during the day, over what we do, over who we have as customers and more, even having the ability on occasion, to decide to do nothing at times and take time off our work tasks.

This possession of such autonomy and independence in our work context, despite the challenges and pressures of running our own show and working more independently, is widely reported and experienced as, in many ways enjoyable and supportive of well-being, proving highly motivating, at least for some of the time, for those working in such businesses, with the high levels of control and autonomy (and indeed power over our own lives) a particular source of enjoyment. Whether this more individualised form of activity and employment where we as individuals frequently have such a sense of control and gain such well-being and fulfillment, can be applied to all of us, all functions and all areas; indeed whether it is wise from the community's point of view for such individually run enterprises to be more generally present, seems open to question on account of the complex processes and high degree of cooperation and interaction involved in much work, much production and much operational, organisational and service delivery. Nevertheless, the well-being and pleasure that can be gained from such autonomy may indicate a route to greater well-being for all of us, including those working within larger organisations.

The reality of our humanity, our human character, means that within the work context and indeed elsewhere, many, if not all of us, are likely to be thoroughly discontented if our own judgments and contributions are excluded from contributions to the decisions and indeed decision-making about the tasks and actions which we are having to undertake. As already indicated, without the capacity to make such contributions we may feel undervalued, and become alienated, cynical and apathetic. We may become hostile to the people and systems directing us, ruling us and constraining us and often, through these approaches, implementing injustice and unfairness. As a consequence, within the range of contexts, but particularly the community and societal context, we may rightly aim to change those systems, and if lacking in power and indeed, powerless to make a direct and expeditious change, while we may choose to make do, understanding and accepting the unwanted constraints and lack of autonomy we may experience, we may determine not to cooperate with such systems and indeed in some cases may determine to undermine and directly oppose them, with the aim that, and such that, one day those systems will change or fall. However, even in cases where we are acting under direct and significantly constraining circumstances we will, at least, most likely, be applying, to some degree, the individual skills and abilities we have in some of our life contexts, and we will hopefully be likely to be making some of our own individual contributions and decisions moment to moment.

That being said, whether or not we are under direction, instruction, or acting in line with accepted, conventional, good practice or under training procedures, the actions that we take in our work and other contexts are our own individual responsibility. Where our actions result in harm and significant harm to others, we cannot use the excuse that we were following instructions from another, acting in line with common practice, or that our actions were a consequence of our education and training. Our actions are, at work and elsewhere, in the end significantly, if not entirely, down to us and comprise our own personal responsibility. We have the capacity to refuse to take certain actions; we have the capacity to foresee and avoid those situations where another might pressure us to act unethically and in a manner that is likely to harm ourselves and others; we almost always have the capacity at some point, even if it is after an event, to act against work systems and component actions which are unfair, dictatorial and oppressive, which inflict harm on others, our community, our societies and the world beyond, even if our actions may sometimes need to be indirect.

Moving beyond the work context and indeed the already discussed family context, in relation to the wider range of broader social contexts in which we live our lives, our freedom, independence and autonomy comprise crucial elements of our well-being and happiness. Indeed issues of freedom, independence and autonomy are often of paramount importance to us.

With regard to our freedom and freedoms, comprising a fundamental element of our well-being and happiness, our freedoms and our discussion and thinking about our freedoms are often approached in terms of what we are free from, and in terms of what we and others, our communities, societies and beyond are not allowed to do in relation to issues of freedom, rather than being addressed in terms of what we are free to do. This is most likely due to the fact that the positive description of what we can and should be allowed to do is probably almost infinite in its scope, there being so many possible positive actions we can take, things we can do, things we can say and more. It therefore does seem reasonable and practical, and indeed is most likely essential in terms of pursuing our well-being and happiness and reducing our pain and suffering, to establish what we, as individuals, should be free from if our well-being, welfare and happiness are to be maintained and improved, and if we are to be free from unnecessary and unwanted pain and suffering.

That being said, in terms of the actions we should be free to take with legitimacy, rather than specifying every positive action we can take, it also seems reasonable in terms of our pursuit of well-being and happiness to identify the most important things we should be free to do and also to establish broad principles which establish what we are and should be free to do. Such a task seems much more manageable than the perhaps impossible task of producing that referred to, almost infinite list of specific actions allowable and legitimate within the framework of core and other principles. And tied to this it is perhaps also practical, realistic and reasonable in relation to at least some areas, to establish broad principles which limit our freedoms rather than being engaged in production of those same lists of what legitimately can be done.

In essence, in the first place, it seems reasonable to suggest that, within the framework of core principles, we are free to do, and should be free to do as we please within the bounds that we cause no significant harm to others, though as described below there are certainly some exceptions to this within the context of our priorities of supporting well-being and happiness and preventing and reducing pain and suffering (such as, for example, forceful self-defence in the face of aggressive violence). Harm here refers to significant physical and emotional damage, significant physical and emotional pain. It does not mean minor inconvenience, or refer to actions that have no substantial negative effect on others. All of our actions will have some effect, and undoubtedly all actions could be argued by someone, somewhere, to be, or could be seen as, being harmful to someone to some degree. Yet minor and insignificant harm to us as individuals, while undoubtedly undesirable is not seen here as being something which, in general, justifies our forcible or legislated prevention from taking the actions.

Determining what comprises significant harm is clearly, however a matter of judgment, and, sometimes, difficult judgment based in precise circumstances and situations. Illustrating this point, winning in a sports competition could be seen as harming those others who lose in the competition, who may be temporarily upset by their loss. This guide views such competitions as, in the main, for the general good, as important for our social togetherness and living, supporting well-being and happiness, and does not consider the emotional pain of those who lose as generally comprising any significant form of harm. That being said, for those who are extremely young, intense competitiveness and pressure from parents and others, focused on competitive events, might be deemed inappropriate and perhaps might reasonably be seen as offering significant harm to such young children.

The simple act of cooking food could be seen as using the earth's natural fossil fuel resources for what might be seen as an unnecessary purpose, as could turning on a light or lighting a fire when it is dark. Again such actions as cooking and using light are seen here as beneficial supporting our well-being and happiness and not comprising significant harm in themselves, though, that being said, clearly, cumulative actions by many hundreds of millions of us, using fossil fuel energy, considering the potential resultant damage to our environment, doing so without reference to potential damage that can be caused, needs to be remedied and other less harmful sources of energy identified. In this case, thus a remedy would need to be found and needs to be found, in order to support our well-being and prevent pain and suffering. Prevention of these acts would comprise curtailing of an individual freedom in some sense and would certainly not be an appropriate first port of call, yet at some point, could certainly be justified for each of us as individuals due to the overall cumulative damage and destruction, the vast levels of harm that are likely to be caused in the absence of remedy.

Similarly, a holidaymaker relaxing on a sunny beach on a holiday could be seen as engaged in harmful conduct since this experience might well have involved travel to that place, and thereby would have utilised some of the earth's scarce resources. While consequences here might reasonably be seen as to some extent being negative, again they are not seen here as representing such significant harm to well-being that these actions should be stopped. Yet solutions in regard to the use of resources need to be found, and, if there are no remedies and threats identified to deal with resource and pollution threats, then there might exist a case for curtailing to some extent our freedoms to travel as holidaymakers in such a manner, such curtailing of our freedom representing something which, overall, in such circumstances, would benefit our well-being and prevent pain and suffering for ourselves and others.

In another type of case, if there is theft of small amounts of money which may have negligible effects on the individual, even to the extent that the theft is not noticed, that theft is still seen as comprising conduct and action which we are not free to do, and which should be circumscribed. Such theft would be seen as damaging to our social relationships, damaging to trust between us in our communities, inaction in the face of such actions having the potential to lead to additional thefts which would have an overall cumulative and damaging effect on us all.

In terms of other freedoms to take actions, there are circumstances, already described elsewhere in this guide, where we, or others, are under threat of physical attack and physical damage. Under such circumstances, we may feel forced to take actions which might hurt or significantly damage others, for the purpose of self- or other- defence. This can certainly be acceptable and legitimate for us to do. It is important to state in the context of our freedoms that we have the freedom to protect ourselves and indeed others from violence and damage and can legitimately use physical force, indeed we have a right to use physical force, at a minimal level necessary, to protect ourselves and others from such harm. Our aim ought not to be in such circumstances to harm others, but to use that minimal force and cause the minimal damage to protect ourselves and others. However, the damage we cause might still be significant, yet comprise the correct level of response, such a level of response being legitimate and reasonable and indeed representing our exercising our legitimate right and the rights of others to be free from physical, violent attack, and significant suffering and pain.

Such a right and freedom to defend ourselves and others with the minimum necessary force remains consistent with the core principles, though clearly conflicts with any statement that we can do as we please, within the bounds that we cause no significant harm to others. This potential to harm others in our self-defence or the defence of others, comprises one of the exceptions referred to above. In such cases, because of the potential physical harm and damage to ourselves and others, because of our obligation and requirement to prevent and reduce pain and suffering for ourselves and others and the fact that we must aim to promote our own well-being and happiness and the well-being and happiness of others, this means that in such cases of self-defence, the defence of others, we can legitimately and indeed have a responsibility where necessary to use physical force for such defensive purposes, even though others may be significantly harmed. That being said, our use of excessive force, beyond that needed for legitimate defence, is not acceptable and must not be adopted.

Such self and other person defence is an example of something we legitimately have the freedom to do. But also, crucially, while we have those freedoms to do, central to our well-being is the range of actions which may impinge on us, that we should have freedom from, actions which should not be done to us and which not only ourselves but all others should have freedom from. These are core and basic 'freedoms from' which we must have and which we must ensure that we and others have, in order to support our well-being and happiness and in order to ensure that we and others do not suffer unnecessary pain, misery, suffering, and distress. Many of these 'freedoms from' reflect and are linked to more affirmative expressions of freedoms and these are all consistent with core principles.

At the core of such freedoms is the necessity of our being free from physical attack, from aggressive violence, the infliction of pain through assault, from gratuitous and other violence and torture, alongside and incorporating the freedom from threats to our personal physical security and any actions which damage us physically, and which in their nature involve the causing of significant physical pain and damage. We, as individuals, working with others, need to act to ensure that as far as possible, we, ourselves are free from such attacks on ourselves and that all others are secure and protected against such attacks. And beyond our more direct individual role, our communities and societies, (and global organisations) need to protect us as far as possible from such physical violence and attack, promoting our individual personal security and the personal security of all. As individuals, it is our responsibility to ensure that our communities, societies and our global and other organisations act to ensure such personal physical security for all of our humanity, for ourselves and all others.

It is unacceptable for anyone as an individual, or for groups, nations or governments to take deliberate actions of aggressive violence with the aim of physically damaging others, causing physical harm, and this means and includes those actions which will physical harm us and others indirectly, through for example actions which might promote starvation, deliberately promoting economic hardship which will result in severe poverty and suffering. Rather we must act to promote the physical security and personal well-being of all.

It has already been said above but it is important to reiterate, that using physical force when acting in self-defence, using physical force at the minimum level necessary, in order to deal with real threats against ourselves as individuals or our social groups, in order to alleviate threats and prevent damage on the moment, and indeed to prevent physical threats into the future, is certainly considered acceptable, and consistent with core principles. Also acceptable is restraining those who offer real threats of physical damage, suffering and pain, or who are in the process of offering such threats and causing such physical damage, such comprising a form of physical force. If we are indeed to be protected from and to protect others from physical threat, where we or others are under physical attack, it is inevitable that such protection will itself involve at some point forceful action in support of that protection. However, as emphasised and reiterated in this guide, our providing such protection needs to operate with minimal levels of force, aiming to preserve as far as possible, the well-being of not only those who might be the victims of those offering threats or engaging in physical attacks, but also, as far as possible, the well-being of those who have offered such threats and are threatening or engaging in such violence.

Connected to the notion of restraint of these individuals is the notion of punishment, the idea implemented in many contexts that damaging actions should receive a response which causes damage to the person doing the action, with the intention of that punishment acting as a disincentive for others to behave badly and providing a response which personally damages those who have done such actions such punishment, this thereby acting as a form of negative 'reward' for their doing actions considered to be damaging and destructive.

Punishment, historically, and sadly still in some modern contexts does means and has meant the infliction of pain, violence and suffering on those deemed to have committed anti-social acts and crimes. It is still widely believed, despite the evidence to the contrary, that such punishment and the prospect of physical pain and suffering or having liberties removed, and the suffering and pain involved, contribute towards ourselves and others not engaging in such violent and other anti-social acts. The reality is that there has been substantive evidence gathered and substantive argument showing the ineffectiveness of punishment as a deterrent with the deterrence proposition being shown to be significantly untrue, our responses as individuals to punishments being considered significantly more complex than this, and our motivations for criminal acts also being complex and varied, and sometimes difficult to immediately rectify.

Such a belief in the efficacy of punishment requires us to believe that people would significantly engage in anti-social behaviour if there were no such thing as punishment, something which seems unlikely to be the case, as many other factors come into play such as moral education, family upbringing, personal circumstances and more. Believing in the efficacy of punishment as a deterrent requires us to believe that those who engage in anti-social acts such as theft and violence are unaware of the possible consequences, unaware of the 'punishments' which may result from their actions and that they will also be deterred by such punishment, something which is clearly not the case for some, if not many. Though many believe, contrary to the likely reality, that they will not be apprehended, and will not therefore face the consequences of their actions.

It also requires us to believe that if punishment were an effective deterrent; and if being identified and found to have committed such anti-social behaviour was a likelihood (and this is often the case), then these people would not engage in those acts, something which may be the case in some contexts and with some of us, but which again does not appear, at least in a significant number of instances to be the case. It requires us to ignore what seems to be the reality that historically in the Western world and in the present day in some jurisdictions, in places and times where punishments were and are far more severe and destructive, the fact is that violent, criminal, anti-social acts which damage others were in the past and still are, present on a much greater scale with violence and criminality deeply embedded when compared to jurisdictions where punishments have been and are less severe, in contexts where there is greater emphasis for example on rehabilitation and restitution.

The balance of argument accepted here is that punishment, even though we may sometimes or often feel the urge for such punishment, is in fact the wrong focus for our responsive actions. Within many of our societies, it is considered that approaches to dealing with those who have committed seriously anti-social acts, which are out of line with the principles put forward in this guide, may need to be revisited and questions asked in regard to the effectiveness and purpose of punishment. It is instead considered possible, if not likely, that such punishments are potentially unnecessary and possibly pointless, failing all of us in many ways.

Certainly punishments and other actions involving direct physical injury are considered entirely unacceptable and inconsistent with core principles, through the physical pain and suffering they directly produce and also because these are seen as being part of, and indeed an encouragement towards a vindictive and punishing society which is unpleasant, damaging, dangerous and destructive for all to live in. Further the actions of physical punishments cannot be undone and this is extremely problematic since the systems through which we judge will always to some degree be flawed and some who are innocent, representing, in reality, substantial numbers of people, are likely to suffer terribly because of falsehoods, malevolence, incompetence and systematic errors in our legal systems. Of course imposition of the death penalty for acts considered highly anti-social, violent, or otherwise is considered entirely unacceptable for the reasons just mentioned, being irreversible and of course involving the infliction of severe violence which is contrary to the core and other principles. Such actions of punishment are seen as encouraging violent and destructive actions and attitudes more broadly by individuals, within family, community and society, encouraging a lack of love and care for others, and encouraging the infliction of pain and violence in our communities, societies and beyond.

Such a view in regard to punishment however, focusing on the well-being of all, does allow confinement and restraint while potential risks to others from criminal and anti-social acts and individuals are dealt with. It takes into account also the likely need to provide reassurance to those of us who are victims and others that such events are not likely to occur to us again and that our fear and personal, perhaps substantially painful experiences have been taken into account and recognised. It does, of course, question the value of punishment. Such a well-being focused view clearly also questions the notion of variable fixed term restraint, fixed term imprisonment, as punishment, a common element of legal and justice systems, as this both allows those who may still be dangerous to others to legally escape constraint and to be free to do harm, cause pain and suffering again, something which seems unjustifiable and untenable, and it also means that those who have committed crimes, but who may in reality be largely harmless and likely to be and able to live well in society, remain with their liberty lost and under constraint, with the responsibility for (and expense of) their daily lives in the hands of the rest of community and society, rather than their taking personal responsibility for their lives, and paying their way themselves. And this denies them and us the opportunity of appropriate and proper recompense and proper and full restitution for their damaging actions, their crimes and anti-social actions.

Many people do feel that the performing of destructive and damaging actions requires such punishment, and it has to be acknowledged that the idea that there is some sense of restraining punishment appropriate in recompense for those of us who have been victims of such actions and as an example to the rest of the community, has deep roots and may be deeply felt. Nevertheless, it is the view presented in this guide that there is likely to be value for us all in moving beyond this, the removal of such a notion of punishment, while retaining the importance of the idea of restraint through imprisonment, combined with education and other personal, developmental opportunities, the latter approaches seeming to be more compatible with core principles of supporting our individual as well as the general well-being and happiness.

Certainly, within this guide, the notion of punishment, if comprising the deliberate inflicting of pain and suffering on an individual in response to damaging and destructive actions, is considered inconsistent with core and other principles. But it is considered legitimate and reasonable to restrain those who are considered to have committed damaging and destructive actions, in particular in order to prevent their repeating such actions and behaviour. This does involve removing important elements of liberty and freedom and inevitably will to some extent reduce quality of life for those individuals restrained. However, that is considered necessary to support the well-being and happiness of all and in order to reduce and prevent pain and suffering more generally.

Thus removing liberties combined with the resultant, likely reduction in the ability to fully enjoy life, is considered a just and reasonably imposed consequence for those engaging in violent and other damaging and destructive anti-social acts. Imposing such restraint is likely to involve, for that individual, the experiencing of a form of suffering, yet such restraint and constraint is likely to be necessary to protect us, to protect other people, community and society from the greater harm that that individual may do. The 'punishment' in such contexts may well mean confinement away from others of us who are at risk, in order to ensure safety and security. In some jurisdictions, in some if not many cases, this confinement is accompanied by absence of access to sources of entertainment, education, luxury and enjoyment, and the removal of important decisions about the individual's lives (bedtimes, meal times). This may not be necessary, however there is an element of consideration which argues that through such minor deprivations, these will act as a form of self-sacrificial recompense which will make it easier for others to forgive those who have done damage and committed crimes. The deprivation of some of the benefits may represent, in effect, a societal desire for punishment, a belief that such punishment acts as a deterrent for people to commit crimes and violent and other anti-social acts, yet it may well act against the optimal goals of such confinement. There is also an important principle of contributing to others and to the rest of the community, which means those confined remain with their responsibilities and obligations to others.

The objective of such confinement, such removal of liberties, must be primarily to protect ourselves, community and society in the immediate present and into the future but it is wise to look to educate, support the development of, and change those who have committed such anti-social damaging and destructive acts such that, where possible and reasonable, they are able to return to community and society acting in a manner, in a sociable manner, consistent with core and other principles.

We also have to be aware that in our systems of constraint and imprisonment, there are clearly, in practice, problems in housing those who are being restrained alongside others who have engaged in anti-social acts and criminal acts. This in itself may be a cruel and unpleasant experience, but further may also result in the incarcerated gaining an education in the knowledge and skills of crime and anti-social acts.

There is much importance in the detail in regard to depriving people of some of their liberties, such as the difficulties in determining if someone remains physically or otherwise a threat to others. In regard to those who offer the possibility for substantial violence or substantial damage in other ways it would seem wise for society to err on the side of caution and maintain their restraint and confinement. Our families, our children, our fellows should not be put at any significant unnecessary risk.

With regard to reducing the level of, and preventing future damaging and destructive acts by those who have committed crimes, as opposed to punishment and deprivation of liberties, it would seem likely that appropriate education, providing opportunities for reflection and personal development (including encounters with victims where victims of crime are prepared to do this) amongst other peaceful and constructive approaches, these embodying appropriate values consistent with core and other principles, are, amongst other things, most likely to be effective, although there may well be other real world factors, such as enabling access to income, a place to live, friends and social support networks, the group and family culture into which they return, which will affect someone's tendency to engage in criminal acts and damaging and destructive acts contrary to core and other principles.

In terms of our own individual personal conduct in our daily lives, in situations where we have personal power, the notion of punishment is undoubtedly, unfortunately so in the view of this guide, at least at the present time, prevalent. Many parents prescribe punishments or sanctions for their children's misdemeanours in the hope or indeed expectation that, for example, taking away privileges, will alter their children's behaviour. While sending out a strong message of parental disapproval, and signaling our view as parents of that particular behaviour, it remains unclear whether such action prevents further bad behaviour or the extent to which such punishments and sanctions are educational, especially when compared to other approaches.

Schools and school teachers certainly prescribe detentions as forms of punishment or sanction, and within schools in some countries, violence is meted out to children who are believed to have behaved inappropriately. In many countries, fortunately, such school based physical punishments have been outlawed. There is little evidence that these punishments were effective in supporting children into more peaceful ways of living in their later lives, with these punishments perhaps, more to the point, representing, sustaining and promoting a culture of oppression and violence amongst people, within institutions and promoting violence amongst those children in those school contexts, with these punishments serving to legitimise violence by those with power over those with lesser power.

This guide certainly sees the removal of these school-based punishments as being an excellent and admirable step forward, with the move to outlawing violent punishments against children in the home, also seen as being a significant positive step, benefiting all concerned in the home and, in the medium and longer term, our whole communities and societies. This is especially the case since youngsters behaving badly will as a consequence experience non-violent approaches to dealing with problems and will therefore, hopefully, to some extent, feel encouraged to seek other solutions to such difficulties and conflict beyond violence. The view presented in this guide is that it is legitimate to restrain youngsters to prevent them from harming others or themselves, but that little is likely to be learnt or gained from the concept of punishment and certainly from violent punishment which causes pain and suffering, and which itself is contrary to core and other principles.

Overall there are a range of good reasons why, and circumstances where, it might be legitimate for us as individuals, communities, societies and beyond, to place explicit limits on the freedoms of others. These restrictions can vary in type and should be implemented where an individual has engaged in significant departures from the principles set out in this guide, in particular where those individuals are significantly damaging others or have clearly damaged other individuals or the community and society as a whole (or beyond) and have the potential or likelihood to conduct such acts into the future.

Core to our freedom and autonomy and overlapping with the protection of our physical well-being, it is essential that we are all free from poverty and destitution. It is very difficult for us to enjoy freedom, independence and autonomy to any meaningful degree if we are suffering in poverty, in destitution and struggling day-to-day to stay alive. Therefore we need to act to ensure freedom from poverty for ourselves and for all, such poverty being damaging to our well-being and happiness, and causing ourselves and others pain and suffering in many ways, including being a cause of persistent illness, sickness, and sometimes, if not often, leading us to premature and substantially premature death. Poverty can be seen in itself as pain and suffering. It undermines our health and reduces or prevents our access to medical care and medical treatments and cures available. Not only this, but poverty leads to, and indeed often means, to an important degree, our powerlessness, which causes a range of other problems in our lives and certainly impinges on our freedom, autonomy and independence.

We need as far as possible to do what we can to ensure that we ourselves are not in poverty, nor are others within our communities, societies and beyond. We need to act in support of generating wealth and well-being. In line with the actions presented in regard to restrictions on our conduct tied to the causing of physical damage to others, it is not acceptable, and we do not have the freedom, to take actions which are aimed at and which are likely to result in placing others in poverty and destitution with the resultant significant harm these engender. Where others are engaged in such actions which promote poverty, it is our role to do what we can to prevent them from doing so, and to do as we can to promote the well-being of those who are under threat of poverty or living in poverty. It is contrary to the core principles set out in this guide to take actions which create poverty, as well as to ignore poverty and to do nothing in response to poverty. Instead we must do all we can to bring an end to such poverty and the suffering and pain it entails.

More specifically, allied to and tied to our need to enjoy freedom from poverty, comprising important, if not integral, elements of working against poverty and the damage to our freedom, autonomy and independence that poverty causes, we all need to work towards and have a responsibility to act to make sure, that there are water supplies, food supplies, medical supplies, supplies of shelter and accommodation available for ourselves and all others. And where we ourselves have generated or have these available to ourselves or have made these more generally available, we need to do our utmost to ensure that both we and the range of others are able to gain access to these basics as well as the other elements we all need for a life of well-being. It is not legitimate to take actions or to follow systems, which willfully or otherwise deny others access to such resources, though as mentioned elsewhere in this guide, it is important that others are themselves committed to, and are prepared to, act themselves to support our personal and the general well-being, as well as being prepared to take action to support their own well-being.

While it may seem an unusual and unnecessary statement to the many of us who live in parts of the modern world where such practices, hopefully, are not occurring to any significant degree, in terms of our relations with others it needs to be stated that no one should be owned by or possessed by others. That is to say that 'slavery' in any form is not allowable and not acceptable.

Not only must we not 'own' others, but others cannot 'own' us, treat us as possessions, treat us as less than human, and thereby deny our humanity and our freedom. This abhorrent practice of slavery having been abolished in many parts of the modern world, such a statement would hopefully be unnecessary, however some individuals and criminal groups or organisations still conduct these practices or conduct practices which represent, in effect, such slavery, and such practice also seems to remain in some communities and groups. Moreover some governments and states are happy to encourage, or turn a blind eye to slavery and to the types of employment which through, for example, lack of payment, the foul conditions of work and hours of work, the use of threats of violence, and other slavery-like practices, are in essence and are in fact slavery. Thus, such slavery-like practices include the payment of pittance wages, vastly overworking people, starving, bullying and coercion of staff through threats and violence and other practices which treat an employee or worker as if they are nothing, of no worth and value, as if they are a slave, someone to be unacknowledged as a thinking, feeling human being. Such behaviour is totally unacceptable within core and other principles, denying our fellows basic human rights and putting them through intense levels of pain and suffering.

Thus, we should never have slaves and no one should be our slave, nor should we hold anyone in slave-like situations or be held in such situations ourselves. None of us should be slaves to anyone else, being at their beck and call, subject to their orders and commands, subject to their moods and violence and subject to oppression from others. In any such situation, we certainly need an avenue for escape to safety and those of us in better off circumstances, are obliged to help any suffering in such slavery and slave-like conditions.

In addition to our receiving sufficient reward for the work we do, in addition to rest and reasonable hours of work, we should, in the vast majority of circumstances, with some minor and necessary exceptions, undertake work which is to all intents and purposes risk free in terms of our safety. We must always have the choice and freedom of moving on from oppressive employers, from violence, from force and coercion. One person cannot and must not, be owned by another. Slavery is abhorrent and contrary to ideas of well-being and happiness.

And linked to this abhorrent idea of slavery and being owned by others is the notion of obeying, doing what others, individuals, societies, state we must do, through coercion or force. Independence, personal autonomy and freedom are of the greatest importance in relation to core and other principles, in relation to living our lives with well-being and happiness. They are needed in order to ensure a healthy society where all can enjoy well-being and happiness. Given this need, we must reject notions of unquestioning obeisance, reject notions of obeying others, and, wherever we can, refuse to obey those who, through force and coercion, wish to control our actions. We must not simply obey others because they are in positions of authority and power. We should, indeed, never unquestioningly submit or obey, as doing so undermines our freedom, independence and autonomy, and importantly and furthermore such obeying actions are likely to lead to wrong decisions and actions. We must have the right to refuse to obey, and where necessary, reasonable and possible, we must take action and refuse to obey instructions and orders, in particular where these do not comply with core principles, but we must also refuse to obey because such commanding and obeying is contrary in itself to the notion of our individual responsibility for our own decisions and actions, and is in itself likely to be damaging of our well-being.

That is not to say that we are not free to decide to do as we are asked, by, for example, a parent requesting our help or protecting our safety, by a boss or manager, with the latter making decisions based in their expertise, hopefully with our input, about what we do, for example in terms of fulfilling our company and client or customer needs. However, while we may simply respect the expertise and authority of our manager or boss, even if we disagree about the value of what we are being asked to do (our acquiescence being on the assumption that we are not causing significant pain and suffering to ourselves and others), we always have the right to challenge and question if we feel these decisions may be wrong, make suggestions, modifications and the like, and indeed, if we are not convinced of the value of what we are being asked to do, we can either go along with those requests anyway, refuse to comply or leave the organisation if we so choose and if we can. Of course, not all managers and bosses have expertise and know what they are doing, and like all of us they may make misjudgments. They, as in fact we should all take notice of, must not command but must request and listen, though sometimes those of us who manage and have responsibility may need to assert our judgment and expertise, and ensure it is put into practice, for the benefit of all.

Further, it needs to be said that in certain contexts, under some present systems, people are required to obey as part of those systems, in particular, as is well-known within the military. The situation of battle where military personnel are engaged in violent life and death conflict or indeed in the context where they are being prepared for battle, is undoubtedly one of the most stressful and challenging situations that can be faced, with lives, the continued existence, not only of those of us who are military personnel but also of those of us they are defending, on the line. Training to follow orders without question in such circumstances generally seems to be seen by military professionals as a pre-requisite for soldiers to operate effectively, in an organised, professional and disciplined manner, to behave automatically in deadly battle and conflict situations. However, it may not in fact be the case that such systems are necessary for optimal military performance and such a system of command and obey might in fact be in place for other more political and systemic reasons related to social control and maintenance of authority and political power, with commands being made on occasion or more often, to conduct reprehensible acts, in the case of some militaries, sometimes against those who are completely innocent. More open and democratic, contributory systems might in fact be more effective even in a battle situation, with more individual actions in the light of circumstances within a battle and on the ground, determined by each individual or by smaller groups representing effective ways of achieving military goals.

Such systems of command and obey would not appear to be consistent with aspects of freedom, independence and autonomy, but given that the defence, the pain and suffering of entire communities, societies, of thousands and millions may be on the line in military conflict, and given that such systems seem to be considered necessary by those who are professionals in military matters, then it may well be legitimate, indeed important or essential for such systems to operate in such military contexts. This guide is not in a position to advocate or deny such systems of military obeisance, command and orders, though would suggest examining and questioning such approaches in terms of military efficacy and considering these matters in terms of overall well-being, effective defence of well-being and happiness for all, and the reduction of pain and suffering, these being the key deciding factors which may or may not, in fact be supported by the military operating through such systems.

Even within such military systems, the individual is always responsible for their actions, even if we, as members of such an organisation, have accepted the notion of such a system of commanding and obeying orders. Where basic values, decency, concern for all others and their well-being and happiness and so forth, contrary to the principles established in this guide, are ignored; where aggressive violence and cruelty and oppression are being implemented by the military or any similar organisation, it is the responsibility of each of us as individuals, however difficult the circumstances might be, within or beyond such a military, to do the right thing and take the correct action in line with core and other principles, as far as we possibly can. Whatever the order or command we might receive, should we carry out such commands, we remain responsible for these actions at the end of the day. We retain our individual responsibility. Whatever others may be doing around us and whatever we may be commanded or ordered to do, it is up to each one of us as individuals to protect the lives and well-being of all others as far as we can, whilst of course aiming to protect ourselves.

While we should not unquestioningly obey anyone; while we should not obey those in authority solely because of that authority, these people being human and flawed like ourselves, and the notion of obeying being seen as one which is almost always if not always detrimental to ourselves, our communities, societies and beyond, it would be remiss to ignore the fact that there may be circumstances where others attempt to physically or otherwise coerce us, threaten us with violence, perhaps with torture, perhaps with death, in order to force us to follow orders and instructions we might otherwise not wish to follow. Such threats may not necessarily be made in the context of each individual command, request or order, but may exist in a broader context, a broader environment, in which all are aware of the likely, if not certain, violent and other consequences of not doing as ordered or commanded.

In the face of threats of severe sanctions against us, sanctions against us which may affect our families, sanctions possibly involving substantial violence against us, our families, those we are close to, and others in general, we may feel we have no or little alternative but to do as ordered or commanded. That is not voluntary of course, and it may be beyond our powers physically or otherwise to resist such threats. Yet even if threatened with violence and death, whatever the circumstances, we can always choose to say no and resist, and we may choose to do so to exemplify resistance and encourage others to resist as well. But our physical suffering and death may well result. In such circumstances many of us will choose to live on if we can, and fight back another day. We may decide we have to follow such commands, some heinous commands, deciding that resistance will serve no purpose except to cause ourselves and perhaps those we love most, great harm. Others of us will resist but may face destructive consequences, though some of us may resist and will succeed in our resistance.

To some extent, our decisions in such dire circumstances may depend on what we are being commanded and ordered to do. However, we need at some time and in some form, wherever we can, to resist such coercion and violence, resolving and acting to end such coercion and violence when the opportunity arises. We are responsible for the things we do, for making our own decisions in regard to our lives and our actions; we have responsibility for our own actions. Within the core principles in this guide, we retain these responsibilities with independence, autonomy, freedom, being essential in enabling us to live out our responsibilities well and being essential in supporting our well-being and happiness.

Importantly, in more every day contexts, while obeying, following and so forth are considered in the vast main, fundamentally inconsistent with individuality, freedom, autonomy and inconsistent with our well-being, as already mentioned, that does not mean that we should never listen to others, follow instructions from others, be persuaded that the suggestions, ideas and recommendations of others are correct, or indeed that we should not follow and act in line with legitimate and agreed upon social, reasonable rules and laws which may govern our conduct.

With regard to laws in particular, in societies with appropriate democratic systems for generation of laws, incorporating consultation, the opportunity for individual contributions and opportunities for voting and decision-making, in societies where there is a sense of equality and fairness in the drafting and implementation of laws, where notions of individual freedom are given important consideration and allowed to significantly impinge on or constrain laws, the law can be said to be, to all intents and purposes, made by the public and have democratic consent, possessing a legitimacy which means we should in the main or indeed perhaps, be completely, prepared to abide by the laws that have been made. The imperfection of even such democratic and open systems may still mean however that illegitimate and unacceptable laws, oppressive in some manner to ourselves and humanity, significantly detrimental to the well-being of ourselves and all others, causing us and others significant pain and suffering, may be introduced. And in these cases, whether laws are democratically made or not, we will have an obligation to oppose such laws, working to remove them and refusing to obey or follow them.

Laws which are inconsistent with core and other principles presented in this guide may be made under many systems, and such laws must not be accepted or followed. For example, laws may be made which legally establish and reinforce racism, which may impose violent damaging punishment, which may present certain groups as second or third class citizens or aim to exclude some from full membership of a community. Laws may be introduced which allow oppression and indeed facilitate oppression through legitimising, for example, theft by the powerful. There may be laws which seek to prevent access to information, thus preventing us from understanding our communities, societies and the world we live in, perhaps preventing us from finding out about corruption, cheating and other law breaking by those with power. There may be laws which directly aim to prevent discussion and debate about important questions in regard to public issues, with regard to key questions about how we live, how our society is organised, about routes to well-being and happiness.

Where such laws exist then it is our responsibility to oppose them in whichever ways we can, optimally peaceful ways, avoiding aggressive violence, but where necessary being forceful and robust, as these laws damage well-being and happiness. In the first place, as far as we can we need to ensure and establish systems and laws which will optimally support our own personal well-being, the well-being of our families, communities, societies and beyond. Where there are laws that are somewhat equivocal in their consequences and which are more debatable in their impact, laws which we may disagree with as individuals, the onus is on each one of us as an individual, listening to others, understanding the rationale for a law, to decide on our actions, peacefully seeking change in such laws where possible, challenging such laws, and where necessary refusing to go along with and accept such laws, bearing in mind the good we are seeking and also our own personal well-being and welfare, the well-being and welfare of the community and society in which we live, as well as considering the well-being of our broader humanity.

In an important sense, we need to feel that laws and the law belong to us, that they are our law and our laws. This can be difficult to feel as we will most likely be born into communities and societies with existing laws which we will not, of course, have contributed to. Moreover, in very large communities and societies, and also with regard to laws and legal frameworks relating to the whole of humanity, we will often not have made a direct or obviously tangible contribution to the formulation of such laws, being one person amongst the many. If born into a system of laws then we must have the freedom, the right to challenge and change those laws, something which should apply to all of us, while at the same time, if those laws are reasonable and just, in the main, we need to abide by those laws.

Yet if we have been a participant in our communities and societies, at whatever level, through our exercising of our personal values and through our democratic choices, we will likely have made some form of contribution to the nature of our laws, and indeed, also through our acquiescence and, in a sense, our lack of voiced opposition to laws in place, we may also be stating our view (or lack of one). Further, through our membership of a society and community, or indeed our humanity, we can express allegiance to, belief in and acceptance of the laws in place. Yet where we disagree with or wish for different rules and laws, as stated, we will need to have the opportunity and will need to take the opportunity to modify, change and add to existing law and laws.

Hopefully our laws, even if made without our substantial contribution and explicit consent, will be satisfactory and will hopefully represent and reflect to a high degree our own personal views of legitimate and illegitimate conduct and will represent the broad view of acceptable and unacceptable personal and social conduct, lying within the frame of core and other principles. If that is the case, it is highly likely that, on consideration, we will agree with many laws, because these laws represent realisations of our own values and beliefs, and we will feel able to go along with the vast majority of laws in place.

Our individual judgment in terms of following or abiding by laws, apart from considering the efficacy of the individual law and its worth in terms of core and other principles, also needs to factor in the value of notion of 'the law' in itself as an asset to community and society, and the potential and possible undermining of the notion of law and social stability if we as an individual make a decision to reject a law or many laws and perhaps encourage others to do the same. In many contexts, there are multiple laws, thousands of detailed laws, and there may well be some laws which are unjust and need more accurate statement and drafting. If some of these are of little effect, then we can hopefully afford to ignore some of these unjust or inaccurate laws as they may have limited effect on our lives. However, as already discussed, there may well be times when refusing to obey a law or a series of laws, especially in systems where law is a vehicle of damage and oppression, is simply of necessity, our refusal to follow the law being simply the just and correct thing to do in support of well-being and happiness and to prevent pain and suffering.

In the event that we are faced with the introduction or indeed continuing implementation of unjust and oppressive laws which significantly damage our own well-being and happiness or the well-being and happiness of others, these being laws which will cause significant pain and suffering to ourselves or others, in the first place, where possible, we must pursue whatever peaceful and legitimate means are available to us to seek amendment and change of these unjust laws, being patient in pursuit of change as far as we can and being patient and peaceful as far as is possible and reasonable.

This pursuit of change may require persistence and patience. Given the realities of our current world and the manipulative and malevolent acts and indeed natures of some systems and individuals, our pursuit of such changes should not be done naively. Individuals and groups, acting in manipulative and negatively selfish ways, may act tactically and strategically to avoid change through delaying tactics, targeting the reputations of opponents, aiming to silence those pursuing justice in a range of ways, engaging in illegitimate efforts to influence and modify the actions of those looking for change. They may offer incentives to desist from our challenges, false rationales and logic as to why our views are wrong or impossible to implement, with their motivation not being the well-being of all, but instead being the interests of themselves or their own groups. Further, rather than being negatively selfish in intention, they may simply misunderstand, irrationally fear change and the unknown and therefore simply be wrong in their judgments. Such people, acting in manipulative ways, may use similar tactics and strategies to avoid the change they fear or the change they have misjudged in terms of its value and impact. We must of course recognise the tactics and strategies such opponents are adopting, aim to recognise their motivations, and act in a proactive manner to counter their actions and approaches, a proactive manner which supports the just and reasonable change we are pursuing which will benefit the well-being of all.

Oppressive systems and individuals acting in oppressive ways, will frequently react negatively and destructively to legitimate and reasonable requests from groups and individuals outside of the power structure, especially if these are seen as a threat to their domination of power, our engaging in opposition to the actions of the powerful being viewed as a challenge to their individual and group power. In highly oppressive systems which use violence and coercion as means to their ends, we need to take great care that we fully understand what we are doing and the risks we are taking should we expose ourselves in opposition to such oppressive individuals and systems. And we need to ensure as far as we can that we will be either safe and protected, or that if we are sacrificing ourselves and opening ourselves to, for example, physical violent attacks, arrest and unwarranted restraint and imprisonment, that we know that this is what we are doing and we are sure and decided that our taking risks is worth it and that we are willing to bear the sacrifice, pain and suffering that may come our way. We do need to ensure as far as we can, wherever we can, that where necessary we have reasonable means of protection and safety, and we must do all we can to make ourselves aware of, and prepared and ready for, the potential dangers we may face. It will undoubtedly be important for us to work with others if we are to achieve the reasonable and just changes we wish to take place.

If we are unsuccessful in arguing for change in regard to what are damaging and oppressive laws through peaceful, discursive and patient means, we may need to move to further non-violent action, at some point in time, and refuse to abide by such laws. Refusing to go along with oppressive and destructive laws which significantly damage the general well-being and significantly damage our own well-being is certainly more than legitimate, indeed it is a responsibility. There may be damaging consequences for us in our refusal to acquiesce to such unjust laws, nevertheless such actions can make government through unjust law unmanageable, adding further pressure for changes to be made.

Even where processes may be legitimate, reasonable and just, the majority, through the democratic process, cannot legitimately impose laws and practices which are substantially damaging, if not destructive, to individuals, their well-being, their lives, for example through banning peaceful beliefs, through acquiring or destroying our homes without sufficient compensation and relief, through imposing unjust and damaging discrimination on ethnic, and other minority groups. The absence of such destructive actions against us is an important element of our freedom, autonomy and independence.

We certainly need to see ourselves and others as important members of our societies, each of us important in ourselves as individuals and worthy of well-being and happiness which cannot legitimately be substantially damaged and destroyed by illegitimate, damaging and destructive laws, contrary to core and other principles. The general well-being must be a priority but that general well-being consists of the well-being of each of us as individuals and all of us as individuals, and thus individual well-being is a foundation of the well-being of the whole.

Of course when we determine our actions in terms of following or breaking laws, there will also be a need for us to make pragmatic decisions based on the direct consequences of our refusal to abide by such laws, for the well-being of ourselves and others. Yet there may well be just reason for us to reject such laws and we may well under certain circumstances, reasonably choose to refuse to follow such laws.

Moreover, our going along with, and following of, laws should never be done unquestioningly, uncritically and we should not, should never, simply follow or obey, without having considered, contributed and assented, as free individuals to that which we are engaging in. We should never put aside our critical faculties, nor should our actions be taken in a manner where we deny our personal responsibility for what we ourselves do, on the grounds that we are following law or on the basis that we are following advice, recommendation and instruction from others, nor should we act in a manner in which we try to deny and exculpate our own responsibility for the actions we take or the consequences of the expression of our thoughts, beliefs and actions.

Whatever laws state; whatever the beliefs, suggestions, ideas of others, even if this is a vast majority of others, our actions and beliefs remain our individual responsibility. We can never place responsibility for our own actions and beliefs elsewhere. Particularly, we should be careful never to absolve ourselves of such responsibility for our individual actions and decide to place such belief in another individual, thereby determining to absolve ourselves of our personal responsibility for what we do and say. And we should be equally wary of placing similar belief in ideologies or belief systems which set aside the value of the individual or indeed set aside the value of community, society and our broader humanity, such ideologies having potential, if not significant likelihood, of doing significant harm and damage to ourselves and others. Through acknowledging and always taking personal responsibility, we, as individuals, will be best serving ourselves, our communities, societies and beyond, and thereby will be optimally supporting and serving the well-being and happiness not only of ourselves, but of all.

While providing others with advice and suggestions, or asking others to do things is not the same as giving others orders and commands, the forms of words which underpin such communication purposes need to be accompanied by the meaning and spirit of requests, advice and suggestions. In other words, these should not be commands by other means, with what are actually commands being hidden through forms of words which are, in form and superficially, open to rejection refusal, but which in reality have no such meaning. We should be prepared and perhaps happy, on occasion, for our advice and suggestions not to be followed and our requests not to be carried out, even if this might cause us discomfort and frustration, and even where the rejection of our advice and suggestions results in wrong decisions being made. Our feelings and responses to such rejection, of course, will likely be dependent on the gravity of the consequences of our advice being ignored and indeed dependent on those people for whom the particular consequences are relevant.

Furthermore if we are experiencing being in receipt of persistent and unsolicited advice and suggestions, we can often feel undermined and insulted, since such persistent suggestions and advice may carry the message that those of us receiving the advice and suggestions are seen by those people giving such advice as incapable and incompetent individuals, perhaps incapable of deciding for ourselves. We all of us need to support the ability of others in achieving their own autonomy and independence, aiming to develop the self-confidence and self-belief of others and giving others, other adults, growing children, some space in which to make their own judgments and indeed misjudgments. This means enabling and allowing others, and of course ourselves, to have the space and time to reach our own decisions and make our own mistakes. And where such mistakes are made, we must also perhaps avoid responding to those mistakes as if a disaster has occurred, or as if their error proves that others should follow our ideas and advice all the time.

We should ourselves also avoid too persistently, or perhaps always, asking others for their advice and suggestions. While in general it may be good to ask others for advice and suggestions, through which we may receive valuable input and ideas, doing so too persistently, leaning too much on others, can undermine our sense of independence and personal responsibility, and can be annoying and burdensome for others. Not only that, it can make us appear weak to others, and if not balanced with our own input, judgments and decisions, it may appear that we have little or nothing to contribute in an adult social or perhaps work context, thereby damaging our credibility with others.

In a similar kind of way to our avoiding overly persistent requests for advice and help, in regard to requesting that others take actions, the doing of which and the responses to which will again be context dependent, the general reality is that constant requests and lists of requests that another, or others, should do things, with an accompanying and embedded message that refusal is not, in actuality, acceptable, may also indicate a relationship where one person is being dominated by another and where one person is not being given sufficient autonomy, something which may cause pain, suffering, hurt and also stress. While it is of course legitimate for us to ask those we love, for example, to do things, to do things for us, this should not be overly persistent and should be a two-way street, in which we are prepared to accept reasonable refusal and we also are prepared to do in turn what we are asked to do.

Of course sometimes, even when advice and suggestions are unsolicited, they may be worth listening to, and may help us improve the quality of our choices and actions, and hence our well-being and happiness. We should not let a feeling of ego and personal challenge turn us away from listening to and taking good advice and suggestions. Indeed it is undoubtedly a useful trait in terms of our personal growth and development, and in support of our well-being and happiness, that we are able to set aside our personal egos, some of our personal barriers, and listen well to the advice and suggestions of others. And it may well be good if we can develop ourselves such that others feel they can approach us with advice and suggestions without fear that we will respond with upset, annoyance and anger.

The notion of responsibility, mentioned here in this chapter with regard to laws, applies in all areas of our lives, within our families, communities, societies and beyond. Within our business, companies and organisations, we as individuals have responsibility for what we do and how we behave, irrespective of organisational culture, management instructions and the actions and beliefs of others. We need to act with integrity and in line with core and other principles. And if, in our social or work context, we are asked to engage in questionable and dishonest practice, it is up to us as individuals to not only refuse to engage in such practice but also to prevent such dishonest action from occurring. While there may be many factors affecting our decisions and consequent actions, there is no legitimacy in hiding behind the decisions of others and those in charge. The actions we ourselves have taken are our actions. The actions of our companies, institutions, groups and teams are also our responsibility even if we are not or cannot be the sole determiners of their actions.

In furthering core principles within our contexts, the possible existence of those who are aiming to simply advance their personal interests or group interests and who may be substantially opposed to the actions we are taking, who indeed in some cases are prepared to behave in malevolent and damaging ways towards us, means that we should be aware that there may be those who may attempt to engage us in forms of entrapment, who may aim, in particular, to lure us into dishonest practice. For example, they may aim to place us in positions where we may feel pressured to act through a reluctance to be controversial and oppose, through a desire and need to conform, or aim to place us in a position where we may be enticed into ignoring poor, dishonest and damaging conduct, enticed into turning a blind eye, through a desire to promote our own success or to avoid trouble and controversy, our thereby becoming an accessory to such conduct, capable, if not likely to be held responsible ourselves for the occurrence of dishonest conduct which we did nothing to stop.

Further and also consequentially to our ignoring of poor conduct and damaging and destructive actions, these people, often powerful people, bosses, owners, managers and manipulators, who may, in some cases, be a font themselves of dishonest and poor practice, these people may use our previous acquiescence or ignoring of poor practice to present us with implied threat, that if we do anything about their dishonesty, mismanagement, bullying or more, if we speak the truth, tell others, then our jobs, careers or even in some contexts our lives may be threatened. And further, through such threats, they may aim to coerce us into poor and damaging conduct ourselves. It is our responsibility to ignore such pressure, to ignore illegitimate enticements and threats, and put paid to these situations wherever we can. We need to run the relevant risks and respond ethically in line with core and other principles, with the benefit of all, our community and society and, of course, our own welfare as our concerns.

Returning to the issues related to our 'ownership' of ourselves, following the mentioning of the reprehensibility of slavery and its incompatibility with core and other principles, in line with our sense of self and rights as individuals, no one, man or woman should be forced or coerced into a marriage, cohabitation or sexual partnership against their will. Choosing those whom we as adults live with is a fundamental element of our personal freedom and autonomy and is central to our well-being and happiness. We need to be able to make choices about our partners and further indeed, we need to be able to choose to leave our partners and to do so legally without punishment or sanction for our choice to leave. We should never be faced with abuse, vengeance and violence from our partners neither during a relationship or on leaving a relationship. Our quality of our life will be significantly determined by our decisions about lovers and partners, and we must have the key role in deciding how we live our lives and who we live with, which means us having a choice of long-term partners and sexual partners, which itself entails the capability of our making the wrong choices as well as the right ones in regard to our well-being.

Thus, children and young people cannot and must not be betrothed or promised by others, by parents or communities, to particular partners or other families. Indeed they cannot, and must certainly not, become part of a marriage or other sexual partnership as children or young people as they are not of an age to fully understand, consent to, or commit to involvement in sexual acts and sexual relationships or a long-term relationship. Marriage or partnership at such a young age cannot support the well-being and happiness of the child, nor is it likely that the selection of brides, husbands and partners by others, by families and communities, support the child's well-being. We, as parents, have responsibilities for our children but we do not own them. Children are not the possessions of their parents to be done with and done to as we, as their parents, wish. Nor should we, as parents, be slaves to tradition and community customs and rules, when these customs and rules damage or are likely to damage our children and where such rules and practices will, in fact, also undermine our communities, societies and the world beyond. We need to bring up our children with care and concern, to educate them and help them gain education, to move towards an adulthood and independence where they can make their own choices about their own lives, based on their own needs, wants and desires.

Consistent with core and other principles, we all need, and must have access to, justice and law, and we need and must have the right to be treated in an equal manner to all others in front of the law. We must all be included within the range of the law, with no groups discriminated against unfairly through laws targeted at our groups rather than being targeted at well-being, justice and fairness for all. And none, no individual and no group, should be privileged above others in terms of those laws, which must be just, equitable and reasonable. We ourselves, and all others, should not be arrested, have our liberty removed or constrained without proper, legal and legitimate grounds, without our having full knowledge of any grounds or charges and certainly not under false charges or false pretexts; we must not be imprisoned and punished for things we have not done, or be dealt with unfairly by individuals, the law and systems, with regard to things we may have done. And if we are arrested and made subject to law and trial, then others must know about this. Our trials and fact of trial should not be kept secret and our trials should not be held in secret, except in exceptional circumstances, justified through legitimate democratic means, consistent with freedom and liberty, well-being and happiness.

If accused we must be tried fairly and justly, on the basis of transparent processes and transparent law, allowed to present our case and employ others to present our case and defend us, in a manner in which outcomes are not significantly influenced by the resources available to us. There must be no undue pressure, physical, emotional or mental, applied in order to coerce the presentation of untruthful accounts of events and happenings. No one should knowingly make up false accounts in order to condemn another or for whatever reason. Such falsehood is reprehensible and totally unacceptable within the core and other principles, even if well-intended, and, if identified, those giving false accounts should be subject to prosecution and trial themselves.

As already mentioned above, there must be no physical punishment should it be found to be the case by the system of law that we have committed a crime, the only acceptable force being our restraint and constraint, our separation from others, our imprisonment, in a manner which maintains our well-being, which supports learning and behavioral change and which prevents such a crime from being committed again and where such restraint removes real threats against others. Physical punishments are entirely unacceptable and the trauma caused cannot be undone. Moreover, as also referred to previously in this chapter, our systems of law will always have a degree of fallibility and while there can be reversal of an order of restraint, with wrongs to some extent righted, physical punishments with their pain and suffering cannot be removed after the event. In particular heinous death sentences or other acts of brutal violence, irreversible acts of cruel violence, such as the severing of limbs are totally unacceptable in terms of core and other principles. Moreover violent punishments through law support a context of violent action, most likely serving to sustain and increase violence in our communities, societies and beyond, and as a consequence causing pain and suffering to many.

In a more peaceful manner, using restraint and constraint rather than violent punishments, the well-being of all will be protected, including the well-being of those who have committed criminal acts. Within the context of our legal systems (and indeed elsewhere) we need to expect and receive justice. Not only this, as individual citizens within our communities and societies, we need ourselves to take responsibility for, and ensure that there are just systems in place which deal with all in a fair and just manner and which serve to protect the well-being of all individuals, our communities and societies.

Considering additional important 'freedoms to', as part of our individuality and humanity, as part of our need for autonomy and independence, we need to be able to move with freedom from place to place, without unnecessary restriction. This desire to travel and move is a core part of who we are as human individuals, though undoubtedly our desire to move and travel is expressed to different degrees by each of us in our different lives. Many of us are movers and travelers by nature, or at least are so at certain times in our lives, and our movement is part of our exploration, our excitement, our personal growth, learning and indeed enjoyment of life. For the many of us, certainly in our modern world, our movement and travel is frequently necessary to pursue our dreams, our achievements, our careers, our economic improvement and indeed our political goals, and sometimes, unfortunately for too many of us, we must move for our safety and security

We need to be free to travel to see family and friends and our freedom of movement is also necessary for our day-to-day survival in the world of work, be it the work of gathering food in an agricultural community, be it the travel which is of necessity to engage with others not simply for social interaction but also for trade and commerce. We need to travel to reach our work destinations in the range of employments, professional and other areas, whichever the work area. Beyond our basic human need for exploration, our human need to roam and discover, all these purposes of travel, illustrate our essential personal and human need for movement and travel.

Our freedom and humanity, our individuality, independence and autonomy, which all support our well-being and happiness, also require that we, as individuals, are free to all intents and purposes to decide who we meet with, talk with, travel with, associate and organise with, and more. With some minor though important exceptions such as that of meeting with others to engage in a joint enterprise to act in threatening, violent damaging and destructive ways contrary to notions of well-being and happiness, or perhaps where there is some real and present danger to us as an individual in associating with another person or other people, it is for us as individuals to decide who are our friends, colleagues, lovers and more. It is not acceptable for family members, legal officers governments or other individuals and organisations to prescribe and proscribe who we associate with. If engaged in political action to support greater justice, we have the right to associate with, meet with, indeed assemble with, the like-minded to pursue our just and reasonable goals, and indeed to pursue goals that might to others seem unjust and unreasonable.

As part of our individuality, autonomy, freedom and humanity, we need to act to, and to be free to, access information in our search for truth, gathering all forms of information and evidence that we can, such that we can educate and develop ourselves, our skills, knowledge and understanding, and such that we can contribute to our own well-being and the well-being of our communities and societies to the maximum. We have a responsibility to seek out information to find out the truth, the nature of events, their underlying patterns and underpinnings, all of which support our determining correct and accurate actions into the future. We have a responsibility to explore, investigate and find out, to counter falsehoods and incorrect information, to counter our own false and incorrect beliefs, and find out the new. And none of us should be denied access to information unnecessarily, and the assumption is that there must be very good reason based in core and other principles to deny access to information.

Each one of us, and in particular each one of us with substantive responsibility and control of information, needs to act to ensure that our systems operate in a manner that such information is, as far as possible and reasonable, available to all so that we all can engage in the pursuit of knowledge and understanding, pursue our education and development, engage in pursuit of truth, improve our understanding of ideas and issues through that information and understanding, enabling us all to support ourselves and others to the greatest degree possible in line with core and other principles.

As part of our need to access information freely, it is beholden on those of us providing information to provide as full and accurate information as is possible, avoiding the provision of partial, incomplete, biased and slanted information which supports our own personal or group view. We must avoid the omission of information and omissions of interpretations of information, which through their omission will leave others with incomplete access to possible understandings and interpretations, leaving them in ignorance and potentially unable to fully understand events, issues and information. Responsibility for acting in such an open manner lies not only with official and government providers of information, but with those who own, manage or work in media organisations. It lies with individual researchers and journalists who must not serve the interests of those who wish to use communication media to support their own ideological view or personal and group interests. It is also a responsibility which lies with each of us as individuals in our own communications, in our conversation and talk with others, when we present our ideas and thoughts, formal or informal, in any context or through any medium. And where we lack sufficient information and evidence to support what we are saying, it is essential that we acknowledge this.

It is our responsibility as individuals to act in an open and informative manner as far as is reasonable and as far as we can, in support of the core and other principles established in this guide. The fact is that this is necessary as part of our individuality, indeed it is needed in support of our own personal satisfaction, happiness and fulfillment. We all of us need to develop and learn not only in support of our selves, not only in order to help us with our making our way in the world, but also in order to help us support others. Almost all of us, if not everyone of us, has a thirst for knowledge, for information, for learning, for finding out the truth, for finding out about our world, wishing to know the truth about the reality of events, for finding out the new, for developing and for improving our skills and abilities. And we need to have the freedom and capacity to fulfill what are such entirely reasonable and desirable thirsts and reasonable and desirable goals, consistent with core principles, the fulfillment of these thirsts and desires acting to support the well-being and happiness of ourselves and others.

That being said, where the free flow of information may significantly endanger safety, the lives of ourselves or others, for example in times of war and conflict, or other circumstances, we may have good reason for certain information to be withheld from those who might use such information with malevolent, destructive and dishonest intent, in order to damage ourselves and others. In these cases, by such withholding of information lives can be protected and saved, and well-being supported and ensured, something which of course is consistent with well-being. It is naive and unacceptable to be ignoring of the existence of those who, for whatever reason, wish to, and will damage others, and even wish and intend to do so in devastating ways. Providing information and knowledge which supports the devastating and damaging actions of such people, is of course detrimental to well-being and happiness and should not be done where at all avoidable.

Our freedoms in regard to access to information and knowledge, must also include and take account of, to an important degree, our personal and human desire and need for privacy and confidentiality, which may also mean not making information available, or denying access to information about ourselves and others when we feel that information is very personal, and where there is no good reason in terms of the individual and common well-being for such information to be available or to be broadcast.

We may well feel that some information about ourselves, for example about our personal beliefs, deepest feelings, our sexuality, personal habits, details of our relationships, our health and medical situation and so forth is highly personal and private – and that others have no need or reason to know about our private lives. We have no obligation to let them know and in terms of our own personal actions and statements, we should not feel personally obliged to tell others or be required to tell others unless there are very strong reasons for doing so, nor should others, organisations with whom we interact, such as governments, employers, be able to demand unnecessary information from us, or where they have personal information about us, should they be able to pass this on to others without our explicit and knowledgeable consent to this being done. Of course we may decide to be entirely open with others, but in those cases, that is a matter for ourselves, our own choice, and our own decision-making.

In terms of the provision of information and secrecy, there are other areas in which there may be a desire, if not an important need for, secrecy and the withholding of information. For example, we may as individuals play a role in various competitive business and other competitive environments. In business environments if we are, for example, developing a new product, then, with commercial systems operating competitively as they currently do in our modern world, we would likely not wish our competitors to know at too early a stage about our product development. In such contexts, we may need to make important decisions about access to information and take steps to ensure information is not freely available. Clearly, for example, where a business or company is involved in the development of new services, processes or products, as yet unfinished and not protected by law and patent rights, in a competitive context, the company has reason to maintain some secrecy, and, as long as there is no significant detriment to the whole, there should be no problem with this, as long as, in the case of potential damage to the community and society, such information is released as soon as possible so that we can all be protected and all of our well-being supported. In certain important cases, at some point, after not too unnecessary a delay, there will also be a need to release information such that we can all benefit from innovations and developments, these important innovations and developments belonging in the round to our human store of knowledge and understanding.

It might be argued that an economic system which promotes such secrecy and lack of communication about developments, developments which might be important to us all, is an inefficient system. This might certainly seem to be a detrimental side of the economic system which is currently in place in many jurisdictions and it may be the case that our development of alternate economic systems would promote the transfer and development of new ideas without such a need for such commercial secrecy. Nevertheless, others argue that such systems promote innovation. At the present time, such a major change in economic organisation and systems seems somewhat distant, though might offer benefits if it were to occur, at least in regard to the sharing of information and cooperation in regard to developments and change which might benefit us all. Nevertheless, in terms of developing the efficiency of our economic systems, it is likely that much more would have to be considered than this single though important issue, for example the potential detriment that might arise through effects on innovation should deleterious effects occur, the related effects on financing of new developments if the potential for their commercial success was reduced, or the issue of whether, should such new economic systems become dominant, there might be detrimental effects from overly bureaucratic or authoritarian and centralised systems which might interfere with both the pace and nature of development and change, and much else.

The keeping of military secrets could also be seen as included within the context of the legitimate denial of access to information to others, with disclosure having the potential to place us, or others, in jeopardy. Nevertheless it is worth mentioning that within legitimate democratic systems in which significant, if not very high levels of freedom and justice are in place for all and in which the well-being and happiness of us all are supported, it is reasonable to keep information from those, those other states and other individuals and groups, that might wish to significantly harm us as citizens and might even wish to destroy our communities and societies. Perhaps with time, with greater togetherness across our world, and greater recognition of our common humanity, the need for the existence of our militaries and indeed perhaps our nation states will be reduced. Such changes may well be desirable in terms of supporting well-being and happiness, but there is a long way to go from the present to such a future, in that respect, with, in the meantime, the presence of militaries, while an unwanted necessity, being reasonable and justifiable for our defence and protection, and linked to this, our keeping of military and related secrets an unfortunate necessity for the same purposes of safety and protection. It is essential not to be naive about the intentions of others if we are to sufficiently support well-being and happiness. It is also of course essential to be understanding of the perceptions of others, to avoid being cynical and overly-suspicious if not paranoid of others, and it is also essential to promote peace and togetherness and to cooperate and work together with others as far as is reasonable and possible.

In terms of decisions not to share ideas and information, in terms of the withholding of information and indeed our withholding of contributions about our thinking, as individuals we may feel a similar need to maintain a level of silence and secrecy when we are conceiving, creating and developing ideas, in particular when our ideas and thinking are at a nascent stage, our being weary of our new, and perhaps unconventional, ideas and thinking, being exposed to others and therefore being discussed prematurely, before we have considered these ideas in depth and until we feel these ideas and thoughts are more fully or fully formed. Apart from the fact that our thoughts and ideas may come across as stupid and naive to others (even where they are excellent ideas), with our potentially consequential humiliation, it is certainly the case that many new and valid ideas may seem shocking and embarrassing to others through their originality, difference and challenge to convention, and we may reasonably be worried about others ridiculing us for our thinking (though, of course, supporting the well-being of others means we should never ridicule people for new and different thinking though we may always be constructively critical – hopefully in a polite manner).

Our ideas may also simply be hypotheses, which need evidence before they can be fully supported and thus it would seem reasonable to gather evidence prior to discussing such ideas as if they were reality. We may therefore choose to keep our thoughts and ideas, indeed our thinking about the world and keep our research thinking, private, until we feel we feel we are ready, and our ideas and state of knowledge, understanding and thinking are ready, for open discussion with the wider world.

Further in regard to our own private thinking, we may have strategies and approaches to living life or which we adopt or are adopting in regard to dealing with specific situations, our aim being to be successful ourselves and to enhance the well-being and happiness of all. As long as we are not acting malevolently, in a negatively selfish manner, or for the purposes of revenge, as long as our beliefs, actions and strategies will not cause significant hurt to others, there is, in the main, no harm in our not sharing such beliefs, strategies and approaches. Whether or not we share these is up to us as individuals. Yet we should as far as possible, with care, be open where we can, sharing such approaches, beliefs and our feelings with those who are honest, who have integrity, whom we trust.

In terms of sharing and not sharing information, we may also have information about others and their lives which we may feel it inappropriate to share with others, private information which might have the potential to embarrass and humiliate or even economically damage people we know and care for. And in these cases it will often be for the best to say nothing and keep our counsel unless there arise significant reasons for this information to be known.

However, if we know that others have engaged in serious breaches of law, conducted actions which have significantly damaged others, our communities and societies locally or more broadly, with regard to which they have not been dealt with by our communities and societies; where we believe that there is a strong likelihood that there are plans for such actions in the future, and believe that these others will continue such breaches then, even in the face of the commitment from another not to repeat what they have done, and where we can do little or nothing as individuals to prevent such future actions, there is an obligation on us to let community and society know, such that there can be appropriate action taken to prevent such actions and there can be certainty that such damaging acts will not occur into the future. Whatever our motivation, our being caring or otherwise, by keeping silent about the crimes and damaging actions of others we are in essence becoming accomplices in silence to the damaging acts which have taken place and the damaging acts which are likely to occur in the future.

Thus secrecy and keeping ideas away from exposure to others may in some, if not many cases, be a bad thing, detrimental to our communities and societies and to ourselves as individuals. Clearly, secrecy and hiding or restricting of access to information may prevent us and other individuals, community, society and our broader humanity, from gaining important knowledge and understanding which might benefit ourselves and the wider whole, and help to keep us safe and avoid pain and suffering. Such actions may prevent access to information about key developments in business and science which could benefit us all, such lack of access to information and understandings preventing cross-fertilisation of ideas between researchers and others and denying us access to the valuable input, suggestions and contributions of others. Having such access might also save us from conducting a great deal of work to no end and might further avoid our wasting large amounts of time repeating research and work which has already been done or pursuing avenues which unbeknown to us, have previously been found to be unproductive or unhelpful.

Undoubtedly there are some other contexts where free access to information may be damaging to individual and general well-being, nevertheless, the principle is one of our being able to gain, and our making available of, complete and free access to information unless there are very strong grounds for preventing such access. Withholding information, withholding access to ideas, withholding access to new understandings, approaches, methods and techniques, where there is no reasonable justification, are all potentially highly detrimental to all of us as individuals, our communities, societies and beyond. Organising or demanding confidentiality and secrecy in order to hide problems and faults or to keep secrets about bad practice is not acceptable, as such actions are clearly likely to be detrimental and damaging to the range of us as individuals and the general well-being and happiness. Using secrecy and confidentiality as means of avoiding embarrassment and preventing the truth from coming out, the truth being something of major concern for our individual, community, society and beyond, is unacceptable.

It is sometimes said to be the case, and perhaps it is quite frequently so, that when there are those of us in official roles, businesses, or indeed elsewhere who are withholding information or making efforts to withhold information, where there are those amongst us who are being secretive, then there is likely to be something of interest and value to us that they are trying to obscure or hide. And if we suspect such important information is being kept from us, then it is reasonable that we should make efforts to find out that information, that we find out what has what is going on, and what has happened. Being aware of such information may help us understand events, policies and actions that have been taken, help us identify corrupt and dishonest dealings and processes and so enable us to take decisions and engage in actions which might help us all into the future. For example, our uncovering of secrets about wrong decisions made may lead us to develop better processes to ensure better future decisions. Our finding out about cover-ups regarding poor individual conduct may lead us to understand corruption in government and how to prevent this. In the vast main, we should be very careful not to allow individuals, groups and group members to cover up their errors and the errors of others, in particular because, as already mentioned that will stand in the way of improvement and development, yet at the same time we should recognise that errors occur and avoid being too harsh with those who make such errors and mistakes, focusing on supporting development and change in a constructive manner rather than acting in a detrimental manner against those who have made genuine mistakes.

In determining whether information is being withheld, we may need to pay close attention to what is actually being said, since apparently open and honest statements may not be full and complete, may be deliberately distracting and focus us on other matters and issues which are those which are not central and important. There are many ways in which our reams of words can be used to hide information which may be of importance. As individuals we need to be as open and honest as we can reasonably be, though as mentioned elsewhere in this guide we are under no obligation to tell all about ourselves. We do need to take account of what others might think of us, consider the notion of our reputation if we go into too much detail about our faults, errors and mistakes. Yet rather than demeaning us, we often find our errors and mistakes are the same as those of others, who may have committed worse mistakes and errors, and as a consequence of our sharing, our faults, errors and mistakes, we can feel greater togetherness with others through such deep sharing. Reputation, while important, is perhaps something which is sometimes over rated and given too much emphasis and prominence in the modern world with honesty, openness and integrity, being higher and more important elements of our overall well-being and happiness, more supportive of well-being than a secretive, false, undeserved ill-founded reputation. A well-deserved and well-earned reputation for integrity and honesty is undoubtedly of greater value.

Moving beyond notions of secrecy and withholding information, in terms of our access to information, fundamental to our freedom is education, access to education and the availability of systems of education to all of us through which we can systematically gain from the store of human knowledge and understanding (and indeed misunderstanding). Without such access we will always be to some extent ignorant, something which will hamper our understanding of ourselves and the world around us and deny us the capacities to develop ourselves and to contribute to our communities and societies around us. Access to education is fundamental to our freedom and fundamental to our well-being and happiness. The importance of education, the role of education and access to education is discussed further in this guide, both later in this chapter and in substantial detail in chapter eleven.

Linked to our openness with information and also linked to our free access to information is our need for the freedom to express ourselves, particularly here in regard to what we say but also of great importance within the context of our other expression of thought, for example through art, music and other forms of expression. From an individual perspective and at the level of our individual daily lives, providing an element of self-regulation of, and personal constraint on, our personal verbal expression, firstly of course, we clearly need to judge what we say and to whom we say it, in order to support our general need for well-being and happiness and our consequent desire to build positive, cooperative and strong relationships. In our speech therefore we should aim to support the well-being and happiness of others, of the whole community and society and the wider world by, as far as we can, speaking in polite, constructive, friendly and cooperative ways. Thus, while we are free to say much, we need to consider what we say and ensure that what we say, as far as is possible and reasonable, promotes well-being and happiness and avoids, again as far as possible and reasonable, causing significant pain and suffering.

Of course in the first place we do need to communicate with others, something which in itself should promote togetherness even if our talk focuses on common and generally uncontroversial topics such as the weather, our food preferences and the like. As part of our communication strategies, especially salient when interacting socially with people for the first time, we tend to look for areas of commonality, common interest and experience which support our togetherness, friendliness and cooperation. Yet at other times, in other contexts we may wish and need to express disagreement, if not strong disagreement with others, sometimes in a robust manner, while at the same time wishing to act in a persuasive manner such that those actions which best support the well-being of ourselves and the well-being of all are adopted at the outcome of our conversation, debate or discussion.

Thus, it is on the whole optimal, wherever this is realistically possible, in terms of building cooperativity and positive relationships which support well-being and happiness, to be polite, friendly and speak and act with kindness to all those we meet, and that includes those with whom we may have important differences in belief and perception (though we should not do so with naivety, with our requiring an awareness of others their motivations and intentions, and indeed our recognising the implications of such other beliefs). Similarly, when others address us, we need to and should reasonably expect similar such politeness, kindness and cooperative conduct which recognises our perspectives. Such an approach, combined with being listening and attentive to the words, meanings and beliefs of others, should allow a process of discussion which has a higher likelihood of leading us towards the optimal decisions and solutions for all and which therefore supports better well-being for all.

A crucial issue for us here relates to the necessity, in terms of well-being and happiness, of our being able to hold beliefs, express beliefs, and express and broadcast them out loud to the many, should we so choose to do. This means amongst other things, expression of our beliefs about the world we live in, the way society operates, about important issues which relate to our personal lives, the way we and others live our lives and our ways of being, such expression of ourselves being bounded by the constraint that such beliefs presage, comprise or offer no significant direct physical threat to others[1].

Our beliefs may contrast with, or be critical of the beliefs of others, perhaps contrast with or be critical of the beliefs of the majority, those holding power and in authority, and may even perhaps be critical of the beliefs of everyone else. The beliefs we express may seem completely illogical and irrational to others. Yet the expression of such peaceful beliefs and opinions is seen as legitimate within terms of core and other principles, substantially supporting our individual well-being and the broader well-being. When we adopt such a stance in regard to self-expression and when we support others in developing and expressing their views and opinions, where these are within the bounds of core principles, this is considered to be to the benefit and well-being of us all.

Unfortunately it is however possible to argue that all beliefs, ideas and judgments can offer threats to well-being and happiness. Those beliefs which are not considered permissible in terms of core principles are those which offer direct threats of physical violence, economic harm and other forms of significant and clear, obvious, direct, damage to others. Thus direct threats of violence aimed, for example, at individuals or racial and belief groups are unacceptable. Where other words, where 'clever' phrasings, and hidden messages, are used to cover up what are, in effect, direct threats to individuals, others and other groups, in the latter case focusing on issues such as claims of racial superiority, or which serve to deliberately diminish the humanity of other individuals or racial groups, which demonise other racial groups, this is not acceptable within the terms of core and other

---

1   The notion of significant physical threat here includes amongst other things, for example, threats to place others in poverty such that they will suffer significant suffering and pain, and also threats to remove key freedoms and impose restrictions which will similarly cause significant suffering and pain. It also includes stages along the road to violence, such as inciting hatred against others, which is invariably done for the purpose of stirring up and encouraging violent acts against others.

principles. Beyond such expression there is in the vast main an obligation for us to support the notion and actuality of freedom of expression.

Such a stance and propensity to support freedom of expression, gives us freedom and power as individuals, enabling us to realise an important part of our personal selves, that is, the need and desire to express ourselves freely and express ourselves largely unconstrained. This approach to expression further benefits us all through improving our communication with others, enabling us to act to solve problems in our more personal lives, but also critically allowing us to contribute our own ideas to others, our communities, societies and beyond, without fear of damage and retribution, enabling us as individuals, communities and societies to discover the important and valuable ideas which others may have, with our interplay of ideas, opinions and judgments enabling debate and discussion, supporting our broader personal learning, education and growth, which will hopefully lead to decisions and actions which will benefit ourselves, our communities, societies and beyond.

Therefore, while others have the ability, and indeed the right to disagree with what we say, to argue with us, to try to persuade us that we are wrong, to criticise the things we say, they have no right to prevent us from speaking our views and arguing our case, from putting our views and judgments in front of others, except in the cases where what is being said provides a direct physical or related destructive, serious threat, to the well-being of ourselves and others (including, for example the dehumanising and demonising incitement of, or promotion of hatred against others). Thus, unless what others are saying represents such a direct physical or other related and destructive serious form of threat to ourselves or others as individuals, we have no grounds in terms of well-being and happiness of ourselves and others, to deny others the right and the space, as well as the ability and opportunity, to express their feelings, ideas, judgments and opinions.

We may disagree, we may feel the ideas of another are outrageous, irrational and unsupported by evidence, which, indeed they may feel about our ideas, nevertheless, in support of individual well-being and the well-being of all, we, and they must have the facility and opportunity for expression of our views; we and they must have the ability to debate and discuss our ideas, aiming to listen, trying to understand the perspectives of others, aiming to learn and develop our knowledge, thinking and understanding, such that we can find the best steps, decisions and solutions for ourselves as individuals, for all others, our communities, societies and beyond, in support of well-being and happiness. In support of core principles, in support of well-being, we, as individuals, need to act in a manner consistent with such an approach supporting open and free expression (within the bounds already stated) and support actions and systems consistent with that approach.

In our own more individual lives, in general, with regard to important issues in our societies and communities, and with regard to other issues as well, we need to encourage those we know and others, to speak their minds, to let us and others know what they are thinking and feeling. We need to encourage our children to speak out with respect, love and care for others, to be sensitive and understanding of others, yet also to speak out their feelings, views, judgments and opinions, and to listen to the feelings, views, judgments and opinions of others, as well to understand the value to us all of so doing.

All of this being said, there is also value in knowing when not to speak out our views and opinions, as there are certainly times when saying nothing, saying little, or listening attentively to others is the best, wisest, most sensitive and caring thing to do. There are certainly times, in practice, when saying nothing or little is the best strategy or option to help us learn, and grow, where our quietness represents the best strategy and course of action to build social relations, to achieve our purposes and support our own well-being and the well-being of others. In particular, we, ourselves, most probably do not always wish to be continually regaled with the strongly held opinions of others and vice versa. There are times for other forms of talk as well, the type of talk which is about simply the pleasure of communicating with others, building better relationships, building cooperation, enjoying fun and togetherness, the kind of talk which sometimes does avoid controversial angst-inducing, charged and controversial issues for the sake of supporting a sense of togetherness, as opposed to our providing opinions and thoughts on such controversial and sometimes painful issues, thereby, potentially exacerbating points of difference and conflict about issues and ideas.

The focus on and discussion of self-expression in our speech, in regard to public issues, as described up to now, to some degree underplays the social complexities of real life in the public space within our communities, societies and beyond. In the public space, there are those of us with power, money and influence whose voices, often expressed in support of their own individual, financial or corporate interest or ideological positions, may be heard more loudly than other voices, our own voices. There are those whose voices may be expressed and heard more loudly than the voices of others of us who lack such power and influence, something which is perhaps difficult to avoid in our complex modern societies. Yet all voices need to have the opportunity for their expression, with the complete drowning out or significant marginalisation of other voices, of other perspectives and approaches, including minority perspectives and approaches, being likely to be detrimental to the whole, to all of us. Such sidelining and diminishment of voices and expression acts to the benefit of those with resources and power, with important voices either left unheard, largely unheard or other voices, if heard, likely to be denigrated in the public space by those with power and influence or their representatives, sometimes, if not often, acting in support of their own views and negatively selfish interests, either with deliberation or otherwise, and thereby with their likely to be damaging the interests and well-being of us all.

Thus, in order to support the well-being of all, we, as individuals, communities and societies, need to speak out ourselves and support others in speaking out, promoting spaces, platforms and channels through which our own and other voices can be heard, and through which other views are allowed to compete on a more level playing field with the voices of those who have easy access to communications channels through relationships, money, wealth and other forms of power.

It is not acceptable, it does not represent freedom, it does not support the general well-being, to have situations where only single voices, single views, only the views of the powerful and influential, the views of powerful individuals, groups, elites and classes are heard. And we, as individuals, need to act against such situations as far as we can. The squeezing out of alternative views and perceptions from the public space is highly likely to damage us all and represents something which serves to demean us as individuals, since we all have differing individual perspectives and views and thus we are all thereby potentially excluded and diminished by the exclusion of non-conformist views. As individuals we need to ensure that there are additional routes to individual expression and larger scale expression to wider audiences, routes which are available, affordable and accessible. All of this should, on the whole, benefit ourselves as individuals, our communities, societies and beyond.

That being said, apart from the promotion of such expression and our ability for such expression, as already mentioned with regard to our more personal interactions and conversations, we must listen to others. In regard to important issues, there may well be those with much greater experience than us, whose views and ideas we need to engage with, listen to and learn from, even if we do not agree. There are those with tremendous expertise, who have investigated and researched areas of life over many years and whom it would be foolish not to listen to in an attentive manner. Suffice to say of course these experts might be wrong in the views they express but they may well not be. For example, in the current age, the substantive scientific community identifies climate change as almost unequivocally occurring and identifies that this climate change has significantly human origins. In particular, given the dangers to the world in terms of climate change, their voices should almost certainly be listened to, their evidence and judgments given substantial weight and policies devised in response to what is known and expressed by these experts. Of course these climate scientists and experts could be wrong but it would seem extremely unwise, to put it mildly, to ignore such experts and evidence. From the individual perspective, unless we have examined the evidence ourselves and understand that detailed evidence, then we are not in a substantial position to argue against such a weight of evidence and expert opinion.

There are a very small number of researchers and others who question the evidence and research on climate change and its origins, and these voices must be heard to and their arguments and concerns addressed with our changing our minds where necessary in line with evidence and reason. However, unfortunately it would seem that more due to social and political considerations, beyond legitimate debate and discussion, beyond consideration of evidence, apparently and significantly in order to support short-term financial and economic interests, substantially unsupported views are promoted and climate experts supporting the human origins of climate change have come under personal attack and their research and findings derided and belittled by those who have no such expertise and no reasonable grounds for their criticisms. This is not indicative of listening and attentiveness, but more indicative of a short-termism for which it seems likely we will all pay in terms of our increased pain and suffering in the future.

Indicating the general imbalance of injustice of our legal systems, it is surely instructive to note that those who steal small amounts, serious as such acts might be and undermining of our communities and societies as such acts might be, may be met in many jurisdictions with harsh punishment, whereas those who, in order to support their own corporate and financial interests, deny anthropogenic climate change which may result in the pain and suffering of hundreds of thousands of us, if not millions, or who, for example, in the past acted to deny the dangers of smoking tobacco, seem to face no similar sanction where there actions have caused or are likely to cause much greater damage to us all.

While, in support of the well-being of all, we must be free to express our feelings, our thoughts, our beliefs, free to express criticism of the opinions and beliefs of others (and indeed criticise others for holding those beliefs), there are things which, as has already been intimated in broad terms, in line with core principles and supporting well-being and happiness as well as reducing pain and suffering, it is not acceptable to say and express.

In more specific terms in regards to our not having the freedom to make physical threats, it is not acceptable to use words or gesture to threaten individuals, groups or others, of all types, with aggressive physical harm or aggressive harmful actions which will damage their physical and indeed psychological and emotional well-being into the future, even where these others may have threatened us. Nor is it acceptable to use words to stir up and whip up violent aggressive action or other destructive action, to incite hatred (a step along the road to the implementation of violence towards others) against other groups of people, those belonging to particular racial groups, or belief groups, those with particular physical characteristics, or indeed other groups on the grounds of their reasonable and legitimate sexual preferences. Promoting such aggressively violent action is not acceptable with physical force only justifiable in terms of our self-defence and the defence of others, with deployment only legitimate in its use at the minimum necessary level to ensure safety, security and well-being. Racist and other words which falsely characterise other groups in an attempt to demonise and marginalise these others, and which may in the end run the risk of violence, and which bolster unfair discrimination, are unacceptable.

So, with the purpose of supporting well-being and happiness and reducing pain and suffering, we may, in some cases, have justification as individuals and as a society and community, as broader social entitles, in restricting to some degree individual freedom of expression. This applies, in particular, in regard to threatening discriminatory and demonising, dehumanising comment against not only ourselves as individuals but also in regard to such discriminatory and demonising or dehumanising comments and actions against those groups, such as those already mentioned, with shared characteristics, including racial and ethnic groups, homosexuals, the disabled, and others. Such remarks are in essence offering physical and related threats, offering threats of violence, damage and destruction to such individuals and groups. Unfortunately, the history of violence and oppression against such individuals and groups demonstrates that efforts to prevent expression of threats and violence are sometimes needed in order to support the well-being and happiness of people in these and other specific groups.

As people with shared characteristics, those who are gay, white, black, disabled, for example, offer no threat related to their characteristics, to the communities and societies to humanity around them. Indeed, it should be recognised that in relation to sexual preferences, both heterosexuality and homosexuality are natural ways of being. Our genetic origins and their influences on our behaviour are, in such respects, simply there and not a matter of choice, and these genetic factors influence, determine or heavily influence our skin colour, sexual preference and other personal characteristics. And whether or not we are kind, caring and acting to support others, we will retain our genetically determined characteristics.

Even if, for example, our sexual preferences were entirely a matter of individual or social choice rather than based in our genetic make-up (and research suggests our sexuality is both genetically, biologically and socially influenced), it would not be legitimate to insult, abuse, demonise and dehumanise homosexuals. All of us, whatever gender we are, female, male, transgender, or whether we are bisexual, heterosexual and homosexual, we need to be supported in terms of well-being and happiness with our aiming to reduce and prevent the pain and suffering of all. Core principles apply to all of us.

If we are significantly disabled then we may have been born with our disability or may have sustained a disability in the course of our lives. Whichever is the case, we may, at least at the present time, are likely to have no way of ridding ourselves of that disability, else we would in all likelihood have done so. Our disability provides no reason for others to belittle and deride us; no reason to discriminate unfairly against us, to dehumanise us.

Indeed it is to the benefit of our communities and societies, and indeed it is a responsibility of us all as individuals, our communities, societies and beyond, operating within the frame of core and other principles to support all of us who are disabled, to make special provision for us, to include us and support us, such that, wherever possible, we can enjoy well-being and such that we can support and contribute to the well-being of others in our communities, societies as well as to ourselves.

None of these various states is deserving or worthy of hatred and abuse. It cannot be allowed that we as individuals, that people, that others, can be abused, insulted, be subject to remarks which threaten us physically, be subject to remarks which deride and demonise us, because we are black, white, gay, because we come from a particular region of the world or a country, because of our ethnicity, because we are disabled. Core principles and values require support for others to the maximum degree possible, and in relation to personal verbal expression, engaging in individually-focused, in racial or other shared characteristics-based verbal threats and abuse, is not acceptable and, where such threat and abuse is occurring, it is the responsibility of all of us to ensure that such threatening abuse is prevented. We must take action in our day-to-day lives and more broadly in terms of our political and social lives against such kinds of abuse and threat.

Nor should threats of violence, forms of abuse which are threatening in nature, expression involving incitement of hatred, be made towards those in belief groups, such as those with particular life stances philosophies or who have religions. As already stated, in pursuit of well-being and happiness, the beliefs of all individuals and all groups must be open to question and criticism, caustic and severe criticism, open to stark and fierce criticism, where necessary or desired. In cases where we as individuals wish to express ourselves critically in such a manner, however, this should never stray into threats of violence or individual or group abuse.

We, as individuals, need to be respected as individual human beings in a sense of identity aside from our particular beliefs or membership of belief groups, although clearly if such beliefs are physically threatening and potentially damaging and destructive to others, then action will need to be taken against such views. Where such groups threaten others, demonise others, are grossly intolerant, promote violence against other belief or non-belief groups or any others; where they threaten to restrict basic and core freedoms, personal autonomy and independence, forcing their beliefs on others, then such views are unacceptable and it is entirely reasonable and legitimate to restrict the expressions of aggressive violence, hatred, physical threat and intolerance by such groups, such that the well-being and happiness of all can be protected. That being said, in some, though not all cases, it may be wiser, where this is reasonable and possible, to allow such expression, and tackle it directly in terms of its intolerance and threatened violence either verbally or through other action.

A key problem with tolerating demonising, threatening, bigoted and destruction-promising speech is that, throughout history, both nationally and locally there have been times when the violent, threatening, racist and murderous have successfully promoted their ignorant, destructive ideas, where they have gained power and put into practice their murderous, destructive ways, in some cases to the cost of many millions, even tens of millions of lives, with the consequence of individual destruction and widespread devastation. Unfortunately our humanity has shown itself to be far from always loving and caring, with many individuals capable of supporting ideas which demonise and dehumanise others, with many threatening and then doing direct violence and supporting violence against others, and many carrying out and supporting destructive, murderous violence and murderous policies at the expense of others, influenced by and in pursuit of foul and murderous ideologies and beliefs. There are strong arguments for preventing such ideologies from being expressed at source in order to protect us all, rather than risk the extreme damage and destruction their views will cause.

The notion of abuse embeds the idea of things being said, sometimes often or persistently, which may in some cases be directly threatening of violence but it also embodies the idea of deliberately hurting another or others deeply, through our causing of deep emotional and psychological harm to others. Verbal and other forms of abuse are unacceptable. Being abusive is certainly not consistent with supporting well-being and happiness. We should likewise also refrain from insult, something which may often in our daily lives represent more of an unplanned intense emotional reaction, but which may also be planned, calculated and aimed to hurt. Not only is insult unwise, inappropriate and reprehensible, it is hurtful and often weak and ineffectual, lacking persuasive capacity, and often alienating others who might be our allies, friends and more.

Both insult and abuse are often signs of subsequent aggressively violent actions, and will often precede violent action, with insult and abuse being interpreted by the recipient of the abuse to be pre-emptive of coming violent actions. Insult and abuse are reprehensible and unacceptable. Where such abuse and insult words are aimed at us, while, understandably we may be shocked, emotionally hurt, worried or even frightened at being on the end of such remarks, we should not respond in kind, but should, as far as we can, ensure our safety, and focus on supporting our own well-being and happiness as well as that of the person giving the abuse. So, as far as we can, we need to ensure we manage the situation, and respond in a non-abusive and non-insulting manner, aiming to de-escalate the situation, reduce tensions and resolve immediate and underlying problems, the angers of those making such remarks, where this is possible, as constructively as we can, acknowledging hurt, pain and anger when this is present in those making such remarks, when such acknowledgement can be done, and pointing out if we can, the innappropriacy and hurtful, damaging nature of such insulting and abusive remarks towards us, turning the situation around if we can, and eliciting regret and, where achievable, apologies. Such is easier said than done perhaps, because of our emotional responses, our personal fear and hurt, perhaps our shock and anger felt in response to such abuse and insult, because those insulting and abusing us may be out of control, even affected by drink and drugs, but we need to try our best, and indeed do whatever we can, given the particular circumstances, to succeed in achieving the resolution of whatever the situation, issue or problem might be, promoting cooperation and peacefulness as far as we can.

While threats of violence and abuse are completely unacceptable, while racist and other language, language of hatred and inciting hatred, aimed at demonising individual others or groups, or which threaten other individuals to groups is entirely unacceptable within core and other principles, we certainly need to exercise tremendous care in that expression which we, as communities, societies, as individuals, disallow and wish to and perhaps act to, prevent from being heard.

Notably, we need to be wary of some others, some groups seeking to restrict the speech of others, there being those, often leaders of belief groups and political groups who, because of their absolute belief in the tenets of their ideology or religion, because there are tenets of their beliefs which condemn non-adherents and non-believers, because of their absolute belief in their ideology, will aim to restrict the expression of ideas which are different from their own, sometimes on the false grounds of claiming offence, not only on behalf of themselves but on behalf of their whole groups, with such people claiming they have been insulted, abused and offended,

It is not, however, legitimate to prevent others expressing themselves because we feel offended or feel we are suffering emotional hurt from others expressing differing views from our own and criticising or even mocking and ridiculing our beliefs. These consequences of expression do not represent serious threats of violence or anything near to that. Frequently such belief group leaders and their followers wish to remove dissension, squash other views, maintain and bolster their own group and power. They see others disagreeing with their views beliefs and ideologies, those acting in ways contrary to their outlook and beliefs, stating things or taking actions which are not in line with their particular beliefs and opinions, or the beliefs and opinions of their groups, as undermining their beliefs (which may well be the case) and therefore representing threats to themselves and their groups. Thus they may wish to prevent others speaking and indeed sometimes wish to damage, and destroy them. Of course, not all those in belief or political groups are of this way of thinking, but some are, and these people represent a danger to us all.

Having stated such offence has been taken, these individuals, often so-called 'community leaders' have sought to, and will seek to, shut down criticism of their beliefs and the beliefs of their groups, seek to shut down ideas and expression of alternative perspectives and ideas, often in order to protect their own power and position and the power and position of their groups, but also sometimes out of ignorance or wrong belief themselves. Often the views and beliefs they espouse may be expressions of intolerance for the ways of others, for example through demonising of homosexuality and demonising of other benign behaviours or ways of being and thinking, with the beliefs and behaviours differing from their own being demonised.

Their views often express the desire for their own privileging above those who are not in their groups. In particular, in modern times, in response to what may be stark and clear depictions of what others see as the irrationality of their beliefs and belief systems, such people may claim that they are mortally offended, that they are being insulted, ridiculed and mocked or that their beliefs themselves are being insulted, mocked and ridiculed. In important cases, some leaders of religious belief groups have argued and called for such actions of self-expression, such statements and depiction of other perspectives, to be met with violence and murder or forcibly stopped, either through violence or stopped by law.

Such calls for violence, murder, repression of those expressing critical views of such belief systems or calling for violence against and the murder of those peacefully criticising, arguing against or even ridiculing and mocking such beliefs, be it through words or other forms of expression, such calls for murder and violence are abhorrent, reprehensible and totally unacceptable in terms of core and other principles.

While those who claim such offence are at liberty to express their feelings; while they have the right to express disagreement with criticisms, and to request of those making remarks or of those taking the actions they see as offensive, that these actions and remarks should be stopped, they are not at liberty, in the light of our need to support the general well-being, to stir up hatred and violence against those who they claim have offended them. They are not at liberty to prevent their critics, those who they claim have offended them or their beliefs, from speaking out and speaking out in clear terms; and they have no right to aim to harm and damage physically or in other terms, no right to engage in destructive and damaging action, against those people whose statements or actions they claim have offended or insulted them.

For what their critics have done is, if claims of offence are in fact genuine (and they are often pretexts and not so) is to have simply offended them, perhaps served to undermine their group beliefs if the grounds for their beliefs are weak, something which is at worst of minimal damage to the general well-being, and which is of no clear and great consequence or significant harm to any individual or to the general well-being. In the face of criticism, mockery and ridicule, those wishing to retain their criticised beliefs can clearly continue to do so and can argue their case for doing so. Criticism, mockery and ridicule, at various intensities, may possibly encourage or enhance a level of disrespect which may feel mildly unpleasant, but they do not incite hatred and do not threaten physical violence, pain and suffering. Indeed in the round such open criticism, such open critical action is likely to be beneficial to the many, including those within such ideological or religious belief groups, not only supporting the general well-being but also serving to support to a more complete humanity, freeing those within such groups whose leaders are most likely highly oppressive and attempting to prevent freedom and openness. The legitimate response to critics, those engaging in ridicule and mockery, within core and other principles is to disagree with them in a polite and constructive manner, arguing our case, stating reasons why we might feel these critics are wrong and listening well to what they have to say. And where beliefs are reasonable and justifiable, those beliefs may well sustain or develop.

Where those who disingenuously or even who truthfully claim such offence, wish to harm their peaceful critics or shut down discussion, sometimes through threat and violent action, it is our responsibility, the responsibility of us all, our communities and societies, our broader humanity, including those within those groups and beliefs which are being criticised, and where it has been said perhaps by community and belief group leaders that offence may have been taken, it is up to us all to stand in the way of those who threaten or act to implement such violence. It is up to us all to prevent any such restrictions on self-expression, supporting the right of critics to criticise and to do so in strong and stark terms. In doing this, we will not only be supporting the freedom of those individuals to criticise, but we will also be supporting the important freedoms of each one of us as individuals, supporting important individual freedoms, independence and autonomy which enhances our individual lives, as well as supporting the broader individual, community and broader social well-being.

As mentioned above, those who claim offence at the expression of judgments and views by other, may also often claim that they and their beliefs are being mocked and ridiculed, and that as a consequence, they and their belief group are being disrespected. They may aim to convince their group members that such mockery and ridicule means that their group and the individuals within that group are under threat and attack, with these terms 'threat' and 'attack' being used to imply real physical threat and real and significant threat to individual and group well-being, where no such threat exists. They may well use this as a basis for fomenting violence against those who they claim are mocking their beliefs or may use this as a basis and reason for aiming to and promoting the banning of such mockery and ridicule of beliefs, as well as aiming to prevent any criticism of their beliefs and group beliefs.

All of this is unacceptable in terms of core and other principles, in terms of supporting our individual freedom of expression and in support of the well-being and happiness of ourselves and others. While it is right that we should not, at least in the main, aim to mock, and ridicule other individuals or groups, and indeed in line with core principles we should be caring, respectful where this is appropriate, aim to persuade, where that is what we wish to do, and be aware of others' beliefs and sensitivities; and while we should show others kindness and love wherever possible, aiming to persuade with peaceful presentation of our views and evidenced and appropriate critique, nevertheless and unfortunately, it is the case that any criticism of a belief and particularly a group belief, can be easily rhetorically presented as disrespectful mockery and ridicule, indeed presented as an accusation that others who share a particular religious belief or ideology, are being accused of being stupid and foolish because they do not accept the view of the person of a different view, of the critic or critics. Such false depictions of criticism and critique are easy to make, and are dangerous and unacceptable, threatening the general well-being, promoting the prospect and reality of restrictions on our important freedoms and threatening potential pain and suffering.

And further, while it may perhaps be possible to draw boundaries between mockery and ridicule as opposed to a well argued, supported case, evidenced criticism or the presentation of different perspectives and approaches, those who represent belief groups can frequently lack respect of such difference, seeking to close down all criticism and critique through portraying any analysis and criticism of their beliefs as being disrespectful of not only particular beliefs but also of a whole group, with such criticism claimed to comprise the mockery and ridicule already mentioned. Yet a stark and clear depiction of truth through argument, evidence, through rhetoric, through vivid pictoral representation, may clearly paint the irrationality of an idea and thereby in itself seem close to or be paralleled to mockery. Thus, for this and other reasons, efforts to limit mockery and ridicule are likely to end up preventing legitimate criticism and self-expression, something which is contrary to core and other principles, and something which will damage our well-being and happiness.

Moreover it may well be that a factor in determining differences between mockery, ridicule and criticism is put down to the degree of hurt, upset and offence by the person claiming their beliefs are being ridiculed and mocked, something which has the potential to place too much power in relation to our freedom of expression in the hands of those individuals claiming they are being mocked and ridiculed. The fact that we, or many in our group, might feel hurt and upset at what another has said or done is not sufficient reason to legally prevent or outlaw others from saying these things or doing such things. Of course we can politely ask others and aim to persuade them to desist or persuade them they are wrong.

Cartoons and pictures, certain clearly phrased and stark expressions of view, which comprise no real insult to others, which offer no real threat of physical attack on others, which are not focused on or aimed at inciting physical violence or other destructive action against other groups or individuals, which are focused in issues and views rather than, for example, races of people, or groups identified through innate characteristics but which make salient to us particular issues or points, may again be claimed to be mockery and ridicule, but they are certainly legitimate in terms of core and other principles in terms of their adherence to our need for the ability to express our views, to exchange and communicate ideas, to raise issues and in support of the general well-being and happiness. There are serious dangers in preventing and outlawing mockery and ridicule of opinions and beliefs, dangers which impinge on our basic freedoms of expression and well-being. That being said, it may well be best and more persuasive to use the more constructive and positive approaches already referred to.

Thus if we are faced in a group belief context, in our communities and societies with our views and ideas being mocked and ridiculed, while we may feel disrespected and upset, our role and responsibility is to speak truthfully and counter untruths, to express our hurt and upset, should we feel that way, but to use evidence, reason, empathy and logic to establish that our case is not worthy of mockery and ridicule, but is in fact true and-or of value and importance in terms of supporting both individual and the general well-being and happiness. Mockery of reasonable beliefs should not be difficult to counter. And through hearing of our hurt and upset, should we feel that way, others may choose to act differently.

Thus, if we are mocked, and held up to ridicule by those who disagree with us, then we need to counter the arguments of those are mocking us with words and arguments. Mockery and ridicule may create laughter and perhaps sometimes express or embody disdain and perhaps a level of disrespect, but they do not express hatred or embody any threat against any person. Indeed mockery and ridicule, while not entirely desirable and possible of causing unwanted offence, can be seen, in some contexts, as to some extent positive when expressed effectively, providing stark and clear demonstrations of truth, demonstrating the lack of veracity, validity, value and truth in certain world views, the hypocrisy and dishonesty of individuals and groups in a way in which more polite speech and persuasion may well not manage.

Such mockery and ridicule, can enable us to see through the puffery, falsehood, hypocrisy, self-serving nature and superficiality of many ideas and many people, reminding us in some cases that those with great power and influence are indeed, in many senses, simply other human beings, likely to have their own faults, who may act in hypocritical ways (for example hypocritically espousing certain forms of morality for others in society while breeching that morality in private themselves); mockery and ridicule can point out in stark terms that people should not simply be respected because they have power, and certainly people should not be followed and unquestioningly obeyed because they have such power, and ideologies should not simply be followed because they are dominant, predominant and prevalent. Mockery, humour and ridicule are forms of our personal expression which notably tend to be the allies of those of us who feel powerless and frustrated and who find it hard to have an impact on events ourselves, indeed who find it hard to hit back in other ways against our powerlessness and humiliations.

However, while perhaps popular with those who agree already with a case, mockery and ridicule are perhaps unlikely to persuade those who disagree and may serve to alienate some of them, alienating perhaps quite caring and good people. And if we wish, of course, in the face of our views and beliefs being mocked and ridiculed, as already stated, we have the power to retain our views and will often have the power to practise the consequences of them (however illogical and unevidenced they may be), because mockery and ridicule do not mean that our views are wrong. Some of the most important ideas of the modern age were mocked and ridiculed by some in the early stages of their proposition and development. New ideas and perspectives, newly encountered ideas and perspectives can often seem rather ridiculous on first experience and encounter, and sometimes we might express such a view, yet in many cases our ideas change as our understanding and knowledge develop and grow.

As suggested through this guide's support for cooperative and caring approaches to our living, and through our recognition of the potentially alienating effects of mockery and ridicule, the statement that mockery and ridicule should not be outlawed and that they can be of value in making vivid, highlighting and emphasising certain points of argument, is not the same as saying that mockery and ridicule are in the main (or perhaps ever) desirable, when we may use other ways to pursue our goals and persuade others. But, for example, difficulties have been pointed out already in deciding boundaries between mockery, ridicule and criticism, including the dangers, if not likelihood, of our banning of mockery and ridicule leading to prevention by the powerful and others of any criticism at all of themselves, their actions and damaging, destructive and wrong beliefs. Thus, while we may choose, and it is likely to be more persuasive to be caring, understanding and cooperative in our approach to other belief groups and beliefs, there is considered to be no significantly justifiable case for preventing the freedom to mock and ridicule, the option to engage in these forms of expression being seen as consistent with our freedoms, our independence, our autonomy and our overall well-being.

Nevertheless, it is generally for the best for us to deal with others and their beliefs in a patient and respectful manner, where such respect is appropriate, with our again, as necessary, finding fault and being critical and starkly so at times, vigorously and persuasively critical if that is required, but also where rational, reasonable and appropriate, also finding value in the perspectives and beliefs of others and certainly understanding their fundamental humanity and individual human needs, while of course being aware of any significant threats that these individuals, groups and their beliefs may pose to ourselves or others, and ensuring as far as we can that such threats to our well-being and happiness cannot be put into action.

Such peaceful, empathetic and respectful behaviour will generally, though not always, provide a better route to cooperation and persuasion, to living together as individuals, communities and societies. It is for the best that others respect us and we respect them, though it should be said that, believing in core principles, the well-being and happiness of each individual, of all, not all world views are commensurate with such a cooperative and caring approach to all others and it may be difficult to feel respect for some such world views, especially those which offer aggressive violence, threats of violence and personal damage to those who do not accept their particular world views and which seek, through violence and threat, to impose their beliefs and views on others. Respect for the humanity, the human identity, the existence, caring for all, the need for well-being and happiness of ourselves and all others, as stated in core principles is essential.

In this context, it needs to be mentioned that statements by any group or individual, by belief groups, using statements quoted from and found in their ancient texts or other texts, to the effect, metaphorically or otherwise, either that others who do not share such beliefs are not fully people, or that on the grounds of holding other beliefs they should be subject to violence or forced to change their beliefs against their desire and will, are totally contrary to freedom, our individual independence and autonomy, and of course destructive and damaging to well-being, being potentially and actually causative of pain and suffering. As already mentioned in this chapter, there is no freedom to threaten those with differing views with aggressive violence, to do aggressive violence or to incite violence against others with differing beliefs and views of the world.

Nor is there a freedom to verbally or otherwise characterise those who express differing views, who have a differing belief, differing beliefs and belief systems, in such a manner that they are likely to, or will by subject to, significantly destructive physical, psychological or other damaging actions against them, with such characterisations often, in essence, dehumanising them, acting in reality as an incitement to hatred and violence. Where those in belief groups make such statements in relation to other belief groups, or other individuals, both within and outside of their belief groups, then in support of well-being and happiness, it is the responsibility of each of us, our communities and societies to ensure action is taken against them to prevent such threats, such coercion and such violence.

Of course, as already mentioned, we have the option of telling people with differing beliefs, in a peaceable manner, that we believe they are wrong, that we have a different view, that it will be to their benefit to change. We can aim to persuade others peaceably to change their beliefs, expecting that if we attempt to do so, such change may take time. But threat, violence, coercion and physical force in support of persuading others to change their beliefs or as a consequence of their different beliefs are not acceptable and stand against the freedom of all of us.

Notably, with regard again to mockery, ridicule and belief, we should take great care, and indeed avoid, and aim to avoid mockery of weak and vulnerable individuals, (and perhaps also weak and vulnerable groups of people) who offer no significant threat to others, those who are powerless and who may be deeply emotionally hurt by ridicule and mockery. We need to take great care of their well-being. The arrogant, oppressive and powerful, the institutionally strong, may be easily criticised, perhaps mocked and criticised, perhaps ridiculed, (though even with some of us who are powerful people, the rest of us will need to recognise that such powerful people may be doing their best to act with justice and care, to support all others in achieving their well-being and happiness). Yet we have a responsibility to be caring, loving and supportive of others as far as we can, and should not engage in conduct which will substantially damage the emotional state, cause significant pain to those who are vulnerable, weak, lacking in power and unable to cope with such mockery and ridicule, whether that be within a home environment or in the public space in front of others, friends and families. That is not to say that we should not express views and disagreement or aim to persuade. However, deliberately humiliating and hurting anyone, in particular the weak and vulnerable, is unacceptable and inconsistent with supporting the well-being of others. It is not consistent with core principles and is not consistent with our supporting our own well-being and happiness and the well-being and happiness of others.

It might be that such mockery and ridiculing of others is indicative in some cases, or is perhaps often indicative, of our feeling a lack of empathy for others, a lack of understanding, love and care. It may be that their use is indicative of powerlessness and impotence. Nevertheless, it is worth reiterating that we should seek no prohibitions on mockery, humour and ridicule, in the public space, particularly in regard to those individuals who are powerful, hypocritical and oppressive or in regard to powerful groups and their leaders, who act in such ways.

Illustrating the importance of this freedom of expression and action, is the observation that within certain communities and belief groups, throughout history and in the current time, those who have engaged in expression of non-conformist beliefs, those critical of powerful political figures, of religious belief systems and political systems, those who have generated new discoveries or who have shown creativity, perhaps seen the world from new perspectives, those who have promoted positive and constructive change socially, politically and otherwise, those people who have promoted togetherness and love, promoted our living well-together, or simply promoted new and different belief systems representing no physical threat, no threat in terms of well-being to any other, despite their peaceful intentions, actions and efforts to support well-being and happiness, these people have been frequently oppressed because of their non-conformity, difference and dissent, and not infrequently, have been deprived of their liberty, tortured and murdered, sometimes in their hundreds, thousands and millions, because of their words, principled actions and beliefs.

In many countries in the current world, those expressing views incompatible with dominant and oppressive political or religious belief systems face the likelihood of severe punishment, torture, legalised execution and murder. Blasphemy laws presented as 'protecting' belief systems or other laws protecting those in power exist, are brought in with the purpose of protecting belief and political systems or leaders from criticism, with severe punishments, incorporating substantial pain and suffering or execution as their consequence. In some cultural groups and religious belief groups, attempting to leave that group, known in the case of religious groups as apostasy, trying to express, even in peaceful terms, ideas contrary to the core beliefs of that group, and acting in peaceful and loving ways though which contrast with the views, beliefs and traditions of such groups, can be met with threats of death and indeed the actual murder of the person expressing these beliefs or wishing to leave that group. Those who think and believe differently are forced to silence or to somehow escape to more free environments.

Making such threats and doing such violence against those with different beliefs, or acting to maintain and even expand such oppressive systems, is appalling and evil, standing fundamentally against the basic notions of personal freedom and belief set out in this guide being entirely contrary to supporting well-being and happiness, causing tremendous pain and suffering in an ongoing manner for all, being entirely at odds with core principles, both generally for all (for none will be free under such circumstances), but also, of course, for the particular person or people faced with the cruel tortures and legalised murder or otherwise which they may well face. Such laws are cruel, callous and detrimental to all and totally incompatible with individual, community and social well-being. It is the responsibility of all of us, of each one of us, to act to remove such laws and support the opening up of speech, action, discussion and debate and the expansion and growth of freedom for all.

In response to what others say, not only should we be prepared and in some cases happy, to be shocked or offended by what people say and do, (where such statements and actions are not abusive, are not threatening of aggressive violence or indicative of support for and promotion of aggressive violence), we should also be prepared to be outraged by what others do within such bounds, and rather than responding with efforts to prevent them speaking and doing as they will (where this does not promote or involve aggressive physical or psychological violence), rather we need to listen where we can, and engage and discuss with these others where we can, to persuade them of our case, and persuade them of our views in regard to that which is necessary in order to optimally support well-being and happiness. Our responses need to be loving, caring and tolerant of those trying the new and speaking and acting in different ways from those which we are used to, while protecting our own life, well-being, happiness and liberty and the lives, well-being, happiness and liberty of others.

All this being said, where there is substantive oppression, where significant damage is being done or threatened to ourselves and others, through violent oppression, through economic oppression which drives us into suffering and poverty, where physical coercion, in some cases torture and other forms of physical and mental suffering are being implemented in whichever context, be such oppression occurring within the home, in the family or in our work contexts, be it more generally in our community and society, where our basic freedoms are being violated, be this unplanned and random, individual or systematically imposed group oppression, then a physical response to such oppression, the use of physical forceful action to remove such oppression may be necessary, advocated, expressed, spoken out, and indeed where necessary for our self-protection and the protection of others, will need to be implemented.

In the vast main of course, those involved in oppression and violent restrictions on liberty, those who torture, push into poverty and oppress, will rarely be inclined to allow others to speak out against them. Yet under such conditions of severe oppression, physical violence and intimidation against us, the restriction of our basic freedoms, such speaking out in favour of forceful physical action against such oppression becomes legitimate. As mentioned in other parts of this guide, many actions should optimally be taken before we reach such a stage, if these are possible and reasonable, and moreover, we should not advocate anything in physical terms, more than the minimum force and minimum physical action necessary to achieve goals of removing such oppression and violence, and ensuring the institution of actions, practices, by other individuals, powerful individuals, government and social organisations, which support our well-being, happiness and freedoms and which support the well-being, happiness and freedoms of others. We should not advocate or practise revenge and violent retribution.

Where our communities and societies, as well as individuals, have strong beliefs in traditions and conventions and have strong tendencies to highly conservative conformity; where there is emphasis or over-emphasis on particular conceptions of family and individual honour, then a significant factor in pressuring people to conform may be the notions of social and group shame, and bringing honour to or dishonour to the family and community. Honour may in some circumstances be a useful and important notion for us as individuals and for the broader community, especially when considered in relation to ideas such as supporting the well-being of others, integrity and honesty, however, in many contexts the notions of family and group honour are inappropriate and can become too central to notions of good conduct, becoming oppressive and destructive such that the concept of honour is substantially at odds with the pursuit of individual well-being and happiness, as well as being at odds the pursuit of wider community and society happiness and well-being. In important respects the notion of such family and group honour takes away from our individual responsibility for our actions and promotes stultifying and oppressive conformity.

In practice such systems have served as oppressive means by which males aim to control girl's and women's sexuality, with girls and women said to have damaged family honour if they have sex outside of marriage, show parts of their bodies, love those from poorer or different caste and class families, or engage in other sex-related and disapproved of behaviours. Such oppression and such male control is totally unacceptable within the terms of core and other principles through its oppressive nature including the oppressive violence needed to maintain such systems, through its illegitimate restriction of women's sexual and relationship freedoms, through its denial of girl's and women's rights to have control over their own bodies and their own relationships, through the pain and suffering it causes to girls and women (and indeed to their whole communities and societies) and for a range of other reasons through which the well-being and happiness of all is damaged.

As an individual within the family or wherever, we must all be free to pursue our own paths, our own beliefs, our own goals in life, which means that we must have the option of not conforming with prevalent conformist social ideas and thinking; we must have the option of identifying, indeed we have an obligation in support of our own well-being and happiness, to develop our own thinking, to develop our own approaches and perspectives, something which will benefit us not only as individuals, but which will benefit all. And whatever the notions of conformity within a community and society, we are individually responsible for our own beliefs, judgments and actions.

If our families feel shame at what we, their children or other members of the family have done, then that shame is for those families to cope with internally in terms of their own individual feelings of shame, rather than taking punitive and destructive action against us or those of us who are not conforming, who have not conformed, against those who are breaking rules, acting out of line with traditions, norms and conventions. And while we may, as individuals, families and communities feel unhappy with someone if they should break such rules, conventions, we should not be and cannot be held responsible for their actions because these were not our actions. And where the actions of others are directly damaging and destructive of others, as long as we did not promote such actions through our actions or our teaching, or do so clearly through our upbringing of that person, then their actions are not our responsibility and we cannot and should not be held to account for what they have done, simply because we are in the same family.

Those with conformist, traditional, conservative views are of course always free to advise us to take a different course of action. Yet our taking of non-conformist, non-traditional approaches, our breaching of oppressive convention is not an excuse for abuse, insult and violent action against those of us who are pursuing or who have pursued their own paths in love, in career, in personal belief, in whichever way they have chosen to go. As parents it is our job and duty to support our children as well as supporting our communities, societies and our broader humanity. It is not our job to suppress and oppress our children or to act violently against them because they have, for example, chosen to love someone of whom we disapprove, whom we consider unsuitable, to take oppressive and coercive action against them because they have expressed a belief with which we do not accord, indeed even because they have done something which might be widely acknowledged as wrong.

Of course, on some, hopefully rare occasions, our children, in their younger years or as adults, may commit crimes, act dishonestly, even hurt and in some cases do serious violence to others. In these cases, it is reasonable and perhaps inevitable for us to be shocked and hurt by what they have done, and wonder perhaps what we might have done during their upbringing to lead to this. Yet, in many cases we will have done nothing wrong ourselves. It is therefore not appropriate in such cases, for us to feel shame for the acts of our children, if we have never and did not ever support such acts. Under such circumstances, our role is to support our children back to an appropriate, loving and caring path, something which in some cases may be a hard task. Yet that is our role as parents – to love and care for our children and to bring them up and look after them, such that they can enjoy well-being and happiness and can care for and support the well-being and happiness of others, our communities, societies and beyond.

Once they are into young adulthood and beyond, our children become increasingly responsible for their own actions, not us as parents. We can do our best to bring them up well such that they pursue their own well-being and happiness and such that they can support the well-being and happiness of others, such that they will have fun and enjoy their lives, becoming fulfilled individuals. However we cannot, as parents, take significant responsibility for the individual acts of other independent adults. We may be upset about the acts done by our children as adults, but we should not feel shame or any significant blame. Their actions do not reflect on us and should not be seen as reflecting on us, unless there are specific and damaging actions which we have clearly promoted or engaged in ourselves, or unless there are specific and damaging, destructive beliefs and values we have promulgated which will have substantially influenced and led to those actions.

Yet shame and perhaps the related idea of honour, do affect all of us as individuals and indeed no doubt any group of individuals, community, any society. If we do something wrong, substantially against the values of our groups, communities and societies, and we appreciate we have done wrong in these terms, then we, as individuals may well feel shame and embarrassment at our actions and we may wish others not to know about what we have done, as we know or believe they will think badly of us, indeed in some cases, they may never forgive us. In a sense that notion of shame allied to our desire to be loved and liked, tied to things like our reputation may act as a motivator for our behaviour and action as well as our inaction, in some instances, where we may address the question, "What will others think if they find out I have done this?" And if we judge that others will think badly of us, then we may think twice about that action.

Most likely, we all have felt shame at some point on the grounds of some wrong action, or we will have been told that we should be ashamed of what we have done. Some parents say this kind of thing frequently or use the notion of shame as a means of teaching their children. Certainly teaching our children that their conduct should be caring and kind, that they should show honesty and integrity and should adopt and implement the range of values consistent with core and other principles is essential. Nevertheless this teaching of personal conduct should not be taught through the notion of shame which, given our social nature as children and adults and our awareness of what is acceptable and unacceptable conduct within our communities and societies, is likely to cause additional pain and may well be superfluous since we are likely to feel ashamed in any case.

There are those who may be described as feeling no shame. Such descriptions will tend to arise when our individual values, beliefs and actions clash with the individual values and beliefs of others or perhaps more often when they clash with what are perceived as the customs and practices of communities and societies. The key thing for us and others to consider is whether our conduct is in line with core and other principles and whether it is supportive of well-being and happiness overall, and results in the reduction or removal of pain and suffering. The possibility of our experiencing potential shame will be something which we may take into consideration in terms of our actions and conduct since shame is likely to be detrimental to our personal well-being. Yet when we are deciding on our conduct and actions, we certainly need to consider broader issues of well-being and happiness not only our own well-being and happiness in all its aspects, but also the well-being and happiness of others, irrespective of what others might think of us should we take a particular action.

And moreover, while others may tell us we should feel ashamed, we may well feel no such thing as we are convinced our actions are justified, moral and correct, even taking into account what such others, perhaps many others, might think. We may believe our actions are honourable, worthy, and are appropriate actions in terms of core and other principles, in terms of the goals of supporting well-being and happiness and reducing levels of pain and suffering. We are of course responsible for our own judgments and actions, but it is reasonable for us to be aware of social codes and norms that we are breaking, and break them with the knowledge of what we are doing. We certainly need to ensure however that the codes of conduct, that our social systems of conduct, are not oppressive, stultifying and constraining of our basic freedoms, which underpin our well-being and happiness.

Issues such as our freedom and oppression are indeed big issues, which quite clearly affect the everyday lives of many, if not all of us, in many ways. Yet there are issues relating to conformity and freedom in our everyday lives which we may hardly be aware of. For example, without noticing and being consciously aware of the fact, in our more everyday terms, in addition to being bound by certain norms of convention which will affect our everyday actions and choices, in relation to our personal expression, as referred to briefly earlier in this chapter ,we are undoubtedly somewhat bounded by the norms and conventions of talk and interaction.

For example, certain things are considered impolite to say and certain subjects are considered inappropriate for conversation, and so we regulate our own talk such that these things are not normally said and such that these topics are not normally addressed. As has already been mentioned, we are required to be and certainly need to be careful and sensitive in our speech, as we would and indeed wisely should be, in the public space, operating through our talk to build cooperation and togetherness, friendship and friendliness with others. Nevertheless it is worthwhile building some conscious awareness of these restrictions, norms and conventions, examining these and perhaps where the need arises, breaking such conventions.

Beyond our every day talk, there are many intricate social behavioural rules, issues of custom and manners, with which we may need to conform if we are to be easily accepted and therefore live more successfully within our communities, and live successfully within certain groups. Our not following such customs and practices may be accepted where people are kind, generous and accepting, or where such customs and practices are not seen as crucial, but can also cause problems for us in some circumstances. This type of conduct refers here to customs such as timekeeping and lateness, certain ways of dressing (which have already been discussed above), cleanliness, personal space, customs and practices regarding eating and drinking, socialising and spending time with others, and more. By contrast to certain key areas, of significant importance to the individual decisions we make in our personal lives, important decisions which may have a significant effect on our direction of travel in our lives and our future well-being and happiness, these being areas where we may wish to and need to breech some conventions and norms, in many cases, where such conduct is of lesser significance, and norms, customs and conventions are of lesser importance in terms of the big picture of our lives, we may choose, on the whole, to follow these customs.

If we break some of these more intricate social customs, we may sometimes be allowed to breech these standard behaviours without any formal sanction, though facing perhaps some social opprobrium, a degree of ostracism from particular individuals or groups, and may also perhaps experience some disadvantage in our work or social lives. Others should not cause us disadvantage on account of our breech of such more minor social conventions nor should we cause others such disadvantage under these circumstances, our all being open to such different ways of behaving and being.

Thus, our decisions as to whether or not to engage in these more intricate and socially acceptable and unacceptable ways of behaving clearly feed into notions of freedom, independence and conformity. In theory, as they may be largely unacknowledged or seen as insignificant, we are free to breach such accepted ways of behaving, and indeed, at times, we may consciously choose to do so, but for the most part it may be wise to recognise some of these conventions and leave our breaches of these conventions either to those occasions when these conventions breach core and other principles, in which circumstances we are obliged to break them, or to leave our breaches of such apparently more minor conventions to occasions where in order to support our freedom and our well-being and happiness, we wish to make a conscious challenge to convention. Of course we may choose to break such norms and conventions as a matter of principle, though as social beings, this may interfere with our interactions with others and our ability to achieve through our interactions with others.

Such norms and conventions of behaviour can clearly lead to difficulties between those of us brought up in different cultures. If we do not understand certain conventions and norms in another culture then we may cause offence unintentionally through our actions. Within core principles, where conventions and norms are just such and cause no significant identifiable harm to others, then, if living in those cultures, it may well be best to recognise and conform to those norms and conventions. If we are part of one culture and we see those from outside our culture breaching such norms, where no identifiable and significant harm or damage is caused then, however uncomfortable we may feel, we must be tolerant and accept such breaches without anger and rancor, and certainly without threat and violence. This is the same attitude we should adopt to such breaches within our own cultures by those who want to go against these norms and conventions and in a sense 'do their own thing'.

As already stated, our self-expression and freedom of expression are relevant to, and, of course, refer to, much more than speech. They refer amongst other things to our freedom to engage without unwarranted and unjustified interference in artistic expression through for example, sculpture, writing in all its forms, poetry, painting, literature and storytelling, music, architectural design, product design, theatre, drama, film, comedy and humour, fashion and more.

Free self-expression and freedom of expression, as applied to the arts and other areas, is almost always of benefit to our society as a whole, enabling us to enjoy the experience of our self-expression and the novelty generated by our self-expression, enabling ourselves and others to see new things, to understand and view the world in new ways, enabling us to experience joy, pleasure and stimulation through new visual and other experiences. Our free self-expression is of key importance to our well-being and happiness and needs to be positively encouraged and promoted.

It is of importance that we are all broad-minded in our responses to such free artistic expression, being welcoming, open-minded and accepting of the new, a new which may sometimes seem strange, but which may engage us in new experiences, understandings and adventures, which may advance our well-being (or may not as the case may be). Such self-expression needs our active support and promotion and should not founder against the painful rocks of social conformity, especially as it supports the benefit of those of us, those individuals, looking to express ourselves or themselves in novel ways, but also acts for the benefit of the wider community, in a sense indicating and supporting our own individual autonomy, independence and freedom.

Within the bounds of self-expression and free expression already discussed within this chapter, painters should be free to experiment and paint as they will; writers and poets should be able to write as they wish to write and about that which they wish to write, and books, literature (fiction and non-fiction), poetry and other writings should not be banned or censored unless they express and offer direct and significant threat to the well-being and lives of others, for example through promoting violence against a particular group or individual, through deliberately expressing and promoting violence *per se* against particular individuals or groups within the bounds already described, and through inciting hatred which will likely lead to aggressive violence (although noting that using our words to promote forceful resistance to oppression is seen as being legitimate).

Not discussed in detail up to now, but also representing the need to promote well-being and prevent pain and suffering, there may further also be a strong case for censoring or banning the publication of falsehoods about individuals and groups, about issues, which may cause such individuals and groups, perhaps all of us, substantial damage through creating false and undeserved reputations, through promulgating misleading and false evidence and through other forms of harm and damage. The mechanisms for determining such falsehoods need to be impartial, independent, just and fair. At the minimum, the opportunity to respond to such claimed falsehoods through legal action or other peaceful means or through the right to respond to published claimed falsehoods is necessary with our being able to appropriately demand and receive, at the minimum, full and prominent retractions and apologies where false and dishonest information is published about us.

Thus, as already discussed in this chapter in relation to false and damaging testimony in court and also in regard to our responsibilities to find out the truth, we have a responsibility to communicate accurate and truthful information, as far as we can. Careless and deliberate false reporting of information is unacceptable within core and other principles. In the present era, there is good reason to believe that certain individuals with financial and political interests have aimed and are aiming to deliberately undermine the case for anthropogenic climate change through selective use of information, through sometimes providing inaccurate or even fake or manipulated data, or through clear and deliberate misinterpretation of evidence available. Those engaging in such false claims are placing us in grave danger, and it the view of this guide that there need to be systems in place to tackle the promotion of such falsehoods, with legal remedies available to us all, and appropriate and serious responses borne by those who promote such falsehoods.

Nevertheless, there is no place within the core and other principles for book burning, for the destruction of newspapers and articles, however provocative and false such books and articles might be. And even in those cases where books and writings may threaten significant damage and violence to others we should take care to ensure that removing or censoring the book or publication is in fact necessary and that it indeed represents the best way to deal with the threats and violence offered by that book and the ideas expressed within, in particular because other approaches and strategies such as argument and persuasion are likely to be available. Discussion and debate with the presented ideas might be the better option and might well have greater influence and effect. Nevertheless, as already discussed in this chapter, none of us is free to make direct threats of aggressive violence against others, to incite hatred and the likely subsequent aggressive violence against others, whichever form we choose to do this in.

Beyond the world of art, in the context of widely available media, such as newspapers and magazines, internet publications and blogs, clearly if we edit or write for such publications, we should be aiming through our work to improve both our own well-being and the well-being of others. Again, newspapers and magazines should be allowed to publish as they wish within the bounds of core and other principles, though as already stated in the chapter on honesty and integrity, editors and journalists must seek out what is the real truth rather than writing to support owner and other interests, and rather than manipulating perceptions and information, or lying and misleading in order to meet the demands and beliefs of their proprietors (which may well of course, for a range of reasons, mirror the editor and journalist's beliefs).

While managers, owners, editors and writers are certainly free to promote and publish their beliefs, what is reported must be truthful and accurate, optimally reporting other perceptions, including the reporting of facts and information inconsistent with an editorial line or journalistic view, and including alternative interpretations of events. Journalistic articles and reporting, indeed other writings and speaking should serve as means of educating and informing, as a means of raising questions and encouraging discussion and debate, and should certainly not represent efforts to discredit those with different views and interests, aiming to present false or skewed information and interpretations designed to mislead, nor should they be used as a means of otherwise damaging opponents.

If we as individuals publish materials, write letters, make statements online, make speeches and provide spoken comments, then yet again we have freedoms to write and speak our views, judgments and opinions and report information as we see it; we have the right and freedom to express ourselves creatively. Yet we also have the responsibility to be truthful, to report events as accurately as we can, to consider other views and indeed present those other views and perceptions where appropriate (those operating within the framework of core and other principles) such that our readers and listeners can gain an understanding of alternative perspectives.

Beyond the area of books, newspapers and magazines, blogs, poetry and the like, those who generate art should be free to produce the art of their choice. Architects should be able to design what they wish to design (though we need not pay for their work); film should touch on the areas that its writers, actors, directors and indeed film corporations and film company owners, wish to touch upon. Theatre and drama should be available to challenge ideas; fashion should attempt to make us look good and also break boundaries. Sculptors should sculpt as they wish to sculpt and so forth.

And none of this art or expression of ideas should be censored on the grounds of taste, its originality, its challenge to a prevailing morality or on many other bases. The only basis for such censorship is if that artwork promises, and threatens violence or significant psychological damage to others, something which is, in the vast main, hard for artwork to do. The production and publishing of images of religious figures, images or other symbols must not be banned by religious or political groups or due to threats from religious, political or other groups, with the exception of where these depictions might reasonably be seen as incitements to others to engage in destructive discrimination and aggressive violence. The production and publishing of images must not be prevented by threats of aggressive violence and intimidation. If a belief system says that an image should not be made, then it is those who wish to adhere to such a belief system who should not make such images. It is not for those with other views to be intimidated and threatened or frightened into not producing such harmless images and representations.

Of course while artists of all kinds are free to produce and promote their work, that being said, none of us, none of our organisations are under an obligation to commission, pay for, fund or buy artwork which we do not like, nor is there an obligation for artwork which is inconsistent with generally acceptable taste, morality and values to be displayed in open public view, though it may well often be a good and challenging thing for such different and new art to be publically displayed and for it to enjoy such exposure. Nevertheless, in the field of art it might certainly be good for us as individuals (if we have the resources), our organisations and institutions, to fund art of all types, to fund education and training in the arts, including in relation to that art which challenges and makes us question our assumptions and beliefs. The value of art in all its forms means that not only should such artwork not be censored but that it should indeed be promoted and supported by us as individuals, by our communities, societies and beyond.

In a similar manner, while we need not pay for and support writers with different views from those which we personally accept and believe in, we may wish as individuals, organisations and institutions to support financially and otherwise, those who think and generate new and different ideas, those who write creatively in new and challenging ways. This can be done by supporting individuals and groups, or by supporting the teaching of effective creative and other writing skills and abilities. This will serve as a means of promoting the diversity of ideas within our communities, societies and beyond, enhancing the freedom of us all through improving our access to thinking and ideas, and enabling and supporting effective and fair consideration of reasonable and rational ideas as opposed to our perhaps being simply exposed to the ideas which the influential, wealthy and powerful are able to promote and promulgate within our communities and societies.

In line with what has already been stated and supporting the well-being of us all, in regard to certain freedoms of speech and action there is a need, in general, though within the types of limits already referred to, for us not only to enjoy our own freedom to speak out our views, judgments and opinions but also for us to be tolerant of others. Indeed we also need to be somewhat tolerant of, and patient with, ourselves and our own actions, weaknesses and inadequacies, accepting our freedom to think, express ourselves, learn and grow.

Yet, tolerance is indeed rather a basic and perhaps minimal level of response in regard to our attitudes to the differences and sometimes challenging actions, thoughts and beliefs of others. Beyond simple tolerance, we must act in a manner which, within the parameters of supporting well-being and happiness, encourages, supports and facilitates both ourselves and others in expressing our own and others' own individuality, judgments and beliefs. That does not mean that such judgments, beliefs and actions are of necessity accepted and agreed upon as representing truth and reality, or that they are or should be enabled into practice. We may disagree and disagree vigorously with some views and opinions, but it does mean that within the context of core principles we are supporting and promoting expression of the self, and supporting and promoting expression of judgment and belief, something which bolsters the value of each of us as a person, and which thereby greatly supports well-being and happiness.

Thus, we need to do more than just be tolerant. We must do our best to appreciate others, support them in their lives, encourage them in their self-expression and support them towards their legitimate and reasonable goals and dreams. It may be that others are wrong in their views and that they have incorrect perceptions and, if we feel this is so, we should, or may choose to, as appropriate, point this out, hopefully in polite, friendly though sometimes where necessary a robust manner, while at the same time encouraging progress in thought and action, and encouraging further personal development, investigation and self-expression. We should seek as far as we can to avoid damaging the broader self-confidence of ourselves and others, encouraging our own and the sense of others, in terms of self-value, while accepting that a realistic assessment of our own current abilities and capacities is something which is always worthwhile, a knowledge and understanding of ourselves being something which in itself will support us to change and grow. Beyond tolerance, we need to appreciate the existence and value of others, appreciate their individual characteristics in terms of both their similarity and differences in relation to ourselves, and appreciate their own need for self-expression, for their own sense of self-value and self-efficacy, representing individual contribution which will support a sense of their own importance.

The presence of many forms of difference and variety provide a vibrancy and excitement in our lives, provide experiences of the new, provide different and novel ways of seeing the world. These forms of difference add to our lives and the lives of the communities and societies, as well as the broader humanity, in which we live. The reality for most of us is likely to be that, through differing personal, community and cultural background, differing histories, through age differences and differing upbringing, we will encounter a vast range of differences in people and personality through our lives, and these different people will hopefully contribute to the joy and pleasure in our lives. In terms of freedom and independence, we need to, as appropriate, in line with core and other principles, enjoy and encourage, indeed celebrate such difference and diversity, which will support not only the more individual well-being and happiness, but also the broader well-being of communities, societies and beyond.

At a more micro and daily level, while many of these broad differences will enrich us, it may be that, in some cases, we find that certain behaviours of others, their mannerisms, their ways of talking to us, their ways of dealing with problems, matters such as their attitude to time (in some contexts this meaning lateness), the things they eat and the way they eat, the distance from us at which they stand, the behaviours, manners and approaches derived from their upbringings, families and cultures, may be sometimes somewhat difficult to cope with and comprehend, and we may in some cases find these problematic, if not, our finding such behaviours annoying, anti-social and unpleasant (though hopefully not generally so).

Where we find such differences, some of which we may not be approving of, we need to remain appreciative and at the minimum be tolerant of others different in such ways from ourselves, understanding that the behaviour and conduct of others will always be, to some degree, different from our own, and that is it is likely that there will always be some element of the behaviour of others that does not, at least initially, meet with our approval. Further, we should also appreciate that not only is it most likely incorrect for us to censure some of this behaviour of others, but we must recognise that our efforts at achieving such change in others may well be ineffective (and indeed perhaps interpreted as very rude). It is essential to recognise, of course, that others have the right to pursue their own well-being and happiness in their own way, to be happy with their own manners and mannerisms, to follow their own cultural and other practices where these do no significant harm to others and support well-being and happiness. We need to understand that such differences are, at least on the whole, of benefit to our communities and societies, providing a diversity of ways of doing things and ways of being, differing experiences, perspectives, actions and talents, and we need to understand that not only do such differences provide an invaluable resource to our communities, societies and our broader humanity, but, as already mentioned, we need to recognise that there is much pleasure and joy to be found in our differences.

On the other hand, it may be that we recognise the tensions that some of our behaviours, some of our lack of adherence to social norms and conventions, are causing around us, and recognising the annoyance, angst and upset arising as a consequence of such apparently minor elements of our behaviour, we may decide to change what we do and how we behave. Though perhaps difficult in some cases, this may well be a generous, appropriate and practical way of making our own lives and those of others easier, facilitating cooperation and togetherness. Given our need to tolerate others and yet the existence of personal tastes and preferences as well as manners, customs, conventions and norms in our communities and societies, we may well need to negotiate our way between appropriate toleration of those tastes and preferences of others, the prevailing conventions and norms in the cultures around us, and our own personal preferences, and the conduct, conventions and norms we are used to from our own more familiar and home cultures.

Tolerance and understanding are of importance to our happiness and well-being in a vast range of contexts. However, one particularly common and important area where difficulties arise and where tolerance and indeed open-mindedness are of particular benefit to us, relates to the relationships between older and younger people, that is, more specifically, the relationships between us as adults and parents with our teenagers, or us as teenage children and young people, and our relationships with our parents and older adults.

Representing the generational differences that frequently arise, it is common for younger people in many cultures to think, behave and dress differently from their parents' generation, and it also common for parents to act in a way which aims to teach, and in some cases aims to impose, at least to some degree, personal, family and social norms and expectations on their children. In our guise as parents, as, optimally, responsible, experienced and reasoning adults, it is wise for us, and indeed beholden on us as parents (and indeed for other adults), to have an understanding of this type of generational difference in behaviour and the desire of younger people to carve out their own niche, to discover and determine their own lives and make their own decisions. In the light of such a reality of younger people's behaviour and indeed what may be the largely unconscious motivations behind as well as the biological and biochemical origins of such behaviour, as parents we need to aim to look after and care for our children while aiming to bring them up well and doing what we can to keep them allied to and caring for others and our families. In the face of what might be seen as, and sometimes is, unpleasant behaviour and conduct from our children, our adopted approach as parents, while maintaining care for our own well-being and happiness, needs to avoid being intolerant and repressive of our children's behaviour and conduct, and needs to avoid being overly critical of our children and other young people around us.

The period when teenagers and young people are moving into adulthood, can be difficult and challenging for both ourselves as parents and ourselves as growing young people. At this time, if we are parents, then showing tolerance and understanding and providing a supportive environment for our children to grow in, are essential, as is doing whatever we can to help them identify pitfalls, though, again, sometimes it may be best to let our children make their own mistakes (as long as the consequences for the children we love will not be too dire). Indeed making decisions and being free to make decisions which may be right or wrong, making friends, having new relationships and coping emotionally and otherwise with our mistakes is an important part of growing up.

Additionally, as parents it is important to recognise that our children need to be supported, listened to and appreciated, especially during difficult times when they are changing and growing towards adulthood. That does not mean from our perspective as a parent that anything goes, (though in some cases events may seem to be beyond our control) but it does mean being aware of the challenges our children may be facing, and being supportive, tolerant and understanding in what can be difficult times.

From the point of view of ourselves as teenagers and young people of course, we need to try to understand our parents, how they feel and what they are going through in their lives. Our parents are dealing with us as we change and grow, and may be having difficulty in making the necessary changes in their behaviour. Where once we may have listened to whatever our parents said and we did as asked, perhaps without question, now we are older and less willing to be instructed, less willing to be told what to do, rightly wanting our own feelings and our wishes taken into account. Our parents may feel insecure themselves in their relationships, in their work, worried about their continued employment and income, their ability to support us as they would like to do.

They are also getting older and may be losing the physical capabilities which they had when they were younger, becoming more aware of their mortality. Our actions, decisions, our words as teenagers and young people need to take this into account with our showing some empathy with our parents where we can do this, sometimes expressing such understanding and empathy to them, expressing understanding of how they may feel and the stresses they are under. This approach can apply not just to our parents, but also to our teachers and other adults who should all consider us as individuals worthy of respect in terms of our fundamental identity as human beings. In important respects we certainly are no longer children.

Another area where we all, whatever age and circumstance, undoubtedly need to exercise tolerance and indeed patience, is in dealing with those who may, or who we believe may, lack the skills and abilities we have (or think we have), those whom we think make wrong decisions or who may be, or may appear to be, slow to learn in a particular moment or perhaps more generally. There are those who have lesser experience than we have on which to base their actions and decisions; there may be those who have difficulty in learning and those who have difficulty in articulating their emotions and feelings and sometimes express themselves in inappropriate ways without any intention of doing harm.

There are those with wrong ideas which, while well motivated, can damage other individuals and the community. All of these people (and more) should, in an important sense be free from receiving abuse and insult or worse, due to our own impatience and intolerance. These people, a category of people which will undoubtedly include all of us at some point in time, need to be dealt with patiently wherever possible. In some contexts we may all be slow to pick up new skills and knowledge; we will almost all, at some level, lack the experience of others; we will almost all at some stage or another hold wrong ideas. And sometimes helping others find the right or better answers, sometimes teaching others, or persuading others can be a long job requiring patience and tolerance, qualities which we all need to develop and demonstrate.

It may be in many circumstances that we are not able to change anything in a situation where we or someone else is not acting as we would wish them to act, for example where they are displaying a lower level of skill and ability than we have or could have, or feel we or they could have, this leading to our resultant frustration. Sometimes we will simply have to put up with what we perceive as slowness or the lack of ability of others, and sometimes of ourselves, recognising that we and others will lack ability and skills in some areas and that others have often had to be patient with us and in the future will need to be patient with us. We will simply need to be tolerant and understanding both of others and ourselves. If we ourselves are feeling incapable, clumsy, stupid or the like, we will certainly need to be a little tolerant of ourselves and our own errors, and should not castigate ourselves to a degree such that we suffer significant emotional pain.

We must control our frustrations and impatience, not only such that we can be ably supportive of others, but also to support our own well-being and happiness, our frustration and impatience representing a form of unhappiness and lack of well-being. In many such situations, whether there be frustration with ourselves or others, we need to gather ourselves, restrain ourselves and be supportive and caring of ourselves and others, looking at how, if possible, we can help others who are having difficulty with our trying to see the world from our and others' points of view. Where possible, in terms of those people (and indeed ourselves) who lack some skills, knowledge and understanding and who need support, we need to help them to grow and learn, listening and observing to find what they can and can't do and helping them progress to the next stage of their learning.

And whether or not their weaknesses, slowness, transgressions and difficulties are accidental and minor in nature or indeed major in their nature, we need to demonstrate support, patience and understanding. If it is a matter of views we perceive to be ill-informed and wrong, these people need to be, as far as is possible and reasonable, patiently persuaded to change their ideas, which as already mentioned can be a long process. And if there is, at least at the personal and local level, nothing we can do to persuade them, then we will need to simply cope with and get used to a situation or move away from that situation. We must not oppress others and do them harm through our frustration and impatience. Of course we could be wrong ourselves!

With more specific regard to mistakes and errors, the reality is that we all make mistakes, if not many mistakes, and sometimes, serious mistakes. It therefore benefits the well-being of ourselves, and indeed all of us, if we are tolerant and forgiving of these mistakes, the mistakes of others, and indeed our own mistakes, in whichever sphere these occur. These may be mistakes in terms of, for example, speaking ill-thought-out and insensitive remarks which we immediately or later recognise as such and then regret (for example, causing hurt through speaking in a fashion we imagine to be a joking fashion but actually causing hurt and upset). We may inadvertently engage in inaccurate reporting of events, make inaccurate judgments such as, for example, the errors we might make while driving a motor vehicle, or perhaps mistakes in arriving for appointments on time, errors in our work duties, or even other much more serious mistakes, some of which may, by accident and unintentional. Some of our errors may have resulted in harmful and sometimes significantly harmful effects on others. Further, there can of course be serious and deadly unintended errors done by others, which it may be difficult for us to respond to in a tolerant and caring way. Yet, that is what we must try and do, in order to support our own well-being and the well-being of others. Angry, intolerant impatience will damage us, affect ourselves and our behaviour in a destructive manner, as well as being likely to damage the well-being of others, causing pain and suffering. Therefore such negative, intolerant and destructive behaviour needs to be avoided.

In regard to the mistakes that we and others may make, we also sometimes, or perhaps often, need to help others to avoid mistakes into the future where we can, doing so in as sensitive a manner as is necessary, and of course we need to understand our own fallibilities. We hope that others will be tolerant and understanding of our ways, our inabilities and lacks of knowledge (which we all have) as well as our mistakes, with others supporting us constructively and positively, as individuals, to improve into the future. And we need to think and behave in a similar way in regard to others. All of this tolerant and caring conduct will support the well-being and happiness of others and of ourselves.

We may sometimes suffer from an impatience, feelings of frustration, anger and intolerance when we are in a hurry to get things done and when others do not support us, impede our progress or stand in our way, in one way or another; in particular, perhaps somewhat dependent on our home culture, at other times we may feel frustrated in regard to time keeping and our expectations that others will do things on time, and may feel frustrated when others state that they will do things but either deliver late or do not deliver at all. In support of tolerance of others and supporting freedom, cooperation, togetherness and diversity, where we feel in such negative and frustrated ways, we need to deal with and alleviate our damaging and destructive internal feelings and thoughts, aiming to tackle our damaging emotional reactions and responses such that they do not become too intense, too angry, too frustrated, or such that they disappear completely.

Yet, beyond our internal selves, should there exist real problems, we also need to resolve the range of those real problems in the best manner we can, especially since it is important and likely to be beneficial to all that we act effectively in that world beyond our internal self. And thus, for example, in many contexts, the fulfilling of expectations in regard to punctuality and keeping to commitments, both of which can be very important things, needs to be tackled. We must therefore do our best to make sure we and others deliver on promises, and stick to commitments and to arranged and agreed schedules and times, our fulfillment of our promises and our efficiency representing important contributors to well-being and happiness

When considering the actions of others, it is usually helpful for us to try to see the world from the point of view of those others, with our attempting to be empathetic and hopefully achieving a good level of empathy, something which can support understanding and tolerance between us. This is also likely to enhance our own freedom, independence and autonomy, as well our capacity to make effective and caring judgments which promote our own well-being and the well-being of others.

Coping with and dealing with difference is an important element of our relationship with ideas and with the realities of autonomy, independence and freedom. Of course, as well as coping with individual differences, we have to recognise the reality of culturally influenced differences reflected through individual action, attitude and belief. These culturally influenced differences may be deep and may also prove challenging to us at times in some respects, with those of us encountering other cultures, other individuals from different cultures in different countries, new organisations, new work environments, new contexts of various kinds, for example, having to understand, indeed tolerate and also adapt to, at least to some degree those individuals and cultures, needing to get used to the different ways of behaving of others compared to anticipated and expected conduct in our own cultures or the cultures we have previously known.

However, in regard to many differences, as already mentioned we need to go further than just toleration, looking to enjoy the many benefits which are frequently gained by encountering such cultural differences. Experiencing such different cultures in all their forms, with all their differing characteristics, can often be enriching for ourselves, building our understanding of ourselves. We can learn new ways of dealing with problems and new attitudes to problems. We can discover more relaxed and laid back lifestyles in which there is more joy found in the every day, where these is more sense of joy and happiness, or in opposite respects, we may encounter cultures and communities with highly constructive and positive attitudes to doing the different and the new, to being efficient, to exploration, and we may encounter cultures with differing attitudes to risk and danger. Across cultures time may be seen and used differently with different perceptions, tastes and expressions of art, architecture, culinary experiences, colour, and more. Our experiencing all of these, our discovery of new ways of seeing and experiencing the world will substantially benefit us, increasing our knowledge and understanding, hopefully raising our sense of empathy and understanding of others even in the event that we return to our own more familiar cultures.

Thus we can gain much even though, on some occasions, or more frequently, such encounters can also be frustrating. While there can be the already mentioned different perceptions of the importance of time, different attitudes to authority, less democratic and more democratic and inclusive styles, different attitudes to gender, to family. these representing conduct which we may find very difficult to understand, which we may find confusing and which may on occasion make us feel angry, our understanding of the nature of such cultures is important. Whether we find a culture difficult to cope with or not, changing other cultures tends to be a lengthy endeavour and thus it is unlikely that we, as individuals, will be able to change another culture, at least in the short term, though we may in time exert a little or perhaps more influence on others in that culture. Of course in the context of business and work environments, such cultures, in some cases, may be in desperate need of change and this change will need to be achieved, and possibly at a rapid pace.

Despite the presence of such cultures, with our primary responsibility for our own individual behaviour and seeking well-being and happiness in line with core and other principles, we are responsible for our own decisions and actions. And while we are highly likely to be influenced by our cultures, we cannot hold such cultures responsible for our own actions, thinking and decisions. Where cultural beliefs, customs, attitudes and actions stand significantly against core and other principles, we need to move beyond those cultures and our cultural influences.

Undoubtedly people from others cultures will influence us. If we are to consider, compare, evaluate, and coexist well with individuals from different cultures, with different cultural backgrounds, then this needs to be done on the basis of core principles, on the basis of supporting the well-being and happiness enjoyed by those individuals within that culture, not simply on the moment, but also in the longer term. We need to show a concern and be concerned with the well-being and happiness of those individuals existing within such differing cultures.

We should certainly take care to avoid intolerance of those originating from other cultures where their individual beliefs and practices offer no significant threat to our individual and social well-being and happiness or their own well-being and happiness, instead developing our understanding, and appreciating the differences between individuals, groups and cultures, and supporting the well-being and happiness of all within the terms of core and other principles.

When such well-being is placed at risk, where other cultures and individuals within those cultures threaten pain and suffering to ourselves and others, including those within such cultures; where our freedoms and well-being are threatened, we will need to engage in action to preserve our freedoms, autonomy, our well-being and happiness. While we must be careful of intolerance, we should also be careful of not being overly tolerant of other individuals and other cultures, cultures in which, for example, others are oppressed, where oppression and aggressive violence, perhaps even torture, are carried out against others, in which social beliefs and personal beliefs are prescribed and proscribed on threat of violence and death, in which individual people may have no voice, in which individual people are made to suffer injustice and pain, at the hands of other individuals acting in line with prevalent and damaging cultural and other oppressive beliefs which create significant pain and suffering.

As well as the cultural differences between national and perhaps other wider geographical and social cultures, we will also face within our more local cultures and social environments what may be described as cultural norms, conventions by which we may feel constrained. These have already been touched upon in relation to ways of speaking such as politeness and our general social behaviour in our daily lives. Yet more specifically, for example, in places of work, there may be certain ways of behaving which are seen as being desirable and more acceptable than others, such as in some Western and other workplaces, for example the acceptability and indeed convention and norm in some work contexts of drinking alcohol after work, engaging in certain topics of talk, for example about sport, (and not speaking about other topics), speaking in certain ways, using certain language, adopting certain attitudes and even common prejudices.

In many work and other cultures, there may be very positive, inclusive and democratic practices, yet in some other contexts there may be pressure to fall in with certain discriminatory, and unsupported beliefs, some of which will be reprehensible, negatively selfish, and damaging in their effects on our communities and societies. Both positive but also more damaging negative cultures may operate in other contexts such as sporting clubs, social clubs, political and pressure groups and elsewhere. As emphasised through this guide, those destructive and damaging beliefs are unacceptable within core and other principles, undermining the well-being and happiness of us all.

It is frequently important for each one of us to be tolerant of individual others who are different from us, but who live in our cultures and social environments. And it is important, within the framework of well-being and core principles, to get along with others and cooperate with them in the range of contexts as far as we reasonably can, enabling us and them to feel an accepted part of the whole.

It may be that our conforming to some degree can enhance the prospects of progress within a work organisation or culture, or even make the day more tolerable in terms of our social relationships. Nevertheless, where we feel this is appropriate, where we feel a need to express our individuality, in particular also where there are substantial departures from core and other principles and where well-being and happiness are not being supported, we should not be afraid, indeed we should be bold enough, to follow our own individual paths, beliefs and instincts, speaking out where necessary, breaking these communication and cultural conventions as we feel necessary, in pursuit of our own well-being and happiness, and most likely in support of the well-being and happiness of others, others who may also feel tension and pain at the constraints, conventions and perhaps unpleasant values and norms being pressured upon them. It is often important to be, as is often said, 'true to ourselves' and in our passion for that truth, it is likely, especially if we pursue our goals in peaceful and cooperative yet firm, determined and robust ways, that we will benefit ourselves and many more of our fellows, through expressing and acting on the basis of that truth.

While tolerance is considered of great importance, we must be careful of being tolerant of those who themselves promote intolerance or who intend to or actually do others harm. Causing significant or substantive harm to others is not acceptable and not to be tolerated. The behaviour of those who are aggressively violent or who engage in other significantly anti-social commit crimes, who cause substantive and significant damage and suffering to others, who incite hatred and violence against others, who threaten or actually do violence to others, cannot be allowed to go unchecked. We must take all reasonable action in our power as individuals, as local communities, as broader human societies, to ensure that such conduct does not arise in the first place, and secondly is prevented from taking place again and repeatedly in those instances where such conduct has unfortunately occurred. This is a necessity to support freedom, liberty, independence and autonomy, none of which can be easily or significantly enjoyed under the threat of coercion, pain, suffering and violence.

It is possible and indeed the reality for some of us to, at least on the surface, appear to be accepting of those who are different, but in fact to act, either consciously or unconsciously, against those who do not conform to our expectations. Thus there are those who wish to deliberately discriminate who will hide their intolerance of others and who will hide their malevolence, intolerance and intention to discriminate. The attitudes and actions of these individuals may show that, by contrast to the words they say and the values they appear to espouse, they in fact believe that those who do not conform in whatever way, should not be respected, supported or achieve advancement in their lives, even though those who do not conform may be successful in what they do, demonstrate good, caring, positive values and engage in good and positive actions which support well-being and happiness and which are in line with core principles set out in this guide, benefiting others through their actions and their words.

Our only window into the actions of those individuals engaging in such covert and deliberate intolerance and discrimination is through careful observation of their words and general conduct and in particular viewing the consequences of their actions. Of course we need to take actions to stop the intolerance and discrimination carried out by these individuals and hopefully persuade them to greater tolerance, fairness and justice.

Yet also for many, if not perhaps all of us, our true motivations may be hidden even from ourselves, and while speaking in a non-discriminatory and even in a deliberately well-intentioned manner, in effect our conduct may indicate deep and discriminatory, even intolerant attitudes which we will need to change. Cultural behaviours, notions of acceptability, norms and conventions that we as individuals may share with others may lead to unfair and discriminatory actions, pursued without our even being aware of our actions and the motivations for them.

Such intolerance and resultant discrimination, whether conscious or unconscious, is not acceptable. And since it is often less overt and explicit, and because it may be frequent and have substantive effect, hidden effects, our unconscious prejudices, biases and discrimination have the potential to be even more insidious and damaging than some forms of overt discrimination, both to those who are on the receiving end of such discriminatory actions, and also in relation to the needs of our communities, societies and our broader humanity.

Further, there may be common practices which we as individuals, which our organisations, communities and societies engage in, which are damaging and discriminatory against other individuals and other groups. Our closeness to others and our general preferences for those we know in terms of providing employment and other opportunities can provide certain individuals and groups with priority access to the range of advantages in our communities and societies. It is important that, while we care about and are loyal to our friends, that we do not serve to undermine our whole communities and societies through unfair, unjust and discriminatory practices.

Further, acting in a manner which supports and enables those who do not conform, yet who act appropriately in line with our core values, towards well-being and happiness; our acting to help these people and all others towards well-being and happiness; our enabling all to participate and achieve well-being and happiness, is a requirement of core principles. Apart from our own decisions and actions with regard to those who might not conform, we also need to argue for and support our communities, societies and beyond in acting in non-discriminatory ways, in ways promoting tolerance and freedom, and in ensuring that within our communities and societies, unfair discrimination against those who operate in line with core and other principles yet who do not conform to some or even many norms and conventions, is not allowed to happen or persist.

As has already been intimated, while it seems to some extent contradictory, the fact is that those who are unwilling to embrace difference within the bounds of core and other principles, and who wish to enforce conformity, not only expressing that wish using words but also promoting and preaching intolerance, hatred and violence towards others, cannot be tolerated. We cannot tolerate those who promote such intolerance and hatred, those who make threats of force and violence, who threaten pain and suffering, destruction of well-being, towards other individuals or groups of others who are peaceful, well-meaning and who express their own views, judgments and ideas without offering any real and significant threat or harm to others. Those promoting such intolerance, discrimination, hatred and violence cannot themselves be tolerated, on account of the threats they pose to the rest of us, other individuals, community, society and beyond. And in taking such actions which may lead to significant pain, suffering and damage to so many, these people are acting against well-being and happiness, promoting pain and suffering and this is unacceptable.

In respect of acting against those people engaging in such threats and harm to ourselves and others, our first steps, dependent on circumstances, if possible, need to involve engaging with these people and their views, making efforts to encourage these people to be understanding and tolerant of others, supporting them in developing the capacity to be understanding of the different perceptions that others might have, helping them to be understanding that they need to and that they should, take the time to listen to and empathise with others, and that their violent and threatening attitudes and actions are likely to lead to pain and suffering for others. Where possible and where safe for us, we need to encourage them peacefully to desist from promoting hatred, violence and intolerance and from expressing such hatred, violence and intolerance. In particular they must be persuaded to desist from making threats of pain, violence and suffering against others and certainly to desist from any threats of, or acts of violence and oppression.

Having mentioned in line with core and other principles, our desire for peaceful and cooperative engagement with those who are promoting and promulgating such hatreds, threats of damage and destruction, threats to freedom and threats to our person, often promoting racism, for us to dissuade them from such threats and action, we are required, in support of our own well-being and the well-being of others to recognise that such individuals and groups sometimes, through their present nature, apart from being threatening and potentially violent, for whatever reason, may enjoy in a perverse manner, causing suffering, pain and being violent and cruel. And therefore our efforts at peaceful engagement when dealing with such people may entail risk in themselves. Optimally we should be prepared to and should take such risks but we should not do so naively, placing ourselves and others in jeopardy unnecessarily.

If such individuals or groups do engage in, and continue to encourage and promote violence and significantly damaging actions towards others, then more impactful action beyond peaceful engagement and persuasion must be taken. It is not reasonable and not acceptable within core and other principles, to be tolerant of those who advocate such violence and destructive hurt and damage against others, to be tolerant of those who are extremely intolerant and who make threats of harm or intend harm against others. We must not behave in such ways ourselves and cannot be expected as individuals to allow or stand by when others behave in such ways. We cannot be indifferent to, or tolerant of those who mean to oppress us, do us significant harm or who will do us significant harm.

Where others threaten us or others with pain and suffering, or intend or carry out acts of violence and hatred against us, or others, whatever their motivation, be it through their own ill-formed characters and anti-social characteristics, their own personal backgrounds, illnesses, false and destructive beliefs, intending violence and violent actions because of our individual attitudes and peaceful and reasoned opinions, our personal characteristics, colour, race, background, beliefs, sexuality, physique, amongst other characteristics, then we are justified in not tolerating these actions and these peoples, and acting, hopefully together with others, where necessary forcefully, to prevent their conduct and to prevent their actions, aiming to move them to more peaceful, cooperative ways of living. Not only is this a matter of supporting our personal well-being and avoiding pain and suffering; not only is it a matter of self-preservation for us as individuals, but it is also necessary for us in protecting others, and is necessary for communities, societies, both local and beyond, for our humanity, in promoting the wider well-being, happiness and togetherness, preventing the implementation and promulgation of destructive suffering, the implementation of anti-social, anti-human values and preventing destructive and heinous actions contrary to core and other principles, actions which will harm us all.

In terms of our freedoms to do and say, it is essential for us to draw the distinction between reasoned proposal, discussion, engaging with, experiencing and arguing about ideas, our promoting an idea as being correct and appropriate using peaceful processes and seeking peaceful outcomes supporting well-being and happiness, with the use of words in deliberate efforts to frighten, intimidate and threaten others. Where words are used in order to stir up hatred and violence against an individual or a group, or where sometimes soft spoken words are used to hide dishonesty and lack of integrity and persuade towards intolerance and violence, then that is not acceptable and is contrary to core and other principles.

The former peaceful and honest efforts to persuade are of course legitimate and the latter promotion of hatred, threat and violence intolerable and unacceptable, requiring an appropriate and robust, though optimally peaceful and hopefully, and necessarily, a successful response. The vast main of us wish to oppose oppression, to achieve and maintain justice and freedoms, which often need to be fought for and won. It may well be necessary for us to encourage others to action, but mindless and vicious words of hatred are not appropriate, and mindless, vicious and aggressively violent acts are not acceptable. Our own ends need to be peaceful and achieved in a measured and appropriate manner which does not inflict unnecessary harm, but which means, on the other hand, that our legitimate goals, in lines with core and other principles, are successfully achieved, and violence and oppression, pain and suffering are removed.

Our requirement for freedoms and independence, and our need to engage in autonomous actions range across a vast range of areas. The issue of sexual freedom has been discussed in other chapters in this guide and in particular represents an essential and core area of freedom for all of us, our freedoms in love, in relation to sex, sexual love and sexual relationships, being a fundamental part of our humanity, a fundamental human need for almost everyone of us, men, women or transgender. We should enjoy and appreciate our loves, our sex, our loving, caring relationships, which are so important for our happiness and well-being at so many points in our lives. Commensurate with well-being and happiness, most things in sex and love should be permissible, with only the most minimum restrictions in terms of our consensual person-to-person loving sexual practices operating within the bounds of core principles, in particular the need for us to seek our sexual, emotional and loving pleasures, joys and happiness, optimally giving great pleasure to our partners but also while not causing significant hurt and pain to others (and optimally achieving joy and happiness and no hurt and pain at all).

Suffice to say, in support of individual happiness and well-being, and in support of the greater well-being, all of us have a right to say yes or no to sex, to agree to or refuse sex; we have a right not to be coerced or forced into sex or engage in unprotected sex, or sexual practices we do not wish to participate in when we do not wish to do so. No law or commonly held belief in any context overrides our personal right to refuse sex if we do not want it. No adult is the sexual possession, or is a possession in any other form, of anyone else. Of the utmost importance, children need to be protected from inappropriate physical engagement in the world of sex until they are of sufficient physical and personal emotional maturity to be able to deal with this world, a sexual world which may indeed be difficult enough emotionally and otherwise, for the many of us who are older to deal with.

That is not to say that as they mature, children should not be told about or be able to find information about the world of sex and love in an age appropriate manner. It is to say that children should not be participating in sex and sexual loving relationships until they are sufficiently sexually and emotionally mature to cope with these relationships, and more than that, mature enough to start to participate voluntarily in, consensually in, and fully enjoy, their sexual and loving relationships. As with adults, children are not and must never be sexual possessions of any other and are never the possessions (in the sense that objects are possessed), of any other in any form.

That is all rather negative in tone. The crucial thing is that sex and love are to be enjoyed and to be enjoyed in whichever way we can within the constraints already mentioned. We should enjoy our pleasures in sex and love and enjoy giving pleasure and satisfaction to others, our partners and lovers, acting mutually and together to achieve our own loving and sexual pleasures and joys, and the loving and sexual joys and pleasures of our partners. Sexual enjoyment can be very individual and we therefore need to be listeners, sensitive to our partners, but also seeking education and learning about sex and love so that we can enjoy and gain the most from our loving, sexual relationships. We also need to be able to and be free to pleasure ourselves through masturbation , discretely and in private when we need to and if we wish to do so, within the bounds already stated and within the range of reasonable cultural conventions operating within our societies. Supporting us in all our sexual and loving practices, adults need to be able to access information and images freely about sex, legitimate adult sexual practices, and about love and its nature, again with the constraint of others not enduring pain and suffering in the generation and other processes tied to such information and images.

Crucially, again supporting well-being and happiness, there is no reason for us, as consenting adults, to be legally or socially restricted in our private sexual conduct, beyond the limits already mentioned, unless there is an undoubted and significant risk to our own well-being and the well-being of community and society as a whole, shown in a clear, reasoned and demonstrable manner, supported by evidence and rationality, the likelihood of private sexual conduct creating such damage and risk being considered here to be very unlikely to be the case. Facile arguments, unsupported by concrete evidence, about unfounded and unsupportable threats to society from minority or even majority sexual practices and sexual choices, arguments based on traditional discriminatory practice, ignorance, lack of imagination and insensitivity to the nature of others, ingrained prejudice and irrational or overly fearful thinking, are not sufficient.

For example, as already stated in this chapter, homosexuality is as natural for some, and is as natural in nature as is heterosexuality for the majority. There are no grounds for the irrational discrimination and oppression of homosexuals and homosexuality, in the same way that there are no grounds for suppression of heterosexuality. Our own specific and freely entered into private sexual practices, the manner in which others of their own free will gain their own sexual and loving pleasures, are, in the vast main, within the constraints already mentioned, none of our business, and not a subject for our external consent or lack of consent, even our approval or disapproval, except where significant pain and suffering is being done to participants or is being done to community, society and humanity, which, in the latter case, as already stated, seems extremely unlikely. Further, given our notions of freedom and autonomy, in line with our goals of supporting well-being and happiness, we all have a right to engage in sexual commerce if we so choose, if all participants do so voluntarily without coercion.

Our overall well-being and the general well-being and happiness are supported by our commitment to individual well-being and happiness, and within this commitment, our component commitment to the freedom, independence and autonomy of the individual within the constraints of core and other principles. Our commitment to individual well-being and happiness helps us all, directly serving each of us as the individuals we are, directly serving our own individual happiness and well-being, but also enabling diverse and different people with diverse and different personalities, lifestyles, beliefs and approaches, with many talents and abilities, differing perspectives and abilities, differing skills and capacities, different ways of living, differing ways of being, to contribute their perspectives, their different skills, talents, opinions, ideas and more, to the whole, something which benefits us all. Indeed in terms of our communities, societies and beyond, it is likely that our supporting of such diversity and difference, indeed our encouragement of such diversity is, in a multitude of respects, essential to the well-being and indeed happiness of our community, social and human whole.

One of our human needs and indeed important freedoms is our freedom to communicate with and be with others as we choose without restriction. As already discussed in this chapter, it is part of our individual well-being and, indeed, the social well-being, that we are able to meet with whom we choose when we choose, within the constraints and context of core principles, and to take whom we choose as our friends, our companions, our lovers and more. Yet beyond the area of our relationships already discussed, this freedom applies not only to our individual and closer, more personal, relationships, it also, importantly, of course, applies to our relationships and actions in our wider society, in particular in terms of acting in concert with others in the pursuit of our political, social and leisure interests, in the pursuit of social change and justice.

With these and other goals in mind, acting to support the well-being and happiness of ourselves and others, it is essential that, within the frame of core principles, there should be no legal restrictions upon our ability to communicate with whomsoever we wish to communicate with; that, in a similar manner, there should be no legal restrictions on communicating with others when we wish; there should be no restrictions on who we choose to meet with, when we organise get-togethers, events, meetings and protests and when we take part in community events, when we act and cooperate together in support of our peaceful, social and political objectives, in order to work for and support changes in culture, practices, systems, law and more.

We also cannot be free unless we have the time and space in which to rest from our various task and labours, both physical and mental. We need time and space in which to rest and recuperate, and time and space to reflect and think about our lives, our decisions, our circumstances, our aims and goals. In our working lives, our employers, organisations, governments, and we ourselves, need to ensure we all have sufficient time to rest and recover from our work and indeed to enjoy time to do the things we need to do outside of work. Our work may be something which is tremendously enjoyable and motivating for us, almost indistinguishable from our leisure, representing something which we find fulfilling and to which we are personally willing to dedicate substantial time and commitment. Nevertheless we will still need to rest at times from such work in order that we can achieve to our optimum. There may also be times of stress, crisis or perhaps extreme emergency in the word context when we need to use more of our time for work-related functions. We may need or wish to work long and hard simply to gain money for survival or to enjoy other pleasures. Even in such contexts we will need to rest and recuperate such that we can perform well at our work and such that we can still take a breath and gain some enjoyment and pleasure from our lives. Overwork, excessive burdens in terms of our physical and mental activity, excessive demands placed on us by others, or even indeed by ourselves, will tire and exhaust us, and as a consequence there is the strong likelihood that we will not only undermine and jeopardise our individual health and well-being, but we will also make poorer and weaker contributions to our families, communities and societies, our fatigue tending to affect the quality and extent of our contributions through its damage to our health, its effects on our state of mind and mood and as a consequence its effects on our actions, behaviour and decision-making.

That is not to say that at times, as suggested above, we may not push ourselves to the limit, working and perhaps playing extremely hard, stretching ourselves to the outermost limits of our capacities and beyond in pursuit of worthy and worthwhile goals that we wish to achieve, with these efforts at the limits of our capacities, substantially enhancing our lives, our experiences of our lives and the lives of others, and thereby supporting well-being and happiness and giving us great pleasure and sense of achievement. But it is to say that pushing ourselves to such limits requires our health and certainly requires rest and recovery after these efforts.

And then there are emergencies at home, times of illness and health crisis, deaths in the family, times when our children are being born when we need to, and indeed must have, leave of absence, maternity, paternity, annual and other leave to deal with these important family matters.

In our time away from work, engaging in those activities which are specifically leisure activities is highly likely to enhance our health. Access to such leisure, and indeed pleasure-time away from the demands of jobs and work represents an important element of our well-being and happiness and indeed an important element of our freedom. We certainly need to be free from the laying of excessive burdens on us from outside, from others incentivising, coercing or forcing us to give excessive amounts of our time to what may be burdensome, tedious or demoralising forms of work, this being highly likely to damage us and damage our well-being and happiness, our freedom, individuality and autonomy.

Clearly, as already mentioned, we may enjoy our work and feel highly committed to our work, and indeed enjoy it and gain great pleasure from it, which will justify time and commitment to that work, though hopefully not at too much expense to those we love or to other important aspects of our lives. Nevertheless, that should be our individual choice, a choice made in the absence of unjust and oppressive coercion. Thus, despite what may be our passion and commitment to our work and the mentioned times where we may need to work intensively in our jobs, hopefully for short periods, for the many of us a life of well-being and happiness will mean we must have and must ensure we have, rest times, days away from work, time for our families, friends and communities, time for other activities, time for holidays where we do something different, the consequence of such rest times and other relaxing times being beneficial not just for ourselves, but also beneficial for our paid work and the quality of work in our jobs, organisations and institutions, as well as being of benefit for our families, communities, societies and beyond.

Yet while needing rest and space, it is also the case that as part of our individuality and humanity, we need to be able to do work, to contribute to our communities and societies, our broader humanity, to have the freedom to perform useful and rewarded work, the access to work which comprises important, valuable and valued work for our communities, societies and beyond. We need to be able to do work which is recognised as of value by our communities and societies, our humanity, to do work in the service of others. We need that freedom to work, that freedom to contribute to our communities, that freedom to do work for which we receive money or a form of return. Such work not only supports us in surviving and thriving, enabling us to have greater levels of autonomy, independence, choice, personal power and supports us in having other freedoms, but it also supports our deep social desire and need to contribute to others, to our communities, realising our want and need to contribute to others and to help others. The absence of our ability to do such work, the prohibition of our engaging in such work, the absence of our capacity and opportunity to gain an income and make such contributions, helping and supporting others, is significantly detrimental to our freedom, individuality, humanity, autonomy, and our well-being and happiness.

Our experiencing and enduring of poverty has already been mentioned as a barrier to freedom. But not only do we need to be free from poverty in order to enjoy freedom, but we also need sufficient resources to be able to participate in an appropriate manner in our communities, societies and as part of our broader humanity. Such participation is key to our freedom since, if we are not involved in the decisions and indeed influential in the decisions which are affecting our lives, if we do not have the resources to support our participation or the opportunity to participate, then we are to an important extent lacking in freedom, independence and autonomy. If there are decisions being made about our lives beyond the decision-making context of our immediate families, we will need the capacity, the freedom to contribute to these decisions which is high likely to require us, as well as our communities and societies, to have requisite resources.

Our consultation and our communication as part of such decision-making processes require not simply money, but need resources of various kinds. Not only will we need time available to us in order to contribute, time itself being an important resource, but we may need to be able to have resources which enable us to travel in order to contribute, resources to send documents, to fund our local representatives, to use a computer or other device in order to be able to contribute to the decision-making process, the resources to enable us to access information, and we may need to do much more in order to make our voices heard.

In other areas, if there are leisure activities and community activities taking place which require resources for participation, then our freedom to participate, and with high likelihood, our well-being, will be reduced if we do not have the resources to take part. If we have family living distant, perhaps living with illness and needing support, then insufficient resources will also mean that we may not be able to travel to see them, perhaps do not have the resources to communicate with them, something which may damage our well-being and happiness and their well-being and happiness too.

Thus, our lack of resources can be seen as representing a restriction on our freedoms, though not one which is necessarily intentionally imposed from outside and not necessarily one which represents substantial and deliberately imposed oppression, though clearly our lack of resources can be a consequence of an economic system and the consequence of malevolent and destructive conduct towards us or the groups we belong to. Of course we cannot demand resources for everything we would like to do, in particular as we ourselves have some responsibility for generation of resources, and further because it will also be a likelihood that there will be insufficient resources available to support us all in all we wish to do.

Within a democratic, open and free context, where there are legitimate, fair, just and open systems of law and justice, our actions in pursuit of freedom must be pursued peacefully (as optimally they should under other peaceful systems) and in support of our own well-being and the well-being of others. In a democratic, free, open context where we are free to influence others, to make contact with others as we choose, to communicate our ideas to others, where there are legitimate and equitable channels open to us through which we can express our views, where there is open and free information and education, and open and free dissemination of information, then there can be no restrictions on our ability and freedom to associate with others, with the already stated exception of our association with the purpose of planning and organising threats and actions of aggressive violence, organising and engaging in aggressive violence, threat and purposeful intimidation.

Clearly, in free and open societies where well-being and happiness are supported and significant pain and suffering is not being inflicted on ourselves and others, we cannot enable and allow people to gather together to organise and implement violence against others. Our activities in such contexts and indeed elsewhere, as far as possible and reasonable, need to desist from such violence, threat and intimidation and be conducted, as peacefully as possible. We certainly should not participate in such activities and need to prevent such aggressively violent actions from occurring.

Where there are undemocratic, oppressive and indeed violent communities and societies in which some important, or where many freedoms are denied, including those relating to free association, free expression within the context of core and other principles, open communication and access to information (within the framework of core principles), then we need to protest against such denial of freedom, and act as peacefully as is possible against such injustice, ensuring such laws and systems cannot prevail. Where necessary and possible, under such circumstances, under oppressive systems, we will be obliged to breach any restrictions on our interacting, meeting, organising and communicating with others as far as we can, such that we can change and remove such oppressive systems. Unfortunately it may be necessary to take forceful actions to remove such oppression.

As already mentioned, our personal well-being and happiness requires that we are not only able to meet with our more political associates but that we are able to decide our companions, friends and lovers, and, while others, our friends and family may have their views, and have the right to try and influence us (if they truly believe that is a wise thing to do), since they are concerned for our well-being, if we are adults and indeed, even if we are young adults, we certainly still have the freedom to choose these friends, lovers and companions. And indeed, if we are that family and those individuals, we must take great care in attempting to determine for our children who should be their friends and companions and, if our children are of such an age, we should take great care in attempting to influence if not determine who our children take as lovers.

And more specifically in regard to issues around our friendships and loves, the fact that someone we might wish as a friend or lover comes from another group, tribe, class, background, has a particular set of beliefs, should never mean we are denied their friendship or love, with the exception of where they may pose a real significant physical, psychological, emotional or other danger to us, which is in the vast main, rather unlikely. These choices are for us to make as adults, as young adults of appropriate age, as individuals. We as individuals have responsibility for the choices we make. It is for us, as individuals, to judge.

Others should not attempt to place sanction or sanctions on us for whom we choose to have as friends or whom we choose to have as a friend, lover, partner or marriage partner. Rather than admonishing or criticising those we love for their choices, instead we should support them and be there for them when we can, supporting their well-being and happiness as individuals. Of course our decisions in choosing our friends and partners may sometimes be wrong, and it is reasonable for parents and family to try to give advice in the light of their knowledge and experience of the world and given their concern for us as their children. But they should not determine our choices of friends, partners or lovers or take steps to manipulate us away from or deprive us of the loves and friends we would wish to have.

Of course, by contrast to our adult years, the later years of our development, our later teenage years, when we are younger children our parents will certainly have the greater responsibility for us and are likely to play an important role in those we have as friends, even if only by dint of the environment which we are brought up in, through selection of the areas where we live (in those cases where parents have a choice), and including through the other parents and adults they associate with, who they are friends with. Certainly these parental actions and choices, will certainly, to a large degree determine or influence who we meet and who we have as friends.

Yet our children will benefit from meeting and communicating with a diverse range of people, through experiencing this diversity developing a greater knowledge and understanding of the world, a greater ability to act effectively should they meet and communicate with a range of differing people, differing children. Hopefully this diversity of experience will help our children in developing learning in a range of forms, developing their communication skills through their relating to a range of others, developing tolerance, knowledge and understanding of other people, developing knowledge and understanding of differing ways of behaving, of differing individuals and their perceptions, differing groups and cultures, together with developing their knowledge and understanding of the wider world and their own place in relation to that world. Our parents and our communities and societies need to help us in meeting with and encountering children, and indeed a range of adults, to support us in experiencing the range of ideas, experiences and cultures which are there to be met, and which are there to be found in our local communities, societies and in our wider world.

As growing adolescents, we also need to be careful sometimes about our choices of who we have as friends and who we associate with, for while we need to have the freedom to choose our friends, in particular we need to be aware of and take care in our relationships with those who might or who perhaps are likely to significantly hurt us, hurt themselves or damage others. And if we do know or associate with such others who engage in activities which may hurt and damage themselves and others, we must surely understand the concerns of those such as our parents with regard to these friends. We must certainly never participate in activities which might hurt others, and must act, as far as we can to stop such activities, something which though difficult to do, since we may be seen as going against friends and therefore may be accused of and appear to be disloyal, we must nevertheless do, in order to protect others from significant damage and harm. That is what we must do for our own benefit, for the benefit of our friends and for the benefit of those who might be hurt by their actions.

Any deliberately imposed restrictions by parents, communities and societies in terms of contacts with other children and indeed adults, meeting and communicating with others, need to be implemented as rarely as possible, and if implemented needs to be put in place with special care given the challenge to independence, personal freedom and autonomy that such restrictions would mean. As mentioned, as parents we need to ensure that our children will meet diverse people and have diverse experiences, but at the same time we must do our best to ensure that they are safe and not significantly and unnecessarily endangered, while being brought up to support their own well-being and happiness and the well-being and happiness of all others. Suffice to say that the idea of danger referred to here does not generally include finding out about and communicating with people with different ideas, from different backgrounds.

Freedom and freedoms in the discussion thus far refer have referred to us as individuals, yet it has to be recognised that groups exist, and that groups of individuals with common and shared beliefs, in support of and commensurate with individual rights and freedoms, need to be able to have certain freedoms themselves as groups. However, these groups and group members must not significantly damage the well-being and happiness of their individual members or damage others outside of the group, and need to act to support the well-being and happiness of all, certainly causing no significant pain and suffering.

Group rights and freedoms are only valid when considered in terms of the rights and freedoms of the individuals who are members of that group, in terms of the freedom and rights of all individuals beyond those groups and indeed in terms of the freedoms and rights of those who are members of other groups, with group rights and freedoms required to be consistent with core and other principles. Group rights do not supersede these individual rights or rights in relation to the freedoms, independence, autonomy and well-being and happiness of the individual and the wider community and society. Nevertheless, such well-being and happiness, includes the notion and supports the reality that individuals should be able to be members of, and should be able to live and act together as groups, should they so wish.

In terms of groups linked by language, groups and group members must be able to speak and teach the language of their choice, should they wish and choose to do so, but nevertheless have obligations to those outside of the group. And, in support of the general well-being and happiness, there is a need for those in these groups to promote and speak the languages of others as well, particularly major language groups, thereby enhancing communication, mutual understanding, cooperation with others and the general social well-being and happiness. Optimal communication and togetherness, optimal well-being, happiness and fulfillment, would most likely be supported by our all using and sharing a common language, yet no individual, no individual within a group and no group should be forced to adopt a language which they do not wish to adopt (though any individual within a group must be able to choose to learn another language should they wish to). And moreover there may be some benefits in having a diversity of languages with the variety of languages providing interest through their diversity, but also allowing diversity of expression. That being said, no group should prevent or put artificial barriers in the way of individual members of their groups who wish to study, learn and adopt other languages, and indeed these groups and the individuals within such groups should promote such language learning and practice in order to facilitate and enhance communication and to support the avoidance of inefficient communication and misunderstanding.

Groups of individuals must be able to practice their rituals and traditions, as long as these do not significantly damage the well-being and happiness of individuals within the group or the whole. Those of us existing within the group need to be able to decide not to participate without significant and damaging sanction or punishment meted out to us. Significant sanction here means we should not be abused, treated with violence, excluded from family, community and other important relations, ostracised because we disagree, do not wish to, or refuse to participate. Of course, as mentioned we all have a right to meet with who we wish to meet, to associate with whom we wish to associate, within the terms of core principles, yet for family and community to ostracise members for non-belief and non-participation is unacceptable, representing in its threat and implementation a form of major coercion, causing or with the potential to cause substantial pain and suffering. We need to tolerate and remain friendly and on good terms with those within our groups who feel differently, who do not conform, who change their beliefs and move on, especially if their new positions remain committed to enhancing the well-being and happiness of all and doing so in an effective, empathetic, loving and caring manner.

Groups of individuals should optimally and in the main, not isolate themselves from the world outside and beyond their group, since they will be denying others their positive contributions as groups and the contributions of the individuals within those groups. They will also be denying their group members access to ideas and interactions beyond that group, actions which might support their well-being. Rather than avoid others, groups and individuals within those groups should engage with and cooperate with the world beyond the group.

Groups may determine their own internal rules and codes of conduct within the bounds that these must be in line with core principles, supporting the well-being and happiness of all. It is contrary to core principles for groups to have rules and codes of conduct that privilege some and which marginalise and oppress certain members of their groups causing substantial hardship to members of such groups, for example, those born in certain circumstances, those individuals who are separated out for one reason or another as different, those with certain status through birth, certain sexual preferences, colour or race.

Education within such groups must be open to and include the provision of knowledge and understanding of the experiences and cultures of those beyond such groups, enabling the individuals born within such groups to have access to options in life beyond their experiences in the group within which they have grown up. As mentioned above, there must also be the possibility of leaving any group without significant and painful sanction, punishment or ostracism, and indeed there must also be ways of joining such groups, a freedom which requires open and reasonable access, and which also requires the possibility of subsequently leaving the group without sanction, pain and suffering, emotional or physical. Where the conduct of groups and cultures and individuals within those groups and cultures is largely, significantly or completely consistent with core principles, the approaches of these groups and cultures needs to be dealt with tolerance, with individuals within such groups and their members being shown respect, perhaps praised and lauded as exemplars, and certainly not attacked, oppressed, abused and denigrated.

As individuals we have a right and the freedom, within the bounds of practicality, to be a member of and join the groups we choose to join, where the objectives and aims of these groups as well as their ways of acting and being are generally and significantly consistent with core principles. We should be able to be part of the nations that we wish to be a part of, within the bounds of practicalities, or belong to the cultural, sporting, political, religious belief or other groups we wish to be a part of, within the same constraints. With regard to being part of other nations, that does not mean that we can just elect to become of another nationality, though hopefully this might be possible. Nor does it mean that, even if we are within the majority within another country, and within an area within another country, we can simply choose as individuals or vote as a group, such that the land area we live in can become part of another country, under another jurisdiction. Complex situations, practicalities, histories, the freedoms and rights of others who may be in a minority, and other factors need to be taken into account in what may be complex situations.

Our freedom to act may be constrained, within the context of core and other principles in legitimate ways by those with power over us. Our freedom may be constrained by our communities and societies, though optimally and hopefully our actions will only be constrained in order to avoid significant pain and suffering. Hopefully such constraints will not involve force, threat and violence, though sometimes coercive and forceful action may be legitimate and necessary in order to maintain and enhance individual as well as the general well-being. There are many important instances where our actions will legitimately and reasonably be constrained.

This chapter has already considered situations where, for example, those who are threatening or have engaged in aggressive violence can be legitimately constrained, separated from others and imprisoned in response to their violent acts, in order to keep the rest of us safe and secure. Further, the legitimate constraints on our self-expression have also been considered, for example, that appropriate action needs to be taken in the face of threats of aggressive violence, the incitement of hatred against others, seen as a key step along the road to the implementation of aggressive violence against others. However there are many other areas where such constraints on our conduct can be reasonably justified in support of well-being and happiness and to reduce pain and suffering.

Thus, as a further illustrative and clear example of where our freedom can be reasonably constrained within terms of core and other principles, where there are outbreaks of communicable and sometimes deadly illnesses, given our primary concern with our well-being and happiness, it is entirely legitimate for our travel and movement, the movement of citizens, to be restricted such that the deadly disease does not spread to others. While, optimally, education and persuasion, need to be the first calls in such situations, time may be of the essence and immediate action may be required to protect the health of the many. Moreover education and persuasion may not be enough since the well-being of all in such situations could be severely damaged by even a single maverick dissenter who refuses to believe, accept and cooperate and who acts in a way which it is reasonably judged have the potential to cause or will cause vast damage to hundreds, thousands if not millions of others.

As caring and responsible individuals looking to promote well-being and support the avoidance of pain and suffering, under such circumstances we should act in a responsible manner, supporting and looking after our communities and acting to stop the spread of such an illness. The vast majority of us will do so without the need for recourse by those we have invested with power and authority for the taking of forceful actions. However, as a community and society, in such a situation we would also have to make provision, in as peaceable a manner as possible, to ensure that without a doubt, that small number of people who do not understand the gravity of such a situation, those who are highly irrational or who are bloody minded and will not listen, cannot act in an irresponsible and dangerous manner, and that they are not allowed to jeopardise the health and well-being of others in our families, communities, societies and our broader humanity beyond. And if we are those people, and restraining action is taken against us, then that action against us, which may need to be forceful but should be as peaceful as possible, involving the minimal force necessary, must be seen and understood by us all as legitimate in such instances. The well-being of ourselves and our communities under these and other circumstances needs to be maintained and supported as far as possible.

Similarly in protection of our health and well-being, those with democratically determined authority and power (or perhaps in some cases otherwise) are likely to be legitimately acting to protect our well-being and happiness if they take steps to legally and if necessary forcibly ensure the safety of our environments, for example through laws relating to pollution or enforcing safe operation and procedures, backed up by necessary enforcing action.

For example, smog and other forms of air pollution can kill thousands (and more), damage health and the quality of life, and it is only reasonable for our communities, governments and other organisations, supported by us, to ensure that we have clean and healthy air to breathe. Our not taking action in such respects in order to protect ourselves and our environments, is unacceptable, irresponsible and contrary to core and other principles. It is certainly legitimate in a range of circumstances where our environment and health are being placed in jeopardy, for laws and action to enforce such laws to be taken.

Damaging and health-threatening pollution generated by others, produced by others (or indeed by ourselves) infringes on our freedom, health and well-being and we should not only ensure that we and our organisations wherever possible, do not generate such pollution but we also need to ensure that, through such pollution, others cannot harm ourselves, our families, communities, societies and the world beyond. No individual or organisation has the right to cause such substantial damage to our well-being or the well-being of others, causing pain and suffering through damaging the environment which we all depend on for our survival and well-being.

In a similar vein, those with authority and power, our governments, encouraged and supported by ourselves as individuals, may need to take other actions in regard to health in order to support the general welfare and well-being, for example, in some jurisdictions and geographical areas where there are mosquito borne diseases which can cause severe debilitation and death, authorities having engaged in largely successful efforts to persuade their populations to remove standing water in which mosquitoes might breed. As part of these approaches, such governments and authorities have also given themselves the power to enter homes and remove standing water, as well as to fine and perhaps even imprison those who fail to protect the community from the scourge of mosquito borne diseases. This is clearly justified in terms of supporting well-being and in terms of reducing pain and suffering.

In such jurisdictions and mosquito-plagued environments, in the first place, as individuals we would need to ensure that we, ourselves, do not facilitate the transmission of such illnesses through allowing such standing water or other mosquito breeding areas to exist in our properties or locally, but we also need to support the efforts of our social organisations through supporting their legitimate and reasonable actions, in order to ensure that tens of thousands, or more, are not the victims of such painful, debilitating and terrible illness. Clearly such measures should never be used as a pretext for following other agendas and as a means of oppression yet clearly in this case there is substantial justification through the need of ensuring our public health and safety. Such circumstances not withstanding, however, our homes need to be, to all intents and purposes, our own space where there must be substantial reasons in terms of core principles, for others to enter our personal living space contrary to our desire and will.

In relation to some other areas related to freedom and health which seem to be controversial in the current age, where significant medical expert opinion as well as other influences, support vaccination as a means of preventing sometimes severely harmful or deadly disease, then we should (indeed we really must) choose to, and allow ourselves and our children to be vaccinated in order to support the well-being and health of both ourselves and others in the community. It is unacceptable to leave others to be severely damaged or to die because we ourselves refuse vaccination or refuse vaccination for our children. The reality of many serious diseases is that some of us may well suffer severely or even die if infected and herd immunity is evidenced as needed to protect us all. Vaccination, dependent on the specific vaccine and its degree of efficacy, is something which has, in many instances, been shown to protect us from illness, and thus we need to take advantage of such vaccination and protect ourselves and others.

That being said, there are real and acknowledged side-effects of vaccination, including deadly side effects in some exceptional cases, which does mean that we require a substantial and solid evidence base to support using vaccination, balanced against the level, frequency and severity of such side effects Nevertheless, as a community, where the evidence supports the overall efficacy of vaccination for us as individuals and populations, we must be willing to take up the vaccination ourselves, and support the implementation of such vaccination as far as we can, within our communities, societies and beyond, using methods of education and provision of information rather than compulsion wherever possible. However, in certain situations, where risk to the general population is severe, a need for compulsory vaccination or some other effective measure (for example isolation) may be justified to protect all of us from such severe illness, disease and premature death.

There are many further examples whereby we might feel it legitimate in terms of core principles for those in power, our democratic governments or otherwise, to act towards us and others as individuals or groups in a perhaps sometimes forceful manner in order to protect our individual well-being, even where there might be no direct and obvious effect on the well-being of others. For example, the imposition of compulsory seat belt wearing for drivers of vehicles, though sometimes perhaps illegitimately argued for on the grounds of cost of treatment following road accidents, has meant that tens of thousands, if not more people, have managed to remain alive and avoid severe disfigurement in car accidents. Of course we consider drivers and passengers responsible for their own actions and safety, yet, following campaigns and persuasion in a number of countries aimed at convincing individuals to wear them, when these campaigns did not reach the desired success level, many of our governments under pressure from their publics and medical professionals legally imposed compulsory seat belt wearing with accompanying prosecution and fines for non-compliance, with the resultant positive consequences of thousands of lives saved. Few would suggest now that it has been wrong to introduce such laws.

The restriction on autonomous choice and freedom in this case has been relatively minor, with no serious and significant damage to ideas of freedom and autonomy, while the benefits in terms of well-being and happiness have been substantial in comparison. Families are able to enjoy the continued living of parents who might otherwise have been killed. Parents have been able to enjoy the continued living of their children, who, without a seatbelt might have died in the accident they were part of. Imposing restrictions on individual autonomy and freedom in this case was clearly right and moral, supporting well-being and reducing pain and suffering in line with core and other principles. There is clearly good reason for us to support such restriction on autonomy and freedom in other cases. Moreover the increased focus on and awareness of health and safety, elicited by this type of measure, may well have had broader effects, raising our individual awareness of own actions in regard to our own safety, and bringing to the fore the fact that our own actions can make a real difference to us, our families as well as others, making a real difference in terms of making us all more safe.

In a perhaps similar way, some of our governments, if not many of them, again under pressure from their publics and medical professionals, apart from engaging in campaigning and persuasion, have introduced restrictions on disease-causing tobacco smoking. In particular, with increasing public support, they have restricted smoking in public places, on the grounds of health damage (that damage including deaths and health damage from passive smoking) and on the grounds of the creation of unpleasant environments for others, clearly a rational policy in terms of supporting us as individuals and the general well-being. However they have not banned tobacco smoking, despite the known damage this does to the health of smokers.

And this is an important issue around which there are some apparently complex arguments. For freedom, choice and autonomy comprise important parts of our life and our well-being as individuals and these require that we are allowed to make wrong decisions as well as right ones; in fact, our well-being and happiness, and indeed our education and learning mean that we must be able to be make stupid and wrong decisions. The issue we face as individuals, community and society, is about where the balance lies in terms of overall well-being. In such cases, like those of smoking, there would be some obvious benefits of banning smoking such as a general increase in lifespan for those who currently smoke, yet this would amount to, as a consequence, a restriction on our choices of how to gain what is seen by and experienced by some if not many, as stimulation and pleasure.

Without attempting to debate the entire question here, we also have to recognise how individuals come to or came to smoke and how the smoking culture arose. The fact is that originally, in terms of wide-scale smoking, individuals and cultures were encouraged to smoke through promotion and advertising strategies. They were misled as to the benefits of smoking and deliberately so, even when the damaging health effects of smoking became known, and such misleading of others, is still continuing today in some jurisdictions. On account of these factors, equally robust policies to end the damage caused by smoking can reasonably be argued for in the other direction, in the direction that is, of prevention.

And yet we also need to consider the consequences of such action for freedom and autonomy for the individuals, most of whom should be capable, despite the addictive nature of tobacco, of saying no to, and stopping, smoking. Despite the issues of autonomy and freedom of choice, the view which seems most in line with core principles would be to ban, perhaps progressively, the production and sale of these health-damaging items and prevent consumption. Gentle persuasion, provision of health information has occurred, and now with the provision of viable non-tobacco-based smoking alternatives, many are desisting from and have desisted from smoking tobacco, yet it is likely more action and stronger action may be needed at some point in the future. When cigarettes are gone, it seems likely that we will simply wonder why such action was not taken earlier. We can gain vast amounts of pleasure from our lives without resorting to the smoking of tobacco and exposing ourselves to the lung, heart and other damage which smoking causes.

The above are areas where there may be and have been efforts which restrain action, freedom and autonomy for clear reasons of improving individual and social well-being. However, our freedoms, independence, our autonomy and our individual selves may be constrained, limited, threatened, challenged and attacked by others who may do so with overt malevolent negatively selfish intention, through indifference and lack of empathy and care for others, through their commitment and belief in perverse anti-freedom, anti-individualistic ideologies, or for other reasons. Furthermore, our freedoms, autonomy and independence, may even be threatened unintentionally by some with the best of motives. They may be challenged and attacked by systems of operation and bureaucracies, attacked simply by the ways of behaving of others, the ways of certain cultures and other factors.

Of course we need to act in support of our own well-being and happiness and the well-being and happiness of others, accepting constraints and limitations where these are reasonable and justified, yet we must act against and prevent unjust limitations, constraints and attacks on our freedom, independence and autonomy. We should oppose unnecessary restrictions on our freedoms and in particular must oppose such restrictions when they threaten, presage or cause significant damage to our personal well-being and the well-being of others, our communities, societies and our broader humanity.

A number of what might be seen as reasonable constraints on our freedoms and actions have already been discussed in this chapter and in this guide, including constraints on speaking in a manner which offers violent physical threat to others. Substantial and where necessary forceful constraints on those who have engaged in or who are threatening to engage in destructively and negatively selfish and damaging criminal actions such as theft have also been discussed along with necessary constraints and restraints on those engaging in, and in response to those engaging in violent, destructive and oppressive acts such as rape and murder. We have also looked at more positive and well-intentioned constraints on our actions in terms of medical interventions such as vaccinations and restricting movement of people where there are dangers from infectious diseases.

It is only reasonable for us as a society, and as individuals to constrain the range of already mentioned viciously damaging and hurtful actions, and to ensure the welfare, the health and well-being of all. Indeed, when faced with actions or the prospect of actions by others who may be malevolent, psychopathic, violent, vicious, callous and cruel, those who may be acting solely in pursuit of their own interests at the expense of and damaging ourselves and others; when faced with destructive systems which will seriously damage our freedom, and autonomy, it is important if not essential to be strong, robust and where necessary forceful in tackling these challenges to our freedoms, independence and autonomy, and indeed it is an obligation for us to prevent others from engaging in such destructive negatively selfish and destructive acts.

In our more personal and individual lives, we may need to respond to restrictions on our selves and our freedoms close to home when those with power in, and over, our more local lives, when those close to us, for example, within our families, as younger people, our parents, try to prevent us through coercive and unjust methods, through force and unjust sanction, from engaging in reasonable actions, for example, preventing us from discussing ideas, speaking out our feelings and opinions, our judgments. Hopefully our parents will allow us some leeway and freedoms in terms of what we say and do, and will discuss things in a reasonable manner with us, but this may not always occur. We may need to respond when they try to prevent us from expressing ourselves in legitimate and reasonable ways, when they try to prevent us from adopting the new or when they try to control what we wear, where we go, what we think, who we meet, what we read, who we talk to, the music we listen to (or whether we listen to music at all) and much more. Such efforts at our restriction are often if not frequently unacceptable and we must, as far as we can, as young people, argue against such restrictions and take other necessary and peaceable action which support our growing independence, autonomy and personal freedom.

In the first place, of course, as parents, members of our families, communities and societies we should be very careful in any restrictions we wish to impose, acting with a propensity to enable and allow others, our children to experiment and experience. As parents we need to be and we are, as already discussed in this chapter, responsible for ensuring our children grow up safely and well, and that they are able to contribute well to, and live successfully in, our families, communities, societies and the world beyond. We do need to protect our children and look after them, and need to do so in an age appropriate manner, yet we should not be zealous in this to the extent that we unnecessarily restrict our children's access to ideas and information, that we stand in the way of their search for truth or obstruct their ability to experiment with, search for, develop and create their own identities. We need to be caring, understanding and responsible, but not oppressive and overly restrictive. However, we also cannot be permissive in a manner which exposes our children to exploitation and significant risk of or significant danger. We need to enable our children to grow, learn, experience and experiment and to do so safely. We need to encourage learning and exploration while helping our children to learn to live in community, society and as part of our broader humanity.

If we, as young people, are living in families where we believe there is unwarranted and over zealous restriction on our behaviour and conduct, then we need to act against and oppose such unreasonable restrictions. Yet also, if we are being restricted in a manner we perceive to be unreasonable and over-zealous by parental action or the actions of others, then we certainly should and certainly do need to reflect on whether some restrictions might be in fact be justifiable and reasonable taking into account the parental perspective.

And dependent on our age, and the fact of parental responsibility up to a certain age, some restrictions may well be warranted. However if, as young people and young adults, we are convinced that such restrictions are not warranted, then in the first place we need to object to and state what we think about these restrictions and ask for reasonable change and accommodation. If that reasonable accommodation is not forthcoming and reasonable negotiation and compromise is not possible with no agreement being reached, we will either need to accept these unjust restrictions or will need to find ways to get around, evade or contravene these unwarranted and unfair restrictions.

Even though, in a family context, as young people moving towards adulthood, our parents have important responsibility for us, our welfare and well-being, and we should aim to be helpful and cooperative, working together with others, our parents, in our families, in our guise as growing and older members of the family, we are not obliged to obey our parents, and accept unwarranted unfair and unjust restrictions and should certainly not submit to violent and other inappropriate actions and punishments. Our parents may be wrong in their judgments, and need to be reasonable and accommodating to us as young people growing to adulthood, while also doing their best to look after our well-being and happiness, a well-being and happiness, which includes the need to make an increasing number of our own choices as we grow. As parents we need to aim to build a context where matters can be discussed, where our growing children are consulted and taken into consideration as appropriate, are sure of their self-worth and value, where they can be sure that we love them and love them in a positive, constructive and supportive way.

The role and job of parenting is a difficult and challenging role for our parents, something which we, as young people, also need to acknowledge. For life is not so simple for parents who love us and wish to care for us and who are very likely to worry about our well-being and happiness. Part of our expression of maturity and part of our growing towards adulthood is an increasing recognition that our parents are fallible, have their vulnerabilities, may have flawed perspectives and have daily challenges in their lives, their own changes in feelings and moods, their own worries and anxieties and threats to their own well-being and happiness. As young people, we need a sense of empathy and understanding with our parents.

Nevertheless, if parents engage in coercive conduct, aggressive violence against us as children and young people, we are entitled to and indeed must resist and act against such violence, protecting ourselves as necessary from such violence, obtaining help where we can, escaping from such an environment if necessary and at all possible, and taking action against such aggressive violence when we can such that this aggressive violence cannot be implemented by these parents on ourselves or on others. Of course we should never use aggressive violence ourselves and should be caring, considerate and loving to our parents as far as we can, yet where it occurs, we should certainly protect ourselves from such violence as far as we can.

Beyond our homes, as adults, we may need to respond to unwarranted and unjust restrictions on our freedom and autonomy in our work environment. As a case in point, if we are subjected to bullying oppression and illegitimate threats, for example being threatened in regard to our jobs and income if we speak out about bad or exploitative practice, then we will need to do whatever we can to counter such oppression and counter such threats both in support of ourselves and others. In such cases, in order to ensure that we are acting in support of the general well-being and indeed in support of the organisation as a whole, we need to act to prevent such damaging and exploitative practice. We should not and must not have our livelihoods threatened because we act with honesty, integrity, care and concern for others, and indeed in support of what may well be the real interests of the organisations for which we may work.

Moreover, we need to be able to freely report bad and oppressive practice within our workplaces. Organisations and companies need to have, available to their staff and managers, systems to deal with this kind of situation with trustworthy mechanisms available to deal with bullying and oppressive bad practice. And where organisations and companies fail in their responsibilities to those employed and to the wider community, there needs to be swift access to redress, and appropriate action available and implemented through means of our wider community and society.

If our group entities, communities and societies, powerful individuals and interest or other forms of group, attempt to impose or impose unwarranted, unreasonable and oppressive restrictions upon us, engaging in unjust, coercive and threatening behaviour to ensure that we conform to unjustly required actions, then again we, as adults will need to oppose these restrictions. Such groups and individuals, often powerful groups and individuals, may try to prevent the discussion of ideas, the exchange of ideas and thinking. They may unjustly try to restrict our abilities to meet up with others, our ability to choose our own ideas and beliefs, our access to ideas and information; they may aim to prevent us from saying certain things (such as criticising those in authority or the prevalent belief system or the principles of government and administration). They may aim to pressurise and coerce others through a variety of destructive psychological, social and physical means, engaging in coercive and violent action against us.

Such coercion and violence is of course, as mentioned throughout this chapter and this guide, entirely unacceptable. It is entirely against core principles of supporting individual and social well-being for our communities to restrict our legitimate and reasonable actions within core and other principles and impose identities, actions and beliefs upon us which are contrary to our legitimate and reasonable individual desires and wishes and which significantly damage our own personal freedom, sense of autonomy and independence, our well-being and the well-being of all.

And we are justified in taking persuasive and where necessary robust and forceful action to prevent oppression and coercive, unwarranted, damaging, destructive restriction, whether by families, communities, societies, organisations, institutions or government.

Where there are coercive efforts to restrict our legitimate freedom of speech through law or otherwise, then we must speak out in contravention of such efforts and act both as individuals and in concert with others to overthrow such restrictions. Where states, communities and societies act outside of core principles to restrict, limit or constrain our rights, our behaviour our conduct, in an illegitimate manner inconsistent with core principles, perhaps on the grounds of the specific beliefs we state, the view of our ideas as a threat to extant power, perhaps due to individual characteristics, background, race, personal and political beliefs; where they attempt to restrict what we wear, what we say, who we meet with, restrict our beliefs, remove our access to information, knowledge and greater understanding; where these entities try to restrict the organisations we can join; where they act to prevent us from opposing injustice through our own campaigning action, where those with power act to promote oppressive action against us and others, through coercion, violence, through laws which are in contravention of core principles and act against freedom, well being and happiness, where they act to restrict our freedoms and access to justice, in all these cases and more we must act and where necessary act robustly against such oppression.

And none of us should cooperate with such oppressive action. None of us should implement such actions or be involved in the implementation of such oppressive and destructive actions. We not only have an obligation to not implement such coercive, damaging and oppressive actions but we have an obligation to oppose such actions supporting cooperative action, cooperative talk and persuasion as optimal in our individual lives, in our communities, societies and our broader humanity. Engaging with others and organising to peacefully prevent such oppression is a necessity, wherever this is viable, and even when it may present significant threats and challenges to our personal well-being.

Efforts at coercion to support such oppressive actions, standing against freedom, and autonomy should be resisted through non-co-operation, through direct resistance, and where necessary through forceful physical action, while aiming to do our utmost to preserve our own well-being and the well-being of others. If we cannot act immediately against such actions, due to threat to our life and limb, due to threats to our families and others, a sadly too frequent situation, then we must act as effectively as we are able to act on the moment, and act as soon as we can, as effectively as we can, to oppose such oppression.

We should avoid physically forceful action as far as we can when acting in our support of our freedom and in our resistance to oppression, aiming to promote peaceful change and peaceful cooperation allied to freedom and autonomy, determining our actions within the context of promoting well-being and happiness for ourselves and for all. It is absolutely necessary to aim to engage in such peaceful and cooperative processes where circumstances allow us to do so. Stating what is needed and wanted, persuasion, argument, passive non-acceptance and resistance as well as other peaceful means need to be our preferred and initial steps and actions, sustained wherever possible, taking into account our contexts.

Unfortunately, however our peaceful actions may not always be successful and, as is too frequently the case, we may realistically anticipate and in fact meet with damaging coercive and brutal, aggressively violent action against those of us who would wish for peaceful change. As a consequence, we become, and are, the visible and open targets of coercive and violent oppression. Where we have pursued non-violent action, in the face of oppression and violence, our non-violence and direct action may become too painful and costly to bear.

In such circumstances, we need to recognise that it is certainly not consistent with core principles to allow ourselves and others to be the physical victims of such violent, destructive and coercive oppression which of course severely damages our freedom, autonomy, well-being and happiness, and which of course promise pain and suffering for us. Where such acts are being taken and enacted against us and others, in these circumstances we may need to take planned and calculated physical and forceful action, against those have engaged in and are engaging in such oppression, aimed at preventing such actions, defending and protecting ourselves and others, aimed at enhancing our own well-being and happiness and the well-being and happiness and others, as well as aiming to prevent pain and suffering.

Such forceful responsive action is not what we desire or optimal, with such action containing within itself the dangers of setting precedents for future conduct even should we triumph against our oppressors, holding the danger of bringing in new oppression. And so therefore, any such action, if taken, should be taken to the minimal level of force to achieve the goals of legitimate freedom, personal independence and autonomy, optimally bringing about freedom and stopping and preventing oppression and aggressive violence without causing any significant harm itself, perhaps a rather hopeful goal in the face of aggressively violent oppression. Nevertheless, such physical action should never be vengeful and disproportionate, or gratuitously violent, but must involve the minimum use of force (which may mean substantial force) necessary to achieve the goals of promoting justice and freedom and removing that oppression and aggressive violence.

Whatever feelings of justifiable anger and bitterness we may feel against those who have done harm, substantial harm to us and others, (those we know and love, and those whom we have never met) through this violence, coercion and oppression, we should not engage in vengeful action but we must certainly disempower those who have oppressed and done aggressive violence, and we must bring to justice those who have engaged in aggressive violence and oppression, exposing their destructive actions for all to see. These purveyors of such violence and oppression must not be allowed to be successful in their actions. Their oppression, their callous negative selfishness, their repression and oppression must never be allowed to win out or allowed to be sustained. If they succeed, the consequences are likely to be terrible, for the well-being and happiness of each of us as individuals and for the well-being and happiness of all.

While opposing and aiming to effectively deal with such oppression, we also need to take care, be wary and rational and reasoned in our thoughts and action, using evidence and logic to determine our conclusions and the actions we take. In particular, we need to be aware that there are those who attempt to falsely portray themselves as victims of oppression, claiming that their freedoms are being violated when in fact that is not the case. Certain belief and other groups, often powerful groups, may claim that others who are speaking out peacefully in opposition to their views and beliefs or who are proposing alternative beliefs and courses of action, represent a threat to them and the whole, with these groups attempting to isolate and demonise, even threatening those speaking out against their views.

Yet well-being and happiness are supported through such diversity of views and opinions, and where such opinions are peacefully expressed, and offer no real significant physical or other aggressive threat to others apart from challenging existing views and beliefs and ways of doing things, which may be outmoded and indeed need change, then those claiming oppression must be seen as acting as self-serving and promoting their own interests rather than the whole. Indeed they are acting in a negatively selfish manner and acting in a manner which is damaging to our community, society and broader humanity.

Peacefully challenging and contradicting existing beliefs cannot be seen as a direct and significant threat to others, with, as already stated in this chapter, speech and action only being open to restriction if it involves threatening abuse, and actual threats of significant psychological, emotional and physical harm and violence. Holding different views than those in the majority or those who are powerful, proposing other ways of looking at the world, putting forward alternate peaceful views or criticising the views of others, however starkly, does not fall into these categories. All beliefs and systems of belief need to be open to challenge, rational discussion, debate and criticism, of course including the ideas presented here in this guide.

Certain groups may state that they are being oppressed because they are unable to exercise and implement their own damaging, discriminatory and hateful views, and because, sometimes as a consequence of their views and beliefs, they are being forced to act in line with ideas and actions which support the well-being and happiness of all. Groups holding views and implementing actions which espouse and promote aggressive violence against others, which are racist, which unfairly discriminate against sections of their own community and the wider community, pursuing actions and beliefs which promise and threaten significant pain, suffering and violence to their members and those outside of their groups, cannot be allowed to act in such ways, and it is the responsibility of the broader community to ensure that such groups cannot act in such ways. In doing so we will be protecting the well-being and happiness of all, and enhancing the broader freedom and autonomy. In practice this means, for example, that we cannot allow groups to make women second class citizens without power, freedom and individual rights, not can we allow groups to discriminate internally or otherwise against homosexuals, or those of different colour, race, family origins or upbringing.

As a corollary to this, if there are those in such groups who are happy in their roles, happy to have less influence for example on decisions, indeed happy to serve in what might be seen by others as second class roles, being free to leave, adopt other roles, having been educated in an open and free manner which presents other options for living, then it is consistent with notions of personal responsibility, personal autonomy and freedom for those people to have that choice and live the life they choose within the bounds of core principles. However, they must not be subject to coercion, violence and emotional or physical intimidation, such representing significant harm, pain and suffering which are unacceptable, inconsistent with well-being and happiness, and contrary to core and other principles. Nor can they be subject to alternative systems which provide the potential for, or in practice significantly damage their well-being and cause pain and suffering.

Poverty has already been mentioned earlier in this chapter as an important and significant influence on our ability to be autonomous, free and independent. To add some further comment to that already presented, in particular our ability to make free choices and enjoy autonomy are almost certain to be significantly damaged by living a life of poverty, something which can damage our lives in almost countless ways. If we are poor, depending on our degree of poverty and the nature of that poverty, then our choices in life will almost certainly be substantially limited. We may have reduced or no access to learning and education, a lack which may have significant ramifications throughout our lives. We may suffer from the range of health issues and health problems associated with poverty, which will mean we are less able to engage in activities which help to make life more endurable, palatable and pleasurable, and furthermore, many choices which are available to others will not be available to us. And these same health issues and problems will tend to indicate that we will die early compared to others who are more wealthy, our maintaining our lives being, of course, a substantial issue in terms of our freedom and autonomy, our well-being and happiness.

If we are poor, then our lack of resources is likely to render us, on some occasions at least, vulnerable to exploitation by others who may attempt to use us, to take advantage of us, for their own purposes. This contrasts with the situation in which we are better able to follow our own purposes and goals through from a position of more equal wealth status, engaging in more equal negotiation in which we can engage in exchanges with others founded on that equality of status and power. Further, our poverty may well mean that we become dependent on others to a damaging extent, with the consequence that they may well aim to, and be able to, place restrictions on our legitimate actions, our legitimate freedom of speech and action, as we may face social and other sanctions in various forms, in particular from those on whom we are dependent and reliant upon. Escape from poverty is certainly something we must all seek for ourselves and for others, to avoid direct suffering from that poverty but also in order to bolster our freedom, independence and autonomy, our escape from poverty not only benefiting our own personal well-being and happiness but also enabling us to contribute more effectively to our families, communities, societies and our broader humanity.

Our living in poverty is also likely to mean that we will be lacking in power in other ways, based for example in our lack of the range of resources, and therefore we will be less able, or unable to deal with those who oppress us. For example, we may be unable to access justice through lack of resources, and even if we can access justice systems, we may be unable to gain equal and fair justice through our lack of resources. Optimally our legal systems, our communities, societies and beyond, as already stated in this chapter, should ensure that equal and fair justice is available to all, and that justice is not something which can be bought. Our poverty may also mean that we are unable to organise with others and protect ourselves, our families, communities and societies from attack by others pursuing their self-interest at our expense, protect ourselves and others from attack by those who will act in malevolent ways, those with cruel, exploitative and bad intention towards us.

Our lack of resources will further form a barrier to our ability to take initiatives which support us and support our families, communities and societies. If we wish to contribute to our communities through developing and applying new skills, starting businesses or providing services which might remove our own poverty and which might benefit others, then our poverty will stand in our way, especially if we are living in a context of poverty where not only we ourselves are poor, but those around us also have few resources.

Thus poverty damages our freedom, independence and autonomy and therefore our well-being and happiness in many ways. The effects of poverty on our freedom, independence and autonomy together with the range of more directly damaging consequences of poverty such as illness, premature death and ongoing suffering in other forms, mean that we must do whatever we can, within the constraints of core principles, to ensure our own absence of poverty and the absence of poverty for all others.

Also relevant to our freedom, independence and autonomy is the ability for each of us to contribute to the organisation and government of our communities and societies, this being one of our essential needs and freedoms. Democracy, though not sufficient in itself for well-being, is nevertheless a crucial pillar of our well-being, recognising our value and worth as individuals, and recognising the right and embodying the capacity and legitimacy for each of us as individuals to contribute to the government and organisation of our lives. Such democracy and contribution does not mean solely the notion of having a vote every once in a while in the choice of those who govern us even though a choice of those who hold positions of power in our governments, local, national and where relevant global, is an essential part of our freedom. Democracy must exist more deeply than that, in general attitudes and ethos wherein we ourselves listen to and value the ideas, take cognisance of the perspectives and contributions of others, and therefore seek out the ideas, opinions and perspectives of those others, and concomitant with this, they listen to us, recognise our value, take cognisance of our thoughts and opinions, the value of our contributions and seek out our perspectives and views.

And in representative democracies, our effective democracies require the continuous accountability of those who we elect to those of us who elected them. In such ways, we can have some capacity to influence the decisions which affect our lives, and others have the capacity to influence any decisions that we ourselves will make which influence the lives of others. This is a crucial element of the notion of government for the people by the people. That being said, the presence of voting democratic systems does not necessarily mean that we can exercise power, as such democratic systems can be distorted by the powerful and well-resourced, holding undue influence over media and communications, over social, political and economic processes. Thus the range of freedoms already discussed, including not only our freedom to express our ideas but also our capacity to be heard, are necessary for the successful functioning of our democratic systems.

Yet democracy, our voting, our contributions to decision-making, our choices of those who are to represent us, govern and our choice of systems of community and societal government, as already pointed out, does not mean a democratic right to dictate to others in all their affairs. It does not mean that our chosen government or authority, or the majority of people, can legitimately do whatsoever it or they like in regard to individual, community and society. Democracy and democratic systems do not mean and should never be taken as meaning such a thing.

Democracy, our ability to select people to represent us and take power, our ability to contribute to decisions about the running of our communities and societies does not trump ideas of individual well-being and happiness, the prevention and avoidance of pain and suffering, freedom, individuality and autonomy and ideas of the well-being and happiness, the freedom of all. Whether or not the majority of us, even the vast majority of us believe in something and have elected a government to do those things, that does not mean that we or our governments have the automatic right to act in such a manner that our actions have significantly damaging effects on others, such that our actions harm others and substantially damage their well-being causing significant pain and suffering.

Moreover, for actions and obligations to be placed on us as citizens in a democratic context, there must be good reason for that being done in terms of core and other principles. And for any of our freedoms to be modified, reduced or even taken away, there must be strong and significant justifications in terms of those core and other principles, such that our individual, such that the general well-being and happiness will be improved, as will optimally our own well-being and happiness. Thus, we certainly all need to appreciate the importance of freedom, autonomy, independence, well-being, happiness and more, alongside and as part of the need for democracy and democratic control, management and contribution. On the other hand, as already discussed, there are frequent obligations for governments to act, and sometimes act in a manner which may limit or appear to limit individual freedom, the freedom of some individuals, in order to support individual, community, societal and broader human well-being and happiness, a number of examples of which have already been discussed in this chapter.

In regard to the decisions made by our communities and societies, it is not legitimate that we should be excluded from debate and discussion because it is said by others that we lack expertise. While there certainly is expertise; while there are highly likely to be experts who have greater knowledge and understanding than we can have as individuals, and while there are certainly many areas which may be extremely challenging for the majority of us in the population to understand, and further, while it is essential that those with specialist knowledge assert their views, present their case with evidence and are attended to, and listened to, it is in fact a responsibility of those with expertise and specialist knowledge to work to inform, enlighten and educate us all as far as is possible in regard to their areas of expertise.

It also has to be acknowledged and recognised that experts may in some cases be financially tied to those who sponsor and pay for their work, those who pay their salaries and maintain their financial well-being. And for this and for other reasons, which may include their own ideological and cultural biases, as well as methodological problems and complexities in some areas of research and expertise, such expert advice may not always be as accurate, impartial and objective as it may seem. And tied to this, it seems to be a common practice in the current age for some of those with financial, political and other interests, to recruit and employ those portraying themselves and perhaps presented as experts, in order to assert the preferred opinions and interests of the powerful, as opposed to those with expertise acting as responsible citizens working with impartial and dispassionate objectivity and independence in the search for the truth, in search of accuracy or optimal courses of actions which are consistent with our common well-being and happiness, and the common good. In some cases false evidence is deliberately presented, irrelevant or insignificant evidence emphasised as a distraction, or existing evidence critiqued in an irrational and biased manner, with use of techniques of debate such as ad hominem attacks, exaggeration, over-emphasising minor contrasts and inconsistencies in data and indeed all manner of tactics. This is all unacceptable since we need the truth, since we need accuracy, impartial judgment and weighing of evidence in order to make those decisions which benefit us all to the greatest degree.

Given the fact that many decisions require expert analysis and expert advice, then where there are decisions to be made which are germane to all of us, germane to the public, to all others, then it is essential that complex ideas, concepts and their implications are made as far as possible, clear and comprehensible and that we are all, as far as possible, able to pass an educated and informed judgment on what may be complex issues. It has already been stated that information and ideas must be mediated in a full, truthful and impartial manner as far as is possible, with the interests of the community, society and our broader humanity in mind, rather than being promoted and mediated with simply the purposes of serving particular individuals, ideological, belief or interest groups. Biases and interests of those involved in advising or making decisions need to be explicitly made known. Without explicit knowledge of personal and group biases, other beliefs and judgments, financial connections and so forth, it is difficult to judge the advice being given and reach the most appropriate decisions.

Some biases and prejudices may, however, be unknown to those possessing them, with their being deeply embedded in culture, society and personal psychological make-up. Such unconscious biases and prejudices may nevertheless have serious negative effects, substantially influencing interpretation of information and being deeply anti-social and destructive. And while the individuals concerned may lack the conscious intent and awareness of the origins of their beliefs and judgments, they can still, through rational and reasoned analysis, through acceptance of observations and evidence which contrasts with their pre-conceptions, biases and prejudices evaluate the consequences of their judgments, and beliefs, and understand the inaccuracy, inappropriacy and the pain and suffering that the views they promote and their resultant actions might have. And these consequences are frequently, to all intents and purposes, equivalent to those arising from the deliberate and malicious presentation of partial and indeed false information, done to support specific personal and group interests. In either case, the consequences are likely to be damaging to the well-being of individuals, of our communities and societies.

Even if such partial information is provided with the aim of supporting the well-being of all in mind, through fears perhaps of misunderstandings about what may be complex issues, the hiding and misrepresentation of information remains unacceptable. It is essential that information is, as far as is possible and reasonable, presented in full, and that full discussion and debate is held. It is not for those with expert knowledge to place themselves above others, the community and society, deciding that they will, in effect, make the decisions for others through partial and biased presentation of information and its interpretation. It is their role, and our role if we have specialist knowledge to support and contribute, perhaps in a leading manner, to debate and discussion, but not to seek to determine outcomes on our own through presentation of half truths, inadequate information or indeed false information. If we are considered experts ourselves, we have to recognise that, even as experts, even as those with years of experience and substantial specialist knowledge, we are ourselves fallible and therefore not only do we need to gain both the views of other experts who may disagree with what we say and who may disagree with our interpretations of what we have observed, but we also need to gain the ideas, views and judgments of those operating from completely different perspectives to ours. It is almost impossible for others to provide sound comment and advice, indeed it is probably not possible or, at the minimum is substantially challenging for others to provide accurate solutions and accurate comments if they are not supplied with full information or are provided with false and partial data and interpretations.

All this being said in regard to experts and expertise, those of us who are making judgments, all of us as ordinary citizens when consulted for our views, sometimes in order to determine important decisions, need to consider the evidence we are presented with in a rational and unbiased manner, in order to support us in reaching the optimal judgments and decisions. Alongside that, we need to analyse and understand our own motives in our decision-making and in our contributions to decisions, examining our own interpretations and considering the validity of other perspectives and points of view. That is, we certainly need to consider the possibility that our current views and judgments may be wrong, and recognise contradictions in our own thinking as well as dealing with that evidence which may clearly not support our current judgments and opinions. Just as those with specialist expertise need to provide us with impartial information, evidence and judgments, we ourselves need to judge that advice and that evidence in a rational and reasoned manner, such that the well-being of all is supported, and in order that we do not cause any significant pain and suffering.

Of course in making democratic decisions in a democratic context, the well-being and happiness of all, the majority, the whole of community and society, needs to be considered, as well as the freedom, well-being and happiness of each of us as individuals or groups of individuals. In the context of our decision-making, we need to hear the range of voices and the evidence they may present. Any unjust and unwarranted suppression and oppression is contrary to ideas of well-being and happiness whatever the source of the suppresion and oppression. Restricting the rights of others because they speak differently, are different, controversial, curmudgeons and critics, because they speak the truth or say things that some may not wish to hear (unless what they say represents a direct physical threat to other individuals, our communities and society) is totally unacceptable and against core principles whether imposed by a democratic form of government or any other form of government.

Restricting the actions of others, the rights of some because they are different, do not fit in, because they are in origin foreign, the wrong colour, have the wrong background, the wrong beliefs (unless these offer direct physical threat), because they demonstrate wrong or unconventional ways of behaving, is entirely unacceptable, and democratic majorities have no more right than any other form of government to engage in such oppression. As individuals it is our responsibility to prioritise core principles, supporting the well-being and happiness of ourselves and all others, to support democratic forms of government, and ensure freedoms, individual liberty and individual autonomy.

Given the threat they offer to our well-being and our freedoms, it is important to consider how we should respond to those who deliberately lie, cheat and mislead, who fabricate information or emphasise false perspectives in order to support their own local desires and wants, in order to support their own personal or group social, economic and political views, in order to support their own financial, economic or other personal interests.

Clearly, we need to point out such lies and deceitfulness where we feel these are occurring and aim to persuade others of the truthfulness and accuracy of our evidence, judgments and opinions. Nevertheless, some of those engaged in such deliberate lying, dishonest, and self-interested policies on the local or more national scales may have substantial economic power and political influence which is likely to have substantial effect in a mass society, where substantial resources may be needed to communicate with millions of others. And thus our efforts at contradicting such powerful figures and groups may not be enough. Further complicating matters, the line between lies, dishonesty and deceit and alternative interpretations of information, alternative perceptions of truth, can be difficult to draw and, moreover, in support of freedom, we are obliged to support others in speaking out, in stating their perceptions and views, this being an element of all of our freedom, independence and autonomy.

However, these things being said, the nature of truth, the presentation of accurate and truthful information in our mass societies cannot be allowed to rest solely in the hands of the powerful and economically wealthy. In addition to combating those who fabricate, falsify and deliberately misinterpret information through stating our own views and interpretations and promoting those, in support of broader freedom, we, our communities, societies, our global communities and societies, need to support and embed organisational structures and institutions which support truthfulness and accuracy, organisations which provide evidence-based, independent perspectives and interpretations to counter those who deliberately lie and mislead, organisations which are open with information, trusted and rigorous in their pursuit of truth, accuracy and effective interpretation, and which also have the power to communicate with the millions of us, organisations which clearly state their paradigms, perspectives, frames of, and methodologies of investigation and interpretation, and which as far as possible are independent from bias stemming from issues such as funding.

Another important if not crucial area where we need to have individual autonomy, independence and freedom is that which relates to the maintenance of, and in particular the endings of our lives. As will be discussed in chapter thirteen of this guide in the context of health and well-being, while the vast main of us have lives which are to some, if not a large extent, interesting, enjoyable and worthwhile experiences, lives which are fulfilling, pleasurable and rewarding, with times of both ups and downs, it is possible that for many of us, in particular, towards the end of our lives, due to illness and general deterioration of our physical and sometimes mental selves, with no prospect of cure and a more healthy life returning, we may end up suffering terribly in pain, and feeling that our lives are no longer worth living. In such cases, taking into account the views of others, in particular those close to us, the ones we love, as well as medical experts who can give appropriate prognoses, we need to have the individual right, freedom and choice under our circumstances of such pain and suffering, with no or almost no realistic hope for recovery, to end the pain and suffering we are enduring, and end our lives.

The escape from pain and suffering in these dire circumstances means that our intense suffering and pain will be removed, something which is in line with core principles. The enjoyment and experience of life is of ultimate importance within the core and other principles and life's existence and enjoyment is also ultimate and fundamental within the core principles of supporting well-being and happiness. However, under circumstances in the modern world, and for all periods in the past, and for the foreseeable future, it has been the case, is and will be the case, that all of our lives come to an end. And there are times towards the ends of our lives when the intensity and extremities of pain and suffering being endured by ourselves, by those we love, by indeed any person, where there is, in effect, no realistic prospect of recovery, mean that as individuals, under such circumstances, we should be able to make the decision and take action or be assisted in taking action to leave this life.

In circumstances, where we are dealing with another who is suffering in such ways, perhaps someone we love deeply or indeed others we may encounter in such a situation, while we may reasonably engage in persuasion and discussion with that person, perhaps aiming to persuade them that their life may be worth continuing with, our first duty is to express love for them, and, where they are in such tremendous pain, suffering in agony, with no hope of recovery or remission, we need to support them in that which they wish to do, psychologically, emotionally and where required physically in assisting them to die, if that is what they wish for.

Indeed it is negatively selfish to allow those suffering in the most intense and severe pain which cannot be remitted, to carry on in such pain, on, for example, the negatively selfish grounds of the pain we ourselves might endure through losing them from our lives. For indeed they will die, most likely soon, and we will feel that pain of loss in any case. If we support those we love in their desire to escape this unremitting and severe pain, then through acting in that manner we will be expressing our love and we will be helping them to escape the excruciating blight of their intense, unremitting pain, which, without appropriate intervention they may have to endure for what to them may seem to be an extended period, until their life finally ends. There is palliative, pain reducing, care, but that may not reduce the physical and mental anguish and pain being endured in its many forms, which may be deepened by our incapability to perform basic functions, inability to move, by the loss of limbs or other parts of our body, rendering us less than physically whole, while being faced with medically certain imminent death. The decision as to what to do under such circumstances must lie primarily with those of us enduring the pain and suffering, supported by medical advice and by those who love us most deeply.

There are circumstances, certainly in our current modern world where many of us have access to advanced medical technology and medical treatment, where there are those who can be kept breathing and alive, while lacking other or perhaps any other normal human capacities. Such occurs with brain injuries in relation to what are termed vegetative or similar states where an individual is surviving but can do nothing and may in some cases, as far as we can determine, be aware of nothing. In some such cases where the person in that state is aware and can be communicated with then, as with other cases, we will need to take the lead from them in relation to their continuing desire for survival where that survival is viable. Over time, there may be the possibility that they recover, though this possibility may be remote to the extent that in reality it is not going to occur. In cases where communication is not possible with someone in such a state, then those closest to that person, knowing that person and taking into account medical advice, with agreement from medical practitioners, under legal decision and supervision where necessary and where there is dispute, after a reasonable period of time, may decide to, and on the individual's behalf, have the right to decide to, end the life support being provided to that person.

This view of our actions in terms of supporting well-being under such end-of-life situations and circumstances does of course ask questions about those in other trying and painful circumstances, perhaps much younger people with potentially long lives ahead of them, who feel that they wish to end their lives, perhaps due to the intense mental or physical pain they might be enduring. Such mental anguish and in a smaller number of cases, severe physical pain and suffering, can affect many of us at different stages in our lives. Some of us may suffer severe physical debilitating injury which means we cannot do the basic things we need or want to do leading some of us to perhaps contemplate suicide. These are terrible situations for us to be in, though we have to recognise, that if we can overcome our mental anguish and pain, even with severe physical injuries, in many contexts, supported by others, we can do much and live life well, enjoying well-being and contributing to others. Precise circumstances will support us in determining our actions.

While undoubtedly, if we are severely physically damaged, mentally of sound mind, in the face of medical advice that we will perhaps never recover, never be independent, never be fully physically well, then we should be free to end our lives under such circumstances, however, we do need to look at what we might be able to do and achieve, how we might still be able to enjoy our lives, how we might manage to enjoy a good level of well-being, how we might change and adapt our thinking such that we can act and achieve in our new circumstances, should that be possible. We should also recognise the love that others feel for us, the joy they will feel in simply having us around, and the pain and suffering they may endure if we determine to leave our lives at such a young age. That being said, their love for us may mean they empathise with our pain and suffering. These choices need to be left with us, as we are the ones enduring and suffering and we are the ones who will have to live on, in some important ways debilitated.

Unconnected to physical pain and suffering, many of us may experience thoughts of intense emotional and mental anguish and pain, and as part of, or through experiencing such intense pain and sometimes despair, we may have thoughts, sometimes serious thoughts of suicide arising from such pain. Our mental pain and anguish may arise from our failures and sense of failure. Such feelings may arise from a deep, intense and painful sense of personal inadequacy, possibly from past traumas, or stem from our deep humiliations or intense confusions about life. Yet our mental and psychological pains and anguish may also arise simply as a consequence of our medical and psychological make-up and identity, as part of a particular phase of our growth and change, as part of our individual human biology and psychology, perhaps being present and arising for no particular reason, but causing us dreadful and terrible mental turmoil, hurt, suffering and pain.

If we are suffering in such ways, then in support of well-being and happiness, we must work to help and take whatever actions we can to reduce our own pain and suffering such that we ourselves can move forward and build ourselves full lives of well-being and happiness, lives in which we will also be able to support the well-being and happiness of others. In the vast main of instances, our pain and the pain of those others who are suffering intense mental pain, anguish, indeed mental illness, is likely to be amenable to reduction and remission though it may not perhaps seem so at the time. Pleasure, well-being and happiness can be regained if lost, and found if they have not been present in our lives. And our lives and the lives of others can be, and indeed are, likely to have times of fun and enjoyment, be enjoyable into the future, and a life of pleasure, fulfillment, of greater well-being can and hopefully will be experienced.

We have a responsibility as individuals and as communities and societies to support both ourselves and those people suffering with mental pain and anguish and perhaps feeling suicidal, into good health, as far as is possible, such that lives can be enjoyed and be fulfilled, even if, at a particular moment or for a period of time, that is not what we as an individual, suffering and in pain, or the individual we are supporting, are hopeful about experiencing.

And we, if we are suffering in such ways, we, remain with a responsibility, if feeling such thoughts of suicide, to do whatever is possible to find a way out of that pain, to find a way to find the pleasure and happiness that we would undoubtedly prefer to enjoy. These ways to health include seeking the help of others, seeking medical and psychological treatment and support, and aiming as far as we and they can to change our feelings and thoughts such that our thoughts and thinking are constructive, supportive of ourselves and support our personal health and well-being. Further, and importantly, those feeling this way, if we feel this way, we have a responsibility to others, those who know and love us, to work to find that well-being and happiness and to live on and provide support and love for others. We must not, and those others suffering or thinking suicidal and self-destructive thoughts must not, impose or be allowed to impose the devastation and misery on others that would arise from our suicide, the loss of someone loved, someone with a future which could be lived in happiness and joy, a suicide which would be something which would be so emotionally devastating for so many, being entirely incompatible with our goals and desire for well-being and happiness which form the basis of the core and other principles.

In essence, therefore, in terms of core principles, in terms of supporting well-being and happiness, those of us who are severely debilitated, who feel suicidal and wish to kill ourselves, yet who have the potential for full and complete lives ahead of us, need to take appropriate actions ourselves and receive appropriate community and social support, to enhance our health, happiness and well-being. We must make all efforts to alleviate our despair and our communities and societies must do all they can to help us recover from our intense suffering and pain. Aside from when we are in the final stages of our lives and are experiencing unremitting pain and suffering, or have the near prospect of such unremittable suffering and pain, we must not commit suicide.

This is all stated, notwithstanding, that to someone who is suicidal, there may seem to be no way out, that mental depression and pain may on the moment seem unremitting, the pain deep and seemingly endless, that in itself such mental pain may hurt intensely and seem insuperable, with death seemingly, the only escape. In cases of such illness, where we or others, as individuals, feel unable to escape such mental anguish, depression and pain, as stated above, we must seek help, and it is also up to the rest of us, as individuals, as communities and societies, to provide help and support, to provide medical and psychological support and treatment where needed, and to ensure systems of medical and psychological help and treatment are available, wherever this is possible. Such mental illness may well be deep in nature, in some cases genetic, biological in origin and difficult to challenge We, as communities and societies, need to conduct research, develop understandings and curative approaches for such mental illnesses and conditions as far as we can, and do whatever we can to alleviate the individual's pain and suffering. And we may need to forcefully impose treatment in order to support the well-being of an individual and prevent their self-harm, their self-destruction, their suicide.

Yet suicidal thoughts may strike us in the range of circumstances. Again with regard to our rights over ourselves and our actions in regard to ourselves and our choices of life and death, more specifically in relations to impulses, feelings of pain, self-harm, self-hatred and suicide, there may be circumstances where we or others are enduring or feeling great humiliation, shame and pain, and because of that shame, as a consequence we may feel, and think, self-harming and self-destructive thoughts. It may be that we may have failed in that which we wished to achieve, proved inadequate in regard to our own standards of success, our own dreams in life, falling far short; we may have been humiliated, or humiliated ourselves in front of our peers; we may have become ashamed of who we are, our inadequacies; feel unwanted and unloved, feel ugly and unattractive to others; feel deficient in our inabilities; feel deeply depressed and unhappy with our personal mundane, unexceptional and ordinary humanity and our human failings. For some of us, under such circumstances, we might also, as a consequence have self-destructive thoughts, suicidal thoughts and feel we wish to end our lives. Yet in these circumstances, as in others where we feel down, depressed, perhaps suicidal, we must avoid harming ourselves or killing ourselves.

Disappointment at ourselves, failure and indeed humiliation are likely to insert themselves into the lives of most of us at some point in our lives, and as a consequence we may (though hopefully will not) feel highly negative about ourselves and feel such self-destructive thoughts. There are many ways in which we can counter such feelings of humiliation. Importantly we need to have realistic expectations in regard to what will happen in our lives and realistic goals. We all need to understand that we are likely to fail at some point in our lives and, indeed, we will probably at some point be and feel highly humiliated in front of others, perhaps feel extremely humiliated. Worse still, we may fail greatly and let others down or even in some circumstances, act dishonestly, destructively and hurt others. Yet these and perceptions of failure and inadequacy provide no reason for self-harm and suicide.

If we have been ambitious in the world, then we may fail to an important extent in front of many others and run the risk of feeling foolish and totally humiliated. How can we expect to live full lives without such pain, humiliation and failure? For the vast majority of us, we most likely cannot. We need to include such an expectation in our preparation, our predictions and plans and be prepared to carry on, move on, to learn from our failures and humiliations. And where we feel pain from our failures and humiliations, then we need to treat this as a normal part of our human experience and a full and well-lived life; because humiliation, failure and pain, are sadly likely to be companions to us all at some point in our lives. They do not uniquely aim themselves at any particular individual though of course we may succeed and fail to differing degrees and our ability to cope with these successfully may vary.

We need in these circumstances of self-disappointment, failure and pain, to look to alleviate our feelings of pain, and be more accepting of ourselves and our inadequacies and failings, aspects of our lives which we all have to put up with. Further, we need to prepare ourselves so that we can reorientate ourselves and refocus ourselves on our sources of pleasure and happiness, perhaps new sources of pleasure and happiness, in the face of such failures, pains and humiliations. And in important ways, recognising this makes us more free, autonomous and independent. Bolstering our sense of self, we need to do our utmost under such circumstances to learn from the past and plan for a different and better future. Whatever the pain of the moment arising from our shames and failings, it is almost inevitable that once we have overcome the pain and perhaps shame of our current situations, there will be moments of, and a level of happiness and enjoyment into the future. If we have lost our job of work, then there will likely be another job; if we have humiliated ourselves then others may well be accepting of this, wisely being themselves aware of their own humanity and vulnerability. And we can do what we can to block out those who demean and criticise us for our past errors and shame, as these people are best ignored in favour of a focus on what we have learned, what we will do in the future, on efforts to reappreciate and focus on the smaller pleasures of life. Many factors can influence our success or failure, many of them beyond our control and there will have been times when we have acted correctly, made the correct judgments and still lost.

We may feel depressed, unhappy, even bereft at events that have occurred in our lives but again, while we may have the freedom, the autonomy, the power to end our lives, that is not the route we should take, such a self-destructive act causing tremendous damage and pain to others, those who indeed do love us, and serving to undermine the experience of life itself. There are almost always other more constructive and positive ways to deal with such situations and such feelings of pain, depression and mental anguish and suffering.

It has been mentioned above that there may be some of us who have acted significantly dishonestly and destructively towards others. *In extremis* there are those who may have committed shameful and repulsive crimes and committed repulsive and abhorrent acts. And in some, if not the significant majority of such cases, these people may be aware of or develop awareness of the gravity of their crimes. In such circumstances, with such awareness, these individuals may be suicidal and quite reasonably, few of us may care much about their lives. The pain these individuals have caused may never be capable of alleviation in any way.

Yet, even in such cases, suicide provides and achieves nothing. These individuals themselves need to have their pain alleviated as far as is possible such that they can contribute to others, to us all. This does not mean diminishing their heinous crimes and responsibility for them. Such people need to be restrained and constrained as appropriate, held responsible for their actions and they need to acknowledge the vile deeds they have done. Nevertheless while denying them significant power and any opportunity at all to repeat their horrendous deeds and acts or to influence others to engage in such acts, they need to be enabled to make contributions to the world beyond, where that is possible, even if these contributions are to all intents and purposes minor in comparison to the gravity of their crimes. Such people need to pay back something in terms of contributing to the broader well-being, if such is possible. They will also hopefully become in important respects someone else, someone better, not the individual who committed these heinous crimes, though it will undoubtedly be almost unconscionable for them to walk free once they have been constrained and restrained, and our capacity to trust them and consider them unthreatening and no longer dangerous after such vile crimes is unlikely to exist and no doubt wisely should not exist, given the potential for their vast criminal and violent acts to be enacted again. Nevertheless, their suicide would represent a further crime and breech of core principles, even though few might regret their passing.

Commensurate with our personal primacy in decision-making in regard to the timing of our own life and death when we are suffering at the end of our lives, as far as we can make such decisions given the illnesses which might afflict our bodies, it is the case that in support of well-being and happiness, we all, as adults, have prime jurisdiction over our own bodies and our own health and can refuse medical treatments if we so wish, as long as we are deemed of sound mind. We, as adults, can refuse operations, medicines, blood transfusions and more because our bodies and minds fundamentally belong to us, and we must be the prime judges of how we feel and what we desire and want when there are treatments and actions available which affect our own bodies alone. Clearly, if there is the possibility of our dying if we refuse treatment, this is an example of something which will affect those we love as well as ourselves, and we need to take the feelings and views of those we love into account as well as our personal situation, personal needs, feelings and desires. And they will need to take into account our feelings, needs and desires as well.

Tied to this control and rights over our own bodies, in a related and very important issue, women have a right and the freedom to have abortions should they wish this, when such abortions are safe and there is no evidence of conscious existence, full formation of their baby. This is because women, like all of us, have responsibilities for, have prime jurisdiction over and rights over their own bodies and their own lives. However much some might disapprove, the foetus, which is far from a full human, is growing in an individual woman's body; it is her body; and again, if of sound mind, she has the right not to proceed with her pregnancy, not to give birth, in order to preserve her own well-being and happiness, the foetus, not being at a stage when it can reasonably be seen as capable of biologically independent existence. That is not to say that in such a case, where it was indeed possible, it would not have been best to avoid pregnancy in the first place. Yet women in some cases can become pregnant through rape and certainly cannot be required to allow the rape of their body to be accompanied by the psychological trauma of bearing their violent rapist's child.

In many cases the avoidance of pregnancy, something which is by far optimal compared to abortion, requires full and proper sex education, full and proper education about love and relationships for both boys and girls, men and women and of course requires the availability and use of appropriate contraception. Even using contraception there can still be pregnancy, and in these cases, if the woman wishes an abortion, that should be sought and carried out at as early a stage as possible.

In relation to a further area closely tied to our freedoms and choices, pressures to conform can act against our desire and need for freedom, autonomy and independence. Our need to avoid, and the validity in our not, conforming to expectations and commonly held beliefs, has already been discussed in this chapter with regard to the pressures exerted on us in a range of spheres, including our choice of clothes, our freedom to express our opinions and beliefs, our sexual behaviour and in other areas. In reality we cannot be other people and cannot conform in all the ways that we behave, with all the behaviour and expectations of others. We are all individual in our nature as well as being part of the social, our families, communities an our broader humanity.

More than that, within the context of our families, communities and societies, there is no obligation or requirement to conform except within the constraint of not doing others significant harm and avoiding causing significant pain and suffering to others. There will undoubtedly, of course, be a certain level of similarity in what we do and how we behave, our all being human and sharing our common humanity. Moreover, hopefully we will have a level of similarity through aiming, for example, to adhere to core principles and indeed hopefully, we will all support and look after the well-being and happiness of both ourselves and others. Nevertheless, the fact of our core individuality and sense of self means that despite the fact that we are likely to behave in similar ways to others in our communities (due to similar educational context, social and environmental context), undue pressure and coercion in order to make us conform to a range of conventions and common expectations outside of our conduct in terms of supporting well-being and happiness and our not causing pain and suffering, is contrary to core principles and is likely to damage our well-being and happiness.

We do not have to conform to certain common beliefs. We should not be slaves to conformity. We are under no obligation to agree with the majority. We do not have to follow the fashions of others, enjoy the music that others like, wear the clothes that are common, that we are expected to wear (except for reasons of safety and some other exceptional reasons); we do not have to do as others do simply because that is what others do; we do not need to live the way others do because that is the way that they live. Nor do we, or should we ourselves implement or accept undue pressure to make us conform in such ways (although in terms of bowing to undue pressure, under certain circumstances where we may be under threat of personal damage or violence, this might be necessary for our well-being). No one must require of us or force us to hold or to follow a particular religion, a particular philosophical approach or life stance or any set of political beliefs, within the bounds that we need to adhere to core and other principles. No one should require of us to conform in terms of our sexual mores (within the bounds of core and other principles). Consistent with core principles, in many areas we can choose for ourselves and must not be forced to conform beyond the terms of supporting that which supports our own well-being and happiness and the well-being and happiness of others, and in terms of that behaviour which avoids causing others pain and suffering.

Of course, allied to our desires and needs to avoid conformity, there are also likely to exist our desires and need on some, if not many occasions, to conform, to be like others, something which is of course acceptable if this conformity operates within core principles and if it allow others to be different, if our own conformity accepts and promotes the rights of others to be different and that we tolerate such difference, even when this contrasts starkly if not shockingly with our expectations.

In regard to conformity, however, as has already been pointed out, we must recognise that on many occasions there are conventions to be followed and our not conforming to expectations can in reality cause significant problems. At a basic level, communication requires certain standard ways of interacting and following such conventions eases communication. There may be conventions in the public space in regard to behaviour. And again, it will ease our lives if we follow such conventions (for example being rude to others may lead to others disliking us with consequent effects on our well-being and happiness). Criticising others directly and openly in public may bring opprobrium upon ourselves – and of course these actions may damage the well-being and happiness of others.

It is certainly worthwhile being aware of social conventions such that, if we break with these conventions, if we do not conform, we understand what we are doing and are doing so knowledgeably, recognising the challenge we may be offering to others and these conventions, and indeed having considered the possible responses of others and possible, desirable and undesirable consequences. It should also be said that there are strong arguments for gaining a deep and practical understanding of social mores, conventions, ways of behaving and cultures. In order to be successful in achieving our legitimate aims, it may be that we do need to be seen to be following norms and conventions, operating in culturally acceptable ways. By doing this we may build allies and friends and avoid the creation of enemies, who may, for example, irrationally dislike us, think us odd and unreliable, because they cannot cope with our non-conformity, even though we may be talented, caring and capable of substantial contribution to the well-being of others.

Social conventions and codes may apply to a range of behaviours. For example, it is not acceptable behaviour in many, if not most, of our human cultures for us to expose our sexual organs in public (though there are certainly some exceptions, for example, as discussed below, in nudist camps and on nudist beaches). And we should as a consequence in our cultures where such is the norm, certainly not do so. Yet some, a tiny minority do this, something which is considered a significant offence in most cultural contexts. Some might masturbate in public, show off their sexual organs to others for their own personal pleasure, contravening the private and discrete nature of sexual activities, with their sometimes being well aware of, but also sometimes perhaps not realising the unacceptability of what they are doing. Such actions are considered to be grossly offensive in almost every society, and are usually illegal and banned leading to legal detention.

To engage in such actions in public is often interpreted as a form of minor sexual assault on another, even if the effect and consequence for us, is simply shock and offence which lies within ourselves, something which should be possible for us to control. Nevertheless, our loving and sexual feelings are deep and important to the many of us, and these are for the many of us kept private, with behaviour of public nakedness being, dependent on precise circumstances, our community and society, challenging and upsetting to some. Clearly, in the circumstances of exposure discussed, there is no direct physical assault and pain for anyone beyond that of seeing something which substantially breaks our social rules, norms and codes, though such exposure might be seen as threatening to lead to sexual assault. Yet, because of the deep, private and personal relationship that we have with sex and love, such actions of exposure can feel for many very upsetting, if not profoundly emotionally and psychologically upsetting.

In the light of such real reactions which seem an important part of our human sexuality, such exposing of ourselves, in almost all social and cultural contexts, is considered unacceptable within terms of core and other principles. By contrast with issues such as our freedom of speech, there is probably no significant community benefit in allowing such conduct and while the individual who is publically exposing themselves might gain their own pleasure, their actions break important sexual codes, relating to our social conduct, our need for private personal sexual space, our desire for real affection and love and our notions of personal privacy, and thus are unacceptable.

That being said, maintaining areas open to the public, open to us, where those of us who wish to be naked with others, can be naked with others, where those of us who are naturists, who see such nakedness as natural and unproblematic, seems a useful way of allowing people to express an important freedom and to reject what they might see as the constricting, unnatural and perhaps suffocating need to wear clothes. And if their nudity is private and away from those of us who do not wish to see such nudity then those people are free to be naked and that is none of the business of the rest of us, and is indeed a valuable expression, representation and indicator of our general and overall freedom. This, to some extent, ties in to what has already been mentioned in regard to sex in which it is accepted that consenting adults engaging in sex with each other is a private matter and as long as no significant harm results to participants (or to the community and society in general, which is highly unlikely), what they do in sexual and loving terms is their own affair and none of anyone else's concern.

Our social groups may restrict our actions as individuals and indeed groups and organisations in other ways. For example, in many societies, quite reasonably we are not permitted to build any property we want, wherever we want, properties which look whichever way we want them to look. Our communities and societies will often, dependent on context, have given themselves a role and they play a role, requiring that there is a social judgment in regard to the design, often demanding that the building is in keeping with the area in which it is located, both in terms of function and look, though that is not to say that some radical and different designs are not approved. The community will frequently also wish to ensure that that which is built is in line with community and social needs, that properties, are built at an appropriate density, with facilities such as water supply available for these buildings, thus ensuring that those occupying relevant properties will be able to live with a good level of well-being and that those already living in the area will not suffer substantial detriment due to new developments. And our social organisations and representatives may also place restrictions on noise levels and pollution, height of the building and other features of the construction as these aspects of a building may be seen as affecting the lives of others in the community.

Our buildings are part of our community and social environment and our communities and societies therefore, with good reason, need, where there are significant buildings and other developments in prospect or proposed, to have that role in approving these elements of our built environment and this is part of supporting well-being and happiness. There needs to be democratic input and consultation in regard to such decisions, and those acting in judgment will need to be professional, expert, yet able to represent those living in an area as well as broader social needs, being open to some extent, to being encouraging and tolerant of the new, and in principle keen on supporting new initiatives. However it must be reasonable for community and society to democratically engage in such advisory, approval and similar roles which are aimed at supporting the well-being of all.

Our communities and societies may also legitimately and reasonably place restrictions on the destruction or modification of older buildings, some of these being seen as representing important elements of our community and social, and in some cases global history. If we do place such restrictions on such older buildings it would seem reasonable to consider whether our communities and societies should contribute to the costs of modifications and maintenance of such buildings, since it is our community and society which is placing restrictions on what can be done with the relevant properties.

With regard to the other side of our own conformity and non-conformity, as experiencers ourselves of the actions of others in terms of conformity and non-conformity, apart from being tolerant and accepting of ourselves and our own non-conformity, as already discussed when considering the notion of tolerance, we do need to be tolerant and accepting of that which is different, and, as already mentioned, what may sometimes seem to us to be shocking and outrageous. We do not have to accept traditional and conventional ways of doing things. Indeed that which is conventional and traditional often needs to be challenged. Supporting the well-being of ourselves as individuals and that of others, we cannot legitimately proscribe behaviour on the grounds that the behaviour of a non-conformist is shocking, outrageous or might cause offence to us, when it offers no direct threat of, does no actual significant physical or psychological harm or causes no substantial pain and suffering.

Particularly heinous and worthy, and indeed necessary of mention in relation to tolerance and in regard to conformity, and already mentioned in the context of our freedom of belief and freedom of speech, are the already mentioned practices of some families, of some groups, of casting out of their communities, ostracising or punishing in other severe ways, and sometimes even murdering, those who say they no longer accept the beliefs of that group. Such punishment and pain for the expression of personal belief, for daring not to conform, for what these groups may refer to as apostasy, is horrendous, evil in the extreme. It is heinous, vastly damaging to those who do not conform or believe, and stands vastly in contrast to core principles of taking care of the well-being and happiness of all others.

In these cases, those speaking out are offering no significant physical and emotional threat to their community and society, to other individuals, to anyone, through their stating that they have different beliefs from those of the family, community and society around them, through their differing views and beliefs compared to those of the family community, society and that often they were brought up in. While such changes of belief and non-belief might be upsetting for some, they should not be, but instead should be seen as representing growth, change and freedoms, which benefit us all.

Open and reasoned exchanges are part of our freedom and well-being which fertilise discussion, personal growth, individual and social growth and development. And conduct in terms of punishing these individuals for their peaceful and heartfelt beliefs, acts as a threat hanging over all in our families, communities and societies, representing oppression, promoting conformity and restricting free thought and expression in the range of areas in which the entire community and society would most likely benefit from such expression, and in most, if not all cases, reinforcing those in power, those imposing oppression, in the places, in the communities and societies where such punitive and destructive actions are being taken.

The absence of conformity and the absence of coercive and sometimes violent and threatening pressure to conform, not only benefits us as individuals, but also benefits our families, communities and societies, benefits us all. The encouragement of diversity, the variety of lifestyles and behaviours, ways of thinking, which we and others can adopt and which can therefore be visible and demonstrated to others, means we can encounter a range of ways of living which we are able to try out, to experiment with and engage in, these actions serving to support our own individual well-being and happiness and acting to the benefit of all others.

Further, and of great importance, non-conformist, imaginative, different and creative thinking present us with new options about how to live life, how to deal with the everyday problems and difficulties which we face, provide ways of tackling the problems and challenges of science and technology, helping us better understand the world we live in. Indeed such thinking and creativity provides us with routes to better organise, participate in and govern our societies. For this and many other reasons, additional to the personal benefits we directly experience from our individual personal freedoms, diversity and non-conformity are important in the vast range of areas in our lives.

As a more specific example, within our work contexts we may be faced with challenges of various kinds which may threaten our livelihoods, the existence of our company and organisation. As a consequence (and indeed even without such pressures and challenges) we may need to think outside of the box, in imaginative and creative ways, some of which are unconventional, leading in some cases to highly unconventional solutions in order to achieve our work and organisational goals and support our business, companies and organisations in sustaining and surviving. Indeed, even if our businesses, organisations and companies are proving successful, we should still be thinking creatively and imaginatively in order to develop new and better ways of being successful (for example improved products, improved processes, better service), providing therefore better experiences to the people we serve, our clients and customers.

More than that, in any context, the skills to imagine the new and develop new ideas, to think creatively, the willingness to go with ideas, the acceptance and the willingness to suspend judgment or to go some of the way with germinating ideas, to support the development of the new, aiming to develop those things and ideas which are nascent or in the process of development, develop those ideas with possibilities and potential but which are not yet proven or shown to be positive in effect; all of these are essential components of effective thinking and acting, which support improvements and positive change in the lives that we live, in our individual well-being and the well-being of others, and in the success of our communities, societies as well as our broader humanity.

The generation of new ideas, new perceptions, new approaches, within whichever context, undoubtedly in some cases requires us as individuals to, not only have developed our confidence and received support through education or training, but also requires us to have support in developing our knowledge and understanding in relevant specific areas. In terms of organisational, community and social success, this also seems to reasonably require an element of, if not substantial diversity of those of us in the positions of decision-making, responsibility and power which enables, amongst other things, the generation of a diversity of ideas.

It would seem likely and reasonable to believe that those who share the same types of background and education, the same or similar attitudes to life, are to some, and perhaps, to an important extent, less likely to be the source of a diverse range of ideas and perspectives when it comes to generating new initiatives or the generation of solutions to problems which might exist in relation to, for example, how we might live, even though of course we are all individuals. And therefore, if we need ideas and solutions, we will likely be damaging the well-being of the whole through the presence of high levels of uniformity and conformity amongst those in such positions of decision-making, responsibility and power, and indeed through the presence of conformist thinking and attitudes elsewhere in any position.

There therefore needs to be an extent to which we as individuals in our own lives and also our communities and societies (and beyond), positively encourage diversity within our own more local lives and environments, and beyond our local communities and societies, supporting diversity in its development, and finding and recognising positives in the range of characters, people and different ideas that we encounter from different contexts and origins. But more than this, we also need to be systematically promoting diversity where we can, supporting individuals, those we know, in moving towards and achieving their goals and dreams, enabling and supporting different life pathways, within the frame of core principles, and undoubtedly showing some openness and tolerance to disagreement about the actions which may best represent the enaction and realisation of the core principles, that is, in other words, about the how of supporting our own well-being and happiness, and the well-being and happiness of all.

Further, we have to recognise diversity, lack of uniformity, as important, worthwhile and indeed enjoyable in its own right, comprising therefore, in itself, an important part of our individual well-being and happiness The stimulus of the novel and new, our encounters with the unfamiliar, the occurrence of invention and creativity are for the many of us, to an important extent, enjoyable in themselves. The enjoyment of new and unfamiliar musics, styles of architecture and design, ways of dressing, ways of talking, forms and expressions of art, the discovery of new and different languages which express understanding of the world in unfamiliar, new and different ways, the encounter with new and different ideas and perceptions, are in themselves stimulating and bring us pleasure (though sometimes challenge), apart from providing the potential to lead us to change the way we live for the better. For the many of us, while often focusing on what we have in common, we often tend to enjoy meeting others with different interests, different educations and different perspectives from ourselves, these perspectives reflecting and developing through freedom, autonomy and independent paths of development, and in many ways themselves serving to enrich our lives. And thus this diversity and difference are important and of value in their own right.

All of this being said in relation to our need for diversity and lack of conformity, and recognising that we should never be aiming to impose conformity for the sake of conformity or because we fear difference, still it can be legitimate under some circumstances, supported in terms of core principles and well-being, as already discussed earlier in this chapter, for us to impose and accept a degree of conformity. Thus the use of uniforms, the need in some cases for consistent work practices to support best practice, have been identified as areas where there may need to be some restrictions in our actions and some level of conformity.

That being said, in regard to best practice, often based in research and expertise, this will often have developed in specific contexts which may well be different from those in which we find ourselves. This research and expertise may not therefore apply to the specific situation in which we find ourselves, and so, while there may be best practice and it may be necessary to ensure certain procedures in order to ensure such best practice, each of us as individuals, often do need to be able to operate in response to those precise circumstances in which we find ourselves, having flexibility to respond to those individual specific circumstances. And, if this flexibility is present we will all benefit from that sense of autonomy and responsibility in terms of what we do, from our ability to make choices and decisions in what we do, from our making of effective choices and decisions which will almost certainly have an impact on the situations in which we find ourselves.

Enabling such flexibility and avoiding overbearing instruction and conformity of action, in addition to its benefits for us as individuals in terms of our personal power and ability to determine our own lives, should also serve to support our organisations, our team and groups, our businesses, our institutions as well as supporting individual well-being.

Having pointed out the need for diversity and indeed the variable situations we find ourselves in, in terms of modern production methods and modern methods of service provision, in large, often multinational corporations, a uniformity, or at least a certain degree of uniformity and conformity of staff behaviours and conduct is often seen as enabling the efficient generation and delivery of products and services as well as helping in the smooth running of the organisation. In such a context, for example in provision of food in cooked food outlets, the standard and quality levels of food and drink for example, through conforming to laid down processes and procedures, can be predicted and anticipated by customers and clients, as being acceptable, indeed can be anticipated to be good, with common high standards across the organisation and few unexpected surprises and disappointments. The standard and quality of manufactured products and other services can as a consequence be maintained. Efficient processes and high quality products and services delivered should be of benefit to all of an organisation's clients, customers and those others receiving the organisation's products and services.

Nevertheless, the need for employees and workers to conform to entirely fixed procedures into which they have no input is to an important extent contrary to our individual human character and needs, and can prove demoralising and debilitating, especially if continuing in the long term, making us as employees feel, to some extent, without value and importance in our working lives, working lives which can take up a substantial proportion of each day and a substantial proportion of our total lives. Thus wherever possible, we need to attempt to recognise the nature of our individual character and humanity and, where this does not occur naturally in our work environments, we need to build space for ourselves and our employees to make decisions of import, to contribute to decisions in regard to their (and our) own actions and indeed enable and engage in input into the broader organisation. As individuals we should not be behaved towards as inanimate cogs in the machine, even though we may be part of a perhaps international organisation. Strategies, tactics, the application of business, organisational and administrative theories need to include consideration of our individual humanity and the consequences of actions for each of us and all of us, including those of us beyond the organisation. Company, institutional and organisational efficiency and success are clearly of great import, providing potential benefits to us all, yet the individual welfare and well-being of each of us is of great import as well.

Technology may be taking over some more mundane roles in industrial production, which has removed some, and may well remove more, of these more mechanical roles. Yet this also raises questions about well-being since there may be declining levels of, or at some point very little production and manufacturing work left for us as employees and workers to do, and as a consequence there will be declining sources of the work we need and the income we need in order to survive and enjoy well-being. We will hardly be free if we have no income and we have none of the work we wish to do in order to contribute to our communities and societies. Thus, we, as individuals, our communities, societies, governments and global organisations, need to ensure that all of us are catered for in terms of our human survival and well-being, including enabling a continued capacity to contribute to others.

Returning to issues of dress in relation to freedom, independence and conformity, within the context of education, in some national contexts, for a range of reasons, some educational institutions impose on children a uniformity of dress, this being undoubtedly an expression of broader attitudes and ideologies prominent in an educational institution, educational system or broader society. A number of arguments are made in favour of this uniformity of dress, for example, a school uniform identifying young people as being of school age, and therefore identifying them as requiring care and protection from others, and such a uniform also associating these children with an institution which has responsibility for them, and which can be contacted if there are concerns about a child's conduct or their well-being. Such a uniform is also argued as providing a common school identity and promoting a sense of belonging, as well as encouraging loyalty to an entity outside of the individual self.

Nevertheless, in many jurisdictions, schools manage to educate their children successfully without any need for such uniforms. Additionally in most contexts wider community and society does not normally require everyone to wear national dress, imposition of which would be seen as standing against freedom and personal autonomy. These facts and a range of further arguments undermine the need for such uniformity of dress in schools, which as a general rule, are not strong. For example, a sense of belonging and a sense of attachment to a wider whole is in fact clearly achievable without the need for such conformity and uniformity of dress, and indeed is considered here to be better achieved outside of such uniformity, which may act against important values of individual freedom and autonomy, and which may serve to hold back education and personal development.

There are in fact more important identities which need emphasis in educational contexts, such as, for example the idea of belonging to the wider community, and a wider humanity, and there are more important issues which schools need to address, such as supporting the development of notions of care and responsibility to all others, as well as responsibility for individual actions, actions and identities, which imposing such uniformity of dress does little to support or indeed actively mitigates against.

Crucially it is as important to support children in developing a respect for the individuality and diversity of others as well as supporting their development of a sense of their own individuality, and their own capacity to respect themselves. In part, through that development of self-respect and that respect for the diversity and difference of others, their importance as individuals, these will develop a sense of commonality, of community and sense of responsibility to others, and responsibility to the social and community whole, along with a sense of community and society loyalty, belonging and membership.

Indeed uniformity of dress for children can be seen as, and undoubtedly is to some degree, a form of suppression of individuality and a means of control, rather than being present to aid the nurturing, caring and supporting of the individual, necessary for true and healthy development towards adulthood, nurturing, caring and supporting approaches which will enable young people to develop their substance as individuals and which will best support them in providing support for others into the future.

Additionally such uniformity of dress would seem to, in general, make little positive contribution towards or alternatively mitigates against the development of a true sense of overall belonging, personal responsibility and community, through that diminishing of the individual. Those cultures containing educational institutions where there is no such imposition of uniform dress in schools show no indication of substantive negative consequences for their communities and societies tied to the absence of such conformity of dress in their schools. Moreover, there is no substantive evidence that children conduct themselves more socially if they are wearing uniforms and there is clearly no particular reason why this should be the case.

It has to be added that there may be circumstances where there might be significant fractures within a school or other institution in which forms of dress chosen amongst school-goers represent group uniforms and emphasise group differences, serving to solidify group-to-group differences and serving to bolster consequent conflict between group elements of a school or other institution. Such differences in dress may be seen as acting against a feeling of membership of a common school and human community.

In such circumstances it might be considered that introducing uniform dress for all might reduce conflict and help to build community, the sense of common humanity, a sense of equality and a sense of shared interests and identity. The introduction of such a common uniform would in effect be replacing the de facto divisive uniforms already in place in such contexts. This response would seem however to be a superficial solution which does not address fundamental issues of difference, tolerance, and conflict, and even if temporarily successful would seem to leave the likelihood of conflict raising its head again over other issues. Imposition of such a school uniform and such uniformity of dress would not be advised as a first port of call or indeed at all. Disallowing any form of group identification dress might be another alternative. However, more complex, difficult and challenging solutions involving talk between individuals and groups, discussion of our common humanity, assertion of core values of peacefulness and cooperativity, perhaps sanctions of some form against those promoting conflict, would seem better options.

Nevertheless, it should be remembered that this text is a guide, and those with responsibility in such situations, as well as we, as the young people, teachers or parents in such situations and others outside of the school or educational institution, need to prioritise and act effectively to ensure the well-being and happiness of each individual and all individuals. And if that were considered, under relevant circumstances, to be supported by the imposition of a uniform dress, then that would need to be the decision. To emphasise, this would be seen here as short-termist and something which would not be likely to work in broad terms in the long term, given the arguments put forward here.

There may be reasons under some less important circumstances where elements of conformity and indeed submission to the management and authority of others may be required. For example in team sports we may be required to follow team strategy, recognise our role within the group, playing one role and ensuring that we do actually fulfill our role such that the team or group can win in competition. In many such sports, we will wear similar clothing to identify us as part of our team and this is clearly useful and appears harmless within such contexts, though clearly some may argue and have argued that team sports through their competitive, non-cooperative and sometimes ruthless nature, are detrimental to the wider whole.

The view put forward here is that such team sports are in fact cooperative and involve team members playing their part in the whole, and contributing to the whole. Nevertheless, there are grounds for debate and discussion in terms of the broader well-being and happiness, since such sports, while bringing people together in some fashions, do frequently involve 'us and them' distinctions, competition and conflict, which clearly on occasion can escalate into more than sporting conflict. In this way, such team competitive sports can be seen as setting aside notions such as togetherness and common humanity, exacerbating conflict and sometimes leading to violence against others in the other team or group, although, clearly in many, if not most contexts, team sports, to an important extent, also bring us together and represent part of our humanity and togetherness.

The laws we have in our communities may well serve, to some degree, to create some conformity of behaviour, being designed to ensure our well-being (or the well-being of some of us) by imposing sanctions for certain forms of behaviour which damage the well-being of others and which cause pain and suffering, and which are seen as undermining our communities and societies. Conformity in terms of avoiding criminal, destructive and damaging behaviour is certainly desirable, though the objective of our laws needs to be to ensure and support well-being and happiness and should have nothing to do with promoting conformity, though that will be to some extent their consequence. However, our systems of law needs to allow for and indeed promote individuality, diversity and difference, and need to be able to take account of such individuality and individual difference in their operation.

Beyond law and the other areas already discussed, there are also ways of behaving which are accepted as representing good conduct within our communities which, as mentioned earlier in this chapter, may not in fact be, necessarily and obviously, components of supporting our human well-being, though they can certainly affect substantially how we feel and think. A number of customs and conventions have been mentioned earlier in this chapter, for example refraining from mentioning controversial or taboo topics and dress codes, which in dispassionate and theoretical terms, our breaching of which would not seem, in some or many cases, to represent significant threats to well-being and indeed might benefit well-being, at least in the longer term. Such conventions and norms of behaviour can be further exemplified by conventional manners at the dinner table (if there is such a table), our ways of expressing gratitude and thanks, ways of talking which support getting things done, or matters as simple as the accepted distance and personal space between us when we are engaging in a conversation.

As already mentioned, it is useful that we recognise the existence of such customs and ways of behaving and it can be very useful and promote good relations and peaceful interaction if we conform to these accepted behaviours. Yet in another way we should be careful about being too rigid or overly oppressive in imposing our own customs and ways of behaving, their representing customs and ways of behaving which really ought not to impinge to a significant and reasonable sense on individual and general well-being and happiness, even though, of course, they may do. It may be that these aspects of behaviour, manners and customs may represent signs of group membership which can serve to exclude others, something which we need to be aware of and careful about doing, as including some within our groups on such a basis means excluding those who may be friendly and able to contribute to ourselves, our groups and the whole.

There are clearly a wide range of areas in which conformity and non-conformity are issues of substantial importance in terms of our well-being and happiness. Perhaps our key area of concern here in regard to such conformity and thence our freedom, is with those individuals, organisations, communities and societies that aim to enforce conformity in an oppressive manner, as a means of suppression and oppressive control or indeed for other reasons, causing pain and suffering through their actions and thereby damaging our well-being and happiness and in the longer term the well-being and happiness of all, of our families, communities, societies and beyond. Such oppression is totally unacceptable in terms of core and other principles through the range of damage it does to us all.

As mentioned towards the beginning of this chapter, but considered worthy of reiteration and further comment, our freedom, independence and autonomy, for the vast majority of us and essential to our well-being and happiness, require a certain level of and access to privacy, the possibility of space for ourselves, a place away from others, not just in terms of our mental space, our headspace and thinking space, but also physical and temporal space in which we can reflect and be alone on those occasions when that is what and where we wish to be. For the vast main of us, if not for all of us, we need such capacity and such space in which to gain some peace, in which to reflect on, think about the world and people around us and develop ourselves. We need space and time for reflection on who we are, space and time in which we can experiment, develop our personal selves, our identity and individuality, time and space in which we can think about our problems and try to resolve them, space and time in which we can absorb the blows of life and perhaps get used to the pains we may feel if we cannot remove them completely. We need space and time to search for and find solutions, for improving our thinking, our knowledge, our strategies in regard to our understanding of the world we live in, our knowledge and understanding of ourselves. We need space and time in which we can plan our lives, determine the directions we wish to take in our lives and in which, we can spend time thinking about and anticipating the consequences of our actions for ourselves and others.

We need to be able to express this desire to be alone, for personal space, without fear of criticism or the interpretation that we are being hostile to others. And we need to be able to achieve this space, if that is what we want. In support of our personal well-being and happiness and the well-being and happiness of others, it is entirely legitimate that we pursue such personal individual space away from others, even though it may sometimes and incorrectly (though perhaps understandably) be seen by others as being somewhat hurtful, unloving, anti-social and unfriendly. Hopefully these others will come to understand that that it is not our intention to hurt, and hopefully many of us will understand anyway, being aware of our own need for space and time, for privacy, for ourselves.

Of course we do generally have a need to engage with others and we have an obligation within core principles and acting in support of the well-being and happiness of others, as well as of ourselves, to interact with and support others. Yet we do also in general, have a personal and individual right in the many cases, not to participate if we do not feel like participating, choosing our own courses of action, setting ourselves aside from others, and selecting privacy and space for ourselves over such participation, at times, if not often. And there should be no problem with this as long as we are offering no significant damage to others through our actions, as long as we have contributed, we are contributing, or we will at some point contribute and contribute significantly to the well-being and happiness of others.

While the vast main of us, perhaps all of us, acknowledge that there are times when we and others do need some space and time to ourselves, sometimes, such space may be difficult to find, and we may have to make do with the private space of our own thoughts and minds whenever we can manage to grasp the opportunity, be that in the quietness of a daytime moment or the peace of night-time prior to sleep. Yet for the many of us, the vast main of us, there is our human need at times, for more space than that, for much substantial personal space away from what may feel like the incessant demands, questions, interactions or too close company of others, company which we may also desire, and demands and questions which we might also welcome and feel rather lost without, at other times. As individuals, families, communities and societies we need to provide and enable as far as we can, all of us as individuals to enjoy such individual space and privacy. Further, our freedom, personal space and privacy need to be respected and we need to protect the freedom, personal space and privacy of others. Others should not impinge on our privacy without our permission and without exceptionally good reason based in core principles and relating to support for our own individual well-being and the well-being of others.

In terms in particular of that personal space, our neighbours must respect our needs for peace and quiet, while we should also respect the sometime reality of commotion and noise as, dependent on our location and circumstances, such noise and disturbance is at some point or other, a frequent and inevitable element of life. Of course we need to respect the needs of others for peace and quiet too. We shouldn't complain too loudly about babies crying (though they may keep us awake at night), nor should we complain about other daily and inevitable sounds of life when produced in a reasonable manner.

Overhearing music which we do not want to hear, from a neighbour, may sometimes have to be endured on occasion, yet our neighbour has an obligation not to play their music too loudly, not to play their music all the time and to avoid inappropriate times to play their music. They need to take into account their neighbours needs and wishes. Similarly and similarly reasonably, they need to avoid inappropriate times to do their home repairs if they have repairs to do, avoiding doing their repairs late at night or times when others are sleeping. Nevertheless, while loud noises of some kind may have to be temporarily endured, especially if they are occasional or temporary, it is consistent with our own personal need for well-being and happiness that, if such noise is excessive and continuous or frequently intermittent, even dangerous, as can rarely be the case, as a consequence we request that the level of noise be reduced, that the noise end completely, or we request some amelioration of the situation, and indeed it is essential that offers of such amelioration occur.

Others should also not encroach upon our property without our permission or without good and justifiable reasons. Such encroachment can be seen as threatening, but our responses to such encroachment need to be peaceful as far as possible, with the exception of where we perceive ourselves to be, and have good reason to believe we are under direct and immediate threat of, for example, aggressive violence. Any physical force we use under such circumstances, as stated throughout this guide, needs to be force at the minimum level to ensure our safety and security and the safety and security of others.

In the case where we are owners of vast amounts of property and land and are denying others access to sources and resources necessary for their survival (for example land for growing crops, access to fishing waters), then our denying such access is reprehensible and we need to offer relevant access. It is not legitimate within core and other principles to allow others to suffer and starve through our actions and inaction, and under such circumstances, and indeed in general, others have a right to access such resources and use them to support their survival and indeed sometimes their leisure.

However, as individuals, in general, we must not impinge unnecessarily on the space of others. And in addition to the obvious physical encroachments we might engage in, by accident or otherwise, as already discussed in this chapter in relation to personal freedom, we must not pollute the space of others with the damaging and poisonous products of our activities. If we smoke tobacco then we must keep the tobacco smoke away from others, as it is known to harm others. But even if it did not, if it were uncomfortable for others to breathe in such smoke and they did not want to breathe it in, then we are obliged to stop our smoking or move elsewhere since we are damaging their well-being in pursuit of a dubious and unnecessary pleasure, which could be carried out elsewhere.

This concern for the space around us and the environment of others applies to a range of other areas of our activities. If we are engaged in harmful activities which significantly damage the well-being of others, then it is the case that others, in support of well-being and happiness are perfectly within their rights to request and then peaceably, legally, perhaps in the end through the use of minimum levels of force, take action to prevent our damaging of their space, of their environment where there is good cause to prevent these damaging actions.

Similarly, our industrial and other neighbours, our own companies and businesses, our publically controlled bodies, should not pollute the air we breathe with uncomfortable fumes, dangerous smoke or dangerous chemicals, or carelessly dump rubbish into our environment. They must not pollute the rivers we walk along, swim in or wash in. They must be good neighbours and good members of our communities, societies and humanity, supporting the well-being and happiness of all, through, in relation to our environment, avoiding the production of damaging effluents, by making safe and, or minimising the effluents and pollutants they produce, and indeed managing effectively their consumption and use of resources.

While our manufacturers and polluters may be generating products or engaging in activities which are of value, if not highly supportive of well-being and happiness, indeed which may perhaps be essential for our well-being and happiness, the fact is that where our companies are involved in production of damaging pollution they will be substantially impinging on all of our individual spaces and our well-being and happiness, on our community, social and global space, and doing this is unacceptable, whatever their contribution might be to our communities and societies in other ways.

Where these are our own organisations and businesses, or organisations and businesses that we belong to or are responsible for, we need to initiate and support actions to reduce and remove any damaging pollution that our organisations and businesses might be causing.

Nevertheless, overall, we are all responsible for issues relating to care for our environment and care for public health and it is our responsibility to promote the avoidance of such damaging pollution. In any case, ways should be found in which all of these organisations and businesses can remove, reduce or substantially mitigate the effects of their polluting actions and processes such that overall well-being and happiness are supported, and pain and suffering arising from these sources is reduced and where possible prevented completely.

In the current, modern world, in addition to our more local neighbours, we also have our international neighbours, who can not only impinge on our freedoms and independence, but who can also damage the freedoms of, and oppress and damage their own citizens. The degree to which other countries, our international neighbours can influence and determine activities and actions of other nations, of our own other nation, is clearly a matter of importance and is a matter of importance in terms of individual freedom, independence and autonomy, but also in terms of group independence, freedom and autonomy. In line with core principles and seeking the well-being and happiness of all, wherever we can, where countries and nations are engaged in actions which cause significant damage to the citizens within those countries, then we as other nations, we as individuals, are obliged to act to protect those individuals who are being damaged and made to suffer, and we as individuals must support our own nations and governments as well as our global organisations, to work together with and support other nations and governments, to support other individuals and groups in engaging in that protection.

States and governments have no rights to cause significant damage and harm to their populations and we, the rest of us, have an obligation to intervene where we can and where it is practicable to improve such situations, to protect life and reduce suffering and pain. Thus, where the government of a nation gives threats and signs of engaging in, for example, mass extermination of parts of its population, engaging in murder of its citizens, oppression and imprisonment of opponents who represent no threat of aggressive violence and who, for example, support well-being, happiness, freedom and democracy, amongst other things, then other just nations which aim to support the well-being and happiness of all and prevent suffering and pain, need where reasonable and possible, where we have the power and capacity, to take appropriate actions to prevent and reduce this pain and suffering and to promote well-being within those jurisdictions and nation states.

Similarly, where such nations represent a threat to the peace, a threat to other nations, promising invasion of other countries, destructive actions to take over those countries, necessitating the physical and violent destruction and oppression of those in other countries, then, in pursuit of well-being, in order to reduce pain and suffering, we as other countries, we as individuals, our communities, societies, our global organisations, all need to take action to cooperate, work together and prevent such invasion, killing, destruction and oppression.

For all of us in such circumstances and indeed other circumstances, the notion of practicality is important. All of this needs to be, and indeed has to be, considered in relation to practicality and the overall effects of acting against such nations. In the first place, hopefully, actions can be taken in pursuit of well-being which do not involve physical force and violence, with hopefully, such non-violent actions, negotiation, perhaps boycotts, sanctions and other means of applying pressure, leading to change and the achievement of reasonable goals, including the protection of those under threat. However, if physical and forceful action is required to prevent such murder and oppression, there will be risks and undoubtedly many lives might be lost if such action is taken with much suffering and pain resulting.

Considering such practicality and reality, a small and just, democratic and free nation on its own, would certainly need to think twice before challenging a malevolent, oppressively governed, but powerful and weapon-rich nation, due to that small nation running the risk of bringing on itself and its citizens, devastating pain as well as enormous levels of suffering and destruction, especially with the potency of modern weaponry. Nevertheless, it might also have to be considered that such a powerful, oppressive and malevolent national government is likely at some time to turn its attention toward that smaller nation and aim to destroy it, with their clearly having no compunction about violent aggression and malevolent violence, given their conduct towards their own citizens. Thus, inaction and non-response to the suffering of others, aside from being potentially contrary to core principles, through leaving others to suffer in pain, may also represent foolish short-termism with aggressive and malevolent powers simply dividing those who oppose them and waiting their turn to attack us and our nation. Nevertheless, where there are larger and powerful nations involved, there will still be times where, at least in the short term, forceful actions against nations doing evil to their populations or threatening others, may not be rational or possible, due to the prospects of even more death and destruction, and indeed overwhelming destruction which may be visited upon us due to our supportive actions of others.

The importance of practicality having been mentioned, wherever possible, wherever practical and reasonable, we should support actions against such oppression, aggressive violence, suffering and destruction, such actions being taken even sometimes where there may be risk of some substantial costs in terms of our own lives, the lives of the good and just, and where there may be damage to our own well-being. This is noticeably the case, not only just to support others but also because those practising such crimes against their own people or threatening those on their immediate borders, are, on the whole, in time, as mentioned above, unlikely to limit their destructive conduct to their own citizens or those close to them geographically. Due to their nature and approach to others, they will be highly likely to aim to cause even broader and wider ranging damage, pain and suffering in pursuit of their goals, ideologies, and interests, or for whatever reason they pursue their violence and destruction.

As already suggested, nations and governments which engage in violence against their own citizens will undoubtedly promise violence and murder against those outside their borders too, especially if those of us beyond their borders seem unprepared or appear to lack the means, capacity or will to defend themselves. Thus, the actions of such aggressive nations and governments must be contained and combated in all reasonable ways possible, and we must be prepared to defend ourselves and our fellows from such violence and aggression as far as we possibly can. Our risks can be reduced through our acting in concert with other groups of individuals, by acting in concert with those existing within such oppressive jurisdictions, and by our acting in concert with other just, democratic and free nations to defend and protect our fellows who are being oppressed and attacked, and through defending ourselves if we become the object or potential object of aggressive assault. We need to work to bring together the powerful, those with similar interests and values wherever possible, such that we can act to protect others and defend ourselves. And we need to ensure that alliances of these individuals, groups and nations are in place and able to respond pre-emptively to threats of such destruction and violence.

Engaging in such cooperation and collaboration should support us in maintaining our own well-being and happiness, and result in the prevention of, or a reduction in suffering and pain, which is undoubtedly our common desire, if not the desire of almost everyone of us. We cannot leave others to suffer without doing our utmost to support them. Through acting in concert with others, we will be protecting the individuality, the freedoms, the lives and the well-being of all.

Finally in this chapter, there is the notion of education to consider in relation to our freedom, independence and autonomy. Education has been mentioned through this chapter in relation to different aspects of our subject matter, including sex education, school uniforms, education as a constructive response to damaging and destructive conduct, as well as in relation to a range of other important elements of our freedom, independence and autonomy. Education and access to education is of fundamental importance, is essential, to our personal freedom, autonomy and independence, and therefore our well-being and happiness. Without formal education and learning encountered in our educational and other institutions, provided through our communities and societies, perhaps sometimes and in the future provided by our global organisations, but also without the education and learning developed through the experience which we gain and the education and learning we are able to pursue ourselves outside of formal settings, without all of these, we cannot enjoy our full freedom, express our true individuality and make the best choices to support our own well-being and happiness and the well-being and happiness of our families, communities, societies and beyond.

Through the formal (and informal) systems of education available to us, we should be able to encounter and be taught the key skills, understandings and knowledge which we will need to survive well in our communities and societies, be they skills, understandings and knowledge relating to reading and writing, be they mathematics, social skills including skills of cooperation, social interaction, technical knowledge and abilities, study skills or be they the skills and knowledge to learn autonomously and develop further and independently beyond these systems of education.

With these skills and understandings, with the range of knowledge available to us and learned by us, we are able to take our full and proper place in our communities and societies, within our humanity, and hopefully survive and more than that, thrive. Denial of access to education, to such common skills and knowledge and indeed more sophisticated skills and knowledge is detrimental to freedom, well-being and happiness, and therefore is contrary to core and other principles. Without those key skills and knowledge it will be difficult for us to be free and to achieve our full potential in the context of our families, communities, societies and beyond. Further, it will be difficult if not impossible to make a full contribution to the well-being and happiness of ourselves and our communities, societies and beyond. It is an obligation for our communities and societies to provide access to such education and we as individuals need to support and make our own positive and constructive contributions so that our communities and societies are able to provide such education for all.

Through our education and education systems, we need to encounter a range of approaches to life, ways of doing things, ways of being, differing beliefs and belief systems so that we are better able to know and understand the world we live in and such that we can make informed and aware judgments for ourselves about not only the things that we believe to be true and which are considered to be true by others, but such that we can contribute in an optimum manner to the maintenance and development of our communities, societies and the world we live in.

We should not be denied knowledge of any series of ideas or set of beliefs, even if they are unpalatable, although those ideas which are clearly inconsistent with core principles, those ideologies which are considered dangerous, destructive and murderous, should quite rightly be presented as that which they are, and shown in the negative light in which they deserve to be held, being presented with substantive truthful and accurate critique and criticism. Yet we should not be denied knowledge of these ideas. Those ideas which are destructive and dangerous in themselves inform our understanding of what is acceptable and what can and can't be done, what does and doesn't work, what is legitimate and illegitimate in terms of supporting the well-being and happiness of individuals, others, our communities and societies and in terms of core principles.

The purpose of our systems of education must be to promote such education, learning and knowledge in the broadest sense, and also to promote a love of learning, a love of the seeking of knowledge, and understanding, and the promotion of the desire to develop our personal abilities, capacities and skills such we are better, more able and stronger in terms of our abilities to support ourselves and support others. While an educational system may favour a particular world-view, it is not the role of educational systems to impose widely held beliefs on others, or enforce particular systems of belief, beyond those fundamental beliefs and needs which involve taking care of and supporting the well-being and happiness of ourselves and all others. Education systems, beyond this, must allow access to a range of world-views and must not restrict access solely to narrowly pre-conceived and in particular un-evidenced and unsupported ideas. They must not attempt to restrict our learner's knowledge and understanding, something which is sometimes done out of fear that our learners, our students, might adopt a different view to that of the community and society or different from those beliefs which are prevalent and common.

Learning and education is a crucial expression of our individuality, and, being a necessity for us to be truly free and enjoy well-being and happiness, education and learning are things which we must pursue throughout our lives, with our aiming to develop new knowledge, new skills and new understandings as we develop and grow in years. We should always be challenging our existing beliefs, existing ideas and conventions in order to develop ourselves and move successfully into the future. The thoughtless and unchallenging acceptance of 'that which is', and 'that which is accepted' is contrary to what is needed for a full and complete life, standing against our personal fulfillment, well-being and happiness, and standing against the well-being of our families, communities and societies.

And, as communities and societies, beyond our formal or other systems for teaching the young, we need to promote learning and education as worthwhile goals through our families, our communities and through our societies. Where it is possible and we have the resources, we need to aim to provide education centres, training centres, libraries, museums, exhibitions, other sources of information (electronic or otherwise), open access to information, support educational talks and educational engagement in all its guises within our communities, societies and more globally. And as individuals we need to be supporting our communities and societies in taking such actions. All of this supports not only ourselves as individuals since we gain from the study and learning we do, but also our communities, societies and our broader humanity, which benefit from our learning, development, knowledge and engagement. And all of this education and learning is part of and supports our personal freedoms.

Moreover, where we can, recognising the contribution of education, learning, of training and skills development, to full human freedom and well-being, we need to be offering our own skills, understandings and knowledge as things from which others can learn. Of course this requires some recognition and confidence that we have something to give, yet for most of us we should have that confidence. Most, if not all of us, do have something important to say, some special skills, understanding and knowledge that we can pass on to others, though passing on such knowledge, understanding and skills and teaching others, can be a difficult art and often needs attentiveness to and patience with those we are teaching and attentiveness and understanding as well as respect for others from those of us who are in the position of learning.

The fact is that we will all be gaining skills, understanding and knowledge throughout our lives and can benefit others by helping them gain those same skills, understandings and knowledge. By supporting others in developing their skills we will be helping them in the development of the range of choices they can make in their lives, increasing their freedom to do, think and act in a manner that will support both their own well-being and happiness and the well-being and happiness of others.

Importantly, as far as possible we need to ensure that, in support of freedom and well-being, there is reasonable fairness and equality of access to such education and learning, with all of us having access to the highest level of educational provision available and possible, and all of us having high quality resources available, with equality of access to facilities and materials needed for personal development and education. This again supports our personal freedom, autonomy and independence and thereby supports our ability to contribute to others, as well as supporting a sense of equity in our communities, societies and beyond, which benefits us all.

Overall in summary of this chapter, our sense of individuality, our sense of uniqueness as people, our personal separateness and autonomy, are fundamental to who we are. Supporting such individual identity, freedom, independence and autonomy is core to our enjoying a life of well-being and happiness. We need to have freedoms from oppression and freedoms of self-expression, freedoms to voice our opinions and ideas, freedom not to conform, freedoms in relation to access to information and education, freedoms to associate with others with whom we wish to be, and many other freedoms amongst the range of other positive freedoms discussed in this chapter.

Yet, of course, as also discussed through the chapter, our freedoms as individuals cannot be entirely unlimited, as we have responsibilities and obligations to others. Clearly we cannot be free to engage in acts, for example, which inflict destructive physical damage on others, or which threaten direct violence and harm to others, excepting that the use of physical force is legitimate when we might be defending ourselves and others from aggressive violence and attack, with our using the minimum physical force necessary in our defensive actions. Aggressively violent and destructive actions and expressions of threat are entirely inconsistent with the core principles of supporting the well-being and happiness of others. Even when protecting ourselves and others, we need to do our utmost to minimise the damage we might do to others, thus again supporting the greater well-being and happiness while also ensuring that we protect our own and others' individuality, freedoms, autonomy and independence, each comprising part of our overall well-being and happiness.

Thus, it is crucial for all of us as individuals to support our freedoms and the freedoms of others, to support our sense of, and the reality of, autonomy and independence for ourselves and others, and to support our own sense of individuality and the individuality of others. Providing such support is consistent with and central to the core and other principles set out in this guide, supporting us in achieving the goals of realising our own personal well-being and happiness and the well-being and happiness of all.

# Eleven
# Upbringing, Education, Learning and Personal Development

Having discussed education specifically in relation to freedom, independence and autonomy, these comprising essential elements of our well-being and happiness, this chapter now looks at education in broader terms in relation to our well-being and happiness, considering amongst other topics, the role and nature of our upbringing as part of our overall education, the importance of learning (and indeed teaching), the teaching and learning of values and personal conduct, and the content of our educational and learning programmes, as they relate to our well-being and happiness.

Effective education, appropriate and effective learning and an appropriate, caring and effective upbringing in our families, homes, communities and societies, are seen here as essential to our appropriate and effective personal conduct and to our enjoyment of a life of well-being, happiness and fulfillment in which there is the minimum of suffering and pain. Without effective learning and education in regard to the broad range of skills and abilities, in regard to the range of knowledge and understandings; without effective learning and education in respect of the broad range of personal conduct and behaviours needed for, and relevant to, our lives; without an upbringing which teaches us and helps us learn so much which is important to our happiness and well-being, which helps us learn and which teaches us about reducing and avoiding where possible, pain and suffering; without effective learning and education which supports us in developing and achieving our capacities to survive and thrive; without all of this we are unlikely to be able to conduct ourselves and act appropriately and effectively in our communities, societies and beyond in support of well-being and happiness. Without such education and learning we will be unable to effectively support and achieve our own well-being and happiness and the well-being of others and we are unlikely to be able to support and achieve the prevention and reduction of our own pain and suffering, as well as the reduction of the pain and suffering of others, stated as the central goals for both ourselves and others through the core and other principles.

The value and positive impacts of our education and learning operate not only through their direct benefits on our lives as individuals and through the development of our skills, knowledge, understandings and more, but also operate through the effects that such learning and development has on our families, communities, societies and our broader humanity. Our personal contributions to the whole are supported by that education and learning with our having the capacity to contribute to the whole based in the skills, knowledge and understandings we can bring to bear in regard to maintaining and developing the quality of life in our communities and societies, as well as through helping others, our communities, societies and indeed our broader humanity deal with the challenges that they face.

In order to support effective education and learning, it is therefore fundamental that we should be supportive of effective education and learning in the home, community, societal and indeed in the global context. And given the complex nature of our communities, societies and the wider world, given the vast array of skills, knowledge and understandings that we as individuals need in order to be successful in our communities and societies as well as the vast range of sources from which our learning needs to come, given the complexity of learning, as well as the vast range of abilities, and complex skills and other needs of our communities, societies and beyond, it is clear that in order to support effective learning and education, we need to develop effective systems of information transfer and exchange, effective systems of learning and teaching, effective systems to support personal development, and effective education and training systems.

Within the context of our communities and societies and within these educational and learning systems, we need to do all we can to ensure that not only do such systems exist, but that we, our children, indeed all of us, have access to such developed and effective systems of education and learning. Where no formal systems of learning and education are available and in place, as individuals and working in concert with others, we need to make every effort to ensure that these are established and developed to as sophisticated a level as possible, in order to support our well-being and happiness and the well-being and happiness of all others, in particular as our education and learning systems are so central to maintaining and improving our quality of life.

In order to support our systems of education and learning, we need to ensure that we as individuals, our organisations, communities, societies and where appropriate our broader humanity, set aside sufficient resources to support education and learning. This needs to start in the first place with providing resources and support for our children and young people in schools but also means providing resources for further stages of education which, in the current era, tends to mean supporting colleges, universities, training institutions and other educational and learning programmes of various kinds which are targeted largely at the young. Each of these forms of educational institution or, in a changing world, whatever entities become, our vehicles for developing learning and education, must be supported. And in turn, our educational systems and processes should serve to support all of us, our communities, societies and our broader humanity, as well as supporting our individual well-being and happiness, which themselves serve to support successful and thriving societies wherein we all can enjoy a high level of well-being and happiness.

Recognising the positive benefits of effective educational and learning systems, it is also important we recognise that the absence of effective forms and systems of education and learning will damage our individual well-being and happiness and the well-being and happiness of all, undermining our capacity to achieve and attain as individuals, and undermining the capacities of our communities and societies to engage in the complex learning, knowledge, skill-based and understanding-based actions and activities which help support us as communities and societies and as individuals within our communities and our more global world.

We, as individuals, as well as our communities and societies need, indeed we must, have effective education and learning and effective education and learning systems in order to survive and thrive, to support our attainment and enjoyment of well-being and happiness. While, on its own, education is undoubtedly insufficient to entirely guarantee well-being and happiness, (there is the possibility, perhaps a distant possibility, but a possibility nevertheless, that we might, for example, be overwhelmed by environmental challenges, irrespective of our education and learning) effective education and learning and systems supporting education and learning are nevertheless an essential to support our well-being and happiness. Without education and learning we are highly likely to endure poverty and suffering; we are more likely to experience threats to our existence which we will be less able or unable to tackle, with all of this making us more vulnerable to the threats and challenges that our changing world is likely to present.

Supporting our need for well-being, happiness and fulfillment and underlining the relevance of education to this need and indeed fundamental goal, each of the actions and decisions we take, our personal conduct and indeed our very thoughts are substantially influenced, if not substantially determined, by the learning we experience through our upbringing in our families, communities, societies, as well as our through more formal education systems. Our upbringing, education and learning in these contexts support us in the situations we face through each day of our lives. In the light of the myriad variable circumstances and situations we face, they support us in being able to plan, react, adapt and change flexibly and effectively, helping us in our efforts to identify and implement appropriate to the circumstances actions and solutions. They support us in our efforts to gain, and support us in gaining a deep, and often deeply embedded, knowledge and understanding of the world around us.

Stated in a more grounded manner, our upbringing, education and learning support us in, amongst other things, the important task of interacting effectively with other people as well as in terms of making a living, earning money, and gaining resources for the purpose of helping us survive and thrive. And allied to these important benefits, they support us in the direct enjoyment of our lives through the direct enhancement of our capacity for personal well-being, happiness and fulfillment. Further they provide a basis for and a framework of thinking, belief and values, which influence our daily decision making and our contributions to our communities and societies, enabling us not only to determine our most effective actions and courses of action, but also enabling us to evaluate and reflect on our actions, decisions and conduct, and enabling us to support our well-being through various acquired and learned procedures and processes such as planning, anticipating, imagining and visualising, in order to support our effective short, medium and longer term strategies and futures, preparing us for challenges to come.

Effective education, learning and upbringing, are crucial components in enabling us and supporting us in our need to cooperate with, live with and work with others, be it in our families, schools, organisations, businesses, communities, societies or within our broader humanity. Alongside our more individual character and identity, we are also innately social in our nature, and through our education, learning and upbringing we develop sophisticated and complex understandings of the patterns and rules of conduct and behaviour followed within our families, communities and other social contexts, patterns of conduct and behaviour which facilitate us in speaking and acting effectively, which support us in responding effectively to others and which therefore enhance our effective cooperation with others, our sense of togetherness as group entities, our personal survival and our well-being and happiness.

Further in relation to our cooperation with others, supported by our education, learning and upbringing, we can learn through reflecting on our cooperative experiences, our experiences of being and working with others, in terms of that cooperation, interaction and togetherness, and act to develop ourselves and learn, such that we can more effectively interact with, cooperate with, deal with, and cope with others in the future, acting as appropriately and effectively as we can based on our learnt understandings and our learning and living experiences regarding others and our social relations. As a consequence, of our better knowledge, understanding and learnt ways of conducting ourselves, we are, on the whole, better able to get through our days in a peaceful and cooperative manner, better able to achieve our personal goals and support social goals, better able to avoid painful and unwanted conflict, better able to avoid threat and damage to ourselves, better able to avoid pain and suffering as well as better able to support our well-being and happiness.

In effect, we hopefully, on the whole, through our upbringing, and through our overall education and learning, become able to survive and hopefully thrive in the social world in which we live, enjoying a good and hopefully an optimal level of well-being and happiness. Our learnt abilities to understand, our understandings in themselves, our various social and interactive knowledge and skills, together with the knowledge that we accumulate about ourselves, others and the world, achieved through our upbringing, through our education, through our learning in all its forms, serve to support our survival and success in our social world.

Our effective education and upbringing give us the range of skills of all forms, from core and basic skills, to the more sophisticated, complex and advanced skills, with both our core and basic, and our more sophisticated skills supporting our ability to survive and thrive, and supporting our ability to contribute to, and play our full roles in, our families, organisations, communities and societies, contributing to ourselves and our own well-being as well as contributing to others and our communities and societies, locally and more globally.

The core knowledge, the basic and core skills we need, include our capacity for effective communication, spoken and written language, our various interactive social skills, including our capacity to listen to others, our understandings of and empathy with others, (including for example our ability to recognise the needs, goals and wants of others and our capacity to identify those who may be friendly and hostile), our abilities to behave with others such that we can gain the things we want and need, and through which we can be part of, and be seen to be part of our families, communities, societies and our broader humanity.

These core and basic skills, in addition to our abilities to read and write, include our counting and other mathematical skills, our capacities for physical coordination, our basic capacities to understand the nature and use of a range of tools and other implements, our skills of thinking, rationality and logic, our planning skills, our understanding of place, geography and space, of time and history, at the minimum some basic musical understanding and artistic skills, our knowledge and understanding of our human and biological environment, as well as the skills related to our capacity for self-protection and personal self-defence as well as many more basic skills. Our capacity to perform almost all of these basic skills, while to some extent these may be influenced by our inherited propensities and capacities, will be substantially if not largely influenced by our education and upbringing, as well as often influenced by our attitude and dedication to, our recognition of the value of, our skills learning and our education and learning. Our core, basic and other skills will need to be learnt and developed, and the degree to which we learn and develop these skills and abilities may be substantially influenced by our family, community and society's, as well as our own, attitude, dedication and commitment to learning, development and education.

And beyond this core knowledge and these basic skills and abilities, as we grow, we will need to and, in almost all cases, will, develop more sophisticated skills, often through our formal educational experiences, but also through other channels of learning. This more adult and expert level learning will take us to significantly higher levels of knowledge and ability, which should benefit us greatly as individuals as well as benefiting substantially others, our communities, societies and beyond. While it may be challenging to acquire high level skills in many areas, each of us is likely to be able to acquire high levels of skill and ability in specific areas.

For example regarding our capacities to speak, read and write it is of great benefit if we can learn and develop our capacities to do so at a sophisticated and complex level, for example through developing our capacities to speak and write in a highly effective and persuasive manner born in evidence, logic and reason, with the accompanying capability of speaking in multiple ways for multiple purposes to multiple audiences. We can, through teaching and learning and a range of means, learn to express understanding of, and execute to a substantial depth, the conventions and requirements of successful communication such that we can communicate our judgments, beliefs, needs and wants with subtlety, effectiveness and sophistication. Our high level communication skills will mean that we can more readily and more effectively and efficiently act cooperatively, avoid unnecessary conflict and argument, and will be able to support others in acting cooperatively and cohesively, enabling us all to support joint enterprises and the success of the teams and groups, organisations, communities and societies to which we belong, as well as hopefully supporting peacefulness and cooperation with regard to our broader humanity.

In addition to these highly important communication skills, which underpin and support success in many, most, if not all of our actions, we are also likely to, and will need to, develop sophisticated technical skills, the ability to use tools, perhaps complex tools, the ability to operate equipment and technology effectively in sophisticated and complex ways for the range of purposes, both more locally within our homes but also tools and devices used in the range of activities in our working lives, in agricultural, technical, administrative, scientific, manufacture and construction domains amongst others.

In this current digital age, even at a young age, dependent on our context, many of us will be developing sophisticated computing and technological skills, even if we perhaps do not appreciate that that is what we are doing. As adults and as we move into adulthood, we will often, dependent on our context, be learning different or significantly more specialised process skills ranging from those of design, often focused on a particular type of design) to complex mathematical skills. Many of us will be learning how to drive vehicles of whichever form are in use in our particular social and technological environment, be they tuk tuks, cars, lorries, buses or new and developing forms of transport.

In terms of our sophisticated skills and abilities in the world of work, some of us may be learning and being taught about areas such as, for example, medical care, in our roles as prospective or practising medical staff, doctors, surgeons or nurses. Perhaps we will be learning skills of research, or selling and persuasion, perhaps organisation and management, accountancy, legal practice, politics, plumbing, roofing, painting and decorating, carpet laying, policing and firefighting and many more skills. Some of us may learn and develop, to a high degree, expertise in complex sporting skills or develop our skills, knowledge and ability associated with the arts, music, painting, sculpture, acting and much more.

Our possession of such skills and abilities, our expertise in particular areas, whichever level of expertise we achieve, means importantly we will have developed talents, skills and abilities which we can use to contribute to the benefit of others, our communities, societies and beyond. And, important to ourselves and our own well-being and happiness, in line with core and other principles, through such contributions we will earn crucial money and resources to support our existence and well-being, money and resources which will support us in surviving and thriving, gaining and enjoying pleasure and fulfillment in our lives. And of course, if our skills and abilities result in us gaining sufficient resources we will be better able, through means of those resources, again in line with core and other principles, to help and support the well-being, fulfillment and happiness of the range of others.

The central terms used up to now in this chapter, namely education, learning, upbringing and in addition the term training, somewhat overlap, but are also somewhat different in their meanings. To clarify what is being referred to in the remainder of this chapter, some consideration will be given to the meaning of these terms, though these considerations are not presented as generating definitive meanings, such precision of meaning often being difficult to assign.

Within the context of this chapter and guide, education is seen as a broad process encompassing the formal systems of teaching and learning that we experience in our lives, but also referring to informal learning and the broad learning that we engage in throughout our lives, all of which sums together to form our overall education. Our education is seen as continuous from the point of view that this continuity represents an inevitable reality in terms of informal learning, even if we do not ever or continuously receive formal teaching or engage with formal educational systems, with our informal learning occurring as a matter of inevitability and necessity, throughout almost all of our lives. In a sense, any form of teaching and learning, including any learning through experience or other means can contribute towards our education. As will be referred to later in this chapter, education as defined in this guide, must incorporate teaching and learning in regard to positive caring values, looking after ourselves and all others, in line with core and other principles, if it is to be considered to be appropriate and acceptable as true education.

Our upbringing is seen here as referring to our education in our families, both our nuclear and extended families, our education in our early social and community environments, our early formal education, combined with our learning experience of all sorts in our younger years. Our upbringing may be influenced by our general social environment during our childhood and youth, the effects of the broader environment, our geographical environments, the political environment, the media, friends, and much more, although our parents, families and carers are usually seen as those who do the bringing up and tend to be those who are most intensively involved and who are most influential in our upbringing.

By contrast, learning will occur both through our education and upbringing and is something we all do throughout almost all, if not all of our lives, with this term applying both to what we gain in knowledge and understanding, in terms of skills and abilities from any new piece of information, any new knowledge, any development of knowledge and understanding, and any new skill we may learn and acquire but also applying to the processes (mental and psychological) through which we acquire these things. Our learning may be about all sorts of things, the world around us, certain specific skills, and may involve finding out about ourselves. We may learn about relationships, other people, about how the world itself works. And learning is something we can do in an effortful way by ourselves as individuals, but is also something which can, in an important sense, belong to our organisations, communities and societies, our broader humanity, representing something social to which we can all contribute. Learning is something which we all do, and need to do continuously, whatever our life style, profession or experiences of life. Learning is and needs to be something which we never stop doing.

Finally, in relation to these descriptions of terms, training is seen as the more direct teaching of specific skills, the teaching of more fixed procedures, knowledge and understanding, which may be subject to lower levels of reflection, analysis and criticism, being taken on board involving lesser levels of critique (though there may be critique and development into the future). Nevertheless, training, while often more fixed and stable in terms of what it is teaching, will often need to enable, allow and teach a level of adaptability and flexibility in us as trainees, enabling us to respond to changing circumstances and situations, thus enabling us to respond and adapt in the face of varying challenges. Again, that which we are trained in needs to be aligned with caring approaches and attitudes, in line with core and other principles, with that which we are trained in not only being supportive of ourselves as individuals, but also supportive of all others, our communites, societies and beyond.

As already mentioned, it is possible, if not likely, that many, if not all, of our skills and abilities are supported to at least some small degree by some form of natural propensity or ability. Nevertheless there will be an important degree to which, in almost all cases, there is a need for some if not almost all of these skills and abilities and the accompanying and required knowledge, to be explicitly developed, taught and learnt. Indeed, without teaching and learning, without some systems of education, some systematic development and training, it is highly unlikely we will be able to exercise these skills and abilities at a high level of competence and expertise. Given the importance of our skills and the importance of our own personal expertise to our well-being, happiness and fulfillment, and the well-being, happiness and fulfillment of others, there can be little doubt as to how important education, teaching, learning and training are to all of us.

Yet our upbringing, training, education and learning provide more in our lives than simply supporting the development of our abilities to cooperate and live with others or the development of the general or the more specialist skills we will need through our daily lives. As well as supporting abilities in these areas, our development of learning, knowledge and understanding can provide us with crucial and substantially greater understanding of ourselves and our place in the world, both in relation to others as individuals and the entities of which we are a part in our families, communities and societies, and from a range of perspectives in relation to the broader world, our humanity, indeed the universe around us.

Understanding the nature of the universe; understanding our sense of place and time with regard to the world around us; understanding how we as people have originated and developed through processes of change and evolution; understanding how we interact with and interrelate to not simply other people, but also with the non-human world, other species, plants, animals, microbes, organisms of all kinds, such understandings provide us with insights into who we are as people and where we sit as individuals in relation to the world beyond our individual selves, our external world, situating our identity and existence in all their different forms, human, community, societal and individual. Having such a sense of position and situation, a sense of place in these regards, seems to comprise a crucial element of our well-being and happiness, not simply providing, perhaps, a sense of our personal place in the world, but also providing us with an important sense of pleasure and wonder at the nature of the world around us, allied to a frequent desire, given our understanding of our position within that world, to find out and know more, to seek greater learning and understanding.

On top of such a sense of wonder, place and position in the world, on top of the range of skills and abilities already discussed, including our social and cooperative capacities, deriving significantly from our education and learning, we often gain pleasure from education and learning *per se*, through simply finding out and discovering the new, from achieving our learning, through the feeling that we are growing in some fashion as people ourselves, understanding more, learning more, developing more, knowing more, becoming emotionally and mentally bigger people, more complete human beings with a better understanding of the world with greater skills and talents.

We, at least almost all of us, frequently find pleasure in our explorations, gaining pleasures and more experiential learning in discovering the new through our explorational, exploratory activities, some explicitly aimed at learning but others not necessarily aimed at enhancing our learning, but rather conducted for the sake of doing the new, through seeking adventure (and sometimes danger), yet still leading to learning. We also find pleasure through a range of other learning activities, which can include the pleasures of being taught, trained or otherwise by others, leading to our further discovering the new and being able to do that which we were unable to do before.

Linked to our exploration and adventure, stemming from our desire for learning and learning experiences and our need to discover the new, we learn and gain joy through our invention and creation of the new, be that through developing new ideas and perspectives or through our experimentation and exploration of new processes and technologies.

We certainly frequently gain pleasure through our developing the abilities to do things that we as individuals previously could not do, abilities which may mean that we have entirely new and useful skills or that we are better able to do the things we previously could not do as we have enhanced the levels of our current skills and abilities. At the same time as gaining pleasure from such learning, we are likely to be better able to contribute to our families, communities, societies, to others, helping to generate ideas or support our groups in resolving problems that we or others have, that we could not previously have helped in resolving. And beyond being able to contribute to the solution of such problems, we may well gain pleasure and a greater sense of self-efficacy through our enhanced status and value in front of others arising from our enhanced qualification and capacities to contribute to others, to the whole.

More specifically, to illustrate the pleasures we as individuals can gain from learning and education, if for example, we are studying a foreign language, whether we have a real and immediate need to learn or whether we are simply learning because that is something we simply enjoy in itself, we are likely to feel pleasure through our everyday acquisition of new vocabulary and language, grammatical and other language knowledge. This will be a pleasure of which we will be greatly aware, through its enhancing of our capabilities and understandings, helping us to articulate our own knowledge and ideas in that foreign language, and being a pleasure which further enhances our potential abilities in real situations to communicate with those from what might previously have been a more hidden culture, and indeed supports us in learning about these cultures. Undoubtedly as a result we will feel a strong sense of involvement in our learning as we study and learn, and we will also feel a strong sense of achievement, often feeling achievement simply though our learning and even before we have had the actual opportunity to apply our new knowledge, understandings and skills.

Yet we will likely feel this sense of achievement from such language learning to an even greater degree when we apply our new language skills and knowledge in actual use in the country and culture where that language is native, experiencing effective communication, achieving our goals and the joy and achievement of such communication success. Of course that is not to say with regard to this example of language learning, and indeed in other areas, that we will not struggle at times, experience frustrations, sometimes substantial, or that we will not have or meet communication problems, nor does it imply that, as with other areas of learning, such language learning and education will always be successful immediately, or that we may not need to work intensively and extensively over time to achieve our goals.

Foreign language learning is just one example area where our learning can bring us pleasure. The same forms of pleasure may arise if we are studying in the vast range of other areas of knowledge and skills where we may feel that we have previously lacked to some extent or another, a level of knowledge, skill and understanding. These areas might include, for example, amongst that vast range, our learning of new agricultural techniques, learning scientific principles or facts, learning new construction techniques or design and architectural principles, new business skills for planning, marketing, selling and negotiation, new creative or other technical skills in computing and engineering, new musical concepts and abilities, new artistic techniques, new research methods and so much else. In such cases, we are likely to enjoy the pleasures of learning, not only through the actual process and doing of learning as we acquire our new knowledge, skills and understandings, but also through that great sense of reward we gain through the application of the new knowledge, understandings and skills we have acquired, and through the new that we can do, the new we can create, through such personal learning.

We also gain pleasure and joy through our knowledge of and through directly observing, the skills and performances of others. For example, if we love sport, then seeing the best performers engaged in their sport, the exceptional skills they can display, seeing the outstanding abilities they possess and demonstrate through their overall skills, seeing their exceptional moments of skills, is likely to fill us with pleasure and sometimes wonder. But we may feel similar ways in the context of the more everyday situations and skills we observe such as the progressive construction of a bridge, the skills of an effective lawyer in court, an exceptional teacher operating in a classroom, a social worker dealing with challenges in a family, a police officer pacifying aggressive individuals, calming down a tense situation through saying and doing the right things. Similarly we may feel wonder and amazement when we observe others expressing their breadth of knowledge and understanding, expressing their more simple every day skills at cooking, gardening, or their clear ability to explain and illustrate important ideas or understand the complexity of nature, or on a more mundane level, their capacity to solve a minor problem which we have been unable to deal with. Underpinning all of these skills, abilities, understandings, performances we admire, will be upbringing, education, learning and training as well as underlying attitudes of dedication and determination, and personal commitment to self-development, education and training.

It can undoubtedly make others feel good about themselves, encourage such others and help our relations with others if we recognise and compliment them on their skills, abilities and achievements, and if we do so in an appropriate manner at an appropriate time. Telling others, letting others know how well they are doing what they are doing, recognising out loud the skills, abilities and achievements of others, such that they know, and perhaps others know of, our appreciation and admiration, is something which benefits us all, and hopefully will benefit ourselves through not only encouraging others to support us and do likewise in regard to our own knowledge, skills, abilities and achievements, but this demonstration of our appreciation should also help us to be more aware of and recognise the skills and abilities we have ourselves and the things we have achieved, building our confidence, our sense of self-value and enhancing our desire to continue with our own personal learning and development.

Of course our compliments to others, while they may be legitimately given for the purposes of encouragement, should not be given for the purpose of gaining favour but need to represent a true and real appreciation and admiration for the skills, abilities and achievements of others. Such false praise and flattery with the objective of our self advancement or achieving other ends represents a lack of honesty, though again, such actions must be considered in terms of core principles and supporting the general wellbeing. Engaging in flattery which results in a powerful person desisting from damaging and destructive actions must be seen as admirable, even if false flattery is used to achieve that goal. There may of course be dangers in pursuing such a course of action, the flattered perhaps being well aware of the manipulation in train. Amongst the skills and abilities we develop through our learning and education should be a skill in valuing and complimenting others, which sits in an important position alongside the ability to understand and critique, privately for our own benefit and understanding, or in public where necessary and appropriate, the conduct and actions of others.

Our pleasures in the attainments, skills and learning of others need not solely revolve around their observed and direct performance. These pleasures can be enjoyed through seeing and experiencing the actual material products of the skills, knowledge, understanding and labours of others, particularly those which reflect the highest levels of skills and abilities. And we may experience the same or similar forms of pleasure or indeed, on occasion, we may experience feelings of wonder and deep joy, on hearing someone performing some beautiful music, our reading a wonderful poem, seeing a tremendous painting, a sculpture or other form of artwork or our reading a well-written work of fiction.

We may also enjoy the technical designs of everyday objects, of motor vehicles, crockery, street signs and more, and admire the skills of those who have produced them. Beautifully designed buildings, exceptional in look or size, grandeur and extent can lead us to such moments of admiration and wonder, hopefully not only giving ourselves such joy and pleasure, but such designs hopefully having given the architects and designers pleasure through their having produced those designs which have left us captured with wonder at their skills and imagination, as well as having given a sense of achievement and pleasure to all those who have been involved in the practical creation, construction and realisation of those designs. On a perhaps less grand level, but nevertheless also of importance, if we have the necessary resources available to us, our enjoyment of a tremendous meal at a restaurant will lead us to appreciate the skills and expertise of our cook and the restaurant staff and wonder at how they managed to produce such exceptional quality in our meal. And we may be moved to learn better to cook ourselves and aim to emulate them, thus adding to the store of skills and abilities in our communities, societies and our wider world.

Moreover, there is beauty and wonder, frequently born in learning and education, to be found in everyday design, be it in the everyday houses and buildings, the lights in our streets, the bicycles we may cycle, the pens and pencils we write with, the cups and saucers, the crockery we use, our everyday furniture, the many things we may simply take for granted. And then there are the more sophisticated technological objects that we encounter and use in the current age, our computers, airplanes, the vehicles we may drive and much more, also contributed to in their development and grounded, at least in part, through our organised processes of acquisition and transmission of learning and knowledge, through our systems of education and learning.

It is only too easy to pass by the wonders which are the everyday consequences of our systems of education, training and learning. It is all too easy to pass by and fail to appreciate the extraordinary achievements, products, services and other consequences that impinge on our everyday lives, almost all of which will have been developed originating in our education, training and learning. Unfortunately, we often take everyday things for granted and may fail to consciously recognise on a daily basis the links between what we as individuals see, the achievements, the things, the products and systems, the services we receive and encounter, and the education, learning, the training which underpin all of these. Given how essential the consequences of our education, our learning and training are to the quality of our lives, it is important that we recognise that almost all of what we do is underpinned by our upbringing, education and training and that our invention and creativity are themselves underpinned by knowledge, understandings and learning from our upbringing and education all of this leading to and having led to the development of so much which supports our well-being and the quality of our daily lives. And through our personal action, conduct and commitment we need to engage in the range of support that is needed for the maintenance and thriving of our educational and training systems and pursue our own personal development, learning and education as a matter of great priority and importance.

Our expression of the range of both more basic and the advanced and developed skills and abilities needed for our lives will thus almost always require learning, training and education, whether those skills and abilities originate through our more formal educational systems, through the more informal observation and learning from others, through our early upbringing within the context of our families, or through more experiential and reflective learning. Whatever the source, as a consequence of the learning of such basic and higher level skills and abilities, we will experience the satisfaction, pleasure and hopefully often enjoy the wonder of practising the skills and abilities we have acquired ourselves, as well as enjoying our experiences of knowing and observing others putting into practice and implementing their exceptional skills and knowing of and observing the products of their skills and abilities.

Yet it is not simply seeking the pleasure of learning and education that motivates us to seek out education, to learn and to develop our skills. Apart from the direct and obvious practical benefits of education, training and learning which enhance our well-being and happiness, for many, if not most of us we have a deep urge to learn, to know, to find out, something which perhaps goes beyond our response to the practical need to respond to the challenges of our everyday lives and situations. Within some of us, if not many or perhaps all of us, there is a deep and almost unquenchable thirst for knowledge and understanding, a thirst to find out, a constant desire to be able to do and achieve more, to develop our skills, and for those of us who feel this way it is very difficult for us to feel satisfied and happy unless we are continuing to seek out and find new knowledge and understandings (or at least knowledge and understanding which are new for us), continuing to make new discoveries, learn new things, develop new skills, solve unsolved problems and more.

But not only that, beyond that thirst for learning, understanding and knowledge, there is for many of us also, to some extent, a pain, a frustration, sometimes a rational or even an irrational feeling of inadequacy in not knowing and understanding things we wish to know and understand, and a sense of frustration and inadequacy in not being able to do things which we wish to be able to do. We may not always try to remedy what we may consider to be our learning and skills gaps and deficits immediately, and sometimes may never do so, in particular as we simply cannot know, understand and do everything and must prioritise and use our time well. However, on many occasions we will, on the moment, or over the longer term, look to develop our knowledge, understandings and skills, and look to develop the capacities and knowledge which we feel we may be missing or lack, in order that we will no longer feel the frustration or indeed no longer experience what may feel like a sense of inability and inadequacy arising from such lacks, from our not knowing and our not being able. Our search for an end to such feelings of frustration and inadequacy at the same time should make us more able and capable of doing the things we wish to do and more able and capable of contributing to others, our communities, societies and our broader humanity.

In addition to the range of benefits of an effective upbringing, of our learning, education and training, there are also benefits from all of these in terms of the support of our safety and in terms of our avoidance of pain and suffering. With the goals of avoiding pain and suffering in mind, our upbringing learning and education, our effective training can more specifically help to reduce our possible injury, pain and suffering. As young children in our homes with our families, we learn about and are hopefully taught about, a range of potential dangers to our health, from sources of heat not to be touched, to the dangers of sharp objects, to the risk-taking behaviours which might lead to painful accidents, to the behaviours to be avoided which might lead to conflict and consequential emotional and sometimes physical pain. At different stages in our upbringing we may learn a range of strategies to avoid threats to our safety and security including means of self-defence and defending others, and when to run and escape in the face of danger. In our schools and also in other contexts including colleges, universities and at work, we may learn safe ways of handling tools, of handling chemicals, of operating machinery and electrical equipment, safe ways of using computers, safe ways of communicating with others and much more.

More specifically in regard to our capacities to protect and defend ourselves and protect and defend others, through our lives we may develop our personal defensive physical skills, for example through study of defensive techniques, tactics and strategies, martial arts such as karate, judo or other means, or by developing our physical strength to ensure we have the capacities for self-protection, self-defence and the protection and defence of others. All of this takes substantial effort, learning and training, and clearly represents in itself a form of social conduct, but also feeds into a capacity of differing personal conduct in the face of challenges and danger. Nevertheless these capacities should as far as possible, optimally, remain capacities or simply be there for sporting purposes. Where possible, words and other means need to be first options to reduce tensions, deal with and end conflict, and thus it is also extremely beneficial for us to have knowledge, understanding and skills in speaking appropriately, to have strategies for promoting peaceful pacifying actions and conflict calming, such that we can avoid violence and ensure the well-being of all.

Of course, where our communities have high levels of knowledge, understanding and skills, then we will all hopefully be somewhat more secure and safe. Clearly, where we have effective, capable, educated, well-resourced, appropriately directed and well-trained policing services, backed by appropriate and just laws and effective legal systems, these police forces acting in line with core and other principles and acting to defend and protect us, we are more likely to be safe and secure from those who might physically attack us, steal from us or engage in other criminal attacks against us. And where for example, we have defence forces which have the appropriate goals, technical and other relevant skills and knowledge as well as the resources and equipment necessary to promote peacefulness, to protect and defend us, as well as capacities to be strategic, creative, tactical and more, we are more likely to be safe against those externally who might attack our communities and societies with the resultant vast damage that may occur to us as individuals and other individuals within our communities and societies.

And there are many other areas where education, learning and training of individuals and where effective education, learning and training systems can incontrovertibly enhance our well-being and happiness and reduce our pain and suffering. For example, while no means a guaranteed consequence due to the wide range of factors involved, it is certainly more likely that in a society which contains specialists, with appropriate and advanced medical knowledge gained in an evidence-based and rational manner, in a society where evidenced medical knowledge and medical skills are taught and valued, and in a society where there is effective teaching and learning in regard to health, we will be more healthy and more able to receive the effective medical care which will support us in prolonging our lives, extending our lives of well-being and enhancing our well-being, with all of this care serving to reduce the level of pain and suffering we experience. Of course such educated individuals need systems behind them, requiring educated and skilled individuals themselves, those involved as medical trainers, those involved in research design, development and application of medicines and medical technologies, those expert in resource management and organisation, those who understand disease, illness, epidemiology, diet, statistics and the vast range of other areas relevant to delivering effective medical care.

Similarly, while recognising the range of factors at play, it is also the case that where we have technical skills, which will be built on education, learning and training, technical skills in terms of design, construction and engineering of our homes, our offices, our factories, our shops, our laboratories, our farms and warehouses, our bridges, our modes of transport, there will be a much greater chance that all of these factories, entities and manufacturing facilities will be more effectively constructed and safe, especially when allied to professional codes of practice, health and safety standards and effective, resourced and implemented law which requires safety.

Equally essentially, where we have expertise, knowledge and understanding, founded in education and training, in the range of areas including agriculture, economics, logistics, planning, food production and food sciences and more, we should be better able to ensure a secure food supply and the constant and appropriate effective supply of the goods we need and wish for, which help to make our lives more pleasant.

Our safety and security is also enhanced by our community possession and effective use of knowledge, understanding and skills in the area of health and safety. Health and safety represents a further important area of skill and expertise which in itself can be seen and is usefully seen as a separate educational, learning and training area aside from, though linked to, the different contexts to which it applies, and clearly serves as a route to maintaining and reducing our pain and suffering and enhancing our well-being. Our individual, community and societal expertise in this area can support our communities and societies in keeping our buildings constructed to safe standards, can protect the preparation and storage of our food, can ensure safe standards in transportation and travel, ensure the safe manufacture and safety of items including household goods, electrical items of various sorts, tools, children's play things, household furniture and a vast range of other products and indeed services be they electrical, roofing, plumbing and other repair work as well. And of course expert knowledge in these areas is built on education, training, and learning in all the forms it can arise.

That being said, there does need to be care taken to avoid creating situations where there is so much focus on health and safety that ordinary, everyday, pleasurable activities and pursuits, which are to all intents and purposes without any significant risk, become almost impossible to engage in due to out of proportion zealousness and bureaucracy regarding health and safety. This over-zealousness, to all intents and purposes, in most contexts, is not a significant problem, especially when compared to the recklessness and carelessness in regard to health and safety which is much more significant and much more often found, and which we certainly need to act against.

All of the skills and abilities mentioned, all of this knowledge and understanding, all of this learning and development, through whichever educational means, whether formal or informal, requires our individual commitment and support. Our education not only supports ourselves, our personal pleasure and joys, and our ability to survive and thrive in our lives, but is crucial in supporting the well-being of others, the well-being of our families, social organisations, our communities, societies and beyond. Our families, communities and societies, both local and global, need us as individuals to develop our knowledge, understanding and skills to the maximum degree possible in order to support others, those local and global communities themselves, and of course with such knowledge, understanding and skills, through supporting ourselves we are also likely to be, to an important extent, supporting our communities, societies and broader humanity, which will likely benefit from our own happiness and well-being.

The promotion of our safety and security and our avoidance of pain and suffering can be seen as, in essence, almost impossible without our appropriate education, our learning, our training and our appropriate upbringing in line with core and other principles, and without our educational, training and learning systems, with even our most basic and core areas of education, our learning and training, underpinning safety and security, and underpinning a vast range of other non-core and more specialist areas of knowledge, skill and understanding. Yet our core and basic areas of understanding are also fundamental to almost every aspect of our community, society and indeed our broader human living.

Clearly, our core and basic skills of reading, writing, effective communication, cooperation and effective interaction, our basic knowledge and understanding, serve to underpin our societies through supporting our personal interactions and our personal contributions to the whole in almost every area of our lives, from our daily experiences and actions in the home and in our more local communities, to our social and employment lives at work and, of course, for many members of our communities and societies, particularly in our modern more connected world, they support us in regard to our broader interactions and contributions to our more global communities.

And in terms of supporting our communities and societies, with regard to more specific and advanced skills, understanding and knowledge, where we have for example technical, managerial and mechanical knowledge, understanding and skills, these will support a wide range of key areas of our community, work and social life, for example through application of our advanced skills, knowledge and understanding in supporting necessary industries operating in essential areas of society, be they in design, computer technology, manufacturing, property maintenance, water, gas and electricity supply and more, all of which support our well-being, happiness and fulfillment.

More specifically and overlapping heavily with the area of our safety and security, which are underpinned by our knowledge, skills and understanding, if we understand the key worlds of agriculture, farming and food, and understand how to practise and act in these areas effectively, then, as already mentioned, we can help not only to ensure the provision of the fundamental food supplies that our communities and societies need, but we can also improve the quality and range of what is provided, and do all of this hopefully with increasing efficiency. Again this will serve to enhance well-being and happiness and support our reducing or avoiding potential pain and suffering.

With effective managerial skills, understanding and knowledge, beyond supporting basic level provision of services for others, our communities, societies and beyond, and beyond supporting effective generation of goods and products, using our managerial skills, using our understandings and knowledge, we can support and enhance administration and organisation of the wide range of services, manufacturing and production, and support the range of business and other functions that our societies and organisations require, all of this serving to support well-being. Of course, in terms of the protection and defence of ourselves, others and our communities, societies and beyond, if we have developed skills in negotiation and diplomacy, our skills in building, supporting and mantaining peace, then we can hopefully act to prevent wars and conflicts. But also with advanced military knowledge and understanding we can help provide the necessary protection and defence such that we we able to avoid the suffering and pain that attends war and violent assault by those who would harm us.

Further, with our learning of high-level research skills and our understandings of research combined with analytical skills and creative thinking abilities amongst other thinking skills, we and our various social entities can think inventively and imaginatively, creating and designing new solutions or enhancing existing solutions in order to help us deal with current problems. And through our research and investigation, we can create greater knowledge and understanding of the world we live in, something which is of the utmost importance not simply in terms of direct and practical applications arising from that which we discover, but also through the enhancement of our knowledge and understanding in itself which, as already mentioned in this chapter, can help us better conceive our position and place within the natural and social world and which, in terms of our actual discoveries themselves, are frequently a source of joy and pleasure. Our high-level research skills support well-being and happiness for all of us in many different ways, in many cases opening windows into new and different worlds, new and different pasts, presents and futures.

Also benefiting our communities, societies and beyond, we can learn and better understand how to explain to others, teach others and help others learn. And with our developed knowledge and skills as teachers, we can ensure that not only is basic and widely used knowledge and information understood, learnt and learnt well, but that core and advanced information, knowledge and understanding is passed on effectively, not only to new generations but also to those of our own generations looking to improve their knowledge, skills and understanding.

With our skills as writers, actors, artists and more, developed and learnt in most cases over years of study, reflection, creativity, experience and practice, we can help others in better understanding the world, and provide pleasure and entertainment as well as insights into our communities and societies, into the world at large and how we see that world, through the works we produce.

These are but some of the vast range of ways through which basic, core and advanced knowledge, understanding, our skills and abilities, provided to us through upbringing, education, institutional learning and training and our own personal learning, support others, our communities, societies and our broader humanity, and thereby support not only our own happiness, fulfillment and well-being but the happiness, fulfillment and well-being of all.

Nevertheless, having noted the vast contributions that effective education and learning can make to ourselves and to others, our communities, societies and the global world, we also need to recognise that formal and also, often, informal knowledge and skills-developing educational processes, training and learning, are not sufficient conditions in themselves for well-being, happiness, safety and security. They are not sufficient conditions in themselves for avoiding and reducing pain and suffering. This is the case especially if the education we receive does not include or sufficiently focus on education and learning of positive human values in line with core and other principles; if our education does not focus effectively on loving and caring for all others and supporting their well-being and happiness; if our education does not emphasise and teach effectively the importance of avoiding pain and suffering for all and our role in doing our utmost to reduce and prevent the suffering of others. Positive caring human values in line with core and other principles need to be taught effectively and taken on board, implemented through our lives, if our learning and our education is to be of full and proper value.

Indeed it would perhaps be best to say, indeed accurate to say, that education without inclusion of such caring values, is not education at all, since an important element of the meaning of this crucial term, as referred to in the already given description of the notion of education earlier in this chapter, incorporates our learning about and as a consequence acting in a manner consistent with core and other principles, acting in a caring, loving, positive intelligent and reasonable way towards others, showing awareness and concern for the well-being and happiness of others. Acting in ways which substantially damage and hurt others represents a lack of education and is by definition a reflection of a lack of education, being contrary to the notion of education and educated behaviour.

We certainly need to know, understand and learn appropriate values of caring and concern for others (such as those represented through the principles and core principles presented in this guide), as part of our upbringing and education, as well as learning the educational content relevant to the development of our understanding and knowledge, our skills and abilities with regard to other areas of education. This does not mean learning 'about' such values in an academic way, though knowledge and understanding of such values in more academic and theoretical terms is of importance and likely to be of value, but our learning here refers to our actually learning in practical, real terms, such that we put into practice and can put into practice values which support not only the well-being of ourselves but also the well-being of all others. Thus, we have to be caring towards others, support the well-being, happiness and fulfillment of not only ourselves but others too, otherwise, amongst other things, we will run the significant risk of being destructive of both our own well-being and happiness and the well-being and happiness of others. And to do that is to act in a manner contrary to core and other principles, in a manner contrary to education, in a manner contrary to that embodied and required for true learning.

Emphasising and illustrating this point in unfortunate and stark terms, we need to acknowledge and recognise that many of those in the modern age, and indeed heading back into the near and more distant past, who have committed and who committed the most atrocious, violent and destructive deeds, those who have been responsible for creating destructive wars, the premature deaths, widespread suffering of countless millions of men, women and children, who have been responsible for heinous acts of individual or more extensive and deliberately imposed cruelty and suffering, many of these cruel and callous people attended 'high level' 'educational' institutions, universities referred to as leading universities, received highly specialised training and indeed learnt much technical knowledge and understanding, much to do with high level skills, organisation, politics and administration. Yet, unfortunately they were not properly educated as shown through the violent and horrific acts they did themselves, organised, or supported.

Tragically, brutal, violent, aggressive actions carried out against the innocent, the murder of innocent, unarmed and peaceful men, women and children, such actions against the strong, weak and disabled, the murder of families, townspeople en masse, genocides, the instigation and carrying out of aggressive, violent wars of all sorts, with intense levels of callous brutality; all of these have been planned, carried out and supported by not only trained leaders, qualified and experienced generals, soldiers, and criminals, but have been underpinned and sometimes, if not often, explicitly supported by administrators, managers, technologists, highly qualified scientists of various sorts, workers with advanced skills and knowledge in construction, engineers, those who have studied politics and economics and social sciences, poets, artists and more. And these uneducated and destructive and violent actions and efforts have been joined with the violent actions and efforts of the many others who might consider and have considered themselves, incorrectly and inappropriately, to be educated people.

Those who commit or support such foul acts cannot be considered to be educated people. They have failed to learn the key values, the love, care for others, the empathy, the tolerance and understanding, concern for others and more that are required of truly educated people. The reality is that those who are less fomally qualified, who lack such high levels of skill and learning, but who know how to care for others, who are concerned for and take action in support of the well-being and happiness of others, who are loving and caring towards others, are certainly more appropriately referred to as educated, even if they have only a little or even no mastery of basic skills of reading, writing, mathematics and the like. They are educated because they have appropriate attitudes, learning and knowledge about how to love and care for others, how to look after the well-being and happiness of others. They are especially, starkly and obviously better brought up and better educated when compared to those who lack concern and care for others, those who have attended the highest institutions of learning, who can talk the most complex talk, those who can design the greatest technological devices and who have achieved the highest levels of skill, yet who use their skills and learning in ways which significantly damage and destroy well-being, cause pain and suffering, and whose actions serve to damage and destroy their fellow human beings.

Recognising the importance of our caring and loving values, our concern for the well-being and happiness of others, it is also important to recognise that our important values and beliefs, as well as our key social skills and understanding, are often learnt or can be influenced to a substantial extent, during our early upbringing in our home and family environments. It is thus essential that caring values, concern for all others and other and appropriate social conduct consistent with core and other principles are encountered and learnt in the home, for the benefit of each individual and for the benefit of our communities, societies and our broader humanity. As parents we have responsibilities for teaching and indeed demonstrating through our own actions, the type of conduct which is appropriate and consistent with those core and other principles, demonstrating love, care, fairness and justice, peacefulness, cooperativity and more.

Beyond the home, but linked to these points about true education and learning, our educational and learning systems will not support our well-being, happiness and fulfillment if they are controlled and managed by those who do not have the notions of supporting our individual well-being and the well-being of our communities and societies, of our broader humanity, as their goals. Nor will our well-being, happiness and fulfillment be likely to be served to the optimal level possible if they are under the management, control and influence of those who, while perhaps sincere in their beliefs, have substantially false and wrong ideas about education, learning, well-being and happiness.

Part of this recognition of the value of education and, reflecting an approach to education consistent with core and other principles, our education and educational systems need to be available and open to all. All of us, whatever our origins, whatever our level of income, personal background, whichever race, sexuality, gender and social grouping we might belong to; whether we are blind, deaf or have other forms of disability, we need to have access to education and need to be facilitated to have such access, and not simply access, but access to the best possible education that can be established, provided and experienced, not only in support of our own well-being and happiness but in support of the well-being, happiness and fulfillment of all.

Supporting such fair and equal access, our educational systems must not promote and pursue unjust discrimination and should not serve to bolster and underpin unfairness in our societies. Each of us, should, as far as is possible, within reason, have the same or similar educational opportunities. Educational opportunity and quality, as far as reasonable and possible, should not be dependent on personal wealth. Yet, in the same breath, we must not sacrifice quality for equality, with education systems, teachers and programmes needing to provide optimal educational experiences and needing to recognise the individuality and uniqueness of each student participating in our educational systems and acting to support each individual in developing their knowledge, skills and abilities to the maximum, yet doing so in a manner which also supports the needs of our communities, societies and the broader humanity. In that way, we should all benefit from our educational and learning systems.

In terms of providing equal access, for those who cannot see or hear or who have other disabilities, we need to provide appropriate support for learning, where necessary through helpers and technological support. For those who cannot walk we need to make our educational facilities accessible through physical features such as lifts and ramps. As a consequence, the joys, benefits and pleasures that education and learning can bring to us as individuals, communities and societies will be available to all including those with disabilities. There should be no racial, gender-based or other systematic discrimination (or indeed non-systematic discrimination) supported and implemented by our educational systems, such actions serving to damage the well-being and happiness of the individuals discriminated against and serving to damage us all.

Amongst the more individual and direct learning pleasures and benefits we gain from education and learning, there are also many social pleasures and benefits we can gain. Through our taking part in formal processes of education, usually organised by others, by our organisations, communities and societies, we have the opportunity to meet others and experience participation, cooperativity and togetherness, often within the context of common and shared individual, community and social goals. In our classrooms, training sessions, seminars, lecture rooms or other forums, as well as before and after our formal periods of learning, we will meet interact, talk with others, sharing ourselves and our experiences, experiencing the perspectives of others and finding out about others and their lives, all of which will comprise a source of our personal development, education and learning.

And even if we are studying more independently in order to boost our knowledge and understanding of the world or for other purposes then, even through the learning process of reading a book for the purpose of learning or through listening to an online class, we are being part of, to some extent, the social world, increasing our meaningful interactions, often finding out about the experiences of others and gaining insights into their perspectives on specific questions, topics and skills, or about life in general. Of course, through our class-based education and through our more independent study, we will be, for the most part, building our personal connection with others and may be reducing what in some cases may be, an unpleasant sense of isolation.

And beyond the direct and immediate social nature of many of the ongoing processes of formal and less formal education and learning, we can gain other individual and social pleasures through and as a consequence of our learning and education. Through having learnt and then applying the skills we have learnt, we are, for example, able to join together with others in projects, work together in teams, working towards and hopefully achieving individual and common goals, making our own, hopefully valued, contribution to our teams. Through such cooperative actions, based in our education and learning, we will therefore have gained the potential to enjoy the enriching experiences of and the positive feelings and pleasure of working in such teams (though, as experience may have taught us, this may not always pleasurable), the pleasures of participating in organisations with valuable purposes; we will have gained the potential to enjoy the well-being that comes from interaction, from effective interaction, from collaboration and working with colleagues in our joint enterprises and projects, something which is without doubt both socially enriching and beneficial for ourselves as individuals. Hopefully we will also gain the pleasures of achievement when our teams and groups achieve their goals. Yet even if they do not achieve broader goals to the extent that might be wished, we will have enjoyed the pleasures of working together and, most likely and hopefully, advances, in some form or other, will have been achieved along the way.

Without our differing combinations of skills, knowledge and understanding, originating in our upbringing, education, training and overall learning, without the sum of our upbringing, education, training and learning as individuals working together, allied of course and linked to our differing perspectives and personalities, much cannot be achieved in our communities, and societies globally. This is because the tasks we as individuals, communities, societies and beyond wish to achieve, the things we wish to do, for example as already referred to, the support of our health systems, our food production and distribution systems, our transport systems, our construction of buildings of various types, amongst other tasks, represent complex tasks and purposes, requiring not simply our individual contributions, skills and expertise but the knowledge, skills and understandings of many.

No, or very few projects are the work of simply one individual person. While there may be leaders and those substantially influencing or determining strategies and approaches, no, or very few businesses, administrative units and organisations can be run and operated by single individuals. No, or few modes of transport in the modern world, can be built by one individual, nor could our systems of transport or various other systems be organised and implemented by single individuals. We need the combination of our varied skills, knowledge and understanding to be available in our societies, along with our individually having the skills, abilities and knowledge to work with and cooperate with others.

And thus, given our need for such complex tasks and outcomes to be achieved, it is clearly the case that our skills, abilities, our knowledge and learning linked to cooperative action are required for our own well-being, fulfillment and indeed happiness as individuals, and also for the well-being, fulfillment and happiness of others. Moreover, our more practical task-focused requirement as human communities and societies, as individuals, for engaging in such cooperative action and collaboration is, in an important sense, inextricably linked to the well-being and pleasure we will experience from our meeting with and interacting with others, through our social experiences of (as well as the pains and strains of) working in such organisations, communities, teams and groups.

Indeed there are a range of pleasures and joys, often a sense of great fulfillment, that we gain through being part of major, substantial or great projects and great achievements. As individuals we are frequently highly motivated by these pleasures, the adventure and excitement of our collaborative and team projects, through our desire to contribute to the whole, by the prospect of achievement and through our direct pleasure in working with others to support worthwhile goals. Our acquisition of core, basic and higher level skills; our development of knowledge, learning and understanding, mean we are able to gain from such community and social participation and contribute to others.

Having considered some of the many and important pleasures and benefits to our well-being we can gain through and derive from learning, education and training, it is perhaps also worth acknowledging that we may not always find our engagement with, and our experiences of education, learning and training to be entirely enjoyable, and indeed some of our experiences may not be pleasant or as pleasant as we would wish. And where our experiences are not so enjoyable we will need to respond to our circumstances in an appropriate manner.

Thus, while in some, if not many, cultures and contexts, many of us, particularly as adults, find education and learning enjoyable, in some situations of formal education, especially when younger, for some, if not many of us, constant hours of classroom-based learning may seem tedious, repetitive and sometimes, if not more often, apparently of little point and purpose, with classroom learning seeming detached from the real world, perhaps ritualistic, uninteresting, abstract, theoretical and perhaps even unnecessary. Further, in a classroom of many others, we may feel that our wishes, wants and desires, our individuality, seem of little value and importance to those teaching or perhaps indeed to anyone in such contexts, where we may be treated, perhaps out of the exigencies of the context, as a minor component of a group or mass, rather than as an important, significant and worthwhile individual.

Moreover, we may not be successful in relation to this classroom learning for various reasons, including those relating to our personal motivation and aptitude. This may also be because the subject matter is not of interest to us, because of the apparent detachment of such learning from real life, because of the social context of education, our status within the classroom, because we lack the required capacity or motivation, or the way in which teaching and learning is approached, with teaching methods and materials not succeeding in engaging and interesting us. As an individual, some of us may see such an education system as oppressive and controlling, and disapprove of and fail to enjoy such education for a range of other reasons.

It is also of course possible that the classes and schools for younger people in which teaching and learning are supposed to take place, can be poorly organised, chaotic and unsafe for children, with teachers acting in dictatorial, unfair and bullying ways, and pupils bullying and oppressing each other, and also sometimes bullying their teachers through anti-social and disruptive conduct. Schools can also be organised and administered in ways in which teachers and other employees of the school are themselves bullied and oppressed in particular in contexts in which school managers and heads are given substantial power and can misuse that power based on false and damaging beliefs about people and management, use power for their own aggrandisement, in pursuit of negatively selfish purposes, manage poorly because of their own fears, or due to their own general inability to manage and incompetence. And beyond that, individuals, governors, systems, politicians, overseeing schools can also be insensitive, and in a way bullying too, sometimes seeking impossible outcomes and accompanying these with threats to employment and well-being. All of such bullying and oppression, by teachers, pupils, heads, governors and systems is entirely unacceptable and contrary to core and other principles.

As teachers, as parents, as communities and societies, we need to be committed to education and learning and do our utmost to ensure that the teaching and learning we provide to young people is presented in an interesting and engaging manner which supports their learning to the maximum degree possible. This can be difficult to achieve on a continuous basis day-in and day-out but needs to be an important goal. This goal can be supported through having appropriate objectives for teaching and learning, through explaining aims and objectives and the rationale for these (though not perhaps always, in order to avoid repetitive ritual), through teaching directed at the precise children or students we are engaging with, through adopting stimulating methodologies and channels for teaching and learning, through teaching in an age appropriate manner with activities which engage, through caring for and respecting those who are learning and recognising them as individuals, and through a range of other approaches and strategies in the classroom, or in whichever context or environment we are teaching.

Nevertheless, whatever strategies and approaches we adopt, reality will mean, as it means in many of our lives, that not all moments in formal education are likely to be as stimulating and interesting as we would like them to be. If we are pupils and students in such situations, then it is our responsibility to participate as far as we can and feed in to classes through our personal interest and contributions, aiming to help make them engaging and perhaps, where we have the opportunity, making suggestions about their development and improvement.

Nevertheless, by and large, as we move beyond our youngest childhood years, and indeed, even to some degree as younger children, our motivation increasingly becomes something which is more, indeed entirely, our responsibility. Certainly as adults and older students, we cannot reasonably land our lack of motivation for learning on our teachers and others. If we feel demotivated that is something we must deal with and if that is affecting our learning we will need to go beyond the classroom to seek learning and knowledge.

It is thus our own responsibility as students and learners to focus on developing our own learning and education whatever the educational context, and to conduct ourselves in an appropriate, peaceful and cooperative manner to enable learning and teaching to take place. Even if we do not feel so interested, we need to behave in a manner which allows other interested individuals to participate and learn. Life is such that not all moments, in education or elsewhere, are likely to be engaging, exciting and full of interest. Tedium and boredom are undesirable, but are likely to occur on occasion (or more frequently), especially in some educational contexts where teaching takes place through a whole day, and of course, in our educational contexts we need to recognise that our teachers are human, with their own frailties, and pressures in their lives, and indeed for some there is a need to develop and somewhat or substantially improve their teaching competence. While such systems might well need improvement and may be responsible to some degree for inducing a level of boredom and disinterest, and while maintaining our interest and motivation through long periods of time may be difficult, nevertheless we have a responsibility to cope with such situations and conduct ourselves appropriately and to engage as much as we can with education and learning.

Hopefully for the many of us, such a sense of boredom and tedium will not be a common element of our experience. By contrast to such a form of experience, our individual, group, classroom and school-based learning will hopefully and certainly should be, overall, a pleasurable and successful experience, where we learn substantially, find out about, and to some extent, gain some experience of the world (and at the minimum certainly the world of school). Schools should be places where we are safe and protected from bullying and oppression of all kinds from whomsoever, and where we are protected, nurtured as individuals and looked after by caring adults with some knowledge and evidence and experience-based wisdom in regard to the wider world.

In our schools, our methodologies and approaches to teaching and learning need to be inclusive and caring, inspiring of learners, interesting and engaging our learners, and helping to support motivation, with these methodologies and approaches also giving us as teachers and students, a sense of efficacy and well-being, a sense of our own importance and value as teachers and learners within our classrooms, schools and within our communities, societies and beyond. Yet we, as learners, as students, also need to take responsibility for ourselves, for our learning, our motivation and dedication within our schools. We need to have and develop a sense of responsibility to all others, and develop, learn and educate ourselves, with support from our teachers, such that we will be able to contribute significantly and substantially to our communities, societies and to our broader humanity.

The study we pursue on our own beyond school and beyond our formal years of schooling, is often, in the main, particularly interesting and engaging, especially because we are likely to be self-motivated in our study and learning. Nevertheless such study can still be challenging and frustrating at times, sometimes because of the difficulty and complexity of the learning that we are trying to achieve, sometimes because there is substantial attention to detail required before we can master certain skills, sometimes because we need help and support which may not be available, sometimes because of the extended period of time needed to develop and master certain skills or the time required to find particular knowledge and information. The fact is that complex skills for the most of us do take time to develop and can be very difficult to acquire and develop without support. And acquiring some forms of knowledge and understanding can require substantive experience and long-term research. Nevertheless, with time and persistence as well as, where relevant, the necessary expert advice, we should be able to make substantial progress and through our efforts we will hopefully enjoy our participation and efforts to learn, as well as enjoying the achievement of positive outcomes of those efforts to learn.

One important factor that is often controversial in the context of many educational systems, in particular those aimed at young people, is that of testing and assessment. Testing and assessment can be seen as oppressing us, seen as comprising an element of oppressive systems which act and serve, through that testing and assessment, to deny opportunity to some of us by excluding us from progress to further study and removing access to certain forms of study, while allowing privilege to others of us. In such a way, testing and assessment can be perceived as serving to damage the individual well-being, happiness and fulfillment of those who are denied such opportunity, and potentially our communities and societies as a whole.

While there can clearly be some argument over this kind of matter, testing and assessment of young people are seen here as, dependent on their form, being broadly positive in their influence, firstly helping those of us who are educators and policy makers, indeed helping all of us, identify what is known and understood already by those of us experiencing education and training, and therefore enabling us to know better what needs to be taught and what needs to be known and understood. Yet secondly and importantly testing and assessment serve in helping guide those of us, in particular those of us who are young, into those areas of education, performance, study and work where we can be most successful and in which we will best be able to serve others, our communities, societies and our broader humanity. Thirdly, this testing and assessment provides a means for guiding our society in meeting its own needs through evaluating our citizens capacity to serve key social roles and functions which support our organisations and institutions, our communities, societies and broader humanity in their activities and which further well-being and happiness.

We ourselves, and our children are likely to have dreams and ambitions for our lives, and our learning and education systems are likely to be a primary channel through which we can move towards these goals and dreams. Nevertheless, where our goals and dreams lie in specific areas that are important to our social entities, these social entities must ensure that those of us who enter specialist areas are truly capable of fulfilling the functions of the job or role required.

Our organisations and institutions, our communities and societies thus, must select those who are able to successfully fulfill the relevant functions available otherwise we will all have the potential to suffer as a consequence or alternatively fail to benefit when we should be benefiting. Few of us would disagree that those who design and build bridges must have the capability to design and build these such that they do not collapse, thus avoiding the consequent suffering, pain and death that would likely result. Incontrovertibly, those who pilot airplanes must be capable of flying those planes effectively and we would all wish to have thorough teaching, testing and assessment to ensure they can.

And at a less perhaps immediately critical level, but nevertheless important, those who cut hair must have the skills to do their jobs well; those who run businesses must have the ability to plan, organise, manage, to buy and sell effectively; those who paint and decorate properties must be able to do so to a high standard if well-being and happiness is to be supported both for their customers and for themselves; those who engage in clerical work, accounts and administration must have an eye for detail and ability to be accurate in all they do; those who are agricultural workers need to be able to generate the best crop possible, are likely to need to have the physical strength to move loads where necessary, produce the best products that a farm or small holding can produce. Skills, knowledge, education and understanding are needed for all of these and the many other jobs and other roles we can play, and all need to be executed effectively for the benefit of all. And of course knowledge, understanding and ability to live well with, and work with others are also needed to support well-being, happiness and fulfillment in our communities, societies and within our broader humanity.

Our testing and assessment should nevertheless exist alongside appropriate opportunities and channels for success for all of us.

Through fulfilling such purposes effectively and in this range of ways, our assessment and testing systems should support our well-being, fulfillment and happiness. The absence of formal and visible testing and assessment of the skills and knowledge would most likely mean the use of invisible systems of selection which were grossly unfair, which would support injustice, inequality and likely unearned privilege. A lack of means of selection might also mean the potential entry of individuals into areas of education and learning or other performance and practice to which they were clearly unsuited, in which they were unable to perform, or alternatively could allow for imbalances or deficits in the skills and abilities available in our communities and societies. In formal systems of education, where education is paid for and supported by the community, either of these latter two problems would run the significant risk of representing an inefficient use of resources, and offering threats to our individual and social well-being. Nevertheless, hopefully and ideally the range of abilities and skills which we all possess will be recognised, and we can and will all experience learning and development, thereby contributing to our communities, societies and our broader humanity.

The importance of testing and assessment being recognised, our communities, societies and systems, we as individuals, have a responsibility to ensure that where such processes of testing and assessment are in place, they occur in an effective, fair, transparent and just manner, as far as is possible, supporting each individual's well-being and serving each of us as individuals, our organisations and businesses, our communities and societies as a whole. We, as individual people, as those involved in learning in education and training systems, as parents and in other capacities, need to ensure that, as far as we can, we have an understanding of such systems, and where they are unjust and oppressive, and fail to serve us well, we need to ensure that these systems are developed and improved, or if necessary in terms of our support for well-being, removed from operation completely.

Any testing and assessment system needs to have flexibility in its purposes and administration. Such systems should recognise their own flaws and the limitations and various problems of testing, for example, the fact that different forms of assessment and testing will produce different responses from different individuals; that some talented individuals may produce well below their capabilities when tested, through nervousness, stress, illness and other factors; and as a further example, the fact that tests will often be unable to mirror real world tasks at which some test takers may excel while performing poorly in paper and other tests.

Such systems of assessment and testing should, for example, recognise and embody the notion that, over time, we change as we grow older, that we may have differing and changing talents, skills, abilities and indeed interests over time, that we develop differently into adults and indeed that we learn and grow through our lives. Therefore a testing and assessment system should make accommodation and provision to enable us, at some point, where we have an interest in doing so and where we are capable of changing direction in our lives, to retake relevant assessments and tests, and use these gateways to move into new fields and areas for which testing and assessment may have previously evidenced that we might perhaps not have the ability to perform in. Our access to tests and assessments should not be restricted by age or other irrelevant factors.

Moreover, the focus of our education systems needs to be the promotion of education and learning. The fact of our community desire and need for testing and assessment should not be allowed to interfere with education and learning and to detract from learning and education. It is testing and assessment which should follow and deal with what has been taught and learnt rather than our requirements for learning and educating changing to meet the needs of testing and assessment.

Of course we also need to ensure, as far as we can, through our support, deeds and actions, that the quality of formal education is as high as it can be. Thus we need to ensure that our systems of education, in addition to being provided with the necessary resources, are supported by appropriate training and education for those involved in teaching in our systems, as well as the appropriate training and education of those involved in organisation and management of these systems. It must be reasonable for there to be monitoring of teachers, teaching quality, individual learning and monitoring of classes to some degree, yet this, in the vast main, should be done in a developmental rather than a punitive manner and this monitoring and assessment should not become the primary focus of teaching, learning and education. If this is the case then, rather than effective teaching, learning and education, focus will move to that of achieving results in the monitoring system which will lead to the possible, if not perhaps likely, lowering of quality and achievement in regard to teaching, learning and education. There does appear to be significant reason to believe that the apparently rational desire for monitoring and oversight can in effect detract to some degree from education and learning, damaging teaching and learning performance.

Our programmes of study, whether we are young or studying at later ages need to be appropriate for and tuned to our learning purposes and the wider needs of our local and more global communities and societies. The development of the range of programmes needs to be informed by those with technical and other situated expertise relating to what needs to be learned in order to be qualified at an appropriate level with regard to a particular skill or subject area.

Thus, clearly, if we are aiming to teach the airplane pilots mentioned above, how to fly planes, we would expect expert pilots, those with substantial experience of flying planes, to have substantial input into teaching programmes with comments and inputs provided by engineers, airline safety professionals, professional bodies, airlines and others, not only in regard to the 'what' of learning but also in some senses with regard to the 'how' of teaching, with educationalists and professional trainers also contributing significantly to the development of teaching and learning programmes. Professional and other specialist programmes need similar ranges of professional experts and others contributing, in order to ensure effective programmes of study and skills development are produced, these benefiting not only the individuals who are trained within such programmes, but also others, our communities, societies and beyond.

In a school context, we need a range of people contributing to the determination of the overall curriculum and syllabuses including those contributing beyond specific subject areas, since school education, in a broader sense, needs to be preparing children in more than just subject-specific ways. For example, we need to teach children as already mentioned, as far as we can, and help them learn, such that they can interact with others peacefully and cooperatively. We need to help them to understand the communities, society and broader world they are part of and will enter and which they need to contribute to, such that they can survive and thrive as individuals and also support their communites, societies and our broader humanity to also survive and thrive. We need to teach our children elements such as morality, responsibility for others and ourselves, health and fitness, tolerance, care and understanding, and much more, though of course much of this will also, hopefully, be taught in the home. Nevertheless, our schools can teach further and reinforce our community, societal and human values in the school and institutional context.

Importantly we need to act to ensure there is a sense of openness and democracy in relation to the determination of the broader curriculum, with all of us having an important level of input into the nature, content and delivery of the curriculum and into the discussion as to what will be studied. Our systems of education cannot and must not be allowed to fall into the hands of negatively selfish, partial and private interests, those aiming to support their own individual or group interests rather than the broader interests of us all. Our education systems must not be allowed to fall into the hands of, or be left in the control, of those whose sole goals are to seek their own well-being, their own wealth, their own power and control, or left to those acting under their substantial influence and control. And these systems must not be managed, controlled or substantially influenced by those who might wish to use our children as tools or vehicles in order to achieve their own ends at the expense of others and at the expense of our children, rather than having the well-being and happiness of each of our children, our communities, societies and broader humanity at heart.

Education and learning need to be lifelong processes and actions. We should not at any stage of our lives consider ourselves to be the finished article. There is always more to learn and discover. And thus having completed formal systems of school-based or college and higher education we will have gained important knowledge, skills and abilities, but there is much more that will need to be learned in our lives, much more to be gained from experience, interaction, reflection, our own self-motivated personal learning and development as well as additional formal education, development and training, if we are to achieve success and support our own well-being and happiness, and the well-being and happiness of all others, to the maximum degree possible.

With regard to our learning as adults, in addition to the practical benefits that such learning can bring, our adult learning can frequently be rewarding for many of the reasons already referred to, including the pleasure of encountering the new, the pleasures of discovery (including for example, perhaps based in evidence, our finding that we are or have in fact been wrong in the past in our views and opinions). Yet our education and learning as adults can frequently help us to overcome problems in our work or other contexts and develop and support us in advancing our careers either through valuable educational content or through acquiring formal and recognised qualifications, the lack of which may serve as barriers to our career progress. The social side of learning, already mentioned in this chapter, may be something we particularly enjoy as adults, with formal adult education sometimes providing us with the opportunity to meet others from different walks of life whom we might not usually meet, or enabling us to share experiences with colleagues and those with similar challenges in their work and perhaps similar interests to ourselves.

Nevertheless, even as adults we may sometimes experience feelings of frustration and unhappiness with our educational and learning experiences. We may for example judge that in formal settings we are being taught the wrong things, studying things we already know, or perhaps feel that we are be being taught badly. Able teachers and coaches, will recognise our adult identity as learners, will take account of our experience and use this as starting point to support learning or to serve as a reference point for determining that which should be taught. Such teachers and coaches will hopefully value us as individuals, understanding our uniqueness and will consider themselves to be on the same level as us as human beings. They will consider us as partners in teaching and learning, as opposed to considering themselves to be superior not only in terms of the relevant knowledge and skill area, but also as opposed to seeing themselves as superior people, superior human beings with more general authority, because of the knowledge and understanding they have (or believe they have) and because of their self-perceived status in their teaching role.

Of course some teachers and coaches may simply not teach in efficient and effective ways. Some may demean us when we are their students or mentees, and criticise us unjustly and unfairly, over-emphasising our errors, drawing attention to our errors in front of others, sometimes taking joy in these mistakes and errors as a means to bolster themselves and their sense of status. If teachers behave in such ways, they will be undermining our sense of well-being, our self-belief, or, simultaneously or alternately perhaps, simply making us angry and frustrated. Such teachers and coaches are well worth avoiding, even though we will need, to some extent, to keep an open mind, and balance that which we may gain from them in terms of skills and abilities, with the level of emotional pain and humiliation we are willing to tolerate. Clearly, in line with core principles, in which we are considered all to be of fundamentally equal human value, no person who is in a position where they are teaching should be aiming to humiliate and hurt their students or should consider themselves as a superior person to others on the grounds of the additional knowledge and skills they possess.

As adult learners, where we are receiving explicit tuition from tutors or teachers, we of course need to be able to listen to them in order to support our learning, but we should not be passive learners, listening mindlessly and learning what teachers, textbooks and other sources say, as if what is said and written represents unquestionable fact and that the classroom teacher is the final word. It is up to us as adult learners to research, investigate and find out, and to listen to and think critically about the ideas we are encountering, what we are being taught and what we are learning, with our teachers and coaches providing one of our possible, and often providing, important routes to learning, knowledge and understanding.

As adult learners we need to not only learn, but learn how to learn in a manner independent from a teacher, trainer, lecturer and the classroom, lecture theatre or training room. We need to take initiatives and set our own learning agendas, establishing our own personal learning goals and the routes to achieve them. As adult learners, we need to take responsibility for our own learning. If we do not take such responsibility, we will run the risk of having learning experiences which are not pleasurable, and we will run an increased risk of not achieving our personal educational goals with subsequent possible reduction in our sense of achievement, happiness and well-being. Through taking such responsibility and, as a consequence, learning in what is likely to be a very effective way, we will be advancing our own well-being and happiness and supporting well-being and happiness in our communities, societies and beyond.

With education and learning being a fundamental need for each of us as individuals, for our communities, societies and for our broader humanity, we each of us need to be prepared to engage in learning and education. We each of us need to be prepared to learn and be ready to learn. And as already mentioned, given that there is always more to know and learn, and always more that we could be able to do, in the light of our often rapidly changing worlds, it is inadvisable in terms of our well-being and happiness to see ourselves as in a sense complete in terms of our learning, to see ourselves as someone who, perhaps following experience of life, of education, perhaps much experience of a particular skill or profession, knows and understands it all and has nothing or even little more to learn. Our organisations, communities, societies, our human world is constantly changing and these changes mean that there are always new learning challenges for us to meet.

Moreover, the probability that we know all that there is to know about something is, in the first place, something which is highly unlikely, especially considering our existence as individuals bounded by our individual capacities and limitations and the obvious fact that we certainly cannot have enjoyed the cumulative benefit of the vast numbers of experiences and learning of others, each other person with their own understandings and knowledge which, more than likely, at least in some cases, could contribute to our own personal education and learning. Any claim to complete knowledge and understanding, or any impression we might have of such complete knowledge in others, is unlikely to be accurate given the constantly changing situations, the new and unexpected circumstances that constantly arise in our complex lives, which bring new challenges, new knowledge and understandings and new ways of doing. Thus, we need always to be open to new learning, whatever age we are, however much we may have achieved, however successful we may have been.

One of the keys to our ability to learn, is in fact our ability to recognise that there are things that we do not know, our recognition that there is more that is there to be learned, that we as individuals are indeed to some degree limited in our knowledge and understandings, and that there are further understandings and insights to be gained about what we do and how we do what we do, as well as further insights to be gained about ourselves, others, our communities, our societies, and about the broader world around us. It is clear that for almost all of us and probably all of us, it is beneficial that we recognise there are always new avenues worthy of exploration and that there exist a multiplicity of skills, knowledges and understandings which, as a single individual, we cannot hope to master *in totale*. In essence there are always things we can learn.

And to do such learning we must be prepared to attend to and listen to others (though that does not necessarily mean we should always, or even often, take on board and agree with what these others say). We must be prepared to explore and research the world around us, the world of knowledge and understanding around us, in particular reading about and listening to the ideas we encounter and experience, the ideas originating from others.

We need to be prepared to take on board new knowledge, alternative, new perceptions and ideas from others that we consider appropriate, ensuring that we are prepared to learn and grow in the light of reason, rationality and evidence, be that experiential, experimental or other forms of acceptable evidence, or through whichever avenue, based in rationality and reason, such information, evidence and new ideas arise.

While persistent personal exploration, persistently aiming to learn can be, to some extent, tiring and moreover, in certain cases, pursuing our self-development and personal change may not be easy, we need to do our utmost to seek and engage in such development, growth and personal change in support of our well-being and happiness and the well-being and happiness of others.

While our recognition of the value and importance of attending well to others in order for us to learn and grow does not mean that we will take on all or perhaps even many or most ideas from others – there are undoubtedly far too many different perceptions and ideas in the world for us to be able to do that – nevertheless, we need to make sure that we have a personal preparedness to learn, a preparedness to listen, a preparedness to consider, accept and evaluate evidence, a preparedness to admit that our current state of knowing and understanding is often incomplete and that indeed in some areas our ideas may be substantially misjudged and incorrect. With such preparedness and recognition, we should be able to pursue our personal growth and development effectively and therefore should more effectively be able to pursue and support our personal well-being and happiness and the well-being and happiness of others.

Yet of course, combined with this openness and desire to attend to others, further, as already briefly mentioned in this chapter, we need the capacity to be critical, the notion of critical being seen in both the positive and negative senses of that term, requiring us to be able to evaluate and find value in ideas, perceptions, events and evidence, but also being able to identify inconsistencies, flaws, irrationalities, biases, false assumptions and other problems in the ideas and information we encounter.

Of necessity to our personal well-being, happiness and fulfillment and the well-being, happiness and fulfillment of others, crucially, we need to be prepared to be similarly critical of our own personal current thinking and ideas, not simply the ideas of others, reflecting on our own beliefs and actions, examining the interaction of our own approaches, beliefs, thoughts and ideas with the world around us, identifying the need for our own change, looking for both the weaknesses and strengths in our own personal perceptions, beliefs, actions and outlooks, exploring the world of ideas and experience, in order to find ways of improving our thinking, knowledge and understanding, and hence our personal conduct and actions.

Through our learning, through reflection and criticality, in these and other ways we will be better able to perform many tasks in our lives, perhaps better able to interact with others, more skilled at the tasks we do and better able to achieve our goals, achieving greater personal satisfaction through being aware of and through ensuring our enhanced personal knowledge and understanding of the world around us. Through a preparedness to reflect on our own ideas and thoughts, through our preparedness to attend to others, to listen, learn and grow, we will be able to better support our own well-being, happiness and fulfillment, and the well-being, happiness and fulfillment of others.

Having stated the crucial importance of our education, learning and personal development, the reality is that our changing of ourselves and our beliefs, our changes of our approaches and actions, in the light of our encounters with new ideas, new knowledge and understandings, new learning, can sometimes require much time and effort, and can be personally challenging and difficult. In particular in regard to enacting fundamental change in ourselves and our fundamental beliefs, behaviour and conduct, such change can be a process which takes time to fully realise itself and may need to occur through a range of stages.

For example, we may first encounter a new approach, a new idea or explanation, which may be at odds with what we currently believe to be true and perhaps at odds with the beliefs and ideas which we were brought up with. Initially, despite its logic and rationality, we may find this new approach or idea, such new perceptions, difficult to accept, or we may at first reject them completely, finding a range of apparently good reasons for rejecting that idea or explanation. That rejection may be valid, but in some cases, with further thinking, with further life experiences, with further experience of reality, with further consideration of the relevant evidence, with further encounters with evidence and arguments, that idea or explanation may start to rear its head as a more plausible view and explanation of our life and experiences, more consistent with our observations and representing a more reasonable origin of appropriate and correct actions.

As time goes by, this explanation or newly acquired framework of thinking, may indeed start to form a more pleasurable and satisfying explanation of the world we live in, providing better and more valid and indeed perceptive explanation of particular ideas and issues we are engaged with. We may also find that this explanatiory framework, as experienced through some initial experiments and actions based on this idea, may lead us to new actions, thoughts and beliefs which we start to recognise as better supporting our own happiness, fulfillment and well-being and the happiness, fulfillment and well-being of others. Indeed as a consequence of taking on board such new ideas, explanations and frameworks we may simply be happier and feel we are enjoying greater well-being.

Unfortunately, in some cases and with some of us, perhaps all of us at times, where it becomes visible to some others that we recognise we have things to learn, this recognition may be interpreted as a sign of uncertainty and weakness, indeed of ignorance, with others developing a lack of confidence in us or adopting undeserved feelings of superiority and authority over us. This is a false interpretation and we need to ensure that we do not allow our reasonable search for optimum actions through our attentiveness and wish to learn from others, to undermine the confidence of others in us.

Our recognising our lacks and need to learn should not and does not represent weakness. Rather it is instead a sign of strength, competence and capability, which facilitates us in our learning and development, in supporting our effectiveness, and enables us to better attend to the ideas and suggestions of other, which in itself helps us in finding out about and helps us in taking those ideas on board when appropriate. Our personal awareness of our lacks in fact facilitates and supports our making those decisions which will best benefit us all. Thus our openness in this regard should in fact help us establish a position of solidity and strength.

Indeed if we are open, listening and attentive, and portray this openness and willingness to listen in an appropriate manner, we will often find ourselves better able to win the confidence of others and, where this is for the best, we should be better able to persuade others to accede to our own ideas, arguments and proposals, others being persuaded by our own openness to their ideas, the evidence and reasons we cite, our interest in finding evidence, our openness and willingness to encounter and consider new information and ideas, and our willingness perhaps to review old ideas encountered again, seen from a new and different perspective. Others may well respect our application of rationality, logic and reason to what is said and our willingness to listen, learn and indeed change.

As a single individual we, based in our own direct personal life experiences, of course, cannot know all there is to know; we cannot gather, analyse and examine all the evidence we would like to have, and imagine all possible solutions to the problems we, others, our communities, societies, locally and globally, might face. We have to seek out ideas, attend to and learn from the knowledge, understanding and expertise of others, and moreover, given the number of, and the complexity of decisions we need to make, we often need to act on the basis of information which may be incomplete if we are to get things right, make correct judgments and the right decisions.

As mentioned already, such a listening approach to our learning and development should not serve to undermine the confidence in us from others, though it may be the case that we are perceived as weak if we prevaricate and are indecisive when important decisions need to be made or if we continually flip flop from one judgment or view, from one policy or action to the other. This is much dependent on specific circumstances, our roles, and the decisions that need to be made, since expressing uncertainty, while entirely appropriate in some circumstances and indeed required (for example in contexts such as academic research) may in some real contexts create nervousness, lack of confidence and uncertainty in others (for example implementing a new business strategy or administrative reorganisation).

In some circumstances, despite our appreciation of our own lack of knowledge and understanding, we may need to and may choose to, communicate an outward confidence and certainty whatever our doubts and concerns about that which we have determined to do. This can be risky in terms of our personal well-being, however, there are times, especially when our judgments and decisions have been made on best evidence, on occasions where we have listened to the ideas and opinions of others, when feeling, having and displaying such a sense of certainty and determination is appropriate and necessary. Furthermore, reality may mean that our own personal effectiveness, the actuality of our personal well-being and the well-being, happiness and fulfillment of others, requires that others do have some sense of confidence in, not only that which we are proposing, but in us as a person, if they are to do what we have put forward, and if we and they are to prove willing to engage in specific courses of action which are necessary for the general well-being, happiness and success.

In the vast main, despite our knowledge that there is always more to learn, we should, and will need to, justify our recommended courses of action with some confidence in front of others such that they fully understand the evidence and rationale for our judgments and beliefs, for what we are proposing. This rationale and reasoning should form the basis for ourselves and others taking necessary actions. However, especially given the lack of information often available to us in regard to some crucial decisions and the ease with which criticisms and unjustified criticisms can be made, we may well need credibility and authority based in previous actions and decisions, the trust that others have in us as people in order to support our judgments and arguments. However, of course, our previous correct decisions will not necessarily mean that our current decisions are correct. Each decision needs to be judged in its own terms.

Moreover as a listener, we should be very careful about taking actions and acceding to and acquiescing in actions, based solely on the notion of trust, without significant evidence to back a decision or course of action. It is often the case where evidence is not present or not presented by others, by decision-makers, that either evidence is weak, problematic and the course of action wrong, or alternatively, that there are those who are deliberately trying to mislead us and who are using the notion of trust in a dishonest and disingenuous manner to enable them to achieve their personal goals at the expense of others.

If we are those presenting courses of actions and decisions, if, due to circumstantial exigiencies, we do not have the opportunity to do so at the time, then following the consequences of our decisions and actions we will need to be prepared to and be able to justify our decisions and actions in terms of reason and evidence, and be prepared to learn from and to be held to account and account for these decisions. The fact that we need to make decisions and act, sometimes in a decisive manner, does not mean that we should not keep listening out for more evidence and information from others, from other sources, which may on occasion be of such significance that we may be obliged to change our decisions, plans and proposals.

There is no weakness in our changing our minds in the face of new evidence. Whatever the context, be it in the family, at work or in the wider public pace, failing to change our minds under such circumstances, on the basis of new information, learning and understanding, will almost always be foolish. While we may perhaps feel reticent to change our minds, concerned and embarrassed about appearing foolish in our previous judgment, concerned about consequent personal criticism, even derision and contempt from others, who may, for example, crow that they were right all along, such feelings of embarrassment can be coped with and our acceptance of change shows us to be well aware of our key priority of supporting the well-being and happiness of others. And fortunately many, quite rightly, will admire us greatly for changing our minds, will admire us for developing our ideas in the face of new evidence, and for not being so foolish to persist in wrong actions, strategies and error. We certainly need to keep observing, learning and listening and, if we are involved in making decisions which affect and have impact on others, we also need to act in a democratic, inclusive and, of course, in a caring manner.

We can develop our learning in many ways, some of these already touched upon. In almost all cases we will need to set aside time for and make a deliberate effort to learn, the effort involved being something which may at times feel somewhat burdensome despite the pleasures that our learning can bring, since our learning almost always requires energy and effort. Indeed learning seldom comes effortlessly. We may be helped if we allocate certain times or a certain amount of time in our days, weeks, months or years, such that we can reflect on events that have occurred, the issues we face, so that we can reflect on our lives, anticipated challenges and more, leading us to better understand events in our lives and determine better actions and strategies for the future, our reflection and more, allied to other thinking and learning tools, being important routes to our learning and personal development.

We may sometimes wish to reflect and explicitly establish what we feel we may have learnt during days, weeks or other periods of our lives, and as a consequence plan ahead, adopt different or modified strategies and approaches for the short, medium and long-term future. Such reflection may not be possible or reasonable to do everyday, as life can be hectic, depriving us of necessary planning and reflection time. Nevertheless regular reflection on our lives, how we are living them and how we may live them better, allied to a conscious effort to identify ways of enhancing our abilities and achievements, looking for ways of doing things better, and supporting our life of well-being and the well-being of others more effectively will be of great benefit to us. And this reflection can be done on a daily, weekly, or that being difficult, on a monthly basis (or even longer periods) and should support our living better and happier lives. Such thought and reflection can also give us a sense of greater control over our lives, thus reducing our levels of anxiety and concern about the future.

Beyond that time for reflection, we should also set aside some time to pursue other forms of our individual learning, aiming to raise our levels of skill, knowledge and understanding wherever we can, whilst also not forgetting to enjoy other areas of our lives, while not forgetting to take rest and seek entertainment and pleasure. We can support our learning, not simply by looking at books or attending training courses and classes, but also by taking action, by doing new things, by pursuing new adventures, then learning from our doing, learning from our experiences.

But we should also set aside time such that we are able to engage in more formal planned study and learning. We may need time to read a non-fiction book or access web-based or other information which provides us with new ideas and perspectives, which informs us about our world or about some aspect of skill which we need to develop. We may decide to acquire new technical knowledge and skills so that we can improve our personal environment, our homes and if doing this we will need to set aside time so that we can master the relevant technical skills. We may need to set aside time such that we can study a new language, perhaps through a textbook or online system at home, or perhaps through classes. Whichever formal or perhaps less formal form or approach to learning we follow, a pre-requisite for our study will be our need to ensure that we set aside the time to focus on that learning.

While recognising the importance of learning and indeed continuous learning, nevertheless, we also need to recognise that there may be times when we decide to place greater emphasis on performance and doing, implementing and executing what we believe we know, rather than engaging in substantive and deliberate, effortful further formal learning, even though, whether or not we deliberately choose to do so, we will undoubtedly be learning through our experiences of doing. For the many of us, hopefully, learning will always be a part of what we do, however, some extensive and long-term projects, through the effort and time involved may be heavily dependent on the learning, knowledge and understanding we have already accumulated. If we are implementing such projects, we may pay less attention at the time to the learning we may achieve or may be achieving through these projects, and focus our attention more on actual implementation and doing.

Furthermore, and importantly, our engaging in learning can be extremely difficult when we are tired and exhausted. Our work and indeed the requirements of our social living in their many facets, can be tiring and exhausting for us, physically and mentally. And since learning, both formally and informally, frequently requires substantial mental effort, there are likely to be times when we really do not wish to engage in effortful, energy requiring and what may be exhausting learning. Our tiredness will clearly have effects in these cases and we will simply have to do our best to find times for rest and recuperation such that we will be able to think about, reflect and learn about our lives and experiences, or engage in more formal learning when we have the time, mental energy and strength available to do so. However it is likely that the absence of such learning and reflection may indicate we are living or having an exhausting and challenging time, an exhausting and challenging life, and that, dependent on our feelings and the circumstances, perhaps something needs to change in order to support our deeper well-being and happiness. Alternatively we may not be giving sufficient priority to our learning and development, something which may reflect on or which is likely to lead to a reduced level of, or a lack of well-being and happiness.

In the vast majority of cases, as far as is possible, however, we should be aiming to engage in continuous learning. And in order to support and bolster our efforts at learning and development, we should take note of and reflect on what we have learnt and credit ourselves for our learning achievements. Where we can, and where this is the case, we must recognise the things we know, the things we have learnt and understand, the personal development and changes we have made in ourselves, the education and learning we have engaged in and our learning achievements. And through this we will be taking time to engage in some kindness to ourselves, through recognising our achievements and contributions educationally and otherwise both to ourselves and others, this recognition supporting our well-being, happiness and sense of fulfillment.

Nevertheless, sometimes, if not often, even though we have our achievements and successes, we may still decide to look at how we might do things better and aim to discover, invent and explore some alternative and more effective forms of action and develop our thinking further. In the event that, alternatively, we are not so happy with our thinking, actions and performance, we will need to look for, study, learn, research, create and invent, new ways of conducting ourselves, and new and improved ways of doing things. All of this represents and should serve to support our learning and personal development, our well-being and happiness as well as the well-being and happiness of others.

Our need to develop and learn impinges on the range of contexts in our lives. In our families we may, indeed we should, wish to improve how we operate in our roles as parents to our children. In the first place, prior to our childrens' births we will undoubtedly need to and wish to seek out information about taking care of our children so that we can do our best to ensure their health and successful birth. We will also need to find out about our children as babies, find out about their needs, their sleeping patterns, their potential illnesses and the symptoms of these illnesses, vaccinations, what they can eat as they grow older, their likely behaviours and so forth. Our learning in these areas and more will give us increased confidence in our care for our babies and help us to ensure they have secure and safe early days, months then years.

Amongst a host of other things relating to our children, we may wish to seek out new ways of helping our children to learn, aiming to understand how children learn and identifying what we should teach and how we can teach them. We may need to seek out actions and strategies which will help us to cope better with the many stresses and demands of parenting, for example when our children behave in anti-social ways. Our learning may come from books, credible internet sources, friends, health professionals, work colleagues with experience with children, and a vast range of other sources.

Of course, if we are maturing and growing children, then as we grow older and become more capable of determining of our own learning, it might be wise for us to investigate how we might best deal with our parents, aiming to understand our parents, their motivations and goals and the ideas underlying their behaviour. As older children we will undoubtedly share experiences of our parents with our friends, but we can also gain advice and ideas about how to handle our parents not only from our friends, but from the range of information sources similar to those from which parents can gain their information, namely books, credible web sources and in some cases teachers and professionals.

Education and learning is likely to be of substantial value to all of us in our relationships. In regard to friendships, we may reflect on the numbers of relationships that we have and, should we wish more friends, we might modify our behaviours to make that possible (although we should be careful with this as fewer, closer and quality friends who truly like us and enjoy our company may be infinitely preferable to high numbers of more distant and less caring friends). Within our various relationships with lovers, partners, those most close to us, we will hopefully learn through the experience of our relationships and find better ways to keep our partners and those close to us happy and satisfied, enjoying our relationships to the maximum level possible. Education about sex and relationships is of critical importance and should be provided both in formal educational settings, by parents and through other media. Again we can consult books, advice columns on relationships, reflect on particular relationships or on our relationships in general, or consult professionals in the area of relationships when we decide to or when necessary.

Professional education programs relating often to our work contexts can be of great value as sources of our development of knowledge and understanding and in terms of developing our skills. In our own areas of need and experience, in our professional areas, we can pursue such formal education programs where they are available, enrolling for programs either dealing directly with developing our skills in regard to the range of working roles we perform or alternatively moving beyond the area of work to areas of our interest and potential need into the future.

In terms of our work and employment based concerns, often in line with the wishes of our employers (though of course we may be employers ourselves), we can and should where possible take courses and programs in the relevant particular professional roles we fulfill or wish to fulfill, (for example professional learning in construction, management, business, sales, accountancy, auditing, law, engineering, computer sciences, administration, nursing and midwifery, to name but a few). Additionally we can seek out educational opportunities relating to specific skills and areas within our professions such as skills of presentations, courses in using specific technologies, software development and computer programming, courses relating to relevant business languages, specific construction materials or techniques, running meetings, dealing with conflict, courses related to promoting our businesses, those describing information about agricultural and farming methods, techniques related to dealing with specific medical conditions and a vast range of other courses and programs dependent on our areas of business and work.

Also in relation to our jobs and work, going beyond formal programs of study and courses, we can attend general presentations, exhibitions, meetings of those of us within a profession or field, and conferences on advances and changes in our fields. Through searching for and encountering promotional publicity in brochures or through advertising in many forms we can find out about new processes and products developed and available which can support us in improving our organisations or our team and individual performance. Moreover, our conferences, meetings and other social gatherings within our professions and areas of business and interest should serve to help us to learn, in particular since we can go beyond formal speeches, presentation and business, and engage in less formal conversations and discussion about new developments of which we need to be aware, also finding out how we can apply the latest findings which relate to our professions, or how to resolve difficulties we are facing ourselves, through listening to the experiences of others in addressing and resolving the same or similar difficulties.

Within our specific work institutions, particularly if we work in those larger companies or organisations, we can attend in-house work training sessions, receive individual support from those more experienced or expert than ourselves, or simply meet with our colleagues formally or informally to share knowledge, understandings and experience. Such exchanges of ideas and information should support all of our learning.

If we can do so, then we can make efforts to seek out those with expertise in our fields of interest beyond our specific place of work, and aim to gain insights and information from them to boost our own activities and our own learning. And of course we can engage in reading about our fields, consult trade magazines, research the latest writings in our professions or areas of interest, looking at research journals, newspapers, consulting online writings blogs and videos in order to develop our knowledge, understanding and expertise, all of which should feed in to our work effectiveness, the effectiveness of our organisations, and support our well-being and happiness and the well-being and happiness of others.

Outside the world of work, should we wish to do so, as adults we can hopefully find formal educational opportunities to develop our understandings, skills and knowledge of the world. There will hopefully be courses and educational programs at local schools, training centres, colleges and universities which we can attend relating to many subject areas, for example courses in languages, in relation to teaching or enhancing our basic skills, for example in mathematics or reading, courses with regard to arts and crafts, accountancy and book keeping, effective use of computers, cookery, martial arts and much more, each hopefully helping us to develop our range of knowledge and skills, but also providing us with enjoyment based in the socialising and social context in which our learning takes place. Yet we may also find online and other sources of courses, find courses through distance learning or other means, which can support us in our learning in a range of different areas. There may be, and hopefully will be, courses and programs relating to areas already mentioned in relation to our family life such as childbirth, helping us prepare for birth and the enormous job of looking after our children, perhaps even courses in building and maintaining effective relationships.

We, as individuals, communities and societies, need to support the organisation and delivery of such courses and programmes which meet and support the educational needs and indeed the educational wants in our communities and societies. Education and learning are of key importance to our individual well-being and happiness, and are key drivers of effective communities, societies and beyond, supporting us all in terms of our well-being and happiness. We therefore need to ensure that we make available sufficient resources to support not only the learning of our children in school-based and other youth-focused education, but also we need to ensure that resources and facilities are available to support the learning of all of us throughout our lives.

In this modern age, in addition to the range of information and courses available through textbooks and other teaching and learning books, in addition to the formal setting of classrooms, the many of us can take courses and gain information available through our televisions, radios and mobile phones, or more frequently perhaps, in this current age, take part in online courses, available though the internet, which may cover any area of interest and skills.

When we take our courses and programs, these may be formal and even certificated, or on the other hand we may simply take such courses to find information and learn out of interest, for our personal pleasure, to find better answers to specific questions and issues, for the experience of knowing and better understanding our world. Of course, as with other more formal sources of information, we need to evaluate the information we are receiving, comparing it with other information, considering its rationality and logic, considering the relevant evidence for what is being said and promoted, and judging its truth value. It is clear that there is frequently significant false information provided through the internet, news and other channels, with this false information provided to pursue personal and political agendas, and sometimes soley to enrich the information providers financially, without regard for truth, validity, veracity and rationality. Thus, as with any source of information and ideas, we certainly need to take care and rationally and effectively evaluate that which we see, hear and read.

Nevertheless there is much useful information that can be gleaned from the range of sources, in terms of the more informal channels of learning already referred to, these representing informal channels through which we can advance our learning, knowledge and understanding. Such channels may include, for example, as prospective mothers, our talking to other mothers who have recently given birth to find out about their experiences and to get advice and information about the things, if anything, we may need to help us through the birth, the things we are likely to experience and the things we may need to do or should not do which may help that experience of birth to be better and perhaps less painful. Of course that information will need to be considered alongside the professional advice we receive from doctors, nurses and midwives, as well as other sources.

In many situations we may turn to our family and friends for advice and information on problems we face in life. Of course if their suggestions are wise and helpful, we will learn from this advice and possibly pass it on to future generations. And, also representing our informal channels of learning, we may discuss a range of matters with our friends and acquaintances gaining advice and opinions and learning along the way. Also, in an equally unplanned and informal, unsystematic way we may gain new information from radio, TV, internet, facebook, twitter and other such social media sources with resultant learning. Our different forms of informal learning may form a substantial part of our overall learning.

Exploration in its various forms is essential for us to learn and grow. Seeking out formal or informal educational and learning opportunities represents one possible form of exploration, but we can also explore through seeking out and enjoying new experiences in our lives, many, if not all of which are likely to boost our learning and education to some degree, as well as providing us with some desirable and desired stimulation, pleasure and excitement in our lives and to some degree the avoidance of tedium. In particular we can take on new challenges which we have not perhaps engaged in or perhaps even considered before, experimenting in terms of what we do and how we aim to achieve things.

For example, it may be that in some area of our lives we have been rather conservative in our approach. Experimenting with a new way of doing things may not only be interesting and stimulating, but may help us operate more effectively. We may feel more prepared to engage in such experimentation if the consequences of error are not so great or potentially damaging. However in many new circumstances and indeed circumstances where outcomes are of significant importance, we may still wish to take the risk of trying something new. Even if our new approach does not work to the hoped for extent, we will hopefully have learnt something new, even if our new knowledge is limited to a greater understanding of that which is not effective and does not work. In many such cases, hopefully our experimentation will be enjoyable in itself.

Indeed experimentation to some degree and doing novel things, apart from adding to our learning, can certainly serve to add to the joys and pleasures of life. In any case, whether or not such experimentation is enjoyable, when we explore and seek out new experiences, we should always aim to learn from our new experiences.

Mention has already been made of being evaluative and critical in our learning. In particular, given the presence of many interest groups, given the presence of negatively selfish self-interested individuals and groups that do not concern themselves with the well-being and happiness of others, given the presence of individuals and groups that aim to influence our opinions, our beliefs, and which therefore in essence are attempting to affect our state of knowledge and understanding, and given the many unspoken assumptions that underpin much communication and much action, it is worth reiterating the great importance of such evaluation and criticality. Such evaluation and criticality is of additional importance for us in the face of the welter of information, opinions and beliefs and their variety, which we experience in our daily lives, these often being put our way in order to meet the goals and intentions of those others, who are aiming to persuade us of the validity of their case or the case of another, or in some instances who are aiming to deliberately mislead us away from fact, truth, knowledge and understanding in order to suit their own goals and interests.

Even if our sources of opinion and information are more local, our friends, families, those with whom we have closer relationships or simply others we meet in our daily lives, we still need to be critical and evaluative. The people we know are likely themselves to have been influenced by others, sometimes perhaps substantially influenced by the agendas of those who are negatively selfish. And these more local and closer people may not be aware of the influences bearing down on them, or if they are aware, they may simply believe that their views are rational and logical views, when in fact, on closer analysis, their views may be unsupported by evidence, may be inconsistent, haphazard and based on principles which are not related to or consistent with supporting the well-being of others. However much we may know and like someone, we need to consider their judgments and views critically, that meaning of criticality being taken in both the positive and the negative sense, understanding, as part of that critical view, the origins of, and influences on their judgments, opinions and beliefs and indeed on our own judgments, opinions and beliefs. We will need to do this in order to ensure that we, and others, are making the correct decisions in terms of supporting our own well-being and happiness, and the well-being and happiness of others.

Thus the capacity to be critical is all-important to much of our learning and understanding of the world. A key factor influencing this need to be critical, and making such a task of criticality somewhat challenging, is the fact that many of us, at least in our current times find out much about the world from a vast multitude of sources, media outlets, newspapers, magazines, online articles, discussion and debates in the media, from journalists and experts in these media, politicians, business people or trade unionists, with our being influenced by other sources from books, to films to internet personalities, bloggers and the like. Many of these sources have their own agendas and motives aside from reporting truth, facts, evidence and events from an independent and indeed multiple perspectives, and aside from supporting the well-being of each of us and all of us.

These motivations and agendas, in some if not many cases, may be based in self-interest and group interests. And those in control of what is expressed through various media and other sources may be pursuing certain agendas irrespective of facts, evidence and reality, these agendas and motivations also sometimes being genuine but misguided, naive and misconceived in thought, or alternatively expressing negatively selfish views and approaches, unconcerned with the well-being and happiness of individuals or the general well-being and happiness. As far as is possible, we need to be aware of the motives of those who are presenting us with such information, their background and level of expert knowledge, their goals and interests, their strategies and the overt and less explicit mechanisms they may use to persuade us to the beliefs and actions they wish us to hold. Our reading, listening and understanding of that which is written or spoken needs to be critical and we need to be aware of when arguments and statements, as is often the case, are faulty in thinking and logic, be aware of where writers and speakers are omitting important facts, changing facts to suit a narrative, have an awareness of where that which is spoken or written is unsupported by substantive evidence and where there are clear patterns of bias (sometimes unconscious), bigotry and prejudice running through the thoughts, arguments and evidence we read and hear.

Notably, as many of us are aware, there are highly sophisticated public relations manipulators, practitioners and organisations, economically interested organisations, political and other forms of organisation, which will seek to act on behalf of their paymasters to influence opinion, our individual opinions and public opinion with regard to important issues, regardless of the evidence and truth in relation to a matter, which they may claim is not their concern. They may act to de-emphasise salient information, distract us from key issues, withhold certain information; avoid or deflect blame in the case of substantive errors; they may in some cases deliberately create false information, false knowledge and in some, if not many cases, will aim to encourage improper and incorrect understanding, avoiding inconsistent facts, rather than presenting balanced and reasonable evidence in support of their case.

To act in such ways is unacceptable and totally contrary to core principles. Those who act in such ways are acting reprehensibly. Their conduct in supporting falsehoods needs to be stopped. Each individual working in such areas needs to take responsibility for that which they are promoting and refuse to mislead and present false or distorted information. We, as individuals and as a general population, need to be aware of such realities, need to be aware of full evidence and facts as far as can reasonably communicated, and we need to be able to address such information with a knowledge and understanding of the truth and reality of what we are encountering in mind. And if we are ourselves involved in activities, or under pressure to be involved in activities which comprise the skewed, biased and dishonest presentation of information to others, it is our responsibility to desist from any such acts of falsifying and deliberately misleading others, and instead provide true and correct information allowing appropriate judgments from others.

Beyond these professional practitioners of persuasion, there are those with certain ideologies, social, religious and political, who wish to ensure that others, ensure that we, hold or speak the exact same views as they do, wishing to ensure that we do and say exactly as their ideologies and beliefs lay down. Their belief systems may require them to not only take action in aiming to convert others to their beliefs, but require them to aim to impose their beliefs on others, pushing aside from themselves any motivation or real intention to listen to others, to learn from others, and to change with evidence, reason, experience and fact. These belief systems often operate in such ways in order to maintain power for certain groups or individuals, aiming to take or sustain power and control which is often in its form and practice, misogynistic, hierarchical, authoritarian and patriarchal. Where such belief groups have power, they will often exercise such power and control in a callous, vile and cruel manner, with those of us not conforming to, or who disagree with the relevant belief systems and ideologies, often being threatened with or subject to physical cruelty and punishment, even murdered because of our different beliefs. Such actions and such intolerance is entirely unacceptable within core and other principles, as is the imposition of such ideologies and belief systems and the requirement, enforced by coercion, that we should conform with such belief systems and ideologies.

Whilst it is legitimate to accept and promote ideologies of various kinds where these can be seen as doing others no substantial harm or injury, many of these groups and individuals have the aim of coercing and indoctrinating us and indoctrinating, in particular, children born into families within these groups, into their world views and beliefs. This indoctrination and inculcational process, often requires that there is restriction on access to other world views, or if presented, such alternate world views and their adherents, are demonised, made other, described in important ways as inhuman, depicted as enemies, actions which are entirely inconsistent with core and other principles and contrary not only to important principles relating to our personal freedom and autonomy but also relating to important principles of education and learning.

These groups and individuals thus frequently wish to cultivate followers and believers who are subservient to the ideology, uncritical and unquestioning of that ideology (in particular its fundamentals) or its implications and systems, believers who will do as they are told by those in authority within that belief system, consistent with this ideology or based on the interpretations of the powerful within those systems. Within such systems, entirely contrary to core and other principles, criticism or disbelief, especially open criticism and disbelief in relation to the key ideas of such groups, are often not tolerated and can be responded to with the severe and violent punishments already referred to, with excommunication and expulsion from a group, social ostracism, or more subtle forms of exclusion and diminution of those who do not believe or dare to question and challenge.

Where these social, religious and political groups and individuals aim to inculcate their beliefs and practices in young children, apart from the mentioned denial to those children of access to alternative views of the world and the mentioned demonising of other belief groups, those children will often be told that the way they are adopting is the only and right way of believing, being and conducting themselves. Even if other groups are not mentioned, it may well be interpreted or implied that there is only one right way or belief and that other groups and individuals are not only wrong in their beliefs but are of lesser value as human beings. This indoctrinative approach to providing information and ideas to anyone, adult or child, is contrary to core and other principles, which see us all as having fundamental and equal value as members of our humanity.

Our well-being and happiness, both individually and for our communities, societies and our broader humanity, requires of us that we make accurate, correct and truthful decisions and this in turn means that we and our children need to have access to differing sources of information and interpretation, understanding our own views, beliefs in terms of the wider world. All of this needs to be joined to our development and possession of capacities to make critical and evaluative judgments about such information and interpretations. Indoctrinative, inculcational and restrictive approaches which deny access to information or which deliberately skew and bias information or which deliberately or otherwise present false information, which coerce belief and indeed coerce into group membership are unacceptable within the terms of core and other principles.

Of course, the presentation of, promotion of, the teaching of core and other principles, founded in the promotion of the well-being and happiness of all and the prevention and suffering of all, in itself, of course, represents a system of values and beliefs. Yet the presentation, promotion and teaching of such an approach to living, is seen as representing pursuit of common and fundamental human needs and goals, and moreover aims to benefit all. Moreover such an approach can incorporate many different ways of realising core and other principles and incorporates broad experiences and education in order to achieve those goals which will benefit all of us. It fundamentally denies a restrictive, indoctrinative and inculcational approach to education and learning beyond the teaching of those clear principles which will support well-being and happiness and reduce pain and suffering for ourselves and others.

As part of their activities, many social, religious and political groups will often engage in the practice of rituals and ceremonies which serve to emphasise individual membership of, participation in, and belonging to the group, emphasising group identity and also serving to exclude others. The reality, practicality and implications of the learning of such rituals and participation in these rituals, along with the often coercive and indoctrinative teaching of identity and beliefs is that, before they have become full adults and developed their thinking and their evaluative capacities, children become bound in to the group, membership of which becomes a substantial component of their identity. However, while coercive and indoctrinative activities are not acceptable in terms of supporting well-being and happiness, the participation in ritual in a manner which is not coercive and which is not indoctrinative cannot be said to cause any substantial and significant harm. As long as growing children and adults have the option to refuse to participate without fear of threat, exclusion, ostracism and punishment, then it is the view here that there is insufficient reason for such ritual to be prevented and that the ability to perform and participate in such ritual is an element of our freedom and autonomy as individuals and is a reasonable freedom for those in groups to possess. A sense of belonging and other positive feelings from participation in such rituals is hardly likely to cause harm and may generate certain benefits in terms of well-being and happiness. Of course those rituals should not involve texts or statements which serve to demonise others, those who do not believe in the same way as the adherents of these beliefs systems.

Nevertheless, it would be optimal if our children, if our human community could share and participate together in the same or similar rituals which would serve to create a sense of togetherness and sharedness of our common humanity. Moreover, rituals and ceremonies which require children to make lifelong or other commitments to their groups and belief systems are not acceptable in terms of core and other principles. It is not legitimate for children to be taken as incorporated within these groups without the space and time for evaluative decision, without the opportunity for open encounters with other groups and belief systems, prior to their development into full adulthood. Such commitments can be made by adults, but children are not the possessions of families or groups and it is not acceptable to persuade or coerce children to make lifelong oaths and promises to belief systems or groups or even offer the opportunity to make such commitments to children, since our children are too young and too inexperienced to make such momentous decisions about group membership and their lives so far into the future. And even where adults make such commitments, there needs to be the opportunity at any stage for those adults, indeed all group members, to change their minds and withdraw from any oath of lifelong commitment to a group, without their fearing or being subject to any significant sanction and punishment.

As already mentioned, criticality and evaluation of fundamental beliefs, especially open criticism, is often, though not always, discouraged or disallowed completely by these groups and individuals, whose goals are not those of promoting well-being, happiness and fulfillment, but instead emphasise, focus on and involve the promulgation, promotion and maintenance of their group, their specific belief system, frequently allied to the maintenance of power and control over their group members and others. In essence these individuals and groups are interested in indoctrination, not education, and are likely to represent a threat to us all, especially where their ideologies and beliefs inculcate a sense of self and group superiority combined with a hostility to those who do not accept the beliefs and ideologies of that particular group, and where such groups suppress and deny the expression of alternative views and act in a punitive and destructive manner against those who disagree with their world view.

While often having the positive individual and sometimes social benefit of a strong sense of group indentity and belonging, those existing within these oppressive belief groups will often suffer, in particular because of our fundamental human needs, amongst others these being our human need to explore, to find truth, to express our judgement, opinions and feelings, to doubt, to be curious, to invent and create, to be free, which combine with our desire and need to be part of a wider whole. Our suppression and oppression, our inability to search for truth, to educate ourselves fully, damages us and overall damages our communities, societies and humanity which cannot gain the benefit of our learning, personal development and education in its fullest sense.

If we find ourselves trapped within such groups, it is our responsibility, as is the case in other more democratic and open contexts, to try to work in whichever ways we can, to develop our own knowledge and understanding, to work to discover new ideas, to find truth, to express that truth to others in order to support their learning and education, to be critical and, wherever possible, to aim to remove from power those engaged in such oppression or, if necessary, to escape from those who are aiming to indoctrinate us into their worldview, who have no tolerance for any significant challenge to their views and world outlook, and who require our wholly or almost wholly uncritical and often absolute obedience to their individual and group beliefs and commands.

In terms of educational institutions, while some, religious and other belief based organisations promote tolerance, openness in education, love and care for others, elements which are entirely in line with core principles, nevertheless, in many jurisdictions, many religious schools in particular, through their control and operation of schools and education, aim to focus mainly or exclusively on teaching their own particular beliefs, aiming to ensure children remain within and accept the relevant group teachings. These entities therefore and thereby significantly control and restrict, indeed substantially close down children's potential experiences of education and learning about their world, something which is unacceptable within the context of core and other principles.

However the practices of such groups through their 'educational' control tend to be at significant odds with the notion of true education and learning which requires access to the range of points of view, presented in an open, discursive, balanced and reasoned manner. Indeed, the reality of the practice of these faith-based schools at the current time, is that, in particular, they frequently engage in skewing or biasing the provision of information in areas relating to the particular faith that they represent. Certainly, for example, in the current age, rarely are atheistic or non-theistic views seriously and credibly discussed in such schools, or if so, this is done with a view to disparagement, if not vigorous condemnation, demonisation and more. Rather than basing teachings in acceptable empirical evidence, rationality and reason, by contrast information will often be presented as true as a matter of faith, because it is reported in an ancient text, or as a matter of community belief, to which children, to which adherents, are required to conform in believing, irrespective of rational evaluation of ideas and evidence.

Moreover, in some, if not many faith schools, within the context in particular of religious education, in addition to frequently ignoring and marginalising other belief systems and world views, inaccurate and false information or misrepresentations, may also be presented in some cases, in order to decry or discredit the range of those who do not believe, who are not religious, not simply atheists and Humanists, but including those from other faith and belief groups.

Indeed, many of such faith schools practice discrimination against different groups within their communities, promote discrimination and unfair practice (particularly against homosexuals and girls), and promote archaic and oppressive views of sexuality and gender roles; and they moreover often encourage a sense of superiority amongst their adherents in comparison to other faith and belief groups with these other groups and their members sometimes being demeaned, if not directly, then by implication. Furthermore, they frequently over-emphasise faith practice in their teaching programmes and curricula, thus skewing the overall curriculum and teaching programmes away other more valuable areas.

Education requires discussion based in rationality, logic and evidence, of the particular and other belief systems, and requires the building of understanding, respect and tolerance towards those of other belief systems, those with differing identities, which operate in a manner consistent with core and other principles. The presentation, indoctrination in and inculcation of a particular religious belief view, or other belief view which dehumanises and demonises others, the promotion of damaging and destructive intolerance and discrimination, are not consistent with education. And groups which control and manage educational systems and institutions in such a manner are not suitable as organisers and controllers of educational institutions.

Moreover, in terms of creating communities and societies where we all live together and get on well with each other, cooperate well together and can live peacefully together with high levels of well-being and happiness, the fact that children born into different belief groups are educated separately from children in other groups creates fissures, often deep and potentially highly damaging fissures, in our communities and societies. And allied to the points made here about the nature of education, this separation of children and young people means that such faith and belief group control of educational institutions can be significantly detrimental to our overall well-being and happiness.

Educational institutions need to be run in line with core and other principles, promoting education, tolerance and understanding. They are best run, controlled and managed by our communities, societies, our local councils, our governments, influenced by teachers and educational experts, parents, businesses, trades unions, charities, those with a range of expertise, and influenced by other social organisations including faith and belief groups. Those who manage and control our educational institutions and systems need to control, administer and manage schools and other educational institutions in a manner through which, in regard to matters of life philosophy, life stance, belief and religions, social and community values and beliefs, as well as in regard to other areas, they pursue open education for their students involving balanced encounters with those of the range of thinking systems, belief and non-belief groups, whose views and values are consistent with core and other principles. Our educational institutions and systems need to promote social tolerance and togetherness, peacefulness, and enable equality of opportunity amongst their students, not practicing unfair discrimination. Our education systems must accord with core and other principles, including those of freedom, justice, tolerance, interaction with and a sense of equality with and care for all others.

That is not to say that individuals with beliefs or belief groups in general should not be able to supplement more general education in values and attitudes, subject knowledge, tolerance, understanding and personal skills delivered in our more community schools, colleges and universities through their own teaching, through their own lessons, through their own classes or indeed supplementary schools. It is to say that these forms of education must be an add-on to our common systems of schooling and education, and moreover they must not act in ways which serve to significantly damage their belief group members or the wider community through demonising other groups or promoting amongst other things, destructive discrimination and intolerance.

Further, as already stated in this guide, children need to meet and acquaint themselves with existing beliefs, belief groups and ideas prevalent in their community as well, indeed, as the possibility of new and different beliefs which currently do not exist. They should be able to hear from practitioners of belief systems, as long as their views are not significantly destructive and damaging, as long as they do not advocate, threaten and promote violence and destructive intolerance and discrimination. Finding out about the beliefs of others forms part of education, but this finding out about is not the same as ensuring children become members of such groups. Should they wish to ally to such groups, this is a decision for them when they are adults or approaching adulthood.

Educational institutions run by communities, our societies, our governments and the like need also to be capable of accommodating difference amongst the children who enter their institutions. Thus where children originate from specific groups which have certain rituals and practices, it is part of their individual freedom that they should, within the reasonable bounds of an institution, be free to engage in specific practices, such as maintaining special diets, praying, having specific days away from school in line with religious holidays and the like. Yet it is also the case that children from within such groups should be able to opt out of such rituals, refuse to pray, eat as they will, should they desire to, without the prospect of coercion, shaming, punishments or other forms of pressure from schools, parents or the wider community. Enabling and allowing such actions is part of our education about and the promotion of our individual freedom and personal autonomy and independence. And moreover, those children who wish to not participate in such rituals and religious practices, must not be socially pressured, coerced, or physically forced to participate if that is not what they wish.

Education and true learning require engagement with different perceptions, views and opinions, presented in as impartial a manner as possible by teachers presenting and explaining the views, cultures, and beliefs of others, or by enabling those who advocate such views to espouse those views and being able to clearly state their own fundamental beliefs and perceptions to those who hold alternative views. Such alternative views need to be presented and explained to children too, by teachers and belief advocates in a manner which is appropriate at a particular age. Children and indeed adults should not be deprived of access to worldviews and beliefs on the grounds that these undermine a group view and ethos, or on the grounds that encountering more than one view is confusing. Of course, however, those who advocate coercion and violence, who advocate racism and destructive discrimination, who demonise others and deny their humanity, should certainly not be allowed to promote such views to children (or for that matter elsewhere).

An open approach to education, learning and discussion, involving engagement with others, engaging with differing ideas, perceptions, culture, views, judgments and opinions, contrasts with the far less useful and, perhaps sadly, far more common occurrence of sources being selected and used for the purpose of confirmation of the opinions, biases, judgments and beliefs we already hold, something which is far often too easy, far too frequent and cannot be seen as optimising our personal development, education and learning, or as being of sufficient benefit to our communities and societies in terms of well-being and happiness.

Consistent with an open approach, an approach in which we are interested in true learning and engagement with different ideas and perceptions, an approach applying in whichever context we find ourselves and acting to support our judgments and efforts to find knowledge, understanding and truth, we need to seek out, be exposed to and identify and select those information sources which have credibility, integrity and openness, those which are interested in evidence and deal with that evidence with integrity. Such sources will optimally acknowledge their own potential fallibility and limitations, their own biases and assumptions, stating these clearly, and also stating the rationale behind and perhaps as far as is possible, the origins of and influences on such judgments, opinions and beliefs.

We may often benefit by studying, reading and listening to those sources which challenge our views and put across alternative views (while retaining awareness of the biases and deeper purposes behind many judgments, views and perceptions), although clearly investing too much time and effort tackling information, sources and texts with which we do not fundamentally agree, may not be an effective use of our limited time. We certainly do need, most of all, to seek out and encounter those ideas and texts that can reasonably be seen as evidence-based, impartial and independent, or at least which are impartial and independent, as far as is reasonably possible and which focus with integrity on establishing truth and accuracy in line with and with the goal of supporting the general well-being and happiness. These latter texts, be they spoken or written, basing their views, perceptions and evaluations in rationality, logic and evidence, engaging in an honest and reasoned search for truth, should be of great value to us in support of our well-being and happiness and in support of our learning and development, incorporating evidenced and supported views which should help us in making our own rational and reasoned judgments and supporting us in determining the most appropriate actions and conduct to be adopted.

However, all texts, all words that people say, in the context of discussion of ideas, debate, and indeed in a range of other contexts[2], do need to be considered critically, for, however rational and reasoned an argumentative or other spoken or written text may seem, it is crucial for us to be aware of assumptions, motivations, biases and prejudices which the writers or speakers we attend to may have, especially since such underpinning features may well influence the evidence, thinking and interpretations that writers and speakers are reporting (this may be unconscious bias, bias stemming from a group, educational, personal or cultural background or other source). We do need to understand the assumptions underlying what writers and speakers are saying or writing, assumptions which may not be entirely visible to ourselves or indeed the writers or speakers themselves.

Furthermore, we need, wherever possible and reasonable, to look at multiple sources of information, in order to gain different perspectives, which support our criticality and which help us to encounter the already mentioned challenge to our beliefs, and to identify additional evidence which may support our current beliefs or perhaps contradict them. We further need to ensure that there is logic and rationality applied in consideration of and interpretation of any evidence presented. And we need to consider the evidence and arguments before us, as far as we can, with impartiality and without bias, as far as that is possible, knowing of and being aware of our

---

2  In our daily conversations and some other more regular interactions, we can and perhaps should consider what is said critically but this may be a tiring, unnecessary and indeed sometimes anti-social thing to do.

own personal attitudes, background, prejudices or biases, something which needs to be supported through a full understanding of ourselves and our own beliefs in regard to an argument, proposition, course of action or issue, before addressing it. In order to achieve this, when addressing any questions or issues, it is beneficial for us to be aware of and make explicit our current state of knowledge and belief and to have a good and hopefully accessible and explicit understanding of ourselves, our views, beliefs, attitudes and judgments, and their origins.

Our search for truth and learning will undoubtedly require much research and effort. The extent of the effort required to resolve the range of questions we may have indicates the importance of spending time on establishing truth and developing our learning. In pursuit of true and deep learning, the processes required may seem lengthy and time-consuming, however in the end, through what can sometimes also be difficult and challenging processes, we will move closer to the truth, closer to real, deep education and learning, a process and movement which supports our own personal development and the contribution we can make to ourselves and others, truly supporting our well-being, fulfillment and happiness, and the well-being, fulfillment and happiness of others.

Our learning, our development of our knowledge and understanding, our skills and abilities, must, importantly, include a focus on understanding ourselves, our personal, individual, social and human identity, as well as our individual and social conduct and what lies behind this. There are aspects of our own personal conduct and behaviour of which we are or may not be not fully aware, which can be difficult to perceive, yet which have been almost certainly shown to be present in many or all of us, as has been suggested, evidenced and demonstrated for example, through focused psychological and social research, research and truths which we really should be aware of and know about ourselves, as part of our learning and the development of our self-understanding.

Such identified and important elements of our human selves include widely acknowledged phenomena such as the halo effect[3], already referred to in prt one of this guide, whereby there is a tendency for us to judge others or make other overall positive judgments on the grounds of an initial positive contact and perception. This is proposed as having the consequence that our judgments in regard to an individual may to an important extent

---

3   Thorndike, E.L. *A Constant Error in Psychological Ratings.* 1920

be inaccurate, with our inaccurate judgments leading to later problems due to, for example the placing of undeserved trust in someone who may be unreliable or even dishonest. Undoubtedly in terms of the real and multifaceted complex lives we lead, there may be variability in how such a principle applies, nevertheless, an awareness of such an effect and other similar elements of our human thinking and psychology are undoubtedly beneficial, serving to focus us on rationality and the broad evidence we have available (and indeed unavailable) to us.

There are other important phenomena which it will help us to be aware of, such as our human tendency to acquiesce and agree with others, or a general tendency for most of us to conform under many circumstances to expectations. The benefits of such acquiescence and conformity may, in the short term, be a more peaceful day and easier cooperation and co-existence, which are important. Nevertheless, while such actions may support the cementing of social relationships and promote cooperativity, such agreement with others, such conformity may not always, perhaps may not often, be the optimal action for us to take as individuals, for the benefit of our relevant groups, or for the benefit of others either immediately or in the medium and longer term. A rational and more considered analysis of evidence, aside from our principles of seeking agreement and acquiescence, may suggest other alternatives as representing better options.

Of course we are all individuals expressing our individual diversity and varying personalities and conduct, and given our individuality there will be greater or lesser tendencies to display these and other behaviours dependent on who we are. Nevertheless, an understanding of our deep selves, our human psychological selves, is of great importance to our well-being. Part of our learning, indeed an essential part of our learning, should as far as possible, include developing a strong knowledge of our individual and more general human psychology as well as our social psychology, and developing an understanding of how these may play out practically, in reality, our reflection and thinking, our learning, heightening our capacity to understand ourselves and helping us to conduct ourselves, speak and act appropriately.

Up to this point in this chapter, the major focus has been on our own individual and personal learning, our personal development and our existence and identity as individuals who are experiencing education and aiming to learn. However each one of us has an important role not only as a learner, but also as a teacher, with this being taken to mean, not exclusively in the formal sense, a role as professional teachers in educational or training institutions, but also with reference to our roles as teachers in our every day lives in our homes and with our families, in our work environments, and in our less formal, more daily interactions. We will all of us, have some knowledge, understanding and skills, some perspectives and wisdom which is likely to be worth imparting to others, especially if we can communicate that which is worth learning with care and skill, at an appropriate time, in an appropriate place, in an appropriate way.

For the many of us, we will have one of our most important teaching roles through our parental role in the upbringing of our children. In addition to the essential daily care we provide for our children, we will need to take the lead role in teaching them, in helping them to learn, in teaching them how to cope with their daily lives as children and beyond, and in helping them to survive and thrive in the home and the world beyond the home, both in regard to the more immediate moment and through their development into the future.

We will need to teach our children and support them in building and achieving amongst other things, a sense of self and self-value, a sense of place, a sense of belonging in the home family and the wider family, a sense of their importance, value and relationship within the family, wider community, social and global family, a sense of purpose in their lives, a sense of place in terms of time and history, a sense of place in relation to other, different groups and cultures, and a sense of place within our biological and physical environment, in relation to the diversity of life around us, our planet, and the wider universe.

As parents, it appears that we are, at least the many of us, in many senses finely tuned in a vast number of ways, through our innate human nature and human character, through our innate patterns of behaviour, and also through the behaviour we have learnt more socially, to teach our children much of what they need to know. And added to this parental teaching, our children will learn lessons and be taught further by family, friends, and our wider communities and societies. Through our parental love and care for our children, we will most likely, and hopefully, spend large amounts of time with them, caring for them and being with them, frequently on a one-to-one basis. And crucially, we spend significant amounts of such time, often through our ordinary and spontaneous behaviour, though also in more deliberate ways, teaching them and helping them to learn. Our children certainly have a natural propensity to learn and indeed they need to and want to learn, and it is essential that we as parents and adults support them in this.

Fortunately, as adults and parents, we do not, in the main, need to be taught the necessary skills in order to be teachers for our children, though as with everything, aiming to improve what we do and how we do it, through advice from friends and family, through reading, research, through expert advice and otherwise, as well as gaining some support and additional knowledge and understanding specifically about teaching and how to teach our young ones can be useful and can add to the natural propensities and skills we have for the teaching of our children.

Even without being taught to be teachers, when helping our youngest children to learn to speak, we are likely to (and indeed probably should and must) start interacting with our children with changing facial expressions, touch, noises, gurgles, burbles and baby language, perhaps saying individual words to represent objects, even when we know the child will not say these words back to us. Indeed we are usually quite expert at tuning our speech to match our children's current state of language development, expanding the complexity of what we say and indeed of what our children say, in a manner which enables them to develop their own language complexity to the right level at the right time. Thus we are crucial as parents in helping our children to learn in so many ways, in particular enabling them to learn language.

Of course as parents, in most, if not all contexts, we spend time helping our children, encouraging them to learn how to walk, encouraging them to crawl to us and come to us in whichever way they can, holding them up, holding their hands as they start to learn how to walk. Again these are things we tend to do naturally without being explicitly taught in a classroom how to help, and without needing any external motivation to do so. Helping our children to learn and grow is part of who we are.

Amongst the very early skills, abilities and areas of knowledge and understanding we may teach our children are very basic ideas such as safety, as well as emotions such as happiness and sadness. We teach about places and people, how to interact with others, things which are allowed and not allowed. We need to teach our children and let them know they are loved and wanted, teach them and help them develop physical skills such as some sense of balance. We need to teach them about the physical properties of common objects in the world around us, how to hold certain things (often through providing experience), basic social customs, opening and closing doors and cupboards, using plates and holding utensils and how to play simple games amongst a vast range of other things which in themselves help our children to learn even more. All of this is of course central to our children's early development, education and learning, comprising some of their initial movements towards the older adult world. As parents, family and others caring for our children, we are of crucial importance to their early development.

And as our children grow older they will become capable of learning more complex skills. For the vast majority of those of us who are parents, contingent on our having the requisite resources, capability and skills ourselves, after, or at the same time as very early capacities such as initial speaking, walking and more have been learned, we will, if we can, aim to teach our children how to read, showing them pictures, telling them stories and reading out loud, perhaps providing our children with picture books, books and playsheets which will help them recognise the sounds, symbols, numbers and letters of our languages, using spelling games, and perhaps special toys, using our fingers and thumbs or other objects for teaching about numbers or even computer programs designed to enhance language abilities if we have access to these.

We will aim to teach our children how to write, providing them with books and activities which will support them in producing the letters of our various languages, moving them through early stages where writing is limited to impressions of letters or numbers, towards the generally later stages where our children may engage in more sophisticated story and even argument writing, although such later development, in the vast majority of cases, is likely to occur within the context of more formal education systems, unless, that is, we teach and educate our children at home.

As our children grow older, in many societies we hand over some responsibility for important areas of their learning to our more formal education systems. Through supporting such formal systems of education, dependent on what is being taught, we can enable our children to develop skills and expertise in a range of areas such that a more sophisticated and wider range of skills can be learnt by our children in comparison to the content, topics and skills that we as parents may be able to ourselves teach. For example, many of us may not know or have a sufficient knowledge of mathematics, chemistry, physics, history and perhaps other languages, to the levels that formal social schooling can bring to our children.

And further we benefit our children through these formal systems because teaching and learning is carried out by those who not only have relevant specialist and field-based knowledge and understanding, but who also have been specifically trained in effective processes of education, of teaching and learning, with children focused on elements of learning skills and knowledge which are determined, hopefully, in the context of democratic and collaborative processes.

As already stated when discussing the content of formal educational programmes, the content of our formal education systems is, and needs to be contributed to by those with educational and other expertise, as well as parents and democratic representatives if it is to be both beneficial to the children themselves and also beneficial to our communities and societies as a whole and our more global world. And wide ranging programmes can be delivered since, while we as parents will to some degree have the restricted knowledge and skills already referred to, while we will perhaps have that mentioned expertise in some areas, our more formal, organised systems of education are able to bring together a range of expertise from a range of different individuals, who are professional in teaching and have expertise in specific areas of knowledge and understanding, something which should enhance our children's learning and benefit our communities and societies.

That is not to say that we as parents may not have some expertise ourselves in teaching and may not be well equipped to teach, especially given the benefit of our close relationships with our children which is particularly helpful while our children are in the younger age range. It is also certainly not to say that we as parents should not have a role in determining what our children learn. Indeed hopefully, and indeed of necessity, we need to be able to contribute to the determination of the content of the programmes and classes that our children can study, this comprising part of our democratic right and serving as an element of our contribution to our communities and societies, our broader humanity and to our children as well.

But going beyond such individual contribution of ideas and opinions to the curriculum and to programmes of study, some parents, through home-schooling, may decide to maintain responsibility for the education and learning of their children for a substantial period of their younger years, in some cases for the entire young lives of their children. This is entirely acceptable in terms of well-being and core and other principles, as long as children are able to experience the full range of required knowledge and understanding; as long as children are able to socialise with and meet others, including those from different communities and belief systems from the one in which they are being brought up; as long as they are able to encounter the range of ideas which are considered germane and relevant to living a life of well-being and happiness; as long as they learn to support their own well-being and happiness and the well-being and happiness of others. Some children, for various reasons, may be better served through being educated at home with their parent or parents, with formal education in schools seen by some, not unreasonably in some cases, in a manner dependent on its organisation, dependent on government, administration and specific implementations, as having drawbacks and not representing the free and open education which children need and which we all need to promote well-being and happiness.

Unfortunately many schools, as already discussed, aim to inculcate certain beliefs into their children denying reasonable access to other perspectives and views, and this occurs particularly in regard to encounters with religions. It is unacceptable, even if schools are formally religious in character (and such actions are also unacceptable if a school is non-religious in character), if schools are giving access to children to particular religious speakers and officials, while denying access to those advocating non-religious philosophies, denying access to those from other religions, and denying access to those advocating the range of other alternate approaches and philosophies. In the context of such schools, religions are being given undeserved status. Unfortunately, these religions are often used as a basis for teaching morality, something which is certainly, at the minimum open to substantial challenge when considered in the context of core and other principles.

It is worth reiterating here that which has already been stated in this chapter, namely that, while children should clearly, at least in the modern age, be taught about religions and belief systems, should know about and understand religions and belief systems, and may, as adults, choose to be in a religion or belief group, within our current formal educational contexts, children should encounter differing belief systems and religions, and be taught about them, hearing from their advocates and hearing different views within the frame of core and other principles, rather than, in the vast main, or solely, receiving the partial, biased and frequently unevidenced or even false accounts that children are often exposed to within religion-based institutions. These religious-belief based schools, as already mentioned, in the main, frequently aim to promote and concretise their own religions, aiming to ensure that children from families within the group will remain within that religious group. Such goals cannot be acceptable as educational and learning goals. It would certainly be reasonable to pursue home schooling to avoid this form of approach or similar approaches to belief and other issues in schools, approaches which are not in line with true notions of education and learning.

Whether at home or in the school context, the general nature of education needs to incorporate the capacity for children to challenge ideas and also needs to incorporate the enhancing of their capacity to provide such challenges, supporting processes of reasoning, identifying inconsistency, internal contradiction, clashes between belief and evidence, belief and action (including the ability to identify hypocrisy), enabling use of evidence, logic, personal social development, self-valuing and more. Where children wish to challenge ideas, their challenges need to be given consideration and accepted or rebutted, dependent on the nature of their challenge, with rational and evidenced responses serving to bolster the role of evidence, rationality and reason, supporting the self-valuing of the child, even if there is disagreement with, rebuttal and rejection of their challenges and views.

By contrast to home schooling, at our organised schools it is likely that children will have much opportunity to socialise and will be able to do so with a much greater variety of other children than might be encountered through home schooling. They will often be able to live in a community with other children and make friends, friends of diverse characteristics, origins, backgrounds and beliefs, which on the whole should be beneficial to them as children but also will be of benefit to our wider community society and our broader humanity. This mixing with others can also be achieved with home schooling, though perhaps it is less straightforward. And schools have an important and added advantage in that, to an extent, we parents are released from the constant need to supervise and look after our children throughout the day, a release which enables us to take on work (often paid work) in roles supporting both the community and supporting ourselves, or which in many cases may enable us to pay attention to younger siblings within the family who will need greater focus and attention.

Whether at home or in the context of formal large scale or mass schooling, our children, through their years of youth, need to study a range of disciplines and subject areas in order that their well-being and happiness and the well-being and happiness of others can be supported. The nature of these areas will most likely change over time with our changing world, as new technologies, new contexts and situations and new understandings, new ideas arise. Nevertheless there are likely to be some fundamental areas which are likely to require study over the generations.

It would, for example, seem an absolute necessity for our children to study the language in use in their culture and community such that they can communicate and cooperate effectively through fluency in talk and through advanced and sophisticated capacities for reading and writing, these being necessary to support well-being and happiness. And these skills need to be developed as far as possible in order to achieve maximal effectiveness of communication in support of such well-being and happiness, and to help in the avoidance of pain and suffering.

Mathematical skills, certainly at the minimum, to a basic level, need to be taught to enable us to survive through the day, to help us to understand the use of money and resources, and participate fully in the lives of our communities and societies. Yet our communities and societies, and often we ourselves as individuals, do require more advanced mathematical skills for a range of purposes and so it is likely to be beneficial for all of us to understand the mathematical principles upon which not only simple but also advanced mathematics is based and through which mathematics is applied. This might include, for all of us, an understanding of proportions, percentages, averages, an understanding of statistical principles in relation to probabilities and possibilities, the use of mathematics in design and engineering, in finance, and in areas such as the various branches of physics amongst other uses.

But further, our children need to be scientifically literate understanding the principles and processes of scientific research, developing an understanding of the fundamental sciences, of biology, chemistry, physics, psychology, geology, physics, geography (also in elements a social science) as well as other science related disciplines, and their related sub-disciplines as well as cross-disciplinary areas.

A strong knowledge of biology gives us insights into our human relationships with the plant and animal world, an understanding of the importance of our environment in sustaining us, an understanding of the mechanisms through which plants operate to utilise energy from the sun to generate the food we eat and through which our food chains are supported, as well as supporting agriculture, animal husbandry and animal welfare. Biological study, amongst other areas where it provides insights and indeed enlightenment, presents us with key information about our biological origins, about the evolution of life, about our historical position in relation to other organisms, the genetic and social factors which influence who we are, about the nature of illness and how illnesses can be treated such that we can live longer and more healthy lives.

And understanding different chemistries and the different forms of and approaches to chemistry means that we are able to utilise natural resources more effectively, or design our own useful chemicals and materials which support our capacities to take action, get things done and thereby enhance our well-being. Chemistry is central to our crucial exploitation of energy resources and our effective use of these resources. In our current world, the raw material of crude oil is converted through various chemical processes to petrol or used to make the plastics which are found almost everywhere in our modern lives, having a vast effect on our daily lives.

Yet chemistry is of value in a vast range of areas, and understanding chemistry is of benefit for all of us. In our current age, sweeteners such as aspartame are chemically synthesised and used in the making of certain drinks. Chemical processes are used in electroplating, the manufacture of inks for our daily writing, for our computer printers, amongst a vast number of other important useful applications as well as the various aspects of chemistry underpinning a wide range of industrial processes. Further, our communities and societies, our broader humanity, need at least some of us to have advanced professional expertise in order to understand, implement and develop these processes, and to be the leaders in developing new chemistry.

And, in order to support such chemistry, which is of such importance to our communities, societies and beyond, it is important that our children, at some point in their education, and indeed that we as adults, gain and possess an appreciation of the importance of this chemistry in our lives. It is important that we all support the development of such chemical knowledge and understanding in our children and throughout our communities and societies. Moreover, an understanding of chemistry and indeed biology should also inform us about the dangers that can arise from chemical and biological sources and therefore support us in making educated decisions about risks from such chemical and biological sources.

Similarly to chemistry and biology we need to ensure our children have a good understanding of the nature of physics. The contributions of physics to our individual lives, to our communities and societies are legion. Key understandings in regard to the generation and distribution of electricity fall within the ambit of physics. Of course electricity and power are fundamental to almost all we do in the modern world. Without these assets, derived effectively from experience, experiment, knowledge and understanding of physics, we, at least the many of us, would find ourselves without computers, cars, without our artificial light in our homes, offices and streets, without air travel, the range of communication technologies, medical technologies, and much more. Indeed our lives would be completely different and much poorer in terms of well-being and overall quality. The range of our communications technologies, from our televisions and radios to our mobile phones and computers, are based in understandings generated through, amongst other things, the study of physics.

Our children, through their childhood and later as adults, clearly need to appreciate the centrality of physics to our modern lives, gaining an understanding of the operation of our communications technologies, understanding electricity and other forms of power sources and generation in our modern world. And not only do our children need to appreciate the notion of electricity in general terms but they need to understand wherever possible the underlying mechanisms through which electricity generation, distribution and utilisation operate.

We cannot afford to have a community and society in which we have no such real appreciation of those essential things which fundamentally underpin our lives, since this runs the risk of allowing substantial misunderstanding with consequential damage to our individual and social well-being and happiness. Moreover, as with other areas of school education, we need to ensure that our education systems develop individuals with the expertise to ensure the continued running, improvement, development or even replacement of such power and energy providing systems in support of our overall well-being.

Yet physics touches many other areas of our lives, from supporting us in an understanding of the nature of what we are composed of as human beings (knowledge and understanding of which also derives from biology and chemistry), to the sub-atomic nature of the components of our environment, to the composition, nature and extent of our universe. Our knowledge and understanding, derived from the world of physics, that we are made up of individual atoms, and sub-atomic particles, together with our knowledge and understanding that we are part of what appears to be an expanding universe, extending for distances of which it is almost impossible for us to conceive, has profound implications for our understanding of that universe and our position within it. These elements of knowledge and understanding, at least in terms of their basic concepts, need to be available to our children and to all of us as adults.

Science also covers areas such as psychology, geology, earth sciences and geography with the range of scientific methods being applied in these and related disciplines. Again, understanding the workings of our minds is of key importance. Through for example scientific study into understanding memory and learning, we can devise ways to enhance our capacity to remember and our abilities to learn. Through an understanding of rocks and their formation we can gain understandings about the history of our planet, and in addition, of crucial importance, we can identify the potential for extracting resources for our human use from our planet, resources which can benefit our quality of life and well-being. Through understandings of physical geographies, the nature of cities and different human landscapes, geographical study gives us further insights into the world we live in.

Key also to our children's learning and education is an understanding of the optimal processes through which we can develop our knowledge and understanding of our world, how in pursuit of scientific discovery we can gather data in a systematic manner, how we can, and do, develop and create knowledge, the manner in which we observe, experiment and collect evidence, evidence as concrete, objective, valid and reliable as possible, in order to reach conclusions and generalisations which are considered true and which are found to be of value to us. We can apply these methods to choices and decisions in our own lives supporting us in making effective, accurate decisions which will enhance our personal well-being and the well-being of others.

Our scientific methods of research and investigation have served to change our world and enhanced our well-being and happiness in a vast range of ways, through their support in so many areas of our lives, including through advancing medical treatment, enhancing our daily lives at home through technological developments, through transport systems, communication systems, enhancing our leisure and entertainment, through helping us to understand the complex world we live in, and in a vast range of other aspects of our daily existence, where scientific study has enhanced the quality of our lives, serving to support and enhance our well-being and happiness and reduce our pain and suffering.

However, it is essential to recognise that our advancements in science and technology have been and can be, in some senses, a double-edged sword, with scientific and technological discoveries having been used inappropriately in ways entirely at odds with core and other principles, being misused for the carrying out of terrible deeds, mass killings and oppression. Furthermore, scientific knowledge and understanding, when not properly understood, not fully researched and not dealt with appropriately, indeed when based in false and flawed assumptions, has sometimes caused inadvertent damage through inappropriate use and application. Thus in certain contexts, our having recognised the immediate benefits of the application of new discoveries and technologies, there have been significant occurrences where the long-term consequences of acting on new discoveries and implementing new technologies have not been fully considered, leading to, in particular, environmental threats.

Moreover, in particular in cases where individual or group selfish interests, in some cases, racist and vicious racist and nationalistic or destructive ideological beliefs have been allowed to prevail, when prejudice, false ideology and hatred have formed the context in which science and technology have been and are being developed and implemented, this has led to, has meant and means a constrained, and in some cases perverted research agenda, with areas of scientific and technological endeavour, development and discovery operating outside the framework of promoting well-being and happiness. Such a perverted research agenda has led to, and has the potential to lead to, enormous damage to health and well-being, the causing of much if not severe suffering, pain as well as death on a wide scale, and the causing of damage not only directly to our humanity but also to our broader human environment with that environmental damage presenting its own consequences for our well-being.

It is clear therefore that our children, in addition to being taught the wonders of science and technology, need to be taught and need to be aware of areas where science and technology can be less strong, with our pointing out the necessity of science and technology operating in a context of values of supporting, loving and caring for others, looking after ourselves and others with the goal of supporting the well-being, happiness and fulfillment of all. Our science and technology and their application must avoid causing any significant pain and suffering and act to prevent such pain and suffering.

Beyond the crucial scientific areas discussed, a sense of history is important for us and our children in terms of our personal, community, social and more global history, supporting us in a sense of place and belonging, contributing to a sense of identity and helping us in our orientation to others, to ourselves and to the worlds we inhabit. And therefore we need some formal education in regard to history. Our historical study must not however be mediated through reporting to our children only issues painted as being simply fact. Instead, crucially there needs to be understanding of history, its role in our current lives and society, its presentation and interpretation, including the role of history itself.

Such an approach is needed because history is always selective, and frequently, if not always, supports a perspective on life, a world view, an ideological approach and set of beliefs about the world. Without a knowledge and understanding of history itself, then there can only be misunderstanding of history, passivity and victimhood in terms of learning. To be truly educated about history (and indeed in regard to other areas of learning), we need to understand that history and learning from history are based in interpretation which will to some degree be constrained by the beliefs we hold about the world, in essence an ideological view of the world which will likely be supporting not only the formation and development of our individual identity but is highly likely to be fulfilling an identity role on behalf of our communities and societies.

That being said, and in itself reflecting the approach adopted within this guide, our history teaching and learning, consistent with core principles and our concern for all people, needs to be, at least to some degree, built on a global perspective, rather than simply focusing on our own family histories, the history of a single culture or our own more local culture, taught with the purpose of creating local social unity and cohesion. As important as the social cohesion of any individual local community and society is, and this is likely to be of substantial importance, the cohesion of our humanity, of our global community needs also to be promoted in terms of core and other principles, and this can be done through appreciation of our common human global history and origins, whatever our differences across the globe. In support of our own well-being and happiness and the well-being and happiness of all, our history should play its role in supporting our appreciation of our common humanity, common origins and in bringing our global communities together such that we are more able to work cooperatively together for the well-being, happiness and fulfillment of all.

The area of geography has already been referred to in relation to geography as a science but more broadly, we as adults and of course our children, need an understanding of social geography, of places, environments and cultures which are different and far away from our own, as well as understanding the more social geography of the places in which we live. In regard to those more distant places, we need some sense of the histories and geographies of the relevant nations and cultures which again serves to help us not only in understanding others but also helps us in establishing our own identity and position in the world, as well as providing us with new and different ideas about living, and can provide new perspectives on, and ways of, living.

Of course one of the best ways of learning about such places is to visit them and directly experience them. However, reality, in the form of the plethora of places available to see and visit, means that, we will generally need to gain our knowledge vicariously through reading books, online articles, magazines and other texts, through the tales of others, through video and film and other means. Our children will, in the main, need to gain much of their grounding and knowledge of geography and places from their classroom experiences, through teaching and learning in the home and also through their own exposure to books and the various forms of media. Yet if they can gain some experience of visiting, living in and experiencing different cultures that will be of tremendous value.

Also expanding their knowledge of the world and of others, our children will benefit from learning languages which is likely to give them a degree of insight into other cultures and an understanding of difference, apart from an initial and, at the minimum, a basic ability to communicate with those from other cultures, although yet again, the optimal way to learn about these cultures and ways of living would be to spend time living in them. If we can provide our children, through schools or formal educational experiences, with the opportunity to actually visit other places and cultures, then that is likely to be enormously beneficial for their learning of languages, their learning about culture and cultures, and their overall education.

Reflecting our communities' and societies' appreciation of the arts and indeed need for the arts in all their forms, we need to teach all of our children about music, painting, sculpture, theatre, film and other forms of art. Engaging in these arts as activities in themselves is an experience, and is likely to be to some degree enjoyable and different in terms of its experiences from much other study, though this will be dependent on our personal level of interest, skill and tastes. But also, as a consequence of their artistic experiences, our children will be better able to enjoy and appreciate art and artistic performance, understanding its qualities, beauty and complexity. Given its importance in our communities and societies, our children need also to gain skills in producing these different forms of art, with those children with the relevant aptitudes and propensities being supported in developing advanced knowledge and skills in the wide range of art forms, gaining the abilities to sing, play musical instruments, write music, produce engaging artworks, participating in theatre and shows and being able to practice whichever art form they wish to study or have a propensity for.

Beyond study of different generally recognised subjects areas, not only do our children need to have a strong awareness of who we and they are as human beings, how our communities and societies operate and can operate, how our communities and societies can work together to benefit their members and benefit all, they also need to know how to cooperate with and work with others, as well as knowing how to support themselves and others in feeling good and living a good and happy life of well-being. Without such values, attitudes, beliefs and values being taught, learnt and implemented; without such cooperative practices, without that knowledge, understanding and indeed implementation in support of well-being and happiness and the avoidance and prevention of pain and suffering for all, they, and we, will not be able to enjoy well-being, happiness and fulfillment.

Thus our children need to be taught to be attentive and caring, be given caring roles, be made aware of the importance of caring for and looking after others and need to have such caring exemplified and demonstrated to them through our actions and words. They need to be faced with a range of examples and models of good caring behaviour, be shown how to be caring and concerned, and understand why we should be concerned with the well-being and happiness not only of ourselves, but also of all others, with their being supported into understanding why such caring approaches benefit us all. Our children need to be taught and shown such approaches, actions and values, that we care for and look after all others, the weak, those who are suffering, ill and in significant need, and that we have community and social responsibilities which must be realised through our words and deeds.

And further, our children need to be shown and also be made aware of behaviour which is unacceptable within the context of a caring and loving approach to life, made aware of behaviour which is unacceptable in the context of a life lived in line with core and other principles, being made aware in the process of the detrimental consequences for us and all, of uncaring, callous, destructive behaviour which damages the well-being and happiness of others.

In support of well-being, fulfillment and happiness, in order to support appropriate personal conduct, our children need to learn how to work together through group activities, play and teamwork as well as learning the value of and the need to be able to act individually, on their own initiative, on their own with persistence and determination, taking personal initiatives in pursuit of their own reasonable and more individual personal goals as well as in support of more social goals. Our children, as they grow, in support of their development and learning, need to be given increasing levels of responsibility, both for ensuring that the daily individual and social functions of their own lives are carried out, but also for supporting others, their family members and those beyond the family. They also need to, more specifically, take responsibility for activities in their communities and societies, adopting where possible organisational and leadership roles in teams and groups.

Each child needs to gain some experience of leadership and taking responsibility for the well-being of others, being mentored and taught during the process or afterwards, sometimes being allowed to make their own mistakes and hopefully learning from their action and their consequences. And as young and growing young people, we need to ensure we gain such opportunities as far as we can. Leadership and coordination roles generally require us to gain understanding and awareness of the existence of the perceptions and beliefs of others, perceptions and beliefs which may well not match our own. Coping with, managing and living with such differing perceptions and perspectives, is something essential for us all to learn and will certainly help us in our conducting ourselves effectively and in terms of supporting well-being and happiness.

Principles of self-sacrifice, of altruistic behaviour, responsibilities to other human beings, our communities and societies, locally and globally need to be introduced and taught, these being fundamental to our appropriate conduct and fundamental to supporting well-being. And again, as young and growing people, we need to ensure that we take on these notions such that we can fully enjoy our own well-being and happiness and support the well-being and happiness of others.

In support of cooperation and working together, our children (and indeed we as adults) need to be taught and to learn how to deal with the range of differences we might encounter, between individuals, cultures and more, and also need to learn how to deal with conflict, conflicting views and perceptions. Tolerance and understanding of difference, where different views offer no direct and significant threats to well-being and happiness, is something which is beneficial for us all. Differences between us are inevitable and our children need to learn how to live with and live well with the differences which exist between us and the differences which may exist between differing groups of people.

Our children also need to develop capacities in terms of dealing with non-ideal behaviour and conduct, such as dishonesty, abuse, violence and more. In particular, the capacity to manage situations, to promote peace and build peaceful contexts, to prevent outbreaks of violence, to reduce tensions and unpleasant conflict, to calm others, to talk appropriately, where this is possible, are valuable assets for all of us and need to be taught and learnt effectively. And beyond that, we need to ensure that our children exist in contexts where they are not subject to violence and abuse and that they understand how such damaging contexts are created and sustained, and how such contexts can be changed and such violence and abuse can be reduced and ended.

It may well be that our children need to be capable of dealing with conflict in their early upbringing in families and communities, but we would hope not and we need to act as individuals, communities and societies to ensure that they do not endure such situations. Through their upbringing and education, it would be as well that our children nevertheless develop the capabilities to protect themselves and where necessary forcefully defend themselves from attack and have the capacity to act forcefully, with minimum harm to others to ensure that they and others do not suffer in the face of those engaging in aggressively violent acts. There may be an important challenge here in avoiding the creation of contexts where the capacity for forceful self-defence, in reality and practice, results in a context where force and destructive violence are too readily adopted. Nevertheless, the absence of an ability to defend ourselves effectively and defend others effectively leaves us all vulnerable and open to substantial pain and suffering.

Our children further need to be taught, shown and learn the importance of truth, honesty and integrity. They need to be shown and need to recognise how honesty and integrity support our well-being and happiness, with such conduct presented as an expectation in their lives. Nevertheless, as disscussed in chapter seven in part one of this guide, it seems that often children will experiment at times with untruth, and that this may represent valuable experiment and is not always such a bad thing, since the reality is that in some instances in our adult lives, being overly direct and truthful in our statements is not appropriate and can lead to poor relationships or exacerbate conflict. But, moreover, indeed as also discussed in chapter seven, there are times when lying is an absolute moral duty and necessity in order for example, to protect others from aggressive violence. Such lying would be demonstrative in some cases of great courage and integrity. Thus, perhaps, in addition to teaching the value of honesty and integrity, we should also teach our children about the differences between integrity and honesty, and exemplify situations where it might be that lying (being untruthful, and in a sense dishonest) is a reasonable and indeed a beneficial or a required thing to do.

To some degree, as discussed in chapter seven, hiding personal knowledge, views, judgments and opinions may, on some if not many occasions, be wise and may benefit personal security and safety, well-being and happiness, through avoiding damage and pain to ourselves and others. Nevertheless, we anticipate integrity and honesty from others in most circumstances, and expect our children to learn this as an expectation, while understanding the mentioned complexities that can arise. It is important for our children to understand that well-being, happiness and fulfillment and the avoidance of pain and suffering are our prime goals, prime goals which we hope are always supported by personal integrity, and which in the vast majority of cases, though not always, are supported by truthfulness. As children and growing young people ourselves, we need to demonstrate integrity and honesty while supporting such well-being and happiness.

All of our teaching and learning to our children must be continued outside formal educational contexts and the home, and as individual parents, as communities, societies and as broader humanity, we must demonstrate the values we teach, for our young children to emulate. Importantly, as adults, we must all be careful of saying and preaching one thing to our children and others, and hypocritically doing another, something which lets us all down, our communities, societies and our children. We will support and achieve our own maximum well-being and happiness through pursuing integrity, and in the vast majority of cases, honesty and truthfulness, and should do our utmost to have and demonstrate integrity and honesty in our conduct, demonstrating this integrity and honesty in real life to our children. The teaching of such conduct and values needs to occur in the home, through our schools and beyond, and needs to occur everyday through each of our actions within our communities, societies and our broader humanity.

Linked to teaching and learning about living together effectively, our formal teaching in schools as well as our informal teaching at home needs to include education and learning about relationships, about loving relationships and sex. At appropriate ages, we need to tell our children explicitly about love and sexual relationships such that they are well prepared for their move into adulthood, the sexual world and sexual relationships. We need to support our children and growing young adults such that in later life they can enjoy sex and relationships to the full, such that these relationships enhance their well-being, happiness and fulfillment. This education needs to include teaching and learning about the mechanics of sex, how we gain pleasure, joy, a sense of self-value, and meaning through sex and love, what makes for an effective partner relationship, our responsibility to love and care for our partners, areas such as childbirth should we wish to have children, and our responsibilities in bringing up our children, amongst a range of other crucial elements required for a full understanding of sex, love and relationships. Such education also needs to tackle the challenges of relationships, varying perceptions of different partners, the common problems that partners and couples can have, the challenges of living so close together and cooperating together, along with approaches to dealing with our relationship problems amongst other areas.

Our children also need a basic education about supporting their personal health, including diet, exercise and other factors affecting their health through their youth and into their lives as adults. They need to be taught the basics about being clean and the links between cleanliness and health as well as being taught about cleanliness and tidiness as a matter of good personal conduct in itself, this being supportive of a pleasant environment at home and elsewhere, the fact of tidiness supporting our organisation and efficiency in living our lives, though perhaps also the need for a balanced approach in terms of tidiness, incorporating the recognition that at certain ages, under certain circumstances, high levels of tidiness in our homes and personal space may be difficult to achieve and indeed may not be a priority. This education also needs to include a focus on the various threats to child safety and well-being such that our children can be prepared to face these and deal with them effectively.

The importance of diet to health needs to be emphasised with the elements of a healthy diet presented to children and indeed to their parents where necessary, as well as the consequences of poor diet. The importance of regular and daily exercise throughout our lives needs to be put across as well, with the threats to our human health from inactivity, threats such as heart disease and obesity, pointed out. Combined with this, there needs to be an awareness of factors in our lifestyles which might encourage us not to exercise and stay fit, as well as provision of education and information about how to counter and overcome these factors. Within the context of their education and beyond, children also need to have the opportunity to exercise, to stay fit and to learn how to incorporate exercise as a regular component of their daily lives.

As already mentioned, the importance of cleanliness to our good health and preventing the spread of illness and disease needs to be taught in school and home-based education, as does the nature of illness and disease, in particular disease transmission, such that our children can better understand the threats to their health and better understand issues related to cleanliness and health. Issues such as the effects of alcohol, drugs and other substances on well-being and happiness need to be discussed at an age appropriate time and in an age appropriate manner. And certainly issues relating to our emotional states, our mental health, such as sadness, depression, suicidal thinking and their origins and remedies, as well as our responses to the different health challenges of various kinds that we may meet in our lives, need to be discussed and discussed openly.

Further, linked to our areas of thinking and emotion, but also tied to our capacities to be successful in achieving our goals and in terms of our well-being and happiness, our children need to be taught and learn a range of thinking approaches and thinking skills. They need to learn thinking approaches, skills and knowledge which support their abilities to be rational, logical, creative, inventive, analytical, constructive, to problem solve, the thinking skills required for design. Our children need to be taught and learn how to think in an evaluative way, to engage in questioning in the search for truth, and also need to learn how to be critical, in both its positive and negative senses, such that they are prepared and able to use evidence, logic and rationality, as well as being able to use inventive, creative, evaluative and critical tools for the purposes of analysing events, situations, information in their various forms, drawing conclusions and designing answers and solutions which are true, of value and which can lead to effective action.

Our children also need to be developing knowledge and understanding of how to be creative in their thinking, for example they need to understand the value of imagining, visualising and indeed how to imagine futures. Not only do they need to understand the how to, but they need to be able to actually engage in and do creative and inventive, imaginative thinking. To support their creativity, inventiveness and our capacities for constructive thinking and design, our children need, as far as possible, to be able to engage in activities and projects which require such capacities, through which they are able and required to generate ideas to meet needs, to solve problems and more. Processes to support such invention and creativity are likely to need to be explicitly taught. The tackling of local and real world situated problems should serve to support the development of these essential abilities.

To support thinking which involves criticality and evaluation, our children need to develop the abilities to identify amongst other things those features which support truthful and accurate statements, judgments and interpretations as well as those features which help us to identify appropriate courses of actions and policies, with our children understanding the need for, as far as possible, acceptable evidence, rational connection and logic between ideas, consideration of alternative explanations and more. Our children need to understand and be able to identify bias, prejudice, absence of evidence, be able to identify false and unsupported assertions, lack of logic, narrow and constrained thinking, the influence of personal and cultural background, of varying perceptions and perspectives on reality, on our thinking, ideas, judgments and opinions. As part of this criticality and evaluation, they need to develop the ability to identify their own motives and motivations but also the motives and motivations of others, understand how others may aim to manipulate and mislead them in support of their own negatively selfish interests, for example, through providing false information, slanted and biased accounts and false analyses of information, culture-bound and limited or illogical statements, and statements based on false assumptions or which are not evidenced.

Our children also need tools for analytical thinking and much more. Such education in effective thinking will support our children in reaching the correct decisions in their lives, in their work and home environments, in regard to the many and various issues they have to deal with and decide upon, these thinking skills enhancing their ability to achieve well-being, happiness and fulfillment and to support the well-being and happiness of all others.

For older children, younger adults, and indeed for all of us, some encounters with key philosophical issues relating to areas such as morality, ethics, the nature of science, the nature of meaning and existence, are likely also to be of value and indeed interest giving us insights into important areas tied to our thinking and living.

There is also great importance for our children in not only understanding that there are different perceptions held by different individuals but that, in support of well-being and happiness, it can be beneficial to recognise and listen to the perceptions and views of others, especially where these perceptions and actions and their consequences, do not involve direct and obvious harm to others. Further we need to help our children in recognising that we may need to modify our perceptions, but also that we can persuade others and lead them to change their perceptions, though it is helpful to be aware that this can take time. As a consequence of recognising and paying attention to such perceptions of others, of additional benefit, we can also develop our knowledge and understanding of the world, identifying ideas and approaches which may support us as individuals in our pursuit of well-being and happiness for ourselves and for others.

Recognising the existence of such varying perceptions and the legitimacy of such differing perceptions within the framework of core and other principles, likewise our children need to develop an understanding and knowledge of the role of conformity and convention in determining that which is accepted as truthful or considered acceptable in the public space, as opposed to the determination of truth through logic, reason and rationality and the determination of utility in terms of what is optimal in terms of supporting well-being and happiness. Notably, there may be prominent and widely held views and beliefs in our communities, in regard to which there is pressure to conform. There may well be views and beliefs which may not in fact be true or useful, which may not indeed serve to enhance our well-being, happiness and fulfillment, yet they are adhered to as norms and conventions. Of course it is likely to benefit us all if such norms and conventions are recognised for what they are and become obsolete.

Younger people by their nature, and many of us through our lives, will have a propensity to challenge, yet our younger people may need to be supported in their challenges and their capacity to challenge through, in the first place, encountering alternative explanations and approaches to the world. They will also benefit from having the thinking and other tools to identify ideas and actions which may be damaging and also the capacity to identify the value and contribution of existing ideas, thinking and institutions, such that change into the future is beneficial and truly supports well-being, happiness and fulfillment. Challenge and change, our rebellion against norms and conventions, while sometimes beneficial, also needs to be thought through in order to ensure as far as possible, that displacement or replacement of that which exists now is accompanied by resultant change which is in reality beneficial, truly supports enhancement of well-being and happiness and does not lead to pain and suffering. We have to be careful about pursuing change for the sake of change when such change may lead in some cases, not to improvement, but to the removal of that which is valuable, and when such change may cause damage to ourselves and others.

Our children, indeed all of us, therefore need to develop understanding of the pressures to conform, and the need to be non-conformist in some or indeed many situations in order to support truth and integrity, and in order to support well-being and happiness. As a consequence of this understanding, they will hopefully more effectively benefit themselves, our groups, communities, societies and beyond. In order to resist pressures to conform, our children need a grounding in ways of independently determining the truth and validity of those ideas presented to them. This requires a grounding in a framework of rationality, reason, logic and evidence already discussed in the context of thinking skills, criticality and evaluation, which will enable us to identify whether the ideas of others and our own personal ideas are indeed true, valid and correct and whether these ideas will effectively support the achievement of well-being, happiness and fulfillment, and the reduction and prevention of pain and suffering.

It is important to recognise that in the range of areas, our teaching, which will vary in its nature with our children's ages, does not necessarily mean simply didactically telling them elements of knowledge and understanding, though of course this can be valuable; it does not mean simply directing them how to behave. It can include helping our children gaining experiences, helping them interpret the experiences they have, as well as providing access to a rich learning environment. It can include discussing the things that we consider of import, feelings, emotions, events, with them and explaining our personal perspectives and our personal stories.

Beyond our formal schooling, we all need, wherever possible, to continue our education and training such that we can achieve the highest levels of expertise and skills, the highest levels of knowledge and understanding possible. And as individuals, communities and societies we need to be supporting the development and achievement of such expertise in our communities, societies and broader humanity, as such expertise has the potential to substantially support our well-being and happiness. While focusing on developing and applying our expertise, for the vast numbers of us developing such expertise, there is a danger of our becoming socially detached from others, from the communities and societies around us, and becoming detached from our connections with and responsibilities to others. To counter this, those who develop such high level, leading expertise and understanding need to ensure they remain servants of our communities, societies and broader humanity rather than ignoring the interests of others, ensuring that they do not misuse their expertise, understandings and knowledge for negatively selfish purposes.

Our personal development to high levels of expertise can be achieved through our formal higher level education systems, colleges, training and expert institutes and organisations, business research institutions and universities, through the training programs already referred to above at work or elsewhere, or though our own self-motivated study and focus on our own personal skills, knowledge and self-development. Again it is beneficial if we are all engaged in and involved in supporting the development of such expertise. Through such learning and educational development and achievement, we will be able to maximally support our own well-being, fulfillment and happiness and also maximally support the well-being, happiness and fulfillment as others. And the contributions of each one of us, not only to ourselves but to our community and social whole, are of the greatest importance if our communities and societies, our broader humanity, are to work effectively, if we are to live well and happily.

We thus all have an interest in promoting high-level expertise and understanding. In regard to the highest levels of expertise that we, or others, might achieve, assuming adoption and commitment to core and other principles and appropriate values as already discussed, it is of tremendous value to ourselves and our communities, societies and to our broader humanity, if we and others achieve such high levels of expertise. For example, in supporting others who have the greatest skills in construction and engineering or through developing such expertise ourselves, we will not only be able to put in place, support and replicate, amend and improve on current systems and designs, but we may also be able to originate or take part in moving our community's, society's, our humanity's engineering achievements forward, to support entirely new forms of engineering and design, perhaps paradigm shifting processes, designs and achievements which will effect the vast range of different areas of engineering, aeronautical, chemical, structural, electrical, electronic, automotive and more.

With the expert knowledge we have, we can support others in developing their expert knowledge. With expertise in the biosciences, we can help to develop individual and community, social knowledge in regard to those biosciences, through which we might, amongst other things, contribute towards supporting an enhancement of the levels, type and sustainability of food production, perhaps better deal with those infections or organisms which can destroy agriculture, with obvious potential benefits for us all. Amongst further areas of crucial biological learning and development, we might be able to contribute to better understanding and knowledge of diseases, the molecular biology and biochemistry of disease causing organisms, the nature of our own immunce systems, the vulnerabilities of our human bodies and the processes of aging, better understanding of our relationships as humans with the other organisms who share our environments as well as our relationship with our living and non-living environments themselves. We might perhaps even take part or lead in the discovery of previously unknown organisms or through paleontology and other means, identify hitherto unknown ancestral organisms that existed in our prehistoric past, thereby helping to trace more precisely the chain of organisms which have led to our human existence.

Through becoming experts ourselves or through promoting and supporting the development of expertise with regard to advanced learning and understanding of conflict and the causes of wars, with regard to skills and expertise in conflict management, in negotiation and diplomacy, we have the potential to be able to contribute to the safety and security of all through having the capacity to act effectively to help resolve disputes between individuals, groups of people, businesses, organisations and nations. The benefits to us all of promoting and implementing the use of such skills are transparent with the likely consequence, in for example the case of the prevention and avoidance of vast military conflagrations, of successfully preserving freedoms and human rights and saving hundreds of thousands if not millions from destitution, intense suffering, injury and death.

In regard to what might seem like a less practical focus, though indeed of great value, a high level of expertise in the examination and analysis of literature can support our enjoyment of that literature, providing new insights into that literature, helping us gain a deeper understanding of the nature of skilful and effective expression through writing, as well as, through our experience of and analysis of that writing, providing insights into the nature of the world around us and our nature as human beings. And developing the capacity and skill to write such skillful literature provides hundreds of thousands if not millions with substantial entertainment, interest, pleasure and indeed education itself.

The above are provided as examples of areas where high level expertise, high levels of skill, understanding and knowledge, developed through our highest levels of teaching and education, supported by our communities and societies at large, will contribute to the well-being, happiness and fulfillment of all. Yet the total sum of areas in which we can develop such advanced skills, understanding and knowledge are vast, including and ranging from skills and abilities in marketing, selling and promoting our products in our local shops, enhancing our skills at painting and decorating such we can achieve the highest standards, skills at planting and supporting the growth of crops, in developing our sporting skills, our organisational, strategic and planning skills, enhancing our knowledge of our social history, the psychology behind our thinking and actions, and the direct development and improvement of our thinking skills amongst others. Some of us will develop our knowledge and understanding of law as practitioners, including as makers of laws, but also develop our expertise in how to administer law in an optimal manner, as well as developing a broader understanding of the role of law, while others will focus on developing processes and actions, as already mentioned, in maintaining peace and cooperation within our communities and societies, and between communities and societies. Others will develop advanced medical, perhaps surgical skills. Further others will develop musical skills and abilities, or advanced expertise and skills in other areas of the arts. There are a vast range of areas in which we can develop our knowledge, skills and abilities, and in which we can, each one of us, do so to the highest level of expertise.

Underpinning much of our knowledge and many of our skills and abilities, and underpinning and indeed a route through which we can learn and implement this high level of expertise, knowledge and understanding, are research and research skills. Research can refer to our talking to and gaining information and knowledge from others through the range of channels, our explorations, reading books, magazines and research papers written by others, our doing new things we have not done before, our learning from our experience, listening to the accounts of others such as experts in our fields or in our areas of activity and interest, or even simply observing the activities and actions of others, with the purpose of gaining understanding and further information, knowledge and skills. Research also includes, and perhaps this is paramount in many important areas, our conducting formal and systematic empirical research, in the sciences, but also social sciences, often involving experimentation but also involving other forms of research, our formal empirical research involving systematic, detailed and often intricate study of phenomena in our world.

Through the range of different forms of research, through the resulting development of our personal knowledge and understanding, and the consequent scientific and social knowledge gained, understood and possessed by our communities and societies, as well as more globally we as individuals, as well as our communities and societies, can make progress such that we can enjoy enhanced well-being and happiness.

For many of us, doing research and finding things out is in itself a pleasurable activity. As individuals, aiming to answer questions and find out novel and new information and answers through research is exciting and stimulating, and not only through the pleasure gained from a developed personal and social understanding which will hopefully be the consequence of our research efforts, but also through the pure joy of exploration, the wonder and pleasure of discovery and, when we manage it, the pleasure of finding answers and even questions which were previously unknown and even previously unthought.

Moreover, to some extent, doing systematic and formal research is something which is valued by many as an activity in our communities and societies, with experimental and other empirical researchers, being often admired, especially by their peers, for their contributions to our world of knowledge, even if in many cases they are not known to the wider public. Those engaged in, and successful in, such research will undoubtedly experience the already mentioned pleasures of discovery, of answering longtime-unanswered questions, will experience the pleasure of ruling out incorrect explanations, or the pleasures of developing new, perhaps elegant, theoretical and other frameworks, or identifying and observing new and sometimes startling phenomena.

There can however, be difficulties, as complex and advanced research may sometimes not be valued and indeed expertise can and has, unfortunately, sometimes been derided, as the views of experts can conflict with common belief, every day perceptions, or additionally may clash with the views, ideas and interests of powerful interest groups, for whom expert and accurate comment is something which can be inconvenient and might act against their desires and interests. For example, in relation to common perceptions, democratically elected representatives may decide to fall in with and act in line with popular belief and opinion which might contradict scientific, rationally argued advice which is accompanied by supporting evidence, since these representatives will fear that if they do not listen to the populus, they will become unpopular and not be elected. Of course that is not acceptable and what is needed is effective explanation and presentation of the relevant evidence.

In other cases, important cases, for example, despite expert evidence on the dangers of smoking to our health, powerful lobby groups representing the tobacco industry attempted and have attempted to discredit, undermine or detract from research on the damaging effects of tobacco. In relation to current issues such as climate change, similarly lobby groups and representatives working on behalf of oil and other industries have engaged in substantive efforts to discredit climate scientists, clearly because climate scientists with predictions of global warming advocate the reduction in use of fossil fuels, something which contrasts with the negatively selfish, short-term, interests of many parts of the energy industry. Such actions by these individuals and groups, is reprehensible and damaging to us all.

In order to free themselves to take the actions they wish to take and, in some cases, in order to support the lobby groups which finance them, some politicians, journalist supporters and others have sought to discredit the notion of expertise in itself, a route which is a very dangerous route to take for us in terms of our support for well-being. Such a task is made easier for these individuals and interest groups by the complexity and extent of much expert advice, making it difficult for many of us to access fully and understand in full detail.

While of course it is correct to say that experts will often have different opinions and can sometimes be wrong, yet that is a capacity of all of us, to be wrong that is. Expert advice must be examined, analysed and evaluated in the same way as any other evidence should be examined, but if not agreed with, if there is disagreement and contradiction, this disagreement or contradiction needs to be on the basis of evidence-based argument, not on the grounds of simply dismissing expert opinion in general or dismissing communities of experts on the grounds that they are individuals with flaws or that expert communities comprise social groups which can be conformist. Such does not comprise an argument or evidence in regard to a specific issue under question and it is that argument and the evidence relevant to such specific issues and questions which needs to be considered above all.

Hopefully, while there may be challenges to those with expertise, those who are highly talented in their areas of work, study, research and practice, those who are indeed experts, they will also be able to communicate their expertise and key ideas effectively. And hopefully, they will gain the pleasure of recognition and acknowledgement by their colleagues, co-workers, clients and customers, our communities, societies and beyond for the work they have done.

It should be acknowledged, however, that in relation to research, much discovery is often the result of substantial effort and research over time, and frequently is the result of the work of teams or the development of thought and ideas over time. In our empirical and other research, we always need to acknowledge that our ideas and thinking are based in the ideas, the research, the experience of others, the history of ideas and thinking. Doing so represents positive, social conduct and helps and supports cooperation between and within our communities of researchers, serving to support and maintain our cohesive, yet diverse, research communities.

Given how valuable research is, both informal and informal, we need to ensure that in all the many areas in which we as individuals, our communities and societies have an interest, we pursue research in its necessary and various forms, in order to support us in developing our individual and social, expertise, knowledge and understanding.

As individuals, with regard to our more daily work, having such personal and research-earned expertise will hopefully contribute towards our enjoyment of our work, our staying secure in our work-life circumstances, and work positions, moving on to better jobs, or perhaps, at some point, our expertise will even support us in setting up our own organisations, charities or businesses. Having research knowledge and expertise, we should certainly be better able to do our daily work effectively and have greater success, taking into account all the other factors affecting our actions and performance. At home, our own private research in terms of resolving technical problems we may face on a more mundane daily basis, or through researching family life, personal health and living well together, as well as researching possible solutions to relationship and family problems is also likely to be of benefit to us. All of this represents education and learning and will of course tie in to our behaviour and general actions, behaviour and conduct.

From the point of view of our communities, societies and beyond research supporting the different forms of expertise already discussed, clearly benefits us all through advancing our communities' and societies' as well as our humanity's knowledge, understanding and expertise in the vast range of areas where our communities, societies and humanity need to operate and operate at maximal efficiency. And in relation to our own more personal actions in support of our communities, societies and the wider world, beyond engaging in our own personal research, recognising the tremendous societal and community benefits of research as an enterprise and activity, means that we as individuals, and as communities, societies and globally, need to be supporting research financially and funding research as a beneficial community and social enterprise which contributes to well-being and happiness.

For example, and clearly illustrating the benefits of research, our support, our efforts and our funding are needed to enable novel and groundbreaking research in medicine and medical technology. This research will clearly help to support the health of us all. More specifically, in terms of what this research can do, supporting research which helps us to understand the mechanisms through which, for example, viruses and bacteria, can attack and damage our bodies, together with financing research into the design of vaccines, antibiotics or other novel cures and remedies, is also clearly of vast benefit to us all. Research on other aspects of health, such as the relationship between poverty and health, lifestyle and health, diet, exercise, and potentially health damaging pollutants, are amongst many areas where research is required. Without our personal commitment and financial support, without the overall commitment and support of our communities and societies, such research will not happen, we will all be at risk, and indeed the health situations within our communities, societies and our broader humanity, may deteriorate substantially due to the continuing advent of new illnesses and diseases.

With regard to the energy industries and energy supplies mentioned already in this chapter, our research underpins our effective generation of the energy which we most certainly wish for, and which we need in order to sustain the complex and technology dependent human communities and societies in which the many of us live. The uses of our energy are of course legion and have been discussed elsewhere in this guide (light, transport, warmth, cooling, communication amongst others), however, in relation to research, in the current age, research has been and is being conducted into a vast range of exciting energy related areas, from efforts to develop solar energy, wind energy, tidal energy, development of battery technology, more effective and safer generation of nuclear energy, the use of other new forms of energy with lower levels of pollution (cleaner energy), new and more effective energy storage mechanisms, new systems for the distribution of energy and a countless range of other energy projects. Amongst other research, we need to be supportive of such energy research to sustain and develop our own well-being and the well-being of all.

In terms of researching other areas such as history, on the more, indeed on the much more personal level, while in some cultures there may be verbally transmitted memories of parentage and ancestry, in other contexts, as individuals we may spend time researching and investigating our pasts, the history of our families, delving into historic records of births, deaths and other recorded events, to find out where we as individuals come from, who was in our families, and perhaps aiming to find out the contributions that our more visible antecedents have made or made to our or their communities and societies in the past. For many of us there is clearly much pleasure in finding out about our ancestors.

We might also feel a connection with the places we were born and the places we live, and therefore research the history of the areas we live in, the people who lived there, their ways of living, the industries, the tools, the daily practices and beliefs of people from earlier generations, in our home cities, towns and villages. And, as individuals, we may have our own particular historical interests, such as an interest in the history of specific subject areas such as engineering or languages, astronomy, music and musical instruments, philosophy, liberty, culture, transport and tourism, amongst others.

Finding out about things through research can be highly absorbing and interesting. It is therefore worth noting for this reason and for others, that research is not simply for those who are known or referred to as experts or professionals in a particular area. The joys and pleasures of exploration and research are available for all of us to enjoy. Moreover, beyond the historical research already mentioned and beyond the kinds of research we can all do for pleasure, interest and personal education, it has been the case in many instances that those who have not achieved the highest levels of university or other education, have contributed in important ways to the world of research. Indeed, much original scientific research was conducted by more amateur experimenters and researchers. For example, the currently renowned Big Bang theory was formulated by a Belgian priest. Amateur astronomers have identified new celestial phenomena such as supernovae and stars. None of us should exclude ourselves from the possibility of our contributing to invention, creativity, discovery and more, simply because we did not attend or achieve the higher levels of formal education. We all have the capacity for tremendous originality, invention and creativity.

However, returning to historical research, those of us who are involved in conducting more formal historical research will be learning about and discovering more about our community, social and global histories, hopefully giving us further insights into the nature of the past and helping us to situate ourselves, provide us with an enhanced and more accurate view of where we belong within these histories and possibly providing us with information and ideas to inform our current individual, community or societal perspectives and decisions. Research in these areas is not, however, simply a matter of finding new information. It requires interpretation; it requires paradigms of interpretation, with effective history benefitting from the application and the capacity to generate such new paradigms of thought in regard to historical matter. The ability to invent or construct interpretations, new paradigms and new interpretations is at the core of world changing research in the range of areas. This requires the ability to invent and think differently (and indeed in some fashion sometimes 'wrongly') in order to enable us to identify that which is correct and true.

Research touches a vast range of other areas. For example, additionally, research in areas such as art, film and theatre helps us to rediscover, invent and create the new, that which is interesting and exciting, providing variety, interest and excitement in our lives, making what may be our sometimes rather mundane lives rather less mundane, and sometimes educating us further in terms of our human understandings, perceptions and capabilities. Research in music may help us understand the composition of music and how talented musicians generated their pieces, tracks, symphonies, operas, operettas, melodies, concertos and more, as well as perhaps suggesting how future writers might compose in effective and imaginative ways.

Research of all kinds in all areas underpins our current well-being, happiness and fulfillment. Of course we also may benefit from research into happiness and well-being and what exactly are the optimal routes to such happiness and well-being. Many ideas are put forward in this guide as to how such well-being and happiness can be achieved, nevertheless, it is certainly useful and will be useful in the future to pursue systematic research in order to identify the optimal pathways to well-being and happiness for each of us and all of us.

Without research into the range of possible areas, our well-being, happiness and fulfillment will not be advanced as they should be, our actions and conduct are unlikely to be optimal, and indeed, our well-being and happiness become vulnerable to future deterioration, in particular as the world changes around us continually and we are constantly faced with new challenges which demand individual and often novel and original responses if they are to be overcome. Notably, in times of crisis, one of the first things our representatives, our communities and societies consider seems to be reducing our commitment, support and funding of far-sighted formal and original research. Clearly there are often multiple factors impinging on any decisions our communities and societies will take, nevertheless the contributions of research, not only to our future and more distant well-being, but also to our current well-being and happiness, needs to be considered, with appropriate weight given to research, weight which recognises its immense value and importance to our well-being.

It has already been mentioned that it is best, if not necessary for us to treat learning and education as a lifelong process. Given the amount that there is to learn, given the variety of specialisms we could learn about, the variety of things we could know and understand in the world, given what for most if us is a constant interest in finding out the new and exploring, and given the always changing and developing state of our societies' knowledge and understanding about the world, such continuous and lifelong learning is essential. Added to these motivations for life long learning, it is valuable for us to know about new discoveries, inventions, new ideas and theories of living, the new evidence that comes to light in regard to currently held and old ideas, some of which shows our current and our former beliefs to be questionable and which thereby leads us towards personal change and new learning.

We also have to take into account our changing selves and our new appreciations of and perspectives on those things which perhaps we previously knew of, but somehow didn't fully know, understand or take on board, alongside our need to deal with the new challenges we may face day-to-day. Given all of these factors and more, it is important that we continue to learn both informally through our own explorations and reflections, through our own self-motivated learning and research, throughout our lives, and through joining in more formal social educational mechanisms and opportunities. Of course, our having such learning will benefit ourselves, others, our communities and societies and the wider world.

While, as already stated in this chapter, we can all of us act as teachers, and indeed we all need to some degree to be teachers, in many cases we may need and it may be wise for us to seek out the help of those teachers, coaches and mentors who have the specialist knowledge, skills and understanding in the particular areas we wish to study and in which we wish to develop our understandings and skills. Their help will be necessary in particular as we, as individuals, might in some cases need to engage in years of research and investigation to find key information and to develop our skills, while teachers and coaches in specialist areas will already have that specialist knowledge, understanding and skills, hopefully combined with teaching and learning skills, which they can pass on to us and many others at the same time, thereby massively enhancing the efficiency of our own learning and the overall learning process. Thus, with their help we should be able to efficiently and effectively develop our relevant learning, knowledge, understanding and skills. Indeed, due to their specialist and deeper knowledge, as well as their skills in helping us and others to learn, it is for many of us almost certain that through the varied stages of our formal learning and education, our learning and education will be supported by, be mediated by, if not led by paid and professional teachers, coaches, mentors and the like.

Indeed, having an appropriate professional and knowledgeable teacher can be crucial if we are to make appropriate and indeed rapid advances in our knowledge, understanding, learning and skills. We should still, however, be somewhat wary and recognise that teachers, as with others in the range of professions, have different levels of knowledge and understanding in their particular fields and different levels of skills in supporting others in learning. Effective teachers and coaches will involve us in the learning process and will need to work collaboratively with us as individuals to ensure we achieve maximum effectiveness and success. While already referred to in this chapter, it is worth reiterating that they should not allocate themselves the position and role of superior person, nor should we accept them or allow them to adopt such a role. These people are teachers and coaches and should not be considered superior beings to whom we should bow down in all matters, and sometimes, certainly as adult learners, we should not even bow down in relation to their subject matter.

Whether or not we have a professional teacher, it is ourselves as individuals, especially as we grow older, who are central to the learning which takes place. We, as individuals, are at the centre of our development and should lie at the centre of our motivation for learning and our practice of learning. That being said there should, as far as possible, be mutual respect between teachers and learners, and we as learners should respect the expertise and knowledge of others, respect our teachers, coaches and others, and we as teachers and coaches should respect those we are teaching, coaching and helping. In that way we will be best able to support learning and best able to support well-being, achievement and fulfillment.

It is important that we recognise that there are many of us who have developed tremendous skills in our own areas of study and practice, but on the other hand, we may for a range of reasons, while skilled and excellent ourselves at practising our skill or art, be on the moment, unsuitable as a teacher, perhaps needing to develop our skills at passing on our own subject-based knowledge and skills to others in certain teaching situations, in particular as teaching and coaching, mentoring others, are tremendous skills in themselves.

But, a truly competent, able and perhaps excellent teacher or coach will be able to give us much, and we, if we are excellent teachers and coaches, should be able to help significantly, in the main, though not always, those we teach. A teacher and coach's specialist knowledge and understanding of their subject or skill area will mean that they will have an understanding of what needs to be known in order to be proficient, excellent or even world leading in a field of performance or study. Their skills as a teacher or coach should mean that they understand their students, their pupils, that they can understand us as an individual, as well as knowing, understanding and being able to practise general and advanced principles in regard to their subject, performance or skill areas. Through their knowledge of their specialism, their skills as coaches and teachers and through their knowledge of us, such skilful teachers and coaches can guide us, point us in the right direction, support us in our understandings, provide us with important insights into not only specific areas of expertise, but sometimes may also provide broader insights into life, into our personal approach to life and even our relationships. A great teacher or coach can support our self-belief and self-efficacy, and more than that motivate and inspire us, sometimes throughout our lives, providing us with not only a thirst for learning and personal development in their own specialist areas, but also supporting and developing within us the thirst and the capacity to more widely explore, investigate, learn, understand and achieve.

If teaching or coaching is our profession then we have substantial responsibilities to those we teach and coach, while of course needing to ensure our own well-being and happiness, which undoubtedly will be contributed to through our support of our pupils and students, through those we teach. We will hopefully gain pleasure from and see them developing and growing and we will hopefully recognise that we are helping them on their way and supporting them in their current and future lives. As teachers and coaches, it will help us to be involved in a constant process of development and improvement of our teaching and coaching skills as well as developing our knowledge and understanding of any specific subjects, skills, performance and knowledge areas where we are responsible for supporting development. Further, as teachers and coaches we need to be continually developing our understanding of other people, those we teach, pupils, students, adults, how they learn, how they operate and cooperate and in a sense live together, either in classrooms, or in more 1:1 coaching, mentoring and learning situations. The effectiveness of our teaching should be enhanced by focusing on all of those whom we teach as individuals, and teaching them and treating each of them as an important individual.

For younger children, we, of course, need to ensure as far as we can, a safe environment in which children can learn, trying to suit our teaching to the manner in which they will best learn. Teaching our children as individuals, we need to be aware of the individual differences, individual skills, individual talents, propensities and aptitudes, and the individual needs of each of the children we teach. We need to be encouraging and supportive, accepting of error, while at the same time being demanding and aiming to help each child reach their maximum potential in the range of areas where they need to develop and perform.

We need to help each child to be excellent, something which they will hopefully achieve in their own way and according to who they are. We must enable them wherever possible and reasonable to have a voice and express their feelings and opinions, expecting increasing and developing levels of sophistication as they grow. We further need to ensure that our children have, as far as we can make this happen, appropriate caring values for others, that they are capable of cooperating with, working with and achieving with others. We need to do our utmost to ensure that the children we teach can put these ways of behaving, these values into practice. And that being said, it is clear and obvious that teachers, school and educational managers, politicians and others should never use children and education to support their own negatively selfish purposes.

When teaching adults, if in the role of teacher or coach, we need to be attentive and listening, aiming to meet the educational and learning needs of our students. We would hope that our more adult learners would be more self-motivated and thus will need lesser encouragement to learn, though that will not always be the case. Representing one of the aspects which can be most engaging about teaching adults is the questions and challenges these students can bring to our classrooms or teaching sessions, which may well serve to enrich us as teachers, enabling us ourselves to learn. As far as we can, we need to be dedicated to our students, supporting them in learning, doing our utmost to help them achieve their goals and dreams. As teachers, in our roles as teachers, we have crucial and fundamentally important roles in our communities, societies and in regard to the world beyond.

Whether a paid teacher, tutor or coach, whether we are a parent bringing up our own children, we have a responsibility to continue our own learning, both within our own areas of specialism but also more generally in regard to the world around us. It is essential for us to recognise as teachers, that a key element of education is to learn that indeed there is always more to learn, that no one can have full knowledge, that we are all fallible, lacking in and continually lacking in, some aspect of knowledge, understanding or skills, and that there is always that need to explore further and find out more.

In classroom situations, if this is the format in which education is taking place, in particular where many children and many young adults are being taught, in addition to the aspect of safety already mentioned, we all have responsibility for ensuring such environments are as enjoyable and enriching as possible, and supportive of learning of all those children present, indeed environments which in themselves support happiness, well-being and fulfillment. As parents and carers we need to do our utmost to ensure that, as far as possible, our children are able to cope in such environments, that our children will not be disruptive of the learning environment, and that our children will understand the nature of the environment and will themselves act in a manner supportive of teaching and learning, a manner which is social and supportive of other children and of teachers.

Whether we are teachers of children or adults, we need to ensure that the education and teaching we engage in is open in its content allowing access to different perspectives and beliefs, particularly those lying within the framework of core and other principles. We should not be depriving our students of key relevant and necessary information and opinions with the purpose of simply promoting our own group and our own group beliefs and perceptions. We should certainly never promote aggressive violence, racist discrimination, and other forms of oppression and abuse nor allow others promoting such ideas to have access to children in order to promote their heinous and destructive views.

Clearly acting as a teacher, being a professional teacher in formal or other surroundings is something which is central to supporting the well-being and happiness of others, and represents an important role for anyone to play in the lives of others and within our communities and societies.

Hopefully those of us who teach professionally will gain a deep pleasure through our work as teachers in supporting others in a manner which, working within the frame of core and other principles, also supports and underpins our communities, our societies and the wider world. As teachers, we will hopefully gain much pleasure in supporting others in developing the skills, knowledge and understanding they need, such that they can survive, thrive and enjoy well-being, happiness and fulfillment in the world.

Thus, hopefully as such teachers, we will gain pleasure and satisfaction through recognising our own contributions to the wider community through our teaching, which range from supporting the development of core and basic skills, knowledge and understanding in areas such as reading, writing, personal relationships, mathematics, social conduct, how to live with others, and more, as well as teaching and leading others to the development of the more complex skills, knowledge and understanding required by our societies, all of which underpin the effective functioning of our communities, societies and the wider world. It would seem fair to say that without effective teachers, coaches, mentors, trainers and more, without their skills in mediating, passing on and supporting the development of skills, knowledge and understanding as they do, we, others, our communities, societies and beyond would not be able to enjoy well-being, fulfillment and happiness to the extent that we are capable of doing.

Our children and young people have a responsibility themselves, differing in degree dependent on their age, to ensure that they are aware of and are caring about others, including their teachers, that they are supportive of learning in the classroom and do their utmost to learn and educate themselves, something that will support their own happiness and well-being into the future. As teachers, as adults in the classroom or in whichever context, we need to fulfill our responsibility in such situations to enhance learning, develop a pleasant environment and ensure the safety and well-being of the young people who are temporarily in our charge. Moreover managers and administrators, head teachers and those beyond, those with broader responsibilities relating to what is learnt and broader responsibility regarding education within our communities and societies, need to ensure that there are frameworks, ways of learning and other systems, most likely flexible in their nature, which not only support effective teaching and learning, but which also support well-being, fulfillment and happiness within the varied environments in which education and learning occur.

Clearly effective teachers can be extraordinarily important in supporting our learning. That is not to say that in many cases we cannot learn without the explicit contribution of professional teachers, coaches, mentors and trainers. Indeed while often important, and sometimes essential, they are not essential in all of our areas of learning. Indeed, sometimes teaching can be ineffective and to some degree detrimental to our learning and education, especially where there are ill-thought-out programs of study, in circumstances where there is encouragement of passivity in learners and learning, or where inappropriate ideological content is taught which is contrary to core and other principles. Incorrect and uninspiring approaches to teaching and learning may not only be ineffective in supporting learning, but they may damage learning to some degree on the moment or even damage our learning and desire to learn in the future.

Over focus on educational systems as means of selection rather than as means to achieving substantive learning, is one factor that can demoralise us and damage our thirst and desire to learn. If we are constantly tested and assessed, the sense of the need to learn for the purposes of learning and for the purposes of contribution to others, to our communities and societies, to the world around us, becomes subsumed under the weight of testing, under the oppression of overly intrusive external monitoring and our desire to learn can, as a consequence, be diminished or lost. While, as already discussed, there most likely need to be such systems of assessment, testing and selection, these should not become the be-all and end-all, and act to diminish learning and demoralise and oppress learners.

That being said, if we have the thirst and desire to improve ourselves and learn, in many instances we may be able to ignore those factors which might demotivate us, and we may well be able to engage in significant learning without having the presence of a face-to-face teacher. Indeed we may sometimes, if not often, achieve deeper and more sustained learning through motivating ourselves and engaging in our own learning using other channels, for example through books, through exploration and experience, through research, through reflection, evaluating our own learning, setting ourselves goals and targets, developing our knowledge of the nature of learning, and working out how to achieve our own learning goals in a more independent manner.

Informal learning has been mentioned a number of times in this chapter. For the youngest children, a key form of informal learning comprises play. Simple actions such as playing with a bucket and spade in the sand, pouring water and getting wet, painting pictures, shaping plasticine, placing bricks one atop the other to build towers, simple playing games of balance involving standing on one leg, skipping, hopscotch or other games are all routes to learning and should be encouraged. They give our children fun and happiness, and at the same time teach important things such as balance, about materials, about texture, coordination, cooperating with others and much more. At many ages play comprises a key route to learning, through fun and pleasure.

Another area already touched upon but which perhaps needs some more discussion is that of learning by our social entities, by our organisations, communities, societies and beyond. For not only do we need to be learning as individuals from our experiences and more formal learning, but our social entities need to be learning from their experiences and indeed from each other. While the world is ever changing and our social entities in their various kinds are faced with different and specific challenges through the years, nevertheless prior experience and expertise based on developing knowledge and experience can feed into our social entities' capacities to make more accurate and appropriate decisions. And this learning and development within our social entities needs to be ensured through systematic processes. In particular organisations should be wary of sidelining or discarding experienced members of their staff, whose wisdom and experience might contribute in valuable ways to discussion and debate, even if those views are not accepted in the face of our changing world with new ways of interacting and the development and introduction of new technologies.

Yet we as individuals need to support our social entities, in particular our broader communities and societies, our governments in particular, in recognising the value of this social learning, pointing out in particular, choices and actions in the past which have led to poor consequences, damage and destruction, with our aiming to ensure that such mistakes are not made again, and that new and appropriate decisions are tried with the aim of supporting well-being and happiness and reducing pain and suffering for all.

Overall, education, and learning are significantly influential if not essential in supporting us to success and achievement in our lives, as well as being essential in terms of supporting our communities, societies and broader humanity in comprising environments in which we can all achieve happiness, well-being and fulfillment. This being the case, in order to benefit us all, we need to ensure that all of our children, and as far as possible, all of us, whatever our age and stage of life, receive the best opportunities possible in terms of learning and education. Since the many of us, if not almost all of us, recognise this importance and influence of education, it is essential that we, as communities and societies, as a broader humanity, invest sufficient resources in supporting our systems of learning and education and do this in a manner such that this optimal education and learning is available to all.

In terms of our education systems and the educational opportunity that we and others are able to receive, we need to promote equality of opportunity in order to benefit us all. It is however, somewhat inevitable that there will be some level of inequality of opportunity in terms of education, with all parents being different, all teachers being different, all learners different, all classes different, with differing access to and differing decisions in regard to resources, and differing strategies adopted for using the resources we have. Some of this educational and learning diversity and inequality may be of benefit in some respects to our communities and societies. However, inequality of opportunity needs to be minimised, though we should be careful that this is not done at the expense of the quality of our educational experiences, and that it is not done at the expense of well-being, happiness and fulfillment of ourselves as individuals and of well-being, happiness and fulfillment in our communities, societies and the wider world.

Yet it is certainly the case that privilege in education, while clearly supporting some, denies capable individuals the opportunities which will not only benefit them as individuals, but denies them opportunities which will also benefit our wider communities and societies. And as a consequence educational privilege serves to underpin unfairness and injustice in communities and societies in a manner which cascades and amplifies unfairness and injustice through our communities and societies, through our lifetimes and over the generations. Thus, the money, resource-based and other sources and forms of privilege in education enjoyed by the wealthy and resource rich, privileges gained, for example, through recruitment of the best-qualified and perhaps in some cases the most knowledgeable and skillful teachers, gained through investment in the best facilities, and perhaps smaller classes, gained through facilitated 'who you know' and status-based access to difficult to enter higher and advanced educational institutions, needs to be countered, for example through redistributive action and similar provision and access for those who do not have access to such resources.

Yet beyond the resource-based origins of injustice and inequality of educational opportunity there can also be, in some contexts, a sense of educational elitism, that is the sense that there are considered to be certain superior forms of learning and education which are determined not on a rational basis in terms of their impact for our communities, societies and broader humanity, but on the basis of tradition, class, culture and convention. As a consequence, those who know about or who are educated in certain areas, in specific ways, at certain specific institutions, are not only seen as more expert and able in their subject areas, but their 'education' in such forms of learning and in such circumstances means that they are considered in some sense superior individuals, more worthy as individuals, more worthy of attention than others, and indeed are considered more worthy of employment in elite professions. Of course this is unjust, irrational and unfair, serving to exclude highly capable individuals, expert in other areas, from contributing and from reaching the heights that their efforts, learning and education deserve.

Yet, in line with core principles, we all need to recognise, respect and understand the value, not only of our own learning and education, of the skills and abilities we possess, but also the learning, education and indeed expertise of others, and we must therefore value and appreciate their attainments, their education and learning, and their contributions as individual human beings. But on the other hand, those of us who attain expert levels of qualification and ability in particular areas, be those advanced expertise in business, home construction and management, research, manufacturing, sports, music or wherever, while needing to be aware of both our own extent of ability, knowledge and understanding, also need to be aware of and understand our own limitations, understanding the achievements and skills of those less qualified or working in other areas, as well as valuing the contributions of those who have achieved different levels of expertise, or perhaps achieved in terms of high expertise in other specialisms.

While in some areas, we may have higher levels of skills, knowledge and understanding than another or others; while we may have enhanced levels of skills, knowledge and understanding in many areas compared to some others, it is a virtual certainty that others will have greater expertise, understanding and skill in some other areas compared to us, especially in those areas with which we are not so familiar. In support of well-being, fulfillment and happiness, we need to respect, appreciate and value the individuality, expertise and contributions of all others.

Thus, whatever our level of education and attainment, where necessary and reasonable, we need to express and act in humility, listen to others and recognise and value their contributions. We will all have, at least to some extent, different levels of skills and abilities in different domains of education and learning, perhaps different capacities for knowledge and understanding, different aptitudes for understanding and knowledge with regard to specific skills and abilities. There are few who can learn and then demonstrate the range of high levels of skills and knowledge in a multitude of areas.

In terms of learning the different skills, knowledge and understanding, if others approach us to seek learning and understanding, to gain information and knowledge, come to us for assistance with learning, we need to be supportive of them and their goals, although that may not necessarily mean providing precise and direct answers to their questions since that may not be the best way to help them learn and develop. And those of us who have lesser qualifications and ability in specific areas and are looking for support and help also need also to be appreciative of those who have the skills and abilities to help us, be appreciative of the help we receive, the skill and expertise of these others. The teaching and learning process should optimally be one of cooperation and mutual support. As individuals with knowledge and expertise, we need to encourage learning and expertise, and if we are those wishing to develop and learn, we should not be intimidated by the knowledge and expertise of others.

We have already discussed in this chapter the fact that there are some who have criticised the notion of expertise *per se*. We should certainly not deride the learning and expertise of others, even where its complexity may seem unfathomable to some of us, due to its intense specialist nature. Yet at the same time those with expertise and knowledge in specific areas need to show their respect for others and do so demonstrably, communicating their understandings and knowledge in as clear a manner as is possible.

Overall, it is essential that we as individuals, communities and societies promote and support a culture which values and supports education and learning, such a culture and such cultures being beneficial to all of us as individuals and to our communities and societies, to our global community.

Recognising the differences that exist in our learning and educational preferences, aptitudes, capacities, abilities and attainment, we need also to recognise that it is as a whole, as cooperative and social communities, societies, as a global community, that we manage and are most likely to generate well-being, happiness and fulfillment for ourselves and for others. Elitism, in an educational, as well as in any other respect, is damaging to our communities and societies and is contrary to the core and other principles presented in this guide, as is deriding the notions of skill development, learning and education.

Within a culture which is supportive of education and learning, we, as parents, as every day ordinary members of our societies, must ourselves value education and learning, our development of understanding, knowledge and skills, and we need to do so openly and explicitly. We need to clearly and explicitly support and encourage our children in terms of their learning and education, helping them understand the need for their own educational, learning and skills development and the need for their own and other's educated, skilled, informed and expert contributions to our communities, societies and beyond, as well as pointing to the range of ways that through education and learning , they can and will be able to contribute both to their own well-being and the well-being and happiness of our communities and societies as a whole.

Their contributions will include not only the more specialist areas of daily work they may enter in their later lives, but their contributions to others through their day-to-day human interactions as friends, parents, member of our communities and societies, through communicating their personal values, perhaps through supporting others directly, or through their contribution to public discussion and debate. Each of our contributions is necessary and the maximal contribution from each of us will most likely serve to benefit us all as individuals, as well as our communities and societies to the maximum.

Through this chapter we have seen that education, learning, training, the development of all our skills and abilities, are central to our own personal well-being, happiness and fulfillment and the well-being, happiness and fulfillment of others, our communities, societies and beyond. As individuals we need to participate in and support education and learning, both informally and through formal educational, learning and developmental systems which enable us to teach and learn, to exchange knowledge, skills and understanding. We further as individuals, communities, societies and beyond, need to invest in and support formal systems of education and learning, with the goal of our both learning and passing on our individual and social learning, and knowledge, and our understanding to coming generations and to those of our own and other generations who wish or need to develop their knowledge, skills and understanding. We need to recognise that it is beneficial to engage in learning continuously through our lives, that learning is a job never completed, engaging in learning through our formal channels, organised programmes and courses and through more informal means, learning and developing ourselves through exploration, experience and reflection amongst the many other ways to learn. With our support for education and learning in our own lives and in our communities, societies and beyond, we will be acting in line with core and other principles, acting to support our own well-being, happiness and fulfillment and supporting the well-being, happiness and fulfillment of all.

# Twelve

# Pursuing Peace and Cooperation, and Avoiding Violence

Our personal well-being and happiness, and the well-being and happiness of others in our communities and societies cannot be experienced and enjoyed in the presence of violence and the resultant pain, both emotional and physical, generated by aggressively violent conduct. Such aggressive violence is reprehensible, evil and entirely contrary to the core and other principles set out in this guide, comprising personal conduct which is entirely unacceptable in every facet. Thus, we need to eschew all aggressive violence and avoid, as far as is possible and reasonable, the use of physical force and violence of any sort, conducting ourselves in a peaceful, cooperative manner in pursuit of our well-being and happiness, and the well-being and happiness of all. This is a central requirement of the core and other principles presented in this guide.

Our human identity is both individual and social, both of these aspects of our identity requiring us to act in a social and cooperative manner. Operating and conducting ourselves in such a peaceful and cooperative manner means that in practice, in our daily lives, we must act in a manner and respond to others in a manner, which recognises the fundamental human value of others, of each individual person and which takes into account, in a manner consistent with core and other principles, their individual identity, their wishes, beliefs, opinions, perspectives and desires. We must act in a manner which demonstrates and embodies care for others, care for their well-being and their wants, needs and desires, and in a manner which recognises those others as separate and independent individuals, unique individuals, who are, however, of course, social in nature, being individual members of our communities, societies and our broader humanity, with responsibilities towards us as individuals, towards others, our communities, societies and our broader humanity.

Cooperation, peacefulness, integrity and sincerity, empathy, understanding, and indeed love for others are key bases through which we, others, our communities and societies, our broader humanity, should be aiming to pursue our goals. And certainly we should not be acting through aggressive violence, threat and intimidation. Aggressive violence and aggression in any form represent actions which, in themselves are, almost by definition, the contrary of the types of action required to support well-being and happiness, and are in themselves, by definition, destructive of our well-being and happiness.

Having stated unequivocally that aggressive violence is totally unacceptable and that we should eschew all violence wherever possible, instead basing our actions as far as possible in peacefulness and cooperativity, it is seen here and proposed here as of great importance and consistent with core and other principles, that we recognise and accept as legitimate the need for us, as individuals and communities, to use forceful action for the purposes of self-defence and the defence of others, physical action which, where used, should involve forceful action at the minimal level as required by the relevant situation and circumstances. The rationale for the legitimacy of such forceful response to aggressive violence will be discussed in detail later in this chapter, though in essence revolves around our responsibility to support the prevention and avoidance of pain and suffering of both ourselves and others in the face of such aggressive violence.

Nevertheless, beyond such use of minimal force for self-defence and protection of others, in terms of core and other principles, our pursuit of well-being and happiness and the avoidance and prevention of pain and suffering means that through our personal conduct and personal actions, we must never employ and must reject and counter aggressive violence, not just aggressive physical violence, but also the deliberate emotional and psychological hurting of others.

As mentioned above, setting out to harm others through aggressive violence is, by definition, inconsistent with the principles set out in this guide, creating suffering and pain, which the core principles require we reduce and, wherever possible, prevent from occurring in any shape or form. And, just as importantly, the use of aggressive violence through our own, out of control, reaction to our own pains and emotions, our responses to trauma, to rejection by another or others, our responses to slights and feelings of being disrespected, feelings of being unloved and unwanted, our jealously, anger, our painful feelings arising through our inability to cope with difficult situations; the use of aggressive violence in these and the range of other such situations is entirely unacceptable.

It is our responsibility to be people who can manage and control our actions and, as a consequence, respond peacefully and cooperatively in the face of difficult and challenging situations, doing our utmost, and indeed hopefully succeeding, in facing and resolving difficulties though cooperative action without violence, through patience, love and determination, and optimally with the minimal emotional pain and suffering to all.

There can be no reasonable contention, and indeed it is further, almost the case by definition, that those on the end of aggressive violence, the victims of aggressive violence, indeed the victims of any violence, will almost always suffer significantly and tremendously, physically and frequently psychologically and emotionally, sometimes, if not often, enduring the most intense suffering, pain, traumatic and damaging injury. At the most extreme end, we can of course be deprived of our lives as a consequence of aggressive violent conduct taken against us. Effects of such aggressive violence can, not only be damaging physically and psychologically in the short term, but can also traumatise and damage us for the rest of our lives.

The core principles stand against all such aggressive violence. We, as individuals, those individuals who are the victims of this violence, certainly do not wish to be victims and on the receiving end of such violence. We do not wish to experience violence, violence which is so destructive of our individuals lives, violence which assaults the lives of all of us as individuals, violence which threatens, intimidates and creates fear. We do not wish to experience such violence, which is so destructive of our local communities, our societies as well as our global community and our humanity as a whole.

Violence damages us not only through the direct personal pain it inflicts, but it also damages us all through destroying the capacities of our communities and societies as well as our global community, to support the well-being of their members. Amongst other destructive effects, aggressive violence serves to promote the already mentioned fear, which damages our relationships and interactions, restricts our actions, and undermines trust and cooperation. It undermines our communities and societies, our global humanity, through the need to take actions, divert resources and engage in activities to defend against this aggressive violence. And aggressive violence often directly damages our physical resources and capacities, our homes, our sources of income, our sources of food and water. Unfortunately, and indeed, for some of those pursuing aggressive violence against others, such actions may be part of their strategies and tactics to achieve their negatively selfish, destructive goals.

Aggressive violence further damages community and society, our broader humanity, through the traumas experienced by those exposed to the sight of such violence, through the traumas who see those they love most being deeply hurt, injured, damaged, perhaps murdered through such aggressive violence. Alongside the incapacitating and traumatising effects of violence on ourselves and others and the effects on those who love and loved those affected by such aggressive violence, we all suffer further through the incapacitation or deaths of those individuals who are the victims of such violence, who also are either no longer around, no longer able, or who are less able to contribute to their families, our communities, societies and our broader humanity. Moreover, aggressive violence means our caring communities and societies, our broader humanity need to provide support and resources for those who have been victims of such aggressive and traumatic violence and who live on beyond their experience of this aggressive violence. While many will be traumatised and damaged by such aggressive violence, hopefully, many, if not, perhaps optimistically, almost all who experience such aggressive violence, will recover to some extent, significantly or fully, and will find at least some level of well-being, joy and happiness. We need to do all we can to help them achieve this recovery.

Of course, we all have the individual capacity to use physical force against others to one degree or another. However the only legitimate occasions when we should use such physical force are where we need to defend ourselves against aggressive physical violence or where we need to defend others from aggressive physical violence. And where we use physical force, as already mentioned, this must be at the minimum level necessary to achieve that self or other defence. Our laws and systems should enable us to use such minimal force and we should operate within legal frameworks.

Such forceful action might be characterised under some, if not many circumstances, as our using of violence, and it might seem like playing with words to suggest that our physically forceful actions, under some circumstances, to prevent others engaging in aggressive violence, might not involve our doing violence. Nevertheless, use of physical force under such self and other protective circumstances is certainly not the same as violent aggression and, dependent on circumstances, using a high level of physical force, even force which might produce fatal outcomes is seen in this guide as being legitimate. For example, in extreme circumstances, disabling someone engaged in a violent murderous assault against ourselves or others, and causing them pain or even fatally damaging them through the use of a weapon or otherwise, must be considered legitimate under such extreme circumstances. That being said, we should be aiming to use the minimal force to retain our safety and the safety of others, and wherever possible should be seeking peaceful and non-violent ways to prevent aggressive violence wherever we can.

Yet for many of us, if not perhaps almost all of us, due to our personal physical capacity for forceful and violent action it may be the case that, where circumstances and situations support it, we might be at risk of engaging in aggressive violence. That is to say that, perhaps, that we all, or almost all of us (or many of us), have the capacity to do aggressive violence. As already referred to, this might occur when we are having difficulty coping under various conditions, including those of severe emotional stress, anger, emotional hurt, jealousy, severe mental and psychological provocation, or in certain circumstances where we may be under threat if we do not engage in ordered and societally, socially or community mandated violence, or when we are under other forms of severe social, peer and other pressure from others, to engage in aggressive violence.

Recognising this capacity for the many of us to use physical force, violence and indeed at times, aggressive violence, it may be wise not to 'other' aggressive violence, by considering it as solely the province of the psychologically disturbed, dysfunctional, defective, vile and evil, but to recognise that many of us, under severe emotional strain, stresses and a range of circumstances including those already mentioned, may have the capacity for such reprehensible destructive and damaging action ourselves.

Nevertheless, while acknowledging that we might find it difficult to cope in certain situations, while some of us might feel highly aggressive, considering thoughts of aggressive violence, and indeed, while we might feel pressured to engage in aggressive violence, we should never engage in such aggressive violence, whatever the perceived psychological, emotional, verbal, violent or other non-violent provocation or pressures from others upon us, and we should prepare ourselves and develop ourselves mentally and otherwise, train ourselves and learn in terms of responses to stresses and pressures, in order to ensure that we will not engage in such violence, such aggressive violence being detrimental to the well-being and happiness of us all, and almost certainly resulting in pain and suffering for all concerned.

While we are fundamentally social and cooperative as human beings, we need to ensure that we develop ourselves to act cooperatively and peacefully, developing our personal strategies and ways of dealing with extremely difficult and stressful situations, developing our approaches to dealing with physically threatening situations, and situations where violent action may already have taken place, developing our true care for others along with the skills, tactics, strategies and abilities to promote peace, cooperation and non-violence. This will enable us to deal with the most severe and challenging circumstances and situations and, as a consequence, we will hopefully never engage in aggressive violence ourselves with the damaging consequences for all that will result. Our families, communities and societies through our upbringing, education and through whatever means possible need to help us develop the personal skills, the emotional and physical self-control such that we will never in our lives engage in such aggressive violence.

Yet, as already mentioned, we do have a perfect right in terms of core and other principles to protect ourselves and others from aggressive violence. In terms of core principles, supporting our personal well-being, we have the perfectly legitimate right to defend ourselves against attack and to do so forcefully, but, in line with core and other principles, we must do this with the previously mentioned minimum force necessary such that we ourselves do not experience pain, hurt, injury or even death and such that those against whom we are defending ourselves, optimally, do not suffer, or suffer at the minimum level necessary for our self-defence and defence of others.

As human beings we all have that legitimate right to defend ourselves and possess different degrees of capacity to act to defend ourselves forcefully. We all have some capacity to hurt others physically (as well as psychologically and emotionally). We are to an important extent, physical beings. Yet, despite our common physicality, we must not use this physicality and capability in order to engage in aggressive violence towards others. We should always look for other alternatives and peaceful responses, wherever we can, sometimes even in the face of aggressive violence. We need to avoid physical, violent and aggressive conduct and physical conflict wherever reasonable and possible.

The impulse for some, or many of us, at certain times, to consider, or feel that we wish to take or to actually take violent aggressive action may originate from many causes, or indeed perhaps no visible and obvious overall cause aside from the situation in which we might find ourselves. But there may be those of us who are simply biologically, psychologically and emotionally more inclined towards aggressive violence than others. It may also be that through being unaware of and untrained in alternative peaceful and cooperative approaches, through being unable to invent peaceful solutions, through being unable to understand the perceptions or feelings of others, through absence of the ability to diffuse tense situations, or perhaps through seeing talk and compromise as being signs of weakness, that some may turn to aggressive violence.

Use of drugs such as alcohol may for some people bring out or exacerbate aggressive tendencies with these drugs used in some cases as excuses for aggressive violence, which distract from real causes and aggressive feelings, thinking and outlook. Some of us may have been brought up in families where violence has been commonplace, in localities and communities where violence is witnessed frequently, perhaps everyday. We may have been brought up in families, communities or societies which lionise violent conduct as something to be admired and look down on cooperative and collaborative conduct. Such backgrounds and contexts are highly likely to support use of aggressive violence by those, and amongst those, who have grown up in these contexts and who have themselves experienced such violence.

Nevertheless, as individuals, whatever our feelings and context, we must put aside any such impulses, feelings and urges to use aggressive violence; we must put aside destructive pressures, urges to conform which support us in becoming part of violent cultures, and we must not engage in aggressive and violent action whatever our feelings, emotional states, drives, urges and impulses. And, as mentioned above, our families, communities and societies wherever possible, need to act against any such tendencies through upbringing, education and other peaceful and effective means.

Considering further the origins of aggressive violence which may lie inside each of us, it is of course a common observation, most likely an observation made by all of us, that young children and child siblings may engage in physical conflict at times (though of course at other times children and child siblings will play together, work together and cooperate). The physical, forceful and sometimes aggressive actions we see among young children, are, of course, the actions of children, not adults, with the youngest children being often unlikely to know, less able to understand or perhaps being less capable of grasping other more complex ways of interacting and behaving to achieve their goals and wants, nor sometimes being able to set aside that which they want in exchange for the longer term benefits and happiness of peaceful cooperation, happiness and friendship.

We aim, and indeed we must aim, as adults, as parents, as teachers, as members of our communities and societies, to prevent such aggressively violent, physical and forceful action amongst young children. We must aim to prevent aggressively violent acts by one child against another, and to steer our children away from taking aggressive physical action. We may aim to restrain them verbally or otherwise, where necessary, looking for immediate effect, such that no one is hurt. 'Otherwise' does not include aggressively violent actions ourselves such as hitting and smacking, but can mean using forceful restraint or moving the child or children away from where they have committed their act, away from those they may have hurt, actions which are of course more easy to implement in regard to young children than adults. We will further, be pointing out to our children in no uncertain terms, what is unacceptable conduct, requesting they apologise and express regret. Moreover we should be demonstrating cooperative, non-violent and peaceful approaches ourselves in response to our own frustrated wants, desires and needs, as well as teaching our children self-control, the need to, and how to put up with, not receiving their wants and desires, many of which may not be quickly or indeed, ever achievable.

That understanding and self-control is part of becoming a full adult member of our communities and societies. And as children grow older, we anticipate and hope that they will always become better able to engage in peaceful and cooperativity activity, helping to build effective social relationships, friendship, love and togetherness, supporting others, our communities and societies, our broader humanity without resorting to unacceptable and heinous aggressive violence to achieve their wants, desires and goals.

Whatever our experiences through growing up, in terms of conduct experienced and violence that may have occurred towards us in the family home or elsewhere, such conduct which may have influenced and affected us deeply; whatever the culture or environment we are experiencing and living in; whatever the other potential origins of our thoughts and actions in relation to enacting aggressive violence, it is our individual responsibility not to support, engage in or take part in aggressive violence against others. While it is likely the case that those of us who experience violence in our family homes or upbringing, or in our local community and culture, in cultures where violent conduct may be frequent, are more likely to engage in violence ourselves, this provides no acceptable excuse or obviation of our personal, individual, adult responsibility for any acts of aggressive violence we might take, with our personal conduct being our own personal and individual responsibility. We must not engage in aggressive violence.

Having mentioned contexts and upbringing, acting with aggressive violence is not and need not be a consequence of such upbringings and contexts. If those backgrounds and contexts have been our experiences, it is our individual responsibility, helped and supported by others where necessary, to go beyond those experiences and act with peacefulness, love and understanding towards others. It is our own personal responsibility to pursue peace and happiness, to change and develop ourselves where necessary and, to do so, however difficult, for the benefit of our own well-being, the well-being and happiness of others, and indeed to support the well-being and happiness of those whose futures are yet to come. That is not to say that this might not sometimes be difficult and challenging, but it is to say that our actions are our responsibility and aggressive violence is entirely unacceptable, destructive and indeed evil.

While the notion of a cycle of violence within someone's life, in which someone who experiences violence then goes on to do violence, seems likely to contain some degree of truth, it is rather a simplistic model, in particular as those people who experience such violence against them will, on the whole, have had many experiences including at least in some cases, hopefully having experienced more peaceful conduct and the more peaceful resolution of problems. Nobody is committed to repeating what they have seen or experienced and it is our individual responsibility not to engage in any such aggressive violence. We cannot hold others in the past, other individuals or generations before us as bearing personal responsibility for our own personal conduct.

There are many who grow beyond bad and violent experiences in their childhood or upbringing, transforming themselves into more peaceful people, engaging in more peaceful strategies in response to their feelings, their moods, their emotions, and finding peaceful solutions to problems. And as parents and adult members of our families, communities and societies, as well as in our position as members of our broader humanity, whatever our previous experiences, we have obligations within those social contexts, to present and promote peaceful models of conflict resolution, to teach people, to teach our children, how to pursue peaceful cooperative solutions, to guide others in adopting and achieving peaceful and cooperative ways to live, and we have obligations to try to help in whatever ways possible, young people and older people, in identifying and supporting more peaceful solutions.

And while a person who has previously experienced violence themselves or who may have been damaged by violence in the past, (though not necessarily so) may have reasons which have influenced them towards aggressively violent conduct, should they be engaged in inflicting violence on ourselves or others, it is likely to be the case that, to those of us who are on the end of such violence, our aggressor's pain and previous hurt and experience is unlikely to be of significant consideration, at least on the moment and in the short term, and certainly will not be perceived as in any way equivalent to that of ourselves as their victim or intended victim. Other strategies having been tried out in order to deal with this aggressive violence, we are obliged to, and must do, and will need to do, whatever we can, at a minimum level of force, to defend ourselves, to ensure we are not hurt and to ensure we ourselves and others, do not suffer physical and other forms of pain and suffering.

While it has been stated that we perhaps all, or the most of us, have the capacity to hurt others and engage in physical and forceful actions, as discussed at some length in chapter four in part one of this guide, we all have the capacity, the propensity and indeed the human need and requirement as adults (and indeed as children), to work with others, to be cooperative, to be positive, caring, loving and constructive, and to refrain from violence and the hurting of others, all of which support our well-being and happiness. We all have the need and capacity to cooperate and work together, and indeed, as part of our human identity, we must cooperate and work together for the purpose of supporting our own individual well-being and happiness and the well-being and happiness of others. Without such cooperation and togetherness, our communities and societies, our broader humanity cannot operate effectively and we, as individuals, cannot enjoy well-being and happiness. Cooperation and working together as peacefully as we can are fundamentals to our individual achievement, well-being and happiness as well as the achievement of happiness and well-being of others, in our communities, societies and broader humanity.

As opposed to violent conflict and aggressive violence, the benefits of our cooperation with others are transparent and legion. In broad terms, without our individual ability to cooperate with others we cannot enjoy well-being and happiness. Yet in more specific personal terms, for example, of course, as partners involved in loving, sexual relationships certainly we need to be able to cooperate peacefully. As loving and sexual partners, we need to cooperate well with each other in our day-to-day lives to support our daily happiness and well-being. And where we have children, we need to cooperate and work together in order to care for and raise our children.

In order to enjoy friendship we need to be able to get along with and cooperate with others, with our friends. At work we need to be cooperative with our colleagues such that work tasks and goals can be achieved and we, in the main, in the context of work and business need to be cooperative with our clients and customers in order to support our winning of effective income for ourselves and our families and indeed to support our clients and customer needs, something which in itself should support satisfaction, fulfillment, well-being and happiness. Anti-social and uncooperative behaviour will damage our relationships and support misery and unhappiness.

Much emphasis is given in public discussions in many contexts to the importance of competition. However, looking around any of our modern, complex societies will demonstrate the vastly greater importance of cooperation in our lives and in our human societies. Our complex, in particular urban societies illustrate starkly the vast need for and benefits of our cooperation, demonstrating not only the fact that we need others, but demonstrating the great extent to which we need those others and the clear and fundamental role cooperation between ourselves and others plays in supporting and enjoying our well-being.

For example, in terms of our fundamental and basic requirements for food, while if we live in less complex agrarian communities or societies, we will most likely grow much of our own food, if we live in modern complex urban societies, then in order to gain our food, of course needed for our survival, we need the producer of seeds, the farmer, the harvester, the collection and distribution systems, the packagers, the sales outlets, the marketers, accountants, the currency manufacturers and more, all to cooperate effectively together.

To enjoy the clean water without which we cannot live, in the context of our urban societies we need the building of effective water collection systems, such as dams (though dams have many other roles). We need the network and pumping systems to transport that water to our homes, the technology to use such water in our homes (water tanks, taps, showers, baths, sinks) and then, once water is used, it needs to be effectively transported away from our homes, cleaned appropriately then recycled back into the environment with any toxic wastes in the water disposed of. All of this requires vast collaboration and cooperation.

To keep our homes warm in the summer (or cool as the case may be) to help us to cook our food, to power our lighting in the dark, we need vast industries of energy production and distribution, sources of metals and minerals, capacities for design, development and research, industrial plants to generate our energy as well as the capacity to manufacture various products which such energy will put to work. And without cooperation and the capacity to cooperate, none of this would be possible.

Our bridges, our roads, our vehicles for transport, our computers and mobile phones, our coffee machines, our chairs, tables, houses, and so much more, all depend on complex interconnections and interactions between us and complex cooperation, which we all need to recognise the importance of. Our administrative systems, our health systems, our transport systems, our sewerage systems, our systems for supplying energy, our pensions and social support systems, our tax systems, our systems for management of resources, our capacity for law, defence and more all require cooperation. Our research and development, our education systems, our systems for government all require vast levels of organisation and cooperation.

And beyond these more materials needs, our cooperation with others is required to support our basic human emotional needs, for our pleasures and entertainments to be enjoyed, be they sex and love, sports, theatre, games playing, dance, comedy, watching television or videos, reading, holidays in other countries and much more. And internationally the peace of the world requires international and global cooperation. And all of this cooperation needs to be as effective and as peaceful as possible, with threats to such cooperation jeopardising the well-being and happiness of us all.

And cooperation, including working together, and both giving help to and receiving help from, others, is frequently needed in the stressful and challenging situations we may face in life. In pursuit of lives of well-being and happiness, we can be faced with many such strenuous and stressful challenges, the nature of these challenges varying dependent on many factors, more immediately, sometimes, depending on factors such as the nature of the living world and climate in our local environment, the type of family, community and society we live in, our particular positions within those communities and societies, our work circumstances, and perhaps changes in the human, social and economic environment around us, as well as other factors relating to the precise circumstances and situations in which we find ourselves.

Whatever the challenges we face, whether these be challenges of natural disaster, whether they be the malevolent, negatively selfish and self-interested actions of others, be they disease, injury and potential death or force of other circumstance, we must do our utmost to act cooperatively and peacefully with others, avoiding violent and aggressively violent responses beyond what is necessary for our self-protection and the protection of others. We must live and work cooperatively and collaboratively with others as far as we can.

Considering more specific situations, at a local family level we may face stress in terms of finding the resources to look after our families, even to feed our children and keep them sheltered and warm. Under such circumstances we will need to do all we can to engage with others and cooperate with others, seeking mutual support such that we can find the food, warmth and shelter that we need. And of course, if we meet families, others in such a situation it is our responsibility within core and other principles to help them out, and hopefully at some point, if we ever need help and support, they will support us.

If we are in conflict with our partners, wherever possible we need to aim to cooperate with them, at least in terms of the practical matters, however upset we might be. If our intensely loved partner has taken another lover and we feel betrayed and let down, indeed perhaps devastated, we may wish to end that cooperative partner relationship, and the decision about that would and should be down to us. While possible as a general principle, it may feel impossible for us to maintain a close cooperative relationship with someone who has let us down so badly. And thus, while we may need to and indeed should nevertheless cooperate in practical matters where children are involved or where possessions and resources need to be shared out, there is no obligation on us to keep a close emotional relationship with that partner and continue our close emotional relationship. Our personal and individual well-being, as well as the well-being of any relevant children, will need to be paramount.

On a broader level, but still tied to our possible personal experiences, there may be some particularly trying circumstances that we might unfortunately face where our desire to be peaceful and avoid violence might be somewhat or heavily challenged. For example, we might find ourselves, and this is not so unusual, falsely accused and the subject of abuse and opprobrium. In more extreme cases, we may be unjustly imprisoned, subjected to physical repression, made to suffer physical, psychological and emotional pain in one way of another. In other circumstances, where there are unjust governments and unjust laws, we may find ourselves, for example, confined to our homes through repressive measures, unable to meet with others, talk to our friends, denied access to education, denied the right to engage in ordinary social and economic activity and political activity in order to support our reasonable and peaceful goals. In all of these circumstances, we will have to, we are obliged to, take action to support our own well-being and the well-being of others, doing whatever we can to prevent ourselves and others from enduring and suffering pain and misery.

Yet we need to do so as far as possible in a peaceful manner, optimally and initially in cooperation with all. Where our cooperative actions, our working with and attempting to persuade those who are oppressing us, are not successful then, dependent on the circumstances and the level of threat to our well-being, we may try peaceful non-cooperation and non-compliance. And our responses to the forms of challenge described, wherever this is possible, and this is not always possible, should as far as possible and whenever possible, not be violent or causing of pain and suffering to others. Importantly, our legitimate right to defend ourselves with physical force where necessary, in the face of direct physical attack, has already been stated, and if our oppressors engage in violent physical attacks against us. threaten or engage in other forms of destructive attack or oppression, such as unjust confinement, removal of basic liberties, casting us into poverty or if we reasonably suspect or expect that such attacks are planned or will happen, then we may have little alternative but to use minimum physical force, sometimes and where necessary, pre-emptively, to defend ourselves and to defend others.

More than that, if we are threatened by poverty and starvation, death from the cold, disease, or other sources of pain and suffering, and there is the capacity available to remove these threats, then we must in the first place, wherever we can realistically do so, take whatever social, independent and peaceful action we can to alleviate our situation, searching out and enacting whatever we can do, to improve our situation. We must also draw the attention of others and other social entities to our situation where this is practical and reasonable, and seek support to alleviate our suffering, where such support is possible, available and necessary. We may seek such support on our own or in combination with others. Further, if we are suffering in poverty and starvation, then those with resources and wealth are themselves obliged, in line with core principles, to help us and alleviate our suffering, helping us out of our suffering and pain, and towards an improved and sustainable state of well-being.

Should we be faced with intense pain and suffering and if our situation cannot be relieved by our own peaceful and cooperative actions; if in the face of our peaceful efforts at persuasion, our protests and perhaps our subsequent deliberate non-cooperation with those in power; if others refuse to help us or place feeble and false excuses in the way of providing the help we desperately need, then it is perfectly acceptable to aim and determine to use physical force to get that which is essential for our continued living, the continued lives of those in our families, communities and societies, from others, defending ourselves from attack, though we must use the minimal force necessary to achieve these ends and make intense efforts to avoid causing significant pain and suffering.

This is not seen as aggressive violence. Imposition of our starvation, extreme poverty and likely death, by deliberation or in a systematic manner, in the presence of sufficient resources which if used to support us would mean that our lives could be preserved, represents a form of physical aggressively violent attack on us, and our response in terms of the use of physical force comprises essential action to preserve and promote our own well-being and the well-being of others. Nevertheless, as far as is possible, wherever we can, we should aim to minimise hurt and injury to others through such forceful actions, nor should these others be deprived of material things such that their own well-being, their own survival is threatened. Forceful actions of this nature should optimally follow much else which has been peaceful and cooperative.

And, as stated we have an obligation to do our utmost in the context of our families, communities and societies working with others, and also where necessary independently as individuals, to alleviate our poverty and potential starvation. But there is no legitimacy in our dying from starvation, no legitimacy in our suffering intensely from easily curable diseases, dying of cold through lack of shelter, and enduring other forms of suffering, when our well-being could be supported by the action of others, our communities and societies, our global entities, which have the capacity and the resources available, but refuse to help us.

And it needs to be recognised that some of those who have acted in truly malevolent and murderous ways have used poverty and starvation as weapons in deliberate efforts to murder many thousands, if not millions, of those they consider to be their enemies, those they consider their inferiors, those who they consider different and 'other', those they consider a threat, deliberately withholding food supplies, cutting off water supplies, chasing people from their homes so that they become destitute landless refugees, being as a consequence unable to grow food or gain income, as well as these malevolent individuals doing much more to achieve their heinous aims. Again we need to make every effort to ensure that such does not happen and need to work against such actions in a peaceful and cooperative manner, as far as is possible, However, of course we must do whatever we can to ensure such murderous and malevolent individuals are not successful in their actions, and we should not be naive in relation to the perceived intentions and actions of such malevolent individuals, groups and organisations. We are certainly justified, when other methods and approaches have failed, in taking forceful action to ensure that we and others do not significantly suffer in intense poverty and destitution, that we do not suffer their violence and that we can live on.

And when those acting in malevolent, negatively selfish, destructive ways or those acting destructively for other reasons, reasons which they may consider legitimate; when these people attack our basic freedoms, again, wherever possible, we need to adopt peaceful means in opposing them and their actions, while maintaining our well-being and happiness, our own safety and security, organising and acting in concert with others, in order to pursue and maintain our legitimate freedoms and our legitimate and reasonable need and desire for well-being and happiness and the well-being and happiness of others.

Yet if we cannot remove the yolk of oppression through peaceful and cooperative means; if we have our basic human freedoms, our reasonable rights to speech, communication, travel, rights in regard to having children, our right to generate an income, rights to fair trial and justice, and many more basic rights removed from us, and if we are being made to suffer in pain, then, wherever possible, having tried those discursive, cooperative and peaceful methods, and indeed having refused to cooperate with and accede to unjust laws and oppression, all other things being considered, including measuring the consequences of our actions, it is certainly legitimate to turn to more forceful means of obtaining justice and removing our pain and suffering.

Those of us suffering under the oppression of slavery, those of us who are imprisoned on no legitimate, just and reasonable grounds, those of us who are physically attacked or suffer significant damage or distress inflicted by others, our communities and societies, because of our race, because of our sexuality, those of us who are denied our core and basic freedoms, then in those cases where peaceful means have produced, are producing and are likely in the future to produce no or minimal alleviation of our situations, then we have a perfect right to defend themselves and fight for our rights using as peaceful a means as possible, using force but employing the minimum level of force, a level of force which causes the minimum level of pain and suffering to others.

Unjust and unfair systems, indeed highly unjust, unfair and discriminatory systems can operate in the organisation, governance and administration of our communities and societies (including within democratic systems), yet these systems and cultures of what may be entrenched and deep injustice and unfairness, may not necessarily threaten the basics of our existence, our basic freedoms, may not visit extremes of poverty and suffering on the many, the few, or even on anyone at all, with these systems not explicitly and openly aiming to destroy or damage opponents of these systems, in some cases even defending their right to protest. Rather than visiting substantial oppression, these systems, indeed cultures, and the individuals within these systems and cultures, will act unjustly and unfairly, indeed discriminate by, for example, privileging some in relation to others, through their actions promoting or sustaining unfairness and inequality of opportunity, for example in the context of education, or through promoting and sustaining unfairness and inequality of living conditions, through promoting and sustaining unfairness and inequality of health treatment, and much more.

This injustice, inequality and unfairness does and will have damaging effects on communities and societies as well as our broader humanity, making our social entities less cohesive, with less sense of togetherness, sense of common interest and purpose, breeding resentment and discontent amongst the many, at least in part because a reality of our humanity and human identity is that our personal status and position within our communities and societies matter to us and we tend to see ourselves and our positions in relation to others within our communities and societies. Seeing others enjoying wealth and privilege to a high degree, feeling that we are denied opportunities available to others, simply because of birth, family, class and privilege undermines to an important degree our sense of well-being and happiness.

Moreover, such privileging of some will have real effects on others. Our earnings, if we are those who are not privileged, our level of resources, our daily quality of life will be somewhat lower. Our access to medical treatment will be poorer. We will, on average, die earlier than the privileged. We will be more likely to be subject to discriminatory and unfair application of law and, as a consequence, injustice. Our schools may be good but will not be as good, will not have the facilities of the schools of the privileged; our access to entertainments and other aspects of life which can enhance our quality of life, will be lesser. Our children will have lesser prospects of achieving success in their lives, though they can still be successful if not, in some cases, highly successful.

For those of us wishing to have better systems of administration and governance, our responses to such situations needs to be, wherever possible, organised, robust, peaceful and democratic. As far as we can, we need to operate through discursive means, cooperating with others, promoting our opposition to such systems and offering real systematic improvements in our systems and cultures such that our overall communities and societies, as well as our broader humanity, are better off in terms of well-being and we and all others are better off in those terms. Such actions may be difficult because there may be deeply entrenched systems of power operating in particular through unbalanced and undemocratic channels of information and media, operating on behalf of those with power and influence; such action may be difficult because the privileged have access to vast resources to support their privilege and can promote and invest in support for those who will argue and fight their case; such action may be difficult because of apathy amongst the many, since without clear, obvious, intense and frequently observed suffering by many, life may seem to be ok, with basic standards of medical care, education and other elements of a good life in place, within the context of such unfairness and injustice.

Nevertheless changing and improving such systems, while difficult should be achievable and possible, and indeed is likely to be in the interests of us all. Discussion, debate, promotion of greater levels of equality would seem reasonable responses to such situations as well as non-cooperation with such unfairness and injustice. Our use of physical force in such a democratic context against systems which are not violently oppressive, in which we maintain a reasonable quality of life, opportunity for success to some degree, reasonable levels of freedom and self-expression, which respect our privacy and individuality would not seem appropriate. Use of physical force and indeed what would be seen here as aggressive violence under such situations would run the risk of causing substantive destruction and undermining what is a reasonable quality of life enjoyed by the many.

However, leaving such systems in place may be a significant risk to the many of us, as, for example, when crises occur, and they will occur, we may find ourselves cruelly dealt with, with the privileged and well-off highly likely to support their own well-being at the expense of our pain and suffering. We run the risk of falling into substantial oppression and substantial injustice through the imbalances of power and their need to maintain privilege and power for a privileged elite. Thus, wherever possible such unjust and unfair systems need to be removed, changed and at the minimum need substantive and fundamental improvement. However we also need to particularly ensure that one form of discriminatory, oppressive and privileged elite is not replaced by another.

Moving beyond such social issues and our responses to oppression and injustice, in terms of peacefulness and issues of conflict, at a more mundane level, in our more daily personal and individual lives as adults, our engagement with others is likely to involve, as well as the warmth of companionship, our joys and pleasures, at least at some points in time, conflict, frustration, emotional pain, the non-achievement of our goals, sometimes feelings of failure, and amongst other things, the inability to gain and have the things which we deeply desire and want, with potential consequent feelings of frustration.

Our responses to these more daily pains and difficulties need to be caring and tolerant, rational and reasonable, focused on taking care of and supporting our own well-being and happiness, but also focused on taking care of the well-being and welfare of those with whom we live, those with whom we are interacting and dealing with in our daily lives, and indeed all others. We need to aim to cooperate and work closely with others, working through conflicts if we can and aiming to resolve our different needs, our differing feelings and our differing beliefs and judgments amongst other differences.

In relation to our non-achievements, failures and our life situations, we may in particular feel bad through our comparing ourselves with others who seem to be more successful than ourselves, be that in terms of relationships or in terms of life achievements, against which we may sometimes feel small, as almost nothing, creating in us feelings of sadness, uselessness and sometimes depression. We are better off, in terms of supporting our own well-being and happiness, focusing on our own happiness and our own achievements rather than engaging in such comparison. Nevertheless of course, we often do not know the true reality of others and how they feel, even if they appear from the outside to be successful and happy. We probably do not know their families, their relationships, their worries, concerns and troubles, and thus our comparison of ourselves with such others is likely to be incomplete. It may be that we are indeed happier inside than they are and indeed they may feel, should they know us, that we are happier and indeed more successful than they are, not knowing of our own feelings in regard to them, not knowing of our sadnesses and comparative sense of non-achievement and sometimes failure.

While comparison with others is undoubtedly inevitable to some degree, we should not and cannot let that lead us to unhappiness and bitterness, and certainly not to aggressive violence. There is no justification in responding to our own lives and our own failures, our some time sense and feelings of failure, our frustrations, our feelings of pain, through resorting to negative, destructive actions, aimed at hurting others and there is certainly no justification for aggressive violence in response to our own frustrations and unhappiness, our personal resentment and perhaps feelings of jealousy at the achievement and success of others. Causing pain and suffering to others on such grounds and in such a manner is entirely contrary to core and other principles, being detrimental to ourselves and others.

Indeed our actions need to involve us in taking care of those who may appear to be, and may in fact be, more able and successful than ourselves in some respects, even with their achieving more in their lives than we are, even with their possessing more power and perhaps more wealth than we do. Through their actions and achievements they will hopefully not only be contributing to themselves and their own well-being, but also contributing to our community's, society's and humanity's broader well-being and happiness.

Rather, as mentioned above, we must focus on our personal objectives, acting in line with core and other principles, focusing on our own lives as far as is possible, our own actions and, even in the face of past failure and non-achievement, act to constructively pursue our goals, our own well-being and happiness and the well-being and happiness of others with peaceful cooperative, persistence, thought, care and love. Comparison with others, while having a positive side in exemplifying what we may achieve and how we might enjoy our lives more fully, is for many of us, if not applied correctly and effectively, with appropriate goals in mind, a route to resentment, frustration and unhappiness. We must respond to our own feelings of frustration, emotional pain with further efforts to support our well-being and that of others, and further efforts, to achieve our goals, overcoming the obstacles in our way, or deciding on a realignment and changing of our goals in the light of the realities of who we are and the circumstances we face.

Overall there is a strong assertion of the need for peacefulness in the context of the core and other principles, requiring support for our own well-being and support for others, our communities, societies and beyond, and the prevention of harm and suffering to both ourselves and others. Within this guide and in line with core principles, the gamut of peaceful and cooperative actions engaged in with others, are favoured in order to pursue our ends peacefully, cooperatively and effectively. And our peaceful and cooperative struggle and effort, sometimes leading to disappointment, are seen as often required and necessary on the route to achieving that which is worthwhile. Indeed such struggle and effort, though perhaps not necessarily desirable in themselves, are seen as providing engagement, involvement, learning and indeed sometimes pleasure leading to a sense of greater reward and fulfillment when we finally achieve our goals.

Nevertheless, as already referred to above, while there is support for peacefulness and cooperative approaches, the view presented in this guide is that while we have an overall desire for and we have goals of being peaceful and cooperative, there may be cases where it may not be possible to realise such desires and goals. Importantly within the bounds of core principles and within the aims of supporting well-being and happiness and avoiding pain and suffering, within the context of this need and desire to be cooperative and peaceful, the core and other principles are seen as meaning, as already described, that we can certainly resort on occasion, where necessary, to physical and forceful action. This has already been stated as being particularly relevant in relation to defending ourselves in the face of potential personal injury and attack, as well as in response to certain circumstances such as deliberate efforts of starvation and other circumstances described above. This justification for physical action certainly extends to preventing harm to and defending others who are themselves facing violent threat and attack, in response to which passive and non-physical responses are seen as sometimes, if not often, insufficient and inadequate, running the risk of leaving ourselves and others open to suffering severe pain and injury, even death.

Thus, while passive non-violent responses to attack may have some rationale behind them and are indeed accepted and promoted by a few, and indeed may be admirable in intention, the principles of enhancing well-being and reducing suffering argue that we are justified in taking physical action to protect ourselves and to protect others when aggressive violence is threatened, when violent attack is in progress, when circumstances threaten us with violence, injury, intense suffering and death.

That being said, within the core and other principles, the case for being totally non-violent can clearly be argued with reference to what is seen as a longer term good, however this case is not seen here as sufficiently convincing within the terms of core and other principles, within terms of supporting well-being and avoiding pain and suffering. In relation to the view put forward in this guide, it is hoped that such occasions when physical force may be a necessity are rare or infrequent, indeed it is hoped that for many of us they may never arise.

While such total non-violence is considered insufficiently convincing as a response to aggressively violent behaviour, the use of non-violence and the notion of turning the other cheek are seen as potentially very powerful and persuasive under certain circumstances. Refusing to respond to aggressive violence and aggressively violent provocation in a violent manner, and talking assertively but in a peaceful and conciliatory way, challenging aggressors with words and a refusal to do as they wish may, under certain circumstances, support us and others in achieving our goals, in particular as such actions may serve to support the breaking of a cycle of violence, often expected by those who are aggressively violent. And such peaceful actions on our behalf have the potential to encourage them to look at themselves, to think further about themselves, their actions and the hurt and damage they are doing. Perhaps much violence is born out of fear and indeed a belief that such violence is acceptable and normal. Non-violence and non-cooperation with the aggressively violent can produce stark and effective lessons for the aggressively violent and support more general peacefulness and non-violent resolution of situations and problems.

Nevertheless, those engaging in violence may simply not have any concern for us and others. They may be ideologically or otherwise convinced in themselves, for example, that damaging, destroying and murdering others from another group, murdering men, women and children is acceptable, possibly the right and moral thing to do according to their perverse and destructive thinking, ideology, belief systems and their system of morality. They may be psychologically ill. On the other hand, they may be trapped in a system where they must do as they are told or face death and injury themselves. Against such thinking and murderous action or the prospect of such murderous action, it may be that acting in a non-violent manner may create some realisation in such people of the horror of that which they are doing, however a non-violent response (as with indeed a forceful and physical response) may well, unfortunately, have no effect at all in terms of the immediate consequence of preventing aggressively violent action, and possibly no effect in the longer term either.

Furthermore and clearly, if we decide to follow such a path of non-violence or decide to act non-violently in situations where we are being oppressed or violently assaulted, perhaps threatened with death, then we are highly likely to be leaving ourselves open to personal damage, suffering in some form, perhaps severe injury or even that threatened death. And further, and importantly, we may well also be leaving others open to aggressive violence and suffering as we will be leaving the aggressor free to hurt and damage others on the moment or in the future. Alternatively it may be that we have no option for physical force available to us, that we are faced with overwhelming aggressive power and so have no option but to adopt a non-violent resistance or a response involving acquiescence (for the time being). Yet if we do have means to defend ourselves and defend others, using physical force for that purpose, we clearly have a responsibility to use such force.

It is argued quite correctly by some, that if we respond to aggressive violence with violent acts ourselves, even if these are not vengeful, but are the minimum necessary to prevent harm and damage, then we will run the risk of creating the already mentioned cycle of violence, potentially extending and deepening this cycle with the consequence of damage and hurt far beyond ourselves. However, by minimising the physical force used in our responses and limiting the hurt and damage we inflict to a necessary level, we are likely, at least to some extent, to be able to reduce the intensity of such cycles. Moreover, those who are aggressively violent and who attack us are likely to have no similar concerns on the moment or at all about such cycles of violence. Nevertheless, we need to do what we can do to reduce the levels of violence and prevent pain and suffering.

Similarly, as in relation to the idea of cycle of violence, notably it can be argued that responding pacifically to attacks and assaults might serve our community and society better in the long run, serving to support a more peaceful context and environment, and with those engaged in aggressive violence, as mentioned above, potentially being dissuaded from their attacks through seeing directly and being shown direct examples of non-violent, non-aggressive behaviour, perhaps even becoming ashamed and regretful when verbally and non-violently addressed about their aggressive violence and the pain, the suffering and destruction they are causing, with others also being influenced towards peace and cooperation by witnessing such peaceful conduct.

Thus, to be able to engage in such pacific conduct might be seen as admirable. However the overall view taken in this guide, while recognising the sometime value and importance of such non-violence and the value of reducing tensions and engaging in non-violence, is that whilst this conduct is in some ways worthy of admiration and we must all aim to practice as far as we can, non-violence and efforts at peaceful collaboration and cooperation, we need to have the option of using the minimal level of forceful and physical action in self-defence and defence of others.

Further, while we must aim to precede any physically forceful action wherever possible by peaceful discursive, verbal and other non-violent actions (such as non-cooperation) to prevent aggressive violence, the fact is that where such actions are not, are not likely to be, and indeed cannot be effective, the person behaving pacifically is too likely to become a victim of aggressive violence, something which is unacceptable within the terms of core and other principles and not seen as admirable in any sense. And others, undefended and unprotected, may well become victims of violence too if, where we have the capacity to prevent such aggressive violence, we do not take appropriate and effective forceful action to prevent such aggressively violent actions.

And such physically forceful responses to aggressive violence will certainly be necessary in some contexts. Apart from being ideologically motivated or forced through circumstances to commit aggressively violent acts, those engaging in aggressive violence may, in some cases, as already mentioned, be temporarily or otherwise, emotionally and mentally deranged, out of control, psychologically ill and therefore be entirely incapable of responding to peaceful, love, care and reason, especially on the moment, due to their illness and derangement. Peaceful talk and discursive actions might work and are, where possible and reasonable, the first port of call, but they certainly will not be effective in some cases, and in these particular cases, physical restraint or even debilitating force must be used, again at the minimal level aimed at protecting ourselves and others, and indeed aimed at protecting those are deranged and ill.

And those engaging in ideological violence or for example, the gang violence that is prevalent in some contexts, those who are captured by false and often inculcated beliefs, misguided group identity and loyalty, destructive nationalism, and racist ideas, drunken by a sense of physical, personal, gender, cultural and other feelings of superiority, and aiming for the destruction of others, other individuals, other groups; these people are not seen as in many cases as likely to respond positively, in many circumstances, certainly in the short term, to such laudable pacific responses, with the consequence that many will suffer, and that these many will potentially suffer in cruel, terrible and terrifying ways. Again efforts should be made to engage such aggressive people in dialogue, conversation and debate, or in other forms of persuasive engagement, but they cannot be allowed to destroy and damage ourselves and others, and we cannot, and we have a responsibility not to, allow them to inflict their aggressive violence, pain, suffering and cruelty on ourselves or others.

These are simply some examples of where forceful and physical response at the minimal level necessary, may be required in answer to those threatening or engaging in aggressive violence. Wherever possible, following attempts to peacefully, verbally and otherwise resolve situations and prevent aggressive violence in a peaceful manner, we may need to engage in carefully considered and optimally calculated and implemented physical responses at minimal, specific, but necessary levels in response to aggressive violence. Such an approach is seen as more consistent with the principles put forward in this guide than entirely pacific approaches and is seen as more capable of serving our individual well-being and happiness and the well-being and happiness of all.

In the first place, we need to ensure however that we are building peaceful, friendly, loving, caring, cooperative contexts, be that in the family, community, in our wider societies or in our more global context. Through our own actions, through what we say and how we deal with others, through our relationships with others, through our cooperation and working together with others in pursuit of peaceful, reasonable and legitimate goals, through searching for constructive, mutually agreed solutions, through compromise, through being giving in nature, through being efficient and effective, for example by establishing standard and other procedures to deal with disputes and difficulties, through a positive attitude towards finding solutions which are, as stated, mutually acceptable (and perhaps mutually unacceptable to some degree), through recognising and taking account of the perceptions, needs, desires, feelings and more of others, we need to aim to and we will hopefully be able to achieve contexts in which aggressive violence is not on the agenda.

Nevertheless, our worlds are not necessarily fully within our control and therefore, in certain circumstances, where we foresee the possibility of and anticipate stressful, difficult and potentially violent situations, involving aggressively violent attack we need to ensure that we are developing and have developed our capacities for problem resolution, our peacemaking and peaceful capabilities, which include tactics and strategies for reducing tension in situations, ways of expressing our fears and our disapproval of aggressive violence, approaches to defusing violence and pacifying those who are involved in, or who are threatening to engage in violence, if necessary through physical force.

In circumstances where it is possible or likely that aggressive violence will be encountered and will take place, and in particular where we are in professions such as security, policing and other professions where encountering aggressive violence is, at some point, a likelihood, it makes absolute sense to prepare ourselves effectively to deal with those who may engage in such aggressive violence against others and against us.

Under circumstances in which we might face such aggressive violence, and in preparation for such circumstances, having developed our capacities and strategies for reducing tensions and diffusing aggressive situations, it is quite reasonable, indeed rational and sensible for us to aim to develop physical defensive capacities which may prove useful in our personal defence or the defence of others.

Additionally, for the many of us, amongst other things, the capacity for us to recognise dangerous situations, to avoid and where necessary escape from them before situations become too dangerous and threatening in terms of aggressive violence, is also likely to be useful. Yet specialist training in self-defence and in ways of defending others is also almost certain to be of great value, if not essential in order to preserve our own safety, the safety of those we may be protecting, as well as in order to protect those who may be engaging in such aggressive violence such that we can respond to them effectively but, where we can, keeping these aggressors safe as well.

Any defensive capacities we develop need to be as far as possible safe for all, involving the capacity to use minimal force wherever possible, teaching us that the notion of safety and minimal force and damage applies to all parties, including those who may engage in aggressive violence against us, our self-defence and our defence of others being the goal. That being acknowledged, our capacities for self-defence and the defence of others need to be effective, and moreover, given the tension, danger and threat in such situations, such effective self-defence and defence of others is likely to be our priority with the well-being being of those who are engaging in or who have engaged in aggressive violence against us, being to an important extent, of secondary importance once we are under attack.

Though it has already been stated, it is considered necessary to emphasise again that we must not see such a physical response as a desirable first port of call – far from it – that is to say that, while core principles can be said to allow such a physical defensive response, this approach is not seen as a desirable first option (though unfortunately it may, in some circumstances, be a necessary and immediately needed option). Non-violent actions, where reasonable and practical, are certainly preferable as our initial and indeed as further adopted courses of action in response to situations where aggressive violence is threatened or even sometimes, when in process, such approaches involving the calming talk already referred to, negotiation, discussion, compromise (where reasonable and appropriate), verbal and other peaceful non-forceful self-protection and expression of understanding and care.

Where possible and appropriate, we should seek the help of others in overwhelming numbers or from those who are better trained than we are, in dealing with threat and aggressive violence and who are given a legitimate role and responsibility in our communities, societies and beyond in terms of protecting us. In essence, this may mean police and other types of safety and security service. Thus, we have the responsibility to engage capable, indeed any other adult others, where necessary in our resistance and defence against violent attacks on ourselves and others, aiming to prevent harm to both ourselves and others, the presence of numbers and overwhelming force and the presence of those qualified and trained to prevent and contain violence, often serving to dissuade those considering, planning or intent on aggressive violence. That being said, unfortunately, and undesirably, the view presented here is that forceful physical action may still sometimes be necessary.

While apparently contrary to core principles there will certainly be occasions, possibly isolated, possibly more frequent, in some of our individual and community lives, when our engagement in physical action against others, to protect others or ourselves, may inflict some, sometimes significant level of pain, hurt and suffering on another or others, or perhaps *in extremis* the actions of some of us, hopefully almost none of us, may, again hopefully in the rarest of circumstances, inflict death on another. Inflicting significant pain on another or killing another are utterly unwanted, totally undesirable, and our forceful actions resulting in such destructive consequences need to represent the final port of call when all else has been tried and failed in a situation where others are in imminent danger of significant and severe, damage, pain and suffering. Nevertheless, such actions may represent in some circumstances an absolute necessity for the protection of the individual, for the protection of others, and for the protection of our communities and societies.

Thus, on account of the reality of the dangerous and potentially dangerous situations that we may face in our world, and the violence, suffering and pain that can be visited upon us, violence, pain and suffering from which we as individuals and we as communities and societies, as a global humanity, may need protection and defence, the use of physical force on some occasions is considered a necessary option. Consistent with core principles, our responses need to be appropriate to relevant situations and circumstances with even the most vigorous and forceful end of the spectrum of our responses to aggressive violence requiring the use of the maximum restraint and minimal force necessary for self and other-protection and to prevent harm and damage to ourselves and others, including as far as possible, those who are acting as aggressors.

Peace, in terms of its meaning as an absence of violence, and in terms of core and other principles and our goals, is clearly and certainly worth pursuing as it is a crucial element of well-being and happiness and core to an absence of pain and suffering. Nevertheless, the absence of overt physical violence is not in itself a sufficiently full description of a peaceful existence. Ordered systems of living, as already suggested in relation to issues in particular of justice and equality, can appear peaceful in terms of there being an absence of violence, but may contain in-built unfairness, injustice, oppression, suffering and pain, substantial poverty, which may not manifest themselves through explicit, obvious and overt daily and visible aggressive physical violence. Such systems do not represent peacefulness, due to their ongoing damaging effects on well-being and happiness and the constant pain and suffering they embody.

As a case in point, as we will, at least the most of us, be aware that there have been and may still exist in some places, systems of slavery or individuals kept as slaves or virtual slaves, treated and trafficked as if they are non-human commodities rather than people, their lives governed by violence, a violence which may in some cases at least, not be externally explicit and obvious on a daily basis. In such situations and systems, undoubtedly the individual slave, the individual under coercion, wishes for freedom, but perhaps through law, tradition, common practice, individual or group coercive and threatening behaviour (not necessarily expressed or visible everyday as violent coercion) or other means, that person cannot gain the freedom and independence they undoubtedly desire.

Living as a slave responsible to the whim of a master, gang master, organisation or other entity, owner or mistress, and not our own individual will, need and desire, with the prospect of violent punishment should we fail to obey these masters and mistresses, cannot be seen as living at peace, or living in a peaceful environment. Clearly such a state is entirely at odds with freedom, independence and autonomy. Daily resistance to this slavery may not be a viable and realistic option, since it will result in severe punishment realising severe physical pain, suffering, cruelty (both physical and emotional) and even leading to death. Coercion and violent force are present in these and other situations, even if not visible or enacted on a daily basis. They are present, if often invisible, in order to make a person do that which they would never have acceded to if they were free to decide, with the aggressive and physical violence in some cases only becoming visible if the slave or individual under threat of violent coercion refuses the order or command or performs a task unsatisfactorily in the view of their master, mistress or other controlling individual. Of course as mentioned in chapter ten of this guide, slavery or similar coercive control of others is appalling, evil and entirely contrary to core and other principles.

And such situations of coercion, oppression and lack of freedom, where pain and suffering is not immediately visible, can exist in many other contexts, similar in principle, some worse in their oppression than the example of slavery in terms of the pain, and suffering caused, some less so.

In some family homes, it may be the case that some girls or women in particular, live in similar conditions of coercive control to the conditions of a slave, yet their situation and suffering may also be difficult to see. In some contexts males in particular, though sometimes females, will control and dominate a household and family, coercively dictating to others their actions, behaviour and conduct, with the threat of significant violence and abuse attached, perhaps with individuals being prevented from leaving the home, being in effect prisoners within their own homes. Those girls and women being oppressed in such situations may fear leaving their home and may be unable to escape this form of oppression and bondage for a range of reasons, most prominently due to fear of aggressive violence (and sometimes fear of being killed), but also through the absence of an income on which to survive outside of their legal marriage, out of fear of opprobrium and abuse that may be received from family, community and others and even perhaps violence or ostracism from the community when they leave a husband, or through fear of losing their children or never seeing them again, amongst other threats. Children in such families may be subject to similar violence and abuse, which again may be difficult to see, with children kept at home or threatened so that they keep silent.

If we are women in such situations, we need to do everything possible to escape, protecting our children as we aim to escape. Remaining in such a place, experiencing violence and abuse, is certainly not a desirable option and should we stay, we risk severe damage to ourselves physically and mentally as well as to our children. Of course in the first place, we should take whatever actions we can to prevent violence against us using words and otherwise, yet this may not be a practical and reasonable strategy in the face of aggressive violence, and coercion and we will need to take whatever care is necessary to protect ourselves and our children. Those who are friends and family who are aware of such situations need to take action to help our daughters, our friends, escape from such situations, aiding their escape and protecting them from harm, providing them with safety from such violence and cruelty.

Beyond such family support and the support of friends, we need to ensure that our communities and societies are also in a position to help women (and on some occasions men) who are in such positions. Our laws and systems need to provide protection and enable safety, bringing those who threaten or have committed such violence to justice. Moreover there needs to be equality in law between men and women with fair, just and equitable, laws enabling and requiring financial payments on divorce and separation which allow partners to survive on with their children, irrespective of the cause of separation, and which will, in particular, enable women who may have never had paid employment or who may have given up work to support their children, to be able to survive outside of their partnership or marriage. Ensuring that women and men, and children, do not have to endure such violent home contexts, is a responsibility for us all, which we need to exercise through our direct support for those who are the victims of such partners and situations and through our ensuring that laws are in place to provide the necessary support and protection for them. Our efforts should wherever possible support peacefulness within a relationship within the home, and if that is not or cannot be achieved, or if remaining in such a home is simply not wanted, then those who are subject to domestic violence in the home should be supported in finding peaceful and safe situations, either in their own home through removal of those doing violence of whichever kind, or they must be enabled and supported in finding more peaceful, safer lives and situations elsewhere.

Prevalent and significant to the many of us in our modern age, in terms of our pursuit of peaceful lives, and in particular, the more general presence or absence of peace, having substantial effect and influence around the world, there are economic systems and cultures, which are highly exploitative and damaging of us as individuals, their characteristics, manner and means of operation, or the systems in themselves, contributing to or causing significant pain, poverty and harm. Yet, again in the context of such systems, there may be no overt aggressive violence present, although there may well be signs of, or indeed much obvious pain and suffering visible and caused by such systems and culture.

In some of these economic systems and cultures, while there may be no daily visible and overt, explicit and obvious aggressive violence, there may well be forms of hidden violence and oppression which reveal themselves to us at the more local level. For example such oppression may become visible and explicit in situations where employees are said to have breached rules, where we as individuals do not conform or refuse to follow inappropriate instructions, where racial, gender or other discrimination is in place and we protest against such injustice, where employees working excessive hours reasonably say they wish to work lesser hours, where workers need more pay to survive and request this or express concern about safety practices in their work contexts, where we as employees suffer injury at work, refuse to conduct dangerous tasks, when we peacefully oppose perceived injustices, where those of us with positions of little power try to pursue economic and other justice and fairness in order to better ourselves and gain greater freedom and relief from our situations.

The response to such transgressions by those in power, be they bosses, managers, sometimes backed by politicians and other supporters, may be to threaten and implement job losses for those who express opposition, who express a desire for better conditions, such actions thereby threatening essential income and poverty against these people, meaning the imposition or efforts to impose poverty and suffering on those accused of transgressing.

Those in power may threaten and implement aggressive violence against their employees or activists in order to ensure that they are not forced to make changes in their employment practices. They may abuse the legal processes that exist to generate false charges of illegality against those they perceive to be their opponents, or alternatively those who are powerful may ensure that laws are in place which privilege owners and the powerful against those wishing for beneficial change, making even the act of protest a form of illegality. Thus, such situations, in which ordinary workers, ordinary people, ourselves and those like us are exploited and put in danger yet can do little about our situations, cannot be seen as in reality peaceful. Similarly, in other situations, there may often be invisible coercion in place, an invisible coercion which exists in various forms in the various situations and circumstances facing us as individuals, with oppressive and aggressive violence only becoming visible when we as individuals refuse to accede to unjust rules and practices or illegitimate (or even legitimate) authority or when we as individuals challenge those rules, systems, laws and that authority.

Moreover in economic systems where we as individuals are valued mainly or solely on the basis of our productive capacities and economic utility, those with less ability, with lower levels of skills, those with difficulties in communications, those suffering with illness, may be left by the wayside, considered of no value, as they are less able or unable to contribute to an economy. This is unacceptable within core principles wherein we need to care for and support the well-being and happiness of all. There, again, cannot be said to be peace when we or our fellows are suffering in such a manner, unable to access work, unable to make contributions to our communities, where we ourselves and others are living in avoidable poverty. And of course, if we are in such situations as individuals, we need to make efforts and commit ourselves to removing ourselves from poverty, cooperating with others to achieve such ends, as well as doing our utmost to ensure the well-being and happiness of others and aiming to remove them from poverty, pursuing our goals peacefully if we can, but certainly ensuring that others are not enduring intense suffering and pain or living in such poverty that unnecessary pain and suffering is inevitable in the future.

Moreover, where our economic systems are inefficient at generating the resources we need, where human incompetence and mismanagement, political ideology or negatively selfish people or other human sources create economic hardship, this is also unacceptable within core principles, with those situations where we and others are suffering badly, living in poverty and deprivation as a result of such actions and attitudes, again failing to represent what could be considered to be peaceful situations.

If we live in such economic systems and cultures, then we have a responsibility, consistent with core and other principles, to support and achieve changes in these systems, to act to remove injustice and oppression and to support economic development and change, with the aim of producing effective economies which support us through their generation of good living standards and high levels of well-being, and which will also generate safe and efficient working environments in which we can all earn sufficient pay, have sufficient resources to survive well, if not more than sufficient, in order to support our well-being and happiness and reduce pain and suffering.

The existence of unregulated or insufficiently regulated economic systems, nationally and globally, which are dependent on unplanned, uncontrolled and unmanaged shifts of capital, which are subject to manipulation and bad practice, holding within themselves the capacity for economic crash and chaos, as a consequence causing pain and suffering to millions around the globe, is also unacceptable. It is not reasonable for us to allow such systems to operate with the threat that such unregulated or insufficiently regulated practices will throw so many of us into significant poverty, distress and suffering.

We have every right to protect ourselves from poverty and suffering through taking the action necessary, optimally peaceful and persuasive, to prevent such systems operating in a manner which is reckless and negatively selfish, which acts to support the interests of the few who are wealthy, and which will likely at some time or other, lead to significant and serious damage and destruction to almost all, if not all of us. We, both as individuals and in the groups which we form or wish to form, have every right within the terms of the core principles to act against those vested interests which act in such negatively selfish ways, sometimes, if not often, criminal in their nature and actions, who would allow us to be exposed to such dangers. Again, peace may appear to be reigning at times if such systems are present and operating effectively as they may do at times, however, it is almost guaranteed that the operation of such unregulated and insufficiently regulated systems will at some point lead to severe economic problems, if not economic disaster, with consequent vast levels of suffering and pain.

More specifically within economic systems, powerful and wealthy individuals, interest groups, businesses and corporations may, in pursuit of their own gain and in pursuit of the gain and enrichment of those within their organisations and those who own their organisations, engage in financial and other practices which push others into poverty, for example creating cartels, fixing prices, forcing down wages, avoiding taxes, worsening pay and conditions, manipulating supply and demand, compromising safety. Indeed, in some if not many cases where larger multi-national companies are involved, there may be attempts to control and manipulate governments and international organisations to support such powerful interests rather than supporting them in fulfilling their proper role of acting to support the well-being and happiness of all.

When such practices and activities are occurring, with their consequent detriment to overall well-being and happiness, again we cannot see this as representing peacefulness and cooperation. And we need to take whatever steps are necessary to prevent such actions which threaten the well-being and happiness of many millions, if not hundreds of millions, if not all of us. This is not to say that all businesses, wealthy individuals or corporations will act in such ways, with some individuals and some businesses and corporations comprised of individuals with the best of intentions. Yet apart from the actions of those who are malevolent, greedy for wealth and profit, there are unfortunately system problems which, for example, may demand that businesses maximise profits and surplus, with no counterbalancing requirements to enhance the well-being of workers and staff or to enhance the general well-being.

Yet beyond the more capitalistic business model, there have been and still exist other economic and political systems which have created and sustained poverty too, in which individual and group freedoms and economic initiatives are, and have been stifled, if not stamped on; systems in which oppressive regimes, governments, and leaderships have attempted to control all, and through their incompetence, bureaucracy, lack of flexibility, ideological blindness, fear of democracy and consultation, fear of freedom, through their conformity, fear of change, corruption, nepotism and more, have created, and are creating poverty and suffering as well as denying basic and important freedoms. Systems where there is such incompetence and denial of our individuality, where there is such corruption, favouritism, nepotism and the like, are unacceptable on account of the damage done to well-being in so many respects, through their standing against basic freedoms, their basic dishonesty, unfairness and corruption, and the economic and other damage they do to individuals and the general well-being.

Of course, if there is justice (including social justice), fairness, freedom and efficiency leading to general all round psychological and physical well-being, leading to economic well-being and happiness, then such economic systems are certainly acceptable. Nevertheless, the presence of controlling, overly-centralised corrupt and bureaucratic systems which deny individual freedom and initiative and which cause poverty and damage cannot be said to represent a peaceful situation. Those of us within such systems need to do our utmost, optimally and as far as possible, through peaceful and cooperative means, to pursue change such that poverty and suffering, absence of freedom, our pain and suffering and more are banished.

Moreover, relating more specifically to our family, our social and political systems, though still in some situations linked to economics, in circumstances where we are disempowered in other ways, for example when we are unable to contribute to those decisions affecting our lives, when we are disenfranchised and marginalised from positions of power and decisions of power, including important decisions relating directly to our own lives, then again these situations are not amenable to description as peaceful contexts and situations. It is almost without doubt that for many of us we will feel frustrated and probably angered or feel humiliated at such situations where important decisions are being made by others about our lives, in particular affecting the detail of our lives, but we have no input to such decisions, where we are not listened to and others are not interested in listening to us.

Through such undemocratic systems and other elements and systems which promote our marginalisation and which deny our individual contribution and value, we will most likely suffer a range of negative consequences in terms of our well-being due to our exclusion from such contributions to decision-making, with most likely those involved in such decision-making often suiting and acting to support their own negatively selfish interests or acting based on their own perceptions or cultural biases, with ourselves reaping the likely damaging consequences. At the minimum, it is highly unlikely such people will be able to truly perceive and recognise our interests, will be able to recognise that which we would perceive as supporting our own individual or family well-being and happiness. In no sense can such exclusion and marginalisation be seen as representing a peaceful situation, and again we will need to do whatever we can, optimally through peaceful cooperation and where necessary non-cooperation to ensure that such systems cannot sustain and better, more democratic, participative systems implemented.

Similar principles apply to social and political systems where uniform beliefs, or at least external appearances of uniform belief are imposed, where our individuality is denied, our individual capacity for personal and independent thought and action is constrained or almost entirely constrained. These contexts can comprise certain political systems or religious and other belief systems where the holding of relevant beliefs are mandated by social and political systems and backed by coercion, law and intensive social pressure to conform. Thus, for example, where there may be a state ideology and all are required to adhere to this by law or through fear of violent and other punishments should they verbally or through other action express disagreement with such an ideology at home or in public, then that does not represent a peaceful situation, even where the streets may seem peaceful and where there is little explicit evidence of violence and conflict. Under such systems there is substantial hidden violence operating through law and coercion and, as a consequence, we may well have to hide our true feelings and beliefs in order to survive, thrive and get through the day. And if we wish to change such a systems we will most likely need to work carefully and quietly to change such ruling and governing systems.

Similarly, in some jurisdictions, the holding of certain religious beliefs and the following of certain religious practices are either compulsory or to all intents and purposes compulsory. In particular, expressing disagreement, either openly or in private, with the mandated religious beliefs and practices, or acting in contravention of religiously mandated laws can lead at best to ostracism and rejection by community and family, but frequently leads to imprisonment, violent punishment and execution.

Such systems represent severe oppression and in no sense can be seen as peaceful. They threaten all who are different, all who have different views, beliefs and practices, be they those who see the roles of men and women differently from those presented in or based in religious texts, be they those of other religious belief systems, those who disagree with violent punishment, those who believe in open expression and freedom, be they homosexual or in other ways contravening of what are seen as social norms and conventions. Again it may seem that these situations are peaceful, but there is highly likely to be violence present, exerted through the punishment of those who do not conform, embedded in general conduct and behaviour or perhaps hidden violence, found in homes and away from the public space. Attempting to change such systems may be difficult and risky, yet we are obliged to seek change in order to support well-being and happiness, and if we cannot seek such change or are under significant threat or at risk, we may well need to escape from such communities and societies in order to preserve our lives, in order to maintain and support our well-being.

If we exist in such repressive systems, while we may be constrained by contexts, cultures and the repressive apparatus, we remain responsible as individuals for the actions we take. We must act within core and other principles to support well-being and happiness for each individual and for all, including those with differing ideologies and beliefs, different social practices from those we hold and practice ourselves. As individuals within such non-peaceful, repressive systems we need to do our utmost to change such systems and support the promotion of well-being and happiness for all.

The range of situations described above cannot be said to be peaceful and are certainly not desirable within the context of the core principles. The presence of such pain, violent coercion, physical threat, suffering, intense poverty, significant lack of freedom of expression, or other significantly undesirable features found in oppressive systems acting contrary to core and other principles, the presence of these and other features of oppression which reduce well-being and which increase or in themselves represent significant and intense suffering, mean that in an important sense these situations certainly cannot be said to represent peaceful contexts and situations.

Clearly, given this rejection of such a range of situations as peaceful, and given the idea of peace and the idea of those peaceful situations which we wish to strive for in line with the values shown through core and other principles, it follows that peace means much more than simply an absence of explicit aggressive violence, even though, of course, this must be an important component of peace. Peaceful situations and peace requires families, communities and societies, a global environment, where there is fairness, justice, absence of poverty and oppression, effective education, the existence of personal autonomy and personal power, personal and substantive freedoms, the opportunity to contribute to decisions which affect our lives, a reasonable level of equality, a reasonable level of wealth, the presence of comfort, safety and security, opportunities for pleasure and entertainment, amongst much else. It requires that each of us as an individual should be recognised and valued, not marginalised and ignored. All of this is consistent with the core principles and the values presented in this guide.

Related to such a conception of peace and peacefulness, in terms of our personal conduct we need to strive not simply to take no aggressively violent action and to refuse to act in aggressively violent ways; we need to strive not simply to act to counter potential and actual aggressively violent incidents in our societies, but we also need to act ourselves in a constructive and proactive manner to support cooperative, peaceful families, communities, societies, a cooperative and peaceful world, and to support peaceful contexts and situations by acting in a manner consistent with and promoting more widely, fairness, justice, care and concern for others, freedom, the absence of poverty and inappropriate and stark inequalities, and more, in order to create those communities and societies, a global community, which truly support the well-being and happiness of their individual members and which are truly non-violent and peaceful.

Aiming in various ways to be peaceful and cooperative individuals ourselves, in terms of our daily actions and thinking, is clearly an important way of promoting peace in the external world around us. Clearly if each of us acts peacefully and pursues the type of peaceful living, peaceful family, community and society consistent with the principles presented in this guide, then this will be an important driver for achieving a peaceful personal life, a peaceful society and a peaceful world.

It would be somewhat naive and simplistic to think that our attainment of a totally peaceful and cooperative existence is a simple enterprise and indeed, due to the complexity of peacefulness, it would be more realistic to think of the achievement of peacefulness as an ongoing and continuous challenge. For example, reflecting the challenges of pursuing peacefulness, it is in the nature of any community and society that there will be differing views, judgments, feelings, opinions and ideas as well as differing personal interests. As a consequence, there will of necessity be some form of conflict between us, between groups of people and organised entities. Such conflict would seem to represent a lack of peacefulness.

Yet of course, the existence of and interaction between differing views, differing perceptions, differing cultures, in the context of discussion and argument, the existence of passionate and committed debate, the presence of difference emotional outlooks, our differing characters, personalities, differing skills and abilities in achieving cooperativity and peacefulness, our differing interpretations of the complex evidence in front of us in regard to the world, the differing legitimate interpretations which are bound to exist within the context of the principles established, and the differing actions which might be taken based on these interpretations and in response to real world events, all are certainly needed and serve to contribute to well-being and happiness, not only through our human desire and indeed necessity for self-expression and interaction, but also through supporting us as individuals and social entities in making the optimal decisions in regard to our personal, family, working, community and social lives.

If such differences, if the presence of conflicting views, differing perceptions and more is interpreted as representing an absence of peace, then our pursuit of peace would mean either aiming to remove such differences or removing the expression of such differences. This is certainly not desirable and indeed most likely not even possible. Such action would not support our happiness and well-being and indeed would cause substantive damage to well-being and happiness. In terms of the freedom, independence and autonomy already discussed in chapter ten, while of course it is reasonable to persuade and aim to reach agreement, it would be totally unacceptable to aim to remove our range of differences as a goal in itself. Moreover, as also stated in that chapter, our well-being and happiness is supported by diversity of individuals, perceptions and more, which in itself is part of our individuality, our freedom and our well-being and happiness. As a consequence of a lack of diversity of perceptions and views we would as families, communities and societies almost certainly not enjoy such well-being and happiness, even though our world might appear peaceful. Our individuality and personal identities would to all intents and purposes have been lost, something which is again fundamentally contrary to our humanity and human nature and damaging to our well-being and happiness.

However, what is meant by pursuing peace here is maintaining the bounds of such debate and discussion, our expression of beliefs and views, and indeed the actions we take, within a framework which avoids aggressive violence, indeed which hopefully and preferably avoids abuse and insult, and which promotes listening, attentiveness to others, rationality and reason, which promotes mutual respect and understanding, care and love, yet which at the same time promotes optimal directions to the future, optimal solutions to problems as well as effectiveness and efficiency. Through such a peaceful approach to hearing, dealing with and benefiting from differences and conflict, we will maintain a high level of peacefulness and cooperation while enabling the exchange of conflicting perspectives, judgments and more, these processes supporting us in optimal decision-making and supporting our personal and social enjoyment and fulfillment. The fact is that there is always likely to be some element of difference and conflict, even within the bounds of core and other principles, but the interaction between our differences, needs to be kept within peaceful and non-violent grounds. A peaceful and cooperative existence, a peaceful and cooperative community, society and wider world which acknowledges legitimate differences and deals with these peacefully and cooperatively in support of individual and the general well-being and happiness is clearly a reasonable and worthwhile goal in line with the principles outlined in this guide.

And through this approach to disagreement, differing perceptions and conflict, and within the bounds of core and other principles, the existence of peaceful disagreements, differing perceptions, differing views on how to act, the discussion of such differences as if they are opposing views, if all of this is seen as representing conflict then such conflict when tackled and dealt with in a constructive and positive manner is seen as good and beneficial for us all. And avoidance of such acknowledgement and expression of conflicting ideas, views and opinions, our personal choice not to express differences, while perhaps sometimes beneficial and necessary to maintain peacefulness (as dealing with different perceptions and arguments can cause stress and anxiety), is also seen as a potential cause of unhappiness and a possible source of potential problems.

Of course, as individuals, we should each of us, aim to conduct ourselves peacefully, attending to and listening to others and promoting cooperation and mutual respect. The manner in which we conduct ourselves refers not only to our actions, but also to our words. We need to consider and use language which, while expressing the ways we feel, the things we think, the beliefs we hold, the judgments we have and more, also itself serves to bring people together, promotes cooperation and creates understanding and a sense of commonality and common humanity, rather than speaking language of disharmony, division, and using language which promotes unnecessary and damaging conflict. We need to ensure that we avoid words and expressions, the range of statements, the range of ways of expressing ourselves, including the manner of our voice and intonation, the mood which we express ourselves, which may enhance conflict and which increase the possibility of angry divisions, aggressive violence, significant pain and suffering. Even with good intentions, however, using inappropriate language and making inappropriate and careless statements can enhance levels and degrees of damaging conflict, reducing peacefulness and cooperativity, increasing the possibilities of aggressive violence and therefore increasing the possibility of pain and suffering and the likelihood of reducing well-being and happiness.

And as listeners and responders to the words of others, in whichever context, be it in the context of a personal relationship or a discussion of important social issues with friends or acquaintances, we have to be careful to be attentive to others, aiming to understand the messages they are putting across. We may often need to listen for and be aware of the underlying and real messages which may indicate the true origins and motivations for an individual's personal views or indeed a group's views, these messages perhaps representing the real origins of the precise ideas and beliefs which they are expressing. We need to do our utmost to understand others and respond in an appropriate manner. This will hopefully mean our producing responses which will enhance well-being and happiness, support the satisfactory resolution of conflict, the resolution of problems, result in diminished tensions and remove potential for aggressive and violent conflict, supporting good, positive and rich relationships, which support togetherness and which will furthermore support the best course of action for us all.

Moreover, it is our personal responsibility and our personal decision as to how we respond to situations where others are using words to express their anger towards us, to provoke us, to insult us, deride and disrespect us and abuse us, where others have breached our trust and hurt us through their actions in other ways. While clearly challenging in many cases, and with our responses dependent on situations, and circumstances, it is almost always best if we can respond to such verbal challenges with appropriate words, aiming to understand and acknowledge feelings, frustrations and indeed anger, our calming situations where necessary, defusing situations where aggressive violence is being threatened, expressing and asserting our own feelings and hurt, aiming to respond with understanding to others, even where that is emotionally challenging for us.

It does need to be pointed out that the notion of peacefulness does not refer here to generating a peaceful world inside ourselves, even though that may be desirable and it may well be the case that a peaceful internal world inside ourselves, a peaceful character and a peaceful mind, help us to be peaceful through our days. Nevertheless the notion of, and indeed the achievement of some form of meditative internal peace (which would be pleasant, though is perhaps very difficult to achieve for the most of us) is seen here as, in fact, likely to be insufficient to support the well-being and happiness of ourselves and others. This is because the external world frequently upsets those of us who are engaged in such searches for, or who claim to have such an inner peace. That such states of personal peace are associated with personal isolation is testament to the difficulties in retaining constant levels of internal and personal calm in a world full of challenges and stresses, which is the type of world that most of us live in.

Too much focus on achieving such inner peaceful states, too much effort over time engaged in aiming to achieve some form of internal 'nirvana', is seen here as being highly and overly self-focused, removing our attention from supporting others in the world, even though some may argue that their claimed inner peace supports them in dealing with that world. Nevertheless, such peaceful states may only be sustainable and effective to the extent that the challenging nature of the external world is avoided or in contexts away from our challenging lives. Thus behaving peacefully and feeling peaceful and relaxed, while certainly pleasant and of value to us, tends to take place aside from the community, aside from others, aside from the many tasks of the day and the real world of getting things done, the real world of helping and supporting others, takes place aside from dealing with multiple relationships, multiple, complex and challenging interactions and conflicts with others and indeed internal conflicts within ourselves. That is not to say that we might not need time to think about, reflect on our actions, our lives, have some personal space, have some rest and indeed sometimes escape from these challenges, at least for a while, so that we can better recognise and understand any pain and suffering we may be experiencing and as a consequence better cope with our lives, living therefore with greater well-being and happiness.

The reality and the real challenge for us is to operate peacefully, cooperatively and successfully in our interaction with the world that really exists outside of a more self-focused internal world of our minds. However, if searches for inner peace indeed are successful in supporting effective engagement with the world outside of us, if they do support our own well-being and happiness and do not detract from our time and the success of our engagement with that real world, with the consequence that the core and other principles are promoted, and such that well-being and happiness are truly enhanced for ourselves and all, then such searches and such states will be worthwhile and beneficial.

While this chapter has up to now dealt with the need for cooperation, the need for peace, describing the reprehensibility and unacceptability of aggressive violence as well as discussing some of the sources and origins of this aggressive violence, we now review the nature of and the extreme damage caused by aggressive violence and consider further the origins of such violence, additionally, and in particular, focusing more specifically and in more detail than previously done, on how we can and should deal with aggressive violence, both when it occurs in our immediate and daily experiences of living, as well as in the context of the broader community, social and indeed broader human context.

Thus, having addressed the need to be peaceful and cooperative it is considered worthwhile reiterating the destructive nature of aggressive violence and its impact in terms of causing pain and suffering. Within whatever context it occurs, aggressive violence is reprehensible; violence kills; violence hurts; violence causes pain; violence damages; both directly through physical injury but also psychologically and emotionally, often causing deep and life changing psychological wounds. Engaging in aggressive violence is the antithesis of promoting well-being in any sense, and causes vast and substantial suffering.

Physical injuries may never be recovered from. Mental scars may never disappear, even with our best efforts and sophisticated medical help and treatments. Aggressive violence in itself, while it should not be the case, and needs to be worked against, can lead to those who have been victims themselves becoming aggressors, cascading the violence, damage and hurt, not only on a wider scale at that current moment and into the near future, but also down through the generations. The existence and doing of aggressive violence and violence in any form can serve itself to perpetuate violence, though fortunately, not necessarily so.

Whatever the context, whether it be in the home, workplace, or elsewhere, the expression and use of aggressive violence is unacceptable and inconsistent with the principles set out in this guide. There are no rights within community, society, families for people, for us, to do and to engage in aggressive violence against each other, against others, against other adults, against children, whatever the strains and challenges of a situation. No parent, employer, government official, person of power, no one of us, has the right to engage in such aggressive violence against others.

Within our families, communities and societies, aggressive violence damages us in many other ways. Even where we as individuals ourselves are not the specific victims of aggressive violence, such violence generates fear which in itself is destructive, unhealthy and damaging to all of us, with that violence often generating mistrust and division. Where there are family members who try to rule and dominate through fear and aggressive violence, where there are violent, political and criminal factions willing to pursue their interests whatever the means and consequences, including through aggressive violence, where there are violent racists, where there is even random and unpredictable violence, the fear generated can undermine our individual lives, our family lives, the whole of our communities and societies, damaging the effective functioning of our families, communities and societies. In particular where there is relevant aggressive violence in our communities and societies, such aggressive violence makes our communities and societies economically and socially weak, and causes additional vast suffering through poverty, fear and destruction, alongside the direct physical and traumatising, shocking effects of violence.

Without doubt, some or many, perhaps most of us, under such circumstances may be afraid to take action, to support justice, to resist attacks on our person and well-being. Where aggressive violence blights our communities and societies, we may even fear to venture out of our homes afraid of potential violence against us. Through such fear, further damage is caused since our contributions and the contributions of others, are reduced or lost, at least temporarily, to our community and society. And if we, and others, do manage to act against the aggressively violent, either individually or cooperatively with others, we may well be taking tremendous risks and, for example, we may well have tremendous difficulty in acting effectively, having difficulty even in being able to talk to others, difficulties in living our lives outside of our homes without wariness and fear.

In such situations, unfortunately, some may reprehensively collude and collaborate with the aggressively violent, with those who are oppressing us, either because they are under personal threat or in order to survive or to benefit their own interests, while others of us may become victims and their victims. There may be systematic observation and spying on our every day lives, with loss of trust in others, causing us more fear and damaging our freedom, independence, autonomy and therefore well-being and happiness further. Those who collaborate in such a manner will be causing destruction, damage and sometimes death. Of course we should never collaborate with such aggressive violence and systems or with individuals and groups promoting such aggressive violence, such systems, groups and individuals acting in such a manner being entirely at odds with our goals of supporting well-being and reducing and preventing pain and suffering. Their actions are entirely contrary to our need for care, concern and love for others, being entirely inconsistent with core and other principles.

Collaboration and indeed participation and non-participation are important issues in other contexts. For example, gangs and gang violence may be prevalent and common, with some, often young people, recruited into participation in local and more wide-ranging criminal gangs, some of these being focused on theft, extortion, drugs dealing and violence, and bound together by gang identity, frequently disputing with other gangs in aggressively violent action. Such gangs often arise in violent and poverty-stricken contexts in which there is an absence of effective law, an absence of effective law enforcement, and inadequate protection for those who are threatened with aggressive violence or who fear they may become victims of such violence. Many, particularly younger people, end up as victims of the violence of such gangs, scarred, injured or even dying in gang conflicts. Such gangs are heinous. Their aggressively violent actions are, as with other activities of this ilk, entirely at odds with the core and other principles. Wherever we can, we as individuals need to out utmost to avoid being coerced into and being forced into membership of such violent and criminal groups, doing our utmost to ensure that we do not participate in any of the damaging and destructive actions of such gangs.

If we are associated with or have influence in such groups then we need to aim to move them towards more peaceful and cooperative actions and living. Similarly if we have a specific formal role in our work, or otherwise, to reduce the violence such groups do, a role which indeed would apply to any of us outside of the work context, then we need to aim to move such gangs towards peaceful and cooperative conduct. Such actions have been taken and have been successful, with gang members turning to more peaceful action and ending their violence, following a recognition of the destructive nature of their actions and the likely self-destruction that will happen where gangs are prevalent and engage in conflict with each other. Our communities and societies as a whole cannot let such aggressively violent and criminal gangs and gang culture exist within our midst, as they will do severe and serious damage to the well-being of us all. Most of all we need to build contexts in which all people are protected from aggressive violence, in which, in particular, there are just laws and systems, combined with enforcement of laws, organised by our whole communities and societies, which give meaningful protection to us all.

While aggressive violence is highly destructive, and while we would certainly prefer that it did not occur in any form and that we did not have to take actions to oppose it, it is also true to say that, apart from the fear, pain and much more that may be experienced, there can be a also be a tremendous sense of togetherness between those of us opposing such violence and oppression, with the strongest relationships required and built comprising great mutual trust and dependence when we face together and attempt to prevent the imposition of such aggressive violence prior to, during or after conflict situations. Opposing those who are carrying out oppression; opposing the aggressively violent, creates the strongest bonds between us, through our shared (though unwanted) danger, through our sharing passionately held beliefs and convictions, passionately shared objectives, the mutual desire to defend others, our families, communities and societies, and sometimes mutual anger and hatred at our oppressors and the vile deeds they are carrying out.

Our struggle against such violence can lead us to make tremendous sacrifices to support our fellows, to support others, to protect others and to achieve our goals of freedom, to achieve an end to aggressive violence, the ending of poverty, ending destruction, ending poisonous and damaging discrimination and more. Thus, even in the darkest times, when we are facing terrible destruction, damage and wars, we can find togetherness, trust and the deepest friendship, as well as having the opportunity to pursue critically important, worthwhile and invaluable goals in our efforts to lift oppression and through working to prevent violence, poverty, war, injustice, death and destruction.

As has been stated in other chapters of this book and as will be emphasised again here, even in difficult and challenging situations, it is ourselves who are responsible for our actions. If we are directed to engage in inappropriate, aggressive, violent actions, then it is our responsibility to refuse. If we engage in such actions then it is our responsibility that we have done so. If we are being coerced and threatened into conducting inappropriate, aggressive violence against our wishes, perhaps on pain of cruel suffering and death, then we must take action against those engaged in this coercion and do so at the earliest point reasonably possible. We must not collude but must use all measures at our disposal to oppose such aggressive violence. Our actions are our responsibility.

And if such aggressive violence is being pursued by a 'loyalty' group, a nation, a belief group, a political or cultural group, then rather than support this loyalty group, it is our first duty and responsibility to protect the well-being and happiness of all and prevent the pain and suffering of all. And if that means being disloyal to our loyalty group, if that means being seen as a traitor to that group, and perhaps being painted as supporters of a discriminated against or hated out-group, then we must still follow our first duty and keep to our responsibility to protect all others, be they in our own loyalty group or another group. In this way we will be acting in a loyal, caring and concerned manner, supporting the well-being of all our fellows, a goal which benefits the general well-being and which is required by core and other principles.

And further, it is not legitimate for us to walk away and allow others to engage in such aggressive violence, without attempting, wherever possible, to intervene in some way to protect others. This is because it is our responsibility as individuals to do our utmost to prevent that aggressive violence occurring and to prevent others from enduring suffering and pain. We may accost those conducting such aggressive actions verbally, accost those who are threatening such action and persuade them or tell them to stop. If we have the physical strength then we can restrain those threatening violence. However, it is also possible that on the moment, we are faced with superior or overwhelming numbers and force threatening such violence, in which case, if we can, as mentioned earlier in this chapter, we need to gather together others in substantial numbers or those with expertise in the use of defensive force, in order to protect us and those others under threat. If no action is possible and achievable at the time, we need to do everything in our power to make sure that those who do, and have done such violence, are held accountable for their actions and prevented from threatening and doing damage to others in the future.

As also mentioned in chapter ten of this guide, it is not acceptable to use the fact that we have been told or commanded to do actions of aggressive violence as an excuse for our actions; these actions are our responsibility. Implementing the principles set out in this guide is the responsibility of all of us. The welfare and well-being of our communities, societies and human community as a whole further requires us to be responsible and accept responsibility for our actions. If our own well-being and the well-being of all is to be improved then such aggressive and violent action must be prevented from taking place.

Clearly this idea of our personal responsibility for our actions can face us with serious challenges, to say the least. In particular, for example, serious difficulties and challenges can occur in certain situations when we are either forced into, or perhaps when some of us choose, either for our life's advancement or perhaps choose in naivety, to join aggressive military organisations or aggressive violent civil forces, under certain regimes and in certain military contexts. Of course we must not, in the vast main, make such a choice.

In the first place we are responsible for making the right and best choices in our lives and should be well aware when a military or civil force is pursuing aggressive violence and oppression. If we mistakenly, out of choice, join such an organisation or are forced to participate, if we find ourselves in such a situation, and aggressively violent actions are commanded then, as we have responsibility for our actions and the well-being of both ourselves and others, we will need to take the required responsibility not only to refuse to carry out, but also to prevent, organise and act against such aggressively violent acts, even though we may well be putting our own lives at risk should we fail to carry out these commanded actions, commanded actions which may be actions of the most brutal and callous nature.

The initial course of action with regard to such situations is of course to avoid getting into such positions in the first place if at all possible. That is, if we as an individual join a military or civil policing organisation, we need to know that that organisation is tasked with and operates to all intents and purposes in line with the principles set out in this guide in that such organisations must be aiming to focus on self and other defence and acting to reduce suffering and promote the well-being of all[4]. In particular, that

---

4   There may be those who argue that military organisations cannot do this because

military must recognise the value of each individual human and our broader humanity. It must be a defender of human rights, an upholder of individual welfare and liberty, a protector of our well-being that aims to reduce our levels of pain and suffering, indeed aims to prevent pain and suffering as far as is possible within its remit. Such an organisation must not demonise those being fought against. It must not demonise those whose aggressive deeds it is combating. It must not depict their families, their children, as lesser human beings, as vile, worthless and sub-human, whatever misdeeds (if any) certain individuals or a group may be accused of, whatever misdeeds may have been conducted by certain individuals or some within the society or group which is being defended and fought against. To be seen as an acceptable, well-being seeking and defensive military, each person, whether in an opposition military or civilian from another country or organisation, needs to be seen as of fundamentally equal worth as a human being. This does not mean ignoring the dangers and threats that an individual from another group or that other group in itself may pose to us or those we aim to protect. Such threats of aggressive violence need to be countered and countered robustly and where necessary forcefully such that we can to the maximum degree avoid pain and suffering.

In relation to those cases when one or more of a group's members has engaged in a heinous and vile act or several such acts, their aggressive violence is never the responsibility of others within their group, can never be blamed on such others, unless those others clearly supported, agreed and agree with the act, unless those others participated and encouraged the act or the ethos of the act, or perhaps knowing of the planned act, did nothing about it, even perhaps if that lack of action occurs in the face of threats or perceived threats. However, inaction by other members of a group or any other in such circumstances where such heinous and vile acts are done or being planned, is an abrogation of our responsibility to others, is itself part of the causation of damage and destruction, and is certainly contrary to core and other principles.

We should, nevertheless, all recognise that, for those of us who did nothing and failed to act in such instances on the grounds of the physical consequences which may or might have resulted for us and for our families

---

of their nature. That is not the view of this guide. As has already been intimated and will be discussed later in more detail, unpleasant reality may sometimes require a vigorous response and a military, a physical force of some sort, may be needed to do this, acting defensively or taking the lead to avoid violent aggression.

and friends, our failure to act is certainly to an extent understandable, if not excusable. Nevertheless, our obligation is to act to protect others against such heinous acts, and even if that were not possible and practical on the moment, steps are required from those coerced individuals or those who took no action in the moment, to ensure that such aggressively violent, heinous and vile acts do not happen again. Under such circumstances, wherever possible, we must actively oppose such acts and actions. Risks should certainly be taken under such circumstances.

In regard to military and policing organisations, the purpose of any military or civil protection or other force must be to support the individual and general well-being and welfare and to prevent harm, suffering and pain. Any particular military or civil protection organisation must not only have appropriate explicit goals within the framework of core and other principles through which well-being is pursued and harm, pain and suffering are stated as goals to be prevented, but also must have an internal culture which ensures that such goals are not mere words and sentiments, but that such goals suffuse the organisation and are the commitment of each individual within the organisation, with all individuals understanding those goals. When these conditions are fulfilled and are fulfilled with confidence, then it is likely to be more reasonable for those of us within these organisations to operate within and follow instructions, commands and orders, though never unquestioningly, these commands being anticipated as being within the core and other principles set out within this guide.

When these conditions or similar are not in place, then we as individuals must not agree to participate in such militaries or organisations in their application of force. And we must take whatever steps we can to oppose and avoid our recruitment into such organisations. Optimally we need to forestall and pre-empt the activities of violently aggressive militaries and militant organisations. If we have been unable to do this, then we need to work against such malevolent forces or militaries before there is military or other forceful action, such that that military or civil force acts consistently with the required values and actions embedded in core and other principles. Where this has not been achieved, and where we are given no choice and cannot refuse, on pain of aggressive violence against ourselves or those we know and love – if we as individuals are placed in a position where we are being forced to cooperate or join such organisations, we must aim to avoid and refuse cooperation, object through whichever channels and means we can, within the context of core principles, and do so as effectively as we can.

And if there is no room for objection and there are threats and coercion anticipated or likely if we should say no to cooperation or joining such a military or other organisation, then we must pursue peace and cooperation as far as we can, wherever we can, within that military, aiming through our individual actions to undermine a coercive and aggressively violent organisation and remove the coercive regime. This may be difficult and challenging. It may take time and may require substantial effort at self-protection, yet this will be necessary in order to support the well-being of all and indeed our own well-being, since we are ourselves likely to become victims of aggressive violence under such systems and in such circumstances.

If we are placed under severe pressure in military or other organisations and groups, facing threats such as torture, cruel acts against us, pain of death of ourselves or family, direct physical injury, in order to make us conduct aggressive and brutal acts, we must refuse, and if we cannot bring ourselves to refuse, through fear of the range of threats against us, it is our obligation to act to prevent such acts as effectively as we can, and certainly at the minimum, take whatever action we can to remove those who have coerced, threatened and forced us into such brutal and aggressive action. We must certainly, at the minimum expose their cruel and brutal intentions and actions, though that may have little or no effect if there are none to listen and take appropriate action.

It is our responsibility at all stages to take action, to prevent significant hurt and harm. And that includes, where we are external to military and civil protection organisations, pre-emptively and continuously engaging in active participation in community and society to ensure that military and civil force organisations act in line with the principles set out in this guide, supporting the well-being and happiness of ourselves and all others, and doing our utmost to ensure that governments and other organisations never appear or never gain power, which act in a malevolent and destructive manner towards others, which act to demonise and degrade others, which promote and realise brutality, aggressive violence and values and ideas entirely contrary to the principles set out in this guide. And we, as individuals, in concert with others, need to act to ensure that that such governments and organisations, should they gain power, are never able to use military or civil force organisations to promote their malevolent conduct. It is our responsibility as individuals and communities to ensure that aggressive violence, brutality, coercion, torture and murder are prevented and avoided, and peaceful situations and peaceful living with well-being and happiness, without substantive and unnecessary suffering and pain are created in places where they do not exist and are sustained and developed where already present.

More personally, in regard to our own actions when encountering incidents of aggressive violence in our locales, in our streets and where we are immediately present and can take immediate action, it is our obligation and responsibility to act to prevent that violence, and where possible and sufficiently safe, that means we need to immediately step in and do what we can to end these incidents. If that is not realistic, if we do not have the personal power and strength to do so on the moment then, as previously pointed out, we need to get help from others available to help, ensure that others, the collective whole of us, our communities, those with more power and physical capacity, our civil safety and protection, our policing services are notified and called upon such that they can step in to prevent such aggressive violence. In some cases, and in some national and cultural contexts, the reality may be that those civil 'safety and protection' forces may not be sufficiently trustworthy in themselves, and in some cases, they may have collaborated with or collaborate with those who are oppressive and do aggressive violence, in which case it might be foolish to request their help and lead us into further pain and suffering. And indeed we have to recognise that others who might help may also be quite reasonably fearful of pain and injury. Yet if we and they, if our civil protection and safety organisations, fail to act to prevent aggressive violence, it is likely that, not only will those under attack suffer pain and injury on the moment, but those who are aggressively violent will continue with their violence and threaten us all, our families, communities and societies with terrible consequences for all of us.

It is in no sense legitimate within core and other principles to take no action in such circumstances, and it is most consistent with core principles to take immediate and effective action to protect others from aggressive violence while aiming to maintain our own well-being and the well-being of others and of our communities. Allowing unchecked aggressive violence is a danger to all of us, ourselves as individuals and all members of our communities and societies, and it is each of our personal responsibilities to ensure aggressive violence is prevented from occurring to the maximum degree possible.

And in regard to matters of our own personal capacities and capabilities, as has already been described, while we might feel fear, while we might be frightened, it is our responsibility to ensure we have the maximum capacities in terms of personal strategies, communication capacities as well as physical skills and capabilities, such that we can act to stop those acts of aggressive violence in progress and prevent the advent of, and continuance of such observed aggressive violence and conflict. Clearly by acting in this manner in more immediate circumstances where aggressive violence is threatened or in progress, or where we are encountering groups supporting aggressive violence, we may be jeopardising our own safety, well-being and welfare, and we do need to do our utmost to ensure our own safety. However in terms of the welfare of others and the well-being of our communities and societies, it is likely to be beneficial if not necessary that we act promptly and immediately in one way or another, to protect anyone in immediate danger and act to prevent violence ourselves or immediately in concert with others.

In terms of those capabilities, we have to recognise that as we get older our physical capacities to respond in such situations will decline, nevertheless in that case, we should be aiming to develop our verbal capacities to respond to such situations, and can use other forms of personal capital to stand in the way of aggressive violence, for example, the immense social disapproval and anger of community and society against those who attack and injure the elderly and the weak, and the often found values within many cultures of the aggressively violent and other criminal groups where violent attacks on the elderly are a matter of shame for those who carry them out (though of course in some organisations and groups there is simply general callousness towards others and no such shame). In situations where we are confronting aggressive violence, we are certainly risking being hurt and hurt badly, especially if we are frail, yet we will hopefully be doing enormous service to our communities, to all others, and hopefully through our words there will be, as a consequence, no violence carried out. Of course where younger and more physically able, and indeed hopefully well-trained individuals in terms of self-protection are available to protect others, then that is a role they should perhaps fulfill rather than leaving such situations to the less physically capable, the frail and elderly to resolve.

We do need to make judgments about the situations in which we are observing aggressive violence and intense conflict. There may be those parties engaging in physical violence in the public or in more private spaces, individuals or groups, who are happy to engage in such damaging and destructive violence, who in some sense have agreed to have such aggressively violent interaction. Irrespective of their agreement, such public or indeed private aggressive violence cannot be allowed to take place. The practice of aggressive violence creates shock and fear, a real sense that that violence can be turned against us, that there are others who are prepared to act in aggressively violent ways which are not under social control and that we will be the next victims. Moreover, the occurrence of such aggressive violence in itself may promote violent conduct in other contexts and support a more general culture of aggressive violence. Thus, while taking care to maintain our own safety and well-being, while taking care to protect ourselves, we must take action to stop all such incidents of aggressive violence, irrespective of the views of the participants, with our seeking to encourage other means of dealing with such conflict.

Beyond these wider social and community contexts, we may encounter aggressive violence in the home, something that is, unfortunately, far from uncommon at this point in time. In particular, women, at least at the present time, too often fall victim to aggressive violence from partners and husbands, although women themselves may also be verbally abusive, coercive, bullying and aggressively violent towards their partners and husbands. None of this is acceptable. Through togetherness and love, through our skills in collaboration and cooperation, our relationships need to be supported and worked at, and aggressive violence avoided in all cases.

There are, unfortunately again, also those who see their partners as possessions or virtual possessions, believing it is their right to control them and deal with them abusively and aggressively should their partner not comply with their desires and wishes, something totally at odds with core principles and principles of well-being and happiness. There are also those who become contemptuous and dismissive of their partners, belittling and insulting them consistently, aiming to diminish them and make them suffer, sometimes on account of perceived insult, events occurring elsewhere in their lives and their own pain, insults and abuse which they heap onto their partner, blaming their partner for their perceived misfortunes, which will almost undoubtedly be more of their own doing. There are also those who lose self-control and may be aggressively violent when taking alcohol or other drugs.

These people need to move or be moved to a position whereby they understand and act in partnership, love, cooperation towards others, supporting others, supporting their partners and working together with them. Where such people take alcohol and other drugs and as a consequence become aggressively violent, they of course need to stop taking such alcohol and drugs, through personal decision, medical treatments or in whichever way that can reasonably be achieved. Alternatively that relationship needs to be brought to an end. Aggressive violence, derisive and dismissive attitudes and insults, bullying and coercion towards a partner, indeed towards anyone, are totally reprehensible and unacceptable. We must support the well-being and happiness of others, look after them, take care of them, not bully, control, dictate to and coerce them through violent threat and aggression or indeed through other verbal means.

Each partner has a right and responsibility to protect themselves from such violent aggression, and it is moreover the responsibility of us all, as individuals and as communities and societies, as a humanity, to protect all such partners, men and women, from violent control and coercion. No one is bound to stay in such a relationship, and as already described in this chapter, as a community and society, we need to provide means to support more effective and positive relationships, and where such is not achieved or achievable, enable safety and escape when non-violent cooperative relationships prove impossible.

Even in the face of the severe stresses which can exist within family life, with our sometimes enduring lack of sleep, with the constant demands of young children (and also the joys of our children), faced with partners who we may feel at times are unreasonable, unsympathetic and uncaring, faced by the requirement to earn money to support and more than support our families, all of this which can serve to make us to some extent stressed, frustrated and tired, there is no acceptable excuse or reason for aggressive violence, for dictatorial and controlling behaviour, for the use of violence, intimidation and threat.

Couples need to work well and cooperate well together, understanding and caring for each other, in an important sense be friends and supporters of each other (something we are not really explicitly taught how to do), And even if we experience frustration and annoyance, feeling that our more personal wants and needs are not being met by our partners, sometimes feeling ill, stressed and pressured by the strenuous and difficult process of cooperative and consensual decision-making, our efforts at give and take, our sometimes giving of ourselves and perhaps we may feel, rarely taking and getting in return, with our, as a consequence, feeling unloved and uncared for, this can be no justification for such controlling, dictatorial behaviour and aggressive violence.

Our homes, for some of us, can sometimes be intense environments where there will be thousands of interactions between partners and between partners and children (should we have children) through the days, weeks and years, all of which we hope would be peaceful. On occasion, however, if not more frequently, in many family contexts, and sometimes persistently in some family contexts, problems may arise with fundamental disagreements, conflict, frustrations and sometimes anger arising between partners. These problems will need to be resolved peacefully in all cases, with, hopefully, partners staying together and continuing to love each other. Nevertheless, tensions and conflict must not be allowed to get out of hand. Whatever the difficulties and tensions, recourse to personal and deeply painful abuse, bullying, character assassination, incessant undermining and vicious criticisms, and of course aggressive violence, all of which undermine well-being and happiness, are unacceptable. They should not occur, and if they do arise, cannot be allowed to continue. No one should feel bound to suffer from these behaviours, for example in order to keep a family together.

And we certainly must not engage in such conduct, in any aggressive, violent, damaging and destructive conduct ourselves, whatever the provocation, and we must support others to prevent these things from happening. Walking away temporarily in tense and difficult situations is reasonable and sometimes necessary to gain peace and space away from argument and tension, in order to provide ourselves with space and time in which to calm down and think. Leaving a partner, at least temporarily, is possible and sometimes necessary to avoid pain and suffering. Talking is possible and indeed necessary if we wish to resolve difficulties to bring relationships back together and resolve conflict, but not aggressive violence and verbal insults and abuse under any circumstances.

Moreover, when our children, as is unfortunately not so uncommon, usually on account of their youth, are provocative, behave in overly negatively selfish ways, are perhaps insulting, rude and disrespectful, perhaps engage in aggressively violent conflict with ourselves as parents or other children, we must not ourselves respond with aggressive violence and physical punishment. Of course, where necessary, we must defend ourselves and defend others. We must prevent pain, hurt and suffering as much as we can. Children have no right to hurt any others, have no right to hurt other children and must be prevented, with appropriate restraint at times, in order for us to fulfill our responsibilities to prevent physical and indeed emotional injury to others. Such restraint should not be so difficult with the youngest children. Yet, while it is legitimate to restrain children from hurting others, legitimate to use physical force to move fighting children apart, legitimate to remove children from a conflict environment thereby reducing the possibility of violence, we must never use aggressive violence with anyone, let alone children.

Hitting children is unacceptable and certainly not educational as is sometimes claimed; spanking and hurting as punishments, as ways of exerting control, teach little other than that aggressive violence is a legitimate response to behaviour we do not like. Their use provides a context where violence appears legitimate and in which violence is part of the family, school or broader social landscape. Children will sometimes, if not often, fail to demonstrate the level of self-control, the self-restraint, the peaceful and cooperative behaviour we would wish for, however, sometimes they may do much worse, failing to share, hurting other children and more. Nevertheless, we must demonstrate and educate, teach cooperation, care and togetherness, empathy and understanding, modeling such behaviours ourselves in order to support the effective upbringing of our children such that they can live well and participate well in our communities, societies and broader humanity.

Further, in terms of our more general interactions with others, more than simply being reactive to situations of aggressive violence when such situations arise, it is our responsibility to proactively promote, as far as is possible, peaceful, constructive cooperation in our own relationships, and between others within our communities and societies, between communities and societies. Our own peaceful and cooperative approaches are likely to serve to enhance well-being not only in our own lives, but in the lives of those with whom we interact on a daily basis, our friends, our colleagues in work environments and those with whom we have the range of relationships, of varying degrees of closeness and intensity.

Interacting with people in friendly, cooperative and constructive ways, is consistent with core principles, with the pursuit of cooperation with others being specified in More Specific Principle two. Even where there are stressful incidents and stressful situations, it is important to deal with these incidents in a manner which is cooperative and peaceful, and to aim to move such situations and relationships to new and different situations where our interactions take place in a peaceful, cooperative and friendly manner. All of this is, of course, part of a life of well-being and happiness.

Achieving and acting towards cooperativity and peacefulness does require each of us as individuals to, first of all, set these as part of our individual agendas and goals. Cooperativity and peacefulness are important goals in themselves, need to be achieved, and, as mentioned, we need to act in a pro-active manner to achieve them. This can be done in range of ways including through, for example, demonstrating a peaceful and discursive, cooperative approach ourselves, through listening and paying attention to the needs, wants, feelings, worries and more, of others, through responding with sensitivity in our words and actions to others.

We also need to let others know, where appropriate and consistent with promoting peacefulness and well-being, what we believe, feel and more, being prepared to state and assert our own thoughts and feelings; yet we also need to be prepared to discuss and negotiate and indeed not achieve all we want, sometimes accepting compromise for the sake of ourselves and others, for the greater good, being prepared to sometimes lose for the benefit of all, yet of course also being prepared to achieve those things which overall support our own happiness and well-being. That being said, negotiations (not simply in terms of formal negotiations but the types of negotiations which might take place over time in a family or small community) can be complex and ongoing, involving give and take and being complicated, with differing perceptions of situations. Nevertheless, we must talk, we must listen, we must empathise, discuss and cooperate and we must not resort to coercive conduct, threats, intimidation and aggressive violence.

Yet, it is also important, if not crucial, in many, if not most situations, that the optimal decisions are reached and taken, and that we do pursue the optimal courses of action, with poor and wrong decisions likely to interfere with and reduce well-being and happiness and possibly result in pain and suffering. We also need to ensure therefore, dependent to some extent on what is being discussed and what actions we plan to take, and to some extent dependent on circumstances and situations, that our desire for cooperativity and peacefulness does not take substantial precedence and operates in a reasonable balance with the reaching of the optimal decisions and determining the optimal actions in order to support well-being and happiness. Taking substantially incorrect decisions, however cooperatively done, can have disastrous consequences for well-being and happiness and lead to substantial pain and suffering.

To illustrate this point in regard to optimal decisions, certainly sometimes, if not often, being as or more important than cooperative processes and procedures, in the presence of problems, perhaps sometimes severe, what is frequently needed, if not needed most of all under many circumstances in order to support well-being and happiness and reduce pain and suffering is correct answers and correct solutions. Thus, in the context of medical treatment, in the face of the need to take action when confronted by illness or disease, while often highly beneficial, the degree of sociability and cooperativity, the interactive capacities of a doctor or researcher may not be of paramount importance if that doctor or researcher, through their individual judgment and personal capacities, can help solve a medical problem and cure a patient. That being said, sociability and cooperativity are extremely valuable and are highly likely to help the doctor or researcher achieve and deliver optimum outcomes, these people needing cooperative skills to identify sources of pain in their patients, to interact with other medical staff who may be delivering treatment, for discussion of the case with colleagues and to deal with others involved in medical analyses and investigations.

In order to solve complex but important mathematical and computational problems, while cooperativity and sociability are undoubtedly helpful, and should contribute to the solution of problems, what is probably needed most of all are solutions and answers, something which individual, somewhat socially awkward individuals, may in some cases, have a greater capacity to deliver. Of course many involved in such areas may be highly competent socially and this supports their success.

Considering these examples (and there may be many other examples which exist), while it is considered here that cooperativity and interactive capacities are of great value, and comprise in themselves elements, if not important elements of much achievement, success and optimal solutions, it needs to be acknowledged that being successful in achieving goals (one of which may be bolstering cooperation and collaboration) finding correct solutions and answers are also of significance in themselves. Both achievement of goals, solutions and answers as well as our cooperativity and collaboration are likely to support our well-being and happiness.

Of course our cooperative actions require us to engage with and interact with others. It is therefore important, if not essential, in terms of achieving many of our own personal goals and supporting the reasonable goals of our communities and societies that we make efforts to meet with and engage with others who might help and support us. Clearly such positive action is an element and indeed a necessity for effective cooperation. Such efforts and actions, if carried out appropriately, frequently proactively, can prevent unnecessary misunderstandings and conflict and avoid our actions causing offence and, in some contexts, impinging on the matters, the areas and responsibilities that others may consider to be within their remit. In particular, we may need to make conscious and deliberate efforts, proactive efforts, to seek out and meet with, not only those people affected by what we do and plan to do, but also with those who have the talents, skills, abilities and indeed the influence and power such that they could be of help to us in achieving our worthwhile goals.

Reality means that we all like to be consulted on matters which are of relevance to us and which might affect us. Indeed we all like to be listened to and certainly taken account of. Further, we, at least the many of us, often like to be offered the chance to help and support others, something which is a recognition of our value, skills, importance and standing. Doing such things, making such requests for help, is a sign of respect for all of us.

Moreover and importantly justifying our need to make contact with and cooperate with others, there are things we do not know and perhaps cannot know. Others have wisdom and knowledge, different thinking, the skills and knowledge already referred to, and can point out the pitfalls in our own thinking, suggest better, more practical and realistic alternatives to the actions we are considering and proposing, point us to others who might help and also advise us in what we are doing. And indeed, if we enthuse others, they may lobby and act on our behalf in order to help us, our communities and societies, our broader humanity, in achieving our goals, helping us to secure the further agreement, cooperation and assent we might need to be successful. The wider the range of others we can know and maintain as contacts, the easier it may be to achieve our goals, though this is of course, somewhat dependent on what we are aiming to achieve. But we can also gain simply from having the benefits of more friendships and other relationships.

Clearly our social skills in terms of getting to meet people and our actual communication once we do meet them, are likely to be significantly critical in helping us achieve our goals, in advancing our own well-being and happiness and the happiness and well-being of others in our communities, societies and beyond, and of course these communication skills will support us in cooperative action and the avoidance of unnecessary disputes and conflict. Moreover, some of us will be more easy with, and enjoy the company of others and be better at building cooperation and contacts than others, yet this form of ability is in reality of importance for almost all of us, whether in the context of work, in terms of our leisure and family activities or in more local community and broader societal environments. Some of us may feel shy and reticent and be less willing to talk, and while in some senses, self-deprecation, modesty and shyness are valuable qualities, it seems reasonable to state that they may, to some extent and in some cases, hold us back in achieving our goals and stand in some cases, though not all, as barriers to important achievement.

Acknowledging this, however, our communities and societies consist of and indeed need all sorts of people, people with different personalities, different constellations of attitudes, knowledge and understandings and different constellations of skills. There are certainly those of us, who may be less adept at cooperating and communicating with others, who to some extent may be more self-contained, more solitary, preferring isolation and solitude away from others where we can think in depth or simply because that is what we prefer. There are those of us who might be described as more thoughtful and bookish, more academic, abstract, theoretical and mathematical, perhaps in some cases we are simply shy; there are those who do simply not greatly enjoy social company, who do not feel sociable or particularly wish for the company of others. There are also those of us who are not so ambitious in terms of our personal achievement, or who are less wanting or perhaps unwilling to engage in frequent persuasive social interactions and relationships in order to present their case, express their beliefs and achieve their goals.

Such people, those of us with this form of character, are of import in ourselves just as any others of us are of import. We may achieve much for ourselves and others through our more solitary approach and through our different approaches and perspectives, providing variability in perspective which may be increased and enhanced through a more solitary, less social form of existence. However, in our education and upbringing, through the development and formulation of our ideas, there will have been collaboration and cooperativity, at the minimum some element of social interaction, even at a distance. Moreover, at some point, to some extent, it is highly likely we will all have to communicate the product of our thinking and actively cooperate with others to do this; we will have to communicate our feelings, our ideas, our thoughts, our discoveries, our reactions and emotions; we will have to do things and do those things in cooperation with others if we are to be significantly fulfilled in our lives, if we are to achieve substantive well-being and happiness.

Nevertheless, the fact is that someone who is troublesome, somewhat anti-social, indeed childish and lacking in many social skills, may in some cases, still be able, through their intellectual and other capacities, in fact by dint to some extent of their differing character and approach, to make valuable, imaginative and creative contributions. Such a person may have high level skills and abilities, or the capacity to find the correct answers to the serious problems we face, answers, skills and abilities, which those who are more cooperative, possessing of all the social skills, the smiles, pleasantries and valued interactive capacities, may not have or may not be able to provide.

And there are those who are eccentric, different and perhaps grating in their approaches to people, yet who are highly skilled in what they do, if not unique in their superior talents and abilities in some respects, who may irritate and annoy, for example through their actions and words, and may even induce substantial hostility from others in their acquaintance groups and teams. Of course their conduct is in many respects undesirable and may be difficult for others of us to cope with. Yet, in order to achieve success and support well-being, we, as a community, society and humanity, may well need these grating people and their different approaches alongside the contributions of those who are more social and cooperative. And where we find such eccentric, different and difficult people, in order to achieve success, we will almost always need to make efforts to incorporate and encourage these individuals to do that which they can do, to participate and contribute to the whole, while helping them to be as social and cooperative as they can be, aspects of behaviour which will hopefully support those individuals in achieving their own happiness and fulfillment.

Indeed, it is not impossible; it may well be possible, for those who are more didactic and less open and democratic in their approaches, to help our communities achieve in the face of challenges and difficulties, although it is unlikely their contributions and achievements will be significantly sustained, since the contributions, ideas and arguments, the perceptions of others are usually necessary for us to achieve success, and certainly necessary to achieve success over a prolonged period. However, such more didactic individuals, for example, as experienced business people and managers, may in some cases have better judgment than others of us, be better able to recognise problems and their solutions, or indeed may succeed simply through circumstances and chance. Of course if such people are in leadership roles within the context of business or elsewhere, they will need to deploy social skills, encourage cooperation and perhaps inspire others. If they are too didactic in their approach and do not encourage peacefulness and cooperation, they will undoubtedly find that hostility arises towards them and as a consequence, find achievement of goals very difficult or impossible.

Didactic, dictatorial leaders seeking total control should be avoided completely, since such individuals will fail dramatically in the end, causing massive damage to well-being and frequently causing substantial pain and suffering. This is inevitable due to their inability to attend properly to others, their intolerance of others, their anti-democratic nature, their sense of their own superiority and rightness, and much more, all of which represent part of their dictatorial nature and approach. Their dictatorial nature will mean that they seek total control, thereby undermining the effectiveness of an organisation, of our communities and societies and damaging us all as individuals. No single individual has such insights and capacities that we should put too significant or our entire belief in them without engaging our own critical and thinking faculties and having the opportunity to express our own perspectives and make our own acknowledged contributions to actions, decisions and decision-making.

Moreover with such power, dictators will, as indeed others do, be unable to see, or frequently ignore the suffering they may be causing, often aiming to control the flow of information such that the truth of their actions (often the truth of pain and suffering) is hidden. All of this is inbuilt in to the nature of dictatorial people, dictators and dictatorships, the presence of whom and which, be that in our organisations (schools, homes, businesses, local councils, our communities and societies or globally) must be prevented, for the benefit of the well-being and happiness of us all. It is cooperative and peaceful action, open and democratic processes, skillfully carried out in support of goals consistent with core and other principles, aimed at enhancing well-being and happiness and reducing pain and suffering, which are desirable.

Importantly, and also relevant to the relationship between collaboration and cooperation, our having great social skills, our being excellent and skilled at interacting with others, our getting others to work together, promoting cooperation and being highly persuasive in our interactions, will not support well-being if we have inappropriate goals, such as pursuing cooperation for our own negatively selfish benefit, using these social skills for the purposes of our own self-preferment and self-advancement, pursuing personal financial gain, at the expense of others or pursuing goals at odds with core and other principles.

We must support cooperation in order to promote worthwhile goals. And for our social skills, our ability to promote cooperation, to be of value, it is essential that, to the greatest extent we can, we have, demonstrated and act on our concern and care for others, use good judgment, strong thinking, knowledge, wisdom, empathy and understanding, creativity, inventiveness, the capacity to self-evaluate in terms of our goals and the goals of others, with the purpose of supporting well-being and happiness.

Without such goals, without these features, cooperative action, while generally much preferable to indifference, isolationism and unpleasant conflict, can be damaging, itself fomenting resentment and intense conflict, leading to damage to well-being and happiness, and causing suffering and pain. All of the social skills and actions and capacities mentioned may seem very demanding, however most of us can manage these, though we need to acknowledge our human frailties and limitations, our human capacity for mistakes and errors, as has already been discussed in this guide. Our optimal efforts and commitment to support the well-being and happiness of ourselves and others are of fundamental importance and we need to do our utmost to be successful in pursuit of such worthwhile and reasonable goals.

However, achieving cooperativity and peacefulness may not be easy. We must acknowledge that there are times when we may find ourselves in situations where our efforts at peaceful cooperation may encounter those who have no interest in such approaches (though sometimes these people may appear to express interest in discussion and negotiation). This difficulty in achieving cooperation and peacefulness can happen when we are dealing with people blinded by ideology and belief, aside from facts, reason and evidence, whose beliefs entail hatred of others or entail the belief that others should be hurt and harmed if not killed, simply for being different or acting inconsistently with their belief systems.

Problems with achieving cooperation are further likely to arise when we are dealing with people who wish to place their personal interest and interests far above that of ourselves and others, being willing to ignore and remove from consideration, our own well-being and the well-being of others. Still others we interact with may simply have no or little recognition of others, of the perceptions of others, may lack the sense of empathy and understanding of others, even, to some extent, may lack the notion of individual separate others of us with our own interests and perceptions, these people being too self-focused, perhaps suffering from mental illness in some form, lost in themselves, indeed perhaps narcissistic, perhaps convinced beyond reason and evidence of their own rectitude and unable to understand, listen to and value the perceptions of others.

In many cases, such individuals will be unwilling and indeed unable to discuss and negotiate in a cooperative and open manner, being unwilling or unable to listen and take account of the desires, perceptions and beliefs of others. Some unpleasant, negatively selfish individuals may deliberately aim to use disingenuous manipulation, perhaps, as already alluded to, aiming to create an impression of integrity and openness to discussion and negotiation, but with no such true intention, with their having the goal of misleading us, pulling the wool over our eyes, playing on our desire to trust others, and our positive assumptions about the integrity of others, treating us as if we are naive and stupid.

Moreover, there are those who may engage in verbal abuse, bullying, nefarious dishonesty, lies and falsehoods and, at an even more extreme end of the scale, there are some who will engage in coercion, threat and aggressive violence in order to support achieving their own goals and interests, using such methods in an effort to impose their own beliefs and perceptions, to support their own immediate personal gain and advantage, brushing aside others, to the detriment of the interests of other individuals, to the rest of us, the group or community, society as a whole. Such actions are entirely unacceptable and entirely out of line with the core and other principles.

Even where we are encountering such people, we need to try to pursue peacefulness and cooperativity, while at the same time pursuing justice, love, care, supporting optimal beliefs, decisions and actions and supporting our own well-being and happiness and the well-being and happiness of others. Nevertheless, where there are such people, unwilling and unable to listen, and unwilling and unable to understand the needs of others, acting solely in their own negatively selfish interests, often in ways which are not peaceful and cooperative, where there are those who are engaging in the range of uncooperative actions, then we may need to have recourse to more robust and firm actions to tackle their conduct, in line with core and other principles. Our actions should be peaceful but firm and robust, as we cannot allow ourselves or others to experience substantial pain and suffering and need to support well-being and happiness.

It needs to be stated and reiterated that pursuing peacefulness and working cooperatively and sensitively with others does not mean weakness in the face of manipulation, threats coercion and bullying. Acting in a peaceful and cooperative manner does require us to demonstrate the required strength in the pursuit of well-being and happiness for all, in pursuit of optimal actions and optimal decisions. Allowing those who are negatively selfish, short-sighted, intolerant, aggressive and aggressively violent, psychologically and mentally ill in a destructive and damaging manner, those who are bullying and abusive or displaying other negative and destructive characteristics, allowing such people to put their attitudes, beliefs and actions into practice and achieve their selfish anti-social goals, causing pain and suffering to others, to those who are caring, empathetic, tolerant, loving, well-intentioned, cooperative and peaceful, and at the expense of the wider community, is not acceptable whatever the context.

Of course there are legitimate differences of interest, perception and view. The fact of disagreement and such different interests, beliefs and perceptions does not mean that those we are dealing with are malevolent or that they are being negatively selfish. Others may be misguided, misinformed, may be thinking irrationally and illogically and may be wrong, as we may be ourselves. Then there are differences of interest, and therefore disputes and disagreements, which are indeed natural and frequent and will need to be resolved through peaceful and cooperative means, through discussion and negotiation, as far as is possible, and certainly not through aggressive violence.

Through talk and discussion, through mutual listening and empathy, we should aim to and will hopefully be able to reach understandings, agreement, compromises where necessary and achieve solutions in response to different views and differing perceptions, beliefs and interests. Where this is not possible and we, or those with whom we are dealing, do not achieve our particular individual or perhaps group goals, then we will have a range of options, our actions being determined by and dependent on the points of disagreement, dependent on that which is being negotiated and the benefits, as well as the costs and pains of achieving or not achieving our goals in a particular set of circumstances and particular situations.

Optimally, if there is no harm to us and others through the presence of a disagreement or varied perceptions, then we may choose, on the relevant occasion, to simply accept that we have not achieved those goals, our wishes and desires, and carry on with our lives, rather than continuing discussion, negotiation, conflict and dispute. If the difference is important and of impact on our lives and the lives of others, yet we cannot agree, we, as differing parties may need to reach some form of compromise which facilitates cooperativity and peace, through which the views of both or many parties are accounted for, compromise which may be to some extent mutually satisfactory but which may also be unsatisfactory in some respects. Being insistent on our own views and perceptions winning the day and overriding the feelings, views, perceptions of others may lead to substantial conflict and unhappiness, diminishing well-being in the medium and long term, leaving a taste of lasting dissatisfaction and resentment. Such insistence on our own negotiating 'triumph and victory' needs to be considered in terms of the relevant context and tempered in the light of recognising that the views of unhappy and dissatisfied others are likely to lead to actions or entail actions which might represent substantial and significant threat to ourselves and others. It is most useful if peaceful and cooperative solutions which are of mutual benefit are pursued as far as is possible.

Unfortunately, although we may be cooperative and social individuals with our possessing many automatic and embedded strategies for securing cooperation with our fellows, and possessing strategies for building and retaining peaceful relationships with them, the fact is that in regard to our individual and personal daily lives there may still be many instances and incidents where unhelpful and damaging, sometimes long lasting conflicts can arise, conflicts with family members, with our neighbours, with our work colleagues and with other members of our communities, societies as well as conflicts within our global social entities.

Given the possibility or even probability of such conflicts, having established cooperativity and peacefulness as a goal for ourselves as individuals, we need, in pursuit of these goals and in order to pursue these goals effectively, to be aware of our daily conduct, how we behave as individuals and how we deal with situations where there may be different beliefs, feelings, interests and perceptions of situations in play. We need an awareness of not only where we consider others are behaving unreasonably, perhaps negatively selfishly, but also an awareness of where we ourselves may be behaving unreasonably and unfairly. Based in our self-understanding, self-observation and self-knowledge as well as a good understanding of others, we will be able to more effectively support the goals of cooperativity and peacefulness and support our own well-being and happiness and the well-being and happiness of others. And often through acknowledging our own faults, our own unreasonable behaviour and perhaps negative selfishness, we will have a route to building peace and cooperativity and better relationships with others.

As part of developing our self-awareness and understanding, we need to recognise that as individuals, many of us may well have automatic behaviours, deeply embedded personal attitudes and ways of acting and speaking that could themselves act against cooperativity and peacefulness. Additionally, we may have ingrained and sometimes hidden biases, prejudices and beliefs of which we, in some cases, may be unaware, biases, beliefs and prejudices which may well mitigate against cooperation and peacefulness in our relationships with others and promote difficult relationships and unpleasant conflict. Not only that, but on the moment, when dealing with others, we may be inclined to or automatically prioritise our own particular goals above the goals of others, listening and attending to others poorly, taking insufficient consideration of the needs and concerns of others, and this itself may cause conflict. We may be sometimes quick to take offence or quick to anger and upset, being overly sensitive, sometimes through overtiredness or stress in our lives, but sometimes being this way more generally. And indeed, often grounded in fear and self-doubt, with no particular intention to do harm or hurt others, we may be overly quick to question the motives of others, being irrationally suspicious of their motives and quick to misunderstand what they are saying and what their intentions and goals really are.

Such behaviour and such problematic thinking is likely to enhance conflict and provoke discord and may even be a starting point for and lead, in some cases, to abusive conflict, damage to relationships and violent confrontation. And so a proper awareness of ourselves, and the ability to know, understand, and reflect on our attitudes and conduct is essential in our efforts to ensure peacefulness, in order to make cooperation happen and in order to promote our own well-being and happiness and the well-being and happiness of others. Such a reflective capacity, such a capacity for self-awareness and indeed for changing our thinking, is essential as is the capacity to act effectively and change our conduct appropriately based on our reflections, with maximal positive effect in terms of the core principles set out in this guide.

Knowing ourselves as well as we can know ourselves is indeed an asset. And as a consequence of our self-knowledge and understanding, these in themselves hopefully, though perhaps not necessarily, will lead us to more conscious and effective management and control of our behaviour such that we are better able to deal with others in what may sometimes be stressful situations. Nevertheless of course, allied to knowing ourselves, as mentioned above, we will likely need to aim to change and in reality change our behaviours in support of the well-being and happiness of ourselves and others. Pursuing our self-knowledge and understanding as well as the consequent effective actions, is and will be, for the most of us, an ongoing task requiring persistent reflection, requiring rationality and decisions to modify our conduct, and may also involve practice in acting as we have decided to act. In itself the possession of such knowledge and understanding is certainly one of the key components towards building a life of well-being and happiness, though this knowledge, understanding and self-awareness, does require combination with the actual capacity to make changes and improve how we conduct ourselves; it does require the capacity to develop ourselves such that we choose more effective actions, and take those actions, therefore meaning we can and do pursue core and other principles to maximum effect.

Peacefulness and cooperation are routes to, and represent in themselves, important elements of well-being and happiness. They require us to engage in continuing dialogue with the range of people in our lives. Such dialogue and communication is essential to the building of new futures, in supporting and encouraging effective involvement, engagement and participation in current and new ventures, in maintaining and building relationships and, of course, in supporting well-being, happiness, and reducing pain and suffering in line with core and other principles.

Our dialogue and communication need to be positive and constructive, caring, conducted in the spirit of friendship and togetherness, cooperative, empathetic, listening, in many cases focused towards goals and shared goals, and hopefully should be enjoyable, enriching and stimulating in themselves on a moment-to-moment basis. Conversation and dialogue, true sharing, true cooperative interactions are, and will be in the main, a pleasure, a real sharing experience from which all of us benefit through the actual conversation and dialogue in itself, and also through the achievement of separate more individual and shared individual, community or social goals. When we are experiencing and participating in such dialogue, this in itself has a knock-on and positive affect on those external to our dialogue, who may receive the benefits of those things achieved through the dialogue and exchange itself, and also experience benefits simply through the presence of those participating in such joyful and enriching communication within our communities, societies and beyond.

That being said, allied to the potential difficulties in achieving peaceful cooperation and negotiation already discussed, not all cooperative dialogue and communication will be positive on the moment, though hopefully all or almost all such dialogue and communication will produce benefits in the longer term. There are times when, for example, we may wish to express our disappointment with others, our unhappiness, express sadness, share difficult experiences with someone, and on the moment the sharing may not be joyful. Hopefully however, in the longer term, expressing our feelings, asserting our wants, needs requirements and desires, telling our stories of joy, happiness, pain and suffering will help to strengthen relationships. We may even wish, and need to, express anger at someone for a range of reasons, particularly those of feeling let down, frustrated, disrespected, unwanted and so forth. Expressing anger may not be seen as cooperative and peaceful, however, rather than containing within ourselves deep anger and frustration, it may be appropriate and for the best to let someone, to let others to whom our anger is directed, know exactly how we feel such that they can respond and perhaps let us know how they feel. The end result may in some cases be deeper love and understanding, and stronger relationships, though of course relationships may well be fractured and forever broken if the expressing of hurt, upset and anger deteriorates into uncaring and callous abuse, or even aggressive violence.

The absence of dialogue – a lack of communication – can be dangerous, often representing in itself the existence of serious problems, or leading to serious problems. While certainly at times, we all need personal space and time to ourselves, sometimes substantial time, desisting from normal communication, refusing to speak to others, particularly those we know and would normally interact with daily, is uncomfortable, with the restarting of dialogue and communication required and symbolic of efforts and of a necessity to repair relationships and deal with what may be deep and difficult problems.

Of course, not speaking and being uncommunicative to someone is preferable to aggressive violence but in itself can be seen as aggressive, being significantly damaging to well-being, indeed often deeply hurtful and emotionally challenging and damaging. Clearly if we refuse to communicate persistently, then those with whom we have stopped communication, and that means meaningful communication, if they can achieve no change in our approach, are likely to feel resentment and more towards us, and may choose to end our relationship. Some periods of non-communication, some moments or periods of silence, may sometimes, if not often, be necessary to absorb emotional shock and pain, to absorb a verbal blow or other form of pain-causing event. We may need time to react internally, to internally express anger. We may also need time for our irrational thoughts and upset to be expressed internally and then reframed for the outside world to hear. Further, we may need time to calm ourselves down and then to have time for reflection and thought, rational consideration, such that problems can be thought about, our own conduct and the conduct of others can be examined and our motives and goals reconsidered as well as the motives, goals and actions of others. In such a period of silence, solutions may be found along with a drive to action, enabling us to address conflict, problems and difficulties, and deal with them as soon as we reasonably can. In most cases, should we engage in them, our periods of silence cannot and should not be allowed to continue for too long and we need to re-open dialogue as soon as possible.

It should be added that there may be circumstances, for example, where a victim of serious abuse or violence does not wish to talk to his or her aggressor or abuser on the grounds of trauma, fear, anger, disgust and sometimes hatred, these feelings being understandable, if not optimal. If dialogue and communication can be started, even under such trying conditions, that may be for the best. However, those who have been hurt and damaged in such extreme ways must not be dictated to in regard to their relationship with someone who has hurt them in such ways. Further communication must be at their behest and is a matter of discretion for them, though where they may benefit from such communication and dialogue, then it might be acceptable, with great care, to provide the gentlest of suggestions, at the right time and in the right place, that such a dialogue might be begun.

Where we live with someone, work in close proximity to them, and need to work together with them and perhaps be together with them every day, then refusing to talk, refusing to interact, is not advisable moment-to-moment and is not acceptable as a medium-term or long-term strategy. Pain and upset might make communication, reasoned and caring communication, difficult for a short period of time, but that non-communication should not be sustained and we need to make efforts at the earliest point possible to re-engage and resolve problems. Dialogue and communication, listening, understanding and a preparedness to change, to act differently by all of us, are essential in the resolution of difficulties and in the building of future cooperation and togetherness, which support well-being and happiness.

Nor is it acceptable to wait for another to take the initiative. It is down to each of us to take the initiative to resolve problems and to establish the route to better cooperation and more peaceful, happy and successful daily lives. Where others refuse to engage and refuse to engage after persistent attempts over time to restore and rebuild a relationship, then, as already suggested, we must give consideration to moving away, at least temporarily, from that relationship, until the other party has resolved their own difficulties and can re-engage (although of course we may have moved on elsewhere in the interim). Where this refusal to engage with us causes us pain and frustration, then we should not put ourselves unnecessarily through the frustration and pain of, in essence, 'banging our heads against a brick wall', but if we can, we need to allow some time; we need to wait for others to become more willing to engage.

Within the context of core principles it is essential that we promote dialogue and communication wherever possible. On the whole, with some exceptions possible, including some mentioned above, it is not acceptable for us to totally withdraw from communication and dialogue with others, in anger, because of conflict and problems, or for whatever reason. There are certainly occasions when perhaps we are in shock, when the moment is not correct for us to engage in dialogue, something which is a matter of personal judgment, when for example someone is tired and stressed, in a context where other problems are already on the table, perhaps where situations are threatening to become more heated and difficult and there may be good cause and reason for us to walk away temporarily, hopefully with the intention to wait for more appropriate moments. That is fine if there is an intention or plan to resolve difficulties at some point through appropriate action, communication and dialogue.

Refusing to speak to others however, on an extended or threatened permanent basis is in the vast main unacceptable. The reality is that even in extraordinary and challenging circumstances, engaging in dialogue, using words carefully and appropriately to promote peace and understanding is likely to lead to better outcomes, will lead to higher levels of well-being and happiness. It may indeed take some courage to overcome the fear of dialogue with those we might mistrust and indeed may dislike, those who may threaten us, may bully us, and even be violent towards us, nevertheless wherever reasonable and indeed safe, core and other principles require cooperative and peace-building conduct, which support the pursuit of well-being and happiness.

As already mentioned, when we engage in such dialogue, discussion and conversation, especially when others are unable or not prepared to listen to what we have to say, and when they have no intention of recognising, or lack the ability to recognise our feelings, there may be substantial difficulties. Such others may hold us in contempt or even mock and ridicule us. They may characterise us, or may have characterised us in a destructive and negative manner such that effective dialogue and communication is highly challenging or even not possible. These represent difficult challenges and situations where we will have to conduct ourselves appropriately and work very hard to enable dialogue in order bring people together and to support our own well-being and happiness and the well-being and happiness of others.

If there is a willingness but a lack of ability to engage, and there is sufficient or a strong desire to resolve differences, then the use of third parties or mediators may help bring us together, support us in the resolution of challenges and problems. Their use should not be seen as a sign of weakness, but as a route to resolving personal and other difficulties which perhaps we are unable to resolve ourselves. The use of such mediators can help in resolving disputes between partners in relationships, other individuals, groups, communities and indeed between societies and nations and thus can represent a highly valuable option, with mediators often better able to provide dispassionate insight into relationships, interests and problems. Indeed, we, our communities, societies and beyond, need to develop and support the provision of professional mediation services, expert mediation insitutions and organisations, available to support the resolution of difficult conflicts and disputes.

Linked to other points, and in relation to the difficulties that there may be in cooperation and peacefulness, as already noted above, there are also those who have their own agendas which they may wish to pursue without the intention of listening and taking into account the goals of others. These individuals, and in many cases, interest groups, may, with deliberate intent, generate false argument, false evidence, hide key information and engage in a range of other strategies and tactics. They may use what is sometimes termed, smoke and mirrors, in order to realise their own interests at the expense of others. Evidencing such approaches from others, amongst other forms of evidence, will be inconsistencies in their words, and contrasts between their words and deeds.

It is important in such circumstances for us to recognise and understand these patterns of conduct and the true motivations and actions of such people at an early stage, disentangling their strategies and tactics. We will need to act appropriately to counter such approaches and may need to talk directly and bluntly where possible and reasonable in response to their words and actions. This will mean to some extent acknowledging their fears, but also pointing out and addressing their falsehoods, tactics and strategies. Our responses will also require our maintaining our integrity in regard to their actions and our conduct, aiming to maintain the principles of cooperativity and peacefulness to the greatest degree possible, while also being effective in achieving our appropriate goals.

While tempting, our mirroring the actions of these people by adopting the false tactics and strategies they use, is not an acceptable option as, in itself, it undermines core and other principles both generally and in particular in relation to integrity, and is highly likely to undermine our well-being and happiness and the well-being and happiness of others. However, all circumstances cannot be accounted for here in this guide. Some groups and individuals may offer such a degree of threat to others, in the form of likely damage and even in terms of aggressive violence contrary to our goals and principles; some may be so disingenuous, dishonest, manipulative, damaging and destructive, for example promising and threatening aggressive violence and oppression on a wide scale, that we may consider it essential that we ensure they are unable to pursue the courses of action that they wish to pursue, with the consequences for us being that in dealing with them, as long as conduct is, and has been consistent with, and supports core principles overall, that robust, forceful and necessarily effective action (incorporating consideration and concern for the well-being of those engaged in such acts) is legitimate in tackling these people and their actions.

For example those pursuing destructive and damaging agendas which threaten the well-being of the community as a whole or which threaten significant damage to the specific well-being of those of us with different views and opinions (operating within the frame of core and other principles), or of other groups, such as racial groups, will need to be dealt with firmly and robustly, if we have the capacity to act in such ways. In addition to such robust and firm action being necessary against those pursuing such threatening and violent agendas, such robust actions may well also be necessary in response to groups which threaten others of us on account of our particular beliefs, sexual orientations, disability, or simply, as we all are, because we are different in individual characteristics. Those of us living peacefully and justly and decently, in accord with core and other principles, must not be subject to such damaging and destructive agendas.

Cooperativity and peacefulness, the well-being of ourselves, our communities, societies and our broader humanity, the avoidance of suffering and pain, will certainly not be promoted by those individuals who revel in causing others pain, those who willfully ignore the pain and suffering of others, by racists, homophobes, bullies, the aggressively violent, and others unwilling or unable to care about others. They will not be promoted by those intent on pursuing their personal interests and perverse, destructive beliefs at the expense of others, those wishing to achieve their heinous goals without concern for others, by those aiming to pursue their destructive ends by gaining physical, political, economic and other forms of power over others. Such people cannot be allowed to succeed in achieving their goals, and where, in our interactions with such people and groups, with such organisations and even states, our peaceful and cooperative approaches are not effective, then forceful and restraining action, using the minimal force necessary may be required to prevent their achievement of their destructive and damaging goals.

Nevertheless, in the vast majority of important contexts, in our daily lives and beyond, it is essential for us to pursue cooperativity, mutuality and peacefulness, and to encourage others to engage in these processes, for the benefit of all. Where specific issues and different initial positions exist with regard to an action, decision, issue or policy, then it is essential that we make an effort to understand the position of the other party or parties and that we are prepared to develop solutions which will meet the needs of all parties where their interests are legitimate and reasonable within terms of core and other principles. And we must be open to the differing perceptions, differing goals, differing evaluations, of others taking these on board and recognising these as valid where it is reasonable and rational in terms of supporting well-being to do so.

Compromise has already been mentioned from the perspective of its value and importance in supporting cooperation and collaboration, yet of course when we are talking with others, discussing and negotiating with others, while we may well need to compromise and make concessions ourselves, we are also likely to need those with whom we are engaging to compromise and make concessions too. The notion of win-win is a very important one. Where possible and reasonable, we all need to be able to engage in, participate in, and indeed walk away from talk, discussion, negotiation, the range of situations, feeling that we have had some kind of gain or win, that the discussion and talk is, or has been, of value, perhaps enriching us, our feeling that our well-being is being enhanced. And we also most likely wish to know that if we have made a concession, one which might in one sense disappoint us in having been made, then at another point we should be able to understand that others have given or made concessions themselves, or that we will receive a concession from the person or people with whom we are discussing or negotiating at a future point in time, and further, overall, that we have taken part in discussions and negotiations in a manner in which we and others as participants have engaged in give and take, with all parties winning overall.

Indeed negotiation is a key word here, with our having many negotiations during our days, not simply formal work and business negotiations, with effective negotiation requiring acknowledgment of what the other person is saying, wishing for, combined with our recognition of the legitimacy of that other person's view, where that view is reasonable, genuine and legitimate. None of this means standing aside from truth and accuracy, from pursuing our own personal goals, the optimal course or courses of action based in evidence and reason. It certainly does mean taking care to listen to others, taking note of them and considering them to be of importance and value in terms of their humanity and individuality.

The need for cooperativity and peacefulness, this effort to reach agreement is necessary even in what might be seen as simple everyday decisions, for example in a family where husbands and wives or partners are making simple decisions about the day, or talking to and dealing with children, or in our community and friendship interactions. Understanding the needs and desires of others, finding common ground and common interests, negotiating, compromising and reaching mutually acceptable and mutually fulfilling agreement in some form or other, is of the highest importance in order to achieve cooperativity and peacefulness, the successful continuance of relationships, successful and happy relationships, successful and happy living, to establish, support and maintain lives of well-being and happiness.

Beyond our own efforts to take account of and listen to others, it is legitimate and reasonable to expect that our own needs and desires should be acknowledged and responded to by others, although our personal needs, as with the needs and desires of others, may not always be capable of being met. It is likely that, in many circumstances, we will not receive and achieve all that we would like to receive and achieve. That is, in a sense, a necessity when we are living with and dealing with others in whatever context, on account of these others having their own individual needs, concerns, interests and perceptions, and with their happiness and well-being being central and integral to our own well-being and of course the well-being of these others.

While we may give up something when discussing, negotiating, making decisions and reaching agreements, for example some element or perhaps much of, our independence, of our time, some of our resources, hopefully, having given these up, we then gain through being a full part of something else, perhaps a relationship, a family, a community, through which we may win the joys and fulfillment of family, the winning of friends, and be accepted as a more complete part of our community. In addition we may simply gain peacefulness and pleasure in our lives through engagement in cooperation with others and that ability to cooperate and engage in give and take with others.

It is not, on the whole, acceptable to subsequently refuse to participate in activities or discussion because our own views, judgments and opinions do not win the day in a discussion or within a group with which we are involved. Our responsibility is to maintain support for others and the group even when decisions go against us, showing our loyalty and care for others and also for the central ideas we believe in. That is the case as long as that which is being implemented is valid and reasonable in terms of core and other principles.

It is certainly legitimate to withdraw from our groups, or be what others might describe as 'disloyal' to our group, community, society or nation, if that social entity is implementing policies and actions which are likely to or will significantly damage others. Indeed it is our obligation within the frame of core and other principles to robustly oppose such actions. As stated already in this chapter, we have a higher and more important loyalty to all of our fellow human beings than we have to any group, including our home groups, where these groups are turning against others, threatening with violence and destruction others whose well-being and happiness we must support. If such groups state that through our actions to protect our fellow human beings, we are being disloyal or traitors, as they sometimes do, that will be untrue. We will in fact be acting in a loyal and caring manner to our fellow human beings.

If such language is appropriate, and such language may not be helpful, nevertheless, to state things clearly, it would be the case in terms of such language, that such individuals groups discriminating unjustly against others, such other groups which operate outside of the framework of core and other principles, which significantly threaten and enact destructive aggressively violent and attacks of various types on others, are showing a lack of loyalty to our humanity and are acting treacherously in relation to our humanity, our human community and society.

Of course complexities may arise in such judgments. In terms of situations where there are serious and damaging threats of violence to others arising from own group, while we might not support the destructive actions of that group to which we are ascribed membership, nevertheless, another group might wish to pursue violence in consequence against our own group and see us, as an individual, as part of that group and a legitimate target for retribution and violence. Hopefully that will not be the case. We must do whatever we can to oppose the aggressively violent destructive actions and policies of any group and of course, of any individuals.

In regard to such serious situations, but also with regard to our membership of groups in situations where matters may not be so grave, it may be that we feel an action or new policy is so at odds with core principles and our own judgments and beliefs about what those core principles mean in practice, that we feel we cannot actively continue to contribute or participate, or even continue to be part of that group. If the decisions and actions with which we do not agree, are clearly and significantly at odds with principles of supporting the well-being and happiness of ourselves as individuals, and all others, then we would be obliged either to oppose such decisions and actions vigorously and continuously from within our group, or determine not to participate and contribute to any actions involving implementation of such a decision.

Nevertheless, withdrawal from groups, in line with what has just been stated, should hopefully be limited, with the many of us having perhaps different views about those decisions which are optimal in terms of well-being and happiness, yet not to the extent of there existing clear and significant destruction and damage arising through the alternate views and approaches, such that our withdrawal, non-cooperation and perhaps continued disruptive disagreement with our group is justified. Where there are different judgments, we certainly need to recognise the perspectives and arguments of others, the possibility that our own perceptions, our judgments and beliefs may in fact be wrong. We certainly need to be prepared to negotiate, discuss, be prepared to change our minds and be, on the whole, prepared to support the group and maintain our cooperativity and commitment to our groups and organisations even where we may disagree with decisions made and strategic directions adopted, especially where is no significant departure from core and other principles. It is quite easy for us to exaggerate our differences out of proportion, when it is the central ideas we believe in, our common concern for the well-being and happiness of ourselves and others, our common and more fundamental points of agreement which we together accept despite our differences, that should serve to bind us together and support our continued membership of a group, a community and society and our continued cooperation and collaboration with others.

It is unfortunately likely that we will all have to put up with decisions and actions which we do not support or with which we disagree and in fact, in the vast main, as long as the actions of others, of the group, are reasonable within terms of core principles and other principles, reasonably conceivable as supporting well-being and happiness and doing no substantial harm to ourselves and others, we should be continuing to support and work with others, work and act within the context of the groups we are in, either living with or accepting those decisions which go against us, or alternatively coming to terms with those decisions and recognising we either may have been wrong or that the matter was perhaps not of the importance we initially ascribed to it.

We may also continue to pursue our own point of view and decided actions, but we must do so in a cooperative and supportive manner, which does not undermine the efforts of the group as a whole. After all, our views and judgments about the optimal way to pursue well-being and happiness might be incorrect. Alternately and worth restating, where the actions and efforts of a group, of others are at clear and substantial variance with core and other principles and are significantly harmful and destructive to others, then we are obliged and must act to change decisions, to alter actions and efforts such that damage and destruction do not occur. We must certainly not acquiesce to or cooperate with such destructive actions.

It is not uncommon for some of those who contribute substantially to families, clubs, societies, organisations and other groups, either in terms of their time, energy and personal commitment or sometimes financially, to wish for, and indeed to expect, their own personal views or judgments to be those which are adopted and accepted by the group or by others, on the grounds of the substantial contribution that they make as an individual to that entity, group or organisation. Indeed, there may be an implied threat in many situations that if such an influential and active person's views are not adopted, such individuals will refuse to continue doing what they currently do, with the potential of resulting detriment to the group. These individuals may be dedicated and passionate about the organisation or group, working day-in and day-out to support the group, with that group in fact being central to their lives. When we are making decisions as a group, the passion, dedication, effort and work, talents, skills and commitment of these individuals have to be acknowledged, and on many occasions, their wishes may reasonably be acceded to.

Nevertheless, while we as individuals, should all be able to influence decision-making, it is an unhealthy situation, though a perhaps too frequent reality, for one person to overly influence or dominate a group in such a manner, the dominance of one or a small number of individuals meaning the group may be vulnerable in itself, in its sustenance and continuation. Additionally, bearing the above discussions in mind, it is not generally acceptable in terms of core and other principles, consistent with notions of well-being, for an individual to refuse to cooperate and work with others because their own view did not persuade others in negotiation, discussion and debate. Unless there are substantial breeches of core and other principles, unless there are substantial threats to individuals and the well-being of all, unlikely in many situations, we should stick with our group, and maintain support for others, rather than pulling up the drawbridge and refusing to continue our role or making such threats, on the grounds of our own importance to the group and because our view did not win the day.

If our judgment and views were correct, then hopefully this will be realised soon enough. But refusal to cooperate with others, withdrawal from the group, hostility to others, who for their own good reason, think differently and interpret things differently from ourselves, is not acceptable, itself being damaging to others and the group. If we withdraw our cooperation, this would in effect be a misuse of power, exemplifying poor conduct, exemplifying an inability to listen, as well as a lack of acceptance of others and their perceptions, something which is not consistent with core and other principles.

As individuals we must be prepared to compromise, tolerate, accept that our views will not always and indeed should not always win out, and carry on with dedication if the rejection of our view occurs. And the group, organisation or entity must recognise the contributions of those who are dedicated, passionate, committed, who give of their time and energy, without needing to cede substantial or total control and all decision-making to those committed individuals. Of course we do wish to be appreciated for all that we do, and given that in such cases, it may be our hands that will do the work, our views need to be given appropriate weight and treated with appropriate gravity and seriousness. Yet democratic principles, involving all in decision-making and contribution, are crucial in supporting the well-being and happiness of ourselves as individuals, in supporting the happiness and well-being of all. We all wish to and need to be valued.

Integrity in the things we say and do, and integrity of purpose, are critical in our relationships and in our communication in order to promote cooperativity and positive relationships. And supporting our integrity and others' perceptions of our integrity, being aware of who we are and how we behave, which includes being personally aware of our own motives and being able to understand and say what these are, both to ourselves and to others, is of great value, in order to avoid any unintended impression of dishonesty or a lack of integrity. Being aware of how our statements and actions affect others is essential as, even if we are acting with integrity, unfortunately others, for a range of reasons which may have nothing to do with ourselves, may wrongly suspect our motives. Misunderstandings and misinterpreting the motivations and actions of others is undoubtedly common, especially if we, and others, are suspicious, are fearful of our personal status and standing, our safety and security, and especially if we have been misled in the past or others are constantly attempting to mislead us.

A reputation for integrity gained through previous honesty and integrity, as well a reputation for success, is of great value in supporting cooperation and peacefulness as well as achieving and supporting our community, social and individual goals. That reputation can be unjustly assailed for a range of reasons by those who disagree with us, by those who mistrust us as an individual for no good reason, by those who mistrust generally through their own experiences and nature, and indeed by those who are malevolent, pursuing their own interests at whatever cost there might be to us as individuals and to others.

And, under such circumstances, we may need a level of self-control and self-restraint when our good intentions are misinterpreted or when we are misunderstood and the response to our comments and actions, rather than being sympathetic, listening, attentive and understanding, becomes one of perhaps anger and dismay, born of unjustified suspicion, mistrust or other factors. It may well take personal strength to deal with such responses, but that is unfortunately sometimes demanded of us and, to some extent, an expectation in terms of acting within core and other principles. It is unfortunately an expectation and indeed a requirement for all of us, that we should try to develop the strength to cope with these situations effectively, cope with unjust, or even cope with just criticisms in a positive reflective manner, cooperatively and peacefully and where necessary firmly and robustly.

Of course we may on occasion, or perhaps more often, suspect the motives of others, sometimes correctly, or perhaps believe that others are not fully aware of who they are and are not fully aware of their own motives and conduct, something which might often be true. Our obligation is to ensure we are aware of our own motives and personal conduct and to ensure that we personally show truthfulness and integrity in these situations in order to support cooperativity, well-being and happiness, though if we suspect deliberate mendacity and dishonesty then, appropriate strategies are likely to be necessary to deal with this. And if we suspect that others are deluding themselves and not aware of their own motives we will need to gently point this out or respond in some other appropriate and peaceful manner. Suffice to say that we should never act in mendacious and dishonest ways ourselves. Such dishonest and mendacious actions run the risk of damaging us personally, damaging our reputation, our well-being and happiness, our ability to act, and run the risk of causing potential harm to others with whom we are dealing directly, as well as causing more general harm to our families, communities, societies and beyond.

A key challenge in building and sustaining our cooperative and friendly relationships, in avoiding damaging and destructive conflict in our often busy and demanding lives, is listening to others effectively. Being able to listen well is undoubtedly a skill that for many of us needs developing. It is easy to be disengaged from what others are saying through, for example, over concern with ourselves and our own desires and wants and through a lack of focus on or an inability to interpret deeper messages that others may be conveying through their words and actions. Moreover, our ability to listen well and interpret what others are saying and doing, may be affected by a range of factors including our tiredness and fatigue, the intense attention levels required for listening, lack of clarity in what is said, hidden emotions and purposes, as well as the much which may be unsaid, which underlies much of our talk.

We may also be unwilling to encounter and acknowledge the meanings and purposes of others, perhaps due to the emotional challenges or the depth of involvement that dealing with others in such depth might present us. And of course our own thinking may interfere with our ability to understand the concerns of others. For example, in our conversations, dialogue and discussions, we may start with assumptions about someone else and their lives or possess a framework of thinking which makes it difficult for us to listen well and take on board the perceptions and concerns of others.

As a consequence of such factors, in order to prevent the advent of destructive and damaging conflict we need to work on our thinking about listening and how we listen if we are to listen to others effectively. Sometimes listening effectively takes time and reflection – we may not fully understand the first time we hear, but after a period of time we may start to begin to understand and value more the perspectives and approaches of another individual or of another group of people. We all have our assumptions, ways of thinking, our own frames of thinking, culture and beliefs and we are all brought up within our families, schools, communities and societies which will undoubtedly engender within us specific and preferred world views, and this may, as a consequence, make other perspectives challenging to both perceive and understand.

Different experiences in our upbringing, for example, may result in different social and economic beliefs and different views of how society works and should work. Such differences can lead to friction and conflict, but need to be debated, discussed and openly dealt with, with each of us listening to others and working our way towards mutual understanding, changes in our beliefs as necessary, and acceptable solutions, within the framework of core and other principles. This can be difficult as there are social and economic ideas which allow or even advocate the significant suffering of others, something which cannot be accepted as this is contrary to core and other principles. Clearly such views need to come into line with the support of the well-being and happiness of all. Others cannot be allowed to suffer and we cannot set up or make do with a system which, in its nature, requires people to suffer significantly. We must conduct ourselves in a manner and advocate and argue for, as well as implement, approaches that support happiness and well-being for ourselves and all.

It is nevertheless inevitable that we will encounter others who will have, at least to some degree, other perceptions, worldviews, attitudes and ideas. Many of these ideas and perceptions will be based in similar principles such as peacefulness and cooperativity, the search for well-being and happiness, but these principles may be seen by different people and different sets of beliefs as being realised in different ways from those we are used to. Of course the alternative proposed realisations may instead be clearly incorrect routes to achieving or entirely inconsistent with core and other principles, for example those views which lionise suffering or which advocate the murder of those who do not hold certain beliefs. Where these perceptions, world views, attitudes and ideas are, in reality, consistent or largely consistent with supporting the well-being and happiness of all, of others, then, however, these should certainly be listened to, discussed, accepted or rejected, as necessary and where accepted and appropriate taken on board and put into practice.

Listening to others does not simply mean listening to others in order to take on ideas, information and justifications for the beliefs we already have. It does not mean funneling and changing the information we encounter, weeding out the information which does not fit what we believe, such that overall we convince ourselves that the evidence backs our thinking when in fact, with dispassionate consideration it does not, or does not do so completely. Listening to others does not mean only listening to and taking note of those who support our beliefs and positions. It does not mean listening to others who disagree with our current views so that we can refute their views. In support of finding appropriate solutions and reducing damaging conflict, in support of well-being, listening well must mean looking for, and where appropriate understanding the value of what others are saying, such that we can advance our own thinking and understanding and such that we will all be able to work for the well-being of all and the prevention of harm and damage to ourselves and all others.

As already mentioned, but worthy of its reiteration as it is likely to be a fundamental influence on who we are and how we conduct ourselves, realistically it has to be acknowledged that we will most likely, in regard to many areas of our lives, have certain values and beliefs, certain frameworks of thinking which will inform our current beliefs, judgments and opinions over time and on the moment, and yet which may also constrain our thinking and our capacity to see the value of and take on board new ideas on the moment. There are also important matters of ego and pride, not wishing to chop and change our beliefs in front of others, something which might affect our standing and credibility with others. And we may further have a deep attachment to certain ideas and beliefs which form a fundamental element of our identity, and therefore are difficult to change and even difficult for us to confront, though confront such beliefs is what we must do. For these and other reasons, listening and changing our views on the moment, during a discussion or debate may be difficult, yet if the evidence and reasoning does not support our position, or if the evidence identifies inconsistencies in our thinking and views then we must re-evaluate our positions and change our views and frameworks.

And of course we all wish that we ourselves will be listened to, acknowledged and valued when we speak. And we wish others to show they are listening. In a conversational and relationship situation, as well as in other contexts, when we are interacting with someone on a personal level, spending time with another and wish to listen to them properly, we will need to give them our full attention and will most likely need to demonstrate that we are doing so, for example by stopping other activities we are doing. This will mean we are giving our friend, partner or colleague the attention that they wish for and deserve, and we will not only be giving them that attention but explicitly showing them we are listening. Being listened to and made to feel of value is an important part of well-being. There is pain in being ignored, in feeling irrelevant and unacknowledged, perhaps isolated, and we should not let that occur to any significant degree to ourselves or others if we can avoid that happening. And by paying such attention we will enhance cooperation and reduce the chances of unwanted conflict.

Many of the positive elements consistent with core and other principles which have already been discussed in terms of building peacefulness and cooperativity can be seen as comprising important components of our effectively daily negotiating with others, since in reality, our engagement in negotiation is something we do every day. As mentioned earlier in this chapter, negotiation is not, as might often be thought, simply something associated with formal situations in business or politics, associated with doing large scale deals over goods, pricing, wage levels, land disputes between countries and other matters with widespread impact. It can occur in situations ranging from those where we have a simple discussion with our partner about where to go on a day out, our discussions about what activity or entertainment to engage in at home, or what we are to eat at a meal, to those situations where there are more major decisions being made in our personal lives, decisions about our children's education, and of course, those major decisions mentioned being made in business or politics.

And so our negotiation skills, our capacity to work with others in a cooperative manner is of great importance. In particular, this is because sometimes, dependent on circumstances, many of our more simple negotiations can prove unnecessarily fractious and unpleasant. We, as those parties involved in a negotiation, need in the first place to recognise that we actually are negotiating and so deploy our negotiating skills. It is easy to fall into a negotiation without actually realising there is a negotiation taking place. We need of course to work together and listen to each other. Moreover, unless we share interests and are able to cooperate, unless we are prepared to engage in give and take, unless we are aware of how to talk in a caring, loving, civil manner, and cooperative manner and actually put into practice our knowledge and awareness, knowledge and understanding regarding negotiation, then we will risk unnecessary conflict and unhappiness.

And what is meant by effective and successful negotiation here relates not solely to what we or another individual, what one individual or party gains from a negotiation, but significantly relates to what all participants feel during and after the negotiation, about their fellow negotiators, those with whom they have been negotiating as well as the outcome and aftermath of that negotiation. In a negotiation with our partner for example, we need to get on with and still love our partner after our negotiation and not feel substantially dissatisfied and unduly pressured into that which we do not want, or not at least without receiving something we wish for in return. We may feel some pain with the outcome of a negotiation, having to do something which is not our preferred option but that should involve more tolerable inconvenience than substantive pain, which would be unacceptable. For example, giving up an evening out with friends so that our partner can go out, while we go out with friends another time is the kind of compromise and outcome of negotiation which surely involves tolerable inconvenience rather than substantive pain and such would be an acceptable result of a negotiation between partners involving give and take, and helping to sustain a loving relationship. If we have negotiated successfully about such a matter, rather than taking this for granted, we need to recognise what we have done and appreciate ourselves for finding our appropriate and mutually acceptable solution.

In addition to the preparedness to listen, negotiate, compromise and take part in give and take, in addition to our granting and acceptance of the concessions that are so important in any negotiation in our lives, it is also advantageous within the home or elsewhere, to be creative in inventing solutions which solve negotiation and discussion problems and which serve to take into account the goals and desires of all parties. Thus, in support of well-being and happiness, in support of cooperation and effective negotiation, we should prepare for creative invention, have a mind set which looks for such solutions and we need to develop the skills to find those inventive solutions where difficulties arise or where there is the likelihood of difficulties. Such inventiveness and creativity is often useful in promoting peacefulness and avoiding conflict, conflict which may sharpen and deepen on some occasions when, by contrast, our efforts to generate, and our success in generating novel solutions and the generation of such alternative solutions might in fact keep all parties happy and better promote agreement, togetherness, cooperativity, well-being and happiness. And we may, on occasion, need to be patient and allow time for such new solutions to be thought of and constructed. Not all negotiations need to be successful on the moment. We can listen, wait, postpone discussions, decisions and even speaking, until we have better accommodated and assimilated the views, feelings and ideas of others and worked out potential solutions to any difficult issues and elements of our negotiation.

As a result of successful negotiation, we can hopefully make sure that all of us negotiating, that all parties involved, gain something of which we want, and, overall, in the round, feel good about the negotiation. Making this negotiation work and maintaining peacefulness and cooperativity during, and subsequent to such negotiation requires, in addition to the listening, empathising, communication and thinking skills which have already been discussed, the ability to sometimes, if not often, live without something we want, at least temporarily, in order to pursue greater togetherness, mutual well-being and happiness, and the greater well-being and happiness.

Core principles, the shared goals of being concerned about our own well-being, the well-being of others, as well as other principles, will support our success, especially if adopted by all those involved in interactions and all participants in negotiations, with the consequence that peacefulness and cooperativity are more likely to be enjoyed and maintained, and our own individual as well as the general well-being and happiness supported. We must ourselves desist from damaging conduct and encourage individuals who are acting in damaging ways to support their communities, others, our societies and beyond, and recognise the personal and social benefits of everyone winning, and all achieving goals in discussion and negotiation.

Cooperativity and peacefulness are worthy goals. However, contrary to what is often said, in reality it only takes the actions of a single person or group to disrupt togetherness and cooperativity, to act to catalyse and generate conflict, be that through small or larger negatively selfish or oppressive actions or even violent actions which damage others and which have the significant potential to upset or arouse the ire and anger of others. Such negatively selfish acts, at a lower, less harmful and damaging level, will optimally be addressed through talk, discussion, negotiation, through peaceful responses aimed at bringing that person or a relevant group or other entity, back to peaceful cooperation. Hopefully such efforts will be successful.

Nevertheless, if there is not a change in conduct and behaviour from that person or from a group; if there is no appropriate statement of regret or apology or some form of step back or perhaps recompense from those involved in the negatively selfish act, then this will result in levels of disagreement and disharmony being raised and the potential for significant conflict and worse to follow. Where those of us who have engaged in such negatively selfish acts, or even unintended acts which appear negatively selfish, wish to rectify the situation, understanding the wrongness of our actions, it is important for us to openly and visibly express our regret at the earliest point possible. That being said, while apologies and statements of regret should certainly be given and we should appreciate their value, demanding apologies and statements of regret can be problematic. Such statements are important and useful, however even more important are changes in decisions and actions such that there is no more damage and destruction, and no more negatively selfish actions.

Yet destructive conflict and a lack of peacefulness can arise where there are no intentions to do others harm. Destructive conflict may arise though misunderstanding, mistrust, suspicion and fear, when in fact there may be no need for these to be present. There exist histories of division and conflict between groups and individuals which can be difficult to overcome, and there are those who live in fear because of past experience of dishonesty, experiences and perceptions of being let down which have damaged them such that they anticipate being let down in the future and thus mistrust those who mean them no harm and who would care for them. Attempts must be made to reduce suspicion and mistrust between people and groups. This can be done in a number of ways including sometimes or perhaps often, through small confidence-building steps. As a consequence of such confidence-building steps, our own well-being and the well-being of all, can be promoted.

Fear is particularly damaging in relationships, being particularly destructive and frequently leading to anxiety, mistrust and painful and unnecessary conflict. While it can be difficult to put deep fears, indeed any fears, aside, putting them aside, while maintaining our own safety and security, is likely to benefit our relationships and help to promote cooperativity and peacefulness. As an example, having suffered deep damaging emotional rejection in the past in love, or perhaps particularly painful emotional experiences, we may reasonably be concerned that, or fear that, such things will occur again in the present and the future. Our fear may mean as a consequence we are slow to return sincere love and affection; that we suspect and mistrust those who wish to love us, care for us or perhaps be friends. And through our fearful, nervous and reticent response to demonstrations of affection and love, this can promote conflict and can damage our prospect of enjoying what might be, on the whole, very positive and enriching relationships, leaving us and others feeling lonely, isolated and sad.

It is certainly difficult to live with constant and intense fear, and at the same time enjoy positive relationships and positive achievements. And at the same time it is difficult for others to live with, work with and deal with those of us who may live with such fear, those of us who are constantly suspecting the motives of others or who place interpretations on actions, interpretations which were never present and arise more from the mind of those of us upset, admonishing or fearful, than in the intentions and minds of others.

Emotional and caring engagement with others can be risky and cause substantial pain. And the reality is that in some cases there may indeed be good reason to suspect the self-focused motives of others, but such suspicion needs some reasonably solid basis for its existence, rather than existing as a constant irrational and damaging fear haunting our lives, such fear being something which may be easier to recognise and to point out than to rectify as a problem. Moreover our emotional pain may be fed into by others who care for us or who wish to care for us, but who simply lack social and relationship skills and empathy, and for other reasons which are not due to any bad intent, but which nevertheless lead to pain, pain which may be just as bad as that caused through others being negatively selfish or deliberately and callously aiming to hurt us.

If we are living with such fears at a minor level, then it may be possible for us to adjust our thinking to be more rational and reasonable in our judgments and to be more understanding of others. If our feelings of fear are intense and destructive of ourselves and others, then we may need some external support to help us with our with thinking such that we can live with greater happiness and well-being. If not countered and dealt with, our fear and suspicion will continue to prevent relationships starting and will undermine existing relationships, leading to substantial damage to ourselves and others, to our communities and societies.

On a wider scale, clearly irrational and unfounded fears between and about other groups, within communities, within societies, and indeed irrational and unfounded fears about other external communities, societies, groups and other individuals, promulgated in different ways, can act as a tremendous sources of tensions, pain and conflict, and lead to war, violence, pain and suffering on a vast level. Fears, concerns, suspicions and worries about the beliefs and actions or potential actions of certain group entities may sometimes be rational and reasonable, can in some cases have some basis, or in others, may be well-founded, but do need to be built on reasonable evidence and certainly should not serve as any rationale or reason for aggressive violence. Yet we need to be very careful to ensure we consider members of such groups as individuals with individual perceptions and outlooks rather than considering all group members to be the same.

And thus, where we have such fears and concerns about group entities (which could include concerns about our own group entities) we need to separate that notion of group entity from the beliefs, views, ideas and opinions, indeed actions of individual members of such groups, individual views and actions which may be entirely different from those views and actions which are presented and perceived as those of a potentially hostile group entity. An individual may well not support their group's views or action and they may act entirely contrary to any prevalent view held within that group, and moreover, those individuals may wish for entirely different actions. To be more specific, this being an important point given human history and the prevalence of destructive actions resulting from such irrational fear and indeed hatred of other groups, regarding all of those individuals within a group, nation or state which is acting in an aggressively violent and destructive manner, we cannot assume that such individuals support such aggression unless there is evidence and good reason to believe that they, as individuals, do.

All those within a social, political, religous or other belief group, a small number of whom, or some of whose members pursue their beliefs through aggressive violence, are not personally responsible for the actions of those who use such aggressive violence. Some, if not many, the vast majority within such groups may believe in peacefully advocating their views, which they are entitled to do, where their beliefs will not cause substantive damage and harm. Where individuals within that group pursue aggressive violence or behave dishonestly, the rest of that group, others in that group, cannot be blamed or held responsible for actions which they did not do, unless there is substantive evidence that they approved of such actions.

Feelings of fear can have another important affect on peacefulness and cooperation. There are those of us who have difficulty imagining the future, imagining futures which will certainly be different. Not only this, we may have an irrational fear of change, change of any sort, in terms of technology, in terms of social relationships, in terms of our own lives and of those changes which are inevitable in our own lives. Rather than move to the future, some of us may try to fearfully cling to that which we have always known, preventing moves to greater justice, fairness and well-being and slowing down, stalling or preventing changes which would protect us from pain and suffering, improve our lives, which would enable us to survive and thrive in a changing world.

While there is undoubtedly a sense in which continuity can be important, a fear of change and a fear of the future is a barrier to progress aimed at improving our lives, and runs the risk of resulting in unnecessary conflict since a degree of change, sometimes drastic change, as well as, in some cases, a degree of continuity, may be needed to deal with problems and to support well-being and happiness. There are certainly reasons why certain changes, dependent on their nature, might not be advisable, and why continuity where possible, might be better, but the proposal of changes, the introduction of new ways of doing things, need to be supported and countered, argued against using reason, evidence and balanced consideration of the benefits and drawbacks of such actions within the context of core principles. Where appropriate, the case for no change needs to be argued as well, rather than responses to change being rejected through lack of our capability and capacity to envisage a better future and through a fear of change *per se*.

Further supporting conflict, irrational beliefs, unfounded in evidence and reason, not grounded in the realities we face; false ideologies which set people against each other, demonising other groups, or placing self-interest or group interest above the well-being and welfare of other individuals and other groups; all of these are likely to be sources of substantial and serious damage and difficulties, promoting pain and suffering and acting against cooperativity and peacefulness. Adherence to ideologies which require the oppression of others, which require that others must adopt those ideologies, which may require suffering and the suffering of others, stating or painting suffering as being a positive route to realisation and success, stand against peacefulness and cooperation between people, within and between communities, creating discord, pain, suffering, conflict and often violent conflict.

Given the reality of who we are as people, wishing for well-being and happiness for ourselves and others, those of us who are the victims of such ideologies, who are poor, weak and suffer because of those ideologies, are hardly likely to peacefully accept our lot as sufferers, as deserving of pain, sitting quietly while others enjoy power, privilege, achievement, success, and opulent wealth under the pretext of a social, political or other ideology. Such situations can only be sustained with coercion and oppression, and will mean ongoing strife, conflict and of course suffering amongst those of us who are required to suffer, those of us feeling our subjugation, those of us under the heel of oppression, those of us who are poor, weak and lacking in a sufficient level of power to resist our oppressors and their oppressive ideologies, at least on the moment.

Anger linked to vengeful thinking (or perhaps little thinking at all) can be a particular cause of aggressive violence, of course leading to lack of peacefulness and lack of cooperation at different levels. Nevertheless, our sometimes feelings of anger, while perhaps best avoided if we can avoid them, are not feelings which, when they occur, we should deny. If we can develop and train ourselves to avoid feelings of anger then that should be a worthwhile thing to do and might support us in behaving and acting rationally. Yet, for the many of us, at least on some occasions, while it is unpleasant to feel anger, our anger is a natural and deep response in some (hopefully not many) situations and represents something that most of us feel at least at some point in time.

Moreover, while if uncontrolled and uncontained, anger can cause much damage and destruction, pain and suffering, the fact is that in some situations, it also has the capacity to serve as a positive motivator, for example motivating us to action in response to injustice and unfairness, in response to oppression and cruelty, in response to the sight of others suffering. And further, our anger may motivate us to take action to defend ourselves and protect and support others. Yet the action we take needs to be the optimal action we can take and needs to be determined, as far as possible, in a rational manner, supporting well-being and happiness and serving to prevent pain and suffering. While a helpful motivator, our anger must not move us to act in ways which might damage ourselves and others.

Moreover, our anger is also, frequently, a somewhat painful and destructive emotion, even though its presence is understandable in some or indeed many circumstances. In its guise as a negative and destructive feeling, which can damage ourselves and lead to the damage of others, the intense and deep anger we can feel needs to be avoided wherever possible, and if not avoided, then managed, acknowledged, understood, but then substantially downplayed, sidelined, removed or reduced within our range of feelings and translated into effective and acceptable words and actions which promote peace and cooperativity in our relations with others and which support well-being and happiness. We need little reminder that intense anger can result in, or is highly likely to result in, out of control behaviour, emotional and possibly physical damage to ourselves and others, sometimes through destructive, hurtful and damaging words and threats and at other times, in other cases, through destructive and aggressive violence which damages all.

Anger is therefore certainly one of our feelings that we that we need to recognise, and at the minimum manage and control. While we may all feel anger, our anger needs to be channeled in positive and constructive directions. However angry we might feel we must avoid this anger turning into aggressive, abusive, insulting and aggressively violent behaviour. And of course, one possible consequence and concomitant of our anger can be a desire to do aggressive violence, to hit back, the desire for revenge, something which is totally destructive and damaging to all who are involved with it. The desire to hurt others because they have hurt us or someone we know – the desire to damage other groups of people because of perceived bad conduct by either another group or a member of that other group, interpreted as being worthy of blame directed towards a group, regardless of individual identity – is destructive in the extreme and entirely unacceptable. Feelings and thoughts of revenge frequently lead to a cycle of violence and pain which is totally at odds with the principles set out in this guide, damaging ourselves, damaging other individuals and damaging whole communities and societies. Vengeful action certainly, in no sense, supports the development of peace, harmony, cooperation and togetherness, our individual well-being and the well-being and happiness of others.

Much anger is intense, momentary or short-lived rather than vengeful and slow-burning over time. It is essential that we control and manage such momentary anger, making sure we are not swept away by our intense anger into shouting, verbal abuse insults, or violent actions which may substantially harm others physically and emotionally. Whether we feel badly let down, upset, put upon, provoked, taken for granted, demeaned and disrespected, particularly by those we love and are close to, such occurrences happening notably in many home environments in which we may live intensely and closely with partners and children, we need to ensure we do not take any such violent actions or use insulting and abusive words, all of which, in addition to the direct harm they cause, may also lead to permanent and irreparable damage to our relationships. If we can, it may be best to walk away in some cases where we are full of anger, and try to deal with the problem, hold the discussion at another time, perhaps with others present. Sometimes others we are disputing with are not prepared to let us refuse to speak and move away, and will continue to harass or chastise us. We must then aim to talk calmly, talk quietly and calmly if we can, and if we cannot, then we need to make even stronger efforts to move away, to escape. Of course, if we are assaulted, attacked, we have the right and obligation to protect ourselves using minimal force necessary, which should mean our using a very low level and minimal level of force.

In our home environment, should we ever feel in such a way, and unfortunately this is considered entirely possible, we should also contain our anger with our children, supporting them and dealing peacefully, cooperatively and constructively with their transgressions. In the same manner that in the home we should never hit, abuse or insult our partners, we should, of course, never hit, abuse and insult our children, though we may restrain them from hurting themselves, other children, other people and ourselves. It is our responsibility to look after and care for our children and bring them up to be peaceful, cooperative and caring individuals, something which aggressive violence, insult and abuse will not support.

Vengeful action, as a realisation of our anger, our sometimes slow burning anger, angry thoughts and more, is totally unacceptable within terms of core and other principles. That is not to say that wishing those who have committed aggressive violence to receive some form of consequence for what they have done, is in itself not a valid feeling to have. Indeed it is a common feeling, and present inside us, undoubtedly, in a sense, so that we have a human motivation to prevent such aggressive violence against us and others, from happening into the future. For those of us who have suffered violence, sexual assault, rape, torture and other forms of attack and injury, or who have endured those we know and love, (and indeed others) experiencing such violence, it is entirely understandable for us to want the liberty of those who have done these things to be restricted such that they cannot repeat those acts and such that those of us who have been their victims can feel we can walk the streets of their villages, towns, and cities in safety and can live our lives in safety, without fear of further attack and assault. That is not the same as any hate-filled desire for revenge. The reality is that the pain, both physical and emotional from such experiences and incidents can be very deep, and that we as individuals, our communities, societies and beyond, need to respond to protect ourselves and others, and to protect all individuals from experiencing such damage and trauma.

Where those who engage or who have engaged in such acts of violence express genuine regret for their actions and are able to commit to, and will not repeat such actions, then that is certainly positive and a step forward towards future peacefulness. Nevertheless, even contrary to the wishes of a victim, some period of restraint and time for reflection may be required for that individual to be seen as having 'paid some price' for their violent misdeeds. Yet all who have the mental capability should be enabled at some point to have the possibility of rehabilitation and rejoining of the community if they are able and capable of doing so, as long as we are convinced that there has been real change such that there is minimal risk to ourselves and others from further destructive conduct, and if that would overall be considered likely to be of benefit to the community. There are however acts of violence which, having been committed, mean that the person or people who have committed these deeds, due to illness or otherwise, remain a likely permanent and significant threat to ourselves and others in the community and society, and for this reason, they may need to be restrained and confined away from society for a very long period of time, if not permanently. Given our current state of knowledge and understanding, we may not be able to be sufficiently certain of their rehabilitation and personal change such that we can all feel safe, and we may decide in such cases, the risk of them doing further severe damage warrants their continued, if not permanent detention away from others.

In particular, where people have committed serious acts of violence including murder of others, there must be significant and substantial action to prevent the possibility of these individuals acting in the same manner again. Extended periods of restraint are undoubtedly likely to be necessary. The real pain of victims and their families needs to be taken into account and there is a strong argument for saying that extended periods outside of society, in some cases permanent exclusion from society are necessary in some, if not many, of these cases. However, even those who commit such acts, with the proviso mentioned above that they no longer represent a threat to others, must be considered at some point for rehabilitation and possible release from restraint should there be reasonable certainty that they offer no further threat to others. State murder through execution of those who have murdered, state imposed violent punishments, are entirely contrary to core and other principles failing to act as deterrents, damaging the relevant individual in a horrendous and final manner, and serving to legitimise aggressive violence in the context of our societies.

Given the level of misunderstandings and misdeeds which can occur, our showing forgiveness, the ability to put past events aside, the ability to not allow past events to sully current relationships and our current lives, the stating to others that we are understanding of their mistakes or their misdeeds and will not hold a grudge, seek revenge or act against them because of such deeds, is a very important tool in promoting cooperation and peacefulness between us, and promoting our own peacefulness, as well as supporting our own well-being and the well-being of others.

Forgiveness is something which can be important in many contexts, in our homes, in our families, at work and sometimes in wider social contexts. In some cases it may be best to not state forgiveness explicitly using the words 'I forgive you' to a friend, partner or work colleague, even when they have apologised for what they have done, since the stating of forgiveness does imply significant culpability in those we are forgiving, and requires the person being forgiven to see us in the morally superior position of a 'forgiver'. And while others may acknowledge they have made a mistake, or hurt us accidentally or even deliberately, they may not feel so culpable as to be in receipt of those words "I forgive you", with other words such as

"It's not a problem" or "Let's move on and forget it" being more appropriate, obviously dependent to some degree on culture and context. Our moving on and not paying attention to or referring to a past error or misdeed can be sufficient enough to demonstrate that we are being forgiving (though not necessarily forgetting).

That being said, if there is no obligation on us to state forgiveness of those who have committed significant misdeeds and, indeed, aggressively violent misdeeds against us. There are those who may have done us serious violence, seriously injured us, raped us, hurt if not killed a member of our family or a friend we love, and whether we feel we can forgive them for the destructive and vile deeds they have done must be a matter for us as individuals. But there is a need, in support at least of our own well-being for us, as far as we can, to perhaps understand these people and their deeds, and not let past events and those individuals who have behaved in such appalling reprehensible ways, poison our lives into the future.

In the case where we have been significantly and clearly hurt and harmed, our uttering of the words 'I forgive you', if we are truly able to do so, can nevertheless be a valuable asset to our well-being and happiness. In doing so, we will be asserting of our own personal power and, perhaps, self-control in the face of what may be or may have been feelings of great anger and hurt. Stating such words may well be valuable for moving life forward for both ourselves and those who truly regret their deeds, moving all of our lives forward in a positive and peaceful direction. Being forgiven by us, may help turn those who have previously done such destructive deeds, to more positive feelings and acts into the future. Engaging in and stating such forgiveness does not mean that pain, and perhaps even anger, ceases to exist, though hopefully they will dissipate or even disappear. It does mean getting on with life without letting our feelings about events in the past damage and poison our lives into the future such that our lives are miserable and devoid of well-being and happiness, or are lived with much reduced well-being compared to that which we could achieve.

Where there have been significant misdeeds, even violence against us as an individual, then it is almost certain that we cannot and will not be able to forget, nor perhaps should we forget. But where possible, once more short-term matters are dealt with, in particular, that we are returned to health as far as is possible, as well as the apprehension and restraint of those who have committed such acts against us, and once, therefore, we are assured of our safety into the future, perhaps through their imprisonment away from us or other means, it will become very useful to focus on other things, on the future and what can be done to make the future better, aiming where we can to put our pain to one side.

We may well need much support from others, from friends and family, from those with medical experience and knowledge relating to dealing with such trauma and injury in order to recover fully. While not always achievable, due to the depth of hurt, pain, trauma and injury that we may have experienced, having a focus on the present, the new, the future, should serve to support us in feeling better, healthier and happier, or at least as happy as we can be given those experiences. And meeting those who have hurt us with their violence, talking to them, discussing with them, expressing our hurt and pain and perhaps uttering words of forgiveness, if we can and feel prepared to, may help us move into that better future.

At the opposite end to forgiveness of those who have hurt us or damaged us, there is the capacity for those of us who have done misdeeds to apologise, say sorry for the things we have done wrong, for the mistakes we have made, something which we must do and do sincerely in order to improve situations, help relationships work effectively, and support well-being and peacefulness. Such an ability to recognise and acknowledge, developing our awareness of and actually openly acknowledging our mistakes, misjudgments, misdeeds and errors is important in supporting peacefulness and cooperation, and therefore in supporting core and other principles.

Acknowledgement to others of our errors, mistakes and even our own more general personal faults can open new ways forward in talk, discussions and negotiations, supporting respect and mutual understanding, demonstrating integrity and building trust, preventing us, for example, from stubbornly holding on to wrong ideas out of a misguided attachment to ego and self-image, out of the fear and shame of acknowledging our human imperfection in front of others. Refusing to acknowledge our errors and faults is likely to prevent our own and more general progress, build resentment in others and encourage unhappiness, conflict and discord.

Acknowledging our errors and mistakes can also have the benefit of being disarming in the most positive sense, building trust through signaling to those with whom we are in relationships, or with whom we are interacting, talking and negotiating, that we have integrity, that we know we have flaws and are fallible and are therefore vulnerable, and that we are open to making mutually advantageous progress, open to solving problems and open to meaningful, caring and cooperative dialogue. Such acknowledgement and admission can sometimes, if not often, lead others to abandon rigid and uncompromising positions which they may sometimes hold, acknowledging as a consequence their own flaws and vulnerability, and again, as a consequence, serve to help our mutual understanding and support better cooperation and peaceful, rather than conflict-filled engagement and interactions between us.

Those who are less ready to admit mistakes and errors are, in many circumstances, concerned about reputational damage, to themselves and sometimes their organisations. There may also be reasonable concerns that others will lose confidence in us if we are known to make errors and to do so frequently. Reputation does matter. However, covering up and failing to acknowledge errors and mistakes generally stands in the way of us developing for the future and making necessary changes to our conduct, with cover-up and lack of openness and integrity itself becoming something which is seen as an element of being successful, even approved of as an element of effective action and management within organisations.

Yet that it is not. Rather, cover-up and secrecy in the face of errors, mistakes and more, instead creates an often poisonous climate of fear, lack of integrity and repression in our lives, in our social entities and organisations, with one secret leading to another, making us and others vulnerable. Many of us will have to keep silent for the cover up of an error, for the secrecy to be maintained, and threat and incentive, the misuse of power, with resultant fear and repression, will often need to be put in place to maintain the dishonest silence. Those with values of integrity, openness and honesty will suffer as a consequence and all will be harmed as individuals, as will our social entities.

Moreover, cover ups and secrecy, and hiding our errors, are likely to help to keep poor systems in place, damage our individual and organisational capacities to learn from mistakes, and indeed, in reality, run the risk of severe damage to reputation, since information about errors and mistakes frequently becomes known at some level, and therefore reputation may suffer even more significantly than if the error or mistake had been acknowledged in the first place, our reputation being doubly damaged through both the error and the efforts at secrecy and cover-up.

That being said, if we are operating in the context of certain social systems, in particular authoritarian, dictatorial and bullying, brutal systems, the admission of error and mistake may result in such damaging consequences for ourselves and others, that it might be extremely unwise to mention our error. Of course it would be far better if such systems did not exist and, as mentioned elsewhere in this guide, we need to aim to change or remove such systems. Nevertheless, whatever the system context, rather than providing severe punishments for mistakes and errors, our systems need to support and enable our reporting of such errors and mistakes so that we all can learn, such that those involved can receive training and development support where necessary, or also where necessary, moved to other jobs or roles which they are better able to fulfill. In that way we will all benefit, and the individuals who have erred will hopefully not lose out. The capacity to acknowledge our errors and mistakes is important to effective operation and cooperation.

Nevertheless of course, where our errors are minor and easily rectifiable, it may be wiser and we may choose, to say nothing, certainly not formally, especially with errors and mistakes being a given in all of our lives. By contrast, in other circumstances, the consequences of saying nothing about our error, for example in key areas such as safety and health, technology and industry, in areas of our social support for those in need, could be deadly or cause substantial damage to others. Under such circumstances we will certainly have no option but to reveal our personal errors and mistakes, for the benefit and well-being of all, whatever the consequences for ourselves.

While we may acknowledge our errors and mistakes, and indeed apologise to others having recognised our mistakes and errors, even sometimes acknowledging them as a means to build trust, cooperation, agreement, peacefulness, we should not engage in such acknowledgment and admission in a manipulative manner in order to disarm others so that our own personal, negatively selfish goals are easier to achieve. Manipulating others in such a way is unacceptable. And others of us must do our best to avoid naivety and need to avoid failing to recognise this and other manipulatory strategies and tactics from those who might be out to support their own interests, at our and others expense, harming us and doing us damage.

There may be those who appear open and friendly, who act as if they are friends, appearing to share information, experiences, appearing to cooperate, appearing to care, apparently admitting of weakness and error, yet they will do these things solely to manipulate us and gain what they want from us with no regard for us as individuals. While being open and caring, prepared to love, give and care, we also sometimes need to be watchful and wary in order to protect ourselves and those we are close and to, as well as to protect others.

An element of such falsehood can be the false apology, made as a tactic for self-protection rather than being made with sincerity. A classic way of doing this is to make remarks such as " I apologise for the fact that you were hurt by what I said", something which in itself is not an apology. Apologies are regrets about the actions that we take as individuals, our taking the blame and responsibility for our actions which led to damaging consequences. They are not about regretting the consequences of what we do and say, but instead need to focus on our regretting what we have done ourselves. If this is not done, then what is said is not an apology, even though the words 'apology' and 'apologise' might be used.

Importantly, nevertheless, apologising and saying those words "I'm sorry", especially in close, loving relationships can serve to relieve pain, indeed make pain disappear completely, both for ourselves when apologising, and for those receiving our apology, Such apology will help those people who may deeply wish to love us, yet who may have been faced with barriers brought on through argument and conflict. Indeed, even when we may feel that we have done nothing untoward or wrong, it may still be of benefit to apologise, as our partner or those we know and care for, may themselves perceive that we have acted badly and incorrectly, whether or not we feel that we have, and we may need to sometimes accept their perspective, even if to some extent we might disagree. By doing so, we may well provide a route to assuaging the pain and suffering of someone who feels hurt by our actions or inaction. Assuaging such pain of course accords with core and other principles in reducing suffering and pain, though should not be done to too great or significant a degree, at too much expense to our own well-being, with the consequence of our own substantive pain and suffering.

Similarly, in a work context, with those we know and trust, apologies can operate in the same way, helping to build relationships, cooperation and peacefulness into the future. Yet as social entities, governments, companies and organisations, even societies and nations, there may well be a need for apologies too; for past misdeeds, for lack of competence, for lack of integrity and more. These may serve to help move our organisation and social entities more effectively into the future if the apologies are sincere and matched by action, as our apologies need to be.

Apologies do need to be sincere and meant when we make them and need to be sincere and meant if we are to feel we can take on board and accept an apology from someone else. Yet if others apologise, then it is important that we take the fact that that apology is being made seriously, even if we are not sometimes perhaps convinced of the sincerity of the apology. Action which matches the apologetic remark is our evidence that the apology was in fact, at least to some extent, sincere and genuine.

However, while apologies, people saying they are sorry, can facilitate peacefulness and cooperation, we cannot and should not require or demand apologies from others as a condition of moving into the future in a peaceful and cooperative manner. Apologies may be suggested by others, but they must really come from inside, be internally motivated, stemming from our internal recognition of error, if they are to be considered of value. They should not be coerced out of others as a result of pressure and given grudgingly, especially since the words of the apology need to be accompanied by specific action which realises and recognises that apology, and which may be unlikely or less likely to follow an apology made insincerely through pressure and coercion.

Of course when the harm and hurt caused is significant and serious, the words "I am sorry" may seem grossly inadequate, though still perhaps we should consider accepting and acknowledging such an apology if we perceive it to be sincere. But an apology will not necessarily be listened to and accepted – indeed there are some acts such as brutal acts of violence where verbal apology will often seem grossly insufficient to those who have been victims of that violence. Indeed the apology may seem like an insult, given the pain endured.

It is particularly difficult to accept apologies when we feel that the apology would not have been given had it not been for the fact that those who have behaved in appalling, destructive and violent ways, had not been brought to book for their actions. Yet even in these cases, those who have been caught out in destructive and damaging deeds, as part of the process of being faced with the open and explicit social disapproval for their actions and the consequences for themselves of what they have done, may actually face themselves and recognise the damage and hurt they have caused, regretting and wishing to recompense and apologise for their actions, committing themselves to a better future.

In any case we do not need to accept an apology. Apologies can be seen as inadequate words which may not even reflect the true thoughts of those apologising, nevertheless these may be words worth hearing and words worth saying. Critical to the value of any apology and statement of regret is the action that follows, which needs to represent some fundamental and visible change, usually underpinned by a change of overall thinking, philosophy and approach which strongly indicates that no malevolent and destructive deed, no substantial oversight and error, will take place again. A verbal apology combined with a statement that no such acts or omissions will occur in the future, is a good starting point for supporting well-being into the future, though is reasonably considered as largely meaningless without accompanying action. Thus, where we are offered an apology, we may choose to hedge our acceptance, expressing gratitude where that is appropriate but emphasising the importance of such action.

Yet in many cases, perhaps in any case, even though an apology may be entirely insufficient in itself, there is often little to be lost by acknowledging our errors and mistakes, poor conduct, and in many cases, in many situations, much can be gained from our apologising. Apologies, and acknowledgment of our own errors and mistakes, are routes to better cooperation, togetherness, peacefulness and the reduction of conflict.

Our need to express regret and to apologise stems, in part, from our need to resolve painful conflict, the resolution of which supports our well-being and happiness. Yet, as already discussed in this chapter, conflict of one sort of another, hopefully peaceful conflict is to some degree inevitable, given our different interests, our differing beliefs and opinions, our differing characters. Hopefully we will be able to keep our conflicts peaceful and our relationships positive in spite of our differences. Indeed, it is not unreasonable to argue, as has already been done in this chapter, that while we must aim to pursue peaceful cooperation, conflict is inevitable and not all conflict is bad. And where the meaning of conflict refers to the existence of differences in our opinions and ideas, the existence of our different perceptions and our various efforts to establish solutions to problems, our various efforts to establish which of those differing opinions and ideas, or which strategies and actions represent the best option to follow, then such 'conflict' is helpful and positive to well-being, though this is perhaps extending the meaning of the word conflict beyond where it should perhaps reasonably be taken.

Nevertheless, as already mentioned in this chapter, the fact is that as individuals, communities and societies, as a broader humanity, we need differences of opinions, beliefs and perceptions, differences in ideas, all of which serve as potential sources of solutions to the problems that we face, support us in making optimal decisions and which provide routes to invention of new ways of doing things. Differences of opinions and differing ideas, differing perspectives, in the main need to be communicated, heard, discussed, built-on, synthesised and more, and should not therefore in general be hidden. Passionate commitment or personal conviction or personal belief in particular ideas as optimal, may lead to discussion and argument, though such passion needs to be accompanied by a willingness to listen and take on board what others say where this is appropriate. Of course, on the basis of evidence, reason and rationale, we are certainly free to reject wholly or partially those ideas we consider incorrect.

Within the bounds of argument, disagreement, and within the context of a passion for pursuing that which is right and best for ourselves, others and for our communities, societies and beyond, enmities may develop, frustrations may occur, anger may even rear its head when our frustrations become too great. Such personal enmities will not support well-being and happiness, and we should all aim to keep our discussion and arguments as far as possible focused on issues, problems, ideas, evidence, knowledge and arguments rather than verbally or otherwise attacking in various ways, other individuals.

Thus, we should, wherever possible, aim to discuss and persuade in a civil manner, with respect for others, understanding their motives and reasoning, acknowledging our own personal weaknesses where those may be relevant and the various weaknesses of our own arguments, such as the need for additional evidence, the limitations of the evidence that we have, the role of interpretation in our formulation of our views, and understanding our own biases and backgrounds. Moreover, we need to set out the assumptions behind our beliefs and opinions as well as the ideological framework or underpinning beliefs behind the things we are arguing, saying and doing.

These actions and approaches will help us, our organisations, communities, societies, and beyond, in identification of outcomes which will have the maximum benefit to all of us, with these actions, interactions and approaches to discussion, debate and decision-making, representing elements of our cooperative and collaborative approaches to determination of truth, which incorporate the range of already mentioned cooperative actions such as attending to and listening to each other and using reason, rationality and evidence to make judgments, incorporating a willingness to change, rather than adopting rigid and uncompromising positions which may be inconsistent with evidence.

Our passions, beliefs and our differences may mean some form of conflict because outcomes certainly do matter in terms of well-being both for individuals and communities. However such conflict needs to be managed within a cooperative framework, maintaining and sustaining relationships wherever possible. Verbal and other disputes, conflicting opinions, and more, need to be dealt with within the bounds of civility, care, love and respect, and should never move to personal abuse or aggressive violence.

Importantly, it is beneficial if our building of cooperativity and peacefulness can be conducted in a pro-active manner by each of us as individuals. Indeed, the reality of relationships is that this is often a need in order to achieve successful cooperation, peacefulness and indeed for finding optimal actions, conclusions, and ways forward. Should we wait for cooperation and peacefulness to arise of their own accord, there is the constant danger that damaging conflict, misunderstanding will arise instead. It is our role to make cooperation and peacefulness happen and it is our role and obligation to do what is within our power to both proactively and reactively where necessary, support peaceful interactions between ourselves and others, peaceful relationships between other people, and peaceful relationships between different groups. We need to take the lead in doing this and making this happen not only in our own immediate lives and our own close families, but also in our local communities, societies and beyond.

Waiting for those who are more dictatorial and authoritarian, who are less able and willing in terms of cooperation and peacefulness, who may be motivated by self-interest and malevolence, or who may not even know their motivations; waiting for these people to take the lead and engender hatred and conflict, as they will, and build the road to discord, build a road to a destination of lack of cooperation and even violence, is an abrogation of our responsibilities and not acceptable within the context of the core and other principles. Such inaction risks our own well-being and the well-being of our communities, societies and beyond, providing a potential route to substantial suffering. If we wish to support well-being and happiness and therefore wish to promote cooperative conduct and peacefulness, well-being and happiness for all, then we need to take the lead in ensuring that these aims and principles are realised, and need to demonstrate whatever boldness, courage and strength is required through our actions to ensure these aims and principles are achieved.

And we may need to show such boldness and strength in a range of contexts. Damaging conflict, violence and a lack of peacefulness and cooperation can rear their heads in various places from within the home and family to social relationships within our communities, to broader societal contexts and beyond, such as conflicts between national and then international interest groups. Within all these contexts the principles presented in this guide mean it is necessary to act proactively to ensure peacefulness and cooperation, to the largest degree possible, in support of well-being and happiness. Our world cannot be left for peace to happen to it. Peacefulness and cooperation are things which need to be worked at in a continuous manner.

Our cooperation is something which is founded on attitudes and approaches which are to some extent part of our human identity and character, based in attitudes and approaches, facets of our individuality, which are significantly part of us in terms of our human identity. Our success as individual human beings, as communities, societies and humanity is dependent on our cooperation and ability to maintain and sustain peaceful relationships. Yet our cooperative attitudes, approaches and actions also need to be fostered and nurtured, and will be supported by the actions of ourselves and others which have the actual and real effect of promoting cooperation and togetherness. Further, our cooperation and peacefulness is to some degree founded in relationships and people who themselves already exist in our lives as peaceful and cooperative individuals, intent on effective social living and togetherness, intent on caring for others and living in caring, peaceful, cooperative communities and societies which support the well-being and happiness of all.

One of the key contexts in which cooperation is needed, and which has already been referred to, though more in the context of the potential challenges and problems present, and as a place where much conflict and indeed violence can occur, as a place in which cooperation tends also to be frequent and frequently necessary, is that of the family, both within the family home and beyond the family home, encompassing our more extended family relationships. For men and women, for partners, to live together, often with children, as recognised in various places through this chapter and guide, can be a tremendously challenging, though highly rewarding endeavour. And while we often have the dream and image painted, and indeed often the hope and expectation that we, as partners, will be able to get along together, cooperate together, indeed love each other deeply over many, many, years, without problem or argument, engaging in cooperation, give and take and togetherness, we know, for the many of us, that the reality of living with a partner can be difficult and can be much more complex and challenging than that, with the likelihood of some level of hurt and upset, pain at different levels, significant emotional storms, sometimes severe, through our relationships.

Beyond our dreams and feelings of passionate love, most of us are hopefully aware of the challenges of love and relationships that we are likely to face, having witnessed such challenges through our own experiences of childhood, our own previous experiences of love, our own previous experiences of partners. And we will have this awareness even though there is little taught to us explicitly about the specific problems that are likely to arise and how we might deal with them, nor is there readily available help should we run into difficulties.

For while love may bring us together, and we may love each other deeply in one way or another (at least temporarily, though hopefully for much longer), that does not mean that we will be able to live together, share each day together, and share almost every experience together cooperatively and lovingly, or even through shorter periods tolerably, especially when the initial excitement and the initial flames of love and passion may, in some or indeed many cases, start to burn less intensely and brightly, and we, as partners, as is often (though not always the case) start to see each other somewhat differently.

Because of these difficulties and challenges and these realities, therefore, in terms of supporting personal well-being and the well-being of others, consistent with core and other principles, in terms of supporting long-term peacefulness and cooperativity, and helping in deciding whether peacefulness and cooperativity can be sustained through all the challenges that will be faced, it is undoubtedly advisable for we as couples to live together for a period before we decide on any long-term commitment to each other, and in particular before we consider having children, children being needy of long-term support and presence, and long-term commitment from their parents. Of course, living with a partner before making a longer term commitment is far from a one hundred percent guarantee of relationship success, as we all change with time. On living with someone we become more aware of the person we love, circumstances change and challenges arise in relationships, not previously met, which can cause strain and in some, if not many, cases lead to eventual separation and break up.

But not only will living together allow partners to get to know each other, there is of course the joy experienced through love, sex, the true closeness of an intense loving relationship which is itself a joy to live through and experience. The sense of being valued and loved by another is wonderful and enriching, and for most of us a central part of the richness of our human lives, our human fulfillment and well-being. Whether or not such a relationship is sustained, the experiencing of such fulfillment, pleasure and joy through a loving relationship enriches our lives, our sense of self-value and self-appreciation, as well as letting us know how much good there is and can be in life. Of course such joy and pleasure is certainly in line with and indeed advocated by the core principles, which state that we should aim for and support well-being and happiness.

Ideally the measure of a highly successful partner relationship is the consistent happiness and well-being of all parties, the sustaining of love and passion, easy cooperation and togetherness sustained over time, and sustained commitment and love for each other such that daily life and daily interaction is as far as possible, a continuous pleasure, if not a source of warmth and joy. Many of us will have successful relationships, which make us feel happy and fulfilled in the round, although sometimes, moment-to-moment things may not always be so pleasurable and there may well be times when, for some or many of us, we have negative thoughts and feelings about our partner and our relationship.

If we, as couples, or as individuals separated from our partners, have children, then that is in itself wondrous, and again while providing significant challenges, the successful and happy raising of children can also be said to be a measure of successful living and a successful partner relationship. If individuals and couples care for and raise children through adoption, that is wondrous too, and if we are able to raise our adopted children successfully, that again indicates a successful cooperative partner relationship and of course successful relationships for the children involved.

Yet successful relationships, caring and cooperative relationships come in many forms. Not all of us, not all partners, wish to have, or indeed can have children. There are many ways to enjoy substantial well-being, a happy and fulfilled life and there are many ways to serve ourselves and our partners, many ways to support our pleasure and enjoyment and that of others, as well as many ways of contributing effectively to our community and society as a whole and the world beyond. All of our successful relationships will however involve us in a substantial amount of working together, most likely incorporating some shared goals and interests as well as, with certainty, cooperative personal conduct and behaviour.

Even though there may often be challenges in our relationships and our effort is often, if not usually, required to make them work, we of course will aim for the best relationship possible, and perhaps will aim for and hope for a situation and relationship which is as close as possible to our ideal. We will wish to sustain our relationships as far as is consistent with our own personal well-being and happiness and the well-being and happiness of our partners, which importantly means that relationships need not be, or should not be sustained at all costs.

Clearly cooperating well and having a peaceful environment, will help both our partners and ourselves enjoy our lives together and will help us in the tasks and goals we have to achieve and wish to achieve in our individual lives and lives together. In the initial phases of excitement and love, such cooperation may seem easy, though is not necessarily so, with passion for each other sometimes carrying us through what might be somewhat complex challenges, this continuing effort being sustained because of love, passion and commitment to each other, the willingness to make sacrifices for each other and to make compromises in order to make our relationship succeed. Indeed partner relationships work in all sorts of ways, with love, cooperation and togetherness pursued in a diverse manner in the many different relationships we have, with different levels of give and take and different perceptions, attitudes and ideas within our partnerships about personal roles within our relationships.

Nevertheless all the factors and issues already mentioned in relation to effective cooperation in this chapter are likely to apply to those in loving partnerships. Hopefully those of us in a loving partnership will already have, to some extent, shared and established our feelings and beliefs about our expectations, wants and desires, and perhaps also our roles in our relationship, either explicitly or implicitly. Preferably our exchanges here would be explicit, though that can often be difficult since our love and attraction for another will not often be grounded in cold, rational, explicit thinking and logic so, for example, we may fear damage to the relationship if we express our true expectations, wishes and desires, and moreover we may indeed not know ourselves well enough to be sure what our wants and desires, our expectations are.

Once there, once together, as with other relationships, we need to listen attentively to our partner and take into account their wants and needs, and we need to act on what we hear and the needs and wants we determine that our partner has. However, while we must always have this other-person interest and focus, this may not, and indeed in many cases will or should not mean giving up all that we might want ourselves as individuals within the relationship and all that we might want as individuals in our overall lives, though our relationship will often likely be an enormous part of our lives.

In order to achieve cooperation and peacefulness, it is helpful if we can speak our feelings appropriately, delicately, though freely where this is appropriate, and have a sure sense we will be listened to. And we need to do some giving but also some taking (though this may be somewhat simplistic as we can in a sense perhaps all gain at the same time without any sense of giving and taking). We should not put aside our own more individual and personal needs and wants all the time, as our own personal needs, wants and desires matter too. We need to take time to think about and work on our relationships. Further, where necessary, we need to assist our partners, recognise their wants, needs, their goals, and support them in working towards and achieving the goals which are important to them, while at the same time being aware of, valuing and pursuing our own, other, more individual goals.

We also need to understand how our partners communicate and keep lines of communication open and dialogue going. Some people are less inclined to speak their feelings, something which is often a barrier to cooperation and togetherness. Some others let their frustrations accumulate in silence and then may explode with anger. That is not optimal conduct. If we are the kind of person who is likely to accumulate pain and ill thoughts and then erupt and explode in upset and anger, them we should look for and are likely to need to find, better ways of dealing with our frustrations.

On the other hand being too open and blunt about feelings (some of which may be momentary) can also serve to damage a partner's emotional state, damage well-being and happiness, and so our expression of our feelings needs to be done with care. Our expression of a dislike of a partner's habit or habits may well be upsetting for them, their having believed previously perhaps that this was not an issue. Possibly deciding to tell them of our dislike is a sign of, or may be seen as, our showing a declining love and affection. Our frustrations at a perceived lack of contribution from our partner may hurt them deeply, as they may well perceive that they are contributing substantially. Nevertheless this sort of issue is likely to need to be addressed to avoid simmering unhappiness and resentment. Having said how we feel, following the expression of feelings from our partner, we will hopefully find it easier to manage the situation and resolve the difficulties we maybe experiencing.

In what would be a more difficult and challenging thing to express and to hear, telling our partner that our feelings towards them have changed, that our love for them has lessened or gone, that our relationship is not working, may be painful and disturbing for them, and is probably indicative of the relationship moving to an end. Alternately saying such things may also begin to lead to solving a problem in the relationship, and even perhaps lead to a rediscovery of the attraction and love that we once felt. Sometimes, unfortunately, relationships become more distant and we do not even exchange words about this and communicate about our changing feelings, our changing relationships and our changing relationship situation, often for fear that that will bring what we are holding on to, to an end, and we will lose a love with which was, has been and is so important to us.

While extremely painful, however much we may feel let down, perhaps distraught, if we are faced with such a situation and such or similar statements or expressions, we need to deal with this as calmly and cooperatively as we can, aiming to support the best future for all of us who are involved. The guiding points for our actions in such situations, as in others, are the core and other principles set out in this guide, the need to support the well-being and happiness of all, balancing our own needs, the needs of others, the needs of our children, including our wider families, our communities where relevant, and viewing our actions and making judgments about our actions in terms of these principles.

Of course, as part of our relationship with our partner we need to desist from behaviour which undermines cooperation, such as being overly judgmental of our partners and overly critical of them. We do need to desist from consistent and persistent undermining criticism, and should certainly never personally abuse them and act with aggressive violence. Rather, we need to take care to nurture our partners, those we love. We need to be concerned for them, understand their needs, and to help them grow and live their lives to the full wherever we can. Importantly, we need to understand that our partners are fallible and human, and cannot perform physically, emotionally at the highest level all day and every day, recognising that for most of us it is difficult or nigh impossible to get near to such a standard.

Our reality is that, as a partner; as a human being, we may wake tired, we may be affected by tensions, pains and swings of mood which we cannot necessarily control on the moment (although we must try to control our consequent words and actions at least to some degree) – we may fall ill, we may feel drained by the demands of our children, for example lacking sufficient sleep due to our need to be with them and look after them; we may have insufficient income, fall into debt – we may face pressures at work and even be threatened with losing our income – there may be decisions about work which need to be taken, such as changing work location, changing jobs, all of which create stress (but which may also create togetherness); there may be stressful situations which need to be taken about our children's upbringing and education. Further and linked to all these areas, we are undoubtedly, at least for the most of us, fallible, imperfect in our thinking, conduct and behaviour, or certainly will be at times. It is too much to expect perfection, or even perhaps high levels of accurate decision-making from our partners or from ourselves, and we need to be forgiving of genuine errors, mistakes and aim to love and support our partners despite their errors and through difficult times as far as we can.

If we or our partner lose our incomes, our home, our land, our sources of the essentials we need in life; if for one reason or another we become no longer able to cope with our job through illness or otherwise, especially if we have children to care for, then there will be immense stress for our families with our survival as individuals and as a family under severe threat. In some circumstances, it may be that we end up without a home to live in, without enough food, warmth or other essentials of a life of well-being. All of this and more, should they occur, will present substantial challenges in themselves and will present substantial challenges to our relationships. During such difficult times we need to support each other and stick together, demonstrating our love, loyalty and commitment, doing our best to find solutions, aiming to support our partners, our family, our children in whichever ways we can.

In better circumstances, though still challenging, as mentioned, our very young babies and children can be very demanding, not sleeping through the night or being ill, demanding constant attention during the day, meaning we ourselves may have no or little sleep. As a consequence we may become irritable and tetchy. And in other or even overlapping circumstances, sometimes, life may become mundane, tedious and repetitive, holding out no reasonable prospects of excitement and interest, just that mundane, dull and daily repetition of everyday tasks, everyday amusements and everyday activities, something which may feel demoralising, with the quality of our lives feeling poor, sometimes leading us to search for excitement, the new, sometimes leading us to look beyond our partner relationship, a relationship within which our partner may be perfectly happy as it is. And then there may be physical and sexual difficulties which may interfere with love and togetherness and, as referred to already, our love changing or even ceasing to exist, being sometimes replaced by annoyance, dislike and even in some more extreme cases, feelings of hatred and revulsion towards our partner, because of who they are, their actions and behaviour, their lack of care and neglect of us, unfairness in the relationship and more, including perhaps sometimes feeling dislike for no easily discernible reason at all.

All of this, and indeed much more, can place severe challenges on cooperation and peacefulness in our closest relationships. Through these challenges we need to work cooperatively to support and care for our partners and to do our best to ensure that our families are sustained and maintained as far as possible with happiness, peacefulness and cooperation. Where, and if, under trying circumstances and difficult relationships, it becomes impossible for partners to stay together, due to the difficulties and challenges being faced, through loss of love (and even the advent of painful hatred and dislike), through difficulties in cooperation, through pain and suffering being endured either on a daily basis or too frequently for happiness and well-being to survive in that relationship, then partners may well need to separate, for the benefit and well-being of children if they are present in the family, and for the benefit of the partners themselves, who may need time apart, time to reflect, time to rediscover the value in their relationship or rediscover the pleasures and joy of living which may have become lost in the deep entanglement of a relationship which has proved constricting, difficult and painful, if not impossible to live well through and impossible to sustain. That does not mean that cooperation and working together should end or even in reality can end as we always retain responsibility for our children. It is our obligation within core and other principles, having brought them into the world, for us to care for, love and look after our children and to provide them as far as we can with the love, the care, our time and attention, as well as the resources, amongst other things they need to grow up well.

Cooperation and peacefulness are relevant to our children, with regard to their personal conduct and happiness while they are children, and of course as they grow older and move into adulthood. Our children need to be taught, in a manner appropriate to their age, to cooperate together and work together peacefully, developing their understanding of the needs of others, developing empathy, being taught how to love others and how to put others first at times in their lives, how to engage in cooperation, engage in give and take, such that relationships and life can be enjoyed in a pleasant happy and cooperative manner.

As far as possible, and concomitant with their age, children need to support and help out, and need to be taught to help out and support their parents in the home as well as supporting others outside of the family and outside the home. They need to be taught to and learn to, attend to and listen to others, demonstrating their care and attention. They need to be taught to and learn to understand the emotions and feelings of others, as far as is possible at their particular ages, and need to develop the ability to be aware of understand themselves, how to communicate their feelings and emotions effectively, when to communicate their feelings and emotions and how to communicate effectively with others.

Yet also our children need to be taught the value and importance of their own well-being and happiness and the need to support the wider world in a loving, social and caring manner. Teaching, as already discussed in chapter eleven of this guide, is sometimes however, a complex endeavour, requiring more than simply telling our children what to do and how to do it, but also requiring children to gain experience and have experiences in their daily lives from which they can learn lessons, requiring them to see and experience the modeling of appropriate peaceful and cooperative behaviour, and requiring them to take part in activities which require cooperation, peacefulness and much more.

As already discussed in this chapter, but of sufficient importance that it is certainly worthy of reiteration in the context of promoting and teaching cooperation and peacefulness, children should never be dealt with using aggressive violence or violent threats. In certain situations, having used talk and other more peaceful means, there may be a need to restrain an angry and violent or potentially violent child and move them away from a conflict situation, or require a child who is being abusive or threatening to move away from a place where they are causing a serious and damaging problem to occur, and if they refuse, we may need to ensure that they do move away using our superior physical force. Children can certainly hurt other children and this cannot be allowed to happen. They can sometimes hurt adults. But, of course, children generally do not have the strength and power to physically hurt to the degree that adults do and so only the most limited and least harmful restraint should be used with children, certainly never with a view to causing pain and suffering. Tremendous care must be taken to avoid causing physical damage or psychological harm to children.

And as already discussed in this chapter, but certainly worth reiterating, punishing children and others through violence is unacceptable. Due to its detrimental effects on well-being and happiness, for all concerned, there must be no smacking, hitting, striking of any kind against children, no corporal punishment, no caning, no aggressive violence of any kind against them. As children, particularly older children, can hurt and inflict damage, we are certainly at liberty to protect ourselves and defend ourselves from our attackers, whatever age and restrain them from causing us and others hurt, pain and suffering. However in such instances, as with adults, we must adopt the minimum level of force necessary to protect ourselves and to restrain that child or young person (or those young people) from hurting others.

In regard to cooperation and peacefulness, and indeed in other areas, as discussed in chapter eleven, it is important in the preservation of peaceful and cooperative behaviour to have realistic expectations of children and their behaviour. This can be a hard thing to do, with many adults seeing adult behaviour as representing the precise standard of how children must behave in the here and now, and with this adult behaviour representing a standard against which children should be held to account. But setting expectations of child behaviour on the moment, at levels expected of mature adults is not a reasonable thing to do. Children are children. Dependent on age they cannot be expected to conduct themselves as adults do, with the maturity, self-control, wisdom, experience and restraint that we expect of adults. And such a realisation should also inform our upbringing and the education of our children.

At young ages children may become frustrated at not receiving things they want and sometimes become extremely upset and angry. However, coping with not receiving is something that most children will have to get used to. Most children will compete with siblings, and have arguments and fights with siblings and others over what, to adults, might appear like minor and insignificant issues and differences, which will sometimes escalate substantially.

And children may also on occasion do the most shocking and horrible things to other children, which they must not do, which they must as far as possible, be prevented from doing. And should they do them, then subsequent to the event, it will be necessary that if they possibly can, they recognise the gravity and seriousness of what they have done. In many cases young children will, to a more or lesser degree, dependent on their age, lack our adult capacities for self-control and self-regulation and, also dependent on their age and state of development, will lack adult abilities, understanding and even in some cases, desires and abilities to cooperate with others and work together peaceably with them. And as these are extremely common facets of particularly younger children's behaviour, we need to be prepared and ready to deal with these behaviours rather than responding in surprise, anger and shock at non-adult behaviour which fails to meet the standards we would expect of mature adults.

Yet children, siblings, child friends, will and do cooperate together peacefully and well, both with other children and with adults. They will play together, enjoy each other's company, talk together and cooperate and collaborate in many other different ways, gaining a great deal from each other and learning important lessons of cooperation, love, care, companionship and togetherness. Such cooperating with others and interacting with others is part of our children's experiences, part of their growing up, part of their human identity.

Sometimes this cooperation and peacefulness breaks down. And it is in particular when there is child-to-child conflict that it is for adults to intervene and deal effectively these situations, being firm and effective in order to ensure no child is hurt while also expressing love and kindness for the children.  Unfortunately, additionally, perhaps in a manner which is difficult to avoid, there may be long periods where from the point of view of parents, confidently expecting children to cooperate continuously and pleasantly with parents, siblings and other children, may be difficult.

As children grow older they frequently need to, and start to, grow away from us as parents, rejecting us in some ways, to some or a greater extent, rejecting in a manner, the complete authority and judgments of their parents which as young children they may have accepted perhaps unquestioningly. In this way children start moving towards the responsibilities of an adult life, no longer wishing, willing or being able to lean so much on their parents, even where they need to lean on their parents, but preparing to become those who are responsible, who may be leaned on and who are expected to contribute to others, to the whole. There is often, though not always, conflict with parents during such periods of growth and change, and such conflict and such difficulties may be intense and fractious. Children in this period need to be developing self-understanding and developing their abilities towards independence from their parents.

And while our children are going through these difficult periods of development, changes which biologically, hormonally, developmentally in a range of ways, may be difficult for our children themselves, at the same time, we as adults, as parents, need to recognise and acknowledge the continuing changes, growth and development of children in this way, giving more authority, responsibility and control to our growing children, to a greater extent accepting our child's perceptions and judgments as well as our child's assumptions, opinions and beliefs about the world as valid and indeed worthy (even if perhaps we might see these opinions, beliefs, assumptions and judgments as incorrect).

This type of acceptance is important, since holding our own independently held, strong beliefs, opinions and perceptions of the world is part of moving from childhood to adulthood and represents a key part of adulthood. Adults need to work to build cooperativity with their children during these periods, being prepared to allow their children to act on their own judgments, and as adults accepting our own personal human fallibility and the emergence of that more independent child, who is moving towards adulthood. In this way it may be possible to maximise peacefulness, togetherness, happiness and well-being as far as possible in the particular adult-child relationships, in the family context, though that being said, these times may be significantly trying.

We, as young people growing into adults, need to be careful to love and look after our parents, who themselves may have challenges and difficulties in their lives. We should be wary of being overly critical and derisive of them, even as we become more aware of their faults and inadequacies, growing to accept their weaknesses and recognising their strengths and their love for us. We should aim to love and support them. Yet if parents are badly behaved and bullying, if they are violent, then we should not accept this and should, as far as we can, refuse to be pushed around by them. And where necessary, where we are not safe, we must make efforts to leave that household as soon as we can.

Even the youngest children have responsibilities to other children and adults. And as older young people growing into adults, we certainly have responsibilities towards children, other young people and adults. As youngsters growing towards adulthood, we need to behave in an appropriate manner in looking after others and looking after all other children and the adults with whom we interact.

Again, as parents and as other adults, as communities, societies and broader humanity, there is a need for us to teach our children how to conduct themselves in regard to others and how to realise their responsibilities, and we also need to ensure that children are protected from other children and indeed protected from adults who are acting or prepared to act in malevolent, negatively selfish, violent, exploitative and misguided ways. Strategies for peacefulness and cooperation, as well as strategies for dealing with conflict, need to be taught amongst the wide range of other ideas and behaviours that children are brought up with.

Relationships outside of the close family can be of great benefit in terms of encouraging togetherness, cooperation and peacefulness as well as encouraging a sense of self-value and belonging; relationships with grandmothers, grandfathers, aunts and uncles, cousins and nephews, nieces and more; these many relationships giving us a strong sense of belonging, a strong sense of being people who matter and who have a place in the world, supporting ourselves in believing that we as individuals matter, that we are of importance, as are those outside of the close family. Clearly these relationships, like other relationships, need to be loving, cooperative and friendly as far as is possible. However, while often friendly and positive, these relationships can present their own challenges in terms of maintaining and sustaining relationships.

Challenges arise because extended families differ in nature, with such extended families perhaps having become, and indeed currently seeming to become, of lesser importance in many parts of the world where greater mobility has meant that members of our families move long distances from their places of birth and origin, from their original family homes, villages, towns and cities. This distance from close family can lead to feelings of isolation amongst family members, feelings of being ignored, feelings of not being of importance in the lives of family, causing unhappiness and sometimes conflict. As older and adult children, if we move away, our parents may feel of lesser importance to us, the children whom they brought up with so much love and care. Some parents and other family members may feel isolated from, and perhaps even angry at their isolation and separation from those whom they had close family relationships when younger. All of this undermines feelings of togetherness and may undermine our potential for acting and cooperating together.

Within core and other principles we have obligations towards all others, and we certainly have obligations to look after our family members, those becoming obligations of a lesser degree under changing circumstances, as our children grow older, as we as children grow older and move away from our families, as our family members become more distant from our own lives, and as our families become more distant in terms of our more nuclear family. Of course the closeness of such relationships will change according to the degree of our contact and experience with these different family members during our own upbringings. Nevertheless we should aim to keep in contact with our families, demonstrate we care and show that we care through practical supportive action, including family visits and financial and other support where we have the capacity to provide it.

While we, as children, as brothers and sisters, and more, have such obligations towards our other family members, those other family members can provide an important source of practical and emotional support for us. While we may not be involved with day-to-day cooperative enterprises with them, our family members can act as sounding boards for us, act as shoulders to cry on, provide us with contacts for advice and support, accompany us when we need company, serve as people to belong with and be with, as well as on occasion providing financial or perhaps material practical support, or support in the form of taking action on our behalf in other ways, pointing us in the right direction, advising us on who to talk to, and even supporting us more directly in, for example, finding employment. Our families and family members can clearly provide us with important means of cooperative support, belonging and togetherness.

It is, of course, hard to maintain the plethora of relationships we have, particularly over long distances, and when we have very busy demanding family and perhaps working lives which take up our time and make high degrees of contact difficult to maintain. Nevertheless, we need to recognise the value of our more extended family and how it supports us and our closer family, how it can help to ground our children and support them in feeling more secure in their upbringing, providing a sense of origin and belonging. And of course, as mentioned already, our more distant family may be helpful to us in practical terms. And so, as far as possible and reasonable, of course to some extent dependent on the nature and extent of our specific individual relationships and our personal feelings, and dependent on our particular circumstances, we need to keep in contact with such distant family and work to promote togetherness and cooperation with and amongst these relatives, acting to promote our and their well-being and happiness as well as acting to avoid discord and unhappiness between ourselves and these relatives and amongst them.

The nature and degree to which we keep up our relationships can affect the peacefulness of our lives and the way others feel. We clearly have differing and sometimes conflicting desires and interests here, with some families and some of us wishing more strongly and feeling more comfortable with having our more extended families close to us, and having a greater wish to be part of a larger family community, while others of us and other families may prefer to have a greater measure of separation from our more distant families, feeling the need for greater independence and therefore more control over decision-making and likely less involvement in our more nuclear families.

Those of us who are more distant members of a family need to recognise that our relatives may wish to have space in which to build their own worlds and their own lives, their own more local and nuclear family lives, separate and distant from the life they experienced within their younger lives. And, in a sense, our movement towards building new lives, perhaps based in new and different ideas about family, may well be beneficial in some ways for those individuals and for those children born into that family, as well as for the broader community, society and beyond, though contact with more distant family is considered here to be of great importance.

Even where family relationships are difficult, or where people move a distance away, it is still worthwhile and indeed important to try to maintain some form of contact and to work cooperatively, or to maintain the potential for cooperativity, as far as is reasonably possible, such that relationships are sustained and the family remains loving and together, whatever strife or difficulties there may sometimes be. Denying or refusing contact over a long period of time, with no effort to renew relationships or re-establish relationships and resolve problems is considered unpleasant and unsupportive of well-being, causing potential emotional damage and hurt to ourselves and others, reducing potential for cooperation and togetherness, the damage caused in itself through lack of cooperative conduct, and the damaging example of shunning those with whom relationships may be difficult, all of these being inconsistent with the principles laid down in this guide.

There may be circumstances where it may be legitimate for a short time to maintain some degree of separation, perhaps in cases where problems have arisen, until problems can be resolved or feelings can calm down, and in some cases it may be legitimate in the longer term to reduce or even stop communication, for example when there is significant danger to participants in the relationship from continued contact. However, such refusal to communicate should certainly be far from the norm. More legitimately, if there is someone we find difficult to deal with, who is insulting, hurtful and fractious, again, while not ideal, if we are unable to resolve this problem, then we might legitimately aim to reduce or minimise the level of contact without refusing to see them and talk to them.

Sometimes it may be the case that others simply don't want to communicate with us and act to resolve problems. They may even say they hate us or act to that effect. In these cases there may be little we can do, at least in the short term. Others should not be behaving in such a way and we certainly should not behave in such ways. Nevertheless, if that is how someone else feels, then it may be wise and reasonable, at some point, where necessary, to desist from our efforts at communication to resolve such difficulties, since there may be nothing we can do, our efforts being an inefficient use of our energies when there are those who will love us, want and who indeed need us, whom we can love, and our continued efforts might potentially result in our emotional hurt and the emotional hurt of others, something which it is only reasonable to avoid under such circumstances.

Beyond our families, within the local communities in which we live, in terms of our neighbours locally and indeed those who we more rarely meet within our community, we need to aim to build an environment of peace and cooperativity. While we may feel sometimes that we have little in common with our neighbours, breaking the ice with neighbours and building some form of relationship should serve to enhance cooperation and peacefulness in the main, though of course there are our individual judgments to be made about others. We are perfectly entitled, to some degree, to maintain our privacy if we want, thereby supporting our own personal judgment of what comprises our well-being and how best to achieve it within the context of our personal selves and our obligations in terms of supporting the well-being of those around us (which feeds back into our own well-being).

Nevertheless, isolating ourselves from others is unlikely to support cooperation into the future. It will provide no basis for action and cooperation should cooperation be needed, and can prepare the ground for misunderstanding and conflict, our distance and isolation sometimes being seen unsympathetically by some others, perhaps seen as rude and anti-social. Cooperation, ice-breaking, conversation and dialogue are thus undoubtedly beneficial given the many possible tensions between us and our neighbours, including potential tensions relating to who owns property, personal space, noise, light, children, pets and other areas of possible encroachment onto our own and our neighbour's space. All of these are best dealt with from a position of already having a form of relationship, knowing our neighbours and understanding them, rather than dealt with from a base of non-communication, silent suspicion, mistrust and perhaps sometimes seething anger.

Illustrating this point, clearly in practice, representing the positive realisation of our initial contacts with our neighbours, where such a need arises it is easier to ask someone who we have some knowledge of, someone who we've already talked to, whose name we know, if they would mind reducing the noise or if they could leave their rubbish somewhere else. And this breaking the ice and having a minor relationship with some of our neighbours is a minimum required. Obviously this should support well-being on all sides. Closer relationships may occur in some cases between neighbours, even though for many of us privacy and personal space may be important.

In some cultures and environments, people are more neighbourly and friendly, but we may not be the kind of person who wants neighbours popping in every few minutes and, what we might consider to be, encroaching on our personal lives and personal time when we have busy lives, families to care for and much to do (including wishing for time alone and peace and quiet). For some of us, it may be that the problem we may have with neighbours is that they are geographically too close to us and can, contrary to our wishes, encroach too much on our lives, causing irritation and annoyance. Most of us can, however, work out the correct form of relationship, in each individual case, with our neighbours. It is certainly useful to maintain harmonious and friendly relationships with our neighbours where we can.

Where we wish for and do establish truly friendly relationships with neighbours and others in our closer communities, this is very likely to be beneficial in many ways, enabling mutual support and cooperation. There might be visits, joint outings, shopping expeditions, shared cups of tea or coffee, support for each other and each other's families when ill or away from home, away on holidays and so forth. And there may be mutual support in terms of safety and security with our neighbours taking care of our property or even looking after our children in times of need. All of this is possible and represents cooperation, underpinning peaceful relationships.

As part of our human character, while in some communities there may be very close relationships between neighbours who may have lived close by each other for generations, in those communities and societies where we are more mobile, we may feel some elements of wariness and suspicion with regard to neighbours, whom of course, other than their location near to us, we may have no real connection with, and we do not know well. More to the point, we may feel reticent about creating relationships and friendships because we do not know the histories of these others, their backgrounds, whether they might have committed crimes in the past, how they operate under stress, and how they may deal with matters in their own households (and nor will they know this about us!). And so in these more urban and mobile societies, some watchfulness, and wariness is indeed justified in the early stages of relationships. But as we get to know people better, then, hopefully we would become less wary and more trusting. Generally our neighbours are, hopefully, likely to be adequately reasonable people like ourselves, and, perhaps tinged with some watchfulness, which perhaps is a reasonable initial approach, over time the extent of trust and the extent of the relationship may perhaps slowly grow, developing in solidity and closeness over time if that is the direction in which we wish to go.

Much of course depends on our actual context. In some more isolated places, geographically close neighbours may be the only people available for us to talk to and to provide us with support, and therefore we must build strong relationships if we can. In some of our farming communities, the help of neighbours may be absolutely essential, especially in times of emergency. In these communities the existence of local community groups and mechanisms for us to meet are absolute necessities for our communities to work at all, facilitating us in meeting with each other, building trust and relationships and enabling cooperation together so that we can help each other when such help is needed.

This need for very close neighbourly relationships may be of great value and indeed essential in a range of different contexts, being particularly valuable in supporting our enjoyment of well-being and happiness in those contexts since we are social as people and need others to socialise with. In more urban and suburban environments, we may have the luxury of choice with thousands of potential friends, including those we work with and those we engage with in recreational and leisure as well as other interest and social activities such as political, belief and charitable organisations. Indeed, simply as a practical fact in such urban and suburban contexts, we cannot make friends with everyone and geographically close neighbours may be of lesser importance amongst the range of potential friends, since we may have little in common with them. By contrast, should we live in villages and more isolated locations, our need for company, our need for a social life, our need to do things together, socially as people, in order to survive, demands that we make friends and that, as far as possible, we and at least some of our near neighbours build relationships and work closely together.

Beyond our more immediate neighbours, we are likely, in some form or other, to need to cooperate with others in our local community and indeed wider society, to achieve certain goals in terms of practical tasks that will benefit both ourselves and others in those local communities. Such engagement with others and cooperation is likely to also support a peaceful local neighbourhood, community and society, through the building of relationships with others and through social actions themselves, which will hopefully support well-being. In terms of actions in our local communities, this might mean more specifically taking part in fundraising activities to support a community need, engaging in various forms of business transactions with others locally, taking part in community activities such as sports, dances, art exhibitions, festival events, parties, local meetings to discuss community issues, helping out in a voluntary and friendly capacity to support those in need, and much else. All of this will benefit ourselves and our local communities.

By contrast, failing to engage with others locally may result in problems within the community. Lack of interaction, involvement and engagement runs the risk of leaving local needs being unsupported and unmet, with the potential for both our local social and physical environment to be damaged, with required social initiatives not even considered, let only being taken. When challenges arise in communities where there is little interaction and engagement, it may be difficult for us to organise and implement responses. Moreover, the fun and pleasure we can gain from local community activities will not occur. Our non-involvement and non-engagement is likely to mean that those with authority and power over and within our community move into a position whereby they are more able and perhaps indeed more inclined through opportunity, to act to suit their own interests without interference from others. Our lack of engagement and inaction will be leaving them in a position to take decisions and actions, to implement policies which are negatively selfish and which are not in the community's, our society's interests, or our own individual interests. Additional problems may arise when the community only behaves reactively in response to such decisions, when proactive and cooperative involvement in the first place is needed to ensure that these challenges do not arise and that effective local decisions, are made.

The existence of democratic local forums such as local councils and representative neighbourhood groups, can channel and focus desire for change, and ensure that where such changes are reasonable, shared and desired by the many, such changes are brought in with the sense of our assent and agreement to whatever those changes might be. Democratic mechanisms provide legitimacy for decision making, at least theoretically, though not always in practice, providing a mechanism through which our views are listened to or taken account of, at least to some extent, enabling all of us to more easily accept and cooperate with decisions. That does not mean of course, that we always agree with or accept such democratic decisions, locally or otherwise, and in some cases we certainly should not accept certain decisions, especially those which substantially impinge on, or significantly damage our important personal freedoms and independence, whether democratically arrived at or not.

Adopting democratic approaches, which accord with core and other principles and which should enable us all to have a voice in important decisions, in the main adds to the stability, quality of life, well-being, peacefulness and cooperativity in our communities and societies. We should, however, not allow such democratic approaches to be confined to simply requesting or delivering of our votes at elections where we select representatives, with our responding to requests for votes every few years. Instead we need to constantly engage in a process in which there needs to be constant consultation and constant involvement and feedback on the many decisions which affect our lives, both the lesser and greater decisions.

Whether locally or more broadly, efforts to subvert or ignore democratic processes, by whomsoever, must not be engaged in or tolerated. Such undemocratic actions marginalise and sideline us, making us, as members of a community or society, feel irrelevant, unimportant, devalued, indeed to some degree for some of us, unhappy and depressed. Where there is little democracy or participation, there can be, as a result, a deep sense of friction, a deep sense of mistrust and a decrease in the quality of life due to a deep feeling that we do not matter, that we are unimportant and irrelevant, and that our feelings, ideas and voices do not count for much or anything. While in societies of many millions of people it is of course unreasonable for us to expect our own view to, in general, count for more than or substantially more than the voices of others, nevertheless, a cooperative and peaceful society requires that each of us has the opportunity to speak, to contribute and be listened to in some shape of form, with that listening not being superficial and ritualistic.

In addition to the friction and lack of trust that may arise where there are those in power making undemocratic decisions, the absence of consultation and contribution is likely to mean that we are not banding together and meeting each other in the type of joint and team-based effort which makes for a closer happier community; we are not cooperating with each other with all the benefits that entails in terms of outcomes; nor will we be gaining experience in learning about and practising cooperation in matters which may be of crucial importance. Our common skills of interaction, negotiation and cooperation are not being used for the benefit of the community and we may fail disengaged and unimportant.

Moreover, undemocratic systems operating to support the interests of those in power, will likely mean that some of us may fall prey to demonisation and othering as individuals, groups and classes by these powerful individuals and also sometimes by our neighbours, who we will have less opportunity to cooperate and collaborate with. Rather than this absence of sharing and cooperation, and a resultant absence of close familiarity and close knowledge of each other, we need to be familiar with each other and know each other as people rather than as caricatures of humanity.

Suffice to say that such demonisation, such othering, can occur even where there are democratic systems, and neighbours and community members do know each other, particularly in cases where those with power and influence present poisonous lies and falsehoods about other groups of people. Even where there are groups whose members hold beliefs which are unacceptable in terms of core and other principles, and which may threaten us, we must demonstrate care and concern for these others, look after their well-being, aiming to change their beliefs, views and outlook, while protecting ourselves from harm. We need to be aware that it is frequently the case that the pictures painted of others, of other groups, such characterisations, are almost always gross simplifications and exaggerations, are almost always, though not always, false, and are frequently if not almost always made for the purpose of supporting negative-selfish interests.

In order to support well-being and happiness locally, and to support cooperation and avoid unnecessary conflict, we need to ensure that we are engaged and involved in local and broader decision-making. And those who are our representatives, those with greater power and influence than we have, need to promote engagement with such decision-making, as well as promoting mutual interaction and discussion and democratic contributions to decision-making. While it is certain that professional advisors and professional expertise are important in decision making, and that we frequently need expert advice from those with experience in the range of matters, we cannot actually be well-served if such professionals operate without our views having been asked for and if our contributions are not wanted, are belittled, or if we are not, as communities, societies or broader humanity, in effect, in reality, through democratic mechanisms, in effective charge of the relevant processes and decisions.

Democratic principles also need to be applied to our broader societies in support of cooperation, peacefulness, well-being and happiness. Similar, though perhaps greater challenges arise in this wider context, compared to the local level in terms of promoting cooperation and peacefulness. An effective, functional society of millions of us, supporting the welfare of all individuals within the society and indeed supporting the welfare of those beyond who are in need, is complex and difficult to establish, maintain and develop, to participate in, contribute to and manage. However, with such systems in place and sustained, embodying in themselves core and other principles, we will be better able to ensure that core principles, and the well-being and happiness of all are achieved to the maximal level possible.

As individuals, amongst millions of other individuals, we may of course feel to some degree somewhat insignificant and lacking in influence. Perhaps we may feel unqualified and unable to contribute on the larger stage, and indeed we may feel, with what may seem like appropriate self-deprecation, that our own individual voice should not be too prominent in a society of hundreds of thousands or countless millions of people. Nevertheless, in spite of what might be our personal reticence to speak and contribute, what is possible if not likely in some contexts if we do not participate and contribute, is that others, some who do not have at heart the interests of all others, who do not have at heart the interests of the whole, will engage in and will participate, acting in pursuit of their own particular and negatively selfish ends. And therefore if we do not contribute, if we do not make the effort, based in core and other principles, using reason, rationality, evidence, love, care and concern for others, as a basis for our contributions, then the field of decision-making, the handles on the levers of power, may end up in the control of those acting in a negatively selfish manner, at the expense and to the detriment of ourselves and others.

The possible if not likely presence of powerful well-resourced, well-organised interest groups in broader society, aiming to serve their own interests rather than those of all others, the community and the society as a whole, and which may indeed operate at the local level as well, means that ensuring justice, well-being and welfare for all can be challenging. Such challenges and the actions of those pursuing their own agendas, and indeed pursuing their own power and successes, as well as perhaps our not having enough information and not understanding what is going on, can dissuade us from participation, with our being perhaps intimidated by their organisation and apparent power. However, whatever the difficulties, we can and must organise and join with others to counter the influence of such negatively selfish, destructive and damaging interests.

As already mentioned, if we are disengaged from society, we leave the way clear for those others of us with specific agendas and self-focused interests to promote their own interests directly and not only sideline the interests of others but damage the well-being of others substantially causing pain and suffering. We must never ourselves promote such disengagement and damage, and should never support powerful groups and powerful individuals in any deliberate efforts to promote disengagement, our disengagement. These powerful groups and individuals, hopefully not represented by ourselves or supported by ourselves, may believe (probably wrongly) that their interests will be better served if they themselves, or their agents, are holding the reigns of power, if they themselves are in place to make social, political and economic decisions, or if those in power have their ear and not the ear of others. We cannot allow those pursuing their negatively selfish interests at the expense of the rest of us, to gain such power and to succeed in pursuing their goals.

So it is essential for each of us to participate as far as we can and as actively as we can in order that core and other principles are pursued, that our own interests and views can be heard and such that the well-being of all will be promoted and safeguarded. Through such engagement and participation, we will gain many additional benefits, having the potential to enrich our own lives through meeting others similarly committed to the welfare and well-being of all, and acting in solidarity with these good, caring and empathetic others to tackle those who may be pursuing their own negatively selfish agendas and who are not acting to support our individual and the general well-being and happiness.

Further, beyond the social pleasures of simply meeting others, our involvement, engagement, participation and contribution enable us to meet a cross-section of people from different backgrounds whether it be in terms of work, beliefs, philosophy of life and more and, in a sense, such meetings and encounters, coming into contact with the experiences, perceptions and views of others, are likely to enrich our lives, being a valuable part of our personal education and development. And of course, in itself, there are the joys and pleasures of interaction with others, arising from our nature as the social beings that we are.

Of course in our modern world we can engage with others in productive and effective ways, supporting our communities, working to promote well-being and to avoid, reduce and prevent pain and suffering, without actually meeting these others face-to-face. Thus, through the Internet, we can join online groups for discussions about shared interests, social and political issues, philosophical and belief matters, gaining social pleasures from our interactions with others and developing online relationships. We can campaign with others to support the political and other goals we believe in, contacting others to promote and discuss our views, recruiting and donating funds for campaigns and organisations we believe in, working to support the outcomes we wish to see in our democratic communities, societies and more globally. Our various electronic outlets, such as for example, the widely used facebook medium, also enable us to some extent to maintain and sustain our relationships at a distance, thereby promoting togetherness and cooperation. Our electronic means thus provide a further way of underpinning our democratic, sharing, collaborative community processes, hopefully acting to support collaboration and cooperation in our communities, societies and beyond.

Our participation and indeed the active participation of others in community and society is something which should be appreciated by others since, on the whole, it should serve to support the general well-being and welfare, due to its and our contribution to peacefulness, cooperation, community and social togetherness. We ourselves should appreciate the participation and contributions of others who are operating to support core and other principles, the general well-being and happiness and the public good, even if we might disagree with them about the route to these goals. And in the way that we conduct ourselves in such contexts in the face of disagreement, different perceptions, backgrounds, philosophies and approaches, as well as where there is agreement and greater harmony, our actions should in themselves serve to promote peaceful and harmonious living incorporating well-being and happiness.

The reality is that in all forums to which we may contribute, be they family discussion and decision-making, in community discussion and decision-making, in wider social discussion and decision-making, the views that we personally have and to which we may be strongly wedded, may not always win the day and, of course, moreover and importantly in any case, our views and ideas may develop and change on hearing the ideas of others. Where these differing ideas are consistent with core principles and are aimed at supporting well-being and happiness, it is best for us to encounter such views where they exist and where possible enjoy and perhaps learn from these alternative ideas and expressions. Rather then repressing or avoiding them, in regard to less palatable views, anti-social ideas, ideas inconsistent with core and other principles, it is where possible and reasonable, most likely best to encounter those views expressed to hear them out, to tackle and deal with those others and their views, though where such views are directly and immediately threatening of aggressive violence, and causing substantial pain and suffering to others, this may sometimes not be possible or reasonable.

In our democratic, work and other contexts, in terms of our experiencing differing views consistent with core and other principles, experiencing such alternative perceptions, can often be far better than surrounding ourselves with those who are in agreement with us, even though it is often pleasant to have others agree with us and support us. Hearing and encountering such alternative perceptions is certainly better than existing in a silent or conformist silo where we may convince ourselves of our own correctness, talk without fear of contradiction, without any other person challenging, engaging with, critiquing, developing our ideas and statements or rejecting our views.

Listening effectively has already been argued in this chapter as central to effective interaction, communication and cooperation. In democratic forums, in work discussions and committees, or other contexts we need to try to engage meaningfully with the ideas of these others, making real attempts to listen, learn and understand the ideas of others. It may be that others are wrong or may have misjudged or miscalculated in their views, but on the other hand, of course, they may have important contributions to make, be expressing important sentiments and feelings, regarding key ideas and issues, and these will comprise valuable contributions to our discussions and may reasonably influence the decisions and actions we need to take. Listening in a caring, sympathetic and empathetic way to all, when appropriate, will serve to enhance well-being and happiness.

As already discussed within a range of contexts, a refusal to engage with others in our community, work and other forums is, in the main, unacceptable. Whatever our views, beliefs and differences, even in cases where others appear to have no interest in supporting our well-being and the well-being of others, if these others are willing to talk and discuss, we will need to engage with them in order to try to persuade those others of the rationale for supporting core and other principles, the importance of taking the correct decisions regarding matters under discussion and the importance of the well-being of ourselves and all. We must attempt to engage, where we can, even with those who promise threats and violence if it is safe for us to do so, since we must attempt to prevent aggressive violence, pain and suffering, and support our own well-being and the well-being of all.

Absence of communication and absence of interaction between us, as well as absence of peaceful constructive cooperation threatens our well-being and happiness. Such situations are unsatisfactory for all of us and so, whenever we can, we, as groups, individuals, organisations, communities, nations and other social entities, need to make efforts to communicate and to resolve problems. That being said, as already referred to in relation to more personal matters, it has to be acknowledged that sometimes breaks in our discussions and negotiations, temporary withdrawals, may be helpful at times, especially when engaged in efforts to resolve complicated and complex problems. Such temporary cooling off periods, time for consideration, thought and reflection, can help us as individuals and, where appropriate as negotiating teams and groups, to reconsider our approaches, to gain perspective, to generate the will and desire to overcome fractures in our relationships with others, enabling us in the case of our taking time outs as individuals, to gain some personal peace and equanimity, as well as providing space for us to generate ideas and possible solutions such that peace, cooperation and well-being can be achieved. Not only do we have to recognise the value of such temporary withdrawals for ourselves but need to be understanding when others seek such time and space.

Nevertheless we do need to avoid as far as possible any long-term breakdowns in communications, proactively aiming to build links between us and others, aiming to build and sustain relationships and communication. Where there are conflicts between our societies and nations, disputes over resources, conflicts over boundaries, or other matters, our previously built relationships should support us in resolving difficulties. And our common humanity, and our recognition of the importance of our common humanity means that we should share and cooperate and seek mutually beneficial solutions, where such disputes do arise. There needs to be talk, negotiation and dialogue with a view to finding such mutually beneficial solutions, beneficial in serving all of us as individuals, communities, societies and globally to the optimum level possible.

It is also important to acknowledge that where there have been threats of, or where there is ongoing violence and intimidation, our involvement in negotiation, discussion and efforts at cooperation, while possibly helpful, at some times may be of no benefit or counter-productive, and there may be a need to withdraw from such negotiation and discussion, and take other actions such as strengthening the mechanisms available to us for self-protection, for our community, society, national and other defence in the face of threatened or likely aggressive violence, something which could indeed be initiated and engaged in by those wishing to violently exert their power, while negotiation and talk is ongoing. Our desire for cooperation and togetherness should not close our eyes to the malevolent intent of others who may engage us in discussion and negotiation with no intention of seeking true cooperation and friendship, but who instead use such communication and discussion as a distraction to mask their true intent.

On the more individual level, and already mentioned in this chapter in the context of discussion of the notion of forgiveness, while we should aim to keep channels of communication open, this being, on the whole, a positive thing to do, if we have been personally assaulted and have been the victim of violence and intimidation, we have the right to refuse dialogue in the short term and longer term and the right to disengage from dialogue altogether, simply because that is what we want, or on the grounds that we have concerns and fears in relation to meeting those who have attacked us. However, if there is room for, and motivation for, resolving problems and drawing back together, the prospect and likelihood of violence and intimidation having receded and our fears dissipated, then, dependent on the situation, the importance of the relationship and the positive effects which might result from resolution, it may well be best to pursue some form of communication and pursue such action and resolution. But that will be our decision as the person who has been the victim of such assault, violence and intimidation.

In the case of communities, societies and nations which have been involved in violent conflict, such non-communication cannot be allowed to be sustained since it will contain the seeds of further conflict, increasing the possibility of misunderstandings, irrational prejudice and hatred, increasing the possibility of further conflict between our groups. Those regimes, those individuals who have pursued aggressive violence and their supporters need to either be removed from power or give clear demonstrations that there is absolutely no prospect of such aggressive violence into the future. Such change will serve as a key element of steps towards peaceful cooperation from which all of us will benefit.

It can be quite easy for relationships within and between groups and communities to encounter difficulties. For this reason it is essential that there are democratic forums available for discussion, dialogue and decision-making, forums through which threats to and breakdowns in relations can be anticipated and tackled. Such forums should not be allowed to dissolve into acrimony and futile conflict. Indeed care should be taken to ensure that such cooperative and democratic groups keep sight of the welfare and well-being of individuals and indeed are concerned with all individuals rather than focusing on perceived group interests or solely the interests of individuals in particular groups, which, if pursued, may end up damaging the welfare and well-being of many if not all individuals within those communities.

Where we have such democratic forums, it is considered here that their membership should not be constructed based on group representation and group interests. Rather they need to be constructed on the basis of individual representation yet enable the voices of groups and their chosen representatives to be heard in such forums. This is necessary to avoid a range of problems including the marginalisation and exclusion of those individuals with no group affiliation, those who wish to have no group affiliation beyond their membership of our common humanity, and indeed those who may have no belief in such affiliations within a community or society. Such more individual construction should also help to avoid problems through those claiming to represent groups not truly representing their group members or only representing some of their group members, or indeed simply representing their own opinions. Situations need to be avoided where those representing such groups are simply involved in pursuing goals which focus solely on the interests of their particular groups at the expense of other groups or at the expense of vast numbers of other individuals who may not have any group affiliation and may not therefore be present or represented.

Indeed the existence of groups, group loyalties and affiliations, group representatives and group interests can in itself serve as a barrier between us, separating us as individuals from others and creating a sense of otherness, which may serve to diminish our sense of common humanity and reduce well-being and happiness, potentially leading to problems, pain and suffering, especially if we do not primarily recognise our common and fundamental humanity. Nevertheless, the reality we face, and perhaps an inevitable reality, indeed part of our human identity, is one of the existence of such groups, our feelings of group loyalties and affiliations and so, rather than ignoring the potential for troublesome and damaging differences and problems between groups, rather than ignoring the real and often irrational resentments that can arise within us as individuals through our group membership, affiliation or identities and through groups pursuing their own interests or aiming to dominate other groups, there do need to be such democratic forums focusing on the individual well-being of all, where difficulties that have arisen between what might be seen as groups and group interests are addressed and resolved.

And where there are breakdowns, indeed optimally prior to such breakdowns, in a proactive manner, community and group members need, in the same manner as occurs with individual relationships, to take the lead and aim to promote peaceful cooperation and togetherness. Efforts need to and should be made by all to resolve differences and difficulties which might lead to painful and intense conflict and to promote, at the minimum, our amicable and friendly co-existence, though hopefully enabling and promoting much more in terms of togetherness, cooperation, friendship, love and more.

Whether they arise from group conflicts or from other individuals, unfortunately, for some of us, on some occasions, reality may involve us in having to deal with threats of aggressive violence or actual aggressive violence at some point or other in our lives, and indeed it is possible, perhaps probable in some contexts, that at some point that we may end up on the receiving end of threats of or actual violence.

Already discussed within the context of peaceful and non-violent responses earlier in this chapter, while this guide does not advocate pacifist approaches, and while we must protect ourselves from violence, if at all possible, faced with potentially violent, as advocated earlier in this chapter, in conflict situations, wherever we can, we need to use words or other actions beyond forceful physical action in the first place to try to prevent the occurrence of such violence. Peaceful, understanding, empathetic and perhaps firm words and dialogue may, in some cases, dissuade those engaged in threats of violence from carrying out their threats.

Nevertheless, our words may not be successful, or in the precise situation they may not represent realistic ways of dealing with the immediate threats we face or the violence we may already have been subject to. For example, those engaging in violent threats and in violence itself may be in no condition to listen, perhaps drunk with anger, hatred, irrationality, psychologically ill (perhaps temporarily) tanked up with alcohol or drugs, and therefore, while asking others to reflect on their actions, reasoning with them, questioning, and making assertive statements in regard to the possible consequences of their actions for themselves and others, may sometimes, if not often, lead to some of those engaged in aggressively violent threats from desisting, where they are not in a fit condition to listen, such words may be sometimes be futile.

Should we decide that under the circumstances, using physical force to defend ourselves and others is therefore a necessity, then this action will hopefully be successful. Nevertheless, even though we have determined it is a necessity under the circumstances, our own response with physical force may run the risk of leading to escalation of violence. Moving away from those making threats may, where possible, also be a better way of, at least temporarily, preventing an outbreak of violence or the continuance of violence. And apart from allowing us to leave a potentially dangerous situation unharmed or less harmed than might have been the case, such action may mean that we are be able to find help, regroup and engage with others in order to collectively prevent further threats and future harm to ourselves and to others. Yet, on the other hand, our leaving a scene where we are under threat or have been subject to aggressive violence, where we have taken no effective action, may mean that others are exposed to violence, pain and suffering, which is itself unacceptable, especially when we are capable of taking action in our own self-defence and the defence of others.

On some occasions, however, the first we may know of violence may be when it is in process, being attacked without warning, unexpectedly, at which point we must protect ourselves and dissuade our attacker if we can from further violence, using the minimum force necessary to achieve that essential goal in an effective manner. We also have to, and are obliged to, make judgments and take action to protect ourselves and others, but we must aim to avoid engaging in physical violence, the use of force ourselves, unless it does comprise a necessity for our own protection and the protection of others, and in the event that we use force it must be at the minimum level to effectively support our protection and the protection of others, although this potentially might involve a high level of physically forceful and indeed damaging action dependent on the circumstances.

The core and other principles presented in this guide do require that we act to prevent our own pain and suffering as well as looking after others, and there may well be times when we need to defend and protect ourselves and others from physical violence, with this becoming a priority above other priorities. If we can prevent someone from injuring us, from hurting us, then, balanced by other priorities (which may include protecting others and protecting our communities) we will certainly need to protect ourselves. Of course we may also consider other priorities as more important, such as protecting and caring for our families, those who are closest to us, those we love and care for most, and indeed those whom we may have never met before. To support these people, while we may not wish for pain and suffering, we may quite rightly in certain circumstances be prepared to suffer pain and injury ourselves, perhaps significant pain and injury, or indeed sacrifice our own lives to protect others. And this is a laudable and admirable thing to do in the defence of others which may benefit those others significantly preventing their substantial pain and suffering, even preventing their deaths.

While being as sure as we can to maintain our own safety, security and well-being, if we can, we also need, as far as is possible and reasonable, to protect those who may wish to do us harm. Of course this may well be challenging, but those who may wish to harm us, who are threatening and attacking us, may be ill, temporarily out of control, may have made an important misunderstanding, may have highly irrational ideas and thinking, and may be considered vulnerable in some ways. That being said, as someone being assaulted and attacked, this is likely to seem entirely irrelevant on the moment and also difficult to see and recognise under such trying circumstances.

Yet, if we can react to these people and their threats through peaceful means, despite the fear that for many of us will almost inevitably be there, doing our best to overcome our fear, then that will provide a stepping stone for building peace and cooperation into the future, and indeed will help out those who are behaving threateningly, aggressively and violently. Having responded peacefully to such an attack, it may be that as a consequence, if we have managed to maintain our own safety as well as the safety of those who have engaged in aggressive violence against us, the problems of those who are threatening or who may intend to assail us may possibly be dealt with, offering both ourselves and such others the possibility of a more decent life ahead and also reducing or supporting the removal of any threat to ourselves and others from these individuals, which might exist into the future. Wherever possible, if we can, we have an obligation to pursue peaceful solutions which work in the short, medium and long term.

However, as already stated, such a peaceful approach may not be possible. Those who are aiming to hurt us, do aggressive violence against us, may be engaging in aggressive violence in a manner which makes it impossible for us to even consider protecting them, in the light of the threat they are offering against us. They may not be rational in any sense, as mentioned above, possibly being consumed with aggressive violence and anger, under the influence of drugs of one sort or another, such that persuasion and talk can do little or nothing to influence their behaviour. Their anger may be so intense and deep that on the moment, our efforts to diffuse anger and violence may be, or are likely to be, ineffective, and may even provoke greater violence and hatred. As a consequence we may need to act immediately and act decisively to protect ourselves and to protect others.

Each situation needs to be judged on its particular characteristics, including our interpretation of the level of threat, the individuals (or groups) involved in the situation, our capacity to physically respond to a threat (which may in itself suggest a non-physical response or escape), our ability to escape the situation and resolve the problem later, and our capacity to resolve the problem through words or other strategies. Those of us who are under real threat will need to evaluate the situation quickly and make our own decisions about what action is most appropriate to take when threatened. Optimally this should be peaceful if at all possible, but none of us is under any obligation to allow ourselves to become a victim of aggressive violence, and indeed this should not be done and does not accord with core and other principles, with the exception of where we are acting to protect and prevent others from suffering, injury, pain and death. In highly dangerous and threatening circumstances, our forceful physical action where required will need to be effective and decisive, though of course should be at the minimal level needed for self-defence and the defence of others.

In some situations we may face defeat and destruction about which we will have the capacity to do nothing. In such circumstances, in support of well-being and happiness of others and in order to reduce the prospect of their pain and suffering, we may determine to use words in order to influence our aggressors actions into the future. Alternately, dependent on the circumstances, we may need to do the maximum we can to damage and disable our aggressor such that in the future they will be less willing to, or will be less able to inflict aggressive violence on others.

As mentioned briefly already in this chapter, ideally we should make ourselves aware of, and learn and practise techniques and strategies to diffuse tensions and verbally disarm those who are engaging in aggressive threats or becoming threatening, as well as our developing awareness of and practising strategies to recognise and try to prevent such situations arising in the first place. This should of course happen as part of our general learning and education. Beyond that, it is quite reasonable to develop personal physical strength such that we can protect ourselves and others from threat. However, this development of physical capacity needs to be linked to developing the mental abilities and self-control not to use such physical capacities unnecessarily and aggressively. Further, if we live in a peaceful context where such violent attack is unlikely, then this development of our defensive capacities may not need to be pursued, though in any case, non-violent approaches should be our first and most important approaches to dealing with aggression and threat.

It could be said that by developing our physical capacities for defensive action we might be encouraging an escalation of physical capacities for violence more generally, and as a consequence we will be providing the potential for generating escalating levels of physical conflict, with each person having in effect a potentially dangerous physical weapon at their disposal. But we will hopefully be aiming to develop effective defensive capacities, not the capacities to attack others, and even though there is undoubted overlap between our defensive capacities and the capacities needed to engage in aggressive violence, where our contexts have a reasonable potential to be threatening and dangerous, we cannot leave ourselves and others open to aggressive violence and attack.

There is little value and purpose in remaining physically weak in the face of the reasonable possibility, indeed likelihood in many lives, of violent action and threats, against us, although if there were no realistic violent threats such capacity would of course be unnecessary and superfluous. If we have the physical capacity to prevent others visiting violence upon us and those we love, on others, then we must, where necessary, use that capacity and consequently it is quite reasonable for us to develop that physical strength and the physical skills and abilities needed to support us in restraining those who may threaten, intend or engage in violence against us, others in our communities, societies and beyond, those we are close to, whom we love and are most responsible to and for.

While it is seen as legitimate here to develop our physical capacities for defending ourselves and defending others, for the most part, dependent on our context, possession and carrying of weaponry for self-defence is seen as, in principle, a bad thing which should not be promoted or done if possibly avoidable. The nearby presence of such weaponry in the context of peaceful societies or indeed in other contexts, provides immediate access, where conflict arises, to extreme and damaging, deadly actions and responses in conflict situations, and extreme consequences which are likely to harm and damage specific individuals and all concerned, permanently. The presence of such weaponry further provides the opportunity for accidental use of such tools with the consequence of injury and death. Yet, that being said, if our context is one where we face a severe and constant threat of extreme violence and death against us, or where there is the possibility of such violent destruction and threat against others, then it may be justifiable for us, or some of us, our civil protection forces, to possess and hold weapons for our own defence and the defence of others.

Further arguing against the presence and general holding of destructive weaponry, the knowledge of the common presence of such weaponry enhances the threat of escalation of conflict and escalation of weaponry, in essence, as a consequence, supporting an arms race between those of us who prefer peace, support individual and the general well-being and happiness and who wish to protect ourselves and others, and those prepared to engage in anti-social acts or willing to engage in aggressive violence to achieve their ends. In the knowledge of the presence of such weaponry for our protection and defence, those who are criminal, anti-social, intent on aggressive violence, may be required and may be led, not only to acquire weaponry but to adopt more developed, sophisticated and dangerous weaponry than might otherwise be used, leading to even more damage and destruction through their actions.

In more precise terms, at the more local and practical level, those for example aiming to steal, while they might be deterred by the threat of violence against them, may on the other hand, anticipating the possibility of a weaponised response, ensure they have weapons and that they deploy these first, before they themselves can come under threat. The reality is, in the main, that in communities and societies where there are deadly weapons which are accessible, which are held carried and held available for the purposes of defence, there are many deadly incidents which would not have occurred had those weapons not been present and available. Peaceful communities and societies, and indeed a peaceful world need to be built and this will not arise if each of us, or even many of us carry a deadly weapon. That of course, and worthy of emphasising again, is not to say that we should not protect ourselves. But it is to recognise that we are highly likely to be more protected and safe in a peaceful, cooperative and weapon-free context.

Civil protection forces should also, in the vast majority of circumstances, again dependent on context, not carry deadly weapons, or indeed weapons which might cause serious harm. In order to protect ourselves if we are in such forces and the public, in threatening situations, dependent on the precise nature of the threatening situation, for our civil protection forces, firstly, we in those forces will need to be well-protected against physical violence, then in terms of action, talk needs to be the first port of call, followed by unarmed physical force aimed at restraint with no aim of causing injury. All of this will support a peaceful social context which in itself will serve to protect us all.

However, if those engaged in threats themselves are likely to have or have deadly weapons, in order for our civil protection forces to defend and protect themselves and others, as they are bound to do, dependent on the precise context and situation, they may have to use weapons of one sort or another, optimally non-deadly, but necessarily effective. In the main, such weapons should not be carried on a regular basis, but should be accessible when needed. If such weapons are constantly carried and widely used, and even if they are used frequently when not immediately accessible, these weapons will support a violent context and serve through their presence, in themselves, to engender acts of violence and a cycle of deadly violence. Even in situations where there is serious and severe violent threat, the goal and end point of having those weapons more available to civil protection forces is that these weapons should no longer be necessary and their availability is no longer needed once threats are removed.

Of course, in terms of relations between nations, the development and acquisition of new weaponry by our own nations, our own allied group of nations or another power, may similarly provide an impetus for we ourselves or the other party to develop new and more damaging weaponry, resulting in an even more intense race to develop and possess greater numbers of, and more powerful weapons, such an arms race appropriating major resources from funds supporting other more peaceful purposes, these other purposes being hopefully, much more worthwhile and much better supportive of our well-being. Increased levels of such nation state weaponry further run the risk of creating violent and destructive damage and war through accident. And, moreover indeed, simply through their existence and possession by different groups, nations, alliances, their presence runs the risk of being provocative of damaging conflict, serving to support the creation of tensions, suspicion and mistrust.

Thus there are too many ways in which possession of weaponry at various levels can lead to tremendous damage, and therefore, wherever possible, the level of deadly and other weaponry needs to be reduced or kept to a minimum. The removal of all deadly weapons, while possibly desirable, is not considered realistically possible, at least at the present time, and might leave us all vulnerable to the actions of those who will act in malevolent ways, but a vast reduction in the level of such weapons in our communities and in the world is undoubtedly desirable and needed to secure both the peacefulness of our communities and societies and the future of our humanity. Yet perhaps the most powerful brake on the use of aggressive violence and deadly violence is all of our cooperative, loving and caring actions, personal conduct and behaviour, aiming to support the well-being and happiness of ourselves and all others, and aiming to reduce and prevent our and their pain and suffering.

Suffice to say, within our communities and societies, we need to be aiming to build the kinds of community and society where aggressive violence and such physical threats of violence, as far as possible, do not occur. We need to be teaching our children to work cooperatively and peacefully with others and, not only that, we need to be teaching them as effectively as possible, how to cooperate, how to work together, how to avoid aggressive violence. We need to be developing our own personal understanding and our communities' and societies' understanding and knowledge of the origins and nature of aggressive violence, such that we can reduce its levels and as a consequence, support us all towards greater well-being and happiness. And, in order to support that greater well-being and happiness, we need to have systems in our society to deal with aggressive violence in an effective manner such that incidents of aggressive violence are prevented from occurring, such that we are protected from hurt and damage from aggressive violence, such that the levels of aggressive violence are reduced or such that such aggressive violence disappears completely, if this is indeed possible.

Through both informal and formal education we need to do our best to educate against aggressive violence, bringing our children up appropriately, yet we should not ignore the realities of a world, at least of our current world and, unfortunately, likely a future world, where there are those who can be extremely violent and will engage in aggressive violence. We perhaps should all be aware that we all, or many of us may, as mentioned earlier in this chapter, under certain circumstances, have the potential for aggressive violence, perhaps due to intense moments where we might have an inability to control our feelings, our anger and emotions. Further, we and others, might possibly commit acts of aggressive violence due to false and damaging beliefs, due to illness or other factors, though hopefully will never do so. Ignoring the reality of our own potential actions (or the potential actions of some of us) and the potential actions of others is not seen as supportive of well-being or acceptable within our principles.

As well as bringing our children up appropriately to be cooperative, loving and caring adults, as well as educating our children in pursuing peacefulness and cooperation, our children also need to be aware of, need to be taught about, and as they grow into adulthood, they need to be capable of, ensuring their own safety in the face of threats which can be real, and will need to develop their capacities to deal with those who may be violent or who threaten violence. For our children and ourselves, it is not considered that there is dignity in being a victim of violence (except when we are protecting others) and there is little dignity in standing by powerless as those we love, or other people in general, are hurt by those behaving in malevolent, aggressively violent and evil ways. We need to act to prevent aggressive violence wherever we can.

Thus, stemming from much of what has been stated above, our aim and priority, within the context of core and other principles is therefore to, as far as we can, develop and ensure a peaceful context in which aggressive violence and incidents of aggressive violence do not occur or are certainly minimised. Building such a context within our communities, societies and more broadly requires us, amongst other things, to focus on, as already mentioned bringing our children up well in manner which promotes peaceful cooperative action and our having effective systems of education, training and development, but also requires us to provide help for those who are ill or in need, requires us to have a concern for all people, ensuring no-one lives in poverty and endures significant deprivation, involves us reducing stark and perverse inequalities, our supporting personal development and achievement for all, promoting non-violence, providing, supporting and building a sense of belonging, self-value, independence and self-efficacy, a sense of freedom and justice in our communities and societies and enabling contribution, valued contribution by all. It is in these ways we will be making the most significant contribution to the avoidance of violence.

Reiterating what has been said already in this chapter, if words cannot be used to prevent violence from another or others then, in a similar manner as to that we would expect from our civil protection forces, if we have the capacity and the opportunity on the moment, we need, in the first place, to attempt to restrain physically those engaging in threatening and violent behaviour towards us and others. To accord with core principles, this optimally needs to be done in a manner which does not leave us open to significant risk of injury. Minimal force should be adopted in order that we protect ourselves and protect others, while as far as possible refraining from injuring the person or persons who are offering significant threat or who are actually attempting to do violence to us or others. And where a low level of restraint is likely to, or is proving insufficient, if necessary in order to protect ourselves and protect others, it may be necessary to restrain an attacker in a more forceful manner.

While hopefully this will not involve any significant injury or damage, we may sometimes need to temporarily injure and hurt our attacker or attackers, though hopefully not damage them to any significant degree, and this should not be shrunk from where necessary, and should be done decisively. Under such circumstances, we must provide the necessary extent of threat, hurt or damage that is needed to protect ourselves and others in that situation. That threat may legitimately be seen as existing not only for the moment of the attack against us, but for the immediate period and indeed longer after the attack on us or others, and we need to ensure as far as we can that we and others will not be subject to further attack.

This necessity under certain circumstances to pursue restraint even injuring another and, as mentioned previously, *in extremis* even using deadly force in self and other-defence, is not seen here as advocating or promoting aggressive violence. Whenever we can resolve things peacefully, that is what we should do, and we should always use the minimum level of force necessary for self-defence, self-protection and the protection of others. Recklessness with the well-being of others; the use of unnecessary and excessive force is not acceptable within the frame of core and other principles, due to the unnecessary pain and suffering caused. As has been referred to already, but is worth reiterating, we need to recognise that those who engage in aggressive violence, may not in fact be, at least on some occasions, deliberately and consciously malevolent but may in fact be, in some cases, under the influence of alcohol and drugs, overtaken with mental illness either temporarily on the moment or in the longer term, illness which may be beyond their control.

They may be in the grip of what, in essence, are mad moments of anger, emotion and passion. These influences may, in many cases, not reduce their culpability for their damaging actions. These possible influences do mean however, that where possible, while needing to ensure these people are unable to do violence to us or others, while we must ensure they do not hurt and harm ourselves and others, such individuals, still need, if possible and practical, looking after, such their well-being and happiness can be supported, again noting that this needs to be done without jeopardising the safety of ourselves and others. So we do need to aim to use the minimal force necessary in dealing with those engaging in aggressive violence, while at the same time protecting ourselves and others from harm. Their restraint and prevention from violence is of course absolutely essential, yet the use of minimal force still needs to apply.

If we can deal with such aggressive violence in the short term, and restraint and constraint has been successfully applied in the short term, then, in order to promote the optimal well-being of all, community-based responses, medical treatments, containment of those who remain aggressively violent, or other relevant means need to then be used in the medium and longer term in order to reduce the threat of violence from that individual or those people into the future. If those who have been ill can be cured, or in regard to those who have intended aggressive violence, if we can have a good level of certainty of their behaving peacefully and non-aggressively into the future, then that is best for us all, though there may be an element of risk that they might again engage in such behaviour into the future (a risk which perhaps may lie to some degree in many if not in all of us).

As communities and societies, as a broader humanity, we need to develop greater understanding of the factors underpinning aggressively violent behaviour. Research is necessary, social, psychological, biological and medical to systematically investigate the nature and origins of human violence, both at the individual and group level with actions taken where possible and reasonable, to reduce this violence. Individuals suffering from psychological conditions which might lead them to commit aggressively violent acts are likely to need medical support.

Moreover in our civil, every day context, we need research into the optimal ways of protecting ourselves against aggressive violence, be those verbal techniques for reducing tensions and disarming those engaged in aggressive violence, be that research into protective clothing such that our civil protection services are less vulnerable to injury from aggressive attacks, be that research into tools which can be used to disable the aggressively violent (or disable their weapons) without causing significant or medium long-term pain and damage.

Those factors which influence and lead groups to pursue aggressive wars need to be understood and tackled and, more to the point we need research into the nature of cooperation and peacefulness and how we can promote such peace and cooperation. At the individual level, based on research, we need to be informed and learn how to adopt and pursue cooperative and peaceful strategies. At the group level, we need to understand how best to pursue cooperation with other groups such that goals can be achieved and be achieved in peaceful and successful manner.

We also, unfortunately, again dependent on the nature of our context, as communities, societies and as part of our broader humanity, at least at the present time, are likely to need research into weaponry, developing more effective and optimally defensive weaponry, since there may be others who are developing new forms of aggressive weapons which could cause widespread destruction and damage, pain and suffering. And we must be in a position to defend and protect ourselves and others.

Optimally, and we have the potential in the modern era, though such action seems challenging, it is possible for our global and regional organisations to themselves organise disarmament or certainly to promote reductions in the levels of arms and a reduction in tensions between different nations. As a common humanity, if we all recognise our common humanity and common interests, there should be no need for weapons and military conflict, and where there are recalcitrant states and other groups, the rest of us can hopefully at some point, band together to protect ourselves from such entities, our combined efforts at defence being likely to outweigh the efforts of maverick, destructive and aggressively violent states. Thus, if we take such actions, then we will have the potential for a much more peaceful world, this being something which we must try to pursue in support of the well-being of us all.

And such action by our global and international organisations to promote disarmament and indeed non-armament; such actions pursuing collaboration and peaceful cooperation; such action to prevent wars and conflicts is critical in our modern age with the massively destructive weaponry, particularly nuclear weaponry, held by many states, weaponry which has the potential, to all intents and purposes, to wipe out our total humanity. As was demonstrated at Hiroshima and Nagasaki, such nuclear weapons have the potential to kill on vast scales with current nuclear weapons far more powerful than those used on these cities. The prospect of nuclear war or the potential for misunderstandings and nuclear conflict arising from such misunderstandings, means that we must aim to remove all such nuclear weapons from our world, along with the mutually assured destruction that their use would entail. We must all do our utmost to pursue nuclear disarmament, as well as the removal of the many other highly destructive weapons that our states possess. We, as individuals, or acting through our groups, need to promote not only nuclear and other disarmament, but also global and international cooperation and collaboration such that nuclear and other destructive weapons are considered superfluous, unnecessary, and are recognised for the catastrophically destructive weapons they are, their being weapons which have caused and which have the potential to cause pain and suffering to untold billions of us and which pose a serious threat to our continued human existence.

There are many circumstances additional to those already mentioned, where it may be reasonable, justified and legitimate to engage in forceful action, subsequent to our having engaged in other peaceful action to achieve our reasonable goals in line with core and other principles. For example there may be situations where we are deliberately oppressed, denied basic human needs in circumstances where there is abundance, and in circumstances where there exists the power to ensure there is enough available to prevent such suffering. There may be situations where we are denied food and condemned to starvation through policy, be it economic or political policies of ruling groups; where we are denied the resources to live, such as for example, the ability to draw water, or to have water at all when there is water available; where we are denied the ability to keep ourselves warm when energy sources are available which would save us suffering and dying from cold; where we are denied basic freedoms, such as the ability to meet others, to have family, to move with freedom, the freedom to earn money or to work and contribute when we have the will and the wish, where we are denied the capacity to speak critically and criticise those who have power over us though we are acting peacefully, and wish to act peacefully in line with core and other principles. In all of these circumstances and those of similar gravity and threat it can be legitimate for us to take forceful and physical action.

As mentioned earlier in this chapter in regard to poverty, the principles presented in this guide, in particular the core principles, do not require that we should stay quiet and starve or die of thirst or cold peacefully, moving silently maybe in our thousands and millions into oblivion. It is not seen as reasonable for us to stand by where the land that we own and rely on for our food is taken away from us such that we will starve or endure other forms of significant pain and suffering. It is not seen as reasonable that we should stand by and 'peacefully' suffer or die when our work is taken away from us, where our well-being and prospects of well-being are removed through the avaricious actions of those acting in negatively selfish, malevolent and manipulative ways, through the systemic and destructive, unimitigated, unrelieved' exigencies of a free market or the deliberate use of unemployment as an ideological and policy goal. Nor is there any requirement to peaceful suffer and die as a consequence of damaging, stupid and foolish, miscalculated ideological, organisational and administrative policies and actions of those in power and control, of those in government, be they well intentioned or deliberately malevolent.

In these cases, there are steps that we need to take initially, democratically and peacefully to pursue and ensure our survival, to pursue and ensure justice. We need to, wherever we can, join with others, make our views known, lobby those with power and influence, identify allies and friends with power or otherwise, who will support us in achieving well-being, justice and fairness. Where it is viable and reasonable, wherever possible, we should refuse to cooperate with injustice and oppressions, refuse to bank roll and support such systems, refuse to act on their behalves, in such a manner that administering such a system of injustice and oppression becomes impossible. Our actions in support of persuasion, our non-cooperation may lead us to endure some pain and some suffering, however, dependent on circumstances, such more peaceful and cooperative strategies need to be tried before resorting to any firmer physical and forceful action, which may be necessary in the face of aggressive violence and brutality against ourselves and others.

Thus, if at all possible, we need to use talk, negotiation, discussion, peaceful pressure and persuasion to achieve our reasonable goals. Nevertheless, when our other cooperative and peaceful methods have failed, if our oppressors are engaged in violent suppression, murders, tortures and more; if they are intransigent in the face of our suffering and pain or cannot be dissuaded from introducing or conducting actions which will cause us and others substantial and significant pain and suffering, then consistent with principles of preventing suffering and harm and promoting well-being, we are likely to be significantly justified in using physical force and physical action to support our well-being, in order to reduce our pain and suffering, this comprising a form of self-defence against what may be destructive, murderous and violent oppression.

Returning to the more individual and more personal level, it is also the case that beyond situations of directly damaging physically aggressive violence and aggressive physical threat against us as individuals, there may also be additional, up-to-now unmentioned occasions when it may be legitimate for us to engage in some form of physical and forceful action in support of our well-being. For example, if our possessions are thieved from us, this is seen here as comprising a form of aggressive violence, since our own personal possessions are being forcibly removed from us against our will and desire, with no legitimate reason behind such theft aside from the wish of the thief to have or make use of our possessions to deprive us of them. In circumstances where minimal aggressive violence is used, such as that person conducting a theft grabbing and running off with our possessions, where we can stop, safely hold and restrain the thief, then it is legitimate for us to do so, though we should use minimal force and should avoid striking blows unless we ourselves are subject to such a response or where we feel these are necessary to protect ourselves from aggressive violence. Where we can gather others to apprehend the thief, including our civil protection forces, it is legitimate for those groups of us and those forces to apprehend and restrain the person who has committed the theft, in as peaceful a manner as possible, using the minimal level of force. Failure to apprehend a person who has conducted such an action against us or others, leaves that person free to thieve again from ourselves and others, thereby threatening damage to all of our lives.

Efforts by strangers at theft and aggressive violence can even occur in our homes where we may face important and serious threats at the individual and family level. The presence of an intruder or intruders in our homes where we are alone or have family, where we have children, with the consequent fear of and the real possibility of aggressive violence against us, may in some circumstances provide good reason for vigorous and forceful physical action, especially if we or members of our families are in fear or are directly threatened or attacked. If we can stay away from such intruders until they are gone, even within our home that may well be advisable, especially if at the same time, we can contact others such as our civil protection services if they exist, contact friends and family outside the home, to come and help us. Nevertheless, if we are fearful of attack, we might aim for escape from our home to further raise the alarm. We might also consider pursuing various means to scare the intruder, who may not wish to engage in physical conflict and may therefore quickly depart, or alternately, we might engage in dialogue with the intruder, though this may be risky, as they may intend violence or be well prepared to use violence against us.

If such routes to safety and such actions are not possible, if others may not arrive for a while then, if we have legitimate fear of imminent aggressively violent attack, or if such attacks are even in progress, then we can quite reasonably take serious and significant action, forceful and physical action to defend ourselves and our families, action to substantially disable our attacker, our potential attacker, such that we, our families, our children are safe. That being said, many of us may not have the physical capability to respond effectively. If there are multiple intruders then it is likely that, in the absence of outside help, either escape or the most vigorous forceful and unforgiving actions may need to be tried, in order to ensure that we and our families are able to survive and enjoy life and well-being into the future.

Ideally, however, it is desirable and indeed necessary, dependent on context and the likelihood of such events, to forestall the possibility of external entry to our homes and properties through proactive measures such as secure entrances, locks. Businesses and those organisations with assets which others may wish to thieve, certainly need to protect their property and facilities, and not simply from theft but also from unwanted entry which might lead to damage of property and indeed injury to the intruder.

Hopefully it will not occur, but we may ourselves, at some point, become victims of aggressive violence. If we are victims of such violence, we may well have suffered significant physical damage which may be shocking, traumatic and disabling, excruciating and painful at the time, and which in the longer term may provide significant barriers to our living well, doing ordinary every day things, those crucial human things which we all need to do. We, if injured by such aggressive violence, will experience pain and possibly ongoing and constant pain, which may never disappear due to the nature of the injuries suffered. And there may well be deeply personally damaging traumatic psychological effects on us, with damage to our sense of self, and to the sense of ourselves as powerful and in control individuals, our potentially carrying a sense of fragility and vulnerability, a sense of powerlessness and victimhood. There may be fear inside us, of the person or people who assaulted us, fear which may stay with us in our dreams and everyday thoughts. And all of this, our injuries, the physical and psychological damage to us, may prevent us from engaging in both the more everyday and the more extraordinary things that we love and would love to do.

Hopefully, however, physical and psychological injuries will not be so bad, and hopefully those of us injured will be able to experience full recovery from such aggressively violent assault, being able to rise above such an incident and, at least to some degree, to put these events behind us such that we can enjoy a good level of well-being and happiness.

If we are the victims of such an assault or of such assaults, while we have responsibilities as far as we can to support our own return to health, it is also a responsibility of those we know, of others, of our communities, societies, our broader humanity, to provide medical care for our physical injuries such that these are healed as far as possible, if not totally, and provide psychological support such that we can come to terms with the events we have experienced and recover fully psychologically. As individuals it is our responsibility to provide what support we can ourselves and ensure that our communities, societies, our broader humanity can and do provide such support, making such help available to all those who have suffered from such aggressive violence.

Whatever the injuries, trauma and pain suffered it will be important, wherever this is possible, to move ourselves onwards and forwards from the experience of being a victim of such aggressive violence. In the midst of our pain, considering our ways forward may be something that is difficult to do, as we may well be lost in the experiencing of our suffering. And in any case moving forward in a positive sense may not be an easy thing for us to do. In aiming to move forward with our lives, that does not mean that we must forget and it does not mean any obligation to forgive, even though such forgetting and forgiveness may help us to recover and move on to a life of improved well-being, at least, at the minimum, improved well-being compared to the way we felt in the direct aftermath of the act of aggressive violence against us, though more than that will be needed.

Part of our recovery may to some degree be dependent on the tackling of and the apprehension of that individual or those individuals who have done such aggressive violence against us, and their being brought to book in terms of facing consequences for their actions and facing such consequences in front of ourselves and others. They will likely face restraint and imprisonment dependent on the degree of violence used, their previous actions and record in terms of violence and crime, and their potential for visiting further aggressive violence on others. Their identification and their facing of the consequences of their actions, their facing justice, may contribute to our being ready to move on with a lesser fear of being subject to such aggressive violence again. Their apology, regret and much more, the feeling and knowledge that they will never do such an act again may also be helpful in making us feel somewhat better, safer and ready to move on to the rest of our lives, as well as, in some cases, the knowledge that they are, at least for a while, restrained and unable to hurt others, receiving treatment if they are ill and where necessary having opportunities for education and personal and other skills development such that their lives can be improved and they can be become happier, peaceful, and more complete and appropriate members of our communities and societies.

Our moving on and recovering from such traumatic and damaging physical attack certainly does mean that we need to identify other things in our lives to get on with, if at all possible. It does mean setting goals for the future which take our minds away from the pain we have suffered and which prevent us, where possible, from brooding, reliving our experiences and enduring further disturbing and traumatic pain originating in what has happened to us. Of course this kind of thing is easy to say and may be far less easy to do if we have suffered in such ways. And there may be real and deep psychological and medical effects on us which are hard to throw off. But establishing new goals provides us with a direction of travel away from our pain, if we can set them and aim to achieve them, which through time will support us in our well-being and happiness, enabling us to better enjoy our lives after such traumatic events. Hopefully for the vast majority of us, if not all of us, we will never have to endure such aggressive violence and pain, but if we have experienced such pain, then we have an obligation to ourselves to recover as much as we can, and we have an obligation to others to regain independence such that we ourselves can become amongst those who support others. This independence is, in itself, part of experiencing and enjoying well-being, and of course reducing and preventing our pain is a deep human desire and necessity for us for which, ordinarily, we will need no or little incentive..

While it is a general principle for all of us to implement, if we are those who have been on the receiving events of such violence or who have witnessed or know others who have experienced such violence, we may feel it is a particularly important obligation for us to ensure that aggressive violence does not occur. And so we may choose to take on a significant role in preventing and reducing such violence into the future. It may be that we may wish to place emphasis on instances of aggressive violence that are engaged in by specific individuals or groups, in order that such individuals or groups do not commit such violence again, and we may take a particular interest in ensuring that these individuals move and are moved towards a more peaceful and cooperative way of living wherever that is possible. This would be an important if not vital contribution for us to make, building and magnifying cooperativity and peacefulness over time in our communities, societies and through our broader humanity.

Also acting against such aggressive violence, as victims and witnesses of aggressive violence, we must report such aggressive violence to others, to our communities, societies and broader humanity where relevant, such that appropriate action can be taken in regard to those who have engaged in such conduct, in particular because those individuals and perhaps violent groups may well represent a continued threat to us, to the person who has been assaulted and to the rest of our community, society and beyond. It is essential that those of us who have been victims overcome our fears, in particular the fear of further aggressive violence from those who have committed aggressive violence against us. If we can overcome our fears and other worries, we will make it more likely that those implementing aggressive violence can be identified, apprehended, restrained as necessary, constrained, and that they can have their own difficulties addressed and helped to go through change where that is possible. Thereby, those who have acted in aggressively violent ways will be prevented or persuaded away from engaging in aggressively violent acts again. Failure to act, failure to report, will leave others, and will leave us, vulnerable to further violence and attack.

The notion of reporting to others mentioned here holds within it the idea that there are those in authority, with power, with integrity, there are others in our communities, organisations and institutions, that there are police forces and systems of justice that can be reported to and called upon, that will support us, and that there are systems and people operating with integrity such that we can achieve and ensure protection, fairness and justice. Unfortunately such people do not always exist. Moreover, our fellows may in some cases be either frightened of, or supportive of aggressors, supportive of those who have done harm and caused significant pain and suffering. In such circumstances we will need to work to both protect ourselves and those we love, as well as aiming to convince others and bring them together to oppose and stop the actions of those who have caused such pain and suffering. This may be very challenging and risky. Where necessary we may need to bide our time and act when the opportunity arises, however we must certainly act.

Of course, an important reality is that, due to the unfortunate fact that reprehensible and false allegations are sometimes made, this being done in order to damage, discredit and hurt, we will almost certainly need to produce evidence, often convincing evidence to others that such aggressive violence has indeed taken place. And such evidence will need to be weighed and evaluated, in particular, as may be likely, someone accused of aggression may state that either they were not involved or that no such incident has taken place. No one can be considered to have committed aggressively violent acts with the serious consequences for them that that entails if there is no substantive and convincing evidence that they have done such acts, for example such as injuries identifiable as a consequence of attack and aggressive violence and credible witnesses, the latter being hard to find particularly in cases where aggressive violence is said to have occurred in the home, but also in other specific circumstances.

Clearly, none of us should make false accusations. Doing so is entirely contrary to core and other principles due, in particular, to the unwarranted damage, pain and suffering to the those of us against whom such accusations are made, but also due to the damage to our communities, societies as well as to our broader humanity. We need to treat such false accusations very seriously, in particular because in addition to the damage and pain caused to those unjustly and falsely accused, such false accusations undermine the experiences of people who truly have been victims of damaging and destructive acts, including aggressive violence and thereby these false accusations endanger these others, our communities, societies and beyond. These false allegations and accusations lead to the casting of suspicion and doubt when we genuinely report real incidents of damaging acts and aggressive violence, evidence which needs to be taken seriously and acted upon if aggressive violence and other destructive and damaging acts are to be prevented and victims and potential victims are to be protected.

Producing evidence may not be difficult for us where there has been significant aggressive violence as our physical injuries will be patently obvious, though there may be some forms of aggressive violence and assault where evidence may be less obvious. In these cases, if we have been victims of such violence, we need to ensure that we do everything possible to retain and record evidence in order to enable action to be taken and our aggressor's conduct to be tackled and addressed. In any case, where there is credible evidence that there has been such aggressive violence it is necessary that some form of action is taken as those engaging in such acts must not be allowed to engage in such aggressive violence again.

We should, of course, never make threats of aggressive violence. If these are made to us or others, then such threats need to be treated with great seriousness. No one should ever make remarks threatening to hurt or injure another, other than perhaps when in some threatening circumstances we are using words to prevent aggressive violence against us, and even in such cases, such language is probably best not used and is perhaps unlikely in many circumstances to achieve its ends, having within it the potential to escalate violence and conflict. Other words will usually be far better at preventing aggressive violence. We should never threaten to kill others. While such remarks are sometimes used angrily by some people, in fits of temper, without thought, we should never use these types of remark under any circumstances, not as real threats or as part of such momentary fits of anger and temper. They should never be used in any form even when we are in tense, argumentative, stressful and difficult situations.

Of course, it will be much better if we can find other positive and constructive forms of expression linked to supporting cooperation and peacefulness, through expression of personal feelings, frustrations, fear and even anger, in order to deal with problems that arise, but we must not make threats to harm others. Such threats harm in themselves and, as mentioned, tend to be counter-productive, promoting discord, argument and perhaps leading to aggressive violence through their use. It might be said that some threats are casual, not meant, said in the heat of the moment. The fact is that such threats must be taken as real, may well be interpreted as real, and certainly can be interpreted as real, by those on the receiving end of these remarks and threats.

As already mentioned, our communities and societies, and also our global community, need to have mechanisms and the power, to ensure protection of individuals and groups from violent threats and from violent aggression and to reassure and support those who have been victims of such violence. Civil protection forces have been referred to, but we also need laws within our social entities, which are clearly set out in regard to what is acceptable conduct and what is not, laws which include within their ambit the outlawing of the range of forms of aggressive violence. We need to have effective bodies, such as our civil defence organisations, to stop, at the point of its occurrence and indeed prior to its occurrence where possible, the implementation of aggressive violence. Systems, processes and procedures need to be in place to systematically protect potential victims of such violence, and educational and restorative capabilities need to be available to turn people away from aggressive violence and crime, and towards peaceful living and cooperation. Further, facilities need to be available to restrain and constrain those who may represent a threat to other individuals, our communities and societies.

And with such laws and systems in position, there is no place for vigilante justice. There is no place for us to seek our own version of justice through aggressive violence, aside from the law in place, We must certainly not engage in vengeful actions against those we perceive to have done malevolent misdeeds which have damaged ourselves or others. If someone within our community or society is believed to have engaged in aggressive violence against others or indeed has committed any other damaging or destructive criminal act, then they must face a proper and due legal process to establish whether or not they have done such deeds, and they must have the opportunity to be represented by those knowing the law, having the chance to defend themselves and bring witnesses in their defence. And if they are judged to have done a damaging and destructive deed contrary to law, then the consequences of their act need to be legally set down, and must not involve punishment through violent action. It is further not for those of us dissatisfied with a judgment or the consequences of that judgment to take our own aggressively violent actions. And certainly we must not do aggressive violence against those who have done misdeeds. Aggressive violence conducted by the mob, by the majority, by anyone, is not acceptable and is contrary to core and other principles. We should never join or support such vigilante action but must, as far as possible, especially where there are just, fair and democratic legal and political systems, operate through legal channels and where desirable, possible and necessary, we must pursue legal change.

That being said, certainly not all legal systems are fair and just. Laws may be introduced and implemented to protect the cruel and malevolent, the powerful, violent and corrupt. Further, laws may be designed deliberately such that they cause pain, damage and suffering, these being mechanisms through which racism and other unjust discrimination can be implemented. In line with core and other principles, we must refuse to cooperate with and oppose such laws. Beyond the letter and statement of the law, whatever those laws may state, systems may be corrupted through their implementation, through the appointment of cronies as judges or civil protection officers, through the use of false witnesses and made up testimonies, through gross dishonesty and lack of integrity in the process. In some instances, such systems can be corrupted through public pressure, fear and prejudice, through situational exigencies which mean that there is pressure to find someone guilty of a crime, and therefore leading to the innocent being convicted.

Such unjust systems and unfairly implemented systems of law cause tremendous damage, pain and suffering, often putting innocent, kind and decent people, sometimes the vulnerable and weak, in prisons or even murdering them through such false systems of law, which often claim to represent justice. In such cases, there is a need to attempt to change and, indeed, to change such systems, in order to support well-being and happiness and reduce pain and suffering. And if democratic, caring, discursive and cooperative means are not successful in changing such systems, then it may be necessary to refuse to cooperate with such systems, and use more forceful means to overthrow such legal and political systems, and indeed where connected to these systems, as is likely to be the case, to remove particular governments or the linked and unjust systems of government.

Where such systems are inflicting misery, pain, suffering and intense harm on our populations, on our communities, societies and beyond, on individuals who share our fundamental humanity, then we will undoubtedly be justified in major protest to change such systems. This should not involve aggressive violence if at all avoidable, but if our efforts to overthrow such intensely damaging, destructive and unjust systems are met with violence against us, we may have no alternative than to use forceful action against such aggressively violent systems, though hopefully this will be as a last resort and our own actions will use minimal violence and avoid vengeance and the implementation of unjust and violent punishments on those who may have harmed us.

Beyond our communities and societies, there should be little doubt that between nations, states and other larger groupings of our human family, we need to have peacefulness and cooperativity. There may be a time where our nation states cease to exist or where they become of lesser importance in the scheme of our humanity, with greater emphasis being placed on our common humanity, our individuality, our individual well-being and happiness, and our more individual and collective responsibilities to each other. Such recognition of our common humanity at the expense of such national and other groupings is seen as a positive development in terms of core and other principles, although the need for us to organise in groups is also recognised and seen as of significant value.

Nevertheless, at the moment of writing, for the time being and for the near future at least, while wishing to move away from our emphasis on such nation state groupings and desiring action to emphasise and develop our sense of common interests and common humanity, our broader human identity, our considerations need to recognise the existence of our nation states and consider the implications of their presence, even though our main focus in this guide is on our individual well-being and happiness and the well-being and happiness of all others from whichever communities, societies and nations they may come.

Thus, while recognising this presence of nation states and their importance for many in terms of identity, we do need, however, to work towards greater emphasis on our common humanity, working with others from other nation states and from other cultures, with a view to enhancing that sense of common humanity and reducing, as appropriate, the emphasis on nation states and, in particular on their divisive conflict enhancing and damaging consequences. Hopefully, as a consequence of our actions such divisions will become of lesser importance in our human relations into the future.

Certainly, with the existence of such nation states in our current world, a focus on supporting peacefulness, friendship and cooperativity between nations is consistent with the principles presented in this guide with such peacefulness and cooperation undoubtedly enabling us at the present time to better pursue our promotion of well-being and the prevention and reduction of pain and suffering. Indicating seemingly necessary and important political and social moves beyond the nation state, in our current times there are now substantial steps to bring nations together, for example through regional organisations which act as forums for states to hold discussions and give consideration to mutual interests. And, in addition there are our world and international organisations, which bring nation states together from all over our planet, for dialogue, discussion and decision-making in regard to the interests and concerns of our nations and the broader affairs and interests of the world. All of this is highly desirable in principle and brings us closer together as a human family.

Few of us as individuals will feel able to have significant influence on such organisations, as these organisations are by their nature, somewhat inevitably distant, and are in practice administered, managed and run at a distance from us as individuals, being overseen and attended far from most of our homes and home communities and societies, by, as is perhaps inevitable, only a few, the leaders and representatives of our nation states, with day-to-day affairs often run by management and other professionals and bureaucracies. Nevertheless, with effective and open systems of communication, we should, both in a practical and in a sense of moral obligation, all be able to access substantive and indeed comprehensive information about these organisations enabling us to support them in principle and in practice if we wish to and indeed enabling us to influence them.

In particular, we can influence these organisations through working with like-minded and committed individuals who support our goals perhaps through our own organisations, which as organisations themselves aim to influence others. As it is difficult for most of us to participate closely on a daily basis in these contexts, our personal responsibilities will therefore lie in our individual action in regard to these institutions and supporting our own lobbying organisations. We will need to support our global organisations through supporting appropriate new global entities in their establishment, through supporting their continued existence, and through supporting them in their work to promote the dialogue, negotiation and discussion, pursuit of shared goals, in the pursuit of the general well-being and happiness, which is an essential part of preventing the misunderstandings between nations, the selfish focus on national self-interests, which can lead to vast national and international conflict, and which can result in substantial damage to the nation states themselves, and more particularly the millions and millions of we individuals, the millions and millions of us, the billions of us, living in these nation states, living on our globe.

As individuals, where we have the opportunity, and where we can make the opportunities, through our individual, group action and global organisations, we need to proactively and actively, support the principles of common fundamental humanity, the value of individuality, the pursuit of individual well-being and happiness, freedom, autonomy, education, an end to poverty, pain and suffering and the pursuit of general well-being and happiness, which must stand before the more negatively selfish interests of nation states and those who govern or rule them, with supranational organisations supported by ourselves, working towards and enabling us and all of our humanity to enjoy our maximal well-being and happiness in all its facets, in all its aspects.

And clearly, we individuals throughout the world have many common interests, be they avoiding suffering from disease, starvation, avoiding experience of disaster of whichever sort, supporting economic well-being, avoiding violence through war and conflict between our societies and nations or internally within our societies. And it is our responsibility to ensure that we and all people, through nation states or through supranational organisations, through whatever other organisational mechanisms are available or could be available, as well as through our own direct personal actions supportive of others, work to ensure that suffering and pain are relieved and prevented wherever possible, and that well-being is enhanced internationally and globally for all individuals, for all of us.

Effective cooperation is of course essential between nations, with our nations, often operating through the already mentioned regional and global organisations. Such organisations through which nations, communities and societies pursue their goals, recognising their own interest in the common interest, will hopefully engage in giving and taking, understanding and responding to the legitimate interests of others, and being proactive in promoting peacefulness and cooperation, in particular and importantly laying aside the legacies of suspicion and hatred which may have arisen between nations and peoples through historic conflict. All this pro-active and positive action is needed to prevent the disastrous and damaging violent wars and violent conflicts which serve to, and which have served to, destroy the lives of so many millions of people through history.

Of course international relationships between societies and nation states, between global groupings, just like community relationships and personal relationships can have difficult periods and can sometimes break down, at least temporarily, with nations, their representatives and people, acting in negatively selfish and destructive, negatively selfish, nationalistic ways which demean and devalue the humanity of others. Thus, our humanity's sense of common human interest, togetherness and cooperation can become much reduced or even cease with damaging effects. This is not a good state of affairs and in itself may represent a sign and indeed a realisation of danger. Such breakdowns in national, international and global relationships and cooperation are likely to represent and present major ongoing and future dangers to those of us, to those organisations and nations, to the citizens of our organisations, groupings and nations, who or which, are no longer cooperating, and also present threats to those of us beyond the location of the breakdown in relations, since local and regional conflicts will have effects on us all, creating a violent international context and threatening to escalate and embroil other communities and nations, as those involved in such conflicts seek allies and supporters.

The presence of global organisations which recognise our common human interests, can lead them to act as mediators involved in identifying problems and their sources, in instituting and catalysing negotiations, supporting and promoting discussion and peaceful solutions, taking actions in a united and globally united way against those pursuing aggressive violence, those who are making threats of invasion of other countries, with global organisations having the capacity to act together to prevent such aggressively violent actions. Our global organisations can support the negotiation of peace treaties and the resolution of problems, helping refugees in war situations, providing aid and protection for those in need, providing peacekeepers to ensure that peace treaties are kept to and, following conflicts, they can act as vehicles to ensure that countries, individuals, communities and societies can rebuild after conflict is over. These many aspects of the work of such global organisations are aspects of their work that we should all support.

And our global organisations, in regard to other matters, can address core global issues that are central to all of our well-being and happiness. Thus, as a clear example, in the current age, a critical problem is that of climate change. Our global organisations have, at the minimum, addressed this issue, which requires international and global cooperation if it is to be dealt with effectively. Yet they have done more than that, bringing countries together and brokering global agreements on fossil fuel production, usage and climate change, even though at the present time, these agreements may seem and may well be insufficient. While there have been global agreements about how to address this extremely threatening climate change, there needs to be much more vision and purpose from our nation states, which together need to take rapid and effective action to address this problem, it clearly being beneficial though insufficient for individual countries to act on their own.

Research has been supported and funded such that the nature of the problems we face is more fully understood and some counter-action has been taken, based on the range of scientific evidence available. In the light of the evidence available, cooperation through our global bodies does give some hope that further appropriate action will be taken. And where we can, as individuals, we need to be supportive of our global bodies and support international and global cooperation, perhaps in particular by influencing our own nation states and governments to take substantive actions and take substantive initiatives and lead on climate change.

Of course, a peaceful life requires not only the absence of violence between individuals, within our families, communities and societies. It requires amongst other things, the absence of war between and within our communities and societies, and it requires the absence of war between our nation states and supranational organisations, with such wars being perhaps the most destructive form of our human violence. Our wars, representing a vile and appalling pestilence, have resulted in and result in the most tremendous destruction and damage, causing and having caused the premature deaths of millions of us, millions of our fellows, in civil wars, in wars between countries, alliances, through world wars, civil wars, religious and ideological wars and other conflicts, creating untold suffering and pain, with such suffering and pain delivered on a vast level to not only vast numbers of individuals but a vast range of our communities, societies and nations.

In addition to the obvious direct effects of violence in terms of visible physical injury and the resultant pain, wars bring vast levels of psychological pain inflicted on men, women and children, combatants and civilians. Wars create tremendous damage to our homes, properties, workplaces, damage to the environment, damage to the provision of basic facilities within communities and societies, such as warmth, medical facilities, food supplies and more. Vast levels of devastation, destruction and destitution have been and are the common outcomes of aggressive wars, both civil and between nations and alliances.

It surely follows from the vastly destructive and damaging nature of wars that without question, the core and other principles require the utmost and strongest actions to prevent wars wherever they may occur, between countries or groups of countries, and within countries, and require the strongest action to prevent vast violent ideological conflicts, vast and violent wars which may possess devastating and destructive power to damage others, to destroy well-being and to promote suffering and pain on a vast scale.

Thus, where there are those who are in their various ways attempting to dehumanise and demonise us or others, be their actions within a community, society or a nation state, or be they the people of another nation state; where there are those who are acting with a view to engaging in aggressive violence towards us or others, our community, society or nation, with the intent of taking over our or others' land, invading homes, taking over peaceful, non-aggressive and free countries, we must ensure we undermine and repulse their efforts and do whatever we can, both as individuals and in cooperation with others, to prevent the war and violence they threaten. And we must do this, where necessary, within our own communities, societies and nations in cases where the groups we are stated to belong to threaten aggressive war. We must not simply focus on preventing the destructive actions of other communities, societies and nations, though this must be done as well when necessary.

As mentioned already in this chapter, but again seen as worthy of reiteration, in line with core principles, we have responsibility for the well-being of all our fellow humans as individuals, responsibility for the prevention of their pain and suffering wherever they are and wherever they come from, whichever group they belong to. Due to appeals to nationalism, racism, appeals to perceived but irrational common interests within our groups, due to words and actions which 'other' or demonise our fellow human beings, it may be challenging and risky for us to oppose such aggressive negatively selfish, conflict-promoting people and their ideas and actions, but we must do so, in order to prevent the vast damage that will ensue in the event of violent conflicts and wars.

If there are differing interests, differing perceptions; if there are competing needs for limited assets and resources, then our communities, societies, nations, supported by us as individuals, need to be pursuing negotiation and discussion for the benefit of all, for the benefit of all of us as individuals such that resources are optimally generated, optimally maintained and optimally shared, based in our recognition of our fundamental common humanity and our common human interests, interests which certainly do not require us to bomb, shoot and maim our fellows and destroy their lives, families, communities, societies, property and resources. Where resources are limited and scarce, we need to focus on collaborative action to generate additional resources and to share what we have, engaging in cooperation and setting up systems of cooperation which will enable us all to live together and live with well-being and happiness.

Such negotiation and discussion may well lead to one or both parties being dissatisfied in some manner or other. Yet we will need to tolerate some level of dissatisfaction and some disadvantage while enjoying the benefits and advantages we gain. Unfortunately, due to misunderstanding, through fear, lack of knowledge and the full facts, through racism, destructive nationalism (or taking advantage of the existence of such feelings and beliefs), it is not hard for some who are seeking their own power, to falsely portray another group as exploitative, as gaining more benefits than we are getting, painting their own group as victims of another, and as a consequence creating mistrust, hostility and hatred against another group. And of course this can lead to oppression, aggressive violence, war and destruction on a vast scale, causing immense damage to us all, aggressive violence, war and destruction which we need to prevent.

Of course our cooperation and working with other communities, organisations, societies and nations need not simply be in regard to our need for resources, but can and should be a means of identifying opportunities for collaborating and working together to achieve better outcomes for all in the whole range of possible areas, supporting well-being, perhaps pooling our resources, financial and human such that more can be achieved, promoting the sharing of ideas, technologies, research with the consequence that we all benefit. Projects with potential positive outcomes which might require too great a resource level for one nation, may be achievable and implementable when several nations, societies, global groupings cooperate together and thus we will all gain. But simply through such cooperation and working together, we will be building bridges with others, becoming more familiar with their humanity and will thereby reduce fears, tensions and the prospect of conflict and wars.

For the fact is that wars, as in our more local and individual conflicts, can occur through fear and misunderstanding which can start at a low level and escalate into aggressive violence. Fear that another group or nation may attack us, a fear which may sometimes be a real and reasonable fear, may lead another group or nation to seek weaponry and arm itself, with the other nation and other nations doing the same. In addition to deliberate attack, in addition to invasion, war and aggressive violence on a grand scale, there is the ever-present risk of unplanned and unintended incidents and accidents which can lead to these wars that are so destructive and damaging. Again wherever possible, we need to de-escalate tensions, reduce levels of weaponry, build understandings and more, through contact, dialogue and interaction such that violent conflict, such that destructive wars do not occur.

That is not to say that we should not, as nation states, be prepared to defend ourselves and our individual citizens, indeed our individual well-being in all its facets, from aggressive and violent attack from other nation states and other individuals who may lead those states. Our human history contains too many records of those who wished to violently seize the assets and resources of others, who considered themselves to be superior to others, racially, technically or otherwise, in a manner which they believed made it legitimate for them to rule over others, to wreak violence on a vast scale against others, to visit the most vile and degrading tortures and cruelties upon others, to commit murderous violence, levels of sexual violence on a vast scale against others. We have no obligation to, and we should not, allow such destructive individuals, groups and the nations and militaries under their control to act so destructively and with such aggressive violence against us. We need to protect ourselves and others against such tremendous pain and suffering.

Thus it is the view of this guide that, while pursuing cooperativity, friendship, togetherness and while recognising and aiming to support the well-being and happiness of all, aiming to reduce pain and suffering, it is yet legitimate under relevant circumstances, in the face of likely war and aggressively violent attack, for us to arm ourselves with appropriate weaponry and prepare ourselves defensively against aggressively violent attack. Hopefully, we will not need to do this and we will never need to use such weaponry. Our modern weaponry is so destructive that its use will almost always cause substantial if not vast damage, pain and suffering, and thus its use should be avoided at almost all costs, perhaps at all costs.

Certainly and more importantly, we need to be proactively working with others wherever possible to build those systems of regional, international and global cooperation such that we will never have recourse to such measures. We need to be building frameworks of international law and international and global cooperation, as well as international enforcement, such that those who might wish to engage in aggressive and violent aggression, are unable to do so, through our persuasive efforts, through pointing out the benefits of cooperation and togetherness, through depriving them of weapons, with the consequence that they are unable to do such damage, and through the potential opposition to them of overwhelming force, And optimally, wherever we can, we need to isolate and remove such vile and destructive individuals and their supporters, such destructive groups and nations from possession of and positions of power, so that their own citizens and all of the rest of us, can be protected from their aggressive violence.

That being said, recognising the vast amount of death, the vast level of misery, the vast level of destruction wrought by war and violent conflict, taking into account the reality of our circumstances and the exigencies of situations, aside from the necessity of our refusing or our doing our utmost to refuse to engage in any aggressively violent conflict pursued by our group, nation state or other entity, we need to give strong consideration to our own personal refusal to participate as soldiers or in other roles, in any form of violent military or similar conflict.

This is because, in the first place, it may be that in some cases, our own simple refusal and the refusal of many of us, to accede to, support and participate in certain wars, may actually serve to prevent that war and thereby reduce violence and aggressive violence, pain and suffering. This may not always be the case, but may sometimes be the case. Secondly, it is not only the righteousness and morality of the cause of conflict that we must consider but the practicality and effectiveness with such a war will be and can be pursued. We need to be sure that we will not be simply participating in wars that will involve us in futile and pointless loss of our own lives as well as the loss of life of others on a vast scale, including those deemed to be our enemies. And we must consider the potential consequences of even small military actions that might lead to escalation of conflict and even more widespread destruction. Thus, in particular, while we must act and are obliged to do whatever we can to defend others from pain and suffering, nevertheless our participation in futile actions, for example, through participation in direct violent conflict with a vastly superior military entity, may simply result in our own immediate personal destruction and the destruction of others. Moreover, our pursuit of a righteous and good cause in terms of core and other principles, if such a pursuit is organised incompetently, or if those managing us and commanding us, have no concern for our well-being, are pursuing war for their own purposes, perhaps seeing us as simple unfeeling, inhuman entities, as pieces on a chessboard, will mean the sacrificing of our lives for little or nothing.

While we may be willing to risk suffering, even perhaps lay down our lives for a worthy cause, particularly to defend others, to prevent pain and suffering, in the pursuit of justice and freedom, given the core and other principles, to sacrifice our lives for no particular good at all, to sacrifice our lives on account of incompetence, or acting in support of the greed and avarice, the destructive, negatively selfish goals of others, perhaps simply sacrificing our own lives and the lives of others for a perverse interpretation of national machismo and glory, is not acceptable.

In particular we need to be careful of being seduced through the use of notions such as our desire to exhibit courage and bravery, or calls for self-sacrifice to support our nation, which have resulted in and may result in our parading and marching off to be slaughtered in our thousands, if not hundreds of thousands on the battlefield, victims of the incompetence of our leaders and sacrificed for reasons and goals which have no or little basis in terms of supporting others, with our being lauded on our deaths as having given glorious sacrifice for the nation, when our sacrifice was in fact futile, ill-directed and pointless, and our physical destruction and the physical destruction of others, nothing like glorious. Millions of European men died or were severely injured and damaged in the first world war , men from many nations, charging at rifles, running at machine guns, blown up by mines, blown apart by artillery, suffocated in chemical gas attacks, in a largely futile and pointless nation state war of power that brought tragedy and destruction on a vast scale. We must do our utmost to make sure that this kind of event never ever happens again. Wherever we can, we must do our utmost to avert such wars, acting to support well-being and happiness, and reduce and prevent pain and suffering.

Bolstering the futility and stupidity of many such notions associated with destructive group loyalties and nationalism, those notions of sacrifice for your group, country, notions of loyalty and treachery, notions which set aside the value of other and all human beings, our whole humanity, elements of the defeated German side in that first world war which cost the lives of more than two million German soldiers, rather than seeing the futility of the entire aggressively violent enterprise, focused on what they decided to perceive as the humiliation of defeat, which they put down to treachery. Sadly such people came to power in Germany, leading to the Second World

War and many more millions of deaths, massacres on a vast scale and the near destruction of the European continent as well as other parts of the world. Given the evidence of their destructive outcomes, such views and the maintenance of such views, must be seen as psychopathic, as characteristic of form of mental illness, with their continuing prevalence, representing a vast and significant threat to us all.

As already mentioned, one key role of the systems of international cooperation that we promote and implement needs to be the initiation, support and implementation of effective international meetings and forums where key issues relating to all of our well-being can be discussed and decided, with our international and global bodies additionally setting out frameworks of international conduct and law which all countries must keep to. Such laws need to establish rules and patterns of conduct between nation states, thereby supporting the promotion of collaboration and cooperation, supporting mediation and negotiation, with the aim of reducing and preventing wars and conflicts.

Yet laws and rules of conduct will frequently not be successful if there is no capacity to enforce them. It is certainly worthy for us to have laws which set out what is illegal conduct between nation states and what is illegal conduct by individual leaders and governments leading those states, but without the possibility of prosecution and enforcement, such laws will frequently be simply futile hot air. Therefore we need to make sure that there are appropriate mechanisms to ensure that laws and rights are enforced. Enforcement of our laws requires bodies which monitor these laws and their implementation, which monitor compliance with such laws, and which, where discussion and persuasion are ineffective in gaining compliance, then prosecute those laws, then prosecute those nations, countries, communities and societies, and those individuals leading such breaking of laws.

Where there is a need, such bodies must be able to bring to book all who are responsible for aggressively violent conduct at the international and global level, and sometimes at the national level, especially where there are vast crimes against populations in nation states or in other areas. As part of these systems of enforcement, again, where there is a need, we must have international and multinational military peace and law policing entities which can be brought in to enforce peace and prevent aggressive violence, conflict and war, thereby preventing wide scale suffering and pain.

Further, where there is a need, there must be systems and bodies for consideration of the evidence surrounding accusations of threat and aggression, of aggressive violence, of invasion and threat of invasion. And these systems and these bodies need to be able to act expeditiously, accurately and effectively in order to prevent conflict, and in order to apprehend those individuals who are promising aggressive murderous violence on a grand scale. Clearly there are issues with regard to the management and control of such international bodies and entities, which, if poorly managed, might themselves represent a danger to well-being and happiness, freedom and autonomy. Such control should be democratic and respect freedom and autonomy, having the overall purpose of supporting well-being and removing and reducing pain and suffering.

But perhaps even more fundamental compared to those systems of laws governing relations between countries, there need to be frameworks of individual rights as set out in the current United Nations Human Rights Charter, which establishes basic rights which we should all expect to receive. Our global and international bodies, as well as concerning themselves with the rights and actions of nation states need to concern themselves substantially with our individual well-being and the protection of each of us as individuals from abuse of our fundamental human rights. Of course, in relation to core and other principles which see each of us as responsible for not only our own well-being but the well-bring of others, it would seem potentially useful if allied to this charter of rights, there was also a charter of broad responsibilities from ourselves and our social entities towards others.

There are undoubtedly many major problems with our international and global bodies, at least in this current age, which need to be dealt with in order for our well-being to be better looked after and for cooperation and peacefulness to be better promoted and guarded. Their distance from our ordinary lives is one issue, but perhaps that is to some extent inevitable. The fact that, for example at the United Nations, nation states are seen as frequently or on the whole acting to support their own narrow national self-interests, even their own imperialistic goals, their own hegemony in some cases, is another problem. Additionally, both the lack of capacity in many instances to find agreement and then the even greater difficulties in regard to wars and potential wars of ensuring enforcement are also particular problems, though the UN provides peacekeepers who have played and can play a valuable role.

Yet our current UN organisation is heavily influenced by powerful countries that are not democratic and which abuse human rights themselves. They do not operate to an agenda which is concerned with our individual well-being and happiness. Indeed nation states which are members of the current human rights council themselves may practice torture of their in-country opponents, deny reasonable freedom of speech (sometimes on pain of death), operate substantially flawed legal systems which fail to protect their citizens from false accusations, support systems which significantly disadvantage and discriminate against women, homosexuals as well as those who do not conform in terms of religious or other belief. Such states may practise the death penalty, violent punishments, and may deny basic human rights to their citizens. Such nation states and their representatives should clearly be barred from any role on global human rights bodies as they are acting in a criminal and destructive way themselves and are severely damaging many of their own citizens, as well as damaging their own communities and societies.

Our current international bodies and organisations clearly need much improvement and development, but while there may be structural or other problems, their faults are often significantly down to the nation states and governments which comprise them. Whatever their current faults and whatever the need to resolve these faults, the fact of their existence and the opportunity for discussion and talk about global issues, wars, conflicts, environmental issues and more, makes these bodies of critical importance to the future of our planet and the future well-being of us all. Through effective global bodies, through effective systems of international law, through enforcement of those laws, through a range of international and global systems backed by the willingness and capacity to take actions to support well-being and reduce pain and suffering, our cooperation and peacefulness can be enhanced to the benefit of the well-being and happiness of us all.

Our international and global organisations need to be able to support our protection beyond national and state boundaries. Where there are those in power in societies, perhaps all powerful in our own countries or states, where such people commit aggressively violent acts, indeed perhaps widespread aggressive violence and oppression against us as citizens within the countries in which they have power, where there are those who kill, injure or torture their own citizens, or deliberately deprive us of the basics needed to survive then, we, each of us as individuals need to do all within our power to ensure, we need to act to ensure, that there are systems in place which will prevent such individuals, countries and states from practising such acts against their citizens and we need to do whatever we can to ensure such people are removed from power.

In practice, dependent on the power, perhaps the malevolence of the individuals, countries and states concerned and other factors including our own levels of power, we may find this difficult, but it is inconsistent with core principles and other principles to leave others to suffer in such ways if there is a possibility for us to act to prevent such suffering. And those who engage in such malevolent, destructive conduct need to know that there are others, many millions of other individuals, other organisations and nations, beyond their state, beyond their reign of power, in addition to their own citizens, who will do their utmost to take action against them should they engage in or continue to engage in aggressive violence and oppression of their own populations or any others.

In a similar fashion, we need to do our utmost to ensure that those who foment war and instigate aggressive violence and instigate those wars against other nations also need to be prevented from acting in such a manner. Acting within core principles of protecting others from suffering and promoting well-being, we need to support our global organisations ensuring, organising and supporting the presence of organisations beyond the local and national, supporting our international and global cooperative organisations which, comprising the embodiment of all of us concerned with the well-being of others, need to act together, as far as is possible, to ensure that those pursuing these aggressive wars and aggressive violence against others are prevented from doing so.

Having such organisations, entities, well-organised, effective, powerful but caring organisations, is a key element of maintaining all of our well-beings, supporting all of our welfares and reducing and preventing suffering, and is essential for us to implement the principles and goals laid out in this guide, such that we can all achieve maximal well-being and can all be protected from those whose actions will cause us suffering and pain.

Fulfilling the responsibilities and goals of our international and supranational organisations, operating within the key framework of core and other principles, requires the taking of proactive actions to bring people together, proactively identifying potential problems such as those mentioned in relation to resources and resource sharing, facilitating cooperation and negotiation in the pursuit of solutions of problems, supporting mutual understanding, principles of equality of our individual humanity, our human freedom and freedoms, and recognising our common human goals in terms of well-being and happiness and avoidance of pain and suffering. Our international organisations need to use, as far as possible, peaceful and cooperative approaches in order to build that well-being and happiness for all and to prevent that pain and suffering.

In some cases it may well be necessary for our international organisations to take physical and forceful, protective, defensive action against those others who are engaging in aggressive, oppressive and violent action, in order to protect the well-being of citizens of other nation states or those being attacked within nation states themselves. And where this seems necessary, just and right in nature, practical and in line with the support of well-being and happiness and the reduction in pain and suffering, then we as individuals need to support, and may indeed need to participate in such actions in defence of well-being and happiness and to support others in avoiding pain and suffering. There are undoubtedly difficult decisions to be made, as acting to support such force-requiring interventions is likely to have some significant cost in terms of suffering for all of us, those of us who are engaging in defensive, protective, and restraining action designed to protect those in danger and under threat, and those who are acting together with us or on our behalf.

Nevertheless, if the welfare and well-being of all is to be supported and there is to be prevention and relief from the extreme damage and suffering of war, violence and oppression, if we are to ensure a better future for our humanity, then these actions must be considered and where possible, reasonable and practical, these actions taken, even though there may well be a level of cost in terms of human lives, human pain and suffering. We may even lose our own lives through taking and supporting such action. Where there are just actions and wars against tyranny, violence, murder and oppression, where these tyrannies have demonstrated their incapacity to negotiate, their incapacity to act cooperatively and refuse to end their aggressively violent actions thereby creating tremendous suffering and pain, we must support our national and international organisations in their actions against such tyrannies, providing support in whichever ways we can, including material and vocal support and, where necessary, actual participation in body. The long-term benefits to all, not only to those suffering on the moment but to our communities and societies, to our humanity as a whole, to future generations will be enormous, if our security, safety and well-being and the safety, security and well-being of others are strongly protected and guaranteed. The establishment of peace developing, cooperation developing, and peace maintaining organisations, at the regional and global levels is without doubt essential for the well-being of each of us and for the well-being of our humanity.

In regard to our group, community and societal self-defence, where we are faced with aggressive violence by our own or other nation states and other groups, where an organisation, nation or group of nations engages in such aggressive violent action against other nations or group of nations, then our violently assaulted nations and groups, where we have it within our power, where we as citizens are under threat, will almost certainly need to take action against our aggressors as far as is reasonable and possible, protecting ourselves and other citizens from threats to our welfare and well-being, protecting us and others from threats of pain and suffering and threats to our lives. Our nations and states under attack, our governments and the like, cannot and should not stand by as countless millions of people, men, women and children face the likelihood of oppression, death and destruction.

Wherever possible, where such conflict is anticipated, we need to seek discussion, negotiation and cooperation, but where such action is occurring or is seen as highly likely or highly probable due to actions or words of those seemingly intent on using aggressive violence, it is only reasonable for our nations and groups to prepare ourselves such that we are safe against such aggression. And in support of such preparations, it may be necessary, dependent on circumstances, as a matter of course, for our groups and nations states to be proactively preparing in an ongoing manner for the likely eventuality of aggressive attack. Ideally and hopefully, there should become less need for this as nation states, as we as individuals show greater recognition of our common humanity and our need to exist, live and work together. Nevertheless we need to be vigilant in the face of potential realities, and therefore need to be prepared in general terms to defend ourselves and to be open to preparing particular, focused and intense defensive actions, tactics and strategies in threatening circumstances.

Hopefully, those of us in nations subject to attack, will be living in democratic, free and just, rather than oppressive communities and societies, but even where we are not, external attack by another nation runs the serious risk of horrendous damage to those of us who live in communities and societies, whatever the form of social organisation, even undemocratic and oppressive nations, through killings, genocide, mass murder, often motivated and supported by unbridled hatred, destructive nationalism and racism, often supported by dehumanising propaganda, implemented and executed by the attacking power against those living in the attacked nation.

Such aggressively violent, war-making attacks on other nations and other groups are of course, contrary to core and other principles, being abhorrent. Nevertheless, there might be circumstances, taking all into consideration, when aiming to gain control of and taking over another nation's geographical jurisdiction might be justified, for example if that nation were attacking, massacring, raping and torturing its own citizens. Such action would represent defence of those being massacred and assaulted, raped, tortured and oppressed and would represent our support within core principles for the well-being of others and the reduction and prevention of their suffering and pain. The principles outlined require the pursuit of peacefulness and cooperation, consistent with core and other principles, yet under such circumstances, we may be obliged to use physical force in relation to the protection and defence of others, in a similar manner to which we might be required to use physical force for our self-protection and self-defence.

Thus, as with other more personal and individual circumstances described in this chapter, the use of physical force by our communities, societies, our nations, our global organisations, at a necessary level is absolutely legitimate if we are under significant threat of aggressive violence and if others are under significant threat of aggressive violence, and even more so if that violence is actually in progress. As with our encounters with more local and personal incidents of aggressive violence, this physical force should always be at the minimum level for self and other protection and should aim as far as possible to restrain those engaged in aggressive violence where possible, seeking to avoid damage even to those engaged in aggressive action, with our minimum force, where causing harm and damage, doing so preferably and optimally only to the extent that those who are aggressively violent are unable to continue with their aggressive action, prevented from further aggressive action, and have their potential for aggressive action substantially or totally removed, and no more. *In extremis* this approach can allow disabling or even killing of others as there may be circumstances where an individual or group offers major and immediate danger to the lives of others and there may be no reasonable alternative to such action.

We need to have good reason and evidence to believe in such a threat of aggressive violence from another individual, group or nation, beyond simply irrational fear. The nature of what constitutes such good reason can clearly be somewhat complex and variable, requiring rational interpretation of actions, stated intentions, and more. In regards to nation states, one nation state may suspect that another nation is organising for military assault, and if the evidence is strong will need to take the necessary steps it can to determine what is going on and to prevent the assault, optimally, initially aiming for discussion, diplomatic activity and other appropriate action in the first place.

There may, for example, be reports from the other nation of soldiers being organised for an assault, observations from within the nation which may be assaulted, intelligence information from the country threatening such attack, and direct threats against the country against which that attack might be directed. But, and unfortunately, that being said, we also have to appreciate and to take into account that false information may be manufactured and disseminated by those wishing for war and conflict, those who are full of hatred, destructive ideologies and desires of imperial and national conquest, such that they will act dishonestly and without integrity to provoke and promote war and conflict to support their own ends. False stories of invasion and attack by others who will be attacked, have not infrequently been the means of starting wars, with populations stirred up by racist lies and stories of such false attack to gain their assent for, or to act as a smokescreen for, aggressive war. Thus we as individuals and social groups, need to be extremely careful in our actions and must be entirely sure of what we are doing and the trustworthiness and reliability of what we are being told, the journey to war being a very grave undertaking. We must do more than simply and naively accept nationalistic and aggressively violent statements from our leaders and governments. We have a duty and responsibility to protect others within other jurisdictions, others within other nations, from unjust, unprovoked attack, unnecessary pain and suffering, inflicted by our own nations.

However, if there is real threat of aggressive war, and indeed imminent threat with substantive evidence of such threat, and if negotiation and discussion, if diplomatic activity is not working, or if the consequences of diplomatic activity are not viewed optimistically then, as a nation or alliance of nations which may be attacked, we will need to raise our level of preparation and mobilise for our defence. Hopefully, much will already be in place for such a defence with, in such circumstances, appropriate weaponry available, with professional skills and strategy accompanying these weapons, which might serve to dissuade a potentially attacking army from any such attack. We will need our nation to organise its citizens, its standing armies, its relevant resources, and prepare to defend itself from this imminent external assault which may well cause vast damage to our populations. Hopefully those aiming to attack us will be dissuaded from their efforts to attack us, and if not we will defeat their violent aggression.

That being said, future wars and conflicts may not be carried out in the same way as the conflicts of our past human centuries. For example, systems of government, our key systems of living may be vulnerable to technological threats from attackers, the consequences of such vulnerability meaning that key life systems may be taken over, threatened and even destroyed. Again, it is hoped that we can live in a world where there are no such threats to us, but naivety and a sense of unreality can have painful consequences. It is wise for those of us interested in peace and well-being, those of us who wish to prevent and reduce pain and suffering, to anticipate and prepare for future threats and potential actualities.

Returning to the common forms of war already experienced through the centuries, aside from the wars between our nations states, there have also been, within our nation states, for various reasons in the past, a number of violent civil conflicts including civil wars, involving conflict between internal groups. These wars are, and have been generally due to conflicts between different interest groups within our societies or different ideological and belief groupings. In particular these civil wars have occurred and may occur when repressive authorities feel there is a challenge to their power and interests, where those in power believe they will lose their power, resources and privilege. As a consequence therefore, they aim to suppress their opponents through punitive, often aggressively violent and other measures.

Our response to this has been and will often be a form of uprising against those in power. In these situations, as in others, it is optimal for those in power to talk and negotiate with their opponents and reach cooperative and peaceful solutions, which may involve giving up some or all of the resources and power they may be desperate not to lose. Those of us campaigning for justice and change may also have to compromise, though if our campaigns are just and reasonable, we should pursue these until our reasonable ends are achieved. However, wherever possible, cooperation and peaceful approaches and means should be adopted, rather than resorting to violent civil war, and substantive violence and internal strife to achieve goals. Terrorism involving attacks on civilians, on ordinary people in order to achieve such objectives is entirely unacceptable.

Referred to already as a motivation for pursuing negatively selfish personal or group goals through war and invasion, not infrequently in the past, but hopefully less so in the modern age, imperialistic powers have invaded, or through other means, taken control of other nations and nation states, often murdering those or many of those in the invaded or controlled areas, sometimes enslaving populations, imposing their rule on other peoples and countries and exploiting the resources of those countries for personal, individual and group economic gain. We as individuals should never participate in or support such imperial actions and invasions and should never support our governments in pursuing such destructive empire building. It is our responsibility to look after all, to ensure the well-being of all, a goal which is not best served by aggressively violent takeover of other countries and peoples.

If it is our country which has been invaded and taken over, and we are faced with oppression and consequent threats to our well-being, threats of aggressive violence against us, then, dependent on the nature of that controlling power, we may well need to take action, again preferably peaceful action but sometimes indeed forceful and as necessary physical and forceful action to prevent the damage being done by that controlling power and remove that controlling power in order to protect ourselves, our families and our communities and societies as far as we can. Our efforts should be directed solely at those who are imposing such aggressive violence on us and their resources and assets, or those collaborating with such aggressors. We should, as in other cases, look to impose the minimum force necessary on our aggressors, even though such military occupiers may well be brutal, cruel and violent in the extreme and therefore, as a consequence our use of force may sometimes need to be substantial.

If that power is more benevolent, something which is unlikely considering their choice to invade and attack us, then we should aim to avoid violence and pursue peaceful cooperation in order to promote well-being and happiness within the context of that invading power or optimally in order to remove the invading power, such that a more peaceful, more democratic situation of well-being is put in place. In the face of overwhelming odds from a cruel and aggressively violent oppressor, we must still do all within our power to end their rule and control.

Linked to such imperialism may be colonisation, often involving the expulsion of local peoples from their homes and lands, often involving the movement of some from the imperial nation to those areas taken over, with these colonisers usually being given high status, power and control in these new lands. Of course, within terms of core principles such colonisation is unacceptable through the harm done to others in their removal from their homes and through the assumption of undemocratic power and control by those colonisers. Even in the event that those colonisers become the democratic majority through mass immigration and expulsion of those who previously occupied that land, this is illegitimate and those who have lost control and had their land stolen, have the legitimate right to do what is necessary to regain their lands and properties. Nevertheless, wherever possible, peaceful means should be used to achieve these reasonable goals. We should note that those who colonise may also have been forced to move against their will. But we should also never knowingly occupy the lands of others in such a manner. If we do so, we are collaborating with theft and oppression and acting contrary to core and other principles.

A real issue with regard to such colonisation in many contexts is the presence of such colonising people, present over long periods of time, even generations. Indeed, perhaps, all of the land that any of us occupy may have been occupied by others at some point in the past. There may be no simple solution to such a problem. Those descendants of the initial colonisers may feel that they are living in what is and has become their home, often feeling no or little affiliation with their family's country of origin. Optimally nevertheless, accommodations will need to be reached whereby all of us can live side-by-side, tolerating each other and creating new communities and societies which operate to support the well-being and happiness of all.

There may also be more complex forms of imperialism whereby powerful nations and groups act through more local agents, with those powerful groups or nations imposing their power at a distance through economic and other means. This form of imperialism substantially contradicts our notions of peaceful cooperation, of democracy and democratic contribution, of fundamental equality of all human beings, and can mean our substantial exploitation by those relevant powers, It is our responsibility to remove ourselves from such a coercive and imperialistic relationship, replacing such relationships with mutually beneficial modes of cooperation, incorporating mutual support such that we can all enjoy maximal well-being, both ourselves and those who wish to trade, exchange, cooperate, collaborate and work with us, this operating to the benefit of the well-being of us all.

Those of us who work within the framework of core principles and act against oppressors, be those oppressors organised nation states or aggressively violent attackers in a range of contexts, can be seen as heroes, people worthy of admiration from our communities, societies and beyond, on account of our actions in support of others.

Heroes come in many forms and may engage in many different acts in support of our communities, societies and our broader humanity. But in regard to our responses to conflict and aggressive violence, as individuals with our commitment to others, our heroic acts may include, in certain circumstances, stepping in directly to help, protect and indeed rescue others faced with immediate violent aggressive attack or with such attack in progress. This is optimally done verbally but using physical force where required. If we step in in such a manner using minimal and reasonable levels of force, then we are certainly heroes worthy of respect and admiration for our protective action, risking ourselves to help and rescue others, and while we will have acted out of a desire to protect others, receiving admiration from others being unlikely to be the motivation for our actions, we are certainly to be admired and given the greatest respect for our courageous actions. Indeed, such forms of heroism and indeed other forms of heroism represent the epitome of our cooperative existence, our cooperative, mutually supportive, human living.

We, our communities, societies and beyond, need to see such actions as worthy examples, representing conduct and actions which we and others should aim, wherever possible, and reasonable, to emulate. Those of us who engage in such actions will hopefully look after and protect ourselves in taking these heroic actions and will leave those situations in which we have courageously decided to intervene, unharmed. The welfare and well-being of all is to be looked after, including ourselves as far as is possible.

And there are those of us who may not intervene directly, our lacking in the personal strength, the capacity and resources to stop the violence and fearing personal harm, or our being faced by impossible odds which would mean our individual intervention on the moment will not be able to protect others. Yet, still we may have the capacity to bring help to protect others and this is also, where possible, necessary, and indeed admirable, as we will hopefully have acted to protect those being subject to aggressive violence. While in some instances, our on the moment, direct physical intervention, may be unrealistic with our being outnumbered or for other reasons powerless, yet we must intervene somehow and at some time to protect others from such pain and suffering. It is unacceptable to stand by and do nothing, although on some occasions, faced with overwhelming force, this may be something which we are unable to avoid on the moment, but must not do over time. At some point, at the earliest point possible where we can be effective, we must act against the aggressively violent.

Nevertheless, it is heroism to intervene directly to protect others and to put ourselves at risk in order to protect others. Our heroism need not simply be in response to attacks on others in the form of aggressive violence. We will be heroes, worthy of the greatest admiration and respect, and worthy of acknowledgment and recognition for what we have done, if we rescue others from dangerous and life-threatening situations, such as saving others from drowning in stormy seas, rivers or even calm lakes or swimming pools. We will be heroes if we rescue others in danger from animal attack or if we provide medical assistance for those who will otherwise die. Indeed our medical systems might, without too much of a stretch, be considered heroic systems staffed by heroic individuals, who in some circumstances, will put their lives on the line to help others, for example, in combating and preventing the spread of deadly communicable diseases.

But there are other heroes, those who take risks in our more social contexts, in order to uncover the truth of those who engage in criminality, dishonesty, corruption, fraud and aggressive violence, with these heroes, often under threat themselves to their livelihood and well-being, even their lives, aiming to bring to book or let the world know about the reality of the heinous conduct of people committing such acts, such that we know about and can take appropriate action and prevent their conduct. As a consequence of their actions therefore, these heroic individuals will be placing themselves in danger from such criminals and their allies, some of whom who may be extremely powerful and threatening.

The work of these individuals who reveal the truth about such conduct, frequently in the role of whistleblowers, professional investigators in our police forces, legal officials, journalists, and other investigators is invaluable to us all. Beyond the dishonesty, criminality, fraud and aggressive violence mentioned, these whistleblowing and investigating individuals may aim to enable us to see or uncover the unpleasant truths of violence in wars and conflicts of the range of types, aiming to reveal falsehoods, lies and realities which some would prefer to be hidden. In that manner those conducting such investigations do us all a great service.

Those people who are engaging in these efforts to let us know, are to be admired as heroes of our communities, societies and our broader humanity societie. They are serving us all in enabling us to find out the truth, to understand reality and promote the well-being and welfare of all. Those in power, those acting for their own benefit or for the benefit of their own closed groups, those who are deliberately operating in service of their own interest and against the general good, cooperating with some but not with those others who have integrity; those who may be threatening violence and suffering against those who attempt to reveal the truth and reveal the reality; these people certainly need to be exposed, removed from their positions of power and influence, and prevented from exerting their malevolent, destructive and damaging influence on society.

As mentioned above, not all of us doing such heroic deeds and taking risks to find the truth are professional investigators or perhaps ever intended to take on such a heroic role. Unfortunately, some of us, by dint of circumstance, by chance, through our daily living and work, stumble across heinous and destructive conduct and patterns of conduct, or indeed ourselves become pressured, sometimes come under severe pressure from colleagues, managers, commanders and bosses, to become involved in examples of poor, dishonest, corrupt or other damaging practice. We may also encounter examples of poor standards, gross incompetence and ineptitude, which may arise through misjudged actions, poor use of resources, the presence of underfunding, inadequate resources, faulty equipment and more. We may identify pathetic levels of service delivery, false recording and reporting of important research results or failing to report key research results (for example on the health effects of drugs). We may observe omissions of key actions and processes, significant negligence in the care of others, poor and dangerous quality of product, and much more, all of these resulting in or having the potential to result in substantial damage to many.

In such circumstances we have an obligation to ensure that such situations are resolved, that such dishonesty, corruption, such levels of incompetence and ineptitude are not allowed to continue with their damaging consequences, that damaging practices are replaced by practices which keep us safe and secure. If we have substantial power in the relevant circumstance, we must use our power to prevent dishonest and corrupt conduct and bring those who have done such dishonest deeds to book. And if we have such power, of course we must put an end to systematic incompetence and ineptitude. If we are a subordinate in a work situation or otherwise, then in support of the general well-being, wherever this is reasonable and possible, we must report substantive dishonest conduct to those who have power such that they can take relevant action to prevent such conduct. And certainly, where there is gross incompetence, we need to, in the first place, point this out to those with power and influence, aim to change such situations, and where necessary inform others more widely such that overall levels of competence and capacity can be improved systematically.

Such reporting to those in power can however be risky to some degree, since those in power may, for example, have instigated dishonest actions amongst their staff and employees, those they manage, or perhaps being connected in some other way to those who are behaving dishonestly. For example, they may have become part of dishonesty and misconduct to support their own finances and well-being, to gain or protect their own position, status and income, or for other reasons. They may also have been aware of dishonesty but turned a blind eye, either not particularly disapproving of it, or not wishing the anxiety and stress of dealing with such a situation and its consequences. Thus we may be putting ourselves at risk if we report, in some cases, incompetence, dishonesty and misconduct to these corrupt, corrupted or dishonest owners, managers or bosses. Similarly with regard to gross incompetence, those in power might prefer not to know and consider us a nuisance for saying something, as this incompetence might be to some degree their responsibility or perhaps might be seen as their responsibility and illustrative of their own incompetence. For if they did not know about such dishonesty or bad practice, then it could be reasonably seen as their job to know about it, and if they did know about it and did nothing then they would certainly bear some important responsibility. In either case those in positions of authority could be seen as being either incompetent or negligent.

In such circumstances therefore, by reporting what we know or have observed, we may put our own job and position, our personal well-being, at risk as well as potentially opening ourselves up to physical and other threats, particularly if those we are reporting to are concerned that we might be jeopardising their positions and roles, their status, position, income and well-being. Nevertheless, we have a responsibility to let others know about such conduct and do our utmost to combat gross incompetence, negligence and dishonesty.

And it may sometimes be the case, that there are those in positions of power and influence who do wish to pursue the general well-being and happiness and therefore will deal with dishonesty and corruption or who will deal with levels of gross incompetence which have serious consequences for well-being and happiness, causing pain and suffering. And since these people may exist, we need to make efforts in their direction to let them know, rather than assuming ill intent from them. Through such whistleblowing we may, having taken such risks, be seen as, and in reality have acted, heroically, putting ourselves at risk to support the well-being and happiness of others, with the potential and consequent ending of such dishonesty, corruption and gross incompetence being a reward in itself, but also serving as a reward for all others.

Engaging in such processes of whistleblowing does require some care and perhaps wisdom. Minor errors and incompetence should not be the subject of such reporting but we should deal with these by talking to people in constructive, cooperative and supportive ways. Indeed, in regard to many incidents and issues, in particular those regarding competence, if we can deal with these effectively directly with colleagues or within an organisation or institution this may well be best, as long as difficulties are resolved and there is no significant damage to the well-being of others.

Yet, it is as well to reiterate that there are those who may not be straight and honest with us, who may seem understanding and sympathetic to the things we say, but who have no real intention of taking any effective action, perhaps urging delay and discretion on us and attempting to bind us into silence through arguments of loyalty, personal duty to others, by contracts and rules of confidentiality and secrecy. They may be bound into a culture of collegiality and authority which is the basis of their appointment and power, wherein they support their friends and colleagues however dishonest and incompetent they may be, their being of the same character and ilk or of similar status and on friendly terms with those who are dishonest, incompetent or corrupt. Indeed such people may even promote courses of action, telling us they are doing things, which superficially appear to address problems, but in reality do not, for example setting up investigations designed to achieve nothing. At the end of the process, they may claim they have taken action and problems are resolved when unfortunately in reality they are not, as these individuals will well know. Their job and role, as they see it, will be to cover up problems, avoid overt conflict, prevent their friends and colleagues from being tackled, damaged through their dishonesty and incompetence, and avoid potential damage to their own and institutional reputation.

In fact they will be prolonging continuing incompetence, creating emotional frustration and anxiety and undoubtedly substantially damaging the organisations and institutions of which they are a member, the communities and societies, the broader humanity to which they belong. They will be sustaining and building around them a culture and cultures of incompetence and dishonesty, something which is entirely unacceptable, damaging of our organisations, community and society, our humanity, and therefore entirely contrary to core and other principles. By contrast, through tackling these people, through dealing with their dishonest and incompetent conduct and aiming to achieve justice and more, especially if we do this in a sustained manner, despite risks to ourselves, we will be acting in a heroic manner to support our communities, societies and beyond (though of course achieving such heroic status should not be our goal).

There are many other ways in which we can act heroically in support of others, our communities, and societies as well as the world beyond. Our pursuit of integrity, justice, working to rid others and our world of poverty, supporting those in need and difficulty, in a substantial and self-sacrificing manner (though too much self-sacrifice is not a necessity), protecting others from oppression, working to ensure others have clean water, acting to promote peace and prevent wars (something which might be unseen by others and effected through intelligent and clever negotiation), identifying and acting to prevent bad and indeed malevolent, damaging actions and practice wherever they occur. Acting in these and many other ways are likely to comprise admirable and worthy heroism, supportive of core principles, supporting well-being and happiness and preventing or reducing pain and suffering, and therefore and thereby being worthy of approbation and recognition from the rest of us.

Being heroic, while often involving significant actions of self sacrifice and dedication in support of others, may also involve our performance of many smaller and kinder deeds which together mean that we are certainly worthy of admiration, even if our actions might not involve the kind of risk to ourselves often associated with acts of heroism. For example, visiting and looking after those who are ill and wish for company and support, those who perhaps can give little to us directly but need caring for, and doing so on a regular basis, can be seen as representing self sacrifice in order to care for others, and therefore, along with being admirable conduct, might also be seen as heroic. Many small acts of giving and kindness might also be seen, in accumulation, as representing heroic conduct.

In any case, as indicated by the actions described as being likely to be worthy of admiration and indeed heroic, this guide certainly argues that such heroic actions are certainly and unsurprisingly more desirable and preferable than neutral and destructive actions. Such actions are interpreted as more desirable than others in terms of the core and other principles, but such preferred and preferable heroic action will certainly include taking the correct and appropriate action to protect others from pain and suffering, and this heroic action in itself may have the potential to involve causing pain and suffering to some others under certain circumstances. Such heroism represents a pinnacle of cooperative action.

While heroes represent those we will admire, respect and indeed perhaps lionise (though also as discussed in this guide, it is likely that our heroes will be real people with all the accompanying faults), by contrast the reality is, and sadly, this may continue to be the reality into the future, (though hopefully not), that there are those of us in the world who are significantly misguided in our actions, while having or perhaps believing ourselves to have good intentions. There are also those of us who pursue our own selfish interests or the selfish interests of our own particularly nation, group or perceived race without regard to the wider interest, without concern for others as individuals, those of us outside of their own group and interest, causing as a consequence, substantial destruction, damage, pain and suffering. That is entirely unacceptable.

There are perhaps a very few among us, though there are certainly some, who may act with simple calculated and deliberate malevolence intending to hurt others. Clearly those who act with calculated aggressive violence and malevolence are worthy of much attention in terms of preventing their actions. They are exceedingly dangerous and their conduct and behaviour needs to be tackled and brought to an end and their capacity to do harm removed in a forceful though hopefully as peaceable manner as possible. Nevertheless, as already discussed, aggressive violence at the more local and immediate level frequently arises from moments of uncontrolled anger, passion and hatred, often, though not always, based in feelings of being disrespected, feelings of being unloved, based in misunderstanding, misguided feelings of group loyalty, an uncontrolled greed for things, or sometimes the need for drugs itself requiring the need for resources, money, in some cases, with those seeking drugs prepared to engage in violence to get the drugs they need.

The consequences of aggressive violence are likely to be no lesser because they have more spontaneous origins. Whatever the provocation in terms of the non-violent behaviour of others, we must control ourselves and not engage in aggressive violence ourselves. Whatever the hurt and anger we might feel against those who may be behaving reprehensibly but peacefully, we must manage and control our responses, be in charge of what we do, and must certainly not turn to aggressive violence ourselves. And, by contrast to our admiration for those who have acted in heroic ways, while perhaps despising the acts of those who engage in aggressive violence, we should try, as far as we can, not to demonise those have done such deeds, or who have done destructive and damaging deeds, but instead we must consistently look to return them, where possible, to good conduct in line with core and other principles, and return them to living, where this is safe to community and society, when they offer no, or no significant threat.

Perhaps, as discussed earlier in this chapter, many of us can be gripped by anger and emotion at times but we must not as a consequence engage in aggressive violence. Yet there are some who have been and are immersed in destructive beliefs and ideology with the consequence that they see others of us who are peaceful, caring, loving and kind, as evil, and indeed malevolent. And as a consequence of their beliefs, they may make conscious plans to engage in violence and aggressive attacks on us and others, and sometimes they may be open about their aggressively violent intentions, issuing open and explicit threats of violence. They will often not see their aggressively violent actions as malevolent, justifying their actions by reference to their beliefs and ideology, their interpretation of the world based in those beliefs and that ideology, however out of kilter with reality their beliefs may be. Of course their aggressively violent conduct is entirely unacceptable, threatening pain, destruction, damage and suffering to others as it does.

Indeed, notably, it is common for those who are aggressively violent to blame those who they intend to attack, are attacking or have attacked, holding their peaceful, non-aggressive victim who may represent integrity and who has done no significant harm to others, responsible for the aggressive violence that these attackers themselves conduct. Such blaming of others when if fact these malevolent and aggressively violent individuals have attacked those who have not engaged in violence, who have acted peacefully, supporting the well-being of others, is vile, evil and reprehensible. Adding to the pain of actual physical and mental suffering and trauma caused by violent attack, such blaming represents an effort to take responsibility away from those who have done such violent acts, placing it on the innocent, and therefore provides further pain and suffering to their victims. It is totally at odds with core and other principles through the danger, pain and suffering it causes to us as individuals and to others.

And then there are those who actually do engage in such violence and attacks, but justify their actions in public, and maybe to themselves, by stating that it was they who were under attack in the first place, even though that is clearly not the case with no aggressive violence against them threatened or having taken place. This further dishonesty in falsely reporting events heaps even more pain and suffering onto their victims and is again, reprehensible and unacceptable. Disagreeing with others, stating differing views, having different beliefs and expressing them, not obeying commands or even requests, these actions and many others, consistent as they usually are with regard to core and other principles, are not acceptable excuses for aggressive violence to be done to others. If others have abused us verbally, this can be painful, if not very painful, yet we need to cope with this verbally and respond and deal with such abuse in as peaceful a manner as possible, bearing the pain and dealing as best we can in a constructive manner with those who have or are, as in this case, verbally abusing us, and aiming to change or end their conduct. We can certainly move away from these people to a safer, more comfortable place if we feel we need to, though we must support our own well-being and the well-being of others, and must not allow ourselves and others to endure pain and suffering.

As already referred to in this chapter within the context of wars, in terms of blaming others, similar to what can occur in more personal and close relationships, it has not been uncommon through history, and indeed is not uncommon in the present, for groups or leaders of groups, contrary to the facts, to falsely paint their own particular group, often the majority or most powerful group, as victims of the aggressive and discriminatory or damaging actions of others, frequently weaker, minority groups. Amongst other things, such leaders and groups often use single or several instances of actions by individuals who are ascribed as members of other groups or who are allocated membership of other groups, to create such falsehoods and lies about an entire group of people.

Individual acts of discrimination and aggressive violence against others by individuals who are part of, or who are associated with, particular groups, may be turned into excuses by the powerful for widespread discrimination, attacks and mass attacks and mass aggressive violence against a whole group of people, none or almost none of whom have been involved with or will have supported the initial act. And otherwise, on some occasions, imaginary and fabricated attacks are constructed, and said to have been conducted by minorities who are painted as representing threats to the powerful majority or individuals within such majority groups, where in fact there is no existing threat to these more powerful groups and certainly not from the minority group as a whole. Such advocates of this notion of victimhood for their in fact powerful and frequently majority groups, are often seeking to advance their own interests as leaders and to advance the interests of their own groups at the expense of these other nations, groups, other races.

As a consequence of such falsehoods, exaggerations and through other motivations, there have been many examples of unjustifiable aggressive violent attacks on certain groups of people, on the grounds of race, colour, belief, sexual orientation, nationality and much more, yet these have almost always been directed at powerless minorities rather than powerful and privileged majorities. These attacks have frequently involved the taking of actions that have perhaps started with smaller damaging discriminatory measures but then move on to actions which substantially harm these others, and which wreak vastly painful and damaging actions on those discriminated against. This might mean discriminatory and destructive actions ranging from reducing access to basic means of survival like food or water, preventing access to work and income, denying people rights as citizens, forcibly removing people from their homes and their countries, mass enslavement, deprivation of liberty in various forms, and usually at their end of these actions, direct and aggressive violence involving attacks on individuals within these groups, or violence against entire groups including mass torture, mass murder and genocide. All of this is often backed by cultural myths, false histories and propaganda aimed at demonising these others, these other individuals, those in these groups, as lesser beings, Core and other principles allow none of these actions which are considered repulsive, evil and entirely contrary to the goals of seeking well-being and happiness for all and reducing pain and suffering for all.

Such aggressive violence against the members of such groups, against individuals, is entirely wrong. And such dishonesty and misrepresentation, such deliberate efforts at over generalisation about others in order to target other groups and cause individuals to endure pain, suffering and violence, are utterly heinous, are totally reprehensible and are almost certain to lead to conflict and violence between groups with terrible consequences, something which is often the plan of those promulgating such lies, such exaggeration, such falsehoods and propaganda.

The concoction of falsehoods in order to pursue a discriminatory and potentially violent agenda against a less powerful group; the knowing exaggeration of unrepresentative or minor incidents in order to bolster and justify discrimination against minorities who, for example, the powerful may believe offer economic or other threats, or whose assets the powerful wish to acquire, indeed even the accidental misunderstanding-generating false conclusions which lead to the threatening of a group or indeed any individual are heinous and unacceptable. We have a responsibility to be aware of the dangers of over generalising with its potential racist and other destructive and damaging consequences and we must all ensure that we show, think and act with integrity. Clearly a lack of integrity and negatively selfish self or selfish group pursuit is entirely contrary to core and other principles.

And sadly, through history, in particular modern history, the machinations of those with aggressive negatively selfish, malevolent intent, especially the leaders of those nations and groups which have engaged in aggressive violence against others, have been exposed, frequently through their dissembling efforts to dress up their own assaults and attacks as a consequence of provocation from another, where in fact no such provocation has in reality taken place. In addition to never engaging in such forms of action ourselves, with their destructive effects on well-being and happiness and the intense violence, suffering and pain resulting; apart from never supporting such actions ourselves, we must all be aware of the potential duplicity of some others, including those within our own groups who may claim to speak for us. We must be wary of such people and take action against such duplicitous and aggressively violent individuals wherever we can, aiming to prevent their actions and remove them from positions of power and influence.

Clearly in engaging in all of this type of action, this dishonest and destructive manipulation and lack of integrity, these individuals are acting contrary to the core and other principles which require integrity and require the support of the well-being of others, and preventing their suffering, which such destructive actions and malevolent malfeasance certainly do not do. Spinning a web of deceit and dishonesty around such malevolent and aggressively violent actions, or indeed around any actions is entirely unacceptable, adding to the pain and suffering of others.

Unfortunately the truth is often not as easy to find as we would like. Dealing with such duplicity and dishonesty and identifying the veracity of claims and reports is often difficult and challenging since we ourselves, being informed of and hearing of such claims and being absent ourselves, may not know the exact facts of incidents or specific cases. Yet, at the basic level we know through the core and other principles how we should behave towards others, and know that we must support the well-being and happiness of others and act to reduce their pain and suffering. We will clearly have to bring to bear the range of evidence we know of in such situations, including our assessment of individuals, political processes, trustworthiness, the potential motivations and objectives on the basis of which those contributing evidence, put that evidence forward. We will need to ask questions and find further answers if we are to fully understand and make the correct decisions for ourselves and others.

Through having developed such understanding it should be clear what we should do and not do, even in the event of hearing the range of lies and duplicity. We should certainly be sure of what we should not do – we must not pursue aggressive violence against other individuals or others as groups, as if they were not individuals, as if they were not our fellow human beings. Rather we must seek truth and justice, not participate in racism, gender discrimination, destructive nationalism, attacks on others and other groups who mean no harm; we must not engage in or act to promote aggressive violence against those in belief groups, engage in anti-gay violence against those who mean and are doing us no harm and who wish to live together with us cooperatively and in peace as part of and as fundamentally equal members of our communities and societies. We, instead, need to promote cooperation, togetherness and tolerance, love and peace, within the framework of core and other principles.

As individuals, in line with core principles, supporting the well-being and happiness of all and wishing to reduce pain and suffering, we have responsibility to protect others from suffering as well as protecting our own interests and well-being, and must recognise that those proposing solutions to problems which involve or incite aggressive violence against individuals, against the individuals in other groups and against groups as entities, are not to be followed, but instead must be rebuffed, and fought against, operating as they are outside of core and other principles, in ways which are likely to be vastly damaging to the many others who are our fellow human beings and who need care and concern, rather than vicious and aggressively violent attack.

Where individuals and groups are accused of organising to support aggressive violence or accused of doing substantive damage to other individuals and the rest of our communities and societies, we need to ensure that as communities, societies and beyond, we have mechanisms in place to establish truth in such circumstances of dispute and in regard to such reported incidents. We need to have reporting systems which are open and democratic, allow different interpretations, enabling reports to be challenged, providing individual capacity to report events in alternative ways, allowing dissent, with the capacity for independent and reliable investigation to determine the realities of events and occurrences. Moreover, if within a group, certain individuals, perhaps even a majority are promulgating and promoting aggressive violence and damage to others, while we must act to prevent their actions and while we must aim to and ensure we protect ourselves and others, we have to recognise and realise that that does not justify action against other individuals in such a group who have no truck with aggressive violence and damaging others. We are individually responsible for our actions and inaction, and cannot be held responsible for the actions of others in our groups through membership of that group through birth or even, in some cases, where we have joined through choice, being unaware of the propensity and support of that group for aggressive violence.

Further, while there is an essential need for us to speak freely, it is difficult to justify an unfettered freedom for those who pursue agendas of hatred, those who aim to incite us and others to engage in violence and oppression of others, and who are willing to lie and foment the spreading of unverified, unverifiable and false accounts of heinous acts, which they may blame on other individuals or entire groups, promoting hatred against such other individuals and groups, rather than promoting peacefulness, cooperation, integrity and truthfulness.

We, being responsible for our communities and societies, having responsibility as individuals for the world we live in, and supporting well-being and happiness for ourselves and all others, need to contribute to the organisation and governance of our communities such that those who might commit acts of aggressive violence against others cannot gain even the smallest measure of power and influence which might enable them to enact their hatreds and violence. Through democratic mechanisms, through our involvement in democratic processes, which encompass much more than simply choosing others to lead, we can make such an important contribution.

Our notion of democracy cannot and does not simply mean government and decision making along with imposition of those decisions, as determined by the majority. It means much more. In particular, our notion of democracy needs to incorporate the ideas that those of us who are in the majority, who hold a majority view, and indeed occupy positions of power on the basis of selection by the majority, have responsibilities to others of us, to minorities, and to all other individuals in line with the stated core principles.

Those in the majority cannot use their majority status as a justification or means for aggressive violence or oppression in its various guises against minorities. Those of us in the majority cannot use that fact and resulting democratic power as reason for taking significantly damaging and destructive actions against other individuals. Instead we have a responsibility to take account of and ensure the well-being and welfare of each individual including those individuals belonging and existing within those minority groups, who must also not themselves be subject to threat of aggressive violence, coercion and oppression within these groups. Democratic societies and indeed any society have a responsibility to protect their citizens from aggressive violence and oppression. Indeed all of our societies and groupings have responsibility to other groups and individuals within those groups and within other groups.

Inflicting aggressive violence and suffering on others is unacceptable. That extends to the infliction of torture, torture being the infliction of pain in order to enhance suffering, to punish others and often used, at least in the explicitly stated purposes of those who torture or use torture, as a route to gain information from those who are deemed to hold such information. Under no circumstances do core and other principles allow us to support others in, or support others to, engage in torture of other individuals for whatever purpose, whatever those individuals may have done, whatever their perceived intentions, whatever they might have been considered to have been involved in doing.

In itself, torture is grossly immoral and totally contrary to core and other principles through its deliberate infliction of pain and suffering. Where it is claimed that such actions may lead to the gaining of important information which might be argued to be supportive of the well-being of the whole, there is little evidence that this is the case, and even were it to be the case, the deliberate implementation of severe pain on any individual for any purpose is totally unacceptable in terms of the principles put forward in this guide, the tremendous pain and suffering imposed on the person being tortured acting in a manner to substantially undermine our notions of care and concern for the well-being of each individual, undermining the foundations of a society in which we can all feel safe, secure and protected from such intense suffering and pain.

Given the individual vulnerability of each of us in the face of power, the acceptance and enabling of torture opens the door to the deliberate imposition of intense pain and suffering with a view to creating the maximum pain and suffering possible, with the potential for such torture to be imposed on anyone in our community or in any community. The use of torture creates a context and, where it occurs, represents a context, in which aggressive violence and the causing of pain is acceptable. Such a context in itself is unacceptable and we must ensure that such contexts do not exist. For these reasons, though principally because of the direct pain and suffering, at the most intense levels that torture causes (which of course it is designed to achieve), the principle of no torture is therefore absolute.

In the context of torture and the infliction of pain, it also needs to be recognised that such practices will likely not only alienate permanently those who are tortured, but will also alienate their families, friends and likely others in their communities and societies, if not alienating and creating enemies of whole communities and societies. Thus, torture, unacceptable in any case, will most likely serve to destroy whichever goal we are seeking to support, alienating and making enemies of those who might otherwise support our causes and actions.

In addition to the social systems of law that we need, as well as our systems and organisations to protect us from aggressive violence, as well as reporting systems for incidents of aggressive violence, we also need systems for caring for those who have been the victims of aggressive violence. Our responsibilities for caring for those who have been the victims of aggressive violence have already been discussed, yet to realise these responsibilities this means the presence of organisations and systems which provide directly the kind of medical care which is of the highest quality for those of us who have fallen victim to such violence. And this includes long-term physical care where this is needed, but it also means having systems and organisations which can provide psychological care into the future where this is needed, alongside focusing on our physical recovery, due to the often intense psychological trauma caused by violent attacks. We should all, as individuals, support the presence of such systems and organisations, both through moral, financial and other forms of support.

Of course as family, as friends and even acquaintances of those who have suffered from aggressive violence we need to be there to love and support those who have been such victims. We may need to provide emotional support, acting perhaps as a shoulder to cry on. We need to be prepared to spend time with them, offer practical support and perhaps also encourage them to rejoin the world if they are having difficulty after their experience. Such support can be an essential part of a full physical and mental recovery.

Where we become embroiled in violent conflicts, wars and the like, even though there may be times when it seems that we as individuals may be able to have little effect, where we can it is our responsibility to act on our own or with others using whatever power and influence we have, to support an end to aggressive violence, to act against oppressive actions which damage our and others' well-being and happiness, and to support peaceful and cooperative actions and relationships, working to end such conflict peacefully, and aiming to minimise the violence being suffered by all parties.

If possible and reasonable, and if we do not accept the purpose, rationale for, and cause or justification of the war or conflict embarked upon by our own nation state or group, our considering such action unjust, unnecessary and inconsistent with the notions of supporting well-being and happiness, then we may and indeed should refuse to cooperate with and take part in, or refuse to take any action to support that conflict, and we may legitimately, reasonably and actively oppose such unjust, destructive and unwanted wars.

Our actions in this way, as stated earlier in this chapter will be supportive of all people with our fundamental concern and care being with the well-being and happiness of all. And while those of a different view may see our actions as disloyal and treacherous to the group, the fact that we have a different view about the embarkation on war and conflict and its consequences in terms of its necessity and the good it will do, does not comprise such disloyalty or treachery but instead comprises our having a different view of the best route to well-being and happiness. Our actions in opposition to such unjust conflict and war represents the greatest loyalty we can show, loyalty which is of more importance than that of supporting any national, belief, racial or other group, it representing our loyalty to our fellow human beings and their well-being and happiness, serving our fellows in acting to prevent or reduce their pain and suffering. If we support another nation state or group or take action to oppose such unjust and unwarranted conflict, then as long as our views and values are consistent with the support of well-being and happiness, then others (and in some cases that will be ourselves), then we, will be acting correctly and in line with core and other principles.

Thus, there is no treachery when we act in a manner which we believe is supporting the well-being and happiness of all, due to our greater loyalty to the well-being and happiness of all and the need to prevent pain and suffering. Our first port of call, of course, needs to be, where this is practical and safe, the honest effort to persuade others that such a war or conflict is wrong, misguided, oppressive, destructive, unjustified and damaging.

If we act in a manner in which we place our well-being substantially above that of all others, act in a negatively selfish manner and follow personal, financial and other gain at the expense of others in a manner damaging to our communities and societies, in such a conflict or other situation, then we are indeed acting in a manner which is damaging to others and which is letting others down, the response to which would quite reasonably be hurt, upset and anger, especially where others may suffer significantly, be injured or die because of our actions. Nevertheless, even under such circumstances, while there must be efforts to prevent and restrain such actions, there should be no aggressively violent response, no efforts to seek revenge, damage, destroy, injure or murder, such actions being contrary to core and other principles, enhancing pain and suffering and being of no support to well-being and happiness.

While as individuals we may seem to be minor, indeed inconsequential players in such major conflicts, the principles presented in this guide mean that each of us is of importance and value, and our individual actions and individual conduct, our individual thoughts and beliefs, can matter greatly, even if the effects of our contribution may not be immediately apparent. Individual refusal to participate in malevolent, oppressive and damaging acts is likely to be important if not crucial, with one individual act of refusal leading to the undermining of those who are unjust and oppressive, supporting a climate of non-cooperation, with one individual act of non-cooperation and refusal exemplifying refusal and, where appropriate, hopefully leading others to perhaps follow or at least leading them to recognise the destructive nature of what is going on and what they are doing.

Even within the context of violent conflicts and wars, with their component vast levels of violence, wars which we need to do our utmost to prevent from taking place, certain specific behaviours are totally unacceptable within core and other principles. As individuals, in line with the principles set out in this guide and in line with the internationally agreed Geneva Conventions, we must minimise violence, and must not take part in the vengeful attacks on, or murderous killings of civilians, soldiers and aggressors. While we may under certain circumstances need to kill others who are attacking us, in the process of defending ourselves, or kill as necessary in conflict and battle as part of a process of removing a destructive and dangerous aggressively violent tyranny, we must not take part in the murder, injury, rape and torture of soldiers and civilians who are offering and offer us no threat. We must not participate in the murder, torture, injury or punishment of captured prisoners and those who have surrendered to us; we must not take part in the vengeful and wanton destruction of property, the looting and theft of possessions. This applies to each of us whatever the orders or commands from those with power above us might be, whatever the anger promulgated in the general context, whatever the heat of the situation, and whatever the pressures there might be in our groups to conform with destructive and violent actions. Such destructive and violent actions will not support well-being and will directly create pain and suffering, also serving to exacerbate destruction, damage and conflict.

It is our responsibility not to do these things, but instead to treat people as far as is reasonably possible in such situations with firmness and dignity, maintaining their safety as far as is possible, while maintaining our own safety. We need to care and look after such people as far as is reasonably possible under the circumstances, while also recognising that the malicious and malign, those ideologically motivated to aggressive violence, possibly present amongst those we have captured, perhaps hiding their true identities, will need to be brought to book for their actions. Moreover it is crucial we also recognise amongst other things, that in some cases, some may falsely surrender, as a means of getting close to us and committing their murders and violence, and that we must protect ourselves against such an outcome while also aiming to preserve the lives of those who are genuinely surrendering to us.

If demands are made on us contrary to core and other principles, commanding us to hurt others, to attack the innocent on the grounds of their nationality, race or other features, to cause them significant and unecessary pain and suffering then we must recognise that the organisation we are fighting for is itself not legitimate, is not acting in a moral manner consistent with core and other principles. Therefore it is our duty and responsibility to refuse to follow such commands, instead acting to prevent such incidents from happening. It is thus our broader duty and responsibility to others to refuse to act in line with these commands or orders and to do whatever we can to remove those giving these orders from their positions of power as far as we can.

In whatever context, what we do with our own hands, our own bodies, through our own actions, is our personal and individual responsibility and we must do the maximum reasonable and possible within our context and circumstances to ensure well-being and happiness and prevent and reduce pain and suffering. In the context of wars, whether we are soldiers, combatants or other actors directly involved in conflict, whether we are civilians and others who have become embroiled in such a conflict against our will, and even within our will; whether we are those who may have become involved through indoctrination, false education, propaganda, and bad judgment, these individuals, all of us, need protection to as great a degree as it can reasonably be given. This will undoubtedly involve all of us with power to do so in aiming to stop the actions of those fomenting and promoting violent conflict, those who are engaged in armed acts of aggressive violence and killing. These people will need to be prevented from implementing such action, optimally in a peaceful persuasive manner but, where necessary through our use of force, optimally through restraining if possible, but otherwise disabling them to some degree or indeed totally, if such is necessary for our self-protection and the protection of others.

Despite the intensity of war and conflict, it is essential for us, wherever possible (and as individuals there may be minimal opportunities for this), to maintain and build positive and cooperative relationships, even with those with whom we are in conflict. Those leading, those with power, need to be ready to talk when this is appropriate. Such talk should aim to lead not simply to an ending of bloodshed and violence, but should support well-being into the future for all parties and should mean the ending of the potential for pain, suffering and bloodshed, into the future. For all wars end, and at the end of wars there is an aftermath. There are consequences, often comprising vast personal physical damage and mental trauma, with personal trauma and damage on a vast scale often affecting thousands, millions and more.

If such conflicts can be ended then, when this eventually happens, there needs to be a basis for cooperation and working together into the future, which memories of cruelty, brutality, rape, torture, murder and revenge do not support. When such conflict ends, in support of future well-being and happiness, we will need to aim to build cooperation, togetherness, shared goals and a peaceful future, which acts of protection of others, expressions of mutual humanity, will serve to support, especially if carried out in such difficult times of war and conflict.

The aftermath of any violent conflict, including that of war is of tremendous importance. It is essential that those intent on, or who were intent on, aggressive violence, aggression and oppression and those who collaborated and cooperated with them in key and leading ways, have their power to repeat such actions removed. Their deeds and the full nature of their crimes against others needs to be exposed and they will need to acknowledge the devastating nature of what they have done. They will undoubtedly need to be kept away from others of us and constrained from any opportunity to wreak their havoc in the future. Their power must never to be returned to them. We need to ensure that we and our fellows are never at risk from such actions again.

Suspicions and fears need to be allayed, with steps taken to build the confidence of those who may have been coerced or forced, on pain of death or otherwise, to cooperate with these aggressively violent people or indeed to allay the fears of those who may have supported those pursuing aggressive violence in more minor ways, with a view to persuading them, and indeed ensuring that they adopt more peaceful and cooperative ways of living. More aggressive violence into the future cannot be risked at any significant level.

Poisonous and destructive beliefs need to be challenged and changed. Ideologies and belief systems which support violence and hatred, which suggest further aggressively violent conflict and war need to put aside with cooperative and peaceful systems and beliefs promoted such that there is little chance of hate-filled and destructive ideologies gaining traction and producing more damage and destruction, further war and conflict. Sadly, certain murderous and destructive beliefs and conduct seem to resurface through the generations, but as a humanity we need to stop this from happening and stop such ideas gaining any currency. While difficult to remove completely, it would be foolish to allow such ideologies to remain in place, such a situation offering danger to us all into the future.

Safety and security for all need to be built, with no opportunity being given for those who might wish to support aggressive violence again. There must be no such opportunity for those who might wish to, or intend to engage in destructive and damaging conduct unsupportive of well-being, who wish to engage in negative selfish conduct aimed at or through its nature creating pain and suffering. There must be no opportunity for those who might engage in racist and other violent and destructive behaviour, or gain power such that they can pursue such murderous and aggressively violent paths and actions again.

In the aftermath of conflict, peacefulness must be demonstrated and the initiative must be taken in aiming to improve the well-being of all. In the aftermath of war, efforts need to be made to help all recover and ensure that such violent conflict does not arise again by, for example, building peaceful mechanisms for resolving differences and encouraging openness and cooperation. Resources need to be identified and actions taken to ensure that all parties to the conflict can regain well-being, with efforts made to take care of, and support those who formerly were considered to be 'on the other side', those who may previously have been considered members or part of an aggressively violent group or nation. Of course many of those on that other side may never have supported aggressive violence and some may have risked their lives in opposition to the aggressively violent.

While those who have encouraged and instigated aggressive violence and conflict need to be brought to account for their misdeeds, for the crimes they have committed, and prevented from having any role or influence into the future, which would enable their violent misdeeds to be repeated; while those who actively supported evil and aggressive actions do need to be held to account for their actions, there should not be any violent revenge sought or practiced, however justifiably angry and disgusted, nauseated, we may feel about these people and their conduct. We must avoid the cycle of killing and revenge, instead building contexts and cultures which support cooperation and peacefulness, something which revenge and killing does not produce.

But once war is done, then support must be given to those who have suffered, including those who were considered enemies or opponents in the war, such that they can rebuild their communities and societies in a form that ceases to threaten others, and which establishes the pursuit of the well-being and happiness of all as the goal of all. As is the case, during any conflict, and indeed at any time, dehumanising others, demonising others, painting others and considering others as worthy of aggressive violence and oppression, because they were a member or part of a group that supported violent aggression, is not acceptable, in particular as individually they may not have supported such aggressive violence. Yet if these people did actively and consciously support such aggressive violence or the ideology behind such violence, while we must not take vengeful action, these people must be seen as culpable to lesser or greater degrees for the conflict that has occurred and may need to be constrained and imprisoned in order to prevent their repeating their actions. They will also need to change their beliefs and optimally clearly demonstrate contrition for their actions.

For it is certainly within the bounds of adult thinking to realise and understand that invasion of other territories, taking the land of other people, bombing, using aggressive violence against, engaging in murder of the citizens of our own and other territories in order to acquire power, dominance, resources and superiority, is criminal, outrageous and totally unacceptable, however uplifted these adult citizens may feel at the notion of power, victory and triumph for their own nation state or group. It is equally within the bounds and understanding of such adults to realise that murder and injury, through direct and indirect methods, of those who are different, those who peacefully disagree with another view, is reprehensible. And all of those who supported or even acquiesced in such action whether through conscious agreement and acceptance of such action, or through a hard to justify naivety, all have some level of responsibility.

However, as referred to above, some of these individuals in such groups or nations may have stood out against such violence and conflict, at great risk to themselves. There will almost always be those who have supported cooperation and togetherness and argued and fought against tyranny, racist and other discrimination, those who opposed or who at some point opposed aggressive war, who oppose or opposed the demonisation of others within their communities and the demonisation of other nations, and who may have suffered for their actions. These individuals are worthy of admiration and are seen as admirable, indeed heroic in the context of this guide and core principles. They are heroes worthy of the greatest respect and admiration in their own struggles and their actions in attempting to prevent suffering and in support of the general well-being, cooperation, togetherness and peacefulness, working against war and violence, and acting against the foolishness and destruction brought about by dehumanising others, groups and nations.

It must be clear to all of us, that war represents a horrendous form of violent conflict, affecting vast numbers of people, damaged directly, killed or injured through weaponry, forced to leave their homes to escape violence, their property and security taken and destroyed, forced into deprivation and death through lack of food and water, warmth, shelter and protection. We need at all levels, locally, nationally and globally to act against those who engage in making moves towards or who wish to engage in aggressive war and any form of aggressive violence, oppressing and acting destructively and damagingly towards others.

In summary, in regard to peacefulness and cooperation, in regard to the avoidance of violent conflict, in support of well-being and happiness and the reduction and prevention of pain and suffering, the core and other principles support cooperation and togetherness between all of us, in whatever contexts, and support the pursuit of peacefulness. Our pursuit of these goals is aimed at serving and aims to reduce suffering and pain, enhancing our well-being and happiness. We must never use aggressive violence against others, and in our immediate and everyday lives we must aim to build peaceful and cooperative contexts. Whatever the provocation, we need to develop the peaceful and cooperative attitudes, approaches and skills in life which will serve to support us in preventing the outbreak of episodes of aggressive violence and which enable us to pursue cooperation and peacefulness, which enable us as individuals to maintain personal self-control in the face of the range of difficulties and indeed threats we may face in our daily lives.

The core principles presented in this guide support us in protecting ourselves and others against aggressive violence and should support us in doing so effectively. When dealing with aggressive violence as individuals, consistent with core and other principles, we must aim to prevent such aggressive violence, aiming at least in the first place, where reasonable and possible, to use words and other strategies in its prevention. Yet where it is necessary, where words and peaceful actions and strategies have not been or are not likely to be effective, we may need to use physical force, at a minimum necessary level, optimally simply physical restraint, to protect ourselves and to protect others from harm.

Our obligations to support well-being and peacefulness and cooperation mean that beyond our direct and individual actions, we are also required to contribute to our communities and societies, as well as more globally as far as we can, to ensure that our social organisations, communities and societies, our broader humanity, our representatives, pursue well-being, cooperativity and peacefulness, both within our societies, within the nations and groups in which we find ourselves, but also in terms of relations between our societies, or more globally.

Embedded in the core and other principles, is the notion that it is the interest of all individuals and of our common humanity which is our priority rather than the goals and needs of individual communities, nation states, individual societies and particular groupings. A crucial end goal for us is that violent aggressive conduct, oppressive and other conduct damaging of our well-being and happiness, causing of pain and suffering, is removed from our personal lives, communities, societies and beyond, and that the horrendous blight of war and violent aggressive conflict is banished forever. The removal and ending of all of such aggressive violence will have the consequences, in line with core principles, of enhanced well-being and happiness and the reduction and prevention of pain and suffering for us all.

# Thirteen

# Supporting Health, Wellness and Well-being

Pursuing our own well-being and the well-being of others in terms of personal physical and mental health, as well as avoiding our own pain and suffering and the pain and suffering of others, are fundamental to the core principles set out in this guide. In the same way, pursuing these goals in line with the core and other principles, supporting the physical and mental health of ourselves and all others and working to reduce their pain and suffering to the greatest extent possible, and doing so in a manner consistent with notions of individual independence, freedom and other principles, are a fundamental requirement of our personal conduct and personal action as set out in this guide.

The core principles require us to support our own well-being and the well-being of others, as well as reducing as far as possible and reasonable the extent of pain and suffering we experience in our own lives and that others experience in their lives. Thus, despite the fact that we know that our own lives and the lives of others will almost inevitably have some level of pain and suffering within them, forms of pain which may be emotional, psychological and physical, forms of pain which may range from minor and annoying to significant and severe; despite our knowledge of such an inevitability, it is our obligation within the framework of the core principles to work to support, maintain and indeed improve our own health and reduce our own pain and suffering. And this we need to do along with our aiming to supporting, maintain, and improve the health of others, acting as far as we can, to reduce the pain and suffering of others.

In regard to issues of our personal health, our concern with this is not simply a matter of our positive and good health being of value to us in itself, with positive health representing positive feelings and the absence of pain and suffering. Additional to this direct experience of positive health as a state or set of feelings, in addition to that absence of pain, it is of course the case that if we are in significant and ongoing poor health ourselves, enduring pain and discomfort in its various forms, if we are suffering from illness and disease, then this pain, illness and suffering will mean we are unable to, or will almost certainly be less able to, enjoy our broader positive well-being and happiness. It is highly likely that with an absence of positive health, with such suffering and pain in our lives, at least to some degree, we will be unable or less able to act and engage in the range of actions we need to take in order to support and achieve our broader personal well-being, happiness and fulfillment.

Clearly our enjoyment of well-being requires, in the main, that we are experiencing good and positive health. While we may be able to experience some elements of well-being and indeed pleasurable and positive, enjoyable experiences while in the throes of some lesser pain-causing elements symptomatic of poor health, or when our pain from significant health threatening conditions is at a lower level or temporarily relieved, if we are suffering in significant pain, if we are in agony, then in essence, by definition, this means that overall we are not enjoying well-being, despite those moments of enjoyment and pleasure. Our own poor health, physical or mental, will to some, or to a greater extent, debilitate us, reducing the quality of our personal lives, reducing our well-being and providing us with experiences of pain and suffering in their various guises that we would certainly prefer to be without.

Yet beyond the important and direct effects of poor health on ourselves and our own lives, if we are in a state of poor health, we will additionally be less able or perhaps not be in any position to support others in maintaining and improving their well-being health and happiness. Moreover, we will be less able, or perhaps completely unable, to help in reducing or removing their suffering. So, with regard to both our own personal worlds and the social worlds in which we live, it is clear that unless we give sufficient weight to issues of personal health; unless we act in relation to prevention and avoidance of illness and disease, in relation to preventing physical injury, then efforts to promote our own well-being and the well-being of others through our own more individual actions and through our more social actions are likely to be less effective than we, others and our communities and societies may need and desire, with the potential or likelihood of our efforts, in many respects, proving unsuccessful and perhaps coming to little.

Not only is it the case that if we are unhealthy, unwell, injured or ill, we will have difficulty, perhaps major difficulty or find it impossible to support others in need and to come to the aid of others who need our help, but of course, if others are unhealthy, unwell in a similar manner, they will be much less able or will find it impossible to help us. Further, through our own ill health, due to our own, injury, illness, pain and suffering, we will not only be less able or unable, to achieve our own personal well-being and happiness, but we will be unable to fulfill the core principle of supporting others; we will be unable to support others in achieving their positive well-being and happiness; we will be unable to help these others in avoiding or reducing their pain and suffering. And moreover, should they be in poor health themselves, those others will be unable to fulfill these core principles as well, proving unable to, or certainly being less able, to support us.

It must be clear to all of us, that we rely on being healthy or being to a significant extent healthy, not only as an integral part of our own personal and direct well-being bound to how we feel physically, emotionally, mentally day-to-day, but we also rely on our being in a fit state of health and well-being in relation to our ability to act to support the well-being of others and support them in avoiding and preventing their pain and suffering.

Further, in line with core and other principles and our need to support the well-being and happiness of others and reduce and prevent their pain and suffering, it is unacceptable for us to leave others to live in pain and suffering, to allow others to suffer with illness, injury and disease, when there are actions we can take to alleviate or remove their suffering and pain; it is unacceptable for us to allow others to endure illness-ridden and disease-prone environments, indeed to allow others to endure physically, mentally and emotionally destructive environments, when there are actions we could take to help alleviate or remove their pain and suffering and their vulnerability to such sources of pain and suffering.

The taking of no action under such circumstances, such indifferent, negligent, indeed callous and uncaring conduct is damaging for all of us, to each of us as individual people, to all others, to those closest to us who we love and care for most deeply. Such inaction undermines our communities and societies, both locally and beyond, through promulgating uncaring and indifferent attitudes within our communities and societies, undermining our sense of reciprocity in our communities, societies and beyond. Such inaction further undermines our communities, societies and our broader humanity through its non-recognition of and indifference to the lost contributions of those who are ill, who are in pain and suffering.

Also, in a perhaps more visibly and directly self-centred and self-focused motivation, such indifference and inaction in the face of illness and disease risks the spread of illness, and not only to those others living in such poverty and disease-ridden conditions and vulnerable to such illness and disease, but to those we know and to all others in the world around us. Indeed uncaring or indifferent acceptance of illness, injury and disease is also likely to undermine our efforts to research and identify cures and treatments, and our capacity to implement those cures and treatments, thus undermining all of our personal healths. And additionally where personal health is jeopardised physically, emotionally and otherwise, by violent and repressive regimes, inaction and indifference can lead to the spread of such destructive, health and well-being damaging behaviours.

Nevertheless, primarily, for the most of us, in response to the pain and suffering we see others enduring, we feel and understand this suffering and pain of others, and we are motivated to help these others through our feelings of love and care, through our empathy with our fellows, our humanity and concern for others. Indeed, for the most of us, we, in the vast main, feel love, care and concern for those who are blameless, indeed for almost anyone, if not anyone, who is suffering in pain, and we wish to help them escape their suffering, pains and indeed agonies. Our deep feelings of care, empathy and love need not only to be expressed but also acted upon in practical terms in support of those who are enduring such pain and suffering. Such feelings are a central part of our human identity; they are of central importance to our humanity and will comprise our central motivations for supporting others to escape their suffering and endurance of pain.

Our deep and caring feelings support and motivate our actions in helping others to escape that pain and suffering and support them in living their own lives of well-being and happiness. Not only does such support for others express our deep need and desire to look after and help others, but our practical actions in their support will, in the main, tend to benefit our own personal health and our own personal well-being and happiness, promoting reciprocity of care in our communities, societies and beyond, as well as promoting health and well-being in the round, within and beyond our societies and communities.

It has to be noted however, that while we are certainly motivated by our deep and caring human feelings, there are those reasons already mentioned, clear and more consciously recognised reasons, more selfish and self-focused reasons in relation to protecting our own health and the health of others around us, which perhaps in a biological sense serve to underlie our feelings of care and concern for others, but which can also explicitly, consciously and directly motivate us and indeed should reasonably and rationally motivate us, to support others who are suffering in pain. Such feelings of care and concern clearly can serve to benefit us all as individuals, can benefit others and serve to benefit us as a broader humanity.

Focusing in more detail on our actions and conduct as influenced by our health, it seems reasonable to say that our personal actions, our conduct and behaviour are likely to be significantly affected by our ongoing state and states of health and indeed our ongoing states of well-being. Our own state of physical health, the suffering and pain we endure when ill or physically injured, as already mentioned will influence all aspects of what we do, indeed it is the norm that they do. And then, beyond our physical health, our mental health, the way we feel and think on the moment, will also certainly affect what we do, how well we can do the things we can or want to do, indeed will determine if we can do them at all. Our mental health will affect how we spend and can spend our time, how effectively we spend that time, how we behave in general during the day, how we engage and interact with others, how we feel about our lives, how motivated we are to do things, how able we are to take the lead and engage in new initiatives, how resilient we are in the face of the problems, stresses and challenges that arise in our lives.

All of our thinking and feeling, conscious and unconscious, is reflected by, and in itself influences, our mental well-being, our mental states, our mental performance and mental alacrity. The decisions we make in all aspects of our daily lives, the decisions we make throughout our lives, will be heavily influenced by the way we are thinking and feeling, by our different and changing states of mind, our emotional selves, our state of understanding and knowledge, our mental capacities, and our positive or negative states of mind (and much in between) which are all central to our mental health. Being central to our well-being, clearly therefore, issues of mental well-being and mental health are crucial in our lives, with good mental health needing to be supported and our mental health needing to be thought about and addressed, not only in relation to our own individual state of personal health, well-being and happiness but also in relation to the effects of mental health on the range of our actions and decisions we take and our personal conduct.

Beyond our own personal and individual states of mental health and mental well-being, in terms of the core principles of supporting others, there is the specific need for us to support others to achieve and maintain positive mental health as well as a need for us to support those who are affected by difficulties with mental health. In regard to those of us with problems in terms of our mental health (which through a lifetime may probably represent a very large number of us), we may endure significant pain and suffering. Under such circumstances of mental pain, these states of mind, the way we feel and think, as with all of us in any situation, will influence, at least to some degree, how we behave and act. Our state of mind will certainly influence how we feel about ourselves and our lives, and how we feel about others and their lives. Along with the more direct pain and suffering that is likely to accompany our own personal mental health problems, our conduct as one of those who is suffering with mental health problems, as well as our needs when suffering mental pain and anguish, will likely present difficulties and challenges for others in our lives and our wider communities and societies, influencing the well-being and happiness of others. Thus, the state of our mental health, as individuals, for each one of us, not only ties in significantly with our well-being and happiness but will also influence the well-being and happiness of others.

And clearly, beyond our mental health and well-being, our physical health and physical well-being tie in to how we feel, our conduct and actions, representing, to some extent, not only a component of our state of well-being as a separate physical health component, but also often influencing how we feel and our personal mental health and well-being. Without doubt, physical injury and physical trauma can be very emotionally upsetting for us, causing many of us substantial mental anguish and pain. Further, and crucially, the physical diseases and illnesses, the physical injury and damage of various sorts that we experience, can be extremely debilitating keeping us confined to our homes and beds, confined to hospitals, feeling awful, in severe pain, even agony, at times, sometimes for long periods. As with our mental health, problems with our physical health influence, to varying degrees, the extent to which we can support others and indeed whether we can support them at all. Of course our own physical state of health influences whether others will in turn actually need to support us.

And with differing and changing physical capacities and abilities, differing resilience and vulnerabilities in terms of health, through the differing phases, age-wise in our lives, we will be, to differential degrees, capable of giving support to others and will have varying and differing needs of support ourselves. Certainly in childhood and almost certainly in the latter years of our lives, we will need more support with our health. In our earliest years we will of course need close, moment-to-moment and everyday support from our parents, families and others. And in our later years we may need substantial support from others such that we can manage our lives and enjoy an acceptable level of well-being and happiness. Hopefully we will still be able to help and support both ourselves and others in our later years and we have an obligation to do so where we can, yet it is of course also the case that we are likely to be more able to give practical support to others in our adult and in particular in our younger and middle to late years of adulthood.

Responsibility for our health and the health of others, as well as responsibility for supporting the avoidance of pain and suffering, lies with each of us as individuals, and with our communities, and our societies in the broadest sense, including those lying beyond the boundaries of our current states and nations. Our common human effort in the face of the various sources of pain and suffering, in the face of the potential illnesses diseases, injury and other threats to our health, a range of threats to our health which can, do and will affect us all, is an obligation and a necessity, reflected in the core and other principles. We need to, and indeed are obliged to act, not only in order to operate directly against these sources of pain and suffering and these various threats to our health, but to ensure conditions where such sources of pain and suffering are less able to arise.

And where we are fortunate enough to live in circumstances, in which, in particular, serious illnesses, diseases and injuries are less prone to arise, develop and spread, at least through the major period of our lives, we need to provide support to others who are facing such threats to their health, be it through directly providing resources to support implementation of actions against such illness and disease (for example through providing drugs and other medical treatments), be it through supporting research or through actually organising or doing research to tackle these threats, be it through communicating effectively with others about the need to counter such threats and through supporting and ensuring implementation of strategies that promote good health and positive well-being, for example through alleviating poverty and promoting good diet, or through other effective measures.

In regard to both our mental and physical health, both our more local and wider communities, societies and beyond, need to be able to act to both identify health needs and to organise systematically to address our individual, community and societal and global health needs. We need to ensure that we have appropriate people with appropriate knowledge, skills and training, appropriate structures and organisations at the community level and beyond, which act to address our physical and mental health needs. And we need to act to implement, where necessary and reasonable, the actions advocated and directed by such organisations and bodies which are aimed at improving health and well-being, as well as supporting those bodies in their legitimate actions to promote health and reduce suffering. As individuals, we need to ensure we act in a supportive manner in regard to these actions and initiatives. And further, we need to identify and use credible and reasoned, evidence and advice, and take actions to ensure and improve our own personal health in all its aspects, with our acting as individuals to support our own health the health of other individuals and to support the health of our local and broader communities and societies, more generally. Part of this is almost certain to involve contributing some of our own personal material resources and indeed where appropriate, contributing our own personal time and efforts, in order to ensure we, other individuals, our local and wider communities, societies and our broader community, are protected from illness, injury and disease as far as is reasonably possible.

Avoiding focus on and failing to give sufficient attention to health, as individuals, communities, societies and beyond, is dangerous in the extreme, with illness, poor health, disease, presenting threats to our well-being on an enormous scale, and allowing the potential for suffering, pain and the greatest of distress for us all. We need therefore, as individuals, communities and societies, to provide sufficient resources, commitment and attention in regard to health. We need to educate about illness and disease, plan ahead for future health threats, conduct research and indeed proactive research in a biological and microbiological world of changing threats that are likely to represent a danger to our health. As individuals, communities and societies, as a broad humanity, we must tackle the environmental challenges to our health arising through waste hazards, pollution and other sources of health threat which present substantial and severe dangers to our health and wellbeing. And similarly, we need to deal with, at an individual, community and societal level, the range of mental health challenges arising through individual psychological and social factors, which also represent a significant threat to us all.

Clearly our maintaining our physical and mental health is central to our well-being and happiness. While there will be much common ground among us as to what comprises positive health, nevertheless, providing a broad and all encompassing definition of what in fact comprises such positive health can be complex and so as with other terminology considered in this guide, this chapter does not aim to provide a formal wide ranging definitive dictionary-like definition of such positive health. Suffice to say that being healthy, enjoying positive health must require an absence of physical and mental illness and debilitating injury, with preferably these being accompanied by comfortable and positive if not pleasant, comfortable and pleasurable feelings of well-being, satisfaction, physical and mental fitness, personal strength (mentally and physically), a sense of self-value self-efficacy and achievement, a sense of belonging, of being respected, wanted and being loved, and indeed perhaps also, at the higher end of positive health, feeling happy, successful and fulfilled. Absence of the more positive elements mentioned may not mean that we are significantly unhealthy but each of these can certainly contribute to our being and feeling healthy. And as demonstrated by what is included here as being part of our positive health, our being healthy will usually, if not always, or nearly always, also involve healthy, positive, satisfying, satisfactory, hopefully happy, enriching relationships with those around us, which is not to say that each moment of all of our relationships will be emotionally positive.

Physical injury, physical illness and disease, conditions which damage our physical selves in particular, certainly damage our personal well-being and the well-being of others around us. Physical injury, physical illness, and disease impair our performance in the things we wish to do. And though often temporary in their effects, physical damage to our selves, to our bodies, can cause us serious long-term damage and of course in some cases death. Not only does such physical injury damage us personally in itself representing painful and negative experience, but the damage to our well-being, to varying degrees dependent on the nature and extent of the damage our physical injury does to us, can negatively influence our capacity to seek well-being and happiness in other areas of our lives and of course, as already mentioned in this chapter, damage our capacity to support and contribute to others, our communities, societies and beyond (something which in itself, of course, is likely to damage us as individuals as well).

The effects of physical injury and illness on our mental health and emotional state have already been mentioned in broad terms, but more specifically, in particular on account of these illnesses, injuries and diseases, we may well find that we become demotivated and dispirited, representing, of course, a lower state of happiness, even depression and affecting our overall mental well-being, all of this being further reason to focus on maintaining and protecting our health. Even with more minor conditions, such as fevers, flu, stomach pains, headaches, and the like, in addition to the direct pain we may experience, these conditions will debilitate us and are likely to lead to tiredness and lethargy, further damaging our capacities to do the things that we want to do. even though they may not, at least for some if not many of us, substantially diminish our sense of happiness.

Of course we should do all within our power, wherever we can, to avoid physical injury, illness and disease of any sort. For many medical conditions and many other injuries, happily and fortunately, if we take care of ourselves in appropriate ways, if we seek and receive the necessary medical treatment, then, for the many of us, at least in the current modern world, though less so for those living in poverty, we will recover after a short period of illness and will hopefully be revived, returning to our normal healthy selves, after our short period of illness.

Similarly, while some if not many physical injuries may debilitate us and affect us emotionally, as well as causing us at times (and perhaps in some cases) persistently, severe physical pains, it is often the case that many physical injuries, if we act appropriately, look after ourselves appropriately and if we are treated correctly, while being painful for a while, after a short or quite a short and unpleasant period of time, our pain will dissipate and disappear, hopefully within a reasonable time, releasing us to return to our normal everyday life. And in many cases of illness and physical injury we may well, to all intents and purposes, forget that the illness or injury actually occurred at all.

But in addition to our more minor physical injuries and encounters with illness and disease, other illnesses, infections, diseases and health conditions damage us more and are more intense and long-lasting, possibly in some cases for some of us, creating an ongoing sense of debilitation and demoralisation, over time affecting what we can do in our lives to a significant extent and significantly damaging our own well-being. And as such longer term conditions, they may significantly affect what we can do in our everyday lives, affect how we can live and how we can enjoy and contribute to our world, with such debilitation affecting us over a lengthy period of time, even permanently.

As with milder conditions, we will in the first place, wherever this is possible (and in many serious cases it may not be possible), need to do our utmost within reason to ensure that we do not acquire such illnesses (which in some cases, for example, where diseases are inherited, or for a range of other reasons, may be impossible to avoid), behaving in safe and personally protective ways in our daily lives, avoiding habits and behaviours which might seem to offer danger or limited danger in the short term, but which for example, might damage us in the long term. Such actions in the current time on an individual level would mean, for example avoiding things like lung damaging and cancer causing smoking, the use of drugs which can damage our health or drinking excessive alcohol (in itself widely considered a drug).

If we are afflicted by serious injury or serious illness, on an individual level, we need to seek out the most appropriate medical treatment available at the earliest opportunity, and take advantage of this treatment, something, of course, for which we may require little incentive. Hopefully such treatment will be available to us though this may be dependent on where we live and the resources we have available as individuals and the resources available to help us which may be available in our wider community and society. In many cases we will certainly need to seek out information about the available treatments and in some cases the personal actions we may be able to take to overcome our injury, illness or disease.

We may well need to show quite a bit of resilience and mental strength in dealing with such serious conditions, but with appropriate medical treatment, the support of others, of those we love, our communities and societies, we will hopefully be able to live with and overcome our health problems and survive such health crises. If our health problems will be long term we need to do our utmost and seek out help to alleviate our pain, to reduce our pain and suffering, such that we can experience the minimum pain and the maximum well-being, happiness and pleasure that we can achieve, even though such more positively focused experiences and outcomes may seem distant if not irrelevant when we are suffering in pain and agony and solely wish for appropriate treatment and an end to our pain.

And of course, as individuals we need to support others who are going through such health challenges and crises, those who are suffering and in pain, supporting them through our emotional support, or through our practical and material support, paying for medical systems, social medical systems which ensure medical care for those who are suffering with such challenging injuries and illnesses.

Of course our most serious illnesses and physical injuries will sometimes lead us, sometimes precipitately, to our deaths. Facing terminal illnesses, in addition to the challenges of coping with the often severe pain we may have to endure, we will also have to deal with and cope with the potential challenge and realisation that we will soon no longer be alive, a potentially traumatic idea to think of and state of being to face, although of course this is for all of us a fact of life which we all should take some time to think about and consider at times. Coming to terms with this reality is a necessity (at least in our current age and for the foreseeable future) and for the sake of our well-being and happiness and the well-being and happiness of those around us, such a 'coming to terms with' and a recognition of our human reality and the inevitability of this reality, is of benefit to us and of great value in supporting us to enjoy a full life of well-being and happiness.

For the vast majority of us, in most circumstances, we do not require significantly convincing arguments to be made in order for us to try to avoid illnesses, disease and injury. In the vast range of circumstances, for most of us that is, at least in the immediacy of our every day lives, taking appropriate actions to avoid pain and suffering is part of our human selves, our human identity. In many if not the vast main of cases and situations, without, in many situations, much conscious awareness and thought, we avoid sources and threats of pain and suffering; we move away from sources of danger, illness and pain. However, there are some ways of behaving which, even in the absence of evidence from systematic research, may be dangerous to our health without that danger being immediately obvious on the moment. For example, systematic research and investigation was needed to establish the link between cigarette smoking, cancer and heart disease.

Yet whatever our personal efforts, through what is to a large extent, the almost inevitability of illness, disease and indeed injury of some kind, originating in our human biological vulnerabilities and deficiencies, through our aging and physical deterioration, through the presence of infection-causing microorganisms in our environments or other environmental factors, we will be vulnerable to illness, disease and injury. Through accidents and natural disaster, indeed through physical assaults on us, through war, oppression and violent conflict we can be exposed to severe injury, illness and disease.

And, more in the range of areas we can take individual action about, through our poor thinking, inertia, through carelessness, through our thirst for risk and danger, through lack of concentration, lack of attention to our health and well-being, we can also increase the risks to our health and well-being. For example through poor hygiene practices, lack of cleanliness, we can be vulnerable and make others vulnerable to illness and infection. Through lack of thought, lack of preparation and lack of due care and attention when entering situations of potential danger, we can leave ourselves open to physical injury. And, at the community and society level, through being unprepared for the real threats our environment can offer us, not only through simple local accidents, but through natural disasters such as earthquakes, heatwaves, droughts, famines, tornados, and flooding, amongst other environmental threats, and also through damage arising from our human pollution and damage to the environment, we can also leave ourselves open to injury, illness and disease.

At the individual level, while we may without much thought avoid many of the more obvious sources of pain and suffering, we certainly do need to motivate ourselves to take more conscious and planned actions in order to protect our health and well-being, and avoid suffering and pain. And we, as individuals and as communities and societies, need information and awareness about threats to our health and the strategies and actions we can put into place to forestall these threats. And sometimes we as individuals will need others, our communities and societies, our global social entities, our social organisations, to point out to us where our behaviours and actions may be damaging our health and indeed perhaps the health of others. Using our own motivation for action to support our health, our own knowledge and understanding, with the advice and information we can gain from others, our communities and societies and beyond, we will be able to act to promote our health in an effective, proactive and positive manner.

Having considered in broad terms aspects relating to our individual health and the individual health of others, in addition to thinking about such individual health, we can also recognise and talk of healthy societies and healthy communities. In using the term healthy communities and societies, we are referring to those communities and societies wherein people live together in one form or another, get on well together, cooperate together, enjoy life peaceably together and of course enjoy good levels of individual health and well-being. Health in this context not only refers to an absence of illness, disease and injury but also significantly to the overall and individual quality of social relationships within these communities as well as incorporating the idea of the general well-being of the individuals within these communities and societies.

In such healthy communities and societies, there may be important differences between individuals, between community and social groups and between community and social group members. These might in some circumstances have the potential to lead to serious and damaging conflict, but in healthy communities and societies, there are likely to be effective and successful mechanisms for dealing with these individual and group differences, with individuals being prepared to accept such mechanisms as rational and reasonable and with serious differences being resolved in peaceful ways. Within these healthy communities, group and individual differences may be seen as ordinary and normal parts of life which are to be enjoyed and which enrich individual lives and the life of the community, with many of such differences not generally being seen as serious issues worthy of generating tensions, intense discord and damaging conflict. Of course where individuals or such a group offers significant threats to well-being and happiness, offer threats of pain and suffering to others, then action will need to be taken, sometimes robust action to counter such threats. Nevertheless, our having such healthy communities and societies, within the overall framework of supporting well-being and happiness and the avoidance of pain and suffering, is a worthy goal and entirely consistent with the principles set out in this guide.

Of course, at the individual level, avoiding pain and suffering and promoting our own health and the health of others requires us to avoid the range of already mentioned major threats to our existence as far as we can, such threats including not only the diseases and illnesses which have mostly been referred to up to now, but also violence in its various guises, as well as natural and other catastrophes and disasters which may arise in the form of the already mentioned flooding, famine, tsunamis, earthquakes, tornados and more. These forms of disaster affect enormous numbers of people every year throughout the world, or at least they do so in our current times, causing damage to health and well-being for a vast number of people,

To some extent, at least at the present time, due to our current lack of knowledge and understanding, as well as the magnitude of and our lack of control over some natural phenomena, there is little that can be done in terms of preventing some of these threats. There is certainly an element of unpredictability given our present state of knowledge and understanding of phenomena such as earthquakes and extreme weather. However some individual and social action can be taken to prepare for and therefore to preserve and maintain our health in the face of such potential disasters, for example through keeping stores of food and water available in anticipation of droughts, varying crops as a protection against disease, building appropriately and safely constructed buildings, flood defences and the provision of early warning systems where possible for earthquakes and tsunamis.

These are important threats to health, well-being and happiness, and we need to ensure that the range of preparatory actions against such disasters and catastrophes are being taken as far as possible, in order to protect all of us who might be affected. It is sometimes argued, frequently by those who are perhaps less likely to suffer the effects of such disasters, that resources are not available to deal with some of these threats. Nevertheless, where we do nothing, and no preparations are made, the consequences of such threats and disasters tend to be much more costly for all when these almost inevitable events take place and the financial costs of such disaster preparation tend to be much smaller when compared to the real financial costs arising from such disasters. But, more importantly, the human cost of such disasters is tremendous and thus we must take appropriate actions, as far as is possible and reasonable, to invest in and act to support our personal protection and defence against such disasters.

Of course, amongst other disasters and forming part of many natural disasters (and in some cases human origin disasters), there is the possibility of degrees of, or absolute starvation through significantly inadequate diet, crop destruction and poor harvests due to lack of labour and other factors, resulting in a lack of availability and access to food, and leading to the pain and suffering of malnutrition and disease. In such circumstances, where there are those of us in other places who have access to more than sufficient or excess food, and where we have the capability to transport that food to those who are starving, or where we are in a position to support the provision of food through allocation and giving of our own resources, then, consistent with the framework of the core and other principles, that is what we must do, ensuring our support for these others and their survival. Given in particular the frequencies of such famines and starvations, beyond that provision once a crisis has arisen, we need to have mechanisms in place such that we are prepared for such crises and ready to help out those in need in a rapid and expeditious manner, reducing as far as possible and as quickly as possible the pain and suffering that might be endured. And as individuals who may ourselves be threatened by such starvation, whether planning ahead or embroiled in such threatening circumstances, we need to do all we can to act to prevent such threats to our own survival, and to our well-being and happiness as well making sure that we support the survival, well-being and happiness of others around us as far as we can in these trying and challenging circumstances, in particular through sharing what we have with others in need.

Many of these famines, many incidents of starvation, some shortages in some places, should be anticipated as natural events which will sometimes occur. Whether natural or not, such famines can and indeed must be prepared for, and those with power and resources in those places where such famines are more likely to occur, as well as within the more wealthy nations and states, those with abundant resources, we all have an obligation to ensure that as far as possible, no one at all suffers, and where this is not possible, where such a goal is beyond our powers, we need to ensure that the minimum number of people suffer to the most minimal degree possible. Arguments which place others, on the grounds of their distance from us, on the grounds of race or other features, as of less value than other individuals, as of lesser value than other peoples, are inconsistent with the principles laid out in this guide, which sees all people, all of us, as being fundamentally equal, of equal value, in terms of our fundamental humanity.

In terms of general living and survival on a day-to-day basis, in regard to food supply, if we are the growers of food, the providers of food, the farmers, the farm managers, the distributors, the bureaucrats and administrators, if we are the sellers, the politicians and governments, it is of course our significant responsibility to carry out our roles in supporting food production, storage and distribution, as efficiently and effectively as possible, maintaining as far as we can a safe and secure food production system and food supply chain, and ensuring that there is sufficient provision for all, for each individual, with none excepted.

Where our individual, organisationa, community and societal activities can influence the agricultural environment in a damaging way; where the economic policies of our communities, societies and beyond, or our own individual or organisational actions might impinge in a damaging manner on the generation and consumption of food and, indeed damage the provision of essential water supplies, in the latter case for example through polluting water supplies, then we have to ensure that such damage does not in fact occur, is prevented, exercising our responsibility to ensure that others do not suffer lacks and the accompanying pain and suffering resulting from such damage, ensuring that we all have access to the necessary clean and healthy food and water essential for our lives. This is of course consistent with the core and other principles set out in this guide.

And on top of these sources of threat from what are the more natural disasters, in terms of threats to our health, there are the also wars – civil, international, possibly global and other – embodying the social conflicts, the range of violent and murderous disputes which threaten and damage severely the health and well-being of so many of us. Again, each of us as individuals needs to act to prevent such violence and such conflict. Consequences of these wars and conflicts of course include premature death, severe physical injuries, mental trauma, destitution, illness and disease, death from severe cold and hypothermia as well the starvation already mentioned, with all of these occurring on a vast scale to millions, and having been inflicted on millions in the major wars and conflicts our humanity has experienced.

All of this, the poverty, suffering, pain and destitution caused by wars, is itself caused by the destruction of the range of other systems which serve to support our well-being and our health in peaceful times, with accompanying destruction of buildings of all sorts, medical facilities, shelter, agricultural production and distribution systems, water and food supply, sewerage, and more, along with destruction and displacement of those of us involved in managing and implementing these systems. The necessity for avoidance of these wars has been discussed at length in chapter twelve, and the necessity of aiming to prevent such wars and conflicts and of supporting cooperativity and togetherness is entirely clear in terms of the core and other principles.

In order to deal with both human-origin and natural disasters we, as individuals all need to make our contributions as far as we can, taking our own individual actions to support those in need, in pain and suffering, ensuring that there are organisations and systems in place for responding to these crises, and using our energies to support our local, national and global organisations in addressing whichever disaster may be occurring. This may involve direct and more individual support or supporting these efforts and organisations at a distance. All forms of support are required and they are required from all of us.

Indeed, the frequent occurrence of one disaster or another, of various types and origins, the disasters of war or disasters caused by natural phenomena, means that while we as individuals (as far as we can), as communities, as societies, as a global community must support and be involved in developing strategies and action plans which anticipate the almost certain occurrence of such natural (and other) disasters, additionally, in our roles as individuals, as communities. societies and global entities through which individual actions are realised, we need also to continually aim to build and strengthen the systems we have in place and set in place, in order to both anticipate and prevent the range of disasters wherever this is possible. Thus in order to prevent destructive wars and conflicts, we need mechanisms for supporting cooperation, peace and problem resolution, and in terms of the more natural disasters, as already referred to, we need to have prepared 'ready to go' systems to support those who may be in desperate need.

And once disaster has struck, we will need to act immediately to ensure the minimum damage, pain and suffering occur, to ensure the minimum level of ensuing problems arise in the more immediate aftermath and in the short medium and long term after the disaster. Thus, we, as communities, organisations and societies, local and global, need to have preventative and reactive systems, actions plans and resources available and on standby, such that we are ready to deal with any disasters, natural or otherwise, which might occur. It is the responsibility of each one of us to ensure that we individually, our communities and societies, our global organisations are prepared for such eventualities.

Turning to consider our health at a more individual level, in terms of our own more personal lives and our more individual day-to-day personal health, it is central to us as human beings that, as far as is possible, we enjoy good health and well-being and support ourselves in having and enjoying health and well-being.

In relation to our personal, general physical health, we all need to have a good understanding of what it means to be in good physical health and what that means for us as an individual in particular. And to pursue our good health, we need to set aside time in our own lives, in our daily lives, such that we can pursue our good physical health, as well as ensuring we have time to plan in regard to, time to think about, to reflect on, monitor and check our own physical health.

Of course, while comprising an element and indeed an important element of our lives, concern with our health should not become such an obsession that it takes up our every waking moment. We have other activities, actions and principles in life to consider and other elements of our life and goals in our lives, other important sources of personal richness, well-being and fulfillment that we need to and wish to pursue, yet of course, as already pointed to in this chapter, it is very difficult to pursue these other elements and goals as effectively as, and as much as we would wish, without enjoying good physical health, though much can still be achieved and done in terms of supporting our pleasure and well-being, if our health is less than optimum. Nevertheless, setting aside too much time to focus on physical activity and health will deny us time to pursue our other important goals.

Of course, by contrast, it is likely that failing to set aside sufficient time to focus on health, and failing to set aside sufficient time to engage in healthy activity, may themselves damage our health and damage the pursuit and achievement of our other desires, goals and priorities. To reduce our chances of experiencing physical pain and suffering, something which the vast majority of us desire, and which is of course in line with core and other principles, and in order to promote our positive health and well-being, there are a wide range of actions we can take.

In the first place with regard to our personal health, given what is known at the current time and given what seems to be strong evidence in the round, we need to pursue our physical well-being and reduce the chances of our enduring discomfort, pain and suffering, through aiming for physical fitness using appropriate physical exercise and physical activity. Such physical activity and exercise is, with quite a high level of certainty, for the vast majority of us, likely to reduce the chances of our contracting a number of health conditions which are thought, if not known to stem from, or be influenced by, too much inactivity, diseases including heart disease, obesity and a range of other health conditions. Yet deliberate physical exercise designed to improve our health, to help us maintain our strength, fitness and athleticism, also makes the daily tasks we have to do and some of the less frequent physical tasks we sometimes have to do, more easy, with our having less chance of picking up painful and unnecessary injuries when we do our more minor physical tasks.

Of course, for those of us in work, and indeed for everybody in all aspects of our lives, our physical fitness, exercise and activity should and does, serve to support, not only our personal health, but also our social lives, our social contributions, and our economic and other activity. Our physical fitness, through supporting our health, in the vast main, supports contribution to the community, obviating against absence from work (sometimes prolonged) and difficulty with work tasks caused by illnesses, as well as supporting us in attending and contributing to activities outside of our paid or otherwise rewarded work. Our strong physical health and exercise in pursuit of such health helps us to avoid periods when we are unable to contribute to others and to our communities and societies, our broader humanity through illness and disease, tied to our lack of physical fitness and health.

Our physical fitness also, in the main, contributes to us having longer lives, enabling us to enjoy our lives, enjoy well-being and happiness, for longer and enables us to contribute to our communities and societies for longer. It is challenging, and certainly less easy, though not impossible, to contribute to our own well-being and the well-being of others while suffering from physical pain, while bearing physical injuries which prevent or damage our ability to our act and contribute. And should we be suffering from physical pain, then we should still do our utmost to gain pleasure and enjoyment when this is possible, and support ourselves and others in whichever ways are possible.

The benefits of maintaining our physical health through exercise of one sort or another undoubtedly support our well-being. Taking time to exercise our bodies at appropriate levels of stress and intensity enhances our personal physical strength and fitness and not only serves to support the prevention of illness and pain, but in itself can be a source of substantial pleasure and well-being, arising through the social nature of much exercise and the various biochemical and psychologically positive effects of exercise.

In practical terms we can take the necessary exercise which benefits our physical health, in many ways. We can take our exercise in the context of what are often more individual activities such as running, walking, and weight bearing activities (although none of these need to be totally individual activities), or through more social exercise such as dancing, martial arts classes, group tai-chi, pilates classes, sports of various kinds such as football, cricket, baseball, American football, rugby, tennis, table-tennis and the range of other sports we engage in in our modern world.

Taking part in individual exercise such as running, swimming, gym training and walking, particularly for those of us living more sedentary lives, can give much needed exercise for our hearts, exercise our muscles and give us great pleasure in many ways, through for example, in the case of running and walking, experiencing the outdoors, the fresh air, natural environment and the feelings induced by the hormones and other biochemicals released into our blood streams through the taking of our exercise. Such individual exercise can also provide us with both time to think and not think, time to escape from our worries and concerns, distracting us from these concerns and worries, forcing us to focus on the minutiae of our exercise, or other less stressful and more minor immediate physical challenges, providing an opportunity to relax our minds, providing us sometimes with much needed space away from others and the demands of these others and the world, and providing some distraction and indeed stimulation, challenge and excitement away from what may be the more mundane, annoying and tedious aspects of our lives.

Supporting our positive health, we can deliberately focus on challenge and the pleasure that challenging ourselves can bring, since in almost all individual sporting and exercise activities, we can set ourselves goals and targets, for example, in terms of distances and length of time spent running, challenging ourselves within reason to lift new weights, to go further or faster with our swimming or walking, developing greater flexibility in our exercises based on movement, pushing ourselves to new achievements and gaining the psychological and physical benefits of having done better than before, having done the new and achieved the new. We can entertain and extend ourselves by trying our best, and we can also focus on winning in more team-based or competitive sports and exercise.

In addition to its benefits in terms of our more direct physical fitness and support of certain more individual aspects of mental health, participation in team sports has related social benefits, encouraging us to get out of the room, house or flat and encouraging us to interact, be with and cooperate with others with some common shared purpose and indeed often supporting a sense of identity (though of course often competing against others who have an opposite purpose, that of defeating our team – yet there can often be cooperation, friendship and togetherness with these others too), providing us with friends and companions, perhaps friends and companions for life and in some cases even life partners.

Through our participation in sports and other forms of exercise we can experience feelings of excitement, joy and exhilaration, experiencing intense moments and times of pleasure through the profound exaltation of sporting victories, achievement and a sense of belonging and togetherness, with indeed in some cases, team sports providing an important anchor for each of us as individuals within our communities and societies, enhancing mental health and personal well-being, as well as providing the important physical health benefits through the actual activity our team sports entail. And thus of course sporting exercise, individual and team sports often, if not for the most part, and in the round, support our well-being and happiness, their pursuit being in line with core and other principles.

Unfortunately, one by-product of sports and physical exercise can be physical injury and this is not infrequent. Our individual health requires that we do as much as we can and as much as is reasonable to maintain and improve our physical condition and health while engaging in our individual sporting and personal exercise activities. However, moving to new more trying challenges in our individual activities, extending ourselves to new levels and achievements, attempting activities which we have not done before, should generally be done with care, incrementally to reduce the risks of physical injury, to ensure as far as possible that we are not temporarily or otherwise injured or disabled.

Moreover, through over-extending ourselves, being too competitive in competitive sports, becoming sometimes carried away with the desire to win, and for some, in some cases being carried away with unwarranted and over-the-top aggression, sometimes this representing violence and in some cases intended violence, it is possible to cause ourselves and others to be the victims of various injuries, sometimes of great severity. Such violent aggression aimed at hurting other team and competitive sport participants is not acceptable within the terms of core and other principles. Each one of us needs to be mindful of balancing the pleasure, joys and indeed thrills of exercise and sporting competition with the potential damage we and others might incur and inflict through adopting overly-competitive attitudes when engaged in such competitive sporting activities. Of course, in physical team sports, at whatever level, clashes and injuries are most likely inevitable at some point in time. There will be risks and small chances of unusual collisions, accidents, bumps and breaks which, though low in probability, are likely to happen to someone, sometime, somewhere.

Those of us taking part in our competitive and other sports need to engage safely in our sporting activity, being physical where necessary and as required by the reasonable rules of our sports, but not being reckless in regard to our own health or the health of others. We need to ensure both that we are safe and that others are safe in the sporting contests and other physical activities we participate in. And that is a priority and is consistent and necessary within the terms of the core and other principles.

In certain sports, to greater or lesser degrees, an element of risk or danger may provide an integral part of the excitement, thrill and enjoyment of the sport. For example motor sports and other forms of racing have the constant danger of crashes at high speed, which will endanger the life, in the case of motor sports, of the vehicle drivers in particular. Those involved in such sports, taking such risks and facing such dangers need to protect themselves and be protected to the maximum, with similar protection provided to those who play other risk-facing roles or spectate in such sports and competitions.

Moreover, in certain physical, competitive sports there is a requirement to deliberately aim to injure the opponent. Such contact sports can only be considered acceptable within core and other principles when each party is sufficiently protected from short and long-term damage. Where such protection cannot be provided then that sport needs to be modified, restricted or banned. Boxers, for example, are exposed to significant risk of head injury through various forms of blow to the head. The effects of blows to the head are known, with damage to brain function likely resulting for many who take part in this sport in the long run and also the threat of more immediate death through traumatic blows and bleeds in the brain. Whatever the level of thrill and entertainment derived from a sport such as boxing it is crucial that those participating do not face or experience such potential brain injury.

Nevertheless, that being said we have a highly significant level, though not complete autonomy, in regard to taking part in such sports and competitions, with the choice of placing ourselves at some risk if that is what we freely choose to do, and within the context that there is a low possibility of being significantly injured, and that all possible steps are taken to ensure our physical and emotional health and well-being. If there is substantial real risk and high probability of injury to ourselves and others, this places a burden on all of us, through our requirement and obligations as fellow human beings, whether this is wanted by the individual facing or experiencing danger or injury or not. The concerns that we all have for others, our human concern for others, is real, part of our humanity and is central to core principles. We others, desire, and are obliged to support and protect those who are in danger or whose health is being or has been damaged and this has to be recognised by those placing themselves in danger and who are placing themselves at risk, with we who are in danger obliged to protect ourselves to the maximum and with obligations placed on others to protect us.

The arguments in the case of each individual sport are complex, but clearly at the minimum, with regard to its specific case, the sport of boxing needs to be made more safe and most likely should be displaced by other safer activities. Yet such sports cannot be taken out of their social context. For some, such a sport may represent their best option for achievement, their best chance to avoid poverty, perhaps to avoid a mundane life and in a sense a way out of poverty. Thus, for community and society, we must not only make sporting activities as safe as possible, but in the case of sports where there is a likely risk, we need not only to make these more safe, but also provide palatable and reasonable options for those who participate such that they will be able to live full lives of well-being, fulfillment and happiness. And for many of us, of course, it has to be acknowledged that we do desire a certain level of excitement in our lives, which is likely to involve our taking some risk, experiencing some challenges and dangers.

Other physical sporting contests can involve our deliberately aiming to frighten and intimidate others. Again we have the autonomy and rights to agree to participate in such sporting and physical contests, but yet again, those participating need to be protected from possible significant psychological harm, in particular as succumbing to intimidation can leave lasting emotional scars on those who have been frightened into submission or into failure. In terms of core and other principles, efforts to intimidate and frighten should not be made, due to the fact of such consequences. Our conduct in sports must at the minimum comply with agreed procedures in the game or sport and must not go beyond such boundaries and procedures without sanctions implemented against those breaching the agreed rules and procedures. Whatever the agreed rules in a sport, violence and verbal threats to injure others in sports such as football, cricket, rugby or any other sport, threats made in various guises, are entirely unacceptable, though passionate and committed sport and play are certainly not.

Beyond those injuries caused through aggression and violence in team sports, our physical injuries during exercise and sport can also occur seemingly spontaneously without any obvious specific external cause, with injuries creeping up on us and becoming more frequent as we age or simply occurring through over-straining ourselves and pushing ourselves too hard. These injuries can be minor in nature but can in some instances have carry over effects into our other aspects of our daily lives. We certainly need to take care in the range of contexts, pushing ourselves to achieve should we wish to do so, but operating physically within the bounds of that which we believe we are capable of, knowing the limits of what we can do without too high a risk of injury. And we should continually revisit these limits and boundaries as we age and change, dependent on our awareness of ourselves, our fitness and condition on the moment, in order to ensure that we avoid what can be painful and unpleasant debilitating injuries.

Our fitness activities and the pursuit of our fitness and health optimally needs to be conducted in line with the best understanding at the specific time of how we can promote and maintain our fitness. With such understanding combined with self-awareness and care and attention in regard to what we do in terms of sports and exercise, we should be able to ensure that we do not run unnecessary risk of injuries, and the accompanying pain and pains that may result.

The purpose of fitness and sporting activity is certainly not to strain ourselves such that we incur injuries that will prevent us taking part in our other activities, thereby preventing or inhibiting our enjoyment of our lives outside such sports and activities. And so we need to take care with our fitness and sport, while gaining the maximum pleasure we can from our sporting and fitness activities. Nor should we exhaust ourselves mentally and physically through our sporting and fitness activities such that we are unable to participate in our ordinary daily lives. Such physical and fitness activities need to be conducted in balance and in line with the other important activities we need to engage in during our everyday lives. Nevertheless we do need to engage in maintaining our fitness, which should support us in our capacity to engage in our other daily activities, whether our fitness activities and exercise involve us in the already mentioned walking, swimming, running, dance, martial arts such as Tai Chi, or indeed any other physical activity or sport. And this applies to all age groups.

Of course in addition to physical injuries we may also, on some occasions, feel down and depressed through failure in both our individual efforts to achieve that which we would like to achieve fitness-wise, and through our failure to achieve in a similar manner in our competitive team sports. In the area of sports and competition we can be upset at our own incompetence and inadequacies, annoyed at the failings of our teammates, angry at the rules, at officials, at our not being selected for the team, angry at our opponents, sometimes because of their superior skills, sometimes because we think, sometimes incorrectly, but sometimes correctly that they are cheating or involved in gamesmanship. These and a range of other negative thoughts and feelings, can accompany competitive team sports. We need to have approaches and philosophies which enable us to enjoy our participation in team sports, respecting our opponents and team mates wherever we can, accepting that there will sometimes be wrong decisions by officials, yet of course being robust and constructive in the face of blatant rule-breaking and cheating.

But not all of us enjoy such competitive team sports. Our preferred sporting activities can be the more individual ones already mentioned, which may in some contexts become competitive but may be competitive to a lesser degree, in different ways, or indeed not competitive at all (though we may in a sense compete with ourselves, challenging ourselves to achieve more, do better and reach our peak performance). Dance for example, can be athletic and enjoyable without the sense of formal competition with others (though again we may well be inclined to compare ourselves with others). In physically demanding sports such as gymnastics we can challenge ourselves, compete with others, and pursue and enjoy fitness. If we walk or jog to pursue fitness, walking and jogging not being in the main, for the most of us, so much sports, then we can challenge ourselves to walk and jog further, but simply fitness and health may be our main goals.

And of course, some of us, at least in regard to team sports, are simply less wishing of participation in, and indeed some of us are even significantly lacking in competence at, some or perhaps most team sports, and may not as a consequence wish to engage in these, wishing to avoid the humiliations and sense of failure we may feel and experience through such social activity and through the public demonstration of our lack of sporting competence (though fortunately we can often enjoy sports even without displaying competence!). Nevertheless, some form of exercise is important for all of us and for those of us who are not so keen on such team sports, we need to build and maintain our fitness through those more individual activities in order to support our health, both physical and mental.

All of this previous discussion is not to say that doing physical exercise is some kind of absolute requirement in order to fulfill the principles set out in this guide. For most of us, physical exercise to achieve physical fitness is of great importance supporting us in achieving lives of enhanced well-being, supporting ourselves and helping others. Indeed we have obligations to family, children, the people we love, to do what we can to ensure we maintain our health, of which physical exercise of some sort is highly likely to be an important part. We need to be around, that is alive, in order to enjoy our lives as they can be enjoyed and fulfilled, to enjoy well-being, in the so many ways in which that is possible. We need to be alive to support the people we love, and indeed to support the communities, societies we live in and in order to support our wider humanity and wider world. And maintaining our physical fitness will, in the vast main, help us in this.

However, that being said, there is no intention to say in this guide that such exercise should be compulsory or is an absolute obligation. There is the possibility that such activity does not fit in with our own particular circumstances, character, inclinations, perceptions and beliefs about well-being, and indeed in certain exceptional cases, in regard to certain medical conditions, particular types of exercise or even exercise in general may threaten and damage well-being and health. Further, our exercise and sporting activities also take up time and so in a sense may sometimes, if given too much focus and taken to too great a length, distract us from other important goals, roles and tasks in our lives relevant to supporting core and other principles, especially in relation to the support of others. While important as social activities, the pleasures of sport and activity are significantly focused on our own personal well-being, fitness and enjoyment, which can certainly be of benefit to others. Nevertheless, we should take care to give appropriate emphasis to pursuing our fitness through exercise and activity, retaining awareness and focus on our other goals in life, our support and care for others, our communities, societies and beyond, something which does not necessarily preclude such an emphasis, sometimes an intense emphasis on exercise and activity.

Our taking of physical exercise is certainly highly recommended and seen as consistent with core and other principles. Those who are unwilling to engage in physical activity and exercise, are on the whole, likely to be engaging in incorrect judgments either to some degree or entirely, though such omission is far from comprising the most significant breach of core and other principles. As matters in regards to what is substantially our own health and our own bodies and minds are highly personal and individual, despite the potential effects on others of our failing to promote our own physical fitness through exercise, it seems reasonable to note that we as individuals, to an important degree, as mentioned with regard to pursuit of more dangerous sports, are significantly, though not entirely autonomous in regard to the actions we take in pursuit of our own health. We must therefore, as adults, in the vast majority of circumstances, be the ones who make the key decisions relating to our fitness and physical health, optimally in the possession of full knowledge of the consequences of our actions and inactions on our own lives and the lives of those around us. It should certainly be added, emphasised and reiterated, however, that those of us who make no or little effort to engage in the pursuit of fitness through exercise and who make no or little effort to develop and remain fit, have a greater chance of becoming unhealthy and as a consequence will thereby place burdens on others in terms of supporting us with our health, something which again would be contrary to core and other principles and detract from our capacity to provide support for others as well as damaging the self. Others, therefore, have some responsibility to persuade us, gently, that exercise would most likely benefit us and others, our communities and societies.

The level and type of physical exercise we can engage in will, to an important extent, be dependent on our age. Yet at all ages some form of exercise is possible for us, be it through repetition of small movements of limbs, stretching of muscles, bending of knees, arms, movement of the head, short walks, gentle dances and the like for those who are more elderly, to much more vigorous and expansive exercises involving long runs, heavy weights, sprints, jumps and extremes of effort for those who are younger and stronger (though those who are older may certainly enjoy and wish to do these activities too). At certain ages of course, some forms of exercise are not appropriate (excessive weights in developing teenagers for example) since they can lead to significant damage and long-term injury. The core and other principles regard us all as of fundamental value and worth, whatever our age, and therefore, given the personal value of each one of us, we do owe it to ourselves to value who we are, what we do and the contributions we make and can make, and as a consequence we owe it ourselves to as far as possible act to maintain our personal fitness and health.

While it is incumbent upon ourselves to set aside time and find some of our own resources if we can to support our physical activity it is also incumbent on our communities and societies, joined with our individual commitment, pressure and support, to aid in the provision of opportunities and of facilities which support such fitness and activity for all. And it is also incumbent on all of us to encourage others to a reasonable degree, to pursue that fitness and physical well-being. To that end, backed by our own support and action, our communities and societies need to ensure that space is available for sporting and fitness activities, be these inside or outside spaces and buildings, swimming pools, gymnasia, tennis courts, parks, cricket fields, sports tracks, open spaces in which to play sports, walk and run, or dance and exercise. And it is also helpful for all of us if we ourselves invest in and provide other resources (sports equipment for example) or for other resources to be made available to support our sports, fitness and exercise.

Those of us who are involved in and contribute to others and our communities through the governance of sports, who promote sport professionally or otherwise, those of us who give of our time for the sports and activities for which we may have a passion, thereby supporting health, fitness, enjoyment and hopefully happiness for others too, need to be proactive where we can, not only in supporting the joy and pleasure of sports and exercise, but also in supporting and ensuring the availability of facilities for sporting activity. Of course we also need to act as effectively as we can and proactively, to ensure the safety of those who play particular sports, and this applies to both the more individual, formally organised activities and sports and those sports involving physical contact. Sports involving direct physical contact such as boxing, wrestling, karate, judo, rugby and so forth are legitimate in training ourselves in self-defence, and in terms of sporting contest can be seen as legitimate and acceptable only as long as the real physical risks to participants are dealt with and reduced to an acceptable minimum, and only where such that participants do not see these as the only viable and reasonable road to success and escape in their lives. It is consistent with core principles, indeed admirable and supportive of the well-being and happiness of others, as well as hopefully being supportive of ourselves, to contribute to and help out with the administration, organisation and management of activities, sports and exercises, both for younger people and adults, which support the health of others and their well-being and happiness.

It must be pointed out that the health benefits we gain from sports, physical fitness and exercise can be undermined by lifestyles which are unhealthy in other ways, with such unhealthy ways of living having the potential to substantially damage our health and shorten our lives. Moreover for some of us, almost our entire lifestyle may be unhealthy.

For example, living a substantially sedentary existence (with a sedentary element of life being common for many of us in the current day and age), even if this sedentary life is punctuated by some level of exercise, such a substantially sedentary life is likely to be damaging to our health. Hours spent in the office sitting at our desks, in front of the computer screen, spending the day largely stationary on a factory production line, or at home or elsewhere watching the television, using mobile phones or computers for gaming, using or engaging in other sedentary activities for prolonged periods, can underpin poor health. As such we need to do our best to reduce our sedentary activity, aiming at the minimum to exercise while sitting, or interspersing our sedentary time with hopefully frequent periods of movement, exercise and activity.

Given the health problems likely to be created by such a sedentary lifestyle in particular, this emphasises the importance ascribed to physical health and exercise, and bolsters the necessity for us to support our social organisations in the promotion of physical exercise, not only in the form of providing information about the health benefits of exercise, but also through providing the necessary facilities and support where possible, such that we can all engage in the promotion of our physical health. As already mentioned, in the current age, for those of us living in cities and towns, this will likely mean our, where we can, paying for and providing publically accessible facilities including swimming pools, gyms, sports fields, public parks, athletics stadia, spaces for dance and exercise, and a range of other facilities which we can use to maintain, develop and improve our health. In passing, yet also an important aspect of such facilities, these will also provide places where we can come together to meet and socialise, helping to make for a more social, together, cohesive and cooperative society. In other contexts, the natural environment, dependent on the climate, may provide opportunities and places for exercise and fitness activities.

Our more sedentary activities do not only take place in our work or home environments. Sitting in drinking establishments consuming large quantities of carbohydrate heavy alcoholic drinks, common in many cultures, in particular in Western countries, but also elsewhere, is certainly lacking in health benefits in regard to physical health (though there will be mental and social health benefits through being with others and alcohol has been found to have some particular health benefits if not taken in excess). And sitting in coffee or tea shops eating cakes or biscuits for hours, if that is what we do, certainly needs to be combined with features more representative of a healthy diet and physical activity at some point in time. Combining poor diet with lengthy periods of inactivity is certainly not a way to ensure good health and instead encourages poor health, disease and obesity.

This guide does not aim to provide detailed advice on what constitutes the good diet that is needed for our positive health and well-being. Such detailed advice would require a book, if not several books, in itself. Nevertheless, with diet being crucial to health it is considered important to mention what are likely to be the components of a healthy diet, at least in broad terms. Of course, as already stated, a healthy diet will serve to support our overall health, which will support our well-being and happiness, and should also serve to support the well-being and happiness of others, our communities and societies.

The basics of what comprises a good and bad diet and the basics of what to avoid seem to be generally clear. At the fundamental level we all need sufficient food to provide us with energy for the day and to keep us at a basic level of health. In practice that means that we all need access to a certain level of fruit, vegetables, protein sources and more. We need sources of vitamins, minerals, carbohydrates, roughage, fats, amino acids and proteins and more. The water we drink must be clean so we must all have access to clean and healthy water. We need to avoid eating anything in excess, anything containing too much fat, avoiding diets containing excessive carbohydrate. Too much of anything seems to have the potential to lead us to illness. As individuals we need to ensure that, if these are actually available to us, we eat the range of the required and different foods needed to maintain our health.

Our food of course needs to be clean and prepared in a manner which keeps us safe, with potentially dangerous microorganisms inactivated or removed from our food in order to support our health. Those foods which are potentially dangerous need to be properly processed, stored and prepared safely prior to consumption. Those selling and providing food need to accurately describe the nature of what they are supplying and selling, ensuring sufficient information about their products, especially as some of us have allergies to certain food stuffs and have a definite if not critical need to know exactly what we are eating. And of course those involved in the preparation of food need to ensure the already referred to cleanliness and the use of procedures which ensure the safety of those who will be eating this prepared and supplied food.

With diet being so important to our well-being and health, we need to take the time and be sure to educate ourselves in regards to what we eat and drink, such that our health is maintained, and keep ourselves up-to-date, as far as we can with new information and research findings about diet. We also need to take the time and make the effort to ensure we eat healthily, consuming the variety of foodstuffs that our bodies need to function effectively. Not only do we need to consult literature, reliable media and research sources, and listen to others about what it is best to eat, as individuals, we also need to support the development of community, society and global expertise in food and nutrition and support research which advances our knowledge of the relationship between diet, well-being and health. The research necessary includes continuing and detailed research into food safety.

We also, as individuals, operating through our social, community international and global organisations, need to ensure that the food produced and provided to us is of quality and promotes our health with standards of food production ensured, education and training in food preparation provided, and standards of food preparation, food storage, food disposal and other food and health related standards properly monitored and regulated. With the quality of our food being of such importance, in support of health and well-being it is almost certain that there will need to be laws and regulations to ensure food is, amongst other things, properly prepared, processed and stored, with monitoring of the implementation of laws and regulations by sufficiently, indeed well-funded organisations, thereby contributing to ensuring our food is safe. Our food production also needs to be efficient to ensure that there is sufficient food for all, and also needs to be engaged in in a manner such that our production of food is sustainable into the future. Our social context, our communities and societies, our organisations and social entities, backed up by our own individual awareness and support, need to ensure that our food supply is as secure as possible and that our food is safe to eat.

Unfortunately it is the case that some of us do not have access to sufficient food we need, and some of us do not have access to the variety and quality of food we need to maintain and support our health effectively. Some of us, hopefully a very small number, and hopefully in the future no one at all, have so little food that we will starve. Others of us may become ill or die due to diseases transmitted through the unclean water, which we may be forced, through circumstance, to drink and wash in. Many potential clean water sources may unfortunately in some cases be used as toilets, leading to the transmission of dangerous diseases which can threaten the health and lives of the many, with similar threats to health presented by ineffective, damaged or aging sewerage systems.

Thus, an essential element of our health and well-being is access to and provision of clean potable water which frequently requires effective sewerage, water filtration and other waste disposal systems. Effective and healthy sanitation systems are essential to our health, well-being and happiness, underpinning our healthy, functioning communities and societies. Where these do not exist we need to take individual, community and social action, global action where necessary, to construct these, to bring these into existence. And where they do exist, we need to ensure their maintenance, development and improvement, thus ensuring, as far as we can, that it is more difficult for water-borne disease organisms to multiply and spread with the consequent damaging effects to the health of so many. We must not take our systems of cleanliness and sanitation for granted, but need to ensure that these are sustained and supported, recognising the massive contributions that these systems make to our health and well-being.

This fact that some of us do not have access to sufficient food to keep us at a basic level of health, that some of us do not have access to clean water, is unacceptable in a modern world where there is in fact plenty, and where we have significant technological capacity and tools to ensure sufficient clean water and food are available. It is a goal of our personal conduct, our activities, of our behaviour as individuals, and it must be a goal of our communities and societies, locally and globally, in line with core and other principles set out in this guide, that all of us, all people, should have access to sufficient food and clean water, such that starvation and ill health due to inadequate and deficient food sources, due to water-borne illnesses and diseases, will become a thing of the past.

For those of us who can access sufficient food, it is possible, and may well be beneficial for us to be vegetarian or vegan. Our health can be maintained and our bodies can grow well with a vegetarian or supplemented vegan diet which contains protein sources and the range of vitamins, minerals and other elements that our bodies require. While meat has been a part of the human diet for many thousands, if not more than a million years, this precedent does not mean that we should not look at the opportunity to desist from the slaughter of animals that must be carried out for our consumption of animal flesh. Prematurely ending the lives of animals through their slaughter, and inflicting unnecessary pain and suffering on animals are contentious in terms of both the core and the subsidiary principles presented in this guide. Objecting to the slaughter and what is considered to be the poor care and factory-like abuse of animals in our human food system, or through simply objecting to the use of animals for food at all, some people may even choose to be vegans, refusing to eat any products derived from such animals. There is certainly justification in such stances. These matters of animal welfare and our human relationship with the non-human world are addressed in more detail in chapter fourteen of this guide.

A good, healthy diet is essential for us, and certainly illness and disease can arise through a poor diet. But additional to disease and illness, and in fact additional to the physical injuries we may receive through violent acts, common additional sources of our pain and injury are what are referred to as accidents, the notion of accident being a concept which incorporates the idea that there is no deliberation in the cause of our pain and injury. Unfortunately, at least to some extent, the notion of accident similarly contains the meaning that little could have been done to prevent that pain and injury and that these 'accidents' were somehow unavoidable chance events. Viewing such events in the sense that little could have been done about them is not helpful, as often there are actions which could have been or could be taken in the future to prevent these accidents and their resultant pain and injury.

Many of these accidents occur within our houses and homes with others occurring outside the home at work; they may occur while travelling on roads or travelling otherwise, or occur in the range of other environments including those used for leisure and pleasure. Within the home, dependent on the nature of our homes, we can suffer from potential burns from fires or cookers, and of course from house fires, as well as suffering harm and potential death due to the possibilities of electrocution from our various electrical devices. We can fall while climbing or descending our stairs, trip over objects, bang heads against shelves and other furniture, cut ourselves on knives and other tools, slip on wet floors, endure splinters from wooden fragments, cut ourselves on broken glass from bottles and much more. To support our health and well-being in the home, we clearly need to be careful to be safe and protect ourselves as well as acting to ensure the safety of others, our families, our children.

In particular, that means ensuring in our homes that, for example, our children (and ourselves) are protected from fires through safety guards around open and other fires, ensure that smoke alarms protect our homes from fires, that broken glass is disposed of quickly and not left lying around as a hazard, that electrical devices are checked for safety with wires properly insulated, that sharp knives are not left lying around such that they can cause injury, that our homes are ventilated and any electrical and other equipment is checked and maintained as necessary to avoid build up of poisonous gases, that passages are kept clear and unobstructed, and floors are kept clean and dry to stop falls and much more. These actions and much more are needed to protect our safety in the home.

And those who design homes, who design materials and equipment for the home, need to ensure that safety is incorporated into their designs such that there is no possibility, almost no possibility or only the most minimal possibility of accident and injury resulting from the designed objects we encounter in our daily lives. Of course these designs need to take into account the realities of our human behaviour, how we are, anticipating how items will truly be handled in the round such that safety can be ensured.

Unfortunately the range of 'accidents' we can endure are legion. In almost any context, as mentioned in the home, we may trip and fall, doing ourselves damage through cuts and bruises, painful and injurious to different degrees. We may bang our heads accidentally through not looking where we are going or knock into someone else. We can trap fingers in doors or windows, break noses and legs and other parts of our bodies in falls or accidentally in the already mentioned sporting contests. The list of sources of painful and damaging incidents and accidents is almost endless.

We need to take the greatest care while in control of our various vehicles. On the road, in our cars or on our bicycles, we may misjudge distance, misjudge the intentions of others in their vehicles, forget to indicate our own driving intentions, lose balance on a bicycle, simply make an ill-considered error, and as a consequence be injured, perhaps severely injured, falling off bicycles, motorbikes, being injured in our cars, and this sometimes through no fault or misjudgment of our own, but sometimes solely through the misjudgments of others. Yet usually, if we have been properly trained, and we are in a rested and healthy state of mind, if we avoid bravado and recognise the dangers our vehicles can hold for others, if we drive with care and attention, such accidents will not happen or will certainly be less likely.

Yet if we are out walking we also need to take care. As pedestrians near roads, we need to, for example, watch out for vehicles when we are crossing the road. And as individuals, communities and societies, we need to ensure that there are safe crossing points for pedestrians. Our systems of car and other vehicular transport need to accommodate those who still walk, who need to walk, ensuring that pedestrians are kept safe but also allowing them to walk, rather than our constructing non-traversable roads through residential areas and other areas where some will need to cross.

In many work contexts we need to take the greatest of care such that accidents are avoided. At work on a building site, an object may strike us unexpectedly; we might fall off a ladder or scaffolding. In a factory, we may be hurt, suffer electric shock or a range of sometimes serious physical damage, even death, from machinery. We can damage our back, neck and our eyes through staring for too long a time at the wrong angle at our computer screens. We can be made ill through the chemicals we might deal with at work, the noise we may experience, the pesticides and fertilisers we might use, not to mention suffering through the stress of work which may lead to the occurrence of illness and accidents. In order to support our well-being and avoid the pain and suffering that result from such accidents, as far as possible, we as individuals and our communities, organisations and societies need to take pre-emptive action to ensure that these accidents do not happen, such that we are all safe, through ensuring that potential hazards in the work environment are removed and dealt with.

Indeed anywhere, be it work, home, in towns, the city or countryside, at leisure, as individuals, communities and societies, we need to make ourselves aware of safety hazards and as far as we can neutralise them or be prepared to deal with them, be they represented by damaged wiring, unstable structures, uneven surfaces, fire safety hazards and many more. In addition we need to anticipate and be prepared to deal with and respond to accidents with protective equipment available. As individuals we need to have first aid kits available, know the numbers of emergency medical services should these exist and be accessible, and we should have other materials and plans in place and available to deal with injury appropriate to the anticipated level of hazard.

In the work environment, we, as individuals, as employees, managers, and organisations, need to ensure that systems are in place to pre-empt and prevent accidents and protect against hazards in all their forms as relates to that specific work environment, as well as having response protocols in place and responsible individuals available and contactable should accidents occur. And as owners, managers and individuals involved, we need to ensure that resources are available to ensure safety, and further indeed, we need to ensure that the health and safety of ourselves and our employees is an integral part of any work, processes or tasks we set or engage in. That is to say that, whatever our context, we must not consider health and safety an optional add-on to what we do. Instead, considerations of health and safety must be a planned component of, and must be embedded in, and an obligatory component of all that we do.

In the work context, if we are owners and managers we will need to take responsibility for safety, but also, of course, we as employees need to make our own contributions to our own health and safety at work and the health and safety of those others with whom we work, adopting and making contributions and suggestions in regard to health and safety and adhering to and putting into practice with diligence and accuracy, regulations and health and safety procedures such that we and those with whom we work, can operate in maximum safety.

And beyond our actions as individual managers or company and company owners, those of us with governmental and political responsibility, at whatever level, with the backing and support of us all, need to ensure that safety standards, regulations, laid down procedures and laws are in place to ensure that we are safe from the wide range of hazards which we may face in the range of home, work and indeed other environments we inhabit. Thus, homes and offices, factories, all forms of buildings and constructions and much more need to be manufactured and built to standards which ensure the safety and well-being of the occupiers and users, such that they can withstand anticipated and probable challenges (be they potential fires in some cases, or for example, this meaning earthquakes in regions where such earthquakes are reasonably likely to happen). Devices used in the home and elsewhere need to meet stringent safety standards. Electrical and gas equipment and the wide range of other products we use, including children's toys, cleaning fluids, paints, and the gamut of other items need to meet safety requirements in order to support our health and well-being. The use of hazardous materials needs to be understood, regulated and monitored such that all of us remain safe as far as is possible.

Underpinning issues of safety, in relevant work environments we need to ensure that staff are appropriately trained to work safely, particularly where health and safety is an issue, and we need to ensure that they are made aware of any relevant work hazards. And we need to make sure that such training, as well as systems and regulations are implemented, and back them up with systems of monitoring and regulation to ensure that we, as employees and employers, are able to work in safety. And in the context of our well-being and health, it is our responsibility as managers, as employees, as organisations, communities and societies to make certain that there are stringent and pre-emptive health and safety procedures in place in our work environments, such that 'accidents' do not occur, with their consequent damaging effects on our well-being.

As individuals, communities and societies, as government representatives and agencies, we also need to make sure, as far as we can, that the environments outside of our homes are also safe. Our pavements, where we have them, need to be safe to walk on without trip hazards and with minimal slip hazards. Our roads should not be full of potholes. Our vehicles, of all kinds, must be maintained in a safe condition, and all aspects of our transport systems need to be efficiently designed, checked and maintained to ensure their safety. Our people managing and operating such systems need to be well-trained and their health, capacities and well-being need to be monitored such that they are capable of acting effectively in their important and responsible roles. We need systems and organisations for identifying potential hazards in our local and broader environments, for example, with dangerous and rotting trees removed from near our highways, such that what are referred to as accidents, do not happen when these trees collapse or are blown on to highways, with potential deaths and injuries occurring as a consequence.

In the broader biological environment, within the limitations of our powers, we need to ensure that our environment provides safe, clean and indeed provides enriching surroundings for us to survive in and also to enjoy. In terms of cleanliness and health, therefore, our human-made physical hazardous wastes and materials should not be dumped in the environment. Sewage and other human wastes must be disposed of safely, cleanly without threatening our health or threatening the quality of our environment. Dangerous and harmful chemical and other pollutants should not be released into the environment, into our rivers and streams, into the air we breathe, at levels which can harm us or which can lead to our harm and which can harm animal and plant life. Not only does such pollution damage our health, but it also makes our biological environments highly unpleasant, difficult to cope with and certainly difficult if not impossible to enjoy.

As individuals, we need to make sure that our own personal actions, the activities that we participate in, do not result in any significant damage to our environments and that we do not, through such activities, threaten our environment and the health and well-being of others. If we are involved in production and manufacturing industries as owners, managers and employees, we are each of us responsible for ensuring our activities do not generate or release hazardous products into the environment which will lead to damage to our human health and to animal and plant life. And we as individuals are each personally responsible for ensuring our businesses and organisations, the businesses and organisations we work in, do not offer such threats and challenges. That being said, some form of potentially dangerous waste may be generated of necessity in key manufacturing and other processes, processes which provide overall benefit and support for well-being. In such cases, the potential danger from any waste and other products resulting from our manufacturing processes requires that we put in place safe storage and treatment as well as planning in regard to the final destinations of such waste, such that there is minimum threat to our human health and indeed animal health and minimal threat to the survival and thriving of plant life.

As mentioned already, we as individuals must be clean and hygienic, doing all we all can to ensure that we are not behaving irresponsibly and allowing untreated and potentially dangerous human waste to contaminate our environments. We need to dispose of the products we use in our daily lives, in our houses and homes in a manner which will not offer potential threats to the health of others. For example glass products must not be left strewn on the ground as hazards for others to cut themselves on. The mess from our pets must not be left on the streets for others to tread in. The paints, cleaning fluids, our medications and other products that we might use and keep in our homes must be stored and disposed of safely, and we must make sure that children cannot access them and be 'accidentally' poisoned through our carelessness. In jurisdictions where soome may keep deadly weapons such as guns in their homes, these must be locked away in places where children cannot access them.

Beyond our homes, with greater relevance to the working environment and manufacturing industry, we need to ensure that processes and actions which may damage or threaten our personal health, the health of others, our human environments, are regulated and monitored, and if necessary stopped completely if the hazard they offer is too great and threatens individual well-being, the health of our workers, the health of community, society and humanity, and significantly threatens the quality of our environment. It is up to all of us as individuals, our organisations, companies, governments, and international organisations, with our individual support and action to ensure that our environment remains one which will support a life of well-being, enjoyment and fulfillment and certainly is not one that will harm or hurt us.

Yet our biological environment is more than a source of potential dangers. An appropriate biological environment is and can be a source of great positive pleasure and an important element of our health and well-being. Our ensuring of a pleasant countryside with pleasant walks, clean and fresh air supports both our mental and physical health. Pleasant clean beaches devoid of litter and rubbish, clean lakes, rivers and seas, can be enjoyed in many ways, whether through swimming, fishing, boating, through providing sites for pleasant walks and other forms of leisure, supporting wildlife and our enjoyment of wildlife, all of this enhancing our health, happiness and well-being. Apart from their intrinsic enjoyment, which boosts our happiness and well-being, these activities both encourage us to achieve, and represent routes to keeping, physically fit and active, as well as supporting our psychological health.

Bearing these benefits of a pleasant environment in mind, in order to prevent our illness and support our health we need to a significant extent to be protecting and maintaining our natural environments such that we can enjoy them and thereby promote our health and well-being. More than that, however, in addition to protecting our environments from damage, to some extent we also need to actively and positively shape as well as preserve our natural environment or elements of our environment, such that they can support our well-being and health. This may mean creating new parks, and other new landscape features, creating waterways, lakes and streams, planting new and different crops, trees and forests, supporting other forms of life and making new wildernesses where this is a possibility. All of this activity, together with our activities in conservation and preservation, should serve to support our natural animal and other populations, enhancing and bolstering the diversity of life on our planet, something which is also of relevance to our well-being and happiness and discussed in greater depth in the following chapter of this guide.

On a somewhat different note, in terms of our physical and mental health, critical to our well-being, this well-being is also enhanced by our having sufficient rest and sufficient sleep. In order to preserve our broader fitness and to ensure that we can act effectively when working and when living and being together with friends and with family, in acting in our communities and societies, we need to ensure that we do get sufficient sleep and rest at a level appropriate to our age and our individual needs. Lack of sleep and lack of rest affects our judgment, our ability to make correct decisions, our moods and behaviours towards others and much more. As a consequence of our tiredness and exhaustion, some of our many decisions which may sometimes need to be made in the midst of intense tiredness and exhaustion, may be inaccurate and wrong decisions that can damage our physical health and welfare. So sufficient sleep and rest needs to be taken by all of us, wherever we can, whenever possible. Such rest and sleep represent, for each and every one of us, essential human needs.

That is not to say that there may not need to be times when we will wish for and take less sleep and rest than at other times. We may be highly motivated to achieve a goal at a particular time, working longer hours and resting somewhat less; we may be under pressure to achieve at work or on behalf of others; for a range of reasons we may be under intense personal or external pressure to perform for extended periods in what may be, in some cases, for some of us, life threatening situations. And therefore under some circumstances we may need to, or choose to, cut down our levels of sleep for a short while and *in extremis* may have to keep on going for long periods with little sleep. Yet overall and in the vast generality, we must not let our own ambition or external pressures force us to lack of sleep, tiredness and exhaustion, all of which can have significantly negative and damaging effects on our health and well-being, and which are likely to damage our achievement of our goals.

Of course we are each of us different and will need different levels of rest and sleep and it is not the role of this guide to advocate specific sleeping and resting time for any particular individual, even if a lack of rest and sleep is likely to influence our actions and personal conduct. Our decisions on our level of sleep and rest are matters which are, in the vast main, for our own individual and autonomous decision-making. But it is the role of this guide in order to support appropriate conduct and in support of our health and well-being, to point out the importance to our health and well-being of adequate breaks, adequate sleep and adequate rest, to which ends we need rests and breaks at work, relaxation and rest at home, sufficient sleep, days or weekends away from work, and holidays at various points through the year.

Recognising the need for sleep, rest and more does not of course mean that we should spend all or excessive time sleeping and resting. Our health and full enjoyment of well-being needs us to engage with others, to make contributions, to take actions, to do things, and it seems likely the case, that in a manner parallel to inadequate sleep and rest, too much sleep, too much lying down and resting, too much sloth, will itself damage our health, both mentally and physically, encouraging a lack of sense of purpose, a lack of activity and lack of physical fitness, as well as, of course, damaging our contributions to others and our opportunities to live complete lives of well-being, happiness and fulfillment. That being said, it seems clear that, for example, in our teenage years, we may have different patterns of, and need different levels of sleep.

Clearly our mental health is core to our well-being, representing and substantially affecting the way we feel, affecting substantially the way we act, affecting our relationships, the effectiveness of our actions, the effectiveness of our decisions and judgments and amongst other things, affecting our ability to grow and learn. Substantial and severe problems with our mental health can significantly incapacitate us and, of course, in themselves can represent substantial and significant pain and suffering. In order to support our well-being and happiness, in order to support our health, in order for us to reduce or avoid pain and suffering due to mental health problems, we need to be looking to promote our positive mental health through a range of different actions and strategies, our positive mental health also being an asset to our physical well-being and physical health.

Such an ability to support the promotion of our own mental health bears the assumption that our mental health is something that we can influence positively through the actions we take and through the ways we think about our lives and life around us. That is indeed considered to be the case in this guide and is considered to be relevant and to a significant extent, true for the many of us. Nevertheless, for some of us, perhaps many however, mental health problems may be deeply embedded, representing deep-seated biochemical and genetic sources of personal pain and suffering which may make our lives very difficult to cope with, at times creating behaviour which is sometimes benign, but also creating behaviour which can sometimes be destructive of ourselves and sometimes destructive of others. Many of us will be aware of conditions such as schizophrenia, depression, bipolar disorders and a range of other serious conditions which can cause extreme anguish, disorientation, pain and suffering.

For those suffering with such deeply embedded mental health conditions, medical treatment, though not guaranteed at the present time to be always successful, will be needed and should be sought by those experiencing such suffering. Where those of us experiencing such pain and suffering are unable to seek this treatment ourselves, it is the responsibility of others, of the rest of us, of friends and family, of colleagues, of us all, to make sure those suffering attempt to and get access to and look to receive the support and the medical treatments that they need, be that through medicine, drugs, be that through cognitive, talking or other forms of therapy aimed at easing their pain and suffering. Of course such treatments and therapies should also, where necessary, be aimed at reducing the pain, strains and suffering which we can cause, through such mental health conditions in others. Mental health difficulties are common and while we ourselves may be afflicted by such conditions, we also need to be caring and supportive of those others suffering with such conditions, as we would be supportive of anyone else with a more obviously physical, medical and health problem.

For all of us, if we are mentally healthy, if we have positive mental health, then we are able to think clearly and rationally with empathy and understanding of ourselves, and others. With positive mental health we can act effectively, within the range of our everyday personal concerns, actions and activities, bounded by some limitations of external factors and our external environments, with our making decisions and deciding our actions rationally and reasonably based on our experiences and rational thinking about the world around us. Our positive mental health is reflected through our lack of negative and destructive and self-destructive thinking, our constructive and often goal oriented approach to the life we live and through our clear thinking, shown for example through the positive way we can deal with relationships, problems, opportunities and more.

If we are mentally healthy, if we are in a positive mentally healthy state, we will be able to experience general emotional well-being, satisfaction and happiness; we will feel good (certainly at times) or at least have a sense of equanimity where this is appropriate (and certainly we will generally lack feelings of persistent unhappiness and depression) at least for much or most of the time, recognising for ourselves that some level of unhappiness at some points in time, or even periods of time, is unfortunately a normal part of a healthy life. That is to say, we recognise that, and indeed know that, while we hope to feel ok or feel good for much of the time, we will not feel joyful and happy all the time, everyday of our lives, for a variety of reasons. We will know that relationships and the like are complex and may well have their ups and downs. We know that we will experience normal everyday frustrations at, for example, our being unable at times to achieve that which we wish to achieve, perhaps because we may feel ill from common infections, perhaps because of pressures at work and at home, and perhaps because sometimes we may feel a sense of emptiness, apartness, loneliness and isolation.

Linked to statements above, of course, while we may be mentally healthy, we may still feel tremendous pain and sadness at events in our lives such as the death of a loved one. Having positive mental health includes experiencing these normal and unavoidable feelings of sadness, grief and indeed perhaps sometimes feeling despair. Such feelings and emotions, if sometimes experienced, would seem to represent a normal and natural part of life for most of us and are likely to be indicative of our living a life of true mental health and well-being, or at least as close to a life of well-being and happiness as may be possible for the human beings we are, leading the lives we lead.

Positive mental health does not mean that we walk around with a possibly annoying and irritating glowing smile on our faces throughout the day. Given our nature as human beings and the insecurity of living, that would most likely, for the most of us at least, be out of line with our true feelings and our responses to the reality that most of us will and are able to experience. Not only do the many of us not always feel strongly positive and good, not only are our positive feelings and sense of well being not necessarily represented by a smiling face, but, importantly, life and living also throw things at us which are bound to make us feel unhappy, stressed and challenged, which will affect the way we feel and which will do so in a manner which may not leave us feeling positive or able to respond with a smile (to say the least).

So, having good mental health does not mean that we will not feel down or will not feel unhappy at times. Yet if we have strong and positive mental health we are likely to feel at least somewhat satisfied with who we are for a large part of the time, or at least contain our self-criticism such that we do not spend our lives obsessing with our inadequacies and faults for too long. And further, positive mental health means that we are, and we will be able to simply get on with life, experiencing life with others, participating in our families, communities and societies with some pleasure and joy and sometimes some pain too; we will try to deal with those challenges which come our way, and in the main we would hope we can tackle them with some level of success. If we have moments of difficulty and crisis, while we may suffer some mental pain and anguish, we will be able to understand these difficulties and get through them without too much mental suffering and pain, perhaps recognising them as the temporary difficulties they are likely to be. Hopefully, with strong and positive mental health we will tend to feel happy enough and healthy enough in our minds for significant periods of time.

An important aspect of positive mental health is our capacity to interact ably with and cope with interactions with others around us, and the wider world we live in, without suffering excessive mental anguish and pain. Such human interactions are necessary for us to live lives of well-being, and our need for these is part of our human nature and character as social beings. Yet certain significant illnesses and conditions can make it difficult for some of us to experience and enjoy such interactions. Again help may be needed to help us overcome such difficulties, such suffering and pain.

That being said, for many of us, from time-to-time, it may well be possible to feel good and enjoy a certain period of time or type of life, to some extent away from the world around us, away from others. Times of peacefulness where we are undisturbed and alone with our thoughts are likely to be valuable for us, enabling us to reflect on our lives, the events in our lives, reflect on others and make us more able to cope with and face the world around us.

Nevertheless setting ourselves up in long-term social islands which avoid interaction with others, which avoid the challenges of living with others, may perhaps allow us some degree of personal happiness, but may also reflect and represent, and indeed lead to deep unhappiness, through our non-interaction with and non-contribution to the world around us. Through such a life of isolation we will lose the joys and pains, the experiences of relationships with others which, for the vast main of us, though perhaps not all of us, we have a deep need for.

For the most of us, to deliberately engage in such isolation, while appropriate under some circumstances, and perhaps useful for short periods of time in order to rest, develop thinking, reflect and escape from, and avoid intense stress, if adopted on a prolonged basis, is contrary to core and other principles as it encompasses disengaging with the world and thereby, in the main, would seem, as a consequence, to involve our not fulfilling ourselves as human beings and not contributing significantly to supporting others in our communities, societies and beyond. This is the case even if as a consequence we might feel for a while, or longer, a sense of equanimity and well-being. Living without any significant interaction with others (no interaction would to all intents and purposes be an impossibility), living without supporting ourselves and others, is considered contrary to the principles put forward in this guide, and most likely will damage our mental health, our well-being and happiness.

Our maintaining and promoting our mental health and well-being can be helped significantly by our engaging in a range of actions, processes and positive strategies. It is highly valuable for us to develop and possess self-awareness, the knowledge of how we are inside, how we behave, how others perceive the ways we behave and conduct ourselves, how we feel, why we feel the way we do, who we are, why we are that way, and also develop awareness of and understanding of the ways in which others respond to us. To gain this latter awareness and understanding, we need to develop our awareness, knowledge and understanding of others too, something which includes focusing on and developing our capacities to empathise with others (which does not mean necessarily agreeing with them, nor does it mean seeing the motives and actions of those who behave badly as valid and acceptable).

All of this awareness and understanding is likely to serve as a useful tool to help us succeed in achieving our well-being and fulfillment, in helping us achieve our goals, in supporting our own positive mental health, helping us to succeed in feeling good and more, since understanding ourselves and others, in itself something to enjoy and appreciate, is an important step on the pathway to and is likely to contribute to us acquiring and executing a greater degree of self-control and understanding in relation to our own actions. Such awareness and understanding will help us to understand the responses we get from others, will support us in deciding more appropriate and effective actions in response to others, and should support and enable us to change our behaviours where such changes are required to suit our goals, the goals of others around us and the goals of our communities and societies. That is not to say that we should always change our conduct and behaviour in the light of others' views of us, since we have our own desires, interests, thoughts, values, beliefs and ideas to take into account, yet understanding others and their perspectives, beliefs, ideas and values, should be of significant worth and help to ourselves in our own pursuit of well-being and in helping us achieve our goals of supporting others in line with core and other principles.

Through self-awareness and understanding and through awareness and understanding of others, we should hopefully also be more able to affect and influence the attitudes, feelings, behaviours and actions of others in regard to ourselves. Such awareness should also help us in relation to supporting and influencing the actions of others in their own lives such they themselves can achieve greater well-being and happiness and support others in doing the same.

If we do not properly understand others and, indeed, if we are unable to understand the systems and cultures around us, this can lead to intense frustration, mental anguish, depression, pain and suffering, with our hopes and expectations of others being disappointed and our having substantial difficulty in achieving our goals. And thus we need to develop our understandings of ourselves and those around us, and also the contexts in which we are living. This self awareness and our understanding of ourselves and others, the organisations, the communities and societies we live in, and indeed where relevant other organisations, communities and societies, is key to supporting us and enabling us to anticipate the responses we will receive from others, such that we can prepare for these responses as fully as we feel we need to.

Having such understanding and awareness means that we should be able to act and react appropriately, with full knowledge of how we may feel ourselves when making such responses and being fully aware of the likely responses to our actions from others, be they positive, negative or in-between. Having the capacity to predict these responses both of ourselves and others, through our preparedness and expectation in dealing with these responses, through awareness of possible consequences, we will be able to act more effectively towards our goals. But not only that, we will most likely feel a greater sense of calm, equanimity, perhaps ambivalence, or a reduction in our anxieties and stress, and a greater level of well-being and happiness. We should further be able to set ourselves realistic and achievable goals, taking into account the nature of ourselves, others and the contexts in which we are living.

We do need to be careful, however, that our self-awareness and concern for ourselves and our mental well-being and mental health does not turn into over-concern, over-focus or even obsession with ourselves and the way we feel, these being in themselves unhealthy and detracting from our capacities to care for ourselves and look after others, something which is a requirement of core and other principles.

Whatever the level of self-awareness and self-understanding we have, as social human beings, the actions of others will almost inevitably influence, to some extent, our feelings, our well-being and our mental health. Developing the ability to cope with negative experiences and those who will be negative, bullying, manipulative, dishonest, disrespectful, indeed spiteful, mean and worse about us, is highly valuable and perhaps something we all need to learn. We may choose to change our behaviours to accommodate these kinds of behaviours and these others; we may aim to change the attitudes of others towards us, thereby building more cooperative and friendly relationships. Clearly in terms of our desires to get on with people, cooperate successfully with others, our desires to be wanted and cared for, to be valued and recognised by others, our need to feel concerned about and indeed loved by others, our building of positive caring and cooperative relationships is the preferable option when dealing with those people who are negative about us. Yet, unfortunately, this may not always be possible.

Where we are acting within the frame of core and other principles, those who are negative or critical of us, who speak and act destructively towards us, may well be acting in a manner or even characterised in their actions by being highly irrational, discriminatory, bigoted, racist, biased, negatively selfish, uncaring, lacking in empathy and understanding towards us or indeed any others. In these cases we must still aim to build positive, caring and cooperative relationships if we can, engaging in all positive and constructive efforts and actions available to us. This can require substantial mental strength, yet is an obligation of our need and our efforts to support others, our communities and societies, as well as in terms of supporting our own happiness and well-being. Seeking such positive, caring, cooperation is almost always for the best in the short, medium and longer term.

Nevertheless, in support of better relationships, as well as in support of our own personal health and psychological well-being, we may need, under some circumstances, when dealing with such people, to develop the capacity to be peacefully robust in response to such people and such actions, pointing out to them in explicit terms their conduct and its effect on us and letting them know in no uncertain terms that we will not accept such behaviour and conduct. While we may listen to such others and take on valid points of criticism we may further in some cases need to develop an iron indifference or ambivalence towards these others who are negative, critical and rude about us. Such an indifference does not mean that in necessary cases where we are being significantly damaged and put upon, we will not respond to protect ourselves and our well-being. Nevertheless, we may well need to develop a high level of psychological resilience, a psychological wall in a sense between ourselves and these others, in order to support our own personal well-being and happiness, to enable us to respond effectively. We need to protect ourselves from the pain and suffering which may result from our taking the unkind and the sometimes calculated and destructive personal attacks that may be directed towards us, as legitimate and deserved by us, or taking to heart the personal, the irrational. Nor can we allow, in support of our well-being and the well-being of others, those oppressing us in such ways to do so without response.

Under such circumstances it is almost always the case that those oppressing us or attacking us have done or are doing similar to others and will be similarly resented and disliked by others. Thus, we are unlikely to be alone in our experiences. And, if we are being substantially oppressed by others in such circumstances, we should be able to talk to others in the same or similar positions and gain their support, hopefully practical support. We should, where necessary not keep silent, but should recruit help where this is possible, so that we are not suffering pain alone and such that we have our own allies who will support us morally or otherwise. And moreover we should recognise in the same manner that with regard to those others who are oppressing and being negative and destructive about us, the seeds of their actions are unlikely to lie with us and we should not allow ourselves to take blame for the actions of these others. The responsibility and origins of their unpleasant, critical and destructive actions, will generally lie largely or wholly within them.

If we are robust and resilient we should hopefully be able to cope with those who are negative, critical and who speak and take destructive actions against us, actions which we ourselves should never engage in towards others, recognising the harm, the deep psychological and emotional damage that can be done to others through callous and destructive remarks about others and actions towards them. Our role and responsibility, in line with core and other principles, is to support and care for others, to support their well-being and happiness and the overall well-being and happiness of ourselves, our communities, societies and beyond. It is certainly not our role to be destructive towards others and cause pain and suffering.

The reality is that life can present us with situations on occasion, where we have to live and work with people who we consider, at least at that point in time, to be unpleasant and unpalatable, and who may perhaps look at us in the same way. In line with core and other principles, certain personal differences and dislikes can and indeed should, in many cases, be put aside in order that greater goals can be achieved. Hopefully, it is possible that through such cooperation and working together, the negativity that exists may turn to positivity and mutual respect and understanding, if not friendship and togetherness. The strength to continue cooperation in a positive goal-oriented manner with those who may be negative about us is a sign of tremendous mental strength, and is supportive of organisations, community and society, as is the ability to make the effort to build bridges and build cooperation with those with whom we may have differences, and who may be negative about us. Through such bridge building and efforts at cooperation it may be possible to largely consign such negative relationship to the pages of our personal histories.

We may need to live, work and cooperate with those who have other unpalatable attitudes and views which we find unacceptable, which are substantially contrary to core and other principles. Again we will need to cooperate where we can with these individuals as far as is reasonable and possible, while attempting to persuade them to change their views and attitudes. Yet if their actions are significantly damaging and destructive, hurting ourselves and others, and causing significant pain and suffering, emotionally, mentally or physically we will need to do our utmost to ensure such actions, behaviour and conduct are stopped.

As already stated, we need self-awareness and self-understanding and the ability to understand others in order to maintain and develop our positive mental health. In order to do this, it is clear that our maintaining, sustaining and developing our mental health requires that we therefore aim to educate ourselves about ourselves, educate ourselves about who we are, that we educate ourselves in regard to and develop our capacities and skills to observe ourselves, to see ourselves as others may see us, that we educate and pursue the development of our abilities to reflect on who we are and how we behave, and also that we educate ourselves about and learn about others, how others, in type and as individuals, conduct themselves, their possible individual and indeed group motivations, and we learn about other cultures which influence personal and social orientations and conduct.

It is likely that for some if not many of us, in some regards we will lack a complete level of personal awareness. Gaining such complete personal awareness is challenging especially since elements of our nature and personal character may be somewhat hidden from our own view and indeed difficult for us to analyse in a dispassionate manner. And this is of importance because our lack of self-awareness may be a contributor to emotional pains and hurts that we suffer and can lead to damage of our emotional health. As a consequence of our deficits in self-awareness, and indeed our deficits in terms of self-understanding, we may unfortunately have ways of behaving, ways of conducting ourselves, perhaps patterns of behaviour and conduct, that we are not fully aware of and do not understand.

These ways of conducting ourselves may cause us pain and may be difficult for us to challenge due to their, in essence, invisibility to us. That is to say for example, we may engage in certain actions or certain talk believing that these ways of behaving are correct and appropriate, yet others respond negatively. And on top of this we may, through our own lack of awareness, misunderstand and misjudge the impression and effects we create in others. On receiving negative and sometimes hostile responses, we may well end up feeling hurt, but perplexed as to why we have met with such antipathy or disagreement. We may also unwittingly say things which are considered offensive by others, yet which we do not, or did not, consider to be offensive, our saying things which may not perhaps have seemed offensive to us, or which may not be offensive in the more individual and personal world or even the group or cultural group we live in.

Because of these 'lack of awareness' behaviours and our inability on some or perhaps many occasions, if not more generally with regard to some of us, to accurately see who we are, and therefore to have the opportunity and ability to rectify our wrongs, our incorrect judgments, it is necessary, if not essential, to seek out and gain the opinions of others about ourselves and our actions, as well as monitoring and listening with care to others, observing their responses to us attentively so that we can accurately interpret the responses of others, and gain other perspectives on who we are or who we are perceived to be. Through this monitoring and attention to the responses to others, as well as educating ourselves about these others, and then moving where necessary and reasonable to act in modified and more effective ways, we will hopefully be taking steps to promote our happiness and well-being and reduce our levels of experiences of unhappiness and pain.

Again, none of this is to say that we must or indeed should always act on what we hear, or change who we are in the face of the perceptions, opinions and ideas that others have about us, or in response to developing self-awareness and understanding of others. Nevertheless, such information and understandings are of value in supporting our mental health, our well-being and happiness and avoiding emotional pain and suffering.

In addition to our self-motivated self-education, personal informal research and, indeed, the study that we can do to support these ends of developing our understanding of ourselves and others, we can also engage in more formalised education and more formal learning about others, about community and society, about people, about cultures, groups, our human characteristics and the world we live in, about the range of influences on ourselves and others. All of this can be important in a multitude of ways to enable us to enjoy strong and positive mental health.

To support our own well-being and avoid pain and suffering, wherever possible and reasonable, we need to find out about, interact with and build positive and constructive relationships with other individuals, other people with differing perspectives, beliefs, attitudes and approaches, from different origins and backgrounds. In order to learn and develop we need to encounter, explore, find out about and, as far as we can, come to know other individuals, communities, societies, cultures, those from other groups. We need to explore and find out about those holding other perspectives on the world. All of this exploration and personal development will serve to support our mental health and mental well-being.

Crucially, to support both our own well-being and the general well-being, to help us in avoiding pain and suffering, we must further do our utmost to understand and cope with the range of relationships we have and develop the capacity to cope with all those other people with their different backgrounds, personalities, life stories and perspectives. That being said, as already stated in different ways, we should not necessarily jettison our own personal perceptions, perspective, opinions and beliefs in the face of the differences we find, but rather it means we need to explore, enjoy and experience the possibility of finding out and learning, of developing ourselves where possible and necessary, of developing beneficial relationships and understanding and appreciating as well as living with, existing in a peaceful manner, alongside the perspectives of others. Our enjoyment of such differing perceptions and perspectives is without doubt useful and valid when the perspectives of others have merit in terms of core and other principles. Our deeper understanding and knowledge will also help us avoid the personal pain, anguish, suffering and frustrations of miscommunications and misunderstandings that we can experience, and will also help avoid the anguish, pain, frustration and suffering of others.

In regard to developing our personal selves, there can be little doubt that educating, training ourselves and developing our skills, developing our knowledge and attributes in the range of the skill areas which are relevant to our lives, doing all of these things, benefits our mental health through, amongst other things, enhancing our feelings of capability, self-worth and self-esteem. Knowing that we can cook a meal and do it well, that we can paint, design, mend a leaking pipe, lay a carpet, deal with electrical faults, build a wall, play a sport, dance, engage in mathematical monetary calculations, do statistics, plough a field, build the roof of a house, engineer a product, write and speak well, discuss issues or plant a good vegetable garden, play a musical instrument amongst other things; all of these examples along with the development and improvement of many, many more skills serves, on the whole, can enhance our feelings of self-confidence and self-esteem, as does knowing that we have such capacities and skills. And of course, through having our own specific skills and abilities as well as a range of skills, we enhance our ability to achieve our goals, providing another potential source of well-being and happiness and reducing the chances of pain and suffering.

Apart from having capacities in terms of the range of skills, our possession of some form of more unique and specialised individual skill or ability, as mentioned above, is also very useful and of value for each of us in many ways, adding to our personal sense of individual identity, enhancing our ability to contribute to our communities and societies and undoubtedly leading to others attributing value if not substantial and greater value to our contributions and, as a consequence, to us as an individual.

Quite obviously, by contrast, being unable to do things, lacking the ability and skills to do that we wish to do, may well make us feel inadequate and dent our self-confidence and self-esteem, as a consequence potentially or likely affecting our mental state and mental health in a detrimental way. Of course we all, or almost all of us, will likely feel some sense of inadequacy at times since we are all unable to do certain things, given the vast array of skill areas it is possible to encounter and develop in life. Coping with our lacks and inabilities is something that we all have to do, our lacks and inabilities being something we all have to get used to, adapt to and live with. It is probable that our self-confidence and self-esteem will be vulnerable if we wish to be the best at everything, if we do not manage to achieve the high levels of achievement and skill we might wish to achieve and if we are destructively critical of ourselves where we are not the best or do not achieve to the levels we wish to achieve to. It is, of course, not possible for most of us to master or even gain high competence at the entire range of skills. Even those of us who have exceptional skills and expertise in one area are almost certain to lack such a level of exceptional skill in other areas.

In terms of our mental health, while aiming to continuously build our skills and knowledge, it is also important, to some extent, to be relaxed about and able to cope with and live with our personal lacks and inabilities (which we may try to remedy), to cope with the fact that we do not and cannot do everything well, that we cannot win all the time and that we are unlikely to be the best all the time. Where we can, we need to move on from our lacks and inabilities, either looking to develop ourselves further such that these lacks and inabilities disappear, or move towards building a sense of equanimity and coming to terms with the reality that we cannot do particular tasks, that we cannot do everything and do everything well. We also perhaps may need to come to terms with the possibility that, even in areas where we are clearly skilled and talented, that in the end, while having such talent and high level skills, we may not be or may not become the best of all in these areas, though still should recognise that we have skills, abilities and knowledge with which we can achieve substantially and can contribute much as individuals without being the best or most skilled.

We do not, in many instances, need to be the comparative best at anything, however nice that night be. And in many areas, determining the best can represent rather a subjective judgment. In terms of supporting our personal mental well-being and indeed in terms of contributing to others, in particular where we are developing our talents, skills and abilities, we are often better off focusing on our own personal development and improvement rather than what may be, at times, painful comparisons with others.

Our skills and talents may, in some if not many cases, take years to develop, and though there may be others who we believe are performing exceptionally well at the skills we wish to gain, giving us a sense of perhaps both wonder and inadequacy, their development will also likely have taken place over substantial time with most likely substantial teaching, support, coaching and experience behind their development, as well as personal dedication, resilience and effort. And behind the successes of these people there will undoubtedly have been many failures, errors and mistakes on the road to their skills development and achievement, failures in the past that will not be visible to the many of us observing their current performance. These past failures are likely to remain hidden from view not only because of our natural viewing of and the saliency of successful performance, but also because of the propensity and in some professions, the necessity, to give the appearance and image of effortless talent and competence in order to be successful, admission of failures and errors being seen as something undermining reputation and image. In fact, however, in an appropriate forum it is highly appropriate and helpful for those of us who have achieved particular successes (and indeed those of us who have not) to describe and talk about the difficult road to achievement, acknowledging failures, challenges and errors along the way.

In the main, it will be difficult for some, if not many of us, to match the achievement and skills demonstration by those who are uniquely and exceptionally skilled and able, without our taking the necessary time and pursuing the necessary development accompanied by the necessary dedication, and effort, and demonstrating the necessary resilience, over a sustained period of time. Yet, noting the skills of others, as we are sure to do, we need to be wary of too much focus on the skills and abilities of others, which can affect our self-image, sense of self-efficacy, self-belief and self-esteem. We need to recognise that we ourselves will have our own unique and individual contribution to make, our own unique perceptions, talents and skills which we can apply in the range of areas of our lives, which will hopefully support us in achieving our own unique success and through which we can benefit others, our communities, societies and beyond. And we need to recognise that others may also perceive us as special, unique and able to make valuable and important contributions.

The education and training, the formal and sometimes less formal components supporting our personal development and change that we require, need to be sought out, and sought out with effort and energy. Where we recognise a lack of skill and ability in relation to our core skills or in relation to the skills and abilities which we wish to have, it is important, even where we are short of resources, that we do what we can to work to develop those skills and abilities and, as is often necessary, that we seek out help and support to develop our talents. Through our searches of information and knowledge from experts, teachers, trainers through conversations, classes, texts or other sources, from the range of sources in our communities, societies and beyond, and through practice, reflection and learning, and explicit instruction and training, we should be able to make progress and support our self-development and self-improvement.

Hopefully we will see ourselves improving, getting better all the time, and as a consequence we will receive some boosts for our positive mental health. Though we should also note that sometimes progress in learning and improving skills and abilities may be somewhat imperceptible occurring in small, almost invisible increments, and further, our development of skills and abilities frequently does not involve us in linear incremental improvement but in processes where, within the context of a general tendency for improvement, there are steps forward and sometimes steps backward, some of the latter providing possible source of demoralisation if we do not understand the complexities of learning and skills development, and also do not understand that backward steps in terms of our performance can be of great value and lead us to understand better the nature of our talents and skills leading to further improvement and development.

In terms of forms of, and the methods through which we seek our skills, abilities and personal development, seeking the help of individual one-to-one coaches, teachers and trainers is of particular value as these individuals can focus on developing our own particular relevant skills and abilities as individuals, identifying our strengths and weaknesses and giving intense focus to our own needs for development. Yet, while coaches and trainers can be of great value, we should be wary of handing responsibility for our development over, to too great a degree, to our coaches, teachers and trainers, since our personal thinking, our personal reflection, our personal evaluations of our progress, based in evidence, are essential for us to develop not only in terms of our skills but as rounded and capable people. And moreover our personal autonomy represents an important element of our overall well-being and happiness. Subsuming ourselves to too great a degree or entirely to the wishes of an overly-demanding coach or teacher may lead to substantial improvement, development and perhaps victory in a competitive context, but it may also damage us, our sense of autonomy and sense of independence as individuals.

A worthy coach or teacher needs to be supporting us in not only developing our skills and abilities, but also supporting us in developing our independence, our capacity to make those appropriate personal judgments which are often required in the specific situations where we put into practice our skills and abilities. As those wishing to engage in learning, we should also be aware of the distinction between those who are capable at what they can do and those who are capable of teaching. It is frequently the case that those who can do, also believe they can teach, but they in practice, while possessing high skills levels, may not have sufficient teaching and coaching ability, may not have sufficient capacity for empathy and understanding of others, or sufficient patience with and commitment to others, teaching and coaching being in themselves specific skills which themselves needs to be worked on and developed. Someone with a lesser level of skill may be more able as a teacher, coach or trainer, in particular through their dedication to the improvement, success and achievement of others.

In order to develop our skills, knowledge and various capacities, all of which will help support our mental health and well-being, we may pursue our learning through reading, reflection, self-observation and practice as well as other means. One-to-one coaching, teaching or training, may be expensive and so we may need to join classes and gain what we can from such classes, which will usually adopt a more generic programme of development aimed at all participants rather than focusing so much on our own individual need. In classes it is often difficult for a teacher to identify and focus precisely on our individual needs. Thus we need to determine our own key goals in terms of our knowledge and skills development, pursue these through our classes, but also do our own additional work and study such that we can gain excellence in what we do. We need to be active and where possible, take the lead in our learning and skills development, in whatever area we work, pursuing our personal learning goals in the learning situations in which we find ourselves.

Of course all of these efforts to develop our skills and abilities require energy and motivation, which we may not always feel that we have, and which, for some of us, we may not feel we have over long periods of time. Feeling demotivated may apply to us in a range of circumstances and if occurring over a long period such feelings are not a sign of well-being or positive mental health. If we do feel demotivated for long periods then we need to look at the sources of our demotivation and try to deal with these, and get back into the joy of trying, doing and hopefully achieving.

Beyond the energy and individual motivation we need, our efforts to develop our skills also require of us that we have the time and the space in which to make such efforts to improve and develop. Yet at times we may feel we are too busy to find the necessary time to develop ourselves, too tired and exhausted to think about and reflect on our lives and actions and to engage in efforts to learn and develop, perhaps due to the variety of the different tasks we have to do, many of which require attention, energy and commitment, due to some of the difficult challenges we face day-to-day and due to what may be for many of us, long working days.

And sometimes, surrounded by others, our families, our children and needing to engage with them, interact with them, relate to them, we may feel it is somewhat difficult, perhaps impossible, to find our own personal individual space where we can reflect on our lives, our days, our skills and abilities, our competencies and competence, and thereby engage in efforts to improve on our skills and abilities. Nevertheless, the importance of our different skills and abilities means we must develop them, keep developing them, and sometimes look to develop entirely new skills and abilities. It is essential for our well-being that, at least at some times, we find time to think and reflect on our lives, the things we do, certainly our personal conduct and general actions, and how we can do them better, set ourselves goals and, as appropriate, focus on developing our skills and abilities.

Beyond the skills and abilities already referred to and the knowledge associated with these skills and abilities, it is, in the main, useful in terms of supporting our health and well-being to be conversant, as far as we can and as far as is practicable, with what is generally known, what is social knowledge, what is accepted as a common cultural knowledge. That doesn't mean that we have to learn everything, but it is helpful to know as far as we can what is considered core knowledge and understanding for those in our cultures and to learn much more if we are able to, and are so inclined. Such core knowledge will help us sustain ourselves as acceptable members within our groups, organisations, communities and societies, being seen as those who can be considered full and conversant members of these groups, organisations, communities and societies. Being aware of such knowledge should enhance our sense of belonging, our well-being and contribute to supporting our mental health.

In terms of avoidance of a level of pain and suffering, having such knowledge should help us avoid being seen as too much of an outsider, help us avoid receiving accusations of significant ignorance or stupidity from others, although such accusations should, of course, never be made. We may well be able to cope without some broader social and cultural knowledge, this being dependent on which groups we belong to, associate with and indeed wish to belong to, and we may well be able to survive and thrive within our smaller, restricted social and cultural groups where we are conversant with the knowledge and understandings of those within our particular groups and cultures.

Within the frame of core and other principles, as those interested in supporting the mental health and well-being of others and supporting them in avoiding pain and suffering, we should never make accusations or insinuations ourselves or use our extent of knowledge to hurt and humiliate others and to put them down. If we are knowledgeable, and others wish to learn from us, then we can teach others what we know. If we are knowledgeable and others do not wish to learn from us, they are under no obligation to do so, though perhaps would be wise to do so. Without a doubt, knowledge and understanding can help us be better people, deal better with others and help us be more successful in achieving our goals. Nevertheless, much more than simply knowledge is needed to achieve well-being and happiness.

There may be those who at times, for a range of reasons, deride us or put us down through accusations about our incompetence, stupidity and ignorance, accusations which can hurt us, perhaps shame and humiliate us, make us feel bad, serve to turn others against us or disrespect us, and as a consequence have negative effects on our mental health and well-being. We probably all need to have strategies for dealing with those people who might look down on us, deride us, who may call us stupid and ignorant on the various grounds that they do, for example, such as the gaps in our knowledge, or perhaps our errors and mistakes of various kinds. We most likely need to be prepared for and inure ourselves against the potential pain arising from those who may call us useless or incompetent because we fail at something, because we lack a particular skill, which they and perhaps we may also deem as important. And as already mentioned in this chapter we may well need to give such people a robust but peaceful response to their offensive, potentially damaging, remarks and behaviour.

However, our preparedness in life needs to take account of the fact that, while these people may be rude and unpleasant, they may also be correct that we do not know, that we do not have the skill and that we lack competence and indeed that we have made errors and mistakes. Thus, though such a response may be a little painful at times, we do have the option of telling them they are absolutely right in what they say (though perhaps not in terms of the way they said it) and state that we will try to rectify our errors, improve, gain help, develop ourselves personally, take greater care on the next occasion and so forth, and perhaps request their help in improving our knowledge, understanding or skill. If criticisms of us are correct, then if our critic conducts themselves in a reasonable manner (and that is certainly not always the case), then it is certainly reasonable to admit our faults and errors. The fact is that learning new things, gaining new information and knowledge, developing relevant new skills can make us feel good both in the immediate moment and in the medium and longer term, and of course will reduce the potential for others to criticise us in the future, though as already mentioned, we cannot know everything and need to be able to cope with a level of not knowing and be prepared to deal with such situations where we do not know and indeed where we may be criticised for not knowing.

Sadly, there are too often those who behave in ways that are simply unkind, insensitive, arrogant or rude. Some of these people who criticise in such ways may do so from perhaps intimidating positions of power and authority, but yet may themselves simply not have sufficient information, knowledge or understanding. Such people and others who are being critical, those acting in these ways, may lack the capacity to evaluate what we are saying in a truly rational and reasonable manner. They may lack the capacity to establish or determine that which is or is not the most effective course of action, because their own knowledge and understanding is in fact flawed, with their addressing us, sometimes however, with a sense of their own superiority, which is often misplaced and undeserved. Their words and actions may be destructive and hurtful to us, especially if they are rude and arrogant persistently.

Sadly, representing a source of such pain and injustice, there are parents, for example, who may persistently criticise, and belittle their children, sometimes seeing this criticism as a source of education, when it is actually, or more likely, largely a significant source of pain, hurt and demoralisation. Bosses at work, drunk with their power over others, can engage in destructive criticism of their employees, establishing dictatorial contexts, diminishing and demoralising their staff, creating environments of fear and establishing environments where all are seen as subservient, acquiescent and dependent on their bosses words and actions.

Those people who criticise destructively in these ways are worthy of criticism and opprobrium and more themselves, due to their destructive talk and clear lack of awareness and concern for the well-being and happiness of others. However, wherever possible, we need to use more persuasive forms of talk and action with a view to encouraging such people to change their approaches to others, such that they are more supportive. Of course they need to desist from such conduct through which they may well be making others feel miserable, stressed and powerless, and through which they will at the same time be encouraging those prepared to act in similar ways to themselves. Of course we need to act to prevent such behaviour, being robust in response to their attempts at criticism and doing our utmost to ensure we and others are not belittled and damaged in terms of our well-being and happiness.

Some managers and bosses have their own personal and ludicrous theories along the lines that that such bullying and dictatorial approaches to leading and management are effective. They have sample sayings such as "If you have them by the balls their hearts and minds will follow". This is foul, bullying, macho and pathetic rhetoric, indicating bravado rather than managerial ability. Rather than promoting effective management and organisation, such approaches promote and spread unhappiness and misery, causing stress and damaging individual health at the same time, as well as promoting inefficiency. There is no evidence or little evidence to support such approaches apart from their personal anecdote and self-delusion. Indeed, such approaches are known in practice to be ineffective and damaging, diminishing the power of others and creating alienation. And even if such approaches did co-occur with company and organisational success, they are unacceptable through the harm they do to the health and well-being of others. In the face of such bullying managers and bosses, we need to act, as far as we can, to prevent their behaviours and stand robustly against bullying and intimidation. If that is too challenging and not possible, then we have no obligation to remain and suffer under such conditions, but should search elsewhere for more amenable employment where that is possible.

Of course, that being said in respect of some managers and bosses, those of us who are employees, colleagues and co-workers need to work cooperatively without such bullying behaviour ourselves and need to actively contribute rather than passively avoiding our own responsibility and placing all responsibility and blame on bosses and managers. We must take care of our co-workers and colleagues; we must not be bullying but need to support others in line with core and other principles, supporting their welfare and well-being and preventing as far as we can, their suffering and pain.

Crucially, in the many contexts in which we may face criticism, we should not accept unquestioningly those criticisms made against us, and we must recognise the human fallibility of those criticising us in these ways. The reality is that we, and that means both ourselves and those criticising us, will all have made mistakes and we will all make mistakes into the future. Additionally, for most of us, we are on a pathway of growing, learning and change. The idea that we will almost always know the correct answers and the best thing to do, particularly at the early stages of our life experiences, perhaps the early stages of our professional experiences, is perhaps rather far-fetched, with our capacities and abilities improving over our years of life, but even then being potentially flawed and inadequate, especially given the contingent nature of many decisions we need to make and the rapidly changing nature of the modern world in which that which we learned when younger can be quickly supplanted by new approaches and new technologies which younger people may be more familiar with and find easier to grasp. Thus even if we are experienced in our fields, in our areas of work, we certainly need to take note of the approaches, ideas and views of those who are in terms of time, less experienced, but who in terms of knowledge, skills and understanding, may have much to offer.

More than that, in terms of the possibility of mistakes and errors, determining the correct course of action, indeed determining many answers to real world questions is often not a simple and straightforward process, with many questions of real import in the world not being open to simple obvious and straightforward answers. If we are reasonable and rational people, we will understand this and tend to be sensitive and understanding, and hopefully kind and tolerant when faced with the errors and misjudgments of others, recognising, after all, that we make and have made many errors ourselves. However with those who are behaving in unreasonable, rude and arrogant ways, those who seem to consider themselves superior to us and others, perhaps bullying others on the grounds of their youth and inexperience, in order to preserve our well-being and mental health, there are a range of options in dealing with such people, which we may need to implement.

For example we can, amongst other responses to such conduct and such people, our operating within the range of core principles and in pursuit of our supporting well-being and happiness, robustly tackle their approach and criticisms directly face-to-face, countering their words and actions with our own more constructive words and actions; then, linked to this, and as a further form of response, we can seek the support of others in dealing with this unreasonable, hurtful and destructive behaviour (undoubtedly we will not be the only person suffering under such a rude and bullying approach, nor will we be the only one who knows of this approach); yet we can also, if absolutely necessary and we can manage it, however undesirable, also quietly tolerate their words and actions, if possible gaining from that person's knowledge and experience, and waiting for an opportunity to take action and improve the environment we are in. With some individuals and behaviours, change may be possible through persuasion over time.

And further, by contrast, as mentioned in relation to other circumstances involving bullying bosses and managers, we can move away from the orbit of influence of this or these destructive behaviours and individuals, such that we do not have to tolerate their criticisms, rudeness, bullying and arrogance. Some of these response approaches can be combined to counter our destructive critics. There are undoubtedly many other strategies that we can adopt which would be consistent with supporting our own well-being and happiness and the well-being and happiness of others. Each of us has to look at the particular individuals involved, the context in which we find ourselves, and our own personal interests amongst others things in deciding how we will act. But we must, in line with core and other principles, support our own personal well-being and the well-being of others.

More broadly, from a more personal point of view, our positive mental health clearly requires us to be, to some extent, emotionally and mentally comfortable with and relaxed with the fact of our making errors, mistakes, comfortable with our lacks, the gaps in our knowledge and understanding. That is not to say that we may not be frustrated, mortified and upset when we make certain errors, some of which may be harmful for others and some of which may make us feel grossly incompetent. The sense in which we need to be relaxed about our mistakes is in the sense of our recognition that errors and mistakes will occur and we will make them, and in the sense that, while we should perhaps remember our errors and learn from them, we should do our best to not let them dent our confidence to too great an extent, and we should not let them bring down our lives in the medium and long term and damage our mental health and our well-being and happiness.

Of course we must aim to minimise our errors and mistakes and aim to rectify them where they hurt others and look to improve and develop ourselves into the future such that these errors do not occur again. Nevertheless, it is essential, while pursuing our own improvement, education and self-development that we avoid too much self-recrimination, self-blame and harsh self-criticism, that we avoid thinking negatively or too negatively about ourselves because of mistakes we make, because of talents we do not have or have not yet developed as far as we would wish, such negativity generally not being deserved.

Further with regard to mistakes and errors, sometimes, if not often, we may fail, or may make mistakes and errors, through no fault of our own. That has to be accepted. We may not have been properly trained; we may have been provided with wrong or false information. Others may not have played the roles they should have done in a team operation. Circumstances may change such that the decision, at the time we made it, was the correct one, but it was inappropriate at the time it was implemented.

Sometimes we will make mistakes and sometimes make big mistakes. That is normal. Sometimes we will get things wrong, and wrong to an extent which, at the time, may seem to be catastrophic. And of course, on rare occasions, we may make really important errors, including taking no action when action is required, which result in harm to others. We hope our mistakes and misjudgments won't be too damaging for others in particular, as well as for ourselves. We certainly have to take responsibility for our errors and mistakes, acknowledge our responsibility. Though if circumstances are complex and decisions have been difficult, we should be careful not to give ourselves too much pain and blame based on the knowledge and understanding gained through hindsight.

The fact is that, as the individuals we are, we are living in a complex world where there are many thousands of judgments that we need to make each day. And the same is true for those other people we deal with and interact with. We simply cannot get it all right all the time, yet many of us can often be very quick to painfully condemn and criticise ourselves, and indeed can be very quick to criticise others. Nor can others get things right on such a scale, like ourselves getting some things right and other things wrong, however well intentioned. While, as mentioned, we can be mortified sometimes by our own errors and incompetence, so can others feel mortified by their own actions and errors. And of course it is very easy to be quick to criticise others when such criticism may well not be deserved. We must simply strive to do whatever we can to perform to the best of our abilities and to get as much right as we can, yet also we need to make efforts to understand others, recognise their humanity and the reasons which may underlie the errors they have made, as well as helping them, where appropriate to make more precise and accurate decisions.

Having made a wrong decision or said something wrong, it is all too easy to recognise this after the event, and that may help us with future decisions and actions. But if we could not have, with reasonable probability, predicted the outcome of our decision and actions beforehand, based on what we knew then, then we are perhaps deserving of some charitable treatment from both ourselves and others.

In support of our mental health and in support of our well-being and happiness, we need to look realistically at the origins of our errors and mistakes and examine the factors which have affected our levels of success or failure. That does not mean to dwell for too long on the things we did wrong, but means we should take a look back to identify problems in our decision-making processes, asking how we could have not only have done differently but how we could have recognised that a different decision needed to be made. This may well be of substantial benefit to us as individuals. And in organisations, communities, societies and beyond, such reflective analysis and thinking is often essential in order to support correct decision-making into the future. Maybe we, or others, made an important mistake. As long as we understand how that mistake was made and how we are going to aim to avoid that mistake in the future, as long as we rectify that mistake where possible, then hopefully, in the many cases, life will be able to continue in a positive sense and we will be able to enjoy well-being and improve our decisions, conduct and actions.

In regard to our more ordinary daily lives, it is further the way of things that because of the numbers of judgments we have to make, because of the range and frequency of our interactions with others, because of our own natural human flaws as a sort of human machine, we will make errors and mistakes. We will have thousands and thousands of interactions with others during our lives and unfortunately, we are therefore highly likely to, on occasion, accidentally offend people, acquaintances, those we love, those we care for, through our making of unintended but inappropriate, clumsy and ill thought out words and remarks.

And, moreover, even though we may make no mistake in our statements, in what we say, yet our remarks may be wrongly and unpleasantly misinterpreted. All we can do is to aim to correct such misinterpretations quickly where they occur, and prior to speaking make our best efforts to be as precise about what we say as we can, anticipating possible misinterpretations, aiming to be as sensitive, caring as we can be, doing our utmost to avoid such clumsy and inappropriate remarks. And when we make a clear mistake, we need to apologise profusely, maybe reviewing our own remarks and conduct, our thinking, reviewing what we specifically said and did, reviewing after the event, such that we reduce the number of such mistakes we will make in the future.

Minor and rational self-admonition may be acceptable with the view to our self-improvement, but to bring ourselves down through false generalisations about our own characters when we have simply done what is likely to be statistically and otherwise, inevitable at some point in time, that is, making some form of accidental mistake or error, is something which is likely to damage ourselves, and cause us unnecessary and undeserved pain and hurt. Our making our own bitter, constant recriminations and put downs against ourselves is damaging to our mental health, affecting our well-being, our outlook on life and, importantly the way that others perceive us, since it can be hard for others to perceive us positively, and for us to think about ourselves realistically, in a positive and a healthy manner, if we are continually negative and destructively thinking and talking negatively about ourselves, which is something that many of us may do.

While our making of errors and mistakes can cause us and indeed others harm, as we need to perhaps acknowledge more often and openly, mistakes and errors are frequently necessary elements on the road to greater learning, helping us to develop our skills and abilities and to choose correctly into the future. However this requires that we recognise our errors, and that we change our processes, our conduct, our behaviour into the future based on these experiences.

It is important for us to recognise that we can almost always come back from our errors and mistakes. It is plain from the history of great events that those who have made great mistakes have often subsequently achieved significantly for themselves and for their communities, societies and beyond. The road to invention and achievement for many is littered with false starts and inventions that did not work. The road to creative achievement is often preceded by rejection by others, even diminishing of our creative work (though in some cases this may not be down to our error). Our ability to cope with failure, errors and mistakes and to see these as simply steps on the road to getting things right and achieving, is an important if not crucial ability, especially if we wish to achieve great things.

And so, while we do not wish to get things wrong, to fail, to make mistakes and errors, when these do occur, rather than engaging in damaging self-destructive thoughts and criticism which can hurt us long term, after we have dealt with what may be some inevitable but hopefully temporary and minor pain of realising that we have acted or spoken stupidly and inadequately, realising that we have not achieved our goal or have made some other form of mistake or error, as already mentioned, we need to focus on moving forwards and resolving any problems our actions have created, developing ourselves so that we do not make such mistakes again.

In order to support our mental health and well-being, if we are engaging at a particular time in tasks which are too extensive, too complex and too challenging for us, and we feel overwhelmed by these challenges, particularly in a manner such that we are suffering from substantial stress, anxiety and our life is being damaged, and especially if we do not need to be facing such complex challenges, then we may, where we can, reasonably downgrade the challenges we are facing and desist from further such challenges, perhaps until we are fully recovered, instead seeking positive pleasure or finding challenges which are more appropriate, challenges that we can cope with, until we feel we are able to revisit the more complex and difficult challenges that we previously could not manage. This might involve breaks of days, months or even years away from a particular and complex challenge. Alternately we can aim to simplify complex tasks, breaking them down into more achievable, smaller tasks with which we can cope technically, emotionally and otherwise, working piece by piece until we achieve our overall goal and can complete the whole task.

To some degree, dependent on our moods and general well-being, we can, at least some of us, sometimes express direct dislike for ourselves and be hyper-critical of ourselves, admonishing ourselves too much and unfairly, causing ourselves pain, and hurting ourselves to a lesser or greater degree. At least for some of us, we can launch into internal tirades against ourselves, extreme and depressing admonishment of ourselves, due to the simple errors we make in our every day lives, be they acts such as accidentally knocking something over or bumping into something (which can sometimes lead us to bitter recriminations against ourselves on account of what we may describe to ourselves as our clumsiness and stupidity), tripping up, mistyping a word on a phone or computer, mishearing the words of another, failing to find something which we later find is within our view, losing things, missing appointments and meetings, and failing at basic tasks. In these and other similar circumstances, it is so easy for many of us to fall into our own largely internal dialogues full of false generalisations about ourselves, which tell us of our stupidity, clumsiness, personal failure and inadequacy. Often we will fail to notice or consider the number of times we get things right, the number of times we do not bump into things, do not knock things over, the number of times we type accurately and the like, thinking intensely irrationally. And how much more are we capable of falling into such unjustified dialogues when we make more serious errors?

The reality is, , that all of such things, such actions, and many many more, are common, statistically likely for all of us and, in the vast main, will reflect nothing more than normal happenings, which reflect nothing negative at all about us and our general efficacy as individuals. Yes, we may well be annoyed at such minor incidents and will be more annoyed at more serious faults. But we do need to act to support our personal well-being and happiness, and it thus would be more wise to consider these to be the minor events and errors they usually are and the kind of stuff of everyday life that we all do now and again. It is up to us to respond constructively in response to some of these instances and simply treat them with equanimity rather than heaping blame on ourselves for things which may be inevitable given our imperfect humanity.

Taking this point further, a minor road accident, and we may condemn ourselves as stupid, when in fact we may be normal and average or even better than average in our driving, but on this occasion we have met the inevitability of chance and statistics amongst those who drive their cars for thousands of miles every year, and made an error resulting in damage. A misplaced word, an inadvertently false statement due to poor memory or inappropriate phrasing, a forgotten meeting, accidentally misplacing the wrong words in the wrong place at the wrong time, and there we (or some of us) are, telling ourselves how awful we might be, how stupid we are, how reprehensible we are, how inadequate we are in dealing with people, in essence suffering pain unnecessarily when most of this should be taken in our stride as part of our ordinary humanity. Such feelings may be seen by some to be useful as motivators to improve ourselves and how we operate, but they are certainly not if taken to the extent of causing us substantial anxiety, stress and pain, with these feelings often interfering with our taking the right steps into the future. Our requirement, having made errors, is to right wrongs, correct errors, and perhaps devise new strategies to reduce the chance of future problems. Such an approach is infinitely preferable to that of making painful statements about ourselves which may make us feel bad, unhappy, or worse, and which may damage us into the future, and indeed damage others as a consequence.

Mistakes and errors, and even major mistakes, are the territory of all of us, with major mistakes affecting the many, in particular those of us living in the realms in which we are making major and influential decisions which have an impact on many others. Of course, incorrect decisions at such levels can have disastrous effects on others and can and should be a source of the deepest concern for those who make and have made them. It is the remit of those who are influential to make correct decisions for which they have an enormous responsibility for others. Yet, major mistakes will be made and must be lived with and learnt from, just as with any other less widely impactful form of error or mistake.

Fortunately those who make major wrong decisions may well follow these with major correct decisions in the future, which may well be lauded. That reflects a reality of life in which we and those others who are making impactful decisions, need to be able to cope mentally, not only with success, but also with responsibility and with our errors. And added to this, we also have to recognise the reality that many of those of us who are admired and lauded as successful and worthy of emulation one day, may be criticised, forgotten and ignored a short time later. Indeed our decisions and work, our achievements, may be later re-evaluated or recognised and interpreted as of less significance than they seemed to have at the time. Conversely, those actions considered incorrect and subject to heavy criticism at the time, and seen contemporaneously as mistakes and errors can sometimes be re-evaluated and recognised as either understandable or appropriate to their circumstances and leading to long-term benefits.

Public and media evaluations of decisions and events on the moment are often based in sectional interests and short-term personal benefit, without much considered thought, and can be made in a short-termist and kneejerk fashion without full consideration of factors influencing decisions, understanding of the perceptions and motivations of protagonists and without much awareness or consideration of the evidence used as a basis for decision-making. Yet these evaluations could possibly affect the emotional state of those making such decisions, those others giving judgments about decisions causing the decision-makers anxiety, hurt and pain, should they not have already developed the thick skins often, unfortunately, at least in our current age, required for exposed positions of power and influence.

For the benefit of our personal health and well-being and the well-being and happiness of others, we need to prepare for the fact that there will be ups and downs that are bound to occur in our lives. And we need to be mentally prepared for, and we need to anticipate these in different areas of our lives. With such preparedness and anticipation we will be better able to cope with these ups and downs which will come to all of us. There are likely to be some higher peaks, moments and times of great pleasure and joy, some periods where life seems positive and even wonderful, yet also some unpleasant and challenging moments, some moments of great sadness and perhaps for some of us, some deeper and extended troughs, some of these latter being significantly challenging and difficult to face and deal with. And knowing that these ups and downs are likely to come to us will help us to face them, to cope better with some inevitable levels of sadness, with greater equanimity.

Where these ups and downs relate to our successes and failures, it is dignified to enjoy our successes but also to treat both failure and success with a sense of humbleness, even disdain, since, in particular, although we may have been personally successful, when it comes to complex endeavours and complex decisions, there may be and may have been many factors influencing our success. The successes and failures in our lives will often be due, certainly considering things in the round and over time, to much more than our own personal efforts, being due to many people, our parents, teachers, trainers, friends, our teammates, managers and co-workers and more, even though it may be our personal efforts, our personal dedication, the quality of our thinking and actions, our own creativity, which are a requirement for success and which make the difference between failure and success. Not only are our successes frequently requiring of the contributions and efforts of others, but they also require favourable contexts and environments in which we can survive, thrive and achieve. And we need to recognise, acknowledge and appreciate the contributions of others and the role of these favourable contexts and environments.

Negative emotions and feelings which damage our personal health and well-being can stem from, at one extreme, unjustified and intense self-criticism, even leading in some cases to self-hatred, and at the other end, a narcissism, a love of self, or vastly over and unjustified self-confidence which, while perhaps insulating us psychologically, at least temporarily, from the criticisms and realities of our social worlds, damages our relationships, mostly likely damages others and in the end is likely to damage ourselves as well.

The former pole, in which we may feel a sense, an intense sense and expression of destructive lack of self-confidence in some cases, of dislike and even hatred for ourselves, is perhaps more common. Such negative self-destructive feelings and the consequent pain and suffering, may unfortunately be deeply embedded in our individual nature and mental selves, arising often from unjustified, deep-seated feelings of inadequacy, feelings of low status and a sense of our low value and unimportance. Our self-dislike and self-hatred in some cases, may stem from our upbringing, perhaps from our being substantially belittled and criticised, when young, through being made to feel inadequate and incompetent, generating feelings of worthlessness during our childhood, perhaps caused by our parents or sibling relationships, or perhaps by our school fellows, our peers or oppressive institutional settings we experience when growing up.

That being said, it may also be that our sense of inadequacy may arise simply because, being young and inexperienced, we do not have the competences we would like, as young growing people, and can therefore feel bad about ourselves as a consequence, especially when we see the standards and qualities of others around us, the things that some older adults seem to manage with ease, the confidence that some will demonstrate, and we do not see the long roads they have taken to be where they are, to achieve what they have achieved and we do not see them as having been young themselves and having had their own difficulties, incompetences and failures.

Many of us feel and engage in this kind of self-criticism intently and sometimes frequently. If such feelings and self-dislike and self-criticism has arisen during our childhood it may be the case that when young, we were, as mentioned above, frequently criticised for our failings and inadequacies in relation to unfairly and irrationally expected adult standards. Such failings and inadequacies can often only be seen as failings in relation to notions of idealised adult conduct set by adults who may sometimes place or have irrational expectations of what we, as young people are actually like, or can realistically achieve. Often when young, our troubles, failures, worries and concerns, our conduct which is criticised as faulty and unacceptable, what are seen as our inadequacies, in fact only represent what normally occurs and what would normally be expected in a child or young child growing up. And we may even have suffered dislike from parents, those we would wish to love and to love us, something which is reprehensible on the part of parents and which no young person should have to suffer and endure.

Our feelings of dislike for ourselves, even, hopefully only in the rarest of cases, self-hatred, should we have them, may also be, for some of us, a more natural and more biological and physiological way of feeling, arising through certain stages of our lives as we grow up, though hopefully these are not inevitable ways of feeling and they will dissipate and disappear. However, for the most of us, in the more moderate elements of the spectrum of how we feel about ourselves, sometimes positive and sometimes more negative, it is rather too easy to be self-critical, to be down on ourselves, to admonish ourselves, make false and negative generalisations about who and how we are, and as a consequence suffer unnecessary pain and hurt. Obviously such mental hurt and pain is contrary to core and other principles, should not be encouraged and, for those of us feeling in such ways, we need to do our utmost to escape from such damaging and painful feelings.

Nevertheless, whichever stage of life we may be at, we may engage in recriminations and significant self-doubt on occasion and we have to acknowledge that sometimes that may be reasonable, warranted and appropriate. Indeed some self-criticism and indeed some criticism from others may be timely, necessary and deserved and may motivate us to improve ourselves. But we should be very careful not be excessive in our self-criticism and create too much unnecessary pain, self-hurt and self-damage, and both we and others should be very careful in our criticisms of others and ourselves, hopefully focusing on the things we have done, taking responsibility and focusing on the inappropriate or wrong actions we have taken, but without inflicting insults and dislike or hatred on ourselves or others and without engaging in deep and personalised attacks.

Unfortunately, even when others are only slightly critical of what we have done or do, even when focusing specifically on our actions rather than ourselves, for some or perhaps many of us, we may interpret this as deep and personal criticism of ourselves, and we may be tempted or actually respond inappropriately and excessively to these others, expanding the most minor criticism to a personal thinking which can bitterly undermine our whole selves and damage others. We should make strenuous efforts to ensure we use other ways of thinking, ensuring we do not engage in self-destructive thinking with its associated damaging hurt and pain, and of course we need to respond appropriately to what we have interpreted as criticisms. We need to think and act with a focus on resolving specific problems, as well as avoiding the broadening of such criticisms to a catalogue or tirade of ill-thought-out and unjustified attacks and recriminations against ourselves or-indeed against others.

Hurting ourselves emotionally through our self-criticisms will not only hurt us, but will also hurt our communities, societies and beyond. Through unjustified self-imposed restrictions on our actions due to overly harsh self-criticism and through damaging our personal confidence, we are likely to be unable to act so effectively in our social contexts, being less able to support those other people whom we might, and indeed, whom we should, be able to support into the future. Our personal health and well-being and the well-being of others is best served by acknowledging that all of us get things wrong and that almost all of us are to some extent vulnerable emotionally and otherwise because of our actual and potential errors and often because of a propensity to be self-critical and sometimes too self-critical. We need to cope with our mistakes without inflicting unnecessary and undesirable emotional and other pain and hurt on ourselves and others.

Having considered being on the wrong end of criticisms and how we might feel in response to criticisms of ourselves, it is also important to say that, in some contexts, we will need to point out what we believe to be the errors and mistakes of others, of those we love, and this can be hurtful, especially if not done with care. If we are in a position as teacher, coach, manager or other authority and allocated that or similar status and role in which there is an expectation that we will support others to improve in terms of what they are undertaking, then it may be easier for us to advise on how things should be done and point out the errors of others without causing so much harm, though still that should be done with great sensitivity. Notably, it is almost always important to focus on ways of getting things right, how to move forward to improvement in a constructive way rather than be so critical of things which are or have gone wrong. In the vast main, we all wish to learn though we do not wish to be personally criticised or have our errors over-emphasised and harped on about, especially once we have acknowledged them, though in some cases reminders of previous mistakes can be instructive and useful.

In the context of more family and friend situations, pointing out what we perceive to be the errors of those we know and love can be difficult, and perhaps should, in the vast main, be avoided unless it is considered of sufficient importance, this being something which will be a matter of judgment. In the majority of circumstances, it is believed here that such pointing out of mistakes in such contexts should as far as possible be minimal, as it can smack of bullying, a perception of personal superiority and oppression. We need to be sensitive to and supportive of those we know and love (indeed of everyone), continuous analysis and critique of others along with the frequent pointing out of their mistakes, being incompatible with support and sensitivity and serving to undermine the confidence and self-belief of others. Such critical conduct will almost certainly undermine our loving relationships.

If we must point out errors, mistakes, faults and the like we should focus, in the vast main, on what has been done, on what is being done, rather than focus our criticisms on the overall person and personality. We can change our behaviours, actions and decisions more easily than we can change our overall personalities and ways of being (though such is also possible). Focusing on actions is in the main, though not necessarily, less hurtful and challenging than broad criticisms and attacks on the whole person which can be deeply undermining. That being said, criticisms of actions may well be interpreted as criticisms of ourselves and who we are. The distinction between criticising behaviour and action, and person, is not always as clear as is sometimes presented. In line with core and other principles we should be looking to promote happiness and well-being, avoiding pain and suffering rather than inflicting unnecessary emotional and other pain.

Yet as has been mentioned elsewhere in this guide, efficiency, our achievement of goals, achievement of success is also important in terms of our personal well-being and happiness and the well-being and happiness of others. Thus in a range of contexts, home, work and other contexts, we are obliged to point out when, in particular serious mistakes are being made, where, for example, at home, we have concerns about family money situations, about the future of our families, about the schools our children are going to, about the safety of our property. At work we may be concerned that policy and strategy are wrong, that people are making practical errors in terms of what they are doing, technical, relationship-wise or in other ways. In such contexts we cannot sacrifice the overall success of our families organisations, institutions, community or other social entity through ignoring or politely ignoring mistakes which could have substantially negative or even catastrophic consequences for ourselves, others, our social entities. Of course we need to act with the aim of improving the quality and effectiveness of our individual and social actions in order to support well-being and happiness.

And as recipients of what may be valid comments, we need to evaluate these comments, criticisms, reflect on whether we are making or have made mistakes and look to improve how we work, how we act. Our first recourse, however we may feel internally, needs to be consideration of whether in fact our critics may in fact actually be correct and we have made and are making mistakes and errors and whether we need to change what we are doing and how we do it. If we are able to recognise our faults and mistakes and learn from them, this is likely to be good for us, improve our skills and knowledge and serve to strengthen relationships and build respect on all sides. We should take care to avoid oversensitivity to criticisms and suggestions and focus on listening to others.

Of course we are not always successful. Our reality is that, whatever successes we may have, there are always moments, periods of time or even sometimes longer periods of time when things don't go so well for us, when we can feel in pain, sad, depressed and even despairing. Sometimes we may attribute our challenge, our feelings to what we perceive as our own inadequacies and failings. Yet, for most of us, in order to improve and maintain our well-being and happiness we need to recognise and accept the reality of errors and mistakes and that we may well have periods when things don't go so well, and indeed that we all have imperfections and inadequacies to some degree. None of us can attain perfection or as already mentioned, attain even a high standard of achievement in all areas of our lives all of the time, and yet hopefully, through the variety and range of people and the diversity of talents in our community, each of us will serve in our own way to complement the talents and abilities of others such that together our families, organisations, communities and societies, our broader humanity are likely to receive the full range of contributions, and work effectively as cohesive and successful entities, supporting those of us living within and beyond them in achieving well-being and happiness.

Unfortunately, we can feel unwarranted and unjustified dissatisfaction, unhappiness and dislike for ourselves in many ways, some of which stem from feelings which go beyond simple dissatisfaction with our decisions and actions. In terms of such additional sources of pain in our lives, as individuals, in relation to our society's archetypal standards, we may lack, or feel we lack amongst other things the level of physical attractiveness, the physical characteristics, beauty and the good looks we wish to have. Rather ironically, some of those generally acknowledged by others as having such good looks and beauty, in a sense representing archetypes of beauty and good looks, often believe themselves to lack such qualities. Such lacks and perceptions of such lacks are likely to be upsetting to us and may well be personally damaging and debilitating, yet in many cases, there may be little or nothing we can do to change our situation with regard to some of our physical characteristics, and even if there were, such changes may well be unnecessary and unwise.

Our feelings about our looks are likely to be influenced by how others look, and what they think of our looks, with our sometimes comparing ourselves to those who are presented in the public space as ideals and archetypes of good looks and fine physiques, something which is bound to cause some anxiety and pain. Indeed comparisons in themselves, though to an extent inevitable, are likely to be damaging to the way we feel, since we will almost always be able to find some who are better at things and considered better looking than ourselves and this may be difficult to face. The archetypes referred to are undoubtedly often not achievable for the many of us and comparing ourselves with such archetypes or indeed anyone close to these archetypes in our more local social environment can be a source of great unhappiness, sadness and even depression. While there may be inevitability in comparing our looks with those of others, it is most likely best to avoid or downplay comparisons of our looks with those archetypes and with the looks of others, as much as we can. Instead, it is better to focus on what we are doing in our lives and the things we can improve and change in our own lives. It is important that, to an important extent, we have some self-belief, however much that belief can sometimes be shaken.

At the minimum, if we insist on conscious comparisons, then we should focus on our own looks in terms of our near environment and those more immediately around us rather than national and international icons of supposed beauty, though if we can, as mentioned, it may be better for us to studiously avoid or downplay comparison with the looks of others around us. And we certainly should avoid denigrating others in terms of their physical appearance (and other characteristics) which is likely to cause such others pain and hurt.

Of course we can in some respects take some actions which will affect our appearance, such as diets if we feel overweight. We can ensure we exercise to maintain our physique and health and to build up our musculature. We can use cosmetics and other devices to help us conform more to the standards of beauty, which others expect, and to attempt to hide our blemishes relevant to those archetypes, should we have any such blemishes. Engaging in such conduct may to some extent be meeting social conventions, which may help us to fit in with others and may make us feel better, and avoid some criticism. Some of this may work to make us feel better about ourselves, feel better about how and who we are, though of course our actions may more truly be reflecting and are, perhaps, even bolstering and legitimising our feelings of inadequacy. We will need to make our own decisions regarding these matters such that our own well-being and happiness is supported.

And in addition to cosmetics and the other more accessible and affordable ways of changing our looks, in terms of changing ourselves physically, in more wealthy and contexts, where modern technology is more available, this now means that it can be possible to change the way we look to some extent, in some cases significantly, by means of surgery which is able to remedy, at least partially, not only required and major medical problems, but also major and also more minor defects against those archetypes, which may affect the way we look and how we feel about how we look.

Where such physical appearance problems are substantial and damage our quality of life, where we have suffered substantially disfiguring injury, and also particularly among the young, then it seems reasonable to make efforts to remedy these problems. Yet for the most of us, the various expensive surgeries available, can probably said to achieve very little. They may also be seen as representing an inappropriate use of personal and community and social resources, given the wider needs of the community and the self-focus, expense and indeed dangers involved in such procedures.

In particular, the changes that come upon us with age, cannot be significantly offset by such surgery, though clearly some can be hidden to some degree. If we are substantially unhappy with our appearance of agedness, then we should consider engaging in some safer and less resource requiring methods of making ourselves look younger, if that is what we wish to do. Yet of course aging is inevitable and whatever the external signs, unfortunately, the rest of the aging process will be going on, invisibly, within our bodies.

In regard to our personal looks in general, more appropriate for the most of us is, perhaps, the sense of a resigned shrug, accepting the way we look, believing in ourselves as having value and importance beyond our looks, getting on with our lives, ignoring those who belittle us because of our looks and physique, or responding politely and robustly to their remarks, however hard this might be, and keeping company with more supportive people who are accepting of themselves and ourselves. Accepting reality as it is; accepting ourselves, in the main, for the way we look, and being significantly satisfied with who and what we are, can be a real asset to our emotional selves and also an asset when we are searching for love and searching for partners in life, a process which may be initially promoted by looks and ideas of attractiveness, but which is frequently dependent on much more than looks.

Turning in on ourselves with self-criticism, bitterness and recriminations about our looks and physiques will simply hurt us, damage ourselves and upset those around us, indeed making it less likely for others to like us and want to be with us. There is little point, and no joy, in spending our lives being unhappy about our physique and our looks. The fact and reality is that, despite what are likely to be our non-archetypal looks, the most of us will find someone we can find attractive and love (of course most of the rest of us will not have these archetypal looks either), and most of us will have at some point the pleasure of a lover who finds us attractive enough and will love us in the same way, hopefully in a deep long lasting and special way which goes beyond our physical looks. And therefore we can certainly achieve well-being and much happiness and joy in our lives, and most of us will manage to achieve such well-being, happiness and joy in our lives without being the most attractive, archetypal male or female beauty.

And as already referred to, contributing to such bad feelings in relation to our looks and in many other areas of our lives, is the activity of spending some time or excessive time comparing ourselves with others, which we may frequently do in negative terms, something which, whether we feel better or worse than others, is likely to cause us emotional pain and suffering in many ways. If rational comparisons are possible, and if we were emotionless beings, then comparison ought in theory to be a neutral and painless process leading us to useful conclusions about who we are and where we stand in relation to others, but that does not tend to be the reality of comparison, a reality in which we are usually emotionally influenced and affected by seeing and placing ourselves next to, above, or more frequently, below, others.

While a certain amount of comparison is undoubtedly inevitable, and perhaps indeed a necessity for a range of reasons (such as pointing us in the direction of new skills we might acquire and seeing examples of how it is acceptable to conduct ourselves), it is surely a better focus in terms of our general health, happiness, pleasure and well-being to focus more on improving ourselves and our own lives, enhancing our own well-being and happiness through our own actions within the context of our own more individual lives, rather than taking part in what is too often the frequently painful process of negative self-comparison.

Too much focus on others and what they are doing, what they have and how they are, too much of the comparison that has already been mentioned as potentially and indeed likely detrimental to our personal well-being, can lead us to focus on the irrelevant and unchangeable, and act as a source of pain, jealousy and envy which works against our mental health, happiness, pleasure and well-being, and indeed the mental health, well-being, happiness and pleasure of others.

Additionally, and importantly, in respect of the effects on us of such comparisons, in factual and rational terms, comparisons with others and their abilities often tend to be incomplete since we will only see part of a picture and usually cannot know the feelings and thoughts of those with whom we are comparing ourselves. That is to say that while another person may appear to us to be supremely capable and competent, perhaps physically beautiful, and as a consequence we may admire and wish to emulate their looks, their skills and abilities, their life *in totale*, we cannot see their whole story, their personal history, and usually do not know the whole person with whom we are comparing ourselves. Their lives may be happy but could in fact be unhappy and we may not be able to see that because of our incomplete comparisons.

Furthermore, and adding more detail to what has already been discussed already in this chapter with regard to skills, knowledge and abilities, the reality is that the apparent competence and achievement of another, with whom we are comparing ourselves, is likely to have arisen following years of struggle and failure, years and multitudes of errors and mistakes, through a long and difficult journey to where they are now, a journey which will frequently not be visible to us. If they appear skillful in terms of what they say, their thinking and actions, it is likely that their personal maturity and articulation of their thoughts and ideas will have been built on not only years of study and dedication, but also years of experimentation and experience, and indeed years of errors and failure. Their skills and abilities may have been generated through practice, training, coaching, sustained effort and struggle and teaching and learning over a long period. Moreover, the person we are interacting with or watching in some contexts may well be that one person who has unique and special attributes or a combination of attributes, which the majority of others of us may in fact not in reality be able to emulate (though we may).

And thus, while admiring that skilled person and wishing to emulate that person and their skills and talents, and working hard to maximise our talents and achievements, we should also realise that it is highly unlikely for the most of us that we can be immediately like them. That achievement, if possible, and it may well be possible, will usually take time, effort, endeavour and struggle. Indeed we need to focus on our being our own unique selves and value our selves. We should not consider ourselves to be failing or a failure, not as good in comparison to that person, that being something which will upset ourselves and which may affect our mental health and well-being. But further this form of thinking is inappropriate since, over time, we may well be able to achieve the standards of the person we are observing and wish to emulate. And further, we should at least be able to develop our talents beyond where we are now, especially if we work over an extended period of time in a dedicated manner to support that improvement and to achieve. We may not all reach the standards of that individual who has achieved to the highest in their field; we cannot all ascend to such a pinnacle of success. Doing our best, aiming to achieve what we ourselves can achieve as individuals, being as good as we can be, in our own journey through life, is enough, is worthwhile in itself and should bring us pleasure, hopefully recognition from others, a sense of achievement in itself, bring us a good degree of well-being and happiness.

So unless it can be used positively and constructively, facilitating us to pleasure, happiness and achievement, something which comparison with others tends not to produce, such comparison can be a source of pain. Comparing ourselves with others is certainly useful in some cases with others potentially serving as exemplars of good values, positive characteristics and also as pathfinders, who show us the ways our lives can be. Others can also provide examples of how not to be and how not to do things, providing society with such negative exemplars representing destructive and unpleasant values and actions and demonstrating actions to avoid and values incompatible with social living, incompatible with core and other principles.

Further, acknowledging another part of our nature, we may feel good, and experience elements of positive mental health when we recognise that we are better in our skills and ability than others. Feeling that we have greater capacities than others can add to our feelings of self-efficacy and self-worth, though clearly there is the downside under such circumstances (for others) that others may feel worse about themselves, and of course if our skills are lesser, we may feel of less worth, though as previously discussed, that should not necessarily be the case and we should ensure our thinking does not lead us to such feelings of lack of comparative worth or feelings of lack of self value and worth.

Winning in competitions against others feels good and the notion of competition is importantly and fundamentally based in our being compared with others, as individuals and groups. It can feel very good to win, to beat the competition, in essence to be better than others, and indeed it can feel not so good, though often not too bad within the gamut of bad experiences, to lose, though persistent defeat and losses can be highly demoralising. Although we may be better at a particular skill than another or others, it is essential to recognise that that does not make us in any way a better person compared to these others or a superior being, nor are we lesser should we be defeated or even if we lose in competition consistently.

Core and other principles state that we have fundamentally equal value as human beings. It is optimal for our own well-being and happiness and for the well-being and happiness of others that we should therefore maintain respect for all, whether or not we have greater ability in a particular area, and we need to speak and act accordingly, demonstrating such respect for others.

While recognising the joys of winning and success, in most if not all forms of competitive endeavour, if we are the ones who have experienced victory and success, we must take care to protect the feelings of those who did not win, where appropriate, aiming to support others to improve and develop their skills and abilities, and to encourage others for the future. If we are the ones who have not been successful, all things being equal, and victory or defeat having been achieved in a fair and reasonable manner, then we must appreciate those who have won, congratulate them, stay on good terms with them, indeed support them, whatever our disappointment.

In competitive contexts we need to accept that the existence of such competitive systems will mean that some will experience the joys and pleasures of victory and success, or will do so to a greater degree, while some others will not be so successful. Hopefully, in some contexts we as individuals will all be able to experience, to some extent, the joys and pleasures of winning and of achievement at some point in time, and we will hopefully be able to avoid feelings of low self-esteem through persistent defeat, though it should be said that after persistent defeat, we are usually compensated in abundance, since the joy of success, achievement, victory can be that much sweeter, indeed produce feelings of ecstasy after persistent struggle, defeat and indeed failures.

Some level of comparison of ourselves with others does seem to be something which is part of our human nature and inevitable in our lives. Indeed comparison with others, as has already been pointed out, is something which can certainly heavily influence how we feel about ourselves and our lives. Nevertheless, as far as we can, we need to be mindful to protect ourselves from the bad feelings that can arise from hurtful comparisons, avoiding a painful focus on the possessions, achievements and talents of others in comparison to ourselves. And we also need to protect others and ourselves from what might become unwarranted jealousy and envy, with the consequence of damaging enmity and bad feeling. The notions of jealousy and envy and their effects on our personal feelings and conduct are discussed in more detail later in this chapter.

It is generally considered positive and useful for our mental health and our well-being, within the terms of the core and other principles, if we have positive thoughts about ourselves and we are positive and constructive in terms of the goals we have and the possibilities of achieving them. Indeed, in terms of our goals and our dreams, it is considered healthy and supportive of well-being if we "reach for the sky" and try our best to achieve our dreams. The fact is that we may well achieve our dreams and as a consequence benefit our lives and achieve great happiness and success, such achievement and success leading to feelings which represent and contribute to our mental health and well-being. Further, in the opposite sense, if we do not try for our dreams, there will always be a sense in our lives of disappointment, that there has been something missed out on, that maybe our dreams could really have been achieved, yet we did not try. Thus we need to have dreams and goals, and aim to realise them. If we do not achieve them, we will have the consolation of knowing we tried. In any case, we may achieve some dreams and not achieve others, enjoying a mix of success and not achieving the success we desire, a mix of outcomes which seems reasonably consistent with a life of reasonable and acceptable well-being.

Of course it is also of great value to be realistic in our lives and in that we wish to achieve. Nevertheless, the notion of being realistic can have quite a negative connotation in our everyday speech, in certain cultural contexts, appearing to communicate the difficulty of achieving our goals, and chasing us away from following our dreams and aiming high. Yet following our dreams and aiming high is certainly something which we should be doing. The problem here exists based in a sense of a commonly found highly conservative irrationality, found in many contexts, which tends to say that possible and indeed some likely and highly possible things are unrealistic, often because that which is aimed for is different, ambitious, perhaps has not been done before (or not by the person giving the advice or by people they know and know of) and is perhaps in particular non-conformist, as many dreams may be. Crucially, many more things are practical and possible than are considered to be practical and possible by the many of us, with unfortunately many lacking the imagination and openness that we need to have about the vast possibilities available to us, and about potential and different futures. Cases in point are the many technological advances in our modern world, which might well have been thought crazy and irrational by 'sensible' people during times of change and development, and not too many generations ago. And social and political advances have also been world changing, yet might have been thought impossible themselves in the not so distant past.

Thus the saying of 'Yes I can' in regard to an ambitious goal is often fine because it happens to be true and realistic in the light of the facts, in the light of rational judgment, and also in the light of the many things which are unknown, which remain to be known, which remain to be achieved and have not yet been explored. Much is possible and we can achieve our dreams and goals and need to try. Further saying 'Yes I can' or 'Yes we can' is likely to launch a journey of exploration, which will encourage both ourselves and others to explore the how of achievement and success, thus helping us develop our knowledge and understandings, even if our final outcomes are not fully achieved.

Sadly there are many naysayers who will put down our chances, who are frightened of the new and say we cannot succeed, that our goals are too difficult and that we are being over ambitious. Yet it is they who are frequently being unrealistic and irrational, lacking in imagination, out of touch with the reality of change, founding their judgments on inadequate evidence and an intensely fearful approach to change and the new. The reality is that we often 'can' succeed and succeed greatly. Their negativity and cynicism and indeed their discouragement may be down to their own fears, their own past failures to achieve imaginative and realistic goals, their perhaps closed minds, a lack of knowledge and experience themselves or a lack of imagination about the possible, for indeed so much which seems difficult or impossible is in fact possible and perhaps within our grasp. And thus the attitudes of these naysayers should generally be ignored, emotionally set aside. Their naysaying may also reflect a lack of love and empathy and an incapacity to understand the joys of goals, dreams and adventure, even if we do not achieve our dreams and goals.

Nevertheless, we can still listen to their words as, in some cases, they may deliberately or inadvertently have contributions to give that can be helpful towards our success, and indeed we may consider elements of what they are saying as being, to some extent rational, reasoned, evidenced, impartial and caring and in such cases, what they say, in terms of content (though not attitude) can inform our goals, our strategies and our decisions. It is also worth considering that even if we may not succeed and we have been informed that this might be the case, the journey of pursuing our goals is often something which we need to take, is something which is enriching and satisfying in itself in a manner which goes beyond the final outcome of our efforts.

And if we are those who may be tempted or requested to give our opinions on the goals and plans of others, it is important, where plans and dreams are within the realms of core principles, that we are supportive, and that if we see problems and serious difficulties, if our experience suggests difficulties or even if we see what we consider to be impossibilities, we point these out, but crucially we must also look for ways in which we can support others in making their plans work, their goals achievable, and support these dreams in coming true, being constructive and supportive, helping to identify routes to success, rather than being destructive and undermining. Even if such plans, such dreams may not work out, dependent on the context and other factors, it is often best that those pursuing their dreams achieve and succeed or fail themselves, rather than their not setting out on a journey due to demoralisation fomented by our cynicism and discouragement.

While it is considered good for our well-being and health to think positively and constructively and to have a constructive and positive outlook, nevertheless such positivity is clearly unlikely to be sufficient in itself to help us in achieving our goals. We must also have a strong focus on the how of achieving our dreams and our goals. Dependent on the nature of our goals and dreams, we may well need to determine actions, way-stages, strategies, pathways of action and perhaps routes for our education and development. We may well need to develop and deploy social and technical skills and much more, such that our goals and dreams can be achieved. We may need to recruit allies and helpers to support us, perhaps accumulate resources so that we can invest to make our dreams a reality.

And of course, while there are important senses in which it is beneficial for us to be positive in regard to ourselves and our actions into the future, we must also be realistic and practical (in a rational sense) in the range of situations if our goals and dreams are to be achieved. In the main, we are most likely to need to move towards many of our goals and dreams in achievable steps, rather than through overextending ourselves and taking on tasks and challenges before we are fully ready. Again, dependent on our dreams and goals, we may well need to realistically look at our personal attributes, social and technical skills and talents, and determine where we need to develop them and then take action to develop them, such that we can meet our various challenges and achieve our goals and dreams.

And to some extent we must weigh our attributes, skills and talents against the goals we wish to achieve and the dreams we wish to realise. Thus, there may be cases where our dreams may not be so easy to achieve. For example, if we are small and lacking in physical strength and slow on our feet, then perhaps aiming to be a leading international player in a sport such as rugby or American football may be to some extent over ambitious and unrealistic (although it may not be), though if that is our dream we should certainly try to achieve our dream and look to enjoy our journey; there are often ways to succeed when others might say our dreams are not possible or likely.

It may be that we have some other specific attributes which we could develop and help us towards success in such a context. Or reframing our dream, maybe our dream might become, rather than being a player, instead to be involved at a top level in such a sport and we might become a coach, sport journalist, sports dietician, or have some other sporting involvement which would maintain our closeness to our original dream.

Of course our dreams may be of different types. Rather than dreaming of achievement and far reaching success, we may simply dream of finding love and having a family and children. This of course will contribute to our own well-being and happiness and the well-being and happiness of others, and for the most of us, while a dream, is also for the many of us highly realistic, rewarding and likely, should we wish for it.

Being realistic about ourselves can also help us avoid some level of pain. Inaccurate thinking about who we are, how others perceive us and how we come across may leave us unprepared when the reality of others' judgments and views of us, when the realities of our true performance and the realities of the world around us, come to pass. When mantras such as 'Yes I can' substantially clash with the realities of what may be, for example, the persistent absence of close, deep and sexual love from our lives, when they are followed by our defeat or non-achievement of what was a premature and unrealistic goal, then we may suffer unnecessary disappointment and pain which would not have occurred with a more realistic self-assessment and more appropriately set targets and goals; which is not to say that we should not pursue our desires, our dreams and our goals, but is simply to say that we may sometimes suffer some disappointments and that in some cases, by setting way stage, realistic goals, and being realistic, we may both better support our happiness and well-being, and better support achieving our goals and dreams.

Thus, as stated already, but certainly worthy of reiteration, while it is considered of value to have a positive outlook, to think constructively and positively, it is certainly considered here, in the vast range of circumstances, to be essential to our well-being that we have an accurate perception of ourselves in terms of both our positive qualities and those areas and qualities with regard to which it would be good for us to pursue change and improvement. Such an accurate and realistic view of ourselves supports us in working out how to make ourselves better, and supports us in determining how to enhance ourselves and our lives, our well-being, supports us in developing our confidence and abilities in all the spheres in which we can engage in such development. And such a realistic view should also help us to feel good about ourselves, understanding that, for the vast majority of us, if not all of us, we have talents and skills, that there is good about us, that there are perhaps, in truth and reality, those who love us and care for us, or who have loved and cared for us, and that there are a range of things about us which make us worth knowing, loving and being with.

That being said, life can be painful and unfair. In terms of our real lives, not all of us have the perfect looks, perhaps far from it, the physique or personality which wins the wonderful, attractive partner we would wish for, the sporting and other attributes which would help us succeed where we wish to succeed, the conversational skills and personality that make others like us and more. It may be that, for some of us, we are able to avoid pains and feelings of being lesser and comparatively inadequate by convincing ourselves that we are better looking, more able and a better person than we actually are or are perceived to be. And that is a way to cope, as is recognising the likelihood of our being successful in many of the ways that we wish to be, irrespective of what may be superficial comparisons with others.

In terms of our conduct, where we can change our conduct and become better then that is optimal, with such change being dependent upon being realistic and understanding ourselves and our effects on others. Yet in some cases we might need to support our well-being and happiness by blocking out or ignoring the realities of, for example, how others percieve the way we look and more, or alternatively learn to respect and admire ourselves and perhaps love our looks even though they may not be consistent with the archetypes that are presented to us as ideal.

It will certainly reduce our pain and maintain and improve our well-being and happiness, if we strive to have a positive perception of ourselves (which of course may sometimes not be entirely deserved), though having argued for this and having stated the benefits of a positive and constructive approaches to living, as already mentioned, we are not obliged to walk round with a constant smile on our faces. That is not the goal. Achieving well-being and happiness for ourselves and others in line with core and other principles represent the fundamental goals, though avoiding a highly negative perception of ourselves is certainly helpful to our well-being and will support our mental health. Moreover the glow of false, planned and deliberate, constant positivity radiated as a general mood and attitude in the public space through glowing and unconvincing smiles, can be an irritant to others, perhaps even depressing to others who may see in it falseness and a reason for mistrust, or see it as representing our detachment from a reality of challenges and problems.

And from our personal perspective, if the external perceptions and our projection of positivity, do not match our own true beliefs and feelings about ourselves, and if we are fundamentally unconvinced in ourselves about what may be an unreal sense of, or projection of positivity, this can itself lead to stresses, pains and tensions, and even severe crashes in the longer term when actual and difficult realities rear their head and threaten or destroy the facade of positivity. However positive we may be, the world presents its challenges and sometimes we may be defeated, with our defeats and life's challenges sometimes difficult to cope with. Thus, while having a positive and constructive attitude and approach to life, we also need to be practical, realistic, open and honest with ourselves (and as appropriate others) about our feelings and emotions, focusing on actions and solutions, dealing with and coping with our pains, focusing on achieving our goals, being solution-focused, and being well-being and happiness-focused rather than being positive in a manner which does not match our own emotional state, our feelings, and the reality around us.

That being said, our overly negative and incorrect, our personally destructive judgments and self-perceptions drag us down, causing us hurt and pain, diminishing our lives from inside ourselves, diminishing our opportunities, through our own actions, for others to love and care for us, and frequently diminishing our chances of achievement, our opportunities for well-being, potentially damaging how others perceive us. By contrast, our overly positive perceptions of ourselves can come across as representing arrogance and rudeness, as covers for insecurity, may lead us to ignore the good advice of others, may lead us to take on challenges which are far beyond our capabilities (with consequent damage to ourselves and others) and may also be seen as inaccurate by others, leading to hostility and resentment.

Importantly having a realistic and accurate view of ourselves may, nevertheless, mean our having a much more positive view of the world than that which we currently have. With a realistic view of our lives, for the many of us we will then have to acknowledge the many often unacknowledged real positives about ourselves, our actions and our lives, thus hopefully decreasing the common tendency, already referred to in this chapter, for many of us to think of ourselves in ways which may be overly full of self-doubt, overly self-critical and negative.

For example, the reality is that in regard to finding a lover, a partner, a husband or wife, something which is important to the vast majority of us, the chances are that almost all of us who want a partner, will find such partner. This may be of little comfort during the search for love, during the search for such a loving partner as there may be times of feeling isolated, inadequate and alone, or feeling that we simply cannot find the right person, yet there may be some comfort in knowing that through difficult, frustrating and indeed, sometimes lonely times, when we may feel unsuccessful, unloved and unwanted, that in the end we will probably find such a partner, it being, most likely, a matter of time before we do.

And such is a positive and encouraging thought for the many if not all of us, though on the other hand, as rational beings, unfortunately we also have to recognise that we are all individual people and the existence of high probabilities for success in anything, the existence of such numbers, does not mean that we as single individuals will all be successful, whatever the generality of events. A reality for people in general, is not a guarantee and may not turn out to be a reality for each of us as individuals. Nevertheless, in the case of finding a partner and a lover, the likelihood will be that, if persistent, imaginative, willing to adapt, and perhaps not overly choosey, we will find someone to love and someone who will love us.

Apart from taking into account the general environment and circumstances around us, realistic thinking in regard to our potential achievements, possibilities and destinations in life does need to take into account ourselves, our personalities and characteristics and our own particular circumstances. And therefore, as mentioned, what is a reality for others, what is the general reality, may not apply to us as individuals. That is not to say we should not follow our dreams and aim to achieve the things we really wish for. We certainly should be doing that, but as a consequence of our combination of positive and constructive attitudes and our realistic assessment of the possibilities available to us, especially taking into account the already stated fact that much that is considered impossible is, in fact, possible and realistic which is often considered challenging or even impossible, we need to, we should recognise, that at some point we may need to adjust or reset our goals to ensure our maximum personal well-being and happiness and the happiness and well-being of others.

As already mentioned, negative unrealistic thinking, where we adopt overly critical thoughts about ourselves or future turns of events is certainly prone to damage our achievement. In many areas, confidence and perhaps more to the point, the appearance of an appropriate level of confidence, will in reality be important for us to take ourselves forward in our own individual actions and efforts, and may be particularly necessary for us to be successful in terms of our achievement at work and in the public space.

And if we engage in the inaccurate negative thinking already referred to, not just in terms of our personal actions but in terms of the world around us, we can damage ourselves. For example if our thinking centres around what might be unhelpful comparisons, disadvantages in our backgrounds, unfairness towards us in life and the privilege of others, while these may possibly represent both specific and general truths (the privileged and wealthy by birth having in general, though not necessarily, a greater chance of achieving in a range of areas), such a focus, while in some ways helpful for us in its recognition of realities, may not be helpful to us in many other ways, particularly if these thoughts lead to feelings of demotivation, frustration, bitterness, jealously and anger, feelings which themselves detract from our feelings of well-being and happiness, and which also, and thereby, distract us from doing what we need to do in our own lives in order to achieve our goals, enjoy well-being and be successful.

While appreciating realities and being aware of tactics, strategies, and appreciating the various actions needed within our circumstances and situations in order to promote our success in the light of these realities, it is realistically the case that as individuals, considering our own nature character, skills and more, if we strive, if we use our specific talents, strong thinking, if we have and develop good skills at getting on with, and dealing with others, and more, then there is a good chance that we will be able to achieve and succeed in achieving at least some of, or many of, our life goals, and attain some or perhaps all of our dreams, despite the existence of privilege and advantage for others. That is realistic thinking and that is what we can do.

Recognising the benefits and unfair advantages of such privilege, we can also realistically aim to act socially and politically to create a fairer system in which there are better opportunities for all, an aim which will require substantial work and commitment and cooperation from others, though yet again represents a realistic and reasonable goal, and a goal which will in fact be of substantial benefit to ourselves, our communities, societies and beyond.

What would be unrealistic would be to believe that without focused political and social action, everyone or even large numbers of people who are disadvantaged and underprivileged, will all or in significant numbers, reach the peaks of success in the short term. This is because, in general, existing systems of patronage and privilege will act against us. Indeed such systems may well act against us in particular as individuals. But it is certainly realistic to think that for ourselves as single individuals, difficulties of privilege and difficulties of unfair and systematic discrimination can be overcome, and indeed, that concerted, focused and dedicated political action and campaigning can be successful in creating fairer systems.

Negative unrealistic thinking, wrong thinking and defeatism, indeed catastrophising, (seeing and speaking of events as disastrous or catastrophic, when they may be normal or simply setbacks), this latter being something that unfortunately many of us undoubtedly do and too often do, such irrational thinking is certainly injurious to our positive mental health, distracts and depresses our thinking and feelings, is personally damaging and destructive, and brings our lives down, making us less able or unable to act rationally to achieve our personal goals and indeed making us less able to support others in achieving their goals. Again we need to be realistic in terms of the import and consequences of events in our lives and, once the shock or surprise of a negative event has been absorbed, we need to respond as positively and constructively as we can, seeking solutions and taking actions to support and enjoy our well-being and happiness and the well-being and happiness of others.

By contrast to the false negative perceptions of ourselves which can damage and hurt us, we certainly, as already referred to, also need to avoid arrogant and inaccurate self perception through which we place ourselves above others. Such arrogance is likely to be self-damaging through its involving too much focus on our selves and our own qualities and the likely consequent damaging of our relationships, such arrogance also having the potential to be damaging to others who must bear the brunt of this arrogance, with such attitudes on our behalf serving to belittle others. A degree of realistic sure-footedness and confidence is helpful in terms of our feelings about ourselves and the ability to get things done, building the confidence of others in us and in what we do and how we are. Nevertheless, none of us is the finished article, however mature, confident, wise and experienced we may be. All of us, each one of us, have learning, development and change to go through, in an almost unending, if never ending process. Being arrogant and dismissive of others and their beliefs and views, stands in the way of our listening and learning from others, and is almost guaranteed to damage our learning and our performance, and as a consequence our own well-being and happiness.

In regards to the many challenges, indeed the significant and difficult challenges that may face us in our lives, some of which at first glance may seem extraordinarily difficult to tackle, we will need to aim to overcome these challenges using the constructive, rational, realistic and systematic thinking already referred to in this guide, being aware of the fact that difficult tasks can be achieved and that the specific challenge in front of us, in particular, through analysing component elements, and tackling them bit-by-bit, one-by-one, through inventing solutions for each element of a task in the case of our more complex tasks and complex goals; through thinking realistically, rationally, practically and inventively on the basis of realistic planning and evidence, can also be achieved. Meeting and overcoming such major challenges will certainly support our mental health and mental well-being.

In the same manner, thinking realistically, we may need to incorporate the possibility of not achieving tasks and goals, not achieving our more distant and complex goals, and in such cases, resetting our aims and goals to be realistic goals, and seeking to achieve what are actually achievable tasks. It is also useful for us to have alternative strategies, approaches and responses prepared and available in response to our not achieving particular anticipated outcomes.

Further, we have to recognise that for many questions, tasks and goals, there may be little or insufficient evidence available to enable us to be certain or even have a significant degree of confidence about our judgments, decisions and goals. There are things that we do not know when we make decisions, when we start out on journeys towards our goals, and indeed there are events and circumstances that are very difficult to plan for and anticipate, even perhaps occurrences and facts that we simply could not know, however much we planned or attempted to see into the future. None of this should stop us setting out on our journeys and attempting to investigate and explore.

Reality is such that circumstances change, people change and we ourselves change through experience and development in terms of how we think and how we feel. As a consequence our goals may change and our desire to achieve may change, perhaps growing and becoming more intense, perhaps in some cases dissipating, our recognising through experience that perhaps our initial goals were not goals that were as important to us as we first thought.

So we need to be comfortable with judgments and decisions which have to be made sometimes based on insufficient information, and we need to be prepared to adjust our goals and change our decisions where necessary, without any or without too much self-recrimination, self-criticism, self-admonishment. Life is complicated, the world is complicated and sometimes it is necessary to be a little charitable to ourselves when we act using our best efforts, when we do our best to support the well-being and happiness of ourselves and others, considering the wishes and feelings of others, with decisions made with the greatest care we can muster and with good intention.

In order to bolster us in moments when we ourselves are suffering through lack of confidence, where things may not seem to be going so well for us, and where we are facing challenges, we may find it useful to record our achievements, the positives about ourselves, the things we have done in our lives, the challenges we have overcome, in order to remind ourselves of our successes, remind ourselves of who we are in a balanced manner, noting the things we have done which have been positive for ourselves, others and for our communities, societies and the wider world. This kind of concrete and explicit self-recognition and acknowledgement may help us to counterbalance the streams of negative irrational self-critical thinking which many of us may experience. Recognising our achievements, reminding ourselves of these achievements, should, at the minimum, help us place any hopefully temporary negative feelings about ourselves in a more accurate, truthful and realistic context. The achievements we have recorded will of course be in our past and may not sometimes, perhaps, seem germane to the moment we are experiencing. Nevertheless such reminders can support us, bolster our confidence and self-belief and help make us feel happier, stimulating memories of achievement and happiness, reminding us of likely or potential joy, happiness and success to come, and enabling us to better face and get on with our current tasks, focusing us away from trains of negativity in our thought, and more on dealing with our current challenges.

In some situations of challenge, in particular, where the relevant and specific problems or challenges are not easy or seem impossible to resolve, we may find it useful under such circumstances to put these problems to one side, temporarily, and to focus on other activities and issues which may distract us for a while. In the midst of tackling an emotionally challenging or other particular form of challenging problem, this may mean our leaving aside this problem for a short period and perhaps working on more everyday tasks, our washing, cooking, cleaning, maintenance, gardening, or alternatively diving into other different challenges and tasks which may substantially distract us and take our minds away from whichever troublesome or difficult problems or challenges we might be facing. While our challenges may not be being solved, at least we will be maintaining our own happiness and well-being, which is important. And while focusing on these other areas, our minds will be working away and while engaged in such distractions, we may well devise solutions to our challenges and problems, we may in a sense become more calm, and may recognise that the particular problem is not so stressful and challenging. Sometimes, fortunately, such problems may, through changes of circumstances or, alternatively through the passing of time, simply resolve themselves or move towards resolution without our contribution and action.

Of course some challenges may be so painful and distressing that it is difficult if not impossible to put them aside. If we cannot put them aside then we may have accept the pain and distress we are enduring, in a perhaps perverse though metaphorical sense, our determining to 'ride the pain and anxiety' we may feel, rather than fighting it and trying to get rid of it. Even such emotional pain and anxiety, however unwanted, if we have to endure it, represents part of the experience of being alive and having a full and complete life. Furthermore, it is almost certain that our emotional pains will at some point dissipate and subside, even if sometimes we don't want them to. And while experiencing such deep emotional pains, while experiencing what in some cases may be our stresses, perhaps humiliations, which we find difficult to put aside, in time it is certain that we will feel better, we will feel good and will be able to enjoy greater happiness again.

Time may not heal all emotional wounds; the pain of some experiences and events may remain with us and do so painfully for a long time, if not for the whole of our lives, but our pain from our emotional wounds, over time, is likely, to some degree, to be displaced by, amongst other things, the concerns of our more immediate day-to-day lives. And perhaps, in a sense, we can get used to our pain, and hopefully we will begin to experience some joys and pleasures moment-to-moment, these joys and pleasures becoming perhaps more frequent as time passes.

When we find others suffering and in pain and distress, whatever form; when we find others struggling with self-admonition, unjustified self-criticism and self-doubt then, in line with core principles and in support of the well-being and happiness of these others, and indeed in support of our own well-being and happiness, we need to act with kindness and care, in a generous and charitable manner to help them through or away from their pain and suffering. In support of well-being and happiness, and in order to avoid such pain and suffering, we must as far as possible be kind, caring, understanding, charitable towards and appreciative of others. While it can sometimes be difficult to support others who are wracked with pain and grief, we are obliged to help them, even if that means just being around, being with them as a friend to talk to, or simply as someone who is just there and through that presence is demonstrating care.

If we know those who are beset with self-doubt, full of such self-admonition and self-criticism, especially to the extent where such thoughts and feelings are debilitating, then we need to support them in whichever ways are possible. Where we can we may need to point out the qualities and achievements of those we know who are suffering in such anxiety and pain, qualities and achievements which may be presented, represented through what they have done, the positive, if not wonderful, things they have achieved and done, that may be represented through who and how they are, their positive effects on others, the positive things they do and say, through pointing out how loved and cared for they are. Indeed, we can sometimes help others to gain a more realistic self-appreciation of themselves through pointing out those positives they have achieved in the various aspects of their lives, much of which may not be seen or appreciated by themselves or others, be it their acting as a good and supportive friend, achieving goals which matter in their personal lives, be it their achievements through their work or achieving other goals outside of work. Doing this requires a care and focus on others, which it is important for us to show and demonstrate to others enduring such emotional pain.

That being said, our support and efforts to help, while appreciated, at least apparently so, on the moment, may not be truly believed by our listener, since many of us may have largely unjustified but deep seated feelings of inadequacy and some of us can almost refuse to know and see our personal value and worth, our importance to others. Thus whatever we might say and whatever might be true, those we are trying to support may still feel bad and lack confidence and self-belief. For all of us who feel that kind of way it might be good to talk, perhaps if we cannot resolve our feelings and thoughts and feel down and depressed, it might be valuable to get some professional medical help if that could be effective, since such deep-seated feelings of inadequacy or even worthlessness represent in themselves poor mental health, aside from the effects they are likely to have on our personal well-being in other ways and their effects on others around us. We have a responsibility to avoid such pain and suffering, and to support our own well-being and happiness and the well-being and happiness of others, and thus we need to try to resolve such problems if we have them.

The pleasure of our being appreciated and our desire to be appreciated has already been considered to some extent in chapter eight in part one of this guide. By contrast to the pleasure we gain from such appreciation, while we may engage with, try hard, and do our best to help our friends, families, communities and others, a lack of appreciation from others can lead to our unhappiness and upset. This lack or sense of lack of appreciation can apply to us in a range of contexts, at work, outside and inside of the home, in the range of social and community contexts we inhabit. It can apply to us as parents caring for our children. It can apply to us all as family members in the home and beyond, where we may try or have tried to help others and where appreciation would be nice, would be pleasant, and where we may feel resentment at being taken for granted, perhaps treated without respect or appreciation. At times we may feel unrecognised and unnoticed as the feeling, contributing and caring beings that we are. Of course, being aware of and recognising our own potential pain at a lack of appreciation and recognition, in support of well-being and happiness, and to prevent others from suffering emotional and other pain, we should do our utmost to recognise the contributions of others, to appreciate them. Hopefully they will in turn try to, and will succeed in, appreciating us.

The need and desire for appreciation also applies to those of us who may be engaged in formal official or unofficial roles in support of our communities and societies. It is pleasant to be appreciated and for us to be recognised for what we do and have appreciation shown to us, even though we are unlikely to be motivated by the desire for appreciation, but instead may be motivated through caring deeply for others, or because we feel that things need to be done in order to support well-being, fulfillment and happiness, through making or helping our communities and societies and beyond work more effectively. As public servants, we may spend significant time and effort working for others, supporting others, trying to make our communities and societies work better. Such public engagement can involve us in significant emotional effort and energy, with our role sometimes involving dealing with troubles, conflicts and disagreements. And acting in such formal roles can sometimes require significant personal emotional strength in motivating ourselves to carry on. Sometimes we may be doing such work unpaid, on a voluntary basis because we care. Thus appreciation from the rest of us is often reassuring, useful and needed.

Such emotional commitment will come from the many of us who help others voluntarily. But such community-based and other supportive activities can take up personal time, if not a great deal of personal time, which we could perhaps be spending on more immediately pleasurable activities, involving less stress and angst (though perhaps in the end generating a lesser sense of achievement and reward). In such roles in which we are supporting others, supporting our communities, it helps us if we are appreciated and if we appreciate the efforts of others. Those people who contribute need to be told of our appreciation, in particular because, on many occasions their achievements may be unpublicised achievements, achievements which may often be hidden from the public view or which at least may not be easily visible as achievements to many others. The efforts and the work done by feeling and caring, by competent individuals, who have supported other individuals in their lives, who have supported constructive policies and actions in the public domain leading to our social and community achievement and development, leading to the betterment of our humanity as a whole, may sometimes not be noticed and appreciated but certainly need to be.

Inevitably, in some, if not many roles, we may expect, to some extent, a lack of appreciation for what we do, in particular perhaps, should we have children, in our role as parents, where we do so much for our children which it is difficult for them in many ways to appreciate, or perhaps also when we are either engaged in daily paid work activities where our work and contributions may be taken for granted, or where we participate in voluntary activities in the public space, where there are different views as to the best policies and actions to take. We would certainly usually wish for appreciation in the things we do. And if that is given, that is also likely to be a positive source and supporter of our well-being, happiness and pleasure. It is without doubt nice to be appreciated and indeed to be told we are appreciated. Indeed we may be lucky enough, on occasion, to be picked out for special recognition of our contributions or achievements, and that can be even more uplifting, creating very positive feelings of well-being and happiness. Hopefully we will all have that experience or receive words and gestures of deep appreciation at some point or points in our lives, for the things we do and the things we have done.

However, the sense that others may not or do not appreciate our efforts in service, others, our communities and societies, our efforts in our jobs, working for the general benefit, is, or can be, significantly demoralising and de-motivating for us. Under such circumstances, in support of our own mental health and well-being, we may need to simply remind ourselves of the value we perceive that the things we do possess, enjoy as far as possible what we do, and gain the most we can from the life we lead, motivating ourselves to do what we do by recognising these gains to ourselves and others. However, we, for the most part, almost all of us, enjoy our efforts being recognised and appreciated.

And recognising our own enjoyment of appreciation, it is therefore our personal responsibility and the responsibility of those of us who are receiving benefits from the efforts of others, in whatever context, to support those making such efforts and to make sure our appreciation for what they are doing or what they have done, is made known to them. And wherever possible we should do this in clear and unequivocal terms.

It is not uncommon for some of us to be quick to criticise but slow to compliment and appreciate, and while criticism is sometimes in order and necessary, the behaviour of being overly critical, diminishing and not appreciating of others, needs to be significantly supplanted by a focus on being appreciative of others and recognising their qualities, contributions, actions and efforts, such an emphasis being something which will benefit us all.

It is particularly important, given the key role of relationships and cooperation with others in pursuing goals and achieving success, that credit is given to all those who have helped us, those to whom we owe and should give credit. Wherever we have achieved or are trying to achieve, we should always make special effort to acknowledge those who have supported us, helped us and contributed to our success or are helping us to success. This of course enhances and promotes cooperation, but also avoids offence to others who may feel bitter, unhappy and unappreciated if not mentioned and recognised for their contributions, and indeed whose sense of mental well-being and mental health may be damaged, with us and them as well, as a consequence, ending up emotionally hurt and under further unnecessary stress with further consequences for our mental health and well-being.

Our own failure to truly acknowledge the contributions of others can also lead to our own feelings of personal guilt and our own personal unhappiness since, in particular, our reputation may suffer significantly if we appear to take credit for things which are not our achievements and where we have failed to give sufficient credit and acknowledgment to others.

Compliments, recognition and appreciation should not wait until the eulogies are given following our deaths and the deaths of the ones we love. We need to be careful that we let others know without equivocation, that we love and care for them, that we appreciate them, that we recognise their talents and contribution while they are actually alive, supporting their well-being and happiness in the one life that we know we have. Tributes following someone's death are fine, desired, and help our memories live on after death, serving also to promote positive values in our communities, societies and beyond, however appreciation and tribute certainly also need to be made while we, the recipients, are alive and able to enjoy them.

It should also be said that we need to be honest and have integrity in our appreciations and tributes, and of course we need to be accurate when we describe someone's qualities and actions. It is worthy and generally warranted and justified to seek out the positives and recognise the contributions others have made in their lives, letting them know of our appreciation and talking about their achievements, complimenting and appreciating them where this is truthful, kind, justified and reasonable. It is not generally worthy to state general appreciation and recognition of others and their contributions when in fact they have generally behaved badly and acted against the general well-being and happiness. This is very undermining for those who have actually contributed, worked hard and helped others, serving to undermine our desire to support others and engage in positive actions ourselves. Moreover such inaccurate remarks, putting a gloss on the actions of those who may have caused substantial pain and suffering, may inadvertently create the impression that either such poor conduct did not happen, can legitimately be ignored or that such conduct might be in some senses acceptable, which it is not.

Unfortunately however, as already referred to, some if not many of those of us engaging in the range of work supporting our families, friends, aiming to support our communities, societies and beyond, may not only find ourselves and what we do to be unappreciated, but we can receive a range of thoughtless and damaging comment and criticism or worse. This may occur to us whether we are voluntary helpers, charity workers, local activists, supporters of human rights and help for those in need (derided sometimes as 'do-gooders' by those wishing for a more negatively selfish short-termist and damaging agenda), parents, or community politicians (derided justly in some cases, but in other cases in relation to things which they have no responsibility for, or no ability to influence). Further, our efforts to help and support can be misunderstood and misinterpreted; we can also make errors and on occasion cause damage despite our good intentions, as a consequence receiving criticism, derision and even worse.

When we engage in our actions in support of others, while hoping for appreciation from others, we should not proceed on the basis or assumption that appreciation will be received. As already mentioned, this is sometimes not received. Our good work, our good intentions, our good achievements may not be noticed or even if noticed, others may not appreciate the quality and positive impact of what we are doing. We need to have other goals rather than seeking appreciation from others in mind, goals of supporting others and supporting ourselves as well as having other positive motivations for our actions.

If our goals are good and appropriate goals, in line with core and other principles, we should feel free to appreciate ourselves, to self-appreciate through our own systems of positive, caring values, appreciating our own actions which are aimed at supporting our own well-being and happiness and the well-being and happiness of others. If others do not appreciate us or cannot see our value and the value of what we do, then we can certainly act to preserve and enhance our own well-being and happiness by appreciating ourselves. Appreciation and recognition by others is pleasant to receive if we can get it, but it cannot be assumed or even expected, and sometimes criticisms and admonition can be more common. Avoiding such unrealistic expectations can help support us in our happiness and well-being and in avoiding unnecessary emotional pain.

Many of the deepest joys, happiness and pleasure we can gain are likely to come, at least in part, from intrinsic pleasures involved in, for example, helping and caring for others, supporting our communities, societies and our broader humanity, from looking after friends, family, children. We can gain pleasures and joys from taking part in community-based activities, from doing a good job, doing things well and from giving to others – and if there is general appreciation, or if there are specific comments from others in gratitude for our efforts, that is nice; that can be supportive, inspiring and uplifting; so be it; but receiving such appreciation in response to our support for others is not the goal. Our personal conduct, our commitment to supporting others and our communities, as in the principles laid out in this guide, should not be influenced by any lack of understanding and lack of appreciation and recognition we receive or do not receive from others. We have our values, our human need to care for and look after others and, whilst being aware of and listening to the comments of others, wanting appreciation, we can judge ourselves against our own internal caring and loving values founded on core and other principles.

That being said, sometimes, if we do feel unappreciated and are finding ourselves being significantly taken for granted with the consequence of us feeling particularly bad and unhappy, we may wish to and sometimes need to take actions in response to this lack of appreciation, as sometimes we have to acknowledge that feeling unappreciated can be a painful blow to our sense of self-value and make us feel taken for granted and of no or little significance or matter to others. If this is affecting us badly and we are finding it difficult to continue as we are, ignored and unappreciated, perhaps derided and looked down upon, then we are obliged to let others know how we are feeling. It may be that these others have made an error in failing to appreciate us and will express regret (and perhaps surprise) at the way we are feeling. Hopefully they will express their appreciation for us. But if responses are negative and insulting then, dependent on our own feelings and the precise circumstances, we may reasonably choose to, indeed we may have an obligation in terms of core principles of supporting our own well-being and happiness, to act to support our own well-being by removing ourselves from such situations and focusing our efforts on helping others out elsewhere, in an alternative context and perhaps focusing more on our own more immediate happiness and well-being.

It is important to recognise, nevertheless, that some of the greatest, richest and deepest achievements we can attain, will often require from us the greatest persistence and the greatest determination. Sometimes achievement may involve enduring some, if not a significant level, of frustration and in some cases, hopefully rare cases, for some of us there may be a prolonged sense of emotional pain and suffering caused in part through that lack of recognition, that lack of appreciation, criticism, and sometimes even our receiving the opprobrium and derision of others. Such frustration and pains can occur in our daily lives as we work and struggle to achieve our various goals, yet hopefully in the end we will achieve our worthy goals. Illustrating the struggles we may have, though on a more well-known and public level, some of the most significant ideas, inventions and discoveries that we accept and think of as key in our societies today, were initially met with substantial criticism, even derision when they were first put forward, with those promoting them, rather than being appreciated by the many for their insights, efforts and far-sighted thinking, being often subject to widespread ridicule and derision by some, if not many, others. Of course, in these cases, in the end, many of these individuals earned success and undoubtedly felt better for their triumph, and hopefully enjoyed reward and appreciation for their ideas and actions.

Thinking realistically involves having realistic expectations about the behaviour and conduct of others in respect of appreciation and reward. Having accurate and realistic expectations in regard to anticipated responses and the efforts required to be successful, in regard to the obstacles we may encounter, can reduce our anxiety and pain substantially. Thus if we take new initiatives, it is sometimes, indeed often the case, that some others will object. They may do this for a range of reasons including general resistance to change, feeling under threat through change, lack of imagination or vision, inertia or lack of energy; they may on the other hand have rational and well-thought out objections to what we are proposing. Expecting such challenges and opposition, and preparing to counter this in a cooperative and friendly, positive manner can ease the way to achieving our goals and help us maintain positive mental health and well-being. Of course as respondees ourselves to such new initiatives, new ideas, new directions and new proposals, in line with chapter five in part one of this guide, we need to act with rationality and reason, weighing up evidence in determining our response to these new challenges and changes.

As already referred to earlier in this chapter, our having realistic expectations of our children is also necessary to maintain our well-being and happiness and indeed to support our mental and general health. Young children will inevitably behave in ways consistent with general young child behaviour. Many young children (though perhaps not all) will have tantrums built out of frustration. That is one of the ways in which very young children can behave. Such behaviour is not desirable behaviour, but it will be something that is likely to happen in the cases of many children. We need to expect such behaviour and prepare for it, being ready to respond in a peaceful and appropriate manner, protecting the child and other children (and ourselves) and aiming to resolve the problem, create a more peaceful context and pointing out, where we can, at some point, the unacceptability of such behaviour.

Very young children may hurt other young children through simply being unable to perceive that their actions will cause pain to another, perhaps failing to understand the existence of pain in others, or even perhaps through 'trying out' giving another pain, however awful that might seem. If it were an adult behaving in such a manner then we would see the person conducting these acts as violent, aggressive and selfish. With very young children, while our hope would be that they do not have tantrums or hurt others, it is unreasonable not to anticipate some form of this kind of behaviour. Thus, our own efforts in response to such behaviours and actions by young children need to be tempered by our understanding of them as children. In regard to our children, it is not reasonable and rational, or helpful, to measure young children entirely or even substantially, by adult standards, even if we are preparing them for the adult world. This is because they are simply not yet adults. Our yardsticks for evaluating behaviour need reasonably to be adjusted for age, which is not to mean that we do not wish for and set high standards, but it is to say that we need to have realistic expectations.

It would also be, in the normal run of things, wrong to label children negatively or blame ourselves unfairly as the cause of such behaviour, to admonish ourselves and consider ourselves shamed in front of others by the more anti-social types of child conduct, such self-admonition and perhaps sense of shame, being perhaps a natural feeling when a child misbehaves in public. But, as adults we need to be practically and mentally ready for and prepared for these and other kinds of child behaviour. Unrealistic expectations are likely to act against our mental health and well-being, and will not support the well-being of others, of our children.

Of course we need to work against any damaging and destructive behaviour being carried out by our children; we need to aim to move them away from such unpleasant and anti-social conduct, and teach them for the future, ensure they learn about acceptable behaviour and conduct. Nevertheless, our responses emotionally and educationally need to be provided in recognition of the reality of child behaviour rather than in terms of a response to unrealistic social expectations of experienced adult behaviour (which indeed unfortunately many of us as adults do not manage to sustain ourselves, at least some of us, for some of the time).

Labeling children verbally or otherwise as in some way individually defective or deficient in character or personality simply because of actions performed while they are a child, is unfair, is irrational and illogical and contrary to core and other principles. Such labeling may damage ourselves as adults, as well as being most likely emotionally and psychologically damaging to the child, damaging to the well-being and happiness of the child, and likely causing them unwarranted and necessary anguish, pain and suffering, which may continue into adulthood.

The same requirements for rationality and realism apply, to an important degree, with regard to our adult dealings with older teenage children who are in the process of building their independence from their adult parents. Our understanding of the often challenging changes and development they are going through is necessary, although this of course can be very difficult and problematic for us as parents and for our teenage children, with our sometimes being embroiled in highly challenging conflict involving difficult situations. As adults we may be going through our own changes into older adult life, and these periods of change and development can also of course, be difficult for the young person. Nevertheless, adopting an understanding, realistic, empathetic and caring approach will help us both as parents and growing teenagers, to avoid suffering and pain, at least to some degree.

Clearly such reasonable expectations should be applied and can provide much benefit in every day life as well. We are much more likely to succeed if, rather than being locked into unrealistic expectations of others, we aim to realistically anticipate the reactions of others to events and occurrences, to the things we are saying and doing. And we are undoubtedly more likely to enjoy better mental health and well-being if we develop ourselves in terms of these expectations and act accordingly. That does not mean that we should not, or that we do not, aim to improve the world around us, that we do not aim to proactively support the well-being and happiness of others and ourselves, that we do not try to shape events into the future, or even that we should not try to persuade and try to influence the ideas and responses of others. Nor does it mean necessarily changing our goals and actions, but it does mean planning and preparing for anticipated reactions in order to support our well-being and happiness. Such preparation for reality will support our mental health, helping us avoid mental turmoil through disappointment, surprise, shock, upset, even anger, at the reactions of others, when these reactions might have been anticipated, prepared for and predicted.

Furthermore and linked to our anxieties and pains which may arise from unrealistic expectations, we can also experience mental anxiety and mental pain by attempting to operate to timescales which are unrealistic, such unrealistic planning leading to frustration and unhappiness. Considering specific and routine examples which affect us all, even on the most simple daily basis, if we attempt to reach our travel destination without taking account of the potential or likely blocks on our journeys, without considering the potential for things to go wrong at a statistical level of probability (dependent on our context, a one in ten chance perhaps of queuing traffic, one in twenty chance of a cancelled or delayed bus or train), linked to an unrealistic and unspoken expectation that we will often or always reach our destination with an unproblematic journey, we are sure to experience considerable frustration and mental anxiety, even deep and irrational anger for some of us, at least on some occasions.

And beyond such a mundane example, this same concern with realistic planning in terms of time is also applicable to our larger projects and more ambitious goals, with many of these plans needing and taking a long time to come to fruition, for us to reach our targets, goals and even our dreams. As far as we can, we need to avoid frustrations arising from unrealistic expectations that things will happen too quickly, that we will reach a certain level in our profession, that we will persuade others immediately, that our social and political goals will be achieved overnight, and indeed in relation to other aspects of expectations, that we may not have problems and difficulties, setbacks along the routes to achieving our goals, which are not only problems in themselves but which may slow our achievement. That is not to say that we necessarily have to put up with problems, setbacks and inefficiencies; but it does mean to say that we should have an expectation that there may be some of these. And it does mean to say that we will be better able to cope emotionally and mentally with those occurrences that we might describe, if that we were unprepared and had unrealistic expectations, as unexpected occurrences, but which in fact should not be shocks and surprises, just perhaps events and occurrences which occur as probabilities and likelihoods, or perhaps statistically infrequent or unexpected events, which certainly do sometimes occur.

As a consequence of having realistic expectations and having also anticipated problems and potential blocks to our attaining our goals and achievements, we should be better able to find ways around these problems when we are faced with such delays, interruptions, frustrations and blocks in time, and other situational features. And if we cannot find ways around them, though having anticipated them, we will still be better able to cope with these blocks emotionally and psychologically.

In terms of our larger and more complex projects, we can, as far as we are able, anticipate problematic areas in terms of time and delay and hopefully prepare for them or design these out of the process, rather than coming across them by accident and surprise, and feeling the stress, anxiety and disappointment at their occurrence when their occurrence was, if not a probability, at least some form of low level possibility. Impatience and stress when faced with frustrations, to an extent, may be an asset in terms of motivating us to get things done, in terms of motivating us to find alternatives, yet it is not beneficial if such impatience leads to significant stress, pain, upset and anger with its consequent effects on others.

Being more specific in regard to our mentalities and thinking, and indeed inextricably tied in to the previous discussion, our mental health does depend to an important degree on our thinking, on how and what we think. In particular, our thinking false thoughts about ourselves (and others) is damaging to our health and to our enjoyment of well-being and happiness. This kind of thinking is also damaging of our efforts to support the well-being of others.

Aside from damaging thoughts such as "I'm no good at…", "I'm such a failure…" I always get things wrong" and the like, which falsely portray who we are, and which falsely describe ourselves, we may engage in particularly damaging and perhaps common thinking which includes reprehensible and almost always irrational thoughts such as "Nobody likes me", "They are all against me", "They all think…". These thoughts are highly unlikely to be true, but they are thoughts we may have, and represent thoughts and thinking which can hurt us emotionally, directly damaging our well-being and happiness. Further they can damage our capacities to achieve well-being through influencing the actions we take, influencing the impression we make on others, as well as the attitudes of others towards us, doing so in such a manner that our capabilities for action, well-being and happiness are damaged with consequent effects on others around us, our communities, societies and beyond.

In the actual and real world, it is unlikely in the first place that the vast majority of people will consider us significant enough as individuals that they will spend the time thinking about us or evaluating us. Often others will simply not have the time or will not consider us of such importance that we could be worth spending time to dislike or deride. Of course most people in our world will not know of our existence at an individual level. This may seem disappointing as we would undoubtedly wish to be of some importance to many or most others, however, the vast majority of other people, just like ourselves, tend have their own busy lives to get on with and while, like us, caring for others and about others, there are billions of people in the world who could be thought about, and likely there are many others closer to the lives of these people, others who these people (a group of course to which we ourselves belong) are much more likely to think about and be concerned about.

Of course there are those closer to us in our lives who almost certainly will care for us and feel strongly for us and about us, probably loving us, though sometimes it may not seem obvious they do. For most people, if they do find the time and are concerned enough about us to have a negative view on who we are and what we are like, then the chances are very small that all others or even many others, will have the same view of us as these people do. If there are those who don't like us, or seem hostile to us, then it is unlikely that all others will share such a view, and if we are decent kind and reasonable, caring people then it is often the case that those who are hostile to us may be jealous and resentful of us for reasons that lie within them, and therefore beyond ourselves and how we are. Such people are likely to be similarly hostile to others and not so liked by others. And thus we will not be alone in facing such hostility and need to ally with our friends to protect our well-being and happiness from those who are behaving unfairly, in oppressive, unfair, unpleasant and hostile ways towards us.

Even if it were the case (and this is very low possibility) that there were many who didn't like us, then that would be a challenge for us to face and we would want to and need to act to change this thinking about us, which we might well be able to do. On occasion, it is true that people may 'gang up' against us or someone else, though most often such a feeling can lie in our inaccurate assessment of what is occurring. But we, ourselves should never do such a thing, and should aim not to give any impression of being part of any such oppressive group nor should we be part of any such group. Rather we need to aim to act in line with core principles which do not support such oppressive actions. We need to support the well-being and happiness of all individuals as far as is reasonable and possible and assert ourselves against others who are acting in unreasonable and oppressive ways. And if others do appear to be against us, and this seems difficult to deal with using rational argument, then as mentioned, we need to seek out allies, of whom there will certainly be some, and do our utmost to support each other and work together against the oppression and poor conduct we are facing. And we need to be careful to consider such hostile groups, should they exist, not as monolithic, but as consisting of individuals capable of independent, loving and caring outlooks who can be changed to see our point of view and to support our well-being and happiness.

From our personal perspective, if we adopt poor, negative thinking which incorporates and accepts as valid what are false negative feelings and thinking that we believe others may hold about us, this is damaging to our mental health. Engaging with others and asking these others what they actually think, rather than relying on false perceptions, often based in our own lack of confidence, fear and uncertainty, asking others what they might think about us, can quickly undermine such negative thoughts and a perception of this kind of 'others against me' thinking. While people are diverse with often complicated and differing opinions and perceptions which we can find out about if we talk to others, if such a negative perception of us is found to be to some extent correct, then asking others about this and listening to them will have provided us with an opportunity to reflect on who we are, how we behave, our personal conduct, and will enable us to decide whether we wish to change and how we might wish to change ourselves.

Alternatively, we may be sure of who we are, our good personality and character, our position and beliefs, and so we may need to take steps to change this situation, and aim to persuade others they are wrong in their view of us, looking for and finding allies to support us in convincing these hostile others as individuals, that their judgment is wrong and that we are a good, worthy and sociable person, intent on supporting the well-being of others. We should not have to put up with the pain of irrational, oppressive and unpleasant attitudes towards us, based in jealously, bigotry, misjudgment and misunderstanding or other destructive factors. And others should support us and we, and others, should provide support such that no one suffers such pain.

Other people's perceptions, in the main, however, do tend to be important to the most of us, both in terms of their practical and emotional effects on our lives, in one context or another, and if others have negative views of us that can certainly make us feel bad and indeed affect us in regard to our practical lives and the achievement of our goals. The most of us simply do care about what others think of us, perhaps not always above all else, but we certainly care, and indeed in practical terms, we sometimes cannot afford to ignore them. Yet paying too much attention to what others think of us, or to what we guess others think of us, can, of course, also be significantly and similarly unhealthy and mentally damaging. Thus, as stated above, given our own positive, caring personal conduct in line with core and other principles, we should do our utmost, where we can, to ensure that the negative remarks of others and negative thoughts about us are not allowed to hurt us and damage us, and are not allowed to prevent us from doing those things which we need to be done in pursuit of our own well-being and the well-being of others.

In particular, as already referred to, others may comment on our physical appearance, our looks and physique, and in reality this usually matters to us and often matters in a major way to many of us as we tend to want to look good so that others find us attractive and good looking, are impressed by us, respect us, or even such that others think of us as someone who is in many ways like them. In terms of personal looks, as already stated in this chapter, we should never be negative and destructive in referring to the personal appearance and looks of others or indeed ourselves. That would be totally out of line with core and other principles and is totally unacceptable.

Additionally, however, while we and others need to make efforts to prevent those engaged in insults of various kinds from being so insulting, destructive and rude, we as individuals also need to have the ability, at times, to treat these kinds of comments with disdain and indifference, to get on with our lives as far as we can, and moreover understand the weakness and fearful if not vulnerable nature of those making those comments. In particular, if they are critical of our appearance in a hurtful and destructive manner, their sense of well-being and self-esteem will most likely and unfortunately be too substantially and closely bound to their own physical appearance, and others' view of that appearance, a potentially dangerous place for these people to be in terms of their mental health and personal well-being and happiness.

We almost always and optimally need to talk in as sensitive and kind a way as we can, given the individual and the circumstances, and where we can, we need to aim to support these people, who are undoubtedly suffering in some ways, perhaps some deep and painful ways. Yet we should also recognise that those individuals who insult our appearance and other aspects of our character will be acting in a bullying and hurtful manner, and may be encouraging negative attitudes towards us in others, marginalising us from our fellows, our communities, and so, as a consequence of their remarks and attitude towards us, we may also need to be verbally robust with them, contradict their abuse and insults, in a non-violent and non-abusive but firm manner. We should not have to put up with hurtful insults about our appearance, and others have a responsibility to aid us and prevent such hurtful remarks.

Nevertheless, an ability to put felt hurt and offence aside, such an ability to display (but perhaps not feel) indifference, may be necessary in some circumstances, for example, in the circumstance when someone whom we might wish to have as a lover, as a partner to care for and be cared for by us, may reject our desire for their affections and love, possibly (perhaps seemingly) on the grounds of our personal appearance and our looks. We may not wish to display excessive hurt, though even a simple refusal may hurt us badly and indeed can feel emotionally devastating, at least for a while, sometimes filling us with feelings of intense inadequacy and worthlessness. No direct insult is necessary for the message to get across that we are, for this person we might love or wish to love, inadequate in some respect, yet of course they may not wish to hurt us. If they can support us through our hurt that can be helpful, and if we can support others through their hurt, that would be supportive of well-being too.

Our senses of who we as individuals find attractive, and who we wish to show affection to, cannot unfortunately be manufactured to suit others. It is the reality that while some will find us attractive, others will not, and similarly we will find some others attractive and others not so attractive. Of course our relationships hopefully will go much deeper than appearance and looks, with personal attractiveness residing in many aspects of who we are, and who others are. Nevertheless, developing a caring and sensitive approach and attitude, looking after and caring for others and supporting their well-being in a loving and positive way, is likely to need to be matched by developing the appropriate thinking and 'thick skin' that may be needed to tolerate or endure the pains that life may throw at us through no fault of our own and through no fault of those whose actions and feelings may, in some instances, lead to us being hurt.

Poor thinking can provide us with inadequate ways of identifying happier and more positive ways in which we can live our lives, can prevent us addressing the issues that arise in our lives in effective ways, and will almost certainly affect our ability to live with well-being and happiness. Amongst other things, effective ways of thinking involve the abilities to imagine and invent new futures, new possible futures for ourselves, these opening up the possibility of new routes to well-being, happiness, joy, fulfillment and achievement. If we feel we need to develop these capacities then we should look for ways to ensure such development and improvement in our thinking, for example through discovering from others their approaches to such thinking, through reading about such thinking and creativity, or through experimentation and application of such thinking. Such exploration, even without consideration of other positive consequences, in itself provides joy through the thinking in itself and our consequent joy of discovery and recognition of the options and possibilities which we can become aware of through such thinking.

Such creative and imaginative thinking can involve deliberate and learnable processes and actions such as lateral thinking and provocative thinking (this latter challenge being done not in a hostile manner but through challenging ideas and thinking in particular, in a rational and procedural manner). Through using such thinking and creative approaches we should be more prepared to think about and imagine, indeed re-perceive ideas and actions which at first appearance, given our more embedded attitudes and approaches, may appear to be the strange and unusual, the odd and weird, the world turned upside down, looking at these strange, counter-intuitive and new ideas without initial instinctive rejection, negative evaluation and condemnation. Such thinking, apart from opening up possibilities, helps us to be freer and less constrained by what are often norms and conventions, products of culture, rather than representing ideas and conduct which are rational in terms of our goals and in terms of core and other principles.

Analysis can be a valuable tool in certain contexts, and may support us in understanding situations, identifying patterns, developing strategies and determining our actions. Nevertheless, we can think poorly by spending too much of our thinking time engaged in analysis, by over-analysing, when what we are likely to need are solutions and the invention to find solutions. While analysis can be necessary, essential in specific work contexts, for example in health care for identification of the nature of an illness or disease, in research of various kinds, for tackling technical problems, and perhaps sometimes when dealing with emotional and social problems at home or elsewhere, yet over-emphasis on analysis rather than the invention and finding of solutions will in many cases be insufficient or lead nowhere, something which may in particular apply in regard to the more personal relationship problems that we might encounter.

Importantly, as thinkers interested in our personal well-being, mental health and happiness, we should aim to avoid waiting for problems to arise before we start addressing our personal or our community, societal or global futures. Imagining futures, identifying opportunities, how our world and the world could be different, is something we should be engaging in often, when we have time, when we can choose to do things of our own volition, when it is an implicit part of an allocated role, for example at work, or when we are requested to or required to do so by others.

And part of our effective thinking, supporting our well-being and happiness, requires our recognising our feelings and emotions, these often being core to how we behave and conduct ourselves. If we are fully aware of how we feel, acknowledge how we feel, understand why we feel that way, if we are aware of who we are mentally and psychologically, and perhaps also our physical state (tiredness, hunger and more) then, even against the background of intense emotions and feelings, we are in a better position to make the rational and reasoned decisions which will best support our well-being and happiness and the well-being and happiness of others. If our judgments are clouded by anger and sorrow and significantly affected by the same; if we are extremely negative about ourselves and our capacities such that we make ourselves unhappy; if we are too excited and lack a sense of rationality and calm when deciding our conduct and actions, then we may well end up making wrong decisions, conducting ourselves inappropriately, engaging in misjudgments and damaging ourselves and others.

There are many other examples of poor thinking which can be damaging to us, to our mental and physical health, our well-being, these poor ways of thinking serving to emphasise the importance of effective thinking. Certainly, realistic, constructive thinking is part of, and is necessary to promote, our good mental health. As already mentioned, the capacity to plan ahead, and to plan ahead in some detail is also something which can benefit our mental health too, with potential problems anticipated and prepared for rather than appearing in front of us as unexpected shocks.

Thus, the notion that we should think well, realistically and effectively in terms of our own thinking processes and in relation to our thinking about ourselves and others, is a worthy and reasonable one which can benefit our personal well-being, our happiness and our mental health significantly. While not in itself a solution to all issues of well-being, happiness and mental health, such realistic and constructive thinking is certainly worth engaging in and adopting wherever this is possible and reasonable. As part of this pursuit of realistic and rational thinking, our ongoing awareness and indeed monitoring of our thoughts to ensure that we are having truthful and rational thoughts should also help serve to support us in maintaining and building our positive mental health.

Our positive mental health also benefits from an adventurous, exploratory, discovery focused nature, combined with the ability to be creative and imaginative in a practical and reasonable and, perhaps sometimes, apparently unreasonable manner (one which breaks norms and conventions). Understanding creativity and being creative, understanding the requirement to be prepared to be wrong in order to develop the new and to be creative in inventing solutions, substantially supports our positive mental health. While the opposite, lack of invention, fear of being wrong, fear of failure, fear of experiment, an inability to be, or a desire not to be creative, stunts us as people, can lead to poor mental health and, importantly, risks a life which to a substantial degree may not have been lived to the full, with maximal well-being and happiness not enjoyed. Adventurousness, the search for and experience of the new, the continuous journey to learn and find out, our constant exploration, and the prospect and challenges of the new are important if not invaluable in helping us develop and maintain our positive mental health.

We also need to maintain the alacrity, effectiveness and skill of our thinking in order to support our thinking, well-being and happiness. Mental games and thinking exercises of a range of types may contribute to such mental alacrity and may also help us with the ability to deal with real problems as well as supporting our mental awareness and functioning. Mental games and exercises, while helpful however and potentially practicing social and other skills which will carry over into our real lives, may also be somewhat distinct from much of our real world thinking and interactions in terms of what they support us in doing, there often being real and important differences between the often more mathematical, theoretical or 'play' nature of many games compared to the more complex often multi-faceted people-centred challenges of our daily lives. Recognising this, while such mental games and exercises may be useful and important, we need to maintain and build our relations in the real world, our real social contacts, deal with and practice meeting challenges in our real worlds in order to support important aspects of our social thinking skills, our interactional skills, our mental health and our personal well-being and happiness.

We have already discussed in this chapter the notion and importance of goals and pursuing our dreams, in particular focusing on setting achievable goals, and considering the setting of goals and following of dreams in terms of supporting our mental health and well-being. Yet it is not only our establishing of the appropriate goals and dreams for our lives, which are in themselves of importance in terms of supporting our own well-being and the well-being of others. Our having such goals and dreams and following such goals and dreams in itself supports our own well-being and health, giving our lives a focus and direction, helping prevent us from drifting through life being unduly pushed and pulled by the desires and wishes of others, by the currents of community and society and sometimes battered and torn by events or by changes in the world around us. Setting ourselves personal goals avoids what may be an accompanying sense of disorientation, malaise, and powerlessness, likely to be injurious to our mental health and mental well-being, which is likely to occur if we fail to set ourselves personal goals in our lives. Again it is best if goals and dreams are realistic and reasonable and that we have some ideas, optimally a thought out plan about how we will achieve them.

Sometimes the pathways to our goals and dreams through our lives may be unclear and a rational and detailed plan may not always be obvious, practical or available to us beyond making opportunities and taking advantage of our opportunities when they arise. Nevertheless, the motivation, desire and energy to set goals is of great importance. Once set, these goals can be powerful supports in helping us live a life of well-being and happiness. We will aim for our goals and hopefully achieve them, but if not, having established and followed our dreams and goals will still have supported our journey through different parts of and through perhaps our whole lives.

And should we have made mistakes or not achieved, it is probably not of benefit for our well-being to spend too much time focusing on regrets for our choices in the past or expressing and feeling regret about events which have occurred in the past. Reflection is reasonable, especially when allied to our making changes for the future, however, of course we cannot change the past, (though we can certainly reinterpret past events) and while we may wish to learn from our pasts and the past, regret is not a positive feeling and, while it is important for us to express our regrets for mistakes if we have hurt others, aiming to assuage the feelings of others and recognising in front of others and to ourselves, our responsibility and indeed guilt when we have done wrong, once such regrets have been fully expressed we will need to focus on making a better future, having learnt from the past.

Allied to such goal setting, and certainly tied to our planning for the future, it is also helpful to make some predictions and estimations or guesses about where we will be in our futures, be it five years, ten years or twenty years or so hence. Making such predictions provides us with a further point of orientation and balance in our lives, removing the uncertainty and anxiety of refusing to look ahead and considering the future to be incapable of prediction.

As discussed in chapter five, there are those who argue that we cannot tell the future, and of course in terms of very high levels of, or one hundred per cent accuracy, dependent on the specific prediction being made, they are undoubtedly correct. However, there are some futures which are more likely, and some futures which are less likely. Through seeing futures in terms of possibilities and probabilities, knowing which are our preferred futures and which are the more or less likely futures, this provides us with a potentially orientating map or provides some points of reference for our future lives, focusing our lives through days, months and years, and to an extent enabling us to cope better with the day-to-day, the ongoing challenges and difficulties we may face in the present and the future, since we have our more distant futures, a future context in mind.

Predicting and imagining such futures does not mean our day-to-day challenges are less worthy of attention, simply that it is helpful to anticipate what they are and might be, and to see those challenges as occurring within the context of a broader vision of our possible lives and possible future lives, in which there are different more likely and less likely possibilities and alternatives. With our visions of possible futures, and having considered the possibilities for our future and the directions we wish to head in, our actions, conduct, progress and successes in the present will hopefully lead us more effectively towards our goals.

But our consideration of, and predictions of different futures, will not simply help to orient ourselves in our lives. They will also support us in finding other routes to our desired futures, and help us in identifying other possible futures for ourselves. Our prediction of futures will enable us to plan ahead and adapt quickly when one of our possible futures becomes less likely. And in the face of our being unsuccessful in our current tasks, our planning and consideration of possible futures will enable us to understand the fact that apparent lack of success in one area may lead to other possibilities in life, increasing the likelihood that we move successfully and achieve success in another direction. Such changes in direction may themselves be beneficial for our well-being and happiness, whether or not we had planned for and previously considered them as high probability directions in our lives.

Importantly, through taking time to envision futures, this can help us better prepare for threats to our survival and well-being. At the level of our individual lives we can look ahead to times of financial difficulty or unemployment and set aside resources and funds to support us in such times. Having made such preparations should support our mental health and well-being. We can predict changes in our relationships and prepare for these. Further, we can predict and therefore prepare for illness, making provision for times when we are ill. Anticipating our eventual death, we can prepare a will so that those we love will have access to our resources once we are dead.

In other areas of our lives, we can further anticipate changes in technology which may affect our opportunities to work and earn a living into the future. Political changes may unfortunately threaten our physical safety and the physical safety of others. It is best to look ahead and be ready for these. As a matter of course it is worthwhile scanning our environment to see whether there are upcoming dangers to our well-being and happiness, and prepare to face and tackle these threats.

Of course, anticipating futures might to some degree reduce the stimulation of adventure and excitement of unknown, unpredicted futures. Adventure and excitement through the unpredictable and unpredicted can certainly bring interest and entertainment. However such unpredictability, excitement and adventure, while hopefully important components of our lives, and while comprising part of our well-being and happiness, these are seen as desirable, present and enjoyable when we are operating within a framework of planning and predicting our futures, with such prediction, anticipation and planning ahead being seen as of crucial value in terms of benefiting our mental health and well-being, our success in life. Though an unfocused, unplanned and overall more opportunistic approach to life might suit some of us, it would seem unlikely, even if it were to benefit the individuals following such an approach, for this to be an effective way to support others, ourselves, our community, society and broader humanity. We can, of course, plan and include this adventure and excitement within our future plans and predictions for our future lives, thereby enabling us to fulfill core and other principles in a planned and more complete manner, and enhance our well-being and happiness.

Our positive mental health is supported by using our time well in pursuit of our goals of well-being and happiness. For many of us, there is so much that we can potentially do in our lives and undoubtedly insufficient time for us to do all we want to do. Each of us will most likely need and wish to spend time with our friends and family (as well as probably some time alone), giving time to loving those we love. We need, and may wish to, spend time on our work, give time to support our local communities and society, our broader humanity, equip ourselves with time for educating and training ourselves and developing our knowledge, skills and talents, set aside time for pure personal pleasure and entertainment, rest and recuperation, and give time to supporting both ourselves and others and the world around us in the range of ways which are possible. We need time to enable us enjoy our own leisure and pleasures, and to fulfill our obligations and commitments to others.

But, given the demands on us and the possibilities available to the many of us in life, there are limits to what we are likely to be able to cope with and we are likely to be able to do, while at the same time retaining our positive and strong mental health. Trying to do too much, exhausting ourselves and pushing ourselves to the edge of what we can cope with in our efforts at work, in our efforts to care for and support others, and in other activities may, on occasion, occur and may be necessary at times, but such exhaustion and stress is likely to place our well-being and mental health at risk. Maintaining and ensuring positive mental health, preserving our mental health and well-being, means we must use our time effectively, do what we can as effectively as we can, but also that we must set aside time for personal privacy, reflection, rest, relaxation and sleep, and personal leisure and pleasure, all of which can and indeed are likely to bolster our motivation, dedication and ability to support ourselves and others.

Enabling us to balance the different needs we have in our lives, it is probably essential that we plan our use of time, at least to some extent, most beneficially in some detail, such that all of our different needs and goals can, as far as possible, be met and such that core and other principles can be optimally implemented. Having a basic laid down timetable for the broad areas we are going to cover on a daily, weekly and possibly monthly basis (and indeed over the years) should enable us to more effectively manage the tasks in our days and support our mental health, though again, what we plan for needs to be realistic. More than this our planning needs to be flexible in nature taking into account the fact that unexpected events may happen, and that we may be unable to achieve all that we wish to achieve. And we should not, in the main, be too critical of ourselves because we have not put into practice or realised our plans. Plans are there to help us to enjoy health and lives of well-being and happiness, not to tie us down in ways which detract from our well-being.

Nevertheless, whether formal and detailed, or more informal, our planning and linked to this our preparedness and preparation, is highly likely to help us to avoid unnecessary stress and worry. In terms of reducing anxiety and stress and being efficient and effective in our lives, detailed plans in terms of what we intend to do, both short term and longer term are most helpful. Of course and somewhat ironically, such planning can of course, take up time, reducing the time available for actually doing the things we wish to do, nevertheless, with appropriate time given for such planning, this planning is almost always worthwhile. Our planning should certainly not be allowed to significantly detract or take too much time from the actual doing of those things we need and want to do, or from our living of the lives we wish to lead.

Setting aside time for reflection on our day or days, on the week or weeks we have had, on specific areas of worry and concern, on particular areas of joy in our lives, or to reflect on life in general, is also likely to be of value in supporting our mental health and well-being. By contrast, not doing such reflection may lead to disorganisation, panic, malaise, a sense of being overwhelmed by the continuous challenges that life may throw at us, with consequential negative effects on our mental health.

The actual thinking about, our reflection on and recording of events from our perspective, can be cathartic and in itself, as a record of our lives and the events we experience, stated and considered from our own perspective, if viewed rationally and reasonably and recognising our achievements, this reflection can enhance our self-esteem. But it is the thoughts arising from such recording, and our reflection on such events in order that we can advance ourselves in terms of our responses to future events, which are of particular value to us. Diaries and the like can allow us to take a more reflective and dispassionate look at ourselves beyond the moments and multiple activities in which we are engaged, in what may be, for some of us, our very busy lives. They can allow us to observe and think about ourselves, concretising and making our lives easier for us to understand, and in that sense enhance our ability to listen to and understand others. And they can further act as an outlet for our feelings, in that manner representing someone to talk to, for what may be our sometimes lonely inner selves. Our reflective diaries can serve as a form through which we can express and also dissipate our anger, upset, our deepest feelings, our emotions which are distressing us, leading us to devise solutions to the problems which we may be facing, this further supporting us in enhancing our well-being and happiness, and as a consequence hopefully, enhancing the well-being and happiness of others. And our diaries can serve as canvasses upon which we can paint in words the environment, the circumstances, the relationships and more around us, helping us to see, know better, appreciate and understand the world around us.

A difficult and perhaps unexpected mental challenge related to goal setting and pursuing our dreams comes from actually achieving our goals and dreams. Of course, achieving our goals and dreams may not be something which happens in a momentary way, with some of our goals being long-term and taking years to achieve. Indeed while there may be clearly discernible moments of achievement and joy, happiness and fulfillment with regard to achieving some goals and some of our dreams, in terms of other goals and dreams it may be difficult to define particular moments of fulfillment and achievement. Nevertheless a significant challenge to us may arise following achievement of our goals and dreams since these may have acted as very important drives to us and motivators for us through our lives. And so, when those goals and dreams are achieved, we can feel a sense of loss, significant emptiness, if not depression, when these goals are no longer there to motivate and drive us, no longer exist for us to follow. And life can, as a consequence, at least temporarily, seem empty, painful and directionless.

A useful and often valuable response to such feelings, after having understood and acknowledged these feelings and their origins, having relaxed, reflected, recognised and coped with the pleasures and then what may be the subsequent emptiness following our goal and dream achievement, is the setting of new goals, our identification of new dreams and, as a consequence, our determining of new paths for the future.

As already pointed out earlier in this chapter, being able to set goals does depend to some degree on how we feel inside. Setting goals and having dreams for the future is not just a paper exercise but needs an important element of ourselves, our deep motivation, something deep within ourselves to be behind these goals. Sometimes we may feel we lack the energy to engage in setting ourselves new tasks for the future. We can feel run down, tired, demotivated and more. Time must sometimes be set aside to recover from achievement, from the challenges we are facing and have faced, time in which we can rest, relax and reflect, and perhaps also enjoy in a more passive sense, such that we can regain our zest for life and our zest and passion for goals and achievement, indeed our passion for living life to the full.

In terms of our mental health, our experiences of stress, which can, perhaps, on some occasions at a certain level in our lives, be healthy, motivating and indeed sought after, can also, when experienced in excess and when stemming from inappropriate and troublesome sources, lead to both physical and mental health problems with some of us unable to work effectively or work at all, unable to enjoy home life, unable to function effectively, with our experiencing suffering and not only poor mental health but poor physical health because of our high levels of stress. While for the most part, the most of us can often cope with the stress and the challenges we face, there may, for example, in some cases, be too much stress and pressure, be it at home, in our situations or relationships at work, in our relationships in our wider communities or in more than one of these different areas at the same time, leading some of us to be unable to cope, and sometimes leading to mental collapse and breakdowns in the face of these intense challenges and difficulties, intense pressure and intense stress.

In the work context, our stresses may originate through excessive workload, being given tasks we feel we cannot achieve, our lack of ability or lack of guidance and training in how to deal with tasks given to us. They may arise if we face facing bullying from managers or even colleagues, if we have to deal with stressful emotional situations with these colleagues and managers, unfair discrimination, a sense of isolation or powerlessness, feelings of sheer tedium, pointlessness and emptiness in regard to the tasks and work we are doing, perhaps feeling under employment threat with potentially, the consequent loss of our incomes. We can be stressed by our inability to progress at our workplace, find ourselves under pressure to engage in dishonest or exploitative practice, or face a range of other work circumstances, some of which may be beyond our control and influence.

If we are self-employed or work alone in our own businesses or operations, then lack of demand for our services or products, market dips and depressions, exploitation and pressure from buyers and suppliers, lack of integrity from others, the existence of competitors who are well organised with better products or superior resources and marketing and promotional strategies, can all result in us being faced with personal and business or financial failure, which represents a threat to our personal status, our sense of self, our financial and other forms of well-being, as well as perhaps threatening, in some senses and circumstances, our personal existence and survival. All of these threats can represent sources of great anxiety and stress.

Apart from such worries and stress about our loss of income which may affect our ability to support our families and live life as we wish to live it, which may affect our ability to pay off loans and debts we have incurred with damaging consequences of bankruptcy and more, significant stresses can also arise in our relationships, in our families. Home life may be argumentative and full of conflict. We may feel unloved, put upon and unappreciated; perhaps overworked and stressed through the need to both look after our children and earn an income; we may be faced with the need to travel for our work on a daily basis which may cause intense tiredness and related stress, or need to move away from family, friends and social support; we may be faced with the stresses of divorce. And on a daily basis we may face the range of minor irritations and stresses which build up to create major stress in our lives. Some of these more family and relationship stresses are discussed below.

Given the range of potential sources of such stress, it would seem reasonable to have an expectation of stress not only in our working lives but also at home and in other areas of our lives. Some of this stress may be normal every day stress, possibly somewhat positive in its nature and perhaps sometimes of our own making, a by-product of our wish to achieve, to get things done and supporting our motivation to do things, as well as comprising a consequence, to some extent, of our relationships.

Yet we should also expect some of the negative elements of and more negative feelings deriving from stress and therefore be prepared for them, having strategies in place to deal with them even prior to their rearing their heads, for example planning out rational strategies for tackling the challenges we face which might lead to stress, including, for example, through our taking proactive action to offset the possibilities of overly stressful events, through ensuring we get sufficient rest, staying physically fit, and through having other interests and foci which may distract us from our stressful situations. In these and other ways we should be more able to cope with our stress.

It is an important component of our responsibilities that we support our own well-being and happiness, and so, as a consequence, we do need to engage with this stress where it arises. This engagement does not mean simply dealing with our own emotional state in isolation from the world around us, but as just stated above, can often mean our adopting proactive strategies to tackle the situations, the circumstances which, and the individuals who, are making us feel stressed and who are in effect making our lives stressful and sometimes intolerable. Many of these problems will need to be tackled with practical interactive responses.

In the work context, if we are leaders or managers in our own or other businesses or other organisations, we therefore need to be prepared for and anticipate sources of stress where we can, not only for ourselves, but for those we manage and employ. And in response to external sources of stress from our organisational or business environments, sources of stress over which we may have little immediate control, then of course, as far as we can, we need to focus on developing new organisational systems, and new business strategies. We need to act as rationally and as reasonably as we can, adopting positive and constructive strategies, working flexibly to develop and improve the products and services we provide, perhaps developing our own new products and services, developing new promotional and sales strategies, identifying new political contacts where necessary to bolster our organisation's success and position, within the overall framework of supporting well-being overall. We may well also need to focus inwards to some degree and aim to improve our organisational and business efficiency, taking a range of other initiatives to ensure our success.

Such stresses with their consequent threat to our well-being, may also be placed upon us in charitable, political or other forms of social organisation and we are likely to need to respond in a similar manner to such stresses, perhaps redoubling our commitment and thinking imaginatively and creatively to solve the problems we face and to achieve our goals.

If we are employees in larger corporate organisations where the levels of anxiety and emotional stress can mean that there is real concern for the well-being of staff and in which there is a working culture which is open, caring and is interested in the well-being of its employees then, if such stress is prevalent for us as individuals and perhaps for others too, then we will need to report our stress to those who are responsible for our workloads or job situations, those who are in charge of, responsible for and perhaps imposing, sometimes without knowledge of the problems being caused, what may be unfair and unreasonable levels of stress upon us. If those who are involved in managing our work are unaware of the stress and pressures we are under and how those stresses are affecting us, then they will not be in a position to take action to support us and cannot be expected to take action to support us. Resentment towards these others when they are unaware of a problem may be justifiable, since of course we might expect them to already be realising a duty of care towards us, being aware, for example, of our workload. However, they may, for good reason, possibly being overwhelmed themselves, or simply through unintended insensitivity and personal fallibilities (which we all have), just not be aware of our stressful situation and how we feel. So we will need to tell them explicitly and unequivocally about our levels of stress, where this is practical and reasonable.

We should expect a supportive response when we are reporting high levels of stress in our work contexts and, if we are in the role of manager, we need to respond supportively to our employees, consistent with the principles established in this guide in terms of looking after others. Unfortunately there are certainly working systems where those in charge place their staff under significant stress, sometimes out of indifference and callous indifference to other people. Such stress may even be imposed as a matter of deliberate management policy (even if unwritten). Those in charge in such situations, where stress is used as a management tool, those with power, are acting entirely at odds with core and other principles, conducting themselves in a negatively selfish, self-focused and indeed callous manner through their actions and approaches, frequently placing too much priority on organisational, company and personal profit and having no or little concern for the mental well-being and happiness of their staff. Such actions and approaches are totally unacceptable. Such management systems need to be changed and colluding owners and managers need to be removed. And if we are managers being asked to impose such systems, then we must ensure such systems are not introduced and imposed.

As employees and managers, sometimes, it may not be possible for us to remove such stressful situations in the short term, and in some cases it may not be possible at all, due to our lack of power and constraints in our situations. And therefore, where we are unsupported and facing stress which is seriously damaging to our personal mental well-being, and where there is no prospect of the situation improving, we need at the earliest opportunity, to move on to a place of work and a way of living that we can cope with such that we can remain healthy. Similarly, when we are being asked to impose or are being substantially involved with organisations and systems which impose unacceptable stress on others, and where we can have no or little effect in terms of changing such organisations and systems, then we must not collude with such systems. Having, where we can, opposed these systems, then where possible we must choose to use our talents, skills and abilities elsewhere. It is the employer and manager, who are likely, in the long run, to be the losers from the imposition of such stress. Indeed emotionally and psychologically they are likely to be losing every day.

Sometimes we may feel unable to leave such a situation due to financial commitments outside of work, our need for money and indeed our need for stability to support ourselves and our families to survive, and sometimes perhaps due to our need to pay off debt. Irrespective of such circumstances, we still need to look for ways to either improve our situations, improve those organisations and systems, or leave. It may be that we need to bide our time, but we ourselves and others will be experiencing pain during that period of waiting and it may be, realistically, that within that context we will not be able to achieve change in a reasonable timescale. If we feel we can cope with the stress, and find ways around it, then of course we may decide to stay, but this should not be at the expense of our personal health and indeed the health of our families and those we love, as there may be knock-on effects on others due to our stressful state of being.

But forms of stress damaging to our well-being and mental health can arise from many other situations beyond the work environment. The family can be a particular source of stress. Relationships with partners, with those we love, can become difficult and deteriorate, and we may experience the pain of this relationship deterioration and breakdown sometimes through argument and conflict through each of our days. Such deteriorating relationships with their embodied conflict can be highly stressful and personally upsetting and damaging. Such situations are difficult to deal with, but we need to act as far as we can, to ensure our individual well-being and the well-being of all in our families under such circumstances.

Children can be difficult to raise and within a loving framework adult-child disagreements may still occur and arguments sometimes, or even frequently, break out quite naturally in some stages of childhood, as our children change and grow, wishing for more independence and asserting their own desires, wants and views, and sometimes doing so in language and through action which causes pain, anguish and stress (and of course they will feel stressed themselves). And of course, we as adults are changing too, as we grow older, becoming in some ways more experienced, but also being faced with gradual, though increasingly visible and largely inevitable physical deterioration, which we need to manage and cope with.

Hopefully, we as adults and as young adults will remain strong and robust under all of these stressful circumstances, taking care of ourselves and providing our love and support for others. However to experience some self-doubt and emotional challenge under such circumstances would hardly be unusual. Individual or close friends can support us, as can a broader circle of friends. But where this is not possible and problems are proving severe, additional counseling, psychological, strategic, and in some cases medical help must be sought to help us through. We should avoid despair, something of course which is easy to say. There will be those who love us, even in such challenging situations. And we need to love and take care of ourselves, support our own well-being and happiness. Help may be needed with partner relationships from those outside of the relationship, and in some cases, the partner relationship may need to end if the difficulties cannot be resolved and the conflict is causing insoluble and substantial stress, unhappiness, mental anguish and hurt.

Of course stress represents a more negative side of our living and mental health. On the more positive side, not only in response to stress, but as a general means of maintaining and enhancing our positive mental health and well-being, there are times when we need to focus on and ensure that we spend time enjoying our lives, not necessarily or simply in the sense of making extra effort to pursue pleasure, but in the sense of taking time to relax and take things easy, enjoying the things we are doing in life, and the environment, the world around us.

We need to allow ourselves and give ourselves time to take a breath and look around us; we need to take time to do nothing, to relax away from our intense efforts to succeed and achieve goals; we need to take time away from what may we may feel are our mundane daily lives, perhaps holidaying somewhere new and different; or perhaps sometimes enjoying the simple activities that we are able to do day-to-day, enjoying the experiences of doing such simple things, be they walking to work, chatting with others, washing clothes, looking out of the window at the world outside our home, gazing at the stars, appreciating the greenery, mountains or other scenery around us, listening to the world around us, breathing the scent of flowers, noticing the small, everyday things in our lives and in our environment that we might not usually notice and appreciate.

Taking such time to simply relax, enjoy and appreciate more closely and intensely the everyday, our realising the basic and inexpensive pleasures that can be experienced through taking our time, through not being hurried and busy, but instead doing little, observing the world about us in a relaxed manner, hopefully substantially unbounded by time, and not deliberately analysing but rather enjoying and appreciating the ordinary and everyday, can enhance our happiness, our appreciation of life and is likely to be significantly beneficial for our well-being and health.

Despite all the measures we can take to live our lives in a mentally healthy manner, there are some, if not many of us, who, beyond the normal ups and downs in our everyday lives, may not be able to enjoy positive mental health throughout our lives and indeed may suffer badly at times through poor and extremely poor mental health, at least with our current level of medical understanding. In some cases such mental illness may well be part of our individual biological self, representing illness which in some cases may be difficult for us to deal with, at least in terms of our personal and independent efforts to control our own thinking and feelings, our own actions and reactions. In such cases, as with other illnesses, we are likely to need medical help and assistance which we should not hesitate to seek if that is what we feel we need. Such medical assistance may optimally help us with positive strategies to help us alleviate our mental distress and comfort and may provide us where necessary with medicines and other forms of treatment which can ease our pain and help us to survive and hopefully also thrive.

At the extreme end, though perhaps not so uncommon, are those of us who may perhaps feel suicidal at times or even frequently feel that way, those of us who feel sometimes, or more often, that life is pointless and not worth living.[5] There are different degrees and levels of such suicidal thinking. It may be correct to say that perhaps almost everyone has had some, what may be described as, passing and 'mild' suicidal thoughts at some point in their lives. Certainly research has shown that many of us do have such thoughts at

---

5   Consideration at this point does not refer to suicide by those of us who are aged and at the end of an extended, long and well-lived life. This will be discussed later in the chapter.

times, but such research may underplay the true levels of suicidal thinking for various reasons, such as our personal unwillingness to admit to others what is frequently perceived as a form of weakness and vulnerability, even if the questions are asked as part of confidential research.

Indeed it may be that having such thoughts is actually quite normal and that unbeknown to us, many of those we see in our daily lives, who seem to be coping so well with their lives, may have such thoughts, and that some if not many of us, may occasionally or perhaps more frequently feel a sense of deep underlying distress and unhappiness. It is certainly likely that some of us will be feeling that way. The existence of these thoughts, given core and other principles, should serve to encourage us as individuals to look at understanding these thoughts better and should lead us to take action as individuals and perhaps also as human communities, societies and beyond, to investigate ways of removing these self-destructive and painful, self-immolating thoughts from our thinking processes and from our own minds, and where possible from the minds of all others suffering in pain with such painful anguish, such self-destructive thoughts and feelings.

While for some of us such suicidal and self-destructive thoughts may be a constant presence in our minds, these suicidal thoughts passing across our minds are, most likely, for the many of us, much more likely to occur during difficult and challenging times, or are likely to be much more intense during such times, when we may ask ourselves what is the point in carrying on with life given the intense emotional trauma, suffering and malaise, and sometimes persistent physical pain or other trials we may be enduring. Such thoughts and feelings may arise the more so during relationship troubles, loss of a loving relationship, the death of someone we love, loss of job and loss of income problems, at times when we have experienced or are experiencing failure, when others are being derisive and contemptuous of us, when we are feeling highly inadequate with low self-esteem. However, some times these suicidal thoughts can, for some of us, arise for no obvious discernible reason at all and indeed can be present or underlie the everyday thinking of some people. Yet for the most part, even though suicidal thoughts may arise, we can certainly override these and cope with these, especially with medical help, and the love and support of friends, lovers and family.

For many of us such suicidal thoughts may perhaps simply represent the minor passing through our minds of a possible suicidal act as an insignificant thought rather than a real possibility with no linked and serious intention of action in our real lives. These passing suicidal thoughts may appear simply in response to larger or smaller anxieties and worries, or perhaps sometimes an accumulation of smaller problems in our lives. In such circumstances, it is important for us to focus on more reasonable and practical strategies to deal with whatever difficulties we face, to allow time for whatever pain we are experiencing to dissipate and disappear, as will occur in almost all such cases of low level suicidal thinking. In such cases these feelings are perhaps more open to being simply brushed aside or ignored though that may not be wise.

Focusing on resolving our feelings, acknowledging our feelings, focusing on that which is good and positive in life, focusing on the things we want to do and achieve, focusing on ways to actually and rationally overcome the problems we are facing – thinking about the love we have or have had from others, recollection of our journeys and achievements in life, perhaps enjoying hugs with people we love, laughter, perhaps even just sleeping and resting. All of these and much more can bolster our spirits and help and distract us from or remove the emotional pains and suffering we are in the process of enduring.

As has already been described and emphasised elsewhere within, and indeed throughout this guide, our lives certainly do have meaning, importance and purpose. However, harmful thinking, depression, grief, sense of failure and inadequacy, distressing mental illness can result in our personal value, meaning, importance and purpose becoming difficult for us to see, can result in our failure to recognise these in our lives.

We can sometimes think, while recognising that our lives do have meaning and purpose, that such purposes and meanings are of no or little importance in the universal scheme of life, and further in some more extreme and painful cases we may come to wrongly believe that we are destined to live in emotional, depressive pain in what we may, irrationally and unreasonably, feel is a pointless world. Such thinking is false and destructive, and we need to make every effort to recognise and think about the near certainty that our emotional pains can be challenged and dealt with, that they are likely to disappear, and that tomorrow may well bring well-being, joy and happiness. We need to further recognise that in our futures we are highly likely, at least the vast majority of us, to enjoy well-being and happiness, which at times can and will comprise the deepest happiness, fulfillment, pleasure and joy. And where we do not anticipate such joys in the future, we need to recognise that for all of us the removal of our emotional pain, our suicidal thinking, can certainly be achieved.

Thus we need realistic and reasonable thinking which recognises and understands our emotional and other pains, thinking which recognises that sometimes things will not go right, that we can and will feel bad and perhaps sometimes depressed and on occasion, perhaps, deeply unhappy and depressed, but this thinking needs to combine with the recognition that we will have significant times of well-being, pleasure, joy and happiness. And it is this thinking and recognition of what is important reality, which needs to be prominent and which we need, wherever possible, to remain prominent.

Thus if we experience suicidal thoughts, and many of us will, we need to make efforts to recognise that, for the vast main of us, most of us, while there is a likely to be a reality of life with some level of pain and suffering, indeed sometimes even deep pits of upset, hurt, depression and despair, we will also hopefully enjoy lives which are generally ok for us, with hopefully prolonged periods of well-being and happiness as well as moments of great pleasure, joy and fulfillment, these sometimes involving our reaching the highest highs of emotion and joy, with all of these positive and less positive experiences and feelings, in the main, being components of a full and complete life. Many of us may experience some periods of extremely negative thinking and feelings, but in the vast main we will recover from such negative thinking and suicidal thoughts should we have them, discovering or rediscovering the daily and other joys of life, the many sources of pleasure, joy, well-being, satisfaction and fulfillment already discussed in this chapter and through this guide.

Those of us who find ourselves in the deepest despair with a deep sense of hopelessness and intense feelings of sadness, pain, accompanied by suicidal thoughts such that we are truly contemplating suicide, need to take action ourselves against such feelings and thoughts, but we also need to seek support, and need to be supported, as far as is possible. We need to be helped such that we can start to think and feel in ways which will lead us towards enjoying well-being and happiness, with real, practical and meaningful steps taken and help provided, medical and psychological help where necessary, such that we can survive day-to-day in the world without enduring traumatic mental anguish and pain, and hopefully and with our enjoying well-being as well as happiness, joy, achievement, satisfaction and fulfillment into and in the future.

If we have such strong feelings and we are thinking about committing suicide then we must ensure we seek help to deal with our self-destructive thoughts and feelings, as part of our obligations to both ourselves and to others. In the vast main, such deep depression and serious thoughts of suicide, in truth, need to be seen as representing a form of illness for which we will need help and medical treatment.

We should not feel ashamed to tell others how we feel and we should not be ashamed or afraid to seek psychological and medical treatment and help. Others of us, including those providing such help, should not in any way encourage such shame or fear. Depression and suicidal feelings are not uncommon and these can best be seen, especially in serious cases, as representing such medical conditions, which can be treated such that we can feel better, such that our pain and suffering can be alleviated and such that we can return to enjoyment, pleasure and, at worst, lives which do not feel intolerable and which encompass moments and times of equanimity, pleasure and joy.

We may feel nervous about putting ourselves forward as ill, as suicidal, but, as said, there is no shame in this and we have responsibilities to ourselves to alleviate and reduce our own pain and to avoid causing others the pain that our suffering and our suicide or attempted suicide will undoubtedly cause. If we are suffering in such a way and we are not seeking such help, then those others of us, aware of our pain, need to lead those of us who are thinking and feeling suicidal to seeking such help, even though, at the end of the day, the condition and well-being of those of us suffering in such a way, are only likely to be improved and our thinking and emotional hurt and despair resolved when accompanied by our own desire to improve our health, our own desire to enjoy life, our own desire to live.

Of course in terms of core and other principles, suicide is not in the vast majority of circumstances considered acceptable. It is the ultimate self-damage and self-harm to ourselves. While there is certainly escape from pain through suicide, such pain is almost always of a nature that, when appropriately addressed, it can be coped with and removed, allowing us to continue with our lives, and gain at least acceptable levels of well-being, pleasure and hopefully happiness too. In almost every case those thoughts, feelings and emotions which are causing such severe unhappiness, such severe depression, those emotions and feelings, those circumstances which are driving our suicidal thoughts and actions, can be dealt with, can be resolved, changed and removed such that good levels of well-being and happiness can be gained or regained.

As already intimated, suicide is, of course, in the vast majority of instances, also significantly destructive of those others who love that person who attempts to, or does commit suicide, and it is also undermining and destructive of communities, societies and beyond through the hurt and pain it causes. All those close to us in our lives, who relied on us, loved us, needed us, cared for us, will have to endure the loss of us, the person who has committed suicide. The family, the ones we love, will likely be in almost inconsolable pain and grief since we have acted and indeed perhaps, in a sense, in some cases, chosen to leave them, rather than having been taken away through accident or common other natural causes, something which would also have hurt them had that occurred. That being said, such severe emotional pain causing such intense suicidal thoughts is undoubtedly a form of illness, as has already been stated here.

Aside from that tremendous emotional damage to others which is caused directly, suicide certainly and terminally means we are no longer able to act to support others, since we obviously cannot provide support for others after we are dead. All those whom we could perhaps have helped through our lives, will now remain unhelped and unsupported, potentially suffering more because we are not there to help them. All those positive actions that we could have taken to love and support others, to help them feel better in their lives, are no longer possible.

And more than that, through suicidal action, our communities and societies themselves suffer through such a loss, their members feeling the pain of loss as a whole, with those of us still alive feeling, in a sense, inadequate through our being unable to recognise the pain that the suicidal person was suffering or through being unable to support and resolve what may have been the cries for help from someone in such deep and intense emotional pain.

None of this emphasis on the effects of suicide on others, on the social effects of suicide, is to underplay the intense pains, the immense emotional trauma, the immense hopelessness which we as individuals may face in our lives, traumas and pains which might lead us to those serious thoughts of suicide. It is to say that under those circumstances it is important to seek help, to try to resolve such feelings, thoughts and difficulties, to find ways through and out of this pain, to endure if necessary, and move onwards and away, if possible, to a more tolerable state of thinking and being, and hopefully move towards a somewhat or significantly better future comprising well-being and hopefully happiness and joy as well.

And at a more personal level, if we know those who are suffering from such deep depression, who feel suicidal, then as already stated, we must support them and help them as much as we can, emotionally and physically where necessary, such that they can recover and think differently wherever that is reasonable and possible. We need to encourage their recovery, point them to medical treatment and stand by them in their suffering until their suffering dissipates and hopefully finally disappears. And within our communities and societies we need to support the provision of medical help and systems for delivering such support and help for those who are suffering in such ways, as well as supporting learning and research into the mind, depression, suicide and other related illnesses and mental health conditions. Giving such support will help us all as individuals, in particular as it is likely that the many of us suffer from such irrational and painful negativity at times. Underpinning core and other principles it is also part of our common humanity and human nature to support others, such actions supporting our own well-being and happiness and the well-being and happiness of others.

There are those who engage in self-harm, which can border in some cases on the suicidal, again representing self-damage which is contrary to core and other principles. There may be a range of reasons for our engaging in this behaviour, which can often represent an outlet for emotional pain and a cry for help. Again this will, in many if not most cases, have its origins in harmful thinking, often contributed to by social situations, relationships, and social pressures, though there may be real biochemical, mental and physical illnesses at work which should hopefully, to some extent, be solvable with care, attention and where appropriate medical treatment. Again, while it is difficult and challenging, those who feel these ways and engage in this self-harming behaviour, need to be open about what they are doing and seek help so that their self-harming can be ended and such that they can escape from their pains and be supported in experiencing well-being and happiness.

It does need to be said that for most of us life is not likely to be, is not to a large extent, a continuously and non-stop positive experience, devoid of downs along with the ups, though some or many of us, hopefully all of us, may enjoy a deep sense of happiness, warmth and satisfaction at times and over time, will hopefully have wonderful and joyous experiences. And when we consider things in the round, often when we are not focusing on the more immediate challenges facing us, we may be aware of and feel overall positively or very positively about our lives.

Of course to have a life that is in all respects a continuous, positive and joyful experience would clearly be wonderful. However, it is not expected or considered realistic in this guide for it to be the case that life will always, or even almost always, consist of those entirely positive and wonderful experiences. It seems reasonable to consider it likely that there will always be challenges in life which may cause us some stress, anxiety and at times unhappiness. And to some extent those challenges, at least some of them, while they might not seem so at the time, are actually important parts of the overall joy of life, these challenges helping to make our lives fulfilling and worthwhile, through the tackling, and in many cases the overcoming of such challenges. Indeed in some respects for many of us we enjoy facing challenges and enjoy taking the risks that facing some challenges involve. Taking risks to achieve can add interest, entertainment and challenge to our lives, and not only that, through overcoming these challenges, our challenges hold out the prospect of providing a deep sense of well-being and achievement which is likely to benefit our lives significantly, both in the shorter and longer term, if not for the rest of our lives.

It is worth reiterating that memories and recollections of achievement, knowledge of achievement in life, memories of our overcoming challenges, in whatever area, from relationships, to travel, to science, to sport, even our overcoming of the health and other problematic challenges and experiences we may have had in the past, can provide useful mental sustenance for us in challenging times. When things are bad, it is often worthwhile spending time recalling the successes we have had, the things that have worked, reminding ourselves of the good we have done, the lives we have changed, the friends we have known who have enjoyed our company, all of this, while probably not solving any immediate problems, can provide a potential useful fillip to our mood, improving our self-belief and perhaps supporting our confidence that current problems can be solved, as well as also reminding us that, having achieved in the past, there is at least a possibility that we will achieve to some degree in the future.

While aiming to achieve, to gain success and attain our dreams, are likely to be sources of well-being, pleasure and joy as well, and at the minimum sources of distraction, on the reverse side our taking risks to achieve, indeed the actual phenomenon of having challenges and goals, does open us up to the possibility of failure and disappointment, even opening up the possibility of our discrediting and humiliating ourselves in front of others, opening us up to opprobrium and potential ridicule in front of others who may directly see, find out about or know about our lack of competence, our failures, our inabilities. And as a consequence, we may, unfortunately, if not robust in our thinking, end up admonishing ourselves and putting ourselves down because of our failures.

We should of course, on the whole, be kind to ourselves, and where we fall short, we need to, instead of engaging in damaging and destructive self-admonishment and criticism, examine our errors and failures to achieve, and invent ways to be successful into the future, without being hypercritical and undermining of our total selves. As already referred to, we may well need to develop a robustness in the face of criticisms or even ridicule by others.

Unfortunately there do exist those who are unsupportive of others, who do not wish us or others to be successful and who will sadly mock and make fun of others who are trying out the new, experimenting with their lives and their life directions, aiming to reach goals which are challenging, trying to achieve. Such experimenting, our making of errors and indeed our failures are, however, essential in many ways to our living a complete life of well-being and happiness. These unsupportive people may mock, deride and even directly insult those of us who are risking our image, self-image and reputations in front of others, those of us who are trying to push our personal boundaries, aiming to develop ourselves, aiming to support community and society, our global world, and who are trying to support others. Their mockery and derision are reprehensible and need to be replaced by support, respect and indeed love.

All of us who put ourselves on the line to achieve for positive purposes in accordance with core and other principles, be it in relation to areas including developing our thought, interpretation, adventure, performance in the range of contexts and skills, in the context of our relationships, through engaging in the range of spheres in invention, creativity and other approaches, need to be supported unequivocally in our efforts. Through our taking risks and trying the new, (which we hopefully will all do to some degree) through our actions and our efforts, important individual and personal, social and human discoveries are made and, as a consequence, we all make progress. Failure and humiliation through such actions of experimentation, adventure and risk, is to be borne to some extent with pride and is to be learnt from, with activities where appropriate persisted in, especially where, in terms of core and other principles, we believe there is a reasonable possibility of success and achievement into the future.

It may be that our approaches, our skills, our thinking and thinking frames, our techniques, our actions, our communication, may need to be refined and developed such that success can be achieved and in order to ensure that any errors, failures, non-achievement and humiliations do not happen again. Nevertheless, sometimes, failure and humiliation, allied to passion, commitment, dedication and self-belief can be important spurs to our development, learning and progress, which in themselves benefit us all as well as benefiting our communities, societies and our humanity as a whole. The risk of success and failure, as already referred to in this guide, can in itself be pleasurable, and once one risk-taking experiment and adventure is over, we can look forward to our next adventure, our next challenge and next risk, all the time expanding our range of knowledge, understanding, skills, abilities and experience, as well as gaining pleasure, deep satisfaction and fulfillment.

Success in all cases, in the face of all challenges, would be wonderful, in particular as it will often feel good to be feted by the many for our achievements and talents, this being something that some, if not many of us may desire. But few of us will achieve such constant success in all we try. Nor will the many of us have the opportunity to be, or actually be able to be feted at a community, societal or even more universal level as exemplary heroes and heroines, much admired by others, even though we may achieve and deserve praise and approbation for the things we do.

And while we may wish for such local or more widespread acknowledgment, appreciation and approbation, along with what may be the consequent additional material and other rewards that such recognition may bring, we should also recognise that, to some extent, for those who achieve the greatest renown and fortune through their abilities, actions or other means, such fame, fortune and success can be a double-edged sword, placing additional stresses and pressures on those who experience these apparent positives with, for example, the possibility of their fallibilities, errors and lives being widely exposed. As a consequence of their renown, they may well face further additional demands, stresses and pressures not faced by the rest of us, and may themselves go through additional periods of significant challenge, self-analysis, unhappiness and perhaps depression, and do so under the microscope of public scrutiny. These individuals may themselves need help and support in their special circumstances.

Our mental health and positive mental health requires being able to cope with all of these situations, success, failure and everything in between, and to deal with the fact that we will feel happy at times, if not very happy and satisfied with life, and at other times we may feel down if not downright depressed. As we know that for the many of us, sometimes life will feel good and wonderful for an extended period, and sometimes we may also feel down for some moments or longer periods (hopefully not for too long), we will therefore need to anticipate and be prepared for these feelings and these situations.

A common and significant source of pain and suffering for us are feelings of isolation and loneliness, perhaps inevitable to some extent because, while we are social beings, we all to some degree, live alone in our own minds, with our own thoughts, our own feelings, our own thinking about others and the world beyond our mind, our own individual perceptions. And within that individual isolation, inside our minds, we will have a deep sense of our own uniqueness, a sense of self, our separateness from others, a sense of our individuality, which, while undoubtedly serving as a fulcrum of our feelings of well-being, positive mental health, happiness and pleasure, can also contribute to a deep sense of loneliness and isolation. Unfortunately, though to some extent inevitably, such a sense of isolation and loneliness can sometimes be our dominant feeling. Our sense of isolation and loneliness can therefore cause us a level of mental and heartfelt pain and suffering.

Yet that is not to say that there are not times when we as individuals may personally wish for separation, isolation away from others, to have peace, to be away from other people and the demands they can sometimes place on us. Many of us will wish to have such personal time for peace and reflection, our own personal space for thought, rest and contemplation. Further, there may be times when others annoy us so intensely that we wish to be away from them, and there may be times when the world seems confusing and overwhelming, when others at home, through work or in other contexts are providing us with upsetting and difficult challenges. Under such circumstances, we may need to give ourselves time apart from others, to consider our feelings, work out what to do and determine our necessary actions in order to support our well-being and mental health. Under such circumstances our desire to be alone, for some solitude, is likely to be entirely justifiable and should hopefully provide a means of reducing the pain and suffering we are experiencing. In such circumstances, separating or isolating ourselves to some degree may, at least in the short term, be a positive course of action, at least for a while.

In other circumstances, there may be projects in our lives which we feel require the spending of time alone, in thought, in planning, in learning and reflection, in pursuing our personal development, acquisition of knowledge and understanding. Taking such time and space for ourselves, away from others, can be tremendously beneficial not just, for example, in terms of providing quiet and space in which to think and explore, to be creative, to find and plan the realisation of opportunities, to find solutions for problems, but also in terms of rebuilding a sense of a strong self in a world in which it can be so easy to be swamped by the multiple external influences, the pressures and challenges we face, the demands and wants of others, all competing for our individual action to pursue their goals, competing for our attention, for influence on and possession of our individual thoughts and minds, creating challenges and difficulties for us, which we can counter if we take the time to engage in reference to our own total selves, our own personal selves, our personal goals, our personal identity, feelings, thoughts, wants, desires and motivations, through which we can determine and prioritise, evaluate and re-evaluate our own personal decisions, directions and goals.

Taking a break from the social, from others, separating or isolating ourselves in such a way in a temporary sense, as referred to in chapter eight of this guide, can at times be significantly beneficial to our own personal well-being, enabling us to think more clearly and re-establish ourselves and who we are, establishing and re-establishing our personal goals, supporting our own satisfaction and well-being, making us better able to cope with tomorrows. And through benefiting ourselves in this way there is a strong likelihood that we may benefit others through our more healthy subsequent interactions grounded in a mentally healthier and stronger self.

In practice, our periods of physical and mental separateness and isolation may be simply short times for ourselves during the day, sitting alone for a few minutes or if we can, a few hours of an evening. We may have some time to ourselves on an individual walk or choose to experience this aloneness and separateness in a range of other ways including, in a broader sense, in some cases, deliberately spend extended times away from our home cultures, something which is likely to give us a better and more clear perspective on who we are.

Yet sometimes during such periods of separation and isolation, and certainly at the end of such periods of separation and isolation, we will hope to be with others again, engage with them, enjoy their company, be with them, speak to them, deal with them and sometimes, when we have spent time in isolation contemplating goals and establishing our goals, perhaps reflecting on the world and writing our thoughts or planning our future, we will be better able to recognise and enjoy the real, many and varied pleasures of being with others.

If our temporary separation and isolation has been a positive decision made in order to develop our thinking and to work on specific projects away from the interruptions and demands of the world, then we may be lucky enough to receive appreciation, recognition and praise from others when the job or task, the product of our time of isolation, contemplation and personal dedication, is eventually brought to fruition.

Nevertheless, despite the positive benefits of having some time aside and away from others, if we isolate ourselves from others for sustained prolonged periods, this may well serve to damage our health, well-being and happiness, in particular through damaging our relationships with others. Others who are close to us, our families and friends, may well wish for and need our company and attention and may feel unwanted, snubbed, saddened if we decline to spend time with them and decline to pay them attention or reduce our levels of attention to them. While we are not and cannot always be at the beck and call of others, we certainly have obligations in terms of supporting the well-being of others.

We certainly cannot and should not, if we can at all avoid it, be too far from or ignore our children who are dependent on us, our partners with whom we live day-to-day, our work colleagues and friends, at least not for overly significant periods of time (though understandably we may need to be away to raise the money and resources that our families, that our children need, for survival). Yet this togetherness with others needs to be balanced with providing us with the space we need for thought and reflection. If others ignored us, snubbed us, then we would almost certainly feel saddened ourselves, though if the individuals concerned explained to us their need for space for reflection and thought, something which we would undoubtedly expect others to want in any case, then our pain would likely not be so intense. We clearly have judgments to make in terms of the degree to which we provide ourselves with the individual reflective and thinking time we feel we need and should have, and in regard to our time for interaction with and engagement with others on a daily or other basis.

Of course, in terms of our feelings of loneliness, with our commonly felt need for company and social life, if we feel extremely isolated and alone, indeed if we are extremely isolated and alone, despite our personal want and need for others, this can be a source of intense and deep pain for us, which can lead to a sense of significant emptiness, inadequacy and perhaps a sense of personal failure, which if not remedied can lead to even greater pain, suffering, isolation and inadequacy. So where we are not seeking separateness and isolation as a means of promoting our well-being, such an undesired lack of interaction with others in self is likely to bring us down, cause us sadness, sorrow and unhappiness, and has the potential to damage our broader mental health.

And the pain and suffering from this unwanted isolation and loneliness occurs primarily because, despite this sense of individuality and separateness, we, with perhaps the rarest exception, are substantially social in our human character. We need others and we know of ourselves and see ourselves in terms of, in relation to, and as part of the social whole. We live largely, if not almost completely through others, gaining almost all of the most important, fulfilling, worthwhile and enjoyable experiences of life through our social selves, be they the joy and pleasures of love, our sense of belonging and being part of a group and our loyalty to others, be these pleasures through discussions and talk with others, through our cooperating with those who share our goals and interests, through our relationships of all sorts, through our sense of achievement and desire to be acknowledged, recognised and considered important and worthwhile by others. And when we lack this social element of our lives, we can feel unhappy, depressed, inadequate, isolated, even bereft. Feeling that way, we will, in the vast main, need to follow the urge go out into the world and be with others, sometime, somewhere, somehow.

Thus, due to our social nature as individuals, as humans, an absence of people to be with on the moment, to talk to, an absence of friends, lovers, family, such absence creating a sense of apartness and isolation, can sometimes be very painful. And if that isolation and loneliness is not a matter of choice, in terms of that painful and undesired apartness and isolation, sometimes, especially among the young, these feelings may be accompanied by self-criticism, or even more extreme thoughts of self-loathing, blaming ourselves, holding ourselves as inadequate and unworthy as human beings, because of our isolation. In some circumstances, at some stages of our lives, especially in our later years, we may simply feel despair, our inability to interact and meet people being down to immobility, illness, the deaths of friends, family and those we used to know and lack of those with whom we might have something in common. And while we may be able to cope, of course this damages our well-being and can damage our mental health.

If we see others suffering such isolation and emptiness, we need to act as far as we can to support them in avoiding this form of pain and suffering. This may be difficult in a world where there is, in some if not many contexts, so much loneliness and isolation. Yet through our individual actions in taking time to show interest in others, in taking time to notice others and value them, to show to them their importance, we can help individuals feel better and help to improve their well-being. Through our individual actions supporting social groups which bring people together who may not in the normal way of things gain much opportunity to talk, to interact, we will be supporting the well-being of others, and reducing their pain and suffering.

Further, by supporting our social organisations, supporting our governments locally and beyond, in pressing these organisations to recognise the importance of such interaction for those who are lonely and isolated, as well as encouraging our governmental and other organisations to act to establish and support groups which promote such interaction, be these organisations established around specific purposes and goals or simply for the purpose of meeting and communicating, we will also be supporting well-being and happiness and reducing pain and suffering. Hopefully such social groups will also strengthen our communities and societies, helping us come together and support each other.

Overall, it is clear that for many of us, our mental health and sense of well-being is substantially affected by, if not significantly determined by, our relationships. As social beings we, at least the vast main of us, need people, wish to and need to interact with people, wish to and need to feel of importance and significance to others, wish to like, love and be with other people, and need to feel approved of liked and loved by others.

In line with the realities of our lives, the shifts and changes in our lives, our changing locations, in line with the changing phases of our lives, perhaps our changing attitudes and feelings too, sometimes we will have many relationships and even many close relationships, and at other points we may be more alone, having few relationships of any sort at all. Where we find ourselves short of relationships, short of relationships which matter; where we feel we are being ignored, isolated, friendless, being treated as irrelevant and of no consequence and no matter, this can damage us, damage our well-being, and may (though not necessarily) threaten our mental health and mental well-being. If we find ourselves in such a position, if we can manage it, we need to aim to set out to either find new relationships or resolve these problems.

While we generally need relationships and positive relationships, it is nevertheless certainly possible to have self-respect, self-belief and strong mental health without requiring approval from others; indeed strong and positive mental health may require us at times as individuals to be of such a nature that we are firm and confident in our beliefs, about life, about what we consider to be right and wrong, about specific issues, about ourselves as individuals, about the world around us, and it is valuable to be able to be able to substantially set aside, disagree firmly with or even ignore the views that others may hold of us and the things we do and believe in.

We can certainly survive and live in a manner which is not so based in this approval of others, instead focusing on our internal values and beliefs as motivators for our conduct, our internal thinking serving to provide our own personal and individual rationales for our actions, irrespective of the thoughts others have about us and the actions others might wish to take against us. While perhaps not what we would prefer, we can indeed survive and manage well at times without the approval of others, even *in extremis* with their ostracising us from family, community and society. For many of us it might be the case that we may suffer greater pain if we betray our internal values and deeply held beliefs, and therefore the path to greater well-being and happiness may involve setting aside our desire to be approved of and loved by others in the short term, with the objective of supporting others, our communities, societies and our broader humanity in the present and future, either hoping to be loved and appreciated in the longer term, or simply willing to be unappreciated and unloved in order to do what we believe is best and right.

In certain cases we may decide to pursue a life away from our communities and societies of birth, even away from our nuclear and more extended families. This may occur on some occasions when these families, communities and societies attempt to impose views, values and ways of living which we, as growing adults, no longer accept. In some contexts, we may wish to leave a religion or belief group and that group reprehensibly go beyond legitimate peaceful persuasion and seeks to prevent us from doing so, threatening punishments, ostracism and perhaps violence. Such groups and families, in the vast majority of cases, are acting contrary to core and other principles, and are certainly not showing their love for us as individuals or their concern for our well-being or showing concern for our broader humanity. Often these individuals, families and groups are concerned about shame being heaped upon themselves for what is seen as their failure to keep someone in the community, when they should feel pride at the freedom and well-being they are promoting. Such individuals, families and groups may be prioritising the maintaining and bolstering of their own group, being willing to severely damage us as individuals to protect their own community reputation and save themselves from the already mentioned shame. No sense of shame, no concern for reputation justifies oppressive action and violence against another.

In other circumstances and situations where often a younger person is drawn to a group which offers threats to them, a group whose practices are contrary to core and other principles, groups which seek to deliberately isolate members from their families, with the purpose of controlling their members, which remove from their members individual freedoms to act, which themselves hold the prospect of ostracism and punishment and place physical and other barriers over departure from the group in the way of those who might choose to leave them, then we are certainly justified in concerns regarding people joining such a group. Under such circumstances we must attempt, in a peaceful but persistent manner, to prevent those in our family and others from joining such groups.

Some families may wish to impose an unwanted marriage on us. We may, as a consequence, having asserted our views where we can, need to leave these groups and pursue our own well-being and happiness as we choose, perhaps in a more isolated manner, away from such families and groups, perhaps joining another group or living independently of any group. That would be a reasonable thing to do in support of our personal well-being and happiness, and indeed in pursuit of the general well-being and happiness.

Healthy relationships with other adults are those which, in the round, benefit us mentally and physically, enhancing our well-being and happiness. Certainly our relationships should not cause us too much pain and suffering, though loving and caring relationships can sometimes cause us pain, if not intense pain. 'In the round' takes into account that there can be difficulties, conflicts and disputes in our relationships yet with those relationships still serving overall to enhance our well-being and being considered healthy relationships. Fractures in our relationships are, in the main, obviously not desirable in such relationships and problems need to be worked out as soon as possible, as far as is possible, to support our well-being and happiness.

Our healthy relationships involve people listening to us, treating us as significant individuals, taking time over us, being aware of our concerns, worries and anxieties, not rejecting us and running away or moving away from us when we are troubled, ill or suffering in some other way. And in turn we need to listen to those others, treating them as significant and important to us, taking time with them and paying attention to and acting on their concerns, worries and anxieties, loving them and sticking with them when the going gets tough, when their lives are challenging, when they face difficulties in their lives and indeed when they make demands on us. In healthy relationships we are likely to do things together, listen to others, share activities and interests, share concerns and worries, share our feelings and problems, share talk of all sorts and we may often work together to support common goals. Hopefully these positive, supportive and constructive relationships will persist over time, causing us great warmth and pleasure, a sense of belonging and bringing us great satisfaction and happiness, whatever the ups and downs during our relationships. Obviously such characteristics of healthy relationships are easier to state and write down than to consistently achieve on a day-to-day basis.

That being said, when relationships become unhealthy, where there is significant conflict which seems insoluble; where we are being bullied and oppressed in a relationship; where our own well-being and happiness is being substantially damaged; when others are being unsupportive of ourselves, and worse, personally destructive of us with their words and actions, being derisive and contemptuous of our very being; where we are suffering violence from a partner; then once we have taken steps, as many reasonable steps as possible, to resolve these problems, in support of our own well-being and happiness, this being central to ourselves and central to core and other principles, then we are obliged to leave that relationship, whatever love we might feel for another.

In terms of finding close and loving relationships in the first place, there is the possibility that it is difficult for some of us to find and therefore to have relationships, causing us some frustration and pain. When we are active and young, thrown together in various circumstances, be it school, sports teams, work and more, then it is likely to be easier for such relationships to be initiated, but realities mean that we move away, leave home areas and home relationships and it may be difficult to sustain these relationships over distance and these relationships may become distant and lost as others and ourselves move on to the new.

Other concerns and priorities often arise in life, such as new loves, families, changes in personality and interest, with the result that sustaining some of our past relationships while possible, becomes more challenging. As a consequence, a more isolated life may well result. If we have partners and children, our more nuclear family relationships may be close, but it can be difficult to find time for friends and more extended family, though it is important that we do try to find such time where we can. Nevertheless, if good relationships can be sustained this can help us maintain our bearings in life, our sense of belonging, involvement and participation, and help to maintain and sustain our mental health and well-being, as well as that of others. These friends and more distant relatives will add a richness and diversity to our lives and to the lives of our closer family.

Some of us may simply find it hard to form many friendly relationships for a range of reasons, or for some of us we may not be so focused on relationships in our lives, perhaps being more interested in ideas, thinking, a particular hobby or interest, academic and intellectual, artistic, scientific or other aspects of life. Even if such is the case for us, we are highly likely to want and need relationships. And for those of us, the vast majority of us, who wish to form relationships, the reality of isolation may result in pain and a sense of being an outsider in community and society and perhaps a sense of personal inability and inadequacy. Moreover, a substantial detachment from others has the potential to lead to substantial difficulty in interacting with others when we do need to interact.

Fortunately at some point in our lives, almost all of us manage to find friends and to build some forms of friendships and close relationships, in particular as those among us who have difficulties in building relationships will most likely, at some point, meet each other and are likely to be happy to build friendships with each other and enjoy each other's company. There are also many avenues of joint enterprise, and co-participation, even for those of us who feel less able in social situations, allowing us therefore to meet potential friends and at least be companions in an activity or enterprise. And where there are fewer friendships and fewer relationships, those relationships may be deeper, stronger and long-lasting, perhaps more reliable than the relationships of the more gregarious and confident, whose relationships may in some cases be more transient and shorter-lasting (though that is, of course, not necessarily the case).

Unfortunately, as already mentioned, as we get older, the friends and relationships of earlier life, in many contexts, are likely to become fewer and fewer, with those of us towards the ends of our lives perhaps finding ourselves increasingly isolated and lonely on account of the deaths of partners and friends, and on account of decreasing levels of mobility, as well as in many cases on account of declining resources. In those societies where there is more geographical mobility in the overall population and in which children may have moved far away, this may create even more isolation for us. To prevent and reduce our isolation, in our older years we therefore need to make whatever efforts we can to remain active and to participate wherever possible in the community, in supporting others, in helping out with children and other jobs and duties we can fulfill, which involve having, maintaining and building relationships.

It is also up to the rest of the community; it is up to the rest of us, to support older people, supporting them in their physical and emotional needs, preventing them from becoming totally isolated from the rest of the world, and thereby supporting their well-being and happiness into their old age. Also of great importance we, of course, need to support the elderly in the latter periods of their lives where they are moving towards death, something which can be a fearful and indeed painful and traumatic experience for some, though need perhaps not be so, death being an inevitable part of all of our lives.

Considering loneliness more broadly, and not simply with regard to those of us who are elderly, if we do feel alone and isolated, unwanted and unloved, we may sometimes say to ourselves in our self-talk, in our invisible personal chatter, reflecting our deeply embedded often irrational feelings and thoughts, or even perhaps sometimes say out loud and visibly, that we must be alone for a reason, that reason being that we are in some way defective and inadequate. "I am different, incompatible with others, inadequate, antisocial in my behaviour, repulsive, too thin, ugly, weird, fat, weedy, thick" or whatever foolishness we might tell ourselves. Whatever the truth, and sometimes indeed we may have characteristics and qualities which some or many will perceive negatively, these being characteristics and qualities that we might need to take concerted action in relation to, it is important for us to get our thinking right, such that we can address any problems underlying our unwanted isolation, and, perhaps more importantly, think in a manner which avoids us doing unpleasant, unwarranted and unnecessary emotional damage to ourselves or indeed others. It seems reasonable to say that, in by far the majority of instances, while we sometimes may be lonely and feel isolated, our own happiness is highly unlikely to be supported by painful, extended and repetitive self-talk statements of our unhappiness combined with persistent and damaging self admonishment and criticism (often unjust) relating to ourselves and our perceived inadequacies.

As part of our efforts to reduce our feelings of isolation and loneliness, rather than unwarranted self-admonition and self-criticism, we often need a sense of self-understanding and self-forgiveness where this is appropriate. We need to make sure we have realistic expectations about the future and future of our relationships, understanding the normality and inevitability of a sense of isolation in our lives at least at some point, as a part of who we are as people (and therefore not blaming ourselves and hurting ourselves about what is general, to be expected, and normal).

We may see crowds of others together and apparently getting on and having fun together; we may see partners and lovers walking hand-in-hand; and, to some degree, that can make us feel more isolated and alone. Yet we need to conceive that each person in that crowd may feel isolated and alone themselves; we need to recognise that at some point we will be a part of such a crowd; we need to enjoy seeing lovers walking hand-in-hand, feel joyful and happy for them, understanding that this is a wonderful time in their lives, and that hopefully, we will also be able to enjoy such love and happiness; we need to understand that such lovers may also have been alone and felt lonely in the past, yet thankfully, they are now, for the moment, feeling happy, joyful and fulfilled.

With reference to our own more negative feelings again, aside from avoiding damaging self-blame and extreme self-criticism, our well-being will, in the main, not be improved by blaming others, holding others responsible for our loneliness and pain, even in the event that that is in reality the case. While there might be some temporary false respite and comfort through wrongly holding others responsible for our own pain and our loneliness, blaming others when responsibility lies primarily with us is clearly inappropriate and will cause damage, upset and hurt not just for ourselves, but also for the others we blame and others beyond that. Where reasonable and appropriate, where possible, and usually for the best, we need to take responsibility ourselves and adjust our own thinking and actions such that we can act to pursue our happiness and reduce our sense of loneliness if that is what we are experiencing.

Nor is harking back to the past, blaming past events, or even current circumstances, of value in order to remove our feelings of loneliness and to improve well-being and happiness. Analysis of the past may help us identify problems and issues, and certainly the past may be relevant to our situation, but we have to focus on the now and the future, seeking change, pursuing happiness and well-being for ourselves and others on the moment, for tomorrow and beyond, rather than dwelling on and re-living the past, perhaps events and happenings which have gone badly. If we feel isolated and alone it is not helpful to be blaming these past events and those involved in them (including ourselves) for the present. We need to focus now on making efforts and taking actions to improve our futures. Nor is it significantly likely that we will act to improve the well-being of others by our focusing largely or exclusively or perhaps indeed at all, on the failings of others or by focusing on situations and circumstances from years ago rather than our own difficulties and challenges in the present.

Clearly, if we can, we need to aim to escape from unwanted isolation and loneliness. If that is our wish and we are unhappy in our isolation and apartness, in order to support our happiness and well-being we need, as far as we can, to make every effort to meet and socialise with others. As an initial step we will need to recognise and decide on our need and want for company and, having done that, we will need to engage in systematic, stringent and planned efforts to locate company, and ideally the right kind of supportive and caring company. If isolated in our homes, farmhouses, flats, wherever, undoubtedly, even in this modern age where many of us are connected to the worldwide web, have mobile phones and can engage in easy electronic communication, we will need to get out and physically try to meet people.

If we are feeling the pains of isolation and loneliness, in order to reduce these pains, along with our making conscious efforts to meet people, we need to do our utmost to make sure we engage with others at the different levels and depths which are appropriate to our need for human relationships. Our engagement in some circumstances and situations may not be so deep and involved, represented, for example, in the form of our daily face-to-face interactions in shops, in the street with brief hellos, through going out to events and dealing with event staff, through the range of more minor business and other conversations on the phone or through a computer if we have one. In other situations we will hopefully have and develop deeper more sharing relationships. In order to develop relationships, ensuring and maintaining a level of physical fitness is of some importance in that it enables us to get out and meet others and supports us interacting with others as individuals, in groups or teams, thus enhancing our well-being and happiness and reducing our sense of isolation and loneliness.

We should have no shame and embarrassment in seeking out friendship, company and even love, and if we feel inclined we should be quite ready to tell others that is what we are doing. Our desire for company (as with friendship and love) is a common if not ubiquitous human need. And wherever we can, if we can, we need to seek the highest quality of interaction possible, friendships, lovers, family, for it is not only the absence of interactions, meetings, with other people which can cause us pain, but it is also our not having the quality of those interactions, not having interactions with those who care for us and will listen to us, those with whom we can share our adventures and interests, our thoughts and feelings, our troubles, sadnesses, our stresses and pains.

Our more extended and deeper interactions with others may simply take the form of conversations with friends in our homes or coffee bars and cafes, talking with others when engaging in charitable efforts to raise money, being with and supporting others locally in the community who may be in greater need than ourselves, conversations with others wherever we can find them. We can find good company, friendships (and indeed even love) through taking part in activities such as watching muscial performances, engaging in sports, joining local history groups, joining the range of interest and activity groups (and if these don't exist starting and organising them), joining political belief groups, reading groups, singing in choirs and other groups, attending local fairs, and taking part in local community activities, festivals, as well as engaging in educational activities (learning new skills, finding out new things), amongst the range of other social opportunities.

We can engage in more distant communications through whatever means are possible, especially in the current age through means such as e-mail, messaging services, facebook, skype and other forms of electronic communication, though this interaction may not be so rich and meaningful (though for some of us it may be the only contact possible).

Our pains and feelings of isolation may occur in part because we have difficulties in talking with others and sharing our feelings about our lives and living. We may in the first place believe that others don't want to listen to us. This may be true in some cases as telling others about our own problems, sharing our worries and concerns, while often reasonable and acceptable, while often an important part of healthy relationships, can become draining for our listeners, especially if our own complaints and problems take up too much time in our interactions, with our being too problem-focused, being too self-focused and our thus giving too little time to listen to the experiences, problems, worries and concerns of others. Moreover, sometimes others may simply wish to do enjoyable things rather than discuss problems in our lives, and indeed their own problems. We most likely need to achieve a balance of sharing our experiences, worries, troubles and problems with listening to the worries, troubles, problems and concerns of others, supporting others, and also getting on with the practical experience and enjoyment of well-being in our lives.

Yet we may also be reticent to share our problems and challenges because we feel these are too private and intimate to be shared. Certainly in terms of sharing some of the private information we hold about others and ourselves, we need to be careful, as those who are our friends may have other friends and may gossip and talk to others, this having the potential to result in the diminution of our sense of self-value and our reputation, with our private information becoming known by many others who may ridicule and deride us.

Such private and potentially embarrassing and humiliating information should be held close and only shared with those whom we can really trust. Yet if we are suffering in silence, then sharing our experiences, pains and more is most likely advisable, and should help, to some degree, to release our stresses and pains, hopefully leading to useful and helpful advice which may, if acted upon, help our situations and serve to improve our own well-being and happiness and the well-being and happiness of others. Such sharing may also place our problems and worries in context, with our perhaps coming to see that what we consider a terrible problem, in fact represents a common problem which many may face, or represents a problem which is in truth insignificant compared to the trials and tribulations of others, which may be much more worthy of our attention and concern.

Our engagement with and interactions with others should optimally not involve simply or solely, passive listening and watching, but instead should require our personal input, involvement, interaction and active participation, with others responding to us, exchanging views and opinions, valuing us and valuing what we have to say, with ourselves valuing these others and what they say. Sometimes we may have to make deliberate efforts, and even reflect, research and deliberately learn, in order to make sure we are doing all of this well, because such actions may not always come easily and naturally to us.

A conversation with a shop assistant, a functional exchange with a waiter or waitress in a café, greetings in the street, may relieve loneliness and pain to some extent, yet while these may make us feel better, noticed and of some significance in the world, they are not the same as a proper chat or conversation with an friend or relative, even if such a chat or conversation might seem to be at a superficial level (though hopefully such conversations will not be superficial). Of course the superficial chat or conversation is preferable to nothing at all, and should be grasped at where there is little else, but it does not match the quality of a conversation with someone who actually and significantly cares for us, who knows us, who believes that we matter and who really wants to listen to us, even if such sentiments are sometimes, if not often, unspoken. The sense of being with such a person, a partner, a family member, friend or whoever, can be deeply warming, uplifting and inspiring, giving us the sense that we matter and taking away, either completely or to some extent, the pain of our loneliness, even if simply, perhaps, temporarily. Such friendships and relationships should not be taken for granted but need to be recognised and appreciated for the importance and value they have.

If many others, including some of those we may know by name, do not talk with us or engage with us extensively, and this may often be the case, we need to recognise that often, if not in most circumstances, the reason for this is not that we don't matter; rather it is because there is simply not the time, space or capacity in the lives of most of us, to actually know and actively care about everyone. It should be easy for us to see that the fact that the crowd on a train, in the street, pay us no or little attention, says nothing about who we are, about our character, even if at times, the lack of attention and acknowledgement, our apparent lack of importance, might make us feel bad. And indeed it is, at least for some of us, sometimes nice to be able to hide in those crowds and be unrecognised and anonymous. In the same way as others may have limited time for us, there are limits to how much attention we can pay to others or that we wish to pay to others. We have our own concerns close to our lives and our own worlds. Realistic expectations, realistic recognitions, such as these, embedded in ourselves, embedded in our thinking and emotions, are significantly helpful in supporting a healthy life for ourselves both internally and in our relations with others.

Those who pay us little attention are not worthy of disrespect and dislike on the grounds that they pay such little attention to us; in the same manner that it would be unreasonable for us to receive disrespect from these others on such grounds. We do need to recognise the practical limitations that may constrain our lives and therefore the extent to which, in terms of time and indeed energy, that we can manage to spend on caring, directly one-to-one, for the large numbers of others for whom we could care, and relieving their particular unhappiness and loneliness. Recognising this we need, to an important extent, to focus on getting on with our own lives, doing the things which keep us happy and supporting our well-being and also the well-being of others.

Our loneliness and isolation can be reduced by our not only joining with groups, but through our participating in purposeful social and group activities. Paid work is often a very important way of being with others, apart from providing a useful form of income which can enable us to do the other things we wish to do and support others. Through our work, we will hopefully, in alliance with others be providing useful service to our communities, societies and beyond. But through voluntary groups we may be able to support those in poverty, those who are having their freedoms challenged, experiencing torture, those seeking democracy, those suffering with illnesses who need financial and day-to-day support. All of this and more can bring us company, enhancing our mental health and well-being, not only through the good we are doing in supporting others, not only through the company and companionship we may enjoy, but also through distracting us from feelings and thoughts of loneliness and indeed feelings of emptiness.

Those of us with extremely busy lives, with intensive jobs, those of us with young children, will spend time and need to spend time on the many things which are the priorities in our lives, our work, our families, our children, all of which will or ought to involve supporting others. But, despite these demands on our time, we still need to find some time to bother about and care for those who may be lonely, while recognising at the same time that our more personal priorities matter, that we ourselves do matter, that we are important to our family and we matter to our friends and need to give them the time they need, indeed demand from us.

We certainly need to take cognisance of those who are close to us, talking to and being with them, and acting in support of their needs. We need to show we care for them. Of course such care and attention should not be too intrusive and encroach too far on people's lives, in ways that perhaps they might not want us to encroach. Yet the core and other principles mean that, reflecting our own human need for others, and the need to support the well-being of others, as well as reflecting our own needs and our own-well-being, we need to provide time and space for others to support them in enjoying well-being and happiness, and in order to help them avoid the pains of loneliness and isolation.

It is important, though perhaps a little irrationally demoralising at times, to accept our, in a sense insignificant position in the world when we as individuals are placed alongside and amongst the millions and indeed billions of other people who currently inhabit our world. This can create feelings of loneliness and a sense of our own unimportance in the world overall (as indeed can feeling our personal position within a human history of millions of years and a universal history of 60 billion years or more), but we need to be accepting of who and where we are as individuals, recognising our centrality in our own lives, in the lives of many others, focusing on our own well-being, our own happiness, our own pleasures, and working for the benefit and well-being of all others as far as is reasonably possible on a daily and longer term basis. In line with focusing on our own well-being and doing what we can to improve the well-being of others, we need to aim to support others in their lives and reduce their suffering, such actions serving to support ourselves and others, and representing a reasonable, rewarding, satisfying, fulfilling and hopefully happy way to live our lives.

In some circumstances, solutions to the pain of our own loneliness and isolation may be difficult to find due to circumstances we cannot change (such as the deaths of friends, partners, other family, the departure from home of our children, illness, immobility in our old age). But in almost all circumstances, some form of solution and respite can be found. By taking actions to meet others, through reasonable examination of our own conduct and modification of our conduct, through modifying our thinking about ourselves and events in our lives, modifying our goals and purposes in life, developing our relationships in an effective way, our sense of isolation and loneliness can significantly be reduced and our health and well-being improved.

Beyond the feelings of isolation and loneliness that we ourselves may sometimes feel, additionally, in pursuing our own health and well-being and the health and well-being of others, it is important, if not critical and essential to think about and be realistic about how others feel and think, recognising their own potential loneliness, the feelings that others may have about their own lives, the possible sense of isolation and loneliness of those who seem self-confident and gregarious. As already mentioned in this chapter, a sense of loneliness and isolation can indeed exist within many who seem to be surrounded by the crowd, who seem from appearances to be popular and loved, but who may feel a sense of performance and distance and who do not actually feel loved and wanted.

To avoid these pains of isolation and loneliness, apart from our systematic and increased efforts to meet others, apart from, but often overlapping with the participation already mentioned, we can set new goals in our lives and focus on personal projects which may help us to achieve things which are worthwhile, but which will also distract us from the negative feelings of loneliness and isolation through focusing our minds and taking up our time in useful, engaging and hopefully productive activities. Through our pursuit of such goals we are likely to need to interact with, participate with others in one fashion or another, something which should serve to reduce our isolation.

Moreover, there is almost always benefit and enrichment in sharing our interests and activities with others. Knowing that others are interested in the things we are interested in, knowing that others care about the things we do, and perhaps knowing that through our contact with them, they begin to care about us, is warming and positive.

We can also take part in a range of more individual activities which will absorb our attention. These include games and entertainments, reading, watching television, listening to radio and of course interacting through our computers. While enjoyable and enriching in their own way, distracting from our loneliness, these comprising in some senses, social activities and in a sense participatory activities themselves in important ways, nevertheless, such activities may still leave us feeling lonely and isolated unless we can share our pleasures and joy in them with others, talking about our books, the shows we watch, or playing games with others in real and present, physically real, social interactions with friends, family and indeed others.

Thus whatever the technologies that may be available, we enjoy and gain from the real presence of others, with us, in front of us, to talk to, sometimes to touch and be with. Thus, the presence of modern communication technologies, be they home telephones, mobiles, skype systems, online forums, messaging services, photosharing applications, social networking sites and other internet-based forms of communication can of course help us to interact with others, assuaging the fact of our being increasingly distant geographically from many others, and our being perhaps distant in other ways, these technologies will in some senses not provide us with the personal communication and personal presence we need and love to have. That being said, while this technological communication may not be as rich and rewarding as having personal face-to-face communication, nevertheless, if we are alone and lonely, it can help to form an important element of social contact and social life, even giving us a sense of belonging, even participation, through such online communication and online group membership which can help in relieving, to some extent, our sense of isolation and loneliness.

However, even with such forms of contact available to us, deep feelings of isolation and loneliness may still strike us at any age. Sometimes connected to, but not necessarily connected to these feelings of loneliness and isolation, we can feel a painful, desperate and deep sense of hopelessness and pointlessness, in some cases comprising total despair and in some cases, the already discussed suicidal thoughts and feelings.

In terms of our thinking and self-talk, after suffering defeat, failure, rejection, injustice or sometimes simply through personal feelings of emptiness, we may dejectedly and depressedly ask ourselves either silently to ourselves or out loud, "What is the point?" and sometimes even more despairingly, and perhaps representing a near encounter with the feelings and expressions of suicide already discussed, we say to ourselves "What is the point in going on?". In many cases, we may make such remarks to ourselves or to others out of minor irritation or minor anger, then quite quickly get back to our daily lives, suffering only momentary and minor upset and pain. However if we are experiencing such feelings of deep despair, in order to support our well-being and happiness, we certainly need to somehow resolve these feelings and this sense of hopelessness and pointlessness.

In some of these moments or times of such deep unhappiness or times of despair, we may see challenges in front of us as insurmountable; we may feel that there are only problems, challenges and difficulties into the future; we may feel overwhelmed by those challenges; we may have lost sight or lose sight of our own value and importance, feeling our pain large and seeing ourselves as being of little worth and as insignificant in terms of others and the world, wondering at the point of our existence at all in the world and universe. We may feel empty and hollow inside. These can at times be desperate feelings, yet in a sense they can also be motivating and indeed reasonable doubts, wonderings and feelings which spur us to re-examine ourselves and the world, which spur us on to find answers and reset our aims and goals. Nevertheless, we need to tackle and resolve such feelings such that our well-being and happiness are supported.

Of key importance in resolving such feelings and despair, as was stated with regard to suicidal feelings, where possible, we need to get our thinking as right as we can. Saying "What is the point?" needs to be recognised as an expression of despair, sadness and frustration, of value to us if we interpret it as saying we have perhaps lost sight of our personal goals and need to refocus on what we are about in our lives, and also of value to us if we use such an expression to establish or re-establish our goals. Interpreted effectively, noting our expression of this question will be helpful and enriching if it moves us towards the recognition of our current sense of a lack of goals and purpose, or if it moves us to devise new strategies to cope with and tackle the problems and difficulties in our lives.

With experience, recognising oncoming feelings of malaise and despair we can act early, establish and re-establish our goals prior to, or at the onset of such feelings and therefore pre-empt and avoid much emotional pain. It seems unlikely that goal-setting will always help us avoid such pains, which in some cases may be a part of our more general mood or affected by other factors in our situations and circumstances, but setting goals and then trying to achieve them can certainly be, at the minimum, a distraction from our pains, and is also likely to be fundamental to making us feel better and happier, improving our mental health and well-being. And deciding on actions and strategies in relation to our feelings of lack of direction, malaise, or in the face of problems and challenges that we face, should either help resolve these senses and problems, or will distract us from our unhappiness while our environment, circumstances and situations change and while we and the world move on, hopefully to happier situations and happier times.

While sometimes difficult to conceive and understand at times, when we feel lost and in despair, in response to the literal question "What is the point?", we do know, to a large extent, what the point is for us as individuals – to enjoy well-being, to live well ourselves, to enjoy our lives, to seek happiness, to be fulfilled, to support and care for, others, our friends, families, communities, looking after them and supporting them in their pursuit of well-being, as well as supporting the well-being of our communities, societies, our humanity as a whole. We know also that we need to act to avoid or reduce our own pain and suffering (including removing the despair and sense of emptiness we might feel which is discussed here) and act to reduce and remove the pain and suffering of others.

That is how our purposes or 'the point' is summarised through the core principles in this guide and in combination with the other principles presented. That is enough, and indeed has to be enough, because that is the answer to the question. If we are prepared to accept such thoughts or similar in answer to the question, then we have rational ways available to us to deal with that sense of frustration and despair, rational ways to improve our well-being and indeed to rid ourselves of such feelings of hopelessness and despair. The question, "what is the point?" in reality, when interpreted correctly, has a real answer, with real solutions, which can be provided and put into practice with resulting actions and strategies which we can use in our own real lives in order to support and improve our own well-being and happiness and to support and to improve the well-being and happiness of others.

And our solutions come more specifically from questions such as "What can I do to make myself feel better, more happy, improve my well-being?", "What do I enjoy doing and how can I make sure I do these enjoyable things?", "What can I do to promote the well-being and happiness of my fellows (which in turn will help improve my own well-being)?", "What can I do to enjoy pleasure and fulfillment, to make today better, to resolve the problem in front of me; to cope?". And then, if the problem or problems and the feelings we have cannot be easily resolved or moved away from where necessary, "What will happen next?" and "How can I [then] ensure my well-being and happiness, and the well-being and happiness of others?".

Addressing these issues, thinking about these types of questions and others, searching for answers and gaining suggestions for answers from others, is more likely to result in achieving happiness, pleasure, fulfillment and well-being and is far more likely to be helpful and life-enhancing than repeating to ourselves the questions and language of despair, which may well serve to increase our feelings of frustration, emptiness and despair.

Again, as with regard to depressive or suicidal thoughts, all this is not to diminish the pain or suffering we may feel in such difficult and challenging circumstances and situations, nor is it to suggest that sometimes removing such feelings might be easy. There may have been tragedies in our lives, the deaths of those we love, our break-up with someone we love deeply, ruptures in our close friendships and disputes with those we love, our abject failure or even marginal failure in some project or task that we set ourselves, which was important to us; there may be threats to our well-being in the work context, perhaps there has been humiliation and embarrassment in front of others, our being substantially let down by friends whom we had trusted, amongst a range of other occurrences which might cause us to feel despair.

In some if not many of these cases, we may need time to absorb and cope with the pain, time to feel grief, sadness and to feel that sense of pain, loss and despair which is perhaps natural for the many of us in the face of such events. It is not in the nature of most of us as human beings that we can suffer difficulties in our relationships, failure or tremendous failure, suffer the loss or death of someone we love, without pain and suffering and without the need for time to absorb the blows. It would be almost unheard of and be uncharacteristic of ourselves as people if within a few moments of such upsetting events, we were to become cheery and move on into the future with no emotional damage and upset.

When such upsetting and bad events happen, the vast majority of us need time to mourn. We need time to cope emotionally with events which may rock our world. Although there may be exceptional circumstances where we need to act immediately and dispassionately in response to traumatic events, especially in the face of threatening circumstances, we, for the most part, need time to absorb the blows, to deal with pain, to deal with the implications of what has come to pass, before we can set ourselves gradually on a course to recover and move forwards again with our lives. Once we have mourned, experienced the pain, then we may well be more easily able to move towards improving our state of being, our mental health, our well-being. Once we have started to deal with our pain, suffering and indeed despair, we can then start to make either tentative or determined steps to move practically forward into the rest of our lives.

Past events will still be with us, but to move forwards we will most likely need to start to set out directions and plans for the future, rather than focusing on the past. That does not mean forgetting the past, or that our pains may go away immediately or in some cases, ever, but it does mean our gradually coming to terms with events that have taken place. Where someone we loved deeply has died, then it may take some time to adjust to our new lives but hopefully we will be able to do so and will do so. If, on the other hand, we have failed to achieve our goals, suffered humiliation and the pain of failure, if we have behaved badly, dishonestly, even violently, then it is likely to be beneficial if we look at and identify where we went wrong in the past (if that were to be the case) and as a consequence or otherwise, design how we can move on with our lives, aiming to be more effective, aiming to be better in terms of how we live into the future.

Following death or loss, we may eventually decide on taking deliberate and concerted actions such that we can meet others, with our joining social groups or putting ourselves in places where we are likely to interact with others. Taking such steps should support us in escaping our pain and loneliness and help prevent us from using to less than best effect, parts of our lives which could instead be used for enjoying and promoting our own happiness and well-being and being supportive of others, rather than living with deep depression and unhappiness, and turning over in our minds our memories of the past, through those thoughts re-living and re-experiencing accompanying hurt and pain (something we may inevitably do to some degree).

If we are feeling down, depressed, unhappy for whatever reason, if we can find the spark of motivation and energy, then we need to use that energy and spark to aim to take some action to improve, more broadly, how we are feeling. If we are of that nature and have such an interest, then we might decide to try to improve the way we feel through some exercise, a walk outside, perhaps even a run or some form of sporting activity. Such activity, even if solitary can make us feel better, through direct positive effects on our bodies, hormonal and physically. And if we can interact with others during such exercise and activity that may help us improve our well-being even more. If we can turn our physical activity from a one-off into a regular walk or activity, that should help our sense of well-being substantially and help to reduce our emotional pain and suffering to some extent.

Alternatively, again if we can gather the energy and wish to move forward, at the same time, we may determine to set new, realistic and enriching goals which can absorb us, our time and energies; we may decide to absorb ourselves in new interests, social or otherwise. Perhaps in the case where a failure or lack of success is the cause of our sadness and despair then we can conduct a detailed analysis of what has occurred and then engage in planning to counter that previous lack of success, and develop our relevant knowledge and skills. Hopefully, as a consequence, our actions will have the outcome that our previous lack of success is turned into success. On the other hand where we have not succeeded in one area, we can choose a new direction or directions, new goals, and aim for success and achievement in these areas.

Further, we may decide to investigate questions and find answers; we may decide to try and find a new love; we may decide to give of ourselves to others through our friendship and companionship or to give to others through charitable or other means, realising our deep human need to contribute to our communities and societies while also making more contact with others, building companionship, common purpose and friendship; we may decide to change the environment we live in through, for example, moving elsewhere to live (though if we do this, we need to be aware that that may not change things, as we, ourselves, our personalities, who we are, travel everywhere with us; we are always present in our own lives and without personal change we may encounter the same situations again and again). Overall, there are endless ways in which we can attempt to move away from our sadness, depression and despair.

Perhaps sometimes linked to the despairing comment already discussed "What's the point?", while not all of us will feel this way, some of us may sometimes feel a sense of pain and hopelessness, in the recognition of our finity, the fact that our lives will end and, as already mentioned, our apparent insignificance in relation to the millions and billions in our communities and societies and the immenseness of our planet, and the millions and billions of planets and stars in our known universe, when we compare this immensity with what may seem to be our own small and insignificant individual lives, our individual existence.

Yet, should we feel this, whatever our sense of minuteness and insignificance in relation to the universe around us, what matters is our value and importance in our own more immediate world, our own feelings, our own perceptions, our own relationships, our own experiences, our own futures, our own well-being and our own happiness which we can gain and regain, and the well-being of our families, of others in our communities, societies, our humanity around us. It is our pains, our pleasures, our feelings, our emotions, our experiences, our anxieties, our thoughts, our beliefs, others, our communities, societies and beyond, and of course our well-being and health which are of crucial importance to us and central to us as individuals. And the feelings, pains, pleasures, anxieties, interests and of course well-being and happiness of others, are crucial to us too, and comprise an essential part of our own well-being and happiness. The point for us, as already stated, lies in our supporting our own well-being and happiness, and supporting the well-being and happiness of others. And in pursuit of these goals there are rational strategies and actions we can take which fulfill our point and fulfill these goals.

However small and insignificant we might feel, for the most of us, in relation to the local lives which are closest to us, we certainly do have influence; we do interact with and affect others, we can and do cause and contribute to change, we do make our local world, and to some extent, despite those sometimes feelings of unimportance and insignificance, we are the ones who make, we certainly are the ones, amongst others, who contribute to the construction of the local worlds we live in and to the wider world around us.

And thus related to 'the point' in terms of core and other principles and our personal significance, we are of significance not only to ourselves in terms of our feelings, emotions, our well-being, but are of importance in our own worlds, the social and physical worlds around us, that certainly do include us and indeed need us as participants and players, acting in support of our own well-being and the well-being of others at whatever level. Further, the undeniable fact is that we are unique and special as individual people, as others are, and without each of us, each of us summing together as individuals to make up humanity, the fact is that our human community, while able to function without us, in itself is less, lesser in existence, less in terms of being, less able to be and less able to do.

For some of us, this sense of our own insignificance within the context of history, the universe and within the context of our human population, can feel positive in some respects. Thus, there may be enhanced well-being and happiness for us in this perception of our insignificance in the vastness of the universe, in the vastness of time, and within the context of our vast human population. Knowing our true size and the true range and limits of our influence in relation to this vast world and universe, and indeed in relation to the vast extent of human, planetary and indeed universal history, can usefully prevent us from becoming too self-focused and too self-centred. And perhaps in some cases it can help prevent us becoming too overblown and arrogant, too full of a sense of self-importance, given the immense forces at play in our world, in our universe, geological, physical and more, and in our human world, the psychological, social, political, some of which forces can damage or destroy our lives in a manner against which, as individuals, and as a humanity, at least with our current level of knowledge and capabilities, against which we may be unable to take any meaningful action.

Such a sense and realisation of our smallness as individuals and as a humanity in relation to the universe can also have benefit in providing ourselves with a pleasurable sense of awe and wonder, and sometimes a sense of calm deriving from this knowledge of our size and significance in relation to this almost inconceivably vast place which is the universe. And perceiving ourselves as part of the vast universe, a vast universe of time, perceiving ourselves as perhaps next to nothing amongst such immensity, an immensity of which we are indeed a part, as part of one moment in time, may, to some extent, provide us with pleasant feelings and enhance our well-being. Our appreciation of ourselves in relation to this vastness and as part of this vast universe can give us a sense of oneness with our material planet and the universe and a positive sense of where we are, a positive sense of our place and a positive sense of true belonging in our humanity, world and universe.

Beyond a sense of isolation and loneliness, other pains, other negative feelings, intense feelings of frustration and indeed suffering, can arise in us from our having a deep sense of powerlessness, something which we can experience in a range of situations, and which may in some cases comprise a constant and nagging daily feature of our lives, though perhaps sometimes being something we are not truly and consistently conscious of.

That being said, there are frequent and clear examples where we may feel helpless and powerless, be it the sight of bad behaviour and poor conduct, sometimes right in front of our eyes, which, in some cases we feel we can do little or nothing about, at least in terms of immediate action. We might endure the sight of others in pain or hurt, the sight of the powerful exploiting those who are powerless, the sight of others lying and cheating dishonestly for their own benefit, yet their not being tackled and dealt with. All of this can be painful and frustrating.

And we may feel powerless, lacking sufficient power in contexts where we are the victims or more directly affected, in our own more immediate lives, when others with authority over us or otherwise, act against us physically or in manipulatory, mistaken, unfair, prejudiced and dishonest ways to our detriment, threatening our well-being, our basic living and subsistence, our families, our jobs and careers, despite our honest efforts to do our best, to care for, to support others and to achieve to the best of our ability. Under such circumstances we can experience intense feelings of resentment, pain and powerlessness, with perhaps the source of our incomes threatened with loss or lost, with our jobs gone. And this can occur when a decision is made by another, in authority or far away (sometimes, if not more often, misguided), which damages our well-being, our incomes, our prospects, our opportunities or jeopardises our personal welfare and the welfare and well-being of those we love. In the face of corporate decisions, organisational decisions (whether democratically arrived at or not), in the face of political oppression and tyranny, we may rightly feel intensely weak and powerless.

Of course in order to support our well-being and happiness and the well-being and happiness of others, we need in the first place, wherever we can, to proactively take initiatives to head off and avoid such situations, to work to prevent such situations arising, and if such is not possible, to act where such situations have arisen, to protect and to defend ourselves against such attacks, defend ourselves against misguided, insensitive and damaging decisions by others, which threaten our well-being, our families, our friends and others, which may threaten our health, happiness and our very survival. Focusing on our sense of powerlessness is unlikely to help us in achieving our objectives. Moreover the reality is unlikely to be that we have no power in any situation. Thus, while we might have feelings of powerlessness, these need to be set aside and we need to identify where we are powerful, the levers we have through which we can exert pressure and use our own personal power in support of our reasonable aims. Those who are taking advantage of us and mistreating us will need to be, in the first place, talked to about their actions and the consequences of these actions for us, and requested to change their minds and their actions.

And if they continue in their conduct we will need to aim to ensure that, where their conduct is unjust and destructive of ourselves and others, we use our understandings and the power we have to ensure we achieve just and reasonable outcomes for ourselves and others. It is likely that in order to oppose such actions and in order to promote well-being and happiness we will need to ally with others and organise with others against such people and such actions. Through working and acting with others we will enhance our individual power and may be able to prevent such oppression, manipulation, dishonesty and the like. Through standing alone and acting in forceful and effective ways we may be able to relieve the threats to ourselves and others, yet through acting together with others, we are often much more likely to be successful.

Our sense of powerlessness may not solely originate from human factors and our human environment. For some of us, on a day-to-day basis perhaps we may feel we are victims of what may be, for example, extremes of natural forces, climate and weather. Highly noticeably for some, that sense of powerless may be felt in the face of nature and the tremendous forces which may result in tsunamis, earthquakes, landslides, floods, storms, tornados, hurricanes, volcanic eruptions and more. And of course we are faced with disease and illness, the inevitability of our old age, that latter against which we can take some action but which seeps through us inevitably reducing our physical and sometimes our mental powers. We can take actions to improve our lives in relation to aging, through exercising, through maintaining social life and social interaction, but at some point, unless we lose our lives early, we will find ourselves physically and perhaps, sometimes, mentally deteriorating too, and unable to continue as before, powerless to prevent such deterioration, though hopefully still able to enjoy and have fruitful, rewarding days of well-being without experiencing significant and unpleasant pain and suffering.

In relation to illness and disease, we may in some cases have the power to take action, either preventatively through the fitness activities, dietary and other approaches already discussed and through seeking medical treatment and supporting medical cures. Yet of course in some cases our illnesses and diseases may be incurable, beyond our power to deal with, and thus we will be left with long-term and unpleasant health problems or recognise that we are more immediately, in some cases, on the path to our deaths. Under such circumstances, it might be useful to recognise and come to terms with the limits of our powers and aim to obtain, as far as we can, the most happiness, love and joy that we can from the rest of our lives, and do our utmost to support the well-being, happiness and joy of others who we will leave behind.

While in some situations we may be powerless, nevertheless, in particular with respect to occurrences more influenced by social and human factors (but also sometimes in regard to natural phenomena), we frequently have some level of power and can take action, sometimes highly effective, to counter our powerlessness or feelings of powerlessness. Indeed, in many such situations, our sense of powerlessness can sometimes be transformed through intelligent action and dedicated effort, such that a minor or even major difference or even total change can be achieved, be that immediately, in the short term, or over the longer term.

Considering some specific situations where we might feel powerless but can most likely exert some power, in circumstances where we, or others are under physical threat or attack, we will need to and indeed are required to take action, where we can. We can and should, if possible, in the first place aim to use the power of our words and other means to diffuse tensions and anger, and to deter and prevent physical attacks on us or others. In preparation for such circumstances, we need to prepare, develop and indeed learn verbal and non-violent actions and strategies which we can put in place in such circumstances, (and indeed it would perhaps be valuable to have these as part of our routine education and training). Having such capacities in itself is likely to make us feel more powerful and more able to protect ourselves.

However, unfortunately there may be circumstances when verbal and non-physical responses to physical threats and actions may not be adequate in themselves to protect us and others from aggressively violent attack. Again, as perhaps a matter of our routine education, development and training, it may be beneficial for us to know and understand how to respond to protect and defend ourselves and others forcefully from physical threats and attacks, and such preparation in itself may lead to us feeling more confident and powerful and less vulnerable to such attacks.

As long as our education, development and training in these areas is focused on defence, physical restraint and using minimal force, including verbal action, as well as being accompanied by training and education in regard to values consistent with core and other principles, in relation to caring for all others, then there should be few negative implications for our communities and societies in having all of us, to all intents and purposes, powerful and capable of using physical force, since that force will be deployed for peaceful and reasonable purposes linked to supporting well-being and happiness, and preventing pain and suffering through protecting ourselves and others.

Consistent with this, if feeling physically powerless and under threat, we can act to develop our own physical capacities such that we can defend both ourselves and others more effectively. We can develop our physical strength and fitness through exercise of various kinds and develop our skills and tactics in terms of physical defence. And further, we can, if we, or others, are experiencing circumstances of physical threat, ally with others in similar positions, working together to protect and defend both ourselves and others against those who are threatening us. We may need, in such circumstances, not only to ally with individuals but also with organisations and groups which will be supportive of us.

Dependent on the particular circumstances under which we are threatened or attacked, we can report threats of violence and violent attacks to those with authority and power, who are able to act legitimately and legally to protect us and others from violence, coercion and other forms of threat. This of course applies when these authorities can be seen as credible and reliable, and this may not be the case in some contexts. It should be remembered that in line with the principles set out in this guide, we are obliged to support our own personal well-being and avoid our own pain and suffering, and have an obligation to defend ourselves as far as we can, from aggressively violent assault and physical threats, and also to protect others from such aggressive violence and physical threats as well. In terms of our capacity to respond to such violence, it is our obligation to be, as far as possible, powerful, not powerless.

That being said, in terms of our individual physical power there are always likely to be other individuals who are stronger than us. In addition to the fact that others may be naturally stronger than we are due to simple physical size and capacities, we will lose physical power and physical skills to some extent as we age, we may be disabled, infirm, lacking our former capacities, or alternatively we may be young and vulnerable, ill or physically weak for other reasons. Moreover, those who threaten us may have weapons and skills with weaponry that we do not possess or have access to. More than those individual comparisons in terms of physical power, irrespective of our individual and personal physical strength, others may come together into criminal groups and gangs, and may engage in criminal violence, which may cause us indirect damage as these groups and gangs engage in pursuit of their anti-social destructive acts or even cause us direct damage and pain when they explicitly target us as individuals and those we love and care for, our communities, societies and beyond.

As a consequence of such a range of threats to our well-being and happiness, we need to support and take part in systems which protect us all from such aggressively violent attack, systems involving law, law enforcement, justice, forceful defensive action against those who are violent, incarceration of those who are dangerous, and protection for all, including the weak and the vulnerable. Of course such systems need to use the minimal level of force to achieve their goals of protecting us, and need to be as far as possible and reasonable, protective of all, including those who might engage in anti-social acts, engage in violence. A prime aim of such systems must be to persuade and support those who are threatening aggressive violence or who have acted with aggressive violence, in desisting from such aggressively violent actions on the moment and into the future, and to ensure as far as is possible that these individuals can reform and change to become peaceful, cooperative and supportive members of our communities and societies.

We may also feel powerless in the face of those who bully us, something which can occur in many contexts and which may or may not be accompanied with the threat of direct physical violence. We need to take action against such bullies, to prevent their bullying behaviour, whatever the context. Bullying, at least at the present time, is unfortunately a source of much pain and suffering. It is entirely unacceptable in terms of core and other principles. It involves hurting others, causing pain and suffering through abusing others from a position of physical, political and social, and sometimes individual mental strength and power.

We may have possessions taken from us forcibly by those engaging in such bullying behaviour; we may be subject to fear and violence, often for the pleasure of those who bully, revelling in their political power, their personal strength and their ability to harm and to get what they want from what they perceive to be a weaker party. But bullies are not simply those of legend found in the school playground, but exist widely in many workplaces, on the shop and factory floor, in the management staff and employees in the range of organisations, in groups on the street, where the loud and aggressive may aim to bully us, sometimes with physical force, or perhaps by means of exposing us to public humiliation.

They may bully in offices and other work contexts where these bullying individuals will take advantage of, dominate and abuse their colleagues and staff, sometimes from arrogant and lofty positions of power, oppressing and abusing those of us who work for and with them. They may take advantage, in particular, in such employment situations because we, in our work context, may be concerned, worried or frightened of objecting against them or dealing with them as we know we ought to, for fear of losing the employment and income, the career opportunities we so desperately need, or even through fear of losing our entire careers. We must ourselves, of course, never bully and must always take actions against those who bully us and who bully others, whatever the context, be it at work, at home or in our communities, societies and beyond.

And there are many ways of dealing with such bullying behaviour, our strategies needing to be dependent on our situations and circumstances. We can, for example, deal with them using words which defuse their bullying actions; we can, dependent on the circumstances and context, report such bullying acts and their perpetrators for their destructive conduct to their own managers should they have them, in an informal manner and if that is not effective, a formal manner. We can, where necessary, act externally to our own organisation and use law to deal with such bullying. We should not shrink from tackling such bullying and exposing such bullying conduct.

Where such bullying behaviour involves giving us instructions which are not legitimate or which are illegal, we must refuse to cooperate with such instructions, refusing to carry them out. If it is too difficult to change their behaviour, we can act over time to marginalise and remove such bullies from their positions, gathering evidence of their vile conduct and bringing it to bear at a time when we can have maximum effect. While taking our legitimate actions, we should be aware of our need to protect ourselves and our own well-being, but inaction and silence in the face of such bullying, in particular, in the face of harmful, bad or illegal practice is not acceptable. Nor must we acquiesce to bullying instructions and commands which will do substantial harm, even if those instructions are legal. The fact that we are following the instructions of someone who is bullying us, who has made threats against us, is not sufficient excuse for us. We need to take actions against such people whenever it is reasonable and possible. In a work context, while not optimal, we could, where possible and reasonable, move to another job, thus escaping such bullying and thereby depriving an organisation of our skills and abilities.

Yet having focused on individuals engaging in bullying behaviour, beyond such individuals, bullying systems and cultures may exist in a workplace or other context, even, and perhaps sometimes especially, those where there are superficial systems which appear to recognise and offer formal means of responding to bullying behaviour. Official procedure and documentation can provide a useful smokescreen to distract victims and to protect those who bully and oppress. In fact, opposition to bullying conduct needs to be deeply embedded in each employee and manager for such conduct to be acknowledged as unacceptable within organisations. This is because, even in the presence of policy and paper, ways of behaving associated with bullying may exist through chains of management and these may be, in effect, seen as acceptable within an organisation, or even seen as good management. And those of us within an organisation may be placed under pressure to conform and behave in the same kinds of bullying ways towards others. Such ways of behaving most certainly are not acceptable.

Sometimes we can feel powerless in terms of our personal relationships with those that we know and are close to personally. This can happen in particular when those we are close to ignore our feelings, emotions and wishes and act with negative selfishness, in uncaring, irrational and unfair, even in horrible ways towards us. Partners can act in these ways towards us causing us tremendous hurt. Children, especially during teenage years, can certainly act in ways which are hurtful and seem incomprehensible to their parents and frequently there may be little we as parents can do about their conduct. Yet parents may act unfairly towards us as young people, behaving towards us as if we are very young children when we are not children any more. As a consequence, as teenagers, we may feel trapped, unable to escape from biased and unfair judgments being made about us, unfair and unevidenced restrictions and punishments, and unfair and unjustified admonition, criticism and more, about and against us.

In our loving, deep and emotional relationships, someone we love may simply decide that they no longer love us and that they no longer wish to be with us, perhaps that now, they may even hate us. We may wish to change that situation but there may seem to be nothing we can do to change their feelings. We may well feel powerless, upset and angry. Faced with such situations in our personal lives, we will need to act in a manner dependent on the situation, the person (and people) and the circumstances. If someone has ceased to love us, there may be nothing we can do to change this. And indeed as long as they are not acting with hostility towards us, then it is perhaps not reasonable to say they are acting badly. Feelings do change and that can be nobody's fault, just a reality. Nevertheless, our sense of powerlessness in regard to that love may be real. Despite what may be our sense of powerlessness, we can be powerful, in a sense, acting as far as we can to maintain our own well-being and happiness, by aiming to ensure that we ourselves behave in a pleasant, kind and civil manner, whatever the hurt, looking to enjoy each day of our lives, getting on with business as usual if we can, but perhaps also separating ourselves from someone who feels so negatively about us, and who is acting badly and has acted badly towards us. In that way our sense of powerlessness should eventually dissipate.

If we are parents with children then we will need to do our utmost to act to protect our children and bring them up well, supporting them while they are growing, supporting them in their well-being and mental health however they conduct themselves. That is our responsibility as parents. Should they behave in rude, aggressive and violent ways, then we will certainly need to tackle their conduct, but we will need to do so in a loving way, in the context of our care and love for our children. Our own violent action is unacceptable, though physical restraint and forceful action, though non-violent action, may sometimes be necessary. There is certainly a sense in which we will lack power to some degree in dealing with our children (for example, as already mentioned in this chapter, many parents will have had to deal with a young child having what is described as a 'tantrum' which can be difficult to immediately resolve; many parents will understand their children becoming upset due to tiredness, to which the resolution is often to get them to sleep). In some situations, all we may be able to do is to love our children as much as we can and take care of them as best we can. Our children will most likely grow older, will develop and change, and as they age in some ways they will become more responsible and able to cope with their own feelings and emotions, and may develop some additional respect for us. If they have developed a negative attitude towards us, hopefully this will change, though some reflection and soul searching linked to changes in our own conduct may sometimes be required in such circumstances.

And if we are those growing and changing youngsters, we need to argue against the approaches of our parents when we feel these approaches are wrong and unjust, and make a stand. We should know that our parents can sometimes be wrong and misguided, not just in individual action, but in terms of their approach, but we also knew that we may also be wrong and misguided too, wrong in approach, and may need to change our own conduct and attitudes towards our parents. Acknowledging our errors and expressing our mistakes and regrets to others is in itself a great expression of personal power, and indeed an expression of love and care for others. And through the relevant give and take, through maintaining love and care for each other, we will maintain healthy relationships and manage to keep our parents and ourselves as healthy and happy as is possible, minimising stress, anxiety, anger and upset for us all.

In terms of broader community and societal issues, if feeling the pain and stress of being politically powerless, for example in situations where others as individuals and groups are oppressing us, we can, again, ally with others with power and influence (or indeed others who appear relatively powerless as individuals), who may help and support us. Together we can often represent an effective level of power. And where others are oppressed, where we are oppressed, it is an absolute necessity and indeed obligation, to take whatever action possible to deal with such oppression and tyranny to the maximum degree possible, within our powers, working with others where possible and helpful (and this is of course normally the case), while maintaining our own well-being and supporting the well-being of others, as far as we can.

In situations of oppression, where we may feel powerless and indeed are lacking in power, there may be immediate action possible, but it is also unfortunately sometimes the case that there may be little we can do immediately. In these circumstances, we are often faced with simply bearing the burden and pain of unjust and unfair decisions, perhaps callous and vicious actions about which we can do little or nothing, We may need to move to try to resolve difficulties in a manner which avoids directly tackling those damaging and oppressive decisions and actions which we feel unable to directly influence and change. Sometimes we may well, in reality, be powerless, at least in the short term, and thus, there may be realities where we simply need to escape, to run away from the powerful and vicious who will impose violence on us.

But where we can, we do need to work to put right individual and social injustices and wrongs, doing all we can to remove such oppression, injustice and tyranny. If we feel powerless in the face of oppressive conduct, aside from the emotional pain and stress we will feel, this can also breed a deep sense of alienation inside us, very likely alienating us from the processes and people involved in governance, whether these are democratically chosen by us or not. And thus our powerlessness can be damaging, not only to us as individuals, but to others, our local and broader communities and societies.

Nevertheless, however, it is important for us to realise and recognise that there is most likely also a rational sense in which it can be said that a sense of powerlessness, felt by many of us through the days of our lives is, to some extent and in some respects, actually a rational and inevitable powerlessness, which stems, at least in part, from the undeniable fact that we are but single individuals in our world of millions and billions of people. We need to recognise, and most of us undoubtedly do recognise, that it is unreasonable to believe that the whole world (or others) should necessarily do as we, a single individual might say, simply because we say it, or for that matter, that the world should place our own individual views on a pedestal above the views, ideas and interests of others. There are millions and indeed billions of others whose views need to be taken into account and listened to as well as our own. What is undoubtedly crucial to each of us, and likely of great importance to our health and well-being, is the ability to contribute and feel listened to in regard to whichever decisions, debates and discussions are taking place, be they in our close relationships, our families, or our local and wider communities, our societies or more globally. It is of importance to all of us to have the opportunity to make some contributions and to feel of value and significance to others. And in recognising that, we should also recognise the responsibility on us to listen to, value and behave towards others in a manner which recognises their significance.

In our own worlds, it is very easy to focus too much on our own views, opinions, perspectives and interests as being paramount and fundamental and above those of others. But in the real society in which we live, in which the interests and beliefs of others have to be taken into account and are likely to have equal weight or in some cases which may have more practical weight than our own (for example due to recognised personal expertise or power of position); in the real world where we understand the principles and necessity of supporting others; then we have to have the understanding and recognition that our personal views are the views of one individual amongst many, however important we see our views to be. Of course we have to recognise that the views of these others count. Others may of course have similar ideas and interests as ourselves. And so if we band together with these others who have similar ideas and interests to ourselves, then we are likely to increase our chances of our individual views and ideas being listened to, influencing others and achieving our goals. So a sense of powerlessness can be changed, (though clearly not always) to become a sense of power and achievement through planning, effort, coordinated action with others, intelligent and persuasive actions and effective organisation amongst other factors.

A sense of our own powerlessness means of course that others may seem to and in fact may have, more power and influence than we do ourselves, which can feel humiliating and maybe to some extent shaming, highlighting our own sense of frustration and feelings of powerlessness and inadequacy. Yet, in a society, in a community, it seems somewhat inevitable that there will be power differences at some level between us, and perhaps this needs to be faced at times with some resignation and equanimity. That does not mean that we should consider ourselves powerless, of no value, of lesser value than those with power, of lesser capability, nor does it mean that we should not seek to effectively exercise the power we have and the influence we can exert, in support of the well-being and happiness of ourselves and others. We should certainly aim to exert the power we have and exert it in a manner consistent with core principles.

In relation to the form of power that comes with position, the reality of our human society, at least at the current time, is that there are roles and positions which carry with them duties and responsibilities, and allied to these, to some extent power, which enables those of us in such roles to more effectively implement actions in support of well-being and happiness (or otherwise). Wishing to implement actions effectively in pursuit of well-being and happiness will, by the nature of our intentions and the need to put them into practice, involve us in the exercise of power. Power to do things, which is likely to include some power over others, however, should not be sought for its own sake, but needs to be sought and used solely in pursuit of supporting the well-being and happiness of others, supporting our communities and societies and the world beyond. Any power we have to influence or determine the actions of others needs to be used caringly and responsibly, recognising the humanity and fundamental importance and value of each person and bearing in mind the well-being of those over whom we might be exercising some power and the well-being of all others.

Also relevant to the feelings of powerlessness and also perhaps the alienation we may therefore feel from our communities, societies and our more global world, is the fact that beyond the numbers of us who can and may wish to practically and technically contribute to the decisions that need to be made, the fact is that there are also millions of judgments required in response to the many complex questions and challenges faced in our complex societies in which there are so many millions of citizens and in which many factors need to be brought to bear to inform our optimal decisions. It is therefore in reality difficult for each of us to have complete and detailed input into the many thousands if not millions of there sometimes complex decisions which are made, yet this may still result in a sense of alienation, powerlessness and a sense of and our own lack of relevance and importance.

Despite the number of decisions that need to be made and their frequent complexity, we can nevertheless have an input into the principles and philosophies which inform decision-making. That recognition of our ability to contribute means that we also need to be sure that our views are considered along with the views of others in fully democratic and accountable systems. In some sense, we should therefore have some sense of power in relation to decisions which are made, and in particular in regard to those decisions which most directly impinge on and affect our own lives, our well-being and happiness. Yet, of course, our role in determining and influencing such approaches brings with it extraordinary responsibility and a dedication to effectively implementing core and other principles. We cannot simply act as consumers, expressing product preferences, but instead we need to act as professional caring citizens responsible for outcomes which will affect both ourselves and others.

The sense of pain and frustration we feel when we experience when we feel powerless is likely to be intensified where those in power have gained their power and influence through unfair means, through inherited wealth and position, through personal or family contacts, through privilege, nepotism and cronyism. While issues of privilege by birth and privilege through inheritance can be somewhat complex, since the reality of family groups and loyalties means we are likely to want to look after those closest to us, our feelings of a sense of unfairness in others gaining privilege through unfair practices is certainly a reasonable and rational source of dissatisfaction and unhappiness. Not only has the receiver of this privilege and preference gained power unfairly and unjustly, in a manner independent or significantly independent of their potentials, abilities and talents, something which can be highly detrimental to our communities, societies and beyond, but the fact is that in doing so, in attaining power through such preference and privilege rather than based in merit, they have also deprived others, possibly, if not likely, who might be more able and worthy of achieving power and influence, and who might be better able to benefit us all.

Our frustrations and pains in regard to such privilege and unfairness may be difficult to remedy in the short term, though sometimes through our own individual efforts, through use of our own talents and abilities, we can break through such barriers put in our way. Allied to that, we can work with others to support improved equality of opportunity, improved systems for opportunity for those who are not privileged, since ideally we should all have, as far as possible, equal opportunity and access to learning and development opportunities, as well as having the same opportunities to reach positions and achieve roles in which decisions are taken and power exercised.

Our communities and societies, supported by our own actions in support of such worthy goals in relation to equality of opportunity, are responsible for ensuring that mechanisms to support equality of opportunity exist, and that these mechanisms exist without damaging the general and broader interests of all. In those unfortunately common situations, at least in the present era, where such undeserved privilege and power continue to exist and exist substantially, we need to work to achieve greater fairness and justice through personal and group action, working with and banding together with others to oppose such injustice and damaging inequality of opportunity.

Notably, in terms of health, there is substantive evidence that inequality in itself within a community and society has health effects on those who are more poor and lacking in resources. It seems that the fact that people recognise or feel themselves as part of the less privileged, as of lower status within a society or community, is in itself detrimental to health, and this seems to be the case aside from the effects of absence of access to specific facilities and lack of resources which accompany such differences in wealth and privilege (see p.299, Guide Part One). Thus it seems quite clear that the promotion of health requires us to promote greater levels of equality within our communities, allowing greater opportunities for all and reducing levels of privilege, particularly unearned and undeserved privilege.

While railing against unearned privilege and promoting greater levels of equality in support of our health and well-being, we also should avoid foolishness and damaging our own well-being and happiness and the well-being and happiness of others. We therefore need to recognise that the privileged person with power may sometimes have a range of skills and abilities developed through their privilege, as well as personal contacts that they have developed or indeed inherited, and at the same time they may have the personal resources needed for achievement, all of these resources, skills and abilities which we ourselves do not have to the same degree. And we should also recognise that some of these people may have good intention and be well-motivated to help and support not just themselves but others too. Further, someone in a position of power may have that power and influence because we, and people like us may simply never have desired or conceived of trying for such positions of power and influence or had an interest in acquiring and exercising such power. There can be no doubt, however, that for the benefit of all of us, our communities, societies and beyond, the availability of reasonable opportunities and life chances need not only to be present for all, but we should all be encouraged to take advantage of such opportunities.

We may also be frustrated by the fact that to some extent, there are natural differences between us as individuals, with some bigger and physically stronger, others better at mathematical calculations, others more skilled at athletics, with different capacities for hand-eye coordination, others more empathetic with better social skills, others bearing archetypal looks seen as more desirable, and others possessing 'natural' abilities and capacities in various other ways which we may not possess and may in fact not be able to possess. While perhaps a source of frustration, or even envy or perhaps inappropriate jealousy at times, and while we should be developing our skills and abilities as far as we can in all areas where we can do so, in general an optimal path in terms of our well-being and happiness is to aim to appreciate the differences between ourselves and others, and value their qualities and skills, this being much preferable to our engaging in unexpressed, silent or perhaps expressed, futile and destructive jealousy.

Such feelings and such jealousy in the face of the reality that in some areas there will always be someone who is more skilled and able than us, is futile and destructive of both ourselves and others. While striving for justice, fairness and greater equality, while striving to pursue well-being and happiness for ourselves and others, while striving to make progress and achieve, it may benefit us to accept the broad principle that there are and will be inequalities and differences, and to some extent appreciating this reality and the talents of others. We are best off emotionally and psychologically and probably materially coming to terms with this reality, appreciating this reality and living accepting this reality, appreciating the talents of such others and indeed ourselves. That being said, it is easier for us to appreciate and value the talents and skills of others when we feel valued and appreciated ourselves. Moreover, with good reason, in support of success, our communities and societies, our broader humanity needs a range of people with the range of different talents and abilities, some with exceptional talents and abilities. And we ourselves, with our own special talents and abilities comprise part of such broader success as well, of course, as our talents and abilities being central in contributing to our own more personal well-being and happiness.

In essence therefore, the talents, abilities and achievements of others are to be appreciated, even though sometimes, if not often, we may feel small or lesser in comparison to these achievers. The fact is that we are all likely to be achievers too in one way or another, worthy of appreciation ourselves on account of what we do as individuals, and we will benefit from an appreciation of ourselves. However, and importantly, spending our lives comparing ourselves negatively with those few individuals out of millions who demonstrate exceptional and extraordinary talents and abilities is likely to be an unnecessary source of pain and frustration. We need to appreciate ourselves in a realistic manner, recognising our own personal qualities and achievements, as well as appreciating these others. And as far as we can, we need to focus on ensuring we are, ourselves, the best that we can be, something which should help us to achieve our own well-being and happiness and support the well-being and happiness of others.

There are many other negative and painful ways of feeling we can experience which influence our health, well-being and happiness. Hatred and intense anger are forms of pain and suffering which we need to avoid as far as we can. Not only is there the emotional pain in our anger and hatred, but there are the practical consequences of anger and hatred in terms of our relationships and the outside world, the alienation of others, the exacerbation of relationship problems, the creation of enemies who may in turn become angry with us and harm us, the broad damage that anger and hatred can do in so many ways to others. Hatred and anger may be an expression of, or lead to, obsession, obsessive hatred and self-destruction in those circumstances where we as individuals become intensely or entirely focused on the feelings of, and the object or objects of our hatred, with some of us becoming so angry and vengeful that we might focus our lives, or an important part of our lives, on destructive vengeful conduct against the person or people who are the object of our anger and hatred, with consequent suffering for ourselves and those for whom we feel hatred, and those towards whom we might act in hate-filled ways.

Such feelings of anger, hatred and vengeance are painful to us, if we experience them, but also dangerous to all. Those around us, if we are the ones who feel and express such hatred, can be drawn into a cycle of destruction, acting in ways which intensify and exacerbate tensions, destructive conflict and hatred, damaging themselves, damaging ourselves and acquiring, for those drawn in to such hatreds, their own role in escalating such destructive conflict, hurt and unhappiness. Those who are the object of such hatred, which of course includes ourselves as potential objects of hatred from others, can of course be deeply hurt, both physically and emotionally, by such hatred, hatreds which are often felt with intense certainty but which, if they were reflected on by the individual feeling such hatred or those of us receiving such hatred, will sometimes be very difficult to understand, representing something which we may find irrational and inexplicable, these representing hatreds of which we or others may be totally undeserving (for example, since many problems arise through misunderstanding).

Hopefully, as individuals we will never feel such intense hatred and anger, or, if so, such feelings will be exceedingly temporary, momentary in nature, and will give way to more rational, caring and constructive thinking. Hopefully we will never experience such burning and painful hatred and anger, and will never engage in reprehensible and unacceptable hateful conduct, this being something which is totally contrary to the core and other principles.

Clearly it is our responsibility at a personal and individual level to avoid such feelings of anger and hatred as far as we can, and if not entirely possible, we need to remove or reduce our feelings of anger and hatred, acting as far as we can in loving and caring ways, supporting our own well-being and happiness and supporting the well-being and happiness of others, which destructive and self-destructive feelings of hatred and anger do not do. It is crucial to our enjoyment of a pleasurable and happy life to avoid, challenge, deal effectively with and turn away from negative and destructive emotions such as hatred and anger.

That being said, nevertheless, while painful feelings of anger, hatred of others, contempt for certain others is clearly outside of the bounds of feeling, thinking, and consequently behaviour and conduct, desirable within the core principles presented in this guide, it must be recognised that under some circumstances, particularly under extreme circumstances, feelings of anger and intense hatred, at least temporary feelings of hatred and anger, may be difficult to avoid. This may be the case in particular where we have been deliberately hurt, put through intense agonies and pain or even, in some cases, accidentally damaged by another, or when those we love have been hurt, damaged, put through agonies and pain, tremendous suffering. Under such circumstances such feelings can be very well understood and indeed sympathised with, and should certainly not be condemned, because they represent real, almost inevitable reaction to real suffering.

If someone feels anger at and hatred for someone who has murdered someone they love, perhaps someone who also shows no regret for their actions, then it is not for the rest of us to pass judgment on the person feeling that anger. Such anger may not be for the best, but it may be in us all of us and represents a natural and understandable response. And there are those in the world who have acted with the most callous brutality towards others, who have engaged in the most heinous acts, assaulting and murdering others, murdering children, deliberately inflicting the most intense pain through brutal torture, engaging in deliberate mass starvations, rape, heinous acts of genocidal murder. If we were a victim of one of these acts, had family and loved ones who had suffered from one or more of these heinous crimes, indeed as an ordinary person hearing of such deeds, then our feelings towards the perpetrators of these acts might well be, at least in part, ones of disgust, revulsion, anger and hatred towards them.

While such hatred may be unhelpful and damaging into the future, being a source of pain for those feeling such hatred, and representing a possible block to resolving problems and promoting overall well-being into the future, nevertheless, there are no grounds for condemning such anger and hatred under such circumstances. That is how we may feel, and that is how some people may feel who have been victims of such callous and heinous crimes. And such feelings are easily understandable. It is easier for someone who is not directly affected and who is not badly hurt and perhaps traumatised, to say that developing understanding is better, that perhaps forgiveness is better, but under these and other such terrible circumstances we all might experience feelings of anger and hatred and cannot be condemned for those reasonable feelings, even if determining on a path of developing understanding of events and perhaps pursuing forgiveness might be better for us as individuals and for others.

Hopefully at some point, hopefully sooner rather than later, such hatred and anger will dissipate such that those affected by such terrible events can begin to carry on with their lives, restart and rebuild again, undoubtedly never forgetting the terrible events they have experienced, but carrying on in any case, with a lessening pain in their hearts, or at least lessening feelings of hatred and anger accompanying their lives.

And in dealing with those who have inspired anger and such undesirable and destructive hatred, and who, while we are responsible for our own feelings, have to some extent created such anger and hatred in us, rather than causing ourselves pain and destroying ourselves in the process of responding to, reacting to and dealing with these people, we need wherever possible to find those better more peaceful resolutions; we need to look for ways of building cooperation and togetherness, acting in positive, constructive ways. Hatred and intense anger prevent or certainly serve to inhibit the solution of problems which, while the search for these solutions may need emotion as a drive to solve them, is likely to benefit more from cool rational thinking, care, empathy and understanding, all of which are inhibited by intense feelings of hatred and anger.

Clearly there are often grounds, dependent on circumstances, for trying to persuade people, those of us who may have been victims of aggressive violence and horrendous crimes, away from such hatred, and indeed being firm in such persuasion. Such efforts at persuasion may be justified through pointing out the damaging effects on those who are experiencing and feeling such hatred and anger, and on account of our aiming to promote reconciliation where that is reasonable and possible, something which is particularly necessary as such hatred, if not dealt with, is highly likely to generate more unwarranted conflict, creating violence and more hatred and destruction into the future, more pain and more suffering. Such destruction is certainly not our goal, is contrary to the requirements of all of our well-being, happiness, and our needs as individuals, community and society, and as such is contrary to core and other principles, but feelings of hatred in response to the most evil of deeds, can and should where they exist, be listened to and perhaps also be expressed rather than being left to fester. They should certainly be understood. And understanding such feelings, it may also, in some cases, be inappropriate or futile for us to aim to persuade others against such feelings, even though in some cases such efforts at persuasion may be a necessity to prevent further violence and conflict, to prevent vengeful destructive action.

If we as individuals are the ones experiencing such feelings of hatred and intense anger at another or others, we need to recognise that hatred is one of those emotions that can and should, wherever possible, and at the earliest point possible, be tackled and overcome by more positive, constructive and conciliatory attitudes and should not be allowed to determine or indeed influence us towards destructive behaviour when we should be focusing on our own well-being the well-being and happiness of others, the well-being of our communities and societies, all of which will not be served by hatred.

Indeed, where possible and reasonable, in particular where those who have done such evil and horrendous acts appear to express genuine regret for their actions and there is no prospect of them conducting such acts again, then it may be best, if we can, to forgive these individuals, to remove the pains of hatred and anger from our hearts and minds and to attempt to move constructively into the future, where possible supporting such individuals. This may be an enormous and impossible ask for many of us. But if possible, this course of action is one which has the potential to benefit us all to the greatest degree.

Nevertheless, in the main it is important that where it exists, we acknowledge our personal anger which, though perhaps unpleasant to feel, may not only be negative in its consequences but can also serve as a positive motivating force in some contexts, for example our anger about how we or others are being mistreated serving to motivate us to take action to defend ourselves and these others; our anger at the horrendous and destructive ways that others have behaved towards us or others, leading us to take actions to prevent such further behaviour; and in our lives more closer to home, our anger enabling us to say the sometimes irrational things we have been thinking, allowing us to clear the air, letting our feelings out (even though perhaps a calmer approach might well be better).

Our anger is certainly not a positive and pleasant feeling, and can hamper our ability to think rationally, but it can be there in the many, if not all of us and can certainly have some positive consequences if managed and used appropriately, motivating our actions, especially if dealt with and expressed calmly and caringly, and used as a basis for acting in a constructive and rational manner. Yet vengeful and irrational, hurtful action based on such feelings cannot be condoned, must not be engaged in, and is inconsistent with core and other principles.

As individuals, as part of our communities, societies and our broader humanity, we need to work to ensure that we ourselves, our families, communities and societies, our broader humanity, act to promote tolerance, understanding, love and care, turning away from angers and hatreds, working against the pain that such angers and hatreds create inside ourselves and cause to others. Through our every day conduct and through our actions within our communities, societies and beyond, we need to act to ensure that such hatreds and angers cannot take hold on individuals or groups within our communities and societies, and outside of them, with the consequent pain and suffering that will bring about.

Hatred and anger can damage our most important and other social relationships which are core to our mental health and well-being. Beyond our partners and families, in terms of our social relationships, our mental and indeed other practical aspects of our health can certainly be damaged in a number of other ways. For example, having and choosing the wrong friends can be detrimental to not only our well-being but also our mental health. There are some who perhaps should be avoided as friends, or at the minimum engaged with peripherally, and whom we should attempt to persuade away from their negative and destructive attitudes and deeds. These people include those who have few principles and have no interest in supporting and helping others; those who act in bullying ways; those who pedal cynical views which focus on looking after themselves, suiting themselves and fighting for their own interests while ignoring the well-being and interest of others; those who live a life overly focused in momentary pleasure which thereby embodies a high degree of negative selfishness (though pleasure is of course reasonable for us all to enjoy); those who joy in their power irrespective of the pain they are causing.

Whichever context we are in, whichever field or profession we are in, whatever our life circumstances at home and in family, whether we are young or old, there is always responsibility to others which lies upon us and our need to be concerned about and act in support of the welfare and well-being of others. There is no doubt that it is important to look after ourselves, to support our own well-being and happiness, but this should not and should never be at the illegitimate expense of others, at the expense of significant damage to others. Our friends need to reflect such care and concern for ourselves and for others and we need to demand that of them. And if they are overly self-focused and acting in ways damaging to ourselves and others, we need to persuade them towards more caring attitudes and actions. And if those we know are behaving in such a negatively selfish manner, being destructive of the well-being and happiness of others, showing callous indifference to others then we need to act to aim to dissuade them away from such actions, and prevent such actions so that we can accept them as worthy friends who will support our own well-being and the well-being of others.

We should be careful of those friends and acquaintances who persistently make us feel bad. Thus, while in terms of our mental health and personal well-being it is best that we take responsibility to an important degree for our own feelings, there are those who certainly may contribute to making us feel bad for a range of reasons. They may be hypercritical of who we are, the way we look, the way we behave. They may criticise us deeply because of our beliefs and values, even our care and concern for others. They may constantly criticise our judgments. Of course, no one, none of us, is beyond reproach or above criticism. We are all fallible and flawed to some extent, but there are those who are friendly in some ways, but in other ways are too critical, negative and verbally destructive of those around them, and there are those who for personal reasons, often relating to fears of personal inadequacy, set out to hurt others, aiming, sometimes unconsciously, without intent, to demoralise others and make them feel bad.

Such critical behaviours and approaches can be dealt with directly through talking to those who are being so critical or by challenging their conduct through understanding their behaviour and pointing out to them how they are conducting themselves. However, if necessary, we may need to deal with them by moving away from them, especially if they refuse to acknowledge their conduct and continue in their ways, refusing to change their uncaring and emotionally damaging behaviour, though such moving away is not optimal. Of course we as individuals should take care that we act to enhance the well-being and happiness of others through being caring and supportive, something which sometimes, though hopefully rarely or not too often, will involve pointing to hurtful and damaging behaviour, as well as the errors and mistakes of others.

There are also those who may make us feel unhappy more generally through their being cynical and negative about effort and achievement, encouraging others in the belief that their efforts to improve and achieve are pointless and futile. It may be the case that sometimes the things we wish to achieve may be extraordinarily challenging and difficult to achieve, but it is living life to the full to set ourselves goals and to try to achieve our personal goals, which may be challenging and difficult goals. And to try to achieve extraordinary goals has the potential of benefiting our well-being, happiness and mental health in many ways. While sometimes we may not achieve what we wish to achieve, our focusing on goals and achievement is often a useful support for our well-being and mental health. And if we have set reasonable and realistic goals then we may well achieve these. And if we have set ourselves highly demanding, stated by others to be unrealistic goals, we may still achieve these through hard work, strong thinking, commitment and dedication. And if we do not, then we will hopefully have enjoyed the effort and the journey.

While trying to achieve our goals, it is usually not uplifting and encouraging to have people around us telling us, perhaps persistently telling us, that our efforts are futile and we are doomed to fail, when in fact our efforts may not be and are not futile, are rewarding in themselves and when we may well be successful and confound their predictions. If we do find such conduct demoralising (and we have to acknowledge sometimes that such conduct can be actually motivating for us, spurring us on to try harder and work better) such people will again need to be addressed in relation to their conduct, and if they intend to continue in that way, or continue to demoralise and undermine us, then it is reasonable to suggest that we should tell these people how they are making us feel and that we wish them to desist. If they continue to undermine us, if we consider it appropriate, then we would certainly be well within our rights to seek out and might well benefit from finding more constructive and supportive company.

That is not to say that realistic comments and support should not be welcomed. Others may help us by pointing out the true challenges and problems we may face, thereby preparing us for such challenges and perhaps they will suggest how we might overcome such challenges. More positively, they may help us and encourage us by boosting our self-belief with rational and reasoned comments about our past achievements and therefore our future capabilities, or even with direct comments regarding the possibility or probability, the likelihood of our success (that is, encouragement).

Many of the more negative comments, which might be described by their users as realistic, in fact fail to fully and rationally evaluate the chances of success for those of us who are dedicated and passionate, their comments over-emphasising the difficulties we may face, or failing to acknowledge our need for and desire to work towards our dreams, even if we may not be successful in the end. In any case, irrespective of such comments, in the vast main, the pursuit of our goals is in itself pleasurable and worthwhile whatever the endpoint of our journey. Striving and struggling, overcoming challenges and obstacles, developing ourselves to the fullness of our capacities is one of the pleasures and joys of life. We need not enjoy complete success in all that we do, though of course some achievement and success in pursuit of worthwhile goals, is certainly good for us, our well-being and mental health.

Ourselves, where we have the opportunity, we should focus on encouraging others and supporting them to their goals and their dreams. Offering advice and support where needed, we should also allow space for others to experiment, achieve and indeed fail, where this is reasonable and does not involve potential danger, It is good to allow others to identify problems in relation to their actions, strategies goals and dreams, and also to allow them space to discover and learn their own lessons. We should certainly not ourselves engage in unjustifiable cynicism and negativity, destructive attitudes, denigrating the efforts of others and undermining others in their efforts to achieve goals which are consistent with core and other principles and which are important to them, nor should others do the same to us. Our own well-being and happiness are supported by appropriate encouragement from those around us, motivating and helping us in achieving our goals and dreams rather than our being faced with often irrational and negative, destructive cynicism. That being said, our support and encouragement should not be mindlessly positive, but needs to be not only supportive in word and deed but also constructive and rational.

We should also be aware that there are those who may make negative comments about us in order to deliberately diminish us and undermine our efforts. They may do this to support their own success and power, simply because they are self-focused, in a perverse sense they are overly competitive, rejoicing in the failure of others, and in some cases simply malicious and uncaring towards others. Great care needs to be taken to protect ourselves from such individuals who may aim to damage us significantly in order to suit their own desire for success, support their own pleasure and their own benefit. Where possible, if these people cannot be dissuaded from their approaches, they do need to be kept at a distance, and certainly set aside from influential positions which they will clearly be using to the detriment of ourselves and others.

Such people may act beyond directly critical and negative comments in order to damage us. Those who are malevolent and anti-social, who wish to damage us and exploit us for their own purposes, who intend malevolence and harm to others, perhaps painting or perceiving their actions as part of a 'rat-race', may conduct themselves in a range of other ways which are detrimental to us. Of course such people need to address their conduct such that it changes or have their behaviour and conduct addressed by us, by others, by our communities, society and beyond, where necessary, such that it is made to change. If such people are unwilling and unable to change their ways then, as mentioned above they do need to be set aside from positions of influence and power. And if, realistically we can have no effect or influence on them, then we would certainly be better off if, as far as we can, we avoid such people, especially if we identify their intentions and understand that they are out to hurt us, use us and exploit us, and there is the prospect of them doing us significant harm. Yet avoiding such people may not lead them to stop their efforts to harm us and others, and therefore more robust action may be necessary in order to prevent the harm they may wish to do.

Where possible and reasonable, we should certainly be prepared to have relationships and friendships with those who have acted against core and other principles in a minor sense or even those who have committed some significant anti-social acts and criminal offences, though of course we should not put ourselves in danger. Through choosing to associate with and be friends with such people, supporting them and enabling them to live as part of our lives, we will hopefully be helping to enable or allow them, or will be actually keeping them within the fold, within our communities and societies and within the remit of our broader civil and social humanity. This is especially desirable where there is good reason to believe that their conduct has changed or will change and they will act to serve and benefit our communities, societies and beyond.

Indeed, the reality is that it is not uncommon for all of us to sometimes act in a less than sociable manner, break rules and sometimes behave in an anti-social manner, or to behave in a manner which might not be sufficiently in line with core and other principles, perhaps to some extent damaging the well-being and happiness of others through our self-focused negative selfishness. There may have been times, or may be times, when our actions are negatively selfish in their nature, in particular as we are growing through our younger adult years and trying out actions and behaviours. Yet some clearly seem to believe in irresponsible, self-focused negative selfishness as a way of living, and this will result in untold damage to others. Reprehensible as some acts may be, we may all need some forgiveness and tolerance in our lives, all of us being capable of making mistakes, misjudgments and errors and almost all of us capable of misjudging the consequences of our actions and behaving to some degree negatively selfishly.

Those who have engaged in perhaps seriously damaging and destructive acts may also be allowed back into the fold, accepted as friends, perhaps with their past serious malevolent conduct put to one side for a while and perhaps forever, contingent to some degree on their having expressed true regret, their having in some manner compensated for their actions, and on the basis of our being convinced that this form of damaging and destructive conduct will not occur again. However, if such people wish or choose to continue with their damaging acts, in their criminal acts and enterprises, and are unwilling to change at that point in time, then we cannot allow them to put into practice or continue in conducting these activities and we must act to change their conduct as far as possible or, alternatively, keep them away from ourselves and others, particularly keeping them away from those who are weaker and more vulnerable, thereby preventing the actualisation and realisation of their damaging behaviour and destructive capacities and intentions, which of course would have consequences for our health and our well-being and the health and well-being of others. In line with core and other principles, we have a responsibility to protect both ourselves and others from significant harm, and so we cannot, as individuals, community, society or as a broader humanity, allow such malevolent and bad intentioned individuals to engage in conduct which damages ourselves and others, causing pain and suffering.

There are many other additional potential sources of pain and unhappiness in our lives which may lead to personal harm and damage to our mental and physical health. For example, in addition to those sources of pain already mentioned, we can also experience anxiety, stress, pain and physical suffering through the discriminatory actions of individuals and through the actions of discriminatory and unfair systems, those systems within which certain individuals, families, racial groups, economic classes, national groups, are discriminated against and in which some are given privilege and preference over us, over others, either deliberately and systematically or though the application of discriminatory systems, some of these systems implementing actions and policies which, even those designing policies, systems and doing the implementation, may be unaware of in regard to their discriminatory nature.

In such circumstances, if we are the ones on the receiving end of such discriminatory and unfair actions, the pain and suffering we experience can be substantial and severe, even deadly with, for example, in extreme cases, lives being directly taken, murder committed on discriminatory racist and other grounds, or our being denied, access to the things we need to survive with the resultant death and destruction that will entail. Such discriminatory systems may deny us reasonable living standards or deny us sufficient resources to live well; they may deny us and our families access to education, representation, shelter, advancement and other important needs and sources of a life of well-being. Indeed we may, as members of a minority group, or simply through being an individual in the wrong place, through speaking truth as we see it, or through being an individual whose face does not fit, be picked out for such disadvantage and personal psychological and physical damage and *in extremis* endure severe personal injury and damage, suffering in some cases physical violence, torture, pain and perhaps death.

In other cases, the effects on us of such discrimination and the effects of systematic unfairness may not be so easily visible or extreme, and we can continue to survive and be to some extent successful despite these actions against us. Nevertheless such actions can be damaging, insidious and personally undermining. We certainly need to protect ourselves from such pain and suffering, and from the sense of unfairness and discrimination which such other individuals, cultures and systems may implement against us and others. We need to do our utmost to ensure that fair, just, meritocratic and non-discriminatory systems are in place, as well as demanding and ensuring that we receive fair and just conduct from individuals, our communities, societies and beyond, in order to support the well-being and happiness of us all.

Our actions against such unjust discrimination need to be taken not only in terms of protecting ourselves and other individuals who suffer such discrimination, but also to benefit all others and the whole of our communities and societies, which need safety, peace, justice, fairness and equality of opportunity for all (and indeed a reasonable level of equality) in order to function effectively. And tied to this effectiveness, it is beneficial for us to have some sense of common purpose and togetherness in our communities, societies and within our humanity, in order to support the well-being and happiness of all.

More specifically, and additionally, it is also the case that the absence of such unfair discrimination is beneficial because we all, as individuals, communities, societies and as a common humanity, need the best, most talented and qualified individuals from our pool of citizens to perform the relevant jobs and roles required to support our well-being and happiness. We need the most talented and able individuals combining their talents with appropriate commitment to ourselves and others. It disadvantages us all if people are selected and chosen for jobs and roles on the basis of their race, gender, family connections, or on the basis of the people they know or other factors irrelevant to those jobs and roles. In such cases, those chosen on inappropriate grounds, have the potential to damage others, community, society and beyond through possible lack of competence, inabilities and the likely higher potential for further consequent discriminatory actions in support of particular groups or cultures.

Those many hate-filled, prejudiced and unfair discriminatory attitudes and beliefs which can generate such harm, are therefore, for the range of reasons given, and undoubtedly for further reasons, destructive and hurtful to ourselves and others, damaging not only those who are the more direct victims of such unfair discrimination but also being damaging to those who hold such discriminatory attitudes, these attitudes and actions being in their nature contrary to the principles set out in this guide and unsupportive of their individual health and well-being.

Those individuals practicing such destructive discrimination will themselves almost certainly deny themselves the range of enriching experiences and the possibility of building positive and friendly relationships with those from other groups, with other individuals who do not conform, those with other outlooks, cultures, sexualities and other differences in self, belief and attitude as well as other forms of background, thereby denying themselves access to sources of knowledge, wisdom, pleasure and fulfillment, such positive gains for us as individuals arising from enlarging and enriching our experience of life and engaging with the experiences of others. Divisive and unfair discriminatory attitudes serve to further damage our society in the broader sense, discouraging cooperation and togetherness, and enabling fissures of misunderstanding between individuals, communities and societies to develop, which will likely lead to conflict and division, most likely violence and more, since most of us will not accept such discriminatory actions against us without taking some form of action to prevent such damaging and destructive discrimination.

Of relevance to both our physical and mental health, importantly and something of major concern in the current modern world, other threats to our health and well-being can arise from the range of mood altering drugs which are available. It is argued that some effects of these can improve our mood, that these drugs can relax us, make us feel good and are perhaps mind expanding. This may be the case for some drugs under some circumstances, though it would seem that the potential benefits of such mood changing drugs, beyond that issue of changing our mood and making us feel temporarily relaxed or good, has not been the subject of the required level of study that such a subject warrants. The possible and actual pleasures, the possible benefits to our mental health that may be gained through using drugs are of significant concern, as are, and certainly should be, the negative and damaging health and mental health affects of such drugs.

In principle, and guided by core and other principles, there should be nothing wrong in gaining pleasure through taking a mood altering or enhancing drug, as feeling good must be an element of well-being. This has the rider however, that such drug taking should not significantly damage our own health and well-being and that it should not detract significantly from our ability to implement our other responsibilities both to ourselves and others. That is to say, use of drugs should not significantly detract from our capacities and actions in terms of promoting the well-being and happiness of ourselves and others, and nor should it result in our own pain or suffering or detract from our efforts to support the reduction of the suffering and pain of others.

Taking a drug to change our mood and make us feel good is likely, however, at least in some respects, to provide a shallow and momentary pleasure compared to the strong senses of pleasure and fulfillment achieved through other more worthwhile and challenging activities, although that being said, there may be some social pleasures, an important form of social bonding, to be gained through sharing experiences of drug taking, though it can equally and perhaps be more powerfully argued that such deep social bonding and connection, such feelings of sharing and togetherness can be obtained in many other deeper and many other better ways.

Indeed our deepest and greatest pleasures are likely to derive from participation, our personal achievement, as well as our service to others, our communities, societies and our broader humanity. We will derive the greatest pleasures from love, from partners, from our children, from a sense of belonging and togetherness with others, from our other more socially-based experiences, which are linked to our desires to support not only our own well-being and happiness but which support the well-being and happiness of others. Therefore, for those seeking a truly enriching and fulfilling life, it is a reasonable position to consider that our lives are of such excitement and challenge in themselves that they can and perhaps should be enjoyed without the use of such mood changing drugs, or alternately, that such drugs, if used, should comprise at best one of the many sources of personal entertainment and amusement in life without exerting undue influence on our lives and certainly without causing undue detriment.

Nevertheless, while medicinal properties have been attributed to some mood altering drugs (and there seems some strong evidence that certain drugs can alleviate pain), it is certainly the case that some, if not many, mood changing drugs, are known to be harmful to their users with potentially serious negative health consequences of using these drugs, including mental illness and harmful, dangerous addiction. Addiction and mental illness lead to deteriorating capacities for self-support and the support of others. For those who become addicted to drugs, these drugs can result in tremendous pain and suffering, with drugs becoming the entire focus of an addict's life, with others frequently becoming, and remaining, of high significance only or significantly in terms of their role in providing the drugs which that person must have, sometimes at almost all costs. In support of their drug addiction, addicts may rob, steal and cheat, thereby damaging others in our families, communities and societies, in a manner and to a degree which is totally unacceptable and entirely contrary to core and other principles. Mental illness can be a consequence of drug taking and addiction and can come in many forms as a result of taking such mood influencing and mood enhancing drugs, this self-damage of course being contrary to the principle of supporting our own individual well-being.

One of the most prominent drugs in many cultures is alcohol. This drug is often unacknowledged as a drug in such cultures where its harmful effects are ignored and where it is taken for granted and considered an ordinary part of the cultural scenery. In these cultures, alcohol is often seen as a relaxant and is widely, if not ubiquitously, used on social occasions or even as a reason for people to get together. Rational cost-benefit analyses both for individuals and society seem rare in regard to alcohol. While perhaps not clearly demonstrated as harmful to all, especially when taken in small amounts (and indeed some evidence has been produced suggesting positive health benefits from drinking alcohol), there is substantial evidence that accompanying what might be seen as its more positive effects, alcohol certainly affects our thinking and can damage our thinking long term through damage to our brains. Moreover it is clear that for some if not many people, alcohol can be addictive and wreck lives. Further there are the increased levels of violence and other anti-social behaviour encouraged by and often excused by certain alcohol cultures, levels of violence and poor conduct which are enhanced by the removal or reduction of limits and barriers in personal conduct when we are under the influence of alcohol, where senses are impaired, and actions less under the aegis of self-control.

Moreover there may be elements of alcohol culture which encourage thoughtlessness and lack of rationality. These elements of course, to some extent, represent motivations undoubtedly for drinking alcohol, in its supporting the breaking down of emotional and psychological barriers between us, supporting people in coming together and overcoming barriers imposed by social constraints and perhaps also supporting escape from the need for what might be energy requiring and energy draining rationality and reason.

Further, in this and many respects, alcoholic intake can be seen, to some extent, as legitimising, or providing a reason for behaviour which breaks social norms, breaks constricting and sometimes suffocating barriers imposed in every day straightened and constraining non-alcohol influenced lives. It may also be the case that alcohol (and indeed other drugs) can provide an important and useful outlet for elements of our psychological self which cannot be expressed without access to some form of relaxant and social lubricant. Clearly, in line with core and other principles, reducing the negative effects of alcohol consumption, engaging in positive and caring social interactions without the need for alcohol or other drugs, and displacing alcohol focused activity should overall support greater well-being for all.

Smoking tobacco is certainly damaging to health, and with tobacco comprising an addictive drug which provides temporary pleasure, but which is known to lead to lung damage, cancer and heart disease amongst other conditions, tobacco is a dangerous substance for consumption. The known effects of smoking tobacco mean that using this drug is contrary to core and other principles. Clearly the promotion of this cancer causing, lung, heart and other organ and tissue damaging, addictive drug, is also contrary to core principles through its known harmful effects, not just to the user but to those who breathe in tobacco smoke. As individuals we should, in the vast main, refrain from using it; as communities and societies, we should discourage or prohibit its use, in particular in public spaces where smoking presents a risk to others. As organisations, businesses and companies we should not be investing in or making money or profits from the promotion of this damaging form of drug use.

Having criticised the use of a range of drugs here, it must be said that context is important. If we are, for example, involved in a war, in violent conflict, where we might soon die, then the smoking of cigarettes would seem less worthy of prohibition than in other contexts. The momentary gaining of what for some might be a minor pleasure before a likely encounter with a life-or-death situation would seem of little worth for prohibition, unless such a stimulant or source of pleasure served to impair our judgment and therefore our likelihood of survival. If we are near the end of our lives, from other causes, cancers or other incurable diseases, then taking such a drug, smoking a cigarette, cannabis, imbibing alcohol, would not seem inconsistent with our requirement to improve our well-being and happiness given the situation we are in, if that is what we wished to do, though there still might be downsides with, for example, alcohol and some other drugs perhaps interfering with our ability to communicate with those we love.

Other so-called 'hard' drugs in the modern age, heroin, cocaine, crack are significantly prominent and present substantial dangers of addiction and damage to mental and physical health in whichever context we find ourselves. Dealing with the consumption and circulation of these prevalent and prominent drugs, which threaten health and welfare, but which are taken for stimulation and pleasure, for highs, by significant numbers of people, is a challenging enterprise, which needs to be considered on the basis of rationality, evidence and reason. Nevertheless, as individuals we should recognise that the taking of these dangerous and addictive drugs is contrary to our responsibilities for our own health and our obligation to support the health and well-being of others.

While this chapter focuses on physical and mental health as well as well-being, the fact that the trade in these hard drugs, deemed illegal in many countries in the modern world, the fact that this trade results in such harm, in part and indeed significant part, through the illegal nature of the trade in these drugs, means that the way in which our societies deal with issues of production, distribution and consumption of these drugs needs to be managed such that minimum harm is done to ourselves and others and to our communities and societies, our humanity as a whole. The reality of the drugs trade, at least in the current time, is one in which its illegality seems almost certain to be promoting crime and violent crime on a wide scale, empowering those ready to engage in violent and malevolent conduct, boosting corruption, damaging democracy and freedom and resulting in murders and violent crime against ordinary people, often by those involved in the drugs trade, but also by governments which in some cases murder through law and legal process and otherwise imprison many involved in the drugs trade. The victims of this violence, those murdered and imprisoned are usually those at the lower end of the scale of criminal operation, with imprisonment being handed out to substantial numbers of individuals for conduct which might better be considered non-criminal in nature. Not only does the drugs trade as it stands lead to violent crime, but the actions of authorities against those in involved in such crime are undoubtedly in many cases, misguided, criminal in themselves and lacking in legitimacy in terms of core and other principles resulting in vast and often untold damage.

Drug taking can be both a result of mental health problems and a cause of mental health problems. Our having mental health problems, in one form of another which make our lives challenging, which may make us partially or almost entirely unable to deal with our individual lives and life in our communities in a successful manner, and which may cause significant personal pain and emotional difficulties, is not uncommon. Though it seems to have been historically the case in many cultures that those with mental health problems were, in the main, badly treated, chastised, and even punished or labeled as evil, and, unfortunately, were given punishments because of their conditions, we now, at least in many jurisdictions, fortunately, have a much better understanding of these illnesses, understanding them as a health issue, understanding how common they are, and in many cases having a greater understanding of how to deal with, cope with and in a number of cases having an understanding of how to alleviate, ameliorate and sometimes cure mental illness.

In addition to the mental health difficulties that may afflict those of us living our ordinary lives, there are also those who are born with significant and sometimes severe mental disabilities and incapacities relative to others of us, unable to a greater or lesser degree to look after themselves independently of others given their illness. There are others who may have been born with certain lesser mental health conditions which may impair their abilities to look after themselves and survive in community and society either generally or at times. And there are those of us affected by violent physical incidents and severe trauma arising from specific or an accumulation of experiences, who acquire or who may develop mental illness during our lives, experiencing mental illness which damages us, in some cases, severely. And there are those of us who may acquire mental illness and suffer mental deterioration as we age.

Fortunately, some of our mental illnesses and mental problems may be curable with appropriate medical treatment and care, and indeed with regard to mental deterioration due to aging, through appropriate drug treatment it may be possible or become possible in the future to delay or even prevent the onset of such conditions. Nevertheless, certainly at the current time, there are severely damaging mental illnesses associated with aging, such as Alzheimer's disease which are devastatingly destructive and currently without cure. However other forms of mental illness may not be curable, at least with our current state of knowledge and understanding, and there is clearly a long way to go for us in our efforts to understand mental illness and our human minds.

Whatever the cause and origins of the particular mental illness, it is our responsibility as individuals, communities and societies to look after those of us experiencing such illness. It is our responsibility to help those suffering, as far as we can, such that they can avoid pain and suffering and live independent, joyful and pleasure-full lives to as great a degree possible.

If we are acting as an individual carer for someone who has mental health problems, then this role may place substantial limitations on other aspects of our own individual lives. Caring for another or others should be, in the round, rewarding and pleasurable supporting our well-being and happiness in itself, nevertheless, we should all ensure that, aside from performing our role as a carer for another, we enjoy as much of the other positive and enriching experiences of life that we can. And therefore, in support of our caring role, we should be helped by the rest of our community and wider society. For those of us whose lives are substantially dedicated day-to-day to those who have mental health problems or who support those who are otherwise incapacitated, as individuals, communities, societies, we need to support the well-being of these carers and ensure as far as we can that we, if we are carers, have access, as far as possible, to other avenues which will support us further in enjoying a full and complete life of well-being and happiness.

We, as individuals, together with our communities and societies as a whole, need to provide sufficient resources and facilities to look after and take care of those who are mentally ill, who have mental health problems.

We also, as individuals and through our social entities, need to support those people who are suffering mental trauma, mental pain and mental ill health, sometime temporarily, sometimes more permanently. Many of us may suffer with mental health difficulties at some point in our lives and we may need specialised support and care. Those individuals around us, as well as our social systems, need to support us as individuals if we are in such circumstances, providing support to those of us in need, with this support including the provision of medical and other specialists with training and understanding of mental health and mental health issues such that we can be helped through what may be difficult times in our lives. And each of us as an individual needs to support the existence of such systems, either though personal financial contributions, through our own direct actions in support of those in need or through other more indirect personal efforts. And further, we, as individuals and communities, need to support research into mental health with a view to finding ways to cure or to alleviate mental health conditions and improve our mental health.

The range of mental health facilities and support we provide should comprise elements of an overall community and society health infrastructure, something which is necessary to underpin the mental health of each of us. Indeed we need to ensure that facilities, including public facilities, should be widely available and easily accessible to support us with our mental health, an element of our health which can at times comprise a significant problem for many of us. The presence of mental health and mental fitness centres aimed at supporting mental well-being, with those centres aimed at promoting our mental health, would undoubtedly be of benefit to many of us suffering with mental health problems.

With regard to those of us who are suffering significant mental health problems, on the whole, wherever possible and reasonable, in line with the health and well-being needs of both those who are suffering mental health problems and those upon whom the demands of substantial or constant care may be placed, we need to do our utmost to ensure that where reasonable and possible, those of us who are suffering mental health problems should be able to be with, and remain with, those of us who are closest to us and love us and who we love and care for. In the most serious cases, where those are ill may be a danger to themselves and others, appropriate, safe and comfortable hospital or other care needs to be available which provides as far as possible for the human needs of those who are ill, and which supports a return, wherever possible, to full health and well-being, and a return to ordinary every day self-supported living should this, as is usually the case, be achievable.

In the case where we become mentally ill ourselves such that our mental health starts to damage our lives, where we perceive ourselves to be suffering from a mental illness of one form or another, if we can, we need to seek help from others, from those of us who hopefully can help us, including in particular medical and mental health professionals. Serious mental illnesses are medical conditions which in the majority of cases will require that we engage with and receive appropriate medical support. Clearly linked to the principles set out in this guide, those of us who may suffer mental illness in one of its forms, be it through breakdowns through stress and pressure or other causes, those of us who have emotional and mental crises in life, those of us who have mental health problems in a more ongoing and perhaps permanent sense with ongoing conditions, need to make our best efforts to seek help and support, as well as making our best efforts to help ourselves in other ways. Nevertheless, we may well need to be looked after and supported through our illnesses and crises, and it is the responsibility of all of us, in line with core principles to look after those who suffer in these ways.

Given historical attitudes to those who are mentally ill, in line with previous statements in regard to looking after and caring for the well-being of others, the core principles state our concern for our own well-being and happiness as well as the well-being and happiness of others. Thus it is not acceptable or appropriate to turn away from those with mental health problems, those who are in such need. Indeed we need to help and support them.

Some, if not perhaps many of us, ourselves may experience a mental health difficulty of some type at some point, and we are highly likely to know someone who will have such a mental health problem, perhaps family or friend, and indeed will be required to support them. Supporting and caring for such others is one of our many responsibilities. These others, those we are closest to, will need us, will rely on us at times, and it is likely that we will rely on others at times ourselves. We must not leave others to suffer in pain through their mental or for that matter their other illnesses, but need to support them through their trials until hopefully they recover and can enjoy the maximum of well-being and happiness.

Beyond mental health issues, illness and disease can plague us in their many guises whatever our age and situation. We certainly need to do our utmost to protect ourselves from the range of illnesses and the pain and suffering they cause, maintaining our physical and mental fitness to the maximum that we can. That of course will not protect us from all illnesses, some of which we may be genetically predisposed towards suffering. Others of the illnesses we experience may be viral, fungal, bacterial, immunological or other origin diseases which affect and infect us, and about which, in some cases, we can do little to prevent acquiring. And yet, others of our illnesses may be preventable and yet others may arise inevitably as we age.

Nevertheless, as far as we can, we need to take action to forestall and prevent our suffering and pain from illness and disease, taking whatever reasonable steps we can to avoid experiencing infections, for example through having necessary vaccinations and other treatments, through cleanliness or through avoiding or reducing contact where necessary and reasonable, with those who are carrying and who may transmit diseases. And if infected, we need wherever available, possible and necessary, to take the range of antibiotics and other medicines which will help tackle the illness and ease our pain and suffering. Similarly where reasonable and possible we need to be prepared to undergo, based on informed medical judgment as well as our own judgments and contribution, the various necessary treatments available which may in the current age include surgery, or lifestyle and dietary change, in order that we can forestall, or recover from our illnesses and maintain our health.

In terms of our sexual and emotional health, we need to seek healthy, loving and caring relationships which make us feel good and happy, not only in terms of sex, which is of course of substantial importance, but also in terms of our broader relationship and relationships. We need, most of all, partners and friends who care for us, care about our well-being, happiness and pleasure, who listen to us, take on board the things we say as being of importance, and who value us and our perceptions. Such partners and friends will give us the deepest warmth and sense of well-being and through their actions and care for us, will benefit and enhance our personal, physical and mental health.

We would hope that a deep and meaningful relationship with our closest partner will sustain and even grow stronger over time as we share experiences and grow together. However that is by no means always the case. The type of passion and love we feel at the early stages of our relationships may fade over periods of mundane every day life, if so, hopefully being replaced by new forms of love and togetherness. However we may start feeling differently towards a lover or partner that we used to love, with our, and their affections dying and sometimes our constant proximity leading to pain and hostility. As a consequence, in support of our well-being and our health, our partner relationship may need to end.

As affections and loves fade, there can be intense pain and when there is a final ending and separation, then the pains and anguish of rejection can be tremendous. If we can maintain our loves then that would be for the best. But sometimes relationships are better ended to avoid the pain that staying together is causing. These are complex and painful situations and circumstances to deal with, which can certainly threaten our health and well-being. Through such circumstances, we need to do our utmost to maintain our own well-being, to support our children if we have children and where we can to support our partners, however much we might feel distraught, unhappy or let down.

In terms of the more positive sides of our relationships, in relation to physical sex, it is wonderful if our partners can meet our sexual needs and desires and we can meet their needs and wants, with such sexual pleasure bordering on or representing the greatest ecstasy, warmth and pleasure. Yet there may be some or indeed many who pursue the physical pleasures of sex with less focus or perhaps no focus at all on the emotional side of sex and no or little interest in an emotional, caring relationship with the person with whom they are having sex. With the pleasures of love and sex being so needed, so impactful on our feelings and so intense, such a sole focus on sex is only acceptable if those having sex are of the same mind.

As previously stated in this guide, we therefore always need to consider the well-being, happiness, and perspectives of those with whom we are having sex, in particular due to that possibility that we may not share the same goals, with one person looking for something deeper and more caring and long lasting than the other. We certainly should not be pursuing our own physical sexual pleasure at the expense of the physical and emotional pain of another who perhaps sees a sexual experience in a more emotional and committed manner than we might do, and therefore who may be deeply hurt and upset at finding they have been 'used' simply for the temporary or momentary physical pleasure of another who does not in fact, or in any sense care for them. And this also means that if we are interested in finding deep, caring and lasting love, then we should aim to ensure that we do not have sex with those we suspect or believe might lack the desire for love and commitment that we have.

Where we have many sexual partners, where we are with a partner whose sexual history we are not sure of, at least in the current age, we should be certain to use condoms and other protective devices, in order to protect ourselves from and reduce and prevent the spread to others of sexually transmitted diseases which are irritating, harmful and painful and in some cases can be deadly, and of course, where we are not wishing to have a child, then we need to use contraception to prevent the possibility of a pregnancy which isn't wanted.

We of course need to take care of our partners and those around us who are in good health, supporting them in maintaining their health.. As individuals, it is also one of our important obligations, in line with the principles set out in this guide, that we not only look after ourselves but, as already mentioned in this chapter, that we also take care of those who are ill, whatever the cause of their illness. That does not mean that we are obliged to put aside entirely all of our personal goals which are needed for our own personal well-being, even though supporting others and supporting those we are close to and whom we love is a worthy personal goal and objective, and will be supportive of our well-being, representing something to which we will wish to devote our time, and to which we may devote almost all or of our time

Thus at times we may reduce our commitment to our more personal goals, indeed perhaps set these aside for a while, in order to support others, allowing our practical support for others to become a major part of our lives. And that is consistent with the principles put forward in this guide. Nevertheless, even when focusing our lives so greatly on the care of others, it is still likely to be beneficial for us to have, during such periods, not only sufficient time for rest and relaxation, but also some time for ourselves where we can think, reflect, enjoy ourselves in other ways and do other things. Total dedication to others is admirable, but even when we get time for rest and relaxation, it can be somewhat draining and indeed demoralising when others are suffering terribly. Thus our pursuit of some distractions and our enjoyment of some pleasures and entertainments are likely to be beneficial in enabling us to support others. Through supporting our own autonomy, joys and pleasures while also dedicating ourselves to the care of others, we will be not only supporting those others in their well-being, but supporting our own well-being to the maximal level possible.

When relatives, friends and even acquaintances are ill, in whatever way, it is important that we care for them emotionally and physically where we can and where our support is helpful and necessary. It will be of importance to them that we demonstrate our care and concern. Those who are ill must know about our love, care and concern for them. Where ill friends and relatives are geographically distant, then we need to ensure that we make contact with them and let them know that we are aware of their situation and that we are thinking of them. Where we can, where it is practical and reasonable, we need to make efforts to see them, be with them and look after them. This is all reassuring to those of us who are ill, reducing our sense of loneliness and isolation, and increasing our sense of personal value, our sense of being thought about, concerned about and cared for. Where financial or other practical support is needed, then this needs to be supplied if we can manage this.

We further need to care and provide support when people we know, and indeed any others, are involved in emotional crises. The fact is that we all are likely, at some point, to go through family crises, such as deaths in their families, family illnesses and accidents, intense family arguments which threaten relationships, perhaps separation from a partner or lover after a long time together (causing major emotional difficulties in some if not many cases), disappointment in love with accompanying feelings of personal inadequacy attached, and other crises such as loss of employment, failing to achieve important personal goals, rejection by others (possibly due to personal mistakes), becoming victims of crime or even receiving social opprobrium through mistaken interpretations of our actions or through having actually committed dishonest and heinous acts which we regret. In many circumstances such as these we may need to give others emotional support and indeed we may need support ourselves.

Indeed, while there are so many sources of potential pleasure in our lives, problematic and challenging situations are likely to arise for almost all of us during the course of a normal life. Our commitment through the core principles and associated values presented in this guide is, in cases where we are anticipating or experiencing such problems ourselves, to do our utmost to pre-empt and tackle these problems such that we can enjoy well-being and be as healthy and happy ourselves as we can. And where others are anticipating and experiencing such problems we must ourselves help and support others, whether these are problems which seem relatively minor to us, whether they are intense crises in the life of another, when they are in need, when they are in pain, when they need help and indeed, including our provision of help in situations when they have done wrong, where we can help them recover and regain their well-being and happiness and their commitment to principles of supporting and helping others.

Of course in this sense we also anticipate support from others when we face troubles ourselves, when we are ill, when we are facing emotional difficulties, short of resources, loss of income, difficult periods in our lives and perhaps other personal crises. And it is disappointing, upsetting and painful, if such support does not arrive or make itself plain. In the same sense that for us, personally making contact with others and supporting others who are known to us, to some degree does not demand a great deal of effort, especially if we have access to modern communications, it should not take too much effort for others who know us to provide us with some emotional and moral support and to keep in contact with us. Failure to keep in touch with us, and failure on our part to look after others we are close to and to keep in contact with them, is unacceptable. Nor should it be too difficult for us as individuals, our communities societies and beyond to provide practical help to those in need.

In such situations, our inadequate inaction may be due to a lack of other person focus in our lives, something which we will need to remedy. But as mentioned elsewhere in this chapter, there are of course some limits here. In our individual lives, it is not possible to talk to and provide direct individual support for everyone in need. We simply do not have the capacity and time to do so. Yet those who are family, our friends, those we know, those who have supported us, with whom we have had reasonably substantial and perhaps long-lasting relationships, whatever troubles and changes have intervened, these people should be receiving our direct care and support and with regard to others, if there is the opportunity to support them, then that is what we should do.

When we, or others, are suffering through the various challenges and struggles of life, personal contact and supportive communication is a minimum level of support we or others can give. But where there is time available to us, and in some circumstances we must make time, we need to provide real support in terms of practically looking after others, in addition to providing that communication which is also of great importance. Be it cooking for someone who is ill, shopping for them, cleaning for them, meeting someone for simple conversation or perhaps spending time to listen to them, to discuss their worries, the upsets, the issues and problems in their lives (which can perhaps sometimes be taxing to listen to if the negative talk goes on and on), through simply just being with them, or through doing the host of other myriad helpful functions that could be performed – all of this is invaluable in terms of practical and emotional support, helping others to survive well, and letting others know that they matter, something essential for well-being and happiness and the avoidance of unnecessary pain and suffering.

Beyond this individual action to support individual others, we can engage in more generally focused and socially focused support to health and well-being. Primarily, as already discussed in this chapter, and representing a very important priority, we can do whatever we can to prevent ourselves and others from becoming ill. In this regard, as part of our responsibilities in terms of personal individual action, we need to maintain the already discussed cleanliness in line with health advice, clean and wash our hands as necessary, bathe and maintain general cleanliness with regard to clothing and personal habits. We need to maintain cleanliness in the environment around us, to an extent which makes it unlikely that illness and disease can develop and be easily transmitted, and this applies to wherever we are, be it in the street, in our properties, at workplaces or other social venues. We can teach others, particularly our children to be clean and do what we can to ensure that others pursue cleanliness. We can ensure as far as possible, that we and others drink clean water (and that we have clean water for other purposes) and eat healthy food, cleaning food as appropriate, keeping food safe (keeping food cool which needs to be kept cool, and maintaining and storing it in edible condition) and cooking it appropriately, hygienically and safely.

And as individuals we need to ensure that there are effective systems which support our health, with our providing our personal resources where necessary to support such systems through our social contributions in the form of taxation and other means, and through our recognition of the importance of such socially organised systems to support our health. And in this context, this means clean water systems, systems for ensuring safe food preparation and cooking, systems for ensuring the air we breathe is clean, systems for responding to dangerous transmissible disease, systems for providing medical diagnosis and treatment, systems for promoting safety and security, justice and much more. Without such systems, without effective systems in these areas and more, our health and well-being will be under substantial and continuous threat.

And as already discussed earlier in this chapter we need to have as healthy a diet as is possible, and support and promote the adoption of a healthy diet by others, by those we know and whom we can influence in that direction. Keeping abreast of the latest information regarding healthy eating is of course important. Certain easily available and indeed, excellent tasting products lacking in quality nutritional value may, if eaten too often, or in too large amounts, promote poor health through obesity, damage to the heart and more, with consequent debilitation, pain and suffering. And there are of course the already mentioned drugs, including alcohol, which are likely to damage our health, as well as the tobacco which almost certainly will damage our health.

Further ways in which we can help others in supporting their health and as a consequence avoid pain and suffering, arise from developing our own personal medical knowledge, understanding and capacity to give medical support and help, indeed perhaps becoming highly skilled and professional in providing such medical support. Clearly there are those of us who wish to dedicate our lives to working as doctors and medical staff, nurses or other medically related staff, supporting the ill directly in the treatment of their illnesses or indirectly through services and management delivered to those who are ill. These are worthy professions and represent activities which clearly and substantially benefit others. If we can engage in this form of work during our lifetimes and work effectively in these fields, we are undoubtedly contributing substantially to the welfare and well-being of others in their lives. And hopefully, at the same time we will be providing ourselves with a rewarding life through helping those others who sometimes, if not often, are in substantial pain and desperate need.

Also related to medical support we can develop our skills in, and take qualifications in providing immediate aid, first aid, so that we can help others as far as we can, even save lives, before those with greater levels of medical expertise, skills and qualification possessing, where necessary, relevant medical technology and equipment, are available to help out further. And moreover, we can educate ourselves about illness and disease such that we build and maintain our personal fitness and health, and such that we can take appropriate action to prevent ourselves and others from developing poor health and illness.

If we are medical staff acting to support others with their health, we do need to operate as far as possible in ways based in systematic research and evidence. We need to be aware of treatments that are proven or strongly evidenced to have effectiveness (though of course not all treatments will be 100% effective) and develop our skills of judgment, our technical skills and abilities at implementing such treatments. Except in circumstances where death or intense suffering is certain, and rational and research-based approaches to treatment have been tried or failed, or where no evidenced treatment is available, we should adhere very firmly to systematic evidence-based approaches to treatment.

On some occasions we can support health and well-being in other ways. For example, there may be occasions where there is significant danger to ourselves and others from transmission of serious, sometimes fatal, illness from one person to another. In such circumstances we all need to follow instructions in regard to quarantine and support medical protection of the many by taking immediate and appropriate action, which sometimes may place us personally in some danger. Nevertheless, if the many will be threatened by our actions or indeed inaction, with transmission of disease supported by our taking potentially irresponsible actions, for example by circulating amongst others, travelling to other countries or jurisdictions when seriously ill, then we must desist from these actions and act in the manner which optimally supports the health, welfare and well-being of others. Thus, in terms of supporting our own well-being and the well-being of others, in terms of supporting social health, as social beings within our human social systems, we also need to take great care in regard to, as far as possible, avoiding and preventing transmission of illnesses and disease, especially serious illness and disease, even though in many or most cases, our own symptoms and suffering may be, at the time, relatively mild.

Thus, in regard to those highly infrequent cases where we are infected with these more severe, deadly illnesses, as an individual, under expert advice, we may therefore need to be quarantined, kept away from others, such that the severe or deadly illness does not spread to others, causing others severe illness or killing them through its effects. In such cases we have a responsibility and indeed must accept isolation and quarantine in order to protect the many others who might be damaged by the illness we are carrying, and indeed should do so willingly and gladly. Medical efforts must be made, as far as possible to save us, to keep us alive so that we can live on and have a future, but the rest of the community, society, our humanity, cannot be put at risk when there is a deadly viral or other threat of illness contagion, and therefore we must accede to isolation and quarantine under such circumstances. Indeed our communities and societies, our human society, have an obligation to enforce quarantine in these cases in order to protect the health and well-being of others, and it is our obligation to gladly acquiesce as part of our individual and personal commitment to supporting the well-being of all others.

General cleanliness has already been mentioned. When we are ill with transmissible diseases, colds, flus, infections of all sorts, it is worth emphasising that we need to take assiduous action and take great care to avoid the transmission of these illnesses to others, through the already mentioned frequent washing of our hands, through sneezing into tissues and being clean generally, gaining medical assistance when such assistance is needed. Acting in such a manner is clearly consistent with our principles of taking care of the well-being of others, our communities and societies and, of course, in terms of taking care of ourselves. Educational systems through families, communities. societal and even global information campaigns need to build understanding of illness and disease and support efforts towards cleanliness and to contain the spread of illness and disease where that is reasonable and possible.

We have responsibilities to others within the context of core and other principles to ensure we do these things to help stop the spread of illnesses. If necessary, based in medical advice and epidemiological advice, based in the gravity of the illness and condition as well as other factors, in some cases of illness where formal quarantine isn't required, we may still need to stay away from others, out of circulation, until we are well, such that the relevant illness is more difficult to pass on, even if this interferes with our work and our passion and dedication for work. The reality for many of us in regard to lower risk illnesses, is that this is easier said than done, when our earnings are essential for us to survive and when we may lose earnings or even a job through our absence, when work pressures, the need to achieve, the need to meet deadlines, and peer and management pressure as well as the pressure we put on ourselves, come into play.

That being said, there may be conditions when we suffer from a more minor illness when there may be no or little harm in continuing with our daily schedules, despite our illness, and further, there are many of us who find it difficult to cope with interruption to our routines, who value and prioritise our work. Indeed there may also be occasions when the presence of ourselves as individuals is absolutely essential if important work is to be done, work which will have substantial benefit for ourselves and our organisation, perhaps our wider communities too. For example, in the agricultural industry, for farmers, where there are crops that need to be harvested, and harvested soon, this many simply have to be done, however ill we may feel. Under such circumstances, bearing in mind the nature of the illness we have and the advice given by medical professionals we may need to continue to interact with and work with others, with our all bearing the risks of acquiring minor infections and illness.

As one of our social and also individual responsibilities, consistent with our core principles, we need to support effective health systems such that effective illness prevention and effective treatment of illnesses and injury can be provided to all. The principles outlined in this guide mean that we cannot allow ourselves or leave others to suffer without making serious, committed, effective and meaningful efforts to counter that ill health, pain and suffering, without making serious efforts to alleviate pain and to deal with illnesses and injuries such that they hopefully are remedied and cured, such that pain and suffering are ended and well-being and health enjoyed. Through our own personal actions, our material, financial and other contributions together with the contributions of others, we need to ensure that resources and funds are available to provide medical treatments, medical training, the provision of and payment for medicines, medical research, medical salaries, medical personnel, medical buildings and facilities, and much more in order to ensure our own health and the health of others, all of this serving to support health and reduce pain and suffering.

In supporting good health and well-being, we need to recognise that the provision of effective health support needs organisation and systems which operate efficiently and effectively. Clearly we cannot all be involved in operating these systems ourselves as there are many other roles, responsibilities and duties to be fulfilled within our communities and societies and indeed in direct service to our broader humanity. In practice, for the most of us our contribution and support is likely to mean some form of payment or other material contribution, involving the social, community and broader creation of resources, necessary funds and funding systems to support whichever system of health is needed or is in place.

Such systems are necessary as supporting our own health care and the health care of others requires planning, organisation, training, development, resources, tools, management, strategies and policies, time and money, and much more. And such funded systems are necessary such that the poor and resourceless are not left to suffer with illness, disease and pain, without assistance from those others of us who are healthier at the time and indeed who are more wealthy and have resources available to give.

It is nevertheless the responsibility of all of us, those of us with resources, wealth and power, and indeed it is the responsibility of those individuals and groups in poverty themselves, to work, as far as possible, as individuals, in cooperation with others, and as much as we all can, to ensure, sustain and work to develop living conditions that support health and well-being, including through creating, ensuring and providing the already referred to clean water supplies, adequate and healthy diets, through providing sufficient shelter, medical support and other important elements of a life of health and well-being. All of these and more need to be brought into existence where they do not exist, and need to be maintained, developed and improved into the future in order to enhance support and to benefit our health.

And our actions to support others, as in many other cases, will also serve to support those of us who are helping out those individuals, communities and societies, those who are struggling with poor public health systems, disease, illness and injury. This benefit for ourselves when helping others occurs in many ways but most practically and immediately obvious is the fact that diseases and illnesses which breed in conditions of poverty can spread easily to those of us in other areas where people are also poor and to those areas and regions where people are more wealthy and generally more healthy. Through acting against disease and illness, through preventing poverty we are therefore helping ourselves and making ourselves less vulnerable to illness and disease. Benefits such as these underpin our individual and social nature as human beings.

There can be not only contagion from such diseases and illnesses, but the presence of desperation for survival and intense pain and suffering amongst those who are poor or relatively poor, can create social schisms, division and conflict between those who are poor or less well off and those who are for example, wealthy, living in better conditions, and who are able to obtain better medical and health treatment. Those of us who are suffering are unlikely to, and indeed should not suffer in silence. And if we are suffering, we may, not be open to explanations, even rational and truthful explanations, for our state of poverty and desperation, explanations which in some cases may serve to foment conflict and violence. Indeed some of us, if not many of us, may choose to blame others for our plight, whether or not that is justified. Of course, if we are suffering in such ways, consistent with core and other principles, we need to pursue escape from our poverty and suffering, but need to do so in as peaceful a manner as possible.

At the minimum, those of us who are poor or relatively so, are likely to demand actions are taken to rectify and improve our situations, which in the presence of severe and damaging poverty and in the face of resistance from more wealthy, powerful and privileged people, can lead to severe, damaging conflict and even civil and other wars. Armed with explanations of our poverty, accurate or inaccurate as the case may be, perhaps understanding the nature of the callous malevolence which in some, if not many cases, has systematically and perhaps deliberately led to our situation, those of us in desperation and in the grips of destructive poverty may need to aim to peaceably but forcefully take hold of the resources we need to alleviate our poverty and suffering, and may face violence and oppression from some of those with power and who are in possession of those resources as they aim to preserve their status, power, resources and privilege.

Of course, rather than such destructive conflict, what is needed is for all of us to support each other, to ensure that no one is in substantive poverty and suffering, something which, at least in our modern world, should certainly be possible. Leaving others to die of starvation and diseases when such situations can be remedied, is totally contrary to core and other principles. While the motivation for our supporting others should not be to avoid such conflict but should originate in our social awareness and our care and concern for others, there are clearly important practical reasons for supporting all others out of poverty and suffering and indeed there are strong practical reasons for reducing levels of inequality.

Underpinning potential problems of poverty and leading to ineffective responses, lack of effective and broad education and other factors may lead to difficulties in understanding the sources of poverty, illness and suffering on all sides, with those of us who are wealthy and privileged blaming what some might ludicrously describe as the feckless poor for their own conditions of poverty, even when the truth is that this is rarely the case. And those of us who are poor may attribute our condition to the wealthy and powerful who fail to act in a social manner and contribute to others as they should do, which indeed is often true, though not always the case in itself, with poverty caused by a range of factors such as poor agricultural systems, lack of technology, social and cultural patterns of behaviour, lack of education, poorly organised economic, social and political systems and much more.

Of course while poverty, with its attendant health consequences, may be to some extent, as mentioned, a product of social systems, in some or indeed many circumstances and situations, those systems themselves can be a product of wrong-headed, incompetent decision-making negatively selfish and malevolent individuals as well as being supported by groups, businesses and organisations operating contrary to the interests of their broader communities and societies as well as against our broader humanity. And individual selfish, acquisitive and greedy actions can also cause vast levels of poverty with ordinary people removed from the land they need for agriculture, with technological advances being used to throw individuals aside, with negatively selfish, short-termist greed-driven financial manipulation aimed at personal enrichment leading to the destruction of businesses, companies and jobs. Such actions will have direct effects on our health and well-being through our inability to fulfill our human needs if living in poverty, through stress and other channels, as well as being likely to have long-term psychological and other effects if we are unable to improve our personal positions and escape from poverty.

We also have to acknowledge that poverty, pain and suffering may also sometimes be a product of nature through poor harvests, drought, natural disasters such as earthquakes, floods and tsunamis. Yet it is certainly possible for us to plan and prepare for such events, for example, setting aside food in case of poor harvests, or putting in place agreements to source supplies from areas where the harvests are good in our times of need. Indeed as already mentioned, lack of effective technology, inefficient organisation and administration, as well as poor systems of various kinds, individual errors in terms of decision-making and much more can also act as very important sources of poverty. Potentially deadly in their effects, we need to consistently work to ensure we have efficient and effective systems in all of these areas and others. There will always be some errors of decision-making but we need to ensure that the minimum errors are made and that these errors can be rapidly compensated for and decisions changed where they occur.

Beyond supporting the basics of health, in terms of our social support for raising general standards of living and treatment of health problems and illnesses, it is also important that we give support as individuals, communities and societies to other strategies for health maintenance and development, such as the already mentioned promotion of healthy eating, engaging in physical exercise and sporting activity, promoting social engagement and participation, adventure and exploration, mental exercise and activity, and creativity amongst other routes to positive health. We can do this through our individual actions in supporting health-focused social organisations, for example by supporting and making available finance to enable these health-based organisations to provide information and education about healthy behaviours; we can do this through providing finance to make facilities available such that people can promote their own health. We can support health improvements by supporting a culture of good health and healthy behaviours as well as through ourselves exemplifying healthy behaviours in our own conduct and using our own individual voices to support the value of such healthy activities and lifestyles.

In terms of the promotion of good health, information needs to be provided about the range of health issues and health behaviours. We all need to have information available and accessible about, for example sex and sexual health. It is not acceptable that young men and women should discover the world of sex and love through unexpected and perhaps unwanted experiences and unwanted pregnancies, through acquiring sexually transmitted diseases or by finding themselves pressured and bullied into unwanted sex because they lack confidence, knowledge and maturity in regards to relationships and sex.

It is further not acceptable, that we should not have information and understanding about how sex and sexual loving pleasure works for ourselves and our partners. Enjoying sexual pleasure is consistent with what are, for the vast main of us, our basic human needs and selves, and of course enjoying such pleasure is consistent with core and other principles representing an important part of our individual fulfillment, our joy and pleasure in life, supporting our well-being and happiness. Falsehoods about sex and sexuality, unhealthy and damaging customs and beliefs which cause unnecessary pain and suffering, need to be combated with accurate information such that those of us engaging in sex are more aware of what we are doing, are more aware of our partners and lovers, more aware of possible hazards from what might be on occasion risky sexual behaviour, as well as of course being aware of the intense pleasures we can gain from sex. Our greater knowledge and understanding will enable us to enjoy sex and love more safely, healthily and with the greatest pleasure possible. Integral to this, we all need education and information about supporting healthy sexual, loving and personal relationships with partners, the expectations, the pitfalls, the joys and pleasures, the realities of relationships, sex and love.

Clearly in terms of customs in some cultures, rituals such as female circumcision involving genital mutilation, are entirely unacceptable, causing physical damage, potential death, potential trauma, presenting risks in childbirth, and damaging potential enjoyment of sexual pleasure for those subject to such rituals. Such rituals serve no purpose in terms of individual or community well-being and represent a violence against girls and women which is entirely unacceptable, as is any such violence.

With regard to male circumcision, the same stricture, in the main, needs to apply to male circumcision, although the physical damage done to males appears to be lesser and there are reported to be some health benefits. Cultures, belief groups and communities may see such male circumcision as harmless, and may see this ritual as marking off individuals as members of their social entity, enhancing a sense of belonging when the child is an adult. Nevertheless this ritual is clearly painful and despite some evidence of health benefits, these benefits are, in most contexts, considered to be relatively minor. Clearly where significant health benefits are considered to be present, then there may be good reason to circumcise males. Nevertheless, it is not acceptable to mark a child off as a member of a culture and belief group, when beliefs and group memberships need to be decided later, when children have reached adulthood, rather than being imposed before a child has reached that stage. Babies, on whom circumcisions are practiced, are in no position to give informed consent to such a ritual which will mark them for life.

As individuals, consistent with core and other principles, we need to support community and social entities and organisations in presenting the range of medical information and education in regard to issues not only related to promotion of physical health and exercise, but also in regard to threats to both our positive physical and mental health. Maintaining our mental health in the face of the emotional challenges encountered in our daily lives in the modern world is of great importance to all of us. Topics linked to our mental health need to be broached, giving us information about the mental, emotional and psychological challenges we may face, though not simply through information provision and awareness raising, but through educational and learning activities such that young people in particular are not caught unawares by mental health problems, which they might consider to be their own fault, which they might consider to be solely their own, unique to them and for which they uniquely blame themselves, leaving them feeling isolated and potentially substantially depressed and unhappy.

In addition to these mental health challenges, information needs to be presented, certainly in our current age, in relation to the dangers of smoking, the dangers of alcohol and excess alcohol, of addictive drugs, and more, with this information being presented in a balanced, reasonable, evidence-based and truthful manner, exhibiting understanding of the history and indeed the origins of desire for such stimulants (the reasons why some if not many people have wanted, want and use these), and basing statements in reason and rationality. Rationality and truthfulness, the use of evidence linked to positive and caring, respectful values within the frame of core and other principles, offers the best hope for encouraging people to accede to, and to adopt behaviours which will benefit their own health and benefit our communities and societies. This is, in particular, because individual autonomy and individual decision-making are of great importance to well-being and happiness, and it is likely and indeed considered reasonable, that it should be within the remit of our individual choice, to an important degree, to determine our own behaviours, so long as our behaviours are not significantly detrimental to others.

Nevertheless there is also an individual, group and social responsibility to ensure that individuals or groups of individuals prepared to act or acting in malevolent, negatively selfish and self-interested ways, who have no or little interest in, and who do not prioritise, the general welfare, who have little or no interest in supporting the well-being and happiness of others, or who operate according to rules and systems which, as a consequence of their operation, embody no or little interest in and which do not prioritise our well-being and happiness, should not be allowed to unduly influence our thinking through for example, presentation of half truths, through depriving us of, or hiding information, through deliberately misleading us away from the truths and realities of events. Of course as individuals we should never participate in any such efforts to mislead others which damage well-being and happiness and which cause pain and suffering.

As evaluators and recipients of so much information, in relation in particular to all those issues tying in to our health, in support of our health and well-being, we do need to learn concrete bases for determining truth and validity through evidence, as well as identifying misleading information and false forms of argument such that we can recognise the optimal pathways to our health and well-being. We certainly need to be able to recognise strategies used to disarm and persuade us in ways which move beyond rationality, reason and evidence. We need to be able to identify tactics and strategies which mislead and distract, recognise untruths and real motivations, such that we are aware of the disinterest in others and falsehoods propagated by those behaving in deliberately or unintentionally destructive ways, and most importantly such that we can deal with them, respond to them in an appropriate and effective manner.

It is also important that in addition to promoting behaviours associated with positive health we support our social entities in combating the promotion of behaviours which will encourage and lead to poor health. Thus, for example in the current era, in many jurisdictions, social action researching, identifying and recognising the dangers of smoking tobacco followed by action to reduce consumption of tobacco, has led to major steps forward in public health, supporting better health and creating a cleaner and more healthy environment. Since the negative effects of smoking tobacco are so well documented, it is indeed reprehensible in terms of the values of supporting others and reducing their suffering, that organisations still promote tobacco products which now need to be moved through an expedited process through which they will be largely and finally removed from production and promotion. It is also reprehensible that governments and those in authority did not, have not taken and in some cases are not taking expeditious action to reduce the levels of smoking consumption even though the evidence of tobacco damage is clear.

While the notion of individual autonomy embraces our rights to make decisions about its consumption, the promotion and consequent mass consumption of tobacco was based on a false prospectus, a prospectus of health and fulfillment, based on inadequate health data and on image-based marketing, aimed at, for example, the association of the product with a healthy and adventurous lifestyle. With regard to such an unhealthy product and perhaps with others too, such marketing is grossly inappropriate. And more heinous were attempts by the tobacco industry to deliberately conceal data which indicated the dangers in tobacco, to fund research promoting tobacco as a healthy product despite mounting evidence of its dangers, and indeed now to continue mass production and promotion of tobacco when the damage it does to health is well-known. We all, and that includes those in the tobacco industry, have a responsibility to support the ending of the consumption of this and related products.

Importantly, however, that is not to say that each of us as individuals should be banned and prevented from smoking tobacco, since we do have significant individual responsibility for our own health. To use such a product, under most conditions, would be clearly self-damaging, damaging to our health, leading likely to an early and painful death, and would have damaging effects on others, who would see how little we value our health and our life. Indeed those who love us dearly, our children and grandchildren may be profoundly upset that we are willing to risk our lives in such a way and damage our health in such ways. Yet if we are fully aware of the damage a product such as tobacco can do to our health, and our use of the product does no others significant harm (our early death of course will significantly harm our close families should we have them and those others we love), then while others may aim to dissuade us to use such a product, it still fundamentally remains our choice about our use or non-use. That being said, the damage to our health from tobacco smoking, means, in almost all circumstances that smoking is contrary to core principles.

In support of our health and well-being, we, our governments, our health organisations are obliged to aim to dissuade us from such use, pointing out in unequivocal terms the dangers of acts such as smoking tobacco, and must ensure such products cannot be promoted to children. Nor should smoking and the like be promoted through devices such as image marketing, associating a toxic product with positive images and positive human concepts, or through other promotional and marketing devices which aim to change or interfere with our behaviour outside of a rational evaluation of the clear danger of such a product to our individual health.

It is worth noting that while some argue that there are financial costs imposed on others of us through tobacco-induced ill health, through the need to treat tobacco related illnesses, resultant cancers and other tobacco effects, these arguments are not accepted here, in particular because it is considered that medical treatments required during our aging and gradual corporeal and indeed sometimes mental deterioration, as well as our upkeep when old if we are unable to support ourselves, all of these can, in themselves, impose costs on others, our communities and societies, costs which may be much higher than those required in treating those dying early through tobacco-induced disease. Within core and other principles it is support of well-being and happiness, support of a complete and full life, replete with well-being and happiness, with the least possible pain and suffering which is our goal, for all people, something which use of toxic substances such as tobacco fails to support.

Given what is known about the toxic effects of smoking, the effects on others of breathing in tobacco smoke and the unpleasantness for many of us of breathing in such smoke, those who smoke tobacco should certainly not be able to pollute our local environment and damage others with tobacco smoke, and thus the prevention and banning of smoking in public places is clearly a necessary thing for us all to support.

In accord with core and other principles, given the importance already described in this guide of our having and maintaining integrity, returning to those who might still be promoting tobacco products, we need to recognise that those who are aware of the unhealthy and damaging nature of the products they are promoting (and there should be little reason for lack of awareness) yet who take no significant action to remedy the potential damage, those who make no significant effort to make others aware of these product characteristics, those who continue to promote such products for daily and regular use and who skews and witheld information, and who take no action to remove these products from public consumption where that is appropriate, justified and necessary (and who take no action to prevent unhealthy products from being sold in the first place), through their inaction are thereby causing damage to those who use the product.

These people are acting contrary to the core principles established in this guide through failing to support the health and well-being of others, and through causing unnecessary pain and suffering. Action needs to be taken in some form against those individuals who promote such damaging products and withhold information about them. Given the potential widespread damaging effects of such products, it is essential that key health-related information about such products is communicated and relevant action taken, such as modifying the product such that it is safe or withdrawing the product so it cannot be bought.

And with regard to this particular point it is essential that not only do we aim as social entities to prevent use of such products, but we support our social entities and organisations in promoting the development of healthy new products and services, new health services of various kinds, which will serve us all, serve our communities and societies and support our health. This is essential in order to enable and support the improvements in health and well-being that we all wish to see and which benefit us all.

Moreover, stemming from our need to support health and well-being, individuals, organisations, businesses and companies developing new products and services need to take responsibility for ensuring the safety of their products and services, ensuring the safety of clients, customers and workers. Our governments, state and other supranational organisations, acting as our representatives, also need to effectively and efficiently monitor and regulate those items and services made available for public use and consumption, such that the health and well-being of the population is protected. And it is our role individually, as communities and societies to ensure that our government, state and other organisations fulfill these essential roles.

Our health, as well as future improvements in health provision and medical treatment, require us as individuals, together with others, to support engagement and investment in the research which underpins those health improvements. This health research includes that technology-based and other medical research which aims to prevent and treat widespread debilitating and deadly diseases such as the current scourges of malaria and dengue fever as well as the technological and other medical research which aims to prevent and treat other prevalent but significant and deadly conditions such as heart disease, breast, prostate or lung cancer, which themselves are responsible for the deaths of many tens of thousands if not millions of us every year. Other crucial health research includes research focusing on mental health as well as research examining social circumstances, diet, environment and other factors affecting health, factors which are of profound importance to the maintenance and promotion of our health as well as illness and disease prevention.

Vaccination, developed in the nineteenth century through research involving hypothesis, experiment and rationality, illustrates the value of systematic research as such vaccination prevents the spread of many killer illnesses, providing protection against the range of dangerous diseases for all of us. Where vaccines have been shown to be successful and to have minimal side effects or side effects at such a negligible level as to be worthy of consideration as insignificant for those of us in the general population, unless there are other rational and reason-based arguments that can be brought to bear, it is our responsibility to protect ourselves, to protect our families and to protect our communities through taking advantage of the vaccinations available, by supporting the development and implementation of vaccination programmes and through supporting the development of new vaccines.

The already mentioned malaria is a widespread killer disease which at this point in time kills hundreds of thousands of people every year and though strategies are already being applied against this disease, malaria still needs to be tackled as a matter of priority in our efforts to support health, well-being and reduce and prevent pain and suffering. Fortunately through research, new treatments and new strategies are currently being developed and hopefully will be developed in the future, in order to deal with the immense challenge of malaria which causes such tremendous pain and suffering worldwide. In addition to efforts to design medicines which will prevent malaria taking hold in our bodies, perhaps making us resistant to infection, efforts are being made to drive out malaria parasite-carrying mosquitoes and replace them with harmless mosquitoes. Hopefully this or other approaches will be successful and will rid the world of this deadly scourge. And regarding dengue fever, another substantially debilitating and dangerous disease, significant research efforts are being undertaken to deal with this. Yet aside from medical and advanced technological and biological cures, some simple measures can be taken in some places to deal with malaria and dengue fever including removing standing pools of water which the various parasite or virus carrying mosquitoes need to sustain their lifecycles.

Research has led to the development of a range of heart treatments whether it be, at the current time, the stents which help keep arteries open so that the heart can continue to do its work and so that our circulation can continue to function; whether it be the statins which many are advised to take to reduce the chances of heart attacks; whether it be the development of implanted defibrillators to restart hearts which are failing and out of rhythm, or be it the pacemakers which maintain the rhythm of the heart, there have been many steps forward in prolonging and extending life through the focus on research and the incredible thinking, creativity and indeed design work of researchers. These are extraordinary developments from which many of us in the current world have benefited substantially.

Cancers, which are the scourge of many, causing the most painful of experiences and many deaths, are being treated with increasing effectiveness in the current age, with systematic research and rational, researched-based treatments enabling increasing numbers of cancers to be tackled and increasing numbers of us to be cured or have our lives extended. While cancers appear to be many, varied and complex in origin, continuing focus on research into these cancers will increase our understanding such that, hopefully at some point, all forms of cancer will be preventable or treatable. It is our responsibility as individuals within the core principles presented in this guide, to support the promotion of research into the vast range of illnesses which threaten our well-being and health, including these cancers. With our support, researchers will undoubtedly develop new and even more extraordinary and surprising solutions to our medical problems enabling us to live longer and healthier lives.

Old age and the increasing numbers of elderly people in many modern countries present us and our communities and societies with many challenges in terms of supporting the maintenance of health and avoiding pain and suffering. These challenges include those of identifying and preventing or slowing the onset of debilitating conditions and symptoms of aging, and responding effectively to the debilitation and deterioration which accompanies the aging process. This is a relatively new area of research in which our modern researchers have a great deal of work to undertake.

Research is further needed in terms of medical treatments for both well-known and newly recognised illnesses and diseases of aging, as well as in relation to our understanding of the ways in which our bodies wear and deteriorate over time, this research hopefully leading to means of slowing or preventing such deterioration. The eventual decline in our mental capacities, which afflicts many older people, is a key area where research is required and through such research we should hopefully gain greater insights into the functioning of our minds, something which should benefit us all, whatever age we are.

Research is also needed into the best forms of care for those living into old age. Those of us who have reduced physical abilities or who are disabled to a greater or lesser degree on account of our age (as well as all of us who are disabled through our lives) need support and need to be provided with support such that we are able to live a reasonable standard of life in which we can enjoy well-being and happiness in later years to as great a degree as is possible.

While much of this is technological or medical research focused on direct treatments for illness, other areas of research have generated key discoveries which have underpinned our improved modern health. These include and have included in particular, the dietary research which has identified the forms and levels of nutritional intake which we need to have in order to grow and in order to maintain and support our health. Such research has contributed substantially and continues to contribute towards our human health and well-being. A well-known example of such invaluable dietary research was the discovery that there is a factor, now known as Vitamin C, found in citrus fruits, required in our diets to maintain health. The need for citrus fruits in our diets was understood for a long time before the actual identification of the vitamin C molecule, nevertheless the need for citrus fruits and hence vitamin C in our diets was initially made through observation and research more than one hundred years ago.

Our increasing knowledge, based on the systematic observation, thinking and practical experimentation behind empirical research, has led to the new knowledge and understanding that dietary factors are not only important in supporting our basic physical health but can also have particular influences on mood and behaviour. Further, allergic reactions to food are now better understood and a greater knowledge and understanding is developing in regard to the effects of excess food intake on the body and on our health. Nevertheless, much research is still needed to investigate amongst other things, not only the dietary factors which influence and promote positive health but also to investigate further the role of dietary factors which might influence behaviour and trigger or influence disease. Overall with regard to our dietary knowledge and understanding, systematic research has been of great importance, identifying a wide range of dietary factors necessary for good health, however our knowledge about our diet and its links to health still needs further development, and we need to be aware of and support further developments in dietary research.

Research is also needed into the mechanisms through which we can act to prevent the advent and spread of damaging infectious illnesses, such as new strains of the flu virus, and other newly arising and newly arrived infectious diseases. Linked to and overlapping with this, we also need research and need to support research into furthering our understanding about mechanisms of transmission and the potential and actual transmission of diseases as well as ensuring effective and speedy responses to the outbreak of disease. It is most likely crucial that we maintain and develop rapid response systems in the advent of new diseases, developing the capacity to rapidly understand and respond to new illnesses such that we can limit the spread of these new illnesses and other illnesses with which we may be more familiar, and quickly develop medical treatments to deal with any new and developing health threats.

Our work environment can be a source of a range of health problems and we all therefore have a responsibility to ensure that our work environments are safe and indeed the broader environments which our work environments can effect, are similarly safe. The medical consequences of uses of new materials, chemicals and indeed old materials and historically used biochemical and chemicals need to be properly understood, for which detailed, in-depth and long-term funded research may be necessary. Where there are potential dangers to health, then the processes, procedures, products and by-products used in work contexts need to be researched and monitored, and modified as necessary, to ensure the safety, health and well-being of all those in the workplace. Of course our work environments also need to be physically and indeed socially safe places to work, and research is needed to ensure that these workplaces are designed effectively in line with safety and our other human individual and social needs.

In our more natural biological environments it is essential that where, for example, pesticides, herbicides and insecticides or other chemicals and biochemicals, are considered necessary to be used, then those used offer maximum safety to all, both to those of us involved in growing and harvesting these foods, and to those of us consuming the food. Again research into optimal biochemicals, chemicals, combined with research and monitoring of their usage and their medical and health effects, their mechanisms of delivery as well as their effects in these contexts, is essential to ensure health and well-being. In the vast majority of cases, such research processes need to pre-empt the introduction of new chemicals, biochemicals into the environment, although it is possible to foresee specific circumstances of threat to our food supplies when more immediate action might need to be taken.

Mental health, as already discussed at some length in this chapter, represents a crucial component of our well-being and happiness and clearly research is needed into how we can maintain and enhance our mental health as well as into the nature of mental health problems. Our well-being in terms of mental health including the mental health problems we may have, is likely to be, to some degree, dependent on chemical and biochemical factors, neural architecture and other more biological, genetic and biochemical factors. Our mental health problems, should we have them, may in some cases be resolved without resort to medicine, through better understanding of the complexity and workings of our mind, through changing the ways we think, as well as in some cases, developing a better understanding of the inter-relation between our individual selves, our individual thinking processes and psychologies, and our social living and relationships in our communities and societies. We certainly need research into our mental health and how best to deal with the range of mental health problems that we can suffer from, with evaluations needing to be conducted on the range of treatments available to us alongside our aiming to develop new treatments and medicines. All of this of course will support the well-being and happiness of ourselves and others.

Systematic, empirical research based in evidence and observation is necessary to underpin our knowledge of health and well-being. While it is clear that our human minds and bodies can give responses to what are technically cure-neutral medicines in the form of placebo treatments which should on other medical grounds in fact have no effect at all, as has already been mentioned, the use of unproven and potentially damaging treatments should not be implemented aside from in those circumstances, where there is little or no chance with our current level of understanding, that life will be maintained. It should of course be recognised by those involved in medicine that our bodies themselves have mechanisms for combating pain, disease and illness and while these certainly do not always work and can importantly be ineffective in the face of the range of biological and other threats to health, it may in some cases be beneficial to take these mechanisms into account, as in some circumstances, with perhaps some help, supporting and enabling these internal mechanisms to operate better, may mean that certain diseases and illnesses are resolved and indeed cured, and complex, expensive and indeed unnecessary medical procedures may not be needed.

The broader human face of health and illness, the nature of our whole selves, our human needs and requirements, our emotional and other needs are also worthy of research in relation to health and well-being. It cannot be assumed that technological and drug-based approaches to improving our medical health are the only route to better health or that they are always optimal, even though they may frequently be so. Technology and drug-based treatments may not only be unsuccessful as treatment options in some cases, and in some cases can result in painful side-effects, but may also distract from more obvious actions in response to illness, pain and suffering as well as detracting from focus on the person who is under supervision, or is ill, thereby causing emotional upset and having detrimental emotional and psychological effects.

This may apply in a range of circumstances and in relation to a number of conditions. The existence of technology and drug-based options in medical care, given the investment and research in such treatments can funnel the thinking of doctors and medical staff into choosing such options when they may not be optimal for the patient. The desire to intervene with surgery and other drug-based interventions needs to sometimes be tempered with consideration of less interventionist options where these may be viable, since these other options may be effective, less costly and be more supportive of those who are ill.

There is certainly a strong case for avoiding substantial medical technological intervention in relation to childbirth, a natural process, where there is ample evidence that not intervening in the birth process may frequently, perhaps in the significant majority of cases, be a reasonable and even the best approach to looking after the baby and mother. The common assumption that drugs must be administered in childbirth, that a mother must be intrusively monitored, is often not correct. In childbirth, the administration of heroin to mothers (referred to as diamorphine) may be standard practice in some jurisdictions, but there is evidence that this may have consequent potentially negative effects on both the mother and child.

Research can tend to become focused on technological and drug-based solutions yet there needs also to be room for other forms of research which, for example, might focus on prevention, which might focus on our human behaviours, and other areas, where research might lead to ideas and cures which might be more effective and less invasive. Research does not always support the technological and drug-based solution, with such a technology and drug-based focus perhaps meaning that medical professionals may not fully see and fully understand, take account of and include ourselves as people and patients in consideration and discussion of treatments. When conducted impartially and systematically with integrity, considering the wide range of potential solutions, as indeed it should do, research will identify the courses of action which are best for those who are healthy and best for those who are ill, and this may not, in some, if not many cases, involve drug-based treatments or surgery, but in other cases, certainly will do if health and well-being is to be maintained and pain and suffering are to be avoided.

Beyond technological and drug-based interventions, the presence of social support and care can be very important in helping to maintain a healthy life and can comprise an important element of our well-being and happiness. Presence in a home environment, despite our need for medical treatment (though perhaps combined with medical treatment), may be a good option in some cases for many of us, due to the familiarity and comfort of our homes, and through being with those we know and love. And further, at certain points towards the end of our lives, when there is little hope of our recovery, we may quite reasonably choose to refuse hospital confinement with its accessibility of medical treatment and doctors, and instead choose to die in a hospice where care and support is available or in those familiar surroundings at home with those whom we love and who are familiar to us, this perhaps comprising a more peaceful and warm, human ending to our lives, which we may find better for us and better for our families and those who care for us.

Systematic research, which is requiring of our individual, community societal and more global support, is necessary in many other areas which might be seen, at first glance, as more tangential to health and well-being, though in fact they are certainly not tangential and are indeed essential to our health and well-being. Thus, given the vast devastation and damage that result, we need to research the causes of aggressive violence, war and international conflict, social, psychological and other, and we need to research the forms of process and action which are needed to build peace and cooperation, enabling us as individuals, communities and states to co-exist and work together. As a consequence, hopefully this will mean we can take steps forward in terms of health, well-being, welfare and development such that we can cooperate to support health and well-being, reducing pain and suffering through our combined and increased understandings and resultant actions. Recognising our common humanity, in support of cooperation, peacefulness and togetherness, linked to well-being and happiness, we may well determine that, to some extent, we need to deprioritise notions of states and countries and look to integrate together in a more cohesive, cooperative and tolerant global human community.

Research is needed into economic development and economic and political systems because poverty, with the pain and suffering, with the damage to health it entails, is an element of under-developed, inefficient and sometimes corrupt economies as well as being indicative in some cases of unstable and corrupt, destructive political systems, which deny the opportunity for improvement and development and which clearly damage our health and well-being. Poverty, and indeed extreme poverty, can also, unfortunately, be a component of more wealthy systems in which it is considered legitimate to allow others to be unfairly exploited and suffer. Such exploitation is entirely unacceptable within the principles in this guide, which requires we research what is needed to develop economic and political systems such that they benefit all of us to the maximum degree possible. Furthermore, economic systems may operate in other ways which are not sufficiently supportive of the well-being and happiness of us all, and we need to look to conduct research which identifies approaches that enable us to maximise well-being and happiness and reduce pain and suffering.

Research is also needed into the effects of our human activity on the environment and on how to optimally respond to the changes which our human activity is effecting in that environment. The phenomenon of global warming and associated climate change are presenting and will present challenges to our world. We need to research further what the real effects of such global warming and climate change will be since there will certainly be impact on the health and well-being of some if not many or perhaps all of us through the droughts, floods, changes in climate and weather and more. We need to determine how to avoid such changes in climate, or support beneficial climate changes (if such is possible), and determine, amongst other things, how to reduce the changing temperatures in our world caused by human carbon emission and other factors, and how to deal with and respond to such changes if they are, in some sense, irreversible in the short term.

We also need to research and develop methods of prediction and early detection when it comes to other natural events and disasters in our environment which may damage our health and well-being, There is little doubt that more research still needs to be done in these areas. Research is required to develop our understanding of, in the first place, the signs of impending natural disasters, and into developing relevant technical equipment required both in detection of and response to such disasters. We need to undertake research to develop not only the most appropriate systems, technologies and equipment in response to such disasters, but we need to know and understand how best to apply those systems and use that equipment and technology in helping people once it is available.

As individuals, communities, societies and as a global population, we remain vulnerable to earthquakes, unpredicted (and predicted) volcanic eruptions, tsunamis, and other global natural catastrophes which may be of extraordinary magnitude. Though perhaps rare in terms of the scale of our individual human lives, the most catastrophic and destructive of these events are likely to occur sometime, these may still occur, and we, as a global community, need to be ready and have a plan. So we need systematic research which proactively examines how we can most effectively prepare for such disasters prior to when they arise, and as they occur, in order to ensure our survival and well-being, and research needs to examine how to most effectively deliver a response in the aftermath of such disasters.

Nevertheless, whatever measures we take in response to disasters and crises, or in efforts to protect ourselves from illness and disease, certainly in the current circumstances and with our current state of knowledge and understanding, but almost certainly into the future, it is inevitable that at least some of us, perhaps a small number of us will experience some form of pain, physical or emotional originating in major natural disasters and crises, whoever we are, whatever life we lead, however good we may be. What we must aim to do is to reduce the level of pain and suffering of any of us, of those who might be affected by such disasters and crises as far as we can.

Considering pain from whichever source it might come, due to its inevitability at some points in our lives, pain is something we must prepare and be prepared to cope with as well as we can, not in the sense of resignation such that we make no efforts to reduce our levels of pain, but beyond the medical systems, medical treatments, and health and safety strategies to protect us from illness, disease and physical injury, we need to have some psychological preparedness and personal adaptation so that we anticipate and expect to deal with and put up with a certain level of pain at some points in our lives, whichever form it takes, until that pain dissipates or is dealt with through medical or other intervention. Encountering pain in our lives should not be a source of psychological shock or surprise to us. In one form or another, it is almost certain, if not certain, to be part of the lives of all of us, though that recognition may not make us feel much better when we experience such pain.

Our physical pain occurs in many forms, varying in terms of, amongst other elements, its intensity and the period for which we experience that pain. Undoubtedly and unfortunately we are likely to have to endure an immediate period following serious injury or other seriously damaging health event, involving significant pain or agony, yet hopefully without too much delay it will be the case that our pain can be somewhat alleviated by medical administration of pain relievers. Of course our own bodies have pain response mechanisms, which may dampen down pain to some degree, but drugs, anaesthetics, sedatives and more in the modern world are fortunately available and used, frequently successfully, to reduce our levels of pain in the short term while physical and illness problems are treated or our bodies respond to repair an injury or fight against a disease or illness. Of course there are side effects of many drugs and pain relievers, one important potential side-effect being, in some cases, addiction to that drug or pain-reliever. We must be careful in our use of such pain relievers and related drugs and our medical advisors and doctors must also show care in their prescription of such pain relievers, avoiding prescription when this is unnecessary. Hopefully pains from our immediate physical injuries, through natural processes and healing allied to appropriate medical treatment, perhaps surgery where necessary, will die down soon or we can be given substantial pain relief such that we need not endure agony, severe or even mild and nagging pain over an extended period. It is a medical responsibility to act to support our health and also where possible and reasonable to reduce our levels of pain, if that is what we as a patient wish for.

Of course there are also milder illnesses, colds and flus, stomach bugs which cause discomfort, headaches, aches in our joints, vomiting and more, which hopefully do not cause us too much severe pain and which after a few days of hopefully less intense discomfort, pain and suffering will disappear. If we have access to them, the pains of these more minor illnesses can be alleviated with appropriate drugs, pain relievers, aspirins, antacids and in some cases, cured using specific medicines and antibiotics, dependent on the infection. We may, in the case of more minor ailments, choose to avoid drugs and medicines, which may in some cases have certain side-effects and instead we may simply choose to endure a low level of annoying, unpleasant, discomfort and pain.

With regard to all of us, all individuals, all groups of people, all of our communities and societies, drugs and remedies for illnesses need to be used in the most effective ways possible. For example, with the development of antibiotic resistant microorganisms, we need to ensure that antibiotics are prescribed in ways which, while preventing illness, will not provide high levels of opportunity for the development of antibiotic resistance which undermines or destroys the efficacy of such antibiotics. Apart from effort being placed into the development of new means of treating illnesses, new drugs, new methods of surgery, new medications and other developments, the benefits of, as well as the potential problems with drugs and their effects need to be anticipated as far as possible and systematically researched as far as we are reasonably able to do so. Of course in regard to dealing with bacterial, fungal, parasitic and viral infections as well as other diseases and illnesses, we, as individuals, communities and societies, need to be supporting the research which will enable us to understand these organisms and these conditions such that we can tackle relevant illnesses effectively. That being said it is not the case that all microorganisms are harmful to our health with some perhaps serving a protective or other useful function.

However, there are also long-term sources of pain and illness which may need to be borne and which may be difficult to bear. Some of us suffer from migraines, intense headaches which recur and recur, and about which there seems to be little that can be done in terms of that recurrence, at least with our current state of medical knowledge, although some medicines can hopefully alleviate some of this pain. Certain illnesses can produce constant intense pains and suffering which need as a matter of urgency to be alleviated.

In these cases and other cases where we face such pains, we may need to look for other ways of coping with our pains, most likely accompanied by medical treatments of one form or another. Of course it is for those who have medical knowledge of our conditions, our doctors, to advise us how best to cope, but we, as those experiencing such illnesses, pains and suffering, must be involved with and contribute to the coping process, given that we are the experiencers of the illness, pain and suffering, and in collaboration with authoritative professional medical advice, we may well need to experiment with and discover the best approaches to relieving our pains. Pain relieving drugs may well be necessary to help us get through the day. Distraction through engaging in demanding activities may help, as may simply trying to sleep such that we do not have to experience the pain.

As mentioned, in some circumstances, it may be considered better to endure pain rather than ingest drugs which might prove to have addictive effects or which might have detrimental effects on our bodies. However, that may depend on the severity of the pain and the endurance that we feel we can show and sustain. It would most likely be unwise to avoid drugs which make our days manageable and ease our severe pains, especially if there are no significant identified prospective side-effects. Some physical pains can be debilitating and long term, requiring difficult and ongoing pain management and pain reduction strategies. Such ongoing pain needs to be accompanied by strategies aimed at enhancing the enjoyment of life through that persistent pain, though it is significantly understandable if ongoing, excruciating, severe and debilitating pain leads us to question the value of our continued living. If we can carry on living positively, with well-being to some degree, enjoying good moments amidst the pains, supporting and caring for others, then that will add strong reason for wishing to continue on with our lives, however, in the face of extreme and continuous unrelievable pain, which damages our lives day-to-day, especially when there is no prospect of relief and we will soon face death from the illness with which we are afflicted, then it is not unreasonable to consider wishing to end our lives early and indeed determining to end our lives earlier than would otherwise happen.

Cancers can be appalling in this regard and while attempts are made to destroy such cancers, we may have to endure what are almost unendurable pains, deterioration in our health and damage to our systems. Various drugs are used to alleviate the intense pains produced by cancers and other serious and painful conditions, though clearly there is room for new developments in management of this pain. Where we are incurably ill, with our, for example, bearing those cancers which cannot be cured, then clearly we would hope that our pain is reduced to the minimum. However, with no reasonable escape from such cancers and their accompanying excruciating and intense pain, our perhaps increasing incapacity, in terms of our living with inability to do the most simple things, and our minimal prospect of surviving on for any significant period of time due to our spreading or deadly cancer, then it is again entirely reasonable for us to consider and where we wish, to take action to end our lives ourselves or to seek help to end our lives through assisted suicide.

As already discussed in this chapter, with regard to our psychological and emotional challenges, our mental illnesses and psychological traumas can also be substantially debilitating, confusing, disorienting and painful. Exemplifying sources of possible short-term pain, there may be feelings of painful depression arising from our biological and biochemical selves, arising from our thinking or arising from specific traumatic incidents and events in our lives. Our sense of isolation and emptiness, our losses in love, our failure to achieve, negatively comparing ourselves with others, may all be severely painful and depressing for some of us, some of such pains and hurts more open to being easily thrown off than others, dependent on our personalities, our feelings, thoughts and attitudes, the extent and depth of our pains.

Moreover, breakdowns in our relationships can cause us severe emotional and psychological pain. This is natural and normal when we may have invested so much in that love, those we love, sharing our passion, cares, feelings and indeed lives with our deepest friends and partners. If we are then rejected, or even if there is mutually agreed separation, there may well still be significant pain for many of us, which in some cases may persist for a long time, hopefully in the end dissipating, perhaps disappearing completely, becoming largely irrelevant as time passes as we move into new lives and new relationships.

There are, however, those of us who may wish to continue to hold our pain of loss into the long term, and indeed, for some of us, though not many, keeping a candle burning for someone we have loved, who is still theoretically available to love, can be a way of dealing with the grief and pain of loss. At some point, hopefully, we will be able to move into a future which will be more healthy and happy for us, since our remaining living in hope for goals and dreams which will almost certainly not happen, will, in all likelihood, represent a source of pain. Such an approach will almost certainly not represent the best way to achieve our own longer term fulfillment, nor will it enable us to best support our own well-being and happiness and to support the well-being and happiness of others.

In life, we all also experience the hurt of some painful disappointments. There may be some moments of disappointment which can be easily thrown off, yet other disappointments which, if not adequately dealt with through effective thinking and action, can be longer term and destructive of us as individuals and those around us. Our level of pain in response to such disappointments may substantially depend on our own ability to think about and resolve our failures and disappointments or our ability, to some extent, to set them aside and even, to all intents and purposes, ignore them, beyond the sense of learning from what we may have done incorrectly. We certainly need some ability to shrug our disappointments off and treat them as an ordinary part of life which we all experience, rather than seeing them as experiences which mark us out as uniquely incompetent and useless, which they are highly unlikely to be. Of course having learned from our experiences and set aside our disappointments then we need to subsequently move onwards to focus on new goals.

The reality is that while we will similarly all achieve at some points in our lives, our being prepared for and ready to cope with, some disappointments, sometimes severe disappointments and our being prepared for, on occasion or sometimes, not achieving that which we might wish to achieve, is necessary for all of us, both in terms of life in general but also in terms of being prepared for and ready to deal with the pain of such disappointments in specific situations.

Being constructive and positive in relation to the tasks we face, yet also having a sense of realism in terms of our chances of success, of achievement, should help us avoid the most severe and painful disappointments. In specific circumstances of potential disappointment, thus it is good for our well-being and happiness if we have prepared for the possibility of not achieving our goals, of disappointment, and that we have already considered realigning our objectives and goals in preparation for the anticipated disappointment of non-achievement prior to experiencing that disappointment, or we have considered other potential routes to achieving those goals should we not achieve them. In the latter event we will try again in different ways, through different strategies, aiming to be more effective and successful in achieving those same goals. That being said, we also need to prepare for and think ahead to the consequences of our being successful and the challenges and joys that success may bring.

Disappointments and failures may come as a painful shock to us, but the approach is basically the same once we have got over the shock, surprise and pain, which is to re-evaluate, reset goals, devise new strategies, and to treat the experience as a means of learning and moving forward. Disappointments and failure are part of life and need to be used constructively to develop our understanding, skills and abilities. Wallowing for a very short while in quiet disappointment, anger and resentment, tears and sometimes louder disappointment may be what we do, and may be legitimate if not inevitable to some degree for a short period, helping us to relieve pain and stress and helping us in coming to terms with what may be a painful emotional shock, but as a short-term, medium-term or other strategy into the future, wallowing, self pity and self-admonishment are damaging to our well-being and the well-being of those around us. Of course we may have made mistakes and errors in what we have been doing, and will sometimes make significant mistakes and errors, including in our relationships. We are human beings and, human beings, are fallible. The point is for us to make mistakes, learn and move on to the next challenge, as a better and more capable individual prepared to learn and learn again if necessary from future mistakes, which themselves are likely to be inevitable.

Having discussed the pain of disappointment, and of severe disappointments and failures, we should be careful of pursuing an unambitious, riskless life, seeking at many or all points to avoid the chance of such failure and disappointment. A life without disappointment and failure is likely to be a life which has not been lived to the full. Experiences of disappointment and failure are, indeed, signs of a good life lived to the full. We tried, we had adventures, we set goals – perhaps ambitious and over-ambitious ones – we pursued our dreams – we took risks, perhaps encountered and experienced dangers, pushed ourselves to achieve greatly, pushed ourselves to the limits of what we could do. That is living. That is a life truly full of well-being, fulfillment and achievement. So we must strive and take disappointment and failure as being part of that life.

One of the most hurtful and painful, if not traumatic, experiences in our lives is likely to be the death of someone we love. The loss of a family member, a lover, partner, perhaps unfortunately one of our children, those who have been our greatest friends, is extraordinarily painful, often, though not always, sending us into the depths of grief and sometimes despair. Many of us, if not most of us, hopefully not those who are young, will have felt the intense pain and grief surrounding such a loss, this being a cause of the most terrible and understandable grief. If we have not yet had an experience in our lives of the death of another, then unfortunately, we almost certainly will.

The precise way we feel under such circumstances may depend on a number of different factors, yet for the most of us, in most circumstances, when such a person dies, someone who has been a living a deeply embedded part of our lives, someone who has been almost a part of us, our mother, father, sister, brother, grandparent, uncle, aunt, our child, our friend, our lover or other family member, we will feel tremendous pain and grief, a deep sense of loss, a sense of being devastated perhaps, of being totally lost, bereft. When this one whom we have loved, who is part of our living selves, who has loved us, as our parent, brother, sister, lover, friend, when this person has gone, is no longer there, when they are no longer someone we can see, talk to, hold, be with, indeed just think about as someone who is here, this is likely to be truly shocking and disturbing for us and extraordinarily painful for us to have to cope with.

The vast hole which our loved one's absence can leave; the total gap and absence of someone who may have filled our life and thoughts, day-to-day, month-to-month, year-to-year, is an immense emotional burden to bear, even if they might not have been continuously with us physically and were simply an ever present in our thoughts. In the space where our lover, husband, wife, child, sister, brother or friend used to be, we are faced with an emptiness which will never be filled with them again, and that hurts, hurts terribly. There are few, perhaps no, written or spoken words, which can alleviate the pain we feel in the face of the loss of someone for whom we feel such love.

Yet of course the death of others, and of course our own deaths are inevitable at some point for all of us. We hope that such deaths will not be premature, that they will not occur earlier than expected, that the deaths of those we love will be from illnesses and diseases associated with longevity at the end of a long, fulfilled, full and enjoyable life, full of well-being and happiness, and we hope that their death will not be painful, long and drawn out.

Those of us who are left behind by those who are and have been well-loved will experience our grief and tremendous loss. And for those of us left behind by our loved ones, it is likely to be very difficult to cope with the shock that someone, our loved one, is no longer there, no longer there to talk to, to hold close, to see, to be with, to smile with, to laugh at, to play with, in the case of our lovers and partners to lie next to, to kiss, to do the mundane in our daily lives with, to be annoyed, angry and frustrated with, to help out, to be helped out by, to go places with, to share our worries and cares with.

In the moments after death, amid the shock of the death of someone we love deeply, particularly if their death is sudden and unexpected, we may experience flashes of memory of our loved one, in the few moments when we last saw them and knew them alive. And soon, through our pain, suffering, through our shock, all those experiences with the one we have loved and still love in our hearts will most likely come to the fore in our memories, as we try to hold them close, reliving our last moments with them, and all the moments we shared before on the road of life, together with the disbelief that they have gone. Our pain in grief is substantial. Our memories and love of the one we have loved and indeed still love, will remain forever, and our pain may, to some degree, our pain will last for the remainder of our lives. Nevertheless, we will hopefully, get used to that pain and it may become a less permanent and daily part of our lives.

For us and our own lives, which are of course of central importance to us, central to us as individuals, whatever the generality and inevitability of death in human life, this death of another, is happening to us, and while we may love other people, at these moments, the fact that such experiences happen to others and have happened to countless others, is likely to be of no or little meaning to us. Our feelings are likely to be so intense that we will be significantly lost in our own feelings. Where we are experiencing feelings of grief, hopelessness and despair, these cannot be easily cast aside or easily turned away, nor is it at all desirable that they should. While it may make us feel better to remember the positives and wonderfulness of the person we have lost, and this is worth doing, indeed a healthy and worthwhile thing to do, we will for the most part still feel grief-stricken, and such thoughts can intensify our pain, though of course we will have such thoughts and we will remember anyway.

Thus, our understanding and acknowledgement of the inevitability of death is not likely to provide any significant alleviation of our own pain. There is often no solution at that moment. We will probably have to endure, carry on, and in time, if we can, we will need to get used to the way things have become and are going to be. We may find a sense of relief and healing of our pains through meeting others who have suffered as we have, through our progressive adjustment to our new reality, through our focusing on new things to do in many forms, setting new goals in our lives, such as helping others, taking up new pastimes and activities, and our pain may dissipate to some extent through the passage of time, as our memories of our loved one are to some extent interrupted by new memories. Grieving is fine and necessary for some time – indeed we may to some extent grieve forever, but debilitating and self-destructive grief needs to be removed if it continues to continuously damage our own lives and the well-being and happiness of others.

Having someone to talk to, to express our grief to, can often be of great importance in helping us to cope with the grief and pain of such loss, especially in the case where the person who has died has been very close to us. The presence of a close friend, the presence of close family to support us in such emotionally troubling times is of great value. At these times, it is important where possible, for family and friends to gather around those of us who are suffering in such pain and grief and give support, hopefully receiving support ourselves in our own grief and suffering. Our giving of practical and emotional support should both serve to help those of us stricken by grief and sadness at the death of a loved one and help us all cope with our own individual pains and sorrows. Our support for others should also help us see value in ourselves through the love and support we are providing to another and through the love and care we are receiving from others, and our coming together will strengthen our sense of family and community, and will strengthen our sense of shared humanity and togetherness. Where we have no one close to, to turn to, in our grief, then we need to seek help from those who are available to give it, either through professional help or from those who will volunteer to help in supporting someone who is suffering intense grief.

In the time around our loss and beyond, we remain with a responsibility, as much as we can manage it in our state of grief, shock, sadness, suffering, pain and undoubtedly sometimes agony, to try to maintain our own well-being and reduce the pain that we are suffering and enduring, as well as acting to support those around us in coping with their pain. For those of us suffering from the pain of bereavement or loss, while feeling, acknowledging and expressing our sense of grief and loss, we must still try to support others who need support and help. We must support our close family and others affected and hurt. We will inevitably focus to some degree and perhaps to a very large degree, dependent on our own relationship with the person who has died, on our own grief and pain, but to focus exclusively on our own pain is likely to be damaging to us, and damaging to all, and possibly self-destructive (though we may feel self-destructive or ambivalent about self-destruction in these and other times). Others still need us.

If we are women who have lost our partners, our lovers, our husbands, or men who have lost our partners, wives, lovers, then, where there are children, in particular young children, our children will need caring for, talking to, as will close friends and others. If we have lost a close friend, then we will have deep grief and pain but will need to try as best we can to support our friend's family and others in grief. Through acting in that way, our friendship and love will in a sense be continuing and we will be doing our duty by our friend, doing as they would wish us to have done.

In times of such pain and loss, we all need to support each other; our conduct will need to be considerate, caring and as sensitive as we can make it. This should be done while not disregarding our own feelings, indeed knowing their importance and being prepared to talk about them, while also showing high levels of consideration and care for others and their feelings. We are bound (in the sense of required) to look after each other, to care for each other and do so with intelligence, wisdom and as much sensitivity as we can muster.

For those of us less connected to those who are suffering such intense grief, those of us who are around those who are suffering pain and grief in these ways, we must also be supportive, caring and sensitive, looking after family, friends and acquaintances, treating them with sensitivity, love and care. It is essential under such circumstances that, even though we may be less directly connected to those suffering grief, we are careful to avoid being overly focused on our own feelings, and that we are willing to accept the love of others who feel they wish to support us and help us, should we need support ourselves. Indeed, in an important way, through allowing others to help and support us, we are helping them and also helping ourselves.

All of this supportive and other conduct is of course compatible with and consistent with core and other principles of supporting others and ourselves, and supporting the reduction of pain and suffering in the world. Yet, at the time, of course, we are unlikely to be explicitly and consciously motivated by such principles, but most likely will be acting in line with our deep-seated nature as caring, compassionate human beings, who understand, love, empathise and sympathise with the pain of others, because we are people who love, care for and are concerned for the happiness and well-being of others, these elements of our nature and humanity, being embodied in these core principles.

While it may seem hard to believe, the pain that we feel when someone we care for and love dies, reflects our fulfilled lives and the wonderful value of the person, the wonderful value of the life which has been lost. Our grief tells us of how much love we had, how much we cared, how much we were loved by that person, and how valuable the person who has died was to us and to others. In the moments and period around their death, thinking of that person is almost certain to make us sad and sorrowful because they have gone. Our remembering them will remind us of our grief and loss.

The only way to avoid such grief in life is never to have loved – to never have loved a partner – to never have loved a child, a parent, a relative, a friend. None of would surely want or set out to have such a life. And while there may be exceptional ones of us who live lives without such love, without such friendship (comprising almost no one), if we are one of this tiny number of people, we will know and understand in that case that our lives are not likely to have benefited from having that love absent in our lives. Such loveless lives may be capable of being lived, but they are not our desire or goal, since such a life would be, almost by definition, a life lacking in important elements of happiness and well-being. In many ways, our grief at loss comes from having loved deeply, having known the best of partners, lovers and friends, having had the joy of our children, and this grief not only demonstrates the well-being, fulfillment and happiness we have had in our own lives, but most likely demonstrates the love, well-being, happiness and pleasure we have given to our loved ones.

Particularly painful is the death of a child. To lose a baby or a young child, someone who we had so many hopes for, someone who was to be such an important person in our lives, someone we had dreamed of holding, loving, caring for, mothering and fathering, hugging, looking after and being with through infancy, childhood and beyond, is grief-causing and shattering for those of us who are parents, brothers, sisters, grandparents, friends and all involved. Such a death of a child is an immense and numbing blow with little to temper the emotional pain, apart from perhaps the hope of having another child, which may well be far from the forefront of our minds at such an immensely tragic time.

Others of us are particularly needed to give support when a baby or a child dies. There may be times when life seems so pointless for those of us struck by such a tragedy. And it is the death of a baby or a child which does count as tragedy. There are probably no words here that could express the pain or provide comfort to someone who has had such an experience. The older child will at least have had the opportunity to live life and have some experiences but that will also be little consolation. That older child will have had a chance to live and their full potential for living a full life will have been visible to all. For them to die at such a young age is certainly an awful tragedy.

All the rest of us can do is to love and support those who have suffered such a loss, be around to be with them, to talk to them, to look after them as best we can. That is all we can do – and while the pain and the severe pain of grief at such a loss is likely to be long-lasting, maybe those people experiencing such a loss will hopefully somehow be able to carry on and gain some further joy and purpose from their lives, bringing up their new or other children, finding other directions in life, fulfilling their responsibilities to family and others if they can. However, the pain of parents who have endured such experience will likely never completely go away.

Of course, as we grow older, not only do we grow closer to death ourselves, but we are also more likely to have experienced the deaths of those around us, including deaths of friends and family. Our age does not inure us from feeling the pain of bereavement and loss ourselves, when our close family or closest friends die. We are likely to experience the same amount and level of grief, sometimes more grief, particularly where our children die before we do. Nevertheless, with age comes a greater familiarity with death and perhaps a greater understanding for us of what death entails in the family, community and beyond. And it may breed in some of us more of a resignation to the fact of death, to which, given its universality, it is a reasonable thing, indeed a certainty to expect around us at some point in time, and a reasonable thing for us to be, to some extent, resigned to, inevitably occurring at some point for others and for ourselves, at least with our current states of knowledge and understanding.

Some deaths will be long and drawn out. There may be a significant time before death when we, or the ones we love, when the person who is ill, has been informed that within a certain period they are likely to die. The expectation and knowledge of our anticipated death or the anticipated death of another may help us cope with that death, with our feeling more prepared for such a death. But the absence of someone who we have loved can still be as hurtful and painful even though we have had time to prepare for losing them. Nevertheless, one of the benefits of such a drawn out process of dying is that there are ample opportunities for reflection together, for final experiences together, for heartfelt exchanges of feelings, of appreciation, of goodbyes to those for whom we care or caring expressions from those we love. And the preparedness for death is likely to mean that positive steps can be taken to relieve the physical and emotional pains of our own dying, where such pain is anticipated, so that those we love may well be able to better cope once we have died.

Once a reasonable period of time has passed, through our grieving, we need to ensure that our grief does not act in an overly destructive manner in our lives, causing us pain which prevents us from living on and living on as well as we can. In a while, we should hopefully be able to start and should start, aiming to find moments of pleasure and joy in our lives again, which does not mean forgetting the one or ones we love, but will hopefully mean taking pleasures and joys from their memory and continuing to love them and hold them close in our hearts. Those we have loved will have wanted us to continue our lives and to live happily, full and complete lives, after they have gone. Which of us does not want that for those we truly love? And so we have a responsibility in terms of the core and other principles set out in this guide, in terms of supporting the well-being and happiness of others and in terms of supporting the memory and self of those who have died, to keep on living as far as we can with well-being and happiness.

Having emphasised the grief we are likely to experience at the deaths of those we know and love, while we will frequently experience such grief when those we know and love die, it is perhaps not the case that we all or will always feel such tremendous grief at someone's death. Our feelings may be influenced by the fact, for example, that those who are aged have lived their lives and had the opportunity to live their lives to the full, enjoying the full experiences that life has to offer. We, their family members, their partners, their friends, may reasonably anticipate their deaths in the near future and may well reflect that they have had almost all they can have, or that could have been had, in their long lives, their lives being more of something to celebrate and be thankful for, which perhaps any life should be. With those who are very elderly, knowing that they are in their later years and are more likely to die soon, on their deaths, while sad at our loss and missing them as we will, we may also be in a position to more greatly appreciate and indeed celebrate the lives they have lived, their achievements, the richness and wealth of their lives, however sad we might feel, however grief-stricken we may be. We know that they could not have lived for so much longer and we know that they had so much in their lives, as much as perhaps could be wanted and more.

Further, there are those who have been suffering with illness and pain for a prolonged period. If we are suffering in such a manner with no prospect of recovery, then we may wish to die and die soon. We, as those who love a person in such a state of pain and agony, may see their suffering and agony at first hand. And as a consequence, when they die, there may be a sense of relief that they no longer have to suffer in such pain, their dying in a sense being a merciful release not just for them, but for those of us who have to witness their pain, their agony, their suffering and more than that their own awareness of their incapacity and suffering, with their appreciating they have no prospect of relief aside from death. Under such circumstances it is indeed totally acceptable for us to help them to escape this pain and agony.

In particular, in the modern age and in more wealthy countries, unfortunately, as we reach our later years we may start to lose, to one degree or another, important elements of our mental faculties, such as our abilities to remember the past, even the ability to recognise others who we have known for many years, including our children; we may be constantly confused, lose our capacity to communicate with others, as well as losing to some degree our physical abilities to look after ourselves. In more extreme, though not in an insignificant number of cases, tragically, suffering from currently identified conditions such as the already mentioned Alzheimer's disease or other disabling conditions, we might become, in essence, a shell of the person we once were, with daily physical needs we are unable to meet without close assistance, unable to communicate in any meaningful way with others, perhaps unable to move beyond our bed or a small number of rooms, largely unable to contribute to others, just in a sense existing and surviving until we die.

Despite how we may appear to others in such severe states, we will hopefully, to some degree, still be able to enjoy, experience, and have some pleasures without too much pain and suffering in our lives. In such a state we can hopefully still enjoy the sunlight and the summer, perhaps the sounds of a garden, of music, and more. As helpers and carers, as family, as others, we need to ensure, as far as we can, the pleasures, joy and happiness of those who are ill in such ways, providing them, wherever possible, with care and love, stimulation, pleasure and happiness. Nevertheless, when someone in such a condition dies, we may not feel the same sense of grief, since in an important sense the person we knew, who may no longer know or recognise us or indeed be sure who they are, had in a sense already left us, and if they were suffering we may indeed feel relief due to the ending of their suffering, and indeed in terms of our own pain in seeing someone who we love and loved in such a situation.

Beyond these groups of people whom we have loved and who we will miss terribly when they die, there are those who, to say the least, we will miss much less if at all. There are those who have been truly evil, malevolent and negatively, destructively selfish in their lives; those who have done the greatest damage and caused the greatest pain to others, never expressing regret, sorrow and sadness for the pain they have caused and never atoning, wishing to atone or being able to atone for their destructive actions. Realistically, we are not likely to suffer pain from or mourn too greatly their dying, however much we wish to care and love all others.

Indeed, with regard to such people, we will often be glad they have gone. Those genocidal murderers who have organised the killings of thousands if not millions of others are not likely to be grieved for by the many of us who have suffered or whose families, friends and others have suffered at their hands, though sadly some, such as the collaborators in their crimes and those misled by their murderous and evil actions, may grieve. Those who have committed murder will not be likely to be mourned by those known to their victims or the rest of our community. Total regret, total change in their nature and attitude, and the performance of positive deeds to support others may mean that they may not be despised forever, and indeed that they may be seen in a more positive light and even possibly forgiven by some, as the new person and better person they have become. Their families may still grieve for them, though perhaps may not given their destructive deeds. Whatever the new person they have become, many others will understandably not do so.

If we love and care for people, if we appreciate them and admire them, who they are, how they are, if we admire their capabilities and achievements, then in line with core and other principles, we should tell them so when they are alive, when they are with us rather than saying little or nothing until after they are dead. Apart from the needs within core and other principles to support the happiness and well-being of all others, apart from the fact that we enjoy being loved and appreciated, factors which clearly support the necessity of expressing our love, admiration and appreciation of others, the fact that we recognise that there are things we have the opportunity to say to those who are involved in a long drawn out journey through illness to death, and our similar regrets in some cases about not saying things to those who have died suddenly, should all indicate to us that, rather than waiting, now may be the time to explicitly state and show our appreciation and love to those we love and care for. Death sometimes strikes unexpectedly and it is surely better to let others know of our love and appreciation of them and let them enjoy our appreciation now, while we and they are alive.

Thus it is essential to tell people, to let them know that we love, respect, admire, appreciate and care for them, that they are important to us, and more than just telling them once, it is important to tell them so regularly such that they do not forget and can carry our love, appreciation, respect and care with them. Friends should be well aware that they are loved, valued and appreciated – we must let them know – not take it for granted that they know. This should of course benefit our friendship relationship on the moment as well as serving to support their and our own happiness and well-being. The form in which such love, appreciation and friendship should be communicated is down to us and may not necessarily involve explicit statement, but often should do so, in order to remove doubt, worry and uncertainty, indeed to remove possible fear, all of which are encouraged by more implicit, unspoken communication, unclear signals, or indeed lack of communication.

Of course, at least in the modern age and undoubtedly into the future, with our current state and likely state of knowledge and understanding into that future, we will all be sure to experience death ourselves, with death arriving in the range of different ways for each of us. As already mentioned, knowing that death is coming to us, and indeed in some cases that death is coming soon, may be difficult to cope with, causing us emotional stresses and problems as well as the physical pain and suffering which frequently accompanies our move towards dying. As stated already above, emotionally and psychologically, it is most likely best to be accepting of the inevitability of our death, though that does not mean we will not do all we can to live on. We will all have our turn, our time to die, hopefully after a long, happy, fulfilled and productive life full of well-being and fulfillment.

The fact that our lives will end is, of course, known to us all the time, but in the passing of our ordinary days, through much of our lives, such thoughts are not likely to be ones that most of us are concerned with through those days or that we will reflect on significantly, focused as we tend to be, on more direct and immediate concerns and tasks. Yet in the background of our minds, the thought of our mortality may perhaps be useful to carry with us in some form every day, however difficult a thought this might be, not to serve as a source of fear and worry, but to serve as a motivator for living life to the full, with the length of our futures always being to some extent uncertain.

For many of us it is the case that, following the death of someone close to us, we find ourselves refocusing our lives and perhaps changing our lives in important ways, as the effect, the shock of this death can often make us much more aware of our own finite nature, and the need to seek our deeper and deepest, our most meaningful goals and achievements with haste, before we in turn, fall out of the world.

Nevertheless, despite the fact that we know of its inevitability, coming close to death, becoming aware of our impending death, being diagnosed with a final illness ourselves, if we have time to consider this, it may still come to many of us as a shock, whatever our previous rational beliefs, preparation and efforts to accommodate ourselves to our finite nature. Even having considered and thought about the inevitability of our deaths, the fact that we will no longer be around can be, and perhaps is likely to be, at least for some, if not many of us, upsetting, comprising a source of stress, pain and emotional suffering.

For the many of us, the painful knowledge that we will no longer be around to love our children, our parents, our friends, our families, to do the everyday things that we do, that we will no longer be able to see the sun rise in the morning, enjoy the warmth of the sun on a summer's day, enjoy the heat of the dry season, enjoy the cold breath of winter, perhaps enjoy the rain, see the snow on the ground, enjoy the taste of life in its richness of experience, that we will never hear the beauty of music, hear everyday sounds, or see the colours of the flowers and of the day, have the pleasure of talking to our friends, playing or watching our sports, all of this can be difficult to come to terms with, though of course for others of us there may be an easy and even perhaps smiling acceptance of death's inevitability. Indeed, and fortunately so, on our journey towards death, if we have the opportunity, there may, in a sense, be a good sadness to be experienced in remembering, reflecting on, appreciating the life we have lived, the things we have achieved, the loves we have known, the journeys we have taken, the things we have done, the places we have been, the joys and sorrows we have experienced.

But in the main we will likely have to cope with death for ourselves and others. And for the many of us, the intense emotional pain and sorrow associated with our own death and the deaths of others, is difficult to avoid. And with our own death, there will be not only the loss of our own lives, but in most cases, there will be the loss and pain experienced by others who will miss us, who will have a gap in their lives because we are not there. And yet they will and must carry on. Even if we feel no particular anxiety at our own coming death then we still need to be concerned for those who might feel our loss terribly.

Nevertheless, our own emotional response to the news of our impending death may still be one of profound upset, even without consideration of the physical pain that we may endure along the way to our deaths, pain which may become so intense that death itself can become a desired relief from painful suffering. Yet, as mentioned, for some of us, the knowledge of coming death and the idea of dying itself may not bring such emotional pain. If we acknowledge and keep with us the knowledge that death is inevitable and will come to us, rather than experiencing enduring shock and pain, for some of us, the idea of our death may be more simple to cope with in principle, in concept, with our passage to death representing another one of life's journeys, yet on this occasion to its end.

For those of us who can and feel more easily able to cope emotionally with the idea of death, it is likely that the difficulties and challenges arising through the physical pain that may be experienced on the journey to our death, the growing demise of our physical and intellectual faculties, is the more worrying and concerning thing that we may have to face and cope with. In some cases we may wish to arrange, if we can, that we should die before we are in the throes of agonising pain, and before we are intellectually and physically disabled by our illnesses of age.

Having mentioned the pains of a long drawn out death, the end of our journey to death may not in some cases be painful for us. Our death can be sudden and unexpected with no time for preparation or thought; can occur as a result of accident, an unexpected and immediately fatal fault in our bodies, through a heart attack or other biological fault. For us, those of us experiencing the moment of death, it may simply involve our existence stopping suddenly, with our having no awareness of our departure from the world, with us as individuals no longer there, no longer able to feel or experience anything.

There are those who talk of death as if it is about the experience of nothingness but this is most likely far from the truth. The reality of our own experience of death is likely to be that our death involves not being there to experience, not existing to experience anything, there being no entity, no 'us' left to think and sense, no us existing to experience, to feel. To be dead really means that we, as a sentient, feeling, conscious being, are no longer there to have any experience, to feel anything. We are simply no more as a person. This does mean that there can be no pain and suffering for us since we no longer exist. We have no longer physical senses to experience anything and no functioning mind remains to make sense of that experience. If we have been experiencing pain and suffering, indeed agony, it will not longer be there, because we are no longer there to experience it and feel it.

If we are involved in a disease and illness-driven, long drawn out journey to death, with accompanying pain and agony, there is of course nothing enjoyable and admirable in such pain, in such repetitive, intense, extreme and extraordinary physical and perhaps psychological pain and misery. Of course there are medical and possibly psychological and other means for reducing pain, which it is, of course, more than reasonable to use to alleviate such agony, in most if not all cases of such physical pain. The core and other principles presented in this guide, as has been stated before, do not advocate the experiencing of pain and suffering, and certainly argue against the endurance of pain at such intense levels especially where there is no prospect of recovery.

If we can, we would no doubt all wish to avoid such an intensely painful, if not excruciating, long drawn out journey to death. The long-term experience of extreme and ongoing pain, agonising pain, which in itself is painful for those who love us (and others) to see us enduring, which keeps us confined to our beds, which presents us doing the most simple things, which humiliates us in terms of our loss of independent humanity, which keeps us confined to a hospital or bed, with little or no hope of recovery, is something to be avoided wherever possible. Hopefully, our pain and suffering can be alleviated to make hours and days tolerable, yet with no prospect of recovery, such pains and agonies can be very difficult if not impossible to tolerate.

Bearing in mind the core principle of reducing and alleviating pain and suffering both for ourselves and for others in the world, if such physical pain can be significantly reduced, that is all for the good. Unfortunately where there is such pain and it cannot be alleviated, then in some cases we may be forced to bear that pain until that pain disappears or we disappear ourselves. Fortunately our modern world has the capacity, and a growing capacity to alleviate the pains of physical suffering, though there is clearly a long way to go in this regard. Particularly, research is needed and progress is needed in order that our pain in such circumstances can be relieved more effectively and so that more of us can have access to the most effective pain relief.

If we can gain additional days to perceive, to see those we love, then that may be good, but there are depths of pain and indeed humiliation (as we may become unable to look after ourselves in basic ways) which may be intolerable or almost intolerable to us, and as a consequence, if we are in such a situation heading in agony towards our death, with no hope of respite or recovery, we may desire to escape our situation and meet our inevitable end at an earlier point, such that we can escape the intense physical and psychological pains we are enduring or even perhaps that we are certain to endure in the imminent future.

In circumstances where there is a negative, fatal prognosis and we are experiencing agonising pain which is almost beyond endurance or beyond endurance, then it is only right that we may choose to, or should be able and allowed to, take steps to end our lives at an earlier point or, if we are incapable ourselves, that we should be able to place responsibility in the hands of others for ending our lives earlier than would otherwise be the case. Within core and other principles, each of us needs to have well-being and we need to avoid and reduce the suffering of others and ourselves. And where there is no realistic prospect of recovery and where what remains to us is largely an almost guaranteed and almost intolerable, or intolerable, pain and suffering, where even our moments with those we love are distracted by our endurance and experience of intense physical pain if not agony, it has to be considered legitimate if we wish to and choose to end our excruciating suffering as soon as we can.

While life is of tremendous importance and we are of tremendous importance as individuals, to ourselves and in important senses to the community and world around us, the balance under such circumstances shifts towards our own more personal experiences, needs, wants and feelings and towards the removal of the excruciating suffering and pain we are enduring. In such a situation, we may no longer wish to avoid death, may no longer be concerned about or fear death, but instead may reasonably see death as a way of escaping such excruciating and insoluble pain. There is service and decency, and indeed it is consistent with core principles that in the face of our intense pain and suffering, close to the point of our death, in others being able to help us in achieving such an escape in as painless a manner as possible. And in a sense that supports not just our own well-being, but our society's well-being. It cannot be supporting another to allow them to suffer excruciating pain which can never be sufficiently relieved, which they do not wish to continue enduring, in circumstances where there is no real and reasonable prospect of recovery.

There are many possible scenarios that are relevant here with regard to seeking help to end our lives early under such circumstances, but there is not enough space here to discuss all of these, with all their individual ins and outs, pros and cons and controversies. Indeed each case is likely to be individual. But the point here is that the principle is established that we as individuals have that significant and substantial if not entire rights over our own bodies, that we have our own experiences and feelings, and that society and community, that humanity as a whole should accept those rights, which incorporate all of us exercising that choice to die early under such circumstances, within the terms set out through the core principles, in which the well-being, interests and concerns of ourselves as individuals are emphasised and prioritised.

Allowing the decision in such trying, near death circumstances, to remain with us as individuals, lies within the framework of core and other principles since we are justified in supporting and have a responsibility to support our own well-being while we are alive, and because the arguments about social harm, harm to others, arising from specific action taken to end our lives early in such circumstances, are weak, and entail our individual experience of intense suffering, pain and agony.

The range of weak arguments presented against allowing us as individuals to take this kind of action under such circumstances of agony, pain and impending death, the arguments made against our ability to take such action in relation to hastening the end of our lives, tend to relate to the well-being of society. For example there are arguments put forward along the lines that allowing us to engage in suicide or assisted suicide in such circumstances might devalue the notion and critical importance of life within society as a whole, taking us down a slippery slope where life becomes less valued and cheapened.

This slippery slope argument is seen here as, and often is, a weak one. There is no reasonable evidence and reason to suggest that there would be such a slippery slope. There would undoubtedly be efforts in places to abuse such a system of assisted suicide, yet that is not the same as widespread and systematic misuse of such systems. What is right and correct is right and correct. If there were a slippery slope, it is those actions down the slope which need to be tackled, not those actions which continue our intense and excruciating suffering and pain. Such an argument is seen here as likely to be founded in irrational fear of the unknown, rather than a realistic assessment of that which will occur, since a properly regulated and overseen system would function effectively, though with undoubtedly some highly controversial cases, with some malevolently acting individuals, at some point, certain to try to take advantage of such a system, and indeed on occasion some bad occurrences. Yet overall the consequence of enabling us to decide our own means of and time of dying in such near death circumstances would be overwhelmingly positive.

Many of the belief systems which argue that suicide and assisted suicide under such circumstances is morally wrong and damaging, possess a faith-based belief that suffering is important in life and even desirable. The view in this guide is that while some suffering and pain are perhaps inevitable in life, they are certainly not desirable and we should be pursuing well-being and happiness, and certainly not allowing and enabling suffering and pain. While the notion of the slippery slope is worth listening to, given the concerns it raises, there does not seem to be sufficient validity in these arguments to warrant a rejection of our right to remove our own significantly unrelievable, intense and extreme pain and agony through preventing us from engaging in assisted or indeed unassisted suicide under such dire circumstances.

It is argued here therefore that within the frame of the core principles, in the context of the intense pain, agony and suffering of those on the road, close to death in circumstances where pain and suffering cannot be substantially alleviated, where there is no or little reasonable prospect of cure and remission, and where the individual concerned has expressed a wish, or wishes to escape life earlier than they otherwise would were events to proceed without medical intervention to end life early, these circumstances change the balance of the ordinary and essential valuing and respect for the continuance of life, to one where the quality of life as determined by the experiencer of that life, becomes of greatest importance. And in this respect the right of the individual to remove themselves from such a physically extremely painful existence, an existence of agony, with no or little prospect of recovery, asserts itself to the extent that such a departure from life, at the wish of the person experiencing this agony and pain, needs to be allowed for, needs to be permissible, needs to be supported and assisted in its implementation. This is seen as entirely consistent with core and other principles.

As has already been stated above, suicide is in the vast generality contrary to the principles established in this guide, denying ourselves happiness, well-being and the full life that we could lead if those problems creating what are likely to be temporary personal psychological and other crises could be resolved, and also denying society and others the benefit of the contributions we can make, through living and caring for others, through contributions we can make in our ordinary lives to others and to our society. In almost all cases suicide causes significant damage, perhaps sometimes almost irreparable damage to those around the person who has committed this act, causing suffering, a sense of helplessness and potentially despair and ongoing hopelessness in those who loved that person. The damage of suicide spreads, can spread wider too, demoralising the many and hurting not only individuals close to the those of us committing suicide, but the wider community and society as well. However in those cases where we are at the end of our lives, suffering in intense pain and agony which cannot be significantly relieved, and where recovery is not in any way likely, then seeking to end our lives and seeking help to do so must be legitimate and allowable.

Additional to those of us who may be in pain and suffering in the final stages of our lives and who wish to die earlier than otherwise would be the case, there are those who, prior to reaching such a state, suffering with disabling, debilitating and progressive neural illnesses, wish to give consent that at a certain point in their lives, when they have become unable to think, unable to move to any substantial degree, unable to look after themselves in any meaningful way, that at this point they should be helped to die. Others may be anguished by the recognition of their moving to a situation where they have all of these characteristics, while others being almost entirely or entirely physically debilitated, remain able to think and remain fully aware of their almost total incapacity to move, speak and act.

It is understandable to feel anguish and pain under these types of circumstances and for some of us, faced with such a prospect, we may want to plan an end to our suffering and pain through preparing for what we know is likely to come in our lives, and in some cases we will wish to prepare to end our lives at the appropriate time. Envisioning ourselves as a potentially mindless, unthinking burden to others, or perhaps a thinking and aware burden to others, destined to lay in a bed, a hospital bed, unable to clean ourselves, unable to contribute to or enjoy the world, unable to do perhaps anything, perhaps our being connected to wires and tubes to keep us alive, yet with no realistic prospect of improvement in health and indeed the prospect of death, or perhaps worse, persistent and terrible pain, with our still remaining in that state for years until death finally comes; envisioning ourselves in this way would reasonably motivate some of us in these circumstances to wish to provide permission to those with responsibility and with the power to do so, to enable us to end our lives early, or to seek to end our own lives before we are too badly damaged by our illness and condition or when we have entered such states of inability, pain and suffering.

It is difficult to argue with those who are ill in such ways who would wish to make such a judgment. Arguments in regard to advances in science and technology, the prospects of cures will seem trivial to those in these circumstances who appreciate the often likely reality that such advances and cures will be a long time coming and will have no likely effect on their circumstances and end.

While it could also be argued that those of us in these debilitating circumstances might serve a social purpose in allowing family and society to engage in looking after us in our damaged state, our being objects for the important responsibility of care by others, it seems wrong in terms of core and other principles to let an individual person live in such pain and leave them to serve such a passive, victim role when that is a role they do not wish for. Similarly, it seems wrong to let that person who is suffering be simply such an object of care when they do not wish to be cared for as such and indeed may well wish others to get on with and enjoy their lives to the full. Allowing someone bearing such pain and suffering to live simply as an object for others to care about would be denying that suffering person their core individual humanity, undermining important principles of individuality, individual responsibility and individual autonomy which accord with core and other principles, such ignoring of our core humanity being damaging to those of us as individuals making the request for the potential to end our lives early.

These debates are perhaps complex, but perhaps are quite simple in terms of core and other principles, since it seems most reasonable that we as individuals should be able to make our own decisions about our own lives and our own bodies under such circumstances and that we should be able, within a regulated and monitored system, under advice from professional medical experts, to seek to end our lives early, where necessary with the assistance of others. While many of us might not make such a decision, hoping for a cure for our illness or hoping that we might somehow recover, it seems also reasonable that others of us should not be making such a decision for such people given the genuine and real lack of likelihood of a cure or a return to good health.

Since this discussion is rather dark in mood and tone, and while it is acknowledged that our lives are likely to contain some suffering and pain, it is worth reiterating and reminding ourselves at this moment, of the wellbeing, the everyday pleasures, as well as the fantastic joys that our lives can bring. There are multitudes of moments of pleasure, happiness, humour, laughter, smiles, peace and tranquility, passion, love, adventure, excitement and laughter, even ecstasy at times. And when we are in moments of pain or even despair, it is likely, for the most of us, that some of these positive moments will be waiting for us at some point in our future lives, hopefully, perhaps, just around the corner. All of this is the pleasure, joy, fun and experience of life and while we are in pain or suffering, our knowledge of the pleasures, fulfillment, of happiness, love and joy and their prospect in the future, will hopefully help to sustain us.

Of course, all of us will age and this will bring notable changes in our later lives. While aging may bring many positives, with our current state of medical and other knowledge, as already mentioned, at some point it is certain to involve physical deterioration (though perhaps our thinking can also improve). Our physical deterioration is likely to affect our speed of movement as well as our ability to move, our awareness of our environment. Our eyesight is likely to decline. We are likely to lose physical strength and have reduced sexual capacities. In our older years, we are likely to find our hearing does not work as well as it used to, and we may be prone to, and suffer from, a range of illnesses and conditions associated with aging. Additionally, while our aging and our level of experiences will hopefully increase our skills at decision making, our knowledge and understanding of the world and help us further enjoy well-being, at some point, for many though perhaps not necessarily all of us, eventually, we may also experience some level of mental deterioration, which should it occur, will undoubtedly affect our capacity for well-being and pleasure as well as potentially causing us suffering and pain,

Whatever physical deteriorations may come our way, as we age into our later years, we need to work to maintain and even improve our physical well-being as far as we can, through activity and exercise. Not only do such activities support our physical health they are highly likely to support our personal mental health and overall social well-being and happiness, in particular as our exercise and fitness activities will help us to maintain our social lives, our engagement with friends and our remaining active within our communities, helping and supporting others even in our old age.

Of course, our communities and societies also need to support engagement of those who of us who are aging and elderly. Indeed, this is a responsibility for each of us to support and adopt ourselves, as individuals, whether young or old, as well as it being the role of each individual and those of us with relevant responsibility within our communities and societies, be they family, friends, or those paid by the community and society, to support those who are elderly and ill or less able. Thinking, discussing, talking, enjoying, meeting, being entertained, but more importantly being active ourselves, doing, participating, investigating, entertaining, researching and exploring, amongst many other things, need to be constant companions in our lives, in order to help us through life, to ensure our continuing physical fitness, pleasures, fulfillment and joys, in supporting our own well-being, and supporting our health.

These activities also serve us in terms of enabling us to find pleasure and fulfillment using avenues through which we are able to support others in the community and beyond, both when we are elderly ourselves and when we are young and supporting the elderly. When young we may not simply be helping those who are older and in some cases somewhat infirm, but learning about helping and caring. It is also possible we will learn from those of us who are elderly, learn about lives and history experienced, that history being something which has led to and which affects and influences our own lives.

But in our older years, social activities and social engagement activities are also likely to play a significant part in maintaining our mental health and our mental capacities. Perhaps more importantly, we can still be supported in our personal growth and development, through gaining thinking and other skills and capacities, through aiming to acquire specialist knowledge and understandings which the young and younger may not have the opportunity to develop. Those of us who are older and elderly have much to contribute and through acting to support the promotion of our own growth and development when in our later years, we will be able to contribute even more to others, our families, our communities and societies.

Whatever our age, we need to take responsibility for and ensure that we are contributing to our communities, societies and to our broader humanity. While in many modern societies it is considered and is indeed law, that there is an age at which we should or sometimes must retire from formal and paid work, as individuals if we can, we should continue to contribute to others, to our communities, societies and beyond. Our contributions are needed and we will have much to offer. We may wish to continue and indeed continue in our paid work roles, making major contributions in business, politics, law, and other important areas. We may be of assistance in helping our children and grandchildren; we may contribute in managerial or individual support and volunteering roles in community groups, charitable organisations, local councils and more, bringing our breadth of knowledge and experience to bear.

Of course as we age further and deeper, our ability to contribute may be affected by our physical afflictions. Moreover, our mental health has the potential to deteriorate with our aging, with, as already mentioned, some of us suffering significant mental deterioration into our much older years. To counter such deterioration, as far as possible, we need to maintain not only our social activities and interactions but also our mental activities, our thinking activities of all relevant kinds from mathematical, spatial and language-based activities to the already mentioned social and indeed sporting activities, in order to help maintain our mental health but also to support our overall well-being and happiness. Engaging in personal and social projects, participating with others of all ages, starting new relationships and continuing the relationships in our lives will serve to support our mental well-being and happiness.

Unfortunately, mental illness and mental deterioration can affect some of us who are elderly to a very severe degree with certain conditions related to mental deterioration such as the mentioned Alzheimer's disease afflicting the elderly in particular. Hopefully with increasing knowledge and understanding of how our body works, how our mind works, and how it sometimes declines, with increasing investment in research and the development of new medical treatments, we may be able to remedy some of these damaging conditions. Suffice to say, and it is of course consistent with core principles, that as far as possible we should engage in total care for those with such mental deterioration and other disabilities, just as we would aim to care for anyone else. It is our responsibility as individuals as community, as society, as humanity, to value and care for all others, which of course includes those who are mentally ill or disabled in whatever respects.

Amongst those of us who are aging, being aware and becoming aware of such physical and mental deterioration may be painful, and may mean our suffering, in some cases to a significant extent, although those of us whose mental deterioration is substantial may perhaps lose some awareness of our situation and condition. If aware, and it seems likely there will often be at least some awareness, then the pain experienced perhaps through possible direct physical pain but also through the realisation of our being in such a condition may be substantial. Doing our best as individuals to avoid as far as we can such deterioration is a necessity. And doing our best as individuals, communities and societies to help all those who are aging and in need, is our responsibility.

Whatever age we are, within core and other principles, those who cannot walk, the aged and all others, need to be helped to walk; those who cannot look after themselves, need to be looked after, those who cannot give themselves basic care due to physical conditions or mental illness, need to provided with such basic care or helped to care for themselves, and those who suffer with mental illness, depression and unhappiness need to be supported, provided with medical care and treatments, and need to be loved through their depression and unhappiness. Wherever possible and practical, we all need to be helpers of others, and if we are in need of help with our health, then we need to be helped as far as is possible, to a more healthy state.

The current discussion has mainly given mention to some of the negative physical and mental effects of aging. However, we should be aware that as we age, we will be developing our knowledge, skills and abilities and will be doing so hopefully into our old age, a period wherein we may have more time and opportunity to learn and develop in some ways. Elsewhere in this guide it has been stated that education and learning are, and should be, continuous. The fact is that we can learn and learn, and learn, and hopefully grow and grow and grow. For many of us, the best we do, some of the highest goals we achieve, the greatest excitements and joys, may be achieved in our later lives, when we are older or elderly. It may be best and indeed reasonable to think and believe that as we grow older the greatest pleasures, happiness and achievement may well lie ahead of us.

Yet, after aging, or sometimes at a younger age, the end of our lives will come to us. It is important for us to realise that while we may be on the road to death and in the end dead ourselves, when we are dead, we do in an important sense 'live on'. We live on through our effect and influence on others through the deeds we have done in our lives, through the effects and influence on others of all the actions we have taken for the good and for the bad, through our influence and effects on the people we know and knew, our communities, societies and our broader humanity. Whoever we are, we will have influenced and had likely significant effects on at least some others, and effects on the world around us.

In our families, if we have had children, then we will have had primary responsibility for bringing up our children who will hopefully contribute much to the world in the future, including perhaps through having their own children and who may then have their own children and so on through the generations. How we have brought up our children, the values, the attitudes, behaviours, skills and knowledge that have stemmed from us, which our children have learnt from us, will pass down the generations, not only through our children but through the other people we have met and influenced and the people our children and children's children will influence.

And of course, particularly for many of us in the modern world, we are likely to have influenced very many others, as well as our communities and societies, and also our broader humanity, through our living and working lives. For example, if have been a teacher, we may have communicated not only the mandated educational content of our programmes to our students, which will hopefully have advanced their lives, but we will hopefully have exemplified and communicated positive and caring values and behaviours to those students as well, which again will affect others in society who those students come into contact with and provide values and behaviours which may be passed down the generations. We will hopefully have helped our pupils and students towards their careers and supported our students on the road to their own successful lives.

The numbers of us influenced and affected by a single teacher, to different extents, may well be into the thousands, with subsidiary effects echoing through from those children to others. The head teacher, the principal in charge of the school, may have influenced tens of thousands of children through their lives, and again influenced many more through the ongoing effects of their actions on those children as those children become adults and deal with thousands of others and have children and families themselves.

Beyond the example of teaching, the range of other work-based contexts and professions also illustrate the effects we can have through our working lives. The architect, though often unseen and unknown to the many of us, will have produced ordinary buildings or perhaps extraordinary buildings, which may have proved to be the homes for tens, hundreds, if not thousands of us, enhancing our lives through giving an environment which is supportive of work and home life. Our offices and workplaces will frequently have been conceived and designed by architects. The life of the architect will, like the teacher, have touched thousands if not tens of thousands or more, considering all those who may have seen or used their buildings or other constructions.

If we are a plumber, we will have installed, maintained and repaired the pipe work, toilets, the water systems transporting water into, around and outside of our homes, and through our work we will have supported health and cleanliness in countless lives, while if our work is as an electrician, then we will have installed, maintained and repaired the lights which enable thousands of others, if not many more than that, to function in the night; we will have installed, maintained, and repaired the cookers and stoves which enable us to cook, and the electrical systems which enable us to use computers in the home, the electrical systems which enable us to manufacture goods in our factories, and which enable us to have warmth and heat in both our homes and places of work amongst a vast range of other useful functions. Without each of us making some such contributions there will be at the minimum discomfort and more likely, much pain and suffering. Each of our contributions matters.

In other ways, our contributions through our work tasks pass through the generations, with the teacher's educational approach, additional to the effects mentioned in direct regard to children, also influencing other teachers who observe, collaborate with and follow them in their profession. Of course the architect is likely to teach and train and have a role in developing other architects with their own individual expertise, knowledge and understanding and their own learning from practice and indeed from knowledge of potential pitfalls and mistakes being passed on to others. The same is true for the plumber, electrician, farmer, software engineer, builder, pensions advisor, road cleaner, waste disposal operative, taxi driver, waiter, tax inspector, clerical officer, HR employee, actor, shop assistant, doctor, veterinary assistant and so on. We all make contributions and have influences through our work tasks that, aside from benefiting us and others directly while we do our job, can pass our knowledge, understanding and expertise into the future.

These are just some examples of how through the skills and jobs that we have, we, the many of us in our modern communities and societies, produce effects and influences on thousands if not tens of thousands of people whose well-being and happiness will hopefully be improved through our contributions through our lives, with the effects and influences of our actions and words passing on down the generations. And in that sense we continue to live on after our deaths.

And beyond our work contexts, beyond the influence and effects we may have through our children, we can have effects and influence through the many other ways in which we have supported others. For example, by helping our friends and others through the difficult times in their lives, we will be demonstrating care for our friends and others, and through the reports of how we conducted ourselves and what we did, we will hopefully be promoting good, caring conduct and values. And of course by supporting others through our various personal actions, through our social and political beliefs, through our charitable giving and donations, we may have had effects in our lives far afield from our own lives, perhaps, for example, through supporting the provision of clean water for those who previously did not have access to safe water supplies, changing the lives of these others and thereby supporting a vast chain of positive effects based on what we, as an individual, have done.

Through supporting charities and research, we may have made one of many contributions which, when taken together, in the end, are likely to result in our human society's improved capacity to treat conditions and illnesses that were previously deadly, be they cancers, heart disease, malaria or other illnesses. Alternatively, we may be supporting those in poverty such that they can live on and do good in the world. And even through simply paying our taxes as we should, we will have supported health care, hopefully defence, civil safety and much more, all of which should contribute to the well-being and happiness of others, and the well-being of our communities, societies and beyond. And the effects of our taking such actions and making such contributions will, as with other actions, pass down the generations.

A small number of us, as individuals, working with others, may make enormous contributions to our communities, society, to humanity, through highly significant contributions, with our influencing thinking and ideas, through creating major positive changes in human lives in the world, for example, through enhancing cooperation and peace in the world using our skills of negotiation, through discoveries in science, through improving systems of management, through improving medical care, through developing new technologies. Others may develop new political philosophies, enable us to better understand the workings of economies such that we can better provide for all, develop insights into the human mind, develop new perspectives on social living, history and politics. And again these achievements and actions will echo through the years.

Of course, if we have behaved badly, acted in ways contrary to core and other principles, committed acts of violence, engaged in cheating, bullying, fraud, theft, corruption, sexual abuse and other destructive acts, then the effects of these actions will sadly also be passed on and have influence and effects, both during our lives and after we have died. The legacy of such misconduct, the damage to community and society are likely to pass on through the generations to some extent. And this indicates and emphasises the importance of ensuring we conduct ourselves well in the now.

So after death we live on, clearly not in the form of a living breathing present organism, but in the form of the our living breathing communities and societies, through the world we have helped to make, in the form of the people we have helped to bring into this world, in the deeds we have done, in the conduct we have shown. We will be remembered by some, by name, through time, but through the years after we have gone, for the most of us it is the influences and consequences of how we lived, of what we said and did, which provide the form in which we are most likely to continue to live on.

There is little good in death, but it is necessary to mention that the death of others can in some cases be positive in changing our lives and motivating us to search in new directions for well-being fulfillment and happiness. As has been briefly referred to already in this chapter, the loss of a loved one, following our grief and mourning, can make us re-evaluate who we are, what we want from life, what we are living for, and how well we are living our lives. Death can remind us of how little time we have left to achieve our goals and to reach our dreams and lead to us changing direction, changing our life strategies and hurrying advisedly, expeditiously, to achieve the things which are really important to us.

We may decide to take up the goals and objectives of someone we know who has died, and do our utmost to make sure that their dreams and goals are fulfilled, thus enabling positive, worthwhile and constructive goals to be achieved. Further, the death of another produces a time when we may reconnect with others, with family, those who we may not have seen for a long long time, hopefully rekindling the bonds of love, friendship, togetherness and family. That of course is not an objective, but a consequence of those who love someone coming together to share mutual grief and sadness, and to support each other.

After someone we know and love has died, it is important that we who are left, celebrate their lives, that we commemorate our loved one together, that we share our experiences of them, celebrate the life they lived, the things they did, the joy and laughter they brought, the love and care they gave, all they achieved, how they were. At our funeral or other coming togethers following the death of a loved one or someone known to us, we who knew the person concerned individually, closely, need the opportunity to tell others about our love of that person, their friendship, their deeds, their connection to us, about the person who has died, to tell stories about them – the moments shared – the adventures had – the feelings, the good times together and the bad. Our sharing in this way and remembering in this way will serve to some extent to ease our pain, in particular the pain of those who were closest to the one who died.

Nevertheless, of course, such occasions can be profoundly upsetting for those who have lost those closest to them. Hopefully such occasions will also be cathartic to some degree. Yet these are also important family and community occasions both for those who have lost loved ones, and for the rest of us in our communities and societies, as we can come together and show our support and love for those suffering in grief and sorrow, as well as recognising and remembering the value and importance to us of the one who has died.

Unfortunately, as already mentioned, not everyone has lived a good life, and some people have aspects to them which may not have been pleasant. When we commemorate and celebrate a life, while these things are a matter of judgment in the circumstances and situations, and sensitivity needs to be shown to those who loved that person, it is probably most often worthwhile for us to broach these negatives where these are widely acknowledged, rather than giving a fantasy commemoration which may leave lasting and remembered unsatisfying feelings of falsehood and dishonesty. The good and not so good need to be dealt with if our feelings towards that dead person are to be properly addressed and if well-being is to be fully supported.

And so, where this is reasonable, and where there is perceived consensus in regard to the not so good, or the bad, dependent on the people and situation, we should consider mentioning important negative events, troubles, traumas and so forth associated with that person. Nevertheless, on occasions where we celebrate a life, significant controversy and argument are probably best put to one side in order that we can mourn without the distraction of anger and conflict. A proper goodbye is needed wherever possible, where we can mutually acknowledge and celebrate the life of someone we loved and cared for and come together as family, a community of people and friends to provide support and love for each other, especially those closest to the one who has died, remembering and appreciating in as full a truthfulness as is possible, the life of the person we have lost.

Consideration of death has comprised the final element of this chapter of the guide and our deaths, the deaths of others and how we cope with death comprise an important element in relation to physical and mental health. But this chapter has focused on a range of other areas in relation to our personal conduct and action in terms of health, happiness and well-being, considering how we can promote our physical and mental health and well-being and how we can deal with the threats to our health and well-being.

Embodying these purposes, the core and other principles require us to promote well-being in both ourselves and in all others, and also to promote the avoidance of pain and suffering wherever this is possible. There are many sources of pain and suffering; there are many ways in which our health and well-being can be threatened and a wide range of key issues in relation to personal conduct and health have been addressed in this chapter. These threats to our health and well-being need to be tackled and tackled effectively in order to support us in a life of health, happiness and well-being.

In particular, we need to ensure, as far as we can, that we and others, our communities, societies and beyond, work to maintain and improve our health, both physical and mental. We are certainly required to avoid and prevent suffering for ourselves and for others. And clearly, poor health is a source of pain and suffering and needs to be avoided in whatever ways it can be avoided.

During the one life that we know we have, we need to avoid and reduce our pain and suffering and the pain and suffering of all others, preserving our own health and well-being and supporting the health and well-being of others. And moreover, closely tied to this, we need to aim to live a life of well-being and happiness, a life which is enjoyable, fulfilling and as far as possible joyful and pleasurable, and we need to do our utmost to ensure that all others in our communities, societies and our broader humanity, all others in our wider world, enjoy the same.

# Fourteen

# Personal Conduct and the Non-Human World

In support of our well-being and happiness and the well-being and happiness of all others, we need to have care and concern for our non-human world, this referring to both our natural inanimate physical and our natural living and wildlife environments, this natural environment including in particular, for the purposes of this chapter, the whole range of living creatures within these environments.

Our concern with the natural physical world and the natural living world arises significantly on the grounds of our dependence on them for our survival and through the direct and obvious benefits to our well-being originating in those physical and natural living worlds. Quite obviously, in terms of our survival for example, our environment is the source of the air we breathe, the source of the water we drink and the food we eat. These and other component elements of our environment are clearly essential and integral to our existence, our survival and our well-being and happiness. We thus need to conduct ourselves in ways which support our natural and physical world such that we can retain the benefits and essentials that our environment provides us with, and such that we can support the well-being of both ourselves and others, as embodied in core and other principles. A lack of concern and inappropriate action in regard to our non-human natural and physical world threatens the existence of ourselves as individuals and our humanity.

Nevertheless our care and concern for our environment also arises because we are caring individuals and we are a caring humanity, our care extending to the living world and living creatures. Not only do we, or at least the many of us in this current world, see the animals and other organisms in our living world as being sources or potential sources of our food, but we correctly understand many living organisms as capable of experiencing pain and suffering, to a greater or lesser degree, in the same or in a similar manner that we ourselves experience pain and suffering as human beings. And similarly and reasonably there may also be good reason to understand many living organisms as capable of experiencing well-being.

As caring beings concerned with well-being, we would wish these living organisms to experience well-being where that is possible and we certainly do not wish those living organisms to endure undue and unnecessary pain and suffering. Therefore, as far as is reasonable and possible, given the realities of our human needs and the realities of the natural world, we need to act with care and concern for these living organisms, aiming to support the well-being of the animals, plants and other creatures with whom we share our world, this being in itself an important requirement of our personal conduct, as embodied and represented through the the sixth Additional Fundamental Principle.

Of course in regard to our non-human physical and biological environments, these are diverse, varying across our local and global environments, and in an important sense we appreciate, enjoy and we therefore have good reason to be concerned about these physical and biological environments which also contribute to our well-being. Not only do our physical environments comprise the sources of many essentials we need for our survival and well-being, but they also constitute the environments which the animals, plants and other organisms we share our world with inhabit and require for their existence. Yet more than this, in an important sense we, as human individuals, as communities and societies, become used to, embedded in and feel, in a sense, part of our physical environments, with our physical environments representing part of our sense of home and belonging, this providing a sense of and form of well-being. And since representing in this manner such a source of our well-being, again there is further substantial reason for us to be interested and concerned with and about the quality and nature of our physical environments.

Along with the vast diversity of our physical inanimate environments, vast diversity is also a feature of the microorganisms, plants and animals living in our natural worlds. In our modern world with its efficient systems of communication, we are almost all aware of such diversity, from the larger animals of the Serengeti plains, the lions, giraffes, buffalo and more, the desert camels of North Africa, the kangaroos and wombats of Australia, the pandas of China, the tigers of Northern India, to the smaller squirrels and badgers of England, and the guinea pigs, snakes and spiders of South America. There is vast diversity. There is vast and varying plant life, from the five thousand year old bristle cone pines of the USA to the desert cacti, to the daffodils and tulips found in temperate climates, the tropical orchids, the algae and other plant life in our vast oceans. And at the microscopic level, there are the viruses, bacteria and other microorganisms which may cause us illness, yet may also be crucial to our health and survival through, for example, their roles in our digestion and in our food chains. All of this vast diversity of creatures needs to be our concern.

And while our more local environments may be more immediate and salient to us, with our having greater awareness of these local environments, we need to be concerned not only about our more local physical environments (which includes those environments of our own making as well as those which are natural in their origins) and the life within those environments, but also those more global environments, our global environment as a whole, and the range of creatures living in those environments distant from us, whose lives and existence may well influence and affect us as individual humans, as communities, societies and as a broader humanity. This wide ranging concern involves, to an important extent, looking beyond the obviously more sentient creatures, beyond our concern for those other more obvious living, visible and motive creatures in our local and global environments, to maintain a concern for plant and other life (fungi, bacteria, viruses), important components of which may support our existence in one way or another, but which, dependent on the precise nature and characteristics of such organisms, at times, may also offer threats to our individual, community, and social, global existence.

As already mentioned, of crucial importance and relevance to our well-being, our human survival without serious contention and doubt, depends significantly on both our natural physical and natural biological environments. It is clearly essential that our environment is suitable for us to survive in, live in and enjoy. And just as clearly, as a consequence of this crucial role of our environment in our survival and well-being, lack of attention, recklessness and carelessness in regard to our physical and living environment, places ourselves and others at risk, providing the potential for substantial pain and suffering and severe damage to our well-being. These dangers apply to both our more current and more immediate generations, but equally and perhaps even more germane, given the sometimes slow but inevitable pace and consequences of much environmental change, these dangers pose a potential, if not likely threat to our future generations, threatening not only the quality of the lives that future generations will enjoy, but also the continued existence of such generations and therefore our humanity. In essence, care and concern for both our physical and natural environment is a necessity for our human survival.

In line with the core and other principles, it is therefore a matter of both self-interest for us as individuals as well as representing part of our concern and support for others, for us to engage in personal conduct which supports an appropriate and healthy, and also enjoyable environment for both our current and future generations. Thus, given our nature and interests as human beings, we must ensure an environment which is not only one which is fit (and more) for us and others to enjoy, live in and survive in, now and into the near future, but one which is fit for our future generations to live, enjoy and survive in.

Overlapping with these points, similarly and importantly, in line with core and other principles, we must ensure an environment which can contribute and indeed which contributes in a significant way, to our well-being, pleasure, enjoyment and happiness. Our environment, particularly our natural environment, is without doubt not only a source of physical sustenance, a source of necessary material resources to support our day-to-day survival, but is also a source of tremendous wonder, joy, beauty, pleasure and excitement for almost all, if not all of us, whether experienced directly or vicariously, providing wonder, joy and beauty which enhances our lives, and which forms an important part of our feelings of well-being and happiness. In support of our well-being and happiness therefore, we, as individuals, communities and societies need to ensure that we take care of our environment. This does not simply mean preserving the environment as it is, though that may be an element of our actions in some if not many instances, but it can certainly mean our acting to develop and improve our environment where that supports our well-being.

With regard to our general strategies, policies, specific decisions and actions in relation to our physical and natural environment, that does not mean that we should ignore other elements of our well-being and happiness and that our natural and other environments should never change. We will certainly need to make use of and change our natural and other environments to support our well-being in the range of ways as required by our situations, needs and through changing times

To take some obvious cases in point, changes in our environments will be needed because we need materials of various kinds to construct our homes for which quarrying and mining, the cutting down of trees, are all likely to be needed. We need to use fields, agricultural and other land to produce the food we require and our use of land for agricultural purposes will likely alter the patterns of land usage or require the conversion of land in its current, original or more natural state to agricultural land (and possibly sometimes vice versa). Our building of dams is most likely needed in some contexts to ensure we have adequate and clean supplies of water and in some cases to generate electricity. And of course this can involve the flooding and drowning of large areas of land, affecting plants and wildlife as well as the physical appearance of our land.

All of these activities and almost anything else we do and need to do, including doing nothing at all, will have environmental consequences. Yet while doing the things we need to do, and indeed have to do, it is essential that we take care of our environment and ensure that we do not cause irreparable substantial or destructive damage to that overall physical and biological environment and carefully consider the various balances and effects of our human activities on our more local environments. As individuals, communities and societies, we also need be sure that we are not adding small elements of local damage which add up to an environmental disaster for ourselves and for the natural world.

Where changes are needed in land usage or for other purposes, we need to be aware of, in particular, the biological consequences of our actions. Where we have the capacity and capability, and where it is reasonable (which should be on most if not almost all occasions), we need to compensate for those changes, for example where trees are destroyed, through growing trees elsewhere, or through moving or establishing wildlife colonies, appropriately supported, in different locations where that is realistic and possible. If such compensatory actions are not possible, then we will need to reconsider our proposed changes in land use.

The consequences of a damaged natural environment for all of us are not difficult to see. If we as individuals, communities and societies are careless with our natural environment, there will be severely damaging consequences for this environment and for us all in terms of our well-being and happiness.

If we pollute our rivers, lakes and streams, if we pollute our water supplies, with untreated waste, chemical and biological or even nuclear, we will be offering a direct threat to our human health through supporting conditions and processes which are highly likely to lead to the development of a range of diseases, illnesses and infections, and which will also create the possibility of direct poisoning in the case that such polluted waters are directly ingested, poisoning effects which may reveal themselves both in the short term or cumulatively over the medium and long term.

On top of this, in terms of the consequences when we pollute our water, there are direct and indirect effects on our health and well-being through, for example poisoning of the shellfish, fish and other water-living creatures many of us would wish to eat. Such pollution will destroy or poison the food that these fish and other organisms eat. Both of these consequences of water pollution run the risk of reducing or destroying our own food supplies thereby threatening and likely leading to food shortages, creating starvation. They also run the risk of poisoning us through our already referred to ingestion of poisoned fish and other water-borne food sources or through our consumption of other foods derived from this polluted water, poisoning us, damaging our health in the short term and longer term.

Moreover the environment around such polluted water sources, the air and land nearby is likely itself to become polluted, in some cases become unusable for crops, unusable for grazing, with animals needing to be kept away from such polluted waters such that they do not become victims of these poisoned water sources. And further, such waters will essentially become out of bounds for us, difficult or impossible to use as sources of leisure and pleasure, for swimming, boating and simply sitting by and enjoying, arising directly from the conditions of these waters or from odours and poisonous fumes arising from such waters, such a loss of leisure in itself being painful and damaging well-being.

Then, if we as individuals, our organisations, businesses, communities and societies generate substantial and damaging air pollution, then many thousands if not hundreds of thousands or millions of us may be damaged as a consequence, in severe cases through direct and immediate debilitating poisoning, but also and perhaps more usually through the immediate or longer term breathing and other problems which are highly likely to result from polluted air. If we allow our forms of transportation, our cars, lorries, planes and other forms of transport to create significant pollution; if our factories leak fumes and gases into the air we breathe, then we are all likely to suffer. If our agricultural or industrial, manufacturing, mining and other activities generate air pollution, then, similarly the quality of our breathed environment will be damaged and our health will be damaged as a consequence.

This type of air pollution is having damaging consequences at the moment of writing due to the gases and fumes emitted from our industries, our vehicles and other sources with many dying or suffering every day from this pollution. Yet remedies and appropriate measures are possible and can have substantial effect if we give these matters the priority they deserve.

As a case in point, such remedy and solution has already been tried and put into practice through the action that has been taken in many jurisdictions to combat the phenomenon of acid rain which damages plants and trees on a wide scale. Acid rain remains a problem, indeed a growing problem in some places and its effects are still measurable and observable even in jurisdictions where legislation and agreement to deal with its causes have been put in place and acid rain has been substantially reduced. But the implementation of regulation has certainly resulted in improvements in relation to acid rain deposition and hopefully, over time, in those jurisdictions in which such regulation has been applied, with some further action and further reduction in the production of acid rain generating pollutants, this will cease to be a problem.

That being said, in other irresponsible, often corrupt and unregulated jurisdictions, the problem of acid rain and other pollution may well be increasing, this failure to take action representing appalling negative selfishness and lack of concern in relation to their local and our global environment, sometimes by the population, more often by those in power. If we are in such jurisdictions, as individuals, it is our responsibility to ensure that action is taken in regard to acid rain and the production of other forms of air pollution such that this pollution is presented or much reduced.

The release of radioactive pollutants into the air, for example following nuclear incidents and accidents (such as that at Chernobyl in the 20th century) demonstrate the global nature and influence of much pollution and the manner in which we as individuals living on this planet must be interested and concerned about pollution beyond the jurisdictions within which we live. As with other forms of pollution, but particularly dangerously with regard to nuclear pollution, the Chernobyl incident led to radioactive pollutants being distributed around the globe by wind and atmospheric flows, providing a wide scale threat to the population of our planet, and offering a potential threat to our health and well-being. While it has been difficult to establish the precise effects of the nuclear pollution produced following the Chernobyl incident, and there have been accusations of efforts to cover up the true effects of this disaster, an estimate of approximately 9000 excess deaths as a consequence of the incident has been put forward.[6] Apart from the specific dangers of nuclear incidents, the incident in itself illustrates the fact that we all have an obligation both to ourselves and others to ensure that such air pollution either does not occur or is minimised such that there is no damage to our health or to our natural environment, such damage to this environment having significant consequences for our health.

Climate change, human or otherwise created, indeed any significant environmental change in regard to the warming of our planet, is likely to offer major threats to us as individuals and to our fellow humans, for example through associated rising sea levels and consequent loss of land for habitation and agriculture, through drought, floods, and other climatic consequences. And clearly we each as individuals, considering our own actions, but also acting through our various organisations, communities, societies and our broader humanity, need to ensure we are not contributing towards climate change, something which is damaging many at this point in time and which will damage us all into the future. We need to do all we can to ensure that we are prepared to act against and tackle the underlying causes of climate change as far as is possible and that we ensure, again as far as we can, that there are no human-made or other changes in the environment which might threaten our own personal well-being and health and the well-being and health of all others.

The core and other principles mean that it is necessary for us to protect ourselves from such threats and dangers. They also mean that not only do we need to protect ourselves, but we need to look after others who may face diminishing well-being and life-threatening situations in prospect or actually caused through damage to the environment in whatever form. Where we can, we are clearly obliged to take appropriate and early steps to remove causes of potential environmental damage into the future or act to prevent actual damage which may be occurring on the moment. We need

---

6   World Health Organisation Report – Health effects of the Chernobyl accident

to protect ourselves against environmental damage and the consequences of environmental damage which may either be occurring now, expected in the short or medium term or which may have significant impact at some distance into the future and affect our children and further future generations.

The interconnections between ourselves as human beings and our environment, further illustrate and highlight the need for us to ensure that we take care of our natural environment. It is clear that due to these interconnections between the environment and ourselves, because of the interconnections between us as humans and other living organisms, any significant level of damage to the environment in its various forms feeds back into our human lives in a vast number of ways.

Beyond the examples of pollution of air and water already given, our existence as part of a web of life in which we interact as a human species with other creatures in our world, in which we rely on other plant and animal life in order to sustain ourselves, means that many of those actions which damage these animals and plants will have a strong probability, in the short, medium or longer term, of damaging ourselves. Thus, we need a functioning and appropriate physical and natural environment where our fundamental needs are met by that environment, and where our interactions with our environment support our needs and support our well-being.

Of course, at the fundamental level of feeding ourselves, of nutrition, essential to our well-being, in the current world the majority of us feed on animals, and all of us feed on plants which themselves form part of our environment and which themselves require their own particular and appropriate environments for their own survival. Animals of course may feed off other animals and plant matter. Our plants when engaged in photosynthesis themselves require, sunlight, water and carbon-dioxide as well as minerals and other compounds and elements found in the environment, while when respiring, plants require water, oxygen and other factors. All of this is required for survival of these organisms.

And more than that, in addition to the positive factors required for growth and survival, certain other factors must be absent for animals and plants to be able to function, for example, the absence (or presence at miniscule harmless levels) of various biochemicals and chemicals damaging and toxic to these organisms.

---

and special health care programmes Report of the UN Chernobyl forum Expert Group "Health" p.106 April 2006

Even small environmental changes have the potential to damage animals and plants, resulting in destructive effects and likely damage all the way along the food chain. And at the top of the food chain, following a cascade of changes influencing the whole food chain, there is the possibility, if not likelihood, consequent on the nature of specific environmental changes, of ourselves being damaged, we humans being damaged, due to lack of food, pollutants in our food, lack of clean water, failure of agriculture, a polluted atmosphere, polluted waters, natural and other enviromental challenges and disasters, and the consequent absence, poisoning of, or destruction of the components which support our basic and essential needs.

Our modern science recognises not only the webs of connection between ourselves and animals, such as those between predators and prey, but it has developed a range of understandings in regard to the environment which we can all know of and share in. These include knowledge and understandings of key biological entities such as ecosystems, biological niches and other environmental concepts and entities where the balance of different species, animals, plants, fungal, bacteria and more, and the resources they require, needs to be maintained if any particular ecosystem is to sustain, with changes in one element of the ecosystem feeding through into all other parts of the system. Changes in these ecosystems can have far reaching effects.

Thus declines in levels of predators may well lead to increases in levels of prey which then may consume high levels of their own food sources (they may be, for example, predators themselves), possibly to a degree whereby these food sources themselves are depleted, with consequences not only for that organism but for other organisms feeding on that source, and additional consequent feedback effects on other organisms, their prey and predators again, and so on. Declines in levels of resources such as the range of food sources, water, microbial flora and plants, the presence of pollutants which damage components of the ecosystem and other factors, will have effects which can severely damage the whole ecosystem and the range of organisms within those often fragile ecosystems.

As a more specific example, relevant to the present day and affecting the lives of many of us in the current age, the absence of specific feeding plants may damage a population of pollinating bees which then, as a consequence, decline in numbers. These bees, in turn, do not engage in the pollination processes in respect of other plants, which they would normally do, or do so to a much lesser extent, and as a consequence there is the probability at some point of significantly less productive fruit-forming by plants and as a further consequence there is the risk of less food for us to eat. It is possible in such circumstances that it is we humans who, unaware of the consequences of our actions, are creating the initial destruction of feeding plants. It is widely believed currently, and there is evidence to support this, that certain insecticides or pesticides are damaging bee populations at the current moment and this may well be generating the declining numbers of bees we are observing, leading to consequential and detrimental effects.

In this and other cases, the evidence supporting the potential damage by such pesticides or insecticides, where this is sufficiently robust, or even where it offers reasonable evidence of such potential damage, needs to result in action such that bee populations, other life and our human selves are protected.

Where evidence is equivocal in regard to the effects of the chemicals and biochemicals we are using, then on the whole, though dependent on circumstances, it is, in the main, undoubtedly best to adopt a precautionary approach, limiting the use of or withdrawing from use those chemicals, pesticides, insecticides and other substances identified as plausibly damaging our environment, until their benign effects or minimal effects are more clearly demonstrated. Where there are damaging effects, then beyond immediate and more obviously detectable effects, there will almost undoubtedly be other effects involving damage to the web of life and food chains, as we see in the specific example of bee populations, due to the vast number of relationships and interconnections within that web of life.

Our role as individuals in terms of our personal conduct and personal action is to ensure, as best we can, that such damage does not occur. Should we work in companies and organisations which design and produce chemicals and biochemicals or other products; should we work in companies which are engaged in genetic engineering and other projects which might affect the environment, our food chains and web of life, then we need to ensure that our products are fully tried and tested and known to be safe for ourselves as humans and for our broader living environment before they are used.

As individuals we can, and most likely need to take action to ensure that our government and legislative organisations have effective safety and testing regimes in place, not leaving such testing and trialing to those with financial or other interests in the development and sale of potentially dangerous products. Through our individual actions and through working with others to ensure that our products, the products we use in society are safe for the environment and ourselves, we will be protecting ourselves and our humanity as well as the plants and wildlife on which we depend.

It is essential that, as shown through the range of examples available, we understand the link between the environment and our own survival and well-being, and the survival of other organisms and life as a whole. Examples of our human action resulting in changes and damage to the web of life, our actions having detrimental effects on our biological environment, are legion. Our overfishing provides an example whereby failing to gain sufficient information and failing to think in broad enough terms, and in a long-term manner, about the exploitative activities in which we are engaged, can damage and destroy the well-being of so many of us and can also damage the livelihoods and well-beings of those engaging in such overfishing. A foolish and short-sighted focus on short-term needs, immediate personal gain or short-term group gain has in this and other cases led to substantial risks and damage to livelihoods and well-being, giving rise to tensions between those engaged in fishing, due to scarce resources and potential substantial damage to oceanic ecosystems.

Clearly, this overfishing has led to the depletion of fish stocks in many seas such that certain fish are no longer available to be caught and eaten. Due to this depletion, significant steps have been required to be taken, through international and regional agreements, and hopefully are still being taken, to return the numbers of fish back to levels that existed previously. Fortunately there is evidence of some positive consequences starting to appear and sustainable fishing becoming viable again under intelligent management of these environmental and web-of-life systems.

As individuals in this type of case, we ourselves must not engage in such damaging short-termist negatively selfish actions with their consequent longer-term damage. We must not pursue our own personal and immediate gain at the expense of others and at the expense of the web of life and damage to our food chains. We also need to work with others to ensure that such damage does not occur, and work to ensure that those who wish to act with such short-term negatively-selfish focus are not able to engage in such approaches. We must further ensure that the environment, in regards to our need for food and other resources, retains a form or develops in form such that it can continually sustain, indeed more than sustain, our lives and the lives of others, not just today, but into the future.

The core and other principles mean of course that we are responsible as individuals, together with others, for the taking of action, to ensure that a safe and livable environment exists for all people wherever they may be. Our personal responsibility in regard to the environment is to ensure, as far as possible, that neither we or others, have to endure pain and suffering through incorrect decisions in relation to our environment, or through careless, negatively selfish, reckless or irresponsible attitudes to the environment, whether those decisions and attitudes stem from ourselves or from others. Thus we need to do our utmost to ensure that neither we or others engage in wrong and ill thought out decisions, or engage in careless, negatively selfish, reckless or irresponsible actions towards the environment, which result in pain and suffering for ourselves and others.

As individuals, in terms of our own actions, we have the power to act responsibly in regard to the environment in our own personal every day lives. As individuals we can also act in concert with others to support the environment, to look after our environment and indeed to protect and improve our environment. We have the power to influence others within our local spheres to be more consciously aware of the physical and living environment around us and to act to ensure an appropriate environment is maintained and improved where this is appropriate.

And we have our capacities, in alliance with others, or acting on our own, if we do not have substantial power of position ourselves, to influence those at regional, national and even more global levels such that they give the environment the prominence and importance it deserves. And if we do have substantial power and influence, we need to act to ensure that our environment is protected and remains capable of supporting our humanity as well as the plants and animals that inhabit our environment.

This needs to be done in line with core and other principles, with the goal of ensuring not only that the environment around us exists in such a condition that it maintains and sustains us, but that it also exists in a manner which supports our broader pleasure and fulfillment, something which we also need our environment to do. The individuals we influence, those who have substantial power and influence, (and also we, ourselves) need to take action to ensure that the global environment is an environment which can help us all survive, thrive and enjoy well-being.

Awareness of the environment and its condition, its fitness for helping us to survive and thrive is of course essential as we rely on our natural environment so much that 'rely on' almost seems an inadequate expression.

In an important sense, the environment is part of us, and in an important sense, we are integral to and part of, our environment. We ourselves, in reality, comprise a part of the biological, ecological and environmental systems in our world. Indeed, it may be the case that there is no or very little sense in which we can be meaningfully separated from those environments upon which we are dependent, and which, due to our powers as organised and powerful humanity, we can support, sustain, damage or destroy.

The food chain and interactive web of life has already been mentioned as central to our survival needs. We have seen the examples of our need for fish from the sea to eat (at least for those of us who eat fish) and the need for bees to engage in the process of pollination such that trees and plants will fruit and sustain, such pollination being of great importance for our human survival. But of course there are a vast range of other areas where our environment is crucial to us.

Water is crucial to our lives. We have a fundamental need for water taken from the environment, for drinking, for industry, for agriculture, for power generation, for manufacturing, washing and cleaning, cooking and much more, and therefore each of us needs to have access to sufficient and preferably copious supplies of clean and utilisable water to supply our individual needs.

But in a world where population is increasing and where there are increasing demands on all resources, we have to recognise and act on the possibility of depletion of our water resources, shortages in the supply and existence of sufficient water (and indeed other resources). At the minimum, as individuals, communities and societies, in particular those of us who have governmental, organisational and management responsibilities, we need to have an overview of the levels of water available, ensure our water and other resources are being supplied optimally and effectively (not wastefully), plan our future needs, plan our use of our water and other resources to ensure use is optimal and effective, and conduct other relevant actions in order to ensure that we all have access to the water we need or that optimally adequate water and more is available to support all of our needs.

As individuals, personally, we need at the minimum, acting in concert with others, including those who do not have adequate water supplies, to take responsibility for ensuring that those without clean water to drink and use for essential purposes, are helped to gain access to the water they need. We also need to ensure that they are able to make effective use of their water supplies. Where water may be unsuitable to drink for reasons of lack of cleanliness, it is our individual responsibility acting where necessary in alliance with others in our communities, societies and beyond, including those needing such clean water, to support the capacity to ensure that such water can be obtained and filtered or cleaned where necessary to make it drinkable.

In circumstances in which it is realistic to expect water shortages, wherever possible, in concert with those facing these situations, and together with others, we need to help those facing such shortages to cope with these situations by helping them to meet their water needs, helping them with water collection and storage for times of drought, promoting efficient water usage, or alternately by helping them to move, perhaps temporarily, to environments where these shortages will not arise. And we also need to ensure, as far as is possible, that those with adequate or abundant supplies of water do not misuse and abuse these supplies to the detriment of others, and ensure we support the sharing of this key resource where this is possible and necessary.

In line with the principles outlined in this guide, we need to use all of our resources as effectively as possible in support of well-being and such that all of us can be supported in our need for resources and no one is required to suffer through various lacks. This means that one of our responsibilities is to ensure that, consistent with core and other principles, amongst other key resources, our land, fundamental to the availability of a range of resources and itself a resource, is used as effectively as possible in order to support ourselves and others.

Clearly our land is crucial, amongst other things for our food supply, and therefore our well-being. If we as individuals and others do not have access to land or the produce of the land, then we run the risk of starvation and death. If land is the possession of a few who are negatively selfish and pursue their own avaricious gain at the expense of others, then there is likely to be pain and suffering on a wide scale, something which is entirely incompatible with core and other principles.

While it may be reasonable for us to have ownership and possession of land, our land needs to be considered as a community and social asset, a human asset, which must be used not only for our own personal benefit but also for the benefit of all. It must not be used solely for the growth of crops which support distant needs but leave a local population in poverty or starvation, when their local needs could be met through alternative use of that land. Our land can serve those more distant needs but local populations and indeed others should not be left facing poverty and starvation. Nor should our land be managed inefficiently and incompetently such that poverty and starvation arise as a consequence of this poor management. Land cannot be shared out equally to all if the consequence is likely to be, or if there is significant risk of low food production, increased poverty and starvation, yet nor should any individuals or groups be able to possess and use land in a manner which damages others. Fairness in land distribution is important, but must primarily support the individual and general well-being and support our effective communities, societies and beyond.

Thus, in terms of food supply, we need to recognise that there are other factors beyond the amount of land used for food production and amount of food produced which influence whether all of us will receive the food we want and need. These factors are derived from and tie in to how our communities, societies and our broader humanity, food and economic systems are organised, our individual and societal belief systems, accessibility of food sources, transport and distribution of food, accessibility of funds for investment, means and capacities for tackling agricultural disease, availability of storage and preservation capacities, social policies and more.

Our communities, societies and our broader global humanity, supported by our own energies and efforts, certainly need to be organised in a manner such we all have access to the food and water resources that we need for survival and, hopefully, we will have access to more than those levels to a degree and extent which will support our broader and substantial well-being, happiness and enjoyment. Nevertheless due to our essential human needs, within the context of the core and other principles, we do need to use our land in the most effective ways possible to support us as individuals, our communities and societies as well as others more globally.

Beyond our need for our environment (and our land) to be used as a resource essential for food production and survival, our needs include the aesthetic, the need for personal space, and the need for recreational and work-space amongst other important functions necessary for our well-being. Therefore, the fact that we need our land to be used as effectively as possible, does not mean that every inch of available land should be used for agricultural processes, even though this use is a reasonable priority.

Further, there are, in addition, in relation to our land use, considerations of biological habitats, local and broader ecosystems, our consideration of those animal and plant inhabitants of the environment whom we wish to thrive and certainly do not wish to drive to extinction. And, moreover, there is our own enjoyment of the environment in its full sense, as well as our need for us to have land use for our homes to live in, and for factories, offices, warehouses, and the rest, for us to work in. Of course this argues against an over-emphasis on the use of land for agriculture and food production. In addition to ourselves and our individual, community and social needs, beyond the avoidance of extinction of animals and plants, in line with Additional Fundamental Principle six, we also need to ensure that there is substantial and sufficient land available such that the range of animals, plants and other organisms inhabiting our environment can live and survive well, in their natural habitats.

Beyond food and water, there are inanimate resources that we require from our environment, inanimate resources which are not inexhaustible. And therefore we need to ensure that we use these with care in relation to their long-term supply and long-term availability. We need metals, minerals, various elements and compounds derived from the earth, which are essential to our lives in this modern age and which will assuredly be required into the future. We need them for a vast range of uses whether they comprise essential elements in bricks and buildings, electronics, everyday tools, clothing, or whether they are needed to support systems of transport and energy production, amongst a vast range of other uses.

Without such resources and their extraction from the ground, our worlds, our personal lives would be substantially worse, far less comfortable in nature, with our well-being substantially reduced and our potential development and security for the future reduced. We need such resources to support us in developing better futures and indeed, we need these resources to be available to act as resources in these better futures. Yet the fact that resources are finite and sometimes scarce, if not increasingly scarce means that we need to continually show care and pay intelligent, considered and calculated concern for our use of materials, as individuals, as organisations, as communities, as societies and globally. We need to gain knowledge and awareness of the levels of resources available and plan their allocation and use such that our well-being is supported into the future.

As a consequence, ensuring appropriate, efficient and indeed also fair levels of use, of such resources (fairness implying a reasonable degree of equality) is of great importance together with recycling and reuse of materials wherever reasonable and possible, such that those materials used can be returned to the chain of usage rather than being disposed of into the ground, sea or air, never to be seen in productive use again.

Many materials can be recycled including metals, paper, fabrics and more, and each of us needs to ensure that we are contributing to this recycling of resources and materials, thereby reducing the levels of requirement for extraction of finite resources and ensuring that these resources and materials are kept in circulation. Wherever we use resources, we need to consider and indeed, ensure, that we design our processes and usage such that, wherever possible, we can recycle and recover our materials then reuse them to the maximal level possible and reasonable.

As an example in relation to our finite resources, in the current and modern world, oil is a key resource providing us with power and energy as well as serving as a raw material for the manufacture of a vast range of products. We need oil and other sources of energy; indeed we need access to energy, whatever the source, for all of us to live a life of well-being, comfort and indeed to support our happiness. In the current age, our energy sources provide us with heat in our homes and workplaces when we are cold. They provide us with light when its dark, providing cooling when it is hot, are required for our transport, for medical procedures, to power our tools and machines, to support our manufacturing and our leisure, to support our communications, in essence to support the vast range of activities we undertake in our modern lives. Undoubtedly we will need to use energy for the range of purposes, some currently unthought of, into the future. And therefore, our power and energy sources are essential parts of our modern lives and modern complex societies.

Yet clearly the oil stored in the earth cannot last forever, and indeed its use on the scale that it is processed, burned or used in other ways at the current time, is having and will have further detrimental and destructive effects on our environment, with a major and particular concern that we know of being the production of $CO_2$ as a product of oil burning and the burning of other fossil fuels, since this is contributing to global warming and damaging climate change. Crucially, given its finite supply and the real dangers of global warming from $CO_2$ emissions, there is a need for planning and research to ensure that there are additional subsequent and alternative forms of power and energy available to replace this oil before this resource is finally depleted, though given the consequences of oil extraction and utilisation in terms of environmental pollution, including the mentioned and well-evidenced occurrence and consequences of global warming, it seems imperative that there is a vast and rapid reduction in the use of this source of energy and of other fossil fuels, or that other measures are taken to reduce the damaging effects of burning these fuels.

We already have many alternatives and more sustainable forms of energy available, including solar power, wind power, geothermal, hydroelectric and tidal power, though some argue, and this may well be the case, that these do not currently, and indeed will not and cannot provide sufficient energy to meet our needs. There is nuclear power, which can provide us with very high levels of energy, yet it is argued to be highly expensive and dangerous in the extreme through its potential for deadly pollution through accidentally released or otherwise radioactive emissions.

New, safer and more effective ways of providing us with the energy we require will most likely need to be developed into the future, and clearly it is critical that our communities, societies and global organisations, with our personal, community and social support, pursue investment and research in this area, committing substantial resources to such efforts. Clearly, both now and in the future, there needs to be substantial forward planning in terms of our requirements for energy and we, as individuals, through our participation in decision-making, through our individual and social influence, need to ensure that such planning and preparation is taking place, and that such planning serves each of as individuals, our communities, societies and the world more globally, rather than the needs of particular interest groups, such as those with ownership and control of fossil fuel resources and those who perceive they will profit from maintaining the unsustainable status quo.

In our modern world, there are still many who would wish to use energy for their various personal purposes but yet do not have access to the energy resources, supplies and power distribution networks they need. There are those who live in the cold but do not have the energy to keep them warm. There are those who could benefit from the power and energy needed to pump, filter and clean water. There are those who live at times in stifling heat who could benefit from air conditioning and cooling. There are those who would like to build, but lack the power for their building equipment, for lifting heavy loads. There are those who could benefit from the protection, safety and convenience of electric light but do not have power and energy through lack of generators and connection to power and energy networks, or whose communities lack the presence of power sources, power stations and other facilities capable of generating, carrying and transmitting the energy and electricity they need.

Not all energy needs may be able to be met practically, at least in the short term. However we all need to make efforts to ensure that none (including ourselves) suffer significant pain and discomfort from the cold, that none of us lack clean water or spend inordinate time in the day carrying water unnecessarily, due to absence of pipe work and water pumps. We need to ensure that none of us are unable to access appropriate medical support through absence of power and energy, such lacks perhaps meaning the absence of medical centres, hospitals and medical care. We need to ensure that there is energy and energy supply and energy access such that we can all, should we wish, enjoy light in the night-time, and such that we can further, all enjoy the range of pleasure and leisure activities which depend on power and energy. As far as possible we need to do our utmost to ensure that power and energy is available to support the many energy supported functions which can enhance and improve the quality of our lives and our well-being.

All of this is not to say that there are not many important things we can enjoy without the use of such sources of energy. We need to make sure, as far as we can, that the means of accessing energy sources and the level of energy available is tailored to our particular social purposes and the particular desires, purposes and locations of energy users. Amongst other things we need to recognise that the production of power and energy is bound to cause, in some form, some level of environmental effect and possibly damage, as also will the means of distributing this energy, at least with current technologies available. Wherever we are supporting energy generation and supply, we need to act to minimise the environmental damage caused to both the physical and living environment, and act in a manner optimal to supporting our own well-being, the well-being of others as well as supporting our non-human environment.

The need for access to the range of resources we wish for and require, something which represents a vast range of resources in our modern technological world, in itself places pressures on our physical and biological environment. Having already discussed our need to have energy for various functions in our lives, we have to recognise that there is a need for a balance to be struck between our acquiring and utilising the resources we need and the sustaining, maintaining and development of our natural physical and biological environment.

Our environment is perhaps our most valuable resource, not only serving as a source of aesthetic pleasure, beauty, adventure and excitement, but also as already mentioned, the source of the commodities and other elements required for our survival and for a life of well-being. Our environment acts as a biological resource, through its sourcing and supply of the oxygen needed for our survival, that oxygen being generated by microorganisms, algae, plants and trees, as well as other organisms found in the biological environment. Moreover our environment acts as a source for developing our knowledge of understanding of life and the interactions between living organisms. The destruction of plants of all kinds, the rain forests, temperate forests, desertification of arable land and much more is likely to upset and damage the delicate biological balance which sustains our existence. Clearly action needs to be taken globally to ensure that our human survival is supported. Thus there are overwhelming reasons for local and global action to support and sustain our physical and biological environment and for avoiding significant damage to that environment.

While we must take care to, at the minimum, sustain our environments, nevertheless that does not mean that we should have an aversive fear of, or even a significant disinclination towards, generating modified or new environments, as these themselves may produce their own environmental benefits. For example, the building of dams to improve water supply or energy production, thereby providing substantial benefits to well-being, while clearly removing land for agriculture and destroying some habitats, also creates new environments. The creation of the dam in itself may produce new, useful and pleasant environments for wildlife, birds, plants and other animal life, and at the same time it may create environments where leisure can be enjoyed in many different ways, from fishing to sailing.

And beyond dams, we can also, through intelligent action and design, create new and beautiful environments, gardens, urban parks, roof gardens, new forests and woodland, which serve to provide new sources of pleasure and well-being, themselves supporting and sustaining wildlife.

Through effective forestry and other land and ecological management we can encourage a diversity of plant and animal life. And through use of new and developed technologies we can enrich soils and land to enable plants to grow where they otherwise would not, to some extent in some cases, enhancing our environment but also making our food supplies more secure.

Our wind farms and windmills, used to generate power and energy, change our environments too. There are some who argue that wind farms and wind turbines are aesthetically unpleasant and should not be built on land. Yet such wind power generates clean energy which can keep the elderly warm, keep our houses lit and warm, this being done in a sustainable and inexpensive manner when compared to other sources of energy. Others argue that these wind farms are, on the contrary aesthetically pleasing additions to the environment.

Working around these arguments, alternatively of course, our wind farms can be built out at sea. However, unless the countryside is made to overflow with wind farms and windmills it seems that wind farms and windmills will produce little damage to our enjoyment of the environment, perhaps to some extent adding some interest and adding to that enjoyment, while providing inexpensive and more sustainable energy which does substantially less damage to our environment compared to other energy sources.

That being said, this guide does not intend to provide detailed arguments and solutions on each individual environmental question that we face or may face in the future, but proposes that we must act in a manner which overall, is based in evidence and which, to the greatest extent possible, supports the well-being of all and prevents significant suffering and pain. In the case of wind farms, the view that these damage the aesthetics of our environment is an element of this argument, as is providing energy as a resource in itself, and providing energy which is clean. Clearly in times where energy supplies are short, then it would seem unconscionable in terms of core and other principles, to allow people to die of cold or to forego emergency hospital treatment because of aesthetic objections to wind turbines. But where there are reasonable, efficient and affordable alternative sources of energy available then aesthetics can clearly play a part in the debate on energy sources.

Our extraction of resources from the land and sea needs, in the vast main, to be accompanied by our returning of the location from which those resources were gathered, as far as is possible, to their original state or to a very similar state such that it appears as it originally did, and also supports plant and animal life as it did prior to the resource extraction. Alternatively that environment, where appropriate, might be modified to become a new environment which supports new and different plant and animal life, new leisure activities, which is a location of fun, adventure and pleasure, and which is enjoyable, clean, and aesthetically pleasing.

This type of land modification, recovery and reuse is also required in many cases for reasons of health and safety with damaged environmental sites being sources of many health hazards in terms of chemical wastes, natural wastes and physical threats. It is unacceptable to leave physical dangers (for example open mine shafts), poisoned landscapes, poisonous and deadly chemicals polluting our land, killing wildlife and plants and threatening our food chain and water supplies and thence threatening the health of our human and other animal and plant populations. This is entirely contrary to core and other principles. In essence and summary, both as individuals and through our social organisations, our businesses, our governmental organisations and other entities, whoever we are, whatever form of organisation we are, where we create a mess it is our responsibility to clear up that mess ourselves, be it locally in our own immediate environment or beyond that local environment.

Beyond its provision of our fundamental and essential needs, our physical and biological environment is something which is, in important other senses, necessary to our well-being. Indeed our environment represents something to be enjoyed, with that word being used in the broadest sense, incorporating its role and use for leisure and pleasure activities but also its wonderful aesthetics, the wondrous sights and experiences that our environment can present us with, sometimes moving us deeply through its immensity and extent, its variety and ferocity, its complexity, colours and shades, its shapes, its gloriousness and wonder.

Sometimes, if not frequently, our biological and physical environments are necessary to us and enjoyed by us in a manner which is foreign to the nature of terms such as use and exploitation, with such terms providing a cold and overly distant and rationalistic sense of our human relationship with our environment, of which in fact we are, as already stated, an integral part. Thus, in fact, the environment in which we live comprises not just a physical and biological environment describable in cold and technical terms, but also represents a familiar home with which we, as humans, in reality have an emotional and psychological bond and attachment. Our familiarity with, closeness to and our bond with our environment as our home, as something which is a part of us, and that we are a part of, may serve to provide us with a sense of psychological and emotional well-being and belonging, arousing in us to some degree a sense of reassurance and a desire and perhaps need inside us for its protection and preservation. In a similar manner, we may well feel importantly bound to both our local and more global world around us, perceiving it as our home both in terms of its physical characteristics and their familiarity as well as on account of its nature as a place where our fellow creatures can live their lives and where we would wish them to continue living free from the harm which we as human beings might do to them, or indeed which natural changes can visit upon them.

Such attachment to our environment and particular environments can occur whether or not we have personal and direct experience of a particular environment in our immediate lives. As human beings we are well able to experience and come to know our various planetary environments vicariously without direct personal contact and experience. Thus the jungles of the world, the rain forests, the deserts of Mongolia, the hills, the vast plains of Africa, the mountains of the Himalayas or the Alps, the temperate forests of Europe and Northern America, the vast rivers of South America and the waterfalls of Victoria, Niagara and more, as well as the ice sheets of the Antarctic and Arctic and the vast oceans of the world, for the many of us, along with the life in these environments, all form part of our experience and part of our known environment, comprising elements of our environment to which many of us will have some feeling of attachment, despite the fact that we have never been physically present within them.

Through our different forms of experience of these places, whether it be personally and practically through visits and travel, or more likely for the many places, through the medium of the written word, television, video and film, art and photography, we are able to enjoy the wondrous if not awe inspiring characteristics of our planets various environmental wonders. And through our experiences of these places, the vast and towering mountain ranges, the beauty of our forests and their wildlife, the vast empty and silent plateaus and deep oceans, such wonders of nature, often entirely different from that which any of us could have seen in our own neighbourhoods and back yards, we can develop and feel a bond, a need to protect such environments, such a protective and caring need, being part of our human selves.

Thus, many of us have attachments, if not deep attachments, to our environments, in particular our more local environments and frequently wish to preserve and keep them as they are. Yet despite our attachments, however, it is also a reality that our environments are ever changing and will certainly change to some extent, even if this is often over the longer term when natural influences act upon these environments. Our mountains suffer erosion; our forests suffer natural fires and then are, in a sense, born again; our trees and plants die, sometimes due to aging, sometimes due to environmental stress, and other trees and plants arise which take over a natural environment, sometimes through their better adaptation to the conditions present in that environment. And certainly an important and major source of change, our human exploitation of natural environments has led to and can lead to enormous changes, often damaging and destructive changes in those environments.

It is clear that we, as human beings, as individuals, communities and societies, as a broader humanity, particularly in the short-term, need to be able to, and often in practice are able to, adapt to changing and newly developing environments, at least within certain limits. We can cope at a greater or lesser capacity with changes in our environments from countryside to urban living; we can cope with changing technologies and changing work environments and work practices; we can cope with changing urban environments; we can cope with the changes in our seasons and to some small degree of changing climactic conditions.

If we are unable to adapt; if we are unable to change ourselves and our actions in response to the changes around us, our personal survival, our personal well-being, is likely to come under challenge, and in some cases, especially with regard to our adaptation to more significant changes, our personal, community, societal and human survival may well be jeopardised.

Given the fact that changes in our environment, social, physical and biological are almost guaranteed to occur at some point in time, even though some of these changes may be slow in occurring, we are likely to benefit from an expectation and anticipation of such environmental change, as well as predicting, managing, preparing and planning for such change. If we do not, we run the risk of being overtaken by such changes, such that our adaptation to these developing and changing environments is not successful and as a consequence we endure substantial pain and suffering or possibly cease to survive.

For some of us, if not many of us, based in our attachment to our environments as homes, these representing contexts in which we have a sense of belonging, there can be amongst some an almost innate sense of conservatism in regard to environments, a conservatism which has the potential to stand in the way of important changes we need to make which may substantially benefit all of us, which will support our adaptation to changing conditions and environments, which will support our changing needs and thereby enable us to better survive and enjoy well-being. Our desire, or the desire of some or many, to avoid and prevent environmental change has to be recognised and appreciated, acknowledged in terms of that desire to look after and protect our environment, to protect our environmental context and home, though where adaptation and change are significantly beneficial overall, where they are required for our well-being and indeed for our survival, then such objections will have to be overcome.

That conservatism being acknowledged, in a broader sense in regard to our human behaviour, such conservatism, at least in the sense of an aversion to experiencing new environments is far from universal. As individuals, exemplifying our capacity to adapt, and illustrating what may be a desire and need for new environments, many people, particularly the young, may move from one country to another, from town to city. Sometimes those of us who move in such ways may have initial difficulties and sometimes potential longer term difficulties in managing or coping in what is a substantially new environment both in terms of its physical and social characteristics. Yet with some awareness of what life in another environment involves, with thought and preparation, with an awareness of our expectations and thinking about what is likely to happen in the new environment, with support from others, that person, indeed most of us who make such changes, will survive and some, if not many of us, will thrive. Indeed in terms of those environments we are often adventurers seeking out new environments both to advance our opportunities and well-being into the future as well simply in some cases looking for new experience, excitement and adventure.

Our human society has indeed, through history, gone through many changes, many of which have arisen out of our own invention, based in our human propensity for creativity and originality, and based in a desire to improve well-being. These changes have had significant effects on the physical and biological environment around us. The evidence suggests that we, as humans, moved historically from hunter-gatherer communities to mainly agricultural societies, from isolated or small village-based communities in the past, to the greater prominence of our modern significantly town and city-based existence. Our physical landscapes have changed vastly accompanying changes in agricultural patterns and processes, accompanying technological changes and other changes in our community and society with, in many contexts, our coming to see many modern agricultural landscapes as in some ways natural in origin when in fact the fields, the paddies, and other aspects of the land we see, displaced vast historic plains, woodlands, swamps, jungles and forests.

Nevertheless, as individuals, as communities and societies, we have survived, adapted and coped with these changes, even though some individuals and communities may have suffered substantially through what have been largely unplanned processes of change, sometimes, if not often, made with little concern for and little thought about the well-being of many individuals affected by these changes. Indeed for some individuals during certain periods of change there has reprehensibly been substantial harm done to them. In more recent centuries we know that there has been illicit and cruel appropriation of land, forcibly removing many people from their source of subsistence, and leading to vast unplanned shifts in population, in themselves leading to poverty and suffering. Such changes were unacceptable, callous and cruel at the time, and if such actions were applied to the modern world, then these consequences would be unacceptable in terms of core and other principles. Yet, of course, that is not to say that we should not pursue changes in some forms, simply that we must pursue changes which enhance our well-being and survival, taking care of each person and avoiding pain and suffering as far as is possible, to ourselves and others.

The changes we have introduced in our human environments have been the consequence of, and have also led to the consequence of, on the whole, significant increases in our capacity to generate the resources we need to support a life of well-being. Thus changes in agricultural patterns, which have changed our environments, have supported the more efficient production of food, and these changes have supported the move to town and city-based living, which itself has, in the main, supported improvements in our well-being. Clearly we as individuals and as human society, must ensure that we have those necessary resources that we need to survive and thrive and must ensure that our physical and biological environment serves us in this same manner, acting as a source of not only resources for our basic survival but also supporting our general well-being and pleasure. Nevertheless, whatever the changes we have wrought, our resources need to be reasonably and fairly available to those who need them, their products generally accessible and used as effectively as they can be used, such that we can all survive and thrive and avoid suffering and pain.

Unfortunately, the fact that there is substantial demand for our world's resources and the fact that the demands on these resources appear to be ever increasing in our changing modern world, clearly comprises a factor which can be seen as a threat to our individual, community, societal and human survival. The possibility of exhaustion of resources, already referred to in regard to our energy supplies in the form of oil and other resources, is certainly present, and is perhaps in fact a grave threat to our future well-being.

This threat will remain unless we either reduce our demands on these resources, make much more efficient use of the resources we have, for example through their efficient reuse and recycling, unless alternative resources are found or unless we use our human inventiveness, our scientific knowledge and understanding, to develop new routes to circumvent resource shortages. In terms of such scientific and technological developments, for example in terms of energy supplies, our scientific and technological research has already led to the development of the already mentioned wind power, solar power, nuclear power, tidal and other forms of power generation, as alternatives to the fossil fuels which will, at some point, be substantially depleted as sources of energy and which are complicit in human-created global warming.

Moreover with the increasing demands on resources arise the concomitant detrimental changes to our environment through damage caused in the extraction, processing and transport of resources, and through increases in levels of waste material which, as already described, in a range of instances, can reduce the quality of our environment, and serve to poison each of us, and damage and poison our planet.

Ignoring the possibility of negative effects of extraction of, and use of our resources, ignoring the negative effects of the production of pollutants and waste products of various kinds in processing and manufacturing, ignorance of the effects of such pollutants or unwillingness to take action to deal with these poisons and pollutants, is damaging to us all. And it is the responsibility of each one of us to take action to reduce the dangers of such environmental poisons and pollutants. As individuals, organisations, communities, societies, as a broader humanity, we need to engage in appropriate actions and strategies which may include reducing our own production and use of products whose component elements, manufacture or use involve or lead to the production of dangerous pollutants. As individuals, we need to act and campaign through our social entities; we need to aim to influence other individuals and take further action, in order to ensure that governments, managers, businesses, social institutions and other relevant entities act responsibly and appropriately in their extraction, manufacture and use of resources.

Achievements can be made and have been made in terms of dealing with issues of anthropogenic pollution. Indeed, if we are to survive as humanity, and enjoy a life of well-being which includes enjoying a pleasant and healthy environment, we have to be successful in our actions to deal with pollution. Fortunately, there are some important, instructive and useful examples of how we, as humanity, have collaborated such that pollution problems which have threatened our environment have been reduced to some degree or which to all intents and purposes have been solved.

The efforts made in relation to tackling acid rain have already been mentioned, and these have had substantial success. As a further example where a global environmental problem has been largely been solved, scientific research identified the fact that pollutants produced from refrigerators were creating danger by reacting with ozone and thereby reducing the levels of ozone in the atmosphere, creating holes in the ozone layer and thus leading to increasing levels of dangerous short wave ultra violet light reaching the earth, with likely significant damage to us in terms of increased risks of radiation-induced cancers and through other mechanisms.

Through individual action, pressures from campaign groups and through the efforts of our national and international representatives, a negotiated international agreement was reached, expressed in the Montreal Protocols, wherein all signatories agreed to phase out the use of the specific refrigerants which were damaging the ozone layer. This has been effective with the key Antarctic hole in the ozone layer predicted to have returned to previous levels by the mid 21st century. Our personal health and to some extent the health of the world has, at least with regard to this threat, been saved.

In another context, similarly when London in the UK, was afflicted by pea-souper fogs resulting in the deaths of thousands in the city from the combination of smoke pollution and fog, the government of the time finally took action and banned the burning of coal in the city. Unfortunately this action came rather later than it should have done, with the change and necessary legislation being substantially motivated by the effects of these smogs on those governing the country in central London. Nevertheless, the result within a short time was cleaner and healthier air as well as reductions in lung diseases and fewer deaths from a range of different causes.

Similarly efforts to clean up rivers have brought fish back to formerly polluted rivers in many industrial countries. Worldwide protection of, and investment in specific natural areas and resources have resulted in the protection and maintenance of threatened populations of wildlife, though despite this, many animal populations continue to decline through destruction of habitat or poaching. And so in terms of such protection we need to make sure that much more is done with many wildlife populations remaining under substantial threat and organisms unfortunately being reported to have become extinct on a regular basis.

While powerful people behaving in negatively selfish, manipulative, short-termist ways, may try to stand in the way of resolving environmental problems, as has been shown above, we can overcome such powerful opposition; we can overcome our own lack of resources; and we can overcome tendencies to inertia. And as a consequence of our effective and cooperative action, threats to human health, well-being and indeed survival stemming from mismanagement, over-exploitation and abuse of our environment can clearly be tackled on that basis of cooperation, common interest, mutually agreed goals accompanied by our will to action.

Change in our climate comprises a natural phenomenon which has proceeded and proceeds through time with a vast range of factors affecting our climate including our changing sun. Research shows that our earth has experienced ice ages and much warmer periods even through the last 20000 or so years, such a period comprising just a tiny part of our earth's history and a tiny part of our human existence on this planet.

Yet in our current age, there is evidence of rapid climate change, at least rapid in comparison to our knowledge of the pace of climate change up to now, something which, for understandable reasons, is a major concern for all of us, certainly in regard to its effects on our human welfare and well-being, with climate change and the current identified global warming representing and exemplifying potentially serious dangers to our environment and our living world. There is substantial evidence of melting polar ice caps, melting and disappearing glaciers and more, all contributing to rising sea levels, which threaten and are threatening the livelihood and survival of those of us who, in particular, live in lower lying areas, though with rising sea levels promising to affect and threaten us all. It seems incontrovertible that our global temperature is rising and that rise is at least in part, if not substantially, the result of our human activity, which, apart from the effects already mentioned, holds the prospects of drought, floods, increasingly extreme weather events and more. All of these changes will have effects on our crucial agricultural systems as well as other important systems which help sustain us, our families, our communities, societies and our global population.

There are those who argue that our humanity should simply adapt to such change and not attempt to try and stop such change happening, since in particular they state that it is too late to change what is happening. Yet it is certainly not too late to take action to reduce the extent of, if not entirely prevent, global warming which will damage our planet, damage our environment and threatens not only the quality of our human lives, but human lives in large numbers and our humanity as a whole. Changes that are likely to occur in the face of increasing global warming cannot simply be left to occur since they may be catastrophic affecting many millions of us and putting us all at risk. Global warming cannot be left to continue on while we attempt to adapt to phenomena, massive floods, extreme weather events, and more which may be beyond the scale that we would comprehend from our everyday lives. Never has our modern humanity, our modern complex human society been under such threat from our climate and we must respond to such change, aim to firstly slow this change and then where possible turn it around. To ignore the peril that our humanity now faces from such global warming is entirely contrary to supporting our human well-being, as individuals, communities, societies and as our broader humanity.

Some of these people also argue that global warming has happened before and is a natural phenomenon (which it has been in the past but which in this case it isn't). If global warming and climate change were a natural phenomenon we would, as individuals, communities and societies, as a global community, need to respond in any case, in some fashion, in order to be able to cope with these changes. However, this phenomenon of global warming is almost universally considered to be significantly the result of our human action, our vast human industry and pollution, with the pollutants, particularly carbon di-oxide produced by burning of fossil fuels, as well as other phenomena such as deforestation, leading to the changes we are seeing. The evidence for the occurrence of global warming and climate change seems incontrovertible and the evidence of a major contribution to this phenomenon arising from human action is also considered by those involved in the relevant fields to be extremely strong.

As a consequence, given this evidence, we certainly do need to take action to slow and prevent this global warming and climate change. That is not to say that we should not take steps to prepare for the consequences of that climate change, some of which is already happening, and which now appears certain to happen to some degree in the future. But our priority must be to act to prevent further increases in global temperature and stop the damaging effects of climate change on our human well-being. And we must take action to reduce and end our human contribution to this climate change, be that through ending the production of pollution, ending or vastly reducing the burning of fossil fuels, the reduction or ending of high carbon dioxide producing forms of agriculture, ending substantive deforestation or through supporting and funding any other reasonable and rational means such that these changes and problems do not become even greater in extent and such that they, optimally, do not continue to occur at all.

Doing nothing while we and others lose the land we need for survival, allowing the loss of our homes and the homes of others due to rising sea levels, due to increased levels of flooding, desertification or other processes; doing nothing in the face of increasing levels of violent weather events, failing to take action which ensures these problems are dealt with as effectively as they can be dealt with, is not acceptable in terms of core and other principles. We must take necessary action in response to these threats, and such action in relation to these threats is the responsibility of each of us. Action must be taken by each of us at the earliest stage possible to do what we can to reduce these threats, visited upon us and others, to some extent visited upon ourselves, through lack of forethought, poor planning and thinking, carelessness, short-term negative selfishness, and disregard for, ignorance about and misunderstanding of our environment and our relationship with that environment.

The identification of substantive evidence of global warming and climate change needed to be followed by immediate action from individuals, communities, our societies, governments and industry, our global organisations and more, from all of us around the globe, in order to alleviate this substantial threat to our well-being. Unfortunately there has been much short-termism, short-sightedness, poor thinking, focus on self-interest, political and economic self-interest and negative selfishness in other ways which has caused and has the potential to produce dire and destructive effects for all of us.

The burning of fossil fuels has already been mentioned as a clear cause of climate change and global warming. However, a further important contributor to global warming and climate change, but also to other environmental threats, is our humanity's voracious destruction of the natural environment. This, in particular in relation to climate change, incorporates the ongoing and increasing destruction of our planet's rain forests, whose destruction and indeed devastation is removing a vast sink for the carbon-di-oxide which contributes to climate change and global warming. Understandable demands for better living, higher levels of income, along with economic pressures from those who are wealthy and wish to be more wealthy, from corporate systems of investment, political and economic interests and others focusing on wealth generation and money-making, mean that for the purposes of producing a range of products, for agriculture, for meat production and for other purposes, vast levels of rain forest are being destroyed, causing, additional to their effects on climate, the destruction of unique rain forest habitats and the plants and animals that live in them.

While for many of us as individuals, such environmental destruction may seem very distant from us, indeed almost invisible on a daily basis, being difficult to conceive of in terms of its extent and nature, this destruction is occurring and occurring on a vast scale. In addition to the objective of this destruction being to generate income for those directly involved in that destruction, to an important degree this destruction is being conducted in order to provide each of us as individuals, with resources, materials and products which support our short-term individual well-being. Whether we consume such products or not, we are involved as individuals and have an important role and responsibility in combating such destruction.

Our growing population levels and the growing demands of those increasing population levels place great strain on our natural environment, with more resources required to be used and extracted from those environments, metals, minerals, timber, stone, food, water and so forth, to serve our needs. This contributes to our natural and sustainable biological and physical environments being increasingly diminished, and diminishing at rapid rates.

Nevertheless, the extraction, processing and use of the resources we need, if we carry these out appropriately, can be done in a much more sustainable manner than is done at the present time and in a manner consistent with core and other principles. Our extraction, processing and use of these resources needs to be planned and managed overall, most likely on a global scale, operating without unnecessary and irreversible destruction of the environment, avoiding destructive pollution of water and air, and incorporating (and requiring) the maintenance of the environment, its return to its original form or involving developing new environments which will be available, in the broadest sense, to support our planetary life in all its forms and to support our humanity. We need to ensure resources remain available such that our wildlife is sustained and that our environment retains its aesthetic and other functions and facets relevant to our human survival (which include our desire to care for, nurture and conserve or maintain the natural environment).

As a consequence of our requirement for increased levels of natural resources, the extent of our natural environment remaining untouched and left undamaged by our human action is continuing to decrease, reaching low if not critical levels with regard to the survival of many forms of environment and for many species. As individuals, focusing on our near environments, we need to be acting both locally and more broadly and globally, wherever we can, taking into consideration the range of other priorities, not only to halt the destruction of the natural environment in our local areas, but also to expand the areas available to form new natural environments. And in these local environments we need to do what we can to ensure that our resources are best used and reused where necessary.

More societally and in particular in our modern world, globally, it is surely essential that we systematically plan our use of resources into the future and systematically research the consequences of our actions in and on the environment, providing resources do this, as well as ensuring that our natural and physical environments are looked after and can sustain our humanity. More specifically, together, as individuals, communities and societies, as a global community, we need to plan and prepare to ensure that not only do we have the resources we need into the future, but such that our use of these resources is not negatively selfish, clumsy, miscalculated and more, and therefore does not damage our individual and human well-being and damage our physical and biological environment to any significant degree.

Clearly we need global democratic organisations planning to support and acting for the well-being of all, in order to ensure that our resources are used in optimal ways and such that, as a global community, we avoid the damaging affects of pollution and environmental destruction. And moreover such global institutions, in line with core and other principles, need to have and need to be given power to enforce actions on countries, regions and other entities to ensure that, in order to support our human survival and to ensure our individual and human well-being our environment is protected and secured. Clearly this implementation of the power of global organisations over other social entities must revolve around the necessity of preventing significant environmental threat and destruction which indeed threatens our human survival and offers the strong possibility of pain and suffering.

Negatively selfish short-term local interests cannot be allowed to significantly damage the local or more global environment, as such environmental damage hurts us all. Those who engage in such damaging and destructive practices will most likely in some senses be damaging themselves in the longer term and so, in order to support their own well-being as well as the well-being of others, need to modify their practices such their own practices are sustainable, but also such that their practices are supportive of others, supportive of us all, forming part of a pathway to development and improvement in well-being and happiness for all.

However there are those who display such a level of greed, such a level of avariciousness, who possess a callous disregard for the individual humanity of others, who do not have sufficient care for others, such that those people when pursuing development through environmental destruction, are prepared to destroy the lives of others, are prepared to significantly damage or even, in some cases, threaten injure and murder those who are acting to defend the environment, who will kill and murder others who wish to defend the land they live on, land which may provide them with their everyday needs. Clearly such murderous and destructive actions are entirely at odds with core and other principles. Such actions are evil and heinous, and wherever we can, we must make all efforts to prevent such murderous and destructive actions by those intent on pursuing their own negatively selfish interests. Our global communities and our global institutions must act against such negatively selfish actions, such attack on those who are defending their own livelihoods and our global environmental systems.

Moreover, our global community, through our global institutions, needs to ensure that destructive and damaging environmental practices are ended. Under circumstances where we, through our international organisations are circumscribing certain forms of environmentally destructive action which might be seen as valuable in supporting livelihoods, our global institutions need to act in support of the well-being of all of us, and provide direction and support, financial if necessary and appropriate, at least temporarily, to ensure those who are being required to change their environmentally destructive practices do not suffer unnecessary substantive damage to their own well-being, through serving the greater global well-being.

As already mentioned, global warming, arising substantially from increased levels of $CO_2$ in the atmosphere, represents one very important form of pollution, probably the most threatening form of pollution we face at this current time. Nevertheless, other pollutants have been released into the atmosphere without due care and concern over a period of many years. In some places, there are very few pollution laws, regulations and standards, and even where these exist there may be limited or no resources for enforcement or no serious effort to support enforcement. Our global action in support of reducing and preventing such pollution in such places is an absolute necessity given the suffering which can be caused to us all through damaging pollution, pollution which doesn't stop at national borders.

For example, while, as has already been described, some smoke-based and other pollution of the air has been eradicated in many cities and towns in the modern Western world, at the current point in time, entire cities in South East and East Asia may be engulfed for days in smogs comprised of and containing dangerous pollutants. Apart from the damage to people locally who must breathe in this polluted air, with likely consequent widespread deaths locally, all of these pollutants are likely to be dispersed and contribute towards pollution in our global atmosphere.

Thus, in addition to dealing with issues relating to our use of our earth's resources, we clearly need our global organisations to aim to influence polluting countries and polluting industries in those countries to reduce such pollution. The reality of these pollution effects on a global level demonstrate that the issue of pollution, indeed the issue of the environment and environments as a whole, is one that reaches across borders and cannot be considered solely as something which national authorities and governments can be allowed to govern, ignoring the effect of the pollution generated in their countries on others.

While it has been stated that global organisations should have the power to intervene in and enforce actions in regard to the environment in more local jurisdictions, there is clearly a case for discussion and negotiation between global organisations and relevant governments in the first place to reach conclusions and determine actions which suit the well-being of us all. Nevertheless, there is also a strong case for limits on sovereignty, sovereign areas themselves being governed and being regulated in order that the global environment and global interests can be protected, such that we do not all suffer from the destructive effects of various forms of deadly pollution.

Clearly multi-lateral, bi-lateral and other treaties may not be sufficient in themselves in this sphere since it is far too easy for signatories, for governments, to fail to follow commitments agreed to, be it for reasons of perceived short-term self or national self-interest or because democratic mechanisms can support those seeking election in promoting the more narrow and immediate interests of their electorates, pursuit of which interests may damage others and damage our global environment. Not only must there be global monitoring and regulation in order to prevent deterioration of, and indeed, improve our global environment, but there needs to be the power to ensure that appropriate and necessary policies are implemented.

More locally, we need, as individuals, communities and societies to ensure that there is planning of the various developments and changes taking place in cities, towns and in our countryside, planning which takes account of both the quality of our lived physical environments but also the quality of the natural environment. We need to ensure that, within such plans, there is a focus on, not only having an appropriate and pleasant built environment within the existing rural and countryside context, but that with regard to urban and suburban development, we ensure that there is an important focus on developing and improving the natural environments within our cities and towns as well as beyond their borders, such that those of us living in towns, cities and their suburbs, can enjoy the natural environment within our town, city and suburban scapes, and such that we can also support and enjoy wildlife and access areas of natural beauty beyond our towns and cities.

By supporting the development and maintenance of such planned environments, by supporting the planning of towns and cities such that they are beautiful and interesting environments for us to enjoy, we will be enhancing our well-being and pleasure. Pleasant and more natural local environments in our towns and cities, mean that close to home in urban areas, and perhaps and hopefully every day, those of us who live in towns and cities, can enjoy the beauty and wonder of nature, will have space in which to relax, run, play sports and games and take exercise, enjoy peace and quiet, fresh air, and will be able to enjoy a variety of biological and other living and leisure environments which can provide us with stimulation, pleasure and interest.

Of course through our ensuring the presence of these open spaces, woodlands, parks, avenues of trees, natural meadows, gardens, squares, or other features in our urban and suburban areas, we will also be providing homes for a range of animal wildlife which would otherwise be unable to thrive in our urban and suburban areas in the absence of such trees, plants, secluded areas, where they can survive and thrive successfully.

It is also the case that by ensuring, through our planning, that we set aside specific land within urban and suburban areas, be those our own gardens or specific allotments of land should we have them, we can also provide some practical additional natural resource for small scale agricultural and horticultural purposes, including fruit and vegetable or plant and flower-growing. Taking part in, and encouraging others to be involved in such small-scale personal production of food or growing of plants and flowers in the context of our town and city environments can also be beneficial for our well-being, as for some, if not many of us, such activities bring substantial pleasure in themselves.

Thus, there is much joy in observing our seeds and plants growing, our plants turning to leaf and flowering, and later enjoying the beauty of, or harvesting the fruits of our labour. Our urban gardening, in an overlapping manner, is also supportive of our well-being and pleasure through engaging us with and providing us with some enriching contact with our natural environment. It further helps our communities and societies to maintain some important agricultural skills and knowledge, something which, while hopefully unlikely and unnecessary, could be of substantive importance dependent on circumstances, in dire circumstances, apart from our urban and suburban gardening providing variety, colour and interest to our close, home and local environments.

Yet it is also of great importance for us to ensure that the areas outside towns and cities, the less populated areas, the countryside, farmland, meadows, beaches, dunes, hillsides, the moorlands, salt marshes, swamps, woodlands, deserts, forests and jungles, are looked after, preserved, maintained, or where necessary changed in a manner which serves to enhance our environment such that it can be enjoyed by us to the full, and such that other animals and plants can also survive and thrive.

Promoting our economic well-being is of course of key significance and this has already been discussed at length earlier in this guide. Yet development which supports economic well-being needs to go hand in hand with our maintenance and development of an appropriate pleasurable, enjoyable and sustainable environment, and indeed this applies to both highly populated and low population areas. In relevant cases, there should perhaps be some reticence in taking actions which substantially change our environments or develop new environments, especially given the potential threats to indigenous plants and animals within what might be complex but stable ecosystems. Nevertheless, we must also support our well-being in terms of having incomes and resources at our disposal. Ourselves or others suffering intense poverty, intense pain and suffering, illness, early death and similar, while preserving a pristine environment, is certainly not an acceptable outcome.

We may also be averse to change due to our human sense of belonging and perhaps comfort that a more constant environment seems to provide for some if not many of us, the conservatism already referred to, as well as the potential unpredictability of the consequences of substantial changes, given our current state of knowledge and understanding. Nevertheless such new and modified environments should not be ruled out as making positive contributions to our survival, well-being, joy and happiness, when this is needed and when this can be done, nor does it mean ignoring the contributions that modified and new environments might make to the supply of resources or the support of existing or newly introduced forms of wildlife. Further, and of great importance, if we fail to act in the face of real or potential and threatening environmental stresses of any kind, if we fail to take action which will provide us with necessary food and other resources required for our survival, then certainly our well-being and quite obviously, our survival itself, will be at risk.

As individuals, we need to act positively and constructively in regard to these issues, negotiating and building solutions which serve the interests of all of us, all parties, ourselves, our families, our local communities, and our more global communities as a whole. As individuals we need to be serving the good of all, and that involves to an important degree supporting both economic sustenance and development and also supporting and looking after our environment. We cannot significantly sacrifice our environment with the vast, varied and complex damage that that involves, in our pursuit of economic benefit. Nor can we sacrifice our important and basic human needs, in particular in relation to our personal, community and social survival, in order to preserve an unchanging environment. Overall it is well-being in all its aspects which needs to be addressed and this means supporting the environment along with and allied with supporting the range of other sources of our well-being and happiness.

In rural and countryside areas, in areas previously less touched by or untouched by more modern construction and development, clearly difficulties can arise in dealing with the range of environmental issues, in particular proposals for new industrial developments, new agricultural developments, new roads, timber felling (with consequent deforestation), warehousing, housing and other similar developments. There may be differing short-term, or more immediate self or group-entity interests, which individuals and groups may sometimes aim to pursue at the expense of the interests of others and sometimes at the expense of the wider interest. Where new developments are proposed, the broad interest along with more individual interests need to be considered in all cases in terms of well-being. And the quality of our environment and the effects of damaging that environment comprise important, if not sometimes crucial elements of that broad interest.

Where there are disagreements in terms of the pursuit of developments in our countryside, and other forms of previously undeveloped or untouched land, it is essential for us all that we make efforts to understand the views and interests of others. And where these are sufficiently reasonable, we need to accommodate these views and opinions to reach a negotiated agreed solution which benefits all. This may not always be possible. Promoting development on pristine natural land and untouched natural environments containing unique wildlife and wildlife systems, will be likely to cause irreparable damage and irreversible change, and in some cases, there may be little room for compromise for those who wish to preserve such environments.

There may be a need on some occasions for those granted the appropriate legitimate authority to act in the best interests of the whole, and to over-ride certain individual or group interests in order to support that greater good. What that good may be is obviously a matter of debate in each case, yet decisions are required to be made and there have to be legitimate, open, fair, democratic mechanisms, representing democratic input to decision-making, incorporating notions of freedom and autonomy, in those instances where such choices need to be made. And overall such choices need to be supportive of the well-being of all. In regard to such choices and decisions, sometimes we will achieve the goals we as individuals wish to achieve and on other occasions we may not. It is important, as far as possible, that all sides should to some extent gain something through such decisions, though all may not achieve that which they wish and some indeed may not attain their key goals.

Increases in our population levels are often seen as a major influence on levels of environmental destruction and pollution. Clearly our population levels would seem to be one factor, and indeed an important factor in environmental change and damage, since the presence of more of us would appear to logically mean we need more resources, more processing of those resources and therefore potentially more pollution and environmental destruction as a consequence of our increased demand for resources. However, population increases need not result in such destruction and pollution. For example, it may be that new and better resources become available; new technologies may be developed to reduce pollution and environmental damage; we may devise ways to access available resources more easily and more efficiently if our processes are improved and resources are used more effectively and if we take, or appropriate regulatory or other measures are taken, such that pollution and environmental damage does not occur or is not allowed to occur. Indeed if those who are, through their existence, increasing population, act to support more effective methods of resource utilisation, help identify new resources or even design such new resources amongst other things, increasing population can at least in theory, result in reductions in pollution and environmental damage.

Despite continuing claims and worries about over-population, there seems little capacity to identify those population levels and densities which are appropriate and acceptable and those which are not. There seems to be little capacity to determine when we have too many people, when we have too few people and when we have just the right numbers. Indeed it would seem reasonable to argue that there is in general, no 'appropriate number' or 'appropriate population density', as such a number of density would have to be substantially dependent on resources available and potentially available, available space, a subjective judgment of the conditions in which we wish to live in terms of crowdedness and personal space, and a vast range of other factors.

It would certainly not seem reasonable to aim to minimise the numbers of us living on this planet, something which would be inconsistent in a multitude of ways with the promotion of well-being and happiness, with increased levels of our populations in principle meaning increased levels of well-being, through the new existence of life, through the well-being these new people can enjoy and through the capabilities provided to society from the unique contributions those increased numbers of us can make. It would seem more reasonable to wish for (or perhaps aim for) an optimal highest level of population, whatever that might be, which would clearly vary with time, technology, available space and the range of other factors.

That being said, crowding and over-population in itself, nevertheless, is likely to comprise something which decreases our level of well-being, putting stress and strain on all of us, individuals, communities and societies, perhaps through the resultant competition for resources or perhaps because overcrowding may be in some deep sense, something which we do not enjoy, with each of us wanting and needing, to some extent, our own sufficient personal space.

Given that, in line with core principles, we would not wish for our population to increase to levels which are damaging in terms of their effects on our well-being and happiness, we do need to note that, as far as current and recent observations are concerned, where there are many of those who are more wealthy, who have a higher standard of living, where there are those who have more resources, better health and also, it seems reasonable to say, greater personal well-being, these people in many parts of the world tend to have lower numbers of children and therefore population growth is reduced, with population actually decreasing in some of the most wealthy countries. There may be a range of reasons for this, including the greater rights and freedoms of women in those more wealthy countries and easier access to contraception, however it seems reasonable to believe and indeed it seems likely that increased levels of wealth and well-being, situated in cultures which do not lionise having large numbers of children, combined with greater power and influence for women and greater access to contraception, will lead to a stabilisation of world population, if such changes continue.

As individuals, considering our more local and personal lives, should we wish to have children (which the many of us are likely to do, at least at this point in our human history), we ourselves need to consider carefully the size of the families we wish to have, and can have, taking into account our own needs and the resources available to us, but also considering the potential needs of our children, as well as the potential demands that increasing population may place upon the planet and other factors. We should certainly try to match the number of children we have, as far as we can, to the resources we have available to support our children as individuals, communities and societies. As part of our thinking and planning, we further need to take into account our human need for personal space, and the consequences for us should the development and availability of resources not proceed at a pace which can meet the new demands of an increasing population.

It may also be the case that in some cultures and contexts we are under pressure, from family, from community, even from the state, to have many children in order to meet family, community, governmental or societal goals. And in some contexts, we may need children in order that we and our family can survive, for example, their work on the land being important for all of us in the family and the community. In such contexts, it needs to remain our own individual and family choice as to how many children we choose to have. It is not the job of the state to demand that we have large numbers of children if that is not what we wish for in order to pursue our well-being. Moreover, we should try to avoid wider cultural, family and other forms of social pressure affecting our choice of family size. For some of course, there may be no or little real choice in regard to family size due to the absence of contraception combined with, for the vast majority of us, our natural and deep instinct and desire to have and enjoy sex.

As a worthwhile goal in itself in terms of supporting our own well-being, but also in order to ensure we have appropriate levels of population, moving from the position where we find ourselves today, we, both men and women, need to promote and act towards the emancipation and empowerment of women in particular, but also men as well, such that in no places in the world are women treated as chattels, slaves, person-less victims of men, treated as objects to whom sex is done, sometimes raped by husbands and others. We need to be implementing changes such that women are able to express and implement with their partners, their own desires with regard to children and childbirth, in particular the numbers of children they wish to have, and with regard to the quality of life they wish themselves and their children to have.

If we think about ideas such as the general levels of population we, as communities and societies would wish to have, in terms of total populations and population densities, arguments about this must be based in reason and evidence and take into account our notions of human well-being, quality of life, as well as the relevant resource context rather than being based in what often, if not nearly always, seems to be an irrational fear by some people of increasing populations.

Population decline is also something which we need to consider. Reductions of population levels may create their own forms of damage through the lack of people available to fill important roles in our communities and societies, for example, those roles where there is human care involved, with nurses, carers and more required to give others help and support. We need to have doctors, engineers, builders, teachers, entertainers, carpenters, plumbers, drivers, and the range of other professions already referred to, and with lower population levels, with fewer people, we will be less able to find people to fulfill these important functions though technological development may reduce the need for some of not many, professions with reductions in populations. As parents we will have fewer children to love or who will receive love from us, though perhaps the smaller number will become more intense and focused receivers of our love. Moreover, lower numbers of people may mean in some respects a lesser level of the store of well-being with those unborn having no opportunity to enjoy the well-being they could have enjoyed through living.

The presence of a quality environment around us does comprise an important element of our well-being. And where excessive population increases comprise a threat to such a quality environment then there is legitimacy in this being a factor in our deciding to have smaller families and wishing to see maintenance or even reductions in populations over the long term, through peaceful, caring and reasonable means which enhance the well-being of us all. Effective use of contraception of course allows many of the pleasures of sex without our producing more children, and this is the most frequent means of avoiding unwanted conception and enabling us to have the number of children that we wish to have, giving them the quality of life that we wish to give them.

Clearly, there are some groups, nationalist, cultural, religious or other, which may see increasing the levels of their own particular group populations as being of paramount importance, sometimes with the driving motivation that their own belief grouping, culture or national group can have greater control and influence over others in a state, region, if not in the wider world. Those in charge of such groupings as well as members of such groups, though often not supported by many individuals within their groups, may well wish their own group to become dominant and powerful over other groups.

This kind of thinking and action is contrary to the principles presented in this guide as it damages society and others through its emphasis on that particular group identity and interests at the expense of the rest of us. Such views and actions in terms of increasing populations of specific groups are also reprehensible through their denial or through their aim to deny our individual capacity to determine our own family and personal needs in terms of our size of family. Such groups and cultures are highly likely to see those of us who are individuals within their groups as a vehicle for the group's sets of beliefs or that group's interests (power maintenance and dominance) rather than as individuals with autonomy, independence, freedoms and a key role to play, indeed, frequently, the key role to play, in determining that which affects their own personal interests and our own personal lives. Thus, it is not considered legitimate within the core and other principles presented in this guide, for groups to use childbirth and population as a means to enhance their influence and power. Such approaches and actions deny our individuality and threaten our well-being.

Whether or not it is considered reasonable for us as individuals, parents and families to decide to have and to have as many children as we want, sufficient resources being available, our aiming to have as many children as possible is a more difficult question as it would seem a fundamental freedom for us as men, women, as families, where we have the biological possibility of choice, to have personal freedom and choice about how many children we, as partners or individuals wish to have, this being a matter which is very personal to each of us and is reasonably, given available resources, within the legitimate range of our own choices. This freedom seems important to apply within the bounds that we as parents and families are responsible for doing our utmost to support a good quality of life and well-being for our children (and indeed for all of us) rather than a life of poverty, suffering and pain.

When we are thinking about our loving and sexual relationships, the issue of the need for the survival of our human species as well as optimal population levels are likely to be far from high on our agenda. While we may have considered the idea of having children, we will much more likely be concerned about our feelings of love and care for our partner and our wish for and desire for sex with our partner. And we will be motivated in our loving relationship by our deep and intense desire for our partner, our sexual instincts, our desire to love and be loved, our desire to enjoy intimacy, closeness to our lover and sex, and also at some points, by our desire to have children. Even though we can choose not to have children, and perhaps even avoid intimate love and sex, few of us choose not to have sex or avoid loving and sexual intimacy. Of course it is not an accident from the point of view of the continuance and survival of our humanity that we feel and act in such ways. It is simply that the continuance and survival of humanity is something we are unlikely to think about and consider in depth, or have as a motivation, when approaching love, sex, intimacy and our deep desires and need to have children.

In terms of our personal conduct as it affects well-being and happiness, we are clearly supporting our personal well-being and happiness through the intense joys and pleasures, our feelings of wholeness and fulfillment, gained through love, passion, through the intimacy of sex and loving relationships. We are also clearly promoting human life and the continuance of our species through our love and sex, leading to the birth of our children. And indeed we will also be supporting our well-being and happiness through the wholeness, fulfillment and completeness that almost all of us as parents gain through nurturing, loving and bringing up our children.

Yet the joys and pleasure of sex and love need not, in this day and age, at least for many of us, result in our having children and thus we, as men and women, can enjoy our loving sexual intimacy without having to, or wishing to have children, and without having more children if we have children already. For the most but not all of us, we do wish to have children at some point in time.

If it is the case for us as partners that, and optimally this is the case, due to the availability of contraception or our want and capacity to avoid sex, we are in the position to decide on the numbers of children we have, then a range of factors will influence our judgments on the numbers of children we choose to have. These factors may include the already mentioned resources we have available to support our children, the norms in terms of numbers of children that others have around us, the amount of time available to us in which we may realistically have children, the views of our wider families, the other activities which are important to us in our lives, the time and space we have available therefore in our lives to dedicate to our children, as well as a range of other cultural and situational factors.

While in some cultures and situations, it may be that children are seen and indeed wanted significantly in terms of their capacity for work, in terms of their capacity to bring in income for a family into the future (sometimes through marriages and dowries) or for bringing some sense of status to the parents and family, this is not seen here as an appropriate way to view children. Seeing children in this way is not seen as beneficial for the child's well-being and happiness, and indeed is seen in many cases, as promising quite a high level of misery. It may be that, if we are very poor, if we are living in dire circumstances, then we may need our children to work for us, and indeed this may be essential and understandable in some contexts, yet our goal needs to be to support our child's well-being and happiness and to help them (and ourselves) escape from such poverty.

Doing all we can to help them to get to school, to acquire education and skills wherever possible, for example, represents the kind of thing we should be doing, wherever possible to help our children, to support their well-being and happiness. We need our children to contribute to family, community, society and more globally, and hopefully they will do this, but it is not acceptable to treat them as, in a sense, semi-slaves, tied to our personal purposes as parents, with the consequent unhappiness and lack of well-being that is likely to involve for the child.

For the many of us, we will have as our goal the wish to ensure maximum well-being and happiness for our children and to do what we can to ensure the minimum of pain, suffering and misery for them. Maximising that happiness seems to mean, for the many of us in the modern and more wealthy world, that we have fewer children and place more resources into supporting the children we have as they grow. As already referred to earlier in this chapter, this has had the broader consequence that population has not grown or has even decreased in the more wealthy countries, and into the future it seems that our populations, at least in some countries, may not grow substantially or that it in some places they might reduce further in level. The lower numbers of children, however, does not necessarily, as a consequence, mean lower levels of stress on the environment and lesser levels of physical and biological destruction, due to the higher resource investment in our children and ourselves.

Our aiming for increasing quality of life and increasing levels of well-being and happiness itself places demands and stresses on our biological and physical environments. Even where we have fewer children and our population levels are stable or even in decline, there can still clearly be higher demand for materials, higher demand for the range of resources and consequent increased environmental pressures. Social attitudes, cultural beliefs and practices, technological development and other factors also play significant roles in these environmental pressures. Nevertheless, it surely must be the case that our increasing levels of population as well as our perceived need to, and our desire to have, increasing levels of materials things, contributes to environmental pressures and environmental degradation, and may well continue to be a key component driving increasing environmental destruction unless we take remedial and necessary steps to alleviate the effects of and repair the damage already done, and reduce potential damage into the future.

Our need for and desire for mobility and to travel, often long distances, brings much well-being into our lives, supporting a better quality of life in a range of ways. Indeed travel and mobility is essential to the functioning of our modern, complex societies. Yet our use of fuels for travel is an important source of dangerous pollution and the manufacture of our means of transport, be they cars, airplanes, trains, ships, or whatever, requires extraction and processing of metals and other materials as well as the fuel consuming transportation of these materials, these processes themselves leading to pollution of and damage to our environment. Our increasing use of these means of transport produces increasing levels of air pollution, in particular, through the polluting products and particles generated from the burning of fuels such as diesel in cars. And of course the fuels we use must themselves, at least in the current age, be extracted from the ground or other sources, processed and transported, all of these processes which in themselves can generate pollution.

Of course, for the many us individuals living in our current modern day technological societies, while we may be well aware of the negative effects, the environmental stress and pollution caused by such travel, because of our work needs, the distance between ourselves and family, and for a range of other reasons, we will still feel we have little alternative but to pursue our capacity and need for travel. Many of us, dependent on where we live, our income and access to other forms of transport, will buy our own car, and if not that, alternatively will be obliged to use some form of public transport and use public transport systems in one way or another. We will thus be participating in this creation of pollution and will feel we have little alternative but to participate and travel if we wish to survive reasonably and enjoy an acceptable level of well-being and happiness. Being unable to work and earn money in a reasonable manner, being unable to visit family members who are important to us as well as our friends, and being unable to do important things such as shopping or going out for entertainment would quite reasonably be largely unacceptable to the many of us.

Thus our travel is and will be frequently, to an important extent, something which we need to do to promote our own well-being and happiness. It is also an important underpinning of our enhancing of our contribution to others through the work we do, and it supports our communities and societies for us to make such a full contribution which in itself will hopefully support others in enjoying higher levels of well-being and happiness.

And our travel and capacity to travel also represents to some extent a need based in community conformity, borne out of our individual need for community participation, our need to be successful in that community and to be recognised as a full member of that community, as well as our desire for the pleasures, the exploration, the experiences that journeys and travel can bring. Without travel and means of transport in a community and society where transport and travel are the norm, we may well, even in modern societies with modern communication technologies, become isolated, lonely and alone, unable to see friends and family, unable to participate in much we would otherwise wish to participate in.

And indeed this more functional consideration of our need for journeying and travel, leaves aside what may be a basic instinct within us as part of our human character, part of our physical selves, which means that we wish to go, that we wish to move, that we wish to explore, that we wish to travel and of course it leaves aside the fact that we need to be with and interact with others, which requires us to go to or be gone to, itself tending to require our significant travel in some form or other.

And if we have the money and resources available to us, particularly in the more wealthy world, but also elsewhere, we will wish to travel, often overseas, for holidays. For the reality is that many of us, as families, individuals, as loving couples, as friends, if we have the personal resources available, will wish to have a holiday, preferably far away from home, perhaps in the sunshine, on the beach, exploring other places and cultures, going somewhere novel and exciting away from our normal everyday working or other environment. Yet of course the travel we engage in on such holidays, the flights, the coaches and buses, the use of a car, the boats, whatever transport, will all involve us in using material resources, energy, forms of transport, which will generate resultant pollution and much pollution, when so many millions of us travel as part of our holidays.

But such holidays support our well-being, providing us with adventure, rest, escape, new experiences, encounters with new cultures, meetings with new people and friends, all of which support us in our well-being. And in the case of our experiences of different cultures and ways of being, these holidays can expand our experiences, understandings, and educate us about the variety of people, cultures, thinking and life and lifestyles on our planet, hopefully supporting a more understanding and cohesive planet, giving us a stronger and clearer feeling of being part of a greater humanity.

Our exploration of the world is positive, enriching and rewarding, often relaxing and beneficial to all of us who have these opportunities, and indeed to some extent shifts some of the resources of those of us who are wealthy to areas where there may be poverty and suffering, providing the potential, if such resources are used appropriately, to alleviate to some degree poverty and suffering, and improve well-being in areas which may be beautiful and exciting to visit, but resource poor. Of course, there are many other ways in which that poverty and suffering can and should be alleviated.

Given that exploration, given that expanding our horizons, engaging in adventure and travel of most and many sorts, are important elements of living a life of well-being, and indeed, given that it is part of our nature to not only explore, but to seek out adventure and to seek out the new, supporting such travel is, under most circumstances, consistent with living with well-being and consistent with core and other principles. We do, however, need to look for ways to minimise the pollution caused by such travel, for example, improving our modes of transport such that the detrimental effects of such travel are reduced.

We should not and cannot ignore the dangers and threats that poor resource utilisation and pollution present to our humanity, to all of us, and the potential destructive consequences for our planet and ourselves which derive from pollution and the effects of our travel and other activities. In reality therefore, combined with considerations about the value and use of energy for these travel and other purposes, linked to the availability and prospective availability of such energy resources, and priorities in terms of energy usage, we need to make sure there are systematic, sustained and effective efforts to minimise pollution in all its forms. Where possible, we need to identify amongst other things, technological solutions to the problems of pollution generated through our travel and indeed all kinds of travel and other activities, such that a suitable solution or suitable solutions to the resultant pollution problems are identified. And indeed, while we will enjoy travel and adventure, we may need to consider to some degree limiting this travel if pollution costs and consequences are too high.

It is up to us as individuals to take actions ourselves to press for technological and other solutions to these problems, and to ensure that the things we do are sustainable over the long term and will be available to others into the future. If we are unable to find solutions to particular problems then, because of the dangers of such pollution to life on our planet, our own well-being and the well-being of others, we will need, in the case of transport and travel, to use alternative forms of transport or substantially curb our travel and adventure. These are very urgent matters at this time. We need to be generating plans of action in order to deal with this specific problem and these types of problems expeditiously.

The endpoint of failing to act on and resolve the problem of destructive and damaging pollution arising from whichever source, is likely to be either a substantial diminution in our well-being, the ending of our human life on earth or a requirement for us to leave our polluted and destroyed planet, something which we are certainly not able to achieve as a humanity at the current time.

Many of our more materialistic needs and desires, and material requiring activities, all involving the use of resources of one kind or another, contain the possibility if not likelihood of our generating pollution at some phase of extraction, production or utilisation of resources and materials. While many of these activities, needs and desires can be reasonably justified in terms of enhancing our overall well-being and happiness, there are also uses and degrees of use of material things which can be seen as being profligate and wasteful use of our resources, these resulting in the unnecessary generation of pollution. The production and possession and use of perverse levels of possessions, material items for minor and trivial pleasure purposes, for example multiple vehicles when only a smaller number are reasonably needed, is a profligate use of our materials and requires unnecessary extraction, processing and utilisation of resources which, certainly if not efficiently recyclable, are likely to be limited in the long run and therefore at some point may become exhausted.

Indeed our societal promotion of energy and resource requiring trinketry and material things, a promotional engine which may in some respects, with or without deliberation, encourage us in what might easily be seen as trivial production and consumption, must provide some weight to concerns over some aspects of our materialism and its effect on the environment. The prevalence of products which are purchased then not used or hardly used, items which are wasted in one way or another, which are so poorly designed and manufactured that even if useful in principle they must be rapidly disposed of, represents an unnecessary and draining use of resources which may contribute to accelerated reduction of the resources available to us. The deliberate identification, if not more accurately in many cases, the invention of material needs by those involved in promotion, marketing and other fields, bolsters the desire and need for consumption and production. Such marketing frequently uses manipulatory emotional appeals to encourage consumption, representing the acquisition of material products as participation, belonging and other deeper human needs. This is clearly effective in terms of marketing and promotion, but is questionable in terms of our support for well-being and happiness, to an important degree trivialising our important human beliefs, attitudes and values. But more relevant to this chapter, the enhanced material demands arising from such promotion of material acquisition clearly places greater strain on our limited resources and further supports unnecessary and increased pollution and damage to our environment.

As individuals we need to recognise the mechanisms and systems that may be operating to promote such unnecessary and significantly damaging consumption and take action to ensure that we either reduce such consumption, particularly our own personal consumption, or work to ensure that our unnecessary or trivial personal consumption is implemented without damage, or with the minimal damage to our physical and biological environment. Stopping or reducing our consumption in some respects, with regard to some items, may be difficult since, as already mentioned, the systems for promotion of material consumption often act to place us under complex social and psychological pressure to engage in such consumption.

As individuals, we need to develop the capacity to cope effectively with such pressures and work with others to counter such pressures, identifying what actually comprises our own priorities and needs with these taking the lead over material items promoted to us. And those of us involved in the promotion of what may be seen as superfluous and unnecessary consumption, which includes not only those involved directly, but also those overseeing political systems which encompass such promotion, need to ensure that our consumption and desire for material things is consistent with the resources we have available to us and the need to maintain an environment which supports us all in surviving and thriving, in enjoying well-being. Indeed it may be that our individual and social action, operating through governments, law and other channels, is necessary to reel in such promotion and marketing, for a range of reasons, additional to our desire to reduce the wastage of resources and the level of pollution.

That being said, this is not to condemn all desire for material things. As discussed earlier in this guide, the possession and enjoyment of material things, beautiful objects, personal items and more, is part of our human identity and expression of that identity. We enjoy our own individual spaces personalised with the things that have meaning to us, our photographs, our ornaments, our souvenirs. The vast main, if not all of us wish, if we can, to have basic possessions, a home, furniture, tables, chairs, beds, books, means of transport and more, things which are ours. And indeed we like our things to look good, to be aesthetically pleasing. We most likely all wish to give gifts and to receive them; most of us would like a little luxury if we could get it and this is part of what might be seen as materiality. Nevertheless, our desire for the material must be balanced with our essential concern for others and relate to our individual decisions and social decisions as to how to meet the core and other principles set out in this guide, which must take into consideration the environmental and resource impacts of our actions and the impact of our desires for material things.

While our resources may be finite, our level of need for specific resources may change, even reduce, as processes and procedures in manufacture change, as technologies change and develop, as our individual and broader human circumstances change and indeed as our needs and wants themselves change. Our invention may mean we can find new ways of achieving objectives, new ways of using resources more effectively, and indeed mean that we identify new and more accessible resources to support our generation and production of material items. Thus, the levels of our available resources change, with new resources identified and becoming available on tap, and alternative resources displacing current resources. Our more effective extraction and employment of resources already in use can also extend the length of availability of the resource supplies available to us. Through encouraging changing technologies, through encouraging efficiency, reduced resource use and more effective resource use, as well as improving processes in a range of areas, we importantly have the potential to reduce the extent and rate at which our resources are depleted.

Added to this we need a focus on reuse and recycling of resources, something which has been referred to already in this chapter, it being something we can all contribute to. Thus, in support of core and other principles, it is incumbent on each of us to ensure that we recycle our resources as far as possible in order to help maintain the level of resources that we as a community have access to. Almost everything can be recycled. Used paper can be reused in the home as scrap writing paper or for wrapping, and then can be recycled to produce further paper once used; metals can be melted down and reused, plant matter can be reused as compost to enrich our soils; old clothes can be passed on to others who need them or recycled to make other clothes. And there is much else which can be recycled. And such recycling is applicable not just to our homes and workplaces, but needs consideration and application in our manufacturing industries with all aspects of production and manufacturing needing to be seen from a potential recycling and reuse perspective.

Not only are there direct benefits of recycling through such material reuse, but there are also benefits in reducing the levels of waste we need to dispose of. Our waste materials in themselves can damage our environment, especially considering the vast levels of waste materials produced by the billions of us on our planet with this waste sometimes, unfortunately and inappropriately just dumped and at other times buried as landfill. We need to avoid this dumping of waste, this being something which represents pollution in itself and which can cause serious and damaging pollution. While some of the processes required to recycle may be energy intensive and in some cases prohibitively expensive, for many materials there may be significant overall substantial benefit in recycling, in particular when considering the maintenance of our available materials and resources, and recognising that this recycling may well extend the life of the finite supply of resources we have available to us.

Unfortunately, the condition of our physical and biological environments is under threat from more than simply population increases and the pursuit of our material and other needs in a manner which lacks sufficient thought and planning. Recklessness and greed, negative selfishness, poor decision-making, short-termist and forms of poor thinking, lack of knowledge and lack of understanding contribute as well. All of these elements may to some extent lie behind the actions of those individuals, corporations and governments which, for example, destroy rain forests for economic gain, even though it is known and the individuals concerned know, that such destruction destroys animal habitats, contributes to the reduction of levels of oxygen generated for the global population and supports the consequent increases in carbon di-oxide linked to global warming. Those of us, those individuals who engage in such exploitation and damage of the environment, those of us who fail to understand and approach the environment in a caring, social and sustainable manner, exploiting the environment without concern for the consequences of our actions, acting without concern for the land itself and its wildlife, acting with concern only for their own negatively selfish, short-term well-being, irrespective of the consequences for the rest of the world and for our global climate, are acting reprehensibly and their actions need to be prevented and action taken against them, where necessary, for the benefit of us all.

Those people operating in such ways, where appropriate and reasonable, must find or be supported in finding alternative ways of supporting their incomes and livelihoods. We are each of us responsible for our actions and the consequences of our actions, and those of us, the corporations, the wealthy individuals, the managers, the individual farmers and agricultural workers supporting significant environmental destruction, with no accompanying significant compensatory and redressing actions in terms of environmental support, as well as those others linked to these activities, need to stop their destructive actions and if not, must be stopped by the rest of us. That is a responsibility for each of us as individuals. It is necessary that we act ourselves to prevent such destruction, that we encourage others to act to stop such damage and destruction and that we work to ensure that our global organisations themselves act to prevent such irresponsible and uncaring destruction wherever it can be brought to an end, ensuring sustainable, environmentally protective and developmental practices which support a healthy and sustainable environment into the future which will serve to support and benefit the well-being of us all.

Beyond our potential and our capacity to exhaust our earth's resources through over-consumption and other means discussed up to now in this chapter, our humanity is capable of presenting and is currently presenting a range of additional and varied threats to our environment and to our human species itself, many of these threats and potential threats originating in our technological developments.

In our current times, nuclear power and nuclear energy generation, through its potential for a range of different forms of destructive impact, provides us with a number of challenges, in particular the dangers of catastrophic accident, the dangers of release of low level poisonous radioactive pollution into the environment during operation of nuclear processes, and the linked and often longer term problems associated with safe disposal of radioactive waste. While technological developments in terms of safety may to some extent be leading to reductions in the level of threat to our safety from such nuclear power and nuclear energy generation, this form of power remains of concern and represents an example of the threat that technology can present to us.

However, it is not the aim or role of this guide to act as a detailed technological digest in which the problems and potentials of nuclear power, nuclear energy and nuclear accident are evaluated in depth. The nuclear industry presents issues and offers potential problems which are stated by some as being unlikely to occur (even the Chernobyl explosion of a nuclear reactor is reported by some as having not caused such vast damage, though as stated earlier in this chapter, 9000 excess deaths are estimated to have resulted from this accident and this must be considered an enormous number of deaths). Others view nuclear power as being a source of great danger (Chernobyl may be considered a very significant accident which itself may be a relatively small scale accident in relation to other possible accidents which might happen in the future).

It seems likely that, while nuclear power generation technology is not monolithic, given where this technology stands at the moment, there must be some risk of nuclear catastrophe arising from such nuclear power generation, through explosion by accident or deliberation. There are certainly dangers from low-level radiation arising from nuclear power generation in regard to health and well-being and known dispersion of radioactive materials and effects on our food chains. Yet such leakage is claimed to be rare or in practice, have little effect, while others claim potentially major effects which are difficult to reverse or indeed irreversible.

Whichever is the case, we clearly have to make decisions in relation to the level of risk we are prepared to bear in relation to nuclear power and the benefits we can derive from this source of energy. And our individual, community and societal decisions, indeed the decisions of our global organisations and global humanity, clearly must be the right ones given the potential existential threat which may be offered by mechanisms of nuclear power generation and the nuclear waste generated from this energy production.

These are questions to be debated to a much deeper and extended level of detail in a forum beyond this guide. From the point of view of this guide however, the questions are clear in regard to the principles of that discussion and can clearly frame such discussion. Is nuclear power acceptable enough as an energy source which can support human well-being and enable short, medium and long-term safety for human kind? Is the use of and development of nuclear energy generation an effective and appropriate use of resources (including in comparison to alternatives)? How likely is it that there will be damage to our human well-being through having nuclear power programmes? Are there alternative forms of power generation which are equally or similarly efficient which would provide lower levels of risk? Is nuclear power acceptable as a source which contributes to the removal and reduction of suffering of individuals in the world or will its use bring significant pain and suffering?

If the conditions of safety are fulfilled, and fulfilled in terms of its safety compared to other energy sources, then nuclear power, in a safe form, is surely valid and acceptable for our use, as long as it is an efficient source of energy production in comparison to other methods. If it is not safe and offers significant threats; if there is evidence to suggest an unreasonable level of risk to the population; if there is reasonable evidence to suggest that nuclear power has the potential to damage our well-being or destroy humankind; if nuclear energy production in terms of its effectiveness and cost is not reasonable and viable, then it cannot be used and expanded, whatever the investment, personal interest, spin offs and momentum behind such a notion.

A key element of this nuclear energy discussion is the link of nuclear energy production to production of material needed for highly destructive nuclear weapons. Issues of weaponry, including nuclear weapons, are discussed in chapter eleven of this guide. But a tie-in between nuclear power generation and nuclear weapons is often drawn. The arguments over the possession by nation states of nuclear weapons are complex with nuclear weapons said to act as a deterrent against others using nuclear weapons against us, with the prospect of mutually assured destruction argued to act against ultimately destructive nuclear war. This seems to be a dangerous argument, prone to fail in the face of mad ideologies, death cults, irrational leaders and irrational governmental systems. Though given the fact that nuclear weapons have only been used against one state, undemocratic dictatorial and imperial as it was, which lacked nuclear weapons, it may be that the non-possession of such weapons itself can impose serious risks.

Optimally we do not wish to have, or wish anyone to have the destructive power of nuclear weapons. Negotiations need to take place to phase out such weapons or for them to be handed over to global bodies. In essence such weapons need to be phased out with ultimate global efforts backed up by real power implemented to ensure that no individuals or states can construct or use such weapons.

Moreover, of course, with regard to the question of optimal energy sources, as already intimated, not only must nuclear power be evaluated in terms of its pollution effects and potential threat to our well-being, but we must also evaluate it against the pollution effects and other threats to our safety arising from other energy sources capable of supporting the energy needs of our communities and societies. Similar to some of the questions already stated, the questions of importance clearly lie in regards to how nuclear power compares with these other energy sources, whether it meets our needs in a better manner than these other sources, whether it is comparatively economic, and whether it offers lesser, similar or increased dangers to the environment and humanity.

We should also recognise in relation to the problems associated with such energy production, that the focus on such problems can take attention away from the need in itself for energy production, with failure to act on and meet our energy requirements holding out the possibility of pain and suffering for many millions (for example suffering through cold, absence of power needed to generate clean water), something which of course must be avoided in terms of core and other principles.

While waste disposal has already been considered in terms of recycling of materials, we also face dangers, as individuals, as communities and societies, as humanity, from a wide range of waste products generated from our human activities, some of which it is difficult to neutralise or recycle. For example, poisonous, polluting wastes may be generated through our abstraction of raw materials. Our mineral extraction, chemical and related industries in their various forms can generate a range of destructive pollutants which can and have poisoned rivers and streams. Such chemical and other wastes may poison our air with sometimes resultant and immediate loss of life, as was painfully demonstrated in the case of Bhopal in India. More often effects arise in the medium and longer term through particles in the air affecting our breathing and affecting our health (for example arising from toxic vehicle exhaust fumes) or through pollutants in our water (such as particulate plastics) which through that pollution, deny us access to important water supplies, cause the destruction of wildlife and ecosystems or damage our health through lung or other organ and tissue damaging illnesses.

But beyond obviously toxic fumes and immediately toxic products there is a range of solid matter or more liquid matter (such as oil, plastics and fuel waste) which may be dumped irresponsibly into our seas and rivers or even left standing around on our land defacing our landscapes and presenting hazards to both animal and human life. Such dumping can poison our rivers, lakes, seas and oceans, in itself damaging our food supplies and also reducing the pleasure which we can gain through enjoyment of our beautiful natural environments.

Adding to the potential poisons and toxins, untreated sewage may be poured through pipes and other means into our streams, rivers and oceans presenting disease hazards, sometimes deadly disease hazards, for any who swim in or use that water, with such sewage changing the patterns of natural life in those waters, destroying some species (though sometimes promoting the growth of others). All of this thoughtless and careless dumping and waste pollution is entirely unacceptable within the terms of the core and other principles offering threats to our well-being and happiness and presenting significant threats of suffering and pain, as well as damaging wildlife and living systems which we need to be sustaining, protecting as well as supporting and developing.

These problems with disposal of our waste products need to be dealt with. While we all have a responsibility to ensure that this is done, especially since we are often involved in polluting processes, being generators of waste or consumers of products which generate waste in their production, manufacture and use, the primary responsibility for dealing with these waste products needs to be taken by those of us who are most directly responsible for generating that waste. In other words if we are the primary people, in effect the ones who make a mess, it is our personal responsibility to clear it up.

Nevertheless, because of our individual, community and societal involvement as consumers and producers of waste, exemplified by our waste producing and resource requiring generation and utilisation of energy, such energy being something which we all need and which benefits us all, there is also a responsibility on the rest of us, to take some action as well. Each of us must, as ever, in relation to core and other principles, assume some personal responsibility of our own in regard to these matters and act accordingly to reduce waste and the dangers from such waste.

Experience has shown, additional to our own more local and personal actions, that dealing with issues such as the disposal of waste requires that we ensure the presence of regulations and laws to govern waste disposal along with effective monitoring and enforcement of such laws and regulations. Thus, we need to have systems, locally, nationally and globally in order to, in the first place act to ensure proper and safe waste disposal, and secondly to deal with those who act in a negatively selfish manner and who do not take sufficient care in regard to their disposal of waste.

As individuals we must all recognise our own responsibilities in regard to the waste we ourselves produce as individuals, ensuring that we aim to minimise the waste we generate, ensuring that the waste we generate is clean or will be cleaned such that it is not a source of infection or danger for others, and ensuring that we recycle and reuse wherever possible, thereby promoting waste reduction.

At an additional basic every day level, we must not litter, that is drop our every day items on the ground, food wrappers, papers, plastic bottles and the like and we must not dump our unwanted items in the public space, but instead must dispose of them in an environmentally friendly manner or recycle them appropriately. Even if such waste seems in a sense safe, offering little damage to the environment and being non-infectious or not capable of promoting illness and disease, its presence can affect the appearance of our environment in a negative and unpleasant manner.

Allied to our own personal and immediate actions with regard to rubbish and litter, and in regard to maintaining a clean and pleasant environment, we should ensure more broadly and as far as we can, that our local environments are clean and tidy, indeed as pleasant and beautiful as we can make them, organising with others, organising as groups, communities and societies to ensure this is the case. We should also take responsibility for ensuring that our broader and more distant environments are healthy and pleasing. As individuals, communities and societies, we need to support the generation of solutions to waste problems and support ongoing research in regard to avoiding the production of damaging or excessive, unnecessary waste and support research into more effective ways of waste disposal and recycling.

Considering other environmental issues, at the current time, many of us are concerned about the introduction of genetically engineered crops into the environment to be used as foodstuffs or for other purposes. Various dangers are seen in such moves. We may worry that there are potential threats to both ourselves, to our human communities and societies as well as to animal populations due to the introduction of modified genes into our food chains, an introduction which many fear may affect our own human health in a damaging manner. While, there is in principle, reason to have cause for concern, and while such damage may be possible, no substantive evidence of dangers arising from this has been presented to date. No substantive evidence has been produced to suggest that such fears are justifiable, though it is understandable that such fears should exist, and it is more than unwise to simply wait for such problems to actually arise before considering whether there is substantive enough evidence to lead to action, since acting at such a point in time may mean acting too late.

We do know that genes can be transferred from genetically modified organisms to other organisms, with evidence of unintended gene transfer between modified and unmodified plants already having been demonstrated, mediated through viral or phage transmission. The uncontrolled and unplanned transmission of specific genes, engineered to enhance growth, productivity or prevent plant death in particular crops, would seem to offer the possibilities of unexpected and unwanted effects (for example certain unwanted plants developing pesticide and herbicide resistance), even though no one has been harmed up to now. We should all be concerned about the potential for harm to our human health through such genetically modified organisms, and substantial further research is needed before we can have full confidence in the widespread use of such genetically engineered organisms. Given the potential risks involved, a precautionary and gradual approach to the use of such genetically engineered organisms seems the wisest approach.

Perhaps a more important concern for us, and perhaps an equally real threat to our well-being in relation to genetically modified food sources is the development of total ownership of food production by corporations which are patenting or have patented and own rights to crops, corporations which claim enforceable property rights over basic food stuffs and the rights to buy and sell these at as far as is possible, at prices which suit them. For example corporations and organisations through market mechanisms, through their control over the seeds they sell, may place hard and indeed unfair bargains on the shoulders of farmers, establishing conditions whereby farmers must use only the corporately supplied seeds and may end up with no alternative but to abide by unfair conditions or lose their livelihoods. There is also the possibility that there may also be corporate efforts to create scarcity and thereby raise prices beyond what the many of us can afford. And we may, as individuals, communities, societies and beyond, reach the stage where there is no independent ownership of food production as there is today, and life or death in terms of food consumption could potentially lie in the hands of the corporate owners of food production capacity.

With food production in the hands of these corporations, unregulated or even regulated, but motivated by financial profit and shareholder interests, as indeed they are bound to be as that is the law in a number of countries at this point in time, those who cannot pay for expensive crops will starve, and those who cannot pay will have no avenue in which to develop their own crops, their own food-based means to survive, as relevant and available crops will be the legal property of a corporation which may pursue legal enforcement of its ownership.

Farmers wishing to grow crops may therefore or alternatively be in the position where they have no choice but to use the crop produced by the corporation and buy and sell the crop at the price determined by that corporation. This type of situation is unlikely to support our overall human well-being. In terms of core and other principles, placing such control of our basic needs in the hands of unelected, undemocratic corporations whose priority, and indeed in many cases, as already stated legally mandated priority, is their shareholders interests and financial profit rather than supporting our general and individual human well-being, is totally unacceptable, and further, any system or outcome which jeopardises our food consumption, the well-being of our communities, societies, global humanity and our individual well-being, is entirely unacceptable.

Thus, while there could certainly be benefits to our well-being through more efficient food production using genetically modified crops, there is danger arising, not only through direct biological threats but in particular through the use of ineffectively regulated market mechanisms applied to our basic food stuffs, as well as with regard to other materials we all require to meet fundamental needs and support our survival. From our individual point of view, in terms of core and other principles, it is our role to support the existence of an appropriate environment which itself supports our health and well-being and which will support the health and well-being of future generations, ensuring that health and well-being is not damaged through the inappropriate generation, ownership and use of genetically engineered crops or other products.

We also have the responsibility to ensure that our resources, including our food, are produced efficiently and effectively such that all of us have, at the minimum, enough to survive, but more reasonably and optimally, that we further can have enough food to support an excellent and varied diet and a high level of health and well-being. We also have the responsibility of ensuring human and community control and power over food production and other areas key to our welfare and well-being, if necessary ownership, and indeed to some degree utilisation, such that no one runs the risk of food shortage and that humanity as a whole, as a democratic, concerned and caring body, has the key influence over agriculture and food production such that each one of us benefits, avoids pain and suffering through starvation or shortages and scarcity, and such that we can all enjoy well-being and happiness.

The advent of the range of new technologies and innovations in agriculture and their potential effects on our environment illustrates the fact that we need to plan and prepare for their possible impacts. Where there are new developments in train in regard to technology and innovation, we as individuals, communities and societies need to encourage forward planning and anticipate the consequences of such new technologies. Those developing new technologies need to ensure that the early developmental stages of a technological or other innovation, where relevant, include consideration of the environmental consequences of that development, with the implementation of that innovation incorporating research which demonstrates any positive environmental effects of the new technology, as well as including plans to deal with any potential changes for the worse, consequent on the introduction of that new technology or other innovation.

Such planning for potential negative environmental consequences will mean that any such negative effects and changes should be able to be remediated or the development stopped from going forward *in toto* if no relevant remedies can be found. Of course this should have a positive benefit on our well-being, as long as our planning, monitoring and oversight does not put such a break on new developments that innovation and change is unreasonably discouraged, and as long as the development of new technologies and other innovations are considered in relation to their effect compared to other futures and other consequences should these technologies and innovations not be introduced. Of course there are certainly substantial grounds for innovation and development of the range of technologies which, in themselves, have as their main purpose, the development and maintaining of a positive environment, for example through tackling pollution.

Where there are schemes involving additional pressure on land use, for example pressures for providing new housing or industrial developments, developments which reduce the land available for agriculture, for leisure and other purposes, we need, in addition to their social and economic purposes and consequences, to consider these schemes in terms of their overall effect on the environment, ecosystems and wildlife. The reality is, at the present time, far too many of these schemes are implemented without our giving sufficient consideration to such consequences, or with developers and planners paying lip service to environmental considerations with a presumption within many of our systems of support for building and industrial development.

Such a presumption is not acceptable within the context of the principles presented in this guide, with broad democratically discussed and accepted plans required, so as to ensure that a suitable environment for all results, and in order that such proposals and changes have broad community support. Yet of course we may well need additional housing; and we may well wish to have, indeed it will benefit our well-being substantially if we do have, industrial development which can support the provision of jobs and income and which will support broader social and community well-being.

Of course, moreover, new buildings, new human-made structures, can serve to improve our environment substantially. Stunning pieces of architectural work can enhance our sense of well-being through their beauty and grandeur, and indeed immensity. Thus our worlds are enhanced by our well-known structures such as the Eifel Tower in France, the Taj Mahal in India, the Great Wall of China, the Pyramids in Egypt and a vast range of other human-made wonders around the world. And, hopefully, wherever we live, there are buildings of subtlety and beauty, town halls, churches, cathedrals, museums, office blocks and homes and houses, some of which are stunning in their beauty, aesthetics and indeed extent. We need to be open to promoting and enabling our own human environmental creations, which will themselves serve to enhance our own personal as well as the general well-being and happiness.

Returning to more general and perhaps more damaging impactful environmental effects, where environmentally detrimental effects are already occurring but were not anticipated, or where they are occurring on the moment due to natural processes (as nature itself can pollute our environment) or due to pre-existing pollutants or technologies, then we must tackle these negative effects in a manner and time frame dependent on and concomitant with the level of the threat to our well-being. In some, if not many cases, this means a requirement for urgent and immediate action.

For example, at the moment with regard to the key issue already discussed of global warming which already is generally accepted as a consequence of human activity, this is starting to result in and will result in significant and unwanted threatening and damaging changes which have the potential to threaten our livelihoods and even the very existence of many of us into the future. Clearly therefore, and representing an illustration of how we need to tackle many other environmental matters, we need to ensure that there is significant and immediate action at the global level to deal with this climate problem, supported by our own appropriate action at the more local level. And such a global focus needs to be promoted and adopted by us all with regard to the environment and a range of other issues. Without our taking such a global approach to and without global agreement on climate action, there is little chance that we will be able to counter in an effective manner what is a grave threat to humanity, with the well-being of all of us being damaged as a consequence.

Of course there are problems in our achieving such global agreements with the range of often negatively selfish and short-termist national and sub-national political and corporate interests often playing a part in the blocking of action which is almost universally acknowledged by those who have conducted research in this area, as necessary. Nevertheless it is one of our responsibilities, as laid out in this guide, within the principles stated, to do our utmost to ensure that environmental threats such as global warming are addressed effectively. And if we do not do so, it seems highly likely that there will be much resultant pain and suffering, with the potential for massive and perhaps terminal damage to our humanity.

If the well-being of others and indeed ourselves and future generations is under such threat, then there is no real choice but for us to take action to ensure that we act to protect our environment such that we have an appropriate environment which supports our healthy living and which provides us with pleasure and enjoyment. As with so many other decisions, actions and areas of our personal conduct, we need to follow the evidence that has been presented, and develop and exercise intelligent and rational judgments and opinions making rational and correct decisions rather than basing them in suspicion, fear, prejudice, superstition, fatalism or negatively selfish self-interest. The evidence in regard to global warming and of its being the consequence of human activity appears highly convincing and authoritative and it seems almost incontrovertible that our human actions are required to tackle and solve this urgent problem.

In terms of what we as individuals can do in practice in regard to these global issues, as individuals, we can raise awareness locally and campaign locally, looking to persuade and exert pressure, both nationally and internationally in order that appropriate policy decisions are made and in order that short term, foolish, ill calculated and inappropriate negatively selfish actions do not prevail with their subsequent damage to our well-being, and resultant pain and suffering in the shorter, medium and longer term.

Without our individual efforts in the direction of supporting the welfare and well-being of all others; without our individual actions in supporting others who pursue the principles as set out in this guide; without our acting ourselves and bolstering others aiming to support a healthy and sustainable environment, who themselves are in need of our support and sometimes our protection, without our consideration of the relevant evidence and reports and as a consequence acting accordingly in line with that evidence, and with boldness, our human society runs the risk of inflicting significant if not permanent and even catastrophic damage on itself, ourselves and others.

Global environmental issues matter and are of crucial importance to our well-being and our care of our environment. Yet within that global picture, within that bigger picture, our more local environments are generally of substantial importance to the lives of each of us. While obviously affected by global issues in terms of pollution and environmental threat, our more local environments have their own identity and importance, their own uniqueness, their own immediacy to our daily lives, in particular in the sense that they are more open to modification and change through our own, more immediate individual actions and the actions of those we know, and those who live in our local areas and neighbourhoods. Our local environments, for example those within the space of our own homes, but also within our villages, towns and cities, represent places where our own individual conduct in regard to the environment can matter in a clearly significant, visible and immediate manner.

In the first place, in those most local of environments, our own more individual spaces, which may be our own personal rooms, our own gardens, our own houses, those spaces in which we can exist as individuals with no, or perhaps the most limited interaction with others (unless they are invited in), we have, in essence, carte blanche to keep our spaces as we will, as long as there is no effect or no significant effect of our actions on others. While in this, our own personal space, there are clearly some social restrictions in terms of, for example, making excessive noise or living in such filth and squalor that our space becomes a hazard to self and others, nevertheless, within our personal spaces, we have the right to be as messy as we wish, to decorate these as we wish, to use these as we wish (concomitant with the other principles) and to call that space private and our own. Each of us needs and benefits from such a personal space, our own highly personal environment, which we can decorate and keep as we will, in which we can think, reflect, enjoy, exist in secret, experiment, invent, contemplate, relax, cry, read, be in control, and do many more things away from the prying eyes and potential criticisms and sometimes laughter and derision of others. In the same way that we might wish our own personal spaces to belong to us and be private to us, so we must respect the privacy and personal space of others.

Yet in our more social spaces we must take much greater account of the wishes and needs of others in line with core and other principles. Linked to the core principles, as individuals, our being careful and caring in terms of our environment means that we can and should act, in support of the well-being of ourselves and others, to enhance our own and their aesthetic and other pleasure in all that which surrounds us locally. By contrast, being careless in terms of our local environment, while in the case of some aesthetic effects, perhaps falling beneath the level of the threshold of causing suffering, in terms of other effects, this can certainly reduce our sense of well-being and the sense of well-being of others.

Local messes will upset others, damaging our aesthetic pleasure and enjoyment of our local environments, bringing down our lives and the lives of others through having that messy environment, and potentially, in some more extreme cases of excessive dirt and mess, promoting disease and more, creating broader damage to ourselves and the environment. Unattractive and damaged, inappropriate, environments, indeed local environments which have been poorly designed in human terms, made more for machines or objects than people, may lead to a sense of unhappiness and perhaps even sadness and depression.

It is fortunately, for many of us, within our power to develop and enhance our local environment, for example, if we have a garden, however small, we can do this through establishing pleasant and perhaps beautiful gardens. We can perhaps plant trees in our gardens, thereby supporting local wildlife, and wildlife habitats; we can construct ponds where perhaps these are in short supply in our local natural environment and where these are appropriate to construct and support. And we can take a range of other actions as necessary to make these environments pleasant, planting flowers, producing beautiful lawns, and more. If we have no garden we can use window boxes to brighten up the outsides of our properties, and with others perhaps develop roof gardens and more. All of this is likely to be beneficial and pleasurable to us as individuals as well as to others through an improved and more beautiful local environment.

We can enhance our local environment through tasteful and perhaps inventive design and modification of our properties. We can support, as individuals and local communities, sculpture, architecture, artworks and other features such as fountains and springs, which enhance the beauty and interest of the places we live, making them distinct from others and therefore of greater interest, worth and note in a characteristic and local sense.

Our built environment certainly needs to be considered, with such aesthetics and a sense of beauty in mind, even where resources are scarce, as appreciation of such beauty is long lasting and beneficial to us all over time. The value and importance of beautiful buildings and other structures have already been mentioned. Our architecture and design need to be of interest and to be valued, but of course, due to our differing sense of taste will of course be controversial and provocative at times (indeed such provocation may be necessary to help us find that which in fact pleases us or does not). While our built environment is important to us, we will also need, on occasion, to be tolerant of that which perhaps does not suit our own particular tastes.

Due to what might be stark juxtaposition with the surrounding more natural world, those significant and challenging building developments which are large scale in their nature, may be more suited to populated areas, although that need not always be the case. Our other needs in terms of well-being, including our economic well-being, may in some cases trump our concerns about preserving a pristine natural environment. However when such developments are being considered, where the new development offers to contribute towards broader environmental damage which may have a significant effect on the quality of our environment as far as health and well-being are considered, then these effects need to be considered as important factors in whether or not we decide to support such developments. Each of our human built constructions, industrial or otherwise, however, needs to have aesthetic and environmental considerations considered and incorporated as far as possible within its design, where necessary and valuable, blending into its surroundings.

Decisions in terms of both some private and some more public developments need to be taken through democratic mechanisms and involve local consultation, since these developments will affect those of us living in the vicinity of these developments and possibly beyond. It is perhaps not always necessary that all, or perhaps even the majority of us, are in favour of any particular development, with radical and new designs sometimes proving controversial, though it would undoubtedly be best if the vast majority of those affected by a new development would support it. Nevertheless, it has often proven to be the case that there is a desire by some, if not many, to keep any new development away from the location where they live, be it new housing, new communication towers, power distribution axes and networks or other. Such concerns should not be ignored and indeed should be able to influence decisions to an important degree. Nevertheless, the overall impact, indeed, the broader impact on well-being for all of us also needs to be a significant factor in any decisions made in regard to such new developments.

Thus, for example, if there is a proposal to build a dam or a power station, a communications transmitter or wind energy generator in a rural area, then there may well be detrimental effects on us if we are part of the local population. These may simply be in some cases what we consider to be visual detrimental effects. But decisions need to be made which take into account our own needs and wants and the wider benefits of such a dam or power station, energy generator or communications mast to the community, for example the potential to reduce deaths from cold, the supply of energy to hospitals, the range of economic benefits through for example, jobs and income. And that being said, if benefits of such a dam or power station are judged as outweighing the disadvantages to ourselves, then we who are disadvantaged by these developments need to be provided for and supported in any transition we are required to make in order for that new facility to be built. In this way the maximal well-being of all will be achieved.

Of course, as previously discussed, we need to make sure that we plan with regard to our local and more global environments. Locally we need not only to ensure that we have a pleasant aesthetic environment, but also that we have ample neighbourhood facilities to support our well-being and happiness, from shops to transport routes, to parks and playgrounds for our children, from schools to markets, to pleasant places of work and more. These facilities need to be accessible and available to all in order to support maximal well-being, and we all need to contribute to ensuring that such facilities are in place. All of these facilities and more are needed in order that we have a healthy and pleasant local environment. And a healthy and pleasant local environment requires effective waste disposal, cleanliness, easy supply of energy to our homes, and effective systems of sewerage and drainage amongst other things.

Relevant to our daily lives and relevant to our local environments and wider global environments, as well as to the future of our humanity, is our relationship with the non-human living world. We have already mentioned the influence of pollution and other facets of our human activity on plants and other wildlife. The previously mentioned reality which we need to appreciate is that microbial, plant, and animal life comprise a part of our lives with which we are intricately bound, whether we like it or not. These organisms support, or are connected to, the air that we breathe, the food that we eat, the water that we drink, the way we feel in terms of our health and well-being, the aesthetics of our environment and many other pleasures of our human living, from our enjoyment of birdsong, to walks through woodlands and forests, from our pleasure in the flowers in our gardens, to the pets that many of us may keep in their homes. As human beings, we are individually and collectively a part of the natural world, indeed an integral part of that living world.

Additional to those pleasures and joys, and our integrated identity in relation to our natural non-human world, we have, as individuals and as a humanity, a broad responsibility to avoid unnecessary pain and suffering to animals.[7] Unnecessary cruelty and hurt to animals is inconsistent with the values presented in this guide as stated in the sixth Additional Fundamental

---

7  We will assume for the moment that plants and other organisms such as bacteria, fungi and viruses cannot suffer.

Principle. It is not acceptable to cause unnecessary suffering and pain to animals, which need to be protected from such harm.

Yet of course animals are a part of the diet for the greater part of our humanity (and part of the diet of each other) across the current modern world. It is considered here in this guide to be possible and indeed desirable for the culture of the world to shift such that animals are no longer eaten, although given our position in regard to animals in this current and culturally varied world, this could only realistically happen in the medium and long term, given the deeply embedded social cultures of animal eating. However, this would seem to be a reasonable medium and long-term goal if, as seems to be in the main the case, our dietary needs can be healthily and sufficiently met from elsewhere. An important bottom line here is our human health, and if it is the case that our nutritional needs cannot be met from elsewhere, that they cannot be met from plants or synthetic sources, something which in the vast main, appears not to be the case, then it would be necessary for us to use the relevant animal sources.

Certainly, at the minimum, where we, and our farmers, have kept animals which are used for food purposes they need to be well-looked after during their lives. They should certainly not experience cruelty and callousness. They must be well fed, their health maintained, such that they do not suffer unnecessarily. If they are to be slaughtered for eating, animals must be killed with minimum pain and suffering. And if their consumption can be avoided, and a healthy and acceptable alternative diet can be provided, then that would be a positive development worth aiming for.

There are also farming practices, designed to create efficient mass production, that are inappropriate and unacceptable in terms of our care and concern for life and living. For example the mass killings of newly hatched male chicks for use as animal feed is unacceptable in terms of our care for life. The confining of animals to crowded and restricted spaces, as is sometimes, if not often, done with battery hens and pig rearing, is undesirable and cruel. Confining young cattle to a restricted and solitary life in darkness, as is sometimes done in the production of veal meat, is cruel and callous. We can all take action in regard to these cruel and callous methods for rearing animals. As farmers and food manufacturers, we can use alternative efficient and more caring farming practices, refusing to use these methods of animal rearing and refusing to support or collaborate with such practices. As individuals, we can act to prevent and reduce such practices by requesting and pressuring, with others, to achieve change and through refusing to eat meat or consume other products which are generated through such cruel animal rearing practices.

That being said, given our human need to survive, to have a positive and healthy diet, while avoiding animal products might be seen as a laudable and worthy goal, it is considered legitimate within core and other principles, at least at the present time, for us to use live animals for the valuable products they provide us with. There may be alternative forms of dietary intake which do not require exploitation of animals for such purposes, and where these are available, it would seem reasonable to develop these, but a symbiotic relationship with the animals used in agriculture, which maintains the health and well-being of such animals, which protects them from the natural dangers they might face as non-domesticated animals, and which at the same time benefits our human health, is seen here as of value and worthy of being maintained.

For, at least at the present time, it would seem impossible for our modern, complex societies, comprising the many billions of us who all need nutrition, who need to eat in order to survive, it would seem impossible for us to continue existing without the use of such animal products. For almost all of us, animal products comprise sources of very important dietary intake, intake which supports our health and well-being. Eggs, milk, cheese and other animal products provide us with important dietary sources of vitamins, fats, proteins and other key nutritional components. We clearly need vast scale production of food to support our dietary needs, our personal well-being and our individual survival. And it is possible, even though some correctly believe that this is not done to a satisfactory degree at the present time, for us to live with our animals and to make use of products from these animals while providing a satisfactory, positive and healthy life for those animals which are the sources of these products.

Thus, without such use of animals and animal products to ensure we all can receive the food we need, our communities and societies, we as individuals, will likely be substantially worse off. While some may argue that it is illegitimate exploitation to use any animal products, our human relationship with animals is seen as a necessary relationship which may also have some benefits for those animals which are in the main kept safe and fed, away from natural predators, with such animals often provided with protection from disease through veterinary care.

Certainly at the present time it would seem impractical and indeed damaging for our health to completely avoid the use of such products. While it seems possible in the current age to have a sufficient diet devoid of many animal products, such a diet certainly needs supplementing with vitamins and other elements, some of which are only found naturally in substantial levels in animals and animal products. In the future, a healthy diet without animal products might be more possible, and again, this may be a worthy goal. Whichever dietary route is taken, animals need to be properly cared for and looked after.

Linked to this, linked to our concern to avoid creating suffering, our concern to avoid hurting and frightening animals, it is not legitimate within core and other principles to use animals such that they suffer in our pursuit of purposes such as sport and entertainment. Thus, the chasing of animals for the sake of human pleasure is not acceptable, nor is the killing of animals for pleasure. We may wish to retain some traditional skills that have been used for hunting, for acquiring our food, but as far as possible, this should avoid killing or unnecessary cruelty to animals. Judgments need to be made in many cases. The pursuit of fishing for leisure is seen as perfectly acceptable if the fish are returned, to all intents and purposes unharmed, to the water, or, within the context of what has already been stated in regard to those of us who eat meat, if those fish are eaten.

It is of course the case that animals can be, and often are, killers themselves, predatory and harmful to humans and other animals. Indeed, we, as humans are embedded in that natural world in which animals eat plants and animals eat each other. The bird eats the worm; the fish eats the fly; the pride of lions eats the wildebeest; the cat catches the mouse. Nevertheless, as humans, as individuals and as human society, we are a different kind of animal, vastly powerful and aware of pain and suffering, feelings, well-being, happiness, and often holding the power to prevent pain and suffering. While animals can be pests to our farmers and damage our crops, cause us injury and disease through attacks, harm us through bites and stings, will attack and eat other animals and can hurt and damage us and other animals in many other ways, despite this, as conscious, caring and powerful human beings, we have a responsibility to look after these creatures, whatever threat they might offer us, while ensuring that we do not suffer any significant harm ourselves.

It is not far-fetched to further state, that our attitudes and actions towards other living creatures are influential in, or reflect, our attitudes and actions towards each other. If we are capable of defining the life of an animal as being meaningless, or see animals as insentient, unfeeling, unexperiencing units of production and consumption, then this may well play in to our own human attitudes towards each other, to other groups, other races, other people and cultures, with consequent terrible effects. It may well be that we need to start unothering the animals we share our planet with. That does not mean that we treat all animals as if they are humans. They are of course not so. But it does mean recognising them as important and sentient life, and caring for them as such sentient, experiencing, living beings.

While caring for animals, our responsibility to protect ourselves and other people, does come above our concerns for other animals. Thus, where animals threaten us directly, or where the food supply or our livelihoods are under threat from animals or other organisms, then, as with other areas, we need to act intelligently but certainly effectively, to prevent this damage wherever possible, acting to use the minimal force and physical action necessary and aiming to avoid as far as we can, any significant harm to those animals doing the damage. Yet our food supply and personal health must be maintained, as must be our lives and livelihoods, consummate with core and other principles, in order to support our individual well-being and happiness and to prevent us enduring suffering and pain.

Wild animals, as opposed to domesticated animals, also comprise an important part, and indeed an essential part of our environment, and as individual animals and individual species, as parts of our interacting ecological communities, we need to look after them as far as we can, making sure that these species are preserved and maintained. This is part of our care for individual animals but is also part of our care for other species, care for our environment and care for ourselves as human beings.

In theory, taking care of most animal species should involve doing little, however the reality in our current age is one of wide scale human ecological and habitat destruction affecting many animals, with food supplies destroyed, predator and prey relationships disrupted, landscapes comprising potential animal homes or acting as sources of protection being destroyed, and in the case of aquatic creatures, wide scale pollution, ocean acidification and warming and indeed over-exploitation of sea creatures as food sources. Therefore we need to take deliberate action to preserve, maintain and enhance our natural environments such that wildlife can thrive. In essence these creatures need looking after.

It is clearly important both to our own well-being and the well-being of animal and plant life that the current levels of habitat destruction are stopped or slowed substantially. Rather than short-termist negatively selfish exploitation and damage of our environment, as already stated in this chapter, our use of the environment needs to be planned on a global scale such that all of us will benefit as individuals, communities and societies and such that our global habitats and the plant and animal life within those habitats are protected. This clearly needs global action and this should clearly be a global priority for our nation states and global organisations. Both we as a humanity and our plant and animal life, are currently under severe threat and there is a need for expeditious action to protect us all.

Being concerned for wildlife raises many important issues for us. By preserving habitats and the range of wildlife, we are preserving existing ecosystems and biological relationships. And as part of this we have to recognise that we are maintaining the reality of animals causing suffering to other animals, and probably intense, extended and painful suffering to some of those animals. Predators kill and eat their prey which may endure intense suffering in the process of being hunted down and in the process of being eaten. And there are a multitude of such predator-prey relationships existing, amongst sea creatures, insects, birds, land animals and more. On top of that there are parasitic relationships where parasites slowly kill their hosts and a range of other relationships through which animals may impose intense pain and suffering on other animals.

If we were to wish to care for all animals precisely in line with the relevant additional specific principle established, then in theory we should intervene to prevent all of their suffering as far as we can. However, the reality is that this is, for the most part, impossible, as predators will not survive without eating their prey, and will face extinction. And, moreover, the absence of predators may mean the explosion in numbers of the relevant prey in that relationship, which itself will have other implications for other animals and plant life. Thus, the consequences of predator extinction will themselves echo down the food chain, the prey most likely expanding to vast numbers in the absence of their predators, eating more of their own prey themselves if they have such prey, or causing destruction on a vast scale of the plants or other organisms they live on.

The reality is that such intervention in animal-animal relationships cannot be seen as a priority, given our other priorities in relation to our own human suffering and other priorities in relation to animals and the environment. Nevertheless, in our desire to reduce suffering and pain, there may be some need for initial investigations and thinking in regard to how we stand and what we might do, if we choose to do anything, in relation to these animal-animal relationships, with the possibility of taking some action into the future, taking into account all possible effects (such comprising a complex and perhaps in the end a potentially impossible and undesirable endeavour). On the other hand determining to take action in regard to these animal-animal relationships might be seen as taking our efforts, care and concern beyond where they should legitimately lie.

Animals are also important to many of us as pets in our households and the well-being of many of us may be enhanced by our keeping of animals as pets. These animals may provide company to those of us who are lonely, becoming objects of our affection and indeed reciprocal affection for ourselves and our children. Our pets can become almost integral members of our families, for some of us providing comfort and companionship in a complex world in which we can feel unwanted, unimportant if not irrelevant, put upon, lonely and isolated from the world around us. Our pets can make us feel better by providing us with attention, a sense of purpose and meaning, warmth and affection. If we have dogs and cats as pets, they can certainly have an attachment to us and show us affection through their various ways of behaving. They can serve as objects for the affection we want to give and that we may be unable to give elsewhere, to other people, even though we might wish and prefer to give and receive that affection in relationships with other people.

Perhaps through their lack of complexity of interaction, their lack of subtlety of response, lack of complex demands, and through the absence of the complex social interactions and give and take required of our human relationships, our pets can often be easier and less demanding sources of comfort and company. We can stroke them and they will often respond with apparent pleasure; we can play with them and they seem to respond with joy and excitement. And, if we are short of other company, our pets can give us something to focus on, rather than the empty space of the day, keeping us busy in looking after them and caring for them and interacting with them, when otherwise our lives might feel somewhat empty. For those who live alone and who are older, it may be that the presence of a pet helps and motivates us to keep up regular activity and a regular regime and exercise, since we are obliged to care for and wish to care for our animals. For some of us, if not many of us, pets can act as a substitute for the more difficult and complex human relationships which we may not have, or may no longer have, providing us with warmth, comfort, company and a human-pet friendship. And moreover there seems to be significant research which indicates that there are health benefits for those of us who keep pets.

There might be those who would argue that such care and affection would be best applied elsewhere, but having pets and taking part in other relationships and cooperative activities are far from mutually exclusive. Indeed caring for a pet might be seen as supporting and allowing the expression of our caring nature as people. We can certainly see that giving practice in caring, and taking care of a pet is one way of trying to teach our growing children to care, and to perhaps act in a disciplined and responsible, caring manner, through giving them their own responsibilities for feeding and looking after a pet.

There are those who point to the level of resources expended on pets arguing this is inappropriate. Indeed, the level of resources devoted to pets can be perverse, with some pet owners spending major sums on their pets, such excessive spending being inappropriate. In a world where our fellow human beings live in poverty, where millions of others suffer from potentially curable illness and disease yet may receive no treatment due to lack of resources, it must be our priority to support those people living in pain, suffering and poverty, to help lift them out of poverty, to reduce their suffering from disease and illness. We must make our utmost efforts to ensure that this is done and this must be a major priority.

Yet at the same time, we do need to be supporting our own well-being and happiness. And for some people, that well-being is significantly enhanced by and includes having pets, animals in the home to look after, to give affection to and, dependent on the particular animal, to receive affection from. As a source of well-being and happiness for those who have pets, such keeping of pets is clearly a positive, yet of course it does require resources which would clearly be beneficial to those living in poverty and suffering in pain. Overall, we need to balance the well-being and happiness we receive from our pets, and the good done through having pets (the care for the animals in themselves, their educational value, their value in other roles such as guards for our properties, their role as sources of interest and engagement in our lives, their roles in a family) with the potential benefits which could be brought to others if we used these resources to support others, including those living in poverty.

Of course there are many economic and other causes of human poverty. The reality of poverty and illness, suffering is complex and the transfer of resources from those who have resources towards those who are poor is probably only one, though an important, element in solving the problem of poverty and certainly not the whole solution. Our not having pets and not devoting resources and money to our pets is not likely to significantly alleviate overall the general levels of poverty and illness that we know exist, though it undoubtedly could help to some degree and make a significant difference to some individuals. Our provision of some resources will thus hopefully help somebody somewhere, and this is something which is crucial for us to do if we have the capacity to do it. Clearly, in relation to the resources we expend on our pets, alleviation of poverty and suffering for people is the priority, and we need to ensure that while enjoying the comfort and pleasures that pets can bring us and our families, we are making sure that we are supporting those people in dire need in our world.

Animals, at least at the present time are also brought to and kept in zoos and wildlife parks. Such zoos and wildlife parks provide us with real experiences of seeing and, in an important sense being with animals rather than the more distant experience of pictures, films and stories. Through providing more real and immediate experiences, these zoos and wildlife parks provide us with vivid, enjoyable and educational experiences in ways which the more distant experiences are unable to do. While there are those who say that such animals would be better off in the wild, that is not necessarily the case due to predation, human hunting and the unwanted destruction of natural environments. As long as those animals in zoos and wildlife parks have sufficient space, sufficient stimulation, the company of others of their species where that is needed; as long as their health and dietary needs are provided for, then their presence in such zoos and wildlife parks is seen here as being beneficial to all. Additionally, the presence of such animals in zoos also provides us with a reservoir of animals which, in the case that natural populations should become substantially depleted, will enable us to repopulate the natural environment with these animals. Moreover their presence in zoos allows some elements of research through which we can learn amore about such animals, their diets and behaviours.

Animals are sometimes used in research experimentation which is designed to improve our health and well-being. Much of this experimentation is harmful, if not deadly to the animals used in these experiments. In line with core and other principles, such experimentation should be ended as soon as is possible and wherever possible replaced with other forms of investigation, research and experimentation such that animals no longer suffer through such experimentation.

That being said, we cannot leave people to suffer intensely, suffering agony, and perhaps lose their lives prematurely, where there are direct or even indirect routes to ending their suffering and saving their lives, even if this involves using sentient animals in experiments. There are illnesses of the brain and other parts of our bodies, illnesses affecting many millions of people which might be alleviated or prevented through our increased knowledge and understanding of disease and illness, knowledge and understanding which has arisen in the past and which can be added to in the future, in order to tackle debilitating and destructive disease and illness.

Therefore, where it is essential and offers significant benefits to human health, saving the lives of babies, children and adults, or where such experimentation offers potential routes to improving health in a major way, or saving lives, undesirable as it is, we need to allow such animal experimentation where it is demonstrably of value, to take place, with the rider that other alternative methods of research must be explored and explored systematically such that inflicting pain and suffering on animals in this way and for these purposes becomes a thing of the past. Such methods and approaches are already in development and some have displaced animal experimentation already. Hopefully many improvements and developments will take place in this area into the future.

If such experimentation is done it should involve minimal suffering, pain and damage to the animals involved. Defining that research which is essential, is in practice difficult as, if we are to make progress with dealing with various forms of disease and illness, it may be necessary to engage in research, the purpose of which at the time is exploratory and quite difficult to justify apart from as a route to exploration. Nevertheless, this research will support long-term developments and greater understanding. Such exploratory research is seen here as being essential, though will optimally not be based in or require animals as experimental subjects.

As a route to preserving and saving human life this guide suggests that, bearing in mind core and other principles, it is allowable for essential medical and health research to use animals in a manner which minimises animal suffering to take place. Clearly this does give humans status above other creatures, and also states that animal suffering, to the minimal degree possible, is acceptable in the pursuit of significantly enhanced human health. However that assumption is accepted here within this guide with the commitment to reducing pain and suffering and supporting of well-being of animals, plants and other organisms as far as is possible, and recognising their integral and essential relationship with our human species.

For some of us, this may be difficult to accept in terms of our deeply held feelings and beliefs, and our upset at any hurt caused to animals in particular. This is recognised here as a difficult and important discussion. Some animals are like us to an important degree, for example chimpanzees, and may well suffer particularly badly as a result of certain experimentation. Moreover, the precedent, the decision that some forms of living organisms are of lesser value than our fellow humans would seem to set the scene for seeing other humans as lesser than us, something which is unacceptable in terms of core and other principles.

For the mean time, this guide is stating that by assumption and definition, our primary concern is with human well-being and happiness. Of course animals, plants and all other research on animals which causes them significant pain and suffering should, as far as possible, be avoided and if possible, end completely. It is the position here that our conduct needs to be aimed at avoiding such pain and suffering amongst animals as a result of our human actions. This almost always needs to be the case, but exceptions are considered to be legitimate where our human health is under significant threat, where we as human beings are suffering in pain or have the potential to suffer in pain, with the rider that any such experiments and investigations should minimise the pain and suffering that animals experience.

Our debates and discussion will continue and we may reach a point where those who wish to see humanity as one of many forms of life of equal worth to other animals, manage to convince others that this is the reasonable position to take. Nevertheless, at this point in time, in the light of our human needs and identity, in the light of core and other principles, that is not the view put forward in this guide, although it is certainly argued, focusing on our desire to reduce pain and suffering for animals, that our research would be optimally performed through other means, and only where considered absolutely essential, should animals be used in experimental research which harms them. And it is also argued that, where this is done, this should be done with minimal animal suffering. This perspective on the role of animals in human life and our relationship with animals is seen as important in all arenas in which other animals and we as human animals engage with each other.

Thus, from what has been already stated and from the core and other principles, we should not engage in non-essential research using animals, which causes, by definition, unnecessary and significant suffering to our fellow creatures. At this point in time, this kind of stricture is not seen as applying to the various microorganisms, bacteria, fungi, viruses, protozoans, and the range of plant life, these not being seen as sentient in a manner similar to humans and other animals. This judgment may seem inconsistent, as these organisms are surely capable of sensing in some ways, for example in their responses to light, nutritional sources and other ways. Yet they are biologically significantly different to animals, lacking nervous systems and brains or similar organs. Thus, it seems reasonable and rational to consider that these organisms cannot 'suffer and feel pain' in the same way that we as humans and other animals can and, indeed, that they are so far away from our understanding of notions of being sentient and having the ability to suffer and experience pain, that we can consider that they do not in fact experience such pain and suffering. It seems equally rational to consider that these organisms do not experience well-being in the same way that we understand the term for ourselves as humans and perhaps for animals too.

Given the centrality of our concerns for our own personal well-being and the well-being and happiness of others, these seem valuable questions with valuable answers which undoubtedly need further discussion. But what is undoubtedly also relevant is the fact that research on these organisms can provide much important information about how living organisms function and, particularly with regard to bacteria, viruses and fungi, this research can provide crucial information regarding disease prevention, since certain bacteria, viruses and fungi are originators and vehicles for many painful and in some cases deadly diseases and illnesses. And thus we certainly need to investigate such disease causing organisms and other microorganisms in order to help protect ourselves against these diseases and illnesses. Our research results in and will result in the destruction of uncountable numbers of bacteria, viruses and other microorganisms, however the pursuit of our human (and indeed animal) well-being is considered here to be by far the priority over the survival of such microorganisms. That is not to say that such organisms are not considered living or open to some concern. They should not be destroyed for pleasure and entertainment, for example, but in support of medical and health research, we need to investigate these organisms, how they live, how they function and how they can cause illness.

Beyond the illnesses and diseases originating from microorganisms which can threaten us as individuals and humanity on a vast scale, as already briefly mentioned, for many of us, dependent on where we live, nature's creatures can face us with a range of threats.

Thus, a range of larger animals can threaten and harm us if we get too close to them or they determine to attack us for various reasons, including, for example, seeing us as food or believing we represent a threat. And these larger animals represent a real threat to many. Lions, tigers, wolves, sharks, wild dogs, crocodiles, bears, elephants, jellyfish, snakes, spiders, mosquitoes and other organisms can all cause us substantial damage. We should of course take precautions against and protect ourselves from such threats should they exist in our local environments, and those of us who live elsewhere, should be understanding of the needs of others to protect themselves, their families and communities from such threats.

In the first place, in such circumstances, if not already known and available, wherever possible, we need to gain knowledge and understanding about the potential dangers to us from such animals. And based in that information, in the first place we should in the main, if we can, and if practical, avoid locations where these dangerous animals live. Of course, rivers which are infested with crocodiles should obviously be avoided, and sea waters teeming with deadly jellyfish or known to be areas of shark attack must not be swum in. Clearly it would be unwise to walk, unprotected, too close to a pride of lions or areas where leopards, cheetahs, wild dogs, grizzly bears or polar bears are known to roam. And if we do, with good and justified reason, enter these areas we should avoid provoking such animals and ensure that we have the means of protecting ourselves or defending ourselves from attack should we need to. Our self-protection here is not just for ourselves, but is also necessary as part of our support for those who care for and love us, who will be deeply upset, possibly traumatised, if we are injured or lose our lives through failure to take appropriate precautions and protect ourselves. Such protection and precautions are also necessary from the perspective of the rest of us, our communities and societies as we are interested and care about others and their safety and well-being.

Beyond such protective action designed to stop ourselves being attacked and enabling us to defend ourselves, medical resources and facilities need to be available to treat us promptly if attacked, and in particular in those areas where venomous and deadly snakes and spiders are known to live, we must ensure that medical facilities are available to provide anti-venoms and thereby reduce the suffering and prevent the deaths of those who are bitten.

While larger animals may be a threat to some of us, it is worth reiterating that by far the most important sources of threat to us from the natural living world arise from sources of infection, the bacteria, viruses, parasites and similar organisms which cause disease and illness, not just in ourselves as humans but in plants and other animals as well. Viral and bacterial epidemics have killed countless millions of people over the years, centuries and millennia, and continue have the potential to decimate the population of the world, having certainly done this in the past. Malaria continues to kill on a vast scale. Flu viruses represent a constant and ongoing threat. New viruses such as AIDS and Ebola have emerged and caused hundreds of thousands of deaths, if not more. And the danger from these diseases emphasises the importance of our continuous substantial investment as national and regional communities, as a global community, in research to tackle these severe threats to our health. The work done in combating AIDS, containing the Ebola virus and dealing with other illnesses illustrates how effective committed medical programmes and medical action can be in reducing the threat to us all when operated in a globally coordinated manner, but supported by all of us, locally and through our nation states.

Beyond their direct threats to our health, viral, bacterial and fungal infections can destroy crops, kill fish, infect the farm animals that many of us eat, and damage our food supply in many other ways. Infection of insects can affect pollination, the level of certain pests and the food supply, and therefore have major ramifications across the food chain with consequences for our human selves. It is essential therefore that these threats are dealt with as far as is humanly possible, and yet again we need research to understand the nature of such diseases and illnesses and such that we can take steps to protect ourselves. In support of our human well-being we need to demonstrate foresight such that these potential sources of threat are addressed before they have the opportunity to do us the substantial harm that they have the potential to inflict.

Thus, as individuals we need to be far-sighted enough to put aside some of our own resources which might be used for more immediate, personal purposes, and use these to support the provision of community, societal and global resources proactively in cases where we as individuals are under more direct threat from such organisms and diseases. But we also need to agree to the putting aside of resources proactively, whether or not we ourselves are directly under threat, in order to prepare for such epidemics of disease which may strike us at some or indeed any point in time, and to support our and other communities in developing effective understanding and knowledge of disease and infection such that we can engage in effective invention and discovery in support of, as well as in preparation for and to support prior action to stave off such threats.

Our environment of course poses more threats to us than simply those which are created by such microorganisms, other animals and the threats which derive from our own human action. Our physical environment also offers substantial potential threats to our well-being and indeed to our survival. Indeed, it is far from being the case that our natural environment is something which can be reasonably or helpfully seen as benign.

In response to changing climate, changing physical and biological environments and the range of environmental threats, during the million years or more of our human history, as a species, as individuals, as communities and societies, our human species has clearly had to adapt substantially in order to enable us to tackle and cope with the problems and threats posed by our natural physical environment. The reality for us is that, irrespective of our own human actions which can clearly change and damage our planet, around the globe, the fact is that as localised human communities and societies, we are, at least somewhere in the world and at some time, beset by floods, droughts, damaging storms, hurricanes and tornados, drought, lightning strikes, excessive periods of cold, excessive periods of heat and much more.

Further, our humanity is always under threat from highly unpredictable (at least with our current understandings), extreme events including volcanic eruptions, earthquakes and tsunamis. And even if such events are predicted, they have the potential to be so catastrophic that our human action, at least at the current time, may still not be sufficient to stave off their destructive effects. There exists even the extremely low probability potential for us (at least within an individual's experience in an individual lifetime) to experience danger and damage from events such as major meteor strikes, which evidence suggests may have had catastrophic consequences at times before our humanity appeared on the earth.

We are in essence a human species living on an enormous complex and vulnerable rock which lies in the midst of a solar system which we anticipate will self-destruct in a few billion years from now. This solar system lies in an almost inconceivably gargantuan universe which itself may contain unknown physical threats to our existence. Clearly it is difficult for us to prepare for threats to our existence which we do not know exist, but we need to continue to develop our knowledge and understanding of our vast universe, for the sake of our enjoyment of knowledge and understanding, for the joy of that cooperative and creative enterprise, but also to protect ourselves and others from such yet unknown threats and dangers to our humanity and life on our planet.

Yet, focusing on our more knowable threats, as individuals and as communities, as societies, as a global community, we need to prepare rationally and wisely for dealing with the range of natural disasters and catastrophic events which may occur on our planet, investing appropriate funds to prevent the damaging consequences of such events, engaging in research to predict and develop our protection against these events, and engaging in planning such that these events can be dealt with, when and if they arise.

Of course the frequency and probability of many of these events is dependent on our location on our planet, the nature of the event in question and a range of other factors. Nevertheless, wherever we are, even if, for example, we live far away from major earthquake zones and volcanoes, even if we are less likely to be hit by a tsunami, it is our responsibility to help those under threat of such catastrophe, not simply after these events but in supporting planned and effective responses before these events occur. And while these events might to some degree be unusual and low probability events, the catastrophe and disaster they bring, the damage to well-being and the pain and suffering they entail, mean that efforts to anticipate, pre-empt and prepare for and then tackle these extreme events need to be made and should be given, where appropriate high priority.

And where context and situation suggest the necessity, we need to make individual and group preparation for the range of naturally mediated and dangerous events, in support of ourselves, our friends and families and also in support of our communities, societies and others more globally, such that others will be secure and safe, and will not have to endure pain and suffering. Engaging in such action is part of our commitment to ensuring well-being and reducing suffering in the world, and it may be crucial to supporting the well-being and happiness and reducing the suffering of those who may not have the resources or technologies available to protect themselves.

The protection of our individual, family, community, societal and global human future in relation to current and potential future threats to our physical and biological environments, requires that we look ahead with significant intensity and thought into our possible futures and the possible futures of our planet, our humanity and life on our planet.

While it may seem somewhat speculative in the minds of some to consider our more distant future as humanity, with perhaps many of us having an inbuilt nervousness about the future, sometimes worried about the dangers that it may hold and its unpredictability, the reality, as has been discussed already in this guide, is that futures can be predicted to some degree, with anticipation and estimation of possible and probable future events and outcomes, and that we must in fact consider possible futures and possible future threats to our well-being if we are to be prepared for those future events, those future threats to our well-being, if we are to enjoy our well-being into the future, and if we, our communities, societies (local and global) and our human kind are to survive and thrive.

Not only do we need to look into the future and consider and prepare for those threats such as the earthly natural disasters already discussed, but we also need to consider the reality that we know there will be a final natural and inevitable ending to our planet, as far as we are aware, at this point in time, when our sun dies, though possibly earlier due to other causes.

Given that, as stated above, we know our planet will come to an end, in one way or another, in order to pursue the long-term survival of our humanity, we need to engage in exploration and discovery, we need to engage in developing our knowledge and understanding, of our solar system, our galaxy, our universe and beyond. As a humanity we have developed different forms of telescope which enable us to see to the ends of our universe, and we are already developing our capacities to travel beyond our earth, having landed people on the moon, placed landers on Mars, landed a spacecraft on a comet and sent probes to the outer reaches and beyond the edge of our solar system, these of course being tiny journeys in relation to the size of our known universe. We have discovered black holes, supernovae, vast numbers of swirling galaxies and much more.

And through our increasing knowledge and understanding, through our developing capacity to move beyond our earth, while somewhat incomplete at this particular time, perhaps uncomfortably incomplete, we are moving towards a reality such that in order to protect our humankind into the future, and in order to support our humanity to survive and thrive, in order to escape from our vulnerability on this one planet considering its apparently inevitable future destruction, we, our human species, at some point in the future will need to have the capacity to leave the earth and inhabit other places in our galaxy and universe, be they other planetary bodies or our own human designed self-contained travelling space stations. Given how far our humanity has come since the 19th century, when travel over relatively short distances of several miles would be exceedingly onerous and uncomfortable, and our state of knowledge in regard to engineering and design as well as our knowledge and understanding of the universe was much lesser than it is today, these possibilities in regard to our living beyond our earth, may not be too distant or unrealistic possibilities.

In our current situation where our humanity occupies only one planet in the universe, in a single solar system, we as humanity are clearly vulnerable to destruction from violent natural and human-created events originating on our earth, and from the distant possibility of violent and destructive events originating from outside the earth. And as mentioned above, we do know it to be the case that, in what may feel like the vast distant future, billions of years from now, our sun will self-destruct, as have other stars, expanding and destroying our earth in its wake as well as the other planets close to us and the entire solar system.

While this prospect lies extremely far ahead in time, at least when considered in relation to our individual life spans, and indeed considered against the time in which our humankind has existed, taking into account the violent upheavals that may occur on our planet, it is clear that we, as humanity, need to move towards a position where we are prepared and able to move off from the planet earth to new places in the universe. And in circumstances as we have now, which may be short-lived, we have an opportunity, due to our technological capabilities, arising due to our relatively stable existence and our current capacity to cooperate on our planet, to make use of this window of opportunity to take steps towards research and development, as well as implementation, and at some point in the near future, if possible, achieve the reality of supporting our human species in leaving our planet and establishing, if possible, substantial and significant human life beyond the earth.

As individuals we need to recognise the importance of this form of venture for the survival of our humanity, for the well-being of our species and indeed for other species. And recognising this, we need to support the provision of resources to enable the long-term planning of such events and adventures, essential for human survival. Exploration of and movement out to other places in our solar system, galaxy and the universe beyond, is also likely to have a range of benefits for our individual well-being and the well-being of our humanity. Apart from allowing us additional safe space in which to live, it may well be possible to obtain important supplies of minerals and other resources to support the well-being of our humanity here on earth or elsewhere should there be other destinations where we can settle as human communities.

Exploration and travel beyond our home planet earth must be an important goal for our humanity if the future of our humanity and indeed the future of life is to be sustained. Moving off to other worlds may involve the creation of entirely new environments in which our humanity can survive, containing the fundamentals needed for our continued existence but also having the potential to be very different from our current earthly environment of trees, plants, seas, mountains and deserts. There may, indeed, be an extent to which familiarity with an environment can make that environment a desirable and homely environment to those who live there. And it may be that some of these environments would become as loved and embedded in the identity and consciousness of those experiencing them, such that those environments would be as valued as those places on earth which are valued and cared for with such great passion by those of us who live here now.

This need for research, exploration and habitation beyond our planet having been argued for, being seen as in all likelihood necessary for the survival and thriving of our humankind, this research needs to be the beneficiary of our resources. And such provision of resources is controversial while there is still suffering on our planet, while some starve, lack basic clean water supplies, accommodation to live in, education and basic freedoms, amongst other things. The reality is that we must support each individual in attaining these basics and these freedoms in order to support their well-being and happiness. Yet to support well-being and happiness overall and its broadest terms, we, as individuals, communities, societies, as a global community, need to pursue and achieve all of our goals at the same time, with our goals and actions running hand-in-hand, aiming to secure our individual and broader well-being in the now and into the future.

Focusing back away from the distant world beyond our earth and the possibilities of leaving our earth, and back to our current biological and physical environments, the fact is that if we are to look after our environments and wish to maintain, develop and improve the environments we live in, then greater understanding of these environments is necessary. In regard to life on our planet, we have a far from perfect knowledge of how our local and global environments function, how the different living and non-living components interact. We have incomplete knowledge and understanding of the full relationships between different organisms, their dependence on each other as individual organisms and as species.

Nor do we understand to as great a degree as we would like, how changes in the physical environment, changes in climate for example, will affect our overall environment, our wildlife on the planet and our human life as well. These things are without doubt crucial for us to know, and though difficult to investigate in some cases, it is essential that we do conduct research and investigate these and related questions. In this way, we will develop a thorough knowledge of our natural and physical environments which will help support our own human well-being, happiness and indeed survival as well as the survival and well-being of the animal, plant and other life that exists on our planet.

Illustrating our lack of knowledge and understanding, there are, at this point in time, environments on the earth which are hardly explored, for example, the deep oceans, and certainly many which are far from being fully understood. It is part of our adventurous nature as human beings to want to explore those places that we do not know, and of course, beyond the knowledge that is generated, our exploration may give rise to our having new understandings which may result in us seeing the world and ourselves in different ways. Our exploration may provide us with learning, with routes and challenges which force us to develop and apply new approaches and new technologies, as well as, of course, providing, in some cases, access to new resources. Such searches for the new bring us a sense of adventure, discovery risk and sometimes danger into our lives, providing us with a focus for our aims and efforts, indeed for our lives, as individuals, communities, societies and beyond, helping us in imagining adventures and goals into the future, for ourselves as individuals and for others, supporting our well-being and the well-being of our communities and human society as a whole.

Beyond that searching of and that research into the environment itself, it would also seem to be of value that we research further to develop a better understanding of ourselves and our own relationship with our environment, our own feelings about our environments since we are, of course, experiencing and living in and as part of our environments. This research and understanding is needed so that we can best ensure that our local environments are pleasing and appropriate for us to experience, live in and enjoy, but also is necessary in terms of supporting the environments in which we live, including in particular, supporting the other living creatures inhabiting our environments. Understanding ourselves better and certainly as part of this, understanding the destruction we can wreak on our environment, sometimes without intention, should support us in acting differently in relation to our environment with the consequence that we can maintain and sustain optimal environments for ourselves and for other living organisms.

Investigation of ourselves as individual and social human beings in relation to our built and planned environments should help ensure we have the best built environments possible in which to live, thereby enhancing our well-being and happiness. As has already been mentioned, our human well-being is undoubtedly enhanced by beautiful and well-designed environments which almost certainly affect our feelings and our moods, but effective design of our environments can also support our safety in a range of ways, which go beyond simply safe design of structures. Building design seems to affect the way we feel. But beyond the design of individual buildings, the layout of our towns and cities is also relevant in terms of supporting our community safety, with good cities and good places to live in containing places which enhance our well-being, requiring the parks and greenery, ponds, lakes, sculpture and art, trees and plants as well as many other things already referred to earlier in this chapter. Greater understanding of ourselves should enable us to ensure the most appropriate countryside, town and city environments for us to enjoy.

Overall, having looked at our well-being and happiness in relation to our biological and physical environments, the principles put forward in this guide require us to take care of our environment in all its forms, maintaining and developing it, improving it where necessary, such that it provides a safe, pleasant, satisfying and enjoyable environment in which we can survive and thrive as human beings, and where other living organisms can survive and thrive. Our environment and environments need to provide the many essentials that we need to enjoy well-being and happiness and to survive. Our environments therefore need to be maintained and cared for so that they can continue to provide for our essential needs, be those needs represented by the oxygen that we require to breathe, the food that we eat, the clean water that we drink, the minerals and other resources needed for our manufacture and industries, or whether these needs are represented through the environment as a place for adventure and discovery or for its provision of the pure beauty and wonder of nature.

Such enjoyment of the environment, considering enjoyment in the broadest sense, means that we need knowledge and understanding of the natural and physical environment to support our well-being. Not only this, we need to act in a proactive and timely fashion in order to ensure that our environment remains suitable for us, the global environment being such a major and interactive phenomenon that, without such proactive and timely action, global patterns which influence climate and other phenomena can escape beyond the realms of our human capacity to exert significant short-term and longer-term influence, and therefore escape beyond the extent of control that we might be able to have if we were to take action in such a proactive and timely manner.

We are also required through the principles presented in this guide to prepare for and counter as far as possible the various phenomena and disasters that may arise both from human action and from naturally occurring threats to our well-being that derive from our environment, which clearly influence and can have a substantial effect on our well-being. Through taking appropriate action we will not only enhance the positive well-being and happiness of ourselves and others, as required by core principles, but we will also be able to contribute towards reducing the substantial pain and suffering that can arise from both devastating natural phenomena and human-induced destruction through the various forms of pollution and other damage that we are currently inflicting on the planet.

Finally for this chapter, and of significant importance in relation to our natural physical and biological environments, we further need to show care, consideration and compassion to the animals, plants and other organisms with whom we share our planet, actions which support the continued existence and well-being of these organisms alongside promoting the well-being and happiness of our humanity.

# Fifteen

# Bringing it All Together – Humanist Personal Conduct, Well-being, Fulfillment and Happiness

Our appropriate individual personal conduct and action along with the appropriate personal conduct and action of others is fundamental to our living lives of well-being, fulfillment and happiness. Based in a Humanist approach to personal conduct and well-being, which places our human nature, needs, desires and experience as central to our thought and actions, this guide has presented core and other principles which are seen as underpinning our personal conduct during our everyday experience of life, such that we can live lives of well-being, fulfillment and happiness, and avoid and prevent our pain and suffering. Through the pages of this guide, the implications, the application and the consequences of putting into practice these core and other guiding principles in relation to our personal conduct, have been considered in the context of different areas of our lives, with the goal of enabling us, as individuals, to live that life of well-being, fulfillment and happiness, and also with the goal of supporting others in achieving their own well-being, fulfillment and happiness, the well-being, fulfillment and happiness of others being seen as inextricably tied to our own well-being, happiness and fulfillment.

The core principles set out in this guide require us to focus, in terms of our personal conduct and action, on supporting our personal and individual well-being and the well-being of all others, as well as, in line with this support of well-being, acting to reduce the level of, and wherever possible and where necessary, preventing pain and suffering, or reducing the level of pain and suffering, being experienced by ourselves and others.

Supporting our own well-being and supporting the well-being of others, as well as acting to prevent and reduce our own pain and suffering and the pain and suffering of others, provide fundamental and essential routes to our personal well-being and the well-being of others.

When referring to our concern and commitment to the well-being of others, as expressed through the core and other principles put forward in this guide, as stated in the fourth Additional Fundamental Principle, we are referring to all others, irrespective of an individual's personal character, gender, race, nation of origin, political opinion or other system of belief, sexual orientation, personal history, past errors and misdeeds or other features of personal and individual character and identity. While it is highly likely that we will have closer relationships and feel different intensity, different levels and forms of love and care for those who we know better and who are closer to us in our lives, such as family and friends, and indeed, perhaps others living close to us in our more local communities, nevertheless, core and other principles require our commitment to the well-being of all people, all others, wherever they are, whatever their individual identities and personal characteristics. Thus, while we will feel important elements of belonging and identity in terms of our families, friends, our organisations, perhaps, for many our countries of origin, our cultures, nevertheless a key and central element of our individual identity needs to be a sense of membership of and a sense of responsibility towards, our broader humanity, all others, all other individuals. Our sense of such identity and its importance is an important contributor to our own personal well-being and happiness, and our avoidance of pain and suffering.

Acting in support of our own well-being and acting to support the well-being of others, do not comprise independent categories of conduct and action, but rather they overlap and interact in a complex manner, with many, though not all of the more self-directed actions we take and the more self-directed conduct we adopt in support of our own well-being, also serving to support others, serving to support the well-being of our families, communities, societies and indeed our broader humanity. By the same token, our actions more directly focused on supporting our families, communities and societies, the wider global world, frequently serve to support our own individual well-being, happiness and fulfillment.

Underpinning core and other principles is a sense of our common human identity through which, as well as being separate individuals with our own individual, unique and special identities, thoughts, feelings, wants, desires and needs, we are also highly social in our nature, having complex and developed social needs. It is almost always, if not always the case, that we need other people if we are to have a life of well-being and happiness. In particular, we are all, or almost all, under all or almost all circumstances, substantially dependent on others for so much in our lives that supports our well-being, fulfillment and happiness. On a daily basis, the many of us, be it within the smallest of hamlets or villages and to a greater extent in our complex towns and cities, we will have some, if not a great number, of interactions with many others, maybe most intensively with certain individuals, those close to us, but also perhaps with tens, hundreds or even thousands of others, dependent on our daily activities, comprising our perhaps more frequent, but less intense, more everyday, transactional interactions.

Our social nature and social identity fundamentally influence our personal conduct and action. In our personal everyday lives, for the most of us, probably all of us, we need others, other people, to interact with us, to talk with us, to be with us, to appreciate and notice us, to be friends with us, hopefully to love us and to love. We, or the vast main of us, wish for and need friends and lovers to care for us, to keep us company, to have conversations with, to act as confidants with whom we can share the stresses and burdens of our days as well acting as people with whom we can share the joys and triumphs we experience in our lives. And of course we need to conduct ourselves in caring and appropriate ways such that we can enjoy and sustain our relationships.

In the complex human societies that the many of us live in, we need others to help us if we are to live a life of well-being and happiness. We simply cannot do, and cannot achieve everything on our own; we cannot, on our own, do all those things that are needed and do all the things that we need to do, in order to provide the diversity of components which make up a life of well-being, happiness and fulfillment.

Others will hopefully love and care for us and we will love and care for them. Yet we also need the many less involved, less personal and more distant interactions and relationships in our lives with so many others; we need interactions and relationships with the multitude of such others. We need the range and diversity of relationships on which we are dependent for so many important elements of our well-being, happiness and fulfillment.

We may not even meet many of these others, those more distant others who may simply, though essentially, support us in receiving and providing us with, at a distance, the many daily basic services, which contribute to our well-being and happiness. Such others, on whom we are dependent, may grow our food, may be involved in supplying electricity to our homes, supporting our communications with others through mobile or other communication networks; they may transport foodstuffs and other goods to our shops, help provide us with essentials for our lives such as clean water; they may drive our buses or trains, make or manufacture the tools, furniture, equipment or other things we use on a daily basis, protect us from dangers, from crime, from attack, look after our health, conduct health and technological research or manufacture equipment and drugs used for healthcare. Others may serve us tea and coffee in a café, support our happiness and well-being with entertainment and amusement at the cinema or theatre or on our televisions or other media channels, and all of these benefit us in achieving our well-being and happiness.

Still others may act as educators and trainers passing on knowledge, skills, enthusiasm and experience, or write books and manuals which provide us with key information or perhaps entertainment, which again all support us in our well-being and happiness. They may act as organisers, managers, and administrators making sure that complex activities and processes required for our individual well-being take place efficiently, managing individuals and ensuring that important and complex jobs get done. They may act as politicians, aiming to build and maintain peace and cooperation or aiming to manage the different interests of those in our community such that the needs and wants of different individuals and different groups are met as far as is possible. And of course we ourselves are likely to fulfill one or many of these roles ourselves, and in doing so, we will be contributing to the well-being, fulfillment and happiness of others.

Through the range of different roles and relationships that we have with others and that they have with us, the many more direct benefits we all gain in terms of well-being, fulfillment and happiness are clear. Yet we also require the general well-being and happiness of others in order to enjoy our own well-being and happiness. And therefore we need to ensure through our personal conduct that we support the well-being and happiness of all others, for its own sake, through the direct pleasure we gain from knowing of and being aware of the well-being and happiness of others, but also recognising the critical interactions between the well-being, fulfillment and happiness of others, the health of families, communities, societies and our broader humanity, and our own well-being, fulfillment and happiness.

Throughout this guide, in line with core and other principles it has been argued that, we must not act in ways which are negatively selfish. That is to say we can, need to and indeed must, act in ways which benefit ourselves, and must also act in ways which benefit and support the well-being and happiness of others. Critically, we must also not act in ways which cause others any significant pain, suffering and harm. Thus, when deciding on our personal conduct, our own actions and behaviour, we need to take into consideration the effect of our actions, personal conduct and behaviour on others, ensuring that others will not suffer to any significant degree from the consequences of what we do. Where possible, we need to consider the range of our possible options for action and their consequences for others, selecting those options which maximally benefit and support the well-being of ourselves and others and which do not cause others any significant harm.

Nevertheless, we do need to take into consideration ourselves and our own desires, needs and wants, being sure, as far as possible, to support our own well-being and happiness in the round, supporting our own personal well-being, happiness and fulfillment. It is fundamental to the principles put forward in this guide that we recognise both the importance of ourselves and our own well-being and happiness, and also recognise the importance of the well-being, happiness and fulfillment of others, as well as recognising the interaction between our individual selves and others, and the interactions between our own well-being and the well-being of others.

In many cases it is quite clear where the boundaries lie between those actions which are acceptable within this framework of core and other principles, and those actions which are not. Examples of both types of action and conduct have been presented and discussed through this guide. Revisiting briefly some sample positive and acceptable conduct described in this guide, these include our acting to pursue our own well-being, pleasures, happiness and fulfillment through our jobs of work, through friendships, through our contributions to our communities, societies and beyond, through acts of kindness, through love, sex, friendships, through enjoying the range of entertainments we enjoy, through taking part in sports and physical activities, through our appreciation of music, art and literature, through supporting and caring for others, developing our skills and knowledge, understandings and learning, through teaching others, through pursuing peaceful resolutions to conflicts in our lives, through pursuing a sense of belonging, following our dreams, goals and ambitions; all these amongst our other individual actions are desirable and acceptable within the framework of core and other principles within the limits of our actions not doing any noteworthy or significant harm to ourselves or others.

Likewise and similarly, representing positive, caring and acceptable if not laudable conduct, supporting the health of others through providing medical support, caring for our friends, loving others, building positive caring relationships, acting to reduce poverty, illness and disease, making our personal contributions to complex community and societal projects and tasks (such as design, construction, administration), where such tasks support well-being, supporting a peaceful and free community and society where we enjoy significant personal autonomy, paying our way in society, supporting our organisation, communities, societies and government, participating in our community activities, doing research to tackle unanswered questions, acting to prevent damage, pain and suffering to others, defending others and our communities against aggressive violence, preventing crime, all of these additional examples of our conduct and behaviour amongst many others, are considered acceptable, desirable and positive conduct and action, again within the limits that we must not inflict any significant harm on others through our actions.

By contrast, clearly unacceptable actions and conduct include those acts which focus on our own well-being and happiness to the substantial detriment of others, taking actions which physically and emotionally damage and hurt others, murderous actions, taking other actions which inflict suffering and pain on others, such as for example engaging in aggressive violence or mental and verbal abuse of others, inflicting torture and cruelty on others, abusing our power and bullying others, inflicting poverty and destitution on others, denying others access to food, water and the basics of survival, destroying homes, acting to destroy our environment, waging aggressive war on others, failing to act and support others when they are in significant or desperate need, aiming to damage and destroy the life of another, engaging in actions which support substantial economic damage to others, discriminating in a destructive manner against others, unjustified robbery and theft, and many more actions or inactions of this nature which, by omission or through their implementation and commission, produce significant harmful consequences for others.

While there are some actions and some forms of conduct which are clearly, in general, positive or negative in their nature, nevertheless, as argued through this guide there are many instances where we will need to determine our conduct and actions and indeed judge our actions and conduct, on the basis of the precise situations and circumstances we find ourselves in. Thus, while normally unacceptable within the terms of core and other principles, if we are starving, freezing from the cold, where other routes to alleviating our suffering and pain are closed off to us, where we have made the utmost effort to take action to provide our own food, warmth or gain our own shelter, where we, perhaps through act of nature, social circumstances, oppressive actions against us, personal incompetence or misfortune have fallen into destitution, poverty, desperate need, and where we have been refused help when help and support in the form of relevant resources is available, then we cannot be chastised or considered to be acting in contravention of core and other principles, if we should take, perhaps remove by force, the food, fuel, shelter or other resource which we as individuals, or our families, communities and societies need to survive. Of course other options are preferable, peacefully requesting help and support, engaging in exchange, sharing of resources and where these alternatives are available they should be pursued first of all, as a priority wherever possible, where our situations and circumstances allow this.

In terms of the notion of others as presented through this guide and mentioned already in this chapter, within the Humanist approach in this guide based in core and other principles, this means all others, encompassing those of all personalities and character, of all races, belief systems, genders, class and type, sexual preferences and more. Others refers to all of us. It includes those who have behaved and conducted themselves badly, in malevolent, damaging and destructive ways such as those just described. And, while this, in relation to people who have engaged in such actions, may perhaps be difficult for us to cope with, given those actions that such people will have carried out, and the damage and destruction they may have done, with our recognising and acknowledging our likely feelings in response to these actions, we still need to consider such people, as human beings of, in essence fundamental equal value, and consider and act to support their well-being, though with a substantial emphasis on preventing their engaging in such destructive and damaging actions into the future, restraining them as appropriate, thereby protecting ourselves and others. While we have concern for such people as human beings, there is no doubt that based in our humanity, our human needs and our human character, and consequently fundamental to core and other principles, we must oppose the heinous, revolting and destructive actions and beliefs of such people with the greatest intensity, preventing them from promoting and executing their damaging and destructive actions and beliefs. Indeed we must respond in a robust manner, demonstrating strength, resolve and where necessary courage and bravery, in response to these people and their actions.

Nevertheless, wherever it is reasonably possible and safe for us and others to do so, we need to act to support even the well-being of those people who have participated in or are implementing such conduct, engaging with them where we can in order to support them in changing their ways, as part of our aim of reducing and ending their aggressively violent and destructive actions and as part of our aim to build peace and cooperation within the context of core and other principles. We all benefit from a context within which the greatest level of peaceful cooperation and peaceful resolution of problems is pursued and implemented.

While we wish for this and hope to support the well-being of such people, our actions must not be naive. We must include realistic understandings of the beliefs, actions, intentions and capabilities of these others, and our thinking and actions must always take place within the context of keeping ourselves and others safe and secure. Thus we need to take whatever action is necessary and whatever action is best to provide well-being, safety and security, both for ourselves and all others, including those who have conducted or who are planning malevolent and destructive actions. This means taking appropriate and effective protective actions in anticipation of, or in the face of, the actions or potential actions of those who have engaged in, are in the process of engaging in or whom evidence suggests are highly likely to engage in violent, heinous and destructive acts.

As a consequence of our approach, where others threaten imminent aggressive violence against ourselves, our families, communities and societies, then having made efforts to use peaceful and cooperative means, in the absence of, and where there may be no other more peaceful options available, we may well need to engage in forceful and physical action in support of our self-defence and defence of others, using preventative and indeed substantially forceful physical action to protect ourselves and our well-being as well as the well-being of others.

Within the frame of the core and other principles, where we have the capacity to take action and intervene, and this includes where we can call or bring others to assist us in intervention, it is not acceptable to allow ourselves or to leave others to endure significant pain and suffering in the face of aggressively violent actions by others or suffer other significantly destructive actions and threats. While it may be difficult, we should, wherever possible, aim for peaceful action to prevent aggressive violence, damage and destruction, and we should aim to restrain such others where possible, and do the minimum in terms of causing pain and suffering to those who threaten us. We need to act, as far as we can, to protect all parties from pain and suffering, including those who have made threats or even attempted to do violence to us. Our use of physical and forceful action thus needs to be at the minimum level, exerting the minimum pain and suffering on any other, that is required to protect ourselves and others.

Supporting such an approach, we need to recognise the reality that a significant amount of harmful and destructive action can arise out of intense momentary and painful anger and distress, and while such violent and destructive action is completely unacceptable, where these others can be calmed, or turned away from their violent and destructive actions, hopefully through words, and without the need for overly forceful physical actions, then we should aim to do this. Moreover we need to recognise, as has been stated in more than one place in this guide, that significantly violent action against such people who have engaged in malevolent, destructive, aggressively and violent actions, our aggressively violent action stemming from our own responsive anger, and perhaps in some cases conducted with the motivation of revenge against those who have engaged in such destructive actions, such aggressively violent action is totally unacceptable within the frame of core and other principles, itself creating further damage and destruction, and promoting a cycle of violence which serves to further damage us all.

We can ignore verbal insulting abuse of course, and this verbal abuse should not be responded to with violence and physical action. However, dependent on circumstances, optimally we would respond with effective words and possibly kindness in response, where we can manage this, aiming to build cooperation and peace, defusing anger and the potential for violence. Inaction and non-response in such circumstances may also be a useful way of deflecting or defusing verbal abuse, protecting ourselves and representing a refusal to participate in a verbally abusive conversation. However such verbal abuse is oppressive and hurtful, being often requiring of a direct response, and this abuse may in some cases presage violent attack for which, under such circumstances, we need to ensure that we are ready and prepared to defend ourselves and defend ourselves as effectively as we can.

To reiterate, for the most part, wherever possible, options other than physical and forceful action would be preferable and indeed should be used in the first place, with a preference for verbal action, listening to and understanding others, combined with efforts at peaceful resolution, discussion and negotiation. If these more peaceful courses of action can be pursued then they should be pursued. However, as already emphasised, and certainly worth emphasising again, we must ensure our own safety and well-being as well as the safety and well-being of others.

Moving away from the issue of our responding to verbal threat, abuse and violence, and considering again the pursuit of well-being, in more general terms, through our lives we need to conduct ourselves in such a manner that we can achieve a sense of balance between those actions which more directly support our own well-being and those which are more directly supportive of others, while recognising that there is interaction between these two different focuses. Through achieving an appropriate balance of appropriate personal conduct and action, we will be supported in achieving a true sense of overall well-being and happiness, spending time both focusing on the more immediate actions in our lives which support our personal well-being and happiness, but also acting in those ways which more directly support others.

As this guide has emphasised and discussed at some length, consistent with core and other principles, the pursuit of actions which more directly support our own personal pleasure and happiness, is entirely justified and worthy. However, if we focus on such more immediate and personally focused actions to too great an extent, then we are likely to lose focus on supporting others, such support for others also representing a source of pleasure and fulfillment, often deep pleasure and fulfillment, which supports our own personal well-being and happiness. Through too much focus on ourselves and our immediate and direct pleasures, we will most likely be denying others and our communities and societies, as well as our broader humanity, the contributions which we can make. And through our inaction in support of others we will be serving to undermine community, society, and the well-being of all others, which will in turn undermine our own safety, security, happiness, fulfillment and well-being.

A further issue addressed in this guide is that of whether we can have too much focus on helping others. An intense focus on helping others can bring us, as individuals, great pleasure and happiness in many ways, through for example our own deep feelings of contribution and worth to our communities and societies, through our own personal knowledge that we have directly supported the well-being and happiness of others and through receiving the gratitude of those we support (though, as mentioned in this guide, we may not always receive this, as our contributions may not always be acknowledged, recognised or appreciated). Importantly, the support we give to others needs optimally to be provided in a manner which does not make others dependent on us into the future. Rather, it needs to enable others to build their own independence and their own ability and capacity to contribute to themselves, their families, community, society and the world beyond, such that we can all benefit from their actions into the future.

It is true that in some cases, for some of us, an over-focus, perhaps temporarily, on others may interfere with our own pursuit of our personal pleasure and happiness. For example, we may sometimes, as a consequence of making great efforts to support others, experience feelings of bitterness and unhappiness where our contributions are unacknowledged, where we feel taken for granted, ignored or we feel our desire to help others is taken advantage of. We may feel resentful of others less committed, who we perceive as spending time on their own leisure and pleasure and who do not do show that same total dedication, passion and commitment to others that we have ourselves. Of course it is important in the latter case that we get our facts right and ensure for certain that it is actually the case that others are not, in a sense, pulling their weight or making the effort to support us and others. They may not perceive things in the same way that we do. And further they may have their reasons – illness, other commitments that we are not aware of, which drink up their time and attention.

But if that is how we feel, then we can either continue to gain pleasure from supporting and helping others, aiming to put aside our feelings towards these others, perhaps overcoming such feelings of resentment with more positive and constructive thinking and thereby supporting our personal well-being and helping others at the same time; we can concentrate on other more self-focused ways of achieving our own more personal pleasure and happiness, while still retaining our commitment to support others; or alternately we can aim to engage these others more and discuss our feelings with them. Nevertheless, neglecting the needs, wants, interests and concerns of others, of our families, communities, societies and beyond, even where we feel our contributions are not being acknowledged and being ignored, is not acceptable. Not only is such neglect likely to damage others, but it is probable at some point that it will damage us as well, for example through seeing an unnecessary level of suffering and pain amongst those whom we are no longer supporting.

Unfortunately, when we dedicate significant elements of our lives to supporting others, it is also possible for others to resent us since they may be unable or unwilling to make such contributions, yet they may also feel a sense of guilt or, for other reasons, feel bad about their own inaction. Such feelings of resentment and such feelings of guilt need to be recognised by us, but, as long as there are no efforts to damage us or others, such feelings are in the end for these others to deal with, optimally by recognising their lower level of contribution and increasing their level of contribution, support and help towards others, something which will benefit their own well-being and happiness. Hopefully at some point they will perhaps recognise and even laud our contribution and our efforts, supporting us in what we do, and adopting more positive and less resentful responses to our personal conduct and personal actions which are aimed at supporting others.

Nevertheless, in the main, as far as this guide is concerned, taking actions in support of others, actions involving a degree of self-sacrifice such that we endure significant and severe pain and suffering, is not considered in general to be desirable as seen through the prism of core and other principles. That being said, however, at times, in certain circumstances, such self-sacrifice may be necessary in order to support others; indeed we may need to and choose to endure intense suffering and pain and, in some cases, we may choose to sacrifice our own lives to support others, those we love and care for and indeed, those we do not know and have never met.

*In extremis*, when those we love, indeed when those others who we may not know at all, are in desperate need, under physical threat and in personal danger, in need of our help, the many of us may well be willing to suffer, to give of ourselves, even as said, give our lives, in support of these others, to prevent their pain, harm, suffering and perhaps indeed to prevent their deaths. Such actions of self-sacrifice, carried out where necessary in order to protect others are certainly considered desirable, laudable and worthy, representing a core part of our humanity and human identity, our social nature, which is part of and underpins the core and other principles. We have discussed the notion of heroes and heroism in this guide and such actions of self-sacrifice for the protection of others are considered heroic.

However, for the many of us, we do hope that such actions of extreme self-sacrifice will not be required in our lives. More common, in areas of less danger and stress, in our more daily lives, we should always be willing to give something of ourselves, our time, our resources, or make other contributions to others, our communities, societies and beyond. In essence, we must engage in some actions in order to support the well-being and happiness of those we love, and of all others, and in the normal way of things, hopefully such social and supportive actions will result in benefit to both ourselves and others and should result in no significant short-term or other harm to ourselves.

Given our need to pursue our own well-being, consistent with core and other principles, it is most likely wise for us to act to serve ourselves and our well-being and happiness in a range of different ways such that we can all enjoy a complete and full life of well-being and fulfillment. Key in terms of our well-being is likely to be our range of relationships with others. In order to pursue that personal well-being, happiness and fulfillment, while we as individuals differ to some degree, we will, almost all of us, if not all of us, gain substantial well-being, happiness and fulfillment tied to our personal relationships, be those relationships with our friends, children, partners, or others in our wider communities.

In terms of our closest adult relationships we would almost all wish to experience the joy of deep love and the passion of a loving intimate passionate sexual relationship. We would almost all wish for and enjoy sexual pleasure, and enjoy and feel enriched by being loved. We almost all, if not all of us, wish to have the pleasure of friendships, of positive, caring relationships, which enrich our lives and support us in feeling good, happy, complete and fulfilled. In terms of other highly important relationships, we gain tremendous and deep pleasure and fulfillment from our children, though our relationships with them as they grow, through our support for them and our joy in them as they move to and attain adulthood. Further, as noted through this guide, we gain pleasure and fulfillment from helping and supporting the range of others as well as the often consequential benefits and pleasures of in turn receiving their care and support. And we gain pleasure from a sense of belonging and attachment within our communities and societies as well as through our sense of responsibility to and belonging to a common humanity.

Yet we also gain well-being, pleasure, happiness and joy from much else. We gain deep pleasure from achievement, from attaining our goals, be those the already referred to goals of finding love, or perhaps having a family, through achieving qualifications, through being successful in our home and working lives, perhaps through our daily service to our communities, through our creation of the new, or through doing research of various kinds and discovering something new, perhaps starting to perceive and interpret the world in new ways, maybe through designing and taking part in the construction of homes or other new buildings, creating and inventing, through painting or drawing pictures, listening to or making music, buying a house to live in, dealing with a difficult challenge or problem at home or in our work, helping those we teach such that they are successful, and further perhaps, for some of us, through providing the medical care which substantially extends someone's life; perhaps for others of us we can gain pleasure through perhaps preventing conflict and building peace, having a successful moment (or even career) in our favoured sport, or perhaps successfully managing a major project as well as through much else in terms of personal achievements.

On top of these pleasures, the vast majority of us love laughter, warm smiles and humour, our feelings of togetherness and belonging which are important components of our healthy and happy relationships. Then we gain pleasure and relaxation from our entertainments, films, music, games and pastimes, dance and dancing, literature, the theatre, simply by socialising with, passing the time with, being with, and talking to our friends. And it is right and consistent with core and other principles that we pursue these many pleasures and joys which support our well-being and happiness.

Many of us have hobbies and interests. For some of us we may enjoy gardening, building radios and other electronic items, studying flora and fauna, collecting of a range of items such as stamps and coins, cooking, fishing. We may have an interest in cars or motorbikes, or enjoy participating in sports and games. We may take pleasure from walking, running and cycling, doing various forms of exercise alone or with others, or we may gain a sense of pleasure through adventures and journeys to new places, perhaps overseas places that we have never visited before. All of these pleasures and joys and many others, are worthwhile for us to pursue and doing so, in pursuing our own personal pleasure and joy through these means, we are also acting in a manner which is entirely acceptable, desirable and consistent with core and other principles.

Of course, consistent with core principles, we should not be pursuing personal pleasures which damage others and we should not be pursuing our personal pleasure to the degree that our taking of action which supports others is forgotten and such that the needs of others, our communities and societies are ignored. Such negatively selfish action will certainly damage others, our communities, societies, and our broader humanity, and will in the end damage ourselves as well.

Of course, we are also obliged, through this guide and in line with the core and other principles, to act to avoid our own pain and suffering and the pain and suffering of others. In pursuit of these goals, we need, for example, to take care of our personal health through good diet, through exercise, through being clean, healthy, hygienic and safe in our actions and conduct, keeping things as clean as is necessary to promote good health and prevent the spread of illness and disease.

And, recognising the social, and recognising our responsibilities to all others, we need to be supporting systems which, as well as serving to prevent the spread of illness and disease, serve to support and provide healthcare to ourselves and others, to our communities, societies and beyond. We further need to be supporting systems that provide the capacity for learning and research such that we are continually developing our knowledge and understanding of our own human health, and in particular illness and disease and its reduction and prevention. This requires our personal awareness of the need for and our personal commitment to investment of our personal and social resources, and may require investment of our time as well.

A further important area of personal action and conduct discussed in this guide, understandably considered critical for the vast majority of, if not all of our lives, relates to our relationship with and actions in regard to material things and money. This guide recognises that we certainly need resources, material things and indeed money (a token of material value) to live a life of well-being, happiness and fulfillment. We need such resources, things and money as individuals, as families, as communities and societies and beyond. In all families, communities and societies we cannot survive and certainly cannot live well without appropriate resources, without money, without material things.

Thus, as already discussed in chapter nine in part one of this guide, at the basic level, we need to have a home, a shelter, materials things in our home to the extent of at least important basics such as beds, crockery, utensils, simple tools, bed sheets, cooking equipment, furniture. And we would like much more and hopefully may have much more. Not only do we need material things for functional purposes but we also wish to have if we can, items which are ornate and beautiful, items of art and beauty which brighten up our home and other environments and which express our identity, helping us form homes, communities, societies and a sense of belonging. Our objects and possessions form part of our well-being and form part of our common culture and human heritage too, supporting our sense of belonging and identity.

More fundamental to our well-being, for many, if not the majority of us in this modern age, we need resources and money in order to have access to the basic energy supplies we need. We need money and resources to have our essential water and food, to pay to our organisations, our governments, and to pay directly for, or through our governments or other organisations, for health care, our personal safety, security and defence and much more.

Then beyond ourselves and our own needs as individuals, our communities and societies need money, material and resources to support our physical and our social infrastructure, be that involving the provision of our medical healthcare systems, support for democratic mechanisms and systems of government, supporting systems of transport, supporting systems for developing investment and enhanced wealth and well-being within our communities and societies, ensuring our protection against violence and crime, supporting research, ensuring effective systems of justice and law, or acting in a systematic and concerted way to support and provide education and prevent or reduce poverty. All of this requires resources and money.

Our organisations, our businesses, our charities, our local and national governments all need to have resources, material things, money in order to perform their functions in supporting others and supporting the communities and societies in which they are situated, as well as providing support beyond our more local communities and societies. And we, as individuals, have a responsibility and indeed a need to contribute money and resources, including our personal effort and skills, to our communities and societies, to our broader humanity, such that these entities can provide resources, support and services which enable us and others to lives of well-being and happiness. In support of our well-being and the well-being of others, be it in terms of our individual well-being or in regard to our community, societal or global organisations, we as individuals, communities, societies and beyond certainly need to possess and pursue a level, preferably a high level, of material things, money and resources. To do so is highly consistent with core and other principles.

It is in the pursuit of perverse personal wealth and opulence, rather than in our ordinary everyday efforts to gain resources for survival or for purposes of our comfort and pleasure, that our acquisition of and desire for money, our wish for resources and material things becomes inconsistent with core and other principles, and this is particularly and starkly the case in circumstances when others are enduring significant suffering and in pain. In such circumstances, in particular, assuming that actual support and help can in reality and in practical terms be provided to those in need, the pursuit and use of perverse levels of money and material things for our own negatively selfish personal benefit and pleasure, to support our own opulent living, becomes even more starkly incompatible with core and other principles, with wealth and resources being, in effect, poorly used to support well-being for others, whether it be in our more local community and society or within the global communities in which we live. Under such circumstances, we, all of us, need to engage in ensuring that such resources are well used and that those suffering in pain, suffering and poverty are supported in escaping their pain and suffering and able to enjoy well-being.

Related to the poor use of resources and the existence of those with perverse levels of wealth and opulence while others suffer in pain, we also need to guard against perverse levels of inequality which are highly socially undermining, which place power and influence in the hands of those with perverse wealth and which, in this and other ways, create divided and fractured communities and societies, situations which act and will act to the detriment of us all.

Apart from in such circumstances of perverse and ill-used wealth and resources, in a broader sense we need to be aware of ways in which poor use of money and material things, our material resources, can cause problems for us all. In terms of finance and markets of trade and exchange, in terms of all kinds of areas tied to finance, poor financial management, poor financial planning, ineffective oversight, allowing those pursuing money and resources in a negatively selfish manner to act without regulation and control over their actions, place large risks not only on those involved in relevant transactions, but also present risks for all of us, as our money and resources may be poorly, if not incompetently used and lost to us, with our financial systems compromised, and destructive and damaging consequences occurring as a result. It is clearly essential that we act to ensure the absence of financial crashes, whatever their causes, considering the tremendous harm and damage such crises have often generated, be these consequences mass poverty and suffering, loss of property and savings, personal or business bankruptcy, mass unemployment, and a range of other forms of our human suffering. Such crises are often fomented through greed and avarice, through false ideologies, but also through system-based faults and errors combined with, supplemented by, or simply independently generated by, perverse human behaviour and simple poor judgment.

Such crashes and financial disasters may often be founded in unjustified belief in the efficiency of unregulated and unconstrained financial markets and sometimes also through dishonesty, negative selfishness allied to gross mismanagement and lack of competence. What cannot be argued about are the destructive consequences of such financial crashes to so many of us. And as a result, based in core and other principles, we need to individually and otherwise, through our community, societal and global organisations and representatives, as well as through our own personal action, do our utmost to ensure that our money, resource and financial systems operate for the benefit of all. We need to ensure that we, and others, take all steps possible to ensure that such financial crashes with their devastating consequences, do not occur.

Moving beyond issues of money and material things, something which is emphasised throughout this guide is the fact of our individual and personal responsibility for the actions and choices we make in relation to our personal conduct and our personal actions. While it is and must be the case that we have been, and most likely are, influenced substantially by the family, social and cultural contexts in which we grow up in and live day-to-day; while it must be the case that we will be influenced substantially by the ideas, ideologies, attitudes, cultures, codes of conduct, systems of education, the behaviours, thinking, actions and conduct of those individuals around us, of our parents, families, our friends, communities and societies; indeed while we will be further influenced to some extent in our conduct by our human characteristics and identity, our human needs and our genetic make-up; nevertheless, whatever these influences, our actions and personal conduct, as adult individuals, are down to us, are considered a matter of our individual personal choice, our own personal decisions and actions, these being matters, choices decisions and actions for which we are individually responsible.

Thus it is up to us as individuals to act appropriately in line with core and other principles; it is up to us to counter any malevolent or negative influences on ourselves; it is up to us to develop ourselves, to engage in learning, to develop our self-knowledge and self-understanding, to develop our knowledge and understanding of community, society and cultures and their natures, of the world around us, to develop our understandings, knowledge and skills such that, where it is necessary, we can make judgments which truly support our own well-being and happiness, and support the well-being and happiness of others. While we may have been influenced, while we may be influenced and indeed be somewhat constrained, by a range of social and environmental factors, we are not able to hold others responsible for the actions which we take. Our actions, our decisions, our personal conduct, are our responsibility.

Stemming from this key and fundamental point, it follows that where pressure is placed on us by others, by organisations, to act in ways which cause pain, suffering and harm to others, in ways which may damage our communities and societies, in ways which may damage our global community; where we are pressured to act in ways which are inconsistent with our pursuit of personal well-being and our support of the well-being and happiness of others; under such circumstances, it is our essential responsibility to resist such pressures, doing our utmost to protect ourselves and others from pain and suffering while also aiming to preserve our own well-being and avoiding our own pain and suffering.

In order to support the greater well-being, the reduction and prevention of pain and suffering to others, as we have responsibility, it may well be the case that we need, in some circumstances, to endure some temporary or even longer term pain and suffering ourselves, as already referred to in this chapter, engage in some self-sacrifice, perhaps giving up some of our well-being for the good of others, our communities, societies and the world beyond. In particular, if we are under threat of physical violence, faced with direct aggressive violence against us, or other coercive threat, then we have the responsibility to give whatever resistance we can, using the minimum force necessary to be effective, at whatever time and place we can, such that those acting to support cruelty, oppression and violence are unable to achieve their goals, unable to harm others and such that they are unable to retain their power and influence.

Related to this notion of our personal responsibility for our conduct and actions, an important human need for the many, if not all of us, recognised through the core and other principles, is that need of a degree, if not a significant degree of personal autonomy and personal freedom. It is a matter of fact that we have our own separate and distinct individual identities as well as our being social in our nature, and as a consequence of the key individual element of our nature, each of us needs to determine, or at least have a major and significant independent ability, to determine or have substantial influence in determining our own actions, beliefs and opinions, in particular in regard to those actions and decisions that influence our own lives and indeed in the actions and decisions we take and make ourselves which influence and affect the lives of others.

In the workplace, we will wish to have some significant influence over our areas of responsibility; in our personal lives we will wish to make decisions about our daily activities. And while circumstances may constrain us to some extent, we will also wish to have significant influence, if not make the final decisions about our journeys in life, our careers, our jobs, our friends, those we love and have as partners, and much else. Indeed for many of us, being someone who is frequently or always told what to do, who is under orders and given little or no independence, freedom and autonomy, will damage our sense of self, our pride, most likely causing us anxiety, suffering and pain, and perhaps giving us a sense of victimhood. Not only will such a situation and such feelings damage us as individuals, they are likely to have detrimental consequences for others, our communities, societies and beyond.

Yet matters are our responsibility and if we are in such a position of being frequently commanded and told what to do and being forced to or expected to acquiesce, we need to change that situation or move on to a less oppressive situation. If we prove unable to achieve that we wish to achieve and are unable to live a life of well-being and happiness on account of our passivity and acquiescence, then the responsibility for having lived that life, especially if we had the chance to move away and move on or change that situation, will be significantly ours, with no one else to be blamed.

Crucial to supporting our well-being and happiness, we need to be able to listen to others, taking note of what they say, valuing what they say where it is reasonable to value their statements and opinions, though not always agreeing or even sympathising with that is said. Sometimes, we will be instructed by others, and in some circumstances, we will need to listen to and pay attention to these instructions, particularly when we are learning, or where it is key to achieving our important goals that we should follow the instructions given. Yet, as autonomous individuals we, as adults, need to be able to choose to follow or not follow those instructions, our being responsible for our decisions and actions.

Of course, should we not follow appropriate instructions, for example, when learning how to do a job effectively, or in implementing a plan, then of course, we may not achieve our objectives or our group and organisation's objectives, and moreover, in some circumstances, we may commit some serious errors. Thus in some, if not many circumstances, while retaining our sense of autonomy and our capacity to make our own choices, it may be wise for us to go along with instructions given.

Not only are we responsible for our decisions as adults, but in the main, we also need to have the autonomy, the personal space, the respect from others and the freedom, which allows us to make many if not all of our own decisions and take actions based on our own judgments, thoughts, beliefs and opinions. As a consequence, dependent to some extent on who we are and the circumstances we are in, we need to observe, bear, experience and learn from the consequences of our decisions and actions.

In terms of our freedoms to act, both at home, at work and in community and society at large, we need to have, and ensure we have, the many freedoms which we need, both positive freedoms to do things, and also in terms of other of our freedoms, we need to have our freedoms from, these freedoms which overall mean our not having unnecessary restrictions on our actions and our not being harmed and oppressed.

Thus we need positive freedoms in terms of a range of areas including our being able to decide on and express our beliefs; we need freedoms in terms of our abilities to meet others and travel; we need freedoms to earn money, to work, to gain the resources and sustenance we need to survive, we need to be able to rest, to have the capacity and space to enjoy our lives, to be alone, and then again to be with others when we so choose (where that is possible). In relation to freedom and justice in our societies we need the freedom to have access to fair and just legal systems and legal remedies and protections. We need to be dealt with, with equality, fairness and justice by our legal systems. Underpinning and tied to, indeed comprising important freedoms and elements of justice in themselves, are the basics we need for survival, our access to food, water, shelter, and more.

In terms of other essential 'freedoms from', we need to be free from oppression, torture, violence, unjust imprisonment and other punishments (including violent punishments), free from poverty, from extra-judicial and indeed judicial aggressive violence, free from kidnap (which may sometimes be deliberately imposed as a matter of policy), forced separation from those whom we are closest to, love and care for, . We need to be free from forced and unjustified removal of our possessions, from being held as slaves, and much more. We need in essence the range of human rights, and, in addition to these, we need systems of protection to ensure that we do have these rights. As individuals we need to work to ensure that all of this and more are available not only to ourselves but that they are also available to all others.

Another key area examined by this guide has been that of the need for rationality, reason, evidence, logic, the use of which are embodied in the core and other principles and serve to underpin our conduct, actions and behaviour. The need to use rationality, reason, evidence and logic represents a principle in itself, but also underpins the effective application of core and other principles. Their use supports our enjoyment of a life of well-being and happiness and the reduction and avoidance of pain and suffering.

The core principles themselves are founded in reason and rationality, representing the reasonable assumption that we wish for our own personal well-being and happiness and recognising our social nature, this social nature meaning we require the well-being and happiness of others in order to support our own well-being and this social nature requiring us to live effectively and well with others, and requiring us to cooperate with others if we are to enjoy maximal well-being ourselves.

Reason, rationality, evidence and logic need to be applied to all areas of our lives, including our decisions about our life goals, our relationships, our actions at work, in the home and wherever. That being said, this guide recognises the importance of our feelings and emotions which are important elements of our individual identity, and which can be powerful motivators for the good, supporting us, for example, in determining goals which are worthy of pursuit through means of our use of reason, evidence, rationality and logic. For example, our care for others will motivate our actions to support the well-being of others and will be optimally implemented through effective gathering and use of evidence combined with using that evidence with rationality, reason and logic. Our anger and hurt at injustice can motivate us to seek and work for justice, with our pursuing our goals of justice through our use of rationality, reason and logic.

Yet also we need to recognise that, if not implemented in a reasonable and rational manner, our feelings of care and love can be oppressive to others and hurt them, and our anger can lead to actions and conduct which damage others. Thus our emotions and our emotional selves are of great importance, but at times, if not often, we may need to manage and control our emotions, such that we can effectively implement and achieve our core goals of supporting the well-being of ourselves and others, and reducing and preventing harm to ourselves and others.

Our actions and conduct in terms of pursuing peace and cooperation, and avoiding aggressive violence are also key to our well-being and the avoidance of pain and suffering, with this comprising another important area discussed within this guide, such actions and conduct being of central relevance to the application of core and other principles. Through peaceful cooperation with others, we are able to achieve great things together, be they simply enjoying our families, be they our establishment of complex systems of medical care and treatment, systems of law and governance, systems for discovery and research, complex systems which enable us to travel far, complex technologies which support us in our communications and other daily tasks, complex systems which enable construction of pleasant and sturdy homes and other structures, and much more.

Conflict has been discussed. Violent conflict is undesired and unacceptable. We must do, in particular, our utmost to avoid wars, civil, international and global, these wars causing vast levels of destruction and damage, having been responsible for the deaths of tens of millions of people and the suffering and oppression of millions more. We need to build global mechanisms for maintaining world peace and security, something which is especially necessary in a world where we have the destructive power of modern nuclear weapons which can destroy cities of millions in seconds. In our every day lives we need to be acting as far as we can to ensure that those who govern us, those we choose as our representatives are responsible, caring, effective and considerate, thoughtful and capable of acting in an appropriate cooperative manner such that threats of war and conflict are reduced. Our failure to do this will result in tremendous personal cost to us all.

Violent conflict having been considered, where conflict refers to our having differences in views, conflicting views and opinions within the framework of core principles, this is seen as capable of being supportive of, if not likely to be supportive of the general well-being, especially if those of us who are parties to such a conflict about and difference of opinions are willing to listen to others, are willing to reflect on the evidence and change our views and opinions where our own views are no longer sufficiently supported by evidence and argument and no longer seem, where relevant to represent the optimal responses to situations. Those of us who care passionately about well-being will be passionate about our ideas and opinions, and we will also recognise the importance of reaching the correct decisions in order that well-being is supported. Exchanges of opinion and perspectives should support the reaching of effective decisions and conclusions with such exchanges of passionate views, avoiding insult, harsh and disrespectful personal criticism and abuse of others, such positive and constructive listening exchanges often leading to stronger and longer-lasting caring, respectful relationships.

This guide has also looked at core and other principles in relation to our health and well-being. Our own actions in relation to maintaining our personal health have been discussed, as have our responsibilities in terms of preventing the spread of illness and disease. Effective and organised systems of medical support and treatment for ourselves and all for others have been identified as crucial to our health and well-being with our having responsibilities not only to those in our own families, communities and societies but also to those suffering in pain and illness further away from us.

Honesty, truthfulness, trustworthiness and integrity, underpin our relationships and cooperativity. Without basic trust in what others are saying and doing, our more personal and intimate as well as our more impersonal transactional relationships will not work effectively and our families, communities and societies, our broader human society, will be at risk of break down. Yet it has also been pointed out that there is a difference between our needing to have integrity and our telling the truth. Situations have been identified in this guide whereby it is a moral obligation, significantly supporting the well-being of others, and preventing their pain and suffering, for us not to tell the truth, and indeed to act in what may be seen from some perspectives as acting in a deliberately untruthful manner. Indeed it was also argued that the ability to not tell the truth, and the full truth, can be a valuable skill which we all need to learn, and which our children seem to need to learn and may need to be taught about explicitly. That being said, it is essential we always retain integrity and act to support our own well-being and happiness and the well-being and happiness of others. And acting with sincerity in such a manner represents the greatest level of honesty and integrity and provides maximal well-being to ourselves and others.

The penultimate chapter of this guide focused on our responsibilities to our non-human world, our need and responsibility to maintain an appropriate environment such that we and future generations can survive and thrive. These environmental threats are of great current urgency and need to be dealt with on a global scale through global cooperation and global agreements aimed at reducing the prospect of catastrophic anthropogenic climate change and the range of other threats of pollution and resource depletion that we face. It is our responsibility as individuals to take our own personal action in response to the environmental threats that we face, including doing our utmost to ensure that action is taken by our local, national and global organisations, indeed by all others, to forestall and prevent these threats to our well-being and to prevent our suffering into the future due to these environmental threats.

Our human voraciousness and carelessness with our environment also threatens the range of other forms of life on our planet, destroying habitats and the ecosystems in which our animal life and other life forms are embedded. Deforestation threatens not only the wildlife living in these forests but also supports climate change and global warming. The expansion of our human settlements encroaches on and destroys natural land where the range of animal species live, with the host habitats of many animal species at the current time eroding away at a rapid rate. And where one animal is threatened with reduction in its numbers, then that has effects on other animals and plants through effects which reach both up and down the various food chains and throughout the various ecosystems. In our personal conduct, we need to be acting to protect our various animals and plants, from reduction in numbers, extinction, protecting their natural habitats as far as is practical, and ensuring that appropriate and substantial environments exist in which the range of plants and animals can survive and thrive. Importantly, of course, we are in many ways dependent on plants and animals for our own survival, and this therefore provides a further crucial and important reason why we need to take action to ensure that not only is our environment suitable for us, but that it is also suitable for our plants and animals.

Further we need to be caring about all organisms as far as is reasonable and possible. Animals are widely used as sources of food, with animals, at the present time, widely, indeed almost ubiquitously slaughtered to provide meat for our human consumption. Clearly these are sentient beings with brains and a range of senses existing, to important degrees, in a similar manner to ourselves as humans. While animals do eat other animals, as humanity it seems likely that we have a lesser need, or can ensure in the future that we have a lesser need for consuming animals, that we can gain sufficient protein and many other essential dietary sources from elsewhere. And further, we are undoubtedly greatly aware of the suffering that our slaughter of animals entails. The slaughter of animals does not incorporate well-being. Clearly we should be aiming to avoid the slaughter of animals for food purposes while maintaining high levels of health and well-being both for ourselves and others.

Much in this guide has been subject of discussion in terms of application of core and other principles, but while discussion is of interest and importance, this is a guide which is about how we act, about how we conduct ourselves, about what we actually do in practice. It is certainly about thinking, beliefs, being rational, logical, using evidence, understanding our emotions and more, yet it is the consequences of our rationality, beliefs, our logic, our thinking, our feelings and our use of evidence that matters. It is how our rationality, how our beliefs, our logic, our thinking, our feelings and our use of evidence affects what we do, how these affect our real actions and performance in the world, which matter. This guide is essentially about doing and taking action, (and sometimes where necessary taking no action), this being our key focus, though, of course, effective doing and effective action frequently if not always, require our thought, planning, rationality, reason, logic and the use of evidence. Yet the key focus of this guide is in regard to that taking of action, effective action, in support of the well-being and happiness of ourselves and all others, and the reduction of pain and suffering for ourselves and all others.

Thus, we certainly need to think, plan, use evidence, reason and indeed discuss and debate how we can most effectively achieve our goals and what these goals are and what they mean. Yet we must be wary of engaging in too much academic and overly theoretical debate such that the taking of action in support of ourselves and others is relegated to a secondary role, with such action moved to the back of the queue, existing behind the understandable interest, pleasure and engagement gained from academic debate and discussion. It also must be recognised however, that academic debate and discussion is something which indeed has value in itself, through the pleasure, understanding and enlightenment it can bring, and that it also has value in terms of its potential consequences in regard to our personal conduct and well-being and the well-being of others.

We must get on with, take action and pursue our goals, and do all of these effectively. We must, for example, in line with core and other principles, pursue our own fulfillment and self-realisation, our own achievement, our own pleasures, aiming to find fulfillment, love, perhaps a sense of belonging if that is what we desire, and the pursuing of the deeper (and indeed sometimes perhaps the more shallow) pleasures of life as well as getting on with supporting the well-being of others.

Additional to our pursuit of pleasures, it is clear that when faced with personal difficulties and personal challenges, be they illness, difficulties in our relationships, criticisms of ourselves; when faced with the threat or actual loss of income endangering our material well-being, and other threats to our well-being, then we must do our utmost to deal with these challenges, pursuing our own well-being and happiness and the well-being of others and protecting all, including ourselves from pain and suffering as much as we can.

It is also clear, in line with core and other principles, that we must act to support those of us who are suffering in poverty, those embroiled in immediate crises, those facing severe illness and needing medical care, those under violent threat from others, and those facing the range of other trying and deeply problematic circumstances. It is essential that we as individuals, through our own personal actions and through our social entities and representative groups, are involved in action to support all those of us in such circumstances.

And our actions must be taken in as an effective manner as is possible. We will be optimally supporting our own well-being, happiness and fulfillment, and the well-being, happiness and fulfillment of others if we act effectively to realise the core and other principles. And in order to achieve that effectiveness, we will generally require and will need to gain the maximal knowledge and understanding of ourselves, others and the world around us. We will in the vast main need to plan, gather evidence, educate and develop ourselves, strategise, evaluate, think about, sometimes, if not often, in depth; we will need to research, investigate, analyse, visualise and imagine implementations of our plans, reflect on our experience, interpret, create, use evidence, reason and rationality and much more.

Exemplifying the importance of research and systematic research in particular, in regard to maintaining and improving our own health, our efforts to support our health are supported through researching and finding out about the best ways to tackle health problems, through understanding, for example our human biology and biochemistry, and devising optimal health responses and treatments. Approaches to enhancing our health arising from research approaches, approaches which can make a significant difference to our quality of life and well-being, often significantly extending our healthy lives and healthy living, may include simple measures involving taking appropriate exercise and having an appropriate diet, or may involve complex and sophisticated treatments in response to serious conditions such as pneumonia, the range of bacterial and viral infections, cancer, heart disease or other conditions. To support such research, which is so central to our health and well-being, as individuals and as communities and societies (and also globally) we need to set aside and allocate appropriate and sufficient resources in a planned manner to support our own health and to support planned and organised systems of medical health care. All of this needs to be done as effectively as possible.

Moreover we can most effectively support those whom we are close to, and whom we love, support others in our own communities and beyond, if we think about and plan our support for them, for example setting aside time to be with them and support them and also setting aside resources to support them in times of need. In order to give the best support possible, we will need to act through not only providing immediate support for those of us who are in need, but through having longer term plans to provide support, such that future difficulties and crises are less likely to arise or, if they do, our responses and solutions are prepared and at hand. Rationality, thought, logic and evidence need to be brought to bear to ensure that we support ourselves and others to the optimal extent possible and we need to ensure that we set aside time to do the necessary thinking and planning where this is required.

We cannot pursue our well-being and happiness effectively or support the well-being and happiness of others without continuous efforts to educate, learn about, train and develop ourselves, and without efforts to support the education, learning, training and development of others. Education, training and other approaches to personal development provide us with increased knowledge, understanding, skills and abilities which support us in pursuing our own well-being and the well-being of others in an effective manner, as well as often representing direct sources of pleasure in themselves. They support us in doing the things we want to do and doing them well, providing us with enhanced capabilities which support our achievement and help us in achieving goals and positive outcomes, for others, our communities, our societies, our global communities.

As an important element of our learning and self-development, in our working, home and social lives, we need, as individuals, to reflect on our actions and experiences, experiment with new ways of doing things and focus on improving how we do things with a view to supporting both our own well-being and the well-being of others. As part of this, in order to support our reflection, learning and development, we also need to take advantage of the knowledge and understanding in our communities and societies, within our broader humanity, taking part in programmes, courses and educational programmes which support us in being as skilled and talented as we can be, in relation to the things we wish to know about and need to know about, understand and do.

Our efforts at developing ourselves in terms of our learning need to be an ongoing part, to all intents and purposes, of the whole of our lives. The fact is that it seems there are always things for us to learn and discover. This is perhaps both fortunate in terms of the novelty, excitement and interest that such learning and discovery provides, yet unfortunate to some extent, in that we find ourselves almost always needing to engage in efforts to find out the new, to learn and develop ourselves. Sometimes making such effort can feel burdensome in its frequent requirement for continual periods of mental effort, despite the rewards and benefits that will accrue through our learning, however our learning itself, as mentioned, is often pleasurable, with our constantly gaining the feeling of knowing and having learned or understood the new. Moreover our continuous efforts at learning and developing may well support our mental agility, as well as supporting our broader capabilities arising directly from our learning. It is certainly optimal and beneficial for us to keep up our efforts in regard to education, training, self-development, self-improvement and learning, and this is the case both within and beyond our work environments, in regard to our family, community, societal and broader human contexts.

Our need for education, learning and development, and indeed our need for effective education, learning and development mean that we need to provide support for systems of learning and education within our communities, societies and beyond, systems where crucial basic skills, knowledge and understanding and crucial social, technical, scientific and other advanced knowledge, skills and understanding can be communicated to others, taught to others, and can therefore be acquired by others and learnt. In this way, through supporting such systems we are not only supporting our own individual personal growth and development, our own personal well-being and happiness but also supporting the education, learning and development of others, of our children, and supporting effective communities, societies, a more secure and effective humanity, all of which can sustain themselves into the future through this transmission of knowledge, skills and understandings as well as through the development of new knowledge and understandings. And such communities and societies, as well as our global organisations and institutions, through their effective functioning, support us all as individuals. All of this education and training and all of these systems require organisation, effective administration, management, resourcing, effective teaching, a commitment to and understanding of learning, and mutual acceptance and cooperation between all of us, both within our communities and societies and, given the global nature of our world and the global generation and acquisition of knowledge and understandings, these require cooperation beyond our more local communities and societies.

Within the context of education and other areas of our lives, within the framework of core and other principles, we need, as far as we can, to ensure the greatest level of equality of opportunity that we can reasonably achieve. Through doing this we are supporting the well-being of both ourselves and others by ensuring we have communities and societies where we all can experience the greatest possible degree of fairness in our lives, with all of us being able to achieve and fulfill ourselves to as great a degree as is possible. Such equality of opportunity means we are ensuring that our communities and societies have access to the talents and potential abilities and contributions of all in our communities and societies, not simply those who are members of elite classes or elite social groups, those born in privileged contexts, those in certain racial, religious or cultural groups, those who know the right people.

The importance of equality of opportunity having been mentioned, we do nevertheless have to recognise that there are factors relating to our individuality, factors influencing our individual character and complexity (such as family influence, genetic background, social and cultural context), factors affecting our level and types of skill and knowledge, indeed our preferences and interests, which mean that, while pursuing equality of opportunity is itself a worthwhile goal, and while preventing overly significant major disparities in income and power between individuals, organisations and groups within our societies, are significantly beneficial to pursue, and indeed these goals need to be achieved, absolute equality and perhaps even near equality of outcomes are unlikely to be attainable or indeed beneficial goals.

Indeed, total equality of outcomes in itself is almost certain to be an undesirable goal given that our aims in terms of core and other principles are that we promote and enjoy well-being, happiness and fulfillment ourselves and work to ensure this for others as well as working to reduce and prevent pain and suffering. A certain level of equality, an important level of equality, may contribute towards these goals, however, pursuing our goals of well-being, while to some extent overlapping with a level of equality, is in important ways distinct from the pursuit of equality. It is important to recognise that there is danger when we advocate and promote overly high levels of equality, economic and otherwise, rather than focusing on our total and overall well-being and happiness to which that level of equality may contribute. It seems likely that too much focus on equality at the expense of a focus on well-being and happiness has significant potential to damage well-being and happiness and increase levels of pain and suffering, not only for each of us as individuals, but also for our communities, societies and beyond, which, as a consequence of such an over-focus, may fail to develop, or lose access to diversity, specialised skills and expertise which benefit us all.

Through this guide, and in line with core and other principles, our acting in cooperative ways has been pointed out as an essential component of our individual well-being and happiness. Our cooperativity and social action underpins not only our own well-being but the well-being and happiness of others in our society. It supports effectively functioning communities and societies, locally and globally, as well as supporting positive and constructive interactions between communities and societies such that the well-being of all is supported.

In our daily lives we need to aim for peaceful cooperative relationships where all of us are able to gain from and achieve happiness, well-being and fulfillment through our relationships, through our interactions with others. In pursuit of such cooperative relationships we have to be clear about our own wants, goals and needs, as well as listening to, and understanding (as well as where appropriate empathising with) the needs, goals and wants of others. Our own actions and our own conduct need to take into account the needs, goals and wants of others, though how we respond precisely is highly likely to depend on the specific and relevant circumstances and situations. On many occasions, though certainly not all, we may need to compromise in terms of that which we personally are able to gain or achieve, in order that we support others and build that effective cooperation which supports us all.

It is important to reiterate, tied in to our pursuit of well-being and happiness and our need and indeed our impulsion to cooperate and work effectively with others, that in line with core and other principles, we must pursue non-violence and peacefulness, recognising aggressive violence, physical, emotional, in whatever form, as being in themselves entirely contradictory to core and other principles. Inflicting violent pain and suffering on others through aggressive violence clearly stands in opposition to the core principles of reducing and avoiding harm, pain and suffering to others. In the presence of aggressively violent threats or aggressive violence itself, we need to take whatever action is reasonable and possible in such situations to prevent such aggressive violence and to avoid outbreaks and continuance of violence, although, as already stated in this chapter and elsewhere in this guide, where necessary we may need to, and may be obliged to, take forceful physical action to preserve peacefulness, our own well-being and the well-being of others.

In our daily lives we must aim to act peacefully, to discuss and negotiate our way through difficulties wherever we can, with our prioritising our finding and implementation of strategies and options for our conduct and behaviour which are cooperative, peace-filled and peaceful though concerned with well-being in all its aspects. We need to adopt conduct which indicates and reflects our love and concern for others, as far as that is reasonable and possible. Even if physically threatened in our daily lives, we need to do our utmost to take steps to pursue peace and resolve such difficulties in as peaceful a manner as possible. However, importantly and significantly in terms of core and other principles, we are not obliged to, indeed we should and indeed must not, as far as we can, allow ourselves to be victims of any significant physical and emotional violence and so we need to take steps to protect ourselves and others from such violent threat and action, doing so in a manner which will minimise and minimises violent and physically forceful action.

Further, in relation to aggressive violence and other destructive and damaging actions, we must never seek revenge. Vengeful actions are completely at odds with core and other principles, through the damage and harm that such revenge inevitably causes to us all, combined with the absence of any good from its pursuit. That being said, as has already been stated, we certainly have legitimacy in protecting ourselves, those we love and indeed all others from violent attacks, and with physical force in some cases. Where necessary, physical force is a legitimate necessity in order to ensure our defence and protection, and the defence and safety of others.

Indeed it is further appropriate that, wherever necessary, we are prepared for and possess the social systems, the physical power and the resources available to defend ourselves such that we and others are not the victims of those who are acting in malevolent and aggressively violent ways. However, should we need to deploy physical force, then the physical force we deploy, as reiterated through this guide and stated again within this chapter, must be at the minimum possible level needed in the circumstances. And we must aim, wherever reasonable and possible to preserve the health, life and indeed the well-being even of those who have engaged in poor conduct and aggressive violence, our actions containing the hope that these people can and will reform and become assets to our communities, societies and beyond with their further serving as an exemplar for the promotion of peaceful and minimally violent responses to aggressive violence, such exemplars serving us all.

While our acting to promote and support our own well-being and the well-being of others are seen as underpinning our personal conduct and action, the ideas and recommended actions presented within this guide are certainly seen as open to discussion modification and change, indeed they must be so. This guide, despite its length, remains a work in progress. While it is indeed hoped that much presented in this guide will be accepted as reasonable and much, if not most of what is stated, is either our current practice or can be adopted without significant disagreement, in reality there are likely to be many different judgments and perceptions in regard to the personal conduct, ideas and actions presented in this guide, especially given changing times and changing communities and societies, and such judgments and perceptions will change into the future.

Not only are the meaning, the balance and the overlap between the core and other principles open to such discussion, debate and change, but along with this, the precise judgments, the precise courses of action which need to be taken in order to achieve these goals and implement these principles are also seen as matters for discussion. Reasonably and realistically, given one's inevitable human frailty and human limitations, it is of course highly unlikely that all of that which is proposed or stated in this guide could be correct. Too much is stated in this guide for such an extent of accuracy and correctness to be likely to be the case. However, there is certainly a strong commitment to core and other principles and it is certainly seen as essential that we do act to support well-being, fulfillment and happiness and we do aim to reduce and prevent pain and suffering as far as we can and we do so for ourselves and for all others. And the range of other principles are certainly strongly advocated in this guide to influence and support our personal action and conduct.

There is certainly a need for greater knowledge and understanding as well as systematic research required in terms of growing and developing our knowledge and understanding about the precise types of conduct and behaviour we need to adopt, this conduct being influenced or determined by the need for actions and conduct which can best support our well-being and happiness and the well-being and happiness of others as well as reducing and preventing pain and suffering for all. We each have to make our own individual choices about our personal conduct and behaviour and should we be accepting of core and other principles, we will ourselves need to take responsbility for determining how these should be put into practice, not only as individuals, but as communities, societies and as a broader humanity. It is hoped that this guide will support all of us in our thinking decision-making, and in the determination and development of our beliefs and opinions as well as our practical personal conduct and behaviour.

Finally, it is also hoped that this guide will help us all in adopting appropriate conduct and behaviour such that our well-being, happiness and fulfillment will be supported along with the well-being happiness and fulfillment of others, such that pain suffering will be prevented or reduced for all of us. While, as has been discussed in this guide, it is considered unrealistic to expect a life of total and continuous happiness, joy and fulfillment, we can certainly enjoy lives with much well-being, happiness and joy within them. And so, while anticipating and expecting some setbacks, some sadness and unhappy times in our lives, occurrences which seem likely to occur as part of all of our ordinary human lives, in line with the core and other principles, we need to aim for, and we will hopefully each of us, achieve a life comprising the highest levels of well-being, the highest levels of happiness and the highest level of pleasure and fulfillment that we can, both for ourselves and for others. These are worthwhile goals in themselves.

As individuals, it is the recommendation of this guide that we therefore all do our utmost in whatever reasonable and possible ways we can, to adopt a Humanist approach which ensures that we engage in appropriate personal conduct and actions, and as a consequence achieve the worthy goals of well-being, happiness and fulfillment, and the avoidance of pain and suffering, not just for ourselves but for all others as well.

# Coda

As mentioned in its concluding chapter, despite its length, despite the breadth of its content and discussion, this guide remains to some extent a work in progress. There is undoubtedly room for development, change, and improvement in its content, and your support in such further development, change and improvement would be welcomed. For the author, as is the case with any of us, is of course unlikely to have managed all things correctly and provided accurate and appropriate answers throughout. I cannot have experienced all there is to experience; I cannot know and understand all there is to know and understand. It would be remarkable if this guide were entirely complete, if there were not flaws in this guide; remarkable if there were no inaccuracies in content or in terms of advised approaches or actions. And while hopefully avoided, despite thorough efforts at editing, evaluation, re-evaluation and revision, there may be, located within the text, unintended inconsistencies or elements which may be perceived as inconsistent, and which might therefore require more effective and accurate statement and better framing. Further, as mentioned at the outset of this guide, all ideas need to be open to discussion and challenge, and that challenge, of course, must apply to this guide.

Your constructive comments, your notions in regard to areas missed out of the text which you feel should be covered, your thoughts and ideas with argumentative and evidential support in regard to, for example, principles which might be added to the list of core and other principles would be appreciated (for instance, I engaged in significant debate about including a principle about protecting all life, but determined that this was sufficiently and better covered by principles referring to the prevention of pain and suffering and the promotion of well-being). Your constructive comments would be appreciated in relation to any areas of this guide, and would be well-received by the author.

If you wish to send suggestions, propose amendments, correct errata, add to arguments and more, then please either post these to the Living

Humanism website at www.livinghumanism.com or address these in writing to the publisher of this guide. I will be happy to hear from you. Unfortunately it may not be possible to acknowledge all comments and suggestions. However, in the event of a second edition of this guide, then any added comments, suggestions, amendments, proposals and more included in that second edition will be acknowledged, as well as some of those proposed modifications which are not included, along with a rationale as to their non-inclusion. I look forward to hearing your comments and suggestions.

# Acknowledgements

I would like to thank the team at Matador, for their support with the production of this book. My thanks in particular go to Heidi Hurst for all of her work in managing and implementing the production of this guide, as well as, in particular, her patience in dealing with the many questions and queries from the author during the process of production. I would also like to thank Lauren Bailey, Chelsea Taylor, Hannah Dakin and Morgan Langford at Matador for their help at various points in time with this project.

My gratitude is also owed to my many fellow Humanist friends. Over the years I have met with you, discussed ideas with you, and enjoyed your company and many kindnesses. In particular my thanks are directed to my many friends at North East Humanists, with whom there have not only been such discussions and the range of exchanges, but with whom I have enjoyed many pleasant and happy times, joyful events, social occasions and more. There are too many of you to mention individually, but I owe a deep gratitude to you all, not only for being there, not only for your support through the years, but for being you, with all your dedication, energy, openness, pleasantness and kindness.

I would also wish to express my gratitude to the many Humanists I have met from other Humanist groups around the UK and beyond, be they either from local Humanist groups, whether encountered through Humanists UK (formerly the British Humanist Association) or indeed whether Humanists internationally, over the years of my association with Humanism. Our discussions, your words, your talks, our meetings and conferences, your friendships, have been enriching, and have all influenced the contents of this guide. For all your support and friendship over the years, I am eternally grateful.

# Appendix: The Principles

### A. Core Principles

*(1) Act to support and promote your own well-being and the well-being of all others.*

We need to work and act to support ourselves in our own lives and to support others, our families, our communities, our societies and our broader humanity. We are individuals with individually focused needs and interests, yet we are also social in our nature with cares, concern and interest in the well-being of our families, communities, societies and our broader humanity. We need to promote our own well-being and happiness, which is inextricably tied to the lives and well-being of others, our families, communities, societies and the well-being of our broader humanity. Indeed, we are all dependent on others, our societies and communities, our broader humanity to support our individual well-being.

Stemming from, but also beyond the obvious personal benefits we gain from our efforts to support others, it is also fundamental to our nature as human beings that we support others, our families, communities, societies and humanity. Acting in a manner which recognises and is supportive of others, needs to be part of everything we do, and is not only to the benefit of those others, of our wider communities, but is also to the benefit of each of us as individuals, this arising through the range of channels including the reciprocal support that others and our social communities give to us, and through the well-being, pleasure and fulfillment we gain through our own provision of such support.

*(2) Act to reduce and prevent pain and suffering for yourself and for all others.*

We need to prevent, remove or reduce, as far as possible, the pain and suffering of others, and prevent, reduce and remove our own suffering and pain as far as we can. Some level of pain and suffering is, to some extent, perhaps an inevitable part of living a full life, indeed a life of well-being, but painful experiences are also, to some extent, by definition, experiences we do not wish to have. None of us set out to or wish to experience significant suffering and pain. More than that, it causes us pain and distress when others suffer and, indeed, the suffering and pain of others damages our own well-being. Acting as far as we can to reduce and remove the unnecessary, preventable pain and suffering of others, improves our own personal individual sense of well-being and happiness as well as such actions supporting the well-being and happiness of others. Where unnecessary pain and suffering is reduced or removed from others, our families, communities and societies, there is greater well-being and happiness overall, which benefits us all.

## B. Additional Fundamental Principles

*(1) Use rationality, reason, evidence then action, to support the achievement of your more personal goals and the goals of your families, communities, societies and of our broader humanity.*

Rationality, reason, involving the use of acceptable evidence, are essential bases for supporting our own well-being and the well-being of others. We need to gather such evidence as far as possible and act rationally and reasonably with the information and understanding we have in support of our goals. Rationality, evidence and reason should be used to help us find truth. When reason, rationality and evidence stand against our current beliefs, we need to change our beliefs. Many actions and decisions in life are made intuitively and rapidly. Nevertheless, rationality, reason and evidence should underpin our decisions and actions in order to support our own well-being and the well-being of others.

*(2) Use your passion(s), emotions and instincts to help achieve your personal well-being and to support the well-being of others.*

We have passions and instincts for many things, for adventure, excitement, challenge, learning and understanding, novelty, decency, fairness, freedom, justice, love, integrity and honesty amongst many other passions and instincts. Our passions, our emotions and feelings, our instincts matter, and can motivate us to achieve things, motivate us to help others, to support our communities, to explore and find the new. We need to acknowledge, understand and respect these passions, emotions and instincts and use them to support our own personal well-being and happiness and the well-being and happiness of others, our families, communities, societies and our broader humanity.

*(3) Acknowledge yourself as both an individual and a social being.*

We are at the same time both individuals with our more personal concerns and interests, and social beings, living through others and dependent on others. We gain pleasure individually, from our individual experiences and actions, which almost always involve others, but we also gain a sense of togetherness, belonging and fulfillment, at least the vast majority of us, from being part of the social, our families, groups, teams, organisations, communities and societies, as well as sometimes from being part of our broader humanity. The reality is that our individual and social identities represent who we are as human beings.

As individual people, we have similarities and differences in our personalities, preferences, beliefs, desires and interests. We have similar and different types of interactions and extents of interaction with others, our communities and societies, and we wish for and experience different qualities and levels of interaction with others at different times in our lives. And the social world interacts with us, influencing us, substantially impacting us. Yet we, as individuals, can exert a positive constructive influence on the social world around us, on our families, organisations, communities, societies and our broader humanity, supporting the well-being of both ourselves and others.

*(4) Treat all people primarily as individuals having equal and individual core value and validity, worthy of receiving equal and individual respect, worthy of receiving equal core individual rights, fairness and justice, and exercising equal core individual responsibilities.*

While we are social beings and may often see ourselves or be seen as part of groups, cultures, races, ethnicities and nationalities, all of us must be considered primarily as individuals in terms of our own individual actions, conduct, beliefs, rights, responsibilities and humanity. As individuals, we benefit from others, from our societies and communities, from our broader humanity, recognising each of us as individuals having essential humanity, having rights and responsibilities, recognising and dealing with us as worthy of individual respect and value. Seeing each of us as individuals in this way also benefits the well-being of our families, communities, societies and our broader humanity. While each individual must be respected and seen as having such common humanity and equal validity and rights, we as individuals, our communities and societies, however, have the right to protect ourselves and individuals where necessary by limiting the freedoms of those who represent a significant danger to ourselves, to others, to those societies and communities and to our broader humanity.

*(5) Take responsibility for yourself, for others, for our communities, societies and for our broader humanity.*

While we are only single individuals within the enormous and complex whole of humanity, and while we are influenced by family, community and society, our humanity around us, we are personally responsible for all of our personal actions, the words we express and the beliefs we hold. Responsibility for our actions cannot be abdicated to our families, communities and societies. We should not aim to avoid blame for conduct and actions for which we are responsible, unfairly aiming to place the blame and responsibility on others. We must take responsibility. And we must take responsibility also, as far as we can, and as far as is reasonable, for the actions of others, for the actions of our communities and societies. We often cannot determine and have absolute control over the actions of others, the social entities to which we belong or are seen to belong, yet each of us has the capacity to influence others, our communities and societies, and indeed the wider world, and as individuals or in concert with others, we all have the responsibility to act in support of, not only our own well-being, but also the well-being of all others.

*(6) Have regard to, be mindful of, and take care of the non-human world.*

Our non-human environment, both physical and biological, is core to our well-being and happiness. We need to have regard to this non-human environment and gain understanding of that environment, which supports not only our physical well-being, but also our psychological well-being. Where necessary, we must maintain, conserve or preserve our environments, but must recognise the need for actions, where necessary, which may change this environment in a manner that supports well-being, happiness and fulfillment, and serves to reduce pain and suffering. We must show care and mindfulness in our conduct in regard to our physical environment, refraining from thoughtlessly damaging that environment and having regard to the environmental future. Non-human creatures need to be cared for and looked after in all circumstances where their care and protection is necessary and within our powers. We need to take particular care, where appropriate, to ensure that we ensure the continuance of those non-human organisms whose existence is under threat.

*(7) Aim to be efficient and effective in supporting your personal well-being and the well-being of others.*

We need to be as efficient and effective as we can in our efforts to support our own well-being and the well-being of others, and to reduce pain and suffering. Having good intentions and appropriate goals represent good starting points, but managing to achieve in practice and reality must be our aim. We therefore have not only to do things to the best of our ability, to conduct ourselves in an optimal manner, but we must also educate ourselves, train ourselves, and develop our knowledge and understanding in support of our goals. While efficiency and effectiveness may not be entirely appropriate in all aspects of our lives (with regard to, for example, having fun), these concepts of efficiency and effectiveness apply to many key aspects of our lives, and most tasks, however small. Furthermore, there is deep pleasure and satisfaction in doing things well, acting efficiently and effectively to support the well-being of ourselves and others, and acting efficiently and effectively to reduce pain and suffering.

## C. More Specific Principles

*(1) Act with honesty and integrity in your personal, family, work and public life.*

Honesty and integrity are keys to good relationships, our cooperating well with others, finding solutions, resolving problems and building a better future for us individually, our families, our communities and societies in general, as well as for our broader humanity. Honesty and integrity help us to build and continue our relationships. They serve to build trust and bring people together. We need to be able to trust each other and believe in each other's words and deeds if we are to cooperate with, work with, survive and thrive with others, and sustain rich, healthy and positive relationships with others, in our families, with friends, at work, in our communities, in our societies and beyond.

*(2) Resolve differences and disputes wherever possible through discussion, cooperation, mutual understanding and respect.*

Dispute and disagreements between individuals, and between and within communities and societies are likely when we pursue the well-being of ourselves, others, our communities, societies and beyond. It is essential that we aim to resolve such disagreements and disputes as peacefully as possible, cooperatively through talk, discussion, listening to others, with a sense of respect for the humanity of others, aiming to understand their points of view (or at least the origins and reasons for those points of view) and that we work to develop our abilities to act cooperatively and find constructive, successful solutions. Where the actions and beliefs of others seriously threaten the well-being of others, ourselves and our communities, and where efforts at cooperation and compromise are proving unsuccessful, then dependent on circumstances and situation, we will likely need to be strong and robust in our responsive actions in order to support the well-being of ourselves and others and to avoid or reduce significant suffering and pain.

*(3) Never pursue revenge.*

Pursuing revenge is destructive for everyone, both for the person or group aiming for revenge and for those who may, or will, be the target of that revenge. While it is a necessity to effectively tackle those who engage in acts that have seriously damaged or that may seriously damage us, other individuals, our communities and societies, the purposes of our actions must be to ensure the well-being of each individual (including those who have engaged or are engaging in such acts), of our communities, and societies, of our broader humanity, and to reduce pain and suffering. Nor we should ever conspire against others over time in self-contained vengeful silence or in secretive and hidden ways. Revenge is by its nature destructive for everyone.

*(4) Do not use aggressive violence; do your utmost to avoid taking physical action against others; and do your utmost to prevent others taking part in and engaging in aggressive violence.*

We must never engage in aggressive violence against others, which is by its nature against core principles of supporting the well-being of others and reducing pain and suffering. Aggressive violent action is heinous and damaging. Where others are planning or engaging in aggressive physical action against ourselves and others, then it is necessary for us to engage in all practical and reasonable steps to prevent such aggressive violence and prevent harm, pain and suffering. Under various circumstances, having engaged in cooperative and peaceful efforts to prevent such aggressive violence, forceful physical action may be necessary for the purposes of defence of ourselves or others against physical threats and aggressive, violent, physical action. This action should be implemented at the minimum level necessary to avert danger, injury, pain and suffering, and should cause the minimum necessary pain and suffering to those adopting aggressive violence. Such physical action should be taken only where there is no reasonable and viable alternative available, and therefore should be taken only once other, if not all other, reasonable and practical alternative strategies for defence and protection, and all other actions and strategies to support the avoidance of significant pain and suffering, have been considered, evaluated, and where reasonable, tried and failed.

*(5) Develop your personal skills, your understanding and knowledge about both yourself and the world around you.*

Learning, knowledge and understanding support our individual well-being, happiness and fulfillment as well as supporting us in preventing, reducing and removing pain and suffering. Thus we must pursue the development of our own personal learning and understanding and support learning and education for all others. There is always more to be learned at whatever stage of life we find ourselves. In pursuit of learning of knowledge, skills and in aiming to develop our understanding, it is generally necessary to engage in conscious, deliberate effort and indeed practical personal research, in order to discover the new, and to verify and ensure the truth of that which we consider we already know.

Mistakes based on inadequate knowledge, understanding and skill are inevitable for ourselves and others, and need to be acknowledged with generosity and patience Where such mistakes are made, they need to be avoided as far as possible into the future through our identification of our errors and our pursuit of new solutions, knowledge, understanding and skills and abilities development. Such development is relevant to the vast range of areas in our working and broader social lives and enables us to contribute better to our own lives, the lives of others, individuals, family, communities, societies, as well as our broader humanity, supporting our own well-being and the well-being of all.

*(6) Be a participant not just an observer.*

We need to engage in an active and practical manner with the world around us, taking part in action to make the world better, both locally and beyond. This is part of living a life of well-being, happiness and fulfillment. We must do what we can in practice, to contribute to ourselves and others, whether it be using our technical or artistic skills to fulfill needs, whether it be using our thinking skills, our experience, our skills in speaking and listening in order to support others with the appropriate advice or to mediate in discussions, consultations and local actions to ensure the correct actions are taken; whether it be using our talents to support others in experiencing interest, fun and joy, supporting our own happiness and the happiness of others. We all seek personal fulfillment and this can be achieved in different ways, nevertheless participation, practical engagement, activity and action are crucial to a deep sense of well-being and personal fulfillment.

*(7) Work to ensure your independence, freedom and autonomy and support the independence, freedom and autonomy of others.*

Our own personal independence, freedom and autonomy are essential for our well-being and happiness and we need to act to ensure that we can enjoy these as far as is possible. Crucially, we also need to respect all others as human beings with a self, with individuality, with their own perspectives and their own human validity. Each of us needs and wishes to feel autonomous, free, and have a sense of independence as far as is possible and we each wish for and need to be viewed by others as having such autonomy, with our having personal freedom and the capacity for personal choices in our own lives, within the context of our responsibilities to others, and core and other principles. Another individual's views and actions may be different to ours, may even in some cases be offensive to our way of seeing the world. Nevertheless, we each of us need to understand who these people are, and understand why they think as they do. We need to aim to understand others in terms of their individuality, their social and psychological background, and of course consider whether, in terms of core and other principles, they may not in fact be correct and indeed more in tune with the promotion of well-being and the reduction of pain and suffering than we are ourselves. This, of course, may not always be the case. Nevertheless, this type of approach respects autonomy, individuality and humanity, which are essential elements of our well-being and happiness.

Thus, wherever possible and reasonable, where there are differences, we must first aim to understand, empathise, discuss and then, where appropriate and reasonable, aim to persuade. That being said, where others through their words or actions indicate or represent substantial and damaging threat to ourselves and others, we cannot allow those offering such threats, those who are prepared to act with cruelty, violence and in damaging unjust ways, to enact their cruelty, violence and injustice or to gain power and control over us and others, such that they are able to damage the well-being of, and cause pain and suffering to, ourselves or our fellow human beings.

*(8) Pursue justice.*

Our well-being requires justice, not just for ourselves but also for all others. Justice requires fairness and fair treatment from ourselves to others and from others to ourselves. It involves respect for others as individuals and respect from others for ourselves as individuals. A life of full well-being requires us to assert our own need for, and indeed our own achievement of personal justice and fairness, and it requires us to act to reduce, remove and prevent injustice, pain and suffering for others. It is our responsibility to work to remove the pain and suffering of injustice from ourselves and others as far as we can, such that pain, suffering and injustice will be reduced or, ideally, be entirely ended. We must work for justice and act against unjust behaviour and conduct that unfairly, unjustly, wantonly, unreasonably, recklessly, callously and uncaringly, damages our own well-being and happiness, and the well-being and happiness of others.

*(9) Be fair to yourself.*

We must do our best, try our best, to achieve our goals, to support our own well-being and the well-being of others, and to prevent both ourselves and others from enduring pain, harm and suffering. Nevertheless there are times when we must be fair to ourselves as individuals and recognise that we are doing and perhaps sometimes have done, all we can, and that, for example, further action at a particular moment may damage our personal well-being and happiness in a manner beyond what would be a reasonable sense of failure and disappointment in being unable to achieve our present goals. Being fair to ourselves, we should be careful to avoid too much self-admonishment and criticism, too many feelings of guilt and inadequacy, imposing too much pain on ourselves, where goals are proving difficult to achieve or are not achieved. In reality we are one amongst many, and while we have power to support change and influence our local and wider worlds for the better, and have responsibility for pursuing these goals, we are certainly not all powerful and capable of achieving everything. But we must do what we can, and this should involve doing much, trying our best, aiming to devise new strategies to support the achievement of our goals, new ways to succeed, even though in some cases we may choose to set aside some goals and temporarily work in other directions. Nevertheless, we must be fair to ourselves in our efforts to live and to achieve, and therefore, in line with our personal, individual nature, in line with our goals and desires, we must allow ourselves (and others), pleasures, entertainments, leisure, relaxation, time to do nothing, as part of our aim of achieving personal well-being and happiness for ourselves (and others).

*(10) Pursue the material things and resources which are necessary for your well-being but don't be greedy.*

Sufficient possessions, money and wealth are a necessity, but material things and money should not be over-valued or become ends in themselves that supplant our search for personal well-being, happiness and fulfillment and that supplant support for the well-being, happiness and fulfillment of others. It is unacceptable to pursue the accumulation of money and goods for the sake of accumulation, for personal aggrandisement or for other reasons, in such a manner that the well-being, happiness and fulfillment of others are significantly damaged. Accumulation of material things and resources for such purposes or in such a manner is not only detrimental to our own well-being, but threatens or ignores the well-being of others. It is, however, reasonable and consistent with core principles for us as individuals to aim to acquire money and possessions so that we can achieve, amongst other goals, a level of comfort in our lives, achieve pleasures and enjoyment, resources so that we can invest in new ventures and adventures, invest in our education, invest in new futures, and such that we can support the well-being and happiness of others.

We also need to ensure that our communities and societies, our social institutional, our global social entities, have material things and resources such that we, through these social entities, can perform those organised social functions which support our well-being, happiness and fulfillment and serve to reduce or prevent our pain and suffering. Nevertheless we have to work to resist, reduce, ameliorate or remove social pressures and actions, social and economic systems which promote personal greed and excessive material accumulation as ends in themselves, at the significant expense of others. And as individuals, together with others, we must ensure we focus on supporting the broader well-being, aiming to reduce and prevent pain and suffering.

*(11) While there are general patterns and rules of thumb that may support our actions and decisions, individual challenges and problems often need individual solutions and judgments.*

The core principles presented in this guide are considered fundamental in terms of determining our personal conduct, and other principles are also considered of central and significant value and import. Our application and manner of application of these principles are of necessity contingent on the varying situations we face in our daily lives, which are frequently complex and individual, being influenced by many different factors, in particular the different people involved in those situations with their different conduct, personalities and behaviours. Relationships vary too of course; we, and other people, vary with time; as do the complex events, series of events and circumstances surrounding situations; the way we personally feel and think also varies with time; and the potential consequences of our decisions and actions vary because of the changing situational factors involved and their interplay.

Thus, while general rules of thumb and our conscious adoption and learning of patterns of conduct and action can make life more simple, providing a sound basis for our decisions and actions, our reality is that varying circumstances and situations often require subtle, individual judgments to support the best decisions, optimal conduct and optimal actions when we aim to pursue core principles and support our own well-being and the well-being of others.

*(12) Maintain regard and care for others, spend time on caring for others and looking after their well-being, but also focus on pursuit of your own pleasures, enjoyment, fulfillment and happiness.*

It is core to our well-being and the well-being of others that we focus on others, care for them and look after them. Engaging in such actions supports our personal well-being in many ways, for example, through our own direct pleasures in supporting others and through the strengthening of our communities and societies as well as our broader humanity as contexts full of well-being and happiness. However, while always maintaining a significant effort in regard to contributing to our families, communities, societies and our broader world, it is beneficial and necessary to our well-being for us to focus, to some extent, on more directly pursuing and enjoying our more personal pleasure, happiness, enjoyment and fulfillment, taking into account the well-being and happiness of others and understanding the relationship between our own well-being and the well-being of others. We have multiple goals and purposes in life, our gaining of pleasure, fulfillment and happiness from serving others being crucial to our well-being. However, our well-being is also supported through a more direct and personal focus on our own pleasures, satisfactions and fulfillments, aiming to experience the greatest pleasures and personal enrichment, finding personal happiness and fulfillment as far as we are able.

*(13) Maintain a sense of skepticism and doubt, where appropriate, about beliefs and statements, but when required, take decisions with commitment and take the necessary action.*

In regard to many important beliefs and statements, it is often worthwhile maintaining a sense of skepticism and disbelief. This skepticism supports us in the finding of effective and truthful understandings and answers that benefit our personal well-being and the well-being of others. Such skepticism enables us to more easily move into thinking in different ways and developing new and effective thinking and ideas. It also enhances our personal autonomy, responsibility and independence. While we certainly do need to listen to, pay attention to, evaluate and sometimes accept the ideas of others, we also need to remain skeptical to some extent about some, or many, of the ideas that we counter. In particular we need to be skeptical about many of the statements made by those with authority and power, due to the propensity of some, if not many of those with authority and power, to use insufficient and false evidence for their own purposes. However, even where there is reasonable authority and substantial evidence gained in acceptable ways, it is important to question, to investigate other perspectives and continually weigh the evidence, adopting those beliefs and actions supported by sound evidence that lead to the most effective and truthful answers. In this respect we also need to be somewhat skeptical about our own thinking, ideas and actions.

Our skepticism is not an excuse for inertia nor is it an excuse to thoughtlessly reject everything. While it is often reasonable to be skeptical, we must also aim to find value in ideas and actions, such finding of value being helpful to us as individuals, communities, societies and beyond, and often being appropriate. And we must also aim to be supportive of others, even if we are concerned about the validity of certain ideas they are expressing. While skepticism is often appropriate, in terms of real life actions, it should be carefully expressed, and should not become negative and destructive cynicism or become continuously and destructively critical.

In reality, there are some answers that are more correct than others, determined by core principles, reason and evidence, and we may under some circumstances need to make choices about what those most correct answers are. In practical daily life our actions and decisions will be best supported by a sense of belief that we are taking the most appropriate actions under the circumstances, nevertheless we need always to be open to alternative ideas and must be prepared to change our thinking and modify our beliefs and actions.

*(14) Aim to achieve in practice.*

We need to achieve in practice, in a manner that has a beneficial effect on both the world around us and on our own well-being. Thinking well and developing our thinking are of crucial importance and can be enjoyable and enhance well-being in themselves. Yet the effectiveness of that thinking must be determined largely through its practical application, through the effects of words and actions, through the effects of our personal conduct, the consequences of which may, in some cases, not be immediate. Moreover the need to achieve in practice means that good intentions and positive feelings towards others are not enough. Practical action, which achieves important goals of supporting ourselves and helping and supporting others, is required to accompany these sentiments. This action may include deeds which may be small but which help ourselves and others. It may mean use of words of inspiration, support and love, to good effect. It may include being part of, contributing towards and realising major achievements and projects that benefit the well-being of ourselves and the many.

*15) Do not discriminate unfairly against others because they are different in innate features such as sexuality, colour, physical characteristics, ethnicity and race. Do not discriminate unfairly and unjustly against others for any reason.*

While there are innate differences between us all, unfair discrimination against others because of their race, gender, sexuality, colour, or other innate or physical characteristics, is unacceptable. Indeed we must not destructively and unfairly discriminate against others for whatever reason, be that reason events past, on the grounds of a poor relationship, cultural background, or their holding of opinions and beliefs consistent with core principles, which do not meet our expectations or conform with social norms. Unfair and unjust discrimination is destructive of ourselves, others and destructive of our communities and society as a whole, damaging well-being and causing direct pain and harm.

*(16) Live life to the full, enjoying all the pleasures and fulfillment that life can bring.*

Tied to More Specific Principle twelve above, we need to live life to the full. There are so many pleasures, so many joys, and there is so much fulfillment that can be gained in life. Pleasures may be as varied as enjoying a mountain view or moments of peace and quiet, the sense of success when a goal is achieved, the pleasure of arriving home after a day's work, sharing laughter with and being with friends, the joy of holding someone close or making love with someone we care for deeply, the wonderful feeling of being appreciated by others, hearing the sounds of our children playing together, the joys of music, the pleasures of beautifully presented and excellent tasting food, relaxing on a holiday beach, and of course much else. All of these pleasures and more should be pursued. They enhance our well-being and happiness. And there is joy and fulfillment from these pleasures and much more. Some of our pleasures are more personally focused, but there is substantial pleasure and fulfillment in focusing on others and in supporting and making their lives better, in supporting our communities, societies, and our broader humanity, as well as being recognised for our contributions to others, where this occurs. We should, if we can, as far as possible, through our lives, ensure we are enjoying and allowing ourselves to experience and enjoy the deepest and richest pleasures of life.

*(17) Be prepared to forgive.*

We undoubtedly all do things wrong and make misjudgments and mistakes in our lives. We may make misjudgments and errors in terms of our personal conduct, sometimes significantly hurting and damaging others. Where appropriate, we need to be able to forgive ourselves and be prepared to forgive others. With regard to the more substantial mistakes and misjudgments of others, some of which may have been conducted with deliberation, some of which may have hurt and damaged us or others, we do need, where we can, to be prepared to forgive those who have done such deeds, especially where those who have done such deeds have committed errors of judgment rather than intending to hurt or where those who have done destructive deeds are transparently, and without significant doubt, committed to never repeating such actions and working to support the well-being and happiness of others.

Our giving and stating of forgiveness may mean greater well-being and happiness for ourselves, helping us set aside feelings of anger, bitterness and resentment. Such forgiveness may support a more peaceful, cooperative community and societal environment. It may also enable those who have substantially damaged and hurt others to move forward and contribute positively and constructively in the future to our communities, societies and broader humanity. Nevertheless, the decision to be forgiving and state forgiveness to another who has substantially hurt and damaged us or others who perhaps we are, or have been close to, is ours alone. We are the ones who have experienced the hurt and injury, and the decision to forgive is down to us. However we must never seek revenge, which is destructive of all.

### D. Additional and related principles

*(1) Be generous, sharing, kind and helpful, but beware of letting others exploit you such that your own well-being and the well-being of others is damaged.*

It is good to be helpful, sharing, kind and giving, with core principles requiring us to support the well-being and happiness of both ourselves and others, this well-being and happiness being supported by our kind, caring, generous and helpful actions. Indeed we are required to and moreover, it is part of ourselves, part of our human character, to wish to be kind to, and to help and care for others. Thus, there is every reason to act in helpful, sharing, kind and giving ways, consistent with core principles and support the well-being and happiness of others and of ourselves. Those in need and in pain, and indeed those without such need and pain, will benefit from our generosity, care and kindness. Our kindness and generosity can support the immediate wants and needs of others, as well as supporting initiatives into the future that may benefit many. Kind and helpful deeds can make others, as well as ourselves, feel good. We can and should try to be generous with our resources, our money, our time and attention, and much more. We need to be prepared to be kind and generous both through our broad actions in support of others, our communities, societies and beyond, but also through small and if possible frequent smaller acts of kindness and care towards others.

Nevertheless there may be some who try to take advantage of our natural human desire and individual inclination to be kind and generous to others. Such advantage-taking actions are reprehensible and contrary to core and other principles. Through taking advantage of others, we will not only likely risk damaging the sense of self-efficacy, personal sense of self-worth of those others of us who have been kind, caring, generous and giving, since we who have been kind and generous will have been taken advantage of, but such dishonest actions risk serving to create cynicism amongst those of us who are and wish to be generous and giving, undermining our want and desire to give and help out. And as a consequence, this risks undermining and possibly preventing those who are truly deserving and needy from receiving help. Of course we should not be put off being kind because of the actions of those of us who are prepared to act dishonestly, without integrity, who would take advantage of us. However, it is important that, while being supportive and giving, we keep our eyes open for those who may wish to exploit us, such that we can prevent their damaging, and destructive actions and the consequences of their actions, which will cause us and others hurt, pain and suffering.

*(2) Pursue cooperation with others both actively and proactively.*

As far as is reasonable and possible, we need to cooperate and work effectively with others, and do this on an everyday basis, acting proactively at the outset of our efforts to achieve goals, doing so as a core element of our daily lives. A major part of our strength as human beings, human communities and societies, as a humanity, lies in our social nature and our ability to act together, yet the search for cooperation should not await the arrival of specific goals to achieve, disputes and conflicts to resolve. Acting cooperatively in an effective manner means being proactive in gaining cooperation. It means acknowledging others, interacting in a positive manner with others, engaging in give and take, compromise, respecting ourselves but also the expertise, experience and knowledge of others, though not necessarily agreeing with them. While some level of cooperation is almost always necessary for us to achieve, there may be occasions where cooperation is not possible with some or many, and a more solitary path may need to be taken, at least temporarily, optimally taken without creating or exacerbating hostility or causing or enhancing the alienation of ourselves or others.

*(3) Accept that mistakes will be made and some things will go wrong in your efforts to achieve worthwhile goals.*

Our making of mistakes and errors represents an important part of learning, development and improvement, having significant value when used properly, not only for ourselves but for our communities, societies and beyond. We cannot get things right all or perhaps even most of the time. Mistakes and errors comprise an inevitable part of our humanity and human living, which render us substantially imperfect. We should avoid inertia, and not be afraid of mistakes or let the possibility of error hinder us from taking actions we judge to be correct. We need also to accept charitably the mistakes of others, encouraging and supporting them in their own learning and development. Openness and admission of errors is of great value in helping us establish better strategies and actions, and in order to discover truth. In regard to moral errors that are contrary to core principles and harm others, admissions of such moral errors, misjudgment and fault need to be genuine, sincere and accompanied by credible resolution and credible commitment not to repeat such errors of conduct and behaviour, if we are to be ready to forgive and move on. This does not mean heinous actions can be ignored or that culpability and responsibility is removed. Nevertheless, sincere admission and acknowledgement of error is an important step forward to supporting the well-being of all.

*(4) Explore, seek adventure, and be open-minded.*

Encountering new ideas, challenging our own thinking, listening to others and being willing to change our opinions and ideas, can all support our own well-being and the well-being of others. We need to actively and positively seek out the new, gaining new experiences, seeking out new adventures, exploring the world, not only in terms of ideas, but also both physically and mentally, through searching for and experiencing what our world around us, both locally and further afield, has to offer in terms of amongst other things, adventure, experiences, knowledge, understanding, ideas, people, geography and cultures. We need to experiment with doing the new and different in order that we learn and develop. While our own personal experience of life will always be to some extent limited, even if it is informed by the many experiences of others, nevertheless, while operating within the frame of core principles, our own well-being and the well-being of others is most likely to be supported through our experimentation, exploration and our encounters and experiences with the new.

*(5) Master communication.*

However capable we are in terms of our more individual attributes, abilities and skills, however brilliant our ideas, however much knowledge and understanding we have, all of this will be of much greater use to us and others if we can communicate effectively with others and cooperate well with these others. We live with others in communities and societies, indeed within a broader global humanity, in which effective communication is essential to support cooperation and promote our own well-being and the well-being of all. Thus, however much we want to help others, however much we wish to achieve for ourselves, and however much we have strong talents and abilities, good understanding and thinking, however much we have great strategies to achieve our goals, unless we can effectively communicate the nature, content and product of our talents, unless we can gain support, cooperation and get others on board with our ideas and projects, and unless we can demonstrate how our approaches and strategies will work in practice, we run the significant risk of a lack of success in achieving our goals and as a consequence, reduced success in enjoying better well-being and supporting the well-being of others.

Mastering communication means mastering the ability not only to persuade others of the rightness or efficacy of what we are doing or saying (in those cases when indeed what we are saying is right and correct), mastering notions of empathy and understanding, and understanding people in depth, but it also requires listening to others, taking on board their concerns, interests and ideas, evaluating (though not necessarily in all cases), and certainly aiming to accurately interpret what they mean to say both from our and their perspectives, perhaps even rejecting our own ideas and opinions where this is appropriate and accepting their world view or judgments. In a world in which many different languages are spoken and used, for those of us who interact or are likely to interact with those from other countries and cultures, with those who use sign language, from an individual point of view, our mastery of communication is likely to involve gaining some, if not expert knowledge and understanding of the languages of others as well as their ways of being and cultures.

*(6) Oppose conformity – Remember it takes all sorts.*

The world is a diverse place comprising people of many different characters, characteristics and beliefs. Achieving our core goals of supporting our own well-being, happiness and fulfillment and the well-being, happiness and fulfillment of others, requires the contributions of many different people with many different perspectives, talents and characteristics. We need to recognise the talents, skills, perspectives and contributions of the range of people with different backgrounds, behaviours, attitudes and beliefs compared to our own. Not everyone needs to be like us, nor would that be a good thing, however good we are, however much we have achieved, however successful we may be.

*(7) Nurture and support the full range of positive human potentials.*

As humans, we are diverse in our thinking, approaches and other personal characteristics. It is important we nurture, develop and appreciate our own range of talents, potentials and abilities and also nurture and appreciate the talents, potentials and abilities of others, supporting them and enabling them to develop and grow. There are those with particular strengths in terms of artistic abilities, design abilities, mathematical abilities, strong communication abilities, literary and language skills, analytical and creative capacities, musical talents, athletic and sporting abilities, personal physical and emotional strength, and so forth and many of us possess a range of many talents and skills. All of these skills and talents, and more, are valuable to us as individuals, valuable to others, to our communities and societies, as well as to our broader humanity, and these skills, talents and abilities, consistent with core principles, need to be valued and recognised in our efforts to achieve well-being and happiness for ourselves and all others.

*(8) Don't let the past, your upbringing, others, family, community and society around you unnecessarily constrain you, keep you from the future you desire, and keep you from your dreams. Act as far as you can to determine your own future.*

Our past and our upbringing are likely to influence us significantly, often positively, though sometimes in such a manner that we feel constrained and restricted in what we can do. In an ongoing manner, our families, communities and societies are likely to influence us too, not only influencing us and also frequently supporting us, but sometimes imposing superfluous and unnecessary constraints on us. We need to aim to surpass and overcome, as far as we can, those constraints we experience and which might be placed on us by our upbringing and the past, as well as, where such occurs, aiming to overcome any destructive and damaging family, community and social influences that may hold us back from living lives full of well-being and happiness. Consistent with core principles, we need to aim to live the futures we desire and live our dreams. We must do all in our power to make our own futures as we would wish them to be, as far as we can. To do this we must take responsibility for our present and our futures, as well as taking upon ourselves responsibility for our communities, societies and the well-being of those around us. We are personally responsible for our own lives and our own futures.

*(9) Don't let others victimise and oppress you, and avoid as far as possible being and seeing yourself as a victim.*

It is essential to act, as far as we can, against those who would oppress or who do oppress us and would make us victims. We must protect ourselves as individuals and protect others, asserting our reasonable, personal wants and needs and asserting and protecting the reasonable wants and needs of others. Through acting individually to protect ourselves and through acting with others against those who are acting in oppressive ways, we will be better able to promote well-being, reduce pain and suffering, and protect ourselves and others. It is important to remember that those who act unfairly and unjustly against us will most likely be acting in the same manner against others, and therefore it is unlikely to be the case that if we are suffering in pain from such oppression, we will be alone in our pain.

That being said, oppression and victimisation can be difficult to see, forming parts of systems and situations where those who are oppressed may find it difficult to understand the origins of their situations and may even see their own oppression as reasonable and normal. Those who wish release from such oppression or wish to change such situations, who wish to protest, express their feelings and take action against such systems and situations, must develop a knowledge and understanding of the origins of their situation and oppression, and must be supported, enabled and allowed to escape from such oppression. Viewing ourselves as powerless victims is self-destructive and stands against well-being, though unfortunately, of course, it is possible that we may, at some point or on occasion, be victims of incidents and the actions of others that are beyond our power, at the time, to prevent or remedy. Still in such situations we must do our utmost to resist such destructive actions against us.

*(10) As far as possible, be open in pursuit of goals, especially when operating in social groups or teams. Wherever possible, avoid aiming to achieve goals in a covert, dishonest and manipulatory manner.*

It is optimal in terms of outcomes and other consequences to let others know where appropriate, what our goals are within our social groups and teams, and to have open, honest and frank discussions about those goals, their value and practicality. Acting in this manner promotes mutual understanding, cooperation, a sense of togetherness and common interest, and enables all of us to contribute to solutions, with our having consequent feelings of being valued, appreciated and consulted. Whether or not goals are worthwhile, adopting covert, dishonest and manipulatory approaches diminishes all, disempowering us, reducing the quality of outcomes, and damaging well-being.

There are, however, sometimes circumstances where it is incumbent upon us to act quietly and covertly to support the well-being of ourselves and others, especially when working to counter the actions of those individuals and systems that act in cruel, inhuman, oppressive and malevolent ways, when we are acting to counter those who would deliberately aim to damage us and others if we expressed ourselves and acted openly, or when countering those who themselves manipulate in a manner which will substantially damage well-being. This covert behaviour however, is not on the other hand acceptable in contexts where there is a sense of human equality, empathy, kindness, justice, fairness cooperativity, attentiveness to others, openness and mutual respect, understanding and acceptance.

*(11) Be robust in the face of disappointment and failure.*

We need to be resilient and robust on those occasions when we are unable to achieve the goals we wish to achieve, that is, in response to failure. While sometimes hard to do, not achieving goals is, to an important extent, an element of all of our lives and must be anticipated and dealt with in a manner that enables us to maintain our well-being, self-respect and our self-belief. All of us may face challenges and fail to achieve goals to terms of our working lives, in our relationships, in our actions in community, society and beyond. Perhaps all of us will face some disappointment at some point in love. Those in politics, business, industry, science, construction and engineering, management and administration, farming and agriculture, writers, those of us in all walks of life, are all likely to have successes but we will also have failures, sometimes substantial, which may create in us feelings of inadequacy, self-doubt or worse.

It is best if we see our failure to achieve such goals on occasion (or even more often) as being part of the expected territory of our lives and as valuable and necessary experiences on our routes to success or on our routes to a full life of well-being and happiness. And thus, it is essential to be robust in the face of such failures, to acknowledge them and learn from them, and following, where necessary and where we need it (and we may not need it at all), time and resolution of consequent feelings, we need to aim to move on to the pleasure and experience of new challenges and the risks of success and failure which serve to motivate us, stimulate us and benefit us in terms of our well-being, and which will likely have significant benefits for the well-being of not just ourselves but also those around us. Our appropriate understanding of the roles of errors, mistakes, failures and the like should serve, in many cases, to reduce our pain and suffering when these inevitably, at least on occasions, form part of our lives.

*(12) Take time to reflect, relax and rest.*

It is essential to take time out, away from the bombardment of information that we can receive from so many different quarters, away from the multitude of experiences we may be having, away from the welter of activities that may fill our lives, away from the multiple interactions and the sometimes challenges of our relationships, in order to have time for ourselves, to rest, relax, reflect and sometimes to do nothing. This helps us to recover from the stresses and strains of our lives, helps us to appreciate and enjoy simply being, helps us to cope with, and perhaps resolve, the welter of information encountered and experiences had. And through our pleasant and restful inaction, relaxation, though our doing of nothing much (at least nothing challenging), this can provide us with space to regain energy such that we are better able to enjoy our lives, enjoy ourselves on the moment, reflect on who we are, work out what we really think, how we are doing in our lives, the extent to which we feel we are achieving our well-being and fulfillment. Doing nothing of any particular purpose is most likely a necessity for us sometimes, so that we can have a full restful recovery from our hectic lives. Rest and relaxation, enabling our effective thought and reflection, help us to survive the fray, to better achieve our own well-being and happiness, enabling us once appropriately rested, to re-establish, modify and recommit to our goals, and better pursue them as effectively as we can. Sufficient sleep and rest, for almost all of us, enhances our ability to think, makes us more healthy and supports more effective reflection about that which has passed and that which may arise in the future.

*(13) Be patient, be prepared for and, where necessary, plan for the long haul.*
Many of the things we wish to do in life can take significant time to achieve. Supporting ourselves and others through our conducting ourselves in ways which serve to improve well-being and reduce levels of suffering can be done in some cases through our actions which have more immediate effects. However, to achieve on a deeper or wider scale, pursuing more challenging goals, will often take time and may require us and others who we cooperate and work with, to engage in much systematic and detailed planning. It is important to avoid frustration through our having unrealistic expectations that goals will be achieved in no time at all, although sometimes we may not fully understand the scale of the tasks we have set ourselves until we are truly engaged in them.

Of course once we understand and recognise the challenges and scales of the tasks we are pursuing, we can set more realistic goals and prepare ourselves for the long haul. Challenges such as being successful in a particular career, pursuing ambitious and transforming goals, creating and building complex structures, indeed building lasting loves and friendships, and much more, are likely to require substantial time. Aiming to promote fairness and justice, and remove injustice, which may sometimes unfortunately prevail for a time, often being difficult to remove, is likely to require determination, patience and long-term commitment allied to concrete plans involving thoughtful action which recognises real barriers to progress and deals with political exigencies. Time will often be needed to achieve our reasonable goals.

We will also likely, and frequently, need to be patient and understanding with other people, others who may well not do exactly as we wish or who may not act in accord with what we want on the moment, others who may disagree with us and do so, to our minds for irrational reasons. We will need to be patient and have understanding with others who might not be as we wish them to be, who may not act as hurriedly or skillfully as we would like them to do, or even have the competence that we feel they should, indeed ought to, have. Our children or others may not learn as quickly as we feel they should, but in teaching and learning we must show great patience. And hopefully others will show us, in all areas of our lives, a similar level of patience and understanding when we do not conform to their wishes and expectations, and do the things they wish us to do. Further, if we wish others to change, if we wish our communities and societies, our broader humanity to change, then pursuing such goals is likely to take time, sometimes perhaps longer than our lifetimes, and is likely to require rational thought-out strategies and substantial patience.

*(14) Be kind not only through your actions but also through your words.*

Kind actions and deeds, both small and large, are of great importance. Our kind deeds of giving, not only of money and material things, but giving others time and attention are of great importance and valued by others. Beyond our kind deeds, our kind and supportive words can make others much happier, help them feel cared for, wanted, noticed and of importance, and so we should be careful to speak kindly and sympathetically to others if we can, even where we are under stress or where others are being rude and unkind to us. Our response to unkindness should, where possible and appropriate, comprise acts and words of kindness. The words we use can have significant effects on the ways others feel and act. While we are, and need to be largely responsible for our own individual feelings, it is likely, for many of us, inevitable that what others say to us and about us will influence the way we feel, sometimes substantially. Understanding how unkind words can affect us, we need to be careful in what we say to others, and this includes what we say to those who may be hostile to us, with whom we need to be aiming to build more positive relationships where this is possible and realistic.

It is also easy on occasions, even when trying to be kind, when we are trying to act with kindness and aiming to show care to others, that we unintentionally make errors in what we say and do; we accidentally misjudge our actions and what we say. And recognising this, there is a need for us when listening and responding to the words and deeds of others, to avoid the over-sensitivity and over-reaction that can start and deepen conflict. While some may try to hurt us deliberately, emotional harm is usually not intended, and we need to rule out deliberate unkindness, clarify and question with kindness where this can be done, and then draw relevant conclusions.

Even where another is attempting to harm us, this does not mean we must give a hostile response, though robustness in the face of verbal assault can be a useful quality and an effective minimal force response to physical attack is often likely to be necessary. Cooperation on a reasonable basis needs to be built with all and kind words support this cooperation. Wherever possible and reasonable, it is desirable and beneficial for us to help others through kind, caring positive, supportive conduct and comments, and to make efforts to reduce tension and conflict, with our kindness to others, what we say and do, serving to support the well-being of ourselves and others, and reduce pain and suffering.

*(15) Take care of your health, both physical and mental, and support the physical and mental health of others.*

Absence of physical and mental fitness in itself represents pain and suffering. It damages our well-being and serves to damage our capacity to give our support to others. Indeed by definition, absence or low levels of physical and mental health in themselves represent an absence, at least to some extent, and often to a significant extent, of well-being, such a state being contrary to the core principles set out in this guide. We therefore need to make maximum efforts to maintain our personal physical and mental health, for example through exercise, appropriate diet, safe health practices, through monitoring of our health and ensuring regular health checks when these are available, through educating ourselves about health. And further, we need to act to support community and social support systems tied to physical and mental health, which help us and others maintain and develop our physical and mental health. Moreover, our physical and mental health affects how we behave and conduct ourselves. Excessive stress, relationship difficulties, tiredness, on the moment, or persistent if not constant physical or emotional pain, can lead us to behave in ways in which we would not normally behave, and which may be damaging to ourselves and others. And thus we need to place substantial effort into supporting our physical and mental health.

*(16) Always be prepared to learn and be prepared to teach.*

Effective education, and learning is essential in support of our appropriate conduct, our well-being, happiness and fulfillment and the well-being, happiness and fulfillment of others. We need to ensure as far as we can, that there is effective education for ourselves, our children and all others. We need to engage in continuous life-long efforts to learn and grow, to develop our knowledge, understanding, our skills and abilities, in order to live a life of well-being and happiness, and in order to avoid unnecessary pain and suffering. There is always more for us to understand, to know, to learn. We can learn through formal education and training where this is available, through our own personal experiences and through the experiences and learning of others, amongst other channels. In support of well-being and happiness, it is necessary for ourselves, our families, communities and societies to aim to provide educational and other developmental and learning opportunities so that all of us can survive and thrive as individuals and so that community, society and our broader humanity can survive and thrive.

Learning is not simply about gaining knowledge and understandings from external sources, such learning being of great importance to us, but learning is also, to an important extent, about learning from our experiences through our resolution, reflection and thinking about the actions, happenings, interactions, events, we participate in and encounter in our lives. To support others and the process of learning and education, as we increase our learning and develop our abilities, it is important that we all, to some degree, become teachers, and develop the skills to be teachers ourselves, becoming able at teaching and able to share the things we know and have learnt so that our children, our fellows, our communities and societies as well as our broader humanity, can benefit from the experiences, understandings and knowledge we ourselves have gained.

*(17) Be prepared to give and receive help.*

We will all need help and support at some points in our lives. As individuals we cannot achieve all, indeed we cannot achieve much without the help and cooperation of others. We cannot know all that is to be known or have the skills to do all that can be done, nor can we solve all problems and meet all challenges ourselves as isolated individuals. It is likewise almost impossible, if not impossible, to achieve our goals, to develop our skills, abilities and understanding, to deal with all situations, to support our own well-being and the well-being of others, to avoid pain and suffering, without the help and support of others. We frequently need the help of others to achieve our personal goals, to maintain and improve our own well-being, to help us in times of need. And others are similarly likely to need our help to support them in achieving their goals and in supporting well-being.

We should do our best to provide such help to others, where we have the capability and where we can support others without the real prospect of significant pain and suffering resulting, and indeed, we should even provide such help and support on some occasions when we might suffer such pain and need to engage in significant self-sacrifice to support others. Whether through giving or receiving direct and immediate help involving advice and action, whether through accessing information, knowledge and skills from others through education and training, whether through enlisting the support of others to directly support our goals and our causes, we will need to receive the help of others. And as social, cooperative beings, in line with and in support of core principles, our own well-being and the well-being of others, we need to give help, where appropriate, to others as well as supporting others and being open to accepting the help and support of others.

*(18) Support democratic values, openness, inclusion and transparency in decision-making.*

In line with our need to support the well-being of others and reduce pain and suffering, through our actions and personal conduct, we need to ensure that others can express their feelings, judgments, opinions, perceptions, their views, ensuring that different voices are heard and that we are all able to contribute and express our own feelings and views as well as listen to the feelings and views of others in an open, honest, transparent, and democratic manner. In our personal relationships, in our families and elsewhere we need to be inclusive of others in regard to our consideration of decisions and decision-making and as open as we feel we can be. And, in the range of contexts, we should expect openness and integrity from others, within the constraints of our desire to support well-being and happiness and not to cause unnecessary pain and suffering to others. It is further essential, in support of our personal well-being, that each of us is able to make important decisions affecting our own lives. Democratic values, as referred to here, include the notion that each of us needs some, if not a significant degree of personal autonomy and personal freedom, including personal space. And thus, importantly, democratic values do not mean therefore that majorities, or those with power, can do whatever they wish whenever they wish to, imposing unfair and unreasonable judgments and actions on us.

Beyond autonomy, our application of democratic values, openness and transparency in group or community decision-making allows us to contribute, allows us to feel valued, and a part of the whole, which is an important element of well-being, while denial of this and marginalisation of ourselves and our voices undermines not only our individual sense of well-being but the quality and effectiveness of our communities, societies and indeed of our broader humanity. Of course there are limitations on what we as individuals can decide to do and limits on what our democratic communities and societies can do since there are always others to consider, with the key notions of freedom and autonomy always needing to be considered. Harming others, causing them significant pain and suffering is not acceptable. Freedom to think and act appropriately where actions do not to any major degree offer direct harm to the well-being of others, is part of living a full and autonomous life in a democratic and free community, and contributes in a major way to a life of well-being. As individuals we must support inclusion, democratic decision-making, openness and transparency which, in themselves, support well-being and happiness, act against pain and suffering, and support our individual freedom and autonomy.

*(19) Be as fearless as you can be – avoid being fearful if you can. Be bold in deciding what you wish to achieve and be bold in your efforts to achieve your goals.*

We need to be bold in deciding what our goals are and in our efforts to achieve our goals, considering how we can be successful and acting, as far as we can, without fear or significant anxiety, in ways to support our success. In order to achieve our objectives, rather than being held back by such worries and fears, our goals being in line with core and other principles, supportive of ourselves and others, when there are things that need to be done, then we must do those things. We must ensure that our often irrational fear and worries, felt in many circumstances, do not interfere with our rational thinking and that they do not serve to paralyse us in regard to action, preventing us from taking necessary and reasonable action. Many of our fears and worries (though not all), felt in more everyday circumstances, are often based in irrational thinking which highlights and exaggerates the consequences of our taking incorrect and wrong actions and the responses of others to our actions. We may for example fear disdain, ridicule, dislike, hatred, rejection and other forms of social disapproval, yet often our fears are not justified and in themselves, can lead us to make errors, mistakes and misjudgments. Irrational fear of others, for example, can lead us to being unnecessarily aggressive, failing to cooperate well with others and even engaging in conflicts with other individuals or another group out of irrational fear which is not justified (that of course is not to say that in some cases our fears may not be justified). Additionally, fear in our everyday lives is almost always an unpleasant feeling in itself. Therefore, wherever we can, we need to ensure that we are thinking rationally and need to do our utmost to avoid feeling fearful with its consequent detriment to our well-being and happiness and its detriment to the well-being of others through its effects on our own conduct and behaviour.

When faced with serious physical threats and substantial threats to our well-being, almost all of us will feel some level of and perhaps, intense fear, and this is probably, for many of us, unavoidable, especially if this is an unusual and shocking experience. Our feelings of fear in such situations will hopefully motivate us to action and help us to defend ourselves from physical and other attacks with the vigour that could be necessary. In the vast majority of situations and circumstances, we need to be as fearless as is possible in addressing such circumstances and the challenges we face.

*(20) Be tolerant of those announcing and holding opinions and beliefs which may astound you or which you may find offensive, unless those beliefs promulgate a real and significant physical threat.*

In general, the opinions and views of others need to be tolerated and listened to. Discussion and cooperation are the ways to find solutions and develop understanding, as opposed to carelessly ignoring and dismissing the perceptions and views of others or aiming to prevent others from voicing their beliefs. Listening to others with such different and other perceptions can be challenging, but where there is no significant threat to well-being and happiness, for example through threats of violence, this challenge needs to be taken on. Our toleration and attentiveness, enables the promotion of well-being and happiness through promoting and enabling acceptance of ourselves and other selves, and enabling that discussion and debate that serves us all and can help to take our thinking and action forwards. Many views and opinions can be painted as offering significant threat. Often these different views in reality do not offer such threat, and need to be expressed and attended to. It is only stating and promulgating views that encourage aggressive violence against others, that promote hatred, and the action resulting from such hatred, views which promote violent action and which encourage unfair and painful discrimination against individuals and specific groups, frequently based in misunderstandings, lies and falsehood; it is only these views that are unacceptable in expression, especially when our goal is to promote well-being and reduce pain and suffering. Failure to tolerate, where toleration is justified, damages us all.

*(21) You can follow the law; you can follow instructions. You can do as you're told or asked. But never obey.*

Obeying is about accepting yourself as a second-class, subordinate citizen of less value and worth than the person or authority demanding your obedience. Thus obeying others is not acceptable. Obeying is about not accepting personal responsibility. There is no merit in obedience. It damages individual and social well-being. Moreover, there is, all things being equal, in the main, no reduction in our culpability for destructive and harmful actions we implement on the grounds of having received orders or instructions from another, although if our lives and the lives of others are threatened or violence is threatened if we do not comply, then we are certainly in a difficult position. We must, under such circumstances, do the utmost to support well-being and reduce pain and suffering and act against those giving such orders and commands. It is ourselves as individuals who have responsibility for our actions.

When authority has legitimacy in terms of representation, justice, fairness, decency, then it is reasonable and indeed incumbent upon us to go along with, for example, laws that make demands on us, or even go along with laws that we may believe are incorrect or wrong, recognising that we are one amongst any. As members of cooperative communities and societies, as long as those laws are consistent with core principles, we must be prepared, where appropriate and reasonable in terms of core and other principles, to give up some of our more direct individual benefits and freedoms of action, and accede to ways of conducting ourselves and accede to law, which support our well-being, the well-being of others, and which reduce pain and suffering for all. Nevertheless, responsibility for our actions still resides with us as individuals.

*(22) Look to the future: Avoid bitterness and harsh regret.*

Things may have gone wrong in the past, events may not have panned out as we wish they had, may have been horrible and unpleasant, and others, for example, may not have acted well towards us. Yet we need to look to the future rather than spending time thinking bitter and angry thoughts about those past events and expressing and thinking about our regrets. Those events are gone. That is not to say they are forgotten or that we will not take action, using the evidence of such past events, to make for a better present and future, in order to achieve a better future for ourselves and others, which represent worthy and desirable goals. But bitterness and harsh regret are forms of personal pain and suffering, and our experiencing of them is therefore inconsistent with core principles. We need to focus on the future, our own future and the future of others, aiming to support personal well-being and happiness for all into that future. And through focusing on that future we will help to set aside the pain of bitterness and harsh regret.

*(23) Feel free to be determined and stubborn at times.*

There is a high probability that during our lives we will need to be stubborn and determined in pursuit of some or many of our goals. We will often meet different forms of opposition to our desires and wants, or find unexpected obstacles in our way. We will need determination and stubbornness to overcome these. That is not to say we should never change direction, give in, or change our minds. There are certainly times when we should reset our objectives, or accept defeat, especially since our relentlessly pursuing burdensome but unimportant, or futile unachievable goals, is not likely to be an optimal way to support our well-being and happiness and spend our lives. However determination and persistence in many instances are important and necessary in support of our goals and in support of our well-being and the well-being of others.

In terms of thinking, beliefs and consequent actions, optimally while all the beliefs and opinions we hold and the consequent actions we take should be based in full and complete rationality and evidence, in reality, not all actions and thoughts we encounter in our communities and societies, or indeed the actions that we perform and the beliefs we hold ourselves, can be always informed by complete and full evidence. Our decisions and thinking can involve complex balances of multiple factors and may need to be developed and applied in very individual, unique situations, taking into account the range of people who may be involved. Moreover, evidence may not be currently available but we may anticipate its appearing in the future. Thus, when we do not have full evidence available and situations may be complex, we may need to, to some degree, make judgments based on what we know and understand at that moment and be dogged and determined in pursuing our judgments and consequent actions.

Moreover, common beliefs and opinions are not always based on pure consideration reason, rationality and evidence. Other factors beyond logic, reason and rationality may determine prevalent beliefs, ideologies and actions in our families, communities and societies including social and cultural assumptions, history and heritage, political goals and social conformity. In some cases there may be substantial social pressures lined up against us, lined up against rationality, reason and logic, which aim to pressure us to adopt a common and conformist stance or behaviour even where the evidence for the value of that stance and behaviour is severely lacking. Indeed there may be punishments if we refuse to adopt such prevalent views and actions. Under such circumstances, despite possible, if not likely, sanctions and actions against us, where it is reasonable, possible and indeed, safe, we will need to be stubborn and reject those prevalent views and behaviours, be determined in the face of such pressures, which are unsupported by rationality, reason and evidence.

It is legitimate, where we judge it necessary and reasonable, that we may also take risks with our safety in pursuit of both the principles of rationality, reason, truth and evidence, and individual cases where truth and veracity based in reason is not being given the priority and the lead role it deserves. Our determination and stubbornness in such cases recognises not only our burning need as individuals, communities and societies for truth, justice and accuracy but also recognises that such truth will most likely in the longer run benefit us all.

Yet in addition to such prevalent social and community beliefs and actions, sometimes we may be faced with what is apparently overwhelming evidence for a truth, yet we retain a hunch, a sense or intuition, a belief, that in some manner the evidence is flawed, that there might be alternative causes or explanations for what is observed, interpreted and believed. In such cases we may choose to be stubborn and stick, at least theoretically, in our thoughts, to our current beliefs, investigating further and developing our thinking about the matter in hand and awaiting evidence which will support our view. The general expectation of the arrival of new thinking and evidence is in itself a rational belief. Our stubbornness and determination in such circumstances needs to openly acknowledge the grounds for our stance, acknowledging the credible evidence against our less or unsupported view and we should not anticipate or perhaps even argue for decisions to be made to reflect our unsupported view since we have at the moment, insufficient reason and evidence for our view. Indeed, in practice where decisions are required, we should support the rational and logical view which is supported by evidence.

Nevertheless, in the long run, it may be that the unpopular view, unsupported on the moment by sufficient evidence, may still be correct due to the accumulation of new evidence and indeed paradigm shifts that alter interpretations of the already existing evidence. In these and other cases, there may be good reason for us sometimes to be somewhat stubborn and for our refusing to conform or change what may be our skeptical and doubting, and on the moment, insufficiently evidenced stance. So a sense of determination and apparent stubbornness, for this and many other reasons may be justifiable on occasion, nevertheless it is crucial that we should listen to and, even when we are not convinced, that we accept in terms of practical applications, the conclusions to which evidence, rationality and reason point.

*(24) Have realistic expectations.*

Realistic expectations about ourselves, others and the world we live in enable us to make more accurate decisions about our actions and our conduct, decisions which support our personal well-being and the well-being of others. Having realistic expectations allows us to deal with our lives effectively on a day-to-day basis and reduces anxiety, worry, frustration and conflict that may arise when our expectations are not met. For example, in regard to children, while we may wish to set high standards and have high expectations for our children, in reality and practice, the common behaviour of children should be expected from children, not the behaviour of adults. Achieving certain goals takes time, and unrealistically expecting immediate achievement, which then does not occur, can be a source of unnecessary pain and frustration, leading to anger, upset, poor conduct, conflict and even violence. Those who move from one culture to another will realistically take some time to understand the new culture and hopefully adapt. To join a new culture (in a working context or elsewhere) and expect those in that new culture to change, at least in the short term, to ways characteristic of our home culture is unrealistic and again can cause pain, frustration and conflict. Moreover, setting demanding goals that are not viable, or setting goals that are too low and undemanding can both be damaging to well-being, though striving for the best and striving to be the best we can be is certainly acceptable as an a goal, as long as it does not lead us to significantly damaging emotional pain and suffering.

*(25) Attempt to see the world from the perspectives of others.*

Understanding the world from the perspectives of others aids our ability to think and act appropriately and promotes our own and the general well-being. We each of us think differently from others as individuals, and our thinking and action will be influenced by our upbringing, family, social, cultural and other factors. Not only this, but it is important to see that others may have their reasons, and their reasons may be correct, being reasons from which we can learn. It may also be that another's reasoning may be correct given their background and perspective, though perhaps may not represent a route to, or represent in itself, the best course of action overall, or for ourselves in particular. Attempting to deal with others without accepting the individuality and value of others and their ideas, their own sense of self-value and need for self-esteem, without understanding the depth and impact of such individual differences can cause us problems in our lives, damaging our well-being, catalysing and enhancing difficulties in our relationships and leading to conflict. We need therefore to understand such different perspectives and take them into account in our thinking and in determining our personal conduct and actions.

*(26) Give love and care.*

In our actions and attitudes towards others we need to be loving and caring of others, considering the well-being and happiness of others, and taking action to support this well-being and happiness. Love should not be suffocating, oppressive and constraining. Love is something which needs to support others, needs to help others find and achieve their goals and dreams. It needs to be something that makes others feel loved, cared for and wanted. Unfortunately, while it would be pleasant, we cannot always expect others to give us the love that we may feel we have earned and deserve. And this can be frustrating and emotionally painful. Ideally, optimally and also hopefully, each of us will receive substantial love throughout our lives, or at least at some point or points in our lives, and we will feel valued, wanted and have a sense of belonging. For most of us, this will happen, but sometimes in our lives, despite our being loving and giving, love may not work like that and we may feel ignored and unwanted. Being giving, loving and supportive of others does not necessarily win the reward of appreciation or even acknowledgement. Nevertheless supporting others and their well-being is part of our human nature as is our deep sense of commitment, dedication and love of others. Giving love and care is an integral part of our individual well-being, happiness and fulfillment, as is receiving love. Hopefully we will all give such love and care and will be receiving of substantial love and care ourselves.

# Index

ability(ies), 1, 2, 3, 5, 27, 30, 36, 37, 38, 45, 76, 115, 116, 118, 120, 122, 133, 172, 198, 200, 323, 343, 356, 370, 378, 380, 435, 436, 458, 459, 530, 574, 577, 578, 579, 580, 581, 582, 586, 589, 590, 600, 603, 604, 606, 611, 613, 635, 649, 650, 660, 693, 699, 700, 701, 702, 709, 714, 719, 730, 745, 757, 765, 767, 779, 780, 901, 908, 910, 936
   developing our, *See* chapter 11, 924, 937, 944
abortion, 175-176
abuse, 32, 71, 91, 92, 94, 106, 120, 142, 288, 331, 357, 388, 413, 489, 490, 557
   of our environment, 816
   freedom of speech and, 158
   in the home, 347, 348, 372, 431
   of power, 349
   sexual, 784
   verbal, responding to, 93, 288, 297, 359, 507, 634, 888-889, 903
   verbal, unacceptable nature of, 90, 91, 92, 93, 143, 309, 374, 383, 424, 885
   at work, 692
accidents, 549, 558-559, 726
   car accidents, 148, 562, 592
   small accidents, 546
   in the home, protecting against, 558-559, 563
   nuclear, 793, 805, 842-843
   from weapons, 459, 461, 485
   at work, protecting against, 559-561
achievement(s)

barriers (and potential) to, 36, 379, 399, 542, 565, 612, 614, 633
cooperation and, 36, 328, 377, 380
determination, persistence, 626, 630
education and, 215, 295, 312, 908
of our groups, communities, societies, 218, 232, 296
of goals, purposes, 196, 613
non-achievement of goals, 7, 336, 337, 338, 578, 610, 618, 660, 757
pleasure of, 215, 231, 232, 236, 545, 598
pursuing, 73
rationality, reason and, 920
recognising others', 216, 314, 604, 606, 607, 619, 620, 621, 623, 701, 765, 767
recognising our, 617, 622, 643, 702, 715, 893
re-living, recording and recollecting, 653, 658
sense of, 126, 135, 214-215, 532, 658, 664, 697
in sport, 545, 547
accuracy and being
   accurate, 166, 167, 303, 395, 489, 561, 592, 913
   with decisions, 271, 282, 431, 589
   expectations, 626
   experts and, 154, 299
   importance of, 237
   need for, 949
   of predictions, 640

of self-perception, 575, 611, 613
statements of law, 65
truthfulness and, 292
of reporting and description,
  75, 112-114,121, 167, 270, 555, 623,
  737, 950
additional and related principles, 932
additional fundamental principles, 788,
  803, 857, 881, 920
adoption, 427-428
advertising (and promotion), 255
and smoking, 149
advice,
  expert, 163, 236, 257, 274, 299, 300,
    446, 730
  following, 67, 68, 69
  giving, 68, 159, 165, 709, 926, 945
  health, 728
  ignoring, 613
  judging and evaluating, 164, 165,
  listening to, 69
  medical, 168, 169, 730, 731, 732,
    754, 776
  negative, 607
  rational and evidenced, 531
  receiving, 253, 945
  seeking, 7, 9, 68-69, 274, 675
  sources of, 254, 257, 439, 537
  unsolicited, 68, 69
agenda,
  damaging and destructive, 393, 439,
    448, 490, 509, 512, 624
  political, 257
  research, 292
  setting learning, 243
aging
  Alzheimer's, 720

mental deterioration, 720, 741, 777,
  779
physical deterioration, 536, 641,
  720, 777, 779
staying fit and healthy, 779
agreement(s), 10, 31, 41, 272, 357, 378,
  384, 395, 397, 406, 407, 419, 423, 444,
  481, 489, 735, 798
global agreement, 852, 904
Montreal, 815
alcohol, 125, 716, 718,
  health and, 291, 534, 554, 716-717,
    729, 738
  violence and, 324, 372-373, 455,
    464
allegations, false, 474
allergies, 555, 745
allotments, 824
altruism, 287
anger, 10, 31, 69, 111, 122, 157, 320,
  322, 353, 371, 386, 389, 390, 400, 407,
  412, 416, 423, 429, 430, 441, 475, 516,
  517, 623, 637, 680, 704, 705, 706, 757,
  785, 903, 932, 950
  channeling and controlling, 412,
    413
  expressing, 31, 388, 389, 390, 643,
    644
  hatred and, 364, 702, 703, 705, 706
  in the home, 374, 413, 435
  mental health and, 629, 630, 702
  pain and, 412, 702, 706
  responding to, 93, 157, 359, 689,
    695, 888
  revenge and, 411, 412
  violence and, 412, 413, 455, 457,
    462, 464, 506, 888

animals, 213
- caring for, 788, 868
- cruelty towards, 857, 858, 861
- diversity of, 788
- eating, 557, 787-788, 795, 858, 905
- the environment (habitats) and, 792, 795, 796, 799, 819, 825, 861, 905
- experimentation with, 866-868
- food chains, 795, 905
- as killers, predators, 860, 862, 869
- as pets, 863-865
- protecting, 556, 788, 792, 795, 799, 803, 819, 825, 857-861, 866, 867, 868, 905
- relationship with humankind, 859, 861, 868
- sport and, 860
- threats from, 861, 869, 870, 871
- in the web of life, 796
- zoos and, 865-866

anti-social conduct and behaviour, 16, 24, 50-54, 117, 126, 164, 192, 233, 253, 328, 380, 384, 441, 450, 459, 460, 628, 671, 691, 710, 711, 716

anxiety,
- our appearance and, 600
- arguments and, 358
- avoiding, 511
- criticism and, 594
- discrimination and, 712
- failure and, 646
- fear and, 408
- reducing, 251, 591, 626, 643, 695
- self-criticism and, 593
- supporting those suffering with, 619
- unrealistic expectations and, 626, 629, 630, 949
- at work, 899

apologising 325, 415, 417, 419, 420, 421, 422, 590

appearance,
- of confidence, 614
- personal, 24, 601-602, 634-635

appreciation,
- being appreciated by others, 399, 620, 621, 622, 623, 660, 663, 666, 667, 701-702, 890, 931, 936, 938
- integrity of, 216, 623, 624,
- lack of, 29, 620-621, 622, 624, 625, 626, 646
- of others, 116, 117, 119, 216, 217, 314, 315, 449, 595, 606, 619, 621, 622, 623, 701, 767,
- of ourselves, 405, 427, 624-625
- of the pleasures of life, 173, 651, 939

approval of others, not requiring, 666

arts (the), 210
- education and training in, 115, 256, 285-286
- engaging in, 286
- and free expression, 111

attention, (paying),
- children demanding, 423
- to detail, 236
- to health, 531, 532, 536, 548
- lack of, 676, 789
- to pets, 863
- to others, 31, 81, 278, 293, 376, 395, 505-506, 575, 663, 659, 891, 929, 932, 941

autonomy (and independence), *See* chapter 10

barriers, 32, 667
  to achievement and progress, 160, 379, 401, 470, 940
  breaking through, 699
  to career progress, 242
  to cooperation, 429, 454
  to freedom, 137
  to education, 142
beauty
  in architecture, 217, 851, 877
  in art and artistic performance, 286
  in our environment, 790, 807, 810, 824, 837, 846, 847, 855, 877, 888
  in our looks and appearance, 600, 601, 603, 760
  in music, 217
  objects and, 839, 895,
belief(s),
  groups, 84, 89, 91, 93, 94, 95, 96, 97, 100, 101, 102, 103, 261, 262, 265, 266, 267, 268, 277, 365, 409, 496, 510, 667, 674, 737, 830
  intolerance of different beliefs, 91, 94, 128
  irrational, unevidenced, 20, 410
  tolerance of different, 25, 104, 115, 116, 117, 123, 125, 134, 140, 142, 177, 180, 181, 183
belonging, 12, 30, 77, 89, 187-188, 263, 265, 273, 284, 437, 439, 463, 532, 536, 582, 664, 668, 669, 679, 687, 715, 737, 788, 810, 812, 825, 839, 881, 885, 893, 895, 906, 920, 951
bitterness and resentment, 31, 32, 157, 347, 602, 614, 890, 933, 949
blame and blaming, 107, 412
  accepting blame, blaming ourselves, 420, 573, 588, 592, 628, 665, 669, 670, 672, 738, 900, 922
  deflecting, 260
  others, 9, 367, 372, 410, 507, 508, 512, 586, 672, 734, 735
  the past, 672
blasphemy, rejection of notion, 103
bullying,
  in the family, 372-374 at school, 233, 235
  at work, 70, 153, 154

carer, being a; need for support, 211, 309, 720, 766, 830
caring.
  for animals, 861, 863, 864
  for children, 273, 275, 620, 761, 774
  for our families, 456
  for others, 19, 100, 118, 226, 234, 284, 286, 425, 505, 514, 625, 631, 635, 690, 720, 722, 754, 884, 885, 929
  for our partners, 373
catastrophising, 615
celebrating,
  difference and diversity, 116
  a life, 765, 785-786
charitable (being), 617, 619, 934
charity(ies),
  involvement in, 779, 783
  setting up, 301
  supporting, 783
cheating, 687
  in sports, 549
  others, 63, 166, 716, 784
childbirth, 256, 290, 737, 748-749, 830, 831

children, (education and upbringing of, *See* chapter 11)
choice, 3, 4, 7-11, 15, 25-26, 36, 37, 58, 61, 63, 72, 77, 90, 109, 114, 133, 136, 139, 140, 141, 148, 149, 153, 159, 160, 167, 170, 172, 176, 185, 198, 201, 281, 312, 358, 366, 368, 443, 497, 512, 547, 639, 665, 738, 740, 772, 827, 829, 830, 832, 849, 852, 898, 900, 914, 926, 931
civility, 424
cleanliness, 109, 290, 291, 536, 555, 557. 562, 723, 728, 731, 782, 801, 857
climate change, *See* chapter 14, 88-89, 112, 299, 750, 751, 785, 792, 816, 818
   anthropogenic, 89, 112, 815, 904
   global cooperation to prevent, 481, 482, 818, 819
   global warming and, 817, 818
   research and, 750
coaching, 242-243, 305-311, 579-581, 597, 601
coercion, 8, 9, 21, 58-59, 61, 62, 66, 70, 71, 72, 101, 104, 106, 131, 133, 136, 141, 144, 151, 153, 154, 155, 156, 157, 159, 176, 182, 261, 263, 264, 268, 269, 346, 347, 350, 354, 355, 372, 373, 383, 411, 421, 511, 519
   responding to, 101, 127, 155 156, 348, 363, 365, 368, 369, 370, 376, 384, 499, 690, 899
cohabitation, 71
collaboration, 198, 231-232, 321, 341, 363, 372, 377, 379, 382, 394, 397, 449, 466, 488, 754
colonialism, 498
common humanity (our), 69, 176, 188, 197, 198, 264, 285, 358, 452, 453, 454, 466, 477-478, 483, 493, 522, 657, 713, 750, 893, 920
communication, 208, 224, 258, 302, 334, 391, 406, 673, 727, 728, 767, 804, 910
   absence, lack of, stopping, 77, 169, 388-391, 440, 441, 451-453
   accurate, open and full, 75, 137
   conventions, 126, 177
   cooperation and peacefulness, 371, 387, 388, 450
   developing, improving and mastering, 85, 140, 142, 208, 209, 215, 279, 660, 936
   effective, 142, 208, 215, 223, 936
   goal achievement and, 377, 387
   integrity and, 400
   the media, 75, 161
   miscommunication, 577
   problems, 215, 350
   promoting, 390, 429, 937
   refusing to engage in, 389
   strategies, 83
   systems, 479
   technologies, 281, 283, 674, 679, 727, 788, 836, 856, 883
community(ies)
   healthy, 537
companionship, 336, 435, 677, 684
   pets and, 863
company, 602, 677, 865
   desiring, 379, 505, 882
   enjoying, 10, 254, 379, 434, 658, 663, 670
   looking for 673-674, 709
   needing, 439, 443, 663, 664, 672

pets and, 863
not wanting, 192
compensation (financial), 66, 712
competition,
  in business, 77
  and cooperation, 328
  overly competitive, being, 710
  for resources, 828
  in sports, 47, 189, 545-547, 549
  winning and losing in, 605, 606
compliments
  giving, 216-217, 622, 623, 624
compromise, 31, 152, 324, 343, 345, 376, 382, 385, 394, 399, 405, 428, 496, 827, 911, 923, 933
confidence, 183, 201, 248, 253
  appearance of, 614
  boosting and building, 216, 407, 519, 568, 611, 616, 618,
  lack of, 247, 248, 617, 632, 736
  outward, 248
  self-confidence, 2, 32, 68 116, 577, 578, 588, 595, 597
conflict(s), 385, 407, 425, 441, 459, 499, 516, 520, 536, 537, 902, 942, 946
  avoiding, preventing, reducing and resolving, 31, 56, 197, 209, 220, 224, 324,327, 337, 356-359, 371, 372, 374, 375, 378, 379, 389, 390, 392, 401-406, 408, 418, 420, 422, 424, 446, 453, 454, 455, 458,459, 469, 483, 484, 485, 488, 489, 490, 515, 518, 519, 528, 520, 522, 541,621, 734, 885, 893, 902-903, 933
  competitive sports and, 189

education and, 207, 254, 288, 374
exacerbating, sources of, 86, 188, 289, 358, 359, 382, 386, 408-411, 461, 475, 486, 509, 517, 540, 702, 705, 714, 734, 941, 950, 951
family, 330, 425, 436-440, 628, 646, 649-650
gang, 363-364
international, 451, 453, 478-482, 750
managing, 297, 424
military conflict, war, 60, 224, 466, 486, 488, 495, 496,501, 514, 518, 521
peace and, 354, 422-424
relationships and, 336, 668
understanding, 297
views, conflicting, 288, 299, 356-359, 385
conformity (see difference), 11, 19, 22, 24, 25, 41, 101, 102, 105, 106, 109, 110, 111, 176, 177, 178, 180, 182, 183, 184, 189, 190, 191, 272, 293, 351, 835, 937, 950
  discrimination and, 128, 181
  of dress, clothing, 41, 42, 186, 187, 188
  law and, 190
  work and, 42, 43
cooperation,
  barriers to, 379, 410, 420, 429, 454, 470
  benefits of, 325, 326, 328, 358, 376, 381, 385, 388, 390, 394, 406, 408, 417, 419, 420, 424, 437, 444, 446, 448, 452, 483, 484, 486, 499
  in business, 328, 351, 352, 125 381, 394, 404, 444

compromise and concessions, 31, 151,
  324, 343, 345, 376, 384, 385, 394, 399,
  405, 427, 496, 827, 897, 911, 924, 934
  democracy and, 335, 336, 352, 354,
    380, 381, 399, 444-447, 449, 450,
    453, 454, 468, 476, 477, 489, 490,
    493, 494, 498, 503, 512
  dialogue, communication and, 342,
    387, 389, 390, 391, 401, 418, 429,
    441, 452, 453, 455, 478, 479, 485
  in the family, 343, 374, 376, 379,
    395, 425, 432, 433, 437, 438, 439,
    440, 450, 477, 478
  integrity and, 319, 383, 392, 400-
    401, 417, 421, 473, 477, 495, 501,
    504, 507, 508, 510, 512
  international and global, 329, 466,
    481, 482, 485, 488, 904
  language of, 358, 359, 396, 467
  listening and, 358, 368, 384, 386,
    388, 390, 392, 400-404, 424, 445,
    450
  win-win negotiation, 394
core principles, 919-920
corruption, 63, 352, 353, 501, 793
  cover-ups, 504
  damage from, 352, 353, 784
  the drug trade and, 718-719
  exposing, 500,
  identifying, 81
  of legal systems, 476, 477
  poverty and, 750
  preventing, 81
  response to, 18, 502, 503
cover-ups, 81, 418
creativity, 111, 184, 221, 659, 662, 744,
  812, 872

developing (our), 215, 218, 225,
  291, 292, 303, 380, 382, 405, 635,
  636, 638, 936
  in thinking, 182, 225, 636, 647
  mental health and, 637, 736
  conflict solving and, 406
  success and, 591, 592
  supporting, 115
crime/criminality, 442, 766
  children and, 106
  drugs and crime, 719
  prevention and protection from, 55,
    883, 885
  punishments, 72
  reporting and responding to, 51-54,
    55, 72, 80, 174, 471, 476, 489, 519,
    520, 704, 705
  victims of, 55, 726
  violent, 126, 719
criticality, 246, 258-259, 264, 270, 283,
  292, 294
culture(s), 103, 132, 149, 315, 316, 442,
  831, 929, 951
  assumptions, bias, prejudice and,
    125, 163, 164, 270, 293, 314, 353,
    402, 898, 948
  bullying, 693,
  changing and improving, 134, 335,
    355, 520, 736, 737
  our common human, 895
  conformity and, 24, 41, 126, 188,
    714
  cooperating with those from
    other, 478
  coping with and adapting to
    difference, 117, 122, 123, 124,
    288, 950

core principles and, 143
damaging and destructive, 126, 503, 509, 714, 737
difference and, 110, 116, 117, 123, 140, 356, 575
discrimination and, 928
drugs, 554, 716-717
eating animals and, 858-861
economic, 342, 351
experiencing other, 123, 124, 140, 178, 214, 268, 269, 273, 284, 285, 303, 571-572, 576, 672, 836, 934, 935, 951
family size and, 829
gang, 364
group, 55
identity and, 881
the individual and, 111, 143, 150, 292, 636, 831, 929
of incompetence, 513
injustice and, 334, 713, 910
common cultural knowledge, 582-583
language and, 214, 215, 279
military and policing, 368, 370
misunderstandings and, 110
norms and conventions, 22-24, 110, 126, 127, 178, 636
poverty and, 735
sex and, 132, 178, 179
superiority, 342
tolerance and, 111, 118, 123
violence, oppression and, 125, 324, 326, 371, 372
work culture, 69, 647
curiosity, 265

death, 135, 330, 332, 339, 340, 364, 493, 623, 665, 682, 689, 726, 730, 737, 768, 770, 771, 784, 785, 794, 801, 807, 823, 825, 843, 844, 848, 870
  by accident, 459, 549, 559, 562, 623
  aggressive violence and, 321, 323, 713
  avoiding and preventing, premature, 147, 227, 246, 456, 458, 519
  causing, 345
  cold and, 856
  coping with bereavement, 568, 652, 683, 758-759
  grief, 758-759, 760-763, 765, 769
  illness, disease and, 146, 535, 540, 744, 870
  inevitability of, 670, 760, 768, 769
  injury and, 533, 535, 540
  life-or-death situation, 718
  loneliness and, 670, 678
  natural disasters and, 540
  penalty, 52, 73, 490
  poverty and, 56, 160
  process of dying (journey to death), 764, 767, 769, 770
  racism and, 283, 712
  slavery and, 347
  smoking and, 148, 740
  suicide and assisted suicide, 168, 171-172, 754-755, 765, 772-775
  threats of, 61, 94, 125, 365, 369, 490
  war and, 60, 197, 297, 482, 486-488, 521, 535, 903
debt, 431, 646, 649
decision-making, 914

compromise and, 399
conformity and, 183, 271
control over, 439
cooperative and consensual, 53, 373, 424
democratic, 10, 62, 170, 353, 381, 399, 446, 453, 827, 944, 945
effective, 175, 594
factors in optimal, 135, 183, 358
global, 478
inaccurate, erroneous and incompetent, 735, 736, 841
space and time for, 33
understanding our, 165, 589
dedication and commitment, 579, 592, 602, 615, 660, 663, 689, 709, 720, 725, 726, 729
    to our children, 833
    to core and other principles, 699, 708
    to learning and education, 208, 216, 235, 602
    to others, 890, 891, 951
    from teachers to students, 398, 581
    to work, 135, 731
defence,
    of others, 48, 49, 89, 220, 319, 322, 341, 344, 455, 456, 458, 459, 494, 888
    self-defence, 46, 48, 49, 50, 89, 208, 220, 289, 311, 323, 341, 344, 455, 458, 459, 464, 468, 493, 494, 553, 888
deforestation, 904
democracy(ies),
    breaking laws in, 62, 66, 72
    consent, 62
    imperfection of, 62
    in the military, 60
    pursuing change in, 138
    styles, 124
    systems, 62
depression, 4, 171, 174, 191, 337, 533, 566, 567, 571, 600, 635, 645, 653-655, 657, 661, 683, 685, 755, 771, 854
despair, 161, 568, 599, 650, 654-655, 665, 680-682, 684, 685, 758, 759, 774, 777
deterrence, 51
dialogue, 469
    absence of, 388, 391
    cooperative, 418
    difficulties with, 391, 401
    encouraging, 342, 389, 390, 429
    importance and value of, 20, 387, 390, 391, 441, 452
    internal, 592
    between nations, groups, 478, 479, 485
    peace and, 387, 389, 455
    refusing, 452
    as a source of pleasure, 388
dictatorial, being, 233, 373, 374, 381, 419, 424, 584, 585
diet, 907, 942
    animals as part of, 858-860
disability(ies), 6, 90, 229, 384, 719, 779
disagreement(s), 384, 385, 397, 575, 621, 826, 913
    with children, 278, 649
    with experts, 300
    expressing, 83, 95, 102, 354
    in the family, 374

peaceful and cooperative, 358, 457
resolving, 407, 423, 923, 924
tolerance of, 192
disappointment, 8, 172, 173, 185, 338, 388, 606, 607, 610, 629, 630, 650, 726, 756-758, 926, 938
disarmament, 466
discrimination, 508, 509
destructive, 114, 268, 269, 309, 714
against the disabled, 90
effects of, 713
gender, 90, 349, 511, 931
laws and, 476
opposing and overcoming, 364, 521, 615
racial, 66, 89, 90, 349, 476, 511, 931
sexuality and, 90, 133, 931
unfair and unjust, 6, 14, 66, 89, 713, 714, 932, 956
at work, 645
dishonesty, 507, 509, 510, 785
dealing with, 401, 688
exposing, 99, 500, 501, 502
identifying, 166
integrity and, 400
learning about, 288
in legal systems, 477
use of, for promoting discrimination and violence, 130
in financial markets, 897
negative selfishness and, 382
in organisations and businesses, 70, 501, 502, 503, 504
past experience of, 407
in systems, 352
diversity, 186, 911

celebrate, 116
diversity of learning, 313
expressing our diversity, 272
importance and value of, 2, 116, 134, 140, 142, 157, 182, 183, 185, 186, 313, 357, 669, 882
of life, 273, 564, 788-789, 808
of relationships, 882
of talents, 600
doubt (and skepticism), 265, 680, 930, 951
false accusations and, 474
self-doubt, 386, 596, 613, 619, 650, 940
dreams (also goals and ambitions), 32, 73, 237, 426, 607, 639, 709, 756, 765, 937, 938
achieving our, 9, 607, 608, 609, 610, 614, 615, 630, 638, 639, 644, 658, 792, 885
failing to achieve our, 172,
supporting others to achieve their, 26, 28, 116, 183, 309, 609, 709, 952
drugs, 534, 883
in childbirth, 748-749
education and, 291, 738,
health and, 531, 567, 715-719, 720, 748, 752-755
hard, 718
mood changing, 714, 715
trade, 718-719
violence and, 102, 324, 363, 372, 373, 455, 457, 464, 506

earthquakes, 527, 529, 561, 688, 735, 751, 871, 872

economic(s)
    beliefs, 402
    circumstances, 6
    class, 712
    crash, 351
    damage, harm, 79, 84, 352, 885
    development, 351, 750
    environment, 330
    equality, 911
    gain and benefit, 497, 841, 856
    knowledge and expertise in, 222, 236
    hardship, 41, 350
    improvement, 73
    independence, 4, 5
    interests and self-interest, 20, 88, 166, 260, 448, 819
    justice, 349
    oppression, 104
    policies, 467
    power, 166, 393, 498, 509
    poverty and, problems, 351
    systems, 77, 78, 137, 349, 350, 351, 352, 735, 750, 793, 927
    well-being, 480, 825, 855
ecosystems
    damage to, 796, 798, 845, 904
    importance of, 803, 825
    management and conservation of, 803, 825, 851, 862, 905
    understanding, 796
education, See chapter 11, 4, 19, 53, 54, 75, 149, 183, 198, 355, 375, 472, 476, 584, 609, 898, 899, 908, 909, 924
    access to (and equality of access to), 18, 55, 82, 85, 199, 201, 331, 335, 713, 910
    against aggressive violence, 324, 458, 462, 690
    about and through animals, 864, 865
    the arts and, 115
    in belief groups, 143
    children and, 71, 404, 431, 435, 628, 833
    conformity and, 176, 183, 186-189
    cooperation and, 329, 379
    effective, 942
    encouraging and supporting, 115, 122, 134, 183, 184, 187, 190
    facilities, 200
    false, 518
    formal and informal, 943
    funding of, 115
    health and, 144, 145, 147, 731, 736, 738
    indoctrination, 261-265, 518
    lifelong, 200, 780
    listening and, 449
    management and organisation of, 909
    personal conduct and, 51
    personal freedom, autonomy and, 3, 26-27, 32, 82, 85, 138, 198, 200, 201, 202, 479
    personal responsibility and, 45
    poverty and, 159, 735, 876
    provision of, 199, 556, 919, 936
    purpose of, 199-200
    and relationships, 176, 737
    school uniform, 186-189
    self-education, 576, 579, 588
    sex education, 132, 176, 737
emotions, 212, 320, 323, 324, 327, 342,

431, 504, 526, 548, 568, 587, 591, 594, 603, 608, 612, 618, 628, 633, 650, 652, 655, 676, 685, 693, 701,703, 705, 717, 738, 758, 838, 902, 905, 911, 912, 919, 937
  articulating, 120
  awareness of our, 637
  communicating, 380, 433
  controlling our emotions, 462, 464, 506, 535
  coping emotionally, 119, 630, 683, 695, 769
  crisis, emotional, 722, 726
  cruelty, emotional, 347
  disconnect, emotional, 20
  engagement, emotional, 408
  harm and hurt, emotional, 16, 19, 40, 46, 92, 93, 94, 101, 102, 158, 159, 179, 319, 322, 323, 324, 361, 375, 389, 412, 413, 430, 440, 441, 533, 573, 597, 623, 628, 635, 655, 670, 702, 708, 755, 885, 950
  hidden, 401
  independence, emotional, 3, 4, 6, 8
  learning about, 274, 291, 295, 433
  needs, emotional, 329, 669, 748
  maturity, emotional, 132
  outlook, emotional, 356
  pain, emotional, 46, 47, 121, 143, 170, 171, 179, 220, 242, 318, 320, 331, 336, 338, 389, 408, 412, 414, 524, 529, 574, 575, 576, 597, 598, 603, 618-623, 625, 626, 653, 654, 656, 657, 681, 683, 696, 702, 724, 751, 757, 763, 764, 768, 769, 951, 952, 953
  pressure, emotional, 72
  problems, 636, 719, 726, 727
  reaction and responses, emotional, 92, 93, 122
  rejection, emotional, 408
  relationships, emotional, 331, 426, 532, 694, 724, 755
  resources, emotional, 5
  stress and strain, 322, 645, 647, 649, 768
  support, emotional, 28, 168, 438, 514, 535, 657, 726, 727, 728, 760
  thinking, thoughts and, 631
  understanding the emotions of others, 433
  well-being and health, emotional, 22, 89, 526, 528, 533, 547, 567, 595, 602, 685, 723, 810
empathy, 40, 89, 100, 102, 119, 123, 124, 129, 142, 150, 153, 170, 208, 228, 319, 375, 376, 382, 383, 384, 388, 406, 408, 433, 448, 450, 455, 527, 567, 570, 572, 581, 608, 629, 701, 705, 762, 911, 925, 935, 938
emptiness, feelings of, 568, 644, 645, 664, 665, 677, 680, 681, 682, 755, 758
energy,
  fossil fuels and, 299, 804 805, 814, 818, 819
  needs, 806, 845
  nuclear, 302, 842, 844
  supply, 806
enjoyment
  of the environment, 790, 808
entrapment, 70
environment, the, *See* chapter 14
  attachment to, 810-812
  biological, 208, 562, 563, 754, 788,

789, 791, 798, 807, 809, 813, 814,
821, 831, 841, 871, 873, 879
built, 180, 823, 855, 877
caring for our, 195, 861
catastrophic threats from, 871, 872
climate change, See climate change
(the) economy and, 819, 825, 826,
841, 851, 855, 856, 865
enjoyment of, 803, 808, 846 852,
854, 878
global warming, 299, 750, 804-805,
814, 817-819, 822, 841, 851, 853,
904
physical, 273, 444, 788. 789, 809,
820-823, 834, 871, 876, 878, 922
pollution of, See pollution
protecting our, 812, 852
recklessness towards, 797, 799, 841
research and, 804, 805, 814, 815, 816,
812, 847, 848, 850, 852, 864, 872
recycling, See recycling, and
resources, 790, 798, 800, 801-809,
812, 814, 815, 816, 819, 820-830,
837-843, 846-848, 856, 865, 875,
877, 878, 886
as a source of well-being and pleasure, 790, 792, 799, 807, 808, 809.
814, 824, 825, 846, 852, 854, 857
waste disposal, 558, 792, 809, 814,
841, 842, 843, 845-847, 857
envy, 603, 606, 701
equality, 62, 355, 492, 701, 804
of access to education, 201
benefits of, 159
educational assessment and 238
health and, 700
impossibility of absolute

inequality and, 313, 314, 326, 700
of fundamental human value, 498
of justice, 346, 348, 910
of opportunity, 267, 313, 699, 713,
910
promotion of, 336, 734, 896
pursuit of
quality and, 229
unattainability of absolute, 910, 911
uniformity and, 188
evidence, 7, 75, 79, 157, 271, 423, 447,
474, 495, 588, 813, 852, 872, 887,
901-902, 905
action and, 395, 421, 905-906
assisted suicide and, 773
belief and judgments, 20, 278, 424
bias, prejudice and, 164-165, 260,
270, 278, 382, 694
challenges and, 616
change and, 410
circumcision and, 737
climate change and, 88, 805, 808,
816-819, 853
critique and, 97
in education, 200, 241, 266, 278,
282, 292-294, 305, 354
the environment and, 797, 798
evaluating, weighing, 245, 246, 257,
266, 474, 489, 594, 627, 930
experts and, 162, 300
false and misleading, 112, 171, 392,
510, 930
faith and, 266
fears and, 409
freedom and, 7
gathering, finding, seeking, 74, 79,
248, 261, 270, 282, 481, 693, 907

GM crops and, 848
insufficient, 616, 950, 951
interpretation of, 270, 357
ignoring, 260, 261, 299, 383
lack of, 259
listening to, attending to, 88, 165, 403, 608, 903
management and, 585
in medical treatment and health, 221, 531, 536, 550, 700, 716, 718, 730, 737, 738, 739, 740, 748, 749
misinterpretation of, 112
negativity and, 608
nuclear power and, 844
personal growth and development based in, 245, 250
in organisations, 166
persuasion through, 97, 98, 166, 209, 247, 249, 299, 423
population levels, 830
punishment and, 50, 55
reliability of research and, 747
responsibility and, 410
scientific, 482
sexual conduct and, 132, 133
testing and evidence, 239
torture and, 513
uniforms, dress codes and, 42, 188
vaccination and, 147
violent conflict and, 903
evolution, theory of, 280
exemplars, human, See role models, 143, 605, 913
exercise, 20, 290-291, 302, 543-546, 548-554, 601, 638, 684, 690, 736, 738, 777, 824, 864, 894, 907, 943

expectations,
realistic, 172, 434, 626-630, 671, 676
unrealistic, 625, 630, 941, 951
expertise, 3, 42, 50, 88, 162, 163, 165, 167, 180, 184, 217, 221, 222, 231, 236, 240, 241, 255, 259, 267, 275, 276, 280, 281, 295-305, 312, 314-316, 365, 392, 446, 555, 578, 697, 730, 782, 911, 933, 934
acquiring and developing, 38, 209, 210, 212, 222
and experts. 50, 88, 147, 163, 164, 240, 260, 274, 580, 730, 776
responsibilities of experts, 59
exploitation, 350, 484, 497, 687, 710, 711, 933, 934
of animals, 859, 861
in business, 645
of children, 152, 437
imperialism and, 498-499
of the natural environment, 798, 809, 811, 816, 841, 862
of those in poverty, 159, 160,
exploration, 32, 608, 638, 736, 876, 934
creativity, 214, 635
experimentation and, 635
learning and, 152, 214, 244, 245, 257, 305, 311, 317
of others, 576
pleasure of, 213, 298
research and, 294
space, 873, 875
travel, 73-74, 123, 836, 837
extortion, 363
failure, 8, 34, 170, 172-173, 336-338, 368, 469, 473, 548-550, 579, 589, 591-593, 596, 604, 606, 608, 612, 631, 638,

646, 652, 653, 659-661, 664, 680, 682, 683, 684, 727, 755, 756, 757, 758, 793, 796, 845, 869, 902, 935, 938-939, 947
    at work, 153-154, 350, 645
fairness, 15, 22, 72, 127, 335, 336, 349, 355, 356, 410, 468, 473, 700, 701, 713, 802, 804, 901, 910, 920, 921, 927, 939, 941, 948
    equality and, 62, 201, 229, 804
    privilege and, 313, 314, 336, 614
    teaching and learning, 228, 229
    unfairness, 45, 229, 334, 335, 336, 346, 352, 411, 432, 614, 699, 713
faith, 773
faith schools, 266-267
fallibility,
    our personal and human, 269, 429, 578
    of legal systems, 73
false
    accusations, allegations 474, 490
    statements, making, 592
    witnesses, 477
family,
    coercion in, 21
    cooperation and togetherness, 343, 374, 376, 379, 395, 425, 432, 433, 437, 438, 439, 440, 450, 477, 478
    divorce and separation, 348, 646
    feeling unloved within, 29
    independence within, 28
    love of our, 29
    maintaining relationships and contact with, 30, 31
    marriage, 71, 105, 139, 347, 348, 667, 833
    mutual support, 330
    nuclear, 438, 440, 669
    restrictions and constraints from, 30
    size, 829-830
famines, 536, 538, 539
farming, 224, 443, 938
    animal welfare and, 858
    methods and practices, 254
fatalism, 853
fatigue, 135, 401
fear, 93, 233, 352, 362-363, 371, 386, 389, 484, 585, 632, 634, 683, 708, 782, 848, 853, 945-946
    acknowledging, 392
    as a barrier to cooperation, 391, 407, 408, 410, 457, 484, 519
    of change, 20, 65, 410, 608
    of crime, 52
    of death, 670, 768, 772
    of difference, 20, 184, 200
    expressing our, 343, 655
    failure, 638
    of job loss, 692
    of financial hardship, 692
    irrational, 20, 133, 409, 830
    of loss of power/status, 20, 299
    relationships and, 408, 420, 767
    secrecy and, 418
    of violence, 320, 347, 354, 362, 363, 369, 370, 372, 452, 469, 470, 473, 499
film, 111, 114, 259, 285, 286, 295, 810, 865, 893
finance, financial
    crashes, 351, 897
    markets, 897
    planning, 897

fines, 148
first aid, 560, 729
fishing, 193
    as a leisure activity, 564, 807, 860, 894
    overfishing, 798
food, 4, 47, 73, 83, 185, 321, 329, 330, 432, 476, 509, 521, 555, 557, 566, 728, 745, 787, 788, 796, 820, 847, 857, 858, 860, 869, 878, 901, 914
    chains, 789, 796, 797, 798, 800, 809, 843, 848, 862, 905
    enjoyment of, 931
    genetically modified (GM), 847-849
    industry regulation, 556
    information about, 555
    preparation and storage, 222, 538, 555, 556, 728, 729
    production and generation, 222, 224, 231, 280, 296, 328, 747, 791, 802, 803, 813, 824, 848, 849, 850, 858, 859, 883, 886
    safety, 555, 556, 728
    science, 222
    supply, 48, 222, 224, 333, 482, 539, 540, 541, 546, 556, 735, 747, 792, 797, 801, 808, 826, 846, 850, 861, 870, 885
force, physical, 48, 49, 50, 89, 101, 193, 196, 202, 318, 321, 322, 325, 331, 332, 336, 339, 341, 343, 346, 365, 374, 434, 455, 460, 468, 494, 499, 522, 690, 692, 912, 913
forgiveness, 415-417, 452, 471, 704, 711, 933
    self-forgiveness, 671
fossil fuels, 299, 804, 805, 814, 818, 819

fraud, 18, 500, 501, 784
freedom, *See* chapter 10
    to access information, 74, 75, 132, 137
    of belief, 21, 181
    conformity and, 11, 19, 22, 24, 25, 41, 42, 43, 102, 105, 106, 108, 110, 111, 128, 176-191
    constraints/restrictions on, 2, 14-19, 20-23, 25, 26, 28, 30, 31, 39, 45, 53, 54, 56, 57, 65, 72, 73, 80, 82, 84, 89, 90, 93, 96, 97, 104, 105, 109, 126, 131-134, 137, 138, 141, 144, 148, 149, 15-155, 158, 159, 160, 165, 166, 176, 179, 180, 181, 183, 200
    democracy and, 62, 64, 66, 72, 78, 126, 128, 145, 147, 161, 162, 165, 166, 180, 195, 196, 197
    education and, 3, 4, 18, 26-27, 32, 45, 54-55, 71, 75, 82, 85, 115, 132, 138, 143, 145, 147, 149, 159, 176, 183, 184, 186, 187, 188, 189, 198-202, 262, 263, 267, 268, 297
    human rights and, 58, 297, 367, 489-490, 624, 901
    of movement, 73
    from poverty, 56-57
    sexual, 131
    supporting freedom, 85, 122, 127
    from slavery, 57-58, 71 326, 346-347
    of speech, expression, 85, 89, 96, 97, 102, 111, 155, 159, 179, 180, 490
    tradition and, 71, 103, 105, 106, 133, 142, 181
    from violence, 20-23, 28, 46, 48-52, 54-56, 58, 61-63, 66, 71, 73, 84,

89-96, 98, 100, 103-106, 111, 113-114, 125, 127-131, 138, 142, 144, 153-159, 177, 189, 193, 195-198, 202
  to work, 136
friendship, 12, 30, 31, 109, 139, 254, 325, 328, 364, 378, 388, 395, 442, 452, 454, 478, 485, 545, 574, 670, 673, 674, 675, 682, 684, 711, 761-763, 784, 785, 864, 886, 892, 917, 941
frustration, feelings of, 13, 29, 31, 32, 35, 40, 68, 120-122, 124, 215, 219, 236, 242, 336, 337, 338, 359, 373, 374, 388, 390, 414, 429-430, 466, 504, 567, 571, 577, 613, 614, 626, 627, 629, 630, 669, 680, 681, 682, 687, 697, 699, 701, 702, 940, 950-951
fun, 86, 107, 170, 444, 671, 777, 809, 922, 925
  learning and, 312
  make fun of, 659
future generations, 257, 493, 790, 795, 849, 852, 904

gang(s),
  violence, 342, 363-364, 691
gender, 124, 342
  discrimination, 229-230, 266, 349, 511, 714, 929
  equality, 90, 229, 881, 886, 929
genuine,
  being, 95, 260, 395, 414, 421, 474, 508, 705, 933
generosity, 118, 619, 923, 931-932
genocide, 227, 494, 507
give and take, 373, 376, 394, 396, 405, 417, 428, 433, 695, 863, 933

giving gifts, 840
global warming, 298, 750, 804, 805, 814, 817-819, 822, 841, 852, 853, 904
GM crops, 839, 848, 849
goal setting, 639, 644, 681
government roles, 896
  education and, 267, 268, 277, 312
  the environment and, 482, 561, 562, 809, 815, 816, 819, 823, 841
  food production, 540
  health and health systems, 146, 231, 732, 733, 740, 742
  pollution, 146
  protection and defence, 195, 493
  resources, managing, 540, 800, 839
  safety, 40, 147-148, 561, 742, 805
  social support, 665
  taxation, 728, 895
grandparents, 763
greed, 352, 487, 506, 735, 821, 841, 897, 928
grief, 568, 619, 653, 656, 682, 756, 758-764, 765, 766, 784, 785
group (s)
  freedoms and rights, 141, 352
  loyalty to, 128, 187, 342, 365, 454, 487, 506, 515, 699
  membership of, 190, 263, 264, 454, 679, 737

halo effect, 271
hatred, 455, 457
  action against, 424
  aggressive violence and, 494, 506
  genocide and, 494
  of oppressors, 364, 389
  of other groups, 409

of a partner, 432
prejudice, ideology, power and, 283, 382, 453, 484, 495
self-hatred, 172
setting aside, 480

health, *See* chapter 13
cancer(s), 534, 536, 717, 718, 741, 742, 744, 755, 783, 815, 907
diet, 221, 290, 291, 302, 531, 554-555, 557, 601, 689, 723, 729, 733, 743, 745, 746, 850, 858, 859, 860, 894, 905, 907, 942
dangerous, mood altering
disease transmission, 146, 291, 556, 730-731, 746
drugs, 291, 324, 372, 455, 457, 464, 534, 715-718, 719, 729, 738
drug treatments, 373, 531, 567, 719, 720, 748, 749, 752, 753, 754, 755, 883
evidence-based medicine, 221
exercise and, 20, 290-291, 302, 543-546, 548-554, 601, 638, 684, 690, 736, 738, 777, 824, 864, 894, 907, 943
healthy society, 59
hygiene and, 536
malaria, 742, 743, 783, 870
mental, 291, 524, 528, 529-533, 545, 564, 566-570, 574, 576-578, 580-581, 583, 587-591, 603, 605, 606, 612, 615, 620, 622, 623, 627-630, 632, 634, 636-640, 642-643, 645, 649-651, 661-662, 664-666, 669, 677, 681, 682, 794, 706-709, 714, 715, 718-723, 738, 742, 747, 778-779, 786, 943
quarantine and, 730-731
relationships and, 532, 537, 566, 567, 569, 572, 576, 595, 598, 599, 616, 623, 635, 641, 644, 645, 646, 649, 650, 657, 658, 659, 663, 664, 665, 666, 668, 669, 670, 671, 673, 674, 675, 678, 682, 685, 693, 694, 695, 696, 702, 706, 711, 714, 723, 724, 726, 727, 736, 737, 747, 755, 756, 757, 779
research and, 527, 531, 532, 536, 555, 576, 636, 650, 652, 657, 675, 721, 730, 732, 739, 740, 742, 743, 744, 745, 746-751, 753, 771, 778, 779, 783
and safety in the home, 558, 559
and safety of products and services, 742, 746, 797
and safety in sport, 553
safety hazards, 560, 562
and safety at work, 560-561
sexual, 610, 714, 723, 724, 725, 736, 737, 744, 777
and sleep, 564-566, 642, 653, 941
smoking tobacco, 89, 148-150, 194, 299, 534, 536, 717-718, 738-741
systems, 231, 329, 732, 733
vaccination, 147, 150, 253, 723, 743
helping others, 32, 120, 121, 122, 136, 204, 225, 500, 527, 550, 619, 620, 621, 626, 655, 707, 727, 728, 729, 733, 760, 890, 891, 920, 936, 943, 952
heroes, 499, 501-506, 512, 660, 892
heroin, 718, 748
heterosexuality, 90, 133
history, 677, 778, 816, 829, 871, 950
and belonging, 273, 284

# Index

global, 284, 285
local, 303, 674
the nature of 284, 304
of ideas and thinking, 300
personal, 604, 881
researching, 302
social, 297
study of, 208, 276, 282
universal, 686
hobbies (*See* also pastimes), 669, 893
homosexuality, 90, 94, 133, 158, 266, 354, 490
honesty, 105, 108, 112, 154, 270, 292, 418, 503, 923, 939, 945
  in appreciating others, 623
  dishonesty, 70, 76, 81, 99, 106, 130, 166, 173, 216, 249, 261, 272, 288, 354, 383, 393, 400, 401, 407, 410, 418, 477, 495, 500, 501, 502, 503, 504, 507, 509, 510, 572, 645, 683, 687, 688, 726, 785, 897, 934, 939
  the media and, 113
  openness and, 79, 82
  about, with, ourselves, 612
passion for, 920
  persuasion and, 131, 515
  in relationships, 904
  reputation for, 82, 400
  teaching and learning, 289
human rights, 58, 297, 367, 489-490, 624, 901
humour, 99, 102, 111
  pleasure of, 777, 893
hunting, 860, 865
hygiene, see also health, 536
hypocrisy, 99, 102, 278, 290

identity, 861, 865
  adult, 242
  belief and, 403
  and belonging, 284
  common identity, 188
  our environment and, 875
  gang identity, 363
  groups and team identity, 1, 263, 342, 545, 831
  history and, 284
  human, 3, 100, 120, 318, 327, 335, 425, 435, 454, 478, 527, 535, 839, 867, 881, 892
  individual, 1, 2, 3, 26, 32, 91, 120, 170, 201, 207, 213, 271, 272, 284, 285, 318, 411, 577, 662, 881, 902,
  material things and, 895
  social, 1, 207, 213, 271, 318, 882
ignorance, 75, 94, 133, 247, 583, 815, 819
illness and disease, See health
image,
  self-image, 417, 579, 659
impatience, 120-122, 630
imperialism, 498
inaction, 46, 891, 940
  in the face of bullying, 693
  causing suffering, in the face of suffering, 193, 196, 526, 527, 727, 741, 885, 890
  in the face of theft, 48
  in the face of violence, 367
  non-participation and, 425, 444
  responsibility for our, 511
incentives, 65, 135, 418, 534
independence (personal), *See* chapter 10

indoctrination, 261-265, 518
inevitability,
   of aging, 602, 650, 688
   of change, 402
   of comparisons, 337, 600, 603, 606
   of conflict, 430
   of death, 535, 670, 758, 759, 760, 764, 768, 769, 771
   of differences, 2, 288, 402
   of the end of our planet, 873, 874
   of feelings of isolation, 671
   of groups, 454
   of happiness, happy moments, 173
   of ill health and injury, 536, 723
   of inequality, 313
   of learning, 211
   of noise and disturbance, 192-193
   of lack of appreciation, 622
   of pain and suffering, 524, 751, 760, 772, 920, 940
   of powerlessness, 696, 697
   of sadness, 594
   of wrong decisions, mistakes errors, 36, 590, 591, 592, 757, 925, 935
information,
   accessing, 74, 75, 132, 137
   accurate, 75, 737
   false and hidden, 164, 257, 260, 263, 266, 293, 495, 588
   sources of, reliability of sources, 200, 257, 262, 270
inheritance,
   of capacities, abilities, 208
   of genetic illness/disease, 525
   of wealth and position, 699-700
injustice, *See also* Living Humanism part 1 chapter 6, 45, 125, 584, 680
   acting against, 138, 155, 238, 336, 349, 351, 411, 468, 696, 700, 927, 941
   anger at, 902
   cultures, systems and, 334, 346, 349, 351, 364
   damage from, 335
   law and, 88
   oppression and, 336, 468, 696
   privilege and, 313, 335
integrity, *see also* honesty, Living Humanism, part 1, chapter 7, 923
   acknowledging errors, 417, 418
   in our appreciation, 623
   assumptions and expectations of, 383
   cooperation and, 904
   conformity and, 294
   evidence and, 270
   false displays, appearance of, 383
   honour and, 105
   information sources displaying, 269
   lack of, 130, 421, 477, 495, 509, 510, 645, 934
   maintaining our, 392, 733
   managers and, 38
   the media and, 113
   openness and, 79, 945
   passion for, 919
   power and, 473, 501
   of purpose, 400
   relationships and, 400, 904
   reputation and, 82, 400
   in research, 749
   self-awareness and, 400, 401
   supporting others and, 504

teaching and learning, 108, 289
truth and, 904
well-being and, 290, 319
at work, 70, 154
interaction(s),
  with pets, 863
  social, 13, 74, 198, 379, 679, 688, 717
international organizations, 178, 344, 466, 478, 492, 563, 814
interest groups, 163, 258, 299, 300, 351, 392, 425, 447, 496, 805
irrationality, 607
  aggressive violence and, 455
  in belief groups, 94
  demonstrating, 97
isolation, 12-13, 31, 379, 382, 441, 569, 662-663, 731, 665, 676, 669, 670, 679
  feelings of, 230, 404, 408, 438, 568, 613, 647, 661, 664, 665, 666, 671-674, 676-679, 726, 738, 755, 863
  isolating ourselves as individuals, groups, 142, 360
  in old age, 670
  isolating others, 157, 667, 669

jealousy, 320, 322, 337, 603, 606, 614, 632, 633, 701
journalists and journalism, 75, 113, 259, 300, 501, 611
justice, *See also* law, injustice, 15, 22, 65, 72, 78, 102, 131, 138, 228, 346, 348, 353, 355, 356, 362, 463, 468, 691, 901, 939, 948
  access to, 155, 160
  and education, 267
  equality (before the law) and, 160
  expectation of, right to, 73, 334
  facing, 471
  passion for, 920, 950
  punishment and, 60
  pursuit of, 74, 127, 134, 157, 334, 349, 383, 410, 448, 487, 496, 504, 511, 700, 701, 713, 902, 921, 927, 941
  systems of, 473, 729, 895
  vigilante, 476
  well-being and, 927

kidnap, 901
kindness, 939
  showing, 83, 97, 436, 505, 619, 884, 888, 933-934, 942-943
  to ourselves, 252

land,
  agricultural, 791, 794, 803, 807
  dams and, 791
  disputes over, 404
  efficient management of, 802
  loss of, 467, 791, 794, 807,
  ownership of, 201, 333, 801, 802, 818, 822
  pollution, destruction and defacing of, 792, 846, 905
  as a resource, 791, 794, 801
  responsible use of, 201
  taking over other's, 483, 498, 520, 735, 813, 818, 822
  use of, 791, 801, 802, 803, 807, 808, 809, 824, 825, 827, 851
language,
  appropriate and careful use of, 358, 359, 396, 475, 650, 937
  of despair, 682

freedoms and, 141-142
learning, 184, 208, 214, 215, 251, 264, 274-276, 279, 285, 286, 303, 936
norms of, 125
racist, 93
sharing a common, 142
sign, 936
of threat and violence, 475
social constraints on, 23
lateral thinking, 636
laughter, 98, 653, 776, 784, 854, 893, 932
law(s) and legal systems, *See also* Living Humanism part 1, chapter 6, 21,132, 134, 145, 148, 189, 190, 321, 329, 346, 348, 475, 476, 561, 691, 778, 895, 902
   abiding by, following, 41, 66, 948,
   access to, 71
   application and implementation, 22, 62, 222, 335
   blasphemy, 103
   breaking, 63, 64, 65, 67, 80
   changing, modifying and opposing, 22, 63, 64, 66, 138
   consent for, 62, 64
   enforcing, 80, 146, 363, 488, 691
   environmental, 822, 846, 847, 855
   equality and, 71, 348, 350
   flaws and fallibility in, 52, 62, 73
   food safety, 556
   formulation of, 21, 22
   human rights and, 489
   ineffective, 363
   international, 485, 488, 490
   justice and, 221
   learning about, 254, 297
   oppressive, unjust and destructive, 22, 64, 65, 67, 95, 103, 155, 331, 334, 335, 354, 476, 477, 719
   principles and, 22
   punishment, 72, 73, 476, 719
   representation, legal, 476
   responsibility and, 67, 69
   transparency of, 72
leadership, 287, 352, 381
learning, *See* chapter 11,
   access to, 699
   arrogance and, 616
   benefits and importance of, 12, 909, 924, 951
   choice and, 149
   cooperative interaction and, 435, 446
   difficulties in, 120
   in educational institutions, 198-199
   effort and, 338, 595, 909
   errors, mistakes, failures and, 590, 660, 756, 933
   experiential, 140, 757, 942
   experimenting and, 908
   exploration and, 73, 152, 876
   formal, 576, 942
   free expression and, 85
   freedom and, 200
   from others, 616,
   about health, 738,
   about helping and caring, 778
   independent and active, 581, 590, 898
   lifelong, continuous learning, 780, 908

language, 142
learning and listening, 900
love of learning, 199
to build peace, 458
personal development and, 576
pleasures of, 584, 909
from practice, 782,
progress in learning, 580, 616
promoting, encouraging and
  supporting learning, 12, 26, 72, 200,
  894, 908, 909
reflection and, 580
reflecting on, 908
research and, 657
self-development and, 909
about sex and love, 132
as a social activity, 674
teaching and, 581, 885
thirst and passion for, 75, 918
legacy, our, 632, 784, 789, 793
leisure, 10, 134, 283, 443, 558, 560, 792,
  804, 806, 807, 860, 890
  access to, 135, 137, 193
  and the environment, 804, 806, 807,
    809, 824, 851
  forms of, 564
  health and, 135
  importance of, 926
  making time for, 642
  work and, 134
libraries, 200
lifestyles, 836
  changing, 723
  diverse, 133, 182
  healthy and unhealthy, 291, 302,
    553, 736, 740
  relaxed, 123

love, 511, 706, 881, 952-953
  acting with love and
    kindness, 97, 325, 383, 912,
  anger and, 388,
  choosing lovers and partners, 106,
    134, 139
  cooperation and, 320, 325, 372
  our children and, 29, 107, 119, 153,
    273, 274, 433, 436, 694, 695
  expressing our love, 619, 768
  our families, 29, 31, 550
  fear and, 408
  freedom in love, 131
  lack of love for others, 52, 102, 608,
  of learning, 199
  feeling loved, 30
  oppressive, 902
  our parents, 437, 438, 596
  our partners and, 28, 29, 31, 71,
    330, 374, 405, 426, 427, 428, 429,
    430, 431, 432, 613, 649, 694, 724,
    755, 756, 770
  passionate, 426, 427, 428
  pleasures and joy of, 715, 724, 777,
    932
  protecting those we love, 459, 473,
    912
  rejection in, 13, 408, 634, 635
  searching for, finding, 602, 610, 673,
    725
  sex and love, 131, 132, 610, 736, 737
  siblings, 435
  supporting those we love,
  supporting others, 168, 228, 514,
    526, 527, 550, 642, 652, 659, 726,
    764, 766, 767, 780, 891, 892, 908
  teaching and learning,

education about, 86, 228, 290
feeling unloved, 29, 172, 174, 320, 373, 506, 638, 671, 678, 684
loyalty, 187, 342, 365, 396, 432, 454, 487, 503, 506, 508, 515
luxury, 54, 840
lying (and lies), 113, 166, 289, 687

malaise, 639, 643, 652, 681
marriage, 105, 139, 347, 348, 833
  forced, 71, 667
martial arts, 220, 256
masturbation, 132, 178
materialism, 838
meat-eating, 557, 819, 858, 859, 860, 905
media (the),
  influence of, 113, 211
mediation, 392, 488
mental health, See health, See chapter 13, 524, 536
  abilities and capacities, 414, 458, 528
  and relationships, 532, 537, 566, 567, 569, 572, 576, 595, 598, 599, 616, 623, 635, 641, 644, 645, 646, 649, 650, 657, 658, 659, 663, 664, 665, 666, 668, 669, 670, 671, 673, 674, 675, 678, 682, 685, 693, 694, 695, 696, 702, 706, 711, 714, 723, 724, 726, 727, 736, 737, 747, 755, 756, 757, 779
  comparing ourselves with others, 549-550, 578, 600, 601-606, 614, 638, 675, 685, 691, 701, 715, 755
  coping with bad experiences, 572
  coping with criticism, insults and abuse, 573
  coping with death, 758, 764, 768, 769, 770, 786
  coping with emotions and feelings, 695, 760
  coping with our errors and mistakes, 591, 597
  coping with failure, disappointment and defeat, 612, 661, 756
  coping with health problems, 566, 569, 650, 719
  coping with our lacks, 578, 584
  coping with pain and grief, 752, 760
  coping with problems, stress and challenges, 630, 642, 645, 646, 649, 681
  coping with relationships, 576
  coping with suicidal thoughts, 652
  coping with ups and downs, 594
  counseling, 650
  depression, 4, 171, 291, 533, 549, 574, 575, 579, 592, 599, 600, 612, 615, 620, 644, 645, 653, 654, 655, 657, 661, 664, 680, 682-684, 738, 755, 780, 844
  derangement, 342
  deterioration, 167
  effort, 252
  fatigue, 252
  goal setting and, 639, 644, 681, 757
  health, learning about, 291
  mental illness, 170, 172, 383, 384, 464, 488
  isolation and loneliness, See isolation, loneliness, 12-13, 31, 379, 382, 441, 569, 662-663, 731, 665, 676, 669, 670, 679

medical treatment, 531, 533, 534,
535, 566, 567, 651, 655, 657, 689,
720, 732, 747, 748, 779
space, mental, 191
positive, 529, 566-569, 574, 576,
580, 581, 587, 605, 615, 627, 637,
638, 641-643, 661, 666
powerlessness, 639, 645, 687-689,
694, 696-698
processes, mental, 211
recording achievements and events,
643-644
recovery, 514
rest, 134
resilience and strength, 252, 323
scars, 361
self-awareness, 386, 548, 570, 571,
574, 575, 576
self-efficacy, 32, 35, 214, 307, 463,
532, 579, 605, 934
self-harm, 172-173, 655, 657
suicidal thinking, 291, 651-654
suffering, trauma, turmoil, pain and
anguish, 104, 168, 169, 170, 171,
174, 507, 518
military, the,
aggressive violence and, 366, 369,
486, 495, 497
commands, obeying and, 60, 61
recognising individual humanity, 367
secrets, 70
uniforms and, 41
value and importance of, 224, 368,
488
minimal force, use of, 48, 145, 319, 320,
322, 332, 344, 346, 393, 413, 463, 469,
690, 861, 943

misinterpretations, 112, 166, 400, 590,
624
mistrust, 37, 362, 391, 400, 407-408,
441, 445, 461, 484, 612
mockery, 94-102, 391, 659
models, *See also* exemplars, 286, 327,
375, 434
money and resources *See also*
materialism, 896
autonomy, independence and, 3, 5
contributing to community, society
and beyond, 896
drugs and, 506, 717
earning, 206, 210
financial systems and, 896
freedom to earn, 467, 901
being generous with, giving 933-
934, 942
healthcare and, 733
importance of, 895, 928
influence and, 86, 95
mathematical skills and, 279
over-focus on, 819, 928
participation and, 136
perverse levels of, 896
pets and, 865
poor use of, 897
privilege and, 313
problems, 599,
raising money for charity, 673
for survival, 135, 210, 373, 649, 663,
835, 895, 928
for travel, 836
monitoring and oversight,
assisted suicide, 776
in childbirth, 749
in education, 239-240, 311

compliance with laws, 488
of our environment, 823, 847, 850
food standards, 556
health, 542, 742, 746-747, 942
of hazards and threats to safety, 561-563, 742, 746-747
of ourselves, 584, 637
at work, 34-35, 38
mood(s), 58, 135, 153, 327, 359, 431, 591, 612, 658, 681
   diet and, 745
   drugs and, 714-716
   the environment and, 877
   fatigue and, 564
motivation, 253, 274, 342, 414, 421, 423, 452, 536-537, 565, 632, 684, 700, 717, 775, 816, 864
   achievement and, 232
   anger as a motivator, 411, 412, 706, 902
   autonomy and, 36, 44
   awareness of, 83, 127, 165, 270, 292, 359, 389, 392, 400, 401, 510, 574, 662, 739
   being appreciated, 621
   being, feeling demotivated, 533, 581, 614, 622, 644
   challenge, risk and, 938
   criticism as a motivator, 593, 596, 709
   death as a motivator, 768, 784
   encouragement and, 710
   enhancing, 642
   fear and, 946
   feelings and emotions as motivators, 902, 918
   for goal setting, 639
   goals as motivators, 644
   for having children, 832
   to help and support others, 527, 528, 621, 633, 734, 762, 902
   for heroic acts, 499
   intrinsic, 666
   to learn, 219, 234, 235, 305, 306, 307, 576
   media, 259-260
   negatively selfish, 14, 20, 65, 423, 497, 527
   problems and, 680
   profit and motivation, 849
   punishment and, 51
   racist, 494
   responsibility for, 234
   revenge and motivation, 888
   self-motivated, 235, 241, 295, 305, 308, 313, 576, 622
   shame and, 107
   speaker, writer motivation, 270
   stress and, 645, 646
   suspecting other's motives, 386, 400, 401, 408, 409
   unconscious, 118
   for violence, 508, 517
   work and, 134
murder, 17, 92, 95, 103, 150, 181, 195, 196, 197, 199, 227, 261, 321, 322, 333, 340, 370, 402, 415, 468, 477, 485, 489, 492, 494, 497, 501, 516, 517, 518, 519, 521, 540, 703, 704, 712, 719, 766, 822, 885
music, 82, 111, 151, 176, 184, 193, 199, 201, 215, 217, 286, 298, 303, 304, 314, 577, 766, 769, 884, 893, 930, 935

mutual understanding, 21, 31, 142, 402, 417, 420, 492, 921, 937

narcissism, 595
nationalism,
　destructive, 342, 483, 484, 487, 494, 511
　racism and, 483, 484, 487, 494, 511
negativity, 574, 588, 608, 609, 657, 710
negotiation, 118, 159, 376, 383, 384, 385, 388, 394, 395, 397, 399, 406, 407, 417, 452, 468, 492, 493, 496, 826, 827, 889
　in business and work, 215
　in our daily lives, 404-406, 912
　at home, 152, 376, 405
　in politics, 196, 224, 376, 479, 481, 483, 484, 488, 492, 815, 823, 844
　as a skill, ability, 297, 345, 395, 437, 451, 504, 783
neighbours,
　international, 195
　relationships with, 192, 193, 194, 385, 441, 442, 443, 446
nepotism, 352, 690
non-human world, the, *See* chapter 14
norms and conventions, 24, 106, 126, 178, 636
　awareness of, 108, 109,
　benefits of following, 178
　breaching and challenging, 23, 24, 25, 109, 110, 117, 126, 294, 353, 354, 638, 717
　conformity with, 2
　conventional beliefs, 294
　culture, 23, 110, 111
　customs, 118, 125

　discrimination and, 128, 932
　in different generations, 118
　manners, 190
　non-conformity, 19
　unwritten, 22-23
　at work, 43
nuclear power,
　dangers of (radiation), 842
　research into, 302
　as a source of energy, 805, 814, 842-844, 845
nuclear weapons, 466, 844, 903

obeying others, 58-63, 65, 67, 99, 152, 347, 507, 948
objectives, *See* aims, 134, 143, 234, 338, 364, 497, 510, 688, 757, 784, 840, 900, 946, 949
objectivity, 163
observation,
　discovery, reason, research and, 164, 745, 746, 747
　informal, 218
　of others, 127
　self-observation, 386, 581
openness, 82, 104, 383, 418, 607, 943
　democracy and, 943-944
　to disagreement, 183
　in education, 241, 265
　encouraging, 520
　about our faults and mistakes, 247, 934, 938
　honesty, integrity and, 418
　to new ideas, 247, 269
　to others, 245, 247
open-minded, being, 111, 118, 934
oppression, 61, 90, 125, 129, 133, 137,

181, 233, 235, 331, 411, 484, 490, 493, 497, 498, 513, 520, 536, 598, 687, 734, 903, 938
  of conformity, 11
  cultures and systems of oppression, 55, 346, 347, 349, 354, 355, 393, 512
  economic, 104
  in education, 265, 283, 309, 311
  freedom from, 2, 201, 901
  by governments and nation states, 166, 195, 196
  law as oppression, 22, 63, 65
  preventing, 104, 112, 131, 139, 155-158, 197, 334, 336, 351, 364, 412, 468, 492, 504, 512, 513, 632, 688, 695, 696, 899, 938
  slavery, 58, 342
  of women, 113
  at work, 152
opulence, 411, 896
ostracism and expulsion, 20, 23 110, 142, 143, 181, 253, 263, 347, 352, 666, 667
othering, 446
overwork, 58, 135, 646

parent(s), 27, 29
  advising children, 139
  aggressive violence, 153, 362, 437
  arranging marriages, 71
  being good, 273
  belittling and criticising children, 584, 595, 596
  caring for our, 437
  child tantrums, 695
  our children's friends, 139-141
  having many children, 832
  coercive conduct, 153
  consulting children, 153
  coping and dealing with our, 253, 695
  death of a child, 763
  death of a parent, 758
  educating our children, 228, 233, 254, 267, 273-275, 276-278, 289, 309, 316, 432
  expectations of children, 436
  fallibility, parental, 153, 695
  improving as, 253
  influence of, 898
  lack of appreciation of, 620, 622
  listening to children, 119
  maintaining independence, 28
  prescribing punishments, 55
  pressure from, 47
  preventing child violence, 325, 327, 373
  protecting our children, 694
  raising and supporting our children, 71, 106, 107, 126, 211, 530
  responsibilities of, 108, 152, 228
  restrictions on our children's actions, 151-152
  separation from children, 438
  shame, 108
  teenagers and, 118, 119, 120, 436, 628, 629, 694
  understanding our, 119, 153
participation, 363, 486, 675, 835, 839
  in our communities and societies, 137, 263, 448

in decision-making, 805
destructive actions, 369
and education, 230, 232, 236, 448-449
freedom and, 137
friendship and, 670
health and, 736
importance of our, 926
law and, 21
non-participation, 142, 192, 445
online, 679
in opposition to tyranny and oppression, 492
as a source of pleasure and well-being, 715, 926
in rituals, 263, 264
in team sports, 545, 549, 550
passion(s), 464, 920
passionate beliefs, 392, 423, 424, 903
in debate and discussion, 356
for the environment, 875
for goals, success and achievement, 645, 709
hatred, anger and, 506
for life, 645
passionate love, 426-428, 724, 755, 776, 832, 892
in sport, 548, 560
for truth, 126
about well-being, 903, 920
for our work, 136, 731
passive, being, passivity, 586, 655, 675, 900
learning, 243, 284, 311,
resistance, 156
as response to

suffering/violence 339, 776
smoking, 148
pastimes, 760, 893
patience, *See* impatience, 65, 66, 100, 115, 111, 120, 121, 122, 201, 311, 406, 581, 630, 924, 931, 940, 941
peace,
building, 288, 343, 386, 404, 457, 520, 522, 750, 887, 893
inner peace, 360
personal space, 11, 12, 19, 32, 39, 109, 190, 191, 192, 291, 360, 389, 441, 442, 661, 802, 818, 829, 854, 900, 945
personal, physical, appearance, 24, 601-602, 634-635
pets, 441, 563, 857, 863-865
physical environment, the, 273, 444. 788-789, 809, 820-822, 834, 871, 876, 878, 922
planning, 697
achievement, success and, 941
ahead, futures, 539, 639, 640, 663
in business, 215
for catastrophic events, 872
education about, 206, 208, 222, 297
effective action and, 906, 908
for energy needs, 804, 805
for environmental change, 811, 818, 850
failure and, 684
financial, 897
flexible, 642,
our health systems, 733
resource generation and use, 823
resources for, 875
technology and innovation, 850
time for planning, 250, 643, 662

realistic, 616, 629
urban and suburban, 824, 829, 841
waste disposal, 563
pleasure, 1, 10, 13, 135, 149, 150, 170, 171, 173, 194, 210, 213, 216, 217, 338, 355, 535, 542, 543, 568, 591, 594, 603, 619, 642, 677, 682, 685, 699, 709, 715, 764, 766, 777, 778, 780, 860, 883, 889, 890, 891, 914, 929, 930, 932
  of achievement, 232, 605, 644, 658, 659, 893, 906
  autonomy and, 44
  of belonging, 893, 906, 921
  of our children, 893
  choice and, 7
  collaboration and cooperative interaction, 231, 232, 337, 388, 395, 444, 664
  of communication, 86
  of companionship and friendship, 336, 769, 892
  of discovery, 241, 299
  drugs and, 194, 715, 717, 718, 720
  education, learning and, 213-215, 219, 223, 225, 229, 230, 241, 250, 251, 256, 257, 659, 908
  entertainments and, 893, 928
  and our environment, 563, 790, 792, 799, 807, 809, 814, 824, 825, 846, 852, 854, 857
  of the everyday, 651, 776
  exercise and, 544, 545, 549, 551, 894
  exploration and, 213, 836
  family and, 29
  giving, 225
  and love, 29, 131, 602, 664, 892, 906
  from drugs, 194
  illegitimate sources of, 178, 179, 692
  inevitability of, 653, 654
  interaction and, 448, 449, 663, 679, 906
  laughter, 893
  leisure and, 135, 928
  literature and, 297
  novelty, originality and, 184, 257
  of partners, 427, 428, 433, 723
  of pets, 863, 865
  pastimes, 893
  play, 312
  of being recognised and appreciated, 300, 620, 622
  relationships and, 29, 30, 427, 668
  research and, 299, 303
  of teaching, 307, 310
  self-expression, 111
  sexual, 131-133, 289, 724, 736, 737, 831-833, 892,
  sports, 545, 546, 549, 551
  through helping and supporting others, 625, 725, 726, 882, 919, 923, 929, 930
  trivial, 838
  variety, difference and, 116, 117
  of victory, 606
  work and, 136
policing, 41, 216, 221, 344, 345, 366, 368, 370, 473, 488, 501
politicians, 233, 259, 300, 308, 349, 540, 624, 883
politeness, 79, 83, 96, 98, 99, 108, 116, 125, 210, 599, 602
pollution, 146, 180, 532, 545 837, 838, 839, 851, 861, 879

air, 792, 793, 815, 816, 820, 822, 823, 835
  chemical, 562
  effective action against, 815, 816, 821, 822, 823, 837-828, 904
  energy generation and, 302
  global warming and, 805, 818
  health and, 145
  industrial, 194, 195, 562
  nuclear, 793, 794, 842, 845
  population and, 827, 828
  travel and, 48, 834, 835-837
  waste dumping, 841, 846
  wasting resources and, 839
  water pollution, 562, 792, 845, 846
population(s), 825, 830, 832
  animal, 564, 816
  decline, 829, 830, 831, 834
  growth, 800, 820, 827, 828, 829, 831, 834, 841
possessions, *See also* Living Humanism, part 1, chapter 9
  having basic, 840
  comparing, 606
  need for, 840, 926
  perverse levels of, 838
  sharing, 331
  stealing, removal of, theft, 469, 517, 692, 901
  treating others as, 58, 71, 132, 264, 372
  well-being and, 895, 926
poverty, 743
  aggressive violence and, 362, 363
  education, learning and, 160, 206, 463, 735
  the environment and, 825
  escape from, alleviating, avoiding, opposing, 56, 57, 159, 160, 332, 333, 350, 351, 356, 364, 467, 479, 504, 531, 547, 677, 733, 734, 783, 832, 833, 836-837, 865, 885, 895, 896, 907
  falling into, 886
  freedom and, 56, 137, 150, 159, 160, 901
  greed and, 735
  health and, 160, 302, 527, 531, 533, 733, 735
  inefficiency, poor management and, 735, 802
  land and, 801, 813
  natural disaster and, 735, 736
  oppression and, 21, 50, 84, 104, 331-332, 349, 677, 885
  peace and, 350, 355
  pets and, 864
  power and, 56, 160
  research into, 750
  systems, cultures and, 346, 349, 350, 351, 352, 353, 750, 865, 897
  technology and, 735, 736
  war and, 540
prediction, 173, 185, 299, 362, 538, 571, 589, 629, 639-641, 709, 751, 811, 871, 872, 873
prejudice, 125, 126, 133, 260, 270, 271, 283, 291, 453, 477, 687, 714, 853
  unconscious, 164, 386
prison and confinement, 52, 53, 54, 66, 72, 144, 146, 195, 331, 334, 347, 354, 417, 471, 477, 516, 520, 719, 901
  privacy, 76, 179, 191, 192, 328, 441, 442, 642, 854

privilege, 411, 496, 614, 615,
　700, 910
　education and, 236, 238, 313, 335
　health and, 335, 700
　inherited, 699
　the law and, 72, 143, 335, 336
　poverty and, 734, 735
　power and, 336, 350, 508, 699
　systems and, 712
　taking away, 55
pro-active, being, 65, 348, 375, 378,
　424, 425, 444, 451, 454, 470, 479, 480,
　485, 491, 493, 532, 537, 552, 553, 629,
　646, 647, 687, 751, 871, 878, 934
profit (business, company), 352, 648,
　717, 849
promises, also see agreements, 123, 264
prostitution, 133
protecting, others, 50, 130, 140, 198,
　289, 331, 345, 364, 365, 368, 370, 371,
　420, 456, 457, 463, 491, 495, 499, 500,
　504, 505, 511, 521, 606, 631, 892, 938
　ourselves, 48, 54, 61, 146, 147, 153,
　　160, 323, 331, 348, 351, 372, 413,
　　414, 420, 434, 454-459, 463, 464,
　　466, 469, 473, 485, 497, 499, 511,
　　516, 522, 547, 548, 572, 606, 689,
　　693, 710, 713, 723, 725, 743, 751,
　　794, 795, 861, 868, 869, 870, 872,
　　888, 898, 912, 922, 938
promoting positive values, 623
punishment, 17, 50-56, 63, 71, 72, 103,
　142, 143, 153, 181, 261-264, 268, 347,
　354, 374, 375, 415, 419, 434, 476, 477,
　490, 515, 667, 694, 719, 901, 949
purpose, sense of, 273, 565, 863

quarantine, 730-731

racial discrimination, racism, 63, 110,
　129, 269, 476, 483, 484, 494, 503
rape, 17, 150, 175, 405, 416, 485, 516,
　518, 704, 830
rationality (reason), *See* irrationality,
　*See also* Living Humanism part 1,
　chapter 5 389, 423, 447, 613, 616,
　628, 632, 637, 643, 666, 703, 705, 709,
　776, 868, 901, 902, 905, 906, 907, 908,
　920, 941, 942, 946, 947, 949, 950, 951
　anger and, 411, 706
　answers and solutions based in, 7,
　　32, 653
　behavioural restrictions and, 133
　bias, prejudice, culture and, 164,
　　259, 277, 314
　being critical and challenging
　　actions, ideas and beliefs, 99, 158,
　　270, 278, 627, 636, 716
　changing conduct, ideas and, 246,
　　248, 387
　comparisons, 603
　conformity and, 293
　creativity and, 115, 292
　education and learning, 208, 234,
　　245, 249, 266, 292
　emotional pain and, 681
　emotions and, 637
　our environment and, 149, 809, 818,
　　852-853, 872,
　escape from, 717, 718
　evaluating action and, 197, 495
　evaluating evidence, ideas and, 165,
　　221, 257, 424, 584
　evidence and, 270

faith and, 266
fallibility and, 272
false rationales, 65
fear, negative thinking and, 408, 409, 615
forceful responses and, 319, 337, 339, 344
health and, 567, 738
judgment, 608
law and, 63
listening to others and, 394
love and, 429
medical treatment and, 221, 730, 741, 743, 744,
misjudgments, errors and, 588, 590
monitoring and oversight and, 240
motivation and, 528
in response to oppression, 157
persuasion and, 451, 739
planning, 646
power, privilege and, 696, 699
poverty and, 734
promoting, 357
pursuing our goals, 639, 685
in response to suffering, 412
finding value in ideas, 99
war, conflict and, 515
at work, 41, 647
realistic and unrealistic thinking, 613, 614, 615, 616, 626
reciprocity, 527, 528, 863, 919
records,
of our achievements, 630, 631
false, 501
historic, 302, 485
keeping, 474, 643
recycling, 329, 804, 814, 838, 840, 841, 845, 847
reflection, 36, 55, 191, 212, 225, 226, 241, 246, 250-252, 305, 311, 317, 387, 389, 402, 414, 451, 580, 581, 639, 642, 643, 661-663, 695, 764, 774, 916, 941, 944
regrets, 93, 121, 175, 225, 341, 407, 414, 416, 420, 422, 471, 626, 639, 695, 703, 705, 711, 726, 766, 767, 949
rehabilitation, 51, 414, 415
rejection, personal, 13, 320, 354, 408, 591, 680, 724, 726, 946
relationships, 413, 598, 599, 615, 616, 623, 625, 664, 678, 693, 694, 711, 714, 881, 883, 885, 900, 901, 902, 903, 929, 943, 945
  acquiescence, agreement in, 272
  aging and, 670
  anger, hatred and, 702, 706
  apologising in, 417, 422
  between parents and teenagers, 118, 437
  building better, 86
  changing relationships, 30, 430, 641
  close family, 438
  coercive, 499
  conformity and, 126
  cooperativity and, 343, 359, 372, 374, 375, 376, 378, 379, 385-389, 392, 395, 424, 425, 426, 428, 429, 433, 513, 518, 572, 911
  education, learning about, 176, 211, 254, 290, 297, 310
  ending, 724
  fear and, 407-410
  finding, 669, 670, 671, 673
  forgiveness in, 415

freedom, independence, autonomy and, 28, 30, 105, 119, 134, 140
give and take in, 433
importance of, 1, 13, 28, 83
health and, 532, 537, 566, 567, 595, 645, 646, 649, 665, 723, 747, 755
healthy, 668, 695, 737
help with, 650
international, 480
joys and pleasures of, 1, 30, 569
listening and, 401, 429
maintaining and sustaining, 256, 439, 440, 882
online, 449
with neighbours, 442-444
problems and challenges in, 426, 427, 428, 430, 432, 451-454, 668, 682, 726, 755, 939, 952
rifts in, 32
sexual, 71, 131, 132, 328, 724, 832, 892
successful, 427, 428
truthfulness, honesty, and integrity in, 289, 400, 904, 923
violence, aggressive, and, 319, 372
well-being and, 13, 83, 576, 668, 892, 911
at work, 34
relaxation (and rest), 123, 136, 360, 544, 565, 642, 644, 645, 650, 651, 714, 715, 716, 717, 725, 824, 836, 854, 893, 928, 932, 940
religion(s),
belief(s), 94, 95, 97, 102, 103, 144, 266, 278, 354
criticism of, 94, 95, 97, 102, 103, 144

ceremonies and rituals, 142, 263-264, 268, 737
education and, 277-278
indoctrination, 261-266
leaving a, 677
oppression of, by, 93, 177
questioning, 91
reputation, 65, 82, 107, 112, 400, 401, 418, 504, 579, 623, 659, 667, 674,
research, 224, 243, 253, 263, 274, 281, 298, 299, 300, 301, 302, 304, 305, 314, 329, 576, 636, 651, 652, 675, 751, 778, 848, 850, 852, 864, 865, 866, 872, 875, 893, 894, 896, 901, 907
accuracy of, 163
for all, 303
on animals, 866-868
climate change and, 88, 816
on cooperation, 482
design, 221
empirical, 298, 747
into energy, 302, 329, 803, 804, 814
flaws in, 283, 501
funding, 301, 731, 742, 746, 779, 783
health and medicine, 172, 301, 377, 527, 531, 532, 536, 555, 657, 721, 730, 731, 739, 740, 742, 743, 744-750, 753, 771, 779, 867, 868, 869, 870, 883, 907
into history, 302-304
on our human selves, 877
institutions, 295
learning about, 279
learning research methods and skills, 210, 215, 224, 225, 298
long-term, 236
openness and, 75, 79, 80

on peace, conflict and
violence, 465
performance at work, 43
personal research, 301, 925
pleasure of, 298
into pollution, 815, 821, 847
as a search for truth, 271
systematic, 304, 536, 730, 907, 914
types of
well-being and, 304
resilience, personal, *See also*
mental health, 530, 534, 571, 579
resources and finances, *See also* money
and resources)
effective (and ineffective) use of, 48,
194, 238, 501, 814, 815, 822, 838,
843, 896
finite resources, 804
generation of, 138
scarcity of, 47, 798
to support space exploration, 875
to support well-being, 7, 896
respect, 25, 97, 98, 100, 127, 248, 314,
336, 359, 374, 499, 500, 521, 572, 583,
676, 738, 903, 920, 922
encouraging and supporting, 266,
417, 599, 903
for difference, 97, 143, 187
feeling disrespected, 98, 320, 388,
413, 506, 620, 659
mutual, 306, 357, 358, 574, 938
for others, 27, 59, 86, 99, 100, 187,
192, 193, 201, 234, 315, 423-424,
549, 606, 767, 854, 920, 922, 925,
926
being respected, 91, 120, 378, 532,
634, 659, 695, 900, 920

self-respect, 19, 187, 611, 666, 933
responsibility,
personal, 5, 45, 53, 67, 68, 69, 158,
188, 326, 359, 366, 622, 799, 846,
899, 948
for, to others, 171, 187, 240, 367,
513, 517, 593, 707
rest (see also relaxation), 134, 360, 569,
645, 646, 653, 661, 725, 901, 939-940
health and, 564-565
learning and, 252
recuperation and, 642
a rested mind, 559
work and, 58, 134, 135,136, 251
revenge, 79, 105, 412, 414, 415, 516,
518, 520, 888, 912, 913, 932
risk-taking, 220, 660
ritual(s), 142, 263-264, 268, 737
robbery, 885
robustness,
acting in a robust manner, 21, 63,
83, 116, 126, 131, 149, 154, 155,
335, 367, 384, 393, 396, 400, 537,
549, 583, 585, 587, 602, 634, 711,
887, 922
personal, *See also* resilience, 151,
572, 573, 650, 659, 938, 939, 941
rules, See also norms and conventions,
21, 22, 24, 39, 43, 62, 64, 71, 106, 109,
143, 178, 207, 349, 350, 488, 503, 546,
548, 549, 711, 739
of thumb, 929

sadness, *See also* depression,
grief, 4, 274, 291, 337, 388, 568, 594,
600, 654, 664, 672, 680, 682, 684,
760, 761, 766, 769, 784, 854, 914

safety, promoting, maintaining and ensuring, 59, 66, 73, 76, 78, 79, 89, 93, 222, 289, 297, 310, 400, 462, 493, 517, 519, 559, 560, 641, 713, 783, 809, 870, 877, 950
  from crime and violence, 54, 193, 220, 322, 333, 344, 345, 348, 370, 371, 372, 373, 414, 419, 442, 456, 457, 464, 469, 887, 889, 890, 912
  education, training and, 220, 223, 226, 240, 274, 291
  of our environment, 145
  expertise in, 222
  fire safety, 560, 562
  food safety, 224, 555
  health and, 752
  in the home, 147, 558
  nuclear power and, 842, 843, 844
  over-focus on, 222
  planning for safety, 560
  of products and services, 742
  regimes and systems, 797
  seat belts, 148
  in sport, 553
  in travel, 148, 562
  at work, 39, 40, 41, 349, 352, 560, 561, 742, 746
sanitation, 556-557
schools, 27, 55, 56, 186-189, 205, 207, 221, 233, 235, 240, 241, 256, 265-268, 276-279, 281, 285, 289, 290, 295, 308, 335, 375, 381, 402, 599, 669, 692, 781, 833, 857
science and technology, *See also*
  rationality, 282, 796
    access to scientific information, 71
    benefits of, 296-298, 783

    creativity and, 181
    flaws in science, scientific systems, 227, 283, 284
    importance of learning, 279, 283, 284, 293
    research in, 296-298
self-criticism
  too much, 568, 580, 587, 595, 596, 597, 602, 617, 619, 657, 663, 664
self-defence, 46, 48, 49, 50, 89, 208, 220, 289, 319, 323, 341, 344, 455, 458, 459, 464, 468, 493, 494, 553, 888
self-development, 216, 245, 295, 580, 588, 908, 909
self-expression, 84, 86, 94, 96, 97, 111, 116, 144, 201, 336, 357
self-focus, 14, 31, 360, 383, 408, 448, 527, 528, 602, 648, 674, 686, 698, 703, 704, 711, 891
self-harm, *See* mental health, 172-173, 655, 657,
self-hatred, 172, 595-596
self-interest, 160, 166, 258, 259, 410, 424, 479, 489, 738, 790, 819, 823, 853
self-sacrifice, 288, 487, 504, 891, 892, 899, 945
selfishness (also see negatively selfish)
sex,
  education, 176, 198, 290
  having children, 26, 290, 328, 334, 374, 427, 428, 431, 469, 622, 724, 781, 829, 832, 833
  masturbation, 134, 178
  sexual assault, 178, 414
  sexual commerce, 133
  sexual freedom, 131
  sexual health, 736

sexual intimacy, 832, 833
sexual pleasure, enjoying, giving and accepting, 132, 724, 736, 737, 892
sexually transmitted diseases,protection against, 725, 736
shame, 105-108, 172, 173, 174, 341, 371, 417, 583, 619, 655, 667, 673
shortcuts, taking, 40
short-termism, 88, 197, 819
skepticism, 929-930, 950
skills development, See chapter 11, See also education, learning)
slaughter, of animals, 487, 548, 557, 858, 905
slavery, 58-59, 71, 334, 346-347, 509, 830, 834, 901
sleep, 253, 373, 431, 432, 564, 565-566, 642, 653, 695, 754, 940
smoking, 89, 148-150, 194, 299, 534, 536, 558, 717-718, 738-741
social action, 444, 538, 556, 599, 615, 739, 839, 911
social conformity, 111, 948
social conventions and codes, 11, 110, 177, 178, 601
social foundations, secure, 13
social identity, 882
social nature (our), 4, 12, 108, 230, 664, 733, 882, 892, 901, 933,
social sciences, 227, 279, 298
solitude, 13, 379, 662
space, 10, 21, 34, 86, 136, 208, 264, 371, 439, 582, 676, 677, 758, 833
  need for personal, 4, 11, 13, 26, 27, 28, 32, 33, 36, 38, 39, 68, 85, 109, 134, 147, 179, 190, 191, 192, 194, 291, 360, 374, 380, 441, 442, 451, 544, 582, 661-664, 709-710, 802, 828, 829, 839, 853, 854, 900, 901, 939, 944
  population and space, 828
  the public, 87, 102, 109, 177, 293, 346, 600, 612, 614, 622, 847, 854
  for recreation and leisure, 552, 554, 824
  at work, 186,
space exploration, 873-875
spontaneity, 273
sport(s), 547, 548, 551, 552
  animals and, 860
  cooperation and, 329
  enjoying, pleasures of 215, 545, 549, 769, 779, 884, 893, 894
  facilities, 553, 554, 824
  fitness and exercise, 544, 545, 550, 551, 684, 736
  goals in, 610
  learning sports skills, 210, 297, 937
  organising and governance of, 552
  participating in, 444
  and physical injury, pain 546, 547, 548, 549,
  safety in, 546, 548, 553, 559
  self-confidence and, 577
  social benefits of, 545
  team, 189, 545, 669
  violence in, 546, 547, 548
stress, See mental health
stubbornness, 417, 949-951
suicide (see mental health), 169-175, 654-657, 680, 774,
  assisted suicide, 755, 773
  suicidal thinking, 170, 171, 172

superstition, 853
systematic, being, 82, 183, 212, 282, 290, 299, 304, 312, 335, 465, 476, 502, 531, 536, 616, 672, 678, 712, 730, 743, 744, 745, 746, 747, 749, 751, 753, 820, 821, 837, 895, 907, 914, 941

tastes, 114, 118, 124, 286, 769, 855
tax(es), 329
    avoidance and evasion, 352
    obligation to pay, 783
    social payment, 728
teaching, See chapter 11, 115
    good teaching, 108
    importance of, 203
    patience and, 120, 201
    shame and, 108
    at work, 37
teams, 9, 70, 185, 189, 230, 255, 588, 938
    cooperation and collaboration, 189, 209, 230, 232, 300, 446
    conflict within, 380
    conflict with other, 189
    negotiating teams, 451
    social benefits of, 545, 673, 920
    in sport, 41, 545-550, 669
    winning and losing, 189, 545
teamwork,
    learning, 287
    pleasure in, 231, 232, 920
teenagers and parents, 118-119, 629, 685
technical skills, 209, 215, 221, 222, 251, 609, 721
tedium, 234-235, 258, 645
theatre, 111, 114, 286, 304, 329, 883, 892

theft, 18, 39, 42, 54, 150, 354, 469, 470, 489, 508, 784, 885
thinking skills, 38, 225, 291-293, 297, 406, 638, 926
thirst for
    knowledge and understanding, 75, 219, 307
    risk and danger, 536
time, using effectively, 642
tobacco and health, See smoking
torture, 49, 61, 94, 103, 104, 125, 360, 361, 405, 459, 476, 485, 490, 494, 500, 504, 513-514, 516, 517, 518, 670, 695, 713, 785, 901
trade, 74, 255, 491, 897
    drugs, 718-719
trades unions, 259, 267
tradition, 71, 103, 105-106, 133, 142, 181, 314, 346, 860
training, 34, 41, 42, 45, 60, 115, 183, 200, 201, 204, 205, 210, 212, 216, 218, 221-223, 225-227, 230-232, 236, 238, 239, 241, 243, 251, 255, 256, 273, 295, 316, 344, 419, 463, 531, 544, 553, 556, 561, 577 579-581, 604, 642, 645, 689-690, 717, 721, 732, 733, 908-909, 944-945
transgender,
    freedom and, 131
    supporting individuals, 90
travel, 47, 48, 64, 646, 730, 902
    accidents and, 558
    air, 281
    benefits of, 834-836, 837
    desire and need for, 834-836
    our direction of (in life), 118, 472
    experiencing the world

through, 810
freedom to, 73, 74, 334, 901
planning our, 629
pollution and, 835, 836
resources and, 137
restricting, 144
safety and, 222
space, 873-875
trust, *See* mistrust, *See also* Living Humanism part 1, chapter 7 part 1, 79, 249, 904, 921
breach of, 359
building, 417, 419, 420, 443
desire to trust, 383
dishonesty and, 48, 174
policing and, 370
in relationships, 443
sharing with those we, 675, 682
undeserved, 272
aggressive violence and, 320, 362-364
at work, 167, 420
truth, *See* honesty, integrity, trust, *See also* Living Humanism part 1, chapter 7 7, 70, 74, 75, 97, 115, 126, 166, 169, 199, 259, 260, 262, 290, 294, 381, 395, 401, 611, 614, 618, 624, 637, 655, 671, 713, 734, 735, 738, 770, 786, 904, 920, 925, 930, 950
conformity and, 293
countering untruth, 98, 99
desire for, 83-84
education, learning and, 289, 292
establishing, evaluating, 257, 270, 424, 510, 511, 935
half-truths, 164, 739
importance of, 163, 904, 950
and the media, 113, 114, 500, 501
searching for, finding out, 112, 113, 152, 163, 167, 265, 269, 270, 271, 292, 500, 501
research and, 271
secrecy and, 81
being true to ourselves, 126
tsunamis, 688, 735, 751, 871, 872
protecting against, 538

uncertainty, 247, 248, 632, 639, 767
unfairness *See also* injustice, 44, 411, 614
powerlessness and, 699
systems, 334, 336, 346, 352, 713
in our relationships, 432
inequality and, 229, 313, 335
unhappiness, 4, 8, 9, 10, 121, 242, 328, 337, 338, 358, 385, 388, 405, 417, 430, 438, 439, 567, 569, 575, 577, 600, 620, 623, 629, 650, 652, 655, 658, 661, 664, 671, 676, 680, 681, 684, 699, 702, 712, 780, 834, 854, 890
uniforms, 41-43, 184, 186, 187, 188, 189, 198
unions, 259, 267
untruthfulness (*See* honesty, truth, integrity, trust)
justifiable
vaccination, 147, 150, 253, 723, 743
veganism, 557
vegetarianism, 557
verbal abuse, 383
refraining from, 413, 885
responding to, 888-889
victims, 50, 55,146, 156, 157, 284, 320,

321, 327, 342, 361,362, 363, 369, 372, 411, 414, 421, 484, 487, 507, 508, 514, 546, 687, 693, 714, 719, 726, 766, 776, 798, 830, 912, 938,
   being, 52, 53, 452, 457, 462, 470, 471, 473, 474, 475, 514, 688, 704, 705, 907
   caring for, 348, 476, 514
   in systems, 11, 938
victory, 606
   in competition and competitive sports, 580
   in negotiation, 385
   pleasure of, 606
   in war, 521
vigilantes, 476
violence (aggressive), 50, 100, 138, 195, 309, 318, 320, 326, 337, 349, 350, 359, 363, 383, 388, 393, 410, 415, 457, 460, 477, 483, 484, 485, 491, 495, 505, 506, 507, 508, 509, 510, 511, 512, 518, 521, 522, 523, 913, 924-925
   acting against/to prevent, 61, 63, 92, 144, 157, 158, 193, 197, 322, 323, 327, 340, 341, 342, 343, 344, 345, 346, 348, 364, 365, 366, 367, 368, 369, 370, 371, 372, 373, 374, 375, 383, 384, 414, 424, 451, 453, 454, 455, 457, 458, 459, 461, 462, 463, 464, 465, 468, 469, 473, 474, 475, 476, 481, 485, 488, 489, 493, 494, 497, 499, 506, 514, 519, 520, 697, 885, 887, 896, 899, 902, 912
   anger and, 410, 412, 413
   against children, 153, 375, 434
   coercion and, 346
   cycle of, 326, 340, 341, 412, 888

   damage and destruction from, 321, 361, 362
   defending others from, 202, 289, 319, 339, 344, 452 485, 500, 513, 885, 887
   education against, 462, 476
   fear and, 409
   freedom from, 49, 101, 901
   in the home, 347, 348, 372, 373, 374, 431, 490
   inciting hatred and, 103, 112, 113, 114, 144, 511, 948
   intolerance of, 125
   the law and, 474, 476
   minimal force, 327, 332
   origins of, 324, 325, 326, 410, 464, 750
   peace and, 355, 357, 911
   using physical and psychological, 319
   psychological consequences of, 320, 323, 361, 434, 470, 472, 482, 514
   research into understanding and prevention of, 465, 750
   self-defence, 46, 48, 49, 50, 89, 202, 208, 220, 289, 311, 319, 323, 339, 341, 344, 455, 458, 459, 464, 468, 485, 493, 494, 553, 691, 888
   threatening, 113, 450, 475
   victims of, 320, 368, 470, 471, 472, 514
visualisation, visualising the future, 206, 292, 907
volunteering, 760, 778
vulnerability, being vulnerable, 13, 101, 102, 159, 206, 289, 304, 399, 418, 456, 461, 465, 473, 477, 496, 527, 536, 578,

597, 634, 690, 691, 712, 733, 751, 872, 874

walking, 671
   as a form of exercise, 544, 550, 684
   as a form of pleasure, 564, 650, 857, 894
war(s), 227, 364, 482, 485, 495, 496, 540
   causes of, 297, 465
   civil, 482, 496, 497, 734, 902
   consequences of, 227, 482 485, 518, 540, 903
   just, 491
   nuclear, 466, 844
   preventing, 224, 466, 480, 482, 483, 484, 486, 488, 489, 490, 491, 504, 514, 515, 516, 517, 541
waste,
   disposing of, 558, 792, 809, 814, 841, 842, 843, 845-847, 857
   radioactive, 842
   recycling, 329, 804, 814, 838, 840, 841, 845, 847
   reducing, 846
   toxic, 329
   water,
   access to clean, 329, 504, 556, 557, 728, 729, 783, 796, 800, 801, 804, 806, 845, 876, 878, 883
   pollution, 194, 329, 562, 792, 816, 845, 846
wealth, 351, 352, 601, 735, 819, 927
   benefits of, 836
   conflict and, 734
   education and, 229, 241, 313
   fragility of, 5
   generating, 57, 819, 895

happiness, health and, 159, 765
inequality and, 335, 614, 700, 734
perverse, 896, 897
population and, 829, 834
power and, 87, 115, 166, 338, 351, 699
poverty and, 411, 750
supporting others, 332, 539, 733, 735, 836
weapons/weaponry, 196, 322, 460-461, 465-467, 484-486, 496, 521, 563, 691
   nuclear, 466, 844, 903
   poverty and starvation as, 333, 458, 459,
web of life (the), 795, 797, 798, 800
win-win negotiation, 394
women,
   circumcision, 737
   coercive control of, violence against, 347, 348, 372, 373, 490
   discrimination against, 90, 105, 158, 175, 341, 348, 354, 511, 830, 931
work
   abuse at, 692
   bullying at, 70, 153, 154
   pleasure of, 136
   and rest, 58, 134, 135,136, 251
   safety at, 39, 40, 41, 349, 352, 560, 561, 742, 746
   trust at, 167, 420
zoos, 865